Policy Applications and Principles of Public Finance

SECOND EDITION

JOHN E. ANDERSON
University of Nebraska—Lincoln

SOUTH-WESTERN
CENGAGE Learning™

Australia • Brazil • Japan • Korea • Mexico • Singapore • Spain • United Kingdom • United States

SOUTH-WESTERN
CENGAGE Learning™

Policy Applications and Principles of Public Finance, Second International Edition

John E. Anderson

Senior Acquisitions Editor: Steven Scoble

Developmental Editor: Ted Knight, J. L. Hahn Consulting Group

Editorial Assistant: Allyn Bissmeyer

Senior Marketing and Sales Manager: Betty Jung

Content Project Management: PreMediaGlobal

Production Manager: Jean Buttrom

Senior Print Buyer: Kevin Kluck

Media Editor: Sharon Morgan

Senior Rights Specialist–Text: Deanna Ettinger

Senior Rights Specialist–Image: Deanna Ettinger

Senior Marketing Comminications Manager: Sarah Greber

Senior Art Director: Michelle Kunkler

Production House/Compositor: PreMediaGlobal

Cover Designer: Patti Hudepohl

Cover Photo Credits:

B/W Image: Getty Images/Rubberball

Color Image: Shutterstock Images/ Ken Schulze

Text Designer: PreMediaGlobal

Library of Congress Control Number: 2011928403

International Edition:

ISBN-13: 978-1-111-52698-6

ISBN-10: 1-111-52698-2

Cengage Learning International Offices

Asia
www.cengageasia.com
tel: (65) 6410 1200

Australia/New Zealand
www.cengage.com.au
tel: (61) 3 9685 4111

Brazil
www.cengage.com.br
tel: (55) 11 3665 9900

India
www.cengage.co.in
tel: (91) 11 4364 1111

Latin America
www.cengage.com.mx
tel: (52) 55 1500 6000

UK/Europe/Middle East/Africa
www.cengage.co.uk
tel: (44) 0 1264 332 424

Represented in Canada by Nelson Education, Ltd.
tel: (416) 752 9100/(800) 668 0671
www.nelson.com

Cengage Learning is a leading provider of customized learning solutions with office locations around the globe, including Singapore, the United Kingdom, Australia, Mexico, Brazil, and Japan. Locate your local office at: **www.cengage.com/global**

For product information: **www.cengage.com/international**
Visit your local office: **www.cengage.com/global**
Visit our corporate website: **www.cengage.com**

Printed in Canada
1 2 3 4 5 6 7 15 14 13 12 11

Contents

PART THREE
Social Choice and Analysis of Government Programs 159

Preface

I am grateful for the opportunity to write a second edition of *Policy Applications and Principles of Public Finance.* Much has happened in the world in general and in the field of public finance in particular since the first edition came out in 2003. In this edition I have updated the data and statistical information, incorporated new policy topics, and revised previous coverage for improved focus and added clarity. I have substantially strengthened treatment of expenditure programs including health care, social security, and disaster response. Here is a list of some of the new features:

- Entirely new chapter on social insurance programs (Chapter 9) covering social security, Medicaid, Medicare, and flood and earthquake insurance. With a unifying theme of insurance against various forms of risk, this chapter is unique among public finance textbooks.
- New appendix explaining the excess burden of taxes and subsidies using indifference curves and budget lines (found at the end of the text).
- Substantially revised chapter on corporate income taxes (Chapter 15) placing more emphasis on global taxation issues (e.g., worldwide taxation, dividend repatriation, and alternative concepts of neutrality in taxation) and moving material on the effects of corporate taxation on the capital structure of a firm to one of the end-of-book appendices.
- Many new policy studies on topics such as:
    - BP gulf oil spill
    - Central London congestion toll
    - Climate change and carbon markets
    - Green taxes and the double dividend
    - U.S. tax reforms and their effects on the average tax rate
    - Medicaid impacts on health outcomes
- Increased international focus with new coverage in several key chapters
    - U.S. taxes in international perspective
    - Individual and corporate income tax rates among OECD countries
    - Social security systems around the world
    - Taxation and dividend repatriation
    - Alternative approaches to international income taxation
- Added topical coverage
    - Incomplete information, moral hazard, and adverse selection as causes of market failure
    - Public insurance programs, including flood, earthquake, and terrorism insurance
    - Municipal bond markets and impacts of the global financial crisis

- Expanding fiscal deficits and national debt in a global context
- Potential tax reforms and their likely impacts
- Green taxes, cap-and-trade programs, and other environmental issues

Thanks are due to the instructors and students who used the first edition and provided helpful comments for improvement. Thanks also to the distinguished panel of professors who provided insightful comments regarding a second edition by way of the publisher's survey instrument. I have tried to incorporate all of their major suggestions. Finally, let me thank Steve Scoble and Ted Knight for their assistance in making this new edition possible.

Radius Images/Getty Images

PART ONE

Overview of the Public Sector and Methods of Analysis

CHAPTER

1

Radius Images/Getty Images

Economics of the Public Sector

LEARNING OBJECTIVES

1. Identify the problems and issues addressed in the discipline of public finance.
2. Discuss ways to think about the role of the public sector in an economy.

Olga is a young woman in her twenties who grew up in a country where the government owned all the means of production, including agricultural land, factories, forests, vineyards, and everything else that had any productive capacity. She went to government schools from elementary school through secondary school and university. When she graduated, she went to work for a state-owned and -operated factory that was required to produce to meet physical output goals according to the five-year economic plan. The state enterprise paid her a very small salary, but because the government provided housing, public transportation, health care, and even gave her two weeks each summer at a health spa on the river, she and her compatriots were not too displeased with their situation. Explicit taxes were relatively low, but implicit taxes were very high. The government took everything and then gave back a little for the people to live on. Olga and her family had very few freedoms in terms of economic opportunity to follow their own pursuits. They joked at work, saying, "The government pretends to pay us and we pretend to work." Once in a while they were even able to buy a smuggled pair of Levi jeans and dress in Western fashion, just like they had seen people dress in foreign movies and magazines. Life wasn't great, but all in all, it wasn't so bad, at least insofar as Olga knew about the alternatives.

Over the last decade of Olga's life, however, the government has changed fundamentally. Land and state enterprises have been sold to private owners who now operate them, hoping to earn a profit. In fact, nearly all the means of production in the form of land and factories have been privatized. Former collective farm workers now own their own plots of cropland and vineyard. They have to find markets in which to sell their products since the government no longer buys them. The government-run health care system is practically worthless because all the good doctors have left the country. When Olga gets sick and needs medical attention, she is better off to go to a private doctor and pay him for treatment. The government-run public transportation

"I like the concept if we can do it with no new taxes."

system is so overcrowded and unpredictable due to frequent breakdowns that when she really needs to get across the city, she catches a ride on a minivan operated by a private company that has purchased the right to provide transportation services on that route from the municipal government. The government is simply doing less these days and Olga must adjust, relying on private providers for some of the services formerly provided by the government. Now, she does not have a government-funded job that pays her even for a low level of work effort.

This example of Olga and her family illustrates a profound change that has taken place in a country that is fundamentally rethinking the role of government. It also illustrates the vast range of government interventions in the economy from which every country may choose. What role should the government play in the economy relative to markets? What services should the government provide, and how should those services be financed? Every society and country has to answer these fundamental questions. These are the essential issues of public finance that we will consider in this textbook.

In most countries the answers have been developed over a long period of time. People have become accustomed to the role their government plays in their economy and have also come to expect that their government will provide certain services and require specific taxes. In transition countries, like Olga's, all of this is up for grabs, and the government's role in the economy is being redefined. Furthermore, the government services provided and taxes required are being re-specified.

In Scandinavian countries like Sweden, Norway, Denmark, and Finland, people expect their government to provide a wide range of services and play a large role both in the economy and in redistributing income and wealth generated by the economy. For example, in Sweden, current government revenues amount to 55.6 percent of GDP (gross domestic product) (*OECD in Figures* 2009). Americans, on the other hand, expect their governments at federal, state, and local levels to play a more limited role in the economy and in redistribution. Current government revenues at all three levels in the United States amount to 34.6 percent of GDP, or just over half of those in Sweden. Individual freedom is highly prized in the United States. People want to be able to pursue their own endeavors, taking risks and earning the reward or living with the loss. Native peoples in places like sub-Saharan Africa, Papua New Guinea, Australia, and the Northwest Territories of Canada are accustomed to living in small tribal or communal societies with no external government, just an internal government established by heredity or custom, yet the reality of the modern world is that they must find a way to live their traditional life within the larger contemporary context that includes advanced market economies with governments.

At the other extreme, there are countries where the government has lost control of its territory and is no longer a sovereign state. Recognized legitimate institution, with authority to make collective decisions, does not exist. Corruption runs rampant. Public services such as public safety and education are nonexistent. Without recognized institutions and leaders, the international community of states cannot recognize the country or its government. Such countries are sometimes labeled **failed states** by commentators in the media, because they fail to provide the basic components required of a government. Countries such as Somalia, Chad, Sudan, Zimbabwe, Democratic Republic of the Congo, Afghanistan, and Iraq have topped the *Foreign Policy* magazine list of failed states in recent years.

Every society must answer the fundamental questions of how comprehensive a role the government should play in the economy, what specific goods and services the government should provide, and how those goods and services should be financed. This is the stuff of public finance.

THE FIELD OF PUBLIC FINANCE

Public finance is the field of study in economics that is concerned with the financial activities of the public sector—that part of the economy controlled by governments. Richard Musgrave says in his classic text (1959) that, "The complex of problems that center around the revenue-expenditure process of government is referred to traditionally as *public finance*." That collection of problems includes both concern for *how much is spent* on government activities and *how we pay* for those expenditures. In public finance, we want to know which activities it is sensible for governments to perform, the quantities of public goods and services that should be provided, and the best method of paying for those services. Furthermore, we care about public sector activity at all levels of government, including federal, state, and local. Because the focus of this field of study is on the economics of the public sector, it is sometimes called **public economics.** The terms *public finance* and *public economics* are interchangeable as they are used throughout this text, however, understanding that the economics of the public sector involves providing public services and financing those services.

In the U.S. economy at present, over one-third of our GDP is allocated by the public sector, including governments at all levels.[1] Although ours is ostensibly a **free market economy**, markets do not allocate all, or even nearly all, of the output the economy produces. From local school districts to state government agencies to the federal government, thousands of governments across the country and around the world are involved in affecting the way income is produced and allocated. This text provides an overview of the many economic aspects of government activity in the economy. It considers government programs and the associated expenditures as well as the financing of those expenditures through various forms of taxation.

The introduction to the *Handbook of Public Economics* (Auerbach and Feldstein 1985), a multivolume summary of the state of the art in the discipline of public finance, says that "Public economics is the positive and normative study of government's effect on the economy" (xv). This definition highlights the fact that public economics includes both the **positive analysis** of the way things are in the public sector and the **normative analysis** of the way things ought to be. For example, a positive analysis of the U.S. income tax may reveal that the average marginal tax rate paid by taxpayers is 20 percent. In a normative sense, however, we would be interested in whether that rate of taxation is too high or too low. The handbook also explains that in public economics:

> We attempt to explain why government behaves as it does, how its behavior influences the behavior of private firms and households, and what the welfare effects of such changes in behavior are. (xv)

Notice the *why, how*, and *what* aspect of this definition. We analyze *why* government behaves as it does in setting public policy, *how* that government behavior provides economic incentives for private companies and households to change their behavior, and *what* the impact is of those changes on the economic welfare of the firms and households. In this regard, public finance is also a field defined primarily by its objectives, rather than by its techniques. The field is characterized by the application of modern methods of economic theory, primarily microeconomic theory, and econometrics to problems that have concerned economists for more than two hundred years. Although those techniques are also used in international economics, labor economics, and other fields of economics, in public finance our objective is to advance the goals of economic efficiency and equity through the appropriate design of public sector programs and financing.

Public finance was a prominent part of Adam Smith's *Wealth of Nations* written in 1776, including his famous tax canon of sensible attributes of a tax system, and continues to be a major focus of both economic inquiry and daily news in the 21st century. Indeed, these concerns are as old as civilization itself. In a more general sense, public finance issues also involve aspects of political science, finance, and philosophy. You will see these influences in the chapters to follow, but the essential aspect of our analysis will always be economic.

In studying public finance, however, it is important to keep a proper perspective. Consider the famous statement by John Maynard Keynes: "Economics is a method rather than a doctrine, an apparatus of the mind, a technique of thinking which helps its possessor to draw correct conclusions." In studying public finance, within the larger context of economics, keep in mind that you are learning a way of thinking, not some prescribed set of answers. This text is not designed to tell you *what* to think about the economics of the public sector, as a political ideologue might advise. Rather, it is designed to teach you *how* to think about the economics of the public sector. You will learn a framework within which you can analyze public policy issues with a focus on their economic aspects. By learning to think the way an economist thinks, you will have a tool that helps you draw correct conclusions.

PRIVATE AND PUBLIC INTERESTS

Public finance is focused on the issues of public expenditure and taxation, yet those issues are only a subset of the larger objectives that governments are designed to achieve. John Maynard Keynes also identified the complex and critical difficulty facing all human societies. In *Liberalism and Labour*, written in 1926, Keynes (1963) said, "The political problem of mankind is to combine three things: economic efficiency, social justice, and individual liberty." A quick look around the world provides easy examples of countries that accomplish two of these three objectives, but there are precious few cases where a political-economic system assures all three. The United States, for example, places heavy emphasis on individual liberty and exemplifies what is arguably the most efficient economy in the history of our planet. But critics are quick to point to social maladies rooted in clear social injustices. Relatively unequal income distribution and employment opportunity lie at the heart of some of the United States's most vexing social problems. Other countries, such as those of the former Soviet Union, placed heavy emphasis on social justice, at least superficially, but did so while at the same time denying individual liberty and sacrificing a substantial amount of economic efficiency. The wrenching saga of Russian transformation from centrally planned economy through Perestroika to a fledgling mixed-market economy in the late 1980s and early 1990s is one of this century's clearest examples of the wisdom distilled in Keynes's observation.[2]

Individual Rights versus Social Responsibility

A more contemporary social critic, Alan Bloom (1987), has provided insightful comment on Western culture's conflicting interests in individual freedoms and community commitments.

> Man is ambiguous. In the tightest communities, at least since the time of Odysseus, there is something in man that wants out and senses that his development is stunted by being just a part of a whole, rather than a whole in itself. And in the freest and most independent situations men long for unconditional attachments. The tension between freedom and attachment, and the attempts to achieve the impossible union of the two, are the permanent condition of man. But in modern political regimes, where rights precede duties, freedom definitely has primacy over community, family, and even nature. (113)

The tension between individual liberty and social responsibility faces us at every turn, and it affects our view of what governments should and should not do. For example, I might wish to reduce the time it takes to travel to Chicago in my car by speeding at 20 miles per hour above the posted speed limit on Interstate 80. That is beneficial to me. My time is valuable. I am willing to take the added risk of an accident at the higher speed. But, of course, my speeding is dangerous to other motorists on the highway and I should also be concerned for their safety. Many of us in this situation, speeding on the interstate, are placing our individual rights over community concerns. A less mundane situation is that of a married couple with children who wish to have the individual freedoms afforded them by their state's no-fault divorce law but then balk at the responsibility to provide child support payments for their children. Again, individual rights are often elevated above community or family concerns. The government may, of necessity, become involved in programs to assure that individuals honor family and community commitments.

Bloom is probably correct in his assessment that in most modern political regimes rights precede duties and freedom has primacy over community, family, and even nature (although one could argue whether the last of these is even possible). Clear consequences exist for the way governments operate. Political uncertainty vividly reflects these issues. The relative balance between rights and responsibilities is often debated in welfare reforms, public education policy, environmental protection regulations and programs, AIDS research, gun control, health care provision, abortion rights, airport security, Internet access for children, and a host of other policy areas.

Stephen Carter has also addressed the issue of personal freedom and social responsibility in his book *Civility* (1998). He states:

> I am not suggesting that personal freedom is unimportant; on the contrary, in a liberal democracy, personal freedom is fundamental. But so is the sense of owing duties to others that leads us to impose limits on our own freedom, not because it is required by law but because it is required by morality—the morality of trying to build a civil community together. And no American soldier, I suspect, ever died for the proposition that none of us should care about one another. (84)

Hence, there is a balance of personal freedom and social responsibility required in a civil society that is neither easy to establish nor simple to maintain. It is often difficult and painful to forgo individual freedom for the sake of civil society, especially if we place primary emphasis on rights rather than on responsibilities.

The terrorist attack on the World Trade Center towers on September 11, 2001, is an excellent example of this dilemma. In the wake of that disaster, Americans have been required to forgo some of their accustomed freedoms in order to tighten national security. Most Americans were willing to put up with additional scrutiny at airports, for example, in exchange for a greater degree of safety on flights. We regularly trade a degree of individual freedom in exchange for social benefits that we value. Americans tend to value freedom highly, however, and have a relatively low threshold of patience with an oppressive government. In European societies, people are somewhat more accustomed to forgoing individual rights in exchange for social benefits. African and Asian societies are often even more willing to trade individual rights for social benefits.

The political debates in this context often turn on the distinction between rights and responsibilities, and this is not a recent development. John F. Kennedy exhorted Americans in his famous inaugural address of January 20, 1961, to be more concerned with community responsibility than individual freedom when he said:

> And so, my fellow Americans: ask not what your country can do for you—ask what you can do for your country. My fellow citizens of the world: ask not what America will do for you, but what together we can do for the freedom of man.

The development of the **republic**—a government based on the **rule of law**, usually embodied in the context of a constitution, rather than the exercise of unconstrained power by a few individuals—has been fundamental to the modern era in Western civilization.

Although governments are necessary, they are also potentially dangerous. As a result, ambivalence toward government is fundamental. People want and need governments in order to assure the rule of law rather than a reign of terror. They want more than just law and order. They want schools, hospitals, roads and ports, communication systems, space research, health protection, and a myriad of other things. At the same time, however, they are suspicious of government activities, motives, and methods of operation. The ability of government to oppress and subjugate has been vividly demonstrated in the 20th century. Fascist dictators like Hitler, Stalin, Mussolini, Pol Pot, and others have subjected millions of citizens to death, torture, and confinement. Ethnic cleansing policies pursued in Balkan States have resulted in the death of millions and the forced dislocations of entire populations.[3] Even more democratic nations have subjected their citizens to high rates of taxation and provided poor levels of government service with graft and corruption of varying intensity over time and across countries. Earlier in this century, U.S. cities such as New York and Chicago were run by corrupt political regimes that undeniably oppressed citizens. People are right to be ambivalent about government. It is necessary but also potentially oppressive. Let's consider the necessary and essential roles of government using the classic statement of Adam Smith over two hundred years ago as our starting point.

Adam Smith's Roles of Government

Developments in 18th-century democracy movements in France, England, and the United States have shaped contemporary notions of what governments are and should do. At the very least, we expect governments to provide national defense, afford law and order and assure the sanctity of contracts, and supply public goods and services that are necessary for the economy to operate at a high level. These three elements are necessary for the conduct of everyday business in a market economy. Adam Smith identified these three fundamental duties of government in his classic study of the nature and causes of the *Wealth of Nations* (1776/1937):

- The first duty of the sovereign [is] that of protecting the society from the violence and invasion of other independent societies (653).
- The second duty of the sovereign [is] that of protecting, as far as possible, every member of the society from the injustice or oppression of every other member of it, or the duty of establishing an exact administration of justice (669).
- The third and last duty of the sovereign or commonwealth is that of erecting and maintaining those public institutions and those public works, which, though they may be in the highest degree advantageous to a great society, are, however, of such a nature, that the profit could never repay the expense to any individual or small number of individuals, and which it therefore cannot be expected that any individual or small number of individuals should erect or maintain (681).

We would call the first duty national defense, the second administration of justice, and the third provision of public goods.

Beyond the essentials of national defense and justice, we in the 21st century expect governments to provide schools, transportation systems, health and safety assurances, and a host of other goods and services. Our expectation derives from our understanding that these provisions are essential to the operation of a modern market-oriented economy and assure a level of welfare acceptable to all.

Musgrave's Economic Roles of Government

Richard Musgrave (1959, 1989) has summarized the essential economic roles of governments with a three-part description of government responsibility that has become axiomatic in public finance. Governments have the responsibility for allocation, distribution, and stabilization.

The **allocation** function of government is that of allocating resources to the provision of public goods and services since they will not be provided efficiently by the private market system. The **distribution** function of government arises from the need to alter the distribution of income and wealth that is generated by the market system but is not necessarily acceptable to society. The macroeconomic **stabilization** function of government assures that output, prices, and employment are being produced at a stable rate by the economy. Because this area of responsibility is largely federal and is associated with the performance of the macro economy, this area of government activity is generally the purview of macroeconomics, not public finance, however. Instead, public finance theory and practice focus on the allocation and distribution roles of government. To a large extent, we are concerned with the provision of public goods like those embodied in education, transportation, research, and Internet systems, along with programs that alter the distribution of income.

We examine the operation of government from an economic point of view. We ask about the fundamental economic incentives that citizens, firms, and governments face in the allocation of resources to provide public goods and services and to alter the distribution of income. In doing so, we are operating within Keynes's broad purview, concerned with the economic aspects of combining economic efficiency, social justice, and individual liberty.

Public and Private Aspects of the Economy: Allocation of Resources

Resources are allocated primarily using markets in the U.S. economy. We rely on the market to allocate scarce inputs among competing uses. **Factors of production** like land, labor, and capital are all allocated by market mechanisms. Who will use the cornfield at the edge of a growing city, a farmer who wants to produce corn or a developer who wants to build a shopping mall? In a market economy, the question of land allocation is settled primarily by permitting land markets to operate. If the developer can convince the farmer to sell the land, by offering a price in excess of what the farmer figures the land is worth to him as a cornfield, the developer will gain the right to use the land. Of course, the market mechanism does not operate in unfettered fashion. The city has zoning regulations, for example, that are designed to prevent busy commercial activities from creating problems in residential areas. The land developer must also gain approval by the zoning commission for the construction of a shopping mall. This example illustrates the interaction of market and nonmarket allocation mechanisms typically used in the modern economy.

The same is true in other factor markets. For example, labor markets are the primary mechanism used to allocate labor, yet those markets are overseen and regulated by federal and state governments. The market is permitted to operate within well-defined limits. Regulations restrain the market in allocating child and immigrant labor and specify minimal safety and working conditions. Similarly, capital markets are restrained in their operation by the federal government.

Institutional Limitations on Market Allocation of Resources

Institutions have been crafted at all levels of government to provide boundaries within which the market mechanism may operate and to limit the outcomes of market allocations. At the federal level, for example, the Federal Aviation Administration (FAA) regulates the behavior of airlines and operates to assure air travel safety, the Securities and Exchange Commission (SEC) oversees the operation of financial markets, the Food and Drug Administration (FDA) provides for safe food supplies and drug development, and so on. At the state level, the Insurance Bureau regulates insurers, the Department of Natural Resources is involved in protecting natural resources, and a host of other state institutions are involved in setting boundaries on the operation of markets. Even at the local level, government institutions abound with the purpose of limiting markets. The local school board provides education in a decidedly nonmarket way; the library district, parks and recreation department, sewer district, and a variety of other local government units all are involved in allocating resources in nonmarket ways.

All in all, the modern **mixed market economy** involves a complex interaction of market and nonmarket forces. A pure market economy would rely exclusively on markets to allocate resources. A mixed market economy relies on a mixture of markets and government actions. Although the operation of markets is the purview of the typical economics course, this course focuses on ways in which governments are also involved in making economic decisions and affecting the allocation of resources, both inputs and outputs.

PUBLIC GOODS AND THE NEED FOR GOVERNMENT

We begin our consideration of public goods and the need for government with a simple example that motivates the primary role of government. The following game theoretic argument for establishing government is both fun and informative. It is based on a classic problem in game theory known as the **Prisoners' Dilemma** and illustrates the provision of law and order, a clear public good and one of Adam Smith's fundamental reasons for government.[4]

A Game Theoretic Motivation for Government

Consider the need for a government to provide a basic public good in the case of two ranchers in the Sand Hills of Nebraska with the payoff matrix in Table 1.1.[5] In each cell of the matrix, the gain (or loss, denoted by a negative number) for each rancher is listed as (rancher X gain/loss, rancher Y gain/loss). If neither rancher steals from the other, the (not-steal, not-steal) strategy combination, each one loses one steer to natural causes. Suppose that one rancher steals from the other, while the other does not steal; either the (steal, not-steal) or the (not-steal, steal) strategy combination occurs. Take the (not-steal, steal) strategy combination, where rancher Y steals from rancher X. In this case, rancher Y will gain 8 steers by stealing 10 from rancher X and driving them across the range to his ranch, which causes two of them to die—a net gain of 8 steers for rancher Y. The payoff matrix entry in this case is (−10, 8) and indicates that X loses 10 while Y gains 8. The situation is perfectly symmetric; if we switch the Y and X roles, the outcome is the same. If rancher X steals from rancher Y, X gains 8 steers while Y loses 10. The payoff listed in this case is (8, −10). Notice that the payoff matrix is symmetric. If both ranchers steal from one another, cattle are driven back and forth across the range causing both ranchers to lose six steers (−6, −6).

In a simple two-person economy such as this, we can define **social welfare**, a measure of how well off people are, as the simple sum of the payoffs to the two persons in the society. This measure takes into account the aggregate wealth, measured in the number of steers, of the two people in the society and can be used to examine how changes in behavior have an impact on social welfare. Adding the payoffs in each of the cells in Table 1.1, we see that the worst possible situation is the one where both ranchers are stealing from one another. In that case, the sum of the payoffs is −12. In all three of the other cells, the sum of the payoffs is −2. Hence, society is better off if at least one person is not stealing. In the two cases where one rancher is stealing and the other rancher is not stealing, the distribution of payoffs is unacceptable, however. In those cases, one person gains 8 cows while the other loses 10 cows. We can attain the same level of social welfare with a much more fair distribution by eliminating stealing. In the case where neither rancher steals, they each lose just one cow to natural causes. Consequently, most people would agree that the no-stealing situation is the best.

How would this hypothetical society get the no-stealing outcome? One possibility is that the ranchers could agree to hire a sheriff and form a local government to provide law and order, enforcing a rule against stealing cows. If the ranchers agree that they will not steal from one another, each will simply lose one steer to natural causes. Yet, in this case, each rancher has an incentive to renege and steal from the other. If I am rancher X and you are rancher Y, and I know that you have agreed not to steal from me, I can increase my expected outcome from −1 steer to +8 steers by stealing from you. Of course, you have the same incentive to steal from me. If we both steal, however, we both lose six steers. We know that we are both better off if we both abide by our agreement and refrain from stealing from one another. Yet that agreement provides an incentive for each of us to violate its terms and steal from the other. We both end up worse off. This situation

TABLE 1.1 The Ranchers' Dilemma

	Rancher Y	
Rancher X	**Steal**	**Not Steal**
Steal	(−6, −6)	(8, −10)
Not steal	(−10, 8)	(−1, −1)

illustrates the difference between the cooperative solution and the noncooperative solution to the problem. The cooperative solution is for us to agree that we will not steal. The noncooperative solution is for us to steal from the other.

So far, we have been thinking of the problem in naive terms where we anticipate that the other rancher will follow through on the agreement, allowing us to cheat and benefit. What happens if we expect the worst of one another? Suppose that we follow a strategy of maximizing among the minimum outcomes possible. If rancher X steals, the worst that can happen is that he will lose 6 steers (rancher Y also steals), whereas if he does not steal, the worst that can happen is that he loses 10 steers (rancher Y also steals). Among these two worst possible outcomes, the loss of six steers is the better outcome (and it occurs when he steals); hence the strategy is to steal. The same is true for rancher Y (prove this to yourself). If both ranchers follow these strategies, they both steal, giving us the strategy combination (steal, steal), and they both lose six steers.

A common solution method used by economists in games is to compute the **Nash equilibrium**. We find the Nash equilibrium by determining each player's best response to the predicted strategy of the other player.[6] In this case, no player wants to deviate from her predicted strategy. A pair of strategies satisfies the condition of a Nash equilibrium when each player's strategy is her best possible response to the other player. In the adaptation of the Prisoners' Dilemma game described earlier, the (steal, steal) strategy is the only strategy pair that satisfies this condition and is therefore the Nash equilibrium.

Let's see if we can improve the situation by hiring a sheriff to uphold law and order. If a sheriff's presence causes both ranchers to uphold their agreements, then the ranchers could agree to not steal, causing each to be better off by five steers. We could levy a tax of one steer each, pay the sheriff, and the ranchers would still be better off by four steers each. This game is an example of the classic Prisoners' Dilemma, which is a positive sum game. With cooperation it is possible for both players to be made better off. It is important as an example of situations in life where government can improve the well-being of citizens through its role of enforcing private contracts. Even the most ardent critics of government activity concede this important role. At the very least, we need government to enforce private contracts.

Although this game theoretic approach provides a justification for government, it does not reveal the optimal size of government. How big a government is needed? What scope of activities should the government be concerned with? The founders of the U.S. federal system of governments were concerned with limiting the size and scope of government. To do so, they constructed a constitutional basis for the role of government that we must consider in order to understand how the U.S. public sector operates.

With this fundamental motivation for government in mind, we now proceed to delineate the specific reasons for government to exist and to outline the role that government may play in each case.

Market Failure and Potential Roles for Government

Markets allocate resources quite well in general, yet we recognize that there are predictable situations in which markets do not provide allocations that are fully acceptable. In those situations, we consider that there is a potential role for government to improve the allocation of resources. Five major reasons exist as to why it is necessary for governments to be involved in the economy: to provide public goods, correct for externalities, assure competition, assure more perfect information, and alter the distribution of income.

Public Goods

Public goods are goods with the unique characteristic that they are **nonrival** in consumption. You and I can both consume them simultaneously without affecting one another's consumption of the good. For example, I can enjoy the view of Halfdome at Yosemite National Park, and there is just as much of the view for you to enjoy. One person's consumption does not limit the amount available to others. The private market will not provide such goods because private entrepreneurs cannot make a profit producing them. As a result, there is a role for government to provide public goods that provide benefits that citizens value but that the private market will not provide. Education, transportation, research and development, and a host of other policy areas may involve public goods that require some form of government intervention in order to assure the proper quantity is provided.

A second important characteristic of public goods is that they are **nonexcludable**. If the government provides a public good such as national defense, making the nation safe for its residents, that safety is provided for everyone. You cannot exclude some from being safe while protecting others. Hence, if the public good is provided to anyone, it is provided to all. This is not true of a private good that can be provided exclusively to those willing to pay for its provision.

Externalities

The term **externality** is used by economists to refer to a benefit or cost imposed on one economic agent by another economic agent when that effect is external to the working of the market. For example, in the process of producing automobiles and computer hardware, the economic system also produces, as a by-product, contamination of air, water, and other natural resources. Pollution is a negative externality. Because these negative externalities occur outside the working of the market mechanism, markets fail to allocate resources properly. In other words, we get too much pollution when we rely on the market mechanism alone. The government's role is to correct for this failure of the market.

Lack of Competition

A natural monopoly exists when an industry is characterized by increasing returns to scale. As a firm in the industry increases its output, its average total cost falls. The natural result is that the industry will be made up of one firm—a monopoly—resulting in a lack of competition and monopolistic pricing and output. The problem of a monopoly is that too little is produced and sold at too high a price, compared to the competitive market outcome. In this case, there is a role for government to regulate monopolies to prevent the ill effects of monopolistic behavior.

Imperfect Information

Competitive market outcomes require perfect information. Buyers and sellers must have complete information about products and prices. In the absence of such perfect information, markets may not allocate resources properly. For example, if the seller of a used car has more information about the quality of that car than a prospective buyer does, he has private information and the market may not work properly. Only poor-quality used cars will appear in the market, so-called lemons. The high-quality used cars, so-called cherries, will not be put up for sale in the market. We get the outcome that some goods do not appear in the market at all while other goods that do appear in the market are all of low quality. In this case the government may be needed in order to enact a **lemon law** that protects buyers in case the car they purchase has intractable mechanical problems.[7] In the absence of such government intervention, a market may not exist or may operate inefficiently.

Distribution of Income

The market mechanism provides an allocation of resources that determines the distribution of income. A society may determine that it finds such an allocation of income too unequal. It may then require government intervention to change the distribution of income through welfare programs, redistributive taxes, and other means in order to bring about a socially acceptable income distribution. For all of these reasons (and more reasons which we will not consider), there is a legitimate role for government to be involved in affecting the working of the market mechanism.

Constitutional Definition of Scope and Limitations of Government

Every country must have a social contract by which the citizens understand the role of the state. In democratic regimes, that social contract is typically summarized in a **constitution** that lays out the basic limits of government and provides the mechanisms for it to function. A constitution also defines the boundaries within which governments may operate. It distinguishes those government activities which are permitted from those which are inappropriate. In so doing, it provides a framework within which to understand the economic role of government as well. Article I of the U.S. Constitution enumerates the powers vested in Congress. Among those powers specified in

Section 8 are the ability to tax and spend. In particular, paragraph 1 states that Congress has the power:

> To lay and collect taxes, duties, imposts and excises, to pay the debts and provide for the common defense and general welfare of the United States; but all duties, imposts and excises shall be uniform throughout the United States.

Paragraph 2 further specifies that Congress has the power "To borrow money on the credit of the United States," whereas paragraph 4 vests Congress with the ability "To coin money, regulate the value thereof, and of foreign coin, and fix the standard of weights and measures."

Section 9 of the Constitution on restraints, federal and state, includes paragraph 4:

> No capitation, [or other direct,] tax shall be laid, unless in proportion to the census or enumeration herein before directed to be taken.

This paragraph was held by the Supreme Court to deny the federal government the ability to levy an income tax because such a tax would not be in direct proportion to the number of people in the country. The Sixteenth Amendment, adopted in 1913, made a federal income tax possible. It specified:

> The Congress shall have power to lay and collect taxes on incomes, from whatever source derived, without apportionment among the several states, and without regard to any census or enumeration.

State and Local Governments and Their Powers

When a question arises as to the appropriate level of government to handle a problem, the U.S. Constitution has a very clear default setting. Unless otherwise specified, the states and people of the United States are authorized to act, not the federal government. The Tenth Amendment, included in the **Bill of Rights**, specifies that:

> The powers not delegated to the United States by the Constitution, nor prohibited by it to the States, are reserved to the States respectively, or to the people.

As a result, the framers of the Constitution draw clear limits on the authority of the federal government, with any remaining unforeseen issues to be handled by the states or the people. The Constitution was carefully crafted to grant a limited set of powers for the federal government, with checks and balances to keep power diffused across the executive, legislative, and judicial branches of the federal government. The rights of the states were preserved, with a blanket default that provided them with the authority to act in the absence of a clear federal responsibility.

State governments each have their own constitutions that prescribe the way in which they go about providing for the needs of their citizens. Local governments derive their authority to govern from the state. For example, a state constitution specifies the rights and responsibilities of a county, city, and township. Within those parameters, counties, cities, and townships are able to govern at the local area.

A FEDERAL SYSTEM OF GOVERNMENT

A federal government system is one where government authority is diffused among the various levels of government (central, state, and local governments). The term **federal** comes from the Latin word *fidere*, which means "to trust," emphasizing the point that the various governments in a federal system must have both an explicit and an implicit trust in one another. The central government in a federal system retains some responsibility but delegates much of its authority to **subnational governments**. State and local governments are empowered with service responsibilities and fiscal independence. The degree of authority retained in the central government level differs across governments.

To some extent, the degree of authority that the citizenry is willing to grant to the central government depends on the history, language, culture, and degree of homogeneity in the population and the presence of ethnic minority regions. Countries with more homogeneous populations, such as France, tend to have central governments that are vested with greater degrees of authority. Indeed, France has a unitary government, not a federal government.

A loose association of states may be formed and called a *confederation*. In this arrangement, the federal government exists only at the pleasure of the member states of the confederation. The central government is quite weak in this situation. The southern states that seceded from the United States during the Civil War formed such a confederation—called the *Confederacy*.

Federal governments are very common in the world. The United States and India have state governments making up a federation. Canada and China have provincial governments in their federations. The former Soviet Union was a federation composed of 15 republics. Other federal governments include Argentina, Australia, Brazil, Mexico, Nigeria, and Germany. In each case, the national government is more powerful than the subnational government units, although the national government allocates clear powers and a degree of autonomy to the subnational government units.

Not all federal government systems have a high degree of diffusion in government power, however. In the former Soviet Union, for example, the federal organization of government reflected ethnic subdivisions among the republics, and the arrangement was designed primarily for administrative purposes. All of the real power was focused at the central government level. The dominant subnational unit of government was the Russian Soviet Federated Socialist Republic. After the breakup of the Soviet Union, the ethnically defined republics refused to accept Russia's rule, however, and subsequently declared themselves independent. Yugoslavia is another example of a federal form of government in a country where the central government authority is no longer accepted by the religious/ethnic regions that have declared themselves independent.[8] In fact, the name Yugoslavia no longer exists because all six of the republics that formerly comprised Yugoslavia are now independent.

Characterizing Governments by Their Level and Reach

A federal system of governments can be characterized by using a two-dimensional scheme of representation. Any unit of government can be classified by its **jurisdictional level** and **reach.** In a federal system of government, the central government is the highest-level government, which also has the widest jurisdictional reach. Below the central government there are many subnational governments at the state (or provincial) and local levels, each with more limited but varying jurisdictional reach. Figure 1.1 illustrates this two-dimensional view of governments in a federal system.

The **central**, or federal, government is assigned the broadest set of powers, giving it the widest jurisdictional reach. Below the central government is a whole host of subnational, or local, governments with more limited reach. We typically think of state or provincial governments as the next step lower in terms of level of government. However, there are some limited policy areas in which government units have been fashioned to operate at a level above state governments but below the federal government. State compacts for the disposal of low-level radioactive waste, for example, operate above individual state governments but below the federal government. Their jurisdictional reach is limited because they only have authority to deal with issues of waste disposal.

Below state governments are county governments, which were formed in the early years of statehood, in many cases, with the express mission of carrying out state government policy in geographically distinct areas of the

FIGURE 1.1 Level and Reach of Governments in a Federation

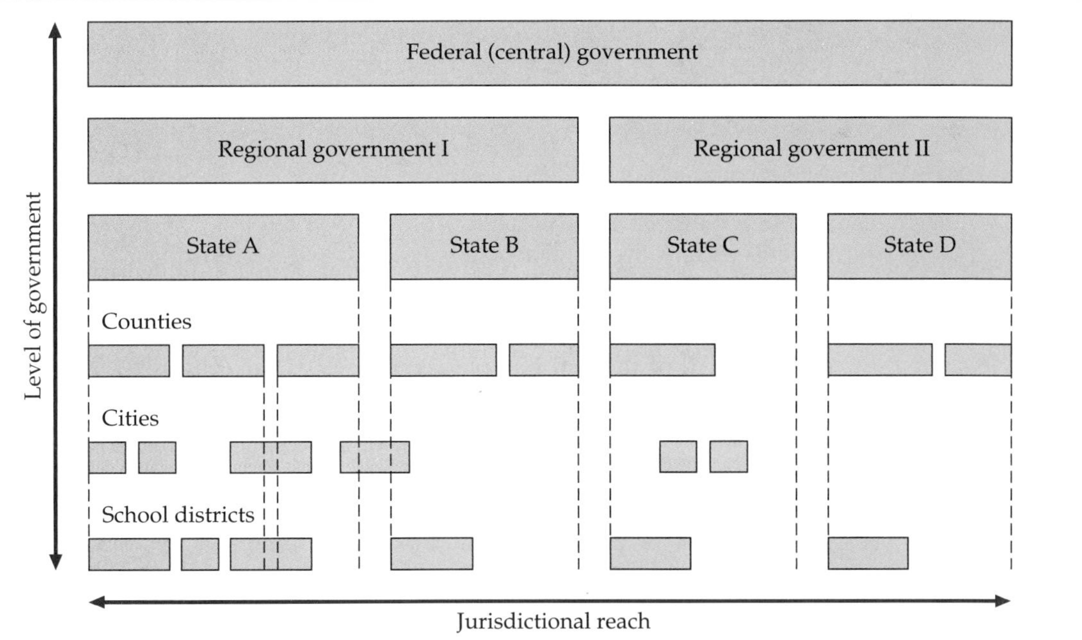

state. Within counties are townships, cities, villages, and other units of local government. At the local level, there are also school districts, library districts, water and sewer districts, community college districts, and many other local governments.

Overlapping Jurisdictions

A system of multilevel governments in which the lower-level governments are not neatly nested within higher-level governments inevitably runs into problems of overlapping jurisdictions. In some systems of government, such as that in the United States, the jurisdictional boundaries may not be lined up in a simple hierarchy, with first-level local governments nested within second-level regional or state governments nested within the third-level federal government. The local public schools all report to an intermediate school district that is in turn responsible to the state department of education, but the boundaries of those educational districts do not match the boundaries of the local municipal governments (such as villages, towns, and cities) or the middle-level governments of the counties that make up the state. Hence, the administration of public education programs may be conducted independently of the administration of municipal and county governments. Such a situation causes problems in the economic efficiency of running government programs, administration of government programs, and data collection and aggregation.

Some city boundaries cross county lines. Indeed, some cities straddle state lines, as in Lake Tahoe, California/Nevada. School districts are not neatly nested within cities or counties. Their boundaries are often independent of both city and county borders. This causes policy difficulties when we consider the provision of local public education, for example. Do small school districts permit schools to be operated at the minimum of their average cost curves, providing education at the lowest cost possible? Perhaps consolidation of small local districts into larger regional districts would permit greater efficiencies. On the other hand, how do we keep governments responsive to the wishes of the people? Do we gain responsiveness by keeping school districts small? We also face the complications of overlapping jurisdictions. Three distinct issues are involved here. First, what is the proper level of government required to solve a given problem? Should the solution be crafted at the local, state, regional, or national level? Second, what is the best-sized government unit for providing a required program or service? Is it best to have a large government unit in order to pursue economies of scale, or is it best to keep the government unit small to provide responsiveness to citizens? Third, how do we conduct research on the public sector when it appears that the government units of observation do not line up properly? If we are interested in public education policy, for example, how do we combine school district data on students' performance and education funding with municipal or census data on population, housing, and income?

In thinking about proper government size and level, there are economic principles to consider. It is not necessary to nest all substate governments neatly within one another, like a set of Russian matryoshka dolls. In fact, there may be good economic reasons to have the boundaries of various government units aligned on the basis of the economics of providing the associated government services rather than for the convenience of data collectors. Consider, for example, the case of an environmental issue where the region affected is a watershed. A political division may run through the watershed because state boundaries are often rivers. In that situation, the river separates two states, but the relevant level of government to consider for solving a watershed problem may be a regional government made up of parts of several states or provinces. We have to consider the proper level and size of government in the context of the policy issue at hand and deal with the messy fact that there are overlapping jurisdictions.

POLICY STUDY

The European Union—A United States of Europe?

The European Union (EU) provides a fascinating example of sovereign states agreeing to sacrifice their independence in exchange for some of the benefits that come from economic and other forms of closer cooperation. After the devastation of World War II, leaders of several European nations searched for a means by which their nations could rebuild, share some forms of sovereignty, and make another world war less likely. At first, six nations began to cooperate in the areas of coal and steel production, international trade, and nuclear energy. The Union has evolved to include a much broader set of policy areas, as the nations of Western Europe have struggled to create a closer form of union among their peoples.

At present there are 27 nations in the EU: Austria, Belgium, Bulgaria, Cyprus, Czech Republic, Denmark, Estonia, Finland, France, Germany, Greece, Hungary, Ireland, Italy, Latvia, Lithuania, Luxembourg, Malta, Netherlands, Poland, Portugal, Romania, Slovakia, Slovenia, Spain, Sweden, and the United Kingdom. Membership has expanded greatly in recent years with the addition of Central and Eastern European countries, and further expansion is anticipated. In order to become a member, a nation must have a "stable democratic government, a good human rights record, a properly functioning market economy, and the macroeconomic fitness to fulfill the obligations of membership." The 1993 Maastricht Treaty, named after the city in the Netherlands in which the negotiations took place, provided for a major revamping of the several existing treaties and agreements that were in place. It provides the current legal and constitutional bases for the EU, creating a structure of the so-called *three pillars.*

The first pillar provides the basis for the European Community. Under the terms of the Treaty of Rome, as revised by the Single European Act, the institutional structure of the EU is established. A single economic market is facilitated, democratic institutions are established, European citizenship is established, and the basis for economic and monetary union is founded. The second pillar provides for common foreign and security policies. Although a common defense policy remains to be realized, it is indeed an eventual goal. The third pillar provides for matters of justice and home affairs in each

TABLE 1.2 A Comparison of the European Union and the United States, 2009

	European Union (27 countries)	United States (50 states)
Population (millions)	492.39	310.23
Labor force (millions)	224.8	154.1
Unemployment rate (%)	9.2	9.3
Gross domestic product (trillions of dollars)	14.51	14.26
Gross domestic product per capita (PPP) (thousands of dollars)	32,600	46,400
World international trade (excludes intra-EU trade)	**Trillions of U.S. dollars**	**Trillions of U.S. dollars**
Imports	1.69	1.455
Exports	1.95	0.995

Source: Central Intelligence Agency, World Factbook, http://www.cia.gov/library/publications/the-world-factbook

country. Closer cooperation is the goal of the union in terms of asylum policy, rules on border crossing and immigration, customs, trade fraud, and other policy issues.

How does the EU compare with the United States? The members of the EU have agreed to combine their sovereign powers in order to pursue unity in much the same way that the United States is a federation of states within the structure of a republic. Table 1.2 provides a statistical overview of the EU and the United States. The European Union is an important case study of the issues involved in forming an association of sovereign states whereby some degree of autonomy is sacrificed in exchange for the benefits of closer association. Clearly, the EU involves a relatively weak role for the central government and is more of a confederation of states than a true federation as in the United States. Monetary policy is a good example of a policy issue in the EU that demonstrates the real difficulty in sacrificing one's autonomy. For example, the United Kingdom has refused to be a part of the single currency, the euro, as it does not wish to forgo its ability to control its own monetary policy. Given the painful history of U.K. monetary policy spanning numerous times of war in Europe, the British fear ceding such authority to the interests of a broader European policy group influenced by the Germans and French. The fact that the EU permits the United Kingdom to be part of the union without participating in the single currency, however, is a signal of the degree of authority vested in the EU government. Member states retain a large degree of autonomy, but that autonomy has been severely tested in recent times when a global recession and fiscal conditions in specific countries such as Greece, Ireland, Portugal, and Spain have required coordinated fiscal policy action by the EU countries. Having a monetary union without a corresponding fiscal union presents the EU with a substantial policy difficulty. Such a difficulty will eventually have to be overcome for the realization of the dream of a single Europe.

PROBLEMS

1. Use Keynes's conception of the tension among the goals of efficiency, justice, and liberty that must be resolved by a political system in each of the following public finance issues:
   a. Designing a new welfare system that would shift away from cash transfers to in-kind transfers of housing, medical care, and food
   b. Considering a type of fundamental tax reform that would be efficiency enhancing but more regressive (requiring a greater share of income paid in tax of the poor than of the wealthy) than the present system
   c. Considering the choice of a municipal water treatment system or private water treatment system for each household
   d. Requiring public education for all children ages 5 to 18
   e. Requiring immunizations for all children entering kindergarten
2. Discuss the issues of public and private interests in the following cases:
   a. Parking on your campus
   b. Sharing the bathroom with your suite mates
   c. Tax evasion
   d. Speeding on the highway
   e. A "Pittsburgh Left" (turning left with your automobile at a stoplight as soon as the light turns green, beating the oncoming traffic)
3. Describe which economic role of government (allocation, distribution, or stabilization) is addressed in each of the following cases of government agencies or programs.
   a. Environmental Protection Agency (EPA)
   b. Department of Defense (DOD)
   c. Price controls introduced by President Nixon in 1973
   d. Federal Open Market Committee (FOMC) policy
   e. Social Security System
4. In each of the following cases, explain the potential causes of market failure (public goods, externalities, lack of competition, or imperfect information) that may be involved with each good or service.
   a. Cigarettes
   b. Education
   c. Urban open space
   d. Pesticides
   e. Roads
   f. Internet access
   g. Research and development
   h. Prostitution services
   i. Handguns
   j. Medical services
   k. Abortion services

5. Using the information provided in the Policy Study on the European Union, compare the role of the central government in the United States and the European Union.
   a. Would you call the EU a federation of states or a confederation? Explain.
   b. Explain how membership in the European Monetary Union (EMU) involves sacrificing sovereignty for the benefits of association with other member states.
   c. Explain how the movement to a single market in the European Community provides member states with both economic advantages and disadvantages.
   d. Using what you know about the need for government, including public goods, externalities, and other causes of market failure, and what you know about the economic roles of government, explain how the three pillars of Table 1.2 are apparently designed to facilitate a substantial improvement in the quality of life for European citizens.
6. Go online and check out Resources for Economists on the Internet at the following website: *http://rfe.org/*
   a. Follow the link to job information and see what jobs are available in the field of public finance.
   b. Follow the link to economic journals and see what journals are available in the field of public finance.
   c. Follow the link to U.S macro and regional data and see what government expenditure and tax data are available.
   d. Follow the link to societies and associations and see what organizations exist related to public finance.

REFERENCES

Auerbach, Alan J., and Martin Feldstein. *Handbook of Public Economics*, Vol. 1. Amsterdam: Elsevier North-Holland, 1985.

Bloom, Alan. *The Closing of the American Mind*. New York: Simon and Schuster, 1987.

Carter, Stephen L. *Civility*. New York: HarperCollins, 1998.

Djilas, Milovan. *Conversations with Stalin*. New York: Harcourt Brace, 1962.

Economic Report of the President 2010, Executive Office of the President. Washington, DC: U.S. Government Printing Office.

Foreign Policy. "The Failed States Index 2010." Available at: http://www.foreignpolicy.com/articles/2010/06/21/the_failed_states_index_2010.

Gibbons, Robert. *Game Theory for Applied Economists*. Princeton, NJ: Princeton University Press, 1992.

Kaplan, Robert D. *Balkan Ghosts*. New York: Vintage, 1993.

Keynes, John Maynard. "Liberalism and Labour." In *Essays in Persuasion*, New York: W.W. Norton and Company, 1963, pp. 339–348.

Musgrave, Richard A. *The Theory of Public Finance: A Study in Public Economy*. New York: McGraw-Hill, 1959.

Musgrave, Richard A., and Peggy B. Musgrave. *Public Finance in Theory and Practice*, 5th ed. New York: McGraw-Hill, 1989, 7–12.

Organization for Economic Cooperation and Development. *OECD in Figures, 2009 Edition*. Paris: 2009.

Remnick, David. *Lenin's Tomb: The Last Days of the Soviet Empire*. New York: Vintage, 1994.

Satter, David. *Age of Delirium: The Decline and Fall of the Soviet Union*. New Haven, CT: Yale University Press, 2001.

Smith, Adam. *An Inquiry into the Causes and Consequences of the Wealth of Nations*, 1776.

Tower, Edward. *Public Finance Reading Lists*, Vol. 2. Durham, NC: Eno River Press, 1990.

NOTES

1. Federal, state, and government current expenditures were 35 percent of GDP in the year 2009 (*Economic Report of the President* 2010, computed from Tables B-1 and B-82).
2. *Perestroika* is the Russian term for the new openness that was embraced during the time of Mikhail Gorbachev and the demise of the soviet system. For a fascinating account of the disintegration process in the Soviet Union, see Remnick (1994) and Satter (2001).
3. For a gripping account of the history of the Balkans, see Kaplan (1994), and for insight into the influence of Stalin in the Balkans and the Yugoslavian resistance to that influence, see Djilas (1962).
4. The Prisoners' Dilemma is an example in which the role of cooperation is important to see. Games are classified as cooperative, where players coordinate their strategies in ways that are dependent upon one another, and noncooperative, where players independently select their preferred strategies. In the Prisoners' Dilemma communication and cooperation are possible, but the stealing strategy still dominates. In other games, the dominant strategy where players are able to cooperate with one another can differ from that where cooperation is not possible. Professor John Nash was one of the early pioneers formalizing the concept of noncooperative games and developing solution strategies. He shared the 1994 Nobel Memorial Prize in Economic Science with John Harsanyi and Reinhard Selten. The Academy Award–winning movie *A Beautiful Mind* is based on the life of Professor Nash.
5. This example is due to Professor Don Fullerton and is adapted from a problem in Tower (1990, 95).
6. For more information on games and solution methods, see Gibbons (1992).
7. This idea is so important that the 2001 Nobel Memorial Prize in Economic Science was awarded to Professor George Akerlof, Professor Joseph Stiglitz, and Professor A. Michael Spence who advanced our understanding of the importance of imperfect information in market failure. Akerlof, in particular, is well known for his article on the market for lemons (1970).
8. The people of the former Yugoslavia are predominantly Slavic in ethnic heritage, but they differ in religious heritage. The Croats are Catholic, the Serbs are Orthodox, and the Bosnians are Muslim. Religious differences are at the heart of each republic's desire for independence.

CHAPTER 2

Methods and Measurements in Public Finance

LEARNING OBJECTIVES

1. Describe various ways the size of the public sector can be measured, consider the applications of each type of measurement, and evaluate its strengths.
2. Analyze the models and quantitative methods economists use to discover truths about the way people, firms, and governments behave.

We learned in Chapter 1 that governments are needed in order to play important roles in the economy. They are involved in allocation, distribution, and stabilization activities. Now in this chapter we turn to important issues of how we measure the size of the public sector and what methods we can use to analyze the effects of public sector activities. First, how can we reasonably measure the size of the public sector? Answers to this question are important so that we know what we are talking about when we refer to the public sector and so that we can evaluate what changes have taken place in the public sector over time. For example, we may wish to have answers to the following questions: How much money is spent for public goods and services provided by governments? How many people are employed by governments? How big is our government (federal, state, local) compared to other governments?

Second, it is important to understand how public finance researchers and policy analysts conduct their investigations of the public sector. It is essential to know what impact public policies have on the behavior of individuals, families, and firms. We may wish to know, for example, how families change their saving behaviors in response to changes in the Social Security system or in response to changes in the income tax rates they face.

SIZE AND SCOPE OF THE PUBLIC SECTOR—FEDERAL, STATE, AND LOCAL

The size of a government can be measured in several ways, each of which provides insight. The most common way to measure government size is by total nominal expenditures or revenues. While this method captures the total of government expenditures, that total can be very misleading when comparing revenues or expenditures over time. As a result, economists often convert **nominal measures** of government size into **real measures** to avoid these measurement problems. A nominal measure of government size, such as expenditures or revenues, is reported in **current dollars** and includes the effects of inflation over time. In contrast, a real measure eliminates inflation by putting each year's information into the same **base year** dollars and reports government expenditures or revenues in **constant dollars.** The conversion from nominal to real requires the use of a price index, usually the gross domestic product (GDP) deflator. For example, real expenditure is computed as nominal expenditures divided by GDP deflator/100. In this computation the deflator is converted from its traditional base of 100 to a base of 1 so that in the base year, the nominal and real expenditures are identical. Nominal revenue and expenditure figures are not so deceiving if the purpose of an analysis is to compare school expenditures per pupil in Wisconsin with those in Minnesota for the year 2000, for example. But they are nearly meaningless if we need to compare U.S. federal government revenues in 1965 with those in 2000. Inflation fundamentally distorts comparisons across time.

Aside from inflation, there are other reasons to consider adjustments to nominal measures of public sector size. Economic growth also distorts the picture. As an economy grows in population or output, we expect the size of the public sector to grow as well. If we want insight about the size of the public sector, holding growth in the economy constant, however, we need to adjust nominal receipts and expenditures. This requires adjustment for population size or GDP. Another form of adjustment is used to control growing populations. By computing government expenditures or tax revenues on a *per capita* basis, dividing by population, we get a picture of spending or taxation per person.

Another measure of public sector size is public sector employment as a share of total employment in the economy. By examining employment in the public sector relative to total employment, we can learn something about the size of the public sector relative to the whole economy—focusing on the all-important labor input. If we further subdivide employment among the various levels of government, we get a picture of the composition of the public sector among federal, state, and local levels.

Finally, public sector size differs substantially across countries as there are different governmental structures and cultural expectations regarding the role of the public sector. It is instructive to consider how the size of the public sector varies across countries. This requires measures of public sector size that control for differences in the size of the economies of the countries examined, such as public sector expenditures as a share of GDP. Cross-country comparisons are among the most difficult of all public sector comparisons due to the many economic and social factors that distinguish countries.

Each of the several methods of computing the size of government has a place, given the purpose of the analysis. We consider each of these perspectives in the following sections and illustrate how each method helps reveal information on the size of the public sector.

Nominal Measures of Public Sector Size

Table 2.1 provides data on government receipts and expenditures (total, federal, state, and local) for selected years from 1960 through 2010. The first three data columns give the amount of receipts, expenditures, and net government saving (surplus or deficit) for all governments in the United States, measured in billions of current dollars. The second set of three columns gives the same data for the federal government and the third set of three columns gives the same data for state and local governments. The last column on the right-hand side gives grants-in-aid to state and local governments. These are transfers of funds from federal to state and local governments for specific programs.

When we consider the size and scope of governments, it is important to recognize government units at all levels. Table 2.1 does this by providing information on total government, federal government, and state and local governments. Consider receipts in 1995, for example. Total government receipts were $2,215.5 billion (or $2.22 trillion). Of that amount, receipts of the federal government accounted for $1,407.8 billion ($1.41 trillion) while state and local governments accounted for receipts of $991.9 billion. You may notice that the sum of federal receipts and state and local receipts is larger than the reported total government receipts. That is because there are intergovernmental transfers that have the effect of causing some receipts to be double counted. Grants-in-aid are grants from the federal government to state and local governments to help provide for programs of assistance or service to the public. If we subtract the amount of grants-in-aid to state and local governments, we get total government receipts.

Table 2.2 provides information on the shares of receipts across government levels over time. In 1960, federal receipts accounted for 69.9 percent of total government receipts, whereas state and local government receipts accounted for 33.1 percent. Again, we need to subtract the share of grants-in-aid to state and local government to make the sum add to 100 percent. We subtract the share of state and local receipts due to grants-in-aid from the federal government and report state and local own-source receipts in the last column on the right-hand side of Table 2.2. State and local own-source receipts accounted for 30.1 percent of total government receipts. Consider how the shares of receipts differed in 2010. Federal receipts accounted for 60.1 percent of total government receipts in 2010, whereas state and local government own-source receipts accounted for 38.5 percent. These figures reveal that a shift in funding has occurred over this period of time. The federal government accounts for a smaller share of total receipts, whereas state and local governments account for a larger share. Notice, however, that there is no smooth trend in these shares over time. Examining the relative shares of receipts and expenditures by level of government, we are able to see changes in the roles and responsibilities of governments at various levels over time.

Table 2.1 also provides useful information about the current surplus or deficit by level of government over time. If you look down the column for state and local government surpluses or deficits, you will see that governments at the subnational level have consistently had budget surpluses. On the other hand, scan

TABLE 2.1 Total, Federal, and State and Local Government Receipts and Current Expenditures (Billions of Current Dollars), 1960–2009

	Total Government			Federal Government			State and Local Government			
Year or Quarter	Current Receipts	Current Expenditures	Net Government Saving	Current Receipts	Current Expenditures	Net Federal Government Saving	Current Receipts	Current Expenditures	Net State and Local Government Saving	Grants-in-Aid to State and Local Governments
1960	134.4	123.0	11.4	93.9	86.8	7.1	44.5	40.2	4.3	4.0
1965	180.3	170.6	9.8	121.0	117.7	3.2	66.5	60.0	6.5	7.2
1970	286.9	295.2	−8.4	186.1	201.6	−15.5	120.1	113.0	7.1	19.3
1975	442.1	510.2	−68.2	277.6	348.3	−70.6	209.6	207.1	2.5	45.1
1980	798.7	846.5	−47.8	532.8	589.5	−56.6	338.2	329.4	8.8	72.3
1985	1,214.6	1,370.9	−156.3	774.4	953.0	−178.6	521.1	498.7	22.4	80.9
1990	1,709.3	1,879.5	−170.3	1,082.8	1,259.2	−176.4	738.0	731.8	6.2	111.4
1995	2,215.5	2,412.5	−197.0	1,407.8	1,614.0	−206.2	991.9	982.7	9.2	184.2
2000	3,132.4	2,906.0	226.5	2,057.1	1,871.9	185.2	1,322.6	1,281.3	41.3	247.3
2005	3,659.3	3,916.4	−257.1	2,290.1	2,573.1	−283.0	1,730.4	1,704.5	25.9	361.2
2010p	4,019.9	5,316.4	−1,296.5	2,416.4	3,760.7	−1,344.3	2,142.7	2,095.0	47.7	539.3

Note: Federal grants-in-aid to state and local governments are reflected in federal current expenditures and State and local current receipts. Total government current receipts and expenditures have been adjusted to eliminate this duplication.

Source: *Economic Report of the President* 2010, Table B-82.

TABLE 2.2 Federal Receipts, State and Local Receipts and Grants to State and Local Governments as a Percentage of Total Government Receipts, 1960–2009

Year	Federal Government Receipts	State and Local Government Receipts	Grants to State and Local Governments	State and Local Own-Source Receipts
1960	69.9	33.1	3.0	30.1
1965	67.1	36.9	4.0	32.9
1970	64.9	41.9	6.7	35.1
1975	62.8	47.4	10.2	37.2
1980	66.7	42.3	9.1	33.3
1985	63.8	42.9	6.7	36.2
1990	63.3	43.2	6.5	36.7
1995	63.5	44.8	8.3	36.5
2000	65.7	42.2	7.9	34.3
2005	62.6	47.3	9.9	37.4
2010p	60.1	53.3	14.8	38.5

Source: Computed from data in *Economic Report of the President* 2010, Table B-82.

down the surplus or deficit column for the federal government and you will see that the federal government has usually run a deficit. A notable feature in the table is the explosion in the federal government deficit in 2010 due to a combination of falling tax revenue and an unprecedented fiscal stimulus.

Total government receipts have clearly risen dramatically over the 50-year period covered in Table 2.1. Total receipts rose from $134.4 billion in 1960 to $4,019.9 billion in 2010. Similarly, total current expenditures rose from $ 123.0 billion in 1960 to $5,316.4 billion in 2010. Such figures give the appearance of phenomenal growth in the public sector. Although there has been very substantial growth, these figures exaggerate the case. Consider total government expenditures in 1960 compared to those in 2010 more carefully. These expenditures are both measured in *current* dollars; that is, the 1960 expenditures are measured in terms of 1960 dollars, and the 2010 expenditures are measured in terms of 2010 dollars. These dollars are not comparable, however, and hence expenditure comparisons using current dollar measures at different points of time such as these can be quite misleading. Nominal expenditures, measured in current dollars, are misleading because they include the effects of inflation over time. In order to remove inflation, we convert nominal expenditures (receipts or surpluses/deficits) to real expenditures using the GDP deflator and then compare the measures in *constant* dollars.

Real Measures of Public Sector Size

The first way to modify government size measures in order to obtain a more accurate view of growth in revenues and expenditures is to adjust them for changes in the value of the dollar over time. A $1,000 expenditure by the federal government in 1960 is quite different from a $1,000 expenditure in 2010. In order to account for that difference, we must convert each of those expenditures into a common dollar measure to make a meaningful comparison. That is, we can use real expenditures as a more accurate measure of the size of governments when we wish to consider how government size has changed over time.

For example, if we wish to compare the expenditures in 1990 to those in 1980 (see Table 2.1), we must divide each of the nominal expenditures by the GDP deflator over 100 in order to convert into constant dollars, or real expenditures.[1] First, we must find the values of the GDP deflator for those two years. One good source of such data is the Appendix of the *Economic Report of the President,* which is issued annually in January. From that source we see that the GDP price deflator (with base equal to 100 in the base year 2005) was 47.776 in 1980 and 72.213 in 1990. Next, we know that in order to convert nominal figures into real figures, we must take the nominal figure and divide it by the GDP deflator over 100. Doing so in this case, we can compute that the real total government expenditure levels for 1980 and 1990 are $798.7/0.47776=1,671.8 and $1,709.3/0.72213=2,367.0, respectively. Use this information to compare expenditures in 1980 and 1990. Although the nominal level of expenditure rose 114 percent over the period 1980 to 1990, the real expenditure level rose by just 42 percent. By comparing expenditures in the two years in constant dollars, we get a more accurate view of the increase as the effects of inflation have been removed.

Notice that the GDP deflator has a 2005 base year; this means that the value of the deflator in that year is 100. In years after 2005, the deflator is larger than 100, reflecting inflation. For example, the deflator was 110.654 in 2010. That means inflation increased prices by 10.654 percent over the years from 2005 to 2010. In years prior to 2005, the deflator is less than 100. For example, the value of the deflator in 1970 was 24.328, indicating that goods and services with the price of $100 in 2005 had a price of just $24.33 in 1970.

Table 2.3 provides data on government revenues, expenditures, and surplus or deficit in real terms, where the data from Table 2.1 have been converted into constant 2005 dollars to facilitate comparison over time. Say, for example, that we want to examine what happened during the 1980s. Table 2.1 indicates that total government expenditures measured in current dollars rose by 122 percent (from $846.5 billion in 1980 to $1,879.5 billion in 1990). We know, of course, that much of that growth was due to inflation, not real growth in government expenditures. Table 2.3 gives us the information we need to remove the effects of inflation and consider the extent of real growth in government expenditures. According to Table 2.3, total government expenditures rose 65 percent in real terms during the 1980s (from $1,373.5 billion in 1980 to $2,305.2 billion in 1990). By using real measures in constant dollars over time in Table 2.3, we get a more accurate picture of real changes in government receipts and expenditures over time.

TABLE 2.3 Total, Federal, and State and Local Government Receipts and Current Expenditures (Billions of 1996 Dollars), 1960–2010

	Total Government			Federal Government			State and Local Government			Grants-in-Aid to State and Local Governments
Year or Quarter	Current Receipts	Current Expenditures	Net Government Saving	Current Receipts	Current Expenditures	Net Federal Government Saving	Current Receipts	Current Expenditures	Net State and Local Government Saving	
1960	722.4	617.2	61.3	504.7	466.6	38.2	239.2	216.1	23.1	21.5
1965	904.8	701.2	49.2	607.2	590.6	16.1	333.7	301.1	32.6	36.1
1970	1,179.3	879.2	−34.5	765.0	828.7	−63.7	493.7	464.5	29.2	79.3
1975	1,316.7	1,067.9	−203.1	826.8	1,037.3	−210.3	624.2	616.8	7.4	134.3
1980	1,671.8	1,373.5	−100.1	1,115.2	1,233.9	−118.5	707.9	689.5	18.4	151.3
1985	1,970.7	1,898.4	−253.6	1,256.5	1,546.2	−289.8	845.5	809.1	36.3	131.3
1990	2,367.0	2,305.2	−235.8	1,499.5	1,743.7	−244.3	1,022.0	1,013.4	8.6	154.3
1995	2,717.3	2,721.4	−241.6	1,726.7	1,979.6	−252.9	1,216.6	1,205.3	11.3	225.9
2000	3,533.5	2,906.0	255.5	2,320.5	2,111.6	208.9	1,492.0	1,445.4	46.6	279.0
2005	3,659.3	3,568.1	−257.1	2,290.1	2,573.1	−283.0	1,730.4	1,704.5	25.9	361.2
2010p	3,632.9	4,804.5	−1,171.7	2,183.7	3,398.6	−1,214.9	1,936.4	1,893.3	43.1	487.4

Source: Computed from data in *Economic Report of the President* 2010, Table B-82, using GDP deflator (2005 base year) from Table B-7.

Consider another example of how the real figures in Table 2.3 provide insight hidden in Table 2.1. The federal government deficit appears to have increased from 1985 to 1995, rising from $178.6 to $206.2 billion, according to Table 2.1 where the deficit measures are in current dollars. But, if we compare federal deficit measures for the same years in real terms reported in Table 2.3, we see that the 1995 deficit was quite a bit smaller than the 1985 deficit. Measured in constant 1996 dollars, the federal government deficit fell from $289.8 billion in 1985 to $252.9 billion in 1995. This simple example illustrates how important it is to eliminate inflation in order to obtain an accurate view of the real changes in government finance.

Measuring the Public Sector Relative to the Economy as a Whole

Even if we find that government expenditures are rising over time in real terms, we cannot be sure that the government is really growing, however. Government expenditures may be rising along with the overall size of the country and the output of its economy. The growth in population or GDP may be outstripping the growth in government expenditures, resulting in a declining size of government relative to the size of the country as a whole. Hence, we need to compare the size of the government relative to the size of the entire economy in order to have an accurate picture of the size of the government. By dividing total government expenditures by population or GDP, we can obtain measures of the size of the public sector that are scaled for the size of the country or the economy.

Consider, for example, the size of the U.S. population that has grown dramatically over the period 1960 to 1995. As a consequence, U.S. government expenditures have grown in part because the nation's population has grown. We know that population growth shifts the demand curve rightward for most goods and services, including government services, other things being equal. Furthermore, consider that real economic growth has been substantial in the United States over the past 50 years, causing the overall size of the U.S. economy to grow dramatically. With growth in output and income, we expect greater demand for government services and hence a larger public sector.

Meaningful measures of the size of the public sector must take into account changes in the size of the country measured by population or changes in the size of the economy measured by GDP in order to obtain an accurate picture of the public sector.

Adjusting for GDP Growth

Table 2.4 reports receipts, outlays, surpluses/deficits, and debt of the federal government over the period 1940 to 2000 as percentages of GDP. This table purposely covers a longer period of time in order to illustrate the dramatic effects of World War II. By computing receipts and expenditures relative to GDP, we are scaling these measures and making them relative to the overall size of the economy. Hence, the receipts and expenditures in Table 2.4

TABLE 2.4 Federal Budget Receipts, Outlays, Surplus or Deficit, and Debt, as a Percentage of GDP

Fiscal Year or Period	Receipts	Outlays		Surplus or Deficit (−)	Federal Debt (End of Period)	
		Total	National Defense		Gross Federal	Held by Public
1940	6.8	9.8	1.7	−3.0	52.4	44.2
1945	20.4	41.9	37.5	−21.5	117.5	106.2
1950	14.4	15.6	5.0	−1.1	94.1	80.2
1955	16.5	17.3	10.8	−.8	69.3	57.2
1960	17.8	17.8	9.3	.1	56.0	45.6
1965	17.0	17.2	7.4	−.2	46.9	37.9
1970	19.0	19.3	8.1	−.3	37.6	28.0
1975	17.9	21.3	5.5	−3.4	34.7	25.3
1980	19.0	21.7	4.9	−2.7	33.4	26.1
1985	17.7	22.8	6.1	−5.1	43.8	36.4
1990	18.0	21.9	5.2	−3.9	55.9	42.1
1995	18.4	20.6	3.7	−2.2	67.0	49.1
2000	20.6	18.2	3.0	2.4	57.3	34.7
2005	17.3	19.9	4.0	−2.6	63.5	36.9
2010 (estimates)	14.8	25.4	4.9	−10.6	94.3	63.6

Source: *Economic Report of the President* 2010, Table B79.

provide insight on the size of the federal government, relative to the overall size of the economy. Consider federal outlays, for example. Prior to World War II, federal outlays were 9.8 percent of GDP. By the last year of the war in 1945, however, federal outlays were 41.9 percent of GDP, reflecting a tremendous growth in the size of the federal government relative to the economy as a whole. By 1950 federal outlays had fallen back down to 15.6 percent of GDP. Since that time federal outlays have grown relative to GDP, reaching a peak of 22.8 percent in 1985 and falling somewhat to 18.2 percent in 2000.

The size of the federal deficit and debt is also put in perspective relative to the overall economy in Table 2.4. The federal government deficit was at its largest in 1945 when it represented 21.5 percent of GDP. Since that time, and until the recession from 2007 to 2009, the annual deficit was in the range of 1 to 5 percent, reaching a peak of 5.1 percent in 1985 and falling to 2.2 percent in 1995 prior to the historic switch to a surplus in 1998 after deficits since 1969. The year 2000 surplus was 2.4 percent of GDP. With the severe recession of 2007 to 2009 and the unprecedented $800 billion fiscal stimulus package implemented to stave off a severe economic downturn, the deficit grew to more than 10 percent of GDP—a level not seen since World War II. In similar fashion, we see that the federal government debt was at its highest in 1945 when it reached 117.5 percent of GDP. Since that time, the debt generally fell to a low of 33.3 percent of GDP in 1980, rose to 67.2 percent of GDP in 1995, and then fell back down to 57.3 percent of GDP with the budget surpluses of the late 1990s. Since the year 2000, however, the debt grew modestly through 2005 and then expanded dramatically in response to the unprecedented fiscal policy actions in response to the recession of 2007 to 2009. In 2010 the debt reached 94 percent of GDP, a level not seen since World War II.

Adjusting for Population Growth

If we use the population of the country as our measure of overall size, we can compute measures of the public sector in per capita terms. Dividing receipts, expenditures, and surplus/deficit data by total population converts the data into per capita terms, the amount per person. Table 2.5 provides information on the same measures of public sector size as we considered in Tables 2.1–2.3, except the numbers in Table 2.5 are expressed in terms of current dollars per capita. For example, Table 2.5 indicates that in 2010 total government receipts were $13,020 per capita, whereas expenditures were $17,219 per capita. The difference, of course, is the deficit amount of $4,199 per capita. What does the per capita data tell us that we could not see otherwise? It tells us the main advantage is that per capita data give us a feel for the magnitude of the public sector as it makes the data comparable on a per-person basis. When we see in Table 2.5 that the federal receipts in 2010 were equal to $7,827 per capita and state and local receipts equal another $6,940 per capita, we get an immediate feel for the size of the public sector that may be lost when the data is expressed in billions of dollars.

Keep in mind that when we consider per capita measures of public sector size, we are controlling for population but not for inflation or GDP. It is possible to take real data such as those in Table 2.3 and divide by population to obtain real per capita data. Such data adjust for both population size and inflation. One would not, however, adjust per capita data for GDP growth. A choice must be made as to which measure of the economy is to be used to adjust the data, either population or GDP, but not both.

Public Sector Employment

Another way to measure public sector size is to examine the level of public sector employment. Table 2.6 reports public sector employment in the United States for the period from 1965 to 2010. Total public sector employment rose from 10.191 million in 1965 to 22,471 million in 2010. Although the overall trend has been one of rising public sector employment over the past 45 years, the composition of public sector employment has undergone a substantial

TABLE 2.5 Total, Federal, and State and Local Government Receipts and Current Expenditures (Current Dollars per Capita), 1960–2009

	Total Government			Federal Government			State and Local Government			
Year or Quarter	Current Receipts	Current Expenditures	Net Government Saving (NIPA)	Current Receipts	Current Expenditures	Net Federal Government Saving (NIPA)	Current Receipts	Current Expenditures	Net State and Local Government Saving (NIPA)	Addendum: Grants-in-Aid to State and Local Governments
1960	743.9	680.8	63.1	519.7	480.4	39.3	246.3	222.5	23.8	22.1
1965	927.9	878.0	50.4	622.7	605.8	16.5	342.2	308.8	33.5	37.1
1970	1,399.2	1,439.6	−41.0	907.6	983.2	−75.6	585.7	551.1	34.6	94.1
1975	2,047.0	2,362.3	−315.8	1,285.3	1,612.7	−326.9	970.5	958.9	11.6	208.8
1980	3,507.3	3,717.2	−209.9	2,339.7	2,588.6	−248.5	1,485.1	1,446.5	38.6	317.5
1985	5,093.4	5,748.8	−655.4	3,247.4	3,996.4	−749.0	2,185.2	2,091.3	93.9	339.3
1990	6,833.6	7,514.0	−680.8	4,328.9	5,034.1	−705.2	2,950.4	2,925.7	24.8	445.4
1995	8,311.5	9,050.6	−739.1	5,281.4	6,055.0	−773.6	3,721.2	3,686.6	34.5	691.0
2000	11,092.7	10,290.9	802.1	7,284.7	6,628.9	655.8	4,683.7	4,537.4	146.3	875.8
2005	12,362.8	13,231.3	−868.6	7,737.0	8,693.1	−956.1	5,846.1	5,758.6	87.5	1,220.3
2010p	13,020.1	17,219.3	−4,199.2	7,826.5	12,180.6	−4,354.1	6,940.0	6,785.5	154.5	1,746.7

Source: Computed from *Economic Report of the President* 2010, Tables B82 and B34.

TABLE 2.6 Public Sector Employment, 1965–2009

Year	Total Civilian Employ-ment	Government Employment				Government Employment as a Percent of Civilian Labor Force				Public Employment Shares	
		Total	Federal	State	Local	Total	Federal	State	Local	Federal	State and Local
1965	71,088	10,191	2,495	1,996	5,700	14.3	3.5	2.8	8.0	24.5	75.5
1970	78,678	12,687	2,865	2,664	7,158	16.1	3.6	3.4	9.1	22.6	77.4
1975	85,846	14,820	2,882	3,179	8,758	17.3	3.4	3.7	10.2	19.4	80.5
1980	99,303	16,375	3,000	3,610	9,765	16.5	3.0	3.6	9.8	18.3	81.7
1985	107,150	16,533	3,014	3,832	9,687	15.4	2.8	3.6	9.0	18.2	81.8
1990	118,793	18,415	3,196	4,305	10,914	15.5	2.7	3.6	9.2	17.4	82.6
1995	124,900	19,432	2,949	4,635	11,849	15.6	2.4	3.7	9.5	15.2	84.8
2000	136,891	20,790	2,865	4,786	13,139	15.2	2.1	3.5	9.6	13.8	86.2
2005	141,730	21,804	2,732	5,032	14,041	15.4	1.9	3.6	9.9	12.5	87.5
2010p	139,064	22,471	2,959	5,175	14,338	16.2	2.1	3.7	10.3	13.2	86.8

Source: *Economic Report of the President* 2010, Tables B-36 and B-46.

shift from federal employment to state and local employment. Back in 1965, federal employment accounted for 24.5 percent of all public sector employment. But, in 2010, federal employment accounted for just 13.2 percent of total public sector employment. There has been a continuing trend of the increasing importance of state and local employment. If you look at the 2010 data, you see that there are fewer than 3 million federal civilian employees but nearly 20 million state and local government employees—probably not what you expected. State and local government employment accounts for 87 percent of total public sector employment. Federal employment peaked in 1990 and fell over the period through 2005, but has risen again more recently. State and local government employment continues to rise consistently.

Table 2.6 also gives total civilian employment in the United States, which can be used to compute the share of total employment in the public sector. The third panel of data columns in the table reports this share, as well as the breakdown of federal, state, and local shares. Over the past 45 years the share of total civilian employment due to the public sector has fluctuated between approximately 14 and 17 percent. The share was lowest in 1965 and highest in 1975, stabilized in the range of 15 percent over the period from 1985 to 2005, and increased to just over 16 percent in 2010.

Measuring the Size of Subnational Government: U.S. State Taxes

Within the United States, it is informative to consider measures of state government size. Table 2.7 gives state government tax revenues (from sales, income and other taxes) and direct expenditures (not including intergovernmental expenditures) per capita in 2008. Total and per capita tax revenues, total and per capita direct expenditures, and population are all listed for each of the 50 states along with the rankings (1 is highest, 50 is lowest). Such data make it possible to consider the degree of variation among states in the size of state government.

Which state has the highest tax revenue per capita? Alaska is highest with taxes of $12,243 per capita, followed by Wyoming with total revenue per capita of $4,512 and Connecticut with $4,167. Which state has the lowest total tax revenue per capita? South Dakota is lowest with tax revenue of $1,642 per person. Other low total tax revenue per capita states include New Hampshire (whose state slogan is "Live Free or Die"), South Carolina, and Texas. The national average among states in total revenue per capita is $2,568, but Table 2.7 illustrates vividly that there is substantial variation among states around that national average.

This type of tax data and ranking is commonly used by politicians and others in the public sector for various purposes. Sometimes, public officials want to demonstrate to potential business leaders who might locate in their state that the business climate in that state is attractive. Of course, there are many other factors that contribute to a beneficial business climate, but taxes are invariably one of the factors considered. Such rankings, although popular, can be quite misleading. Reconsider the case of Alaska, for example. Why do you suppose that total tax revenue per capita is so high in Alaska? Is it

Wisconsin Governor Scott Walker speaks to the media about state budget problems.

because total taxes collected are high or because there are not many people living in Alaska? Remember, for a ratio to be high requires that the numerator be large or the denominator be small or both. In the case of Alaska, taxes per capita are high for both reasons. But there is still more to the story.

One reason the ratio is high is that Alaska collects a great deal of severance tax revenue from oil produced there. Severance taxes are taxes levied on natural resources extracted from the ground (severed), such as oil and coal. Who pays those severance taxes, Alaska residents? Probably not. Oil produced in Alaska is sold to buyers outside of Alaska who pay the severance tax and may then pass it (or part of it) along to their customers in the form of higher prices, employees in the form of lower wages, or shareholders in the form of lower dividends. In any case, most of those who ultimately bear the burden of the Alaskan severance tax are outside Alaska. They are not counted in the denominator when we compute the per capita taxes in Alaska. As a result, we are not very concerned about Alaska's high tax revenue ranking. It does not mean taxes paid by Alaska residents are the highest in the country.

A relatively high total tax revenue per capita is found in a state like Connecticut, ranking third in the country. Although some of the tax burden there too is probably exported out of the state, most of the tax in Connecticut is made up of state income and sales taxes. Unlike the Alaskan case, Connecticut residents truly face a relatively high level of taxation. So too do residents of Vermont, Hawaii, and other states with high ranks in total tax revenue per capita.

If tax revenue is high on a per capita basis, is that reason for concern? Perhaps so, but then again, perhaps not. Consider the case of Connecticut. Should we be concerned on behalf of Connecticut residents that they pay high taxes per person? Does it matter that they have one of the highest per capita income measures in the country? Shouldn't we expect people with

TABLE 2.7 State Revenues and Expenditures per Capita ($ Thousands), 2008

	Tax Revenue ($1,000)	Direct Expenditure ($1,000)	Tax Revenue per Capita	Rank	Direct Expenditure per Capita	Rank	Population	Rank
UNITED STATES	781,647,244	1,256,776,878	2,568.04		4,129.04		304,374,846	
ALABAMA	9,070,530	18,171,925	1,939.20	42	3,885.00	33	4,677,464	23
ALASKA	8,424,714	8,628,265	12,243.00	1	12,538.80	1	688,125	47
ARIZONA	13,705,901	20,537,003	2,108.80	39	3,159.84	47	6,499,377	15
ARKANSAS	7,530,504	11,263,413	2,625.91	19	3,927.59	31	2,867,764	32
CALIFORNIA	117,361,976	153,040,151	3,208.33	12	4,183.67	26	36,580,371	1
COLORADO	9,624,636	16,578,390	1,950.20	40	3,359.20	44	4,935,213	22
CONNECTICUT	14,597,970	19,297,498	4,167.36	3	5,508.96	10	3,502,932	29
DELAWARE	2,930,955	5,979,858	3,345.03	11	6,824.68	3	876,211	45
FLORIDA	35,849,998	57,492,367	1,945.84	41	3,120.54	48	18,423,878	4
GEORGIA	18,070,032	30,749,733	1,863.31	44	3,170.78	45	9,697,838	9
HAWAII	5,147,569	10,396,098	3,998.17	5	8,074.76	2	1,287,481	42
IDAHO	3,651,917	5,637,576	2,390.77	28	3,690.71	38	1,527,506	39
ILLINOIS	31,890,924	48,618,172	2,483.15	24	3,785.59	35	12,842,954	5
INDIANA	15,116,208	22,813,823	2,366.23	30	3,571.18	42	6,388,309	16
IOWA	6,892,026	12,379,777	2,301.96	35	4,134.88	28	2,993,987	30
KANSAS	7,159,748	10,754,336	2,559.45	21	3,844.44	34	2,797,375	33
KENTUCKY	10,056,293	20,720,560	2,345.26	32	4,832.30	17	4,287,931	26
LOUISIANA	11,003,870	26,981,138	2,471.94	26	6,061.12	6	4,451,513	25
MAINE	3,785,719	6,815,572	2,868.64	13	5,164.52	14	1,319,691	41
MARYLAND	15,713,987	25,520,815	2,776.98	15	4,510.05	21	5,658,655	19
MASSACHUSETTS	21,908,599	36,383,133	3,348.10	10	5,560.11	9	6,543,595	14
MICHIGAN	24,781,626	37,356,409	2,477.55	25	3,734.71	37	10,002,486	8
MINNESOTA	18,320,891	23,094,713	3,502.66	8	4,415.34	23	5,230,567	21
MISSISSIPPI	6,770,880	13,531,213	2,302.85	34	4,602.12	20	2,940,212	31
MISSOURI	10,965,171	21,150,162	1,840.93	46	3,550.87	43	5,956,335	18

MONTANA	2,457,929	4,819,020	2,539.09	23	4,978.15	15	968,035	44
NEBRASKA	4,228,800	6,461,189	2,373.13	29	3,625.91	40	1,781,949	38
NEVADA	6,115,585	6,985,139	2,337.97	33	2,670.39	50	2,615,772	35
NEW HAMPSHIRE	2,251,179	5,149,678	1,703.02	49	3,895.75	32	1,321,872	40
NEW JERSEY	30,616,510	47,611,602	3,534.01	7	5,495.72	11	8,663,398	11
NEW MEXICO	5,645,649	11,444,598	2,841.63	14	5,760.42	8	1,986,763	36
NEW YORK	65,370,654	104,576,875	3,357.89	9	5,371.79	12	19,467,789	3
NORTH CAROLINA	22,781,202	33,511,468	2,463.60	27	3,623.98	41	9,247,134	10
NORTH DAKOTA	2,312,056	3,320,569	3,604.58	6	5,176.89	13	641,421	48
OHIO	26,128,377	49,682,964	2,266.50	37	4,309.74	24	11,528,072	7
OKLAHOMA	8,330,786	15,125,933	2,286.15	36	4,150.89	27	3,644,025	28
OREGON	7,278,718	16,745,890	1,924.06	43	4,426.63	22	3,782,991	27
PENNSYLVANIA	32,123,740	53,834,040	2,556.33	22	4,283.98	25	12,566,368	6
RHODE ISLAND	2,761,356	6,442,088	2,621.12	20	6,114.93	5	1,053,502	43
SOUTH CAROLINA	7,979,367	21,874,379	1,771.90	48	4,857.43	16	4,503,280	24
SOUTH DAKOTA	1,321,368	3,018,467	1,642.41	50	3,751.83	36	804,532	46
TENNESSEE	11,538,430	19,743,961	1,848.97	45	3,163.87	46	6,240,456	17
TEXAS	44,675,953	73,969,186	1,838.19	47	3,043.46	49	24,304,290	2
UTAH	6,109,256	11,243,496	2,240.00	38	4,122.51	29	2,727,343	34
VERMONT	2,544,163	3,729,401	4,096.56	4	6,005.00	7	621,049	49
VIRGINIA	18,408,276	28,732,897	2,361.42	31	3,685.87	39	7,795,424	12
WASHINGTON	17,959,833	30,546,049	2,735.25	16	4,652.10	19	6,566,073	13
WEST VIRGINIA	4,881,908	8,466,365	2,689.94	17	4,664.99	18	1,814,873	37
WISCONSIN	15,088,662	22,536,947	2,681.18	18	4,004.71	30	5,627,610	20
WYOMING	2,404,843	3,312,577	4,512.06	2	6,215.19	4	532,981	50

Source: U.S. Census Bureau, State Government Finances: 2008.

high income to pay high taxes? Definitely. This issue raises a concern with tables of tax burden per capita. They do not take into account the ability to pay of the residents of those states. One might want to consider state taxes as a share of income in order to avoid this problem. Furthermore, such rankings ignore the fundamental issue that the residents of each state have expressed their desires for public services, and the differences we observe in taxes and expenditures may reflect the varying demands for public goods and services.

Table 2.7 also provides information on expenditures per capita. As you scan down the rankings, you see that states that have high taxes per capita tend also to have high expenditures per capita. A high correlation between revenues, taxes, direct expenditures, and total expenditures per capita exist. However, some variations are worthy of mention. A state such as South Carolina is unusual in that it has a relatively low rank on total taxes per capita, ranking 48th in the country, whereas it has a much higher rank on total expenditures per capita, ranking 16th in the country. How is this possible? Well, one factor to take into account is intergovernmental transfers, generally from the federal government to the states, so the difference does not necessarily involve deficit spending. Another part of the difference in ranking may be due to differences in nontax revenues the state may earn, such as utility revenues for state-run utilities, charges and fees, liquor store revenues in states with monopoly liquor store distribution systems, and such. When you look at rankings such as these, you must be mindful of the complexity of state budgets and their interaction with the budgets of both higher and lower levels of government.

An International Comparison of Public Sector Size as a Share of GNP/GDP

It is also revealing to compare the size of the public sector across countries of the world. A useful measure of government size can be derived by taking total tax revenue and dividing by GDP. This measure can range from zero in the case of no government to 1.0 in the case of a government that takes everything produced in nation's economy in the form of taxes. Of course, neither of these two extreme values is observed in the world. Countries vary widely in the share of GDP that their governments collect in tax revenues. The measure of government size listed in Table 2.8 is total government tax revenue divided by GDP, expressed as a percent and denoted G. This measure varies considerably among OECD countries, with total government revenues being smallest in Mexico ($G = 18.3$) and largest in Denmark ($G = 48.7$). Hence, governments account for 18 to 49 percent of GDP in the various countries of the OECD.

The United States's measure of government size is $G = 28.2$, indicating that total tax revenue collected by governments at all levels accounts for about 28 percent of GDP. Although the United States places a relatively strong emphasis on allowing markets to operate free of government intervention, it must be recognized that the government revenues collected in that free market–oriented system still account for more than a quarter of the total value of the economy's output.

TABLE 2.8 International Estimates of Public Sector Size: Total Tax Revenues as a Share of GDP for OECD Countries, 2007

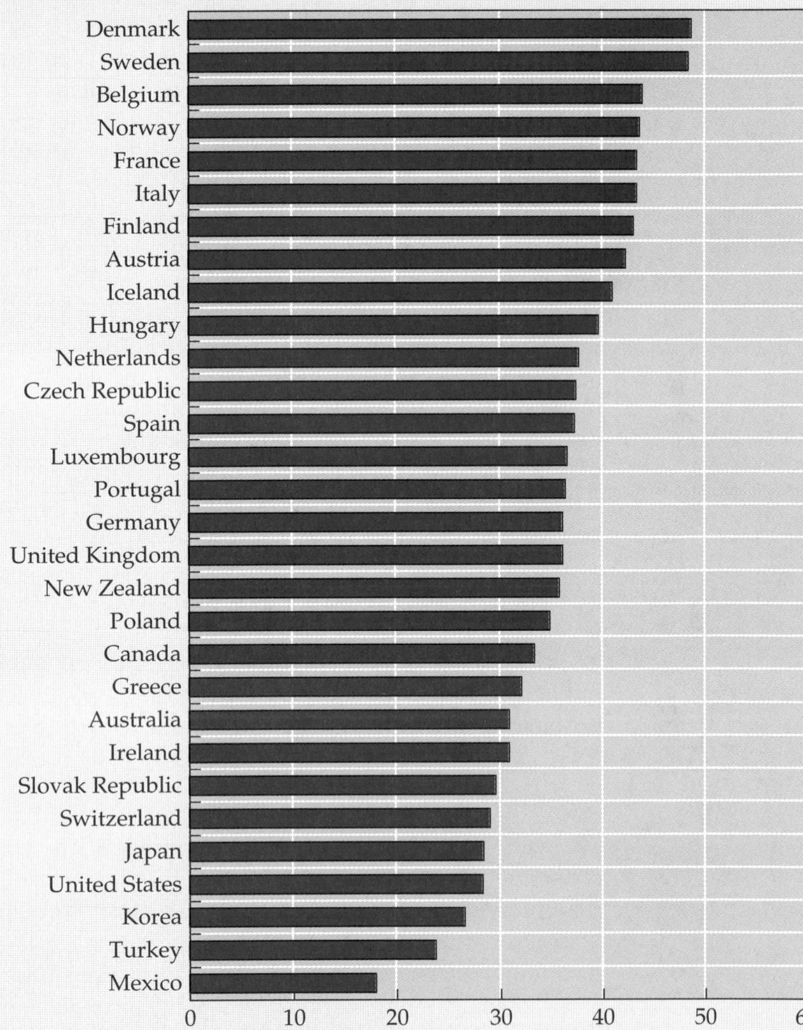

Source: Based on data from Public Sector, Taxation and Market Regulation, OECD. Stat Extracts http://stats.oecd.org/Index.aspx.

METHODS OF ECONOMIC ANALYSIS[2]

In this section we consider the methods that are used by public finance economists as they conduct economic and policy analysis of the public sector. First, we examine the ways in which economists go about discovering truth in their discipline. Then, we examine particular methods of quantitative analysis such as econometric models. Finally, useful references are suggested.

Economic Epistemology: How We Know What We Know

Epistemology is the study of how we know what we know. Over the course of thousands of years, philosophers have debated whether we know about the world around us on the basis of pure reasoning or on the basis of empirical insight due to our senses' providing perceptions of the world. The philosophical school of thought known as **rationalism** held that truth is attained through pure intellectual reasoning. With the mind alone, people are able to reason their way to truth, thought the rationalists. A very different school of thought based on **empiricism** held that we cannot simply reason our way to truth; we must rely exclusively on the inputs provided by our senses. Empiricists held that we can only know about the world around us through our sense perceptions; hence, empirical observations based on those sense perceptions provide the only proper basis for knowing.

The revolutionary nature of the **scientific method** is rooted in the fact that it combined these two methods of knowing. When we apply the scientific method, we begin with a set of assumptions from which we draw inferences on the basis of pure reasoning (rationalism). We then subject the predictions of that theoretical model to empirical testing (empiricism), using real-world data. If the data support the prediction of the model, we have reason to believe that the model may capture truth, but if the data refute the predictions of the model, we reject the model.

The discipline of economics is a social science that employs the scientific method to understand how people, firms, and governments react to changes in prices, income, and other key variables of interest. The subdiscipline of public economics is concerned with the application of these methods to the problem of providing public goods and paying for them.

The Economic Method

We must begin with an understanding of what it means to develop an economic explanation for an event that we observe. Consider, for example, the observed trend of increased female labor force participation in the United States over the past 50 years. Many potential explanations for this trend exist, but how does an economic explanation differ from a sociological explanation, a psychological explanation, or a political explanation? The paradigm of economics, which is distinct from the other social sciences, has been summarized by Silberberg (1990) as follows:

> In terms of methodology, economics is that discipline within social science that seeks refutable explanations of changes in human events on the basis of changes in observable constraints, utilizing postulates of behavior and technology, and the simplifying assumption that the unmeasured variables ("tastes") remain constant. (6)

The economic view of the world is one of constrained optimization. People, firms, and government agencies are all seen as optimizing some objective function (utility, profits, costs, etc.) subject to some constraint or set of constraints. First, we study the properties of the optimum, looking to be able to identify the best that can be done in a given set of circumstances. Then, we investigate how the economic agents react to changes in the constraints. For example, how does a family respond to a change in taxable income that follows an increase in their income tax? How does a firm respond to a change in its taxable income due to an increase in the research and development tax credit? How does the local public school district respond to a reduction in its allocation of state education aid?

Economic research begins with the construction of models of behavior that depend on economic factors, at least in part. Those models are based on theories developed to explain how economic factors affect behavior. A theory consists of three essential components. First, we begin with a set A of assertions about the behavior of various agents (individuals, households, firms, government agencies). For example, we may assert that a firm acts so as to maximize profit, or a family acts so as to minimize expenditures on market goods consumed in order to attain a given level of satisfaction from those goods. Second, we need a set of test conditions C that are observable. For example, the variable R may represent the central government's share of total tax revenue in a country. An observation that $R = 0.61$ in Bulgaria in 1992 is such an observable test condition. Finally, there is a set E of events that are predicted by the theory. All together, we then can characterize this system of thought using the symbols A → (C → E), where → means "implies." The set of axioms A implies a system (C → E) within which the test conditions imply a set of events predicted by the theory.

It is important to remember that a theory is a matter of logic and is therefore unprovable. It can be confirmed or refuted, but not proven. The only theories that are useful in economics are those which can be wrong; that is, theories that are refutable. A theory that says it *may* rain tomorrow or it *may not* is no theory at all. Because the theory cannot be refuted, it is of no use to us. A theory that says it *will* rain tomorrow is refutable. We can wait and see if it does rain, and then either confirm the theory's prediction or, in case of no rain, refute the theory. In economics, a theory that says people will save more when income taxes are reduced is an appropriate theory because the theory's predicted event is refutable. For example, we can collect data before and after an income tax reduction and see whether people alter their saving behavior in a predictable way. In other words, any theory must assert that events E will occur, and it must be possible that those events do not occur.

The paradigm of economics, when applied properly, provides refutable hypotheses that are then subjected to empirical testing. In practice, the mathematical method of comparative statics is used to investigate whether a refutable hypothesis can be developed from a theory. That method investigates how sensitive the optimum solution may be to changes in the values of **parameters** in the model. Typical parameters in economic models are price and income. For example, how sensitive is the consumer's choice of the optimal quantity of gasoline to purchase to changes in the price of gasoline or to changes in the consumer's income? If the theory indicates that the consumer's optimal quantity of gasoline falls as its price increases, we have a refutable hypothesis. If no refutable hypothesis is forthcoming, there is no point to collecting data and engaging in empirical examination of the results. No data can ever refute a theory that fails to produce refutable hypotheses.

Consider three alternative hypotheses about the behavior of firms. First, firms act so as to maximize profit π, the difference between gross sales and total cost. Second, firms act so as to maximize some utility function of profit $u(\pi)$, where the utility function is increasing in profit π. We can denote the marginal utility of profit as $u'(\pi)$, and typically assume that it is positive.[3] Profits are not desired for their own sake but for the utility they provide the firm's owners. Third, firms act so as to maximize total sales (revenue). Now consider the refutable hypotheses that may be implied by these behavioral assertions. One such hypothesis is that a firm will reduce its output level when a tax is applied to its output. This is certainly a refutable hypothesis because it is possible that the firm increases output or leaves it unchanged, either of which refutes the hypothesis. Marginal analysis embodied in the typical principles of economics courses provides the result that a profit-maximizing firm will produce that output where **marginal revenue** equals **marginal cost.** When a tax is imposed, the firm's marginal revenue is decreased accordingly, because the additional revenue to the firm from selling another gallon of gasoline is the price of that gallon less the tax that must be paid to the government. Hence profit maximization is expected to lead to the result that a tax will reduce the output of the firm. Figure 2.1 illustrates the situation.

In the absence of the tax, the firm would produce output level Q_1, where $MR = MC$. The imposition of the tax, however, causes the marginal revenue curve to shift downward to $MR - t$ and thus causes the firm to reduce its output to Q_2. In this case, the postulate of profit-maximizing behavior, which is unobservable, leads to the refutable hypothesis that the firm's output will be reduced from Q_1 to Q_2 in response to a tax of t on its output. We

FIGURE 2.1 Effect of Tax on a Profit-Maximizing Firm's Output

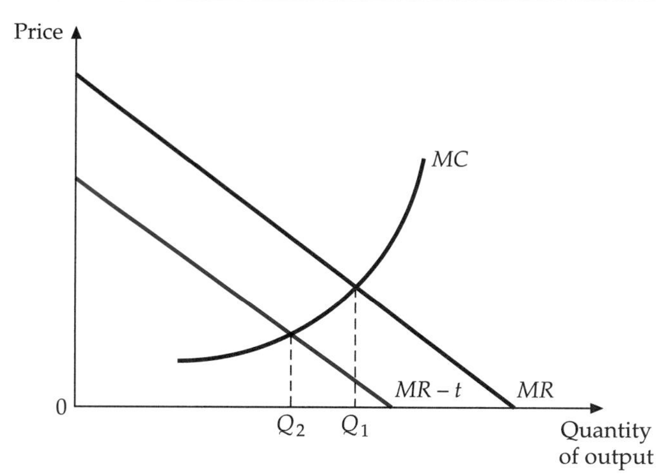

have a prediction concerning a choice variable (output) in response to a change in a parameter facing the decision maker (marginal revenue after tax). Deriving this type of prediction is the purpose of comparative static analysis. We compare the equilibrium output of the model with and without the tax. The second hypothesis, that firms act so as to maximize some utility function of profit, yields the same predicted outcome as the profit maximization model. Hence, there is no way to distinguish between the two theories. No amount of empirical analysis can tell us which theory is correct. This situation reminds us that observed facts can sometimes be consistent with more than one explanatory theory.

The third hypothesis, that firms act so as to maximize sales (revenue), leads to the prediction that the firm will reduce output in reaction to the tax. A sales-maximizing firm will produce that output where marginal revenue is zero. Figure 2.2 illustrates the case. Recall that marginal revenue is the slope of the total revenue curve. If the firm's objective is to maximize total revenue, or sales, then it will sell that quantity of output where its total revenue is at its peak, which occurs where marginal revenue is zero.[4] Hence, the firm will produce output Q_3 in the absence of the tax and reduce output to Q_4 in the presence of the tax. This theory predicts that the firm will respond to the tax by reducing output.

It would appear that this theory is indistinguishable from the profit-maximizing theory, because both predict that output will be reduced in response to the tax. We may be able to distinguish between the two theories, however, if we have information about the revenue and cost functions of the firm. If we know exactly the position and shape of the marginal revenue and marginal cost curves, we can tell the difference between the reduction from Q_1 to Q_2 predicted by the profit maximization model and the reduction from Q_3 to Q_4 predicted by the sales maximization model.

FIGURE 2.2 Effect of a Tax on a Sales-Maximizing Firm

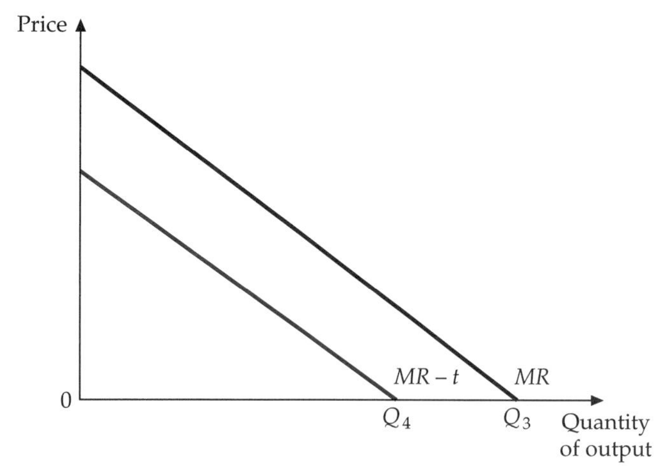

Empirical Methods Used in Economic Analysis

In order to test refutable hypotheses in economics, we need reliable data on economic variables. Fortunately, advanced industrialized nations have been collecting reliable and useful economic and public sector data for several generations. Data on output, prices, interest rates, housing starts, and a myriad of other economic variables are available. In the public sector, data on tax revenues, expenditures by functional category, deficits, and other data are also available.

Induction and Deduction

Economic analysis relies heavily on both probability theory and statistical inference. Key differences exist in the way these tools assist us in analyzing economic events, however. Probability theory is based on **deductive reasoning**—reasoning from knowledge of a known population to the likely characteristics of a sample drawn from that population. For example, if I know that a federal government mandate will affect public elementary schools and I know that 68 percent of all public schools are elementary schools, I can then conclude that there is a 0.68 probability that any public school drawn at random will be affected by the mandate.

On the other hand, statistical inference is based on **inductive reasoning**—reasoning from knowledge of a sample to the likely properties of a population. Suppose that I conduct a survey of public elementary schools and find that 67 percent of the schools surveyed have been affected directly by a particular federal mandate. Due to the sampling process, I also know that there is a 2 percent sampling error. From this information I can conclude that approximately 65 to 69 percent of all public elementary schools are affected by the federal mandate.

There Is More Than One Way to Be Wrong

Of course, there is always the possibility that I have drawn an incorrect inference when applying statistical reasoning. It is important, however, to recall that there is more than one way to make an error in statistical reasoning. Table 2.9 illustrates the two types of errors that can be made. We typically denote the hypothesis being tested as H_0. This is called the **null hypothesis,**

TABLE 2.9 There Are Two Ways to Make a Mistake

	State of Nature	
Decision	**H_0 True**	**H_0 False**
Do not reject H_0	Correct decision	Type II error (probability β)
Reject H_0	Type I error (probability α)	Correct decision

and it typically is a statement of what we do not expect is true. We hope to collect empirical evidence that indicates the null hypothesis is false, leaving us with the alternative hypothesis. For example, suppose that our hypothesis is that a federal mandate will not affect elementary schools: The null hypothesis H_0 is, No fiscal effect is felt from the mandate. The **alternative hypothesis,** denoted H_A, is a fiscal effect felt from the mandate.

Two possible states of nature exist: The null hypothesis may be true or it may be false. Two possible decisions can be made: We can choose to reject the null hypothesis, or we can choose not to reject the null hypothesis.

Suppose that we are interested in reducing federal spending on some particular welfare program that we believe goes to undeserving recipients. Our null hypothesis is that the recipients are deserving of the federal assistance, H_0: Recipients are deserving of continued assistance. The alternative is that they are undeserving of the assistance, H_A: Recipients are undeserving of continued assistance. If the recipients are deserving and we cut the program because we think they are undeserving, we have made an error, a **Type I error.** However, there is another way to make an error in this policy situation. If the recipients are undeserving and we continue the program, we also make an error, a **Type II error.** One of the most difficult aspects of policymaking is taking care to consider both Type I and Type II errors. Political rhetoric on public policy topics often strenuously emphasizes one type of error or the other, but rarely is there consideration of both types of error.

Econometric Models

A simple **regression model** begins with a relationship between two economic variables determined by a theory that predicts a causal relation. Suppose that our economic theory predicts that a variable x will influence a variable y. In particular, because we are interested in explaining the size of the public sector in this chapter, suppose that we want to explain what determines total government receipts. Our dependent variable y is total government receipts, including federal, state, and local government receipts. The explanatory variable x is the output of the economy, or GDP. We hypothesize a linear relationship between the variables

$$y = \beta_0 + \beta_1 x + \in \tag{2.1}$$

where β_0 is the y intercept, β_1 is the slope, and $\in$ is an error term. This equation is a model of total government receipts (federal, state, and local) that says receipts have three components: a component β_0 that is independent of GDP, a component $\beta_1 x$ that depends on GDP, and a random error component $\in$. We do not know the actual values of either of the parameters β_0 or β_1, but we would like to estimate them using a sample of economic data we have collected on the two variables x and y. We do not expect that our estimated relationship will be determined exactly. For any value of x, our predicted y may differ from the true y corresponding to x by some error. We expect those errors, however, to be entirely random and unrelated to x.

FIGURE 2.3 Fitting a Regression Line to Data

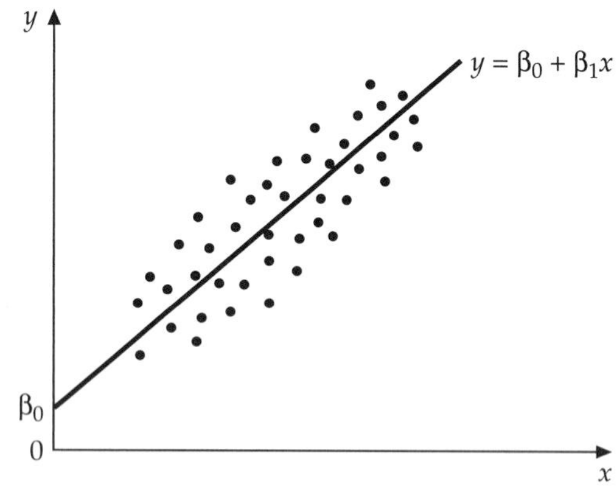

Figure 2.3 shows a hypothetical set of data points collected. Plotted in two-dimensional space, the information appears as a cloud of data. Through the scatter of data points is a line that represents the causal relationship underlying the sample data. This is called the **regression line.** Regression analysis typically fits a line to a data set in such a way as to minimize the sum of the squared distances from each data point to the regression line. This method of fitting a regression line is called the **ordinary least squares (OLS) method.** In this sense, regression methods produce the best fit with the data that is possible. Applications of this method appear frequently in economic analysis. In fact, regression analysis is the primary analytic tool used to test economic theories using empirical data. Regression analysis, usually taught at the end of a first-semester introduction to statistics and covered in more depth in a course called econometrics, is the most important tool used in conducting applied economic analysis.

Returning to our model of total government receipts, we would expect that y would rise with x; higher government receipts are caused by higher GDP, reflecting the fact that as the economy grows and produces more output, there is more taxable income, resulting in more federal and state income taxes, and there are more taxable transactions, resulting in more state and local sales tax revenues. As a result, we would expect the parameter estimate β_1 to be positive. We would first collect a sample of annual data on total government receipts and GDP and estimate the regression equation. Then, we could test the null hypothesis H_0: $\beta_1 = 0$ (GDP has no effect on receipts) versus the alternative hypothesis H_A: $\beta_1 \neq 0$ (GDP does affect receipts). In order to conduct such a hypothesis test, we must have an estimate of the standard error of the coefficient estimator as well—a measure of the variability in our coefficient estimate due to sampling error. If we denote the standard error as s and assume that we have a large sample (roughly speaking, a large sample is at least 30 observations), we can test the hypothesis by constructing the ratio of our estimated value of the coefficient to its standard error: β_1/s. If this ratio

TABLE 2.10 Regression Models of U.S. Total Government Receipts 1980–2008

Variable	Model 1 Coefficient Estimate (Standard Error)	Model 2 Variables Transformed to Logarithms Coefficient Estimate (Standard Error)	Model 3 Variables Transformed to Logarithms Coefficient Estimate (Standard Error)
Constant	−13.084	−1.604	−1.557
	(17.965)	(0.041)	(0.057)
GDP	0.294	1.043	1.041
	(0.003)	(0.005)	(0.005)
Unemployment Rate			−0.017
			(0.023)

is greater than 1.96, we can reject the null hypothesis. This test has a confidence level of 95 percent, meaning that we have a 5 percent chance of making a Type I error. If we want to be more confident of our result, say with a 1 percent chance of making a Type I error, the critical value of the ratio is approximately 2.5. Regression results are generally reported in research papers with coefficient estimates, standard errors, and the ratio of the coefficient estimate to its standard error, known as a *t* statistic. When we have fewer than 30 observations, we use the critical value of the **student-*t* distribution.**[5]

Using annual data for the years 1960 to 2008 for the United States, the estimated regression equation coefficients for this model, labeled model 1, are standard errors reported in Table 2.10. The estimated regression equation can be written as

$$y = -13.08 + 0.29x \tag{2.2}$$

where y and x are both measured in billions of current dollars. The estimated value of the slope coefficient β_1 is 0.29, indicating that an additional billion dollars in GDP results in additional government receipts of \$290 million. In other words, for every additional dollar of GDP produced in the economy, government receipts rise by about \$0.29. When the data are measured in levels, the estimated slope coefficient β_1 gives us the rate of change of y with respect to x.

The constant term is the intercept in the model and has no particular economic meaning in this context. You might be tempted to interpret the constant as that level of government receipts when GDP is zero. That is correct, but keep in mind that the data for the period 1960 to 2008 did not include any observations where U.S. GDP was anywhere near zero. In fact, GDP ranged from about \$526 million in 1960 to about \$14.4 trillion in 2008. Hence, the constant term is the projection back to the vertical axis where GDP is zero, but that is not a meaningful economic concept here because our data range for GDP goes from \$526 million to \$14.4 trillion.

We can test the hypothesis that GDP has no effect on government receipts by taking the ratio of the estimated coefficient on x to its standard error: β_1/s. In this case that ratio is 107.08, which is far larger than the critical value of $t = 2.01$ (for a 5 percent probability of a Type I error) and indicates that GDP definitely has an effect on government receipts.

Another way to specify the regression model is useful. If we transform the variables x and y by taking their logarithms, then our estimate of β_1 will be the elasticity of government revenues with respect to GDP. Recall that the elasticity is the percentage change in receipts divided by the percentage change in GDP. Thus, by transforming the data into logarithms and estimating the regression, we obtain the estimated elasticity. Model 2 in Table 2.10 reports the coefficient estimates for the case where the data have been transformed into logarithms. In this case, the estimate of β_1 is 1.04, which indicates that total government receipts are approximately unitary elastic with respect to GDP. That is, a 1 percent increase in GDP results in approximately a 1 percent (1.04 percent) increase in total government receipts. Hence, we see that the U.S. tax system generates revenues in proportion to the nation's GDP. Problems are rarely so simple in the real world of policy. Consider, for example, the prospect that government receipts are also affected by the unemployment rate. We might expect that the higher the unemployment rate, for any level of GDP, the lower the total government receipts would be. In this case, there are two independent variables: x_1 representing GDP and x_2 representing population. The regression equation is then

$$y = \beta_0 + \beta_1 x_1 + \beta_2 x_2 + \in \tag{2.3}$$

and we must estimate the three parameters β_0, β_1, and β_2. In this case, we would be interested in the policy question of whether the unemployment rate has an effect on government receipts, aside from the effect of GDP on government receipts. In order to test the null hypothesis H_0 that the unemployment rate has no effect on GDP, $\beta_2 = 0$, versus the alternative hypothesis H_A that it does have an effect, $\beta_2 \neq 0$, we would construct the ratio of our estimate of the unemployment rate coefficient to its standard error, β_2/s_2, and check whether it exceeds the critical value, given our level of confidence. Table 2.10 reports the results of this model 3 estimation. Notice that the unemployment rate variable has an estimated coefficient of -0.017, indicating that as the unemployment rate rises total government receipts fall slightly, holding GDP constant. Because this variable is measured as the logarithm of the unemployment rate, this estimated coefficient can be interpreted as the unemployment elasticity of receipts. A 1 percent increase in the unemployment rate leads to a 0.017 percent decrease in total government receipts, other things equal (specifically GDP). The impact of the unemployment rate is not significant, however, because we cannot reject the null hypothesis of no effect. The ratio of our estimated coefficient to its standard error β_2/s_2 is -0.767, which is smaller than the critical t value of 2.06. Notice also, that after we add the unemployment rate variable to the model, the estimated GDP elasticity increases to 1.041, indicating a somewhat less elastic relationship between GDP and total government receipts. The addition of the unemployment rate to the model does not add explanatory power, however. The reason is that GDP captures the effect of changes in the economy having an impact on government receipts, and the addition of the unemployment rate to the model adds nothing to the explanatory ability of the model.

Economic Literature and Data Sources

The literature of economics is vast, but there are several predictable places to look for quality research on topics related to public finance. The top-quality academic research journals are highly technical, requiring a solid background in mathematics and statistics in order to read and comprehend. Among the best academic journals where you can find good research on public finance topics are:

American Economic Review
Review of Economics and Statistics
Journal of Economic Perspectives
Brookings Papers
Southern Economic Journal
Economic Inquiry
Journal of Political Economy
Quarterly Journal of Economics

These are general interest journals that publish articles on a wide range of topics, including public finance. More specialized journals also exist, with a specific focus on public finance. They include:

Journal of Public Economics
Public Finance/Finances Publique
National Tax Journal
Public Finance Review
International Tax and Public Finance

For more general views of public policy analysis and public sector management issues, see the following journals:

Journal of Public Budgeting and Finance
Journal of Policy Analysis and Management
Policy Studies Journal
Policy Studies Review

Issues in local public economics at the urban and regional levels are covered by the following journals:

Journal of Urban Economics
Regional Science and Urban Economics
Journal of Regional Science
Land Economics

Two general purpose sources of good economic information on the U.S. economy are the *Economic Report of the President,* written annually by the Council of Economic Advisers (published by the U.S. Government Printing Office) and transmitted to Congress in February each year, and *The Statistical Abstract of the United States.* The President's report has extensive data tables at the back, which are very useful to the student of economics. The statistical abstract is a vast compilation of data which are very useful.

ON THE WEB

For more on the methods economists use in analyzing behavior, see the Policy Study "Voting for an Increase in the Local Property Tax" on the companion website (www.cengage.com/international).

Statistical data on the U.S. income tax are available in the *SOI Bulletin* (Statistics of Income) published quarterly by the Internal Revenue Service. Of course, the *Census of Governments,* published by the U.S. Department of Commerce, Bureau of the Census, is also very valuable for state and local government data. For a general website where you can find many federal data sources, see the Fedstats site at *www.fedstats.gov.*

For international data providing expenditure and tax information for most of the world's countries, see the *Government Finance Statistics Yearbook,* published annually by the International Monetary Fund (IMF). The IMF website can be found at *www.imf.org.*

The World Wide Web (WWW) has a number of sites with specific public finance information. See, for example:

Federal Budget Information: *http://www.gpoaccess.gov/usbudget/*
Internal Revenue Service (IRS): *www.irs.ustreas.gov*
Census of Governments: *www.census.gov*
U.S. Treasury: *www.ustreas.gov*
Congressional Budget Office: *www.cbo.gov*
Congressional Quarterly: *www.cq.gov*
National Tax Association (NTA): *www.ntanet.org*
National Conference of State Legislatures: *www.ncsl.org*
National Bureau of Economic Research (NBER): *www.nber.org*

Finally, there are many other resources useful to students of economics available on the Internet. A good place to start a search of resources for economists is at the Resources for Economists (RFE) website, *http://wuecon.wustl.edu/other_www/EconFAQ/EconFAQ.html. http://rfe.org*

PROBLEMS

1. Use the figures in Table 2.1 to answer the following questions:
   a. For which decade did federal government current expenditures rise more, the 1980s or the 1990s?
   b. During the period 1995 to 2005, which grew faster, federal government current expenditures or state and local government current expenditures?
   c. Compute the rate of growth in state and local government current expenditures for the periods 1995 to 2000 and 2000 to 2005, and explain whether there was been a significant change.

2. Use the figures in Table 2.3 to answer the following questions:
    a. For which five-year period listed in the table was the rate of growth of federal government expenditures greatest?
    b. For which five-year period listed in the table was the rate of growth of state and local government expenditures greatest?
    c. For which five-year period listed in the table was the rate of growth in grants to state and local governments greatest?
3. Use the figures in Table 2.4 to answer the following questions:
    a. For the period 1970 to 2005 compute the rate of growth in federal receipts (as a percentage of GDP) for each five-year period. Identify the five-year time period over which receipts grew fastest as a percentage of GDP.
    b. For the period 1980 to 2005 compute the rate of growth in federal debt (as a percentage of GDP) for each five-year period. Identify the five-year period over which federal debt grew fastest as a share of GDP.
4. Use the figures in Table 2.5 to answer the following questions:
    a. For which five-year period listed in the table was the rate of growth of federal government expenditures per capita greatest?
    b. For which five-year period listed in the table was the rate of growth of state and local government expenditures per capita greatest?
    c. For which five-year period listed in the table was the rate of growth in grants to state and local governments per capita greatest?
5. Find the state of your residence in Table 2.7. Note where it ranks in total taxes per capita and state taxes per capita.
    a. Can you explain why your state ranks as it does? Are there particular features of your state's economy that affect its ranking?
    b. Find the ranking for a neighboring state in Table 2.7. Explain why there may be similarities or differences between your home state and the neighbor state.
    c. If you are originally from a state other than your current state of residence, look up both states in Table 2.7 and see if you can explain, on the basis of your knowledge of the two states, why their rankings may differ.
6. Use the GDP deflator reported in the table below to convert the nominal expenditure per capita figures in Table 2.5 into real terms, answering the following questions:
    a. Explain how real per capita federal expenditures changed over the period 2000 to 2010. Compare this to the change in nominal per capita federal expenditures.
    b. Explain how real per capita state and local government expenditures changed over the period 1995 to 2005. Compare this to the change in nominal per capita state and local government expenditures.
    c. Explain how real per capita grants to state and local governments changed over the period 1980 to 1990. Compare this to the change in nominal per capita grants to state and local governments.

Year	GDP Deflator (2005 = 100)
1960	18.604
1965	19.919
1970	24.317
1975	33.563
1980	47.751
1985	61.576
1990	72.201
1995	81.536
2000	88.647
2005	100.000
2010p	110.654

Source: *Economic Report of the President* 2010, Table B-7.

7. Use the population figures reported in the table below to convert the real government receipts and expenditures in Table 2.3 into real per capita terms, answering the following questions:

Year	Population of U.S. (Thousands)
1960	180,671
1965	194,303
1970	205,052
1975	215,973
1980	227,726
1985	238,466
1990	250,132
1995	266,557
2000	282,385
2005	295,994
2010	308,746

Source: *Economic Report of the President* 2010, Table B-34.

a. Explain how real per capita federal expenditures changed over the period 2000 to 2010. Compare this to the change in nominal per capita federal expenditures.
b. Explain how real per capita state and local government expenditures changed over the period 1985 to 1995. Compare this to the change in nominal per capita state and local government expenditures.
c. Explain how real per capita grants to state and local governments changed over the period 1970 to 1980. Compare this to the change in nominal per capita grants to state and local governments.

8. Use the information in the following table on receipts by the federal government and by state and local governments to support your evaluation of the following proposition: *During the period 2000 to 2010, federal government receipts grew more in real terms than state and local government receipts.*

Fiscal Year	Federal Government Receipts (Billions of Current Dollars)	State and Local Government Receipts (Billions of Current Dollars)	GDP Deflator (2005 = 100)
2000	2,057.1	1,322.6	88.648
2010	2,416.4	2,142.7	110.654

REFERENCES

Economic Report of the President 2010, Executive Office of the President. Washington, DC: U.S. Government Printing Office. Available at: http://www.gpoaccess.gov/eop/.

Rubinfeld, Daniel L. "Voting in a Local School Election: A Micro Analysis," *Review of Economics and Statistics* 58 (1976): 30–42.

Silberberg, Eugene. *The Structure of Economics: A Mathematical Analysis.* New York: McGraw-Hill, 1990.

NOTES

1. Readers may be more familiar with the Consumer Price Index (CPI) as a measure of inflation. We do not use the CPI to deflate nominal revenues and expenditures, however, as it is a rather narrow measure of inflation. Think of the GDP as consisting of consumption expenditures (C), government expenditures (G), investment (I), and net exports ($X - IM$). The CPI only measures inflation in the prices of consumer goods and services—the C part of GDP. The GDP deflator is a broader measure of inflation that takes into account prices of all the components of the GDP.

2. The material in this section involves modeling and statistical analysis, typically covered in the introductory statistics course in an economics curriculum. Readers with a strong background in economics and statistics may wish to use this material for a quick review or skip it entirely, whereas readers with less background in economics and statistics will find the information here useful.
3. The expression $u9(x)$ denotes the first derivative of the function $u(x)$ with respect to x: $du(x)/dx$. In the context of this application the derivative is the marginal utility of profit.
4. This is also true at the minimum of total revenue, so we also need rest assured that the second-order condition holds, that marginal revenue is declining.
5. Technically, the critical value of 1.96 applies when we know the sample data are drawn from a population with a normal distribution or from a population of unknown distribution of sufficient sample size that the normal approximation applies. That sample size is generally 30. When the sample size is less than 30, and we do not know that we are drawing from a normal distribution, we use the student-*t* distribution. In that case, another parameter is used, called the *degrees of freedom*, which is the sample size minus the number of estimated coefficients in the model.

Radius Images/Getty Images

PART TWO

Market Efficiency, Market Failure, and the Need for Governments

Radius Images/Getty Images

CHAPTER 3

Welfare Economics and Public Goods

LEARNING OBJECTIVES

1. Describe how the market mechanism provides for an efficient allocation of resources.
2. Describe the nature of public goods and how they differ from private goods.
3. Analyze how public goods can be allocated efficiently.

Entrepreneurs are quick to respond to opportunities in the marketplace, taking risks and producing goods or services that people want. Consider the origins of the personal computer industry, for example.[1] In the mid-1970s, 19-year-old Bill Gates wrote a high-level programming language based on the BASIC computer language to run on the Altair hobbyist computer. Although the Altair designers thought their machine too primitive to run such software, Gates and his friend, Paul Allen, thought otherwise and proved themselves correct. Dropping out of Harvard University after his sophomore year, Gates founded the Microsoft Corporation. Meanwhile, Steve Wozniak, an engineer at Hewlett-Packard, built the Apple computer simply to impress his friends in the Silicon Valley Homebrew Computer Club. His friend, Steve Jobs, who worked a part-time job for a video game company, saw the commercial potential in the Apple computer. He offered a Volkswagen Microbus and the use of his parents' garage in exchange for a share of what was to become the Apple Computer Corporation.

These PC industry pioneers continued the legacy of famous prior entrepreneurs. Henry Ford of Dearborn, Michigan, for example, thought that people of even relatively modest incomes would be willing to pay for an automobile if he produced a model and marketed it at a reasonable price. Through assembly line innovation he was able to mass-produce the Model T Ford, which sold very well. Sam Walton, another modern-day entrepreneur, thought discount retailing was a concept whose time had come back in 1962 when he established his first Wal-Mart retail outlet in Rogers, Arkansas. He was betting on the willingness of shoppers to patronize his retail store if he provided convenient service at rock-bottom prices. In all of these famous cases, entrepreneurs took risks in order to provide goods and services to consumers, and they were successful. In each case, the entrepreneur provided an innovative private good or service, and the market rewarded that innovation handsomely.

We have no folktales of entrepreneurs doing similar things, however, with public goods or services—things like national defense, clean air, community safety, public health, and other public goods. To understand why, consider for a moment the legendary story of Moses leading the Israelites in the wilderness. At one point during their wanderings, the disobedient people found themselves surrounded by fiery serpents sent by God. The serpent bites were lethal, and people were dying left and right. God instructed Moses to craft a bronze serpent, put it on a pole, and lift it high in the air. Anyone bitten by a serpent could simply look to the serpent on the pole and live.[2] Incidentally, this is likely to be the origin of the serpent-on-a-pole symbol frequently used to this day by the medical profession.[3]

Now, if Moses were an aspiring entrepreneur in the mold of Bill Gates, Steve Jobs, Henry Ford, and Sam Walton, he might have thought there was an opportunity to cash in on this situation. Just imagine what people would be willing to pay for an immediate cure of a lethal serpent bite! The problem, of course, is that once he put the bronze serpent on the pole high in the air where it was visible to everyone and effective with just a glance, he would have no way to enforce payment. It would be impractical to extract payment from those people using the service. Furthermore, he would have had no way of withholding the service from those unwilling to pay. Deliverance from the fiery serpent calamity by a simple act of faith expressed in a glance was a public good. Moses was doomed. He would never be cited as an example of an early entrepreneur.

Consider the contrast between private goods like automobiles, computer software, and low-priced retailing services, and public goods like the healing provided by a glance at the bronze serpent on a pole. This comparison reveals that markets are perfectly capable of providing private goods very efficiently but are likely to fail miserably in the case of public goods. Given that fact, there is a need for governments to assure that public goods are provided—and in sufficient quantities.

PUBLIC AND PRIVATE GOODS

Rivalry and Exclusion

Public goods are fundamentally different from private goods in two important ways. First, they are **nonrival** in consumption. Two or more individuals may use the public good and benefit fully from its provision simultaneously. A classic example of a public good is national defense. You and I may simultaneously be safe because the federal government has provided a national defense. The provision of that safety to me does not in any way diminish the amount of safety left for you. A given amount of safety is provided to all residents of the country. Private goods are not like that. They are characterized by rivalry. If I consume a gallon of gasoline while driving my car, there is one less gallon of gasoline for you to consume in your car. My consumption and your consumption are **rivalrous.**

The nonrival nature of a public good can also be viewed as jointness in the supply of the good for everyone. The production costs are all fixed, and

Matt Hart/Shutterstock

A lighthouse is a classic example of a public good.

the marginal cost of provision is zero. A further consequence is that a private competitive market will not provide the public good. After all, what private producer operating in a competitive market—where price must equal marginal cost—will provide a good that must be sold at a zero price?

The second important characteristic of public goods is that they are **non-excludable.** If the public good is provided to anyone, it is available to everyone. You cannot exclude some people from using the public good while permitting others to use it. Consider the classic case of a lighthouse used for navigation. If a lighthouse is built on the coast, it is there for everyone to see and use for navigation while sailing. It is not possible to make the lighthouse visible to some (perhaps those willing to pay taxes to pay for it) while making it invisible to others (those unwilling to pay taxes for it).

The lighthouse example raises another important point, however, related to exclusion, as the state of technology is essential to our understanding of public goods. With new technology it is possible that an individual boat owner could buy a sensor that activated the lighthouse beam. This technology would then make lighthouse services a private good. The exclusion problem is solved by selling the sensor-activator. The definition of a public good is dependent on the state of technology. Goods once considered public may become private with technological advances. Hence, the classification of goods as public or private may change over time with technological change. A corollary to that principle is that government provision or production of public goods may also have to change over time as technological advances change the menu of goods and services that governments should provide.

Various exclusion mechanisms exist. They may be technical as in the previous example. The use of technology for exclusion is very apparent in the provision of television programming. The primary exclusion mechanism used in this context is the cable. Cable television subscribers receive the benefits of all the programming available from the cable service. Nonsubscribers receive none of the benefits. Through the use of fixed cable technology, the private firm providing cable television services is able to invoke an exclusion mechanism that makes it possible to be in business and provide services, hopefully at a profit. In the early years of satellite television reception, viewers could tune in to signals without paying. As a result of that lack of exclusion, limited programming was available. Providers subsequently found the technological means to scramble the signal and thereby eliminate the problem of nonexclusion. Now you can receive the signal using your satellite dish, but you must pay a fee for a descrambler that makes the signal intelligible.

However, when a local public radio station puts its signal into the air, there is no technically feasible way for that station to exclude listeners who do not pay for the service. We can all listen to the classical music, news, and other programming whether we contribute during the station's on-air fundraisers or not. The station has no way of blocking the signal to those listeners who have not paid.

Excludability may be obtained by controlling it at a different point to a different group of people. The local private rock-and-roll station does not rely on fundraisers to solicit listeners for support. Instead, it sells the property rights to its signal in 30-second increments. Advertisers can buy time slots in which to inform listeners about their products. This is where exclusion occurs. No advertiser may use the radio station's signal without paying, although all listeners can still listen to the broadcast and not pay for the services of the station. It is easier (cheaper) to apply an exclusion mechanism at the source of the signal than at the receiver.

We may be physically or technically able to exclude people from using a good or service and to provide the good or service to those willing to pay for their use. But that exclusion may be more costly than the owner of the good or service wishes to pay or can recover. Consider the simple case of a city park. It is technically possible to exclude all children from the playground equipment at the park unless they pay a fee, but it is expensive to do so. It would require fences, monitoring, and enforcement, all of which are costly. As a result, the city does not implement an exclusion mechanism. The park is available to all who wish to use it.

Of course, there are also equity, or fairness, considerations. Our sense of fairness may be violated if a fee is required and we know that the fee would act to exclude some people from using the city park because they could not afford to pay.

We take a number of things for granted in everyday life that are public goods. Take honesty and integrity, for example. If my friend, Arthur, is honest in his dealings with others and they come to count on him as a person of high integrity, they benefit from that public good. They can trust Arthur as they deal with him, and that trust translates into lower transaction costs. Honesty and integrity are nonrival in consumption and nonexcludable. That is the nature of a public reputation, for good or ill. In contrast, BP, the global energy company whose deep water oil-drilling activity in the Gulf of Mexico resulted in the largest oil spill on record in 2010, is currently dealing with the serious problem of a tarnished reputation. (A policy study in Chapter 4 provides additional information on this event.) Information about the oil spill and the company's response was available in the news and on the web to everyone interested. Although investigations into the causes of the oil spill spread blame widely, nevertheless BP must deal with the fact that there is a public perception of impropriety. That information and its implications for BP's reputation is nonrival in consumption and nonexcludable. A reputation should be guarded carefully, precisely because it is a public good.

Impure Public Goods and Club Goods

So far, we have considered the case of a pure public good where there is no rivalry. In some cases, however, the public good is subject to congestion. When that is the case, the public good is not a pure public good but rather an **impure public good.** Figure 3.1 illustrates a continuum from pure private goods on the

FIGURE 3.1 Private and Public Goods

right to pure public goods on the left. A Big Mac is a pure private good because if I eat it, you cannot. That is the essence of rivalry. On the other hand, a lighthouse involves no rivalry whatsoever, as we discussed previously. In between are goods that are impure public goods. They have elements of publicness about them, but they are congestible. For example, an interstate highway is a public good, providing a fixed quantity of transportation services to all. As long as the highway is not busy, my use of it does not affect your use. No rivalry is involved. However, once traffic builds to a high level, congestion sets in and rivalry results. My presence on the road slows you down or perhaps precludes your use of the road altogether. Hence, the highway has attributes of a private good. Public goods with this characteristic are termed *impure public goods*. They are public goods subject to congestion. Other examples of impure public goods include parks, schools, and other public facilities such as the Internet.

Public goods that are excludable and subject to congestion in use are sometimes called **club goods.** Think of a health club that provides the services of weight-training equipment and a pool. The club has an exclusion mechanism: a membership requirement. But the equipment and facilities are also subject to congestion. The more members who join the health club, the harder it is to get time on the weight machines or find an uncrowded time to swim in the pool. Clubs of many types exist. For example, NATO can be considered a defense club, for example, and a suburban community a residential club.

Implications for Public Policy

If public goods are provided and efficient quantities of those goods, government action is necessary to assure provision. Private markets will not provide adequate amounts of such goods, if they provide them at all. It is easy to see why that is the case. Suppose you are willing to pay $20 for the navigational services of a lighthouse where you enjoy sailing during the summer. You are willing to pay that amount because without the lighthouse, there is a greater chance of running aground and damaging your sailboat or of colliding with another ship on a foggy morning. Although there is a small chance of such an event, the loss to you in such a circumstance would be large. Your sailboat is worth $20,000, and there is one chance in a thousand that it would be destroyed (a probability of 0.001). The following matrix lists the probabilities with and without a lighthouse.

The expected loss is zero when there is a lighthouse. But if there is no lighthouse, the expected loss is $20. To compute the expected loss in the case of this risky situation, we must take the weighted average of the two outcomes, a loss of zero in the case of no accident and a loss of $20,000 in the case of a collision with another ship, where the weights are the probabilities of each outcome: $EV = 0.999(0) + 0.001(\$20{,}000) = \$20$. In general, the expected value (EV) of a risky situation is the weighted average of the potential outcomes, where the weights are the probabilities of each outcome. In this particular example, you are willing to pay $20 per summer for the services of the lighthouse, because that is your expected loss.

No private firm will supply lighthouse services, however, because there is no easy exclusion mechanism. Even if you pay, I will not. Why should I pay

TABLE 3.1 Sailing, Expected Outcomes

	No Lighthouse	Lighthouse
No accident	0.999	1.000
Accident	0.001	0.000

for a lighthouse? I do not sail. Even if I do sail, why should I indicate my willingness to pay for lighthouse services if I can get them for free because people like you are willing to pay? Such is the dilemma we face with public goods. People have an incentive to be **free riders,** receiving the benefits of the public good without paying for the provision of the public good. Let's face it, we all free ride. Have you ever watched public television without contributing during the station's fundraiser? If so, you have been a free rider (and so have I).

The problem of the free rider effectively inhibits private markets from working. As a result, we get too little of the public good provided. After all, some of the public good is justified because people would receive positive marginal benefits from the public good's provision. If the good were private, the market would provide that quantity where the marginal cost equals the marginal benefit. Because the good is public, the quantity that should be produced is where the sum of residents' marginal benefits equals the marginal cost of provision. It falls to government to provide the public good that benefits everyone and to prevent free riding by requiring everyone to pay for the provision of the public good.

ALLOCATION OF PUBLIC AND PRIVATE GOODS

The essential difference between public and private goods results in two different means by which the goods are allocated to users. Private goods are allocated by markets where prices are the fundamental allocation mechanism. The number of Big Macs each student in your class purchases during the semester is determined by each student's willingness to pay the price. Each student has a sense of the additional satisfaction or benefit that he would derive from consuming an additional Big Mac, called the **marginal utility** in economic theory (the additional utility provided by consuming one more Big Mac), denoted MU. Consumers whose marginal utilities at their current level of consumption are in excess of the price of a Big Mac, $MU > p$, will purchase additional Big Macs. As more Big Macs are consumed, however, a person's marginal utility typically declines. Each additional Big Mac provides added utility, but the additional utility per Big Mac declines as the quantity consumed rises. The third Big Mac just doesn't taste as good as the second, which wasn't as tasty as the first. In fact, eventually the marginal utility of additional Big Macs turns negative as the consumer becomes uncomfortably full and then positively sick of eating Big Macs. A person will continue to buy Big Macs until her marginal utility has declined to the point where it is equal to the price of a Big Mac: $MU = p$. At that point, she buys her last Big Mac and stops because the marginal utility of one more will be less than the price. Another one just isn't worth it. Of course, there are some students who will not buy a single Big Mac during the semester. They either don't like them (low marginal utility) or don't consider them worth the price ($MU < p$). The hamburger market allocates Big Macs via the price mechanism. Consumers willing to pay the price get the Big Macs. Furthermore, they can have any quantity for which they are willing to pay. In contrast, public goods are not allocated on the basis of price. Rather, they are provided in fixed quantity for all. For example, national defense is supplied in a fixed quantity for all residents of the country. No individual choice is permitted in selecting the quantity of national defense. Public goods are quantity rationed. Private goods are price rationed. This distinction is critical to understanding how public and private goods differ and why governments do not behave as firms in providing public goods.

Private Goods

In the case of a private good, we aggregate individual demands for the good by horizontally summing the individuals' demands, thereby deriving the market demand for the good. We take a given price for the good and ask ourselves: How much of the good will each consumer demand at that price? We find those individual demands from each person's demand curve and add them up to get the total amount demanded in the market at that price. We could do the same thing for all other possible prices in order to trace out the whole market demand.

Consider, for example, a three-person case. Wilt, Bill, and Shaq are all residents of Springfield and all demand basketball shoes. Their basketball shoe demand curves are shown in Figure 3.2. The market demand for basketball shoes is derived by horizontally adding the individuals' demands. At price p_1, Wilt's demand for basketball shoes is x_1^W, Bill's demand is x_1^B, and Shaq's demand is x_1^S. Market demand at that price is $x_1 = x_1^W + x_1^B + x_1^S$. We do

FIGURE 3.2 Market Demand for a Private Good

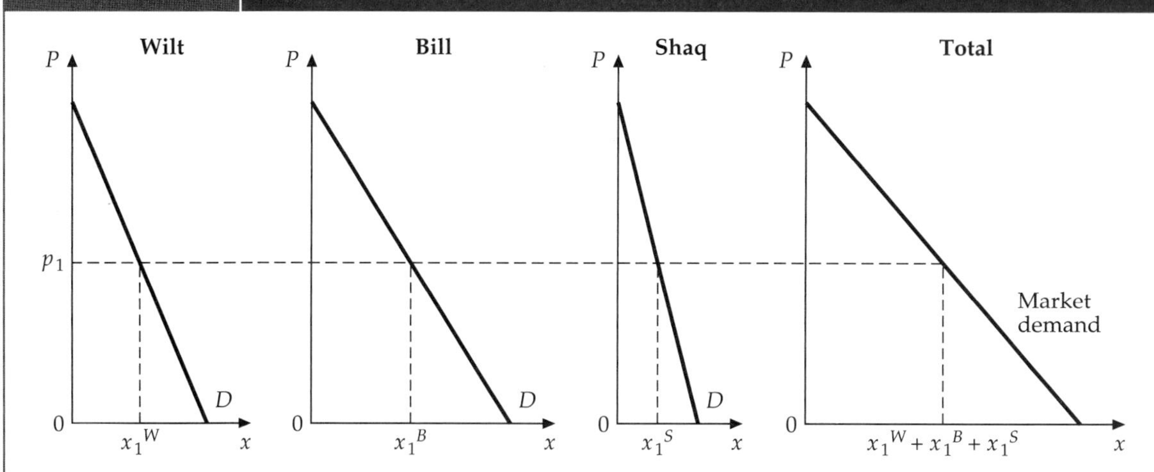

the same at other prices and trace out the market demand curve shown in Figure 3.2. Notice that the market demand curve is more elastic (flatter) than the individual demand curves. Also notice that at price p_1 all three individuals are demanding different quantities.

Public Goods

In the case of a public good we cannot follow the procedure we used for the private good because we cannot ask how much an individual will demand of the good at a given price. Because we must provide the same quantity of the public good to each individual, we must ask a different question: For a given level of the public good provided to all individuals, what is their willingness to pay? We must stack the individuals' demand curves and sum them vertically in the case of a public good. Consider, for example, another three-person case. Diana, Florence, and Mary are all residents of Motown, each with preferences for snowplowing as given by their individual demand curves in Figure 3.3. We consider each person's demand curve for snowplowing to illustrate her willingness to pay for various quantities of snowplowing services. That willingness to pay is based on the person's **marginal benefit** derived from additional units of the public good or the additional benefit from the last unit of the public good provided.

In order to determine the proper amount of snowplowing to provide the community, we begin by summing their marginal benefits vertically, as shown in Figure 3.3. For example, at quantity x_1, Diana derives the marginal benefit MB_1^D, Florence derives the marginal benefit MB_1^F, and Mary derives the marginal benefit MB_1^M. The sum of their marginal benefits is then:

$$\sum MB = MB_1^D + MB_1^F + MB_1^M. \tag{3.1}$$

Notice that in this case we must fix the quantity of the public good at some level and then determine the aggregate marginal benefit for that quantity of the public good. We can do so for each quantity of the public good, tracing out the sum of marginal benefits for each service level. Notice in this case, unlike the private good case, we provide a fixed quantity of the good, and each person has a different marginal benefit. Also note that if we wish to determine the total benefit of the public good received by any individual, we can sum the marginal benefits for each unit of the good provided. That quantity is illustrated graphically as the area under the demand curve. The efficient level of snowplowing service to provide in Motown is determined by finding where the sum of the residents' marginal benefits ΣMB equals the marginal cost MC of providing the snowplowing service. That is the efficient level of service, denoted x^*.

EFFICIENCY IN PUBLIC GOOD PROVISION

One Public Good

Suppose that we wish to know how much of a public good x to provide in an economy with several individuals. Individual i derives the marginal benefit MB^i of an additional unit of the public good. The marginal benefit curve is

FIGURE 3.3 Demand for a Public Good

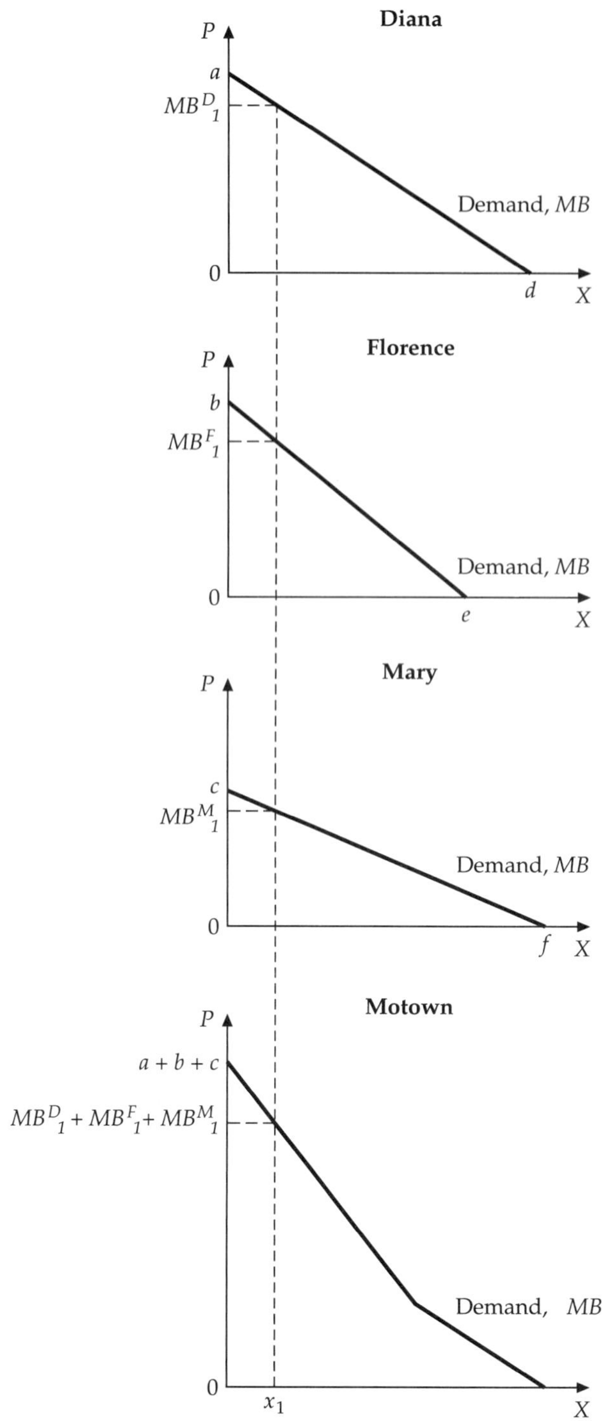

also the individual's demand curve for the public good. To aggregate marginal benefits over community residents, we vertically sum the marginal benefits for all n individuals in the economy. That gives us the sum of marginal benefits for any given level of the public good: $\sum_{i=1}^{n} MB^i$. In order to have the efficient level of public good output, the sum of the residents' marginal benefits must be equal to the marginal cost of producing the public good:

$$\sum_{i=1}^{n} MB^i = MC. \tag{3.2}$$

This condition is the rule for efficient provision of a public good and is often called the **Samuelson rule** in honor of Professor Paul Samuelson, the noted 20th-century economist and first U.S. Nobel laureate, who popularized this formulation of the public good problem. Figure 3.4 illustrates the marginal benefits to the community residents and the determination of the efficient level of a public good to provide the community.

ON THE WEB

For more on how economists estimate the demand for public goods, see the Policy Study "Estimating the Demand for Public Goods" on the companion website (www.cengage.com/international).

For example, suppose that three individuals in a community, Joseph, George, and Michael, have the following marginal benefits for streetlights:[4]

$$\begin{aligned} MB^J &= 100 - .5x, \\ MB^G &= 200 - .5x, \\ MB^M &= 200 - x. \end{aligned} \tag{3.3}$$

The sum of marginal benefits for these three community residents is $\Sigma MB = 500 - 2x$. If the marginal cost of streetlights is \$300, $MC = 300$, and we can compute the efficient level of streetlight provision. Setting the sum of marginal benefits equal to the marginal cost gives the solution $x = 100$. Hence, the optimal (efficient) number of streetlights to provide in this community is 100.

At this level of streetlight provision, each of the community residents has positive marginal benefits. We can calculate those benefits by substituting

FIGURE 3.4 Optimal Quantity of a Public Good

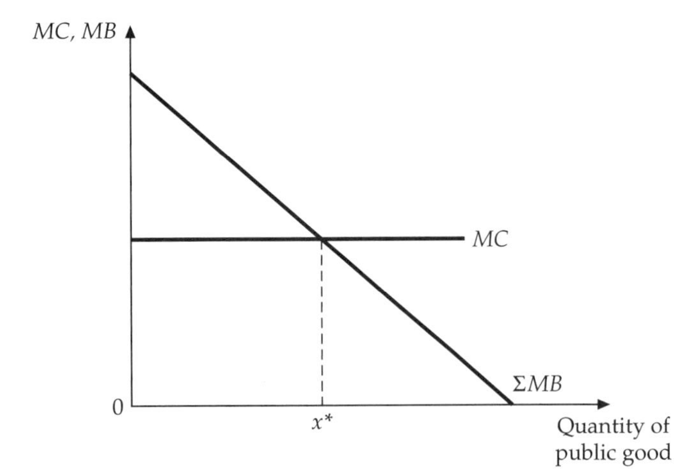

$x = 100$ in their marginal benefit functions. Doing so gives $MB^J = 50$, $MB^G = 150$, and $MB^M = 100$. Notice that the three residents have quite different views on the usefulness of the last streetlight provided. Joseph derives a marginal benefit from the 100th streetlight of just \$50, whereas George derives a marginal benefit of \$150, and Michael \$100. All three residents of the community are provided the same quantity of the public good, 100 streetlights, but they differ in the marginal benefit each derives at that quantity. This situation differs from the private good case, where all consumers pay the same price for a good and each consumes the quantity he desires. Recall that in the private good case the price is given by the market and each consumer selects the quantity of the good where $MU = p$. It is also useful to notice that when we select a level of streetlight provision, because all residents will be provided the same number of streetlights in the community, it may be the case that no resident will agree with that particular level of provision; that is, no one may be satisfied with the provision level of the public good.

We will talk about financing the public good later, but for now notice that if we fund the provision of 100 streetlights with a fee of \$100 per streetlight for each of the three residents, each paying one-third of the *MC* of provision, we will have three very different desired levels of streetlights. Joseph would want no streetlights at that price, because when we equate *MC* with *MB*, we have $100 = 100 - 0.5x$, which has the solution $x = 0$. George would want 200 streetlights because $100 = 200 - 0.5x$ has the solution $x = 200$, and Michael would want 100 streetlights because $100 = 200 - x$ has the solution $x = 100$.

Now, suppose that we change a parameter in the problem. In particular, let's change the marginal cost of streetlights and see what happens to the optimal number that the community should provide. If the marginal cost of streetlights were reduced to $MC = 100$, the optimal number of streetlights to provide would rise to 200. Notice that at this level of provision, $MB^J = 0$, $MB^G = 100$, and $MB^M = 0$. This example illustrates that it is not necessary that the marginal benefits be positive for all the individuals; that is, they do not all have to value the public good in order for it to be provided. All that matters is that the sum of the marginal benefits equals the marginal cost.

We can also establish that the efficient level of public good provision is welfare maximizing. The marginal cost line in Figure 3.5 represents the additional cost for each unit of the public good provided. If we sum the marginal cost for each additional unit, starting from zero, we have the total cost of providing the public good. Graphically, the total cost of providing a given quantity of the public good is represented by the area under the marginal cost line from zero up to that quantity of the public good. Similarly, the sum of marginal benefits ΣMB represents the additional benefits for community residents for additional units of the public good. We can represent the total benefits derived from the provision of a given level of the public good by summing the marginal benefits for each unit from zero up to the quantity provided. Graphically, the area under the ΣMB curve represents the total benefits derived by community residents. At the efficient level x^* of provision for the public good, total benefits to community residents are represented by the area $0bex^*$, whereas total costs are represented by the area $0aex^*$. Total benefits exceed

FIGURE 3.5 Welfare Effects of Public Good Provision

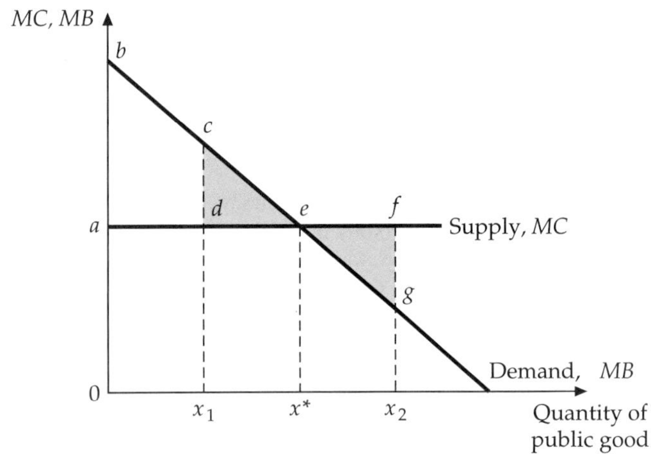

total costs by the triangle *abe*. By providing the efficient level x^* of the public good, we can be sure that we obtain the maximum excess of benefits over costs. At x^* the welfare of the community is maximized.

In order to assure ourselves that x^* is the best quantity to provide to maximize social welfare, consider providing either more or less. If we provide x_2 units of the public good, total benefits are $0bgx_2$, whereas total costs are $0afx_2$. In this case, total benefits exceed total costs but by an amount smaller than we had at x^*. If we assume that triangle *efg* is approximately the same as triangle *cde*, the excess of benefits over costs at x_2 is *abcd*. On the other hand, if we provide a quantity of the public good less than x^*, such as x_1, we can also show that social welfare is smaller than it is at x^*. Providing x_1 units of the public good brings total benefits of $0bcx_1$ and total costs of $0adx_1$. Here, the excess of benefits over costs is again the area *abcd* which is less than *abe*, which x^* provides. Thus, we can be assured that the efficient quantity of the public good provided by the Samuelson rule is the quantity that maximizes social welfare. It is the quantity that assures that total benefits in excess of total costs are the largest possible. No other level of public good provision is as good.

Two Goods: One Public, One Private

If we wish to know how much of two goods to provide, both a public good y and a private good x, in an economy with several individuals, we must generalize the analysis discussed previously. When there are two goods, the individual's marginal benefit of an added unit of one good in terms of the other good is given by that person's **marginal rate of substitution** (*MRS*). Recall from your principles of economics course that individual *i*'s marginal rate of substitution of good *x* for good *y*, denoted MRS^i_{xy}, is the ratio of the person's marginal utilities for the two goods: $MRS^i_{xy} = MU_x/MU_y$. This ratio reflects the rate at which the person is willing to give up y in exchange for additional x while maintaining the same level of total utility.[5]

Similarly, the marginal cost of producing the public good must be expressed in terms of the amount of the private good that must be forgone in order to produce the public good. That trade-off is captured in the ratio known as the **marginal rate of transformation** ($MRTxy$). MRT is the ratio of the marginal costs of producing two goods: $MRT_{xy} = MC_x / MC_y$.[6]

Having generalized both concepts, marginal benefits and marginal costs, for the case of two goods, one public and one private, the Samuelson condition for the efficient provision of the public good becomes $\Sigma MRS_i = MRT$. We have the efficient level of the public good provided when the sum of the marginal rates of substitution for all community residents equals the marginal rate of transformation. In Figure 3.4, we can re-label MB as MRS and MC as MRT, and then we can interpret the optimal provision of the public good, relative to the private good, using the same figure we used in the one-good case.

For more on the theory of public goods, see Oakland (1987) and Cornes and Sandler (1996).

MARKETS AND EFFICIENT ALLOCATION OF RESOURCES

Welfare Economics

Economists hold that markets are capable of allocating resources efficiently. They then use competitive market allocation as a benchmark to judge the efficiency of other allocations, including the provision of public goods, the effects of taxation, the distortions of externalities and, importantly, economic welfare under various circumstances.

Fundamental Theorems of Welfare Economics

The market mechanism is known to provide an efficient allocation of resources under certain circumstances. Those circumstances include:

- Households and firms acting competitively, taking prices as given
- A full set of markets for inputs and outputs
- Full information on the part of all buyers and sellers

Given this set of conditions, the foundational result with which we begin in welfare economics is the **First Fundamental Theorem of Welfare Economics.** A nontechnical statement of the theorem is that under these circumstances a competitive market equilibrium is **Pareto efficient.** This type of efficiency, named after the Italian economist Vilfredo Pareto, is achieved when no one can be made better off without someone else's being made worse off. Keep in mind that in the context of public economics, the term *welfare* has nothing to do with government programs to assist the poor. Rather, it has to do with the well-being of people in the economy.

These required conditions also alert us to the situations where we may find inefficient allocations arising in market-oriented economies. In cases of **imperfect competition,** either monopoly or oligopoly situations, the first requirement is violated. The problem in this circumstance is that firms are not price takers but rather have a degree of control over the price of the product they produce. Second, we can expect inefficiency when there are **missing markets,** as in the case of pollution. When a company produces both steel and air pollution, the absence of a market for clean air results in air pollution. Finally, whenever there is **imperfect information** on the part of buyers or sellers, there will be inefficiency. Indeed, the three Nobel laureates whose first names were used in the streetlight example won their joint prizes for contributions to our understanding of the effects of imperfect information. George Ackerlof, in particular, is famous for his analysis of the used car market where the seller has more information about the product than the buyer. The result of that informational asymmetry is that the used car market is dominated by low-quality products: so-called lemons.

Another foundational result in economic theory provides an answer to the question of what happens if we look at the problem the other way around (the converse). Suppose that we have a particular Pareto allocation of resources in which we are interested. Can we be assured that the market mechanism can support or get us that allocation of resources? The **Second Fundamental Theorem of Welfare Economics** says that any given Pareto efficient allocation is supported by a competitive market allocation. Of course, these foundational results in economic theory assume that the goods being allocated are private goods, that the markets are perfectly competitive, and that there are no externalities. For a more detailed description of the fundamental theorems, see Cornes and Sandler (1996).

Consumer Purchase Principles

We assume that the consumer chooses to purchase that quantity of a private good where the marginal utility (MU_x) of the last unit purchased equals the price of the good (p_x) in the marketplace: $MU_x = p_x$. At price p_1, illustrated in Figure 3.6, the consumer will purchase up to x_1 units of the good x. The consumer stops at that point because additional units of the good provide marginal utility less than the price p_1 that must be paid in the marketplace. If the price were lower, say p_2, the consumer would purchase a larger quantity x_2 because at the lower price it is worthwhile to purchase additional units that generate smaller marginal utility. Because the consumer is following the rule to purchase that quantity of the good x, where $p_x = MU_x$, the marginal utility curve is thus the demand curve for good x.

The consumer problem can be generalized to the case of two or more goods.[7] Consider a consumer desiring to purchase the combination of goods x and y that will maximize utility subject to a budget constraint. The **budget constraint** that the consumer faces is written as $m = p_x x + p_y y$, where m is money income available for the purchase of the two goods in quantities x and y at market prices p_x and p_y. The budget line is illustrated in Figure 3.7 as a downward-sloping line segment with vertical intercept m/p_y and slope $-p_x/p_y$. The consumer is constrained to operate within her budget set formed by the budget constraint, a triangle with base m/p_x and height m/p_y. In order to derive the greatest possible utility given that budget constraint, the consumer

FIGURE 3.6 Demand for a Private Good

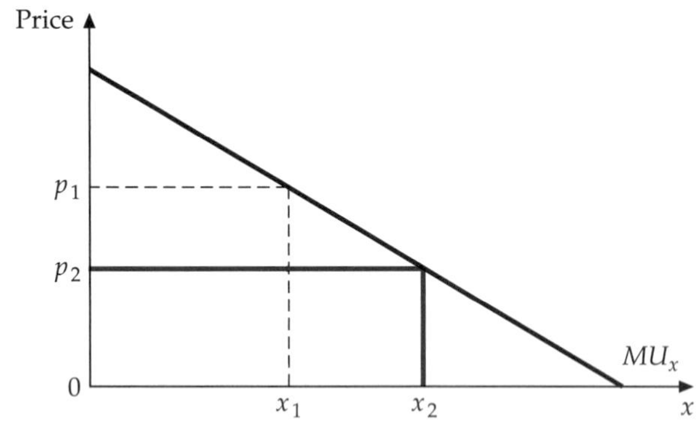

must operate on the downward-sloping line segment from m/p_y to m/p_x. It is inefficient to operate inside the budget set triangle. The consumer must be on the boundary of the budget set in order to be consuming efficiently.

The consumer's preferences are represented by the utility function $u(x, y)$.[8] A well-behaved utility function has indifference curves that are convex to the origin, illustrated by the indifference curve I in Figure 3.7. An indifference curve with this shape reflects the diminishing marginal utility of each of the goods on the axes. As you move southeasterly down the indifference curve, consuming more x and less y, the marginal utility of x falls and the marginal utility of y rises. The slope of the indifference curve (in absolute value—ignoring the minus sign) is $MRS^i_{xy} = MU_x/MU_y$, the ratio of marginal utilities. That ratio falls as we move southeasterly along the indifference curve. Another way of thinking about the indifference curve is to focus on the set of x-y combinations that are considered better than any combination on the curve I. That is a *convex set* or a set with the property that two points in the set or on its boundary can be connected with a line segment that lies entirely within the set. People generally have this type of preference function. Most of us prefer intermediate combinations of goods to extreme combinations. As a result, we have convex better sets. Here is a practical way to think about convex preferences: Which would you rather have: four MP3 players and no MP3 music files, or one MP3 player and three MP3 music files? If you answered the second combination, you have convex preferences and your indifference curves have the shape illustrated in Figure 3.7.

The consumer will maximize utility while satisfying the budget constraint by consuming the (x^*, y^*) combination of goods illustrated in Figure 3.7. At the point of tangency between the budget line and indifference curve, the slopes are equal. That requires minus the ratio of prices (the slope of the budget line) to be equal to minus the ratio of marginal utilities (the slope of the indifference curve): $-p_x/p_y = -MU_x/MU_y$. If we multiply both sides by -1 and define the ratio of marginal utilities on the right-hand side as the

FIGURE 3.7 Optimal Consumption

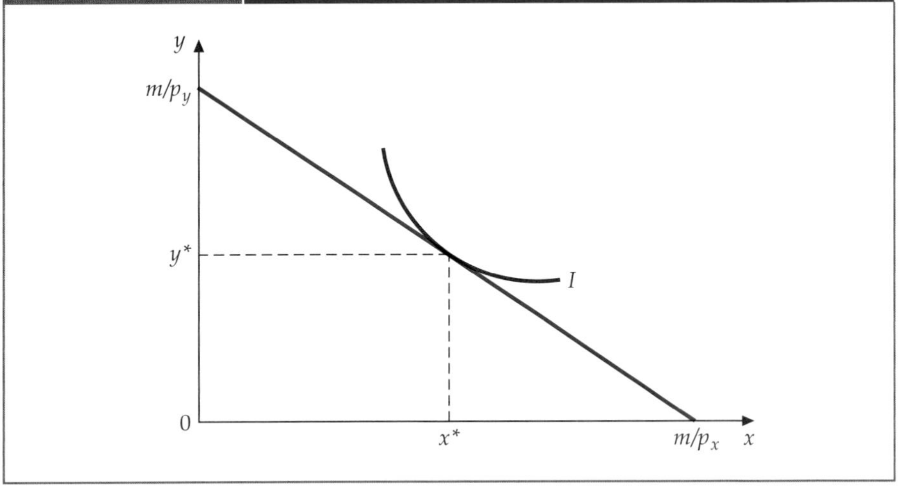

marginal rate of substitution (MRS_{xy}), we have the familiar optimality condition $-p_x/p_y = MRS_{xy}$. In order to maximize utility subject to the budget constraint, the consumer should purchase that combination of goods in quantities x and y such that the marginal rate of substitution MRS_{xy} equals the ratio of prices p_x/p_y. The marginal rate of substitution indicates the rate at which the consumer would be willing to trade one good for the other (trading units of y for additional units of x) while maintaining the same total utility level. The ratio of prices indicates the rate at which good y may be traded for good x in the market place—the relative price. The consumer will be optimizing when she is consuming the combination of goods where the two rates are equal. Table 3.2 summarizes the necessary conditions for efficiency in consumption in both the one-good and the two-goods cases.

Efficiency in Exchange

Now suppose that we have two consumers and we are interested in the optimal allocation of two goods between them. Efficiency in exchange is characterized by equal rates at which two consumers are willing to trade commodities: equal marginal rates of substitution. Let's consider the case of Dominique and Caesar, two individuals who must decide on an allocation of pizzas and cokes. Suppose that Dominique is willing to trade cokes (denoted c) for additional pizzas (denoted p) at a rate of 6 pops per pizza, whereas Caesar is willing to trade 10 pops per pizza. Dominique's marginal rate of substitution of pops for pizza is $MRS^D_{pc} = MU_P/MU = 6$. She is willing to trade six pops for an additional pizza. (Recall that the marginal rate of substitution is the ratio of the person's marginal utilities for the two goods.) We do not have to measure her utility; all we need to know is the *relative* size of the marginal utility of a pizza compared to the marginal utility of a pop. The marginal rate of

TABLE 3.2	Efficiency in Consumption
One-Good Case	**Two-Good Case**
Consume the quantity of good where the marginal utility equals the price: MU = p.	*Consume the quantity of goods* x *and* y *where the ratio of marginal utilities equals the ratio of prices:* $MU_x/MU_y = p_x/p_y$.

substitution is equal to the absolute value of the slope of Dominique's indifference curve. If we plot pizzas on the horizontal axis and pops on the vertical axis, Dominique's indifference curves are downward sloping and flatten as we move from left to right. The reason her indifference curves flatten as we move downward to the right is that such movement involves her trading pops for pizzas. As she trades more and more pops for pizzas, the marginal utility of pops increases because she has fewer of them, and the marginal utility of pizzas decreases, because she has more and more of them. Because marginal utility declines as we have more of any good (total utility rises but marginal utility declines), the ratio of the marginal utility of pizzas to the marginal utility of pops declines.

Dominique's friend, Caesar, has a marginal rate of substitution $MRS^C_{pc} = MU_P/MU_c = 10$. He is willing to forgo 10 pops for an additional pizza. Because Dominique's and Caesar's marginal rates of substitution are unequal, there is clearly not an efficient allocation of pizzas and pops because efficiency requires them to have equal *MRS*s. They need to trade with one another. What is wrong with the current allocation of pizzas and pops? Because Dominique's *MRS* is smaller than Caesar's, her *MRS* needs to increase while his needs to decrease. Because the *MRS* is the ratio of the marginal utility of pizzas divided by the marginal utility of pops, we need to reallocate in such a way as to increase MU_p and decrease MU_c for Dominique while doing the opposite for Caesar. Dominique should have fewer pizzas and more pops while Caesar needs more pizzas and fewer pops. They should arrange a trade of some of Dominique's pizzas for some of Caesar's pops in order to bring about efficiency in exchange. They can both be made better off with a different allocation of pizzas and pops.

Using symbols as shorthand, we can state the problem as one where $MRS^D_{pc} = MU_P/MU_c = 6$ and $MRS^C_{pc} = MU_P/MU_c = 10$. Because $MRS^D_{pc} = MU_P/MU_c < MRS^C_{pc} = MU_P/MU_c$, we must increase MRS^D_{pc} while we decrease MRS^C_{pc}. That requires re-allocating pops to Dominique and pizzas to Caesar, which drives Dominique's MU_p/MU_c upward and Caesar's MU_p/MU_c downward.

This concept is illustrated in an **Edgeworth-Bowley box diagram**, as in Figure 3.8, in which both persons' preferences are represented by indifference curves.[9] The size of the box reflects the total number of pizzas and cokes available. The lower left-hand origin is for Dominique, whereas the upper

FIGURE 3.8 Exchange Possibilities

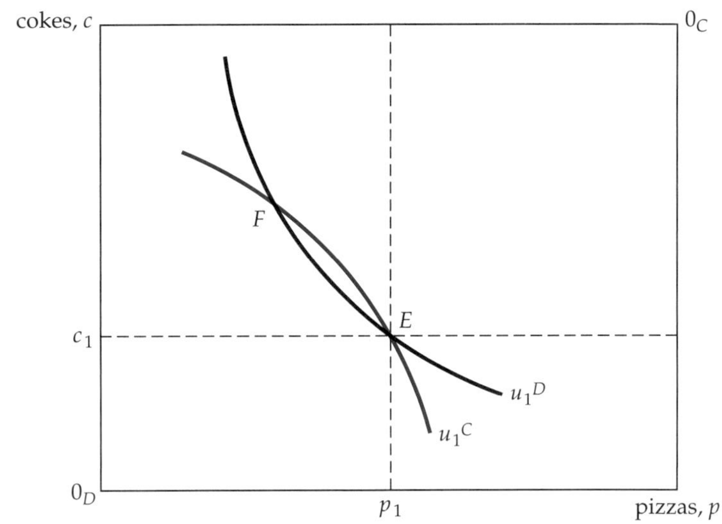

right-hand origin is for Caesar. We have p total pizzas and c total pops to allocate between Dominique and Caesar. Suppose that we have the initial **endowment point** E, illustrating an arbitrary gift to each consumer. At point E, Dominique has p_1 pizzas (so Caesar has $p - p_1$ pizzas) and c_1 pops (so Caesar has $c - c_1$ pops). Dominique and Caesar each have an indifference curve that goes through that endowment point E, as illustrated.[10] The lens formed by their indifference curves between the two points of intersection E and F represents the set of allocations that can make at least one of them better off without making the other worse off. If we hold Dominique on her original indifference curve, we can give her fewer pizzas and more pops, moving along her indifference curve in a northwesterly direction while at the same time enabling us to put Caesar on an indifference curve farther from the origin, making him better off. If we followed Caesar's original indifference curve, we could hold him at his original utility level and make Dominique better off. The interior of the lens represents the set of allocations where they are both better off than they were at point E. Efficiency in exchange requires reallocation of pizzas from Dominique to Caesar in exchange for cokes being transferred from Caesar to Dominique.

Figure 3.9 illustrates an efficient allocation of resources where the marginal rates of substitution are identical for the two consumers. When the two indifference curves are tangent, the marginal rates of substitution are equal and no further reallocation of resources can improve the situation. The set of all such allocations where we have Pareto optimality is illustrated by the **contract curve,** a line going from the bottom left-hand origin to the top right-hand origin. The contract curve consists of all of the points of tangency between the individuals' indifference curves—all of the points where their

FIGURE 3.9 Efficiency in Exchange

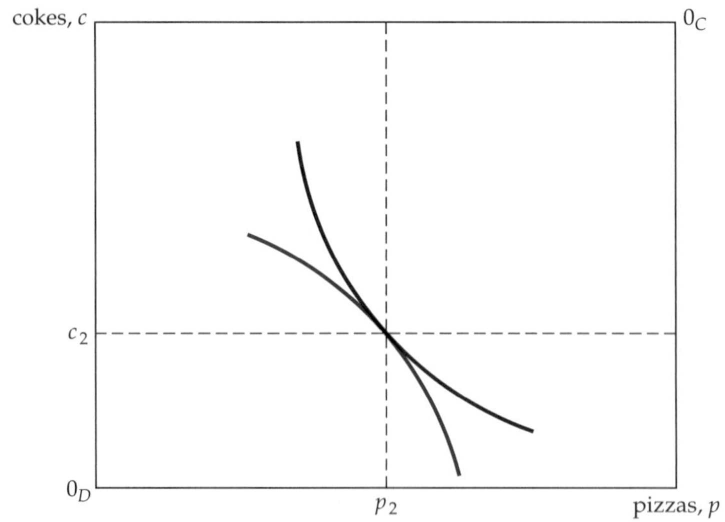

FIGURE 3.10 The Contract Curve

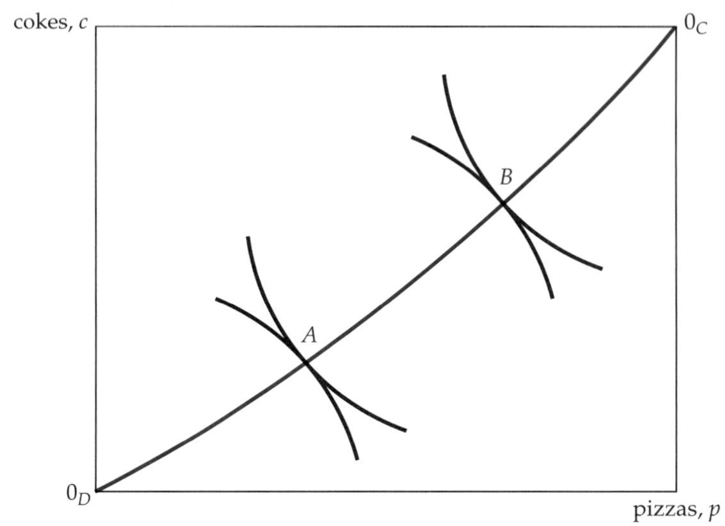

marginal rates of substitution are equal. Figure 3.10 illustrates the contract curve. Any allocation off the contract curve is inefficient in the Pareto sense. The goods could be reallocated to make at least one person better off without making anyone worse off. Once we have exchanged goods to reach the contract curve, no further Pareto improvement is possible. Any further reallocation along the contract curve makes one person better off and the other person worse off.

Points on the contract curve have the property of being Pareto efficient, but that does not mean that they are fair in an equally shared sense. Think about a point like *B* in the diagram. This allocation of the goods provides the majority of both pizzas and pops to Dominique. That is not fair in an egalitarian sense that counts fairness as equal proportions of the goods allocated to each person. The concept of Pareto optimality does not involve an equal allocation of resources. Rather, Pareto optimality involves a concept of fairness that means we cannot make one person better off unless that can be done without making the other person worse off, regardless of the magnitudes of those welfare changes. It could be the case that a move in the southwesterly direction away from point *B* would make Dominique better off by an amount greater than Caesar's loss in welfare. Pareto optimality does not consider such a possibility. It refrains from making any such interpersonal comparison of changes in utility. A weaker concept of efficiency is the **Hicks-Kaldor compensation criterion**, which says a reallocation is justified if the gain to those made better off is larger than the loss to those made worse off; there is a welfare improvement. In our example, the gain to Caesar is larger than the loss to Dominique; therefore there is an improvement in the allocation.[11] The compensation criterion does not require actual compensation to be paid; rather, it suggests that if compensation could be paid in such a manner, we would have a welfare improvement.

Finally, note that our choice of an initial endowment point *E* determines in large part where we end up on the contract curve. In an extreme case, we could begin with an endowment point at the origin 0_D. That point would also then represent the final allocation because no move from 0_D would be a Pareto improvement. Although this outcome is efficient (in the Pareto sense), it is manifestly unfair because one person has everything and the other person has nothing. Pareto efficiency does not imply fairness in an egalitarian sense.

Efficiency in Production

We must also consider how the market allocation mechanism works to allocate resources in production. Firms use resources to produce products. We need to consider both the allocation of resources in the use of productive inputs, and the production of outputs (or products). Let's begin on the input side of the production process to examine how the firm uses inputs. Every firm is engaged in a production process whereby it takes inputs of land, labor, and capital (machinery and equipment) to produce goods or services. Recall that in the single-input case, the firm uses the quantity of the input where the value of its marginal product is equal to the price. The value of the marginal product is the additional revenue earned by the producer from using one more unit of the input. Consider the labor input, for example. A firm will employ labor, measured in hours l, up to the point where the value of the marginal product, $p \cdot MP_l$, equals the wage w paid for an hour of labor. Note that the value of the marginal product of labor is made up of two components: the price of the product being produced and the marginal product of labor. An additional hour of labor is used to produce an additional product, and that additional product is sold at the market price of the product. Hence, the principle for proper input usage is to use that quantity of labor where $p \cdot MP_l = w$.

TABLE 3.3	Efficiency in Production, Inputs
One-Input Case	**Two-Input Case**
Use the quantity of labor where the value of the marginal product equals the input price: $p \cdot MP_l = w$.	*Use the quantity of capital* k *and labor* l *where the ratio of marginal products equals the ratio of input prices:* $MP_k/MP_l = r/w$.

In the case of two inputs, the firm will use the quantity of labor l and capital k where the ratio of marginal products of the inputs equals the ratio of input prices: $MP_k/MP_l = r/w$, where r is the price of capital. Suppose that the price of capital falls, for example. How does the firm adjust its use of capital in response? Well, when the price of capital falls (relative to the price of labor), the ratio r/w shrinks. Then the ratio of marginal products must also shrink. In order to accomplish that, the firm can use more capital, which drives its marginal product down, and use less labor, which pushes its marginal product up. The combination of these two changes results in a new ratio of marginal products that is smaller. Hence, the firm's reaction to a reduction in the price of capital is to use more capital and less labor to produce its product. Table 3.3 summarizes the necessary conditions for efficiency in the use of inputs in production for both the one-input and the two-input cases.

The market mechanism leads the firm to use the efficient input combination. Efficient in this sense means the input combination where the firm's **rate of technical substitution** (RTS), the ratio of the marginal products of the inputs, equals the input price ratio. The RTS measures the rate at which the producer can substitute one input for another in the production process, holding output constant. Although this explains the use of inputs, it is also important to consider how the firm makes decisions about the quantity of output to produce.

A profit-maximizing firm should produce that quantity of output where the marginal cost of the last unit produced equals the price of the product.[12] Table 3.4 summarizes the necessary conditions for optimal production of outputs for both the one-good and the two-good cases.

TABLE 3.4	Efficiency in Production, Products
One-Product Case	**Two-Product Case**
Produce that quantity of a product x where the marginal cost of production equals the price: $MC = p$.	*Produce that quantity of products x and y where the marginal rate of transformation (ratio of marginal costs of production) equals the price ratio:* $MRT_{xy} = MC_x/MC_y = p_x/p_y$.

TABLE 3.5 Market Efficiency

	Efficiency in Exchange	Market Prices	Efficiency in Production
One-Good Case	*MU*	*p*	*MC*
Two-Good Case	$MU_x/MU_y(MRS_{xy})$ *Identical for all consumers*	p_x/p_y	$MC_x/MC_y(MRT_{xy})$ *Identical for all producers*

Efficiency in the Relationship Between Exchange and Production

Finally, we must consider the relationship between exchange and production to see how the market mechanism provides for the allocation of resources. The power of the market mechanism is that in the presence of competition, it assures efficiency in exchange, production, and the relationship between exchange and production simultaneously. This is the essence of the fundamental theorems of welfare economics discussed previously. Table 3.5 illustrates that market prices lead consumers to purchase combinations of goods and to produce efficient combinations of products where the *MRS* equals the *MRT*. Consumers make independent choices about the goods they desire to purchase, looking only at market prices and making their consumption decisions in such a way that their *MRS* equals the price ratio. Firms make independent choices about producing products, looking only at product and input prices, in such a way that their *MRT* equals the product price ratio. The effect of the market mechanism is then to bring the two sets of decisions together, assuring that resources are allocated efficiently with $MRS = MRT$. The market mechanism, however, does not necessarily provide the efficient level of *public* goods.

Measurements of Economic Welfare

Economists use approximate measures of changes in welfare by using the standard model of a market, summarized in the familiar demand and supply diagrams. First, consider the case of consumers whose demand for a good is captured in the market demand curve shown in panel A of Figure 3.11. At price p_0 consumers wish to purchase x_0 units of the good. Of course, the demand curve reveals that for all quantities smaller than x_0, consumers will be willing to pay a price larger than p_0. The difference between the price consumers were willing to pay and the price they actually have to pay in the market for a given quantity of a good is a measure of their welfare known as *consumer surplus* (*CS*).

Similarly, we can measure the welfare of producers in the market by defining the concept of *producer surplus* (*PS*). It is the amount producers are paid for x_0 units of the good, over and above that which would be necessary in the market to induce them to produce that quantity. Graphically, *PS* is

FIGURE 3.11 Consumer and Producer Surpluses

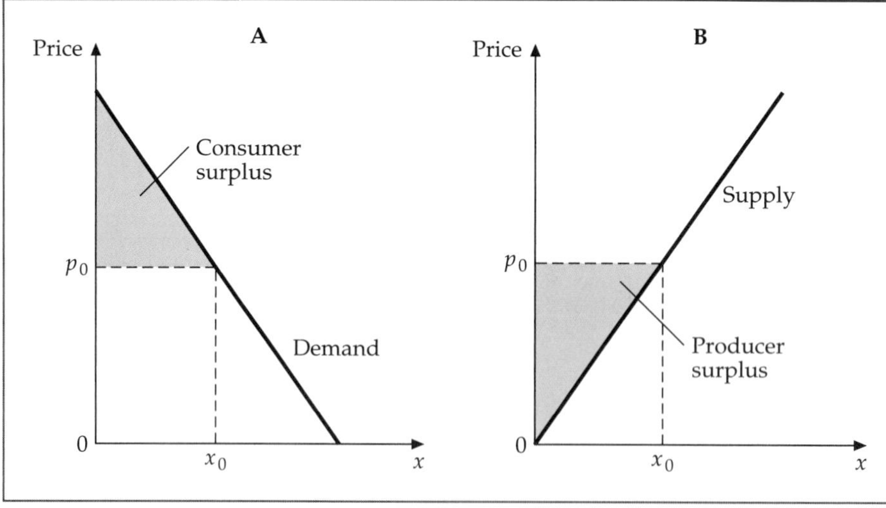

illustrated in panel B of Figure 3.11 as the area above the supply curve but below the market price p_0 associated with the quantity x_0.

Because we have drawn the demand and supply curves in a linear fashion, *CS* and *PS* are both represented as triangles. Hence, it is easy to compute the size of *CS* and *PS* as the area of the corresponding triangles. Recall that the area of a triangle is half the base times the height. We will have occasion to compute *CS* and *PS* using this simple geometric property later in the text. For example, when we want to measure the welfare loss due to a tax increase, we will be able to compute the change in *CS* that results from the tax and have a specific measure of the impact on consumers.

A change in price causes *CS* and *PS* to change also. Consider, for example, what happens when the price of a good rises in the marketplace. As a consumer yourself, you know intuitively that a price increase hurts you. When the price rises from p_0 to p_1, Figure 3.12 illustrates how *CS* shrinks. The reduction in *CS* is given by the area *abcd* in the left-hand panel of the figure and is a measure of just how much consumers are hurt by a price increase. On the other hand, the right-hand panel of the figure illustrates how an increase in price benefits producers. *PS* increases by the area *efgh* when the price goes up.

It is important to understand that the market mechanism, which provides the equilibrium quantity and price (x_0, p_0) that clears the market, also assures that welfare is maximized. Combining *CS* and *PS* gives us a convenient measure of total welfare. The market-clearing equilibrium assures that the sum of $CS + PS$ is as large as possible. Figure 3.13 illustrates the sum of $CS + PS$ at the market equilibrium. To convince yourself of this fact, try any other price in Figure 3.13. You will find that the sum of $CS + PS$ is smaller at any price other than p_0.

FIGURE 3.12 Changes in Consumer and Producer Surpluses

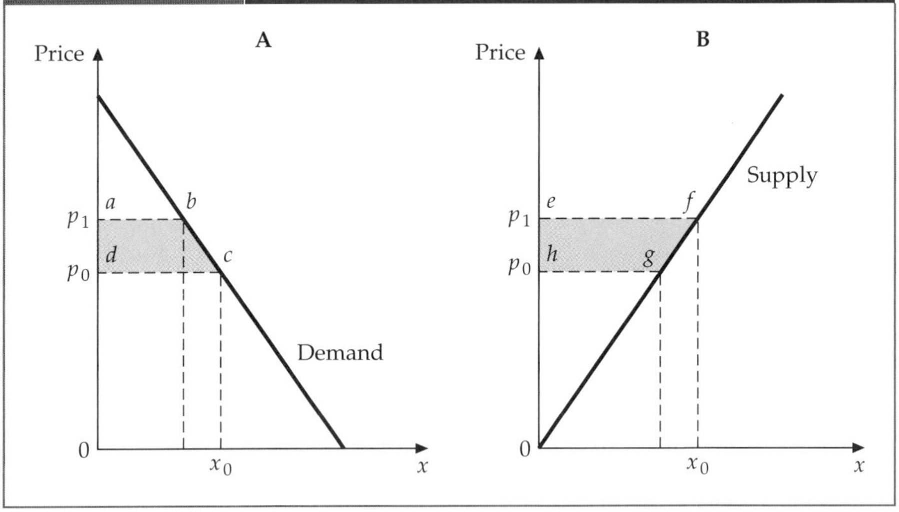

FIGURE 3.13 Welfare Is Maximized at the Equilibrium Price and Quantity

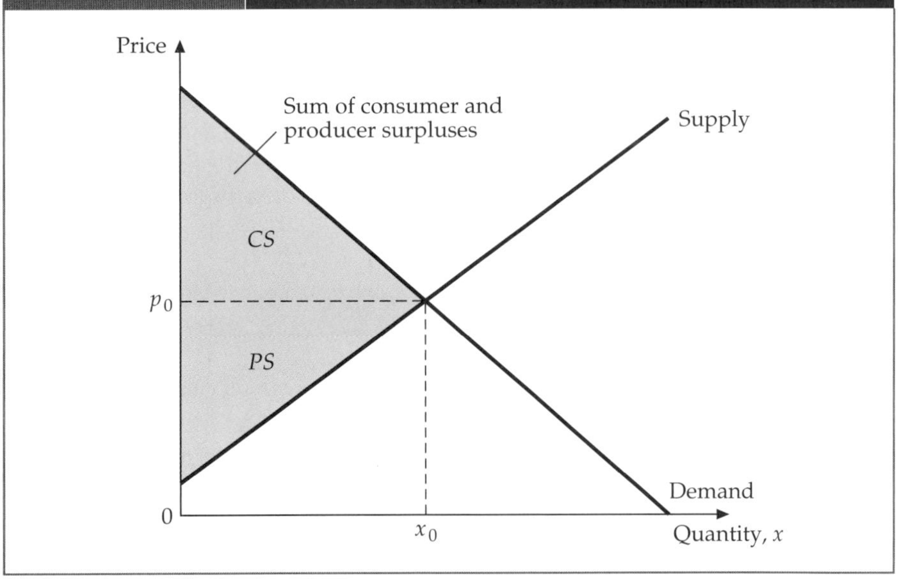

The Theory of the Second Best

The theory presented previously indicates that markets will provide efficient allocations of resources. Efficiency concepts here mean that the market outcome is consistent with the efficiency conditions sketched in Tables 3.2 to 3.5. What happens if for some reason one of these efficiency conditions cannot be met? Is it still advisable to attempt to fulfill the remaining efficiency conditions, or does the impossibility of meeting one condition mean that there is no reason to attempt to meet the remaining conditions? Common sense might indicate that we should try to fulfill as many efficiency conditions as possible, despite the fact that one efficiency condition is unfulfilled.

Consider a simple example. Suppose we live in a two-good world where we know on the basis of economic theory that the goods should be allocated in such a way that their price ratio equals the marginal rate of substitution for all consumers (Table 3.2). During a period of war, however, the government is forced to ration the amount of good x so that all consumers have an equal amount of it. Sugar, gasoline, and other goods were rationed during World War II. Rationing of good x prevents consumers from buying the amount of that good where $MU_x = p_x$. This situation prevents fulfillment of the efficiency condition that the ratio of marginal utilities (the marginal rate of substitution) equal the price ratio. Given this situation in the market for good x, does it still make sense to attempt to allocate good y in such a way that marginal utilities equal price? This is the essence of the question of second-best policy.

Economic theory provides the rather surprising result that when one efficiency condition is unfulfilled, there is no particular reason to try to fulfill the other efficiency conditions. In fact, a better solution may be obtained by breaking the remaining efficiency conditions. This is the so-called **theory of the second best** that was developed in this form by Lipsey and Lancaster (1956). Most of our discussion in this text will involve first-best economic policy; that is, we will assume that it is possible to achieve all the efficiency conditions required. There will be situations, however, where we will also address the circumstance where the first-best policy cannot be achieved and we must consider the second-best policy.

PROBLEMS

1. Trash collection is a typical service provided by most local governments. But is it really a public good?
   a. Analyze this service according to the characteristics of a public good.
   b. Explain the implications of your analysis for local government policy.
   c. Should the city be engaged in trash collection activities?
   d. Could it contract with a private trash collection agency?
2. Consider each of the following goods and services and explain whether it is purely private, purely public, or a public good subject to congestion:
   a. Security guard services
   b. Police services
   c. Physician's services
   d. Immunizations
   e. Lawyer's services
   f. Supreme Court services

3. Suppose that the community of Twainville consists of three people with the following marginal benefits (MB) for streetlights provided in quantity x:
   Tom: $MB = 1{,}500 - 5x$, for $0 \leq x \leq 300$, $MB = 0$ elsewhere.
   Sally: $MB = 2{,}100 - 7x$, for $0 \leq x \leq 300$, $MB = 0$ elsewhere.
   Huck: $MB = 2{,}100 - 5x$, for $0 \leq x \leq 420$, $MB = 0$ elsewhere.
   a. If the marginal cost of streetlights is \$3,150, what is the optimal number of lights to install in the city?
   b. Compute each person's marginal benefit at the optimal number of streetlights. Check to make sure that the marginal benefits for the three residents sum to the marginal cost.
   c. If we finance the streetlights with a lump sum tax of \$1,050, where each resident pays one-third of the marginal cost, how will each resident react? (Hint: Compare each resident's MB to the tax price of \$1,050.)
4. Suppose that the (inverse) demand for a good is given by the equation $p = 100 - 4q$.
   a. Compute the consumer surplus corresponding to a price of \$80.
   b. Compute the change in consumer surplus corresponding to a change in price from \$80 to \$70.
5. True, False, or Uncertain. Explain.
   Pareto optimality requires a private ownership economy with well-defined property rights so that goods are allocated among consumers according to a pricing mechanism.
6. True, False, or Uncertain. Explain.
   a. As a fiscal conservative, I maintain that it is always good to reduce government expenditure by providing smaller quantities of public goods.
   b. As a fiscal liberal, I maintain that if government provision of a public good is helpful to residents of a community, we should expand the provision of the public good as long as anyone benefits.
7. Suppose that we have a simple two-person exchange economy with two goods: sunglasses and capes. At the present allocation of goods in the economy, Clark is willing to exchange three pairs of sunglasses for a cape, whereas Lois is willing to exchange just one pair of sunglasses for a cape.
   a. What is wrong with the current allocation of goods in this economy?
   b. How should goods be reallocated in order to move to a more efficient allocation?
8. Suppose that we have a simple two-firm production economy with two goods: software and movie videos. At the present allocation of resources in the economy, Bill is producing software at a marginal cost of \$20, whereas Michael is producing movie videos at a marginal cost of \$10. The current market price of software is \$100, whereas the market price of movie videos is \$40.
   a. What is wrong with the current allocation of goods in this economy?
   b. How should resources be reallocated in order to move to a more efficient allocation?
9. Suppose that we have two inputs that are used in the production of sports entertainment: Mac's hitting and Tommy's managing. At the present

allocation of resources in the economy, the value of Mac's marginal product is $5,000, whereas the value of Tommy's marginal product is $4,000.

a. What is wrong with the current allocation of goods in this economy?
b. How should inputs be reallocated in order to move to a more efficient allocation?

10. In many transition economies, it is still the case that the price of electricity provided by the state utility is well below the marginal cost of production. Describe what is wrong in such a circumstance and provide a policy recommendation for fixing the efficiency problem. Does the solution to the efficiency problem have any other impacts that you may want to consider? If so, what are those impacts?

REFERENCES

Cornes, Richard, and Todd Sandler. *The Theory of Externalities, Public Goods, and Club Goods,* 2nd ed. New York: Cambridge University Press, 1996.

Cringely, Robert X. *Accidental Empires.* New York: HarperCollins, 1993.

Lipsey, R. G., and K. Lancaster. "The General Theory of the Second Best," *Review of Economic Studies* 24 (1956): 11–32.

Oakland, William H. "Theory of Public Goods." Chapter 9 in *Handbook of Public Economics*, vol. 2, edited by Alan J. Auerbach and Martin Feldstein. Amsterdam: North-Holland, 1987.

NOTES

1. The PC industry entrepreneur examples in this paragraph are taken from Cringely (1993).
2. See Numbers, ch. 21.
3. In later classical mythology the caduceus, as it was called, was the rod borne by Hermes or Mercury. In that context, the caduceus represented authority, quality, and office.
4. In honor of the three recipients of the 2001 Nobel Prize in Economic Science: Joseph Stiglitz, George Akerlof, and A. Michael Spence.
5. We can write the utility function as $u(x, y)$. Taking the total differential gives $du = u_x dx + u_y dy$, where u_x and u_y are the marginal utilities (MU_x and MU_y) of the two goods. Along an indifference curve there is no change in utility; $du = 0$. The slope of the indifference curve can then be computed as $dy/dx = u_x/u_y$. The marginal rate of substitution is the absolute value of the slope of the indifference curve—the ratio of marginal utilities.
6. This ratio is also the absolute value of the slope of the Production Possibilities Frontier (*PPF*). We can derive the MRT_{xy} as follows: Assume that we have a fixed quantity of a productive resource like labor and

the resource cost of producing the two goods is given by the function $c\ (x, y)$. Total differentiation gives $dc = c_x dx + c_y dy$. Holding total cost of production constant, as it would be along an isocost curve, we have $dc = 0$. We can then solve for the slope of the *PPF*: $dy/dx = -c_y/c_x$. Hence the slope of the *PPF* is minus the ratio of marginal costs. If we take the absolute value of the slope of the *PPF*, we have the marginal rate of transformation, or MRT_{xy}.

7. The two-good case is discussed here. The principles are similar for three or more goods, although it will be sufficient to consider the two-good case. In order to avoid the complexity of more than three goods, economists often use a Hicksian composite good as one of the goods. It is useful to consider that composite good as "bread," meaning all other goods but the one being considered.
8. If you are concerned about how we measure such mythical utility, do not worry. Economists do not need to actually measure utility in order to use the utility function.
9. This diagram is named for the British economists Edgeworth and Bowley who devised this method of viewing efficiency in exchange between two consumers.
10. One of the characteristics of well-behaved preferences is that given any point in commodity space, the consumer has an indifference curve that goes through that point. That is, the consumer is able to rank any conceivable combination of goods.
11. This criterion is named for Sir John Hicks and Nicholas Kaldor, the two British economists who proposed this standard for welfare comparison.
12. This is also true for a cost-minimizing firm.

CHAPTER 4

Radius Images/Getty Images

Externalities

LEARNING OBJECTIVES

1. Describe the nature of externalities, both positive and negative, and how markets misallocate resources in the presence of externalities.
2. Analyze remedies for externalities, including both market and nonmarket solutions.

In this chapter we consider another major reason for governments to exist—to reduce negative externalities and facilitate positive externalities. Although the private market mechanism works very well in the allocation of resources generally, it fails to allocate properly when there are externalities present. In the presence of a negative externality, such as pollution, the market mechanism allocates too many resources to the production of goods in that sector. On the other hand, in production processes where there is a positive externality, as in the case of research and development, the market allocates too few resources. Thus, the government plays an important role in helping to facilitate the proper allocation of resources in an economy with externalities.

THE ECONOMICS OF EXTERNALITIES

The classic definition of externality is given by Meade (1973):

> An external economy (diseconomy) is an event which confers an appreciable benefit (inflicts an appreciable damage) on some person or persons who were not fully consenting parties in reaching the decision or decisions which led directly or indirectly to the event in question.

The key concept in this definition is that the external benefit or damage occurs outside the market mechanism. After all, if these effects were subject to the market, they would be priced and there would be no allocation problem. It is precisely the absence of a market mechanism that causes these effects to result in an inefficient allocation by the market. For this reason the problem of externalities is also said to involve the absence of markets.

Categories and Examples of Externalities

Externalities can be either positive or negative. **Positive externalities** confer benefits to those not party to the decision. Consider education, which provides private benefits to the person who decides to pursue a degree program and learns, and that decision leads to new ideas, products, services, and programs that confer many benefits to many other people, none of whom were involved in the decision of the person to pursue advanced education. Consider another simple example. On Arbor Day, many people plant a tree. Besides the direct benefits to the family planting the tree in their yard in the form of esthetic beauty, benefits flow to many others in the neighborhood, such as the oxygen output of the tree over the years of its life. The family probably does not take those external benefits into account, however, when it decides to plant the tree to beautify their yard.

Negative externalities confer costs due to damages and are commonly known as pollution. Water, air, noise, and other forms of pollution are all examples of negative externalities. Two distinct types of negative externalities exist: **point source pollution** and **nonpoint source pollution**. Point source pollution originates from discrete sources such as factory smokestacks or effluent pipes. When you drive along the Lake Michigan coastline through Gary, Indiana, for example, it is not very difficult to identify the source of the air pollution you are breathing. The steel mills are the clearly identified point source of pollution. Nonpoint source pollution originates from many places, none of which is easily identified, as the pollution comes from diffused sources. When you drive along the Santa Monica Freeway in Los Angeles, for example, there is no clearly identified source of the smog you are breathing. Of the millions of sources, many are cars, but there are other sources as well. Here is how the U.S. Environmental Protection Agency (EPA) describes nonpoint source pollution:

> Nonpoint source (NPS) pollution, unlike pollution from industrial and sewage treatment plants, comes from many diffuse sources. NPS pollution is caused by rainfall or snowmelt moving over and through the ground. As the runoff moves, it picks up and carries away natural and human-made pollutants, finally depositing them into lakes, rivers, wetlands, coastal waters, and even our underground sources of drinking water. These pollutants include:

- Excess fertilizers, herbicides, and insecticides from agricultural lands and residential areas;
- Oil, grease, and toxic chemicals from urban runoff and energy production;
- Sediment from improperly managed construction sites, crop and forest lands, and eroding stream banks;
- Salt from irrigation practices and acid drainage from abandoned mines;
- Bacteria and nutrients from livestock, pet wastes, and faulty septic systems;
- Atmospheric deposition and hydromodification are also sources of nonpoint source pollution.[1]

Many types of pollution are classified according to the polluted environmental medium. For example, air and water pollution are two major categories of pollution. The EPA describes its air pollution division as follows:

> Air pollution comes from many different sources such as factories, power plants, dry cleaners, cars, buses, trucks and even windblown dust and wildfires. Air pollution can threaten the health of human beings, trees, lakes, crops, and animals, as well as damage the ozone layer and buildings. Air pollution also can cause haze, reducing visibility in national parks and wilderness areas. EPA protects human health and the environment through the regulatory process and voluntary programs such as Energy Star and Commuter Choice. Under the Clean Air Act, EPA sets limits on how much of a pollutant is allowed in the air anywhere in the United States. Although national air quality has improved over the last 20 years, many challenges remain in protecting public health and the environment. EPA's goal is to have clean air to breathe for this generation and those to follow. (*www.epa.gov*)

The Beekeeper and the Orchardist

A classic example of externalities is the case of a beekeeper whose apiary is next to the orchard of a person who cultivates apple trees. The presence of the apple orchard nearby helps the productivity of bees in making more honey than they would otherwise. Similarly, the orchardist will have a better apple crop due to the presence of the bees who facilitate the pollination of the apple blossoms. Each producer will have lower costs due to the presence of the other. But there is nothing in the working of the market mechanism that compensates either producer for the positive externality conferred on the other. The price of honey, apples, and all of the inputs in the two production processes fails to capture the effect of the externalities.

Consider the case of the beekeeper whose marginal private benefit (*MPB*) and marginal private cost (*MPC*) are illustrated in Figure 4.1. Ignoring the positive externality she provides for the orchardist, she will choose to produce a privately efficient amount of honey x_p, which falls short of the socially

FIGURE 4.1 The Beekeeper and the Orchardist

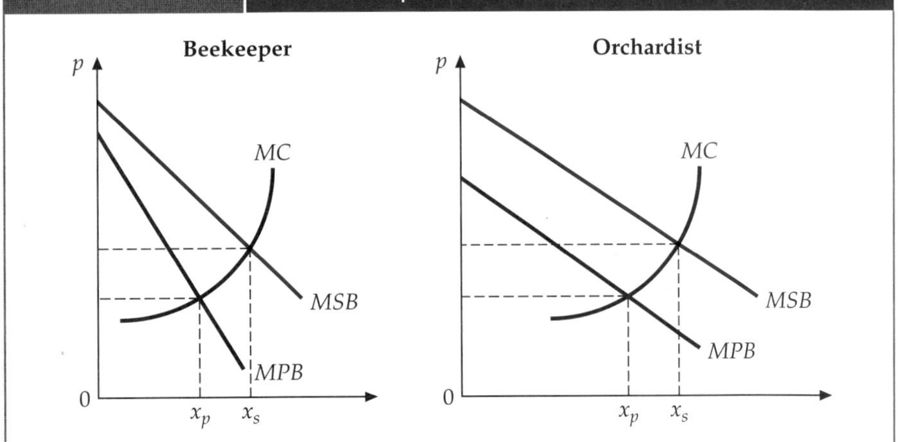

efficient level of honey production x_s. If the honey market would somehow compensate her for the external benefit her bees provide for the orchardist, her marginal benefit curve would be *MSB*, reflecting the marginal social benefit of honey production, and she would produce a larger amount of honey. As it is, the honey market ignores the positive externality, and the beekeeper produces too little honey.

Similarly, the orchardist looks at his marginal private benefit and his marginal cost and makes the decision to produce the privately efficient quantity of x_p bushels of apples. If he were somehow compensated for the positive externality his apple blossoms provide for the beekeeper, he would equate his marginal social benefit (*MSB*) with the marginal cost and produce the socially efficient output level x_s. As it is, the market for apples leads him to allocate too few resources to apple production.

In both of these cases, the private market mechanism fails to price the external benefit each producer confers on the other. Because there is no market for bee pollination services or for apple blossom pollen services, the honey and apple markets fail to allocate resources properly. In this sense we have market failure. Private markets allocate resources improperly when they ignore the externalities that exist. In the absence of externalities, they operate efficiently.

Game Theory Version of the Beekeeper and the Orchardist

We can look at the classic problem of the beekeeper and the orchardist using game theory as well. Table 4.1 gives the payoffs to a beekeeper and an orchardist. If each produces a low quantity of output, each will earn 1 unit of profit (perhaps $1,000). If both produce a medium level of output, they each earn 4 units of profit, whereas at high levels of output, they each earn 18 units of profit. Notice that if we hold the output of the orchardist constant at a low level, increased output by the beekeeper raises profits for both producers. The same happens if we hold the output of the beekeeper constant and increase the output of the orchardist. Each produces positive externalities for the other.

The social welfare maximum occurs when both the beekeeper and the orchardist are producing at high output. But private markets may not assure this outcome. Notice, for example, that the beekeeper's marginal benefit from increasing output from a medium to a high level is only 3 units when the orchardist is producing at a low level but increases to 8 units when the

TABLE 4.1 Beekeeper and Orchardist Payoffs

	Orchardist		
Beekeeper	***Low Output***	***Medium Output***	***High Output***
Low output	(1, 1)	(2, 3)	(3, 6)
Medium output	(3, 2)	(4, 4)	(6, 12)
High output	(6, 3)	(12, 6)	(18, 18)

orchardist is producing at medium output and to 12 units at high output. The beekeeper makes a private decision about whether it is economically sensible to increase output from a medium to a high level. The beekeeper compares the marginal cost with the marginal benefit. If, for example, the marginal cost of increasing output is 6 units, the beekeeper will not expand output unless the orchardist is producing at medium output or higher. The market mechanism fails to capture the effects of the positive externalities each producer confers on the other. In the absence of some way of internalizing those externalities, each producer will consider only the private incentives and may not produce the socially optimal output level.

Fertilizer Usage and Groundwater Contamination

Another example will help illustrate the problem. Consider the case of a farmer who uses fertilizer to produce corn. The application of fertilizer on the cornfields causes groundwater contamination, however. The nitrate levels in groundwater are high, exceeding the recommended safe threshold established by the EPA of 10 parts per million. The negative effects of drinking water with high nitrate levels are most injurious to small children whose ability to absorb oxygen may be inhibited by the nitrates. This situation is illustrated in Figure 4.2.

The corn-producing farmer makes the rational choice to produce the privately efficient level of output x_p where the farmer's marginal cost of producing corn equals the marginal benefit of corn production. This level of output provides the greatest possible profit from corn production. In making this decision, the farmer has considered only the private benefits and costs to him.

The corn production involves fertilization, however, which contaminates groundwater drinking supplies with nitrates. This fact means that the private solution for the farmer ignores the external costs imposed on others. The typical water-drinking household finds that the marginal cost of clean drinking water is higher as a result of the presence of the high nitrate levels. The

FIGURE 4.2 Corn Production and Water Contamination

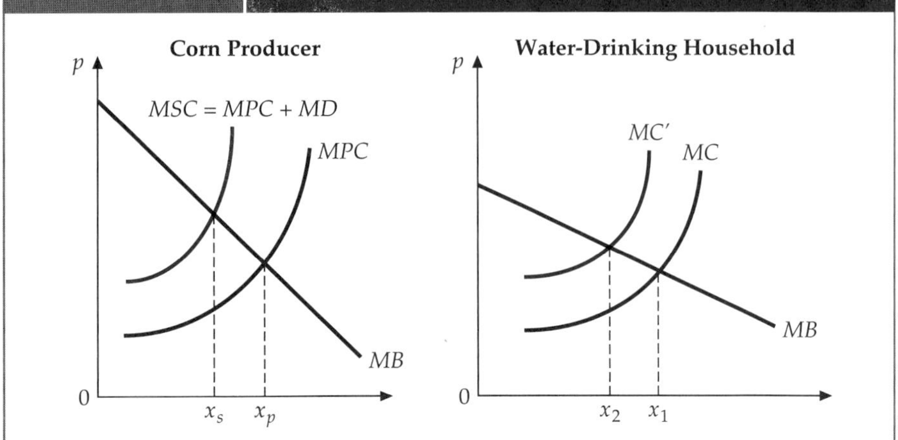

household incurs the costs of filtering the water to assure that it is safe for drinking. Graphically, the extra cost is illustrated as the vertical difference between MC' and MC. For any given quantity of drinking water, the marginal cost is higher due to the externality. These higher costs are the marginal damages caused by the fertilization involved with corn farming. If the farmer were asked to pay those costs, as well as the private cost of the fertilizer and other inputs used in the production process, he would face the marginal social cost (MSC) curve rather than the marginal private cost (MPC) curve. When confronted with the full cost of corn production, including the marginal damage caused to groundwater supplies, $MSC = MPC + MD$, the farmer would wish to produce the socially efficient output rate x_s.

Externalities and the Absence of Markets

Externalities exist because of poorly defined **property rights**. If property rights were well defined, it would be possible for people and firms to negotiate solutions to the problems caused by externalities. A polluting firm could compensate people adversely affected by its pollution. Alternatively, a group of consumers could band together and pay the firm not to pollute. Market solutions are possible when property rights are defined and it is clear who has rights. But, in the absence of clear property rights, these private solutions are not possible. Hence, we can consider the case of an externality as a situation that arises in an absence of well-defined property rights. Recall that the fundamental theorems of welfare economics hold as long as certain conditions prevail. One of those conditions, stated in Chapter 3, is that there must be markets for all inputs and outputs. In the case of externalities and the absence of well-defined property rights, there can be no market. Hence, there is a fundamental problem to be solved that requires the establishment of property rights and the potential development of markets. In some cases there may be a private solution to the problem, where property rights are designated and markets are formed and allowed to solve the externality problem. In other cases it may be necessary for the government to solve the problem using nonmarket solutions.

Consider the example of Steve and Cheryl who are serious birders and dedicated members of the local Audubon Society in their hometown. They dedicate a great deal of time, effort, and personal expense to attracting a wide variety of birds to their home feeders, and they enjoy categorizing, counting, and observing the variety of species they observe. They are especially fond of the Eastern Bluebird, which was once nearly extinct but now thrives and visits their home each year in the summer. This species of bird was nearly driven to extinction due to pesticide usage, DDT in particular. If Steve and Cheryl owned the bluebirds, they could have sued those pesticide users who killed off the birds. But, there is no ownership of the wild birds, no property rights to wild birds, and no market for the birds or rights to the birds. The absence of a market for bird-watching rights or bird attraction rights means that Steve and Cheryl must be satisfied with indirect means of assuring the presence of birds. If they could buy bird rights from local farmers who overuse pesticides, they could more directly increase the supply of Eastern Bluebirds in their area. But that is not possible because there is no market for rights to wild birds.

Public Goods as a Special Case of Externalities

Public goods are a special case of externalities. They are goods that provide positive externalities to all community residents. Public goods provide benefits to all residents of a jurisdiction, with the same quantity of the public good available to everyone (the definition of a public good). A city park, for example, provides beautiful views, open space for enjoyment, picnic facilities, bicycle paths, and other amenities that city residents can enjoy. One way to view this public good is that the park provides positive externalities to all the residents. From this point of view, the essential publicness of the park lies in the positive externalities it generates for all residents of the city.

Education is at least partly a public good because the creation of skills and knowledge benefits others. You and I benefit from Dr. James D. Watson, Dr. Maurice H. F. Wilkins, and Dr. Francis H. C. Crick having been well educated in Britain, for example. Together they studied the nature and structure of deoxyribonucleic acid (DNA) and won the 1962 Nobel Prize in Physiology and Medicine for the discovery, and we benefit from that discovery in many ways as it has advanced modern medicine considerably. National defense is also a public good in that it confers positive externalities to all residents of the country. We all benefit from the national security provided and the opportunity to pursue our life's interests undeterred by foreign invasion. Our judicial system, legal structure, patent and copyright laws, and a host of other features of our national institutional setting provide positive externalities as well.

NEGATIVE EXTERNALITIES: ANALYSIS OF MARGINAL DAMAGES

Negative externalities, as described earlier, confer costs due to external damages caused by some activity. Assessing the extent of damages can be difficult; cases are often divided into constant marginal damages cases and variable marginal damages cases.

Constant Marginal Damages

A private firm acting in such a way as to maximize its profit will want to produce that level of output where the **marginal private cost** (*MPC*) equals the **marginal benefit** (*MB*) of production, which is the marginal revenue; hence the usual rule for the efficient level of output is to produce where $MPC = MB$, illustrated in Figure 4.3. The marginal private cost curve is drawn as upward sloping, the usual case, reflecting decreasing returns to scale. The marginal benefit line is downward sloping as we would expect in the case of

FIGURE 4.3 Privately Efficient Level of Output

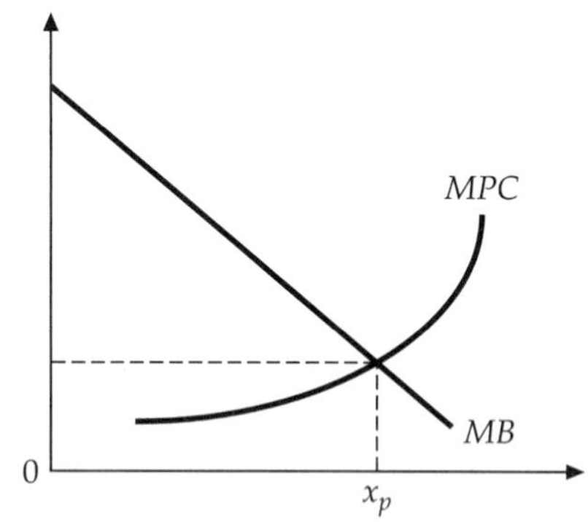

a linear demand curve.[2] At the output level x_p, we have the privately optimal output where the firm is maximizing its profit.

If a negative externality is associated with the production of this product, there are also **marginal damages (*MD*)** that must be considered. Although the firm incurs costs of *MPC* and takes those into account as it makes production decisions, the marginal damages to others in the economy are ignored because they are external to the workings of the market mechanism. If we were to take both the firm's marginal private costs (*MPC*) and the marginal damages (*MD*) inflicted on others into account, the solution to the production problem would be different.

First, construct a measure of cost that reflects the full cost to society of producing the product. That includes the firm's marginal private cost (*MPC*) plus the marginal damages (*MD*). Adding these two together provides a view of the full cost to society of the production of the product. We define **marginal social cost (*MSC*)** as $MSC = MPC + MD$. In this case, the marginal social cost (*MSC*) lies above marginal private cost (*MPC*) by a constant amount equal to the marginal damage (*MD*), as shown in Figure 4.4. From the firm's private point of view, the efficient level of output is x_p, the output level that maximizes profit. From society's point of view, including the marginal damages in the consideration, the socially efficient output rate is x_s. Taking the marginal damages into account results in an efficient output rate that is smaller. The manufacturer should produce less: $x_s < x_p$.

Beverage Bottles and Cans

People enjoy beverages packaged in bottles and cans. Whether it is a cold bottle of Budweiser consumed on a hot summer day or a can of Mountain Dew slipped into the backpack for enjoyment during economics class, the convenience of bottles and cans is an ordinary part of life in the affluent United States. Unfortunately, another part of ordinary life in the affluent United States is litter. Bottles and cans litter roadsides, parking lots,

FIGURE 4.4 Socially Optimal Output with a Negative Externality

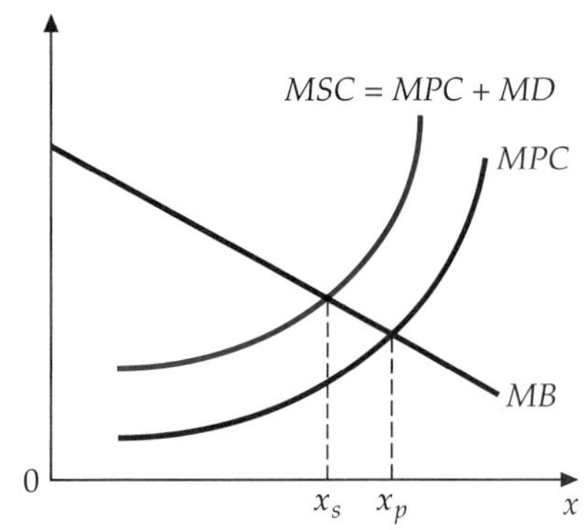

classrooms, and most any area where people go. In this case, the production of bottled beverages brings with it the negative externality of litter and the associated marginal damages.

Litter is a type of marginal damage that is proportional to the quantity of output. For each bottle or can of beverage produced, we obtain one empty bottle or can generating a damage of constant amount. That is, total damages are proportional to the number of bottles and cans; hence the marginal damage of each additional bottle or can is constant.

Given this situation, it is clear that the socially optimal number of bottles and cans of beverages is lower than the privately optimal number of bottles and cans. The reason, of course, is that the private decisions of bottlers and consumers do not take into account the damages caused by improper disposal of the bottles and cans. Taking these marginal damages into account, we should produce fewer bottles and cans of beverages.

Automobile Batteries

Another example of a negative externality involving constant marginal damages is automobile batteries. The production of automobile batteries causes a fixed amount of damage per unit of output regardless of the firm's output level. Each battery produced eventually fails and requires disposal. Even the Sears Diehard battery eventually dies. The name put on the battery is intended to communicate that killing this battery is difficult, but the fact remains that it *will* die. The damage caused by improper disposal of batteries is a given amount of pollution per battery. The amount of marginal damage each battery causes is independent of the number of batteries produced by the firm. Of course, the more batteries produced and sold, the more total damage, but marginal damage is constant. Here again, if we take the marginal damages into account, the socially optimal quantity of batteries is smaller than the privately optimal quantity of batteries. We should produce and consume fewer Diehard batteries and have fewer disposal problems with dead Diehards.

As new hybrids and electric vehicles that rely on batteries for power storage, such as the Toyota Prius and the Chevy Volt become more common, the marginal damages related to all of the additional batteries must be taken into account. If consumers ignore the marginal damages from these batteries, too many will be consumed. One way to address this situation is to require a prepaid disposal fee, refundable if and when the battery is recycled. Consumers in states with a "bottle bill" are familiar with this concept as they are required to pay a bottle/can deposit of 5 or 10 cents per container of soda bought. When they return the container, the deposit is refunded. The concept of disposal deposits will be discussed further in the section on remedies for externalities.

Variable Marginal Damages

Unlike the examples of pollution involving constant marginal damages, some forms of pollution cause increasing marginal damages. In these cases, the marginal damages grow larger as the output of the firm or industry increases. Figure 4.5 illustrates the case. The marginal social cost (*MSC*) lies above the marginal private cost (*MPC*) by an amount equal to the marginal damage (*MD*). Because marginal damages are rising with the output level x, the vertical distance between *MSC* and *MPC* grows with x. We can think of marginal damages as an increasing function of output $MD(x)$, where $MD'(x) > 0$. The effect of the externality is to cause the firm to produce too much output, and hence its product causes too much pollution. The socially efficient level of output requires scaling back the privately optimal output rate. In the process, there will be less pollution created.

It is important to notice, however, that the socially efficient output rate still involves some pollution. It is not economically sensible to eliminate all pollution. Even at x_s, the socially efficient output rate, there will be marginal damages $MD(x_s)$, and hence total damages equal to the sum of all the marginal damages from $x = 0$ up through $x = x_s$ output levels.

FIGURE 4.5 Analysis of a Negative Externality When Marginal Damages are Variable

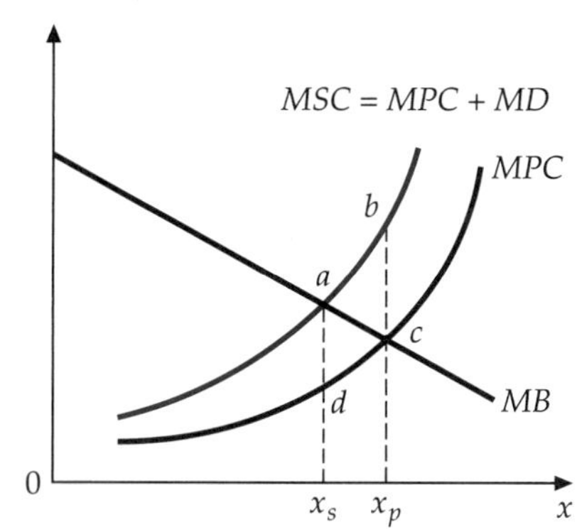

If we restricted the firm to producing an output rate x_s rather than its desired rate x_p, wouldn't the firm be worse off? Of course it would. We can measure how much worse off the firm would be at x_s by computing its lost profit. The marginal profit ($M\pi$) on each unit produced is the difference between the marginal benefit and the marginal private cost: $M\pi = MB - MPC$. Graphically, it is the vertical distance between MB and MPC for each unit by which we require the firm to scale back output from x_p to x_s. Thus, the lost profit to the firm would be the (approximately) triangular area *acd*. No question, the firm is hurt by this requirement. As a result, some combination of the firm's customers, workers, and shareholders will be hurt by the environmentally based requirement that the firm scale back its business. Consumers may have to pay higher prices for the product produced by the firm, workers may earn lower wages, and shareholders may receive smaller dividends.

The other side of the coin, however, is that society benefits from a reduced level of environmental damage. When output is scaled back from x_p to x_s the total environmental damage is reduced by the amount of the marginal damage times the number of units of output no longer produced. In Figure 4.5, the reduction in total environmental damage is given by the (approximate) parallelogram *abcd*. This area represents the summation of the marginal damages avoided over each unit of output no longer produced.

The net effect of scaling back production from x_p to x_s is to impose a loss of *acd* on the firm while conferring benefits of *abcd* on all of society (including the customers, workers, and shareholders of the firm). A clear net benefit is associated with reduced output because the firm's loss is smaller than society's gain. The net gain is the (approximately) triangular area *abc*.

This result is general. Whenever a negative externality causing marginal damages exists, reduction of output from the privately efficient level x_p back to the socially efficient level x_s will result in a positive net benefit. The private market mechanism allocates too many resources to the production of goods when that production process involves a negative externality. It is socially efficient to produce less of the good, using fewer resources and producing less of the externality.

Nuclear Power Plant Cooling Towers

Consider the case of a nuclear power generating facility that uses lake water to cool its generators. A nuclear plant located on the edge of Lake Michigan, for example, can draw cool water from the lake into the power facility. That water is used to cool the hot generators, being warmed in the process of generating power, and the warm water is then returned to the lake. Environmental damage may be caused in this process as warm water returned to the lake kills delicate forms of aquatic life that cannot live at the higher temperatures of the water. In this scenario, the more power generated by the facility, the more lake water is used to cool the generators, the more damage is done to the aquatic life of the lake in the region of the facility. The diffusion properties of heat in the lake water are such that high temperatures are maintained in the coastal area near the power facility and are not sufficiently dissipated.

As a result, several species of aquatic life are threatened. Each additional kilowatt-hour of electricity generated produces an increasing amount of damage. In this type of externality, the marginal damages rise with the output of the firm.

Debating the Extent of the Damages

Environmental debates are often subject to sharp disagreement over the extent of the damages involved. Environmentalists claim that the world is ending unless we wake up to the problem and do something right away. Business interests claim there is no problem. In the face of such disagreement, is the previous analysis of any use at all? How can we possibly apply such a model when the two sides of the debate have such different views? Actually, the model introduced previously is very useful in such a situation because it helps us define the range of policy options worth debating. Consider a case where the environmentalists claim that the marginal damages are MD^e while the business interests are claiming that the marginal damages are MD^b. Of course, $MD^e > MD^b$. Figure 4.6 illustrates the situation.

The business community admits some small amount of environmental damage and concludes that the efficient output rate is x_b. The environmentalist community believes the environmental damage is large and concludes that the efficient output rate is x_e. What are we to make of the difference of opinion? Are the resulting policy recommendations regarding output level for the firm or industry of any use? They are, and the reason why lies in the very biases we expect undergird the recommendations. We would expect the business interests to have a downward bias in their estimate of the marginal damages caused by the production of their product. We would expect the environmental community to have an upward bias in their assessment of the potential damage caused by production of the product. As a result, the two views of the marginal social cost (*MSC*) probably bracket the range of all

FIGURE 4.6 Debating the Size of Marginal Damages

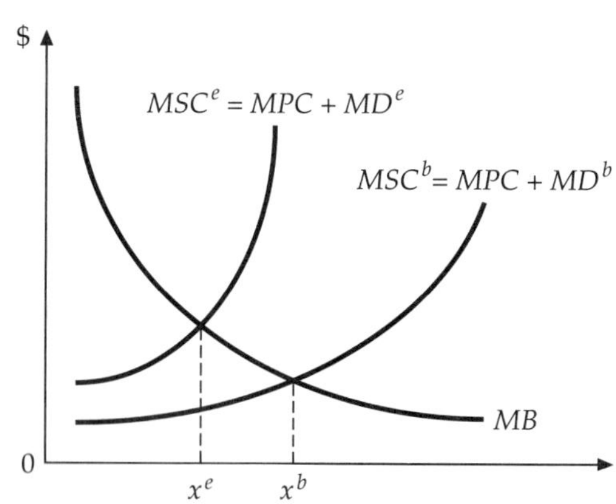

feasible outcomes. The range of policy debate over how much output should be permitted is narrowed to the range $[x_e, x_b]$. We can eliminate all policy options less than x_e and more than x_b. The differences of opinion help specify the appropriate range for reasonable policy consideration. What is needed, then, is more precise estimates of the marginal damages caused by the production of the product. Environmental economists are called on to provide just such estimates because they specialize in the estimation of marginal damages.

Pollution Abatement

Another way to view the problem of pollution is from the point of view of cleaning it up. **Pollution abatement** is the process by which pollution is reduced. The question is to determine just how much of the pollution ought to be cleaned up. Does that notion sound strange? Why not clean it all up? Should we be satisfied with anything less than a pristine environment? From the economist's point of view, there is an economically efficient level of pollution. To attempt to reduce the level of pollution below that quantity is costly and foolish.

Figure 4.7 illustrates the problem. The horizontal axis measures pollution abatement—the amount of pollution cleaned up. P is the total amount of pollution that exists. If $a = 0$, none of the pollution is abated. If $a = P$, all of the pollution is abated. Abatement technology is such that the marginal benefits of abatement are declining. For the first few units of abatement, marginal benefits are large, but those benefits decline as the environment becomes cleaner and cleaner. Abatement is always helpful, $MB > 0$, but it is less and less helpful as we have a cleaner environment. On the cost side, the marginal cost of abatement activity is rising. The first few units of abatement are easy and cheap. All we need to do is clean up the big chunks of pollution that are

FIGURE 4.7 Pollution Abatement Analysis

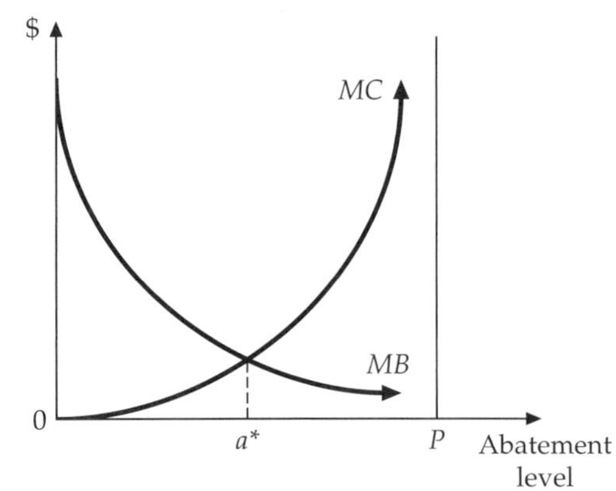

easy to retrieve. As we clean up more and more of the pollution, however, it becomes more expensive to eliminate additional units of pollution. The last few traces of pollution are very expensive to abate.

The efficient level of pollution abatement is where the marginal cost of abatement equals the marginal benefit of abatement, the level labeled a^*. We should abate exactly that quantity of pollution, no more, no less. If we were inclined to abate more pollution, we would find that additional units of abatement beyond a^* involve marginal costs that exceed marginal benefits. It simply costs more to abate those units of pollution than it is worth. We would use more resources than it is worth to clean up the added pollution. Similarly, if we were inclined to abate less than a^* units of pollution, we would be making a mistake because added abatement would bring more in marginal benefits than it would take in marginal costs to abate the pollution. In an economic sense, we can make either mistake: too much pollution abatement or too little. The efficient level of pollution abatement is a^*. That leaves $P - a^*$ quantity of pollution unabated. It is not economically sensible to clean it all up. Consequently, we would not support a public policy to clean up all the pollution. An optimal amount of pollution is not generally zero.

We should consider the comparative static effects of changes in the parameters of the pollution abatement problem, however. What would happen if new technology reduced the marginal cost of pollution abatement? The marginal cost (*MC*) curve would shift downward, and the efficient level of abatement would increase. It would be sensible to abate more pollution if the marginal cost of abatement were reduced. What would happen if we discovered new medical evidence that the pollution is more harmful than we believed previously? In that case, the marginal benefit of abatement would be higher than before. The marginal benefit (*MB*) curve would shift upward, and the efficient level of pollution abatement would be greater. It would be sensible to clean up more pollution understood its harmful effects.

Additional pollution abatement is justified if there are reductions in the marginal costs of abatement or increases in the marginal benefits. Reduced abatement levels are justified if there are increased marginal costs of abatement or lower marginal benefits.

POSITIVE EXTERNALITIES: ANALYSIS OF MARGINAL EXTERNAL BENEFITS

Consider the case of a firm engaged in the production of high-technology equipment. As a part of its production process, the firm has a team of researchers actively engaged in cutting-edge research in the field. New ideas generated by the research team can be transformed into profitable new products by the firm. But those new ideas cannot be kept exclusively for the firm's application. Once they become generally known, others will benefit as well. The firm's expenditure on research and development brings with it a positive externality in the form of new knowledge that benefits others.

Economic Analysis

The private decision on how much research and development (R&D) in which to engage is determined by the firm's usual rule of efficiency. The firm will engage in that amount of R&D where the **marginal private benefit** (*MPB*) equals the marginal cost (*MC*). In this case, however, since there is a positive externality, the **marginal social benefit** (*MSB*) exceeds the marginal private benefit (*MPB*) by the amount of the **marginal external benefit** (*MEB*). Figure 4.8 illustrates this. The privately efficient level of R&D is labeled x_p. It is that amount of R&D where the marginal private benefit equals the marginal cost. When the marginal external benefit of R&D is taken into account, the marginal social benefit of R&D is higher, and the socially efficient level of R&D is x_s. The private firm will engage in too little R&D on its own. If we expanded R&D from x_p to x_s, total benefits would increase by the area labeled x_pbcx_s whereas the additional costs would be measured by the area x_pacx_s. The net benefit of expanded R&D would be the area labeled *abc*. Although the firm would be spending more than is privately profitable on R&D, society would benefit by an amount larger than the firm would have to spend.

This result is general. When a positive externality exists, the private market mechanism allocates too few resources to the production of the good involved. It is socially efficient to produce more of the good, using more resources, and hence produce more of the beneficial externality as well.

Xerox Corporation's Palo Alto Research Center

Consider the case of the Palo Alto Research Center (PARC) of Xerox Corporation.[3] In 1970, leadership of the Xerox Corporation had a sinking feeling that the prospect of electronic communications and a paperless office environment would not be good for a company specializing in the paper-based photocopy business. To avoid such a grim future and assure corporate

FIGURE 4.8 Analysis of a Positive Externality

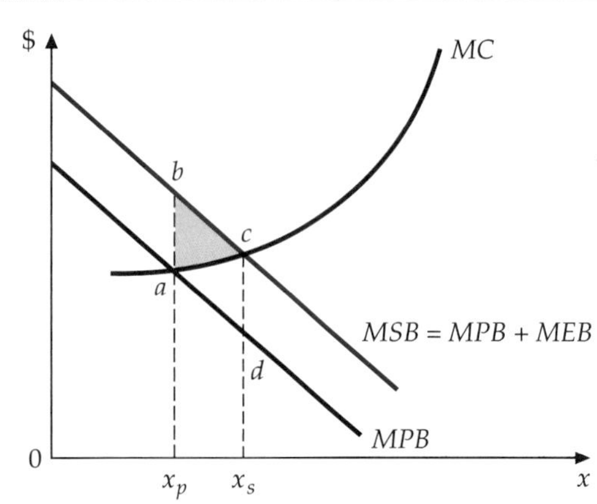

profitability long into the 1990s, Xerox assembled a team of scientists at PARC in California with a broad mandate to generate innovations that would benefit the firm. Consistent with their vision of the corporate office environment, Xerox wanted innovations that would be beneficial for office workers with minimal training. Part of the research generated in this effort was focused on the issue of the computer-user interface. Doug Engelbart, working at the Stanford Research Institute in Menlo Park, examined how users interacted with a computer system and pushed the frontier of ways to make computers easier for people to run and obtain more useful results. At the time, data were being entered into computers via punch cards, one line at a time, with up to 80 characters per line. Engelbart saw that people do not normally write letters or complete office forms one line at a time, however. Rather, people think in terms of a page and use their pens and typewriters to scroll back and forth along a line as well as up and down the page. Engelbart saw that a page metaphor was much closer to the way people actually do their work than was the line-editing capability of the mainframe computer of the day. He worked out a mechanism whereby users could see a page of data at a time on a terminal, with full text-editing capability. With bit-mapping technology for the screen and a small mechanism the size of a cigarette pack on wheels attached by a cord to the computer (now known as a mouse) that provided a way of moving around the screen, he had a much more natural user interface. The PARC leadership developed more-advanced systems of networked computers that used mice, full text page editors, and bit-mapped screens. This is the type of computer system we all use today, although neither your system nor mine is made by the Xerox Corporation. The pioneering PARC ideas were later adopted by both Apple in the development of the Macintosh, and Microsoft in the development of its Windows operating system. The private research activities of Xerox generated huge positive externalities in the form of advances in knowledge about computer system design.

REMEDIES FOR EXTERNALITIES

How do we remedy the problems caused by externalities? Do we take a hands-off approach and rely on the market mechanism to fix the problem, or do we have governments step in and fix the problems? Although markets are known to misallocate resources in the presence of externalities, it might seem hopeless to rely on the market mechanism to resolve the problem, but there are some ways in which we can use markets to solve externality problems. At other times, however, when the market failure is so severe, government action is needed.

A Private Solution: The Coase Theorem

Consider how one economic agent's actions affect another economic agent. Take the classic case of a railroad using steam-powered locomotives to pull train cars through rural areas where the land along the tracks is used for

TABLE 4.2 Railroad and Farmer Payoffs When the Farmer Has Property Rights

Railroad: Trains per Day	Farmer: Fields Planted *0*	*1*	*2*
0	(0, 0)	(0, 150)	(0, 160)
1	(100, 0)	(40, 150)	(−20, 160)
2	(150, 0)	(30, 150)	(−90, 160)

Source: Adapted from Roy J. Ruffin, "Externalities, Markets and Government Policy," from *Federal Reserve Bank of Dallas, Economic Review* Third Quarter, 1996. Reprinted by permission.

farming. The steam locomotives are fired by wood or coal, and on occasion a spark flies out of the smokestack, landing on a farmer's field, starting a fire, and destroying the crop. In the absence of the trains, the farmer can make \$150 on the first field planted and a total of \$160 if two fields are planted. The railroad makes \$100 on the first train it runs and another \$50 on the second train. When trains run through the area, however, each train causes \$60 worth of damage per field planted along the tracks. Table 4.2 illustrates the payoffs to both the farmer and the railroad, assuming that the railroad is liable for the damage caused by the fires. Each cell lists an ordered pair where the first entry in parentheses is the railroad's payoff and the second is the farmer's payoff.

If the farmer has one field planted and the railroad does not run any trains, the farmer will make \$150 in profit from farming activity. If the railroad runs one train, however, there is \$60 in damage due to the fires, and if the railroad is liable for that damage, its profit of \$100 is reduced to \$40. If it runs two trains, the railroad's profit of \$150 is reduced to just \$30. Assume that the railroad directly compensates the farmer for the damage caused by the fires its locomotives start.

Social welfare can be approximated in this situation by the sum of the farmer's and the railroad's profits. We can establish that social welfare is maximized when the farmer plants one field and the railroad runs one train. That is the cell with the largest sum of the two payoffs: \$190. In all other cells of the table, the sum of the payoffs is less than \$190.

How might the outcome be different if we assigned property rights the other way? Rather than assigning the farmer the right to a fire-free field, we could assign the railroad the right to create fires. This may seem peculiar, but there is always more than one way to assign property rights. Table 4.3 illustrates the payoffs when the railroad may start fires in the farmer's fields.

In this case, the farmer receives no compensation for the damages caused by the trains. For example, when the farmer has planted two fields and there are two trains run per day, the farmer's income of \$160 is changed to a loss of \$80 because each train causes \$60 in damages per field planted. What is

TABLE 4.3 Railroad and Farmer Payoffs When the Railroad Has Property Rights

Railroad: Trains per Day	Farmer: Fields Planted *0*	*1*	*2*
0	(0, 0)	(0, 150)	(0, 160)
1	(100, 0)	(100, 90)	(100, 40)
2	(150, 0)	(150, 30)	(150, −80)

the social welfare–maximizing allocation in this case? The sum of farmer and railroad payoffs is maximized when the farmer plants one field and the railroad runs one train; social welfare is $190. Notice that this is the same combination that maximized social welfare in the previous case, when the railroad was liable for damages. This outcome is not a coincidence. In fact, this outcome is of general significance and is known as the Coase theorem in economic theory.

The **Coase theorem**, named after Nobel Prize–winning economist Ronald Coase, states that the welfare-maximizing outcome is unaffected by the assignment of property rights, as long as someone is assigned property rights. Although the distribution of welfare among the parties is certainly affected by the assignment of property rights, the efficient outcome is not affected.

The obvious policy implication of the Coase theorem is that the government is not needed to guide the economic agents to the social welfare–maximizing outcome. Rather, all that is needed is a clear establishment of property rights and enforcement of those rights, and the market mechanism will guide the economic agents to the social welfare–maximizing outcome.

This result might make it appear as though there is no scope for government because the market mechanism yields the efficient outcome, but the Coase theorem requires further examination. The theorem is based on several strict assumptions which we may question. First, Coase assumed no transactions costs were involved. The farmer and the railroad are able to identify, negotiate, and compensate one another at zero cost. If there are positive transactions costs, however, the strong result of the theorem will not hold: the assignment of property rights will affect the social welfare–maximizing outcome. Second, the number of parties involved in the example is very small: one farmer and one railroad. If the number of parties affected by the externality is large, the result of the theorem is affected. In reality the Coase theorem is likely to hold only in those cases where transactions costs are low and the number of parties involved is small.

Another Private Solution: Emissions Permit Trading

Another way to use markets to solve pollution problems is for the government to place a limit on the total amount of pollution permitted, and then allow polluters to trade the pollution permits. The issue of emissions trading is especially important because it is a policy option being used in a number of environmental contexts. These programs are sometimes called *cap-and-trade* programs if they are designed to put an overall cap on the amount of pollution permitted, combined with an emissions trading provision. In this way, the program can reduce the overall level of pollution, but permit the emitters to do so in the most efficient way by trading emission rights.

The emissions permit trading idea is based on the concept that the marginal cost of emissions reduction may be different across firms, regions, or countries. Suppose that the marginal cost of reducing emissions is relatively high in country A and relatively low in country B: $MC^a > MC^b$. The total cost of a given level of emission reduction can then be minimized by shifting the emissions reduction, as much as possible, to the low-cost country. The problem, of course, is that emissions reductions may be relatively costly in highly developed countries. The consequence of an emissions trading policy is then to permit highly developed countries to continue emitting greenhouse gases while emissions reductions are accomplished in developing countries. The policy question that arises with permit trading is whether such a policy solution is fair. Another design issue of importance is the mechanism used to provide the initial allocation of permits. One option is simply to hand out the pollution permits free of charge. This option provides a windfall to the polluters, however. A better design option is to auction the initial permits to polluters, thereby avoiding the problem of giving windfalls to polluters. In addition, the action can generate revenue that can be used to advance abatement technologies. Paltsev et al. (2007) provide a good overview of the design issues in cap-and-trade programs. On the issue of the allocation of allowances, they point out that if allowances are auctioned, the overall distributional effect of the program depends on what the government does with the auction revenue. On the other hand, if the allocations are distributed using some kind of "grandfathering" principle, the firms that receive the allocations are being given the asset value or scarcity rent.

A Public Solution: Regulations and Controls

The natural inclination of a government faced with a pollution problem is often to pass a law making pollution illegal, with corresponding fines and penalties for those polluters caught in the act of polluting. Consider the case of a regulation that outlaws all pollution above the quantity P'. If we put such a regulation into effect, the economic situation can be illustrated in a diagram like Figure 4.7. If P' is chosen by the regulatory agency at a level less than a^*, too little abatement and economic welfare would be enhanced by making the regulation more stringent. On the other hand, if P' is chosen by the regulatory agency at a level greater than a^*, there is too much abatement mandated by the regulation, and economic welfare is reduced (as compared to the maximal welfare possible at a^*).

This dilemma illustrates the difficulty of regulating pollution abatement directly. How does the regulatory agency select a^*? Scientists may be able to tell the agency about the pure science of the effects of pollution. Businesspeople may be able to tell the agency about the regulation's impact on profits. The best way to bring all the relevant information to bear on the situation, however, is to subject the analysis to the marketplace where the marginal benefits and marginal costs of abatement activity are balanced against one another. Regulatory agencies often select an ad hoc physical limit on the amount of pollution permitted or an ad hoc physical limit on the amount of abatement required of firms. Oftentimes economists fear that the physical limits selected are not the optimal quantities. A command approach to the allocation of resources is not likely to lead to the economically efficient level of output or attendant pollution. For this reason, economists have been recommending market-based approaches for reducing pollution. One of the most promising approaches is the emissions trading permit scheme discussed previously. Although this approach does begin with a limitation on the total amount of pollution permitted, it does permit firms in the marketplace to allocate resources according to their individual marginal costs and provides a more efficient means of reaching a given level of pollution abatement than does the command approach.

Consider this example. The State of California recently debated a complete ban on plastic shopping bags at supermarkets and retail stores. Supporters of a statewide ban claimed that 19 million plastic bags are used every year in California, harming the environment and costing the state $25 million in litter cleanup. Although the statewide ban did not pass, several California cities have enacted their own bans, including San Francisco, Palo Alto, Fairfax, and Malibu. Clearly, plastic bags create negative externalities in the form of litter which lasts a very long time as the half-life of a bag in a forest or landfill is exceedingly long. They are also responsible for the death of some wildlife. Even so, a statute to completely ban the dissemination of plastic bags is not an appropriate economic solution to the problem. The economically optimal number of new plastic bags to distribute is not zero. As Figure 4.4 illustrates, the socially optimal number of new bags is less than the number that are distributed when the externality is not taken into account, $x_s < x_p$, but it is not zero. In this case the command-and-control approach of banning plastic bags will seriously distort the market and result in a large welfare loss.

Another Public Solution: Pigouvian Taxes and Subsidies

An important public solution for the problem of externalities is the use of a **Pigouvian tax** or **subsidy**. Originally suggested by the British economist A. C. Pigou, the idea is to tax a firm producing a negative externality or subsidize a firm producing a positive externality in order to correct for the effects of the externality. In the case of a negative externality, Pigou suggested applying a tax on the firm's output equal to the amount of the marginal damage: $t = MD$. The firm would then face a private marginal cost curve that would shift up by the amount of the tax. Because the tax is equal to the marginal damage at the socially efficient output level, $t = MD(x_s)$, the firm's private marginal cost curve including the tax, $MPC + t$, would be the same as the marginal social cost curve at x_s. As a result, the firm would select x_s output, which is exactly the output that is efficient socially. The Pigouvian tax leads the firm

"I've always felt that my role as a beaver transcends any political changes at E.P.A."

to make a private decision that is socially efficient. Figure 4.9 illustrates the application of a Pigouvian tax to correct for a negative externality.

If the tax can be set equal to the marginal damage (*MD*), the firm will voluntarily change to the socially efficient output rate. This is one of the strengths of the Pigouvian tax solution.[4] Government action is limited to setting the tax. Once the government sets the tax equal to the marginal damage, market forces solve the problem. No government agency tells the firms what to do. They simply react to the tax, seeking their own best interest, and in the process they are led by market forces to the socially optimal solution. In addition, the tax generates revenue equal to the area *abcd*. The practical difficulty with implementing this solution, however, is determining an accurate estimate of the marginal damage at the socially efficient output rate in order to set the tax at the appropriate level.

In the case of a positive externality, a subsidy is required. We must set the subsidy s equal to the marginal external benefit (*MEB*) at the socially efficient level of output x_s: $s = MEB(x_s)$. Figure 4.10 illustrates this case.

FIGURE 4.9 Pigouvian Tax Corrects Negative Externality

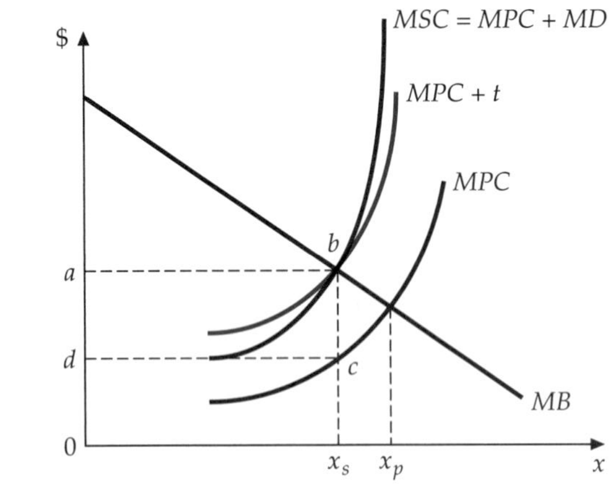

FIGURE 4.10 Pigouvian Subsidy Correction for a Positive Externality

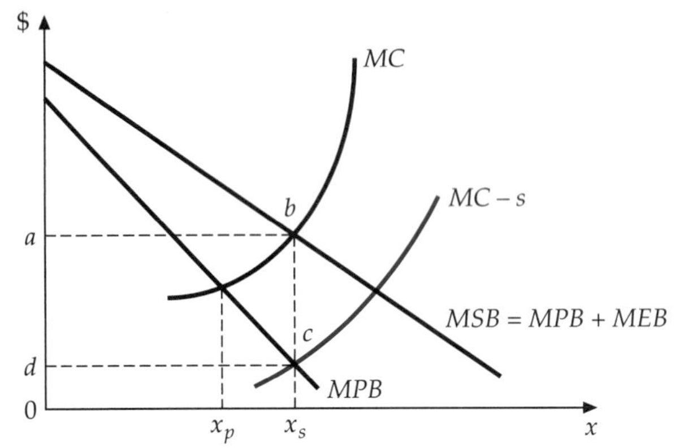

Public policy debates about pollution are often characterized by sharp disagreements over the extent of marginal damages. Listening to a public hearing on a pollution topic, one typically hears environmentalists stressing that unless the pollution source is stopped and the existing pollution cleaned up, life as we know it will end (literally and figuratively). On the other side, business interests often minimize the damage, saying that the pollution does very little harm, if any at all. And besides, it would be very expensive to clean up. How are we to deal with such a divergence of views? Do we simply

FIGURE 4.11 Dolphin By-Catch Debate

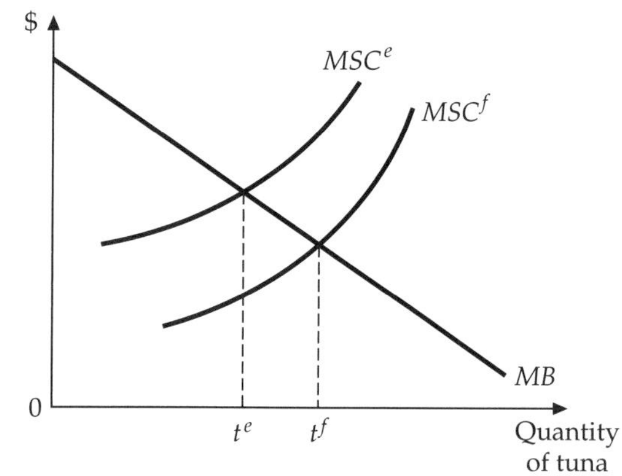

throw up our hands and say take a point of view, one or the other, depending on your beliefs and biases? That is not an economist's response. From an economics point of view, the divergence of opinion is helpful to narrow the range of policy debate.

Let's examine this situation using the example of dolphin by-catch, as illustrated in Figure 4.11. Suppose that the environmentalist estimates the marginal social cost of tuna fishing as MSC^e. Due to the problem of dolphin by-catch, the environmentalist sees the *MSC* as being very high. On the other hand, fishermen don't view the problem of dolphin by-catch as very problematic. They estimate the marginal social cost of tuna fishing as MSC^f. Given the fishermen's estimate, we should harvest t^f tons of tuna per year. Given the environmentalists' estimate, we should harvest a smaller quantity t^e. Rather than see this as a conflict where the two estimates provide different socially efficient harvesting rates, we can observe that the two views have narrowed the range of feasible solutions. No harvesting rate less than t^e is efficient, just as no harvesting rate in excess of t^f is efficient. Public debate on the policy should be confined to harvesting rates between t^e and t^f. What is really needed is more objective evidence on the marginal damages of tuna fishing caused by dolphin by-catch. Environmental economists are trained to estimate just such damages and use them to provide policy.

POLICY STUDY

BP's Deepwater Horizon Gulf Oil Leak

On April 20, 2010, a Deepwater Horizon oil drilling rig operated by BP in the Gulf of Mexico exploded, touching off the largest oil leak in history. Some of the oil floated to the surface of the water and drifted to south Louisiana coastal areas, and some of the oil remained submerged, following ocean currents to distant destinations. Tropical birds along the coast were coated with thick gooey oil residue. Critical fisheries were damaged and may take years to recover. Damage to the Gulf of Mexico ecosystem and to the livelihoods of those who depend on economic activity in the Gulf region is a major concern.

Figure 4.12 illustrates the National Oceanic and Atmospheric Administration (NOAA) map of the oil spill and their discovery of oil as far as 3,300 feet below the ocean surface 42 miles northeast and 142 miles southeast of the oil rig site. Samples of contaminants revealed low concentrations of subsurface oil and PAHs (polycyclic aromatic hydrocarbons) at depths ranging from 50 meters to 1,400 meters. The samples indicate that concentrations of hydrocarbons generally decrease with depth, with limited exceptions. Although the concentration of contaminants in the ocean is low, the extent of the marginal damages involved is uncertain. Estimates indicate the total cost from the leak could rise to a total of $20 billion. BP has committed $20 billion to a claims escrow fund, out of which payments are being made to those negatively affected by the oil spill.

FIGURE 4.12 BP's Deepwater Horizon Oil Leak, 2010

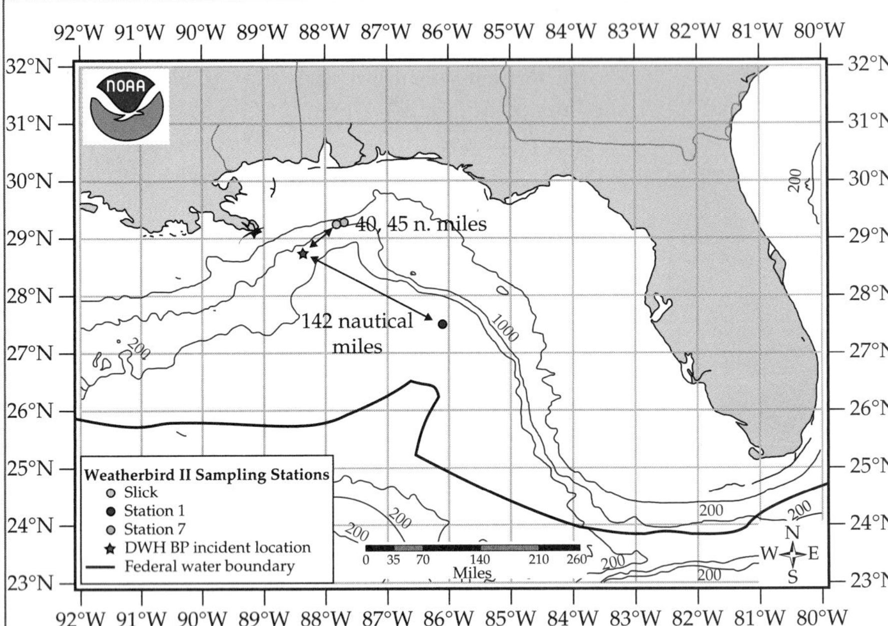

Source: NOAA.

The costs associated with this historic mess are clearly marginal damages associated with exploring for and producing oil. For each additional barrel of oil discovered and produced, a marginal cost is associated with the damages caused to the environment in the process. Even though an event such as the BP situation is a low-probability, high-impact risk that is an inescapable part of deepwater drilling, the expected value of the damage must not be ignored. By ignoring the marginal damages, we get too much drilling, too much oil spilled in the process of exploring for more oil, and too low a price for oil.

In the wake of this disaster there are calls to halt all offshore drilling. Is that the right conclusion? In terms of the analysis of this chapter, it is not. What is required is to properly assess the risks involved and the expected value of potential damages and take those into account in making decisions about exploration and drilling. Doing so rationally will result in less drilling, but not a complete halt to all drilling.

References

Koch, Wendy. "NOAA: Tests Confirm Oil Spreading Deep Below Surface," USA Today, June 8, 2010, http://content.usatoday.com/communities/greenhouse/post/2010/06/tests-confirm-deep-gulf-oil-plumes-are-spreading-far/1.

"NOAA Completes Initial Analysis of *Weatherbird II* Water Samples," NOAA website, June 8, 2010, http://www.noaanews.noaa.gov/stories2010/20100608_weatherbird.html

Crooks, Ed. "BP 'Not Prepared' for Spill," *Financial Times*, June 3, 2010.

POLICY STUDY

Climate Change

Concern has grown in recent years that human activities are responsible for increased concentrations of greenhouse gases such as carbon dioxide and methane in the earth's atmosphere. Higher concentrations of such gases are believed to be responsible for observed higher temperatures all around the globe and may eventually lead to serious impacts such as higher sea levels and changed weather patterns. The Stern (2007) review of evidence reports that the overall costs and risks of climate change in the absence of any action may be equal to a loss of at least 5 percent of global GDP each year in perpetuity. With such serious potential consequences, the world's leading industrialized nations studied the issue and came to an agreement in 1997 known as the Kyoto Protocol, more formally as the United Nations Framework Convention on Climate Change (UNFCCC). The UNFCCC represents an international coordinated effort to develop and implement policies to reduce global warming or more generally address climate change. Follow-up meetings of the UNFCCC have taken place annually, such as the meeting in Copenhagen (2009) and Cancun (2010), with the objective of developing monitoring systems and compliance mechanisms.

This agreement commits its signatories to reduce their emissions of greenhouse gases. The United States signed the agreement in 1998 and committed itself to reducing emissions of such gases to a level 7 percent below its 1990 level during the commitment period of 2008 to 2012. The way gases are measured and counted toward the target reduction, and because of the way gas-removing sinks are counted, the actual reduction in the United States was expected to be less than 7 percent. Although the United States signed the Kyoto Protocol during the Clinton Administration, the Senate did not ratify the treaty. Subsequently, the United States withdrew from the Kyoto process in the year 2001, questioning the underlying science and citing the high cost of compliance and an "ever-tightening straightjacket" of regulation.

Specific aspects of the most difficult issues involved in the Kyoto Protocol were not included in the initial agreement and are subject to ongoing negotiation. Issues still being debated and negotiated include:

- The size of required greenhouse gas reductions and those gases covered by the agreement
- Whether developing nations should be part of the agreement and be required to reduce their greenhouse gas emissions
- Whether to permit emissions trading among countries, allowing credit to be given to a country that provides either funding or investment in another country which actually reduces emissions but where such a reduction can be accomplished less expensively

An important mechanism that is part of the Kyoto agreement as well as a suggestion of the Stern (2007) review is emissions trading.[5] This mechanism, discussed in the chapter, is important because it is a suggested policy option that is being advocated in a number of environmental contexts. The idea is based on the concept that the marginal cost of emissions reduction may be different across regions or countries. Suppose that the marginal cost of reducing emissions is relatively high in country A and relatively low in country B: $MC_A > MC_B$. The total cost of a given level of emissions reduction can then be minimized by shifting the emissions reduction, as much as possible, to the low-cost country. The problem, of course, is that emissions reductions may be relatively costly in highly developed countries. The consequence of an emissions trading policy is then to permit highly developed countries to continue emitting greenhouse gases while emissions reductions are accomplished in developing countries. The policy question that arises is whether such a situation is fair and proper.

Although the United States participated in the development of the Kyoto Protocol under the leadership of the Clinton administration, the subsequent Bush administration has flatly rejected the protocol and argues that it puts the United States at an economic disadvantage. In light of this situation, discussions among the remaining Kyoto signatory countries have resulted in an agreement to proceed with modified terms of the protocol, allowing for more emissions trading and crediting forest planting and other activities that reduce atmospheric carbon dioxide.

The point of this policy study is to illustrate just how difficult it may be to recognize the presence of negative externalities, incorporate them into the economic analysis, and appropriately scale back production of output. The reality of doing what Figures 4.4, 4.5, and 4.9 illustrate is very difficult. First, there is serious debate about whether there is damage at all. Second, there is debate over the size of the marginal damages. Third, controversy surrounds the need for a Pigouvian tax. Finally, there is resistance to scaling back the output of goods and services that produce the harmful pollution.

PROBLEMS

1. In which of the following situations is the Coase theorem likely to apply? Explain.
   a. The neighbor who lives below you in the apartment building loves to play old John Denver records at loud volume early in the morning. In fact, his favorite song seems to be "Thank God I'm a Country Boy." You hate old John Denver songs and this one in particular.
   b. You have just moved to Beijing and quickly discover that you are allergic to smog. It causes you great pain in breathing and limits your ability to work. Furthermore, you have medical expenses related to treatment for its health effects on you.
   c. Medical research in the 1990s has revealed a specific cause of birth defects related to a certain drug prescribed for pregnant women in the 1960s (thalidomide).
   d. The water in the huge underground Ogalalla aquifer in the Great Plains region of the United States is being nitrate contaminated due to agricultural fertilizer use throughout the region. As a homeowner in this region, you find that your water must be treated in order to be safe for drinking.
2. One of the most striking aspects of cities in the former Soviet Union is the poor condition of public places. Streets, parks, libraries, museums, concert halls, and public gathering places of every description are all in very poor condition, revealing years of neglect and lack of maintenance. Explain this phenomenon in light of the definition of property rights and the transition from socialism to a market economy.
3. Suppose that the marginal benefit associated with corn production is $MB = 2.5$. The marginal private cost of production is $MPC = 2 + 0.1Q$, where Q measures bushels of corn produced in thousands. The marginal damages caused by pollution in corn production are given by $MD = 0.05Q$.
   a. Compute the privately optimal output and the socially optimal output.
   b. Compute new solutions for an increase in MB to $MB = 3$. Explain what has happened and why.
   c. Demonstrate the effects of an increase in MD to $MD = 0.075$ compared to the solutions in part a.
4. Policy analysts in the Department of Natural Resources have estimated that the marginal benefits from water pollution abatement are given by the function $MB = 0.90 - 0.03A$, where A is a measure of the abatement intensity. Industry experts have estimated that the marginal cost of abatement activity is $MC = 0.30 + 0.09A$.
   a. Determine the optimal level of abatement activity.
   b. Explain what happens when new technology reduces the marginal cost of abatement to $MC = 0.25 + 0.06A$.
5. Write a one-page memo to President Obama outlining a Pigouvian tax solution to the BP oil leak problem described in the Policy Study, "BP's Deepwater Horizon Gulf Oil Leak."

6. Consider the pollution reduction mechanism known as emissions trading.
   a. What is the economic rationale for permitting emissions trading?
   b. If the objective is to minimize the cost of emissions reductions, explain what economic principle should be followed in allocating emissions reductions between two countries.
   c. Suppose the marginal cost curves for emissions reductions in countries A and B are $MC_A = 10 + 0.04q_A$ and $MC_B = 5 + 0.02q_B$. What is the most efficient allocation of an emission reduction of q_0 between the two countries? (Assume that the emissions reductions of the two countries must add up to the total emissions reduction: $q_0 = q_A + q_B$.)

REFERENCES

Fletcher, Susan R. *Global Climate Change Treaty: The Kyoto Protocol.* Washington, D.C.: Congressional Research Service, 2000. Accessed from http://ncseonline.org/nle/crsreports/climate/clim-3.cfm

Hoffman, David. "A Puzzle of Epidemic Proportions." *Washington Post*, December 16, 1998: A1.

Meade, J. E. *The Theory of Economic Externalities, The Control of Environmental Pollution and Similar Costs*. Geneva: Sijthoff-Leiden, 1973.

Paltsev, Sergey, John M. Reilly, Henry D. Jacoby, Angelo C. Gurgel, Gilbert Metcalf, Andrei P. Sokolov, and Jennifer F. Holak. "Assessment of U.S. Cap-and-Trade Proposals." MIT Joint Program on the Science and Policy of Global Change, 2007. Report Number 146.

Ruffin, Roy J. "Externalities, Markets and Government Policy." *Economic Review*. Dallas, TX: Federal Reserve Bank of Dallas, 1996, 3rd quarter.

Stern, Nickolas. *The Economics of Climate Change: The Stern Review.* Cambridge, UK: Cambridge University Press, 2007. Electronic version available at http://webarchive.nationalarchives.gov.uk/+/http://www.hm-treasury.gov.uk/independent_reviews/stern_review_economics_climate_change/stern_review_report.cfm.

NOTES

1. *http://epa.gov*.
2. With linear inverse demand $p = a - bx$, the marginal revenue line is $MR = a - 2bx$. The marginal revenue line has the same intercept as the demand line, but it is twice as steep.
3. This example is based on Cringely (1993).
4. If you like the Pigouvian tax/subsidy solution for externalities, you may want to join Harvard Professor Greg Mankiw's Pigou Club. See his economics blog at *http://gregmankiw.blogspot.com/*.
5. For more on the Kyoto protocol see Hoffman (1998).
6. This material is based on Fletcher (2000).

CHAPTER

5

Radius Images/Getty Images

Income Distribution and Transfer Programs

LEARNING OBJECTIVES

1. Describe the income distribution of an economy and explain how it is measured.
2. Explain the nature of poverty and its measurement.
3. Describe the economic theory of income redistribution.
4. Discuss the government programs designed to redistribute income.

The world economy is becoming simultaneously wealthier and less equal in the distribution of that wealth. According to *Forbes* magazine and its "rich list" there are currently 1,011 people worldwide with assets of at least 1 billion dollars (Miller and Kroll 2010). Americans account for 40 percent of those billionaires, but the second-largest number of billionaires is now from China. Eleven countries have at least twice as many billionaires as they had just a year ago, including China, India, Turkey, and South Korea. Is this a problem or a sign of a healthy global economy? At the same time, 27 countries of the world have an income per capita of less than $2 per day, a key World Bank measure of extreme poverty (*World Development Report 2010*, Table 1, pp. 378–79). Furthermore, there are 52 countries where the share of the population in extreme poverty, earning less than $2 per day, is at least 30 percent. (*World Development Report 2010*, Table 2, pp. 380–81). Poverty is a reality around the world. No one would question that this situation is a problem, but it is a very difficult problem to resolve. This chapter examines income distributions and their measurement, poverty and its measurement, and transfer programs designed to change income distributions and alleviate poverty.

Market-oriented economies, in particular, are effective in generating income, but the distribution of that income among a nation's citizens may not be acceptable. Wide disparities of income among the wealthy and the poor can contribute to discontent and social unrest. Concerns for economic justice are voiced and motivate government action to redress the situation. Although societies vary in the extent of the income inequality that is socially tolerable, all societies have some mechanisms to help them avoid extreme inequality. Of course, there is always heated debate over redistribution programs as they take income or wealth from some people and give it to those with less. This is the proverbial problem of Robin Hood—robbing the wealthy to benefit the poor. It may seem that the process of redistribution is a zero-sum situation where what one gives up another gets, but the classic situation of "robbing Peter to pay Paul" is not the case.

The very process of redistributing income and wealth alters the incentives to produce income and wealth and thereby affects the total amount of income and wealth in the economy. As a result, it is important to keep in mind that redistribution is not merely an issue of equity. It also affects efficiency. It is certainly possible that redistribution programs can result in less distributed income. If income and wealth are destroyed in the process of altering the distribution, a fundamental problem must be resolved. That being said, there are also ways of redistributing the produce of an economy without destroying wealth in order to assure a more equitable distribution. It is imperative to understand what types of redistribution mechanisms are efficient, not destructive of wealth. Increasing the income and wealth of an economy is the purview of growth theory, which is not a direct part of public finance. Rather, we focus on issues of how redistribution of existing income and wealth affect people's lives.

Efficiency issues related to these programs are considered in greater detail in later chapters. Equity issues are the focus here.

MEASURING THE INCOME DISTRIBUTION

In order to begin thinking about an **income distribution**, we must first array the income data from the minimum observation to the maximum observation. Think of arranging all of the families in the United States along Interstate 80, beginning on the East Coast in New York City with the wealthiest family and ending on the West Coast in San Francisco with the poorest family. The median family is that family in the middle, with half of the families having lower income and half of the families having higher income.

Table 5.1 reports **median income** (along with the 90 percent confidence interval) for households with selected characteristics in the United States in the year 2008. The median income for all households in the United States was $50,303. That means that half of U.S. households earned more than $50,303 while the other half earned less. It is useful to note that the mean income for the same year was $68,424, about 36 percent higher than the median. This difference reveals an important characteristic of income distributions. Recall from your statistics course that the mean and median are both summary statistics measuring the center of a distribution. The mean is more sensitive to extreme observations than the median, however. If a distribution is symmetric, there is no difference between the mean and the median. In this case the difference indicates that there are high-income households that pull the mean up, making it substantially greater than the median. Clearly, the income distribution is not symmetric. Consequently, we usually use the median as our measure of the typical household income because it is not so affected by the presence of relatively few high-income households. Simply looking at the median income, however, glosses over very important differences in the earnings of various different types of households. For example,

TABLE 5.1 Median Income for Selected Household Characteristics, United States, 2008

Household Characteristics	Median Income ($) and 90% Confidence Interval (±)
All households	50,303 (±225)
White households	52,312 (±250)
Non-hispanic white households	55,530 (±370)
Black households	34,218 (±725)
Asian households	65,637 (±2,280)
Hispanic-origin households	37,913 (±799)
Type of household	
Family households–Married couple families	73,010 (±540)
Family households–Male householder, no wife present	49,186 (±1,092)
Family households–Female householder, no husband present	33,073 (±620)
Nonfamily households	30,078 (±306)
Male householder living alone	36,006 (±436)
Female householder living alone	25,014 (±383)
Age of household	
15 to 24 years	32,270 (±617)
25 to 34 years	51,400 (±536)
35 to 44 years	62,954 (±944)
45 to 54 years	64,349 (±933)
55 to 64 years	57,265 (±875)
65 and over	29,744 (±370)

Source: *Income, Poverty, and Health Insurance Coverage in the United States: 2008*, Table 1 p. 6. U.S. Census Bureau, September 2009. Available at: http://www.census.gov/prod/2009pubs/p60-236.pdf.

White households earned a median income of $52,312, whereas Black households earned $34,218, Asian households earned $65,637, and Hispanic-origin households earned $37,913. Households composed of a married couple had a median income of $73,010, which is clearly higher than that for single-parent households. Male-headed households with no wife present had a median income of $49,186, whereas female-headed households with no husband present had a median income of $33,073. Single-person households earned even lower median incomes. Median income also differs substantially depending on the age of the householders. The median income rises with age, reaching a peak in the 45- to 54-year-old bracket, and falling thereafter. Both very young and very old households earn substantially lower income than do middle-age households. This pattern reflects the fact that wages rise with experience, at least up to a point.

Confidence intervals are reported in Table 5.1 in order to provide a measure of the variability of income. Recall from basic statistics that an income sample and its standard error enable the construction of a confidence interval. A 90 percent confidence interval is constructed by taking the income sample estimate and adding and subtracting 1.645 times the standard error. Notice that the confidence interval is $225 for all households but ranges from a relatively low figure of $250 for White households to a much larger $2,280 for Asian households. Across ages, we also see substantial differences in the confidence intervals. Among the elderly (65 years of age and older) the 90 percent confidence interval is a relatively low $370, but among prime-aged workers (45 to 54 years of age) the standard deviation is a much larger $933. Income distributions are described by both the center of the distribution, reflecting the typical income for a household, and the fatness of the tails of the distribution, reflected in the standard deviation. The more variability in the income data, the higher the standard deviation and the fatter the tails of the income distribution.

The Lorenz Curve

In order to visualize the income distribution, think of plotting a graph with the cumulative proportion of the population plotted on the horizontal axis and the cumulative proportion of the nation's aggregate income plotted on the vertical axis as shown in Figure 5.1. If income were equally distributed in the economy, we would follow the line of perfect equality from the lower left-hand corner of the box to the upper right-hand corner as in Figure 5.1. The bottom 20 percent of the population would have 20 percent of the income, the bottom 40 percent would have 40 percent of the income, and so on. In reality, however, income is not equally distributed. The bottom 20 percent of the population has less than 20 percent of the income, whereas the top 20 percent of the population has more than 20 percent of the income. As a

FIGURE 5.1 A Graphic Illustration of the Income Distribution

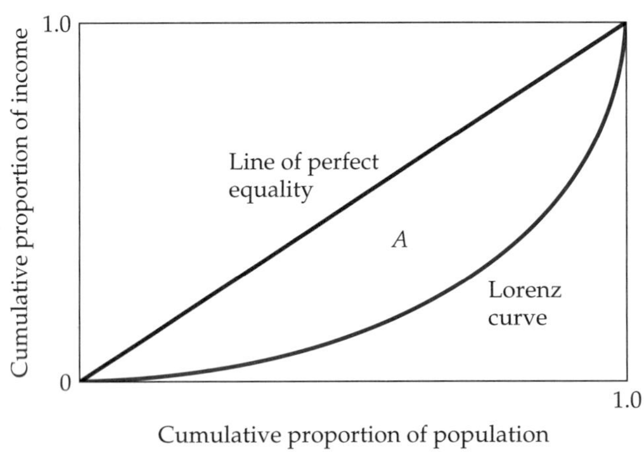

result, the actual income distribution, when plotted on a graph such as that in Figure 5.1, will follow a pattern first observed by Lorenz; hence the income distribution plot is known as the **Lorenz curve**. It sags below the line of perfect equality whenever the income distribution is such that the lower-income individuals hold less than an equal share of the income while the upper-income individuals hold more. (The Lorenz curve would bow above the line of perfect equality if the lower-income individuals held more than an equal share of income while the upper-income individuals held less.)

It is useful to consider the two extreme possibilities that the Lorenz curve can follow. The first is the most egalitarian possibility that each of the n individuals in the population has the share $1/n$ of the income. In this case, the Lorenz curve will follow the line of perfect equality. The other extreme possibility is that one person holds all of the income, whereas everyone else has nothing. Imagine what would happen if Bill Gates eventually earned all of the U.S. national income in a given year. The Lorenz curve would follow the horizontal axis as we accumulated everyone's zero income, until we got to the last person, Bill Gates. When we added his income to the total, our cumulative total would jump from zero to the full proportion, 1.0. The Lorenz curve would follow up the right-hand vertical axis, with an overall backward-L shape.

The Gini Coefficient

A numerical measure of the extent to which the income distribution departs from perfect equality has been developed and is useful in judging changes in income distributions over time or across countries. The **Gini coefficient** is derived by comparing the Lorenz curve to the line of perfect equality. If we denote the area between the Lorenz curve and the line of perfect equality as A, the Gini coefficient is $G = 2A$. Notice that if the income distribution is perfectly equal and the Lorenz curve follows the line of perfect equality, the area $A = 0$; hence $G = 0$. The Gini coefficient takes on the value of zero when the income distribution is equal. On the other hand, if the income distribution is perfectly unequal—Bill Gates has it all—the Gini coefficient is $G = 1$. That is because the area between the backward-L-shaped Lorenz curve and the line of perfect equality is 0.5 (a triangle with base and height of 1.0), so $G = 2A = 2(0.5) = 1.0$. The Gini coefficient takes on a value between 0 and 1 (inclusive). The more unequal the income distribution, the higher the value of the Gini coefficient.

Empirical Evidence on the Income Distribution

Table 5.2 provides information on the distribution of U.S. income since 1970. For each year listed in the table, the percentage of aggregate income earned by each income **quintile** is reported. Suppose we have arranged all of the households from poorest to richest. The first quintile is the bottom 20 percent of the income distribution: the poorest 20 percent of households. The second quintile is the next 20 percent of households, and so on. The fifth quintile is the wealthiest 20 percent of households. The top 5 percent of households is

TABLE 5.2 Share of Aggregate Income Received by Each Quintile, 1970 to 2009

Year	First Quintile	Second Quintile	Third Quintile	Fourth Quintile	Fifth Quintile	Gini Coefficient
2009	3.4	8.6	14.6	23.2	50.3	0.468
2005	3.4	8.6	14.6	23.0	50.4	0.469
2000	3.6	8.9	14.8	23.0	49.8	0.462
1995	3.7	9.1	15.2	23.3	48.7	0.450
1990	3.8	9.6	15.9	24.2	46.5	0.428
1985	3.9	9.8	16.2	24.4	45.6	0.419
1980	4.2	10.2	16.8	24.7	44.1	0.403
1975	4.3	10.4	17.0	24.7	43.6	0.397
1970	4.1	10.8	17.4	24.5	43.3	0.394

Source: DeNavis-Walt et al (2010), Table A2.

also reported in the next-to-last column of the table. Gini coefficients are reported in the final column of the table.

For perspective, in 2008 the bottom, or first, quintile included households with income of \$20,712 or less. The second quintile included households with income of \$20,713 to \$39,000; those in the third quintile had incomes of \$39,001 to \$62,725; those in the fourth quintile had incomes of \$62,726 to \$100,240; those in the top quintile had incomes of \$100,241 or more.

Over the last nearly 40 years, the first quintile of the income distribution, or the poorest 20 percent, has generally earned about 4 percent of the income in the United States. The wealthiest 20 percent of U.S. households, or the fifth quintile, has generally earned about 45 percent of the income. Such evidence clearly indicates that the U.S. income distribution is not equal. If we had an equal income distribution, each quintile would earn 20 percent of the income. In fact, the top 5 percent of the income distribution earns about 20 percent of the income in the country.

The Gini coefficient calculated for the income distribution in a given year provides a summary measure of the income distribution, whereas changes in the Gini coefficient indicate whether the distribution is becoming more or less equal. The U.S. Gini coefficient has ranged from about 0.39 in 1970 to 0.469 in 2005. This change indicates that since 1970 the U.S. income distribution has generally become more unequal. When did important changes occur in the distribution? The bottom quintile's share peaked at 4.3 percent in 1975 and has fallen since. The top quintile's share was at its minimum at the same time in 1975 and rose to a peak of 0.469 in 2005, falling slightly since then. If we were to define the middle class as the third quintile, we could say that their share of U.S. income has fallen steadily over the entire time period, with the exception of a slight improvement from 2005 to 2008.

If we take a longer view, say over the entire course of the 20th century, we would see that the relatively recent increase in the share of income earned by the top quintile is nothing new. In fact, in the 1920s, the share of income earned by those in the top decile (top 10 percent) was about 50 percent, as it is today. Atkinson and Piketty (2007) chronicle the changes in the U.S. income distribution over the 20th century and illustrate that the share of income earned by the top decile peaked at about 50 percent in the late 1920s, fell precipitously during World War II, stabilized at about 33 to 35 percent throughout the 1950s to 1970s, and then accelerated over the period of 1980 to the present.

One of the challenges economists face is to understand the dramatic increase in income inequality over the past 30 years. The basic cause, as it is currently understood, is that the returns to skill acquisition accelerated at the end of the 20th century. Why that happened is still being investigated. Federal Reserve Chairman Bernanke (2007) has surveyed the potential sources of changes in the level and dispersion of economic well-being, and summarizes them as including: (1) productivity gains, (2) human capital acquisition (education and training), (3) technological advances, (4) globalization pressures, and (5) international trade.

Descriptions of the income distribution such as this are quite sensitive to the measure of income used in the analysis. Table 5.2 reports **aggregate money income** as its measure. This measure of income includes all money income from earnings, unemployment compensation, workers' compensation, Social Security, Supplemental Security Income, public assistance, veterans' payments, survivor benefits, disability benefits, pension or retirement income, interest earnings, dividends, rents, royalties, estates and trusts, educational assistance, alimony, child support, financial assistance from outside the household, and other income. Despite this exhaustive list of money income, this measure excludes all forms of non-money income (e.g., medical benefits, insurance, food stamps, and other forms of income that are provided in kind). It is an aggregate measure in that it adds up all money income for the entire population, before taxes.

How different is the income distribution after taxes? Because the personal income tax is progressive and is designed to redistribute income, and the estate tax and several other forms of taxation are intended to alter the distribution of wealth (and thereby income), it is insightful to examine how the tax system affects the income distribution. Table 5.3 illustrates the effect of the U.S. tax system on the distribution of income for the year 2007. The U.S. tax system increases the share of income distributed to the bottom four quintiles, whereas it decreases the share for those in the top quintile. Households in the top quintile earn 55.9 percent of the pretax income, but after the tax system has its way with them, they have 52.5 percent of the income. The income taken from those in the top quintile is distributed to households in the bottom four quintiles, with each quintile gaining about a 1 percent increase in its share of income due to the tax redistribution. Obviously, the U.S. tax system redistributes income, but in comparison to the highly redistributional tax systems of the Scandinavian countries, for example, the U.S.

TABLE 5.3 Shares of Pretax and After-Tax Income, 2007

	First Quintile	Second Quintile	Third Quintile	Fourth Quintile	Fifth Quintile
Share of Pretax Income	4.0	8.4	13.1	19.3	55.9
Share of After-tax Income	4.9	9.4	14.1	20.0	52.5

Source: Congressional Budget Office. "Average Federal Tax Rates in 2007." June 2010. Available at: http://cbo.gov/publications/collections/collections.cfm?collect=13.

system is relatively modest in the extent to which it redistributes income. Furthermore, the extent to which the tax system is capable of substantially redistributing income is an important technical question, and the extent to which it should redistribute income is a lively political question.

This simple comparison of pretax and after-tax distributions illustrates that your view of the income distribution is crucially dependent on how you define income. A limited view of income as current money income may give an impression of the income distribution that is inaccurate. If other forms of compensation such as health care benefits, government transfers, and implicit returns to homeowners were to be included, it would significantly alter the appearance of the income distribution, and thereby affect the thinking of policymakers wishing to alter the income distribution.

POVERTY

As the income distribution in Table 5.2 illustrates, a large portion of the population has an income level below an equal share. The bottom 20 percent of the population earns 4 percent of the pretax income generated in the economy. The second 20 percent of the population earns just over 8 percent of the pretax income, and the third 20 percent earns about 13 percent. When a large portion of the population earns relatively little, a number of social problems may arise. In the first place, we are concerned that people in such circumstances are not able to realize their potential and represent a vast waste of our society's most valuable resource. Beyond that, problems of poor-quality housing, illegal drugs, and urban crime arise, which impose great difficulties for society.

Definition of Poverty

Poverty is hunger. Poverty is lack of shelter. Poverty is being sick and not being able to see a doctor. Poverty is not being able to go to school and not knowing

> how to read. Poverty is not having a job, is fear for the future, living one day at a time. Poverty is losing a child to illness brought about by unclean water. Poverty is powerlessness, lack of representation and freedom.

This is the World Bank's definition of poverty—not a technical definition but a practical sense of what it means to be impoverished. In developing countries, these aspects of poverty are daily realities for hundreds of millions of people. Even in highly developed economies millions of people lead impoverished lives described in these terms. In the United States, the world's most advanced economy, nearly 40 million people lived in poverty in the year 2008. That number represents over 13 percent of the total U.S. population.

Poverty is the term used to describe the state of being poor or having a very low level of income. Because large numbers of households live in poverty and poverty brings with it a multitude of social problems that require attention, it is useful to have a systematic way of describing the state of poverty and classifying impoverished households. The U.S. federal government defines poverty in terms of a level of family income, depending on the family size, below which the family is considered to be impoverished. The Census Bureau defines poverty this way:

> [The] U.S. Census Bureau uses a set of money income thresholds that vary by family size and composition to determine who is poor. If a family's total income is less than that family's threshold, then that family, and every individual in it, is considered poor. The poverty thresholds do not vary geographically, but they are updated annually for inflation using the Consumer Price Index (CPI-U). The official poverty definition counts money income before taxes and does not include capital gains and noncash benefits (such as public housing, Medicaid, and food stamps). Poverty is not defined for people in military barracks, institutional group quarters, or for unrelated individuals under age 15 (such as foster children). They are excluded from the poverty universe—that is, they are considered neither as "poor" nor as "nonpoor." (Dalaker and Proctor 2000)

The threshold below which the Census Bureau considers a family to be in poverty is sometimes called the **poverty line**. The **poverty gap** refers to the amount of income it would take for an impoverished family to lift them to the poverty line. This distinction is important as we consider government policies to relieve poverty. The simple notion of the poverty line only identifies households that are in poverty, falling below the line, but it does not measure the degree of their poverty, that is, how far below the poverty line they fall. The poverty gap measures the depth of a household's poverty, as it captures the amount of income necessary to lift the household from their current income level all the way up to the poverty line. Antipoverty programs with limited budgets face a difficult policy dilemma. If they focus on maximizing the number of households lifted out of poverty, the best way to accomplish that goal is to focus on households that fall just below the poverty line. They could maximize the number of households lifted out of poverty by giving assistance to those closest to the poverty line. Although the assistance is just a marginal improvement in the households' situation, they are officially lifted out of poverty and make the program look effective. On the other hand, they could choose to focus on the households in deepest poverty—those with the greatest poverty gap. Because those households are farthest from the poverty line, however, the limited antipoverty program funds would lift a smaller number of households out of poverty; those lifted out would be assisted dramatically.

Both absolute and relative measures of poverty are useful in considering antipoverty programs. An **absolute measure of poverty** specifies some particular level of income or expenditure below which a person is considered to be impoverished. That measure is applied to anyone regardless of circumstance. For example, we could define an absolute measure of poverty as $2 of income per day. This is a measure of poverty used by the World Bank in its annual *World Development Report.* According to the 2010 *World Development Report,* the following countries have poverty rates of over 50 percent of the population falling below the $2-a-day level:

Angola	70.2 percent
Bangladesh	81.3 percent
Benin	75.3 percent
Burkina Faso	81.2 percent
Burundi	93.4 percent
Cambodia	68.2 percent
Cameroon	57.7 percent
Central African Republic	81.9 percent
Chad	83.3 percent
Congo, Democratic Republic of	79.5 percent
Congo, Republic of	74.4 percent
Ethiopia	77.5 percent
Ghana	53.6 percent
Guinea	87.2 percent
Haiti	72.1 percent
India	75.6 percent
Kyrgyz Republic	51.9 percent
Lao PDR	76.8 percent
Liberia	94.8 percent
Madagascar	89.6 percent
Malawi	90.4 percent
Mali	77.1 percent
Mozambique	90.0 percent
Nepal	77.6 percent

Niger	85.6 percent
Nigeria	83.9 percent
Papua New Guinea	57.4 percent
Rwanda	90.3 percent
Senegal	60.3 percent
Sierra Leone	76.1 percent
Tajikistan	50.8 percent
Tanzania	96.6 percent
Togo	69.3 percent
Uganda	75.6 percent
Uzbekistan	76.7 percent
Zambia	81.5 percent

Using this absolute measure, the World Bank considers people all over the world who earn less than $2 a day to be in poverty.

Although no one will argue that $2 a day reflects serious poverty, what if we increased our absolute measure of poverty to, say, $8,000 per year for a single person? In the United States that level of income might well be considered to reflect poverty, but what about in Zambia? In that country, an income of $8,000 is a very high income relative to the country's income distribution. This comparison reveals the need for both absolute and relative measures of poverty. A **relative measure of poverty** specifies some particular percentile of an income distribution below which a person is considered to be impoverished. For example, we might define the poverty line as the tenth percentile of a country's income distribution. This measure of poverty takes into account the country's income distribution and defines poverty relative to the distribution of that country.

Although any definition of poverty is bound to be problematic and arbitrary to some extent, the attempt in the United States is to define poverty in a systematic way, linking its definition to dietary need. Minimal food expenditures are computed for families of various sizes on the basis of government estimates of dietary need. Suppose that we call this minimum required expenditure $E_f(n)$, where n is family size. Then the proportion of income that families of all different sizes actually spend on food is estimated using budget surveys. We can denote that proportion as $\rho_f(n)$. The so-called poverty line is then determined by multiplying $1/\rho_f(n)$ by $E_f(n)$. The product gives us an estimate of the level of income required for a family of size n to have a minimally sufficient diet, assuming that they spend their income as do other families. Early research on U.S. poverty in the 1960s revealed that families spent about one-third of their income on food. Subsequently, definitions of poverty were developed using that benchmark, estimating the cost of a minimal food

TABLE 5.4 U.S. Poverty Thresholds ($), 2008

Size of Family Unit	Related Children Under 18 Years of Age (For Householders Under 65 Years of Age)				
	0	*1*	*2*	*3*	*4*
1	11,201				
2	14,417	14,840			
3	16,841	17,330	17,346		
4	22,207	22,570	21,834	21,910	
5	26,781	27,170	26,338	25,694	25,301
6	30,803	30,925	30,288	29,677	28,769

Source: *Income, Poverty, and Health Insurance Coverage in the United States: 2008*, p. 43.

budget, then multiplying that food budget by the inverse of one-third, or three. Adjustments can be made for size of family, regional cost of living, and other factors, but the essential means of estimating a poverty threshold is this procedure.

Table 5.4 reports the U.S. poverty thresholds (or the so-called poverty line) for families of various sizes in the year 2008. For example, a single-person household had a poverty threshold of $11,201. That means that a person with income less than that amount is considered to be living in poverty. For a family of four with two children, the poverty threshold was $21,834. These estimates are adjusted each year to compensate for the effects of inflation.

Distribution of Poverty

How many families are impoverished, and what types of families are more likely to be impoverished? Because the government has a systematic way of defining poverty, it can then use that definition to study patterns of poverty.

Table 5.5 reports the number of persons and families in poverty classified by several characteristics for the United States in the year 2008. A total of 38,829 million people lived in poverty in 2008, which represented 13.2 percent of the total U.S. population. Although the overall poverty rate is 13.2 percent, the incidence of poverty differs dramatically across racial and ethnic groups. The poverty rate is well over 20 percent for both Blacks and Hispanics and about 11 percent for Whites. Poverty rates also vary dramatically across types of families. Although the poverty rate is just 5.5 percent for married couples, it is 28.7 percent for female-headed households with no husband present. Finally, poverty rates also vary by age. The lowest poverty rates are among families headed by prime-age householders (18 to 64 years

TABLE 5.5 Persons and Families in Poverty by Selected Characteristics, 2008

Characteristic	Number (Thousands)	Percentage
Persons		
Total	39,829	13.2
White	26,990	11.2
Black	9,379	24.7
Asian or Pacific Islander	1,576	11.8
Hispanic origin	10,987	23.2
Family status		
Married couple	3,261	5.5
Female householder, no husband present	4,163	28.7
Age		
Under 18	14,068	19.0
18 to 64 years	22,105	11.7
65 years and over	3,656	9.7

Source: *Income, Poverty, and Health Insurance Coverage in the United States: 2008*. Table 4, p. 14.

of age). Poverty is much more prevalent among the young, and to a lesser extent among the elderly.

Internationally, the conventional wisdom for much of the 20th century was that poor people live in poor countries. For example, in 1990, over 90 percent of the world's population in poverty lived in the poorest countries of the world. As a consequence of this situation, global aid agencies focused their efforts toward the poorest countries. More recently, however, researchers are finding that a large proportion of the world's poor live in middle-income countries. Sumner (2010) finds, for example, that nearly three-quarters of the world's poor living below the $1.25-per-day-day level, numbering some 1.3 billion persons, live in middle-income countries. The policy impact of this type of finding is captured in the reaction of Mr. Robert Zoellick of the World Bank, who was quoted in the *Economist* (2010) saying that such evidence should "change how we conduct development research." Sumner's research implies that efforts to fight poverty may be more focused appropriately at the national level rather than the international level. Middle-income countries may be more effective in using their own means-tested cash and in-kind transfer programs to help their own poor than has been the case with international agencies providing directed aid to the poorest countries.

REDISTRIBUTING INCOME IN THEORY

Redistribution can be attempted in two fundamental ways. One is to transfer money income from the wealthy to the poor; the other is to transfer goods and services from the wealthy to the poor.

Utilitarian Model of Redistribution

Utilitarianism is a philosophical school of thought from the 19th century that holds that intrinsic worth of a person or thing is rooted in its usefulness. The more useful a person or thing is, the more he, she, or it is worth. Of course, this leads to very difficult philosophical questions about what makes people and things useful. We will not follow a digression into that set of issues. Rather, we will follow the basic concept of utilitarian thought and define a **social welfare function** as the simple sum of individuals' utilities. Using a utilitarian approach, the welfare of society is the sum of the welfare levels of each of that society's individuals. Let us define social welfare, using the symbol W, as the sum of the n individuals' utility:

$$W=\sum_{i=1}^{n} u_i(m_i), \qquad (5.1)$$

where each person's utility is a function of his or her money income. Hence, we simply add up the utility derived by each member of society from the money income he or she earns. The arithmetic sum of individuals' utilities is defined as social welfare.

In a two-person case, we can illustrate the fundamental issues using marginal utility functions as in Figure 5.2. The marginal utility functions for

FIGURE 5.2 An Equal Distribution of Income

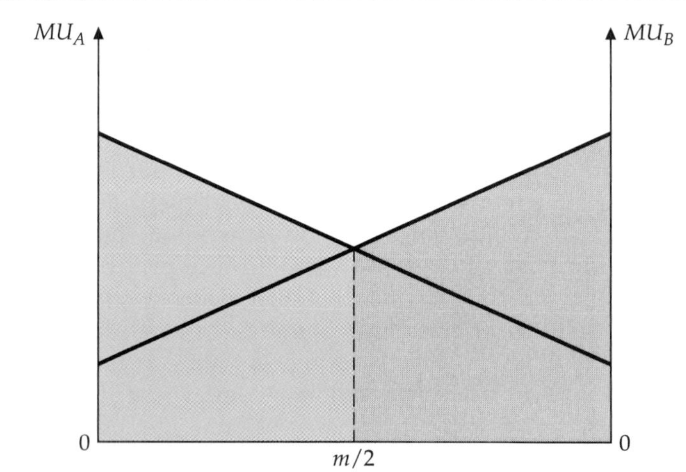

person A and person B have been drawn using the same horizontal axis, because that axis measures income which we desire to split between the two individuals in some way. Read money income from left to right for person A but from right to left for person B. These two people are identical in the sense that their marginal utility functions have the same intercept and slope. They value each additional dollar of money income in the same way.

In order to maximize social welfare *W*, we must allocate income to the two people in such a way as to make the sum of their total utilities the largest possible. That occurs at $m/2$, where each person receives half of the total money income the economy has available. If we give $m/2$ dollars of money income to person A, her total utility is illustrated by the area under her marginal utility function from 0 to $m/2$ dollars of income. (Recall that total utility at a given level of income can be viewed as the area under the marginal utility curve.)[1] Person A's total utility is illustrated by the vertically shaded area under her marginal utility function from income of 0 up to $m/2$ dollars. Person B's total utility is illustrated similarly by the horizontally shaded area in Figure 5.2. The combination of their total utilities, added together, is the entire shaded area.

Consider a different allocation of income between the two individuals. Suppose that we allocate more income to person A and less to person B, as Figure 5.3 illustrates. If we allocate three-quarters of the total available money income to person A, she will have $3m/4$ income, whereas person B will have $m/4$ income. Person A's total utility is vertically shaded, whereas person B's total utility is horizontally shaded. Notice that the sum of their total utilities is now less than the total we had with equal distribution of income to each person. Social welfare is reduced by the amount shown in triangle *abc*. The allocation of three-quarters of the income to person A and

FIGURE 5.3 An Unequal Distribution of Income

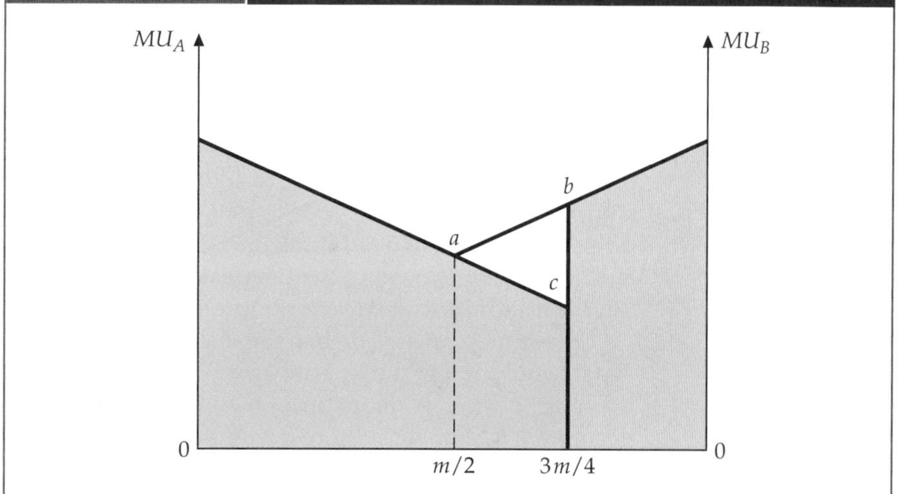

FIGURE 5.4 Optimal Income Distribution When People Are Different

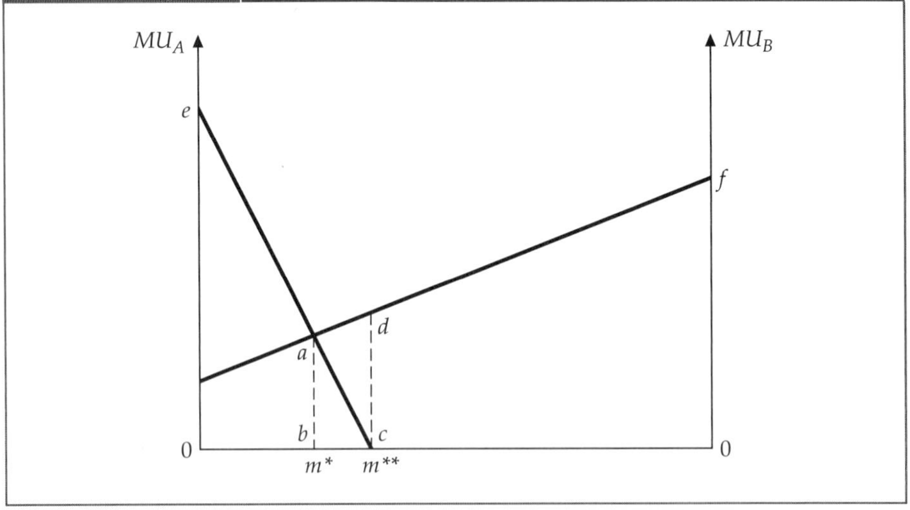

one-quarter to person B results in a lower level of social welfare than the equal allocation of half of the income to each person. An important general principle is that social welfare will be maximized with that allocation of income where the marginal utilities of the individuals are equal.[2]

What if the two people are not identical? Because diversity is a fact of life, we expect that people will differ in their assessment of their marginal utility of income. The model of income distribution works just fine even if people are different. Consider Figure 5.4, where person A and person B are clearly quite different. Person A has a very high initial marginal utility of income. The first few dollars of income are valued very highly by person A. But the slope of her marginal utility function is relatively steep, indicating that her marginal utility of income declines quickly. Each additional dollar of income is worth less and less, and the rate at which her marginal valuation declines is steep. Person B has a lower marginal utility of income to begin with, but the rate at which his marginal utility declines is slower. In this case, the optimal distribution of income is to allocate m^* dollars of income to person A and the remainder, $m - m^*$, to person B. At m^* dollars of income allocated to person A and $m - m^*$ dollars allocated to person B, we have equal marginal utilities of income. An unequal income distribution is best in the sense that it maximizes social welfare, the sum of the individuals' total utilities.

If we are concerned that this income distribution is unequal, we can see what would happen if we allocated more income to person A. Suppose that we give person A more income. Let's go all the way to m^{**} dollars of income. It is not sensible to give more than m^{**} dollars of income because person A's marginal utility is zero at m^{**}. Additional dollars of income are not valued at all by person A. The increase in income from m^* to m^{**}

FIGURE 5.5 Social Welfare Function Contours When Individuals' Utilities Are Perfect Substitutes

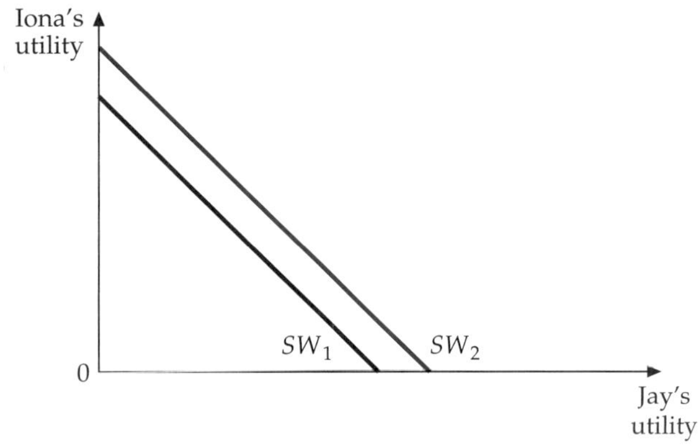

makes person A's total utility rise by an amount represented by the triangle *abc* in the diagram. The problem is that this reallocation has taken income away from person B, and his loss of total utility is given by the area *abcd*, which is larger than the triangle *abc*. As a result of the income reallocation, person B is made worse off by an amount that is larger than the additional utility we were able to provide to person A. Social welfare is reduced by an amount represented by the area *acd*.

In the two-person utilitarian model when individuals are identical, one person's utility is a perfect substitute for the other person's utility in terms of contributing to social welfare. Because social welfare is simply the sum of the individuals' utilities, it makes no difference whether a bit of utility is enjoyed by Iona or Jay. All that matters is that the sum of their utilities is as high as possible. If we were to plot the social indifference curves in the simple utilitarian case, where the utility of Iona and Jay is perfectly substitutable, the social welfare contours would look like those in Figure 5.5. The contours are downward-sloping straight lines where the slope is -1. We can trade off one person's utility for the other person's utility at a constant rate of 1 for 1.

Of course, we do not expect that the trade-off would actually be constant. Suppose that we began to redistribute income away from Iona and toward Jay. Her marginal utility of income would likely rise as she had less and less income, whereas his marginal utility of income would fall as he had more and more. As a result, the trade-off, which is the ratio of the marginal utilities of the two people, would decline and the social welfare contour would flatten out as we move downward to the right. Similarly, if we redistribute the other way, the social welfare contour would steepen as we move upward to the left. Hence, we expect that the slope of the social welfare contours will not be constant as utility is not perfectly substitutable between people. Figure 5.6 illustrates this case.

FIGURE 5.6 Social Welfare Function Contours

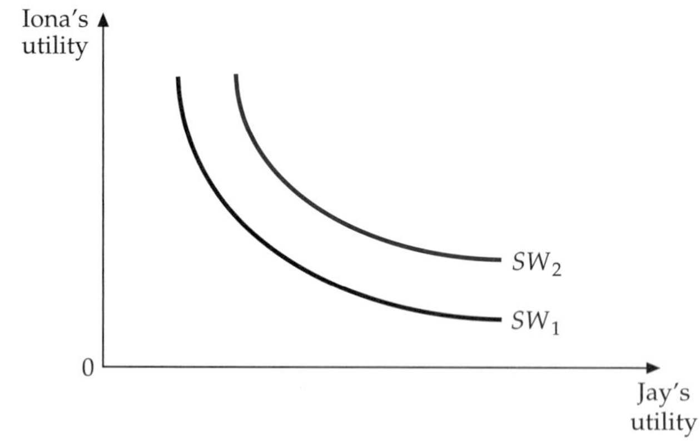

Rawlsian Model of Redistribution

What happens if we care specifically about the well-being of the least well-off person in the economy? Suppose that the only way we are all made better off is to assure that the least well-off person is made better off. We want to take the entire income distribution, keep an eye on the income rankings for each person, and shift the whole distribution upward. Suppose that in our two-person economy, social welfare is defined as the minimum of the two persons' welfare:

$$W = min\ \{u_i,\ u_j\}. \tag{5.2}$$

You can make Jay as well off as you like, but until you make Iona better off, social welfare is not increased, and vice versa. In this case the social welfare function's contours are illustrated in Figure 5.7. The L-shaped contours

FIGURE 5.7 Social Welfare Contours in the Rawlsian Case

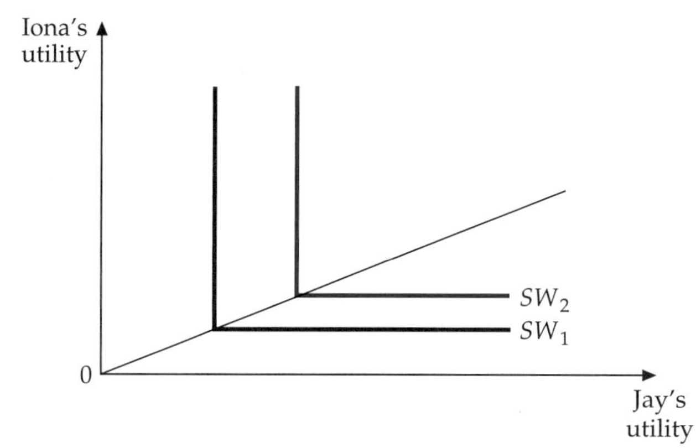

indicate that increasing one person's utility while holding the other person's utility constant has no effect on social welfare. The only way to move to a higher social welfare contour is to increase the utility of both. In this case, the utilities of the two people are perfect complements (like a left shoe and a right shoe, neither is useful without the other). Notice that the slope of the expansion ray connecting the corners of the L-shaped contours need not be 45 degrees. We do not have to have equal proportional increases in utility to move up to higher social welfare contours. This social welfare criterion has been examined in the work of contemporary philosopher John Rawls (1971).

Determination of the Efficient Allocation

If we take the intermediate case where social welfare contours are concave as in Figure 5.6, we can determine the efficient allocation between Iona and Jay. First, we plot the **utility possibilities frontier (*UPF*)**, illustrated in Figure 5.8, which shows the combinations of utility that the economy is capable of providing given its resources and technology. We then maximize social welfare by selecting a combination of utilities that is on the *UPF* and simultaneously puts us on the highest social welfare contour. Point (u_i^*, u_j^*) in Figure 5.8 is the efficient combination of utilities to allocate to Iona and Jay. At this point of tangency between the *UPF* and the social indifference curve, the rate at which we can transform one person's utility into another person's utility (the slope of the *UPF*) is identical with the rate at which we can swap one person's utility for another person's utility while maintaining the same level of social welfare (slope of the social indifference curve). We are reaching the highest level of social welfare attainable with the constraints of our economy given by the *UPF*. In theory, this is the way we can determine the optimal distribution of utility among members of a society. In practice, of course, it is difficult to accomplish this task as we struggle to determine our collective preferences and the shape of our social indifference curves.

FIGURE 5.8 Social Welfare Maximization

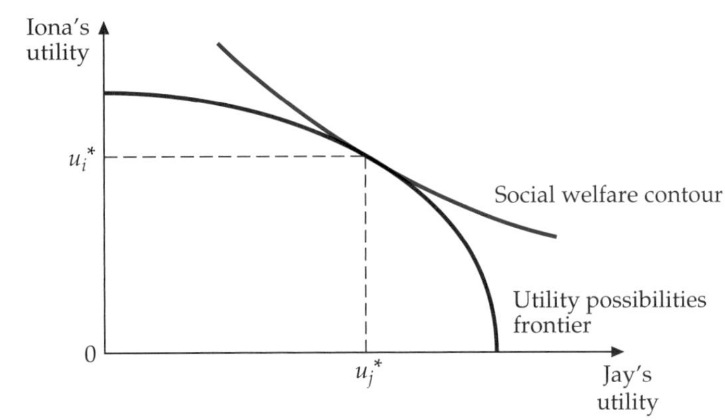

Economic Analysis of In-Kind Transfers

When an **in-kind transfer** is provided, the recipient is given a quantity of some good or service instead of cash. Let's analyze the effect of such a transfer using the graphical framework we introduced previously. Suppose that we are interested in the effect of a food program that provides families with food, not cash. Figure 5.9 illustrates the effect of a food transfer. The household is in initial equilibrium, consuming F_0 units of food and G_0 units of other goods, on indifference curve I_0. The government food program provides F^*

FIGURE 5.9 Analysis of In-Kind Transfer of Food

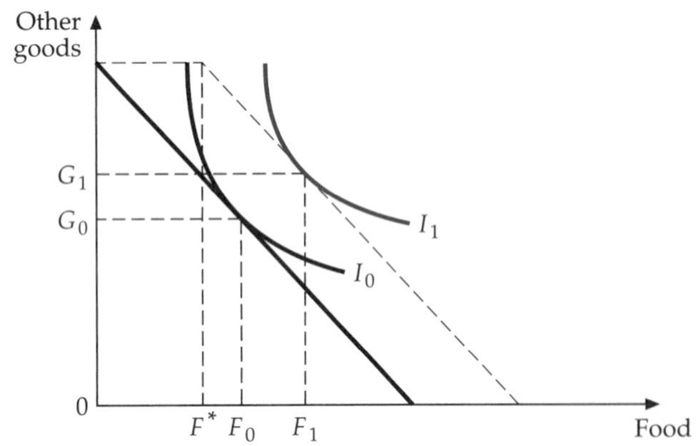

AP Photo/Paul Beaty

Food stamps are a common in-kind transfer.

units of food to the household. Because the in-kind transfer does not affect the relative prices of food and other goods, the slope of the budget line (the downward-sloping straight line) is unaffected. Rather, the in-kind transfer shifts the budget line rightward by the amount F^* of the food transfer. The new budget line is the dashed downward-sloping line to the right of the original budget line. As a result of the in-kind transfer, the household adjusts its purchases to F_1 units of food and G_1 units of other goods, attaining a new equilibrium. The household moves out to indifference curve I_1, consuming both more food and more other goods; this clearly makes the household better off than before the transfer.

We notice several things about this transfer. First, the household is clearly better off, so the food transfer is effective in improving the welfare of the household. Second, the food transfer induces the household to consume more of other goods. When households are given food, we cannot prevent them from adjusting their spending patterns in such a way that the food transfer frees them to consume more of other things at the same time. In fact, that adjustment is part of what makes the in-kind transfer beneficial to the household. Third, the increase in food consumption is less than F^*; the amount of the in-kind transfer is $F_1 - F_0 < F^*$. Giving the household F^* units of food induces them to reduce their food purchases, increasing their overall food consumption by less than the transfer of F^*. Just because we give the household F^* units of food does not mean that we will cause their consumption of food to increase by F^* units. Fourth, the new budget line involves a horizontal line segment from the vertical intercept of the original budget line rightward to the quantity of food F^*. This part of the new budget line reflects the fact that if the family spends none of its money income on food, it can buy the same maximal quantity of other goods that it could buy before and have that quantity of other goods along with an amount of food up to F^*. From that point on, however, purchases of food in excess of F^* require the family to forgo other goods. Consequently, there is a **kink** in the family's budget line at the point where the horizontal segment meets the downward-sloping segment. At that point there is a dramatic change in the rate at which the family must trade off other goods for food, reflected in the abrupt change in the slope of the budget line.

What if the household values food as relatively unimportant compared to other goods? Figure 5.10 illustrates such a case where the indifference curves are relatively flat. Recall that the slope of the indifference curve is minus the ratio of the marginal utility of food to the marginal utility of other goods. In this case the in-kind transfer induces the family to increase their food consumption up to the amount F^*, the amount of the in-kind transfer. Notice that the family is now consuming at the kink point of the budget set. Here, again, we have a case where families may tend to cluster at the kink point of a budget set, where the kink is created by public policy, in this case the in-kind transfer.

If this household could cash out their food transfer, they could operate on the portion of the budget line above the kink point as illustrated in Figure 5.11. The cash-out enables the household to attain utility level I_2, rather than being

FIGURE 5.10 Clustering at the Kink Point

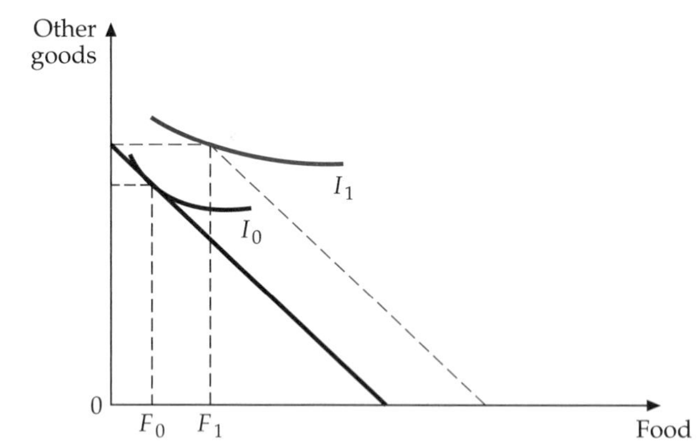

FIGURE 5.11 Analysis of Household Cashing Out an In-Kind Transfer

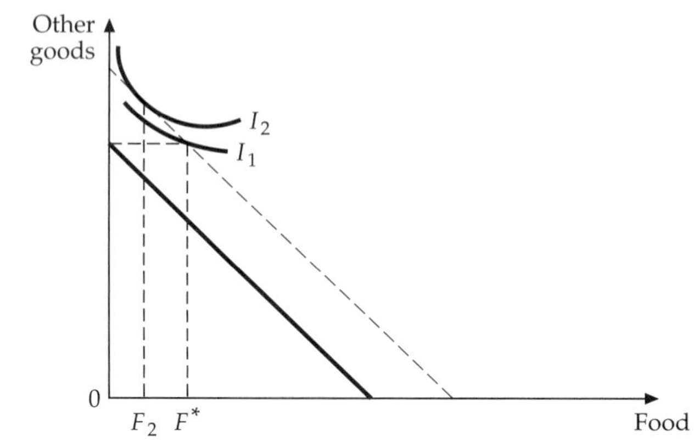

forced to consume F^* units of food, which results in utility level I_1. This is exactly why food stamps have a street value and serve as a medium of exchange, much like ordinary currency, in many inner-city areas.

Economic Analysis of a Price Subsidy

As an alternative, consider a government assistance program that reduces the price of food with the intention that the lower price will enable families to buy more, rather than simply giving food directly to families. Figure 5.12 illustrates the effect of a food subsidy program on the family and their consumption choices. The family's initial budget line is drawn as downward

FIGURE 5.12 Analysis of a Price Subsidy

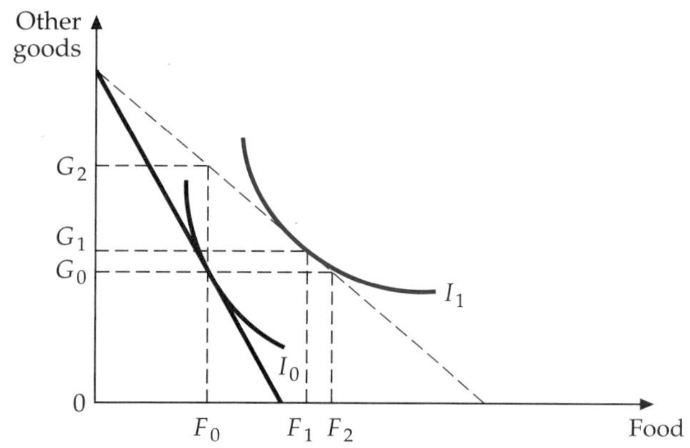

sloping, with a slope reflecting the relative price of food compared to other goods: slope $= -p_f/p_g$. Given their initial budget set, the family selects combination (F_0, G_0). A food price subsidy program has the effect of altering their budget set, however. With a lower price of food, their budget line rotates outward in counterclockwise fashion, expanding their budget set. They now have an expanded budget set over which to select in such a way as to make themselves as well off as possible. Considering the new alternatives, they select point (F_1, G_1) on the new budget line, enabling them to attain a higher indifference curve and making them better off.

Of course, the movement from the initial point of equilibrium to the new point involves two distinct effects that are induced by the food price reduction. A substitution effect arises because the food price subsidy program makes food cheaper than other goods. Hence the family will purchase more food because its relative price has fallen. An income effect is caused by the food price subsidy because the purchasing power of the family's income is enhanced by the subsidy program. The increased food purchase $F_1 - F_0$ is the combination of both of the substitution and income effects produced by the price reduction.

Notice that the price subsidy program has the effect of inducing the family to purchase additional food, as well as other goods. Policymakers funding this food subsidy program might like to force the family to maintain the same level of consumption of other goods and adjust their food consumption only, moving rightward along the dotted line at level G_0 and increasing food consumption to F_2. They have no way to constrain the family's choices, however. The food price subsidy program will inevitably cause some increase in the consumption of nonfood items. In fact, it is possible that a family with different preferences than those illustrated in Figure 5.12 (represented by a flatter indifference curve I_1) would move vertically upward at level F_0, taking advantage of the food subsidy program by purchasing the same quantity of food at the new lower price and spending all of the benefit of that lower price on other goods, increasing consumption to G_2. As a result of this reality, policymakers sometimes do not use price subsidy programs because they cannot be sure that the benefits of the program will be directed in the way that they wish. Of course, even if they force families to take food, and food only, they still cannot be assured that the benefits of the program will be directed as they wish, as we saw in the previous analysis of an in-kind transfer program. Like the food transfer program discussed previously and illustrated in Figure 5.11, the family could decide to trade the food for cash or other goods. A policy study at the end of this chapter provides fascinating evidence on just such a situation where families engage in illegal trafficking in food stamps. Ample evidence indicates that families in fact trade food stamps for cash or other goods.

Analysis of a Cash Transfer

A third form of assistance to families is to provide a **cash transfer** and let the family choose how to spend the assistance check. What are the efficiency effects of a cash transfer, and how do they compare to the effects of a price subsidy? Figure 5.13 illustrates the effect of a cash transfer. The family's budget line is shifted outward in a parallel manner because the cash transfer has no effect on the relative prices of the two goods. An expanded budget set permits the family to select a new combination of food and other goods that maximizes their well-being. In Figure 5.13, the family moves from the combination (F_0, G_0) to the new combination (F_1, G_1). Because the cash transfer does not affect relative prices, there is no substitution effect; only an income effect is induced.

How does this situation compare to the case of an in-kind transfer? Comparing Figures 5.13 and 5.9, we see clear similarities. One difference between the two cases, however, is that the cash transfer program, shown in Figure 5.13, shifts the entire budget line outward in a parallel manner, including the portion of the budget line above the original vertical intercept. Hence, the cash transfer

FIGURE 5.13 Analysis of a Cash Transfer Program

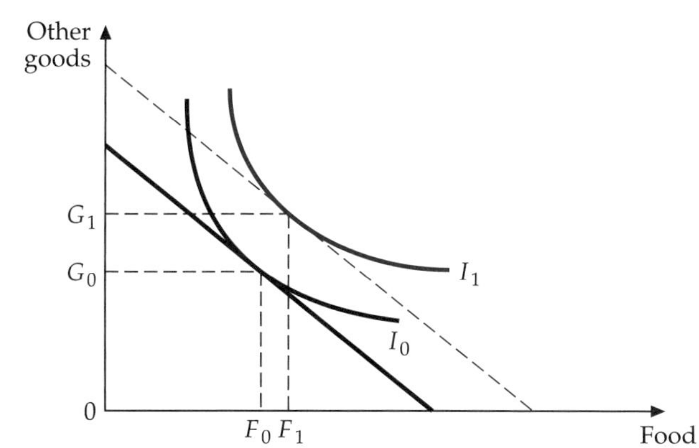

program automatically adds the choices on the upper part of the new budget line, whereas the in-kind transfer program does not. Although families may choose to cash out their in-kind transfer, the street value of that transfer will reflect **transactions costs** involved. For example, food stamps worth \$20 at a grocery store may only fetch \$15 on the street. The food stamps are not worth the full \$20 to the purchaser because of the time and effort involved to obtain them. The transactions cost includes the time cost and inconvenience, not to mention the chance of being caught in the midst of an illegal transaction, making the street value of the food stamps worth less than their face value.

How does the cash transfer compare to the price subsidy? Figure 5.14 illustrates both forms of assistance programs. The price subsidy rotates the budget line outward in a counterclockwise fashion, and the family responds by moving to the new combination (F_1, G_1), putting them on indifference curve I_1. A cash transfer with the same cost to the government would shift the budget line outward in a parallel fashion and go through point (F_1, G_1). The family would adjust and move to the consumption combination (F_2, G_2), which enables them to be on indifference curve I_2. It is possible, indeed likely, that the family will be better off with the cash transfer than with the price subsidy. Of course, the effects on food consumption differ. The food price subsidy will induce the family to increase food consumption by a larger amount than the cash transfer: compare $F_1 - F_0$ to $F_2 - F_0$.

Which method of providing assistance is better? Well, if we care about families purchasing additional food, the price subsidy is better than the cash transfer. If, instead, we care about making people as well off as possible, the cash transfer is preferable because it puts the family on a higher indifference curve. In order to answer the policy question, we must have a specific concept of what *better* involves—food consumption or welfare? It is in this sense that policymakers must define their criteria for policy evaluation in order to make sensible decisions.

FIGURE 5.14 Comparing a Cash Transfer and a Price Subsidy

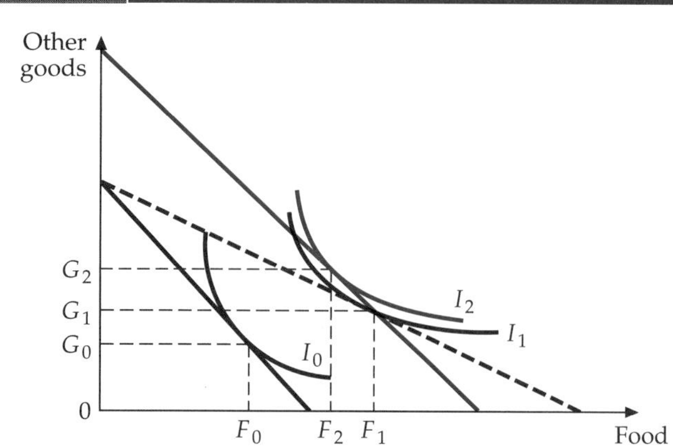

We might be concerned, in the practical reality of policymaking, that some households will use the assistance program benefits to purchase goods that are harmful rather than helpful. For example, what if the benefits of an assistance program are used to purchase cigarettes, alcoholic beverages, pornography, or drugs? Keep in mind that the previous graphical analysis assumes that the other goods on the vertical axis are indeed *goods*, as far as the household is concerned, not *bads*. One limitation of this form of analysis is that the household defines for itself what is good rather than appealing to an external absolute standard of goodness. Policymakers may wish to provide that external standard of goodness, or at least try to, but their success in doing so may be quite limited. As we saw previously, even if policymakers define food as good, they cannot prevent families from using food assistance to purchase other things that the families consider even better than food.

REDISTRIBUTING INCOME IN PRACTICE

Redistribution programs can be categorized conveniently as providing either cash transfers to the recipients or in-kind transfers. In-kind transfers are provided in a host of programs covering housing, food, medical care, insurance, and other goods. For example, the Medicaid program provides health care services to poor individuals and families, the Food Stamp program provides food for individuals and families, and housing assistance programs provide housing units to poor families.

Brief Descriptions of Selected Federal Programs

Federal programs targeted at helping the poor can be divided into cash transfer programs and in-kind transfer programs. We begin with brief descriptions of three major cash transfer programs.[3] The newest program is **Temporary Assistance to Needy Families (TANF)**, a federal block grant program giving money to states for most any purpose that will provide assistance to poor families, end dependency of needy parents on government benefits, prevent and reduce out-of-wedlock pregnancies, and encourage the formation of two-parent families. With the introduction of this block grant program, family entitlements to cash assistance were ended. The TANF block grant program replaced Aid to Families with Dependent Children (AFDC) in the welfare reform of 1996. The AFDC program originated with the Social Security Act of 1935, providing cash assistance to families with dependent children that had an absent parent, or two-parent families where one parent was disabled or unemployed. The AFDC program primarily provided assistance to single mothers with dependent children. Because the program was jointly funded by the federal and state governments, eligibility requirements and benefits varied from state to state.

The largest federal program that provides cash transfers is the **Supplemental Security Income (SSI)** program. This program provides cash to aged, blind, or disabled persons subject to a means test. Many states also supplement SSI payments with additional payments of their own. Payments received under the SSI program vary with the recipient's income from other sources.

A fundamentally different type of cash transfer program operates through the personal income tax, providing assistance to low-income people by providing tax reductions. The **earned income tax credit** (EITC) and the **child tax credit** (CTC) are two major mechanisms by which low-income households are provided with federal cash transfers. It provides assistance to working families with children. A family of four (parents filing a joint return with two qualifying children) in 2009 was eligible for the EITC as long as their income was less than $45,295. The maximum amount of credit available in 2009 was $5,028. The credit reduces the income tax owed by low-income families, and may even provide a cash refund if the family does not owe any income tax. Since its expansion in the early 1990s, the EITC has become a major cash transfer program. The child tax credit can reduce federal income tax liability by up to $1,000 per eligible child in the family.

In addition to these cash transfer programs, four major programs provide in-kind assistance to the poor: Medicaid, food stamps and child nutrition, housing assistance, and education and job training. A brief description of each follows. The **Medicaid** program originated in 1965 and is designed to provide medical care to the poor. A companion program, **Medicare**, provides medical services for the elderly. Medicaid is a joint federal-state program with funding provided by both federal and state governments. Low-income families that receive SSI payments automatically qualify for Medicaid. Others, passing a means test, may also receive Medicaid benefits. Individual states set their own eligibility requirements and reimbursement policies for health care providers under the Medicaid program. With fast-paced increases in the cost of medical care in recent years, Medicaid expenditures have been a growing concern for state governments. The **Food Stamp** program, begun in 1971, is financed federally through the Department of Agriculture budget and is administered by state governments. The food stamp program has recently been renamed the Supplemental Nutrition Assistance Program (SNAP). Benefits are means tested and provided via an electronic benefits transfer (EBT) card to recipients that can be redeemed for food items at grocery stores. The benefit amounts depend on the recipient's income. A variety of **housing assistance** programs provide subsidies to low-income families. Public housing is provided where rents are subsidized at below-market rates, depending on the family's income; rent supplements are paid for low-income families to enable them to rent private housing; and subsidies are provided to housing producers who rent units to low-income families at below-market rates. Both demand- and supply-side assistance programs are provided by both federal and state governments. A variety of **education** and **job training** programs are provided by federal and state governments in order to enhance the earnings potential of low-income workers. The federal government provides assistance from Head Start, aimed at enhancing the educational success of four- and five-year-old students, to Pell Grants for college students. In the area of job training, a variety of programs exist as well. For example, the Job Opportunities and Basic Skills (JOBS) program provides education and training,

TABLE 5.6 Expenditures for Selected Programs Designed to Benefit the Poor, 2010

	Estimated Expenditures (Billions of Dollars)
Cash Transfers	
TANF	17.059
SSI	47.217
EITC	49.539
Child Tax Credit	23.355
Making Work Pay Tax Credit	20.476
Unemployment Compensation	157.751
In-Kind Transfers	
Medicaid grants to states	275.924
Food stamps and nutrition programs	68.681
Housing assistance	61.672
Education, training, employment and social services	84.518

Source: *Budget of the United States Government, Fiscal Year 2011, Detailed Functional Tables FY11.* Available at: http://www.gpoaccess.gov/usbudget/fy11/fct.html.

whereas the Summer Youth Employment and Training Program (SYETP) is designed to enhance the employability of high school and college students. State governments also provide a variety of education and training programs.

Table 5.6 illustrates the magnitude of federal assistance programs of both cash and in-kind types. Most federal aid is provided through in-kind transfers rather than cash. The cash transfer programs such as TANF and SSI provide far less assistance than do the in-kind transfer programs that assist people with medical care, housing, food and nutrition, and education and training. Consequently, it is clear that the U.S. federal system is specifically designed to provide most of its assistance through in-kind transfers rather than through cash transfers.

Welfare Reform

A major reform of welfare programs was enacted in 1996. The official name of the legislative bill was the Personal Responsibility and Work Opportunity Reconciliation Act of 1996. Welfare reform had the effect of limiting cash support to families, mandating stronger work requirements, and giving states more control in program design and implementation. The fundamental goal of welfare reform was to transform the former federal-state joint AFDC program into a new block grant program in which the federal government sends money to states that design and implement the assistance programs.

Although AFDC was funded as an open-ended, matching grant program, TANF provides a fixed amount of funding, equal to the level of funding states received in the early 1990s. With the TANF funding level fixed in nominal terms, the real value of funds provided to states will decline over time with inflation. Furthermore, the states now bear the financial risk that accompanies rising poverty or unemployment rates.

Work requirements and time limits are important features of welfare reform. A parent receiving assistance through a TANF-funded program for 24 months must be working or be in a work program in order to continue receiving assistance. Starting in the year 2002, at least half of all families receiving assistance were required to be working at least 30 hours per week. Time limits also apply. A family is ineligible to receive funding if an adult in that family has already been receiving support for 60 months over his or her lifetime. States may even apply shorter time limits.

Supporters of welfare reform expect it to reduce reliance on public assistance to the poor, increase both employment and wage earnings, and eventually reduce out-of-wedlock birth rates and increase the marriage rate. Opponents of welfare reform expect it to make already poor families even poorer and pull the public safety net from beneath them.

INCOME INEQUALITY AND THE EFFECTS OF TAX AND TRANSFER PROGRAMS

Tax and transfer programs have an impact on altering the income distribution, but the size of that impact is not as great as you might expect.

Tax and Transfer Programs and Their Impact on Poverty

How do government transfer programs and the tax system affect income inequality? Recall that Table 5.3 provided alternative measures of income inequality for the official measure of income used by the Census Bureau as well as for five alternative measures. These alternatives are useful as we seek an evaluation of the effectiveness of tax and transfer programs. The first row of the table reports that, using the current measure of income, the bottom population quintile earns 3.6 percent of the income in the economy, whereas the top quintile earns 49.7 percent. These income shares reveal a substantial inequality of income. One of the frequent criticisms of such data, however, is that government transfers and taxes are not taken into account in computing these shares. The third row of the table presents income shares that reflect after-tax income, and the fifth row of the table reflects the correction for cash transfers. Income shares reported in the fifth row indicate slightly less income inequality but still reveal substantial inequality. The Gini coefficient has been reduced from 0.447, using the current measure of income, to 0.411, reflecting a somewhat more equal distribution of income. The U.S. transfer and tax systems do have some impact on reducing measured income inequality, but that impact is very modest.

How does the U.S. tax system affect poverty? The U.S. Census Bureau provides annual estimates of U.S. poverty thresholds. For example, in 2009, a family of four with two children was then considered to be in poverty if their income was below \$21,756. A single mom with one child was considered to be in poverty with an income below \$14,787. An important relationship exists between the poverty threshold and the tax threshold that should be considered as well. An Urban Institute analysis, using 2003 data, indicates that a family of four with two children faced a tax threshold of \$33,328. The poverty threshold for that family was \$18,660. Hence, the tax threshold was 179 percent of the poverty threshold. With the income tax threshold above the poverty line, it is clear that a family with income at the poverty line will not face a federal income tax liability. For a single parent with two children, the 2003 tax threshold was \$39,700, whereas the poverty level was \$14,810. In that case the income tax threshold was 268 percent of the poverty level. In general, the U.S. income tax system does not subject families in poverty to taxation. Those families are subject to the payroll tax used to fund Social Security, however. It is important to note that the EITC, CTC, and other credits on the income tax clearly offset substantial payroll taxes required of low-income families. Although the payroll tax is a flat-rate tax applied to all payroll earnings, with no exemption at the low end, credits on the income tax help to reduce the combined impact of the two federal taxes.

Effectiveness of Antipoverty Programs

How effective are the U.S. tax system and transfer programs in reducing poverty? Table 5.7 provides information on the antipoverty effectiveness of tax and transfer programs in 2006 for three types of households: persons in units with unmarried head and related children, the elderly, and children. The table lists poverty reduction due to a variety of government programs including social insurance programs (Social Security, unemployment compensation, and workers' compensation), means-tested cash transfers (AFDC, SSI, and general assistance), and means-tested noncash transfers (food stamps, housing benefits, school lunches). Table 5.7 provides alternative estimates of poverty, reporting counts of the number of people in poverty before any government assistance programs; after each type of benefit is added to income; and after government cash, noncash, and tax-related benefits are added or subtracted from income. Table 5.7 also provides estimates of the poverty gap and the reduction in the poverty gap due to various sources.

In order to understand Table 5.7, it is useful to follow a column as you move from the top to the bottom of the table. First, consider persons in units with an unmarried head of the unit and related children. There were 40.7 million such persons in 2006, of whom 16.1 million were in poverty, if we simply consider cash income before any transfers. Social insurance programs other than Social Security reduced the number of persons in

TABLE 5.7 Effectiveness of Antipoverty Programs, 2006

Category	Group: Persons in Unit with Unmarried Head and Related Children	Elderly	Children
Total population (thousands)	40,749	36,035	73,727
Number of Poor Persons (Thousands)			
Cash income before transfers	16,118	16,785	14,673
Plus social insurance other than Social Security			
Plus Social Security			
Plus social insurance	14,721	3,743	13,372
Plus means-tested cash transfers	13,992	3,394	12,827
Plus means-tested noncash benefits	12,192	2,961	11,200
Plus EITC and CTC, less federal payroll and income taxes	10,654	2,965	9,419
Percent of Persons Removed from Poverty Due To:			
Social insurance	8.7	77.7	8.9
Means-tested cash benefits	4.5	2.1	3.7
Means-tested noncash benefits	11.2	2.6	11.1
Federal taxes (including EITC)	9.5	0.0	12.1
Total	33.9	82.3	35.8
Poverty Gap (Millions of 2006 Dollars)			
Cash income before transfers	53,613	97.7	43.6
Plus social insurance	45,035	12.7	36.8
Plus means-tested cash benefits	38,607	10.0	32.3
Plus means-tested noncash benefits	27,023	8.9	23.6
Less federal taxes (including EITC)	24,038	8.9	20.3
Percent Reduction in Poverty Gap Due To:			
Social insurance	16.0	85.1	15.6
Means-tested cash benefits	12.0	2.7	10.2
Means-tested noncash benefits	21.6	1.1	20.0
Federal taxes (including EITC)	5.6	0.0	7.7
Total	55.2	88.9	53.5

Source: *Green Book* 2008, Tables E-29, E-30, E-31, pp. E67–E76.

poverty on the basis of cash transfers alone to 14.7 million. Means-tested cash benefits reduced the number in poverty to 14.0 million, and means-tested noncash benefits further reduced the number to 12.2 million. Finally, tax-related benefits further reduced the number in poverty to 10.7 million.

Table 5.7 also lists the percentage of persons removed from poverty by each category of benefit. For persons in households with an unmarried head and related children, social insurance programs removed about 8.7 percent of such persons from poverty. Means-tested cash transfers removed another 4.5 percent, whereas means-tested noncash transfers removed another 11.2 percent from poverty. Tax-related benefits including the EITC removed an additional 9.5 percent from poverty. Altogether, antipoverty programs removed 33.9 percent of these people from poverty.

Estimates for the elderly and children are also provided in Table 5.7 in succeeding columns, with similar interpretations. It is notable that among the elderly antipoverty programs are dominated by social insurance programs which alone remove 77.7 percent of the elderly from poverty.

Although such information on the number of poor removed from poverty by various programs is useful, it does not give us a sense for how antipoverty programs reduce the depth of poverty experienced by households. The lower part of Table 5.7 reports estimates of the poverty gap (in millions of 2006 dollars) and the percent reduction in the estimated poverty gap due to antipoverty programs. For persons in units with unmarried head of household and related children, the poverty gap amounted to $53.6 billion in 2006 if we consider only cash income before transfers. The poverty gap is reduced to $45.0 billion after we take into account social insurance programs. Means-tested cash benefits reduce the poverty gap to $38.6 billion. Means-tested noncash benefits reduce the poverty gap further to $27.0 billion. Tax-related benefits reduce the poverty gap to $24.0 billion. These poverty gap estimates give us a much fuller sense of how antipoverty programs affect the depth of poverty, not just the number of people affected. Finally, Table 5.7 provides estimates of the percent reduction in the poverty gap for each of the sources listed. A total of 55.2 percent of the poverty gap is estimated to be removed by antipoverty programs for persons in households with an unmarried head and related children. Hence, 45 percent of the gap remains after all antipoverty programs are taken into account.

Which antipoverty programs are most effective? First, the notable effectiveness of social insurance programs (primarily Social Security) for the elderly has already been mentioned. Second, it should be noted that federal programs are most effective in reducing measured poverty among the elderly as compared to children and persons in household units with an unmarried head of household and related children. A much larger percent reduction exists in the number of persons removed from poverty for the elderly (82.3 percent) than for children (35.8 percent) or persons in households with an unmarried head of household and related children (33.9 percent). In this sense, federal antipoverty programs work much better for the elderly than for other poor persons. However, notable programs appear to be quite effective in reducing poverty for nonelderly persons. Consider means-tested cash transfers, for example. These transfers are far more effective in reducing poverty for persons in households with an unmarried head and related children and for children than for the elderly. Means-tested noncash transfer programs appear to be quite effective in reducing poverty for both children and persons in households with an unmarried head and related children. In fact, it is these noncash transfers which are the single most effective category of antipoverty programs listed in Table 5.7 for these groups of the poor. Tax-related benefits, including the EITC, are not at all effective in reducing poverty among the elderly but are quite effective in reducing poverty for persons in households with an unmarried head and related children and for children.

POLICY STUDY

Does Inequality Matter?

The New Rich May Worry About Envy, but Everyone Should Worry About Poverty

"It's the same the whole world over, It's the poor wot gets the blame. It's the rich wot gets the pleasure." What would the have-nots who penned this lament long ago make of today's world?

There are more rich people than ever before, including some 7m millionaires and over 400 billionaires. From sipping champagne to taking trips into space, they are getting plenty of pleasure—though as our survey of the new rich in this issue shows, these sad souls have worries, too, not least about the damaging effect their wealth may have on their children. As for the poor, the gap between them and the rich is rising, even in the industrialised countries where for much of the 20th century the gap had narrowed. In America, between 1979 and 1997 the average income of the richest fifth of the population jumped from nine times the income of the poorest fifth to around 15 times. In 1999, British income inequality reached its widest level in 40 years.

That was then, you (or your financial adviser) might say, but this is now and the rich are getting a little poorer once more. Share prices have fallen and much of the industrialised world is heading either for recession or for slower growth. At such times, inequality of wealth tends to narrow, though not necessarily that of incomes. But such times also tend to be those when anger about inequality comes to the fore, and starts to have political and social consequences. For in good economic times, even the poor feel better off. In bad ones, the rich may lose the most money but the poor lose their jobs, their houses, even their families. And then their acceptance of the way the system works?

Questions of Justice

That, certainly, is the danger. But how much should people (rich or not-rich) worry about it, these days? In the past, in many countries periods of the greatest widening of inequality coincided, more or less, with periods of democratic reform, as the franchise was extended and the discontented thus gained a channel through which to express their ire. That is no longer necessary. Yet although democracy may well mean that a backlash by the less-well-off will not become literally explosive, there are still plenty of ways in which it could be harmful. Past backlashes have, for example, been bought off through trade protectionism, job-guarantee schemes, extending welfare benefits even to the middle classes and, most notoriously, draconian taxation of the wealthy. All such measures sap an economy's strength and make everyone worse off.

The first question to ask about inequality is this, however: If the have-nots are angry about it, are they right to be? In societies where advancement is on merit and seemingly open to everyone, regardless of class, race, creed, or sex, unequal outcomes ought not to be a cause for concern. No one thinks it outrageous that Tiger Woods is the best golfer in the world and rich to boot; we all had the chance to do what he did, but he had the skill and personality. Nor should it be thought outrageous that Bill Gates has made so much money. But where opportunities are not genuinely equal, governments must do what they can to make them so, chiefly by improving public education and ensuring it is open to all.

There is, though, a second way in which anger about inequality could be justified even if opportunities were equal and education were both universal and universally good. It is when power, even power initially gained in a meritocratic way, is abused to raise prices or exclude competitors. That, in a previous backlash, is what gave rise to antitrust laws in America and elsewhere, as governments sought to restrain monopolies and cartels. Difficult economic times, for companies and for consumers, often give rise to accusations of gouging. The temptation at such moments is for governments to be kinder to companies, for fear of job losses. When genuine abuse occurs, however, that is the wrong reaction.

This issue of abuse of power could also apply to individuals. Resentment at "fat-cat" salaries for bosses has been strikingly muted during the boom years. Partly this reflected a new realism about capitalism, but it was also helped by the fact that everyone was becoming better off. In Britain, the poorest fifth enjoyed real annual income growth of 1.9% under John Major and 1.4% under Tony Blair. In America, the average real income of the poorest fifth fell by 3% during 1979–97, but it has since also moved into positive territory, jumping by 5.4% in 1999 alone. Yet during a recession, companies cut costs, which mainly means firing people.

As Hemingway might have said when Scott Fitzgerald said the very rich "are different from you and me": "Yes, they get three years' salary and a protected pension and fully-compensated options when they lose their job. I get a month's notice and a black plastic bag." There will be little that governments can do about resentment at the different treatment given to sacked bosses and to sacked workers, but companies themselves—especially their shareholders—should pay heed. Unjust and unequal treatment is poor corporate governance and, in the longer term, is likely to hurt productivity.

... But Really of Poverty

Liberal democracies and well-run companies ought to be able to find ways to deal with any justified grievances about inequality, and to win the argument against unjustified ones. There is, though, a bigger problem that exists regardless of the gap between rich and poor, but is made starker as a result of it: pure, sheer poverty. Unlike inequality between the few haves and the many have-lesses, this is not readily channelled and defused by democracy, for the truly poor, the underclass, are a small minority. Their interests risk having no democratic means of expression, and can easily be overlooked.

Helping the poor, the truly poor, is a much worthier goal than merely narrowing inequalities. If the rich get poorer thanks to high taxation, some people may feel pleased but few are better off. If the poor get richer, however, the whole country will benefit. Focusing resources and policy on poverty would be worthwhile simply on humanitarian grounds. But also, the disadvantages of growing up in extreme poverty pose a challenge to a belief in equality of opportunity. And helping the underclass rejoin society is in the interests of all.

The main task here is for governments: to provide a proper welfare safety net; to provide and protect public education in the poorest areas; to provide remedial training and schooling; to provide adequate incentives to help the poor get back into (or just get into) work through which they can support themselves. Yet today's many rich individuals can also play a role.

For if they are wise, the rich will behave in ways that help to reassure the rest of the population that rising inequality is not, by itself, a problem. The rich of Victorian Britain helped build great municipal buildings and galleries for art and science. The rich of early 20th-century America used philanthropy to distribute some of their wealth, salving their consciences as well as defusing some of the criticism. Today's rich would do well to follow that example. America's new rich are already beginning to do so, but mostly (with Mr. Gates a notable exception) on a small scale. Their compatriots, and the rich elsewhere, ought now to do more. The more they give away to help the poor, the less anybody else will care that the rich have so much money in the first place. And, who knows, it might even turn out that philanthropy is wot gives the rich pleasure.

POLICY STUDY

Trafficking in Food Stamps[4]

Food stamps are intended as a means to get food to poor families. Some families may choose to illegally sell their food stamps, however, in an attempt to cash out the in-kind benefit that food stamps provide. The U.S. Department of Agriculture, which administers the Food Stamp program, tracks illegal trafficking in food stamps. Their most recent report on trafficking provides estimates of three key measures of trafficking activity: the store violation rate, the overall trafficking rate, and the estimated amount of trafficking. The store violation rate measures the proportion of all authorized stores that are found to engage in trafficking. The rate of trafficking measures the proportion of total food stamp benefits that are found to be trafficked. The total amount of trafficking is the total dollar amount of trafficked food stamps. This measure depends on the total food stamp benefits issued and the rate of trafficking.

Table 5.8 summarizes the most recent USDA estimates, based on some 10,000 investigations, many of which were conducted by undercover agents. According to this study about $657 million in food stamp benefits were diverted during the period 1996 to 1998. Although that sounds like a large amount of money, and it is, it represents just 3.5 percent of all food stamp benefits. Table 5.8 also provides a breakdown

TABLE 5.8 Trafficking in Food Stamps, 1996–1998

Type of Store	Store Violation Rate (%)	Trafficking Rate (%)	Estimated Trafficking Amount ($1,000)
Supermarkets	5.3	1.9	279,163
Large groceries	9.8	3.2	35,255
Subtotal	6.7	2.0	314,418
Small groceries	14.4	15.8	154,109
Convenience	11.7	10.8	66,809
Specialty	10.7	8.1	55,782
Gas plus grocery	12.8	9.7	21,784
Other types	16.2	9.4	43,892
Subtotal	13.0	11.5	342,376
All stores	11.7	3.5	656,794

Source: Macaluso 2000.

by type of store that is quite revealing. Supermarkets and large grocery stores have relatively low store violation rates and trafficking rates, whereas small grocery stores, convenience stores, specialty stores, gas plus grocery, and other stores have much higher store violation and trafficking rates.

Table 5.9 provides information on store violation and trafficking rates by neighborhood poverty measure. Neighborhoods with over 30 percent of the households in poverty have store violation and trafficking rates that are substantially higher than the rates in neighborhoods with low poverty rates. This occurs, despite the fact that the poorer neighborhoods have smaller shares of total stores and total food stamp

TABLE 5.9 Trafficking Is More Frequent in Poor Neighborhoods, 1998

Percentage of Households in Poverty in Zip Code Where Store Is Located (%)	Store Violation Rate (%)	Trafficking Rate (%)	Percentage of All Stores (%)	Percentage of All Redemptions (%)
0 to 10	9.5	2.0	26.5	23.2
11 to 20	10.7	3.1	40.5	40.1
21 to 30	13.2	3.3	20.5	21.6
Over 30	16.8	7.1	12.4	15.1
All stores	11.7	3.5	100.0	100.0

Source: Macaluso 2000.

redemptions. Grocers are more likely to locate their stores outside central cities to attract more customers and reduce the risks of theft, arson, and other problems associated with inner-city locations.

In order to reduce trafficking in food stamps, and to more efficiently administer the food stamp program, the USDA has converted from printed food stamps to electronic benefit cards much like debit cards. The program is now called the Supplemental Nutrition Assistance Program (SNAP). By requiring a personal identification number (PIN) to use the SNAP card, fraud and trafficking have been reduced but not eliminated. All one needs to do is search the Internet for advice on how to convert SNAP benefits to cash and there is plenty of advice available free of charge on how it is done.

This Policy Study is based on Macaluso (2000).

POLICY STUDY

The Samaritan's Dilemma

The Samaritan's dilemma is a fascinating way of looking at the question of providing in-kind transfers to the poor.[5] Although the conventional wisdom in economics is that cash transfers are more efficient than in-kind transfers in terms of making the recipient as well-off as possible, there are some situations in which that general rule may be violated. Such is the case of the Samaritan's dilemma. The context of the Samaritan's dilemma is one of insurance in the face of uncertainty or risk. The rich are assumed to care about the well-being of the poor. The poor face a risk of loss due to unanticipated medical expenses, crop failures, or flooding. The government is assumed to represent the rich and make transfers on their behalf. The analysis of the Samaritan's dilemma, following Coate (1995), follows four steps:

1. When government makes an unconditional transfer, the poor may have an incentive to not buy insurance and rely on private charity to bail them out in the event of a loss.
2. The rich are unable to commit to not help out the unlucky poor even if the government is making the *ex ante* (prior) desirable transfer.
3. The poor's failure to take out insurance in anticipation of private charity has adverse efficiency effects stemming from the fact that the rich (rather than the poor) choose how much protection against loss to give the poor.
4. To restore efficiency, the government needs to ensure that the poor obtain insurance. The optimal transfer policy is therefore to provide in-kind transfers of insurance.

Here we have a case where the optimal policy is an in-kind transfer of insurance. Hence, depending on the context of the risky situation, the appropriate government policy is to provide crop insurance, flood insurance, hurricane insurance, or other forms of insurance. The key reason for this unexpected policy outcome lies in step 3 listed previously. It is the failure of the poor to insure in anticipation of private charity provided in an amount after a disaster by the rich that leads to an inefficiency. The poor choose a level of insurance that is below the optimal amount (zero) in anticipation of assistance in case of a disaster. It is the rich who select the amount of protection to provide after a disaster, not the poor. The mismatch in the amount of insurance leads to an inefficient result. The solution is for the government to provide disaster insurance to assure a more efficient outcome.

Consider the following example. Suppose you are poor and living in southern Florida. You live in a mobile home that is susceptible to serious damage in case of a hurricane and its attendant tornadoes and flooding. You know that you should insure your mobile home and its contents against the possibility of damage due to a hurricane, but the insurance premium is high, and besides, you expect that in case of a big storm, the federal government is likely to provide low-cost loans and other assistance to those who lose their homes. Hence, you underinsure. In the aggregate, we get too many people living in mobile homes with too little hurricane insurance coverage given the risk and the expected damage. The market misallocates resources in this way. When a hurricane eventually blows through your trailer park and destroys your home, the federal government provides assistance in an amount chosen by the government, not you. If you had known in advance what the level of coverage might have been, you might have made a different choice in your decision about how large a mobile home to buy and fill with household goods.

PROBLEMS

1. Consider a hypothetical economy with 10 people, 8 of whom have income of $30,000, 1 of whom has income of $100,000, and 1 of whom has income of $500,000. Sketch the Lorenz curve for this income distribution. Describe the distribution by comparing the Lorenz curve to the line of perfect equality. Can you approximate the Gini coefficient? (Hint: Use graph paper and count blocks to approximate areas.)
2. Consider a hypothetical economy consisting of you and Bill Gates (the CEO of Microsoft, a billionaire). Draw the Lorenz curve. What is the approximate value of the Gini coefficient?
3. Suppose we broaden our definition of the *middle class* to include the middle three quintiles combined. Using this definition and the data in Table 5.2, explain what has happened to the *middle class* since 1980.
4. Compare the first rows of Table 5.2. Explain what happened to the income distribution from 1995 to 2000.
5. The following table provides information on the distribution of money income among families in the United States.
   a. Explain the concept of a quintile in the distribution of income.
   b. Suppose that we define as poor those in the bottom two quintiles of the income distribution. Explain what happened to the share

Year	First Quintile	Second Quintile	Third Quintile	Fourth Quintile	Fifth Quintile
1989	3.8%	9.5%	15.8%	24.0%	46.8%
1999	3.6%	8.9%	14.9%	23.2%	49.4%
2009	3.4%	8.6%	14.6%	23.2%	50.3%

Source: DeNavas-Walt et al. (2010), Table A-2.

of money income earned by the poor from 1989 to 2009.

c. Suppose that we define the middle class very broadly as those in the second, third, and fourth quintiles of the income distribution. Explain what happened to the share of money income earned by the middle class from 1989 to 2009.

d. Explain two significant factors that a table of information such as this ignores.

6. Suppose that an economy consists of two people: Ted and Jane. Their marginal utility functions are given by $MU_T = 600 - 3I_T$ and $MU_J = 600 - 2I_J$, where I_T is Ted's income and I_J is Jane's income. A total income of $I = 500$ is generated by the economy.

a. Compute the optimal income distribution for the two people, assuming that society values each person's utility equally (i.e., $W = U_T + U_J$). Explain why this income distribution is optimal.

b. Draw a graph and identify the welfare loss to society of an egalitarian income distribution where Ted and Jane are each allocated income of $250. Explain why an egalitarian income distribution is typically nonoptimal.

c. Explain the assumption made in this type of analysis regarding the relationship between the income distribution and the total income in the economy.

REFERENCES

Blank, Rebecca M. "The 1996 Welfare Reform." *Journal of Economic Perspectives* 11(1997): 169–77.

Bernanke, Ben S. "The Level and Distribution of Economic Well-Being." Speech before the Greater Omaha Chamber of Commerce, Omaha, Nebraska, February 6, 2007. Available at: http://www.federalreserve.gov/newsevents/speech/bernanke20070206a.htm.

Coate, Stephen. "Altruism, The Samaritan's Dilemma, and Government Transfer Policy." *American Economic Review* 85(1995): 46–57.

Committee on Ways and Means. *Green Book 2008*. Washington, DC: U.S. Government Printing Office, 2008. Available at: http://democrats.waysandmeans.house.gov/singlepages.aspx?NewsID=10490

DeNavas-Walt, Carmen, Bernadette D. Proctor, and Jessica C. Smith. U.S. Census Bureau, Current Population Reports, P60-238, *Income, Poverty, and Health Insurance Coverage in the United States: 2009*, U.S. Government Printing Office, Washington, DC, 2010.

Economist. 2010. "Measuring Global Poverty—Whose Problem Now?" October 2, 2010, p. 65.

Macaluso, Theodore F. *The Extent of Trafficking in the Food Stamp Program: An Update*. Washington, DC: Office of Analysis, Nutrition, and Evaluation, Food and Nutrition Service, U.S. Department of Agriculture, 2000.

Miller, Matthew, and Luisa Kroll. "World's Richest People: Bill Gates No Longer World's Richest Man." *Forbes*, March 9, 2010. Available at:

http://www.forbes.com/2010/03/09/worlds-richest-people-slim-gates-buffett-billionaires-2010-intro.html.

Office of Management and Budget. *Budget of the United States Government, Fiscal Year 2011*. Washington, DC: U.S. Government Printing Office, 2011.

Piketty, Thomas, and Emmanuel Saez. "Income Inequality in the United States: 1913–2002." Chapter in A. B. Atkinson and T. Piketty, editors, *Top Incomes over the Twentieth Century*. Oxford, UK: Oxford University Press, 2007.

Rawls, John. *A Theory of Justice*. Cambridge, MA: Harvard University Press, 1971.

Sumner, Andy. "Global Poverty and the New Bottom Billion: Three-Quarters of the World's Poor Live in Middle-Income Countries" Institute of Development Studies, University of Sussex, UK, 2010. Paper available at: http://www.ids.ac.uk/index.cfm?objectid=D840B908-E38D-82BD-A66A89123C11311F.

World Bank. *World Development Report 2010*. Washington, DC: World Bank, 2010. Available at: http://www.worldbank.org/wdr.

NOTES

1. Of course, the same principle holds for total cost, total revenue, and all other total marginal entities. Total cost can be viewed as the area under the marginal cost curve, total revenue is the area under the marginal revenue curve, and so on.
2. This principle can be demonstrated mathematically. Social welfare is

$$W = u_A(m_A) + u_B(m_B),$$

where the sum of income allocated to each person must add to the total income available:

$$m = m_A + m_B.$$

We can include this constraint in the welfare maximization problem by writing the welfare function as

$$W = u_A(m_A) + u_B(m - m_A).$$

The choice variable is m_A, the amount of income to allocate to person A. The remainder, $m - m_A$, is allocated to person B. Differentiating W with respect to m_A, setting equal to zero, and solving gives the condition

$$\partial u_A / \partial m_A = \partial u_B / \partial m_B,$$

which requires that the marginal utility of income be equal for each person.
3. This material, and that in the welfare reform section, is adapted from Blank (1997).
4. This policy study is based on Macaluso (2000).
5. The original use of the term *Samaritan's dilemma* is due to James Buchanan. The current research on the Samaritan's dilemma is summarized in Coate (1995).

PART THREE

Social Choice and Analysis of Government Programs

CHAPTER

6

Radius Images/Getty Images

Collective Decision Making

LEARNING OBJECTIVES

1. Discuss the nature of collective decision making and how it differs from individual decision making.
2. Identify the various collective decision-making rules in a direct democracy, including majority rule and the median voter model.
3. Discuss collective decision making in a representative democracy.

In this chapter we examine how groups of citizens make collective choices regarding the quantity of public goods that they want their governments to provide. Although we all know our own individual preferences quite well and could easily tell the government leaders what we want, in a democratic society we face the additional problem of making collective decisions that take into account the preferences of all citizens. This is no small problem. How do we somehow aggregate the very disparate views of thousands of city residents or millions of national voters to obtain a coherent set of collective preferences that will guide government leaders in making allocation decisions? After all, you may well understand that it is tough enough for a group of three college friends to agree on what pizza toppings to order on a large pizza they plan to share. We will examine a number of properties of voting mechanisms and then consider some of the practical problems that voting confronts us with in a direct or representative democracy.[1]

INDIVIDUAL PREFERENCES AND COLLECTIVE DECISION MAKING

Every person has preferences. You may like Eminem's music or you may hate it. Maybe Shontelle is more to your liking. You may prefer a Pepsi to a Coke, or a Mountain Dew to either. Although you may readily recognize that you have preferences, you may not have thought much about how to describe those preferences. It is important to understand some basic properties of individual preferences in order to analyze collective preferences for public goods. Individual preferences are typically described using properties that are assumed to be basic descriptors of people's desires.

Individual Preferences

Consider two sets of public good expenditure and tax combinations. The first set is denoted x_a and consists of a high level of expenditure on local public schools and a high property tax rate. The second set is denoted x_b and consists of a low level of expenditure on local public schools and a low property tax rate. A person's preferences for public goods and taxes can be described by the following four characteristics.

First, there must be **comparability** in the person's preferences. Comparability means that any two public good and tax combinations, x_a and x_b, can be compared.[2] Either x_a is preferred to x_b, or x_b is preferred to x_a, or the person is indifferent between x_a and x_b. In other words, either the person prefers that the local governments provide public good combination x_a with high expenditure on local public schools and high property tax rate, or she prefers the combination x_b with the opposite combination, or she is indifferent between the two options and does not care which combination is provided. In any case, she is able to compare combinations of public goods.

Second, her preferences must be characterized by **transitivity.** This characteristic of a person's preferences involves a basic type of consistency. If policy combination x_a is preferred to policy combination x_b, and x_b is preferred to another policy combination x_c, then it follows that policy combination x_a is preferred to x_c.[3] Indeed, we would think it quite inconsistent if a person said, "I prefer a big budget for local public schools to a medium budget, and I prefer a medium budget to a small budget, but I prefer a small budget to a big budget." Such a preference is inconsistent and we call this type of inconsistency *intransitivity*.

Third, the person's preferences must be characterized by **nonsatiation.** This characteristic means that the person does not become satiated (where marginal utility is zero) with respect to all goods simultaneously. That is, the person does not have so much local public education and other public goods that her marginal utility is zero for all public goods simultaneously.

The fourth and final characteristic of the person's preferences is that they be **convex.** Convexity of preferences means that the person prefers mean combinations to extreme combinations.[4] That is, the person prefers an average (or intermediate combination) of the extremes to the extremes themselves. In the context of our example, convexity means that the person would prefer an intermediate combination between x_a and x_b. If we offered the median combination x_m, which consists of the median level of local public education expenditure and the median property tax rate from combinations x_a and x_b, the person would prefer that median combination to either extreme combination x_a or x_b. This characteristic is not hard to understand. Would you rather have two Big Macs and no fries, no Big Macs and two orders of fries, or one Big Mac and one order of fries? Because McDonald's offers value meals that involve one Big Mac and one order of fries, it must be that most people have convex preferences and prefer a mean combination to an extreme combination.

The point of describing the person's preferences with these four characteristics is that such a set of preference characteristics is sufficient to assure that the person's demand for public goods has the conventional downward slope.

This is important as we are then assured that we can use the conventional economic theory with demand curves to describe individuals' demand for public goods. We often summarize a person's preferences for a public good x by assuming the person has a utility function $u(x)$, and we draw the person's indifference curves for the good with the usual shape.[5] Assuming the existence of a utility function is equivalent to assuming the above four characteristics of the person's preferences. If people have these preference characteristics, we can work with utility functions and more importantly demand curves for public goods and services. When we draw an indifference curve, we are simply drawing the person's preferences for the two goods measured on the axes.

So far, we have focused on individual preferences. We need to move from individual demand for public goods to collective demand for public goods by residents of the community. Because a community is made up of many individuals, we must find a way to combine all of the individual preferences into a collective, or community, set of preferences.

Moving from the Individual to the Community

Although each individual has preferences, as described previously, the challenge facing the community is to devise a method of collecting these individual preferences into a collective decision about what the government should do in a particular policy setting. For example, you and I and everyone else may have an opinion about the appropriate level of government spending for the Food Stamp program, which provides subsidies for low-income families to purchase food. We may only have a vague opinion that the current level is too high, about right, or too low, but in any case, we have an opinion. How do we take all of these individual opinions and turn them into a collective decision about contracting, expanding, or leaving the current Food Stamp program unchanged? How do we move from individual preferences to collective preferences? That is the challenge of a democracy which lives to fulfill the desires of its people.

In the United States, we have adopted the national motto *e pluribus unum,* which is Latin for "out of many, one." The motto is intended to reflect the fact that out of many varied groups of immigrants with widely differing national origins, ethnic backgrounds, points of view, and life experiences, we have become one people—Americans. Although this notion is more a reflection of what we would like to be than what we are, it captures an essential concept for collective choice. Out of many individual preferences, we must construct one collective preference for our government.

COLLECTIVE DECISION MAKING IN A DIRECT DEMOCRACY

Collective decision making can occur in either a direct democracy or a representative democracy. A statewide referendum on an environmental cleanup program is an example of the former, whereas a congressional vote on the budget for the next fiscal year is an example of the latter. In this section we consider collective decision making in the direct democracy context. We will examine the representative democracy case in the following section.

Voting Rules

A number of voting rules can be applied in a direct democracy where voters are voting directly for candidates or on issues. The most common rule applied is the majority voting rule where the candidate or issue receiving the majority of the votes cast is the winner.

Majority Rule

Majority rule occurs when each voter writes the name of exactly one candidate on his ballot and the candidate with the **plurality** of votes is declared the winner. In a two-candidate race, it takes one vote more than 50 percent to win. In races with more than two candidates, the candidate with the plurality of votes wins. This would seem to be the quintessential democratic method of collective decision making. Put the issue to a vote, and the proposal that wins the greatest share of the votes wins. Obviously, this is the best outcome, right? Believe it or not, it is possible for the plurality to violate the wishes of most voters. Consider the following example with four candidates and 21 voters.[6] Voter preferences are summarized in Table 6.1. For example, column 1 indicates that three voters have the preference ranking A, B, C, D. The second column indicates that five voters have the preference ranking A, C, B, D, and so on.

If we follow the principle of plurality, candidate A wins the election with 8 votes from the 3 voters in column 1 and the 5 voters in column 2. That result occurs by counting the first choice of each voter. Candidate A wins because he receives more first-choice votes than the other candidates. Notice, however, that candidate A is actually the worst candidate for a majority of the voters because 13 voters rank candidate A as their least-preferred choice, 7 voters in column 3 and 6 in column 4. In fact, this set of voters prefers *anyone else* to candidate A. Thirteen voters also prefer candidate B to candidate

TABLE 6.1 Plurality Results in the Election of the Least-Preferred Candidate

Ranking	Preference Ordering (Ranked from Most Preferred in the Top Row to Least Preferred in the Bottom Row)			
First	A	A	B	C
Second	B	C	D	B
Third	C	B	C	D
Fourth	D	D	A	A
Total	3 voters	5 voters	7 voters	6 voters

A, 13 voters prefer candidate C to candidate A, and 13 voters prefer candidate D to candidate A. Despite the fact that a majority of voters want anyone but candidate A, he is elected.

Alternatives to Majority Voting

The weakness of plurality as a collective decision-making rule has been known since the time of Condorcet in 1785 (Condorcet 1785). Who should be elected in this case? The **Condorcet rule** says that the candidate who defeats all other candidates in pairwise comparisons using majority voting wins. Her procedure calls for consideration of all possible pairs of candidates (or ballot issues) with plurality's determining the winner of each possible pair. In the example of Table 6.1, the Condorcet rule would declare candidate C the winner. Because there are four candidates, there are six possible pairwise comparisons: A-B, A-C, A-D, B-C, B-D, and C-D. In the A-B comparison, a majority prefers B. In the A-C comparison, a majority prefers C. In the A-D comparison, a majority prefers D. In the B-C comparison, a majority prefers C. In the B-D comparison, a majority prefers B. In the C-D comparison, a majority prefers C. Considering all possible pairwise comparisons, with the winner of each pair determined by plurality, candidate C wins.

Another alternative rule for collective decision making was suggested by Borda (1781). Decision making using the **Borda rule** requires each voter to report his or her preferences by ranking the top n candidates from first choice to nth choice. No ties are permitted. The candidates receive $n - 1$ points for being ranked first, $n - 2$ for being ranked second, and so on. No points are allocated to a candidate ranked last. The candidate with the highest point total wins. Applying the Borda rule to the voter preferences in Table 6.1 results in candidate B as the winner. Why? The candidate point totals would be as follows: A is 24 points, B is 44 points, C is 38 points, and D is 20 points. The outcome of the Borda rule differs from that of the Condorcet rule because the Borda rule takes into account each voter's entire ranking of all the candidates. In this sense, the Borda rule uses more of the information available in voters' preference rankings.

Both the Condorcet rule and the Borda rule have advantages over simple majority rule, yet most elections in a direct democracy use majority rule. Why is that? Shouldn't we use the more superior rules that overcome the shortcomings of the simple majority rule? Well, yes, but the complexity of the Condorcet rule and the Borda rule makes them less appealing in a direct democracy. A powerful intuition is shared by most voters that the majority opinion is most representative of the wishes of the electorate. Perennial calls to abolish the Electoral College system in the United States are witness to the powerful attraction of the simplicity of the majority rule, despite its weaknesses.

Unanimity

Consider an extreme case where we require an absolute unanimous choice in order to implement a public decision. **Unanimity** requires all voters to agree on the issue or candidate. This rule is applied by the United Nations Security Council, for example. All members of the council must agree on a proposition for the council to support the proposition. Each member therefore has the equivalent of veto power and is able to block a proposal by voting "no." With this collective decision-making rule in use on the Security Council during the Cold War, the United States and the Soviet Union regularly used their veto to block initiatives of the enemy. As a consequence, the United Nations Security Council was stymied for many years, finding it difficult to come to a collective decision on any issue about which the United States or the Soviet Union had a strong opinion. Without this decision-making rule, there would have been no forum in which the United States and the Soviet Union would have jointly considered any initiatives, however. Given their adversarial relationship, unanimity was the only feasible decision-making rule that would have elicited participation by both countries.

It is not generally possible to provide public goods using a unanimity rule, because by the nature of public goods, the same quantity of the good must be provided to all individuals. In the market for private goods, each individual selects the quantity desired on the basis of the price. If we could somehow adjust prices to the individuals so that they would desire the same quantity, we might have a solution to the public good provision problem and at the same time have unanimity among voters. A method of doing this was devised by Swedish economist Erik Lindahl in the early 20th century. Figure 6.1 illustrates **Lindahl prices,** where George's and Linda's demands for streetlights are plotted, with Linda's vertical axis flipped upside down. Doing so enables us to think of the vertical distance in the figure as the full cost of providing a streetlight and then to consider George's and Linda's shares of that total cost per streetlight. Equilibrium is determined where George's and Linda's demands for streetlights are equal; that is, at the cost shares where the two residents would desire the same level of streetlight provision. At the quantity L^*, George and Linda are unanimous in desiring the same quantity of streetlights. In order to accomplish this outcome, however, we must charge the two residents different tax prices for streetlights. George must be confronted with a tax price of S^* of the cost of a streetlight, whereas Linda must be asked to pay a tax price of $1 - S^*$ of the cost. Obviously, the **Lindahl equilibrium**[7] requires that each resident be charged a tax price for the public good that is related to that person's demand for the public good, reflecting the benefit received. For this reason, Lindahl prices are sometimes called **benefit prices.**

This mechanism has two problems. First, it requires specific information on each resident's demand for the public good. That information is difficult to obtain. Recall the problem of the free rider and the difficulty of eliciting information on true preferences, especially if that information is going to be used as the basis for unique tax computations. Second, community residents may perceive that the tax prices are unfair. After all, everyone is getting the same quantity of the public good, but some people are asked to pay a larger share of the cost while others are paying a smaller share. A fundamental sense of fairness may be violated by application of such a mechanism.

FIGURE 6.1 Lindahl Prices

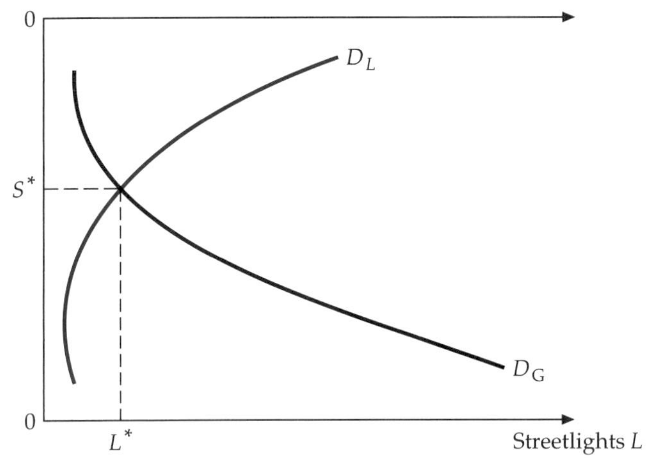

Let's add another dimension to the collective decision-making problem. In addition to the opportunity to vote for what he or she wants in the jurisdiction, what if the voter has the option of leaving the jurisdiction if he or she does not like the choices available?

Exit, Voice, and Loyalty

When a citizen is confronted with a situation in which her opinion clearly differs from that of others in the community, what options does she have? Say, for example, that she desires a larger expenditure on local public education (and is willing to pay for it) than most of her neighbors. She has more than one alternative means of responding to this situation. First, she may **exit** the community, simply pack up, leave, and look for a different community where people have preferences more like hers. A second alternative obviates the need to leave the community. She can get involved on the local school board, organize a group of like-minded parents, and **voice** her opinion, hoping to influence the community to provide the level of education expenditure she desires. Finally, she can choose to be **loyal** to the community's decision, despite the fact that it is not consistent with her desires. This characterization of the citizen's **trilemma** has become a classic since the work of Albert Hirschman (1970).

MEDIAN VOTER MODEL

In the case of the majority rule method of collective decision making, we know what outcome will occur. The **median voter theorem** tells us that the median voter is decisive. Consider a budget bill in Congress. Line up all the members of Congress in order of their preference from the member wanting the smallest budget to the one wanting the largest budget. Pick the middle voter and ask him what he wants. That will be the outcome of a majority vote. This result might sound amazing, but it is true, at least under certain circumstances.

Consider a situation where the distribution of voters favoring increasing levels of expenditure by their local school district is as follows: 4 percent favor expenditure level E_1, 12 percent favor E_2, 23 percent favor E_3, 31 percent favor E_4, 18 percent favor E_5, 10 percent favor E_6, and 2 percent favor E_7. What will be the expenditure level favored by a majority of the voters? The answer is expenditure E_4, the median expenditure level. Why? Well, start at the lowest expenditure level E_1 and ask yourself what share of the voters prefers that level of expenditures? The answer is that just 4 percent prefer the smallest level of expenditure and the remaining 96 percent of the voters prefer a higher level of expenditure. At expenditure level E_2, we still have a majority (86 percent) that would prefer a higher expenditure level. Continuing in this fashion you can determine that the median expenditure level E_4 will be the outcome of majority voting. A majority will not support expenditures either less than E_4 or in excess of E_4. The amazing result is that the preference of the median voter will be decisive in a majority voting context. In this section we will describe the median voter model and the fundamental result that follows from that model—the median voter theorem.

Competition and the Median Location

Harold Hotelling was the first economist to explore the properties of **median location** in his paper "Stability in Competition" (1929). We can illustrate his insight by referring to a political continuum from a liberal position denoted L to a conservative position denoted R in Figure 6.2. Suppose that there are two political candidates who are ideological purists at the beginning of a campaign for public office. Voters are distributed uniformly along the continuum. The liberal espouses views that are at the far left of the political spectrum, and the conservative espouses views at the extreme right. After a few weeks of campaigning, one of the candidates, let's say the liberal, wises up and recognizes that if she moderates her rhetoric and begins to sound a bit more conservative, she will retain the voters to the left of her on the political spectrum and pick up voters on the right. Of course, the conservative candidate is equally bright and figures out the opposite plan works for him as well. Competition for votes drives the two candidates to the center. By the end of the campaign, they end up sounding very similar. Both locate at the

FIGURE 6.2 Political Ideology

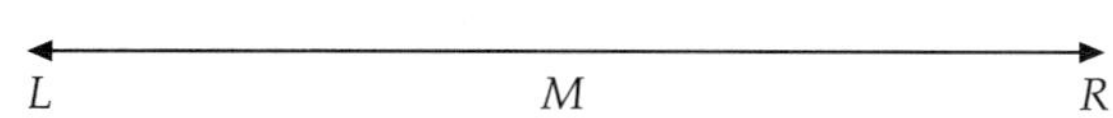

FIGURE 6.3 Two Candidates' Positions

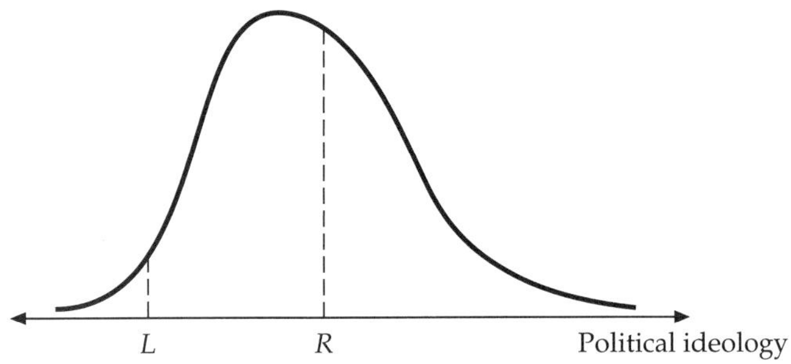

median of the political spectrum. In so doing, they are assured that voters with more extreme political preferences will stay with them, because such voters are unlikely to cross over and vote for the candidate whose views are further from theirs. The candidates' moderation in espoused views has been driven by a desire to secure at least 51 percent of the votes. In the end, it is the median voter who decides which candidate will win the election. For every liberal voter, there is a conservative voter on the other end of the spectrum. Each liberal vote cancels out a conservative vote. The median voter decides the election, in other words.

This characterization of the median voter result is, of course, very naive. Voters are unlikely to be uniformly distributed along a political spectrum. Let's suppose that the distribution of political opinion is as illustrated in Figure 6.3. In this case, a liberal candidate with views that are represented by *L* will certainly lose to a conservative candidate with views represented by *R*. The conservative will win over half the votes easily, even though his position is probably right of the median. If the liberal candidate moderates to a set of views closer to the middle, or that of the median voter, her chances of winning the election increase dramatically. If you are a political candidate, the key is to make sure that more than 50 percent of the distribution of voters supports you. But, just joining the candidate with views *R* at the point of his views on the political spectrum will not necessarily win an election for the candidate with original views *L*. If the candidate with views *R* had views slightly to the left of the median voter's to start, the candidate with views *L* would have to push the candidate with views *R* to become more conservative during the election, following him to the right with her views. Only in doing so would the candidate with original views *L* have any hope of winning a plurality of votes.

This view of the critical role of the median voter also explains why political parties engage in massive efforts to *get out the vote*. They call registered voters to encourage them to vote and even offer transportation to the polls. Is all of this effort worthwhile? Well, if the median voter is decisive, efforts to turn out the vote can affect who the median voter is, making sure he is *one of ours*. If the Democrats can turn out an extra voter on the left, given

FIGURE 6.4 Choices Along a Continuum

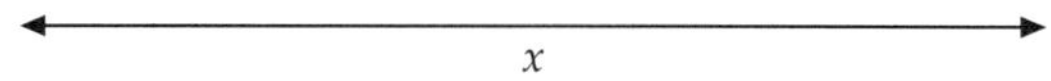

any number of voters on the right, the median shifts leftward. Hence, election day is often rife with speculation about voter turnout. Political pundits speculate about the day's weather and its effect on voter turnout. Conventional wisdom holds that bad weather favors the Republicans because poor Democrats are less likely to get to the polls in such circumstances. The motor-voter bill, which permits people to register to vote when they are at the Department of Motor Vehicles office to get their driver's licenses, was hotly debated in Congress because of the clear implications for making it easy to register to vote. Republicans were fearful that additional registered voters obtained in this way would be more likely to be Democrats, thus shifting the median voter in that party's direction.

Suppose that we are interested in a single issue where choices that voters face, like expenditure on a government program, involve a variable x that can be represented along a continuum, as illustrated in Figure 6.4. In addition, the nature of a continuum is that between any two values of x we consider, such as x_a and x_c, there is an intermediate value x_b. That is, the set of choices between x_a and x_c is continuous.

A person's preferences over various possible choices may be illustrated as well. Consider the choice of three levels of public expenditure for a project: x_a, x_b, and x_c, where $x_a < x_b < x_c$. If the person's preference ranking, from least preferred to most preferred, is x_b, x_a, x_c we can illustrate her preferences as in Figure 6.5. Values of x are plotted on the horizontal axis, whereas her preference ranking is plotted on the vertical axis. It is important to notice that this person has **single-peaked preferences.** Her preference ranking has just one peak in the graph, and it occurs at the expenditure level x_b.

FIGURE 6.5 Single-Peaked Preference Ranking

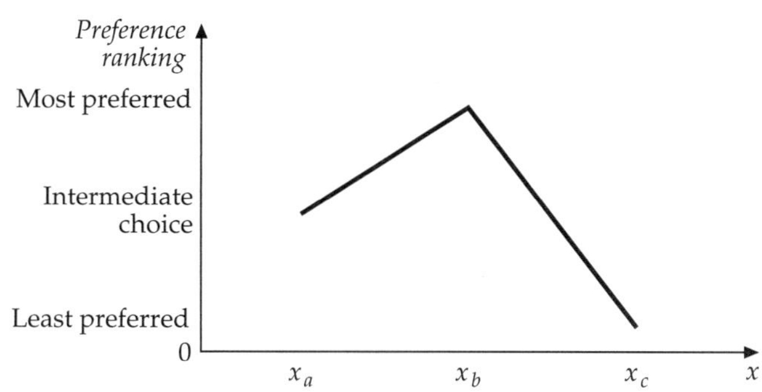

FIGURE 6.6 Double-Peaked Preference Ranking

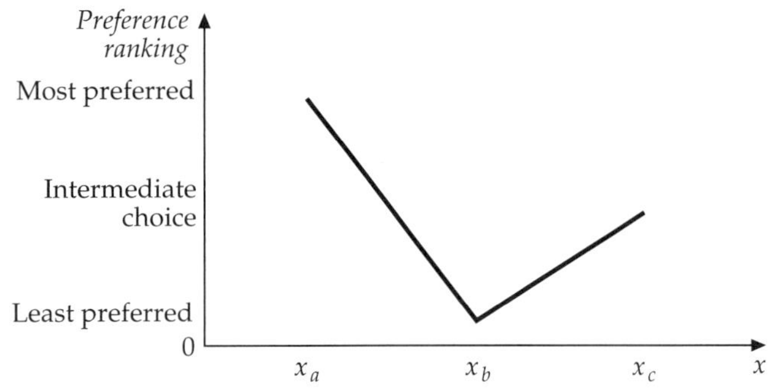

Not everyone's preferences look like those shown in Figure 6.5 when plotted. Consider, for example, the case of a person who likes extremes. Gus is a fellow who prefers the smallest possible government expenditure, because in general he believes that governments are unnecessary. But if he cannot have the smallest possible government program, he would pick the largest possible program as his second choice. He figures that if he can't have the small program he wants, he'll choose the huge program hoping that it will eventually fail and be reduced to the small program he wanted in the first place. His least-desired choice is the intermediate-sized program. Gus has **concave preferences** for government programs; this results in his preference map having two peaks. His preferences are described as **double-peaked preferences** and are plotted in Figure 6.6.

If voters' preferences are single-peaked and if voters express their true preferences when they vote, then the choice selected by majority vote will be the median outcome. This result is so important in public finance that it is a theorem—the *median voter theorem*. A more formal statement of the theorem can be given.

Statement of the Median Voter Theorem

> If x is a single-dimensional issue, and all voters have single-peaked preferences defined over x and vote according to their preferences, then x_m, the median position, cannot lose under majority rule. (Mueller 1989, pp. 66)

This theorem assures that the median voter is decisive in an election, as long as the conditions of the theorem hold. Hence, the outcome of majority voting is predictable—the median voter determines the outcome of the election.

Real-world elections are more complex, of course, than the basic statement of the median voter theorem. In real elections there are often choices that are not single-dimensional. What if the state ballot has a proposition that would eliminate the personal income tax while simultaneously applying the sales tax on services? This two-dimensional ballot proposition is more complex than the simple unidimensional case of the median voter model.

What if there are some voters who have double-peaked preferences (concave preferences rather than convex preferences)? Will the presence of some voters with this type of preferences nullify the median voter result?

Characteristics of the Median Voter Result

Aside from outright violations of the necessary conditions of the median voter theorem, there are still problems with the median voter result, even if all conditions hold and the median result is realized in an election. First, there is inherent dissatisfaction with the result. Because the only person who may be satisfied with the outcome of majority voting is the median voter, there is likely to be dissatisfaction with the result. Those who desired an outcome either above or below the median may well be quite disappointed with the result. The majority of voters may be dissatisfied. Second, the median outcome is not necessarily the efficient level of public good required by the Samuelson rule. The outcome of majority voting is the desired outcome of the median voter. Efficiency in the provision of public goods, however, requires that the Samuelson condition be fulfilled: provide that quantity of the public good where the sum of the residents' marginal benefits equals the marginal cost. No assurance exists that the median voter's desired level is the same as that required by the Samuelson condition.

Voting Paradox

Suppose that we have three voters: I, II, and III. They must choose among three public projects, x_a, x_b, and x_c, which are listed on the ballot in order of their size (measured by the government expenditure necessary for each project). Project x_a is the smallest, x_b is an intermediate size, and x_c is the largest project. The three voters have the following transitive preferences for ballot propositions x_a, x_b, and x_c, as illustrated in Table 6.2.

These preferences can also be plotted, as illustrated in Figure 6.7.

What is the outcome of majority voting in this case? Will the median be the outcome, or does the presence of a voter with double-peaked preferences nullify the median voter result? Compare ballot measures x_a and x_b. Two out of three voters prefer x_a to x_b (voters I and III); hence the majority favor x_a over x_b. Compare ballot measures x_b and x_c. Two out of three voters prefer x_b to x_c (voters I and II); hence the majority favor x_b over x_c. Because the

TABLE 6.2 Voter Preferences

Voter	First Choice	Second Choice	Third Choice
I	x_a	x_b	x_c
II	x_b	x_c	x_a
III	x_c	x_a	x_b

FIGURE 6.7 Voter Preferences

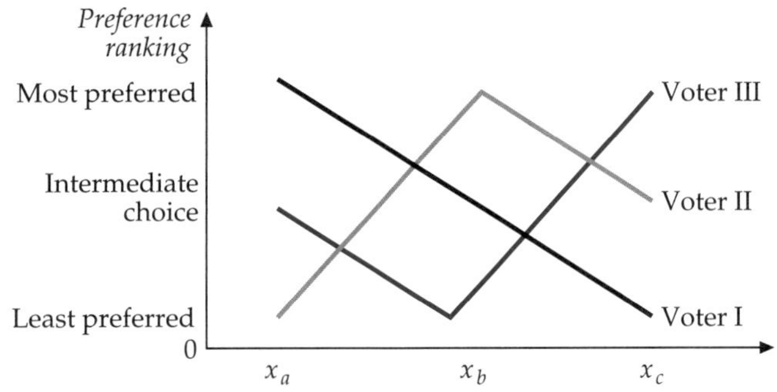

majority prefer x_a to x_b and the majority prefer x_b to x_c, it should follow that the majority prefer x_a to x_c, right? Well, let's check and make sure. Voter I prefers x_a to x_c, but voters II and III prefer x_c to x_a. Thus, a majority prefer x_c to x_a. Despite the fact that all three voters have transitive preferences, the outcome of majority voting is intransitive. A majority prefer x_a to x_b, a majority prefer x_b to x_c, but then a majority prefer x_c to x_a. A contraction of this type is called the **voting paradox.** It is a violation of logical consistency we would hope would hold. As you can see, majority voting can sometimes lead to a nonsense result.

What makes this example turn out intransitive? Notice that although all three voters have transitive preferences, one voter has double-peaked preferences. Voter III is the culprit. He likes the largest project best, but if he has to take his second choice, he wants the smallest project. The intermediate option is his least preferred. As you can see from Figure 6.7, this voter has concave preferences, unlike voters I and II and most of us who have convex preferences, preferring the intermediate-sized project when compared to the least preferred of the smallest and largest projects.

This example has illustrated how the presence of one voter with double-peaked preferences can cause the outcome of majority rule voting to be inconsistent. It is important to consider whether it is possible to devise a decision-making rule that will satisfy basic properties that we would consider essential to any sensible rule by which we make collective choices.

Properties of a Good Collective Decision-Making Rule

Kenneth Arrow, a Nobel Prize–winning economist, has studied collective choice and proposed that a good collective decision-making rule should satisfy the following six reasonable criteria:

1. It can produce a decision regardless of the nature of voters' preferences. For example, it cannot fall apart just because some voters have multi-peaked preferences.

2. It must be able to rank all possible outcomes. Hence, it will be capable of providing a preference ranking for all contingencies facing the community.
3. It must be responsive to individuals' preferences. That is, if every individual prefers option x_a to option x_b, then the collective decision-making rule should indicate that society prefers x_a to x_b.
4. It must be transitive. That is, it must have the property of logical consistency where if x_a is preferred to x_b and x_b is preferred to x_c, then x_a must be preferred to x_c.
5. The collective decision-making rule's ranking of x_a and x_b should depend only on individuals' rankings of x_a and x_b, and not on other alternatives. This property is known as the *independence of irrelevant alternatives.* For example, the rankings of defense expenditures and medical care do not depend on how people rank either of those with respect to transportation.
6. Dictatorship is not permitted. That is, the collective decision-making rule cannot simply be represented by the preferences of one individual.

All of these properties of a collective decision-making rule seem reasonable, and we would hope that any decision-making rule used in a society would embody all of these properties. It turns out, however, that incorporating all six properties appears to be impossible. This result is so important that it has theorem status, known as *Arrow's impossibility theorem.*

Arrow's Impossibility Theorem

Arrow's **impossibility theorem** states that it is not possible to find a collective decision-making rule that satisfies all six of these criteria. If all six conditions hold, phenomena like the voting paradox can occur. Arrow showed that dropping any one of the six criteria permits a proof of the existence of a collective decision-making rule. But then, the important question is which of the six reasonable criteria outlined previously would you be willing to sacrifice? How about accepting the inconsistency of intransitive preferences? Worse yet, how about accepting a dictator like Stalin in order to assure the existence of a collective decision-making rule? The impossibility theorem makes it clear that collective decision making will not always be easy, consistent, or rational.

COLLECTIVE DECISION MAKING IN A REPRESENTATIVE DEMOCRACY

Many situations in a democratic society involve representative, rather than direct, democracy. For example, the voters in each of the 50 U.S. states elect senators to represent them in the U.S. Senate. You and I as voters have no ability to vote directly on bills that come before that body, but our representatives do. Hence, we engage in communication activity to let our elected representatives know our views on issues important to us. We expect our senators to represent our interests. Senators from farm states had better stand up for farmers when farm bills are debated. Senators from highly urbanized states had better stand up for their urban constituents on mass transit bills and welfare reform bills. With representative democracy comes a whole set of issues related to the indirect nature of the democratic process in that setting. We will consider two sets of issues in particular: political parties and logrolling.

Political Parties

Consider the case of a two-party representative democracy. Elections in this context occur in two steps. First, there is competition among candidates for the party's nomination in a primary. In this process, candidates are pulled toward the median view of the party. The second step of the election process is the competition among the two parties' candidates in the general election. In this process, the candidates are pulled toward the median of the population of voters. Notice the distinction here. In the primary the candidate has to move to the center of the party, but in the general election the candidate must move to the center of the wider electorate. This transition from primary to general election is fatal to some politicians who are successful at the first stage but fail miserably at the second stage. Barry Goldwater and Michael Dukakis are good examples of this problem in U.S. presidential elections.

Figure 6.8 illustrates the distribution of candidate positions along a continuum. The upper dashed line in Figure 6.8 represents the distribution of voters in the general election. The candidates are both forced to move in the direction of *P*, the median voter view in the general election. If each of the political parties' candidates takes the other candidate's position as given in the general election, the equilibrium will generally fall between the party position and population median voter position. That is, the Democrat will move from the *D* position she took in the primary and moderate toward the *P* view during the general election. The Republican will move from the *R* view that was successful for him in the primary and moderate toward the *P* view during the course of the campaign. As we near election day, we should not be surprised to find that both candidates are effectively at point *P*.

FIGURE 6.8 Distributions of Political Views

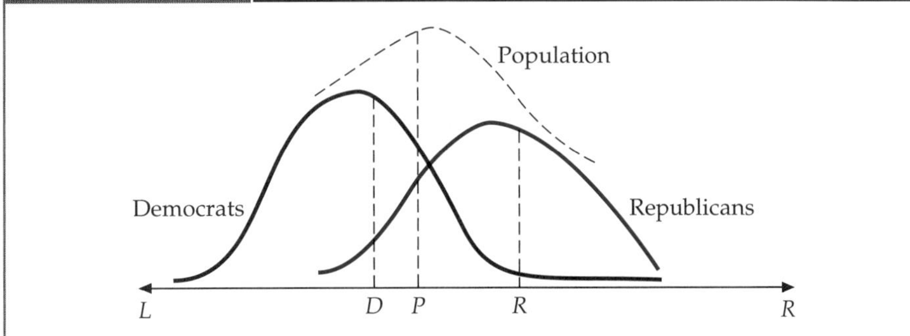

Besides forcing candidates to move to the center, as indicated by the median voter theorem, other aspects of representative democracy are important to consider. We examine two issues in the following sections: logrolling and rent seeking.

Logrolling

A fundamental economic reality is that exchange can enhance welfare. That applies in the world of representative voting as well as in the world of economic exchange. Whenever person A's marginal utility of good X is very high compared to person B's, it is welfare enhancing for A to trade some of good Y to person B in exchange for added units of good X. In the context of representative voting, if A and B are senators, it may be welfare enhancing for them to exchange votes on critical issues. Although there is no market permitted for votes, that being considered unethical, senators may effectively trade votes by voting in favor of a colleague's proposal when the marginal utility is small in exchange for that colleague's support on another bill that is much more critical. The process of representatives trading votes with one another is called **logrolling.**

Consider the following example. Senator Wheatly from South Dakota cares intensely about the outcome of a bill that would provide subsidies to wheat growers in his state. However, he does not much care about the outcome of a vote pending on a mass transportation bill that would provide funds to cities with subway transit systems. His state does not have subway transit systems. On the other hand, Senator Metro from New York cares intensely about the outcome of the mass transit bill because it would mean millions of dollars in aid for the rapid transit system in New York City, whose voters she represents. She does not represent any wheat growers, so she does not care about the wheat subsidy bill. A third voter exists as well. Senator Smith from South Carolina cares neither for the wheat subsidy bill nor for the mass transit bill. It may happen that Senator Wheatly is willing to trade his vote on the mass transit bill in exchange for Senator Metro's support on the wheat subsidy bill. This is logrolling, and it can be welfare enhancing, despite the possibility that it is a violation of the intent of representative democracy.

Consider the following example.[8] The columns of Table 6.3 illustrate three representative voters' payoffs (measured in billions of dollars of net benefits to constituents) resulting from the passing of two legislative bills. If the bill is defeated, there is no payoff. The voting procedure is based on majority rule. Notice that voter B cares strongly about bill X's passing, as does voter C about bill Y's passing. Otherwise, the passing of bill X results in small losses to voters A and C, whereas bill Y's passage results in small losses to voters A and B. Now, if voter B votes in favor of bill Y in exchange for voter C's support on bill X, both are made better off. Voter B is willing to incur the loss of 2 billion required in voting in favor of bill Y in exchange for a vote that assures the passage of bill X, which provides a payoff of 5 billion. By trading votes, voter B is made better off by 3 billion. The same occurs for voter C.

TABLE 6.3 An Example of Logrolling

Voter	Bill X	Bill Y
A	−2	−2
B	+5	−2
C	−2	+5

Of course, logrolling has been an ever-present feature of voting patterns in the U.S. Congress since its inception. Is that bad? Not necessarily. The essential feature of logrolling is that the intensity of voters' preferences can be considered, not just their preference rankings. This makes logrolling efficiency enhancing.

Lobbying and Collective Action

Individuals realize that there are potential gains from influencing public policy and band together with others with a common interest in order to do exactly that. Farmers with an interest in keeping commodity prices high, textile workers interested in retaining jobs in their region, insurance companies interested in limiting liability, and countless other examples illustrate the tendency to form groups with an interest in collective action. Often, such groups will hire professional lobbyists to influence policymaking on their behalf. **Lobbying** is the act of attempting to influence public decision making. Organizations do that by informing public decision makers of the implications of legislative bills being considered. Beyond simply informing the policymaker of the implications for the organization, there may be pressure brought to bear in order to increase the likelihood of obtaining the legislator's support.[9] For this reason, organizations are sometimes called **pressure groups.** Although the role of lobbyists and pressure groups is often decried, it should be noted that they provide very valuable services for their clients. Beyond that, they may also provide valuable services to society in general.

Olson describes the origin of this more general view that lobbyists and pressure groups are beneficial.

> It would be difficult to trace exactly the development of the view that pressure groups are generally beneficial, or at least benign. But one type of thinking that has probably helped create an intellectual climate favorable to the growth of this view is that known as "pluralism." Pluralism, to be sure, deals with much more than pressure groups: indeed it deals with them only tangentially. It is the political philosophy which argues that private associations of all kinds, and especially labor unions, churches, and cooperatives, should have a larger constitutional role in society, and that the state should not have unlimited control over the plurality of these private associations. It opposes the Hegelian veneration of the nation state, on the one hand, but fears the anarchistic and laissez-faire individualistic extremes, on the other, and ends up seeking safety in a society in which a number

> of important private associations provide a cushion between the individual and the state. (1965, 111–12)

The critical insight in this view is that private associations have a role to play that is distinct from that of the individual and the state. Public goods are provided at this intermediate level that cannot be supplied properly at other levels.

Groups formed for a common purpose clearly provide a public good to their members. Whether it is a labor union negotiating better working conditions or an industry trade group negotiating better economic conditions for its member companies, the goal is to provide a benefit for all members of the organization through influencing public policy. They also often provide private benefits in order to encourage membership (coffee mugs, bumper stickers, low-interest credit cards, travel services, etc.), but their primary role is to provide a public good for their members. Indeed, it is common that large economic groups with substantial lobbying efforts are organized for some other primary purpose. Consider, for example, the American Medical Association, the Association of Trial Lawyers, the Federation of Teachers, the Farm Bureau, and other such organizations. They all exist for a primary economic reason and also find it beneficial to engage in lobbying efforts. If all they provided to members was a public good, they would have no rewards or incentives to offer members. Rather, by providing both a private benefit and collective benefits, they can induce membership.

Rent-Seeking Behavior

Lobbyists and pressure groups exist because in a representative democracy there is an inherent incentive to rent-seek. Government regulations often lead to monopolies or forms of monopoly power. When monopoly power is created, strong abilities to earn above-normal returns are generated as well. An economic return to a factor of production such as land, labor, or capital that exceeds the return necessary to draw that factor into market usage is called **economic rent.** When the opportunity to earn a large economic rent exists merely because of a government regulation, there is a clear incentive to try and convince the government regulators that your firm should be granted that monopoly power, rather than some other firm. In such a case, resources may be expended to lobby government officials to get them to grant the monopoly rights to your firm or to firms that will in some way pass a portion of those monopoly profits along to you. This activity is called **rent seeking.**

First, consider the nature of an economic rent. In normal economic terms, an economic rent is a return to a factor of production above that return required to draw the factor into production. In competitive factor markets for inputs such as land, labor, and capital, economic rents are zero. Inputs are paid just what is required to draw them into production. When the market setting is less than fully competitive, however, there are economic rents earned. That is, the inputs earn a return in excess of the minimum amount necessary to draw them into the market. In the extreme case of a unique factor of production (like Tiger Woods), the return paid to that factor may far exceed that necessary to draw the factor into production. (What do you suppose is the minimum salary that would have been required to draw Tiger Woods into professional golf?)

Consider the case of ethanol made from corn.[10] Farmers grow corn and earn a return for their efforts, although the size of the return to the farmer's labor, land, and capital (machinery) depends on the price of corn. In a competitive corn market the return is relatively low and is just enough to draw farmers, land, and capital into production. Now suppose that the government considers passing a law mandating that corn be used for ethanol production to enhance gasoline, making it burn more cleanly. The regulation would increase the return to farmers' labor, land, and capital, generating economic rents, or returns in excess of those necessary to draw those inputs into usage. In addition, ethanol processing facilities could be constructed that would earn economic rents. The potential economic rents encourage large agribusiness firms to engage in lobbying efforts in Congress and at the state capitol in support of the ethanol legislation. It matters not that the process of growing corn to turn into fuel is itself an energy-losing activity, requiring more energy to make the ethanol than is derived from it. Economic resources are expended in order to obtain the economic rents generated by the regulation. This is the essence of rent seeking.

Figure 6.9 illustrates the situation of a firm producing a product in a monopolized market. The competitive price and quantity are p_c and q_c, determined where price equals marginal cost, the pricing relationship provided in a competitive environment. In this case, there are no economic profits earned by the firm because its total revenue (p_c times q_c) is equal to its total cost, illustrated as the rectangle $0p_cbq_c$. When the firm is a monopoly, however, the price and output will be p_m and q_m. As a result of the lack of competition, the firm will price the product too high, produce too little output, and earn

FIGURE 6.9 Social Costs of Monopoly Provision

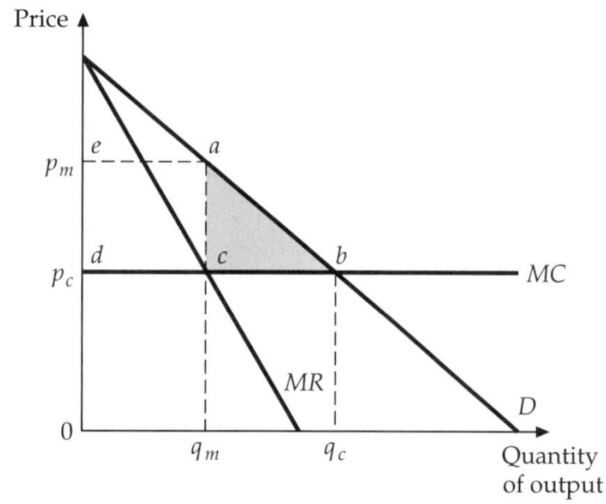

economic profits equal to the amount represented by the rectangle *acde*. The monopoly power of the firm creates the transfer of *acde* to the firm as increased profit. This is a clear benefit to the firm producing the product. But there is a loss to the economy as a whole that is larger than the gain to the firm. As a result of the reduced output produced by the monopoly, there is a loss to the economy of the amount represented by the triangle *abc*. This loss represents the value of the lost output from the monopoly. Scaling back production from q_c to q_m causes a reduction in cost in the amount of the rectangle q_cbcq_m. At the same time, however, the total benefit to consumers is reduced by the area q_cbaq_m. The difference is the triangle *abc* which is the deadweight loss due to monopoly.

When a monopoly such as this is created by government regulation, say for example that the firm is Cablevision providing cable television services to a community via a monopoly granted by the city council, a deadweight loss occurs as expected, and the firm is profitable as expected. This profit is a prize known as a rent and the pursuit of such a rent is known as rent seeking (Mueller 1989, 229). Another firm such as Community View may engage in activities designed to convince the city council to grant the monopoly right to it rather than to Cablevision. Such activity may include the promise of better service, lower prices for residents, free access to a channel to broadcast city council meetings, and all kinds of other benefits. The key insight of rent seeking is that the resources spent in the pursuit of this rent are actually a social cost, not just a redistribution from one group to another. Because the government has created the monopoly, there are incentives to expend resources, up to the amount of the rent, in order to be granted the monopoly right. Hence, the loss to society is not just the deadweight loss triangle *abc* but may also include an amount up to the full rectangle *acde* as well.

Another example of rent-seeking behavior is the lobbying activity on the part of a special interest group seeking favorable tax treatment. Say, for example, that you and I head companies that are engaged in the production of customized software for the medical care industry. We might jointly hire a high-powered lobbying firm to encourage the legislature in our state to adopt a sales tax exemption for our products. Such an exemption would generate rents for us and we would be willing to expend resources in the pursuit of those rents. Rent seeking is often also found in the policy areas of regulation, tariffs, and quotas. Physicians lobby Congress for increased professional standards that keep the supply of new physicians low. The airline industry lobbies Congress for regulations that enable each firm to monopolize a hub in the spoke-and-hub system. Organized labor lobbies Congress for trade restrictions in order to increase the return to domestic labor. Steel firms lobby Congress for trade restrictions on imported steel in order to increase the return to domestic producers. Sugar beet farmers lobby Congress for trade restrictions on imported sugarcane in order to increase the return for domestic producers.

Posner (1975) has estimated the social cost of regulation for selected regulated industries. Table 6.4 reports his estimates for several regulated industries in the United States. The table reports estimated price increases in these industries due to regulation in the first column. Then, two sets of estimates

TABLE 6.4 Posner's Estimates of the Social Cost of Regulation

		Estimates Based on Price-Increase Data		Estimates Based on Independent Studies	
Regulated Industry	**Percentage Price Increase Due to Regulation**	***Estimated Elasticity of Demand***	***Costs as a Percentage of Industry Sales***	***Estimated Elasticity of Demand***	***Costs as a Percentage of Industry Sales***
Physicians' services	40%	3.500	14%	0.575	31%
Eyeglasses	34%	0.394	13%	0.450	24%
Milk	11%	10.000	5%	0.339	10%
Motor carriers	62%	2.630	19%	1.140	30%
Oil	65%	2.500	20%	0.900	32%
Airlines	65%	2.500	20%	2.360	19%

Source: From "The Social Costs of Monopoly and Regulation," by Richard A. Posner in *Journal of Political Economy*, Vol. 83, No. 4, August 1975, Table 2, p. 818.

of the elasticity of demand and the social cost of regulation as a percent of industry sales are reported. The first set of such estimates is based on industry studies of the price effects of regulation. The second set of estimates is based on independent studies of the elasticity of demand in those industries. Together, the price increase due to regulation and the two sets of regulatory social costs give us a sense of the potential inducement to engage in rent-seeking behavior in industries such as these.

Consider the market for physicians' services reported in the first row. This is a highly regulated industry, as entry is limited and advertising is restricted. Prices in this industry are estimated to be about 40 percent higher than would be the case in a competitive industry. If that is the case, imagine the incentive for physicians and organizations representing them to engage in rent-seeking behavior. Individual physicians, professional associations, lobbyists, and others can potentially benefit from regulations that increase the price of services provided. Posner estimates that the social costs of regulation of this industry result in a loss to society of anywhere from 14 to 31 percent of the gross sales in the industry.

Price increases due to regulation in other industries range from a low of 11 percent in the milk-producing industry to a high of 65 percent in the oil and airlines industries, as reported in the first column of Table 6.4. These figures indicate that rent-seeking opportunities are substantial in all of these industries. Milk producers, oil companies, and airlines all have incentives to be active in attempting to influence the regulations imposed by the government in their industries. Posner's estimates of the social cost of regulation range from a low of 5 to 10 percent of sales in the milk (dairy) industry to a high of 20 to 32 percent in the oil industry, as reported in Table 6.4. These costs are quite substantial. Of course, the existence of social costs due to regulation does not necessarily mean that the regulations are inappropriate. Citizens may benefit from the regulations to an extent that justifies the costs. What Posner reports are simply cost estimates, with no corresponding estimates of the valuation of benefits.

Monopoly/Agenda Control Model

ON THE WEB

For more on the growth of government, see the Policy Study "What Is a Leviathan? Is There One in Your Backyard?" on the companion website (www.cengage.com/international).

A government agency is sometimes in the position of being a monopoly provider of a public service. For example, the Department of Defense is the only provider of national defense. As a result, it has a large degree of monopoly power. What would happen if the public debate over appropriate funding of the Department of Defense were limited to a set of two choices, one of which is much too large, resulting in a tax increase, and the other of which is much too low, making the country vulnerable to attack? If voters are given a choice between supporting a defense department that is larger than they want or a defense department that is so small that it cannot assure even basic protection and economic freedoms, it is likely that they will select the large defense department budget, even though it is too large. The alternative is even worse. This form of manipulation is called **agenda control** because it limits the choices put before voters.

The situation is illustrated in Figure 6.10. The efficient level of public good to provide is q^* because at that quantity the sum of the marginal benefits equals the marginal costs of provision (recall the Samuelson rule). But the agency wishes to provide a larger quantity of public service, say q_m, reflecting its monopoly position. Of course, if quantity q_m is provided, social welfare is reduced. People in the community are made worse off by an amount equal to the area of triangle *cde*. If we put the two options q^* and q_m to a vote by the residents, they would select q^* since that is the quantity that makes them better off than q_m. But what would happen if the public agency were to manipulate the agenda in such a way that the voters do not have a choice of selecting q^*? What if the agency were to give the voters a choice between q_m and some

FIGURE 6.10 Monopoly/Agenda Control Model

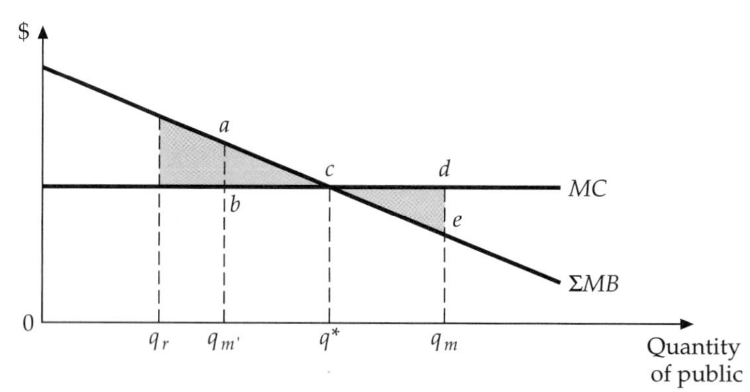

other level of public service that makes the voters even worse off? We can find such an alternative easily. Quantity q_m' makes residents worse off by an amount equal to the triangle *abc* which is equal, by construction, to the triangle *cde*. As a result, we would expect voters to be indifferent between q_m and q_m'. An amount less than q_m' would make voters even worse off. Suppose that the agency selects a reversion amount q_r designed to knowingly be worse than q_m. If voters have to choose between q_m and q_r, they will select q_m. Thus, by controlling the agenda and giving voters a limited choice, the agency is able to manipulate the outcome of the vote and entice voters to support a level of public service provision that is larger than the efficient level.

The key to making this strategy work is selecting the reversion amount q_r in such a way that voters clearly understand that if the agency scales back to providing q_r, they will definitely be worse off. Consider the example of a public school district that wants to control the outcome of a district consolidation vote. The district may threaten to shorten the school day, eliminate sports, music, art, transportation, or other programs if the consolidation does not pass. If the threatened reversion level of service is low enough, voters may be induced to support the consolidation even though it would not have been supported directly.

Although the monopoly/agenda control model makes it appear as though a public agency can easily manipulate voters into supporting anything it wants, that is not necessarily the case. Consider for a moment the information required in order to make this procedure work. The agency must have perfect information on the demand for the public good, ΣMB, the marginal cost of providing the public good, MC, and the areas of triangles *abc* and *cde*. What would happen if the district has imperfect information regarding voters' demand for education and it selects a reversion quantity that is larger than q_m'? The result is that voters turn down the millage vote for q_m, favoring the reversion quantity. Consequently, the district provides too little education compared to the efficient level q^* which the voters would have supported.

The information requirements of the monopoly/agenda control model are quite demanding. Very few public agencies know the demand for their service with the degree of precision required to make the reversion threat work.

PROBLEMS

1. True, False, or Uncertain. Explain.
   a. Using a majority voting method, a public good will be provided only in the quantity desired by the majority of the voters.
   b. An increase in the transactions cost involved in voting reduces voter turnout.
   c. In a two-party primary, candidates should moderate their views, anticipating the median view they will likely face in the general election.
   d. If x is a single-dimensional issue, the median position cannot lose under majority rule.
   e. Jay has political preferences that are transitive. He likes candidate A better than candidate B, and he likes candidate C better than candidate A. Therefore, we know that he likes candidate C better than candidate B.
   f. Iona has political preferences that are intransitive. She likes candidate A better than candidate B, and she likes candidate B better than candidate C. Therefore, we know that she likes candidate A better than candidate C.
   g. Hank is really angry about some aspects of the education his children are receiving in the public school system in his hometown. After the latest incident that raised his ire, he concluded that his only option is to pull his children out of the school system and send them to a private school. Hank's conclusion is correct.
2. Suppose that there are three groups of voters in Scholarville where there is a school district expenditure vote coming up soon to determine the level of public school expenditures per pupil. The choices are a high level

of expenditure, \$10,000 per pupil per year; an intermediate level of expenditure, \$5,000 per pupil per year; and a low level of expenditure, \$3,000 per pupil per year. Three equal-sized groups of voters can be identified in the community with preferences summarized in the following table.

Voter Group	Most-Preferred Choice	Second Choice	Least-Preferred Choice
I	10,000	5,000	3,000
II	5,000	10,000	3,000
III	3,000	10,000	5,000

a. Plot the preferences of the three groups on a graph.
b. Determine whether the outcome of majority voting will be transitive. Use pairwise comparisons. Will it result in a voting paradox? Why or why not?
c. Determine the result of the vote.

3. Suppose that there are three groups of voters in Northtown where there is a vote coming up soon to determine the number of old-growth trees to protect from logging in order to save the habitat for the rare checkered owl. The choices are a high level of protection, an intermediate level of protection, and no protection whatsoever. Three equal-sized groups of voters can be identified in the community with preferences summarized in the following table.

Voter Group	Most-Preferred Choice	Second Choice	Least-Preferred Choice
Tree huggers	High protection	Medium protection	No protection
Ditto heads	No protection	Medium protection	High protection
Convexers	Medium protection	High protection	No protection

a. Plot the preferences of the three groups on a graph.
b. Determine whether the outcome of majority voting will be transitive. Will it result in a voting paradox? Why or why not?
c. Determine the result of the vote.

4. Suppose that we know the demand for schooling in Scholarville is given by the equation $p = 7{,}500 - 75q$, where p is price per pupil and q is the quantity of schooling measured in hours per day per pupil.

a. At what price will voters desire a seven-hour school day?
b. Suppose that the price is given as computed in part a, but the school board wants an eight-hour school day. How can the board exercise agenda control in order to obtain a favorable vote on an eight-hour-day proposal? Explain.
c. What is the welfare loss due to the agenda control?

5. Consider the following set of voter preferences:

Preference Ranking		
A	B	C
B	C	A
C	A	B
8 voters	7 voters	6 voters

a. Compute the plurality winner of the election.
b. Compute the Borda winner of the election.
c. Compute the Condorcet winner of the election.
d. Explain the problem that arises with the Condorcet rule in this case. (A voting paradox occurs due to cycling.)

6. Consider the following net benefits (measured in billions of dollars) that will result from the passage of two legislative bills X and Y:

	Issue	
Voter	X	Y
A	+6	−3
B	−1	+4
C	−2	−3

a. Identify the logrolling opportunity present in this situation.
b. Identify the potential gains to voters.
c. Explain why logrolling is efficiency enhancing.

REFERENCES

Birnbaum, Jeffrey H., and Alan S. Murray. *Showdown at Gucci Gulch*. New York: Random House, 1987.

Brennan, G., and J. M. Buchanan. *The Power to Tax: Analytical Foundations of a Fiscal Constitution*. Cambridge, MA: Cambridge University Press, 1980.

de Borda, J. C. *Mémoire sur les élections au Scrutin, Histoire de l'Academie Royale des Sciences*. Paris: 1781.

de Condorcet, Marquis. *Essai sur l'application de l'analyse à la probabilité des decisions rendues à la pluralité des voix*. Paris: 1785.

Hirschman, Albert O. *Exit, Voice, and Loyalty*. Cambridge, MA: Harvard University Press, 1970.

Hotelling, Harold. "Stability in Competition." *Economic Journal* 39 (1929): 41–57.

Jones, Philip, and John Cullis. "Is Democracy Regressive? A Comment on Political Participation." *Public Choice* 51 (1986): 101–7.

Krugman, Paul. "Reckonings: The Unrefined Truth," *New York Times*, May 9, 2001.

Lindahl, Erik. "Just Taxation—A Positive Solution." Reprinted in *Classics in the Theory of Public Finance*, edited by R. A. Musgrave and A. T. Peacock. New York: St. Martin's, 1958.

Moulin, Hervé. *Axioms of Cooperative Decision Making*. New York: Cambridge University Press, 1988.

Mueller, Dennis C. *Public Choice II*. New York: Cambridge University Press, 1989.

Oates, Wallace E. "Searching for Leviathan." *American Economic Review* 74 (1985): 748–57.

Olson, Mancur. *The Logic of Collective Action*. Cambridge, MA: Harvard University Press, 1965.

Posner, Richard. "The Social Costs of Monopoly and Regulation." *Journal of Political Economy* 83 (1975): 807–27.

Saari, Donald G. *Decisions and Elections: Explaining the Unexpected*. New York: Cambridge University Press, 2001.

Zax, Jeffrey S. "Is There a Leviathan in Your Neighborhood?" *American Economic Review* 79 (1989): 560–67.

NOTES

1. For an entertaining, but somewhat more advanced, treatment of voting issues and unexpected results that can occur, see Saari (2001).
2. Comparability can be stated as follows: Either x_a is preferred to x_b, denoted $x_a > x_b$, or x_b is preferred to x_a, denoted $x_b > x_a$, or the person is indifferent between x_a and x_b, denoted $x_a \sim x_b$.
3. Transitivity can be stated as follows: If x_a is preferred to x_b, $x_a > x_b$, and x_b is preferred to x_c, $x_b > x_c$, then x_a is preferred to x_c, $x_a > x_c$.
4. The convexity of preferences is defined in a technical way as follows: Let $x_m = \alpha x_a + (1 - \alpha)\, x_b$ be a mean policy bundle representing a weighted average of x_a and x_b, where $\alpha \epsilon [0, 1]$. If x_a is preferred to x_b, that is, $x_a > x_b$, then x_m is preferred to x_b, $x_m > x_b$. Thus an intermediate combination of x_a and x_b is preferred to the less desirable bundle of x_a and x_b: $x_m > \min \{x_a, x_b\}$.

5. We cannot measure utility directly and have no need of doing so. A set of preferences such as these is sufficient to guarantee the existence of a utility function with the conventional properties.
6. This example is adapted from Moulin (1988).
7. The Lindahl equilibrium is not, however, incentive compatible as it does not completely solve the free rider problem. An incentive compatible mechanism requires that all parties do best by truthfully revealing any private information.
8. This example is drawn from Mueller (1989, 82–83).
9. For a humorous account of the intense lobbying effort surrounding the Tax Reform Act of 1986, see Birnbaum and Murray (1987).
10. This example is drawn from Krugman (2001).

CHAPTER 7

Radius Images/Getty Images

Benefit-Cost Analysis in Program Evaluation

LEARNING OBJECTIVES

1. Explain the essentials of benefit-cost analysis and its uses in public finance.
2. Analyze the economic valuation of benefits and costs.
3. Discuss project evaluation criteria.
4. Discuss the effects of risk and uncertainty on benefit-cost analysis.

The evaluation of public projects is very important and requires a method by which a number of complex issues can be considered simultaneously. One method often used to evaluate public projects is **benefit-cost analysis**, which combines the dollar value of all the project's benefits, subtracts all the project's costs, and then determines whether the project is feasible given the net benefits that the project is expected to generate. For a project to be feasible, it is necessary that it provide positive net benefits. That is not sufficient, however, for the project to be funded and implemented. There may be other projects that can be reasonably expected to generate greater net benefits. Benefit-cost analysis is useful both for determining the feasibility of public projects and for ranking the attractiveness of competing projects. As public projects are subjected to increasing public scrutiny, benefit-cost analysis is becoming increasingly important in policy analysis. In fact, in some cases, a public project must be shown to pass a benefit-cost test in order to be considered by legislators or administrative agencies.

BENEFIT-COST ANALYSIS AND ITS USES[1]

Policy analysis often benefits from, indeed requires, the analysis of benefits and costs involved with the policy application. Benefit-cost analysis is necessary for two purposes. First, it establishes priorities among public projects or ranks the relative merits of projects. Suppose, for example, that we are contemplating the implementation of either a housing subsidy program to aid poor families in obtaining adequate living quarters or a nutrition supplement program for single mothers with young children. If we have funding for only one program, which do we select? While there are many criteria that may be used in making that choice, it is certainly helpful to know which program would generate the greatest net benefit. Second, benefit-cost analysis analyzes single projects to determine whether they are economically feasible. Suppose that the city council is contemplating funding a parking structure downtown to help solve the problem of a shortage of parking places. We need to know if the parking structure proposed will generate benefits in excess of its cost. If so, the project is feasible. If not, the city council should not consider the project. Benefit-cost analysis serves both of these purposes. It is useful for establishing priorities among, or ranking, various alternatives and for determining the feasibility of individual projects.

Basic Assumptions of Benefit-Cost Analysis

The application of benefit-cost analysis presumes certain underlying assumptions. First, we assume that public projects have economic value because people need or desire the services that are provided by the project. Second, we assume that any public project that is implemented should be developed at the scale that generates a maximum of net benefits. Third, we assume that the government should follow the development priorities established by ranking the net benefits associated with those projects; that is, begin by developing the project promising to generate the greatest net benefit and continue through subsequent projects in order of their desirability, as indicated by their net benefits.

Defining Benefits and Costs

The place to begin estimating benefits and costs is the **tangible material benefits** and costs associated with a project. Tangible material benefits are those benefits we can see, touch, feel, and smell. Further, these benefits can be measured in material (dollar) terms. Consider a flood control project, for example, where the tangible material benefit of the project is the value of flood protection provided to residents of a flood-prone area. They benefit from avoiding periodic floods that would damage their houses, automobiles, and other material possessions. The tangible material benefits generated by an urban mass transit program, for example, include the transportation services provided to riders.

There may also be **intangible benefits** generated by a public project. For example, the flood control project may involve construction of a reservoir that provides beautiful scenic views. This is a benefit, but it is not a tangible material benefit in the sense that we find it difficult to place a material value on the benefit. Similarly, an urban mass transit system may provide some urban residents with a greater sense of freedom and mobility. That benefit is also intangible.

A third category of benefits we must consider is secondary benefits, or **spillover benefits**. These are benefits that are not directly associated with the project but arise secondarily because of the existence of the project. Consider the flood control project again. A reservoir is built which is attractive for recreational purposes. Boaters, water-skiers, hang gliders, picnickers, and others enjoy the direct benefits of the reservoir. Secondarily, however, the people who own and operate marinas, convenience stores, and other businesses that cater to those enjoying the public facility also benefit since their businesses are made more profitable by the presence of the reservoir. Similarly, the urban mass transit system creates economic activity in the urban area, especially near the transit system stations. These are secondary benefits. We can measure the value of secondary benefits by examining the change in net income earned by proprietors or by measuring the change in property value that occurs when the public project is built.

On the cost side, we begin by considering direct costs of the public project. Land acquisition costs, construction costs, and project operation costs are the primary cost factors to consider. Suppose that we are contemplating the construction of a new light rail (aboveground) transit system in Capital City, for example. We begin to assess the cost of the project by considering what we will have to pay the property owners to purchase their land along the transit system routes. Then we must include the cost of construction for the system. At this point it is worth pausing to provide a warning about the labor costs involved in such a project. Politicians invariably want to trumpet the virtues of such a project and do so by touting that it will create jobs. The construction jobs created represent a cost of building the system, not a benefit. Capital expenses such as rail stations, rail lines, administrative offices, and maintenance facilities must be built. Beyond construction costs, there are also the costs of the daily operation of the system. Fuel costs, personnel costs, security costs, and a host of other direct costs must be included as well.

Secondary costs also arise with public projects. Those costs may be associated with the secondary benefits discussed previously. For example, the flood control project which creates a beautiful reservoir attractive to many people wishing to use the area may also generate new crime in the community and the need for police patrols. The cost of crime and the cost of providing additional public security services are secondary costs that must be considered.

Net Benefits

Once we have identified all the costs and benefits and measured them as accurately as possible, we must combine them in an overall evaluation of the net benefits associated with the project. **Net primary benefits** are calculated by subtracting the direct costs of the project from the primary benefits of the project. This is a narrow measure of the project's net benefits because it includes just the primary benefits and the direct costs. It ignores all of the secondary benefits and costs that the project may bring with it. A broader view of net benefits can be obtained by including **net secondary benefits**. Net secondary benefits are computed by subtracting the secondary costs from the secondary benefits. Table 7.1 illustrates the benefits and costs most important in conducting benefit-cost analysis.

@ ON THE WEB

For more on the application of benefit-cost analysis, see the Policy Study "Benefit-Cost Models for Tax Policy Evaluation" on the companion website (www.cengage.com/international).

TABLE 7.1 Taxonomy of Benefits and Costs

Benefits	Costs	Net Benefits
Primary benefits Tangible material benefits: Measured by use value, or the value of the project to those who use it directly Intangible benefits: Benefits arising due to security, safety, opportunity, or aesthetic beauty of the project. In the case of an irreversible project, we may include option value and existence value.	Direct costs	Net primary benefits = primary benefits − direct costs
Secondary benefits	Secondary costs	Net secondary benefits = secondary benefits − secondary costs

ECONOMIC VALUATION OF BENEFITS AND COSTS

How do we measure the value of direct benefits conferred by a public project or policy? The conceptual method is to compute the change in consumer surplus. You may recall that consumer surplus is the amount that consumers are willing to pay for a given amount of a good but are not required to pay. For a public good, we know that the sum of the residents' marginal benefits, ΣMB, represents the community marginal benefit from each possible quantity of the public good that may be provided. We can call that marginal benefit function $b(q)$, where $b(q) = \Sigma MB$. The sum of the residents' marginal benefits for all possible quantities of the public good, $b(q)$, for $q > 0$, is then considered the community demand curve for the public good.

In order to estimate the total benefits derived from the provision of a certain quantity q_1 of the public good, we can sum the marginal benefits for all units from $q = 0$ up to $q = q_1$.[2] That gives us our needed estimate of the direct benefit residents derive from the provision of q_1 units of the public good. We can see the total benefits in Figure 7.1. The area labeled $0abq_1$ is the total benefit of q_1 units of the public good. Let us call that amount $B(q_1)$ to represent the quantity of total benefits derived from q_1 units of public good provision.

We can also use this approach to estimate the benefits that flow from *changes* in the quantity of the public good provided. Suppose that the government is currently providing q_1 units of the public good and is contemplating an increase to q_2 units. The increase in public good provision will increase

FIGURE 7.1 Measuring Benefits Provided by a Public Good

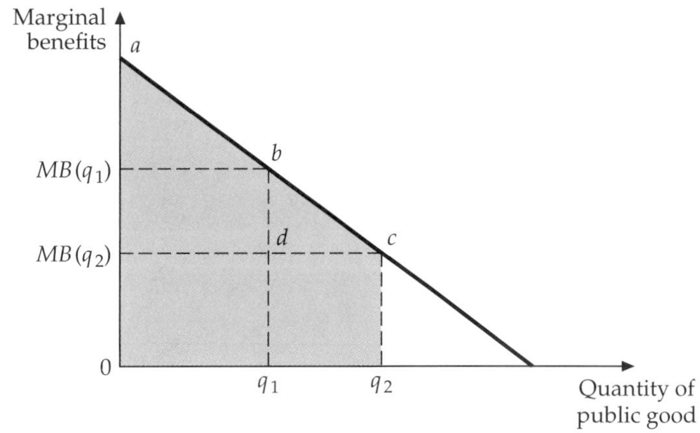

the total benefits received by the residents of the community. But by how much? We need an estimate of the increased benefits that will be realized from the expanded public good provision. The increase in total direct benefits from $B(q_1)$ to $B(q_2)$ is a measure of the increased direct benefit derived from increased provision of the public good. That is, for $q_2 > q_1$, we have $B(q_2) > B(q_1)$, and our estimate of the increased benefits will be $B(q_2) - B(q_1)$.

In Figure 7.1, the benefits received from provision level q_2 is labeled $0acq_2$. The increase in total benefit received from the expanded public good provision is illustrated graphically as the area q_1bcq_2. In order to compute the amount of this increase, we need to calculate the area of the rectangle q_1dcq_2 and add to it the area of the triangle *bcd*. Of course, the area of the rectangle q_1dcq_2 is measured by $MB(q_2)$ times $q_2 - q_1$. The area of the triangle *bcd* is half its height times its base, or $(1/2)[MB(q_1) - MB(q_2)](q_2 - q_1)$.

The increase in total benefits can easily be computed from marginal benefits. Suppose that our marginal benefit function is a downward-sloping straight line written as $MB(q) = \alpha - \beta q$, where α is the intercept and $-\beta$ is the slope. When $q = q_1$, we have a marginal benefit of $MB(q_1) = \alpha - \beta q_1$. After an increase in public good provision up to the level q_2, the marginal benefit rises to $MB(q_2) = \alpha - \beta q_2$. In this case, we can calculate the area of the rectangle q_1dcq_2 in Figure 7.1 as $(\alpha - \beta q_2)(q_2 - q_1)$. The area of the triangle *bcd* can be computed as $(1/2)[(\alpha - \beta q_1) - (\alpha - \beta q_2)](q_2 - q_1)$, or $(1/2)\beta(q_2 - q_1)^2$. Thus, knowing the intercept and slope coefficients α and β of the marginal benefit line, we can compute the increased benefit.

On the cost side, we must know the marginal cost of producing the public good for each quantity of public good provision. Suppose that the marginal cost function is written as $MC(q)$, indicating that the marginal cost may vary with the level of q. In the typical case, the marginal cost curve is U-shaped because there are likely to be increasing returns to scale in the production of the good initially, eventually turning to decreasing returns to scale as

FIGURE 7.2 Average Cost Curves for Public Goods

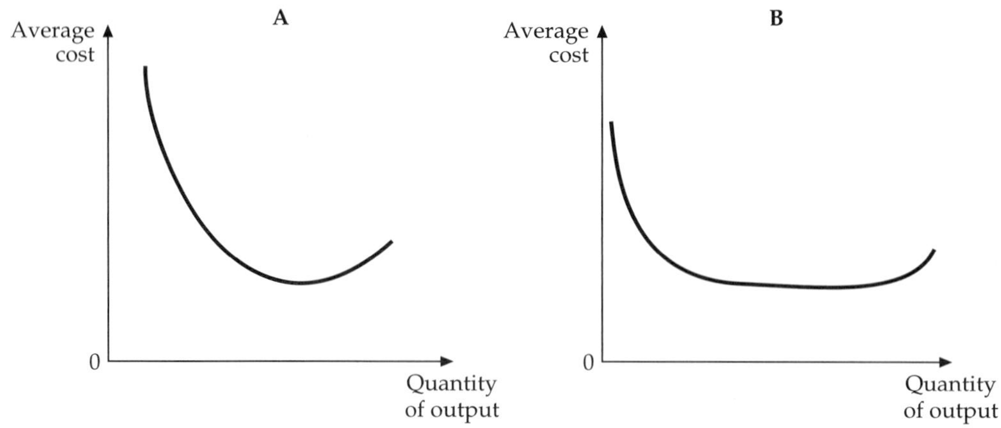

production reaches high levels. Panel A of Figure 7.2 illustrates this case. For many public goods, however, there is a wide intermediate range over which there are constant returns to scale. Constant returns to scale means that the marginal cost function is constant over that range. Graphically, the U-shaped marginal cost curve is horizontal over the constant returns range of output. Panel B of Figure 7.2 illustrates this case. Although the overall marginal cost curve is U-shaped, there is often a wide flat bottom on the U. As a result, we often simply draw a horizontal marginal cost function, knowing that to be a good approximation over a wide range of feasible levels of output.

Total direct costs are then computed by summing the marginal costs.[3] If we want the total cost of producing q_1 units, for example, we need to sum the marginal costs for all units of output from $q=0$ up to $q=q_1$. Call the total cost of producing q units of the public good $c(q)$. Figure 7.3 illustrates

FIGURE 7.3 Measuring the Cost of Public Good Provision

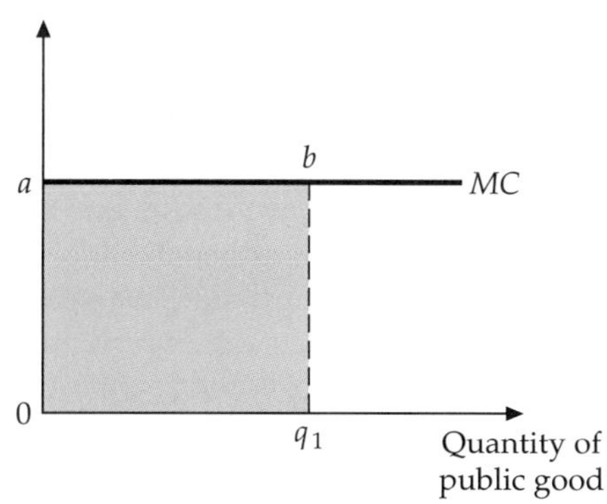

the derivation of total direct costs for the quantity of public good provision q_1 in the case of constant costs. The total direct cost of providing q_1 units of the public good is the area $0abq_1$.

We also know that the optimal quantity of the public good that should be supplied by the government is that quantity where the sum of the residents' marginal benefits equal the marginal cost of producing the public good: $b(q)=\Sigma MB=MC=c(q)$. Thus, we know that we should be providing the quantity of the public good where $b(q)=c(q)$. Of course, that also implies that the difference between total benefits $B(q)$ and total costs $C(q)$ is maximized. Hence, we know we will have maximum net benefits by providing that quantity of the public good where $b(q)=c(q)$. These quantities are critical for determining the proper level of public good provision and for the policy analysis of proposed changes in the level of public good provision.

In the case of a linear marginal benefit function ($MB=\alpha-\beta q$) and a constant marginal cost ($MC=\gamma$), equating the two requires providing the quantity q of public good where $\alpha-\beta q=\gamma$. Solving for q provides the solution $q=(\alpha-\gamma)/\beta$. For example, suppose that the demand for education in a school district is $10{,}000-1{,}000q$, where q is measured in hours of schooling per child per day during a school year. Hence $\alpha=10{,}000$ and $\beta=1{,}000$. Assume that the marginal cost of providing schooling is $\gamma=4{,}000$. In this case, the optimal length of the school day can be computed to be $q=(10{,}000-4{,}000)/1{,}000$, which is $q=6$. Hence, the school board should provide a six-hour school day for the students.

DISCOUNTING

Suppose that a project generates a stream of benefits over time where B_i represents the benefit in year i. The project runs from now, $i=0$, to its end, $i=n$. Costs are also associated with the project. The cost in year i is denoted C_i. In any given year I, the net benefits generated by the project are given by the difference between benefits and costs: B_i-C_i. Of course, we cannot just add the net benefits over time, because the value of a dollar's worth of net benefits is not constant over time. A dollar in net benefits earned in the distant future is certainly worth less to us than a dollar in net benefits today. As a result of this reality, we must discount properly the net benefits over time, converting them into today's equivalent dollars. The conversion requires use of a **discount rate** denoted r that expresses our rate of time preference.

Discounting works in the following way. Net benefits generated during year 1 are discounted at the rate $1 + r$ because the net benefits are presumed to have been realized at the end of the first year. Consider a benefit of B dollars realized today. Denote that amount by B_0. Over a year's time that amount would grow to be worth $(1 + r)B_0$. Call that benefit, earned a year from today, B_1. The relationship between the benefits in the two years can be written $B_1=(1 + r)B_0$. If we solve this expression for B_0, we have $B_0=B_1/(1 + r)$. Thus, in order to convert a benefit of B a year from now into today's value, we simply divide by 1 plus the discount rate. If the benefit were not earned until two years from today, we would have to discount for both the loss of the opportunity to use the benefit the first year but also the second year, and, in addition, we would have to account for the compounding of interest on the interest. A benefit of B_0 would grow in value over a two-year period to be worth $(1 + r)^2 B_0$. As a result, a benefit B_2 earned two years from now is worth $B_2/(1 + r)^2$ in today's terms. The second-year net benefits are discounted by the factor $(1 + r)^2$ because we have waited two full years to realize those net benefits and each year we apply the discount rate r. We must divide the net benefits by $1 + r$ for the first year and do so again for the second year. We can generalize this approach by saying that the benefit in year k must be discounted by the factor $(1 + r)^k$. The same process must also be applied to the costs incurred over time as well.

Assuming that the discount rate is r, the discounted flow of net benefits over time can be expressed as

$$V = \sum_{i=0}^{i=n} \frac{B_i - C_i}{(1+r)^i} \tag{7.1}$$

Table 7.2 provides a simple example of discounting of net benefits. A program with a 10-year life has the net benefit stream given in column 2 of the table. In the first two years of the program, costs exceed benefits and we have negative net benefits. In subsequent years the net benefits are positive, rising to a maximum in year 7 and declining thereafter. If we simply summed the net benefits, with no discounting, we would find total net benefits of \$104 million. Of course, that sum is not usable because the net benefits in each year are measured in different dollars. If we discount at a 5 percent rate, we

TABLE 7.2 Discounting Net Benefits

Year	Discounted Net Benefit	Discounted Net Benefit $r = 0.05$	Discounted Net Benefit $r = 0.07$	Discounted Net Benefit $r = 0.10$
1	−10.00	−9.52	−9.35	−9.09
2	−5.00	−4.54	−4.37	−4.13
3	2.00	1.73	1.63	1.50
4	7.00	5.76	5.34	4.78
5	13.00	10.19	9.27	8.07
6	18.00	13.43	11.99	10.16
7	22.00	15.63	13.70	11.29
8	21.00	14.21	12.22	9.80
9	19.00	12.25	10.33	8.06
10	17.00	10.44	8.64	6.55
Total	104.00	69.58	59.42	46.99

obtain the discounted net benefits reported in the third column of the table. Consider the year 1 entry, for example. The net benefit of −10 is divided by 1.05 to yield the discounted net benefit of −9.52. In year 2 we take the net benefit of −5 and divide by $(1.05)^2$ and obtain the discounted net benefit −4.54. The remaining entries are obtained with similar computation, raising the power in the discounting term each year. The sum total of discounted net benefits is $69.58 million, a dramatically lower figure than the original undiscounted total of $104 million. The difference in the two figures is that the present discounted total has put each year's net benefit into the same dollars, or units of value, those of today or the present, rather than naively summing net benefits measured in dollars with very different values over time. The present discounted value of the net benefit stream generated by a project is also called the **present value** of the project, often denoted *PV*.

What happens if we discount at a higher rate? What does it mean to discount at a higher rate? Let us answer the second of these questions first. A higher discount rate involves a greater discount of future net benefits. That, in turn, reflects a stronger preference for net benefits realized in the relatively near future, compared to those realized in the relatively far-off future. That is, it reflects greater impatience. Table 7.2 reports the net benefit stream discounted at 7 and 10 percent, as well as the original discounted stream. Discounting at 7 percent yields the sum of discounted net benefits of $59.42 million. If we discount at an even higher rate, 10 percent, the present value of net benefits is even smaller: $46.99 million.

As a general rule, the higher the discount rate, the lower the present value of discounted net benefits. Similarly, the lower the discount rate, the higher the present value of discounted net benefits.

Discount Rate Determination

What determines the discount rate used? As the examples in Table 7.2 illustrate, the discount rate fundamentally reflects our patience or impatience. The more impatient we are, the higher the discount rate we should use. The more patient we are, the lower the discount rate we should use. But what determines the degree of patience we have? In the first place, the opportunities available to us determine our patience. If there are many highly beneficial alternative opportunities, reflecting a high opportunity cost of funds, we should use a high discount rate. Most fundamentally, the discount rate reflects the opportunity cost of funds, as does any interest rate. That includes inflation. The higher the rate of inflation we expect, the higher the discount rate we should use. A nominal interest rate is always equal to the real interest rate plus the expected rate of inflation. The discount rate is a nominal rate of interest and includes both the real rate of interest and the expected rate of inflation over the lifetime of the project we are analyzing.

The Special Case of a Perpetuity

A special case arises when the flow of net benefits is constant at the level B_i each year, continuing in **perpetuity**. In this circumstance, the net present value can be approximated with a very simple version of the formula: $PV = B_i/r$. Simply divide the annual net benefit by the discount rate to obtain the value of the discounted net benefit stream. Suppose, for example, that a project generates net benefits of $80,000 per year in perpetuity. Discounting at a 5 percent rate, the value of the net benefit stream will be $V = 80{,}000/0.05 = 1{,}600{,}000$. This project has a discounted present value of $1.6 million over its lifetime. Although the perpetuity formula is an approximation, it is a very handy tool to provide quick estimates of discounted net benefits for long-lived projects.

Internal Rate of Return

Benefit-cost analysis can also include the computation of the project's **internal rate of return (*IRR*)**. In order to find the internal rate of return, we need to find the implicit interest rate at which the present value of the net benefits of the project, PV in equation 7.1, is equal to zero. Setting $V = 0$, we solve the problem backward, finding the rate of interest r at which the stream of net benefits would be zero. In this way, we find the rate of interest at which the discounted benefits equal the discounted costs; hence the net benefits are zero. That rate of interest is called the internal rate of return.

The *IRR* then provides a way of assessing the feasibility of the project. First, if the *IRR* is positive, we know that the net benefits of the project are positive; hence the project is economically feasible. Second, we can use the *IRR* as a means of ranking alternative projects. Projects can be ranked by their *IRR*s, and we can proceed through a list of projects in order, starting with the project providing the highest *IRR* and proceeding to projects with lower *IRR*s.

EVALUATION CRITERIA

It might seem sufficient to observe that benefits exceed costs and therefore to conclude that a project or policy is justified and consider the analysis finished. That would be a mistake, however. In order to design sensible policy, our evaluation criteria must be more sophisticated. Just because a project is expected to generate benefits in excess of costs does not mean that that project is the only one capable of doing so, much less that that project generates the highest net benefit possible or that the scale of the project that was analyzed is the optimal scale. For these reasons, we must consider the criteria by which projects are evaluated in more detail. Several criteria are used in benefit-cost analysis. We will discuss two of the most common criteria: maximizing net benefits and maximizing the ratio of benefits to costs.

Maximize Net Benefits

Just as a private firm is not satisfied to know simply that it can operate at a profit because it wants to earn maximal profits, so too in benefit-cost analysis we want to know when we are generating maximal net benefits. Figure 7.4

FIGURE 7.4 Maximizing Net Benefits

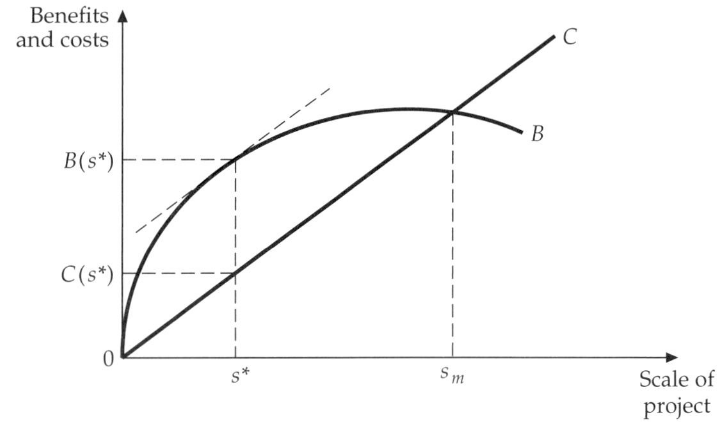

illustrates benefits B and costs C associated with various scales of a given project. Benefits exceed costs for projects smaller than s_m, which we can consider the maximum feasible size of a project. For project scales larger than s_m, costs exceed benefits and the project becomes infeasible. Of all the feasible-sized projects up to scale s_m, which scale would we consider the best? We want the scale s^* that will give us the maximum of net benefits: $B-C$.

The scale that maximizes net benefits $B-C$ is that scale where the marginal benefit equals the marginal cost.[4] Just as a profit-maximizing firm will want to sell that quantity of output where marginal revenue equals marginal cost, a net-benefit-maximizing public agency will want to operate at the scale where marginal benefit equals marginal cost. Although there are many scales for which benefits exceed costs, there is only one scale where net benefits are maximal.

The net-benefit-maximizing scale is illustrated in Figure 7.4. It is that scale s^* where the slope of the total benefit curve is equal to the slope of the total cost curve. A dotted line drawn tangent to the total benefit curve B illustrates the slope, which is equal to that of the total cost line C. The vertical distance between B and C is maximum where the slopes are equal; thus net benefits are maximized.

In policy analysis, it is often the case that supporters of a project will produce estimates of benefits and costs demonstrating that the project generates positive net benefits. Although that information is of some use, it does not assure that the project has been designed to provide the maximum of net benefits. Policy analysis of public projects should do more than simply show that the policy can generate positive net benefits. Good policy analysis is also sensitive to the scale of project implementation.

Figure 7.5 illustrates a more complex case where the benefits are initially rising at a decreasing rate, and then switch to rising at an increasing rate. In this situation, only project scales of at least s_1 but less than s_2 are feasible.

FIGURE 7.5 Scale Choice for a Public Project

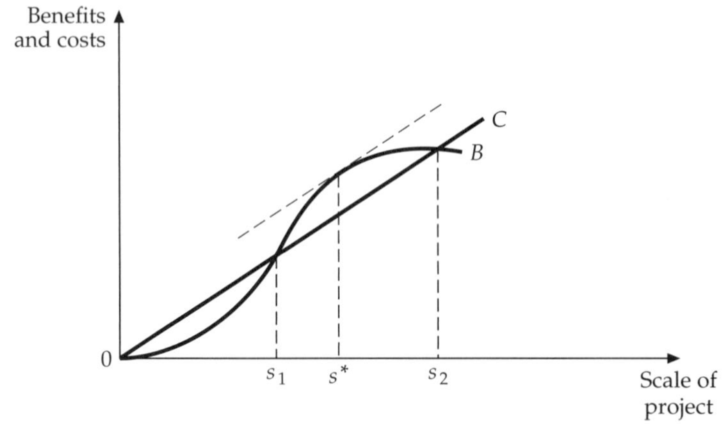

All other project scales result in negative net benefits and are infeasible. Again, the net-benefit-maximizing scale s^* will be the one between s_1 and s_2 where the vertical distance between B and C is maximized.

Maximize the Benefit/Cost Ratio

Because many project analyses are discussed in terms of the **benefit/cost ratio,** rather than in terms of net benefit, analysts often presume that the optimal scale is the one where the ratio of benefits to costs is maximized. It might seem that this is the same scale that maximizes net benefits, but it is not.[5] The scale that maximizes the ratio of benefits to costs is the scale where the slope of a line segment from the origin to the benefit curve is steepest. Figure 7.6 illustrates this case. Scale s_r is the one that maximizes the ratio B/C, whereas scale s^* is the one that maximizes net benefits $B - C$.

Case Study: Yangtze Dike-Strengthening Project

The world watched the news coverage in disbelief as pictures of flooding due to torrential rains in China were broadcast in 1998. A large region in the central part of the Peoples Republic of China was flooded. Twenty-one million people and 3.3 million houses, factories, and commercial centers were affected. Four million people were displaced from their homes, and 1.3 million buildings were destroyed completely. One of the causes of the vast flooding was the poor condition of the dikes along the Yangtze River. In response to that disaster, the World Bank was asked to fund a $210 million loan for a project of dike repair to protect people from subsequent flooding episodes. As a routine part of its evaluation of a loan request, the World Bank conducted a project review and published a report that included a benefit-cost analysis

FIGURE 7.6 Scale Choice Depends on Criterion

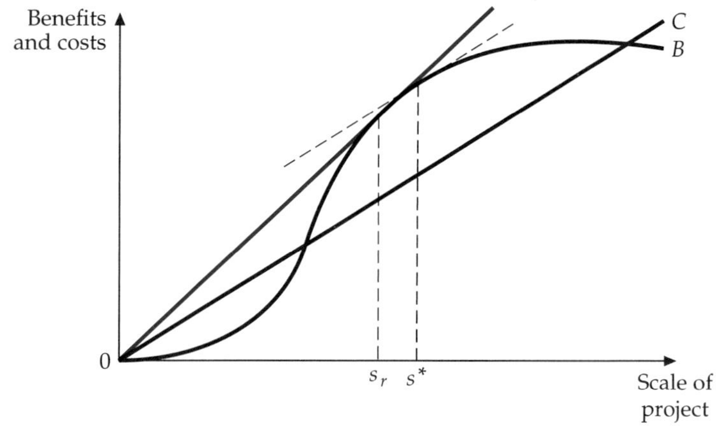

of the proposed dike project. The highlights of that benefit-cost analysis are presented here to illustrate the ways that the principles presented previously are implemented in practice.

The World Bank identified the main project objective as enhancing the protection of the riverbank against erosion and improving critical sections of the main dikes along the river in Hubei and Hunan Provinces to protect property and lives behind the dikes against floods. Economic benefits of the dike-strengthening project included the benefits due to flood alleviation, incremental cost savings from flood fighting, incremental cost savings from the use of detention basins, reductions in flood-fighting costs, and reductions in the cost of using detention basins. Notice that these are primary benefits in the form of tangible material benefits, as identified in Table 7.1. Secondary benefits and costs were not included in this analysis. Consequently, the analysis was narrowly limited to primary benefits, reporting estimates of net primary benefits.

Table 7.3 summarizes the benefits and costs of the project. The incremental capital costs of the project were 4.85 billion yuan for the two regions involved.[6] On the benefit side, the World Bank estimated total benefits of 16.80 billion yuan. Both the benefits and the costs had to be discounted, resulting in net present value estimate of 11.96 billion yuan. Because the net present value of the net primary benefits is positive, the project is economically admissible. Consideration of this project was justified on this basis. Whether it should be funded by the World Bank is an altogether different question, however. Keep in mind that there are many other potential projects around the world vying for World Bank funding. The Bank should use its resources strategically. Because its primary objective is poverty alleviation, it should consider whether this particular project is justified and ranks high on the list of alternative projects. The fact that the net present value of the net

TABLE 7.3 Yangtze Dike-Strengthening Project Benefits and Costs (billions of yuan)

Costs and Benefits, discounted	Habei Province	Hunan Province	Total
Cost	2.87	1.98	4.85
Benefits			
Flood alleviation	10.39	4.22	14.61
Other benefits	1.84	0.35	2.19
Total net benefits	12.23	4.57	16.80
Net present value of net benefits	9.36	2.59	11.96

Source: Cost and benefit data from the World Bank *Project Appraisal Document on a Proposed Loan in the Amount of US $210 million to the People's Republic of China for the Yangtze Dike Strengthening Project*, May 31, 2000. Report No: 20204-CHA.

primary benefits is positive merely indicates that the project is economically admissible.

The World Bank report provides two additional summary measures of the project: the benefit/cost ratio and the *IRR*. The overall benefit/cost ratio was estimated to be 3.5, indicating that the project was justified economically. With benefits 3.5 times the costs, this would appear to be a very useful project. Once again, however, the bank should allocate its limited resources to those projects with the highest benefit/cost ratios. It would have to check whether this project benefit/cost ratio of 3.5 is high relative to alternative projects. The *IRR* for the overall project was estimated to be 49.2 percent, indicating that a discount rate of that amount would be required in order to make the project have zero net present value of net benefits. That means the project pays an implicit rate of return of 49.2 percent, which can also be compared to other projects to determine whether this project should be funded.

EFFECTS OF RISK/UNCERTAINTY

So far, we have treated the problem of program or policy evaluation as if we operate in a world of certainty, knowing precisely what the benefits and costs may be and designing programs based on that certainty. Of course, the problem we face in the real world of policy analysis is that there is uncertainty about the way things work. Take the flood control problem as an example. Although we may be quite sure of the costs of a flood control project, we are fundamentally unsure of the potential benefits because we cannot know with certainty when or how often we will experience floods. Do we know the likelihood of a major flood in the next three years with

TABLE 7.4 Wealth Affected by Uncertain Net Benefits

	State of Nature	
	No Flood (1 − *p*)	**Flood (*p*)**
No flood control project	W	$W - D$
Flood control project in place	$W - C$	$W + (B - C)$

certainty? Certainly not. How can we take such uncertainty into account in our analysis?

A Framework for Analysis

Suppose that the situation is described in Table 7.4. A probability p exists that a major flood will occur over the next three years. Consequently, the probability of no flood is $1-p$. If we do not build the flood control project, we will suffer damages of D in case of a flood. If we do build the flood control project, it will cost C and provide benefits of B.

Suppose that we start with wealth W. With no flood control project and no flood, we will still have wealth W. That outcome will occur with probability $1-p$. In case of a flood, our wealth will be diminished to $W-D$ with probability p. Graphically, we can represent the situation as illustrated in Figure 7.7. With wealth W, we derive utility $u(W)$, but in case of a flood,

FIGURE 7.7 Analysis of Risk

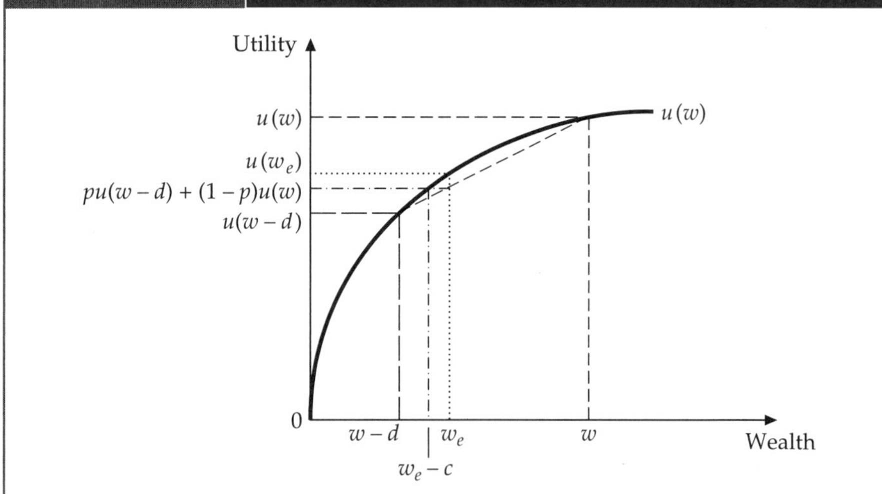

our wealth is diminished to $W-D$, from which we derive utility $u(W-D)$. Because the outcome $u(W-D)$ occurs with probability p and the outcome $u(W)$ occurs with probability $1-p$, we can compute our *expected utility* of this uncertain situation as the probability-weighted mean of the two possible outcomes: $pu(W-D) + (1-p)u(W)$. This expected utility is shown in the graph as well. If we connect the two possible utility outcomes with a line segment, we can consider the probability of a flood occurring. If there is no flood, we will be at the right end of the line segment. If a flood does occur, we will be at the left endpoint of the line segment. Because there is a probability p of a flood and a corresponding probability $1-p$ of no flood, the odds of a flood, $p/(1-p)$, indicate the point along that line segment where we expect to be. Our expected utility of the uncertain situation is read as the utility level corresponding to the point along that line segment reflecting the odds of a flood.

A concave utility function, like the one drawn in Figure 7.7, reflects risk aversion. A risk-averse person is willing to pay for insurance. A convex function would reflect risk-loving behavior where the person is willing to pay a premium just to have the thrill of bearing risk. Most of us are risk averse, especially when it comes to things like being flooded out of our homes. Of course, it is possible to be both risk averse and risk loving. In fact, many people display this paradoxical situation when they buy both fire insurance for their home and lottery tickets. In this case, the person has a concave function as drawn in Figure 7.7 over an initial range of outcomes, but over a much larger range of outcomes, including the possibility of winning the Power Ball jackpot, his or her function turns convex. Although this type of complex set of attitudes toward risk is acknowledged, we will focus on the simpler case where the person is simply risk averse, and we will consider the payment such a person would be willing to make in order to avoid risk.

Certainty Equivalents

We would like to rid ourselves of the uncertainty associated with this situation. How does the graph reveal this preference? Notice that the utility of a *certain* wealth equals $W_e = p(W-D) + (1-p)W$, the expected wealth given the probability of a flood, is above the expected utility of the uncertain situation $pu(W-D) + (1-p)u(W)$. Hence, we are better off with a certain outcome with wealth W_e than with a risky situation with the same expected outcome. How much would we be willing to pay for flood control? Well, a certain wealth level of $W_e - C$ would leave us just as well off as the uncertain case with wealth W_e, so C is the maximum amount we would be willing to pay for flood control. The quantity of wealth $W_e - C$ is the *certainty equivalent* of the risky expected wealth W_e. Now, for a benefit-cost analysis of a flood control project, we should take this into account. The possibility of a hundred-year flood (a level of flooding likely to occur once every hundred years) is quite low, yet risk-averse residents of the floodplain would be willing to pay for protection against such a flood.

The benefits of providing flood control by way of a public project should measure this willingness to pay for protection and take into account the riskiness of the flood event.

Another issue to consider is whether people have accurate perceptions of the risks they face. Take an example from recent history. Numerous lawsuits have been filed in state and federal courts by smokers who claim that they did not accurately know the riskiness of smoking cigarettes. They claim that the tobacco companies producing cigarettes systematically concealed information on the risks of smoking. The producers, for their part, point out that research on the health risks of smoking was publicly available, and, furthermore, they complied with government regulations in placing warning labels on their products explicitly stating that smoking causes health problems. The question is whether smokers accurately perceived the health risks of smoking and made their own rational decisions about whether and how much to smoke on that basis, or whether the information available to them resulted in an underestimate of the riskiness of that behavior.[7] Policy Study, "The Benefits of Smoking," considers some of the issues involved in assessing the benefits and costs of smoking from the government's point of view.

POLICY STUDY

The Benefits of Smoking[8]

A recent study commissioned by Philip Morris, a major tobacco products company that markets its products worldwide, has caused quite a stir. It seems that the study intended to show both the benefits and the costs of tobacco products for the government of the Czech Republic. Philip Morris hired Arthur D. Little International, a consulting firm, to study the impact of smoking on the finances of the Czech Republic. The study concluded that the benefit of smokers' early deaths combined with revenue generated by cigarette taxes outweigh the economic costs of health care and other costs associated with smoking. The conclusion that smoking provides net benefits that are positive, in part due to the fact that smokers' lives are cut short thereby reducing the cost of their medical care, has caused a vigorous public policy debate.

The study was conducted for Philip Morris's Czech Republic unit in response to claims by the Ministry of Health in the Czech Republic that the costs of smoking exceed the fiscal benefits of smoking. Contrary to that view, the Philip Morris study found that smoking in the Czech Republic generates a net benefit of 5.815 billion Czech korunas (about $159 million at the current exchange rate of 36.5 korunas per U.S. dollar). The largest part of the net benefit is due to tax revenue from tobacco products, primarily cigarettes. The study also reported that the Czech government saved between 943 million and 1.2 billion korunas ($26 million to $33 million) from health care, pension, and public housing cost savings due to the early deaths of smokers.

What is wrong here? In this study the early death of a smoker is identified as a benefit of smoking! Although that may be true from the point of view of the Czech treasury, because a shorter life reduces state health care expenditures, pension outlays, and subsidized housing costs, it is certainly not true from the person's point of view or from society's point of view. It is a rather strange view that sees shorter lifetimes as a benefit. From the larger social perspective, we should consider the shortened lifetimes of smokers as a cost of smoking, not a benefit. A cost-benefit study conducted from a social point of view would consider first the direct benefit of the pleasure of smoking. It would also include the tax revenue to the treasury, but not in isolation of the cost incurred by smokers. After all, smokers pay a price for a package of cigarettes that includes the tax. The tax is a cost to a smoker. Presumably, a smoker will continue to smoke as long as the expected net benefit exceeds the costs, including medical costs and the cost of a shorter lifetime. The flaw in this logic, however, is that smoking is an addictive activity over which smokers do not have complete control. That is no excuse, of course, but it is hard to believe that the act of smoking is a completely rational economic calculation of benefits and costs. For more on this topic you could consult the research by Viscusi (1990) on whether smokers properly perceive the risks of their behavior, which is fascinating.

POLICY STUDY

Benefits and Costs of Preserving Old-Growth Forests

One of the most contentious issues in environmental public policy in recent years has been the question of preserving old-growth forests in the Pacific Northwest. Preservation of the forests is deemed desirable not only to avoid cutting trees that are hundreds of years old and increasingly scarce but also to preserve habitat for the northern spotted owl. This threatened species requires the remaining old-growth forests in order to survive. Beyond concern for the spotted owl, the condition of old-growth forests also has implications for fisheries, recreation, scenic value, water quality, and soil stability.

In order to assess the potential benefits that would follow from preservation of old-growth forests, Hagen, Vincent, and Welle (1992) conducted a national survey to elicit market-like valuation responses from households for a conservation policy that would preserve the northern spotted owl. They used the responses to the survey to estimate the average household **willingness to pay (WTP).** With existing estimates of the cost of conservation, they were able to compute the threshold prices required for the policy benefits in order for the policy to be efficient. Benefit/cost ratios were calculated using both best and lower-bound estimates of the conservation policy benefits. They found that under all combinations of the assumptions that could be made, the benefit-cost ratio exceeded 1. If that is so, the benefits of preserving old-growth forests exceed the costs and preservation is a sensible public policy.

The survey instrument used by Hagen, Vincent, and Welle questioned households on three components of value. First, household estimates of recreational value were solicited. These represent a subset of **use value,** which also includes use for scenic enjoyment, fishing, and improved water and air quality. Households were also questioned on **option value** and **existence value.** Option value represents risk premium some consumers might be willing to pay to assure that the forest resource will be available in the future. Once the forest is cut down, we no longer have the option of cutting them down available. The existence value is the value attributed to the forest and its ecosystem arising in the minds of some consumers from the mere knowledge that the forest and the spotted owls exist. Such knowledge is valuable to some consumers even though they may never go hiking in the woods or see a spotted owl through their binoculars.

The method Hagen, Vincent, and Welle used to survey households is called the **contingent valuation method (CVM).** The CVM involves questioning people directly about the values they place on goods—preservation of old-growth forests in this case. Direct questions ask for the dollar values that people would assign to the policy benefits, including the option value and the existence value. The contingent nature of the survey arises because people are asked to respond, given a hypothetical situation, so their valuation response is contingent on the situation described by the questioner. The person administering the questionnaire describes the policy change contemplated, the impacts on the respondent's household in terms of any monetary costs involved, and the forms of payment that would be required. Although this method of eliciting willingness to pay from respondents certainly has its limitations, it is the most widely used method.[9]

The CVM survey used by Hagen, Vincent, and Welle elicited a willingness to pay on the part of the respondent households that was measured in annual terms. They then estimated a stream of willingness to pay over time based on future annual WTP, income, and assumed growth in the national economy.[10] A threshold price was then computed. That price is the one which when used as a starting value for the stream of estimated benefits over time, discounted over the infinite time horizon, yields a present discounted value equal to the cost of preservation. As such, the threshold price is the initial price a household would be willing to pay that just covers the cost of preservation. The threshold price can also be considered a kind of *break-even* price where the initial annualized value of average household WTP would equal the cost of preservation.

A conservative *lower-bound* estimate of the threshold price was derived assuming that WTP remains at a constant fraction of real income over time. With a 3 percent real rate of growth in income, the resulting threshold price is $3.39. This amount is the net present value of the stream of benefits due to preservation that would just equal the costs of preservation. We could assume that the demand for goods yielded by preservation would grow disproportionately over time. If we assumed that there is no growth whatever in WTP, which implies that WTP is a falling percentage of income over time, we can establish an *upper-bound* estimate of the threshold price of $13.56. These two threshold prices are the low and high threshold prices listed in the two columns of Table 7.5.

Another issue of concern is how to handle nonrespondents in the CVM survey. Two approaches were used in handling nonrespondents. The *upper-bound* approach

TABLE 7.5 Benefit-Cost Ratios Under Various Assumptions

	High Threshold Price	Low Threshold Price
Assumptions		
Best estimate of benefits	10.64	42.56
Upper-bound approach to nonrespondents		
Implied benefits $144.28		
Assumptions		
Best estimate of benefits	6.37	25.46
Lower-bound approach to nonrespondents		
Implied benefits $86.32		
Assumptions		
Lower-bound estimate of benefits	3.53	14.14
Lower-bound approach to nonrespondents		
Implied benefits $47.93		

Source: Table 1, p. 21 from "Benefits of Preserving Old-Growth Forests and the Spotted Owl" by Daniel A. Hagen, James W. Vincent, and Patrick G. Welle in *Contemporary Policy Issues*, Vol. X, April 1992. © 1992 Western Economic Association. Reprinted with permission.

assumed a positive benefit value for nonrespondents on the basis of extrapolation from the data. A *lower-bound* estimate assumed that all nonrespondents derived no benefits whatsoever.

Table 7.5 reports the estimated benefit-cost ratios for various sets of assumptions. The two columns of the table correspond to the high and low threshold price assumptions, whereas the three rows of the table correspond to sets of assumptions regarding nonrespondents and benefit estimates. The benefit-cost ratios range from a low of 3.53, indicating that the benefits of preserving old growth forests are expected to be 3.5 times the costs of preservation, to a high of 42.56, indicating that benefits are expected to be more than 42 times costs. The low benefit-cost ratio arises from assuming the high threshold price and lower-bound estimates of benefits and nonrespondents. The high benefit-cost ratio arises from the assumption of a low threshold price and higher estimates of benefits, including an upper-bound estimate for nonrespondents.

Regardless of the assumption set used, this analysis indicates that the benefits expected from preservation of old growth forests will exceed the costs of preservation by at least 3 times, and perhaps as much as 42 times. Preservation of old growth forests in the Pacific Northwest, as a public policy option, is justified on the basis of this analysis.

POLICY STUDY

Cost-Benefit Study of Disaster Mitigation Measures in Three Islands in the Maldives

The Maldives is an island nation in the Indian Ocean comprised of more than 1,000 islands which are at risk due to the possibilities of tsunamis and potential consequences of global climate change bringing extreme weather events and raising sea levels. Following a devastating tsunami in 2004, the Maldives government raised the concept of a Safer Islands Programme (SIP) intended to:

1. Protect the islands from natural and other hazards,
2. Rebuild and improve existing infrastructure and economic facilities, and
3. Develop capacity to plan and implement measures to reduce natural hazard risks and build the community resilience to disasters.

Table 7.6 reports the UNDP estimates of both the benefit/cost ratio and the net present value of net benefits (NPV in Rufiyaa, RF). The full SIP program, if implemented for the island of Thinadhoo, would only generate a benefit cost ratio in excess of unity and positive NPV under the maximum hazard occurrence scenario or the maximum hazard climate change scenario. Under the minimum hazard occurrence scenario the benefit-cost (B/C) ratio is less than unity and the NPV is negative. A more selected SIP program similarly only generates B/C ratios in excess of unity and positive NPVs for the maximum hazard and climate change scenarios. The most restrictive limited protection option is capable of generating a B/C ratio in excess of unity and positive NPV under

TABLE 7.6 Cost-Benefit Findings for the Islands of Thinadhoo and Viligilli

Protection Type	Minimum Hazard Occurrence	Maximum Hazard Occurrence	Maximum Hazard Climate Change
	Island of Thinadhoo		
Safe Island Protection	B/C ratio: 0.39 NPV: −161,077,586	B/C ratio: 1.35 NPV: 93,714,442	B/C ratio: 1.40 NPV: 105,180,640
Selected Safe Island Protection	B/C ratio: 0.52 NPV: −89,909,427	B/C ratio: 1.79 NPV: 149,251,980	B/C ratio: 1.85 NPV: 160,185,167
Limited Protection	B/C ratio: 1.13 NPV: 9,731,053	B/C ratio: 3.54 NPV: 191,202,975	B/C ratio: 3.65 NPV: 199,823,621
	Island of Viligili		
Safe Island Protection	B/C ratio: 0.28 NPV: −179,159,791	B/C ratio: 0.93 NPV: −18,202,523	B/C ratio: 1.00 NPV: 1,002,046
Selected Safe Island Protection	B/C ratio: 0.29 NPV: −153,708,573	B/C ratio: 0.89 NPV: −22,941,082	B/C ratio: 0.96 NPV: −8,403,115
Limited Protection	B/C ratio: 0.42 NPV: −58,696,320	B/C ratio: 1.23 NPV: 23,529,219	B/C ratio: 1.33 NPV: 33,690,198

Source: UNDP (2009) Tables ES4 and ES10.

TABLE 7.7 Cost-Benefit Findings for the Island of Viligili

Protection Type	Minimum Hazard Occurrence	Maximum Hazard Occurrence	Maximum Hazard Climate Change
Safe Island Protection	B/C ratio: 0.28 NPV: −179,159,791	B/C ratio: 0.93 NPV: −18,202,523	B/C ratio: 1.00 NPV: 1,002,046
Selected Safe Island Protection	B/C ratio: 0.29 NPV: −153,708,573	B/C ratio: 0.89 NPV: −22,941,082	B/C ratio: 0.96 NPV: −8,403,115
Limited Protection	B/C ratio: 0.42 NPV: −58,696,320	B/C ratio: 1.23 NPV: 23,529,219	B/C ratio: 1.33 NPV: 33,690,198

Source: UNDP (2009) Table ES10.

the minimum hazard occurrence scenario as well as under the maximum hazard scenarios. These estimates indicate that the limited protection option may be the most cost-effective option. The more elaborate protection options are only economically feasible if the maximum hazard occurrence scenarios are likely.

For the island of Viligili, the benefit-cost analysis is less encouraging, as Table 7.7 reports. The SIP program has benefits that do not exceed costs for any of the scenarios. Hence, the SIP program would not be feasible for this island. The selected SIP program is even worse, with B/C ratios less than unity under all three hazard occurrence scenarios. Only the limited protection plan shows the potential for benefits to exceed costs, but only under the maximum hazard occurrence scenarios. Hence there is no clear financial justification for implementing anything but the limited protection option under the extreme hazard occurrence assumption—an unlikely situation.

United Nations Development Programme. 2009. Cost Benefit Study of Disaster Risk Mitigation Measures in Three Islands in the Maldives. September 2009.

PROBLEMS

1. Suppose that the annual marginal benefit of crime prevention program that puts police walking the beat on the streets of Crimeville has been estimated as $MB = 500{,}000 - 1{,}200q$, where q is the number of police employed in the program.
   a. What is the total benefit of the program when 200 police are employed?
   b. What is the change in total benefit if we increase the number of police from 200 to 250?
   c. If the marginal cost of employing a police officer is $80,000 per year, what is the optimal number of police officers to hire?
   d. If the optimal number of police officers is hired, what is the expected net benefit of the program?

2. The total benefits of the COMMIT program, which is designed to encourage schoolchildren to commit themselves to a life free of drug addiction, has been estimated to be $B = 800q - 4q^2$, where q is the number of days the program is run in local schools. The total cost of running the program is $400 per day.
   a. What is the maximum number of days that the COMMIT program can be run before net benefits turn negative?
   b. What is the optimal number of days to run the program in order to maximize net benefits ($MB = 800 - 8q$)?
   c. At the optimal number of days, what is the net benefit of the program?
   d. If the cost of running the program were to rise to $500 per day, how would that affect the optimal number of days the program should be run?
3. Use the perpetuity formula to estimate the value of the following projects generating net benefits in perpetuity.
   a. $B_i = 5{,}000$, $r = 0.06$
   b. $B_i = 10{,}000$, $r = 0.06$
   c. $B_i = 10{,}000$, $r = 0.05$
   d. $B_i = 10{,}000$, $r = 0.04$
   e. $B_i = 5{,}000$, $r = 0.035$
4. Sketch the conceptual outline of how you would conduct a cost-benefit analysis of the 55-mph speed limit law implemented in the United States during the 1970s and 1980s.
   a. Identify benefits, both direct and indirect.
   b. Identify costs, both direct and indirect.
   c. Suggest an evaluation criterion and its application.
   d. Suppose that you had the option of determining the appropriate scale for a general speed limit law; that is, you could select any speed limit, not just 55 mph. Explain how you would determine the most economical speed limit.
5. Analyze the Philip Morris study of the public finance consequences of smoking discussed in the Policy Study "The Benefits of Smoking." Do so by answering the following questions:
   a. Identify the primary benefits and costs of smoking.
   b. Identify the secondary benefits and costs of smoking.
   c. Should the cost savings due to smokers' early deaths be included?
   d. Are there other costs that the study ignores?
6. A cost-benefit analysis of a new irrigation project indicates that the net benefits of the project in each of the first four years will be –$2 million. That is, $B_i - C_i = -2$ million for $i = 1, 2, 3, 4$. Thereafter, the project will yield positive net benefits of $750,000 each year for the next 21 years; that is, $B_i - C_i = 0.75$ million for $i = 5 \ldots 25$.
   a. Calculate the present value of net benefits when the social rate of discount is 10 percent. (Assume that the net benefits in year i are received at the end of year i in this and other problems.)
   b. Explain whether the program merits approval on the basis of this information.

c. How is the present value of the net benefits changed if the social rate of discount is 5 percent? Explain why.

7. Calculate the present value of each of the following income streams using a 5 percent discount rate:
   a. An income stream of $1,000 per year for 20 years
   b. An income stream of $1,000 per year for years 1 to 10 followed by an income stream of $500 per year for years 11 to 20
   c. A net income stream of −$1,000 per year for years 1 to 3 followed by an income stream of $2,000 per year for years 4 to 10
   d. A perpetual income stream of $1,000 per year
   e. A perpetual income stream of $10,000 per year
8. Suppose that a proposed government irrigation project lowers the marginal cost of producing food and thereby lowers the market price of food. If the market demand for food is given by the estimated inverse demand equation $P = 3 - 0.2Q$, where P is a food price index and Q is the quantity of food measured in millions of pounds per year, and the irrigation project reduces the price from 1.4 to 1.2, compute the benefit of the project reducing food prices that must be included in the cost-benefit study.
9. (optional advanced problem) You work for the State Department of Labor and have been given the task of evaluation a state job-training program. In order to conduct the analysis, suppose that the typical client for the program has the following utility function of income I.

$$U = (I + \alpha)^{\beta}, \quad \textit{where} \quad \alpha \geq 0, 0 < \beta < 1.$$

   a. Sketch the typical client's utility function and explain the person's attitude toward risk.
   b. Suppose that you must evaluate a proposed job-training program that would have an unpredictable effect on the typical client's income which is currently $20,000 per year. The program will leave his annual income unchanged with probability 0.3, or it will increase his income by $10,000 with probability 0.7. Calculate the benefit of the program to the typical client assuming that $\alpha = 5{,}000$ and $\beta = 0.5$.

REFERENCES

Bartik, Timothy J. *Who Benefits from State and Local Economic Development Policies?* Kalamazoo, MI: W. E. Upjohn Institute for Employment Research, 1991.

Diamond, Peter A., and Jerry A. Hausman. "Contingent Valuation: Is Some Number Better than No Number?" *Journal of Economic Perspectives* 8 (1994): 45–64.

Gramlich, Edward M. *Cost-Benefit Analysis of Government Programs*. Englewood Cliffs, NJ: Prentice Hall, 1981.

Hagen, Daniel A., James W. Vincent, and Patrick G. Welle. "Benefits of Preserving Old-Growth Forests and the Spotted Owl." *Contemporary Policy Issues* 10 (1992): 13–26.

Hanemann, W. Michael. "Valuing the Environment Through Contingent Valuation." *Journal of Economic Perspectives* 8 (1994): 19–43.

Portney, Paul R. "The Contingent Valuation Debate: Why Economists Should Care." *Journal of Economic Perspectives* 8 (1994): 3–17.

Viscusi, W. Kip. "Do Smokers Underestimate Risks?" *Journal of Political Economy* 98 (1990): 1253–69.

World Bank. Project Appraisal Document on a Proposed Loan in the Amount of $210 Million to the Peoples Republic of China for Yangtze Dike-Strengthening Project, World Bank Report 2024-CHA, Rural Development and Natural Resources Sector Unit, East Asia and Pacific Region, May 31, 2000.

NOTES

1. The classic text in benefit-cost analysis applied to government programs is Gramlich (1981).
2. In the case where the marginal benefit function $b(q)$ is nonlinear, we must integrate under the function in order to derive total benefits. Total benefit for q_1 units of the public good are derived by computing

$$B(q_1) = \int_0^{q_1} b(u)du.$$

3. Again, if the marginal cost function $c(q)$ is nonlinear, we must integrate in order to compute total cost. The total cost of providing q_1 units of public good is computed as

$$C(q_1) = \int_0^{q_1} c(u)du.$$

4. If we write total benefit and total cost as a function of the project scale, $B(s)$ and $C(s)$, we can then maximize net benefit $B(s) - C(s)$ by differentiating with respect to the choice variable s. The first-order condition for optimal scale is then $B'(s) - C'(s) = 0$, which can be rearranged as $B'(s) = C'(s)$, indicating that marginal benefit must equal marginal cost.
5. The ratio of benefits to costs can be written $B(s)/C(s)$. If we maximize this ratio with respect to choice of s, we must set the derivative of the ratio equal to zero to obtain our first-order necessary condition for a maximum. The derivative is $[C(s)B'(s) - B(s)C'(s)]/C(s)^2$. When set equal to zero, we can rewrite the necessary condition as $B'(s)/B(s) = C'(s)/C(s)$. Thus, maximizing the ratio of benefits to costs requires that we equate the ratio of marginal benefit to total benefit with the ratio of marginal cost to total cost. This requirement is clearly different from what we obtained in the case of maximizing net benefits.

6. For reference, the exchange rate used in the study was 8.3 yuan per U.S. dollar.
7. For an interesting study of this issue, see Viscusi (1990), who conducted a national survey of individuals, which examined perceived risk of lung cancer. Viscusi found that both smokers and nonsmokers generally overestimated the risk of getting lung cancer. Those risk perceptions reduced the likelihood of smoking. He also computed the lung cancer risk equivalent of the excise taxes applied to cigarettes. In other words, he calculated what endowment of lung cancer risk perception that would be equivalent in its effect on smoking probability as the cigarette excise tax. His conclusion was that even if people had no perception of lung cancer risk, the excise taxes applied to cigarettes generally reduced the likelihood of smoking by more than the effect of an accurate risk perception of lung cancer.
8. *http://edition.cnn.com/2001/BUSINESS/07/16/czech.morris/index.html?iref=allsearch*.
9. A number of good articles on the subject of contingent valuation methods were included as a symposium in the fall 1994 issue of the *Journal of Economic Perspectives:* Paul R. Portney, "The Contingent Valuation Debate: Why Economists Should Care"; W. Michael Hanemann, "Valuing the Environment Through Contingent Valuation"; and Peter A. Diamond and Jerry A. Hausman, "Contingent Valuation: Is Some Number Better than No Number?"
10. In studies of environmental pollution, researchers also estimate consumers' **willingness to accept (WTA)** various environmental damages.

CHAPTER 8

The Pricing of Public Goods and Services

LEARNING OBJECTIVES

1. Explain the economics of government production of public goods and services.
2. Analyze the cost of producing public goods and services and discuss the implications for provision.
3. Calculate the price of public goods and services, including user fees, tolls, and two-part tariffs.

Governments sometimes produce public services themselves, whereas in other cases they merely oversee the provision of those services by private producers. For example, a city may actually produce garbage collection services by purchasing trucks, hiring employees, and running a refuse collection service for the community. Alternatively, the city may merely contract with a private refuse company to provide collection services, subject to city-specified terms and conditions. Governments are increasingly looking at ways to contract with private producers for the provision of goods and services in order to reduce costs. The government is not always the most efficient producer of goods and services. In some cases there may be an efficiency gain in privatizing city services. In other cases, it makes sense for the city to be the producer of public goods and services.

Consider the realm of education policy where public school districts have traditionally been involved in the direct production of education. The school district builds the school buildings, hires the teachers and support staff, and produces education. In recent years, however, some public school districts have experimented with contracting for the services of for-profit private educational firms as an alternative. The objective in doing so has been to obtain either a higher level of educational services at a given cost to the district or a given level of educational services at a lower cost than the school district was able to achieve itself. Mixed evidence exists on the success of for-profit educational firms contracting with public school districts. It is not yet clear whether they are either more effective in teaching or more efficient in cutting costs than public school districts were on their own. Nevertheless, more and more school districts and other government units are looking to find ways to provide services more effectively or more efficiently.

Governments are also looking for more effective ways to fund the provision of public goods and services. Increasingly, they are turning to user fees rather than general taxes in order to pay for specific services provided to constituents. When they do so, how should they price the public goods and services? Price determination is an important policy issue in order to assure adequate revenues to the government to pay for the public good or service provided.

PRODUCTION OF PUBLIC GOODS AND SERVICES

Suppose that we know the optimal amount of a public good or service that should be provided in a community. We obtain that information from application of the Samuelson rule discussed in Chapter 3. Knowing the optimal level of a public good or service that should be produced in a community, we then need to know how best to produce that quantity of the public good or service. In particular, suppose that we are concerned with providing public education in a school district and the school board needs to know how many teachers should be combined with classrooms to provide a specific level of public education for the district's children. The mathematical description of the relationship between the minimum quantities of each input required to produce a given quantity of the output is known as the **production function.** This is the critical starting point for analyzing the production of public goods and services. For a review of the important economics of production functions, see the appendix to Chapter 8 located at the end of this textbook.

Consider the case of producing public schooling. We can express the production function for schooling as $q = f(k, l, n)$, where q is the quantity of output and k, l, and n represent quantities of the inputs capital, labor, and land. Output would be measured using some quantitative description such as the number of students educated, the credit hours produced, the graduation rate, or student achievement on a standardized test. The **variable input** of interest in this case is the number of full-time equivalent teachers used in the district. The top panel of Figure 8.1 illustrates the total product of public education that can be produced with various quantities of teachers, the variable input. Two important quantities of labor are labeled: l_1, where the total product curve has an inflection point, and l_3, where total product reaches its maximum.

If our objective were to maximize the output of public education, we would use l_3 units of labor because the total product curve reaches its maximum with variable input quantity l_3 combined with the **fixed inputs.** Using a smaller quantity of labor would not enable us to produce as much public education because we are combining that labor with a fixed amount of capital. With too little labor, our output suffers. Similarly, using too much labor also reduces our output. With quantities of labor in excess of l_3 units, output also falls below its maximum level. Because there is a fixed amount of the capital

FIGURE 8.1 Product Curves for Production of a Public Good

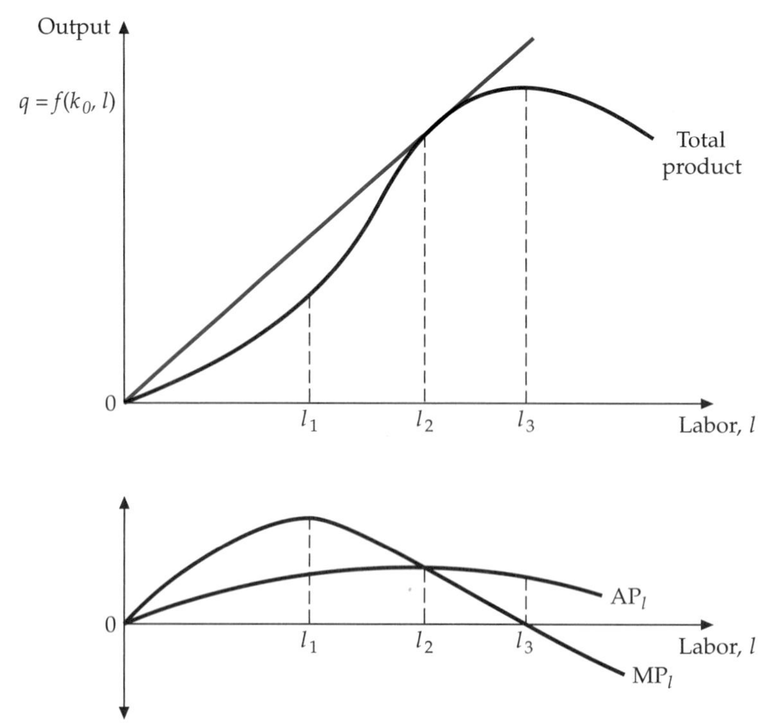

input being combined with labor to produce education, using too much labor relative to capital is also inefficient. The additional units of labor beyond l_3 have negative marginal product because they must share a fixed amount of capital. Consequently, we can rule out use of labor in excess of l_3 units. That would simply be foolish because we can maximize output using l_3 units.

The corresponding marginal product curve is illustrated in the lower panel of Figure 8.1. Marginal product is rising initially but reaches its maximum at the quantity of labor l_1. Because the marginal product is the rate of change in total product with a change in labor, we can think of it as the slope of the total product curve. For quantities less than l_1, the marginal product is rising, and for quantities greater than l_1, it is falling. Hence, the marginal product is at its maximum at l_1, the same point where the second derivative of total product changes sign—the inflection point. Additional units of labor initially provide increasing returns as each additional unit of labor employed results in increased output and the rate at which output increases is rising. That experience ends once we have employed l_1 units of labor. After l_1 units of labor, each additional unit of labor employed adds to output but at a decreasing rate. That is true of all units of labor employed up to l_3, where the marginal product reaches zero. For units of labor employed in excess of l_3, the marginal product of labor is negative, reducing total product.

So, what is the right number of teachers to employ, given the fixed physical plant we have in the school district? We can eliminate all quantities of labor on the interval $(0, l_1)$ illustrated in Figure 8.1 as possible solutions to the problem because over that range too little labor is being used when combined with the fixed amount of capital k_0. How do we know too little labor is being used? Over this range, the average product of labor is rising, indicating that the productivity of labor is improving as we use more of it. Therefore, we do not want to be satisfied using l_1 or fewer units of labor. If we use at least l_1 units of labor, but less than l_2 units, the average product of labor is still rising because the marginal product is above the average product. In this interval, we have the potential to use the proper quantity of labor relative to capital. If we were to use more than l_3 units of labor, the marginal product would be negative, clearly indicating that we were using too much labor with the fixed capital. By scaling back our labor usage, we can actually produce more output. Hence, the optimal amount of labor to employ is somewhere in the interval (l_2, l_3).[1]

For the physical aspects of production only, we can narrow the range of options to consider. The exact quantity of labor to use, however, is an economic problem that requires additional analysis. We need to know something about the price of labor relative to other inputs like capital, and we also need to know something about the trade-off between inputs that is embodied in the production function. That is, we need to know both what the trade-off is between teachers and computers in producing education and what additional teachers cost relative to computers.

Isoquants and Isocost Lines

A given quantity of public good may be produced in many different ways. In our schooling example, we can consider a rural school in Nebraska, such as Oak Valley School just a mile and a half from the author's home, that has a total of 18 students in grades 1 to 6 and employs two teachers in a one-room schoolhouse (even in the 21st century!). Such an approach to producing schooling is very labor intensive. Very little capital is used in the form of structures and equipment in the production of schooling. At the other extreme one might imagine a school on the Internet, called CyberSchool, where students study at home using computers, modems, and Internet access providers to supervise their studies. Such an approach is very capital intensive. Ignoring the question of the quality of either form of education, we can consider the input combinations used in the production of schooling.

Figure 8.2 illustrates the input combinations that are capable of producing a given quantity of schooling, call it q_1, from an extremely labor-intensive school like Oak Valley School to a very capital-intensive school such as CyberSchool, and combinations in between. The locus of input combinations capable of producing the same output level is known as an **isoquant.** The prefix *iso-* means the same, indicating that along such a line we have the same quantity of output. Recall that if we increase the quantity of schooling produced, perhaps due to an increased number of students, we

FIGURE 8.2 Schooling Production Isoquants

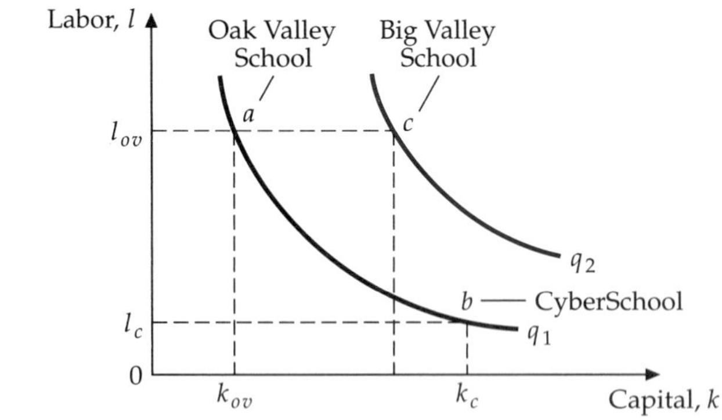

move to an isoquant that is farther from the origin. Isoquant q_2 represents combinations of inputs capable of producing quantity q_2 of schooling. The slope of the isoquant is the ratio of the marginal products of capital and labor and is known as the marginal rate of technical substitution: $MRTS = MP_k/MP_l$. As we stated in Chapter 3, the *MRTS* measures the rate at which we can technically substitute capital for labor and retain the same level of output. It measures a technical relationship and captures the trade-off between inputs that we have available to us as we consider how much of each input to employ.

In the schooling context, an important statistic that is compiled for school districts all over the country is the **pupil-teacher ratio:** the number of pupils in the school divided by the number of teachers. In terms of Figure 8.2, suppose that we are measuring output q in terms of the number of students educated per year. The pupil-teacher ratio for a given enrollment q_1 in the two schools would then be q_1/l_c for CyberSchool and q_1/l_{ov} for Oak Valley School. This ratio essentially tells us how labor intensive the district is in producing schooling. But the enrollment at the two schools may be quite different. Assuming a given quantity of capital (and technology embodied in that capital), the higher the pupil-teacher ratio, the more labor intensive the school district. We are moving up the q_1 isoquant. But if the enrollment differs at two schools whose pupil-teacher ratios we wish to compare, then the pupil-teacher ratio does not have such a clear interpretation. Say there are q_1 students at Oak Valley School and CyberSchool, but there are q_2 students at Big Valley School, where $q_1 < q_2$. If we compare the pupil-teacher ratios at the three schools, we would find that the ratio for Big Valley School is larger than that for Oak Valley School since they both use the same number of teachers, but Big Valley School has a larger enrollment. But how would the ratios for CyberSchool and Big Valley School compare? It is not obvious. Big Valley School has more pupils; this raises its ratio. But CyberSchool uses fewer teachers, and this raises its ratio. It is not at all clear which would have the greater pupil-teacher ratio. In fact, it is possible that the two schools would have identical ratios. Thus, when we consider pupil-teacher ratios, we cannot simply conclude that the ratio is a straightforward measure of labor intensity in production.

The curvature of the isoquants tells us the degree of substitutability of the inputs and reflects the **elasticity of substitution.** That elasticity is the ratio of the percentage change in the ratio of inputs to the percentage change in the input price ratio. Consider the two extreme cases. When the inputs are perfect substitutes, the elasticity of substitution is infinite. In that case a very small change in the input price ratio will lead to a very large change in the combination of inputs used in producing a given quantity of the output. Take, for example, the case of male and female junior high school teachers. Because male and female teachers are likely to be perfect substitutes in the production of American history at a junior high school, an increase in the price of male teachers relative to female teachers will lead to a large substitution of female teachers for male teachers.

The isoquant in this case is drawn as a downward-sloping straight line. The slope of the isoquant indicates the rate at which one input is substituted for the other input. In this case the trade-off is -1. For each male teacher we lay off, we hire a female teacher. Figure 8.3 illustrates this case. We can produce quantity of education q_0 using 10 male teachers and no female teachers, 10 female teachers and no male teachers, or any combination of 10 male or female teachers. In order to produce the larger quantity of education q_1, we must use 20 male teachers and no female teachers, 20 female teachers and no male teachers, or any combination of 20 male and female teachers. Quantity of education q_2 requires 30 teachers, male or female. In each case, there is a perfect one-for-one trade-off between male and female teachers. Because gender does not matter in the production of education, male and female teachers are perfect substitutes and the isoquants are downward-sloping line segments with a slope of -1.

FIGURE 8.3 Production with Inputs That Are Perfect Complements

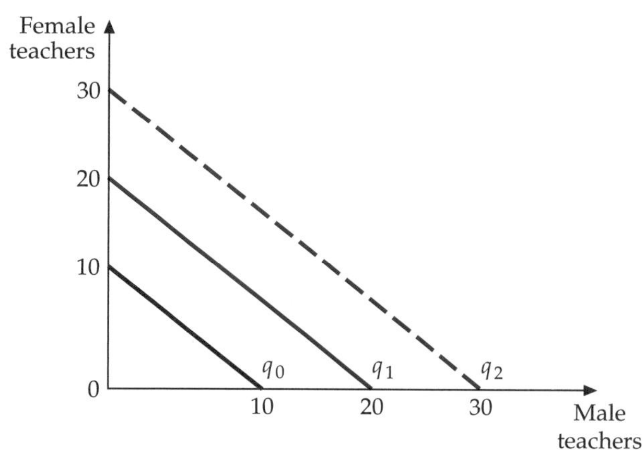

The other extreme case is that of perfect complements. In this case, the inputs are required in a fixed ratio. In order to produce a given quantity of output, a fixed ratio of the two inputs is required. No scope exists for substitution of one input for the other. Consider the example of a laboratory classroom with 20 stations. The teacher of that class can work with 20 students and no more due to the capital constraint embedded in the fixed number of stations. Hence, if we want to produce 20 graduates with training in that lab science, we need one teacher and one laboratory classroom. The only way to produce more is to use two teachers and two laboratory classrooms with a total of 40 lab stations. No scope exists for substitution. In this case, the elasticity of substitution is zero. A given change in the input price ratio leads to no change in the ratio of inputs employed. The isoquant in this case would be L-shaped, as illustrated in Figure 8.4. For a given quantity of one input, increasing quantities of the other input do not enable production of any different quantity. Quantity of education q_0 can be produced using one teacher and 20 lab stations—the (20, 1) combination. Additional lab stations have zero marginal product because they must be combined with additional students and a teacher. Because that is true of both inputs, the isoquant has both a vertical segment and a horizontal segment along which the marginal product of the input is zero.

Most production situations are in between these two extremes of perfect substitutes and perfect complements. Production technology is usually such that there is some scope for the substitution of inputs. As a result, elasticities of substitution are usually greater than zero but less than infinity. The isoquants are downward-sloping curves convex to the origin, as illustrated in Figure 8.2. The smaller the elasticity, the less substitutable the inputs; the larger the elasticity, the more easily substitution can occur.

Now we turn to the essential economic question. For any given level of schooling we care to produce, what is the optimal combination of inputs to

FIGURE 8.4 Fixed Ratio Production Technology

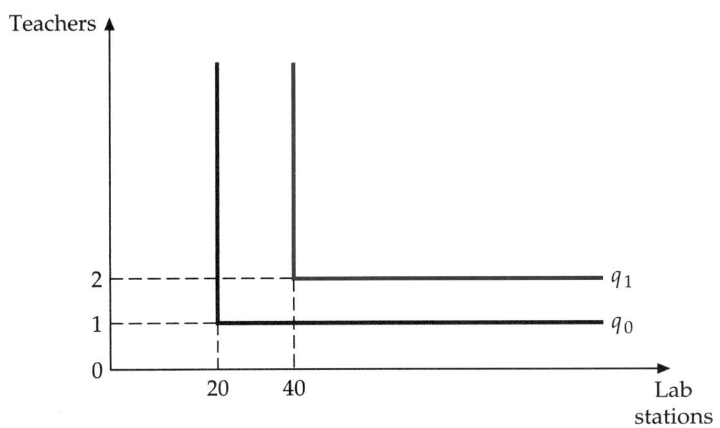

FIGURE 8.5 Schooling Isocost Lines

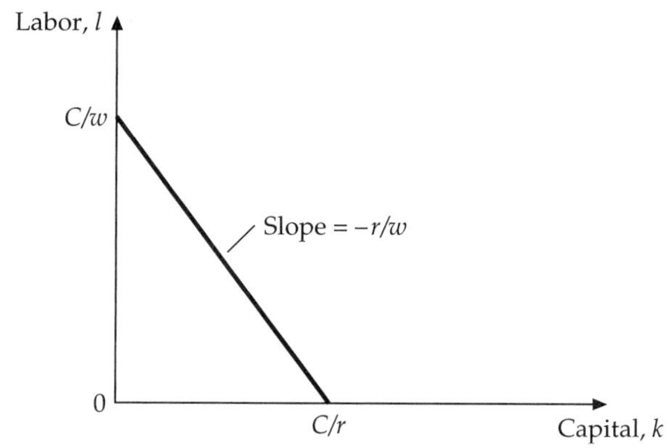

use? Should we produce schooling in a labor-intensive way, a capital-intensive way, or perhaps use a mix of labor and capital in between those extremes? In order to answer this question, we must consider not only the technical possibilities given in the isoquants but also the costs. It will make a difference whether teachers cost \$20,000 per year or \$40,000 per year and whether computers cost \$500 per child or \$5,000 per child.

If we consider the variable inputs labor and capital, which can be purchased at market prices w and r, respectively, the cost of producing schooling can be written as $C = wl + rk$. If we rewrite this cost relationship, solving for l as a function of k, we have $l = C/w - (r/w)k$. This relationship is plotted as a downward-sloping line in $k - l$ space, as illustrated in Figure 8.5. The vertical intercept is C/w and the slope of the line is $-r/w$. This line is known as the **isocost line** as it illustrates the combinations of capital and labor that have the same total cost. The higher the cost of capital, relative to the wage, the steeper the isocost line. Similarly, for low-wage rural school districts, w is small relative to r and the slope of the isocost line is steep. Urban school districts where w is high relative to r have much flatter isocost lines. The slope of the isocost line is minus the ratio of input prices, $-r/w$, and represents the economic rate at which we can substitute one input for the other while retaining the same total cost. It represents an economic trade-off.

Optimal Input Combinations

Determining the optimal input combination requires that we bring together both technical and economic information. The optimal combination of inputs to use, for any given level of output produced, is that combination where the $MRTS$ equals the price ratio: $MRTS = MP_k/MP_l = r/w$. Graphically, the optimal input combination is that where the isoquant is tangent to the isocost line. At that point of tangency, the slopes of the two relationships are equal and we have the efficiency condition $MP_k/MP_l = r/w$. This expression can also be written as $MP_k/r = MP_l/w$. Hence, the marginal product per dollar paid must be equal on the last unit of each input used. Returning to our schooling example, this would mean that in order to be using both teachers and computers in the optimal quantities, it must be the case that for the last teacher hired and the last computer purchased, the marginal product per dollar paid must be equal. If not, we are not using the right quantities. Suppose for a moment that the marginal product of labor per dollar paid in wages is larger than the marginal product per dollar paid for computers. If that were the case, we could improve the production of schooling by hiring more teachers because we get more additional schooling per dollar that we spend with teachers than with computers. Doing so, however, drives the marginal product of teachers lower and the marginal product of computers higher, and that restores the balance required in the optimality condition.

Figure 8.6 illustrates the efficient combination of inputs of capital and labor to use in order to produce quantity q_1 of the public good. The efficient combination is that point where the isoquant is tangent to the isocost line, assuring that we can be on the isoquant producing q_1 units of the public good but simultaneously be on the lowest isocost line. Using the input combination (k^*, l^*), we are able to produce q_1 units of output at least cost.

Returning to the special cases of perfect substitutes and perfect complements illustrated in Figures 8.3 and 8.4, we can see how important the shape of the isoquant may be in determining the optimal input combination used to produce a public good. Consider the case of male and female teachers as in Figure 8.3. The isoquant in that case has a slope of -1, reflecting the fact that there is a one-for-one trade-off between male and female teachers in the production of education. Now combine that information on the production technology with the economic information on the price of teachers. If the price of a male teacher is higher than the price of a female teacher in the labor market, then the ratio of the male teacher price to the female teacher price is greater than 1, and the slope of the isocost line is steeper than the

FIGURE 8.6 Optimal Input Combination

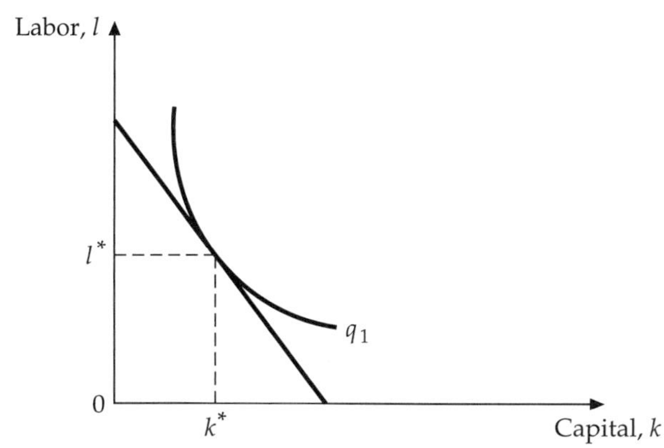

slope of the isoquant. If that is the case, the school district should specialize in hiring all female teachers. Because the inputs are perfect substitutes, the school district can produce a given quantity of education at lower cost by hiring all female teachers. In such a situation the school board is highly sensitive to even small changes in the relative price of the inputs and will switch gender in its hiring practice.

In the case of inputs that are perfect complements, however, the school board will not be sensitive at all to changes in the relative prices of the inputs. Consider the isoquants illustrated in Figure 8.4 where teachers and lab stations are complementary in the ratio of 1 to 20. The isocost lines in this case reflect the relative prices of teachers and lab stations, but for any downward-sloping isocost line, variations in the relative prices of the inputs are unlikely to have an impact on the combination of inputs used. Suppose, for example, that the price of lab stations falls relative to the price of teachers. In that case, the isocost line becomes flatter. Because the optimal combination of inputs occurs at the point of tangency with the L-shaped isoquant, however, there is no response on the part of the school board to a small change in the relative price. Only when there is a very large change that flattens the isocost line sufficiently to justify a second lab will the district be responsive. In this case, the school board is unresponsive to small changes in input prices.

These two examples illustrate the importance of production technology in the public sector. The underlying technology of producing public goods and services is critical to our understanding of the input combinations used by public agencies. Furthermore, the responsiveness or unresponsiveness of the public agency to changes in relative prices depends crucially on the production technology as well.

Returns to Scale

An important question that arises when we consider production is the effect of a proportional scaling of all of the inputs. If we hire 10 percent more teachers and buy 10 percent more computers, will we get 10 percent more schooling? If we are fortunate, perhaps we will get 12 percent more schooling. On the other hand, if we are unfortunate, perhaps we will get only 7 percent more schooling. We need to know what kind of **returns to scale** exist in schooling. The consideration of returns to scale is a long-run concept because we must be free to scale input usage for all inputs. In terms of the production function $q = f(k, l)$, the question is, what happens when we scale up our use of both k and l by the proportion t, where $t > 1$? Do we get the same proportional increase in output, more than that, or less than that? That is, what do we get from using tk units of capital and tl units of labor? The output resulting can be written as $t^r = f(tk, tl)$. If $r > 1$, we have **increasing returns to scale,** where proportional increases in all inputs yield a greater than proportional increase in output. On the other hand, if $r < 1$, we have **decreasing returns to scale,** where proportional increases in all inputs yield a smaller than proportional increase in output. The case where $r = 1$ is called **constant returns to scale,** where proportional increases in all inputs yield that same proportional increase in output. It is essential for governments to know the economies of scale they face as they plan their output of public goods and services.

Consider the case of a growing city where population projections indicate that there will be a 30 percent growth in the number of high school students in the public schools over the next 20 years. In order to plan for a 30 percent increase in high school output, we must know the technology of the schooling production function and its returns to scale. It is essential to know whether a 30 percent increase in output will require 30 percent more teachers and computers, more, or less. Without knowledge of the returns to scale in schooling, the school district will be lost in its planning process. It can blindly plan to hire 30 percent more teachers and buy 30 percent more computers, but that may not be the optimal combination of inputs for producing 30 percent more schooling. If they can get 30 percent more schooling with less than a 30 percent increase in teachers and computers, the average cost of educating a student will fall, but if it takes more than a 30 percent increase in the inputs, the average cost will rise. Because there are important budgetary implications, the school district must know about the economies of scale. This is true for all public goods and services and means that cities, counties, states, and central governments everywhere require the essential knowledge of the production technologies by which they produce public goods and the associated implications for the cost of providing those services. In the next section we turn to an explicit consideration of the cost of providing public goods and services. Keep in mind that the cost curves that are discussed have embedded within them the production function properties we have just discussed in this section.

In the context of Figure 8.6 we are also interested in what happens as we move out to isoquants farther from the origin. Do we follow a ray from the origin with a fixed input ratio as we scale up production? The set of all optimal input combinations (points of tangency between isoquants and isocost lines) as we scale up output is called the **expansion path.** That path may be linear, meaning that we simply follow a fixed input recipe as we expand output. On the other hand, it may be nonlinear, either concave or convex, requiring us to adjust the input combination as we expand. If, for example, the expansion path in Figure 8.6 is concave, then as we expand output, we use proportionately greater and greater amounts of capital relative to labor. That means we will be buying more and more computer equipment relative to teachers as we expand the capacity of the school district to teach more and more students.

Education Production Functions

Since the Coleman Report in 1966, a benchmark study of education in the United States, there has been a blizzard of studies estimating educational production functions. Some 147 such studies were reviewed in a major survey article by Hanushek (1986). Hanushek's initial finding is that "teachers and schools differ dramatically in their effectiveness." That being said, however, he provides an overview of the specific characteristics of teachers and schools that have been thought to be important in producing student attainment. Further, he reports on a comprehensive review of the studies that have estimated educational production functions. Although the specific measures used differ from study to study, each measures student achievement in some way as the output of the schooling production function. The studies all attempt to explain student achievement as a function of the quantities of inputs used in the production process.

Studies of the economics of schooling can attempt to estimate the production function either directly or indirectly by estimating the cost function. If the cost approach is used, the study examines the various determinants of the total cost of schooling. The largest cost is that for instructional expenditures, which makes up the lion's share of school expenditures—about two-thirds of total expenditures. The other one-third of school expenditures goes to operational expenses such as utilities (electric and heating) and custodial expenses. Instructional expenditures are determined primarily by teacher salaries and school district average class size. Salaries in turn depend primarily on the educational attainment of the teachers and years of teaching experience. As a result, the fundamental factors affecting school district expenditure are teacher experience, teacher educational attainment, and average class size. Studies then analyze the effect of such expenditures on student achievement. Performance on standardized tests such as the Iowa Basic Skills Test, the California Achievement Test, graduation rates, or other measures of educational outcomes are typically used.

Table 8.1 provides Hanushek's summary of the results of 147 studies of educational production functions. The table lists five important inputs thought to have a positive effect on student achievement: teacher-pupil ratio, teacher educational attainment, teacher experience, teacher salary, and school expenditures per pupil. Hanushek tabulated the sign and statistical

TABLE 8.1 Summary of Estimated Expenditure Parameter Coefficients from 147 Studies of Educational Production Functions

		Statistically Significant		Statistically Insignificant			
	Number of Studies	Positive	Negative	Total	Positive	Negative	Unknown Sign
Teacher/pupil ratio	112	9	14	89	25	43	21
Teacher education	106	6	5	95	26	32	37
Teacher experience	109	33	7	69	32	22	15
Teacher salary	60	9	1	50	15	11	24
Expenditures per pupil	65	13	3	49	25	13	11

Source: From "The Economics of Schooling" by Eric A. Hanushek in *Journal of Economic Literature,* 24, No. 3 (Sep. 1986): 1161. Reprinted by permission of American Economic Association.

significance of these factors in the studies he surveyed. The sign of the estimated relationship should be understood as a partial effect of that input on student achievement, holding constant family background and other inputs.

Consider first the teacher-pupil ratio input in the production function of schools. We expect that the higher the teacher-pupil ratio, the greater the educational attainment that should be achieved. Teachers are important inputs in the educational process, and the more teachers per pupil in a school, the greater the personal attention students receive. Hence, we would expect a positive and significant relationship between the teacher-pupil ratio and student performance. The effect of teacher-pupil ratio was tested in 112 of the 147 studies Hanushek analyzed. Among those 112 studies just 9 found the expected positive and statistically significant effect. It is disturbing that so few studies found a significant relationship between the teacher-pupil ratio and student performance. Even more disturbing, a greater number of studies, 14, found a negative and significant relationship, indicating that the higher the teacher-pupil ratio, the lower the student performance. This is disturbing because the obvious policy implication is that teachers not only do not aid in educating students, they actually seem to deter student learning. Overall, however, these 112 studies provide very weak evidence that the teacher-pupil ratio has any effect whatsoever. A total of 89 studies found that the teacher-pupil ratio is statistically insignificant; this means that one cannot reject the hypothesis that there is no effect whatever. Thus, the vast majority of studies indicates that the teacher-pupil ratio has no effect on student achievement.

The second educational input examined in Hanushek's survey is the education level of teachers. One hundred six studies include this input in their estimation of the educational production function. We would expect that more-educated teachers would be more effective in teaching students, resulting in a positive relationship between teacher education and educational achievement. Of those 106 studies that include teacher education in the production function, 11 found the variable to be significant. Six studies found a positive relationship as expected; the other 5 studies, however, found the relationship to be an inverse relationship where higher teacher education was associated with lower student achievement. The remaining 95 studies found no relationship at all between teacher education and student achievement.

Similarly, we would expect that teacher experience would be positively related to educational output. More experienced teachers should be more effective in teaching. Of the 109 studies that included teacher experience in the educational production function, 33 found a positive and significant relationship, as expected. Just 7 studies found a negative and significant relationship. The other 69 studies found no relationship between teacher experience and educational output. Although the majority of studies indicated there is no relationship, this input provides the strongest evidence, among very weak evidence in general, of a relationship between an input and student achievement.

Teacher salary is expected to be directly related to educational achievement. The higher the salaries of teachers, the better their quality and the more effective they are expected to be as educational inputs. Teacher salary was included as an input variable in 60 of the production function studies surveyed by Hanushek. In 10 cases it was found to have a statistically significant effect on educational output. Nine of those studies reported the expected positive effect and the remaining study reported a negative effect. The other 50 studies indicated that there is no relationship between teacher salaries and educational output. Most studies indicate that teacher salary has no effect on student achievement.

Finally, expenditures per pupil are expected to be positively related to educational achievement as well. The more a school spends on educating students, the more educational achievement is expected. This variable was included in 65 studies surveyed by Hanushek. Thirteen studies reported the expected positive and significant relationship that indicates a positive and significant relationship between expenditures and educational output, and three cases reported the opposite. In the remaining 49 studies, there is no relationship found between expenditures per pupil and student achievement. Most studies indicate that expenditures per pupil have no effect on student achievement.

Hanushek cautions that without systematic tabulation of these results, it would be tempting to conclude that the results are inconsistent. He indicates that there *is* a consistency to the results: "There appears to be no strong or systematic relationship between school expenditures and student performance." His policy analysis indicates clearly that there is no predictable relationship between measured inputs and outputs. Hanushek concludes that "the expenditure parameters are unrelated to student performance." Looking back at the accumulated evidence, Hanushek (2008) concludes that, "The existing research suggests inefficiency in the provision of schooling. It does not indicate that schools do not matter. Nor does it indicate that money and resources never impact achievement. The accumulated research surrounding estimation of education production functions simply says there currently is not clear, systematic relationship between resources and student outcomes."

Production of Police Protection

In order to see the application of these economic principles in the production of a specific public service, consider the case of public safety. Gyapong and Gyimah-Brempong (1988) studied the production functions of 130 Michigan police departments serving cities of 5,000 population or more during the years 1984 and 1985.[2] Seven distinct measures of output were examined in their study: arrests for robbery, burglary, larceny, motor vehicle theft, arson, personal crimes (murder, negligent manslaughter, rape, and aggravated assault), and a nonarrest measure of police department efforts in directing traffic, investigating accidents, providing emergency first aid, and attending to domestic arguments. Inputs in the production of police department services included police officers, civilian employment, and capital equipment. Police accounted for 79.84 percent of the cost of output on average, civilian employment accounted for 6.6 percent, and capital equipment accounted for 13.56 percent.

TABLE 8.2 Elasticity of Substitution Estimates for Inputs Used in Producing Police Services

	Police	Civilian Employees	Capital Equipment
Police	−0.1149	0.9032	0.2368
	(0.0298)	(0.0427)	(0.1693)
Civilian employees		−6.9984	−1.9609
		(5.0371)	(2.4961)
Capital equipment			−0.1591
			(1.5454)

Source: From "Factor Substitution, Price Elasticity of Factor Demand and Returns to Scale in Policy Production" by Anthony O. Gyapong and KwabenaGyimah-Brempong in *Southern Economic Journal* 54, No. 4, April 1988: 873–874. Reprinted by permission of Southern Economic Association.

The diagonal elements of Table 8.2 report the substitution elasticities for the factors of production used to produce police services. These elasticities are negative, as we would expect, reflecting the fact that as the price of an input rises, less of it is used.[3] Notice, however, that the elasticities are less than 1 for police and capital equipment, indicating a relatively unresponsive demand for those inputs, whereas the elasticity for civilian employees is much larger than 1, indicating a very responsive demand. Apparently, policy departments are far more sensitive to changes in the price of civilian services than to changes in the prices of police services or capital equipment. Off-diagonal elements in Table 8.2 are the elasticities of substitution for pairs of inputs used in producing public safety services. The first elasticity of substitution to consider is that between police and civilian employees. That estimated elasticity is 0.9032, indicating a relatively high degree of substitutability between police and civilian employees in public safety departments. An elasticity near 1 indicates a nearly proportional response on the part of the police department. In this case, a 10 percent change in the relative price leads to a 9 percent change in the ratio of inputs used. Recall that an elasticity of substitution of 1 would indicate perfect substitutability.[4] As a result, we know that the isoquants for police and civilians are very gently sloping curves, concave to the origin. It is relatively easy to substitute civilians for police in public safety departments and produce the same level of protection services.

The second elasticity of substitution to consider is that between police and capital equipment. That elasticity is 0.2368, a positive number, indicating that these inputs are substitutes. Police manpower can be replaced by capital equipment to some extent. Computers and electronic surveillance equipment reduce the need for police officers' time to a rather substantial degree. Finally, consider the elasticity of substitution between civilian employees and capital equipment. The estimated elasticity is −1.9609, a negative number, indicating that these inputs are complements. Civilian employees operate computers,

AP Photo/Carlos Osorio

A Flint, Michigan, officer uses capital equipment in producing police services.

word processors, and communications equipment. It is logical that civilian employees and capital equipment would be complements. It would be tempting to say they are strong complements because the estimated elasticity is apparently so large, far exceeding 1 in absolute value. Take care in interpreting that estimated coefficient, however. Notice that the estimated standard error is 2.4961, which is larger than the estimated elasticity, indicating that this elasticity is not estimated with sufficient precision to make such an inference.[5]

Own- and **cross-price elasticities** were also estimated for input demands in this study, with the results reported in Table 8.3. Notice that the price elasticities of demand for all three inputs (the diagonal elements) are relatively inelastic. Most of the cross-price elasticities are small, near zero, indicating that the demand for each factor is relatively insensitive to changes in the price of other factors. For example, the cross-price elasticity of demand for capital and police is 0.0321, indicating that when the price of police rises by 1 percent, the demand for capital equipment used in the production of safety services rises by 0.0321 percent, a very weak degree of substitutability.[6] An economic implication of those inelasticities is that despite the input substitution possibilities, total expenditures on providing police services are likely to rise at a faster rate than the demand for law enforcement.

TABLE 8.3 Own- and Cross-Price Elasticities of Input Demand for Police Services

	Police	Civilian Employees	Capital Equipment
Police	−0.0917	0.7211	0.1891
	(0.0230)	(0.0001)	(0.0229)
Civilian employees	0.0596	−0.4548	−0.1295
	(0.0343)	(0.3326)	(0.3384)
Capital equipment	0.0321	−0.2658	−0.0216
	(0.1352)	(0.1652)	(0.2101)

Source: From "Factor Substitution, Price Elasticity of Factor Demand and Returns to Scale in Policy Production" by Anthony O. Gyapong and Kwabena Gyimah-Brempong in *Southern Economic Journal* 54, No. 4, April 1988, pp. 873–874.

This study also tested for the presence of economies of scale and scope in the production of police services. The safety services they examined included robbery, burglary, larceny, motor vehicle theft, arson, and personal crime. They found no evidence of economies of scale in the provision of police services. That implies a relatively flat long-run average cost curve for police services. Police departments can be scaled up or down in size and the average cost of providing police services stays the same. This implies that there is no economic reason to consolidate police departments in two small adjacent cities in hopes of reducing the cost of providing police services. Two small departments will have the same costs as one large department of twice the size.

The study did find significant economies of scope, however. Economies of scope exist when combining production of similar outputs reduces the per-unit cost of production. The hypothesis of no economies of scope can be rejected in only 5 of the 21 pairwise cases. The presence of economies of scope indicates that consolidating public safety functions can result in large cost savings. Joint production of these various outputs will reduce the cost of production. The policy implication is that public safety departments should be configured in such a way as to coordinate all of the efforts to reduce crime, rather than being split apart in specialized crime-fighting units.

This type of economic analysis is valuable in providing the public safety department a very clear set of implications for how it should use its inputs to produce public safety and how it can organize itself. Without such analysis, public agencies have no clear idea how best to produce their public service.

PRICING OF PUBLIC GOODS AND SERVICES

Governments produce public goods and services and deliver them to their constituents, but how should these goods and services be priced? If they were private goods and services, we would hope that the markets in which they were provided were competitive, yielding price equal to marginal cost. That is our ideal concept of the best price. User fees are an increasingly important source of revenue for governments; hence, it is essential that they get the prices of their services right.

Marginal Cost Pricing

Economic theory assures us that the best pricing policy in a competitive market environment is to set the price equal to the **marginal cost,** called **marginal cost pricing.** At that price, we expect to obtain the efficient level of output. Where possible, it is wise for public agencies to price their products at marginal cost. Consider the example of a public university that provides education in two distinct programs, one in the music department and one in the history department. Suppose that the demand for the services of the two departments is identical, as illustrated in Figure 8.7, but the marginal cost of providing education in the two departments is quite different. The marginal cost of educating students in the music program is relatively high due to the need for one-on-one lesson time for music students with their professors. In contrast, the history students can effectively learn their discipline in large classes with little personal attention from the professors, resulting in a relatively low marginal cost of educating those students.

If the university were to use marginal cost pricing, the price of tuition would be high in the music department and low in the history department: $p_m > p_h$. This pricing scheme would allocate scarce resources optimally, resulting in small enrollments in the music department where costs are high and large enrollments in the history department where costs are low. In this case, the price would accurately signal scarcity and provide the optimal allocation of resources. If the university were to charge a common tuition rate for all students, regardless of major, the resulting allocation of resources

FIGURE 8.7 Marginal Cost Pricing at the University

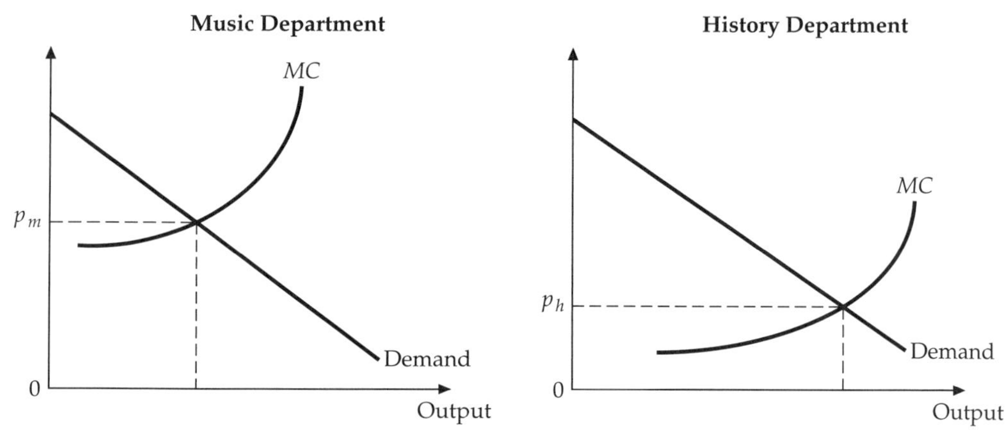

would be inefficient. A price below p_m would encourage too many students to major in music. A price above p_h would encourage too few students to major in history. A misallocation of resources would result from improper prices being charged. The music department would be too large and the history department would be too small.

In the public sector, however, we are often confronted with situations where marginal cost pricing simply will not work. We need to examine those cases and consider modified pricing rules that can be used by governments. Consider first the case of a public transit authority that produces transportation under conditions of increasing returns to scale. The implication of increasing returns to scale is that the long-run average cost curve, *LRAC,* is falling as output increases, as discussed previously, as illustrated in Figure 8.8. For simplicity, we have assumed a perfectly elastic demand giving us a horizontal demand curve. Under this circumstance the demand curve is not only horizontal but the price is equal to the marginal revenue *MR*, which is also identical to the average revenue *AR*. If the transit authority prices its fare equal to the marginal cost of producing a trip for a passenger, $p = MC$, it will generate revenue equal to the area $0q_1ab$. The total cost of producing those q_1 rides is the area $0q_1dc$. Thus, the transit authority will find itself in the situation where its revenues fall short of its costs, resulting in a deficit of *abcd*. In this case, marginal cost pricing with $p = MC$ results in a deficit, presenting the transit authority with a difficult situation. It will not be able to be economically viable in the long run with such a pricing policy. Here is a case where the usual efficiency rule from a perfectly competitive setting simply will not work. The city may decide that the transit system is so important that it will subsidize its operation and cover the deficit with a subsidy from its general fund. Those funds must come from some other source supported by general tax revenues paid by all taxpayers, not just the users of the transit system.

FIGURE 8.8 Marginal Cost Pricing Results in a Deficit When There Are Increasing Returns to Scale

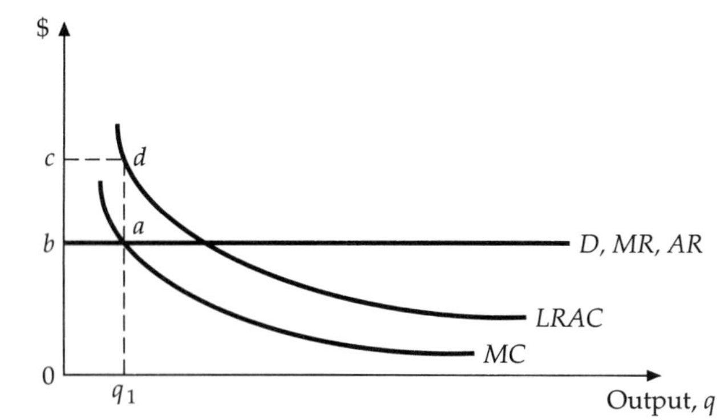

The problem is that marginal cost pricing is incompatible with a situation where the public good being provided is subject to increasing returns to scale. The fact that there are increasing returns to scale is not a problem. After all, we should appreciate the fact that average cost is falling, making transit rides less and less expensive as more and more rides are provided. The problem is that marginal cost pricing is not compatible with this situation. We must find an alternative pricing scheme. One viable alternative is a two-part pricing mechanism: the two-part tariff.

Two-Part Tariffs

With a two-part pricing scheme, we can achieve the efficient result without requiring a subsidy from the government. Transit riders will be asked to pay two fees. First, a subscription fee equal to one rider's share of the deficit *abcd* must be charged in order for the transit authority to cover the deficit. Second, a variable fee per ride on the system must be charged where the fee is equal to the marginal cost of production. This type of financing mechanism is called a **two-part tariff.** Users are required to pay a fixed fee for the privilege of using the facility plus a variable fee based on the extent of use. Two-part tariffs are used either to fund publicly provided services that involve high fixed costs, as indicated above, or as a way to price discriminate, charging different prices of customers with distinctly different elasticities of demand.

Although this kind of pricing scheme may seem a bit peculiar, reflect for a moment on a number of contexts in which you have seen just such a scheme applied. When you join a health club or racquet club, you pay a membership fee and then pay a court fee per use of the facilities. Country clubs work the same way. Even an amusement park applies a two-part pricing scheme where you pay an entry fee and then pay additional fees for each ride you take. This pricing mechanism is often applied to a public good subject to congestion. The variable fee allocates use of the facility in order to reduce congestion.

In the context of a transit system, this pricing mechanism could be applied in such a way that passengers are required to pay a price $p = a+bq$, where a is the flat fee charged each rider for the privilege of using the transit system that is designed to cover the deficit and b is a marginal cost fee charged for each of the q rides the passenger takes. This type of pricing scheme is easily implemented by selling the passenger a card good for a specified number of rides that includes the flat fee a, plus the variable fee of b times the number of rides q. The passenger's card is magnetically coded to provide the q rides for which the passenger has paid. In this way, the marginal cost pricing gives the efficiency result we want, $p=MC$, with price equal to the marginal cost of providing the trip combined with the flat fee that helps cover the deficit associated with marginal cost pricing.

Two-part tariffs are used in a wide variety of public finance contexts. Perhaps the most common situation is that of a public utility providing electric power or other form of power. Customers are typically charged a flat monthly fee plus a fee per unit of power used. Meters effectively measure the quantity of power used and a charge per kilowatt-hour is added to the flat monthly fee. Large industrial users of power are charged lower fees per kilowatt-hour, reflecting the declining *LRAC*. This pricing mechanism is also often used by municipal water and sewer departments.

User Fees

For public goods that have well-defined benefits flowing to the user, governments are increasingly relying on **user fees** to finance the provision of the good or service. A user fee is a specific fee charged of the user of a public good or service. Rather than rely on general tax revenues to fund the provision of this public good or service, the government charges only those who directly use the good or service. This approach is based on the **benefits-received principle,** which holds that those who receive the benefits of a publicly provided good or service should be the ones to pay for that good or service.

Consider the example of public highways. It is reasonable to expect that trucking companies using the interstate highway system extensively should pay fees for the use of those roads. The gasoline excise tax approximates a user fee in that it requires payment in proportion to the number of miles driven. The more you drive, the more gasoline you use, the more you pay to maintain the roads. The same principle may be applied to any number of services provided by state and local governments.

Tolls

One particular form of user fee often used by governments for the use of specific facilities is the **toll.** A toll is a user fee that is required per use of a public facility such as a highway, bridge, or ferry. Congestion is a problem on many highways, bridges, and other forms of networks. Tolls have a potential role to play in relieving congestion. Consider the problem of a public facility, say, a bridge crossing a major body of water, with the cost curves illustrated in Figure 8.9.

Suppose that T is the number of vehicles entering the bridge per hour and the average cost $AC(T)$ is the cost per vehicle per mile of travel from entry point on the bridge to exit point from the bridge.[7] The average cost is constant up to T_1 trips per hour, which is the design capacity of the bridge. When the number of trips per hour exceeds T_1, the average cost per trip rises sharply. Of course, when the average cost is rising, we know that the marginal cost is above the average cost. The marginal cost $MC(T)$ represents the increase in travel cost to all travelers due to an increase in the number of drivers on the bridge. This is an external diseconomy, or a marginal damage as we called it in Chapter 4. When the number of drivers on the bridge exceeds the design capacity T_1, the speed of each driver falls and the average cost per trip rises. All drivers on the bridge must go slower; hence the addition of another driver past T_1 imposes increased costs on all drivers. The marginal cost of the Tth

FIGURE 8.9 Congestion Toll Application

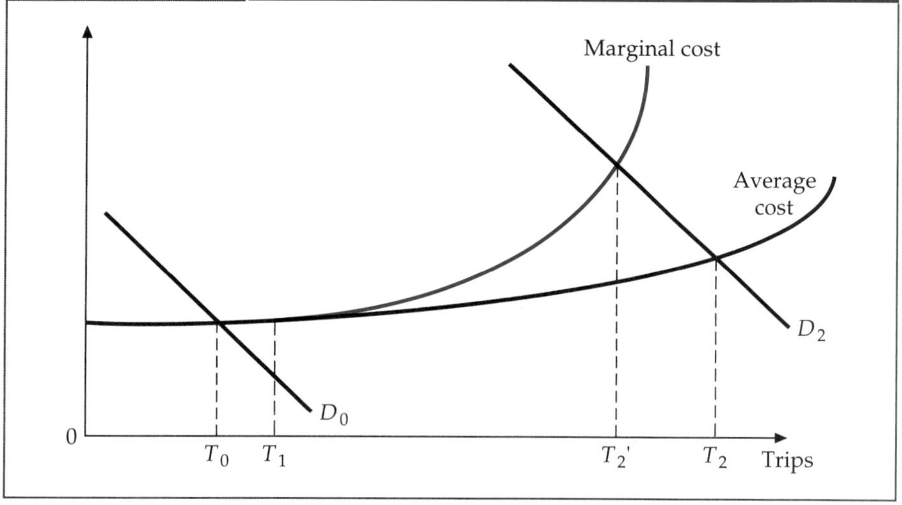

trip is the increase in the total cost with an increase in the number of trips. The increase in **total cost** (*TC*) is the average cost of that trip plus the increase in the average cost for all the other drivers times the number of drivers on the bridge. As the number of drivers on the bridge increases, the external diseconomies (marginal damages) grow and the vertical distance between marginal and average costs grow.

The marginal private cost curve captures the cost to a particular driver of operating her car to cross the bridge. That includes the gasoline, depreciation, time, and other private costs to her. When there are a lot of people trying to cross the bridge at rush hour, however, each person's presence imposes time costs on everyone else. A social cost exceeds the private cost. The marginal social cost curve captures the time costs of congestion in addition to the private costs. For any given number of trips across the bridge, the vertical distance between the two curves represents the marginal damage in the form of congestion costs.

At a low level of demand such as D_0 during an off-peak time, there is no congestion and there is no difference between marginal cost and average cost. Drivers demand T_0 trips. At a higher level of demand for crossing the bridge during rush hour traffic, represented by the demand curve D_2, the marginal social cost is well above the average cost because additional trips have associated with them congestion costs imposed on others. Drivers demand T_2 trips as they consider the average cost of a trip. Each individual driver perceives that the trip has a cost of $AC(T_2)$, but the true cost, taking into account the congestion costs imposed on others, is $MC(T_2)$. The private decisions of drivers will result in T_2 trips demanded, when the socially optimal number of trips is T_2'.

A congestion toll can be used to solve this problem. During rush hour when the demand for trips across the bridge is D_2, a toll t can be charged, where $t = MC(T_2') - AC(T_2')$. Requiring each driver to pay this toll increases the driver's perceived cost of a trip across the bridge, raising the average cost curve and internalizing the externality. When faced with the toll, drivers demand fewer trips, T_2', thus reducing congestion. With the toll we get the efficient number of trips.

This example is illustrative of a broad range of situations in the public sector where we have a **peak-load problem.** During off-peak times, the demand curve is to the left and there is no congestion problem. But during peak demand times, the demand curve is far to the right and there is substantial congestion. In order to eliminate congestion, we would have to expand the design capacity of the public facility to meet the peak demand. That would be very expensive, especially because the peak demand is only present during a portion of the day. We could save a great deal of expense if we could redistribute demand from peak times to off-peak times, eliminating congestion at no cost. One way of doing that is with **time-of-day pricing.** Under this pricing scheme, the tolls vary with the time of day depending on demand. Consider a simple example of time-of-day pricing for a public facility—parking meters along the street. In most cities that have parking meters for on-street parking, a fee is charged per minute of parking. A quarter may buy you 15 minutes of parking, for example. The meters are often only enforced during weekday business hours, however. The off-peak price is zero for evenings and weekends. Another example of time-of-day pricing is the fare charged on the Washington, D.C., metro system, which varies with time of day. During peak commuting hours, the fares are higher than during off-peak times.

Extending this principle to other units of time besides the day, we can think of examples of time-of-year pricing, or **seasonal pricing,** of public goods and services. Public electric utilities usually charge higher prices per kilowatt-hour during the summer when there is peak electricity demand for air conditioning.

Limiting Government Monopoly Behavior

Increasing returns to scale in the provision of public utilities and other services have traditionally led governments to grant monopoly rights to a single provider of the service in order to take advantage of the declining average cost. Two problems exist with monopolistic provision of a good or service, however. The monopoly provides too little of the good at too high a price. Where economies of scale dictate that a natural monopoly exists, governments often grant the monopoly rights to a single producer of the good or service but then also regulate the behavior of the monopolist to eliminate one or both of the problems inherent in monopoly provision. For example, the state government may grant monopoly rights to a power company to operate in a region of the state, providing electric power to both residential and commercial users. To prevent the utility from implementing a monopoly pricing scheme for electricity, however, the state regulates the utility through its **Public Service Commission (PSC).** The role of the PSC is to regulate prices as well as service quantity and quality. Ultimately, the state wants the advantages of the monopoly's producing electricity at lower average cost per kilowatt-hour, without the disadvantages of the higher price and lower output an unregulated profit-maximizing monopoly would want.

In recent years there has been a movement away from regulated monopolies to **deregulation.** Federal, state, and local governments have all been active in removing regulations in industries such as airlines, trucking, electric power, and telecommunications.

Price Discrimination

Another problem that arises when monopolies are created by governments for the provision of public goods and services is the tendency of the monopolist to price discriminate. It is natural for a monopolistic firm to want to engage in **price discrimination** where it charges high prices to customers with low elasticity of demand and low prices to customers with high elasticity of demand. Doing so maximizes revenue. The monopolist will attempt to identify segments of the market that have distinctly different elasticities of demand. It will then design its price mechanism so that it charges a higher price to the submarket with the less elastic demand. In fact, this tendency is so strong that government monopolies may be tempted to price their services in just the same way.

State attorneys general and public service commissions are often on guard, watching for evidence of price discrimination among regulated utilities and other government-sanctioned monopolies. Finding evidence of such pricing, the attorney general or the PSC will often prosecute the offending monopoly in order to end price discrimination.

POLICY STUDY

Central London Congestion Charge

Department for Transport

A congestion toll can be an effective way to reduce traffic congestion in a central city. Figure 8.9 illustrated that effectiveness. You might ask, "Has any city actually done this?" The answer to that question is a definite "yes," with London being the more relevant recent case. London implemented its congestion toll in 2003 and the result has been a substantial reduction in congestion.

Drivers of vehicles that park on public roads within the Congestion Charging Zone between 7:00 am and 6:00 pm on weekdays in central London are subject to a congestion toll. If you pay the toll on or before the date you travel to London, the toll is 8 pounds. If you pay before midnight the following day, the charge is 10 pounds. If you do not pay the toll appropriately, there is a penalty charge of 120 pounds that is sent to the Registered Keeper of the vehicle. That charge is reduced to 60 pounds if paid within 14 days.

They make it easy for drivers. You do not need to buy a ticket to enter the congestion zone; there are no toll booths or barriers either. They just take your picture. Cameras are mounted at entrances to the congestion zone and they read your license plate. Computers check whether you have already paid the toll, or whether your car is exempt from the toll. In case of a match, the picture of your license plate is automatically deleted from the database. If not, you get a penalty charge notice.

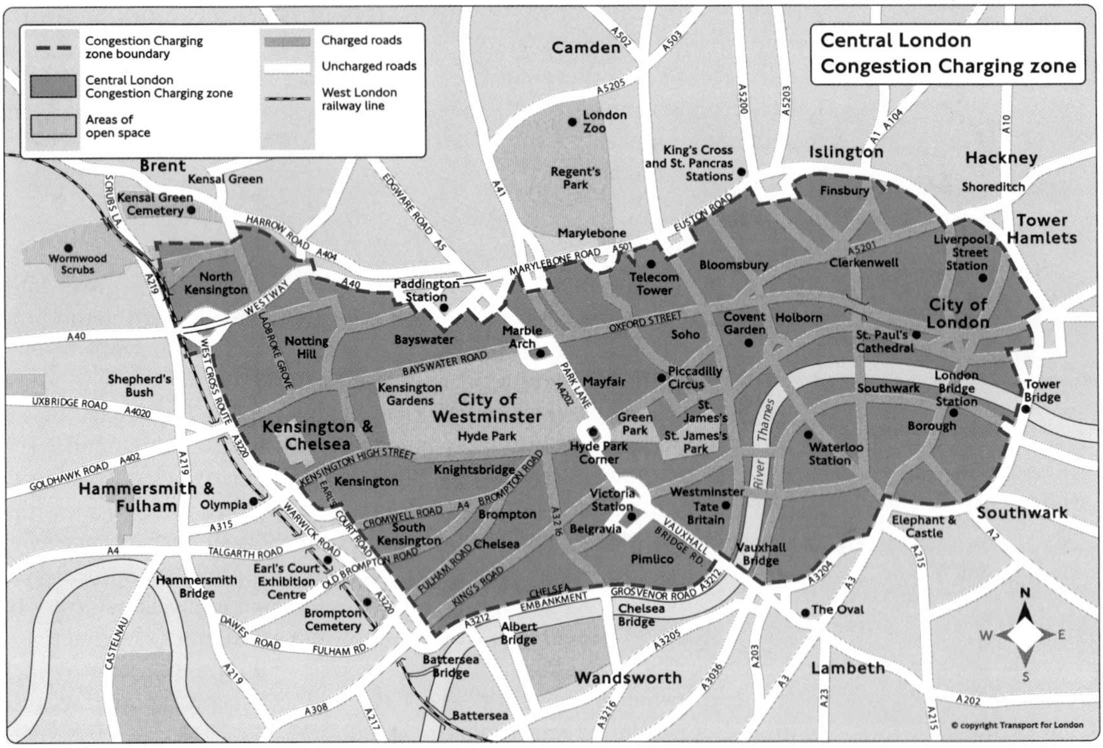

Map © Transport for London

Since London introduced its congestion toll in 2003, a number of other large cities have considered a similar charge to reduce central city congestion. For example, Mayor Bloomberg of New York City proposed such a charge in 2008 for traffic entering the congested island of Manhattan, but found that there was not sufficient political support to make it feasible. For more on the implications of London's toll for other cities, see Litman (2006).

Discounts and exemptions are provided for certain types of drivers and vehicles. The following is a list of exemptions and discounts.

- Residents
    - Residents living within the congestion zone have a 90 percent discount
    - Registration is required
- Blue badge holders
    - Individuals and institutions in the European Economic Area holding a valid Blue Badge may receive a 100 percent discount
    - Registration is required
- Accredited breakdown
- Vehicles
    - Alternative fuel vehicles
    - Electronically propelled vehicles
    - Vehicles with 9 or more seats

- Motor tricycles
- Roadside recovery vehicles

Source: Information on the Central London Congestion Charge can be found at: http://www.tfl.gov.uk/roadusers/congestioncharging/6733.aspx.

POLICY STUDY

Economies of Scale in Health Insurance Coverage

Health care reform has been a major policy issue for the past several years. Debate has raged over whether to change the current U.S. system whereby most people receive health insurance coverage through their employers, rather than buying coverage directly as individuals. This distinction lies at the heart of plans to reform the health care system. Should we consider switching coverage from employer-provided coverage to individual or government coverage? The policy issue to consider is why employer-based health care plans have become the standard. The answer lies, in part, in the fact that there are significant economies of scale involved in providing insurance on this basis, and that leads to much lower per-unit cost.

One advantage of employer-based plans is that they permit workers to buy health insurance coverage as a group, rather than as individuals. Group coverage provides significant savings in the cost of administration of the plan. Table 8.4 demonstrates the

TABLE 8.4 Administrative Expenses for Health Insurance Plans, as a Percentage of the Cost of Providing a Benefit

Size of Firm (Employees)	General Administration	Sales Commissions	Claims Administration	Risk and Profit	Premium Taxes	Interest Credit	Total
1 to 4	12.5	8.4	9.3	8.5	2.8	−1.5	40.0
5 to 9	11.2	6.0	8.6	8.0	2.7	−1.5	35.0
10 to 19	9.2	5.0	7.2	7.5	2.6	−1.5	30.0
20 to 49	7.6	3.3	6.3	6.8	2.5	−1.5	25.0
50 to 99	4.8	2.0	4.3	6.0	2.4	−1.5	18.0
100 to 499	4.0	1.6	4.1	5.5	2.3	−1.5	16.0
500 to 2,499	3.2	0.7	3.9	3.5	2.2	−1.5	12.0
2,500 to 9,999	1.4	0.3	3.8	1.8	2.2	−1.5	8.0
10,000 or more	0.7	0.1	3.0	1.1	2.1	−1.5	5.5

Source: U.S. House Committee on Ways and Means 1990, 12.

various sources of cost savings. General administration costs decline from 12.5 percent of the cost of providing a health care benefit for a firm with one to four employees to 0.7 percent for a large firm with more than 10,000 employees. Significant economies of scale are inherent in activities such as billing, advertising, sales commissions, administration of claims, and overhead costs. Sales commissions decline from 8.4 percent of the cost for a small firm to 0.1 percent for a large firm. Claims administration declines from 9.3 percent of the cost for a small firm to 3.0 percent for a large firm. Pooling of risk also reduces the percentage of cost from 8.5 percent for a small firm to 1.1 percent for a large firm.

This study illustrates that there are plainly significant economies of scale in the production of health insurance coverage. As a result, it is important that insurance coverage be available to large groups of people in order to take advantage of the lower costs afforded by economies of scale. Public agencies need to take advantage of this fact and combine employees from various departments and branches of the government to assemble the largest groups possible that can be covered at lowest cost achievable. As a practical matter, that might require city and county employees to be combined under coverage in a city-county employee group, for example.

In the larger context of health insurance coverage in society, whether the best way to provide group coverage is through the employment base or some other form of grouping based on membership in professional organizations or geographic association remains to be considered. Employment-based insurance coverage is only one of many ways to group and assure the cost savings afforded by economies of scale in insurance coverage.

PROBLEMS

1. Set up a diagram like Figure 8.6 and analyze the potential effects of the following:
   a. A reduction in the price of capital used to produce schooling
   b. An increase in the price of labor used to produce schooling
   c. A state law that forces small schools to consolidate with larger school districts
   d. A state law that requires that schools have a pupil-teacher ratio of no more than 20
2. Suppose that you serve on the city council of Larcenyland, a suburban community adjacent to the central city Burglarytown. Individual efforts to fight crime in both cities have been very expensive in the past. Both cities have come to the point where they are desperate to try something new in order to reduce crime. Write a policy proposal for a joint crime-fighting effort of the cities, and support your proposal with evidence of economic advantages based on the work of Gyapong and Gyimah-Brempong (1988) based on the experience of cities in Michigan.

3. Use the information in Table 8.4 to construct a graph of the long-run average cost function for health insurance administration. Assume that a particular benefit costs $1,000 to provide. Use the total percentages in the table to compute the dollar cost of administering that coverage.
   a. Plot the administrative cost of coverage as a function of the number of employees. (Use the midpoints of the first eight cells. For the unbounded cell of 10,000 or more, just plot the cost at 10,000.)
   b. Explain what the graph of administrative costs indicates regarding scale economies.
   c. Suppose that you are a state senator confronted with two policy proposals. Proposal A would shift health insurance coverage from being employment based to being entirely individual. Proposal B would shift coverage to communities with each city of your state providing coverage for its residents. Compare the economic aspects of the two proposals in terms of the costs of administering insurance plans under the two options.
4. The following table provides data on elementary and secondary school enrollment and the number of classroom teachers for each of five years in the United States.

	1960	1965	1970	1975	1980
Enrollment (thousands)	42,181	48,473	51,272	49,791	45,949
Classroom teachers (thousands)	1,600	1,933	2,288	2,451	2,439

Source: Hanushek (1986), 1144.

   a. Plot the five points on the total product curve where the variable input is classroom teachers and the output is enrollment.
   b. Find the point at which the total product is maximum.
   c. Plot the average and marginal product for classroom teachers.
5. Does the university where you study charge the same tuition rate for students in all majors, or does it differentiate tuition according to major? Is there evidence of marginal cost pricing? Even if your university charges the same tuition rate for credit hours, does it charge other special fees of students in particular programs such as laboratory fees or computer fees? Analyze the pricing structure of your university in light of the marginal cost pricing ideal, and explain how the allocation of resources may be improved by more explicit marginal cost pricing.
6. Suppose that the Department of Transportation has advanced a proposal to install scanners along roadsides and IDs on the sides of cars and trucks, much like universal product codes used in grocery and department stores. The scanners would sense the presence of cars and automatically charge the registered owner of the car or truck the appropriate congestion toll when congestion is present. In the absence of congestion, no toll is charged.

a. Use a diagram like Figure 8.9 to explain what congestion toll should be charged.
b. Explain how this proposal solves the problem of congestion.
c. Discuss how you think this proposal would be received by drivers.
d. Anticipate ways that drivers would try to avoid paying the congestion toll (both legal and illegal).

7. For each of the following education production functions, determine the returns to scale:
a. $q = (40)\ l^{.8}k^{.2}$
b. $q = (40)\ l^{.9}k^{.15}$
c. $q = (40)\ l^{.7}k^{.25}$

8. Suppose that the marginal cost of producing a public service is $MC = 100 - 2q$, whereas the average total cost is $ATC = 100 - (3/2)q$.
a. If the optimal quantity of the public service is $q = 20$, compute the MC and the ATC at that quantity.
b. Compute the revenue that would be generated by charging a price equal to marginal cost.
c. Compute the total cost of providing $q = 20$ units of the public service.
d. Compute the deficit that results from marginal cost pricing.

9. The Policy Study on the Central London Congestion Tolls includes a list of discounts and exemptions that are provided for certain types of drivers and vehicles. Analyze whether each of those discounts and exemptions can be justified on the basis of public finance theory.

REFERENCES

Coleman, James S., et al. *Equality of Educational Opportunity*. Washington, DC: U.S. Government Printing Office, 1966.

Gyapong, Anthony O., and Kwabena Gyimah-Brempong. "Factor Substitution, Price Elasticity of Factor Demand and Returns to Scale in Police Production: Evidence from Michigan." *Southern Economic Journal* 54 (1988): 863–78.

Hanushek, Eric A. "The Economics of Schooling." *Journal of Economic Literature* 24 (1986): 1141–77.

Hanushek, Eric A. "Education Production Functions." In S. N. Durlauf and L. E. Blume, editors, *The New Palgrave Dictionary of Economics*, Basingstoke: Palgrave Macmillan, 2008.

Litman, Todd. 2006. "London Congestion Pricing: Implications for Other Cities." Victoria Transport Policy Institute. Paper is available at: http://www.vtpi.org/london.pdf.

Mills, Edwin S., and Bruce W. Hamilton. *Urban Economics*, 4th ed. Glenview, IL: Scott, Foresman, 1989.

U.S. House Committee on Ways and Means, Subcommittee on Health Insurance. *Options for Reform*. September 20, 1990.

NOTES

1. The quantities l_2 and l_3 are called the extensive and intensive margins, respectively. The intensive margin is where the marginal product of the variable input first turns zero, reflecting the fact that beginning at that level of usage, the variable input is used too intensively relative to the fixed input. From this point on there is too much labor being used compared to capital, so much so that the marginal product of labor is negative. The extensive margin is where the average product of the variable input is at its maximum, reflecting the fact that up to that level of usage the variable input is small in comparison to the fixed input that is being used too extensively. Prior to the extensive margin there is so much of the fixed input capital relative to the variable input labor that the marginal product of capital is negative. Quantities of labor less than l_2 or in excess of l_3 are not sensible merely on the basis of the characteristics of production.
2. Two hundred sixty observations were in the authors' data set.
3. The numbers in parentheses below the elasticity estimates are standard errors. In all three cases we can reject the null hypothesis that the own substitution elasticity is zero.
4. In this case, we can reject the hypothesis that the elasticity of substitution is equal to one (take the ratio of 0.9032 − 1.0 divided by the standard error of 0.0427 to obtain a t ratio of 2.27); hence we know that police and civilians are not perfect substitutes. But they are very close substitutes.
5. The null hypothesis that the elasticity of substitution is zero cannot be rejected. To see why, form the ratio of 21.9609 − 0.0 divided by 2.4961 to obtain a t-statistic of − 0.79 which is less than the critical t value of 1.96 for a 5 percent test. Thus, we cannot reject the hypothesis that civilian employees and capital equipment are independent of one another in the production of police services.
6. Table 8.4 includes all of the off-diagonal elements because the model used by the authors permits the cross-price elasticities to be nonsymmetric. That is, the price elasticity of demand for capital with respect to a change in the price of police can differ from the price elasticity of demand for police with respect to a change in the price of capital.
7. This analysis is adapted from Chapter 12 of Mills and Hamilton (1989).

CHAPTER

9

Radius Images/Getty Images

Social Insurance Programs

LEARNING OBJECTIVES

1. Describe the major forms of social programs used by governments around the world.
2. Explain the forms of social insurance programs typically used.
3. Describe and analyze the economics of medical programs.
4. Describe and analyze government programs to deal with disasters.

SOCIAL INSURANCE FRAMEWORK

Social programs provided by governments are most often motivated by a desire to hold citizens harmless from various economic disasters that may befall them. When the private insurance market fails to provide appropriate policies, the federal or state government may step in and provide that coverage. The government is essentially insuring against risks for which the private markets fail to provide coverage. For example, the social security program can be viewed as a form of insurance against low income in retirement, or the Medicaid program is a form of insurance against health risks for those otherwise unable to purchase coverage. In this chapter we examine a number of social programs that provide benefits to citizens in special circumstances where there is a risk of loss and the government provides coverage in the absence of (or in addition to) private coverage.

The first national-scale mandatory social insurance programs were instituted in Germany in the late 1800s and included health insurance, workers' compensation, and pensions for the elderly and invalids. Austria and Hungary followed suit soon thereafter with similar programs. Great Britain first adopted its national health insurance program in 1911 and greatly expanded that program in 1948. Since then, there has been an ever-expanding role of governments in providing social insurance for many of life's risks.

Governments provide many forms of social insurance due to market failure in private insurance markets. The main cause of market failure in these markets is the existence of **private information**, which subverts the ability of an insurance company to provide insurance against risky events. A competitive market outcome requires the existence of perfect information on the part of both buyers and sellers, among other requirements. When the buyer of an insurance contract has more information than the seller of insurance, as is often the case, it is not possible for the insurance company to provide an insurance product. In the absence of insurance, the market fails. Suppose, for example, that as a homeowner you know that your home lies in a flood-prone region, but the insurance company does not have access to that information because the local flood map has not been updated to reflect this reality. In that case, the insurance company will underestimate the likelihood of having to pay for damages and will thereby underprice the insurance policy. In the long-run they cannot provide viable insurance due to the lack of information regarding potential flooding.

If the insured individual is able to change the odds of the insured event occurring, there is *moral hazard* involved, which can cause market failure. Consider the example of automobile insurance. Suppose that drivers begin to take more risks after they obtain auto insurance than they took previously, either by leaving their keys in the unlocked car or by driving more recklessly. Knowing they have insurance that will repair or replace their vehicle if stolen or damaged, the drivers change the odds of theft or accident by their own behavioral change. This form of moral hazard creates a real problem for the insurance company, which based its computation of the necessary premium on the basis of incorrect information regarding the odds of theft or accident. In the extreme case, the insurance company goes bankrupt and the automobile insurance market fails. The same thing could happen in the context of a social security program that provides income to retirees. Knowing that there is social security coverage at retirement, a worker may deliberately save less during his working life, increasing the probability of being poor in retirement and therefore needing to rely more heavily on social security payments. In this case, the market for savings is affected by the moral hazard.

A related private information insurance problem is **adverse selection**. Consider the case of health insurance coverage for a broad population of citizens. Suppose that the federal government requires private insurance companies to provide compressive coverage at a high fixed premium level. In this case many healthy individuals will choose to take no coverage, figuring that their chances of becoming sick and needing the coverage are low and that they can save money by not buying the expensive comprehensive coverage. On the other hand, many unhealthy individuals will take up the coverage, figuring that it is a good deal at the premium rate offered. They know they are very likely to need expensive health coverage. The net effect is adverse selection, with all of the healthy people opting out and all of the sick people opting into the system. Public insurance programs commonly face the problem of adverse selection because they often attempt to proscribe a uniform premium level across individuals with highly varying need for the insurance.

Social programs of many types are largely aimed at helping people cope with life's risks that may leave them in dire circumstances when private insurance markets fail. We can use the analytic framework of decision making under risk as our analytical starting point. Suppose that the situation is

TABLE 9.1 Wealth Affected by Loss-Inducing Circumstance

	State of Nature	
	No loss-inducing event $(1 - p)$	Loss-inducing event (p)
No social insurance	w	$w - d$
Social insurance in place	$w - c$	$w+(b - c)$

described in Table 9.1, with no social insurance in place. Consider a person with wealth w and a probability p that a major problem will occur in the future, with a corresponding probability $1 - p$ of no problem occurring. If the problem occurs the person will suffer damages of d, reducing her wealth to $w - d$. Hence, the expected value of the person's wealth is,

$$E[w] = p(w - d) + (1 - p)w = w - pd. \tag{9.1}$$

Clearly, her expected wealth is less than w by the amount pd reflecting the expected damage. The government may think that it is necessary to protect citizens in such a circumstance against the risk of such an outcome, if no such insurance is available in the private market.

It is also important to consider the expected utility that the citizen would derive from her wealth under both potential states of nature. Graphically, we can represent the situation as illustrated in Figure 9.1. With wealth w, the citizen derives utility $u(w)$, but in case of a loss-inducing event her wealth is diminished to $w - d$, from which she derives utility $u(w - d)$. Because the utility outcome $u(w - d)$ occurs with probability p and the utility outcome $u(w)$ occurs with probability $1 - p$, we can compute her **expected utility** of this risky situation as the probability-weighted mean of the two possible outcomes: $pu(w - d)+(1 - p)u(w)$. This expected utility is shown in the graph as well. If we connect the two possible utility outcomes with a line segment, we can consider the probability of a loss-inducing event occurring. If there is no event, she will be at the right end of the line segment. If an event does occur, she will be at the left endpoint of the line segment. Because there is a probability p of an event and a corresponding probability $1 - p$ of no event, the odds of an event, denoted $\frac{p}{(1-p)}$, indicates the point along that line segment where she expects to land. Her expected utility of the risky situation is read as the utility level corresponding to the point along that line segment reflecting the odds of an event.

Recall from our discussion in Chapter 7 that a concave utility function like the one drawn in Figure 9.1 reflects risk aversion on the part of the citizen whose preferences are drawn.[1] A risk-averse person is willing to pay for insurance. There are risk-loving citizens whose utility function would be drawn in a convex manner. In general, however, we are concerned with the risk-averse situation as it describes the aggregate preferences of society.

FIGURE 9.1 Value of Social Insurance to a Risk-Averse Society

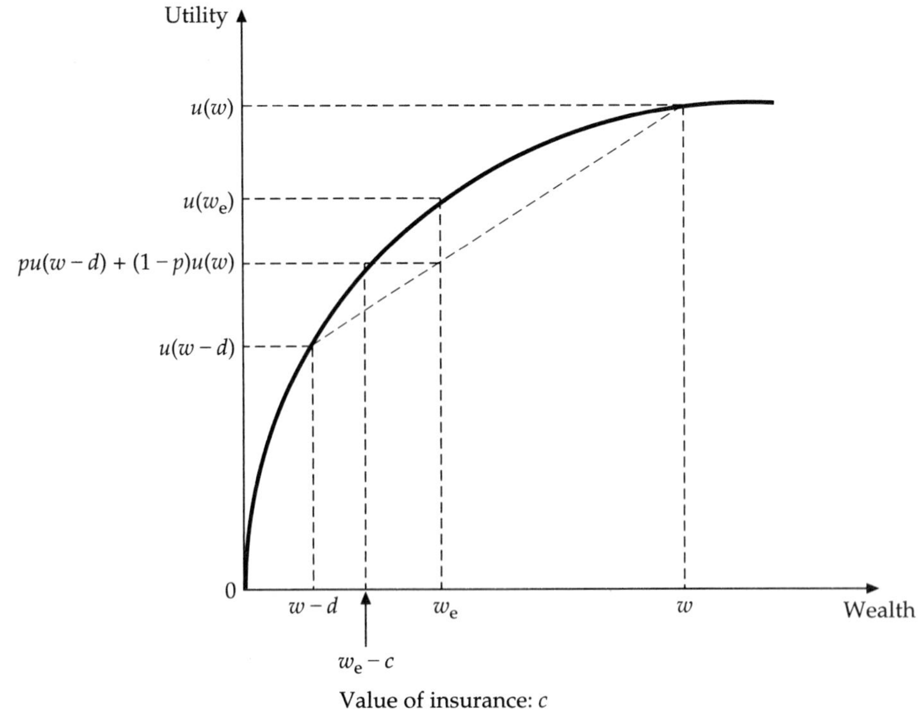

Certainty Equivalents and Insurance Premia

The citizen would like to rid herself of the risk associated with this situation. How does the graph reveal this preference? Notice that the utility of a *certain* wealth equals $w_e = p(w-d)+(1-p)w$, the expected wealth given the probability of a problem, is above the expected utility of the uncertain situation $pu(w-d)+(1-p)u(w)$. Hence, she is better off with certain wealth w_e than with a risky situation with the same expected outcome. How much would our citizen be willing to pay for social insurance? Well, a certain wealth level of $w_e - c$ would leave us just as well off as the uncertain case with wealth w_e, so c is the maximum amount she would be willing to pay for insurance against the loss-inducing event. The quantity of wealth $w_e - c$ is the *certainty equivalent* of the risky expected wealth w_e. Using the certainty equivalent we also know that the amount c is what the person would be willing to pay for insurance. If this characterizes social preferences, not just individual preferences, then we know that social insurance is valued and therefore justified.

SOCIAL SECURITY PROGRAMS

Rationales for Social Security Systems in General

Why would a country decide to implement a social security system? The usual rationale for government intervention, as we saw in Chapter 1, is the existence of externalities or market failure. In this case, it is both the traditional insurance problem of asymmetric information and the lack of a market for real (inflation-adjusted) annuities that are the primary motivations for government intervention. The traditional insurance problem is caused by asymmetric information between the insurer and the insured: the insurer knows much less about the insured than the insured knows about herself. For example, a car insurance company knows very little about a driver's ability and driving habits, whereas the driver knows those attributes intimately. The challenge for the insurance company is to use readily available public information, such as the driver's address, age, and history of moving violations, in order to assess the risk of accidents and provide a policy on which it can expect to earn a profit. Also, the lack of a market for real annuities presents a serious problem. After all, if people could insure against the risk of job loss or poverty in old age by buying a real annuity in the private market there would be no need for a social security system.

Feldstein and Liebman (2002) list the three possible rationales for the existing U.S. Social Security system as: (1) paternalism on the part of the government due to an individual's life-cycle myopia (nearsightedness), (2) avoidance of counterproductive gaming of the welfare system by the elderly, and (3) desire to redistribute income among individuals on the basis of their lifetime income rather than simply their annual income (which the personal income tax system does). The first of these rationales is a condescending attitude that the government knows better what the citizen needs than he knows himself. Being like a benevolent father, the government sees into the future with clarity, whereas the citizen is nearsighted and improperly discounts the future more heavily than is appropriate, excessively preferring immediate gratification to deferred gratification. Therefore, the government must step in to assure that there will be future income for the individual because he will not provide that for himself via saving. The second rationale recognizes that a citizen may purposely spend down her assets early in life in order to qualify for welfare benefits in the future, gaming the system which requires the government to spend more on welfare benefits than should be required.[2] Finally, there may be a rationale for a social security system if the desired amount of wealth transfer from the rich to the poor is not accomplished by the annual progressive income tax system. Taking a lifetime income view rather than an annual income view, there may be a role for a social security system to reallocate wealth in addition to the reallocation accomplished by the income tax system. Whether these rationales are sufficient to justify implementation of a social security system and a particular level of social security benefits is the stuff of lively current debate both in the United States and many other countries around the world.

Social Security in the United States

In 1935 President Franklin Delano Roosevelt signed the Social Security Act and had this to say about the fundamental purpose of the program:

> We can never insure one hundred percent of the population against one hundred percent of the hazards and vicissitudes of life, but we have tried to frame a law which will give some measure of protection to the average citizen and to his family against the loss of a job and against poverty-ridden old age.

The original system created in 1935 was designed to help workers prepare for retirement with specific features intended to assist retired workers with low incomes. In terms of risk mitigation, the system was designed to reduce the risks of both job loss before retirement and poverty in old age.[3]

In crafting a system to accomplish these goals, creators had to balance a desire to provide high enough benefits for retirees with the need to distribute benefits in proportion to the contributions made by those workers. In this regard there is a fundamental policy trade-off underlying the social security system between adequacy and equity. Low-income workers receive benefits that exceed their payments into the system, but at the same time, higher-income workers receive greater benefits than lower-income workers. An element of redistribution exists in the system. It is not simply a private retirement fund where each worker receives benefits based on her own contributions plus interest earned on those contributions over the years.

A helpful way to think about pension programs in general is to classify various programs based on two key characteristics: whether the plan has a defined contribution or benefit, and whether the program is funded or pay-as-you-go (PAYGO). Table 9.2 illustrates the four possibilities and suggests examples of each type of system. A funded **defined-contribution** pension plan is typically one where a company's employees have individual retirement accounts into which the employee and/or his employer make regular contributions. The retirement plan specifies the maximum amount that can be contributed to the account and the matching rate at which the employer may also make contributions. Upon retirement from the company the individual makes withdrawals or receives an **annuity** based on the value of the accumulated assets and the return on those assets in the individual's account. An annuity is simply a regular stream of payments over a fixed period of time. As noted in Table 9.2, Argentina, Australia, Chile, and Mexico also use this type of system for their national social security programs.

If the funded pension system has a **defined benefit** rather than a defined contribution, the company accumulates assets in their pension fund and the plan defines specified benefits that retirees obtain. Those benefits typically reflect the number of years the employee has been with the company and the employee's earnings prior to retirement. The benefits proscribed by the plan are independent of the value of the pension fund assets and the company is

TABLE 9.2 A Taxonomy of Pension Systems

	Funded, Based on Accumulated Assets	Unfunded, Pay-As-You-Go (PAYGO)
Defined contribution	Private pension plans and social security systems of Argentina, Australia, Chile, and Mexico	Social security systems of Sweden and Italy
Defined benefit	Older U.S. corporate pension plans and most U.S. state pension plans	U.S. Social Security system

Source: Adapted from Feldstein and Liebman (2002).

responsible for providing any additional funding necessary in order to provide the required benefits to retirees. In recent years as health care costs have regularly risen at rates exceeding the overall cost of living and the rate at which pension fund assets have grown in value, companies have been hard pressed to make good on the defined benefits required. Consequently, many companies have switched to providing newer employees with defined contribution plans rather than defined benefits plans.

If the pension system is unfunded, relying on a PAYGO method of financing, you have a system like the U.S. Social Security system. Although the U.S. system has some accumulated assets that are held in trust funds, it is primarily financed via a PAYGO payroll tax. Under this system, the payroll tax revenues collected from workers this year pay the social security benefits for retirees this year. This method requires sufficient revenues collected from current workers to pay all of the retirees currently receiving benefits.

The fourth type of system is an unfunded defined contribution system such as the social security systems of Sweden and Italy as described in Social Security Administration (2008). In this type of system, PAYGO financing is used to provide benefits linked to defined contributions. An alternative name for this type of system is a **notional defined-contribution** plan. In this type of system an individual's account is credited with the taxes the person pays into the system plus interest earned on the account balance. This type of system has no real investments, however, so the interest rate is an implicit rate, or a notional rate. At retirement, the individual receives benefits or an annuity based on the accumulated amount in their account, including the notional amount of interest.

The U.S. Social Security system has always been financed primarily with a payroll tax levied on workers and their employers and secondarily by general government revenue. Payroll taxes have been used primarily so that retirees would feel that they had earned their benefits (regardless of the reality that this is not fully the case). In the early years, there was a distinct desire to portray the social security system as a method by which a worker provided for her own retirement, rather than to portray the system as a form of welfare. In those days, there was a strong stigma against welfare and it was necessary to package the social security system as a self-help program in order to engender public support. Ironically, the misleading concept that the social security system operates like a private retirement fund is still with us and is a fundamental stumbling block to the needed reform of the system.

After its initial creation, the social security system was expanded in several important regards. First, benefits for spouses of retired workers and for survivors of deceased workers were added in 1939. This change transformed social security from a strict worker-based program for funding retirement benefits into a family-based benefit program. Second, an insurance program was added to provide disability benefits in 1956. The so-called disability insurance (DI) component of social security provides insurance for workers against the possibility that they become disabled. Finally, the social security program was expanded in 1972 when automatic cost-of-living adjustments were added for benefits. Prior to that time Congress had to approve benefit increases across the board for all recipients. With the advent of cost-of-living adjustments (COLAs) the social security system started providing annuities indexed for inflation.

How the U.S. Social Security System Works

Benefits are paid to retired or disabled workers based on their income earning history. **Average indexed monthly earnings** (AIME) are computed for each worker. For a retiree, AIME is based on the highest 35 years of earnings on which he paid social security payroll taxes. A progressive formula is then applied to compute the primary insurance amount (PIA), or the monthly amount the retiree will received when he is first eligible to receive benefits. For example, the formula in 2010 for a worker retiring at age 62 is given in Table 9.3 and illustrated in Figure 9.2. This formula assures that initial benefits replace a larger share of pre-retirement earnings for low-income workers than for high-income workers.

Workers begin to receive social security retirement benefits when they retire. The **normal retirement age** (NRA) depends on the year of birth of the worker. Workers born before 1938 have an NRA of 65 years of age. Younger workers have NRAs that are two months later for each additional year of birth, reaching a maximum of 66 years for workers born in 1943. That maximum NRA applies to workers born between 1944 and 1954. Workers

TABLE 9.3 Primary Insurance Amount (PIA) Computation

If AIME is over:	But not over:	PIA is:	of the AIME over:
$0	$761	90% of	$0
$761	$4,586	$685+32% of	$761
$4,586		$1,292+15% of	$4,586

Budget of the United States Government: Detailed Functional Tables Fiscal Year 2011, Table 32.1 Budget Authority and Outlays by Function, Category, and Program. http://www.gpoaccess.gov/usbudget/fy11/fct.html

FIGURE 9.2 Computation of the Primary Insurance Amount (PIA), 2010

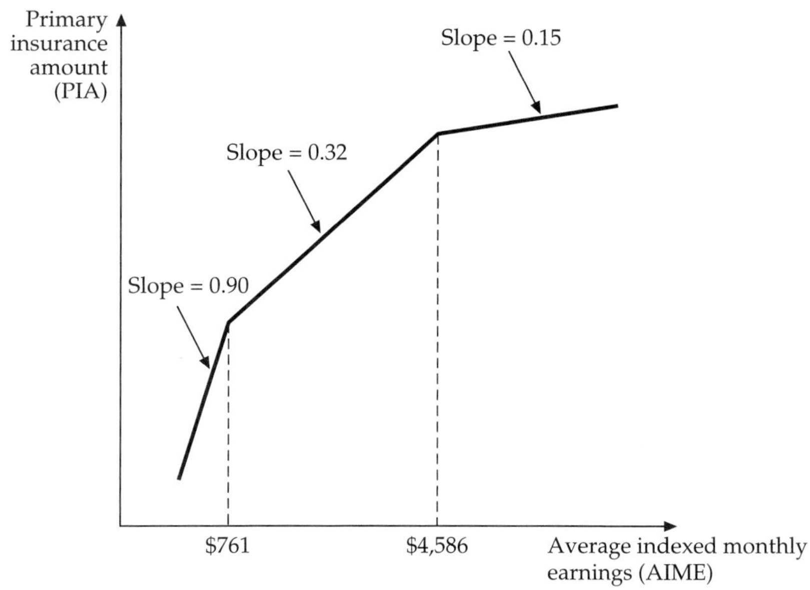

born after 1954 have NRAs that increase by two months per birth year until a maximum of 67 years is reached for workers born in 1960 or later. All workers can choose to take early retirement at age 62 and receive permanently reduced benefits. With an NRA of 67, for example, the reduction in benefit level is 30 percent. Early retirement involves a trade-off between the date at which benefits begin and the size of the annual benefit. Some workers are willing to accept lower benefits in exchange for starting the benefit stream earlier. Others prefer to start later and receive larger benefit checks. For example, a person who retires early at age 62 rather than waiting until age 67 accepts a 30 percent reduction in her benefits each year in exchange for starting the benefit stream five years earlier. Over the past decade more than two-thirds of all retiring workers have accepted a reduction in their benefits in order to retire early.

The average monthly social security benefits paid in 2010 for various types of recipients are listed below:

- Retired worker: $1,164
- Retired couple: $1,892
- Disabled worker: $1,064
- Disabled worker with a spouse and child: $1,803
- Widow or widower: $1,123
- Young widow or widower with two children: $2,391

Source: SSA Publication No. 05-10024, January 2010.

Financing the Trust Funds

As you will see in Chapter 14, the payroll tax is the major source of revenue for the social security system. Employer and employee pay a combined rate of 12.4 percent of payroll up to a maximum amount of earnings that is indexed for inflation.[4] In 2010 the maximum taxable earnings amount was $106,800, resulting in a tax of $13,243.20 split between employer and employee (12.4 percent of $106,800). For an employed worker, the employer pays a tax rate of 6.2 percent of the employee's earnings up to that maximum and the employee pays another 6.2 percent. A self-employed worker would pay the full 12.4 percent tax.

There is a second and smaller tax revenue source from the income tax that some social security recipients pay on their benefits. Beneficiaries must pay tax on part of their benefits if the sum of the adjusted gross income (AGI), nontaxable interest income, and half of their social security benefits exceeds a taxable threshold. In 2010 that threshold for an individual taxpayer was $25,000. For income between $25,000 and $34,000, 50 percent of the social security benefits received are subject to income tax. For income in excess of $34,000, 85 percent of the social security benefits are subject to income tax. For a couple filing jointly, the corresponding income figures are $32,000 and $44,000, respectively. About one-third of all social security benefit recipients must pay income tax on a portion of their benefits.

Revenues from the payroll tax and part of the revenue generated by the income tax on benefits are deposited into trust funds; the **Old Age and Survivors Insurance Trust Fund**, and the **Disability Insurance Trust Fund**.

The Medicare tax requires both employer and employee to pay 1.45 percent of earnings. In this case, there is no limit on the taxable earnings that are taxed. A self-employed worker would pay the full 2.9 percent tax rate on all earnings. The Obama health care program will require for the first time, starting in 2013, another 3.8 percent tax applied to unearned income in the form of realized capital gains, interest, dividends, rents, and royalties. This additional Medicare tax will apply to individuals with incomes of more than $200,000 or to married couples filing jointly with income of more than $250,000.

OTHER SOCIAL INSURANCE PROGRAMS: MEDICARE, MEDICAID, AND SSI

In the United States three related programs are important to consider along with social security: **supplemental security income** (SSI), **Medicare**, and **Medicaid**. Each of these programs was implemented by amending the Social Security Act, although each is distinct from the social security system. Table 9.4 lists the expenditures for each of these programs in 2010, as well as each program's share of total federal outlays. Social Security is the largest of the three programs at $723.5 billion, whereas Medicare and Medicaid cost $462.1 billion and $292.7 billion, respectively. Social Security accounts for about 20 percent of

TABLE 9.4 Federal Government Outlays for Social Security, Medicare, and Medicaid, 2010

Program	Expenditures (Billions of $)	Percent of Total Federal Outlays (%)
Social security	723.5	19.45
Medicare	462.1	12.42
Medicaid	292.7	7.87
Subtotal	1,478.30	39.73
Rest of federal government	2,242.40	60.27
Total outlays	3,720.70	100.00

Congressional Budget Office, The Long-Term Budget Outlook 2010, Table 1.2 http://www.cbo.gov/ftpdocs/115xx/doc11579/06-30-LTBO.pdf.

total federal outlays, whereas Medicare and Medicaid together make up another 20 percent.

Medicare

Medicare is a national health care benefit program for the elderly or disabled, providing benefits for those receiving social security benefits. The Medicare program was created in 1965 and is comprised of two major components: the **hospital insurance** (HI) program and the **supplemental medical insurance** (SMI) program. HI pays for hospital care and some forms of nursing home care, home health care, and hospice services. SMI pays for services provided by physicians, medical suppliers, outpatient facilities, and some home health care services. Funding for the HI program comes from payroll taxes. The SMI program is funded partly (about one-quarter) through monthly premiums paid by enrollees and partly (about three-quarters) through general federal government revenues. Medicare beneficiaries pay less than 15 percent of the current level of Medicare outlays, indicating that the program provides a heavy subsidy for health care.

Nearly everyone over 65 years of age is automatically eligible for Medicare Part A coverage. Part A coverage provides inpatient hospital services, up to one hundred days of post hospital skilled nursing facility care, limited home health care services, and hospice care. A patient making use of the hospital coverage must pay a deductible ($1,100 in 2010) for each hospital admission. Part B coverage is voluntary and provides physicians' services, laboratory services, durable medical equipment, hospital outpatient services, and other medical services. The Part B premium for individuals with income of $85,000 per year ($170,000 per year for a couple) or less is $96.40 per month in 2010. For those with higher incomes, the premium can be as high as $353.60/month. Generally, Part B coverage pays 80 percent of Medicare's fee schedule after the patient has met the annual deductible ($155 in 2010). Medicare Part C combines Parts A and B and covers all medically needed services. Private insurance companies are approved by Medicare to provide this combined coverage and often do so at lower cost and/or with greater coverage than the original Medicare plan. Many times, this coverage requires the patient to use participating health care providers within a proscribed network (for example, a preferred provider organization [PPO], or a health maintenance organization [HMO]). Part D coverage was added in 2003 and provides prescription drug coverage.

Medicaid

The Medicaid program, also created in 1965 as part of the Social Security Act, provides medical assistance to low-income people. The program is a joint federal-state program, with the federal government paying from 50 to 83 percent of the cost, depending on the per-capita income of a state's residents. States are free to specify which medical procedures are covered under this program, so benefits vary from state to state. Each state administers its own Medicaid program. The federal Centers for Medicare and Medicaid Services (CMS) monitor those state programs to assure quality, eligibility requirements, and other service standards. CMS is an agency within the U.S. Department of Health and Human Services (DHHS). Although state participation in Medicaid is voluntary, all 50 states participate. Some states use private companies to administer some of their Medicaid benefits, often through managed care programs that contract with the state to provide services at a fixed cost per enrolled participant.

States are finding the expense of Medicaid to be an increasing burden as medical care costs rise faster than the general rate of inflation and faster than the rate of increase in the state's revenues. This has caused many states to limit their covered services over time. The state budgetary pressure is especially strong during an economic downturn when more people become eligible due to income loss.

Supplemental Security Income (SSI)

SSI was created in 1972 as a backstop for the social security system. It is a means-tested cash transfer program that provides benefits to low-income elderly, blind, or disabled people. SSI provides benefits for those who do not qualify for social security, or only qualify for very low benefits. The intention when the SSI program was created was to establish a national income maintenance system. The SSI program was created as a replacement for the Federal-State Programs of Old-Age Assistance and Aid to the Blind, which were originally established by the Social Security Act of 1935, and the Program of Aid to the Permanently and Totally Disabled, which was created as part of the Social Security Amendments of 1950. Previously, the federal government provided matching funds to states so that they could provide cash payments to recipients. Each state established its own criteria for recipient qualification; that is, its own definition of needy. With the creation of the SSI program, a federal program was created with uniform eligibility requirements administered by the Social Security Administration.

In order to be eligible for SSI benefits, a person must meet the criteria for age (at least 65), blindness, or disability. The person must also have limited income and limited resources. Individuals and married couples are income eligible if their incomes are below the federal maximum monthly SSI benefit. Sources of income counted include money earned from work, money received from other sources such as Social Security benefits, workers' compensation, unemployment benefits, veteran's payments, transfers from friends or family, or the value of free food or shelter received. Resources considered for eligibility include cash, bank account balances, land, vehicles, personal property, life insurance, and other assets that could be converted to cash. SSI limits for resources counted are $2,000 for an individual or child, and $3,000 for a couple. The maximum SSI benefit in 2010 was $674 per month for an eligible individual or $1,011 for a couple with no other income (Source: http://www.ssa.gov/OACT/COLA/SSIamts.html). For more information on the SSI program see Committee on Ways and Means (2008).

Long-term projections for the three largest social insurance programs (social security, Medicare, and Medicaid) indicate that they will pose serious challenges for funding the U.S. federal budget. The Congressional Budget Office (CBO) currently projects that under the extended baseline scenario (reflecting current law) social security will grow from its current 4.8 percent of GDP to 6.2 percent by the year 2035. Medicare spending will grow from its current 3.6 percent of GDP to 5.9 percent, and Medicaid and other health spending will grow from 1.9 percent to 3.8 percent. All together, these programs which now consume just over 10 percent of U.S. GDP will grow to nearly 16 percent. Under the CBO alternative fiscal scenario, which incorporates changes to current law that are widely expected at the present time, the share of GDP taken by these programs is anticipated to grow to more than 17 percent, primarily due to additional anticipated spending growth in the Medicare program. Table 9.5 provides the detail of CBO's long-term budget scenario projections.

INSURING AGAINST DISASTERS

In advanced industrialized countries governments insure their citizens against a wide range of potential disasters. In this section of the chapter we consider the ways in which governments provide social insurance against natural disasters such as floods, hurricanes, and earthquakes, as well as insure against terrorist attacks and wars.

The Case of Hurricane Katrina

Consider first the case of Hurricane Katrina that hit New Orleans in August of 2005. Vigdor (2008) examines the economic impacts of Hurricane Katrina on New Orleans and in so doing provides a rationale for expecting recovery

TABLE 9.5 Projected Spending Under CBO's Long-Term Budget Scenarios (percent of GDP)

	2010	2020	2035
		Extended Baseline Scenario	
Primary spending			
Social security	4.8	5.2	6.2
Medicare	3.6	4.1	5.9
Medicaid, CHIP, and exchange subsidies	1.9	2.8	3.8
Subtotal	10.3	12.1	15.9
Other non-interest spending	12.5	8.3	7.8
Subtotal, primary spending	22.9	20.4	23.7
Interest spending	1.4	3.1	3.9
Total spending	24.3	23.5	27.6
		Alternative Fiscal Scenario	
Primary spending			
Social security	4.8	5.2	6.2
Medicare	3.6	4.3	7.0
Medicaid, CHIP, and exchange subsidies	1.9	2.9	3.9
Subtotal	10.3	12.4	17.1
Other non-interest spending	12.5	9.7	9.3
Subtotal, primary spending	22.9	22.1	26.4
Interest spending	1.4	3.8	8.7
Total spending	24.3	25.9	35.2

www.ssa.gov/OACT/COLA/piaformula.html

after recent catastrophes. He compares the historic population trajectories for cities hit by disasters, including Chicago, Dresden, Hamburg, Hiroshima, Nagasaki, and San Francisco. Cities that were growing before disaster struck (e.g., Chicago hit by fire in 1871) continued to grow in the post-disaster period, albeit with a temporary impact due to the disaster. Declining cities, however, are generally expected to continue their decline after the disaster.

Vigdor provides an argument in favor of a degree of optimism in the case of New Orleans, however. His argument is that although historically governments responded to disasters with ad hoc relief measures, the United States now has a formal disaster assistance program since the establishment of the Federal Disaster Act of 1950. Furthermore, federal emergency preparedness and related efforts were consolidated in the Federal Emergency Management Agency (FEMA) in 1979. With these institutions in place, there should be a more coordinated and systematic disaster relief response. In terms of the

Samaritan's dilemma discussed in Chapter 5, the formation of these institutions would provide optimism that the optimal combination of in-kind transfers of relief could be provided along with cash assistance in order to attain the welfare maximizing outcome. In the wake of the Hurricane Katrina event in 2005, however, critics are skeptical about the government's institutional responses being either coordinated or systematic, much less optimal in any sense of the word.

New Orleans was a declining city for a long period of time prior to the catastrophic event of Katrina. After the hurricane, however, there were loud political calls to rebuild the city to its former glory. Attempts to override the natural progression to a smaller city, however, would require large subsidies to alter the behavior of those who would otherwise decide not to rebuild their homes in the city. The Road Home program, implemented after Katrina, was designed to do just that. This program was intended to offset costs that were not covered by insurance payouts. In addition, the Congress implemented the Gulf Opportunity Zone Act that provided favorable tax incentives for businesses operating in the Gulf Coast areas hit hard by hurricanes Katrina, Rita, and Wilma.

Hence, in the case study of Katrina responses, we see that relief was provided in several forms, in addition to the subsidized flood insurance that was available throughout the metro area prior to the hurricane. Indeed, the Samaritan response was swift and strong after the disaster, if not coordinated and comprehensive.

Based on the implications of the Samaritan's dilemma, we know that after a catastrophic disaster:

- Any aid provided can have negative efficiency consequences.
- Exclusively cash aid is not necessarily the best form of aid. In-kind aid in combination with cash aid may be preferable.
- Any aid provided can cause sub-optimal levels of insurance among the poor.

Federal and State Catastrophe Insurance Programs

Federal government assistance to victims of disasters of various types has been provided throughout the history of the United States. Prior to the mid-twentieth century, however, that assistance was provided on an ad hoc basis with Congress responding to a disaster, deciding whether and to what extent to provide assistance. Acts of Congress passed in 1947 and 1950 have regularized the process, providing a mechanism by which the federal government extends disaster assistance to communities. Subsequent legislation has clarified and expanded federal disaster assistance in numerous ways.

A major problem with federal relief programs is that they can make it much more difficult for private insurance companies to sell policies for catastrophic hazards. Potential victims have less incentive to buy insurance, especially at prices reflecting the underlying risk, if they expect to receive federal aid when a catastrophe strikes. This problem of moral hazard has prompted policymakers to respond. The federal government provides insurance for selected catastrophic hazards at prices well below those that would be charged by private insurers. In this way, the federal government provides in-kind transfers of insurance. In some cases, the federal government requires individuals to purchase insurance policies. In other cases, it requires that private insurers offer policies for sale in selected markets.

In the following sub-sections we review three major forms of insurance market interventions by federal and state governments. Program descriptions in this section are taken from the Council of Economic Advisers (2007). In each case we examine the characteristics of the in-kind transfer of insurance in light of the Samaritan's dilemma.

National Flood Insurance Program

Established in 1968 in order to make flood insurance more available to homeowners and businesses, the U.S. National Flood Insurance Program (NFIP) encourages communities to prepare for flood hazards. The program also is intended to reduce reliance on federal disaster relief after significant floods. Property owners in approximately 20,000 communities are eligible to purchase flood insurance under the program, either directly from the federal government or through local insurance companies selling NFIP policies. These local insurance companies selling NFIP policies under their own name pass their risk along to the federal government. Premiums are remitted to the NFIP, which bears all of the risks associated with the insurance provided. The NFIP program is administered by the **Federal Emergency Management Agency** (FEMA).

FEMA uses Flood Insurance Rate Maps (FIRMs) to underwrite flood insurance. Such maps identify areas with at least a 1 percent chance of being flooded in a given year. These areas are designated as 100-year floodplains. The concept of a 100-year floodplain is widely misunderstood, however. In reality, a 100-year floodplain is an area over which there is a one percent chance of a flood in any given year. The implications of a 1 percent chance of flooding in any given year are direr than might be expected. For example, if we consider the probability of flooding in any given year to be independent of the probabilities in other years, we can view the situation as a series of **Bernoulli trials.**[5] In a 10-year period, using the Binomial probability distribution, we know that the probability of having zero floods is 0.9044. That implies the probability of at least one flood year is 1 – .9044, or 0.096. Hence, there is nearly a 10 percent chance of at least one hundred-year flood in a decade.

FEMA makes flood insurance available in communities that adopt zoning ordinances, building codes, and implement other planning processes that reduce potential damage caused by floods. One difficulty with the program is that not all structures covered under NFIP meet the standards of the program. Structures built before the community begins participation in NFIP, or prior to the publication of a community's FIRM, are eligible for insurance even if they do not meet FEMA standards. Structures built or renovated after 1974 or after the community's FIRM was published, whichever is later, are charged actuarially fair premiums. About one-quarter of NFIP structures covered were built before 1974 or prior to the publication of the community's FIRM, however. These properties pay subsidized premiums that are not actuarially fair. Due to higher risk associated with these properties, they pay higher premiums than newer properties, but despite this fact the premiums are not sufficient to cover the expected losses on these properties. Estimates indicate that on average premiums for pre-FIRM properties are about 40 percent of the actuarially fair rates.

The result of the NFIP pricing scheme is a severe problem of adverse selection and moral hazard. In many cases, property owners simply have no flood insurance. FEMA estimates that one-half to two-thirds of the structures in floodplains are not covered by flood insurance. In other cases, very high risk properties have NFIP insurance coverage at heavily subsidized rates even though they have been flooded many times over. Repetitive loss properties account for about 38 percent of all NFIP claims historically.

There are conflicting economic effects of the NFIP. As the NFIP only provides coverage in communities taking steps to adopt and enforce flood mitigation measures, it likely reduces flood damage. On the other hand, by providing flood insurance at subsidized rates for pre-FIRM properties NFIP discourages property owners from relocating or renovating their structures that are at high risk of flooding. With flood insurance, it is easier for the property owner to obtain bond financing for property investment in locations that are highly vulnerable to flooding. On balance, it may be the case that the NFIP actually increases federal spending on flood disaster relief due to its encouragement of development in high-risk areas.

Since 1986 NFIP premiums exceeded losses in most years, but the story was entirely different in 2005. That year the combined impacts of hurricanes Katrina, Rita, and Wilma resulted in \$16.3 billion in NFIP claims. Figure 9.3 illustrates the NFIP number of policies in force and number of losses paid over the period 1978 to 2009. Figure 9.4 illustrates the historic impact of the 2005 hurricanes on NFIP losses paid. If this insurance program were being run by a private firm, the company would have to accumulate surpluses (premiums more than covering claims) or purchase reinsurance in order to pay the claims. But, the NFIP is able to borrow from the federal government. On the eve of Hurricane Katrina striking the Gulf Coast, the NFIP had a cumulative debt of \$300 million it owed to the U.S. Treasury. Estimates indicate that the program will need to borrow a total of \$21.2 billion in order to pay claims that were filed in 2005. The NFIP should pay back this amount over the coming years, but that is very unlikely to occur. Although the NFIP premium revenue was able to cover claims in much of the program's recent history, prior to 2005, the subsidized insurance program exposed taxpayers to a massive financial liability that hit home in 2005. Taxpayers will be feeling the effects for many years to come.

Flood insurance was a particular issue related to the catastrophic impact of Hurricane Katrina in New Orleans in 2005. Vigdor (2008) provides a comprehensive overview of the economic impacts of Katrina on

FIGURE 9.3 National Flood Insurance Program, Number of Policies in Force and Number of Losses Paid, 1978–2009

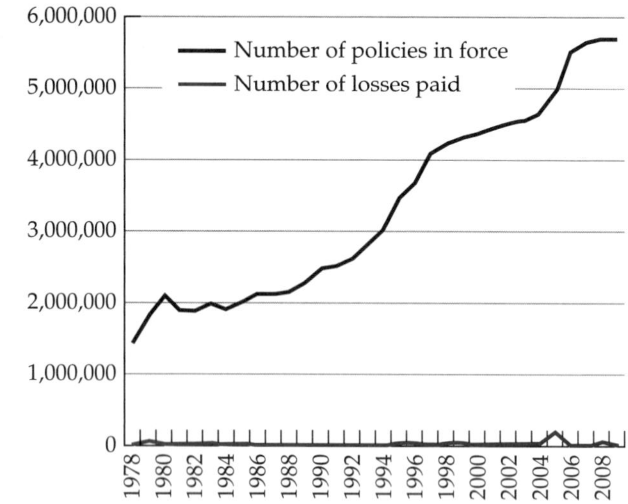

Source: http://www.fema.gov/business/nfip/statistics/

FIGURE 9.4 National Flood Insurance Program, Premiums and Losses Paid, 1978–2009

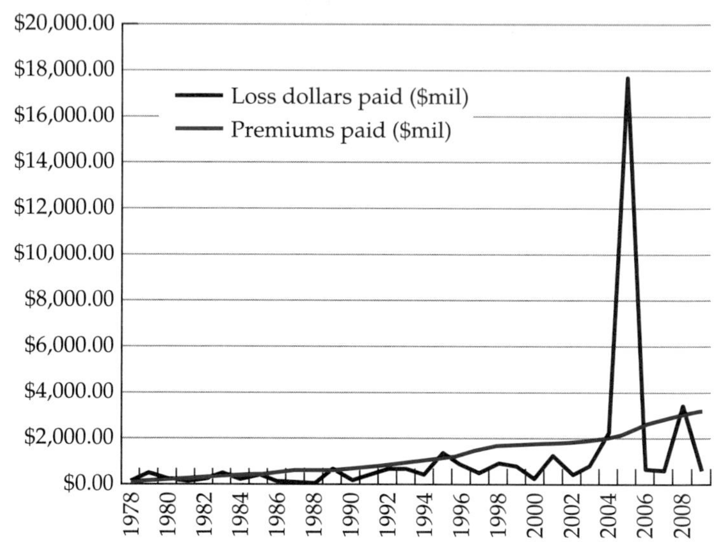

Source: http://www.fema.gov/business/nfip/statistics/

the city and the metro area. He argues that the New Orleans housing market, left to its own devices, will not return to its pre-Katrina equilibrium.

Although the Samaritan's dilemma provides an efficiency rationale for the in-kind provision of flood insurance, it is not clear that the NFIP provided the appropriate level of insurance. In the aftermath of that catastrophe, it would appear that the NFIP provided insurance that was too heavily subsidized, encouraging the location of far too many families in flood-prone areas of the New Orleans metro area.

Terrorism and War-Risk Insurance Programs

After the terrorist attacks on the World Trade Center of September 11, 2001, the U.S. federal government provided substantial support in disaster assistance. That assistance included $4 billion in aid to the airline industry and another $20 billion to the New York City region. By 2005 private insurance companies had paid about $36 billion in loss claims resulting from the terrorist attacks. These losses do not represent the total losses caused by the attacks, however, because many losses were not insured. Nevertheless, those losses far exceeded any such losses from previous terrorist attacks.

Soon after the 9/11/01 attacks private property and casualty insurance companies began to re-evaluate their terrorism risk exposure. Companies began to cancel policies, exclude terrorist attacks from coverage, and raise premiums substantially. With this contraction in supply of private insurance, the federal government stepped in to provide insurance for airlines and commercial real estate. The Federal Aviation Administration (FAA) began to provide insurance policies to airlines to cover third-party liability. These policies covered potential harm to both individuals and property on the ground that might result from terrorist attacks on planes. In November of 2002, the Department of Homeland Security expanded the FAA insurance program to also include loss of aircraft and passenger liability. By 2006, this insurance program provided coverage to 75 airlines with covered losses ranging from $100 million to $4 billion per airline.

Also, in November of 2002, the Terrorism Risk Insurance Act (TRIA) was adopted with a much broader program encouraging private firms to provide terrorism risk insurance coverage (United States Department of Treasury, 2005). Although the original program was intended to expire after three years, it has been renewed and extended in 2005 and 2007. TRIA 2002 established a three-year temporary program providing shared public-private compensation for losses resulting from terrorist acts. The purpose for this program was to ensure widespread availability of insurance to cover terrorism risk. In addition, the program was intended to help private insurance markets stabilize after the 9/11/01 event. The basic structure of the TRIA program can be thought of as providing federal terrorism risk reinsurance at no cost, on top of company-specific deductible. Under TRIA, firms that sell property and casualty insurance are required to make available policies that do not exclude coverage of losses from terrorist acts. In addition, TRIA authorized the U.S. Treasury Department to provide re-insurance to cover loss claims from terrorism. An act of terrorism is defined under statute as having the following characteristics:

- a violent act that is dangerous to human life
- resulting in damage within the United States or outside of the United States in the case of an air carrier or vessel, or on the premises of a U.S. mission
- has been committed by individuals acting on behalf of any foreign person or interest
- as part of an effort to coerce the U.S. civilian population or influence the policy or affect the conduct of the U.S. government by coercion

The act of terrorism must be certified by the secretary of treasury, with concurrence of the secretary of state and the attorney general. In addition, the act of terrorism must result in property and casualty loss of at least $5 million. The TRIA liability limit for the federal government and insurers is a total of $100 billion per year.

TRIA 2002 was extended and amended by the Terrorism Risk Insurance Extension Act of 2005 (TRIEA). Then, at the end of 2007 the Terrorism Risk Insurance Program Reauthorization Act of 2007 was approved, extending TRIA through 2014. This law extends the temporary federal program providing shared public-private compensation for insured losses due to acts of terrorism.

State Property Insurance Markets

Most families and businesses find their first line of insurance protection provided by local property insurers. Insurance companies provide property and casualty policies to cover homeowner and business risks (fire, wind, burglary, etc.). Wide variation exists across states, but all states regulate the insurance industry in terms of who is permitted to sell insurance products, the terms and conditions of the insurance policies, and the rates that can be charged for insurance products. Insurance regulations are intended to assure protection for consumers buying the insurance products. Regulations are designed to avoid fraud and poor risk management practices in the insurance industry. The other side of state regulation, however, is that ill-conceived state regulations have the potential to create difficulties for the operation of catastrophe-risk markets.

Regulations limiting rates can make it difficult or impossible for insurance companies to set premiums for policies that accurately reflect the risks involved with the insured events. If the rates do not accurately reflect risk, problems of moral hazard and adverse selection are worsened. The regulatory process may prevent rapid adjustment of rates in light of new information available regarding catastrophic events. It may also discourage insurers from proposing complex pricing schemes that may more accurately reflect risk, but are difficult to explain or justify to state regulatory boards. This may especially be true for insuring particular hazards.

If regulators are successful in keeping rates artificially low, it may become difficult for households and businesses to obtain insurance coverage in private markets. Insurers may simply stop writing policies in those states. A recent example of this situation is that of the State of Florida where regulators declined a rate request by State Farm Insurance, hit hard by losses related to hurricanes in 2005. Consequently, State Farm Insurance has announced that it will no longer write household insurance policies in Florida. Insurers may respond to this type of situation by providing catastrophic coverage only in areas where the risk is low. Alternatively, insurers may exclude specific (named) events from coverage.

In states with a high risk of catastrophes, such as hurricanes or earthquakes, special entities have been created to provide insurance to those who are unable to obtain coverage from private firms. For example, the State of California created a quasi-public company in 1996, the California Earthquake Authority, designed to sell earthquake insurance to California residents.[6] The Authority is backed by private insurers that operate in California.

Other states have established residual pools to cover wind damage (tornadoes, wind storms, etc.). These entities operate much like traditional insurance companies, but they sell policies covering property in very high-risk areas. Additionally, they are given the ability by the state government to apply surcharges on primary insurers that operate in the state. One characteristic common to all state programs is that they provide insurance coverage exclusively to those who will not or cannot get coverage in private insurance markets. Consequently, these programs attract policy holders that are unattractive to traditional private insurance companies.

When a state-sponsored insurance program finds itself in financial difficulty following a major catastrophe, it has several options it can pursue. First, it may obtain funds from the state government to shore up the insurance program. This course of action passes the cost of covering losses to the tax payers of the state. Second, the state may levy an additional surcharge on premiums sold by private insurers in the state. This course of action forces property owners in low-risk areas to subsidize those in high-risk areas. A consequence of this course of action is that some policy holders in low-risk areas, when confronted with a higher premium, will choose to go without private insurance coverage, thus making them likely to seek insurance from the state-sponsored residual pool. Hence, the state-sponsored residual pool is more vulnerable to higher losses in the future.

Fundamentally, government policies that keep insurance prices artificially low in high-risk areas have substantial inefficiency effects. Such policies encourage excessive economic development in risk-prone areas.

Worldwide, earthquakes are a major cause of injuries and loss of life. According to the U.S. Geological Survey (2011) about 227,000 people were killed by earthquakes in 2010. The vast majority of the fatalities were caused by the magnitude 7.0 earthquake that hit Haiti, killing 222,570 people. In contrast, the largest 2010 quake was of magnitude 8.8, hitting Chile and killing just 577 people. What accounts for the difference in loss of life, and therefore risk to residents? Clearly, the risk is not solely due to the magnitude of the earthquake. In addition, the quality of building construction and other factors play a major role in the actual risk borne by a population living in quake-prone areas. Aside from the question of providing and funding national earthquake insurance programs, governments can take other measures to reduce the risk of property damage and loss of life. Governments can substantially mitigate risk through thoughtful zoning restrictions and building codes. Japan is a prime example of a government that takes earthquake risk seriously and goes further than any other national government to minimize risk.[7]

Recent Developments in the Catastrophic Insurance Market

Bond issuers sell so-called **cat bonds** (catastrophic bonds) to provide protection against natural disasters. The buyers of those bonds demand higher yields than other bonds due to the risk of losing their investment in case of an extremely large catastrophe. The demand for cat insurers bonds dried up in the fall of 2008 as investors retreated into the safest possible investments. With the fall of the Wall Street firm Lehman Brothers in September of 2008, the market for catastrophic bonds was dealt a severe blow. Cat bond sales are reported by Unmack and Suess (2009) to have fallen to half of their previous (2007) level. Catastrophe bonds provided a 2.9 percent return over the period January 2008 through January 2009, based on the Swiss Re Cat Bond Total Return Index. Corporate bonds with similar ratings provided investors with a loss of nearly 22 percent over the same period, based on Merrill Lynch & Co. data. Some of the bond deals relied on the bank to guarantee assets that were pledged to make bond coupon payments. Several bond issuers defaulted on their interest payments. In addition, some reinsurers are disbanding their financial markets units as part of a larger strategy of reducing company risk exposure. Despite the difficulty in the cat bond market, the situation in 2009 improved. The improved market situation was due to the fact that insurers needed alternative capacity and investors looked for assets whose values were decorrelated.

POLICY STUDY

Efficiency and Effectiveness of Medicare

In this policy study we examine whether the Medicare program is (a) efficient and (b) effective. To provide insight on these questions, we examine evidence from two studies published by the National Bureau of Economic Research (NBER).

In order to assess the efficiency of the Medicare program, Skinner et al. (2001) examined the question of whether the marginal social benefit of the last dollar of Medicare expenditure is equal to the marginal social benefits of spending on alternative programs. If the Medicare program is efficient, its marginal social benefit should be at least as large as that for alternatives. If not, the money spent on Medicare would be better spent elsewhere. In order to estimate the marginal social benefits of Medicare expenditures Skinner et al. (2001) used data on survival rates across 306 hospital referral regions in the United States. Their conclusion is that, "Our best estimates of the incremental value of Medicare spending with regard to survival are essentially zero across all regions."

Table 9.6 reports their regression estimates of factors affecting survival rates across regions. The key variable of interest is Medicare expenditures, reported in the second row

TABLE 9.6 Regression Estimates of Factors Affecting Survival Rates

Variable	Coefficient Estimate (t-statistic)
Constant	94.53
Medicare expenditures ($1,000)	0.005 (0.1)
AMI rate (per 1,000)	−0.014 (1.7)
Stoke rate (per 1,000)	−0.035 (3.7)
Gastrointestinal bleed rate (per 1,000)	−0.050 (2.9)
Colon cancer rate (per 1,000)	−0.013 (0.4)
Lung cancer rate (per 1,000)	0.087 (1.3)
Hip fracture rate (per 1,000)	−0.034 (2.3)
Fraction living in poverty	0.029 (3.4)
Average Social Security income ($1,000)	0.198 (2.9)
Effectiveness index	0.021 (4.2)

of the table. Notice that although the estimated coefficient on Medicare expenditures is positive (0.005), the associated t-statistic is very low (0.01) which does not permit us to reject the hypothesis that there is no effect. Hence, according to this result additional Medicare expenditures have no statistically significant effect on the survival rate. Other estimated coefficients indicate that a higher stroke rate, gastrointestinal bleed rate, or hip fracture rate all reduce the survival rate significantly. Higher poverty rate, social security income level, or effectiveness index has the effect of increasing the survival rate.

In order to assess the effectiveness of the Medicare program, Finkelstein and McNight (2005) examined both the impact of Medicare on health outcomes and on risk exposure for the elderly. They found that in the first 10 years of the Medicare program's existence, "...the establishment of universal health insurance for the elderly had no discernible impact on their mortality." They did find, however, that the program, "... was associated with a substantial reduction in the elderly's exposure to out of pocket medical expenditure risk." This was particularly true for the elderly in the top spending quartile. For them, the introduction of Medicare reduced their out-of-pocket spending

TABLE 9.7 Changes in Average Medicare-Eligible Expenditures

	Out-of-Pocket Spending	Private Insurance Spending	Total Insurance Spending (Public Plus Private)	Total Spending
All spending	−117.3	−507.1***	259.0*	142.3
	(106.5)	(97.0)	(150.2)	(204.7)
Hospital, Part A	−44.7	−465.9***	127.5	85.3
	(89.8)	(87.6)	(133.84)	(171.1)
Physician, Part B	−72.58**	−41.2*	131.5***	57.0
	(34.1)	(23.3)	(32.3)	(53.9)

*Standard errors reported in parentheses with asterisks *, **, and *** indicating significance at the 10, 5, and 1 percent levels, respectively.

Source: Finkelstein and McNight (2005), Table 4, p. 36.

by 40 percent. Finklestein and McNight's estimates indicate that the welfare gains from that risk reduction for those elderly may be large enough to cover between one-half and three-quarters of the cost of the Medicare program. The importance of this finding is that the direct insurance benefits of the program are substantial, in addition to the indirect benefits derived from improved health.

Table 9.7 reports the Finkelstein and McNight (2005) results on average Medicare-eligible expenditures. The presence of Medicare Part B coverage reduces the out-of-pocket spending for physicians' services, in particular. Medicare coverage has a significant effect in reducing overall spending on private insurance. Notice, however, that total spending on insurance (public plus private) rises and does so most significantly for physicians' services under Part B. Total spending rises (out-of-pocket plus insurance), but not significantly.

POLICY STUDY

The Fiscal Sustainability of the U.S. Social Security System

The Congressional Budget Office (CBO) updated their long-term fiscal analysis of the U.S. Social Security program in 2008, providing projections for 75 years into the future. Although all such long-term projections are subject to a high degree of uncertainty, it is useful to consider the CBO study to get a sense for the prospects for fiscal sustainability of social security. Figure 9.5 provides the CBO estimates of the potential ranges of social security outlays and revenues, expressed as a percentage of GDP, under the scheduled benefits scenario. The dark blue lines report the expected outlays and revenues, with the light blue shaded area representing the 80 percent certainty range of outcomes that may occur for both outlays and revenues. Outlays are projected to exceed revenues starting in the year 2019, but there is a good deal of uncertainty in that estimate as indicated by the 80 percent shading for both outlays and revenues.

FIGURE 9.5 Potential Ranges of Social Security Outlays and Revenues as a Percentage of GDP Under the Scheduled Benefits Scenario. 1985 to 2082

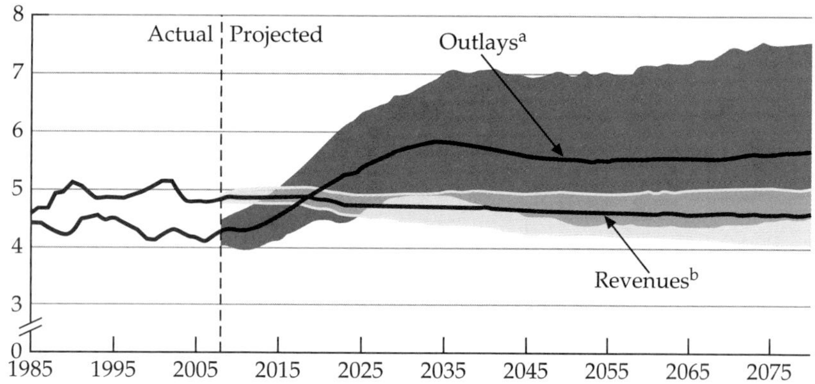

[a]Includes scheduled benefits and administrative costs.
[b]Includes payroll taxes and revenues from the taxation of benefits.

Source: Congressional Budget Office

Notes: The dark lines indicate CBO's projections of expected outcomes. Shaded areas indicate the 80 percent range of uncertainty around each projection based on a distribution of 500 simulations from CBO's long-term modal. (An 80 percent range means that there is a 10 percent chance that actual values will be above that range, a 10 percent change that they will be below it, and an 80 percent change that they will fall within the range.)

In the scheduled benefits scenario, workers each year receive full benefits as calculated under the current law.

CBO projects that under current law, outlays will begin to exceed revenues in 2049, scheduled benefits cannot be paid in full.

GDP = gross domestic product.

Figure 9.5 illustrates the potential path of benefits over time. If the currently scheduled benefits are paid out according to schedule, the outlays will rise to nearly 6 percent of GDP in 2035 due to the retirement of the Baby Boom generation. That ratio is projected to fall slightly to 5.6 percent for the next 20 years as the Baby Boomers begin to die off. But, with anticipated increases in life expectancy, the ratio is projected to rise to 5.8 percent in 2082. The figure also illustrates a potential scenario of what could happen when the trust funds are depleted if benefits are cut to match projected revenues. Under that scenario, benefits are constrained at a level of approximately 4.6 percent of GDP—a substantial reduction compared to currently scheduled benefits. Whether Congress and the president would agree to such a dramatic reduction is debatable.

Ultimately, some combination of reduced benefits and/or increased revenues will be needed to make the Social Security program sustainable. Benefits can be reduced for eligible beneficiaries, or eligibility can be tightened to provide benefits for a smaller

FIGURE 9.6 Social Security Outlays as a Percentage of Gross Domestic Product Under the Scheduled Benefits and Parable Benefits Scenarios, 1985 to 2082

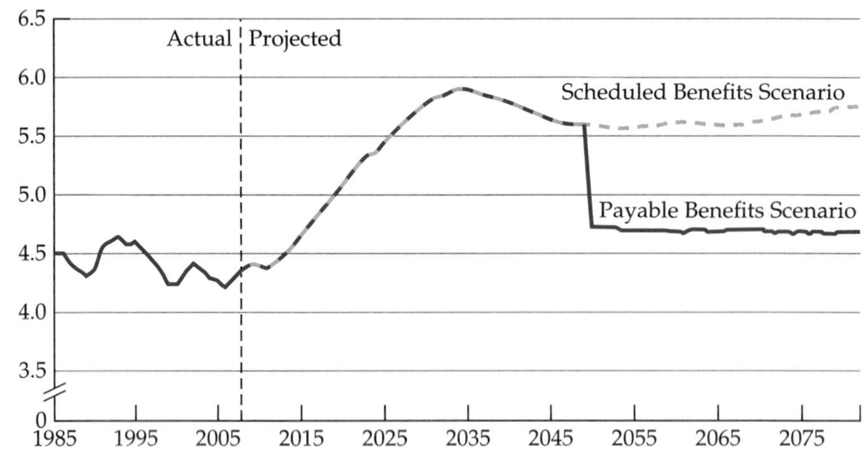

Source: Congressional Budget Office

Note: In the scheduled benefits scenario, workers receive full benefits as calculated under current law. In the payable benefits scenario, workers receive full benefits until the trust funds are exhausted. Then benefits are subjected to an across-the-boardcut each year so that total projected benefits equal projected revenues.

share of retirees. Revenues can be increased via payroll tax increases (either raising the rate, or increasing the income cap thereby expanding the tax base) or some other revenue supplement such as a value added tax (VAT).

Figure 9.6 illustrates the CBO projections for the Social Security trust fund ratio. This ratio is the balance in the Social Security trust funds divided by the projected outlays in a given year. The ratio in the year 2008, for example, was 3.6 indicating that the trust funds had sufficient balances to pay out that year's benefits 3.6 times over (or roughly 3.6 years' worth of benefits at the 2008 level). That ratio is expected to peak at 4.1 in the year 2016, then fall rapidly reaching zero in the year 2049. The 80 percent certainty range of projections illustrates the highly variable set of potential outcomes, however. According to those CBO estimates, there is an 11 percent chance that the trust funds will be exhausted before 2035, a 54 percent chance that they will be gone by 2050, and an 86 percent chance they will be zero by 2082.

For additional insightful analysis of the current state of the U.S. Social Security system and suggestions for reform options, see Diamond (1996, 2002, 2004).

FIGURE 9.7 Potential Range of the Social Security Trust Fund Ratio Under the Scheduled Benefits Scenario, 1985 to 2082

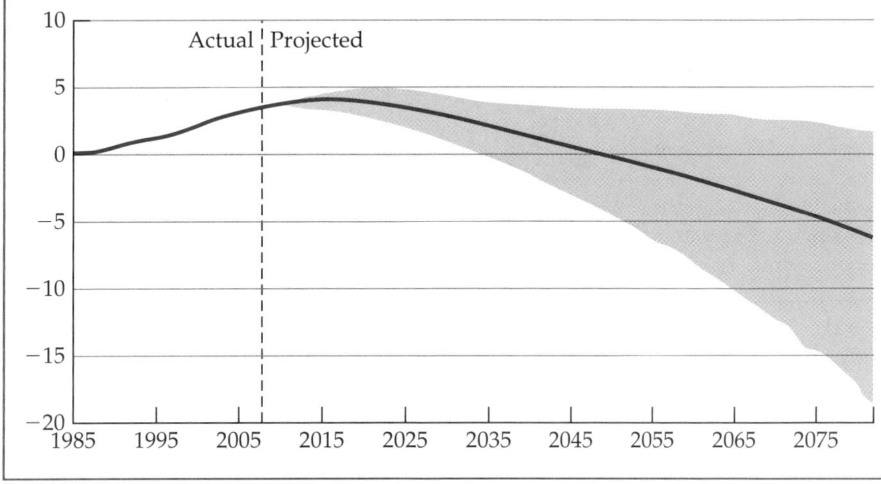

Source: Congressional Budget Office

Notes: The trust fund ratio is the total balance in the Social Security trust funds (the Old-Age and Survivors Insurance and the Disability Insurance Trust Funds) at the beginning of a calender year to total Social Security outlays during that year.

The dark line indicates CBO's projection of expected outcomes; the shaded area indicates the 80 percent range of uncertainty around the projection based on a distribution of 500 simulations from CBO's long-term model. (An 80 percent range means that there is a 10 percent change that actual values will be above that range, a 10 percent chance that they will be below it, and an 80 percent chance that they will fall within the range.)

In the scheduled benefits scenario, workers each year receive full benefits as calculated under current law.

PROBLEMS

1. Compute the tax owed in each of the following cases:
   a. Social Security tax (employer and employee portions) for a pre-retirement worker with income of $50,000
   b. Social Security tax (employer and employee portions) for a pre-retirement worker with income of $150,000
   c. Social Security tax (employer and employee portions) for a pre-retirement worker with income of $250,000
   d. Compare the above three answers and explain the average tax rate pattern

2. Compute the Social Security primary insurance amount (PIA) for a retiree in each of the following cases:
   a. Average indexed monthly earnings (AIME) of $1,000
   b. AIME of 3,000
   c. AIME of $6,000
   d. Compare the above three answers and explain the pattern you observe.
3. For tax year 2011 the Social Security tax rate applied to pre-retirement employees is reduced from 6.2 percent to 4.2 percent. Compute and explain the tax savings for workers in each of the following situations:
   a. Annual income of $50,000
   b. Annual income of $100,000
   c. Annual income of $150,000
   d. Annual income of $250,000
   e. Compare the above four answers and explain the pattern you observe.
4. Using a figure such as Figure 9.1, illustrate and explain the effect of a reduction in the degree of risk aversion (which makes the utility function less concave).
5. Feldstein (2005) points out that a large volume of research over the years confirms the conclusion that the Social Security system depresses private savings. Explain the economic and policy implications of this research finding.
6. The U.S. Social Security program is funded on a PAYGO basis along with a trust fund. Explain what rationales might account for this hybrid method of financing.
7. Using the information in the Appendix on PAYGO systems, found at the end of this textbook, explain the politics of the initial adoption of a social security system funding using a PAYGO financing mechanism.
8. In 2009 the State Farm Insurance Company withdrew from writing homeowners insurance policies in Florida, claiming that state regulations prevented it from charging premiums sufficient to cover expected losses.
   a. Explain the economic perspective on this issue, covering points on both sides (state insurance regulator and insurance company).
   b. Explain what impact the Florida Windstorm Mitigation Discount Program might have had. That program was a state-mandated program requiring all insurers to double insurance premium discounts for homeowners who shored up their homes against hurricane potential hurricane damage.

REFERENCES

Committee on Ways and Means, U.S. House of Representatives. 2008 Green Book. http://democrats.waysandmeans.house.gov/singlepages.aspx?NewsID=10490

Congressional Budget Office. 2008. Updated Long-Term Projections for Social Security. Available at: http://www.cbo.gov/ftpdocs/96xx/doc9649/08-20-SocialSecurityUpdate.pdf.

Council of Economic Advisers. 2007. "Catastrophe Risk Insurance." Chapter 5 of *Economic Report of the President, 2007*. Washington, DC: U.S. Government Printing Office.

Diamond, Peter A. 1996. "Proposals to Restructure Social Security." *Journal of Economic Perspectives* 10, no. 3 (Summer): pp. 67–88.

Diamond, Peter A. 2002. *Social Security Reform*. Oxford, UK: Oxford University Press.

Diamond, Peter A. 2004. *American Economic Review* 94, no. 1 (March): pp. 1–24.

Feldstein, Martin. 2005. "Rethinking Social Insurance." *American Economic Review* 95, no. 1 (March): pp. 1–24.

Feldstein, Martin, and Jeffrey B. Liebman. 2002. "Social Security." Chapter 32 in Alan J. Auerbach and Martin Feldstein, editors, *Handbook of Public Economics*, Volume 4. New York: Elsevier.

Finkelstein, Amy, and Robin McNight. 2005. "What Did Medicare Do (And Was It Worth IT)? NBER Working Paper 11609. Available at http://www.nber.org/papers/w11609.

Shlaes, Amity. *The Forgotten Man: A New History of the Great Depression*. New York: HarperCollins. 2007.

Skinner, Jonathan, Elliott S. Fisher, and John E. Wennberg. 2001. "The Efficiency of Medicare." NBER working paper 8395. Available at http://www.nber.org/papers/w8395.

Social Security Administration. 2010. Publication No. 05-10024, January 2010, ICN 454930. Available at: http://www.ssa.gov/pubs/10024.html.

Social Security Administration. 2008. "Social Security Programs Throughout the World: Europe, 2008." Available at: http://www.ssa.gov/policy/docs/progdesc/ssptw/2008-2009/europe/ and http://www.ssa.gov/SSA_Home.html

United States Department of Treasury. 2005. Assessment: The Terrorist Risk Insurance Act of 2002. Washington, DC.

United States Geological Survey. 2011. "Haiti Dominates Earthquake Fatalities in 2010." Available at: http://www.usgs.gov/newsroom/article.asp?ID=2679

Unmack, Neil, and Oliver Suess. 2009. "Scor Sells First Catastrophe Bond Since Lehman Demise (Update2)." Bloomberg.com, February 17, 2009. Available at: http://www.bloomberg.com/apps/news?pid=newsarchive&sid=aXEQqFHe6r30

Vigdor, Jacob. 2008. "The Economic Aftermath of Hurricane Katrina." *Journal of Economic Perspectives* 22, no. 4 (Fall): pp. 135–54.

NOTES

1. A convex function reflects a risk-loving attitude, which may characterize some individuals (e.g., skydivers). It is possible, of course, that an individual may both buy insurance and gamble, reflecting both risk aversion and risk

loving. The usual explanation of that combination of behaviors is that over a relatively small range of wealth outcomes the individual is risk averse, wishing to ensure against bad outcomes, but when given the opportunity to win a very large prize (e.g., a $200 million Powerball jackpot) may exhibit risk-loving behavior and buy a lottery ticket.

2. An example of this behavior is the common practice followed by many elderly Americans who spend down their personal assets in order to qualify for Medicaid care.
3. For a good description of the larger context of the government reforms and programs implemented in the 1930s in the United States, see Shlaes (2008).
4. For the year 2011 only there is a temporary 2 percent reduction in the employer-paid payroll tax as part of the compromise agreement between President Obama and Congress to extend the 2001 and 2003 tax rate reductions.
5. A Bernoulli trial in probability theory is one repetition of a random experiment where there are two possible outcomes that are labeled "success" and "failure." Consider the example of a coin flip where a "head" is labeled a success and a "tail" is labeled a failure. A key feature of Bernoulli trials is that the probability of success on any given trial is independent of the outcome of all other trials.
6. For more information on the California Earthquake Authority, see: *http://www.earthqukeauthority.com/*.
7. For more information on earthquakes and preparedness in Japan, see the Japan Meteorological Agency website: *http://www.jma.go.jp/en/quake/*.
8. For more on these possibilities see Feldstein and Liebman (2002).

Radius Images/Getty Images

PART FOUR

Efficiency and Equity Effects of Taxes and Subsidies

CHAPTER

10

Radius Images/Getty Images

The Structure of Taxes

LEARNING OBJECTIVES

1. Discuss the structure of tax systems, including the importance of the tax base definition and the role of tax rates.
2. Explain alternative tax bases, including income, sales, and value added.
3. Analyze the effects of exemptions, deductions, and credits in a tax system.

Taxes are important. They account for a large share of our income, and as a result we care about them intensely. Some of the most heated discussions at the Thanksgiving dinner table when the entire family is gathered together arise when Uncle Joe starts railing about the latest absurdity in the tax law he heard about on talk radio. Differing opinions are expressed as individuals have differing views on the appropriateness of the government programs being funded by that tax system, as well as on how best to fund any given set of programs. Uncle William, a wealthy investment banker from the East, thinks that we should trash the federal income tax system and replace it with a consumption tax. Aunt Florence and her husband, Robert, run a large farming operation in the Midwest and think that the local property tax is extremely unfair and should be replaced with greater reliance on sales taxes. Cousin Katie works in a big city and dislikes the income tax she must pay to that city when she doesn't even live in the city. Francine and Robert just bought a house in California and cannot believe how much larger their property tax payment is than their elderly neighbor's who owns an identical home. These are the typical tax policy issues we live with, but in order to understand these issues and consider how best to respond or reform the tax system, we need to know how these tax systems are designed. The purpose of this chapter is to provide a foundational understanding of tax systems, how they are designed, and how best to evaluate whether they work the way we would like them to work.

The sheer size of the tax system makes these issues important. Beyond that, however, we have an innate concern that the tax system be fair and efficient.[1] We want a system that treats people fairly. Roughly speaking, we want a tax system that taxes on the basis of ability to pay. Those with greater ability to pay should be required to pay more. We also want a tax system that distorts the economic system as little as possible. Most of us recognize readily when a tax provision encourages changes in behavior that are wasteful. We make fun of Aunt Sally for driving across the state line, incurring both gasoline expense and time expense, to shop at an outlet mall where she can save a few dollars on the sales tax, for example. We also worry about the efficiency effects of large companies that employ thousands of people when they uproot their activities from one community and relocate to another state in response to a tax incentive provided by that state's legislature. In order to evaluate such concerns, however, we must first have a framework for analysis. This chapter begins to build that framework by providing foundational instruction on how tax systems are designed.

Table 10.1 summarizes the receipts of U.S. federal, state, and local governments. In the year 2010, total receipts of federal, state, and local governments totaled $4.5 trillion, or nearly 31 percent of GDP. If we net out federal government transfers of $525 billion to state and local governments, to avoid double counting, the total amount of receipts is approximately $4 trillion, or about 26.3 percent of GDP.

Where do we get $4 trillion to pay for the public goods and services provided by our governments in the United States? What do we tax? Despite the amount and importance of taxes, most people have little sense of how a tax system works. Sure, they have an impression of how the tax works—it takes their hard-earned income—but they really do not have a clear sense of just how the tax system works. They naively think that a 5 percent sales tax is really a 5 percent tax when variations in the definition of the tax base can easily make the effective rate of taxation 3 percent, or even 15 percent. They believe that a proposed flat tax has a flat rate when its true effective rate is anything but flat. In order to get a clear view of how a tax system works, it is essential to understand how the tax base is defined; how deductions, exemptions, and credits work; and how the tax rate structure is applied.

Government receipts are reported in Table 10.1, measured in billions of dollars. The term **receipts** implies that both tax revenues and nontax revenues are included. Federal government receipts in the year 2010 were $2,378 billion, or about $2.4 trillion. State and local government receipts amounted to $2,113 billion, or $2.1 trillion. As indicated previously, some of the state and local receipts are transfers of funds (e.g., grants-in-aid) from the federal government and we do not want to double-count those receipts. At the federal level, personal taxes are clearly the most important sources of revenue, including both personal income taxes and contributions for social insurance (payroll taxes) which together account for 71 percent of federal receipts. Taxes on corporate income account for 13.7 percent of federal receipts. At the state and local levels, current tax receipts account for 62.5 percent of total receipts. Among the most important sources of tax receipts for state and local governments are sales taxes, property taxes, and income taxes. Note that the second-largest source of state and local government receipts is transfer receipts. This receipt category includes federal government transfers

TABLE 10.1 Overview of Receipts of U.S. Governments, 2010

	Receipts (Billions of Dollars)	Percentage of Receipts at that Level of Government	Percentage of GDP
Federal government current receipts	2,378.30		16.3
Personal current taxes	856.60	36.0	5.9
Taxes on production and imports	106.60	4.5	0.7
Taxes on corporate income	325.60	13.7	2.2
Taxes from the rest of the world	12.60	0.5	0.1
Contributions for government social insurance	978.10	41.1	6.7
Income receipts on assets	43.90	1.8	0.3
Current transfer receipts	59.10	2.5	0.4
Current surplus of government enterprises	−4.20	−0.2	0.0
State and local government	2,112.80		14.5
Current tax receipts	1,321.10	62.5	9.1
Personal current taxes	279.60	13.2	1.9
Taxes on production and imports	950.40	45.0	6.5
Taxes on corporate income	91.10	4.3	0.6
Contributions for government social insurance	22.40	1.1	0.2
Income receipts on assets	118.40	5.6	0.8
Current transfer receipts	659.80	31.2	4.5
Federal grants-in-aid	525.00	24.8	3.6
Other	134.80	6.4	0.9
Current surplus of government enterprises	−8.90	−0.4	−0.1

Source: U.S. Bureau of Economic Analysis, U.S. Department of Commerce, Government Receipts and Expenditures, Second Quarter 2010. Federal receipts from Table 2, state and local receipts from Table 3. GDP from U.S. Bureau of Economic Analysis, U.S. Department of Commerce, Gross Domestic Product: Second Quarter 2010 (Third Estimate), News Release, September 30, 2010.

to state and local governments in the form of grants-in-aid. Total government receipts at all levels account for just over 26 percent of GDP (netting out the federal transfers to state and local governments in order to avoid double counting). That is, the sum of all of the taxes, charges, fees, and other sources of revenue used by governments at all levels in the United States generates receipts equal to 26.3 percent of the value of all goods and services produced by the domestic economy. U.S. federal, state, and local governments have tax systems that generate large amounts of revenue. In order to understand how those tax systems work, we must begin by examining the tax bases that are used and then consider how exemptions, deductions, and credits affect the tax system.

A tax system is characterized by its base definition, rates, exemptions, deductions, and credits. Every tax you can imagine, whether it is applied to income, consumption, the value of property, or anything else, works in the same way. By understanding the definition of the tax base, the rate structure, and the effects of exemptions, deductions, and credits, you will know how the tax works.

WHAT IS TAXED? DEFINING THE TAX BASE

In order to understand how a tax system works, we must first consider what is taxed. The **tax base** is the item or activity that is taxed. Defining the tax base involves specifying both what is taxed and what is not taxed. An income tax, for example, is applied to certain forms of income such as wages but not to other forms of income such as interest earned from municipal bonds. A sales tax may be applied to certain transactions, like the purchase of a good, but not other transactions, like the purchase of a service. Specifying what is taxed and what is not taxed determines the tax base.

Some Useful Distinctions and Examples

It is useful to distinguish between **factor taxes** and **product taxes**. A factor tax is a tax applied to a factor of production such as land, labor, or capital. A product tax is a tax applied to a final product—either a good or a service. For example, the income tax on wages is a factor tax because it is applied to labor, an input in the production process, whereas the sales tax applied to a restaurant meal is a product tax.

Another useful distinction is that taxes are applied to firms as either buyers or sellers. For example, when Wal-Mart sells its products, it is liable to pay the state sales tax in most states where it operates. As a seller of products, the retailer must pay the state sales tax to the state Department of Revenue. Of course, the retailer attempts to pass that tax along to the buyer of the product by adding a sales tax charge to each purchase. The firm also must pay excise taxes on the cigarettes, liquor, gasoline, tires, and other products for which federal and state excise taxes apply. In addition, as a buyer of factors such as labor and capital, the firm must pay an employer's payroll tax on its labor and a corporate income tax and property taxes on its capital.

Households are liable for taxes as well. As a buyer of products, the household may be subject to an **expenditure tax** on the value of all expenditures for goods and services purchased or **excise taxes** on the manufacture or sale of specific goods or services such as long-distance telephone calls, cigarettes, automobile tires, and airline tickets. As a seller of labor resources, the household is liable to pay an employee's share of the **payroll tax** on wage and salary income and an **income tax** on broad sources of income including labor income and capital income (interest and dividends).

When the tax base is the value of a good, the tax is known as an ***ad valorem* tax**. For example, a property tax is an *ad valorem* tax because the tax base is the value of the property. If the tax base is defined as a unit of the good, we have a **unit tax**. For example, an excise tax of $0.40 per package of cigarettes is a unit tax; each unit (package) of the good is taxed at the rate of $0.40. Table 10.2 provides additional examples of both *ad valorem* and unit taxes.

In this text we begin our discussion of a tax system by first specifying the tax base and then discussing the rate structure of the tax. The reason for this

TABLE 10.2 *Ad Valorem* and Unit Taxes

	***Ad Valorem* Tax**	**Unit Tax**
Tax Base	**Value of the Good**	**Unit of the Good**
Examples	Sales tax applied to the value of a commodity purchased (e.g., Illinois state sales tax of 6.25%)	Amusement device occupation tax (e.g., city of Lincoln $10 tax per kiddie amusement ride machine)
	Franchise tax applied to business property (e.g., North Carolina corporate franchise tax $1.50 per $1,000 of value applied to corporate property in the state)	Wheel tax (e.g., city of Chicago wheel tax $75 per automobile per year, $45 per motorcycle per year)
	Property taxes applied to the value of real estate (e.g., Massachusetts property tax rate is limited to a maximum of 2.5% of land value)	Housing impact fee (e.g., city of Alameda affordable housing fee $0.66 to $3.79 per square foot of new commercial or nonresidential construction in the city)
	Estate tax applied to the value of an estate or inheritance tax applied to the value of inheritance (e.g., Kansas inheritance tax 1 to 5% of bequest, in excess of a $30,000 personal exemption, left to a child, depending on the size of the bequest)	Excise taxes (e.g., Colorado tax of $0.22 per gallon of gasoline, New York State excise tax of $2.75 per package of cigarettes, and Florida tax of $0.48 per gallon of beer)

pattern lies in the fact that the tax base definition is the most critical aspect of defining a tax. The rate structure follows after the fundamental definition of the base. Then, we can consider exemptions, deductions, and credits and their impacts on the effective rate of taxation.

Income Tax Base

The essence of any tax lies in the definition of its base, but in order to understand the U.S. income tax it is essential to consider its base definition. Figure 10.1 shows the tax form that is used for the U.S. income tax—Form 1040.[2] Let's examine important aspects of that form to determine how the tax base is defined. The process of defining the tax base begins on line 7 of Form 1040 by asking the taxpayer to list wages, salaries, tips, and so on. Taxable interest received is added on line 8a (tax-exempt income is listed on line 8b). Dividend income is added on line 9. Business income net of business expenses is added on line 12 (or line 18 if the business is a farm). Capital gains or losses are added on line 13. Unemployment compensation and taxable social security benefits are added on lines 19 and 20. The sum of all these amounts and other income is recorded on line 22. This total is called **total income**. The taxpayer is then allowed to make certain adjustments to total income, deductions for retirement or medical savings, moving expenses, and other purposes, resulting in **adjusted gross income** recorded on line 37. On page 2 of Form 1040, the taxpayer lists deductions (either itemized or standard) on line 40 and subtracts personal exemptions on line 42. The final income measure used for the computation of the tax liability is **taxable income** on line 43. Notice the structure of this tax base definition:

$$\begin{aligned} \text{Total income} &= \text{wages, salaries, and tips} + \text{interest income} \\ &\quad + \text{dividend income} + \text{business net income} \\ &\quad + \text{other income} \\ \text{Adjusted gross income} &= \text{total income} - \text{adjustments} \\ \text{Taxable income} &= \text{adjusted gross income} - \text{deductions} - \text{exemptions} \end{aligned}$$

Or, equivalently,

$$\begin{aligned} \text{Taxable income} &= \text{wages, salaries, and tips} + \text{interest income} \\ &\quad + \text{dividend income} + \text{business net income} \\ &\quad + \text{other income} - \text{adjustments} \\ &\quad - \text{deductions} - \text{exemptions} \end{aligned}$$

Are there any sources of income missing from this definition of the tax base? Yes, several forms of income are missing. For example, tax exempt interest paid by state and local governments to bondholders is missing. But there are even more important forms of income missing from the definition of income used in Form 1040. For the most part, only monetary forms of income are included. A worker's compensation consists in part of money income but also includes a range of benefits such as health insurance, dental insurance, life insurance, retirement contributions, and other forms of

FIGURE 10.1(a) U.S. Income Tax Return, Form 1040, Page 1

Form **1040** Department of the Treasury—Internal Revenue Service
U.S. Individual Income Tax Return **2010** (99) IRS Use Only—Do not write or staple in this space.

For the year Jan. 1–Dec. 31, 2010, or other tax year beginning , 2010, ending , 20 OMB No. 1545-0074

Name, Address, and SSN

See separate instructions.

PRINT CLEARLY

Your first name and initial | Last name | **Your social security number**

If a joint return, spouse's first name and initial | Last name | **Spouse's social security number**

Home address (number and street). If you have a P.O. box, see instructions. | Apt. no.

▲ Make sure the SSN(s) above and on line 6c are correct.

City, town or post office, state, and ZIP code. If you have a foreign address, see instructions.

Checking a box below will not change your tax or refund.

Presidential Election Campaign ▶ Check here if you, or your spouse if filing jointly, want $3 to go to this fund . . . . . ▶ ☐ **You** ☐ **Spouse**

Filing Status

Check only one box.

1 ☐ Single
2 ☐ Married filing jointly (even if only one had income)
3 ☐ Married filing separately. Enter spouse's SSN above and full name here. ▶
4 ☐ Head of household (with qualifying person). (See instructions.) If the qualifying person is a child but not your dependent, enter this child's name here. ▶
5 ☐ Qualifying widow(er) with dependent child

Exemptions

6a ☐ **Yourself.** If someone can claim you as a dependent, **do not** check box 6a . . . . .
b ☐ **Spouse** . . . .

Boxes checked on 6a and 6b ____
No. of children on 6c who:
• lived with you ____
• did not live with you due to divorce or separation (see instructions) ____
Dependents on 6c not entered above ____
Add numbers on lines above ▶ ☐

c **Dependents:**

(1) First name Last name	(2) Dependent's social security number	(3) Dependent's relationship to you	(4) ✓ if child under age 17 qualifying for child tax credit (see page 15)
			☐
			☐
			☐
			☐

If more than four dependents, see instructions and check here ▶ ☐

d Total number of exemptions claimed . . . .

Income

Attach Form(s) W-2 here. Also attach Forms W-2G and 1099-R if tax was withheld.

If you did not get a W-2, see page 20.

Enclose, but do not attach, any payment. Also, please use **Form 1040-V.**

7	Wages, salaries, tips, etc. Attach Form(s) W-2		7
8a	**Taxable** interest. Attach Schedule B if required		8a
b	**Tax-exempt** interest. **Do not** include on line 8a . . .	8b	
9a	Ordinary dividends. Attach Schedule B if required		9a
b	Qualified dividends	9b	
10	Taxable refunds, credits, or offsets of state and local income taxes		10
11	Alimony received		11
12	Business income or (loss). Attach Schedule C or C-EZ		12
13	Capital gain or (loss). Attach Schedule D if required. If not required, check here ▶ ☐		13
14	Other gains or (losses). Attach Form 4797		14
15a	IRA distributions . 15a	b Taxable amount . . .	15b
16a	Pensions and annuities 16a	b Taxable amount . . .	16b
17	Rental real estate, royalties, partnerships, S corporations, trusts, etc. Attach Schedule E		17
18	Farm income or (loss). Attach Schedule F		18
19	Unemployment compensation		19
20a	Social security benefits 20a	b Taxable amount . . .	20b
21	Other income. List type and amount		21
22	Combine the amounts in the far right column for lines 7 through 21. This is your **total income** ▶		22

Adjusted Gross Income

23	Educator expenses	23	
24	Certain business expenses of reservists, performing artists, and fee-basis government officials. Attach Form 2106 or 2106-EZ	24	
25	Health savings account deduction. Attach Form 8889 .	25	
26	Moving expenses. Attach Form 3903	26	
27	One-half of self-employment tax. Attach Schedule SE .	27	
28	Self-employed SEP, SIMPLE, and qualified plans . .	28	
29	Self-employed health insurance deduction	29	
30	Penalty on early withdrawal of savings	30	
31a	Alimony paid **b** Recipient's SSN ▶	31a	
32	IRA deduction	32	
33	Student loan interest deduction	33	
34	Tuition and fees. Attach Form 8917	34	
35	Domestic production activities deduction. Attach Form 8903	35	
36	Add lines 23 through 31a and 32 through 35		36
37	Subtract line 36 from line 22. This is your **adjusted gross income** . . . . . . ▶		37

For Disclosure, Privacy Act, and Paperwork Reduction Act Notice, see separate instructions. Cat. No. 11320B Form **1040** (2010)

FIGURE 10.1(b) U.S. Income Tax Return, Form 1040, Page 2

Form 1040 (2010) Page **2**

Tax and Credits	38	Amount from line 37 (adjusted gross income)	38
	39a	Check if: ☐ **You** were born before January 2, 1946, ☐ Blind. ☐ **Spouse** was born before January 2, 1946, ☐ Blind. **Total boxes checked ▶ 39a** ☐	
	b	If your spouse itemizes on a separate return or you were a dual-status alien, check here ▶ **39b** ☐	
	40	**Itemized deductions** (from Schedule A) **or** your **standard deduction** (see instructions)	40
	41	Subtract line 40 from line 38	41
	42	**Exemptions.** Multiply $3,650 by the number on line 6d	42
	43	**Taxable income.** Subtract line 42 from line 41. If line 42 is more than line 41, enter -0-	43
	44	**Tax** (see instructions). Check if any tax is from: **a** ☐ Form(s) 8814 **b** ☐ Form 4972	44
	45	**Alternative minimum tax** (see instructions). Attach Form 6251	45
	46	Add lines 44 and 45 ▶	46
	47	Foreign tax credit. Attach Form 1116 if required	47
	48	Credit for child and dependent care expenses. Attach Form 2441	48
	49	Education credits from Form 8863, line 23	49
	50	Retirement savings contributions credit. Attach Form 8880	50
	51	Child tax credit (see instructions)	51
	52	Residential energy credits. Attach Form 5695	52
	53	Other credits from Form: **a** ☐ 3800 **b** ☐ 8801 **c** ☐ ____	53
	54	Add lines 47 through 53. These are your **total credits**	54
	55	Subtract line 54 from line 46. If line 54 is more than line 46, enter -0- ▶	55
Other Taxes	56	Self-employment tax. Attach Schedule SE	56
	57	Unreported social security and Medicare tax from Form: **a** ☐ 4137 **b** ☐ 8919	57
	58	Additional tax on IRAs, other qualified retirement plans, etc. Attach Form 5329 if required	58
	59	**a** ☐ Form(s) W-2, box 9 **b** ☐ Schedule H **c** ☐ Form 5405, line 16	59
	60	Add lines 55 through 59. This is your **total tax** ▶	60
Payments	61	Federal income tax withheld from Forms W-2 and 1099	61
	62	2010 estimated tax payments and amount applied from 2009 return	62
	63	Making work pay credit. Attach Schedule M	63
If you have a qualifying child, attach Schedule EIC.	64a	**Earned income credit (EIC)**	64a
	b	Nontaxable combat pay election **64b**	
	65	Additional child tax credit. Attach Form 8812	65
	66	American opportunity credit from Form 8863, line 14	66
	67	First-time homebuyer credit from Form 5405, line 10	67
	68	Amount paid with request for extension to file	68
	69	Excess social security and tier 1 RRTA tax withheld	69
	70	Credit for federal tax on fuels. Attach Form 4136	70
	71	Credits from Form: **a** ☐ 2439 **b** ☐ 8839 **c** ☐ 8801 **d** ☐ 8885	71
	72	Add lines 61, 62, 63, 64a, and 65 through 71. These are your **total payments** ▶	72
Refund	73	If line 72 is more than line 60, subtract line 60 from line 72. This is the amount you **overpaid**	73
	74a	Amount of line 73 you want **refunded to you.** If Form 8888 is attached, check here ▶ ☐	74a
Direct deposit? See instructions.	▶ b	Routing number ▶ **c** Type: ☐ Checking ☐ Savings	
	▶ d	Account number	
	75	Amount of line 73 you want **applied to your 2011 estimated tax** ▶	75
Amount You Owe	76	**Amount you owe.** Subtract line 72 from line 60. For details on how to pay, see instructions ▶	76
	77	Estimated tax penalty (see instructions)	77

Third Party Designee

Do you want to allow another person to discuss this return with the IRS (see instructions)? ☐ **Yes.** Complete below. ☐ **No**

Designee's name ▶ Phone no. ▶ Personal identification number (PIN) ▶

Sign Here

Joint return? See page 12. Keep a copy for your records.

Under penalties of perjury, I declare that I have examined this return and accompanying schedules and statements, and to the best of my knowledge and belief, they are true, correct, and complete. Declaration of preparer (other than taxpayer) is based on all information of which preparer has any knowledge.

Your signature	Date	Your occupation	Daytime phone number
Spouse's signature. If a joint return, **both** must sign.	Date	Spouse's occupation	

Paid Preparer Use Only

Print/Type preparer's name	Preparer's signature	Date	Check ☐ if self-employed	PTIN
Firm's name ▶			Firm's EIN ▶	
Firm's address ▶			Phone no.	

Form **1040** (2010)

compensation. The U.S. income tax only taxes the money income part of compensation. Why should that be the tax base definition? Consider two workers each with total compensation packages of $40,000 per year. Alfred receives a salary of $30,000 and benefits with a value of $10,000, whereas Bettina receives only a salary of $40,000. Both have the same total compensation, yet the U.S. income tax will treat them very differently. Alfred will have a tax base of $30,000, whereas Bettina will have a tax base of $40,000. Clearly, there is an incentive to convert taxable salary into nontaxable benefits and legally avoid paying so much income tax. Consider another example of the limited tax base used for the U.S. income tax. Suppose that Alice puts her savings into a bank account that pays interest. Her interest income is taxable, and she must report that interest income on Form 1040, adding it to her wage and salary income in the definition of *total income*. Boris prefers to buy a life insurance policy, which is another form of savings because the policy has a cash value after a certain amount has been paid. Form 1040, shown in Figure 10.1(a), does not ask taxpayers to report the implicit interest on savings in life insurance policies, so this form of income is not taxable. It might make sense for an individual to save by buying an insurance policy rather than by putting money into a bank account, given this difference in the tax treatment of interest. Differential tax treatment such as this can lead people to alter their behavior. Notice, too, that the change in behavior is driven by the definition of the tax base.

The definition of income for the purposes of the U.S. income tax is not what an economist would call total income, including all sources of income. The tax base definition of income emphasizes money income and omits in-kind transfers (such as health care benefits provided by employers), unrealized capital gains (only realized gains are included in the tax base), and imputed income (such as the implicit rental value of homes for homeowners). A more comprehensive definition of total economic income is provided in the **Haig-Simons definition of income as described in Simons (1938).**

Haig-Simons Definition of Income

The Haig-Simons concept of a person's income during a particular time period includes consumption plus the change in the person's net worth. This concept of income includes the total accretion to a person's wealth. Musgrave and Musgrave define this comprehensive measure of income as follows:

> All accretion to wealth should be included, whether it is regular or fluctuating, expected or unexpected, realized or unrealized. No consideration should be given to how the income is used, i.e. whether it is saved or consumed. (1989, 322)

Notice that this definition of income is a net measurement, not a gross measurement of income; that is, it requires that the costs of earning income be subtracted. For example, a comprehensive measure of income should permit that the gross interest income a person earns on a savings account be reduced by the fees on that account, resulting in a net interest income that is less than the gross income. Another feature of this income definition is that it is blind to the source of income. It does not matter whether income is due to capital or labor; it is income. Under the current U.S. income tax base, capital and labor income are sometimes treated differently. For example, capital gains are taxed differently than wage income. A capital gain is the difference between the sale price and purchase price of a stock, representing the increase in value over time. (Capital losses are also possible if the value of the stock fell.)

This taxable income definition is also based on accretions to wealth, not realizations of wealth. That difference is important. Anything that gives a person increased wealth counts, whether that increase is realized or not. For example, a homeowner whose home is appreciating over time has increased wealth that represents increased ability to pay. The fact that the capital gain on his home has not been realized, because he has not sold his home, does not diminish the fact that his ability to pay has increased. Another issue that arises in a comprehensive definition of income relates to **imputed income**. Some forms of wealth result in cash income and other forms of wealth result in imputed income, but a comprehensive income definition should include both. For example, one person may have a bond worth $100,000 that provides interest income which is cash income, but another person may hold her wealth in the form of a home worth $100,000. The home does not pay any cash income to its owner. Rather, it provides implicit income that can be imputed. We could consider the homeowner as any other landlord who rents the home and reports the rental income for tax purposes. In the case of the owner-occupant, she is her own landlord. In this sense, the imputed rental value of her home would be included in income under a comprehensive income tax base.

What are the implications of defining the income tax base more broadly? First, a broader definition of income would result in lower tax rates with the same revenue being generated. Further, lower tax rates result in less distortion to the economy in that they provide taxpayers with less incentive to change their behaviors due to the tax. Second, a broader definition of income assures more equity in the tax system. Similarly situated individuals are more likely to be treated similarly under a comprehensive tax base than under a narrow tax base. Thus, the equity of the tax is improved.

Sales Tax Base

Sales taxes are applied by federal and state and provincial governments in many countries. Some states permit local governments, including cities and counties, to apply a sales tax as well. Although the tax base definition varies quite widely, most sales taxes are applied to the final sales of goods. Notice two things about that definition. First, the sales tax is typically applied to goods, not services. Although states are increasingly looking to expand their sales tax bases to include selected services as well, for the most part, sales taxes are applied to the purchase of goods only.

Second, the sales tax is applied to final sales, not intermediate sales. Intermediate goods are not generally taxed, in order to prevent **cascading** of the tax. Consider a good produced in four stages. Firm A takes raw materials and applies labor and capital to produce a good that is worth \$100. The good is then sold to firm B for further processing. Firm B applies more labor and capital to the good, improving it, and sells it to firm C for \$200. Firm C applies further labor and capital, making the good worth \$300, and sells it to firm D. Firm D finishes the good and sells it to the customer for \$400. If we applied a 5 percent sales tax at each stage of production, firm A would pay a tax of \$5, firm B would pay a tax of \$10, firm C would pay a tax of \$15, and firm D would pay a tax of \$20. The total tax on the good would be \$50 which would be equivalent to a 12.5 percent tax (50/400 = 1/8 = 0.125). Hence, the 5 percent tax would cascade to being a 12.5 percent tax. In order to avoid this problem, the tax is generally applied only at the final stage, resulting in a tax of 5 percent of the value of the good produced. Most state governments apply industrial and agricultural processing exemptions in order to avoid cascading the sales tax. Under these exemptions, a good used in industrial or agricultural processing of other goods is not subject to the sales tax.

Aside from issues of a cascading sales tax, due to a poor definition of the tax base, there are essential issues of *what* to tax. Although the sales tax is designed to apply to all final goods, many states provide an exemption for certain goods such as unprepared food and prescription drugs. The Federation of Tax Administrators reported that as of January 1, 2010, a total of 31 states provide a full exemption of unprepared food. In addition, 7 states tax food at a reduced rate. On prescription drugs, 45 states provide a full exemption. Thus, the sales tax base varies in its definition from state to state, with some states having a broad base and others narrowing the base to exclude unprepared food and prescription drugs. The narrower the tax base, the less revenue is generated from a given tax rate applied to that base.

Another important base definition issue is that most state sales taxes are applied only to goods, not services. Hence, the tax base is the final value of goods produced. If the tax base were expanded to include services, either more revenue could be generated at the existing tax rate or the existing tax rate could be lowered to generate the same revenue. Fox and Murray (1988) estimated that potentially taxable services were 29.3 percent of consumption expenditures in the United States. As a percentage of personal income, the potentially taxable services amount to 23.2 percent. Clearly, taxation of consumer services would expand the sales tax base greatly.

On a state-by-state basis, taxing selected services would generate not only large revenues but also highly varying amounts of revenue. Fox and Murray (1988) report that the greatest revenue potential lies in the taxation of construction services, followed by business and business-related services and health services. Across states and the District of Columbia, there is a wide variation in a total services tax as a percentage of state tax collections. Taxing services is estimated to generate revenue in excess of present sales tax revenue in the District of Columbia. With total tax as a percentage of state tax collections at 103.49 percent, the District could more than double its sales tax revenue by including services in its tax base. States where that percentage is in excess of 60 percent include: Maryland, Massachusetts, New York, Pennsylvania, Rhode Island, Texas, and Vermont. For other states, such as Hawaii and West Virginia, adding services to the sales tax base would generate only a modest amount of added revenue. Fox and Murray (2005) also outlines a number of tax base coordination issues that would be involved with the implementation of a national sales tax.

Value-Added Tax Base

A **value-added tax (VAT)** is a tax applied to the difference between the value of a product at sale and the cost of the raw materials used in its production. That difference is known as *value added*. Although VATs are not often used in the United States, they are a very common form of tax in the rest of the world. Canada, Mexico, Russia, Australia, New Zealand, and most South American and European countries all have VATs. In fact, the World Bank and the IMF make a VAT a required part of the package of reforms countries must adopt in order to receive aid.[3] The VAT is attractive because it is a broad-based tax and can generate substantial revenues at modest rates. The key to understanding the VAT lies in understanding the definition of its tax base.

If you recall the definition of *national product* from your macroeconomics course, you may recall that national product, and hence national income, can be expressed as the sum of consumption expenditures C, investment expenditures I, government expenditures G, and net exports $(X - IM)$; that is, $Y = C + I + G + (X - IM)$. For the moment, let us ignore government and the rest of the world, so that national income and product can be simply expressed as $Y = C + I$. With this context, we can characterize two types of VAT: an income-type VAT that taxes Y, including both C and I components, and a consumption-type VAT that taxes Y net of I, $Y - I$, which is equivalent to taxing consumption C. The difference between the two types of VAT lies in the treatment of investment expenditures.

A simple example will illustrate the VAT tax base.[4] Consider a bakery that produces baked goods for sale to customers. Table 10.3 defines the essential concepts required to understand how a value-added tax would work if applied to the bakery.

In this example, the bakery's costs include expenditures for labor, materials, capital, and credit. The firm's revenue is spent on paying the costs of labor, the cost of materials, depreciation, and interest. What remains is profit. If we define a tax base based on profit, we take revenue, subtract costs, including depreciation and interest, and are left with profit. A value-added tax, however, is not based solely on profit. Rather, a value-added tax is based on the difference between revenue and the cost of raw materials used to produce baked goods. That quantity can be identified in two ways. First, we can obtain the value-added tax base by the **subtractive method**, whereby we begin with gross receipts, or revenue, and subtract the cost of materials. Second, an alternative method of obtaining the value-added tax base is the **additive method**, whereby we add the cost of labor, interest, profits, and

TABLE 10.3 Value-Added Bakery Example

Concept	Example or Definition
Costs	
Labor	Baker, salesclerk
Materials	Flour, sugar, spices, utilities
Capital	Building, mixer, utensils, oven
Credit	Interest paid on loans
Revenue	= Cost of labor + cost of materials + depreciation+ interest + profit
Value added	= Revenue − cost of materials
	= Cost of labor + interest + profit + depreciation

depreciation and obtain the value-added tax base. The equivalence of these two methods of computing the value-added tax base is apparent when one realizes that revenue minus the cost of materials is just equal to the cost of labor plus depreciation, interest, and profit.

Applying the VAT

Value-added taxes are applied in two ways. The first and most common method is the credit-invoice method. According to this method of application, the firm at each stage of production is liable to pay a tax based on the full value of the product. But the firm is given a tax credit for the value of the goods it purchased from the previous stage of production. Table 10.4 provides an example of a credit-invoice VAT applied at a rate of 1 percent. The first stage of production is raw material extraction where the cost of extraction is \$100. Because no other raw materials or intermediate goods are involved, the whole \$100 is value added. A VAT applied at 1 percent requires the extractor to pay a tax of \$1. The second stage of production is raw materials processing where once the good is finished, it sells for \$200. The value-added tax base is the difference between the \$200 sale at the end of this stage and the \$100 cost of raw materials in stage 1. Thus, the value added in the second stage is \$100. Similarly, the third stage of production (component fabrication) and the fourth stage of production (product assembly) each add \$100 in value added as well. The fifth stage (national distribution) and the sixth stage (regional distribution) of production add \$50 each to value added for the product. The final stage of production (retail sales) adds another \$100 to value added.

One of the attractive features of this method of application of a VAT is that reporting and auditing efforts are reduced. The tax is presumptive (applied to the full value of the sale) unless the firm has an invoice to prove otherwise and receive the credit. Tax compliance is thus built into the system.

TABLE 10.4 A 1 Percent Credit-Invoice VAT Example

Production Stage	Sale Amount	Value Added	Gross Tax	Credit	Net Tax
Raw material extraction	100	100	1.00	0.00	1.00
Raw material processing	200	100	2.00	1.00	1.00
Component fabrication	300	100	3.00	2.00	1.00
Product assembly	400	100	4.00	3.00	1.00
National distribution	450	50	4.50	4.00	0.50
Regional distribution	500	50	5.00	4.50	0.50
Retail sale	600	100	6.00	5.00	1.00
Total		600			6.00

Source: From "Closer Look at a State Invoice-Credit VAT," by James Francis from *1992 Proceedings of the Eighty-Fifth Annual Conference on Taxation.* Reprinted by permission of National Tax Association.

This consideration is especially important for countries where compliance levels tend to be low. Even so, there are sometimes problems with VAT compliance in eastern and central Europe, evidenced by the fact that there are more claims for credits than VAT paid.

The second method of application for the VAT is the declaration method and requires firms report to their value added at the end of the tax year, as is typically done with a corporate income tax. The firm reports its VAT tax base, receives whatever exemptions and deductions are permitted, applies the tax rate to the taxable VAT base, and then receives whatever credits may be provided to obtain their VAT liability. This method of applying the VAT requires auditing the firms to assure that their reported value added is accurate and that deductions and credits are taken appropriately.

Comparison of Income, Sales, and Value-Added Tax Bases

A simple way to compare the tax bases for the alternative major taxes that are applied in modern economies is to consider the traditional circular flow diagram for the economy. Figure 10.2 illustrates the circular flow of income and product in the economy.[5]

A personal income tax is applied at point *A*. The tax base is the combination of wage and capital incomes received by households. A tax on the profit of firms is applied at point *B* of the circular flow. A sales tax applied to consumer goods or a VAT of the consumption type is applied at point C. Finally, a VAT of the income type is applied at point *D*.

So far, we have defined three major types of tax bases: income, sales, and valued added. The differences between these tax bases are clear, as we have seen previously. Yet, once the tax base is defined, each tax system is further

FIGURE 10.2 Taxation in the Circular Flow of Income and Product

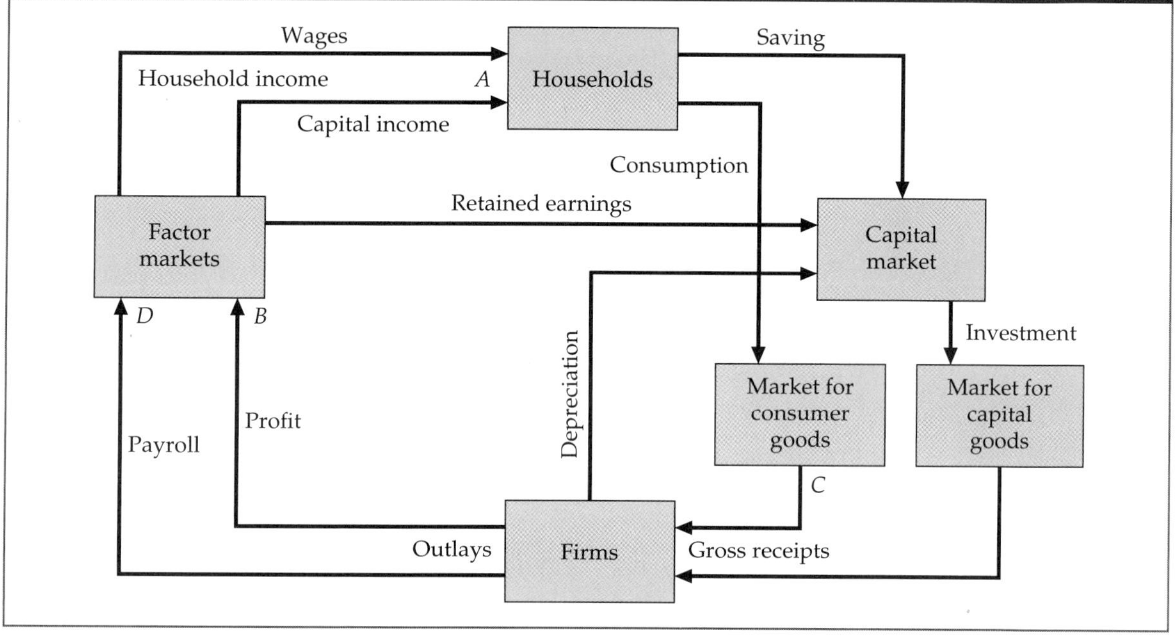

specified by the presence of certain exemptions, deductions, credits, and the tax rates that are applied to the tax base.

HOW IS THE TAX APPLIED? TAX RATES, EXEMPTIONS, DEDUCTIONS, AND CREDITS

Once a tax base is defined for a tax system, exemptions, deductions, and credits that have an impact on the effective rate of taxation are typically applied. Although a nominal tax rate may be applied to the tax base, the effective tax rate may be quite different, due to the deductions and credits.

In order to make the effects clear, we begin with a simple model of the tax base. The amount of tax to be paid (denoted by T) is determined by the product of the tax rate (r) times the tax base (b): $T = rb$. As a result, the amount you pay in taxes is a combination of the definition of the tax base and the tax rates that are applied to that base. If we rearrange the relationship, we can write the tax rate as the ratio of the tax paid to the tax base: $r = T/b$. For example, suppose that you are required to pay a property tax of 2 percent of the value of your home to the local governments in your area. If your home has a value of \$100,000, your tax liability is $T = (0.02)(\$100{,}000) = \$2{,}000$. Thus, the tax you must pay is simply the product of the tax rate and the tax base. We can flip the relationship and discuss the tax rate as the ratio of the tax liability and the tax base. If your tax is \$2,000 on your home which is worth \$100,000, the tax rate is 2 percent,

FIGURE 10.3 A Graduated Rate Structure

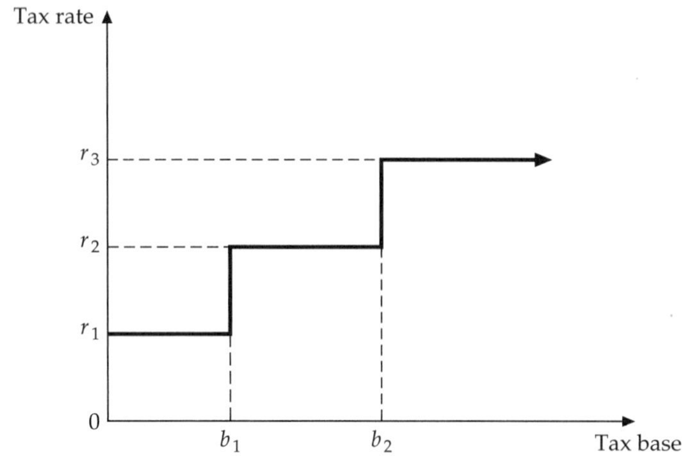

because \$2,000/\$100,000 = 0.02. An understanding of these fundamental relationships is critical to working with issues of taxation and tax policy.

The rate of taxation may not be constant, as was the case in the property tax example in the previous paragraph. An example of a tax with graduated rates is the U.S. income tax, which has approximate rates of 15, 28, 32, 36, and 39 percent. In such a case, we say that the rates are **graduated.** Figure 10.3 illustrates the case of a graduated tax with three rates. For values of the tax base from zero up to b_1, the rate r_1 is applied. For larger values of the tax base from b_1 up to b_2, the rate r_2 is applied. For values of the base equal to b_2 or more, the top rate of r_3 is applied. The intervals defined by the base amounts 0, b_1, and b_2 are often called **tax brackets.** They are intervals over which the specific tax rates apply. When the tax base increases past one of the interval's end points, the taxpayer is said to move into the next bracket.

How do we compute the tax due with a graduated rate structure? Well, if the value of the tax base is between zero and b_1, we simply take the product of the base and the rate: $T = r_1b_1$. If the value of base b is between b_1 and b_2, we must compute the tax, realizing that the rate r_1 applies to the first b_1 units of the base and the rate r_2 applies to the base thereafter: $T = r_1b_1 + r_2(b - b_1)$. If the value of base b is in excess of b_2, we must compute the tax, realizing that the rate r_1 applies to the first b_1 units of the base, the rate r_2 applies from the b_1 to b_2, and the rate r_3 applies thereafter: $T = r_1b_1 + r_2(b_2 - b_1) + r_3(b - b_2)$. Consider the example of a graduated income tax structure (actually a simplified version of the U.S. personal income tax), as defined in Table 10.5. Given this tax structure, we can compute the tax liability for several income levels in order to illustrate how the graduated rate structure works. Table 10.6 provides three examples of tax liability computation.

TABLE 10.5 A Hypothetical Income Tax Rate Structure

Tax Rates	Tax Brackets
$r_1 = 0.15$	Zero to \$25,000
$r_2 = 0.28$	\$25,001 to \$40,000
$r_3 = 0.36$	\$40,001 or more

TABLE 10.6 Example Tax Computations for the Hypothetical Income Tax Structure

Income	Tax Liability
\$16,000	$T = 0.15(\$16{,}000) = \$2{,}400$
\$37,000	$T = 0.15(\$25{,}000) + 0.28(\$37{,}000 - \$25{,}001)$
	$= \$3{,}750 + \$3{,}360$
	$= \$7{,}110$
\$68,000	$T = 0.15(\$25{,}000) + 0.28(\$40{,}000 - \$25{,}001) + 0.36(\$68{,}000 - \$40{,}001)$
	$= \$3{,}750 + \$4{,}200 + \$10{,}080$
	$= \$18{,}030$

Exemptions, Deductions, and Credits

Taxes can be reduced in three ways: exemptions, deductions, and credits. A **tax exemption** is a provision in the tax law that makes a specific class of taxpayers or specific type of activity that would normally be taxable exempt from the tax. For example, many states exempt farmers from paying the excise tax on gasoline used in farm equipment because that tax is used to provide road maintenance. Because farmers use gasoline to drive in fields rather than on roads, they are exempt from paying the excise tax.

Tax deductions are subtractions from the normal tax base that are permitted for specific purposes defined in the tax law. For example, the U.S. individual income tax permits a deduction for tax preparation expenses. If you pay an accountant to prepare your tax return, that expense may be deducted from your taxable income, thereby reducing your tax.

A **tax credit** is a reduction in the amount of tax owed. For example, the U.S. corporate income tax provides a credit for foreign taxes paid. A company that is obligated to pay tax to a foreign country on its income can receive a credit on its U.S. tax for that foreign tax paid, thereby assuring that the company's income is taxed once, not twice. A **refundable tax credit** is a credit provided in its full amount, even if it exceeds the person's tax liability.

ALTERNATIVE DICKENS

SCROOGE IS AUDITED.

For example, a person may have a tax liability of \$167 and a refundable tax credit of \$200. In that case, the person would receive a check from the government for \$33. The tax credit is fully refundable and is paid despite the fact that the person's tax liability is less than the amount of the credit. A **nonrefundable tax credit** is a tax credit that is usable only up to the amount of the tax liability. In the previous example, if the \$200 credit were nonrefundable, the taxpayer would have no tax to pay but would not receive a check for the \$33 difference. The credit is usable only up to the amount of the tax liability.

Table 10.7 gives more examples of exemptions, deductions, and credits as they are often applied on income, sales, and property taxes. How do these mechanisms alter the rate of taxation? Because each reduces the tax to some extent, the effective rate of taxation is lower than the nominal rate of taxation. The **nominal tax rate** is the rate named in law that applies to the taxable base, whereas the **effective tax rate** is the rate of taxation that effectively applies after exemptions, deductions, and credits are taken into account. To see how exemptions, deductions, and credits reduce the effective tax rate, we use a simple model of the tax base, applying the nominal tax rate, making adjustments for these features, and then computing the effective rate of taxation.

First, suppose that part of the tax base is exempt from taxation. That exemption may apply to a class of taxpayers, as in the case where all agricultural producers are exempted from paying a sales tax on new machinery, or

TABLE 10.7 Examples of Exemptions, Deductions, and Credits

Tax	Exemption	Deduction	Credit
Income tax	Personal exemption for each dependent ($3,650 per person in 2010)	Standard deduction ($5,700 for a single person or $11,400 for a married couple in 2010)	Earned income tax credit (EITC) for low-income working persons (Form1040, line 61a)
	Exemption for interest income earned from municipal bonds	Itemized deductions:	Education credits (Form 1040, line 49)
	Exemption for compensation paid in the form of health care benefits	Deduction for home mortgage interest and property taxes paid	Credit for child and dependent care expenses (Form 1040, line 48)
		Deduction for charitable contributions	Credit for a portion of local property taxes paid (circuit-breaker).
		Deduction for medical expenses in excess of 2.5% of AGI	
Sales tax	Exemption from sales tax provided to nonprofit organizations		Sales tax credit for tax paid on intermediate goods
	Exemption for intermediate goods sold to businesses		
Property tax	Exemption provided to government property (e.g., national forests are exempt from local property taxes)		Open space and prime agricultural land given a credit in exchange for nondevelopment
	Exemption provided by some states for owner-occupants, exempting a portion of home value from taxation		

the exemption may apply to a class of goods or specific activities, as in the case where intermediate goods are exempted from the sales tax. Take the case of unprepared food (purchased at a grocery store) that is exempt from a state sales tax, as is practiced in the majority of U.S. states. Of the total tax base b, we can denote the taxable part as b_t and the exempt part as b_x, so $b = b_t + b_x$. The effect of this exemption is to reduce the effective rate of taxation. If we divide the tax paid by the total base, the effective tax rate (denoted r_e) is given by

$$r_e = T/(b_t + b_x) = rb_t/(b_t + b_x). \tag{10.1}$$

Exemptions reduce effective tax rates. The ratio $b_t/(b_t + b_x)$ in the expression for the effective tax rate is less than 1, because $b_t < (b_t + b_x)$, so the effective tax rate r_e is smaller than the nominal tax rate r. The larger the exemption, relative to the taxable base, the smaller the effective tax rate.

Take the example of a sales tax exemption for unprepared food, or groceries. Suppose that the state sales tax is applied at the rate $r = 0.05$, a 5 percent tax. Suppose that the Ricardo family has an annual income of \$45,000, of which it spends \$40,000 and saves \$5,000. Of the \$40,000 the family spends on goods and services, suppose that they spend \$10,000 on groceries. The effective rate of taxation can be computed as $r_e = (0.05)(\$30{,}000/\$40{,}000) = 0.0375$. The grocery exemption reduces the effective rate of taxation for the state sales tax from 5 down to 3.75 percent. Compare that to the Mertz family with an annual income of \$25,000, of which it spends \$23,000 and saves \$2,000. Of the \$23,000 the family spends on goods and services, suppose that they spend \$10,000 on groceries. The effective rate of taxation for this family is $r_e = (0.05)(\$13{,}000/\$23{,}000) = 0.0283$, or 2.83 percent. Thus, the grocery exemption reduces the effective rate of taxation more for the Mertz family than for the Ricardo family. The reason, of course, is that both families spend the same amount on groceries so that the grocery exemption is worth proportionally more to the lower-income Mertz family than to the Ricardo family.

Deductions also reduce effective tax rates. Suppose that we provide a deduction of amount d to a taxpayer. That deduction reduces the amount of the taxable base to which we apply the tax rate in order to compute the tax, as shown in the following tax computation:

$$T = r(b - d). \tag{10.2}$$

Taking the deduction into account, we compute the effective tax rate r_e as

$$r_e = T/b = r(b - d)/b \tag{10.3}$$

The ratio $(b - d)/b$ in this expression is less than 1, because $b - d < b$, so the effective tax rate r_e is less than the nominal tax rate r. Deductions reduce nominal tax rates. The larger the deduction d, the smaller the effective tax rate. Consider the effect of the standard deduction on the U.S. income tax. The standard deduction for a single person for tax year 2001 was \$4,550.

Compare the effect of the standard deduction for two individuals. Keisha works at a bookstore and has taxable income of \$25,000, whereas Marquis is a professional musician with taxable income of \$50,000. Suppose that the nominal tax rate for both individuals is $r = 0.20$, a 20 percent rate. Taking into account the standard deduction, the effective tax rate for Keisha is actually $r_e = (0.20)(\$25{,}000 - \$4{,}550)/\$25{,}000 = 0.1636$, an effective tax rate of 16.36 percent. The effective tax rate for Marquis is $r_e = (0.20)(\$50{,}000 - \$4{,}550)/\$50{,}000 = 0.1818$, an effective tax rate of 18.18 percent. The standard deduction has the effect of reducing the nominal tax rate from 20 percent to something less. How much less depends on the size of the deduction relative to the tax base. The larger the deduction relative to the tax base, the greater the reduction in the effective tax rate.

A tax credit works in an entirely different way. Rather than reducing the tax base as an exemption or deduction does, a credit reduces the tax liability.

For example, the U.S. individual income tax has several credits, including the child credit (Form 1040, line 46), the foreign tax credit (Form 1040, line 43), and the credit for the elderly or disabled (Form 1040, line 45). The effect of each of these credits is to reduce the tax liability of a taxpayer, after the tax has been computed (see Form 1040 in Figure 1(b) and note that the tax liability is computed on line 40, with each of these credits reducing liability after line 40).

If we provide a credit (denoted c), the tax becomes $T = rb - c$. The effective tax rate is then

$$r_e = T/b = (rb - c)/b. \tag{10.4}$$

Credits reduce effective tax rates but do so more powerfully than exemptions and deductions. It is important to notice, however, that a credit reduces the effective tax rate in a more powerful way than an exemption or deduction does. Because the credit reduces tax liability, rather than simply reducing the base, it has a greater effect in reducing the effective tax rate.[6] A \$1 credit reduces the tax owed by \$1, whereas a \$1 deduction reduces the tax owed by the marginal tax rate times that dollar, which is substantially less than \$1. Consider the example of the Nixon family with taxable income of \$70,000 and two children. If the tax rate is $r = 0.20$, or 20 percent, their tax liability would be $T = (0.20)(\$70{,}000) = \$14{,}000$. The child tax credit of \$600 per child would reduce their liability by \$1,200 to \$12,800. That would make the effective rate of taxation $t_e = (\$14{,}000 - \$1{,}200)/\$14{,}000 = 0.1829$, or 18.29 percent. Notice that the child tax credit has reduced their effective rate of taxation from the nominal 20 percent down to 18.29 percent. Now, consider the Kennedy family with the same income but five children. Their tax liability would be \$14,000 less the credit of \$3,000 (5 times \$600), making their effective rate of taxation $t_e = (\$14{,}000 - \$3{,}000)/\$70{,}000 = 0.1571$, or 15.71 percent. The Kennedy family faces a lower effective rate of taxation due to the credit.

In recent years a number of high-income **phaseouts** have been introduced in the U.S. income tax system. For example, the personal exemption of \$3,650 permitted on the year 2010 tax return is phased out for single persons with Adjusted Gross Income (AGI) in excess of \$166,800 or a married couple filing jointly (separately) with AGI in excess of \$250,200 (\$125,100) (Form 1040, line 42). If your income is above the phaseout threshold, you must reduce the dollar amount of your exemptions by 2 percent for each \$2,500 (or part thereof) that your AGI exceeds the threshold. This phaseout reduces the personal exemption for high-income families and has the effect of raising the effective rate of taxation.

Similarly, itemized deductions for income and property taxes paid to state and local governments, interest paid for home mortgages, gifts to charity, job expenses, and other miscellaneous deductions are subject to a **deduction limitation** based on income. If your AGI is more than \$166,800 (\$83,400 if married filing separately), your deductions are subject to limitations. These phaseouts and limitations are an indirect means of making the tax rate schedule more steeply graduated. Rather than directly raise the tax rate on high-income taxpayers, however, the phaseout or deduction limitation is an indirect means of raising the tax rate without making it appear as though the tax rate has been raised. The reality, however, is that a phaseout or deduction limitation raises the effective tax rate. This is yet another example of how things are not as they may appear in the realm of tax policy. Whatever the top marginal tax rate listed in the tax table, the effective tax rate for a family in that income bracket is higher because exemptions are phased out and deductions are limited for taxpayers in that bracket. The true effective rate of taxation is not what it appears to be.

Statutory and Effective Tax Rates

Exemptions, deductions, and credits all have the effect of reducing the rate of taxation. In order to get a more accurate picture of the rate of taxation, we need to divide the tax actually paid by a full measure of the tax base. That rate of taxation is called the *effective tax rate*. The effective tax rate can differ quite substantially from the statutory tax rate that appears in the tax statute, or law. Economists define the effective tax rate as the ratio of the tax actually paid to the full tax base. The numerator of that ratio is affected by credits and the denominator is affected by exemptions and deductions. Because the tax actually paid is net of any credits, we divide that net tax paid by the tax base to compute the effective tax rate. On the other hand, because the tax base is reduced by exemptions or deductions, we include the full tax base in the denominator to compute the effective tax rate.

An example helps to illustrate the difference between the statutory rate and the effective rate. Suppose that a person has a home with a market value of $100,000 and lives in a community with a property tax rate of 2 percent. The state government provides an exemption of $20,000 worth of home value in order to reduce the property tax burden, making the taxable portion of the home value $80,000. The property tax paid is then 2 percent of $80,000, which is $1,600. The effective tax rate is the $1,600 tax paid divided by the full value of the house, $100,000, which is a rate of 1.6 percent. Although the statutory tax rate is 2 percent, the effective tax rate is 1.6 percent which is fully one-fifth less. Tax rates are never as they appear. Consequently, be careful to consider effective tax rates, not statutory tax rates, when evaluating tax systems.

Average and Marginal Tax Rates

Tax rates can be defined on either an *average* or *marginal* basis. Suppose that we ask the question, What portion of the taxpayer's total income is required by the tax? To answer this question, we would compute the **average tax rate (*ATR*)**: the ratio of the tax paid to income (the tax base). For example, if a person with an income of $50,000 pays an income tax of $7,500, the average tax rate is 0.15 (since $7,500/$50,000 = 0.15). The tax bill, averaged over all the person's dollars of income, is 15 percent of that income. The average tax rate is the tax divided by the tax base: $ATR = T/b$. The ATR represents the share of the total tax base taken in tax, averaging all the dollars of the tax base. The tax rates discussed previously are average tax rates, both statutory and effective.

Another conceptual way of thinking about tax rates follows from asking the question differently: What portion of an *additional* dollar of income will the taxpayer be asked to pay? If an additional dollar of income results in an additional tax of \$0.30, the marginal tax rate is 0.3. The **marginal tax rate (*MTR*)** is the ratio of the change in tax ΔT to the change in tax base Δb:[7] $MTR = \Delta T/\Delta b$. The MTR represents the fraction of an additional dollar of tax base that is taken in tax.

In order to illustrate the potential difference between average and marginal tax rates, consider a simple progressive income tax with two brackets. Income up to \$30,000 is taxed at the rate of 20 percent, and income above \$30,000 is taxed at the rate of 30 percent. Now consider a person with an income of \$50,000. That person will pay a tax of \$12,000 (\$6,000 on the first \$30,000 of income and \$6,000 on the next \$20,000 of income). The average tax rate is the ratio of tax paid to total income, in this case \$12,000/\$50,000, which is 0.24. On the margin, however, the person pays a tax rate of 30 percent because an additional \$1,000 in income will raise the person's tax liability by \$300. The marginal tax rate is 0.30, whereas the average tax rate is 0.24.

What is the relationship between average and marginal tax rates? In the previous example, the marginal rate is above the average. Is that always the case? Not necessarily. If the tax rate applied to the upper-income bracket were 15 percent, the person's total tax bill would be \$9,000, resulting in an average tax rate of 0.18 and a marginal tax rate of 0.15. Well, when will the average tax rate be below the marginal rate and when will it be above? The answer to this question is clear if we think for a moment about something every student has: a grade point average. A student's grade point average is an average like an average tax rate. It is the ratio of the total honor points earned to the total number of credit hours taken. But the student's performance this semester will increase both the number of honor points and the number of credit hours. The ratio of the two is the student's grade point average this semester, a marginal grade point average. The overall grade point average will rise if the performance this semester is above the average. It will fall if it is below. Tax rates work the same way. The average tax rate rises if the marginal tax rate is above the average, and it falls if the marginal tax rate is below the average.

Beyond our concern for the average and marginal rates of taxation, expressed in terms of the tax base involved, we may also care about a tax in relationship to income. We may care, for example, that a sales tax that is expressed as a simple percentage of consumption expenditure actually takes a larger share of income from poor people than it takes from high-income people.

Taxation and Income

We are often concerned about how a tax affects people of different income levels. Consequently, we may want to examine the tax paid as a fraction of income to see whether low-income people are paying a lower or higher share of their income in tax compared to high-income people. Although the tax base may be consumption, property, or some other form of expenditure or wealth, we are concerned about how the tax affects people across the income distribution.

Consider a state sales tax as an example. Suppose that a person's consumption function is given as $C = \$5{,}000 + 0.8Y$, where C is consumption expenditures per year and Y is annual income. In this linear consumption function, the constant \$5,000 is autonomous consumption or that portion of consumption independent of income. If $Y = 0$, we have $C = \$5{,}000$. Even with no income, this person consumes \$5,000 worth of goods and services per year. How is that possible? Positive consumption is possible even when income is zero because the person may have savings that she can draw up or because she can borrow. The slope term 0.8 is the marginal propensity to consume. It represents the portion of an additional dollar of income that is allocated to consumption expenditure. In this case, the person allocates 80 cents of each additional dollar of income to consumption.

Table 10.8 illustrates this person's consumption expenditures for several levels of income. Insert the income numbers into the consumption function and convince yourself that the consumption levels listed in the table are correct. Table 10.8 also lists the tax that the consumer would pay in a state with a 5 percent sales tax that applies to all consumption.

The fourth column of the table lists the average tax rate paid by the consumer. This is the fraction of her income that she pays in sales tax. The average tax rate is undefined at an income level of zero because division by zero is not defined. The average tax rate falls from 6.5 percent at an income level of

TABLE 10.8 The Relationship Between a Tax and Income

Income (\$)	Consumption (\$)	Tax (\$)	Average Tax Rate	Marginal Tax Rate
0	5,000	250	NA	0.04
10,000	13,000	650	0.065	0.04
20,000	21,000	1,050	0.053	0.04
30,000	29,000	1,450	0.048	0.04
40,000	37,000	1,850	0.046	0.04
50,000	45,000	2,250	0.045	0.04
60,000	53,000	2,650	0.044	0.04

\$10,000 to 4.4 percent at an income level of \$60,000. Notice that as income rises, the *ATR* falls.

The last column of Table 10.8 lists the marginal tax rate, which is the rate of tax applied to an additional dollar of income. The marginal tax rate is 4 percent throughout. This may seem incorrect because the tax rate is 5 percent, but keep in mind that the consumer spends just 80 cents of each additional dollar of income; hence the 5 percent tax rate applies to 80 percent of an additional dollar of income. Because 80 percent of 5 percent is 4 percent, the marginal tax rate is 4 percent over the entire range of income in the table.

This example can also be described more generally using the consumption function $C = a + bY$, where C is consumption, a is autonomous consumption (independent of income), b is the marginal propensity to consume, and Y is income. If the tax rate applied to consumption is t, the consumer will pay a tax $T = tC$, where

$$T = tC = t(a + bY) = ta + tbY. \qquad (10.5)$$

Notice that the tax on consumption has two components. The first term is independent of income and the second term depends on income. The average and marginal tax rates are

$$ATR = ta/Y + tb, \qquad (10.6)$$

$$MTR = tb. \qquad (10.7)$$

Notice that the average tax rate and the marginal tax rate have one term in common: tb. The *ATR* is larger than the *MTR* by the amount of the second term in the *ATR*, ta/Y. As Y increases, however, this term shrinks toward zero and the *ATR* approaches the *MTR*. Hence, for large income, the *ATR* will be approximately equal to the *MTR*. Notice also that the usual relationship between average and marginal quantities holds in this case. We know from our study of cost curves and other applications in economics, as well as from our understanding of grade point averages and baseball batting averages, that when a marginal quantity is below the average, the average must be falling. The same relationship applies to tax rates. In just the same way that if Alex Rodriguez goes 0 for 4 in tonight's game in New York, his batting average will fall, if the *MTR* is below the *ATR*, the *ATR* will fall. Figure 10.4 illustrates this case. The marginal tax rate is below the average tax rate, and hence the average tax rate is falling with income.

When the average tax rate declines with increasing income, we say that the tax is **regressive**. The tax requires a smaller share of income for a high-income person than for a low-income person. If the opposite situation holds, with the average tax rate rising with income, we say that the tax is **progressive**. These two terms tell us how a tax is related to income. Of course, a third possibility exists. If the average tax rate is unrelated to income, we say the tax is **flat rate**.

FIGURE 10.4 Average and Marginal Tax Rates for the Sales Tax

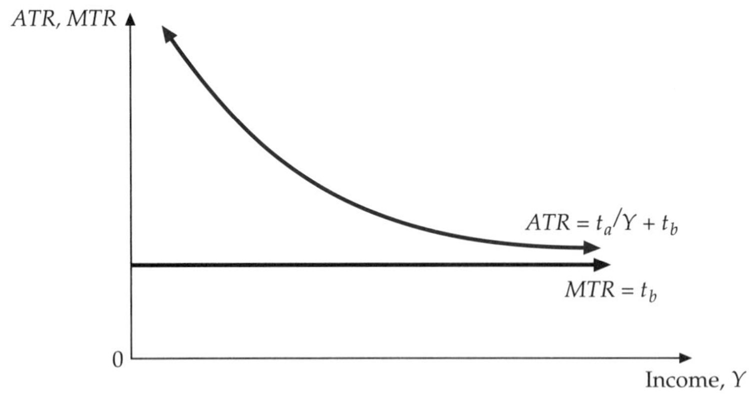

In order to see the impact of an exemption on the degree of regressivity of a tax, we can reconsider the sales tax example previous. Suppose that we exempt the first $3,000 of consumption from taxation. This is what a number of states do when they provide exemptions for expenditures on food or prescription drugs. The table is modified, as shown in Table 10.9. The exemption has the effect of reducing the tax at all levels of income and hence reducing the average tax rate at all levels of income. Notice, however, that the average tax rate falls by a larger amount at lower-income levels. That is because the $3,000 exemption is a larger fraction of income at the lower-income levels.

TABLE 10.9 The Relationship Between a Tax and Income—with a Tax Exemption

Income ($)	Consumption ($)	Tax ($)	Average Tax Rate	Marginal Tax Rate
0	5,000	100	NA	0.04
10,000	13,000	500	0.0500	0.04
20,000	21,000	900	0.0450	0.04
30,000	29,000	1,300	0.0433	0.04
40,000	37,000	1,700	0.0425	0.04
50,000	45,000	2,100	0.0420	0.04
60,000	53,000	2,500	0.0417	0.04

POLICY STUDY

The Flat Tax

One of the more interesting proposals for reforming the U.S. tax system in recent years has been the proposal to implement the so-called flat tax. The term *flat tax* is used to describe several forms of taxation. First, some advocates of a flat tax simply want an income tax with a single flat tax rate above some exemption amount. In that case, the tax has an exemption E, above which a single strictly positive marginal tax rate t is applied to labor income. The tax paid T is a function of income Y, where $T(Y) = \max[t(Y-E),0]$. A number of countries have adopted such flat taxes in recent years, as illustrated in Table 10.10.

Although the name of the tax might indicate that its principal feature is a flat tax rate, the more important issue is what the flat tax would tax; that is, defining the tax base. As it turns out, the flat tax is not at all like our current income taxes applied to households and corporations. In fact, the flat tax is a completely different kind of tax than is currently used in the United States.

The flat tax is a value-added tax (VAT). Hall and Rabushka (1995, 2007) and Hall et al (1996) have the objective of taxing consumption, not income. So, their proposal is to replace the present personal and corporate income taxes with a VAT of the consumption type. Recall that in a macroeconomic sense, income is consumption plus investment: $Y = C + I$. Because they want to tax consumption, they begin by thinking of their tax base as income minus investment: $Y - I$. The simplest way to tax consumption would be to have each firm in the economy pay a tax on the amount it generates minus its investment expenditure. That is how a VAT would be applied, as in all European countries. Hall and Rabushka, however, do not propose a traditional VAT. Instead, their conception is to break the consumption-type VAT tax base into two pieces: one part paid by firms and the other part paid by individuals. Their proposal is to have

TABLE 10.10 Flat Tax Adopters

Country	Year Flat Tax Adopted	Personal Income Tax Rates		Corporate Income Tax Rate, After Adoption
		Before Adoption	After Adoption	
Estonia	1994	16–33%	26%	26%
Lithuania	1994	18–33%	33%	29%
Latvia	1997	10 and 25%	25%	25%
Russia	2001	12–30%	13%	37%
Ukraine	2004	10–40%	13%	25%
Slovak Republic	2004	10–38%	19%	19%
Georgia	2005	12–20%	12%	20%
Romania	2005	18–40%	16%	16%

Source: Keen M, Kim Y, Varsano R (2006). The "Flat Tax(es)": Principles and Evidence, IMF working paper, available on www.imf.org, Washington, Table 1, p. 6.

firms pay tax on all the income they generate net of investment, except the amount the firm pays to workers. That part would be taxable for the workers. By doing this, Hall and Rabushka say they want to introduce more progressivity into the proposed tax than would be possible under a traditional VAT. They propose that the part of the tax paid by workers be taxed progressively. Hall and Rabushka describe their objective this way:

> But a value-added tax is unfair because it is not progressive. That's why we break the tax in two. The firm pays tax on all the income generated at the firm except the income paid to its workers. The workers pay tax on what they earn, and the tax they pay is progressive. (1995, 55)

The flat tax should be viewed as an integrated tax system. It is integrated in the sense that all income is taxed. Keep in mind that the business tax portion of the flat tax would apply to all businesses, not just corporations. Hence, all business income (net of investment) would be taxed, not just the net income of corporations as with the corporate income tax. The flat tax also taxes all forms of interest income, not just the part of interest income taxed under the personal income tax as in the present situation. The objective of the flat tax is to tax all forms of income at the same tax rate. The wage tax portion of that tax system is made progressive, however, by including large exemptions.

Figures 10.5 and 10.6 illustrate the proposed postcard tax returns that Hall and Rabushka would use to implement their flat tax. There is a postcard-sized return for the individual wage tax (Form 1, Figure 10.5) and another for the business tax (Form 2, Figure 10.6). What is the tax base for the individual wage tax? Form 1 asks the taxpayer to record wage and salary income on line 1 and pension and retirement benefits on line 2. The sum of those amounts is total compensation, recorded on line 3. Personal allowances are then subtracted before the tax is computed.

Form 2 asks businesses to record gross revenue from sales on line 1. Then allowable costs are listed on line 2, including purchases of goods, services, materials, wages, salaries, pensions, and purchases of capital equipment, structures, and land. Line 3 sums the allowable costs and line 4 takes gross revenues minus allowable costs to obtain taxable income. Except for the deduction for labor income (wages, salaries, and pensions), this tax would look very similar to a consumption-type VAT. Of course, as Hall and Rabushka point out, the labor income is taxed at the household level, so in effect; this *is* a consumption-type VAT.

The name *flat tax* would seem to imply that this is a tax with a flat rate, right? Hold on, things in the murky world of taxation are not always as they appear. The proposal for a flat tax to replace the current progressive income tax in the United States has gained a good deal of public attention, in part because people are attracted to the simple notion that the tax rate is a single rate that would make tax liability proportional to income, or so they think. The main idea embodied in the so-called flat tax is to define a broad-based tax and apply a flat rate to that base. That much is true. It takes little analysis, however, to demonstrate that the effective tax rate embodied in the proposals that have been suggested in recent years does not have a flat rate. The effective tax rate rises with income, making the flat tax progressive. The Hall-Rabushka version (1995) of the flat tax would tax a family of four at a 19 percent flat rate on income in excess of $25,000.[8] With such a large amount of

FIGURE 10.5 Flat Tax Individual Wage Tax Form

Form 1	**Individual Wage Tax**	**1996**
Your first name and initial (if joint return, also give spouse's name and initial)	Last name	Your social security number
Home address (number and street including apartment number or rural route)		Spouse's social security number
City, town, or post office, state, and ZIP code		Your occupation
		Spouse's occupation

1 Wages and salary	1	
2 Pension and retirement benefits	2	
3 Total compensation *(line 1 plus line 2)*	3	
4 Personal allowance		
(a) $16,500 for married filing jointly	4a	
(b) $9,500 for single	4b	
(c) $14,000 for single head of household	4c	
5 Number of dependents, not including spouse	5	
6 Personal allowances for dependents *(line 5 multiplied by $4,500)*	6	
7 Total personal allowances *(line 4 plus line 6)*	7	
8 Taxable compensation *(line 3 less line 7, if positive; otherwise zero)*	8	
9 Tax *(19% of line 8)*	9	
10 Tax withheld by employer	10	
11 Tax due *(line 9 less line 10, if positive)*	11	
12 Refund due *(line 10 less line 9, if positive)*	12	

exempt income, we should expect to find that the effective tax rate is anything but flat. Consider the structure of the flat tax using the concepts of this chapter, in particular the effect of the generous exemption on the effective tax rate. Table 10.11 shows that the effective average tax rate is zero for families with income below the taxable threshold, due to the exemption. The effective *ATR* is positive at 3.2 percent for a family of four with income of $30,000 and rises from that level to 16.2 percent for a family of four with income of $100,000. Clearly, the so-called flat tax is quite progressive as the average tax rate rises with income. The flat tax does not have an effective tax rate that is flat.

What is the current status of the flat tax proposal? After several years of intense interest in some form of comprehensive tax reform during the 1990s, Congress and the administration seem content at this point to tinker with the existing tax system rather than replace it with an entirely new tax system. The President's Advisory Panel on

FIGURE 10.6 Flat Tax Business Tax Form

Form 2	**Business Tax**	**1996**
Business name		Employer Identification Number
Street address		County
City, State, and ZIP code		Principal product

1 Gross revenue from sales	**1**	
2 Allowable costs		
(a) Purchases of goods, services, and materials	**2a**	
(b) Wages, salaries, and retirement benefits	**2b**	
(c) Purchases of capital equipment, structure, and land	**2c**	
3 Total allowable costs *(sum of lines 2(a), 2(b), and 2(c))*	**3**	
4 Taxable income *(line 1 less line 3)*	**4**	
5 Tax *(19% of line 4)*	**5**	
6 Carry-forward from 1994	**6**	
7 Interest on carry-forward *(6% of line 6)*	**7**	
8 Carry-forward into 1995 *(line 6 plus line 7)*	**8**	
9 Tax due *(line 5 less line 8, if positive)*	**9**	
10 Carry-forward to 1996 *(line 8 less line 5, if positive)*	**10**	

TABLE 10.11 Effective Tax Rates for a Family of Four at Various Income Levels Under the Hall-Rabushka Version of the Flat Tax

Income ($)	Taxable Income ($)	Tax ($)	Average Tax Rate
10,000	0	0	0.000
20,000	0	0	0.000
30,000	5,000	950	0.032
40,000	15,000	2,850	0.071
50,000	35,000	6,650	0.133
60,000	45,000	8,550	0.143
70,000	55,000	10,450	0.149
80,000	65,000	12,350	0.154
90,000	75,000	14,250	0.158
100,000	85,000	16,150	0.162

Source: Adapted from Hall and Rabushka 1995.

Federal Tax Reform (2005) proposed two alternative tax systems, neither of which was a so-called flat tax. Although Steve Forbes, Dick Armey, and other prominent advocates of a flat tax system have faded from the political landscape, the underlying discontent with aspects of the income tax system has not gone away. Currently there are several proposals for fundamental tax reform, some of which are based on the insights of the flat tax. We will discuss tax reform proposals in greater depth in Chapter 14.

POLICY STUDY

Average Tax Rates for the U.S. Income Tax[9]

Analysts at the Statistics of Income (SOI) division of the IRS have developed a consistent measure of income for the purpose of examining changes in the distribution of individual income over time. This measure of income can be used to examine the changes in the average tax rate (ATR) over time. Substantial changes have occurred in the past 25 years in both tax rates and definitions of taxable income, but the overall impact of those changes can be summarized by looking at the ATRs over time.

In order to analyze changes in income and taxes over time we must have consistent measures of both income and taxes. The most common measure of income is adjusted gross income (AGI), but the definition of AGI has been subject to numerous changes over time. That means it is not a suitable measure as a basis for analyzing changes in average tax rates over time. To remedy this situation, SOI has developed a comprehensive and consistent income measure they call the *1979 Retrospective Income Concept*. Strudler, Petska, and Petska (2004) and Petska, Studler, and Petska (2003) provide background on this income concept and its measurement. It is designed to include the same income and deduction items available on the individual income tax returns over time. Using the tax years from 1979 to 1986 as base years, they identified income and deduction items that were then applied to later years. This measure of income includes several forms of income that were partially excluded from AGI in the base years. The most significant of these inclusions is the full amount of all capital gains. In addition, all dividends and unemployment compensation were included in the calculation of income. Total pensions, annuities, IRA distributions, and rollovers were also added. Social security benefits were omitted because they were not included on tax returns prior to 1984. Depreciation in excess of straight-line depreciation that was subtracted from AGI was added back. Several important limitations of this income concept are acknowledged in Petska and Strudler (1999). They note that cash, in-kind public assistance, and Earned Income Tax Credits (EITC) are omitted from retrospective income.

Retrospective income has been computed for all individual returns in the annual SOI sample files for the years from 1979 to 2004. Returns with negative income were omitted and the remaining returns were tabulated into income size classes based on the 1979 Retrospective Income measure. For each income size, class average tax rates were computed by dividing total taxes paid by total retrospective income. SOI publishes the computed ATRs at various points of the income distribution. In this policy

FIGURE 10.7 Average Tax Rates, 1979–2003

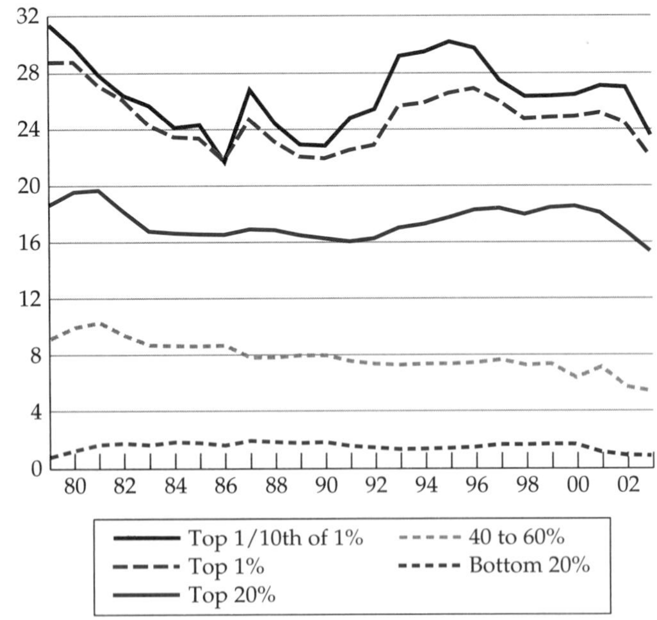

Source: Author's compilation using SOI data. See Anderson (2007).

study, we can analyze the following income groups over the period from 1979 to 2003, for which consistent data are available: Top 0.1%, Top 1%, Top quintile (top 20%), Middle quintile (40th to 60th percentile), Bottom quintile (bottom 20%).

Figure 10.7 illustrates the ATRs for these income classes over the period from 1979 to 2003. Notice that the ATR is higher as we move up income quantiles. For the bottom quintile the ATR has been in the range of 1 to 2 percent over the past 25 years. In the third, or middle, quintile (40 to 60 percent) the ATR has declined from about 10 percent to about 6 percent. In the top quintile, the ATR has fluctuated in the 16 to 20 percent range. For those in the top 1 percent of the income distribution, the ATR has fluctuated from a high of nearly 32 percent to a low of about 22 percent.

PROBLEMS

1. For the hypothetical income tax rate structure defined in this chapter, compute the tax liability and the average tax rate for each of the following taxable incomes:
   a. \$10,000
   b. \$29,000

c. $84,000
d. $242,000

2. Recompute the income tax liability and the average tax rate for each of the income levels in problem 1, assuming that the first $8,000 of income is exempt from taxation. Explain the effect of the exemption on the average tax rates.
3. Recompute the income tax liability and the average tax rate for each of the income levels in problem 1, assuming that there is a $500 tax credit. Explain the effect of the credit on the average tax rates.
4. Suppose that you are the chairman of the Library Board of Governors in Bookville. Your library system has been authorized by the voters to collect a property tax in order to pay for the services provided. The current value of property in Bookville is $100 million. The Library Board has authorized a tax rate of 0.5 percent. The village charter specifies that the tax base is the market value of property in the village, and it permits the Library Board to select any tax rate it wishes.
   a. How much revenue does the Library Board collect?
   b. If you were to raise the tax rate to 0.75 percent, by how much would revenues rise (assuming no change in the tax base)?
   c. If a disgruntled group of homeowners were to succeed in changing the village charter, so that assessed values for tax purposes are just one-half of market value, what change in the tax rate would generate the same revenue as we had in part a?
5. This problem is an exercise in computing average and marginal tax rates. The objective is to understand the difference between average and marginal rates and further understand the effects of exemptions, deductions, and credits on those rates. It is best to use a spreadsheet program such as Excel to complete this exercise. If you do not know how to use such software, you may compute the exercise by hand.

   Assume that a taxpayer has a linear consumption function $C = \$4{,}000 + 0.8Y$, where C is consumption expenditure and Y is income.
   a. Set up a table with income in the first column and consumption in the second column. Fill in the columns for incomes from 0 to $100,000 in increments of $5,000.
   b. In the third column calculate the tax, assuming a 5 percent tax on consumption expenditures.
   c. In the fourth column calculate the average tax rate, dividing the tax liability by income.
   d. In the fifth column calculate the marginal tax rate, computed as the change in tax liability divided by the change in income.
   e. Graph the average and marginal tax rates as a function of income.
   f. Now assume that the government exempts the consumption associated with the first $5,000 of income from taxation. Repeat steps 2 through 5. Explain the effect of the exemption.
   g. Go back to the original tax without the exemption and assume that the government provides a credit of $500. Repeat steps 2 through 5. Explain the effects of the credit.

6. Consider each of the following deductions currently permitted on the U.S. income tax. Explain whether each would be retained if the tax base were broadened to a Haig-Simons definition of income.
   a. Medical expenses
   b. Housing mortgage interest
   c. State and local income taxes
   d. Charitable contributions
   e. Unreimbursed employee business expenses
7. Consider each of the following forms of income not presently included in the definition of income used on the U.S. income tax. Explain whether each should be included if the tax base were broadened to a Haig-Simons definition of income.
   a. Value of health insurance provided by employer
   b. Value of parking benefits provided by employer
   c. Cash value of life insurance policies
   d. Implicit rental value of automobiles owned
   e. State lottery winnings

REFERENCES

Anderson, John E. "U.S. Tax Reforms and their Effects on Average Tax Rates." *National Tax Association—Proceedings of the One Hundredth Annual Conference 2007.*

Fox, William F., and Matthew Murray. 2005. "A National Retail Sales Tax: Consequences for the States." Paper presented at the Symposium on Federal Tax Reform and the States, National Press Club, Washington, DC, May 18, 2005. Available at the Federation of Tax Administrator's web site: http://www.taxadmin.org/fta/fs_symposium/fox-murray.pdf.

Fox, William F., and Matthew Murray. "Economic Aspects of Taxing Services." *National Tax Journal* 41 (1988): 19–36.

Francis, James. "A Closer Look at a State Invoice-Credit VAT." *Proceedings of the Eighty-Fifth Annual Conference, 1992*, National Tax Association, 1993, 142–48.

Hall, Robert E., and Alvin Rabushka. *The Flat Tax,* 2nd ed. Stanford, CA: Hoover Institution, 1995, 2007 available at: http://www.hoover.org/publications/books/8329.

Hall, Robert E., Alvin Rabushka, Dick Armey, Robert Eisner, and Herbert Stein. *Fairness and Efficiency in the Flat Tax.* Washington, DC: American Enterprise Institute for Public Policy Research, 1996.

Keen, Michael, Yi Tae Kim, and Recard Varsano. "The 'Flat Taxes': Principles and Evidence." Working Paper WP/06/218. Washington, DC: International Monetary Fund (IMF), 2006.

Musgrave, Richard A., and Peggy B. Musgrave. *Public Finance in Theory and Practice.* New York: McGraw-Hill, 1989.

Simons, H. *Personal Income Taxation.* Chicago, IL: University of Chicago Press, 1938.

Slemrod, Joel, and Jon Bakija. *Taxing Ourselves: A Citizen's Guide to the Great Debate Over Tax Reform,* 4th ed. Cambridge, MA: MIT Press, 2008.

Steuerle, C. Eugene. *The Tax Decade: How Taxes Came to Dominate the Public Agenda.* Washington, DC: Urban Institute, 1992.

The President's Advisory Panel on Federal Tax Reform. 2005. *Simple, Fair, and Pro-Growth: Proposals to Fix America's Tax System.* Washington, DC: U.S. Government Printing Office.

NOTES

1. Steuerle (1992) shows how these concerns came to dominate the public agenda during the 1990s in the United States. Slemrod and Bakija (2008) provide an excellent overview of the U.S. tax system and proposals for reform.
2. The IRS Form 1040, the so-called *long form*, is presented here. Some taxpayers use Form 1040A, Form 1040EZ, Form 1040EZ-T, or other forms.
3. The full package of IMF suggestions on tax policy will be discussed in Chapter 21.
4. This example is taken from *Analysis of the Michigan Single Business Tax*, Taxation and Economic Policy Office, Michigan Department of Treasury, January 1985.
5. This figure is adapted from Musgrave and Musgrave (1989).
6. The mathematically precise way to compare the impacts of exemptions, deductions, and credits on the effective tax rate is to take partial derivatives of r_e with respect to b_x, d, and c. The derivatives are as follows:

$$\partial r_e/\partial b_x = -rb_t/(b_t + b_x)^2,$$
$$\partial r_e/\partial d = -r/b,$$
$$\partial r_e/\partial c = -1/b.$$

7. For small changes, we can use the concept of a derivative to write the marginal tax rate as $r = dT/db$.
8. For a more-balanced consideration of the concept of the flat tax, see Hall et al. (1996).
9. For additional insight on how tax reforms over the period from 1979 to 2003 have affected average tax rates at various points of the income distribution, see Anderson (2007).

CHAPTER 11

Efficiency Effects of Taxes and Subsidies

LEARNING OBJECTIVES

1. Discuss the efficiency effects of taxes and subsidies.
2. Discuss how taxes and subsidies distort economic decision making and reduce welfare.
3. Describe how tax systems can be designed to minimize the welfare loss involved with taxation.

Taxes and subsidies are essential to fund the provision of public goods and services, correct for externalities, and alter the income distribution, but they are also responsible for causing inefficiencies in the economy. People generally hate taxes, or at least love to say they hate taxes. Good reasons do exist as to why taxes elicit such a response. Most fundamentally, taxes and subsidies cause people to change their behavior. In the absence of a tax people choose to behave in the way that is best for them. When the tax is introduced, people are forced to adjust their behavior and consume a different quantity of the taxed good than they would have otherwise chosen. Because the tax causes changes in behavior, it also causes a reduction in economic well-being, alias welfare. A subsidy also causes changes in behavior that most likely reduces the overall well-being of people. It is these efficiency effects to which we turn in this chapter in order to better understand just how taxes and subsidies cause inefficiencies in the economy and design tax or subsidy systems that minimize the inefficiencies created. As a result, we must be concerned not only with the revenue generated by a tax but also with the extent to which that tax alters taxpayer behavior. In this chapter we learn the methods economists use to estimate the welfare loss imposed by taxes, over and above the revenue that they generate.

EXCESS BURDENS OF TAXES AND SUBSIDIES

Whenever a tax is placed on a good, service, or form of income, people in the economy are burdened. Not only do they have to pay the tax, which is the first form of burden, but they also are induced to change their behavior as a result of the tax. That change of behavior causes a second form of burden that we call the *excess burden* of the tax. The **excess burden of a tax** refers to the welfare loss caused by the imposition of the tax, over and above the revenue the tax generates. In a similar way a subsidy causes an excess burden, measured by the welfare loss to those paying the subsidy that is in excess of the benefits received by those receiving the subsidy. Such welfare losses are caused by inefficient allocations of resources in the market. Excess burden is alternatively called **deadweight loss**.

Concept of Excess Burden

A simple example illustrates the concept of excess burden. Suppose that one of life's small pleasures for you is eating a bag of Doritos each week—a total of four bags per month. At the current relative price of Doritos and given your income, tastes, and preferences, you make the optimizing decision to buy one bag per week. Now, suppose that your state decides to implement a new snack food tax (as California did a few years ago). The new tax is \$0.25 per bag of chips. The tax changes the relative price of snack foods and confronts you with the need to make a decision about your consumption of Doritos. Suppose that your reaction is to reduce consumption to one bag every other week, thereby paying a tax of \$0.50 per month. Although you must pay \$0.50 to the state each month, reducing your welfare by that amount, you are worse off by an amount that is even larger. The tax reduces your welfare by an amount in excess of the actual tax you pay. Beyond the tax you pay, you have been forced to adjust your consumption pattern. Other things equal, you prefer to buy a bag of Doritos each week. But, due to the tax, you have reduced your Doritos consumption and suffer a welfare loss due to that adjustment.

To put the example in extreme form, suppose that you steadfastly refuse to pay this absurd new tax, as you see it. Your response is to adjust your consumption of Doritos to zero bags per week and pay no tax whatsoever. Where is the excess burden of the snack food tax? Well, having reduced your consumption to zero bags of Doritos per week, you are clearly worse off than before, even though you do not pay any tax. Your preference is to buy a bag of Doritos each week, but the tax has led you to change your behavior, making you worse off. This simple example illustrates that a tax creates a welfare loss that exceeds the amount of tax revenue generated by the tax itself. The welfare loss in excess of the revenue is called *excess burden*. The tax creates an excess burden if you reduce your consumption in any way. Only if you do not change your consumption of Doritos will there be no excess burden, only the direct burden of paying the tax.

Excess Burden with Demand Curves

The excess burden of a tax can be illustrated easily using demand curves, rather than indifference curves and budget lines, as long as we use a specific type of demand curve called the **compensated demand curve**. We can use the compensated demand curve as a tool to examine how people change their behavior in response to a price change, holding their income constant. Doing so gives us a clear picture of the substitution effects at work, without clouding the picture with income effects as well. In order to understand this special type of demand curve, it is helpful to recall the precise meaning of an ordinary demand curve. When we construct an ordinary demand curve, we solve the problem of the consumer maximizing utility subject to a budget constraint that holds her money income constant. The resulting demand function, illustrated in a demand curve, tells us the amount of the good that she will demand at various prices, holding income constant. Of course, as the price of the good rises, she demands less of the good, *ceteris paribus,* and the utility she is able to derive from consuming the good is reduced. Hence, along an ordinary demand curve, money income is constant and utility is variable. One of the things held constant in the *ceteris paribus* phrase is money income. (Recall that the other things held constant are tastes or preferences, prices of related goods like substitutes or complements, and population.)

What would happen if we reversed our treatment of income and utility? What if we changed her money income in such a way as to compensate her for the price increase in the good and to enable her to maintain the same level of utility? Doing this, we derive the compensated demand function. The compensated demand function tells us the amount of the good a consumer will demand at various prices, provided we compensate the consumer for changes in price in such a way as to maintain a constant utility. Thus, along a compensated demand curve, utility is held constant while money income varies—just the opposite of what happens along an ordinary demand curve. Along an ordinary demand curve, money income is constant and utility varies.

Another way to characterize the difference between the ordinary and compensated demand curves is to notice that the compensation mechanism we have described previously has the effect of removing the income effect of the price change. Ordinarily, when the price of a good changes, there are two effects: a **substitution effect** and an **income effect**. If the price of a good rises, the consumer buys less of the good because it is now relatively expensive compared to substitutes available in the market and because at the higher price the consumer's purchasing power of income is reduced, thus diminishing her demand for all normal goods. Recall that a normal good is one that a person buys more of as income rises; an increase in income shifts the demand curve rightward. If we compensate the consumer, holding her utility level constant, we are removing the income effect. Thus, a compensated demand curve reflects only substitution effects.

To illustrate the difference, both types of demand curves are drawn in Figure 11.1. We begin with quantity x_1 demanded at price p_1. Ordinarily, if the price were to rise to p_2, the quantity demanded would fall to x_2 due to both the substitution and income effects of the price increase. If, however, we compensate the consumer with added income to offset the decrease in welfare that would normally accompany a price increase, the reduction in quantity demanded will be smaller. The reduction in quantity demanded is from x_1 to x_2^c, reflecting the reduced quantity demanded due to the substitution effect with the income effect removed. The income effect would have been to reduce

FIGURE 11.1 Ordinary and Compensated Demand

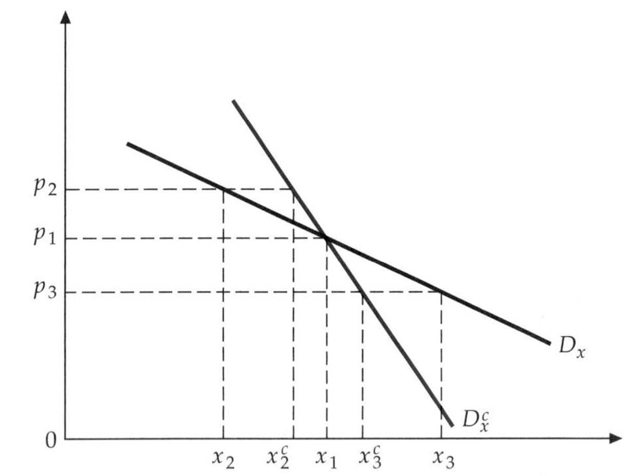

the quantity demanded by the amount $x_2^c - x_2$, but this reduction in the quantity demanded has been removed by the income compensation provided the consumer in order to keep her at the same level of utility she experienced at the original point (x_1, p_1).

Similarly, if the price were to fall from p_1 to p_3, we would ordinarily expect the quantity demanded to rise from x_1 to x_3. That increase in the quantity demanded occurs due to both the substitution and income effects. At the new, relatively lower price, the consumer substitutes good X for other goods that are now relatively expensive in comparison. In addition, the quantity of good X demanded is increased due to the fact that at the lower price the consumer's purchasing power of income has risen, leading to increased quantity demanded for all normal goods. If, however, we remove the income effect by reducing the consumer's income in order to maintain the same level of utility as was derived at (x_1, p_1), the increase in quantity demanded will be smaller with the new compensated quantity demanded, rather than x_3, as would be expected along the ordinary demand curve.

Using the compensated demand curve, illustrated in Figure 11.2, we can derive a method of measuring the excess burden of a tax. At the original price p_x, consumer surplus is the triangle *fbd* in Figure 11.2. This represents the amount consumers were willing to pay for x_1 units of the good but did not have to pay. Consumers are willing to pay the amount illustrated by the area under the demand curve up to quantity x_1, but they only have to pay p_x times x_1. Hence, consumer surplus is the area under the demand curve but above p_x, summed over the x_1 units. It is a measure of welfare that is very useful in conducting efficiency analysis of taxes and subsidies.

Now, when a tax is applied at the rate t_x, the price of good X rises from p_x to $(1 + t_x)p_x$ and the quantity demanded falls from x_1 to x_2. Note that we

FIGURE 11.2 Excess Burden of a Tax

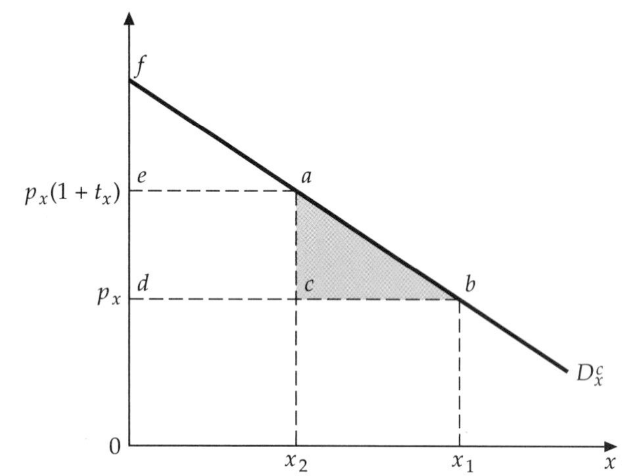

are assuming perfectly elastic supply in this case—a horizontal supply curve. That keeps the issue simple for now and puts the emphasis on the experience of the consumer when confronted with a tax. We will bring the supply curve into active consideration later and see how the tax affects the producer of the product as well. At the higher price, consumer surplus is reduced due to the triangle *efa*. It is quite intuitive that a higher price reduces consumer welfare. Consumers pay tax in the amount of area *deac*. But, their welfare loss due to the tax, measured by the reduction in consumer surplus, is the amount *abde*. Consumers' welfare loss due to the tax is larger than the tax revenue paid by the consumers. Thus, the tax has created an excess burden, or a welfare loss in excess of the revenue generated.

The excess burden of the tax is the area of the triangle *abc*, illustrated in Figure 11.2. That triangle has area equal to one-half of its base times its height. The height is the change in price, which is $(1 + t_x)p_x - p_x$, or $t_x p_x$. The base of the triangle is the change in the quantity of x demanded, denoted $\Delta x = x_1 - x_2$. In order to compute the change in x for a given change in price p_x, we must know the elasticity of demand. Recall that the elasticity of demand is defined as the percentage change in the quantity of x demanded divided by the percentage change in price p_x:

$$\eta_x = (\Delta x/x)/(\Delta p_x/p_x). \tag{11.1}$$

Using this relationship, we know that the percentage change in x that will result from the application of the tax is given by

$$\Delta x/x = \eta_x(\Delta p_x/p_x), \tag{11.2}$$

and the change in x is given by

$$\Delta x = \eta_x(\Delta p_x x/p_x). \tag{11.3}$$

Because the change in price is $t_x p_x$, this expression can be written as

$$\Delta x = \eta_x t_x x. \tag{11.4}$$

This change in x is the base of the triangle *abc*, illustrated in Figure 11.2.

Now we can put together an expression that enables us to measure the size of the excess burden. The area of the triangle is one-half the base times the height. The base of the triangle is $\eta_x t_x x$ and the height is $t_x p_x$. The area of the excess burden triangle is then

$$EB_x = (1/2)\eta_x x p_x t_x^2. \tag{11.5}$$

It is important to notice that the size of the excess burden created by a tax is determined by two factors: the tax rate and the elasticity of demand. First, consider the effect the elasticity of demand has on the size of the excess burden. If the compensated elasticity of demand is zero, reflecting a situation where the same quantity is demanded regardless of price, the excess burden of the tax is zero. Hence, there is no excess burden of taxation when demand is completely inelastic. As the compensated elasticity is larger, however, the excess burden is also larger. A tax on a good with a larger compensated elasticity of demand will generate a larger excess burden, other things being equal. As a general rule, the larger the compensated elasticity of demand, the larger the excess burden of a tax. If we are concerned about designing a tax system that creates as little excess burden as possible, then we should consider taxing goods whose compensated elasticity is small. The worst taxes, in terms of generating large excess burdens, are those applied to goods with large compensated elasticities of demand. What goods have small compensated elasticities of demand? Coffee, gasoline, cigarettes, and physicians' services all have small elasticities that make them logical choices for relatively high rates of taxation. What goods have large compensated elasticities of demand? Consumer durables such as automobiles, refrigerators, television sets, fine china, and crystal all have relatively large elasticities that make them logical choices for relatively low rates of taxation. Most importantly, what about Doritos? If the demand for Doritos is relatively elastic, due to the fact that there are many close substitutes (such as potato chips, pretzels, and popcorn), then a tax on Doritos is not a good idea!

Second, consider the effect of the tax rate on the size of the excess burden. Notice that the tax rate appears in the excess burden equation (11.5) in squared form. Thus, an increase in the tax rate will have a squared impact on the excess burden of the tax. For example, if we double the tax rate from t_x to $2t_x$, we can expect that the excess burden of the tax will be quadrupled from EB_x to $4EB_x$. We can illustrate this relationship graphically, as in Figure 11.3 where we illustrate doubling the tax rate. The effect of doubling the tax rate from t_x to $2t_x$ is to increase the excess burden of the tax from triangle *abc* to triangle *bdf*. Because triangle *abc* is equal to triangle *aef* and rectangle *acde* is twice the size of triangle *abc*, this new excess burden triangle *bdf* is four times the size of the original excess burden triangle *abc*. Hence, doubling the tax rate quadruples the excess burden of the tax. This illustrates the general principle that the excess burden rises with the square of the tax rate.

FIGURE 11.3 Excess Burden When a Tax Is Doubled

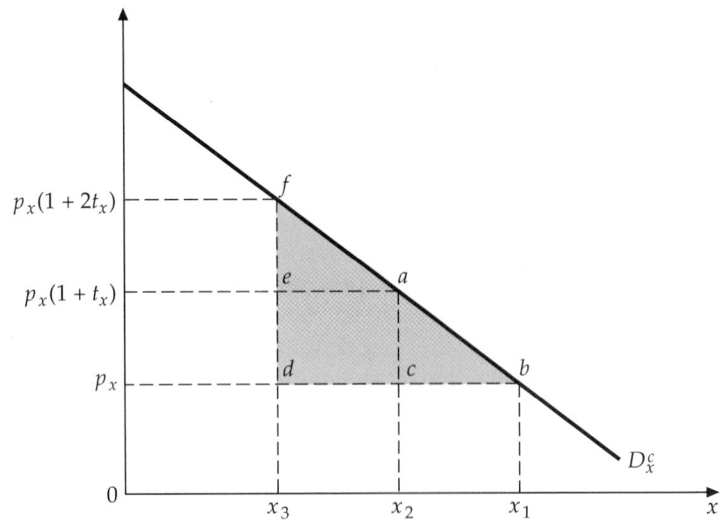

Marginal Excess Burden

When a preexisting tax is changed by a small amount it causes a **marginal excess burden** (*MEB*)—the increase in excess burden associated with that tax increase. Although we might expect the *MEB* of a small tax increase to be small, that is not necessarily the case. Consider the situation depicted in Figure 11.4. The original tax on good X creates an excess burden equal to

FIGURE 11.4 Marginal Excess Burden of a Tax Increase

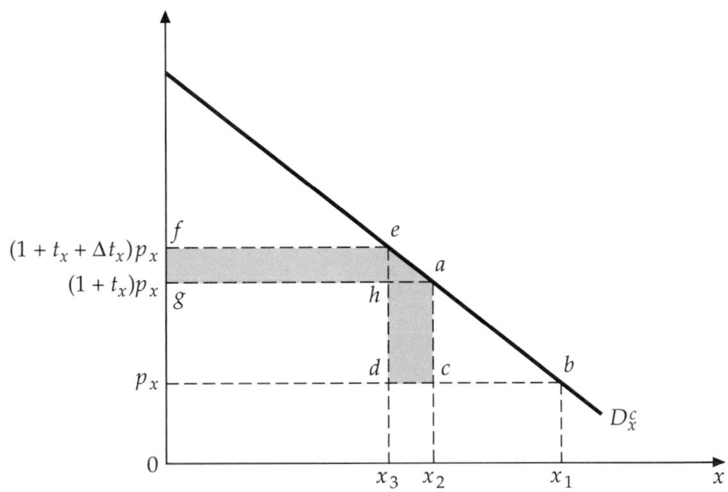

ON THE WEB

For more on measuring the efficiency effects of tax increases, see the Policy Study "The Marginal Welfare Costs of Taxes in the United States" on the companion website (www.cengage.com/international).

the area *abc* in the figure. An increase in the tax on good X, denoted Δt_x, increases the excess burden of the tax by the amount *acde,* which is large in comparison to the tax revenue generated by the tax increase, area *efgh*. The amount of the *MEB* may be a relatively large share of the added tax revenue. Some evidence indicates that a 1 percent increase in taxes can cause a *MEB* of anywhere from 17 to 56 cents per dollar of revenue generated.[1] That means for every dollar of additional tax revenue raised, we throw away 17 to 56 cents due to the welfare loss of the additional excess burden. If marginal excess burdens are that large, we should be very careful about proposing tax increases. We would do well to increase taxes in those cases where the *MEB* is small but to avoid tax increases in those cases where it is large. The *MEB* of a tax increase varies with the type of tax and level of taxation applied.

Excess Burden of a Subsidy

The excess burden created by a tax is somewhat intuitive because we all have a sense that taxes are harmful. What about a government subsidy, rather than a tax? Is there an excess burden in that case, too? It would seem that a subsidy is beneficial, so your intuition may lead you to believe that subsidies do not entail excess burdens, but they do. For example, European countries with substantial agricultural subsidies for their farmers experience an excess burden due to those subsidies. U.S. state governments that subsidize the production of ethanol experience excess burdens from their subsidies. Federal housing subsidies for low-income families cause excess burdens in housing markets. Could it be (perish the thought) that subsidies for higher education involve an excess burden also? Sad, but true. We turn to consider the efficiency effects of such subsidies in this section, showing that the concept of excess burden is perfectly general and can be applied to both taxes and subsidies.

Figure 11.5 illustrates the effect of a government price subsidy. Consider, for example, the case of a federal subsidy in the market for prescription drugs. At price p_x, quantity x_1 is demanded by consumers. Suppose that the subsidy pays a share of the price denoted by s, where $0 < s < 1$. The prescription drug subsidy reduces the price to $(1-s)p_x$, and the quantity demanded increases to x_2. At the subsidized price, consumers are able to buy more prescription drugs. That would seem to be a good policy, making much-needed drugs available to those who would not otherwise be able to buy them. Before concluding that the subsidy is unambiguously good, however, stop to consider the welfare implications of the subsidy. We can measure the additional benefits to consumers by the additional consumer surplus due to the lower price. That additional benefit is the area *abde* in Figure 11.5. Now, compare that benefit of the subsidy program to the cost of the subsidy program. The cost of the subsidy program is the portion of the price that is subsidized, sp_x, times the quantity x_2. The total cost of the subsidy program is therefore rectangle *ecbd*. Notice that the cost of the subsidy is larger than the benefit conferred. The difference between the cost of the subsidy and the

FIGURE 11.5 The Excess Burden of a Subsidy

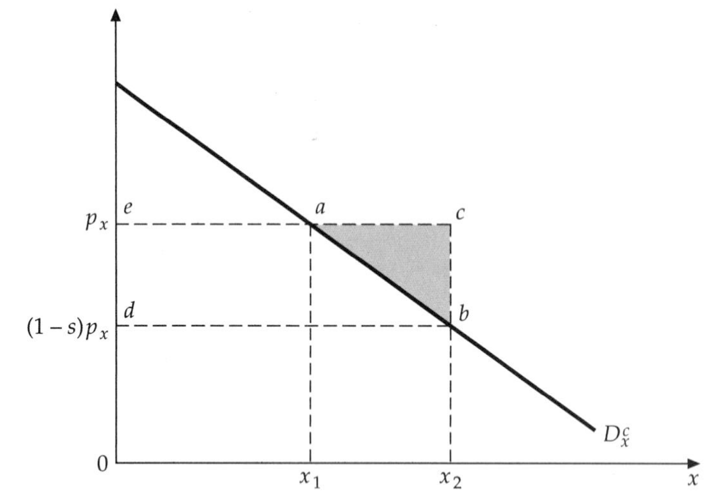

benefit conferred is measured by triangle *abc*. Although the subsidy program confers benefits on consumers of prescription drugs, those benefits are smaller than the cost of the subsidy program. Hence, the subsidy creates an excess burden, just as a tax does.

Here again, the size of the excess burden depends on the size of the subsidy and the elasticity of demand. The larger the subsidy or the more elastic the demand, the greater the excess burden created by a subsidy. It may be that in some policy applications, the elasticity of demand is small and the excess burden of the subsidy is minimal. In other cases where the demand elasticity is large, however, a subsidy program will create a large excess burden and an overall welfare reduction.

Connect the concept that subsidies involve excess burdens with what you learned in Chapter 6 on collective decision making. Suppose that the federal government does not presently provide a prescription drug benefit for senior citizens. Seniors want subsidized prescription drugs, however, and are active in lobbying their representatives to include such a provision at the federal level. If the median voter were a senior citizen, the prescription drug subsidy program would pass without question. Given present demographics, the median voter is not a senior citizen, however, and a prescription drug subsidy for seniors is not likely to pass on its own. Combine that program with some other programs benefiting younger voters, however, and you might find a logrolling scenario in which such a subsidy would pass. The senior citizen prescription drug subsidy is welfare reducing but might be adopted if deftly combined with other proposals as part of a package. Include, for example, a proposal to provide subsidized health insurance for children of low-income families (also a welfare-reducing subsidy), and you might find that the package of two proposals would garner sufficient support to pass in Congress.

Adding the Supply Side to the Story

Corresponding to the consumer surplus effects of a tax, there is also a story to tell about producer surplus on the supply side. We conveniently assumed perfectly elastic supply (or a horizontal supply curve) in the case presented previously, but in reality the supply curve in a market is typically upward sloping, as illustrated in Figure 11.6. Producers of a product are enticed to provide a given quantity of the good at the price indicated on the supply curve. But for quantities of the good up to x_1, they receive price p_1 in the market, which is above the price necessary to entice them to produce. Hence, they earn an amount in excess of that required, resulting in a welfare gain called *producer surplus*. Producer surplus is illustrated as the area below price p_1 but above the supply curve, up to the quantity provided in the market.

In this case, the tax has an effect not only on the welfare of the consumers but also on the welfare of the producers. Figure 11.6 illustrates a situation where a tax is imposed on a good in a market with upward-sloping supply. Compared to the original price p_1 and quantity x_1, the tax causes the market price to rise to p_2 and the market-clearing quantity to fall to x_2. For consumers, welfare is reduced by an amount equal to area *abde* in Figure 11.6. This is the change in consumer surplus from the original amount *bdf* to the new reduced amount *aef*. Consumers pay a tax of an amount equal to area *acde* and incur a welfare loss of area *abc* over and above the welfare loss due to the tax. Their remaining consumer surplus is labeled area *aef*. For producers, their producer surplus is reduced due to

FIGURE 11.6 Excess Burden with Upward-Sloping Supply

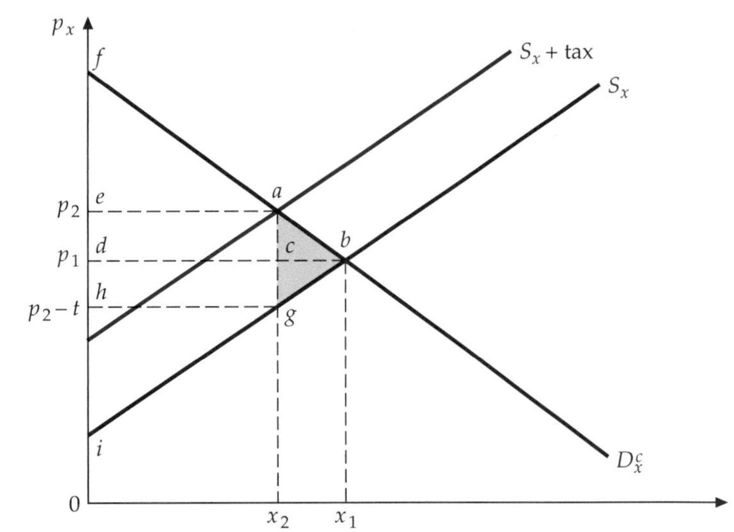

TABLE 11.1 Welfare Effects of a Tax

Economic Agents Affected by Tax	Welfare Reduction Due to Tax	Welfare Gain Due to Tax
Consumers	*abde*	
Producers	*bghd*	
Taxpayers		*aghe*
Society as a whole	*abg*	

the tax by an amount equal to area *bghd*. They pay a tax equal to an area *cghd* and have a welfare loss in excess of that amount of tax paid, illustrated by area *cbg*. Their remaining producer surplus is labeled area *gih*. Hence, the welfare loss due to the tax is the combined amount paid *cghd* and the excess burden *cbg*.

Of course, taxpayers benefit from the expenditure of tax revenues on their behalf for public goods and services that benefit them. This point is important to keep in mind when you consider the welfare effects of a tax. Although the tax creates a burden on taxpayers, the revenue generated is spent on public goods and services that are valuable to taxpayers. Consequently, there is a welfare gain to taxpayers in the amount of the revenue generated by the tax: *aghe*. The net impact on society of the tax is a reduction in welfare of the amount of the excess burden *abg*. Table 11.1 summarizes the welfare impacts of a tax.

With linear demand and supply, as illustrated in Figure 11.5, the excess burden is triangle *abg* that can be computed using the equation

$$EB_x = (1/2)xp_x t_x^2/(1/\eta_x + 1/\varepsilon_x), \qquad (11.6)$$

where ε_x is the elasticity of supply. Notice that as ε_x approaches infinity, its inverse approaches zero and this expression becomes identical to the excess burden equation we had previously for the case of perfectly elastic supply. The size of the excess burden of a tax in a market with an upward-sloping supply curve depends on the elasticities of demand and supply. The greater the elasticities, the greater the excess burden. Hence, as a general conclusion, we observe that the efficiency cost of a tax will be crucially dependent on the price elasticities of demand and supply for the good being taxed.

Having established that taxes and subsidies create excess burdens, we now turn to consider special cases in which those excess burdens are zero. It would be very useful to know under what circumstances the excess burden of a tax or subsidy is zero, because in such a circumstance the tax or subsidy could be implemented without the welfare reduction usually created. Even if we cannot confine the application of taxes and subsidies to cases where the excess burden is zero, we would like to limit their application to cases where the excess burden is as small as possible.

Special Cases of Inelastic Demand and Supply

First, consider the case where demand is completely inelastic, reflecting a willingness on the part of consumers to purchase the same quantity of the good, regardless of its price. In this case, the demand curve is vertical and the excess burden is zero. Hence, if we apply a tax to a good whose compensated elasticity of demand is zero, no excess burden is generated by the tax. We derive revenue and in the process create no excess burden. In this case, the tax is efficient in the sense that it generates no excess burden. The left-hand panel of Figure 11.7 illustrates this case. The tax is shown in the upward shift of the supply curve. With vertical (inelastic) demand, however, there is no change in the equilibrium quantity in the market. The revenue generated by the tax is identical to the change in producer surplus. The burden of the tax is simply the revenue that is paid. No excess burden above and beyond the revenue exists. This result is verified in Equation 11.6 for the excess burden. As the elasticity of demand approaches zero, the denominator of the equation blows up and the excess burden shrinks to zero.

What type of goods and services have small elasticities of demand? Typically, goods such as gasoline, coffee, and cigarettes have very small compensated elasticities of demand. In each case, consumers are addicted to these goods, either due to physical or psychological addictions, as in the case of coffee and cigarettes, or due to the fixed nature of the transportation system that requires using automobiles, as in the case of gasoline. An excise tax applied to any of these goods would generate a small excess burden. The more price inelastic the demand for the good, the less excess burden is created by a tax on that good. From an efficiency point of view, taxes on goods like cigarettes and gasoline that have low price elasticities are relatively efficient, creating little excess burden. The essential reason for this result is that the

FIGURE 11.7 Excess Burden When Demand or Supply Is Inelastic

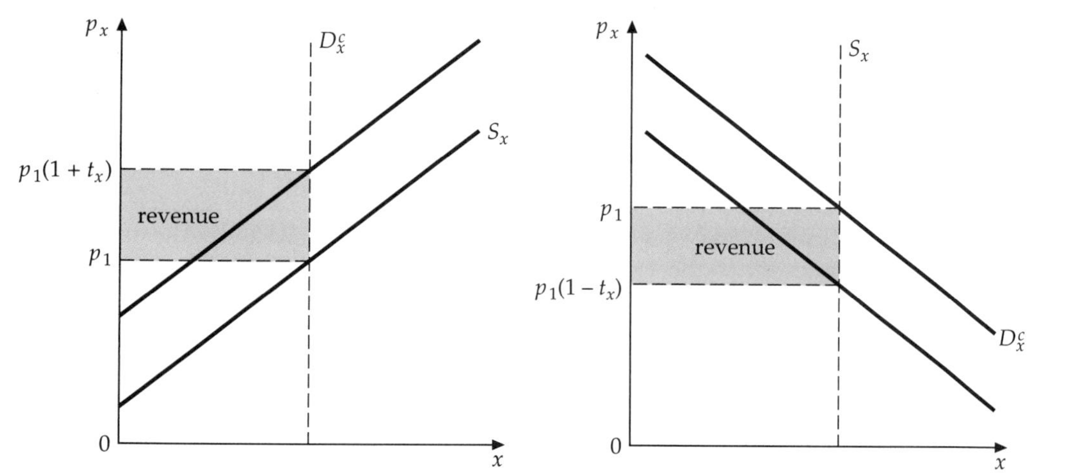

tax raises the price of the good, but the consumer response is only a small reduction in the quantity of the good demanded. Because the tax does not change behavior much, there is little distortion in the market and therefore little excess burden.

Second, suppose that the demand curve is downward sloping, as we would normally expect with a nonzero value for the compensated elasticity of demand, but now suppose that the good is fixed in supply with a vertical supply curve. The right-hand panel of Figure 11.7 illustrates this example. In this case, a tax applied to the good will also be efficient because no excess burden is generated due to the tax. The tax is shown by shifting demand downward in this case, lowering the price of the good from p_1 to $p_1(1-t_x)$. With vertical (inelastic) supply, however, there is no change in the equilibrium quantity in the market. The revenue generated by the tax is identical to the change in consumer surplus; hence there is no excess burden. This result is verified in Equation 11.6 for the excess burden. As the elasticity of supply approaches zero, the denominator of the equation blows up and the excess burden shrinks to zero. Having considered the extreme cases where the excess burden is zero, we now turn to a more general discussion of when the excess burden will be small (or large).

Determinants of Excess Burden

Taxes and subsidies create excess burden, as we have established, and the size of that excess burden depends on three critical factors: the size of the tax (or subsidy) and the elasticities of demand and supply.

Size of Tax or Subsidy

The excess burden of a tax (or subsidy) rises with the size of the tax (or subsidy), but the relationship is not linear. Notice that in the excess burden equations (11.5) and (11.6), the excess burden of a tax rises with the *square* of the tax rate. As a result, the excess burden of a tax is very sensitive to the tax rate. For example, if we double the tax rate from t_x to $2t_x$, we will quadruple the excess burden of the tax. To prove this to yourself, simply put $2t_x$ into the simple excess burden equation (assuming perfectly elastic supply) and see what you get:

$$EB_x(2t_x) = (1/2)\eta_x x p_x 4t_x^2 = 4EB_x(t_x). \tag{11.7}$$

The outcome is four times the excess burden of the tax t_x. This result confirms what we saw in Figure 11.3 when we doubled the tax rate and got four times the excess burden. In general, with a linear demand curve the excess burden of a tax is proportional to the square of the tax rate.

Of course, this relationship works in the other direction as well. If we reduce the tax rate to one-half its former level, we can expect that excess burden will fall to one-fourth of its former level. As a result, the size of the excess burden due to a tax is very sensitive to the tax rate. Other things equal, the lower we can make a tax rate, the smaller the excess burden we create with the tax system.

Elasticity of Demand

The excess burden of a tax is also affected by the elasticity of demand for the good or service being taxed. From the excess burden equations (11.5) and (11.6), we know that the larger the elasticity of demand, the larger the excess burden, other things being equal. We also know that if the elasticity of demand is zero, indicating that consumers are unresponsive to price, the excess burden of a tax is zero. But as the elasticity rises above zero, the excess burden also rises in direct proportion. Goods with price-inelastic demand such as cigarettes and gasoline will have small excess burdens created by excise taxes applied to those goods. But goods like television sets and fine china, which have price-elastic demand, will have very large excess burdens if an excise tax is applied.

Elasticity of Supply

The elasticity of supply also affects the size of the excess burden of a tax. The excess burden equation (11.6) illustrates that the elasticity of supply is directly related to the excess burden of a tax: the larger the elasticity of supply, the larger the excess burden of taxation. Here again, we know that in the special case of an inelastically supplied good, there is no excess burden of a tax. But as the elasticity of supply rises, so does the excess burden of taxation. For example, a tax placed on land that is inelastically supplied will generate no excess burden. Similarly, a tax applied to workers who continue to work the same number of hours regardless of the tax, has no excess burden. But other workers, who are sensitive to the tax and decide that because of the tax it is no longer worth working, have a large elasticity of supply, and a tax on their labor will generate a large excess burden.

Policy Implications of Excess Burden

If excess burden is very sensitive to the tax rate, we should tax in a manner that recognizes this fact. First, because the excess burden is zero for goods inelastically demanded or supplied, we know that taxation of such goods generates no excess burden. As a result, we know that taxes on inelastically supplied labor or land will have no efficiency effect to worry about. Second, because the excess burden of taxation is small for goods whose price elasticity of demand is small, we know that taxes applied to commodities such as cigarettes and gasoline will have very small excess burdens and thus have small efficiency effects to worry about. Third, for all other goods and services whose elasticities of demand or supply are not zero or small, taxation will generate significant excess burden and thus create substantial efficiency effects. The proper policy rule to follow for such goods and services is to keep the tax rate as low as possible in order to minimize the excess burden of taxation. As a general tax policy rule, we should keep tax rates as low as possible (on all but inelastically supplied or demanded goods and services) in order to minimize the excess burden and the efficiency effects of taxation.

Consider the case of the excise tax on cigarettes. This tax is currently a popular funding mechanism for many public policy proposals, due in part to the political and social vulnerability of the tobacco industry. But there are sound economic reasons to have high taxes on cigarettes, quite apart from the political and social issues. Because the price elasticity of demand for cigarettes is approximately -0.15, we know that demand for cigarettes is relatively inelastic. We also know that an excise tax applied to cigarettes will have a small excess burden. Why is that? Well, with such a small price elasticity of demand, smokers are not very sensitive to the price of a package of cigarettes and will not respond very much if that price rises due to a tax increase. For example, with a price elasticity of demand of -0.15, we know that a 50 percent increase in price will lead to a 7.5 percent reduction in the quantity of cigarettes demanded. With that small reduction in the quantity demanded, there will be a small excess burden. Hence, if our policy objective is to generate tax revenue by taxing goods that create small excess burdens when taxed, cigarettes are a good policy choice. Is that the reason cigarettes are a popular target for increased taxation? Probably not, but the reason is probably related to the inelastic demand.

Cigarettes are an easy target for increased taxation.

Because smokers will reduce their consumption of cigarettes by only a small amount when the tax is increased, their behavior does not change very much. Many smokers are inconvenienced by the tax increase, but the additional tax paid by each smoker is relatively small. As a group, smokers are not well organized and represented by lobbyists, at least not as well represented as the tobacco industry. Cigarettes are an easy target for increased taxation due to the nature of the political clout of the consumers relative to the producers of the product. Smokers do not put up much political resistance.

Proponents of higher taxes on cigarettes often cite another policy justification for higher taxation. They argue that a higher tax on cigarettes will have a beneficial public health effect by discouraging smoking. Although this policy justification sounds good, stop for a moment and think about the price-inelastic demand for cigarettes. If the demand for cigarettes is price inelastic, the quantity demanded will not fall very much when the tax is increased. As a result, there is not much of an effect of discouraging smoking. Hence, this policy argument is weak. There may be certain groups of smokers who are more price sensitive than others, however. Some empirical evidence indicates that teenagers, in particular, have higher price elasticities of demand than older smokers. If that is the case, then a tax increase may have a more forceful effect on discouraging smoking among teenagers.

OPTIMAL TAXATION

If taxation of some goods or services creates large excess burdens while taxation of other goods or services creates small excess burdens, why not design the tax system to generate revenue by taxing the former more heavily than the latter? This approach is called *optimal taxation.*

Optimal Commodity Taxation: Ramsey Rule

Suppose that we have the problem of designing a tax policy in such a way as to tax two goods, X and Y, to generate a given amount of tax revenue but to generate as little excess burden as possible. Our objective is to minimize the excess burden for a given amount of revenue generated. This is the classic problem of **optimal commodity taxation.**[2] We want to find the taxes t_x and t_y that will generate a given level of revenue but create as little excess burden as possible, thereby minimizing the distortions in the markets for the goods. If the demands for the two goods are independent, that is, the cross-price elasticities are both zero, and the supply curves for the two goods are horizontal, it can be shown that the optimal combination of tax rates is the ratio where

$$t_x/t_y = \eta_y/\eta_x. \qquad (11.8)$$

This is the classic result known as the **Ramsey rule** first derived in Ramsey (1927). The optimal commodity taxes should be inversely proportional to the compensated elasticities of demand for the goods. Hence, goods with low elasticities of demand should be taxed at high rates, and goods with high elasticities of demand should be taxed at low rates.

Another way to view this result is to say the Ramsey rule requires that the demand for each good be reduced in the same proportion, relative to the pretax situation. It is sometimes said that optimal commodity tax policy requires that the tax system should raise the prices of all goods by the same proportional amount in order to minimize the excess burden of the tax system. This suggestion is not correct. Rather, the optimal commodity tax system should reduce the demand for each good in the same proportion, as Figure 11.8 illustrates. In this case, good X has relatively inelastic demand, whereas good Y has relatively elastic demand. Suppose that we applied a 100 percent excise tax on each good that doubles the price of each good. Application of a 100 percent tax on both goods would result in an excess burden of an amount equal to the area of triangle *abc* for each good. The Ramsey rule tells us how to improve on that situation. Rather than apply taxes that increase prices proportionately, we should apply taxes that reduce the quantity demanded proportionately. Applying taxes of t_x and t_y, which reduce demand to one-half their original levels in Figure 11.8, we can reduce the total excess burden. With taxes t_x and t_y as illustrated, the excess burden created in each case is $a'bc'$. Although this requires a higher tax on good X, which increases its excess burden by the area $a'acc'$, it permits a lower tax on good Y, which reduces its excess burden by the amount $aa'c'c$. Clearly, the total excess burden is smaller with the taxes that reduce the quantity demanded of X and Y by equal proportions.

It should also be noted that the Ramsey rule, as described so far, ignores issues of equity or fairness in taxation. It is simply an *efficiency* rule: in order

FIGURE 11.8 Illustration of the Ramsey Rule

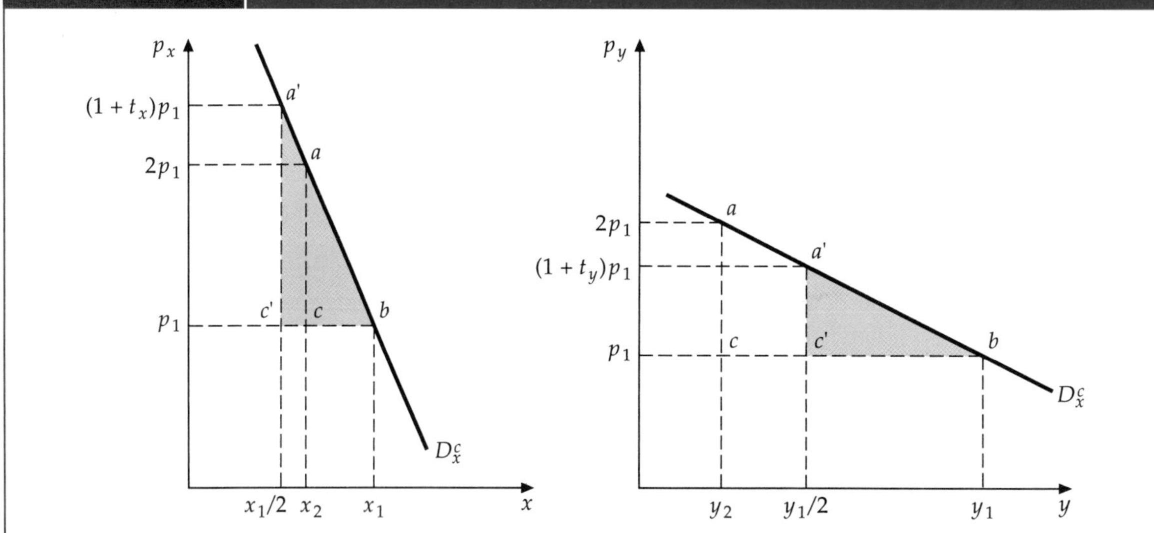

to minimize excess burden, tax goods inversely proportional to their elasticities of demand. There may be a concern of equity reasons about a tax applied to a commodity with relatively low elasticity of demand. Consider the excise tax on gasoline, for example. If the excise tax on gasoline is regressive, due to the fact that gasoline consumption is relatively high in comparison to income for the poor, then by taxing gasoline at a high rate, we are taking money from those least able to bear the tax burden. The Ramsey rule does not consider equity.

Optimal Income Taxation: Combining Equity and Efficiency Concerns[3]

Modern public finance is concerned with both efficiency and equity in taxation. The concept of **optimal income taxation** explicitly combines these two concerns within the context of a model that includes labor supply. The seminal research on this important topic is that of Diamond and Mirrlees (1971). Mirrlees won the Nobel Prize in Economics in 1996 and Diamond won the prize in 2010.

Suppose that labor is supplied to the market by individuals, and it is taxed. Recognizing an efficiency cost of taxation, the model captures the effect of the tax on labor as it affects labor supply. The higher the tax rate, the less labor is supplied and the less output is produced and the more excess burden is created. With this effect in mind, we wish to design an income tax that will maximize social welfare. This is the focus of the optimal tax literature.

Suppose that labor (hours of work) L is supplied by workers according to a constant elasticity formula:

$$L = L_0[w(1-t)]^{\varepsilon}, \tag{11.9}$$

where w is the gross wage per hour, ε is the elasticity of labor supply with respect to the net wage, L_0 is the time endowment, and t is the tax rate. In this formulation of the problem, the labor supply curve is upward sloping, assuming that we have a positive value of ε. Revenue generated by the tax is given by $R = twL$. For a value of $t = 0$, no tax revenue is generated. As the tax rate is increased, however, there may be revenue generated, but the general relationship between the tax rate and revenue is ambiguous in sign. It is possible that an increase in the tax rate will reduce revenue if the labor supply response is strong enough.[4] As the rate of taxation initially rises above zero, revenue is generated. But at larger values of t further tax rate increases reduce revenue. We can determine the maximal revenue that can be earned in this case.[5] Doing so provides the tax rate $t = 1/(1+\varepsilon)$. At tax rates above this level, revenue falls with increased tax rate. At rates below this level, revenue rises with increased tax rate. If ε is 0.3, for example, the maximal revenue is generated with a tax rate of $t = 0.77$.

Equity aspects of taxation are also included, as the social marginal value of income is permitted to vary through the use of a parameter that captures society's taste for redistribution. In this formulation of the problem, the optimal tax rate can be expressed in a form that reveals both the efficiency and equity aspects of the problem:

$$t/(1-t) = \varepsilon^{-1}[1-(1-\eta^2)^{-\gamma(1+\varepsilon)}] \tag{11.10}$$

(Atkinson 1995). The parameter t is the tax rate, ε is the elasticity of labor supply with respect to the net wage, η is the coefficient of variation of the gross hourly wage distribution, and γ is a parameter capturing our taste for redistribution. A zero value of γ indicates distributional indifference (equal social marginal value of income for all), whereas a value of γ approaching infinity captures the Rawlsian objective of maximizing the welfare of the least well-off person in the income distribution.

Now, consider the decomposition of the right-hand side of the previous equation. The first term, ε^{-1}, measures the efficiency aspect of the problem, whereas the second term in brackets measures the equity aspect of the problem. Notice that the efficiency aspect of the problem is determined entirely by the labor supply elasticity. The larger the elasticity of the labor supply, the larger the efficiency cost of redistribution through a linear tax mechanism. This result is expected if we recall the simple Ramsey rule from the policy world of indirect taxation. According to that rule, tax rates should be set inversely proportional to elasticities in order to minimize excess burden of taxation, for a given amount of revenue generated.

The equity part of the decomposition in Equation 11.5 is more complex. It depends on all three parameters: ε, η, and γ. First, the wage dispersion measured by η is involved; as the degree of inequality in wages rises, the optimal tax rate required rises as well, other things being equal. Second, the elasticity of labor supply with respect to the net wage ε is involved because the gross wage w depends on this parameter. The larger the elasticity of the labor supply with respect to the net wage, the more gross wage earnings rise with w, causing the income tax rate to be more effective in redistribution. Third, the value of γ, which indicates distributional preference, also affects the equity term in Equation 11.5. If we attach no weight to redistribution, only caring about total income, $\gamma=0$ and the optimal tax rate is subsequently zero. For positive values of γ, the greater our preference for redistribution, the larger the optimal tax rate, other things being equal. For example, if we assume that $\gamma=0.5$ and $\varepsilon=0.3$, then the equity term in the previous equation is 0.092 and the optimal tax rate can be computed as $t=0.23$. As γ approaches infinity, the equity term in the previous equation approaches 1 and the optimal tax rate approaches $(1+\varepsilon)^{-1}$. For a value of $\varepsilon=0.3$, the optimal tax rate is $t=0.77$, for example.

Table 11.2 illustrates the optimal tax rate for various values of the parameters. Retaining the same values for ε and η, we can examine the effect of increasing γ. As γ rises from zero to 0.25, the optimal tax rate rises from 0 to 14 percent. Additional one-quarter increases in γ raise the optimal tax rate to 25, 32, and 38 percent. Further increases in γ cause the optimal tax rate to asymptotically approach the rate of 77 percent. These examples illustrate the sensitivity of the optimal tax rate to the distributional parameter. The more income inequality we are willing to tolerate, the lower the

TABLE 11.2 Optimal Tax Rates for Various Parameter Values

Labor Supply Elasticity (ε)	Wage Dispersion Measure (η)	Distribution Preference Parameter (γ)	Optimal Tax Rate (t)
0.3	0.4	0.00	0.00
0.3	0.4	0.25	0.14
0.3	0.4	0.50	0.25
0.3	0.4	0.75	0.32
0.3	0.4	1.00	0.38
0.3	0.4	5.00	0.68
0.3	0.4	10.00	0.74
0.3	0.4	100.00	0.77

Source: Atkinson 1995.

optimal tax rate. The more income equality we desire, the higher the tax rate required.

We now must specify an objective function that will enable us to select the best tax rate from among the many possibilities that exist, as described previously. A simple objective function that is often used in the optimal tax literature is to specify that the social marginal value of income to a person is proportional to her wage rate: $w-\gamma$. By specifying the value of the parameter γ, we can characterize a number of alternative views regarding redistribution of income. For example, a person who is completely indifferent to alternative distributions of income, let us call him Milton, would have a value of $\gamma=0$. That would result in a constant unitary social marginal value of income. On the other hand, a person who considers it most important to make the least well-off person as well off as possible, let us call him John, would have a value of γ approaching plus infinity. In this case, the social marginal value of income for a person with a high wage approaches zero, whereas that for a person with a low wage is very large. As an intermediary case, consider the person who has a value of $\gamma=0.5$. This person, let us call him Arthur, would compare a high-income person whose wage is nine times larger than that of a low-income person and attach a weight of one-third as much to a dollar increase in the low-income person's income.

An important early study of optimal taxation is Mirrlees's (1971), whose results are reported in Table 11.3. He estimated the optimal tax rates, both average and marginal, by income class for two cases of redistribution preferences. The upper panel of Table 11.3 gives the estimated consumption levels, average tax rates, and marginal tax rates in the case of utilitarian preferences for redistribution. His simulated marginal tax rates start at a high level, beginning at 23 percent for the lowest-income class and rise to 26 percent

TABLE 11.3 Optimal Tax Rates by Income for Two Cases of Redistribution Preference

Income	*Consumption*	*ATR*	*MTR*
	Utilitarian Case		
0	0.03	N.A.	0.23
0.05	0.07	−0.34	0.26
0.10	0.10	−0.05	0.24
0.20	0.18	0.09	0.21
0.30	0.26	0.13	0.19
0.40	0.34	0.14	0.18
0.50	0.43	0.15	0.16
	More Concern for Equity in the Income Distribution		
0	0.05	N.A.	0.30
0.05	0.08	−0.66	0.34
0.10	0.12	−0.34	0.32
0.20	0.19	0.07	0.28
0.30	0.26	0.13	0.25
0.40	0.34	0.16	0.22
0.50	0.41	0.17	0.20

Source: From "An Exploration in the Theory of Optimum Income Taxation" by J. A. Mirrlees in *Review of Economic Studies* 38 (April 1971): Tables 2 and 8, 202–203. Reprinted by permission.

for the next-lowest income class, then fall as income rose, reaching a low of 16 percent for the highest-income class. The average tax rates are negative for the two bottom income classes, indicating that people in these classes receive payments from the government rather than pay taxes. The *ATR* rises to a maximum of 15 percent for the highest-income class. The lower panel of Table 11.3 provides the estimated results for the case where society has more concern for equity in the income distribution. In this case, more redistribution is evidenced by more negative *ATR*s in the first two income classes and larger positive *ATR*s in the higher-income classes. The *MTR*s are uniformly higher in this case as well. Notice also that the consumption levels are higher for those in the first four income classes and lower for those in the top income class. Needless to say, the equity aspect of this type of result has been very contentious. Most people do not think of a fair tax as one in which the marginal tax rate falls as income rises! As a result of this counterintuitive outcome, there has been a continuing debate over whether the optimal tax literature provides policy direction that is politically feasible.

Redistribution Pessimism

A heavy pessimism surrounds contemporary discussions of redistribution through the tax system due to research that indicates the marginal excess burden of taxation is large. This pessimism, sometimes called **redistribution pessimism,** is grounded in the belief that marginal reductions in income inequality through the use of a more progressive income tax are very costly in terms of efficiency effects. Most notable in this regard is the work of Browning and Johnson (1984). Using the case they describe as most plausible, which embodies a compensated elasticity of 0.312, they derive estimates of the gains or losses of net equivalent income from a 1 percentage point increase in the linear income tax rate. Table 11.4 provides a summary of the dollar gains and losses measured in terms of net equivalent income that would be experienced by the five quintile groups as a result of a 1 percent increase in the marginal tax rate used to finance an increase in basic income. Taxpayers in the bottom two quintiles gain the equivalent of \$47 and \$33 dollars each for a total gain of \$80. But taxpayers in the upper three quintiles lose the equivalent of \$279 in income. The source of those losses, of course, is the distortion the higher marginal tax rate causes in labor markets, resulting in lower income. This loss of income must be considered as well as the benefit of redistribution for low-income households. Browning and Johnson conclude that "the marginal cost of less income inequality is surprisingly high even when labour supply elasticities are relatively low" (1984, 201). Evidence such as this has led to a very substantial resistance to income redistribution through more progressive taxation.

Is Redistribution Pessimism Justified?[6]

We should consider whether such pessimism regarding income redistribution through more progressive taxation is justified. In fact, a number of reasons

TABLE 11.4 Gains and Losses from Increasing the Income Tax Rate

Quintile	Gain/Loss (\$) Resulting from a 1 Percent Increase in a Linear Income Tax Rate
First	+47
Second	+33
Third	−11
Fourth	−72
Fifth	−196
Total	Gains: +80
	Losses: −279

Source: Browning and Johnson 1984.

exist to question the prevailing pessimism in this regard. The previous analysis is based on just one form of tax effect on economic decision making: labor supply. Changes in the tax system affect a wide range of other activities in addition to labor supply. For example, a change in the marginal tax rate will potentially affect savings, investment, and risk taking as well. Suppose for a moment that the tax rate increase has the effect of increasing taxpayers' willingness to hold risky assets (because the higher marginal tax rate provides a greater subsidy to potential losses); this fuels increased entrepreneurial activity, which stimulates growth. It may be that the subsequent growth in the economy provides a type of dynamic efficiency that is not considered in the static view of efficiency employed in the literature referred to previously. The criticism here is that existing models that led to redistribution pessimism are extremely narrow in their focus. The sole supply-side effect is typically a labor supply response. All other forms of responses to changes in the tax system are typically ignored. Some of those potential effects move in the opposite direction.

Although labor supply has been incorporated in the models used in the optimal linear income tax literature, the particular form of labor supply response included is limited. The models generally incorporate labor supply response in terms of hours of work. Effects on labor force participation rates do exist. Suppose for a moment that we have a linear income tax system, with a basic income guarantee and a single marginal tax rate. Such a tax system may reduce the disincentive to work that exists under the current U.S. tax and transfer system. If so, the labor supply response—measured in terms of labor force participation—may be greater than we would otherwise have expected. But a person who returns to work moves out of a position of receiving the income guarantee and moves into a position of paying a positive income tax. We cannot simply assume that other dimensions of responses to changes in the marginal tax rate will operate in the same direction.

The empirical evidence we have on labor supply responses is voluminous but limited. The literature is voluminous, with a plethora of studies each providing a view of labor supply responses, taking into account a myriad of econometric issues that provide more accurate estimates. Most of the studies in the labor supply literature are cross-section studies based on subgroups of the population. For example, the work of Hausman (1981) excludes workers who are self-employed, under 25 or over 55 years of age, farmers, single women without children, and the disabled. Each group excluded makes the remaining sample more homogeneous; this has the effect of making the estimated labor supply responses less representative of the entire population.

Potential problems can arise due to the often wide confidence intervals on the estimates of labor supply elasticities that reduce our confidence in the results. Finally, our estimates of labor supply elasticity suffer from the inevitable problem that cross-section estimates are not properly derived from a controlled experiment in which a control group has no change in tax treatment, whereas an experimental group experiences a change in tax law. Time series studies suffer from the weakness that there are confounding events that occur and that distort our picture of the partial effect of the tax law change. In all, there are a number of reasons to be cautious regarding the efficiency effects of redistribution. These concerns do not suggest that studies that indicate the efficiency cost of redistribution is large are systematically biased or otherwise unreliable. Rather, these concerns are intended to provide a cautionary note so that the estimates can be understood within a specific context. There may indeed be a reason to believe that the efficiency cost of redistribution through the tax code is large, but our models are not yet sufficiently comprehensive and robust to allow us to draw that conclusion with certainty.

Charles Ballard (1988) has estimated the efficiency cost of increased progressivity as well. In his most preferred estimation, he finds that the efficiency cost of transferring $1 from upper-income groups to lower-income groups has an efficiency cost of $0.50 to $1.30. Although this estimate is for the same type of demogrant simulated by Browning and Johnson, Ballard also estimates the effect of an alternative redistributional mechanism, which he calls a *notch grant*. Using this mechanism, a grant for low-income groups is financed through an increase in the marginal tax rate for higher-income groups combined with a wage subsidy for low-income workers. Both high-income and low-income taxpayers are assigned exogenously and both face linear budget constraints. The efficiency cost of both of these redistributional methods is found to be far lower than that for the demogrant. The *demogrant* is a funding mechanism whereby the marginal tax rate is increased by 1 percentage point for all households and the resulting revenue is distributed in equal per capita cash grants.

Another policy alternative is to provide increased progressivity through an expansion of the earned income tax credit (EITC). Robert Triest (1996) estimates that the efficiency cost of improving progressivity this way is less than $0.20 per dollar of income redistributed if the redistribution is financed through tax rate increases for middle-income taxpayers. His assessment is that the efficiency cost of redistribution "varies considerably with the type of tax reform considered." He also makes a particular note of the fact that he is only modeling one distortion due to taxation: individuals' hours of work decision. He cautions that "I may be missing the most important distortionary effects of taxation affecting very high-income households." Despite these caveats, he concludes that

> the simulations do suggest that the efficiency cost of increasing progressivity by raising the marginal tax rates faced only by very high-income households is likely to be much greater than if the progressivity-increasing reform were instead financed by raising the marginal tax rates faced by moderate income groups. (1996, 167)

The conventional wisdom on labor supply elasticities for the past two decades has been that prime-age men are quite unresponsive to wage changes, whereas women are quite responsive. That view was based on the research of Hausman (1981, 1985), Burtless and Hausman (1978), and others. That literature is briefly summarized in Bosworth and Burtless (1992).

Corlett-Hague Rule

The essential distortion caused by an income tax is that it affects the labor/leisure choice, with a tax applied to hours of labor. If it were possible to tax both labor and leisure hours, we would have a nondistortionary tax that would generate no excess burden. Hence, if it is possible to tax both labor and leisure rather than just labor, we can improve social welfare. If we are considering the choice of two possible taxes, the better tax to implement or increase would be the tax that applies to goods or services complementary with leisure. The income tax is equivalent to a tax on all goods and services, except leisure. An excise tax applies to a single good only. The sales tax applies to all goods but generally does not tax services, labor time, or leisure time. Because these taxes all apply to goods and services other than leisure time, they have the effect of encouraging leisure time, relative to all other goods and services.

The idea of Corlett and Hague (1953–54) was that the least distortionary taxes in this context are those taxes that apply to goods or services complementary with leisure. This idea is known as the **Corlett-Hague rule**. The policy implication is that we should tax goods such as television sets, video cassette movies, hiking boots, mountain bikes, snowboards, romance novels, supermarket tabloids, and other goods that are used along with leisure time. Consumers use these goods, along with leisure time, to produce entertainment that they value. None of these goods is useful by itself. All must be combined with leisure time in order to be useful. Hence, these goods are all complementary with leisure time and would be appropriately taxed. Doing so would reduce the excess burden of the tax system as we move away from a complete tax exemption for leisure time.

Optimal Taxation in Theory and Practice

So where does all this optimal tax theory leave us as we consider the practical world of implementing tax policy? Are policymakers actually following the proscriptions of optimal tax theory and reforming tax systems? Mankiw et al. (2009) assess the state of progress in the field of optimal taxation and its practical application in the policy realm as follows.

They suggest that on balance tax policy has generally moved in the directions that have been suggested by optimal tax theory, with some notable exceptions. The trend of the past 30 years among OECD countries, for example, has been for top marginal rates to decline with a flattening of marginal income tax schedules, and a movement toward more uniform commodity taxes applied to final goods (and not intermediate goods). In the field of capital taxation, however, the impact of optimal tax theory has been less successful. Tax rates are still well above the zero level recommended by theory. Beyond that, the more subtle proscriptions of optimal tax theory, such as taxes based on personal characteristics (e.g., tax on stature, or tax on IQ), asset-testing, and history-dependence, have not been generally implemented. Mankiw et al. also observe that, "Where large gaps between theory and policy remain, the harder question is whether policy makers need to learn more from theorists, or the other way around."

POLICY STUDY

Green Taxes and the Double Dividend

Environmental concerns have bred intense interest in tax policy, believe it or not. One important policy option proposed in recent years is to implement new environmental taxes such as a carbon tax that will not only discourage harmful environmental damages, but can also be used to replace other existing distortionary taxes such as income taxes. The so-called **double dividend hypothesis** is that new environmental taxes will not only benefit the environment but can also reduce the distortions of the existing tax system, yielding two benefits, or a double dividend. An environmental damages tax can be corrective, as we learned in Chapter 4 about Pigouvian taxes, helping the market price externalities. Beyond that, if the environmental tax is a replacement for an income or sales tax that creates an excess burden, as explained in this chapter, there is the potential for efficiency enhancement.

Here is an excerpt from the abstract from the Brookings Institution and World Resources Institute's Greening the Tax Code publication, which suggests some specific environmental taxes and fees.

> Analysis indicates that taxes on air and water pollution could generate substantial revenue for the U.S. Treasury while improving environmental quality, stimulating technological innovation and enhancing energy security. Reducing tax expenditures with adverse impacts on natural resources could do the same. As lawmakers explore ways to reduce federal budget deficits and reform the tax code, they should consider measures that shift more of the tax burden onto activities—such as pollution—that make the economy unproductive or reduce quality of life.... This policy brief examines fiscal instruments that both raise revenue and help improve environmental quality.

Table 11.5 lists their suggested pollution taxes along with estimated revenue.

Parry and Bento (2000) review economic studies of the potential for double dividends with various environmental taxes and fees. The early literature on this topic found that there was little reason to expect double dividends with environmental tax swaps because they exacerbate the costs of the existing tax system. Examining the issue more carefully, however, Parry and Bento extended the existing models by including several important consumption goods that receive tax preferred status in the existing U.S. tax system. In particular, housing and medical care sectors were included in the models. With this modification the efficiency gains from implementing environmental taxes are larger due to the preexisting distortions created by the income tax preferences. Both the markets for consumption goods and factor markets involved in producing those goods are distorted by the tax preferences. Parry and Bento found that with this model innovation a double dividend is more likely to occur.

Parry (1998) provides some important advice on when to expect a double dividend, and when not to have such an expectation. If the tax system is fully efficient, applying only optimal taxes in the Ramsey sense, then the prospects for a double dividend are nearly completely eliminated. If inefficiencies exist in the existing tax system, he suggests that it would be more economically appropriate to reform the tax system than to indirectly address the inefficiencies by adopting new environmental taxes. Furthermore,

TABLE 11.5 Possible Pollution Taxes

Tax	Tax Base	Possible Charge Rate	Estimated Revenue (over five years)
Carbon	Carbon content of fossil fuels for energy	$12 per metric ton, rising $0.50 per year	$100 billion
Volatile organic compounds	Volatile organic compounds (VOC) emissions from stationary sources	$2,100 per ton	$49.5 billion
Water effluents	Effluents from water treatment, pulp and paper, food processing, and chemical plants. Based on effluent's biological oxygen demand (BOD)	$0.65 per pound of effluent	$11.2 billion
"Superfund" tax	Petroleum and chemical feedstocks; corporate environmental income tax (reinstatement of expired tax)	$0.097 per barrel of oil; rate varies by chemical feedstock; 0.12 percent of corporate income over $2 million	$8.0 billion
Fertilizer	Nitrogen fertilizers	$0.20 per pound	$3.3 billion
"Gas guzzler" tax	Light trucks, minivans, and SUVs up to 10,000 pounds (extension of existing tax beyond passenger cars)	Varies by vehicle fuel efficiency up to $7,700 per vehicle	$2.9 billion
Mercury emissions fee	Mercury emissions from industrial boilers, waste incinerators, and chlor-alkali plants	Varies by source: $3,000-$40,000 per pound	$1.1 billion

Source: Hanson and Sandalow (2006), available at: http://www.wri.org/publication/greening-the-tax-code.

Parry cautions that in the real world of policy it is unlikely that all of the new revenue generated by environmental taxes and fees would be poured into reductions of existing taxes. If that is so, then the prospects for a double dividend are substantially reduced.

PROBLEMS

1. True, False, or Uncertain. Explain.
   a. A tax imposed on a good with zero elasticity of demand has a large excess burden.
   b. A tax imposed on a good with zero elasticity of supply has no excess burden.

c. A tax imposed on a good with a large elasticity of demand has a small excess burden.
d. A tax imposed on a good with a large elasticity of supply has a large excess burden.

2. Calculate the excess burden of a tax of 10 percent for a good with compensated elasticity of demand of 0.5 (in absolute value), a price before tax of $1, and a quantity demanded of 1 million units. Explain what happens to the excess burden if we consider a tax of 20 percent instead.
3. The short-run price elasticity of demand for gasoline is 0.15 (in absolute value) while that for television sets is 1.50. Explain what the optimal commodity taxation for these two goods would be using the Ramsey rule. Is this the pattern of taxation that is actually applied by the federal government? Speculate as to why or why not the Ramsey rule is being followed.
4. In the case of a consumer with a given level of income and the choice of spending that income on commodities X and Y, evaluate whether an excise tax on X or an equal-yield income tax will impose the least excess burden. Write the consumer's budget constraint. Incorporate each tax separately and evaluate the tax effects on the budget line and the consumer's utility-maximizing commodity combination. Use a graph to demonstrate.
5. Comment on the following statement: If the compensated demand for a single commodity is completely inelastic, the most socially desirable *ad valorem* tax rate on this commodity will be higher than the tax rates on other commodities.
6. Use the Ramsey rule to compare two alternative tax policies. First, suppose that we apply two small taxes at the rate t to a commodity. Second, suppose that we apply one tax at the rate $2t$ to the same commodity.
   a. What are the efficiency effects of the two policy options?
   b. Is there a reason to prefer one policy to the other on efficiency grounds? Explain.
7. True, False, or Uncertain. (Use graphs to explain.)
   a. Equal proportional taxes imposed on all market goods have no excess burden.
   b. A tax on a product with zero elasticity of demand has no excess burden (or is "neutral").
   c. The excess burden of an excise tax on a product with close substitutes is lower when the substitutes are initially taxed than when the substitutes have no initial distortions.
   d. A reduction in the income tax rate will induce greater labor supply.
   e. A reduction in the income tax rate will induce greater private savings.
   f. A reduction in the income tax rate will induce greater risk taking.
8. Illustrate graphically and discuss the excess burden of each of the following policies, taking into account your estimation of the elasticity of demand or supply that may affect the size of the excess burden:
   a. An excise tax on coffee
   b. An excise tax on fine china and crystal

c. An excise tax imposed on the product produced by a monopolist
d. An excise tax on health care services

9. Use the expression for excess burden $EB = 0.5p_x x t_x^2/(1/\eta + 1/\varepsilon)$ (where η is the absolute value of the compensated price elasticity of demand and ε is the supply elasticity) to estimate the annual excess burden of a tax on cigarettes using the following information:
   a. The excise tax is \$0.20/pack.
   b. The compensated elasticity of demand for cigarettes is $\eta = 0.5$.
   c. The elasticity of supply is $\varepsilon = 0.75$.
   d. In the absence of the tax, the equilibrium price of cigarettes is \$1 per pack and the equilibrium quantity is 500 million packs.

REFERENCES

Atkinson, A. B. *Public Economics in Action: The Basic Income/Flat Tax Proposal.* New York: Oxford University Press, 1995.

Ballard, Charles L., John B. Shoven, and John Whalley. "General Equilibrium Computations of the Marginal Welfare Costs of Taxes in the United States." *American Economic Review* 75 (1985): 128–38.

Ballard, Charles L. "The Marginal Efficiency Cost of Redistribution." *American Economic Review* 78 (1988): 1019–33.

Bosworth, Barry, and Gary Burtless. "The Effects of Tax Reform on Labor Supply, Investment, and Saving." *Journal of Economic Perspectives* 6 (1992): 3–26.

Browning, Edgar K., and William R. Johnson. "The Trade-Off Between Equality and Efficiency." *Journal of Political Economy* 92 (1984): 175–203.

Burtless, Gary, and Jerry A. Hausman. "The Effect of Taxes on Labor Supply: Evaluating the Gary NIT Experiment." *Journal of Political Economy* 86 (1978).

Corlett, W. J., and D. C. Hague. "Complementarity and the Excess Burden of Taxation." *Review of Economic Studies* 21 (1953–54): 21–30.

Cornes, Richard. *Duality and Modern Economics.* Cambridge, UK: Cambridge University Press, 1992.

Diamond, Peter A., and James A. Mirrlees. "Optimal Income Taxation and Public Production." *American Economic Review* 61 (1971): 8–27, 261–78.

Hanson, Craig, and David Sandalow. "Greening the Tax Code." Washington, DC: The Brookings Institution and the World Resources Institute, 2006. Available at: http://www.wri.org/publication/greening-the-tax-code.

Hausman, Jerry A. "Labor Supply." In *How Taxes Affect Economic Activity,* edited by Henry Aaron and Joseph Pechman. Washington, DC: Brookings Institution, 1981.

Johansson, Per-Olov. *An Introduction to Modern Welfare Economics.* Cambridge, UK: Cambridge University Press, 1991.

Mankiw, N. Gregory, Matthew Weinzierl, and Danny Yagan. "Optimal Taxation in Theory and Practice." *Journal of Economic Perspectives* 23 (2009): 147–74. Available at Digital Access to Scholarship at Harvard: http://dash.harvard.edu/handle/1/4263739.

Mirrlees, James A. "An Exploration in the Theory of Optimum Income Taxation." *Review of Economic Studies* 38 (1971): 175–208.

Parry, Ian W. H. "The Double Dividend: When You Get it and When You Don't." *National Tax Association Proceedings of the Ninety-First Annual Conference, 1998*, pp. 46–51.

Parry, Ian W. H., and Antonio M. Bento. "Tax Deductions, Environmental Policy, and the 'Double Dividend' Hypothesis." *Journal of Environmental Economics and Management* 39 (2000): 67–96.

Ramsey, Frank P. "A Contribution to the Theory of Taxation." *Economic Journal* 37 (1927): 47–61.

Triest, Robert K. "The Efficiency Cost of Increased Progressivity." Chapter 5 in *Tax Progressivity and Income Inequality*, edited by Joel Slemrod. New York: Cambridge University Press, 1996.

NOTES

1. See Ballard, Shoven, and Whalley (1985).
2. The formal derivation of this result follows from the optimization problem. The objective function is the total excess burden. With the independence assumption, we simply add the excess burdens of the two commodity taxes:

$$EB = EB_x + EB_y = (1/2)\eta_x x p_x t_x^2 + (1/2)\eta_y y p_y t_y^2.$$

The constraint is that we generate a given amount of tax revenue:

$$R^0 = t_x x + t_y y.$$

Minimizing total excess burden subject to the revenue constraint using the method of Lagrange yields the following two first-order conditions:

$$\partial L/\partial t_x = \eta_x x p_x t_x - \lambda x p_x = 0,$$
$$\partial L/\partial t_y = \eta_y y p_y t_y - \lambda y p_y = 0,$$

where λ is the Lagrangian multiplier. Solving these two equations for λ and setting equal, yields the Ramsey rule:

$$t_x/t_y = \eta_y/\eta_x.$$

3. The material in this section is adapted from Atkinson (1995).
4. The derivative is given as:

$$\partial R/\partial t = wL_0[w(1-t)]^{\epsilon} + twL_0\epsilon[w(1-t)]^{\epsilon-1}(-w).$$

As the rate of taxation initially rises above zero, revenue is generated because for small t the above derivative is positive. But for larger values of t, the derivative is negative, indicating that further tax rate increases reduce revenue.

5. We do so by setting the above derivative equal to zero and solving for the tax rate.
6. This section is based on Atkinson (1995, 12–13).

Radius Images/Getty Images

CHAPTER 12

Incentive Effects of Taxation

LEARNING OBJECTIVES

1. Explain how taxes create incentive effects that lead people and firms to change their economic behavior.
2. Discuss the effects of taxation on savings, labor supply, risk taking, and tax evasion.

As we said in the previous chapter, taxes affect the activities of individuals and firms in every economy because they provide incentives for people and firms to change behavior. Those changes in behavior induced by the tax system are the source of inefficiencies that we need to consider. In this chapter, we will consider four of the most important ways that a tax may provide incentives for people and firms to alter their behavior. A tax can affect the amount of work that people are willing to provide in labor markets, the amount of savings they wish to set aside for the future, the amount of risk they are willing to bear, and their inclination to engage in tax evasion. Keynes addressed the importance of these issues in his *General Theory of Employment, Interest, and Money* (1935/1964) where he spoke of the potential for raising tax rates being deterred

> partly by the fear of making skillful evasions too much worth while and also of diminishing unduly the motive towards risk-taking, but mainly, I think, by the belief that the growth of capital depends upon the strength of the motive towards individual saving. (372)

Notice that Keynes identified three ways that high tax rates might provide adverse incentives: to evade taxes, to reduce risk taking, and to depress individual savings. He identified the main concern as that of capital formation that is made possible by savings. Recall that equilibrium in the macroeconomy requires that savings be equal to investment. If we want to have a high level of investment in the economy, we must have a high level of aggregate savings. If the tax system discourages private savings, it will not support a high level of investment. Because investment in this context means productive machinery, equipment, factories, and buildings, we are talking about capital inputs. The other, and more important, input is labor. For a high level of economic output, an economy requires a high level of labor input to be made available for productive use. After all, labor is by far the most important input used in the production of goods and services. In the year 2009, for example, U.S. employee compensation was $7,812 billion out of a total national income of $12,225 billion, or 68 percent.[1] Consequently, the individuals' labor supply decisions in response to the tax system are critical to examine. For a good summary of how taxes affect labor supply, savings, and investment, see Bosworth and Burtless (1992). Keynes also identified risk taking and tax evasion as important issues to consider as high tax rates provide incentives for people to change their behavior.

TAXATION AND LABOR SUPPLY

Each person is endowed with time and is confronted with the problem of allocating time to competing uses. Students understand this problem acutely. They need to spend time being in classes, studying, conducting library research, working on the computer, developing a social life, attending sporting and artistic events, and possibly working at a part-time job. And then there is a need for some sleep, too. How do people make decisions about allocating their time? Does economics have a role in this process?

Analyzing the Labor/Leisure Choice

Time allocation is fundamentally an economic problem. We will develop a model that will permit us to analyze not only a person's decision about how much to work but also the person's response to a tax on the wages earned from that work. The problem is to allocate scarce time to the competing activities of leisure and work, where it is work that generates income. The person values both income and leisure and must decide how to use her time. Figure 12.1 illustrates the economic time allocation problem. Suppose that a person has a

FIGURE 12.1 Labor/Leisure Choice

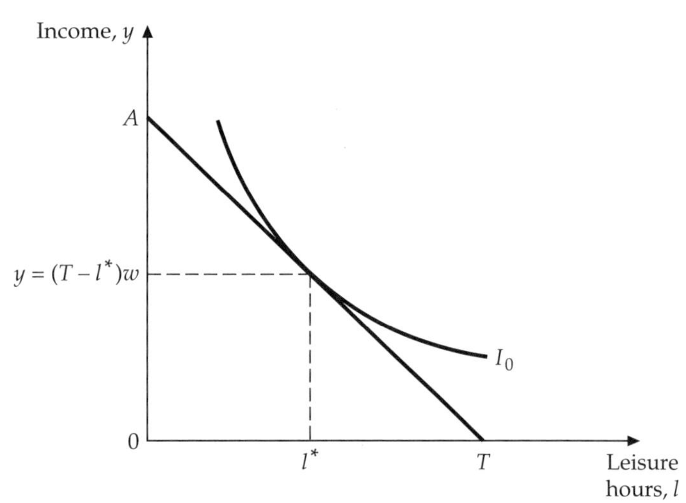

time endowment of T hours per week that represents the total amount of time she has to allocate to competing activities. She has two alternative uses for her time: she can use her time for leisure activity (l hours) or she can work ($T - l$ hours). Work pays her a wage income of w dollars per hour, so her wage income y will be the product of the number of hours of work times the wage: $y = (T - l)w$. Initially, we can think of the person at point T on the horizontal axis where she has time but no income. For each hour of time she allocates to work, she loses an hour of leisure but earns the wage w. As she moves northwest along her budget line, her income rises at the rate of w per hour of work. At the extreme point A on the vertical axis, she is spending all of her time at work, with no leisure whatsoever, earning the maximum possible income of wT.

The person has preferences for income and leisure captured by her utility function $u(y, l)$. Her marginal rate of substitution (MRS) is the ratio of her marginal utility of leisure to her marginal utility of income and represents the rate at which she is willing to substitute leisure for income: $MRS = -mu_l/mu_y$. The optimal choice of time to allocate to leisure activity and the corresponding income earned is illustrated by the point of tangency in Figure 12.1. At that point the slope of her indifference curve, her MRS, equals the slope of her budget line, $-w$.[2] That is, the rate at which she is willing to substitute leisure for income while maintaining the same utility level (being indifferent between the two) is equal to the rate at which she is able to trade leisure for income in the marketplace, earning a wage w. Of course, with the amount of leisure determined, we also know the amount of labor she will provide in the marketplace, $T - l$, and her income level, $w(T - l)$. At the optimal allocation illustrated in Figure 12.1, she uses l^* hours for leisure activities and the remainder of her time, $T - l^*$ hours, for work. She earns a wage income of $y = w(T - l^*)$. The combination of l^* hours of leisure and a wage income of $y = (T - l^*)w$ makes her better off than any other combination that is available to her.

If the wage is reduced how will the person react? Will she decide that at the lower wage she needs to work more in order to maintain her income or will she decide that at the lower wage work is just not worth it? This is a critical issue we need to examine. The effect of a reduction in the wage is to flatten the budget line from AT to BT, as illustrated in Figure 12.2. The person will react to that change. Initially, the person faces the budget line AT with the slope $-w_0$. A reduction in the wage to w_1 flattens the budget line to BT, reducing the vertical intercept to B because the total wage income the person can earn is lower at the lower wage. The new flatter budget line has slope $-w_1$, where $w_1 < w_0$. Notice that the horizontal intercept T, the time endowment, is unaffected by the change in the wage. The person reacts to the reduced wage by moving to the point of tangency b on indifference curve I_1. This point requires her to allocate more time to leisure: $l_1 > l_0$. Hence, the person reacts to the lower wage by working less and spending more time in leisure activity. She also has lower income, $y_1 < y_0$, and reduced utility, reflected in the lower indifference curve I_1.

Why has the person reacted this way to the reduced wage? She could have decided to work more in order to offset the wage reduction, but she did not do that. Why? In order to answer this question, we must consider two distinct effects in her decision to work less. The reduction in the wage has

FIGURE 12.2 Labor Supply Effects of a Wage Reduction

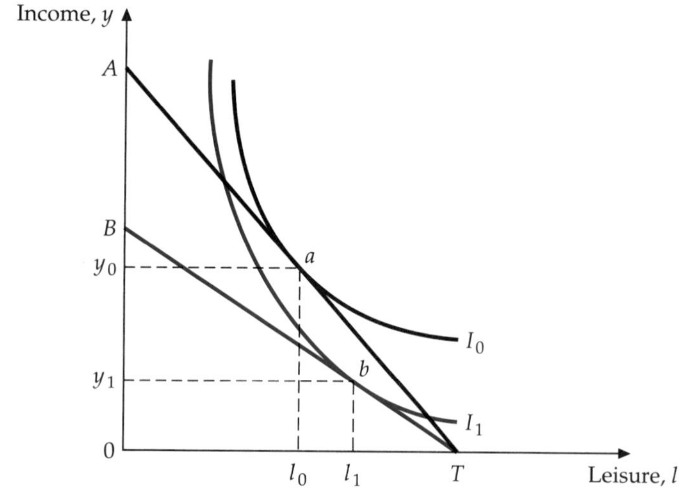

lowered the price of leisure and, like any price change, has created a substitution effect and an income effect. The substitution effect comes from the fact that the wage reduction has reduced the price of leisure and that price change will induce the person to substitute in favor of the lower-priced good—leisure. After all, the price she pays for an hour of leisure activity is the forgone opportunity to work an hour and that price falls when the wage goes down. When the price of leisure is reduced, other things equal, she will want to have more leisure. She will substitute leisure for work. But there is an income effect as well. At the lower wage her income is reduced. When her income falls, she will consume less of all normal goods.[3] Because leisure is likely to be a normal good for her, she will consume less leisure. With less time spent in leisure, she will work more. Thus, the reduced wage has two distinct and opposing effects. The substitution effect encourages her to work less, whereas the income effect encourages her to work more. Table 12.1 summarizes the effects of a wage reduction on labor supply.

TABLE 12.1 Effects of a Wage Reduction on Labor Supply

Substitution Effect	Income Effect	Total Effect
Price of leisure falls.	Wage income falls.	Price of leisure falls and wage income falls.
At lower price of leisure, person desires more leisure and *works less.*	At lower income, person desires less of all normal goods, hence desires less leisure and *works more.*	Effect on labor supply depends on relative strengths of the substitution and income effects.

FIGURE 12.3 Substitution and Income Effects of a Wage Reduction

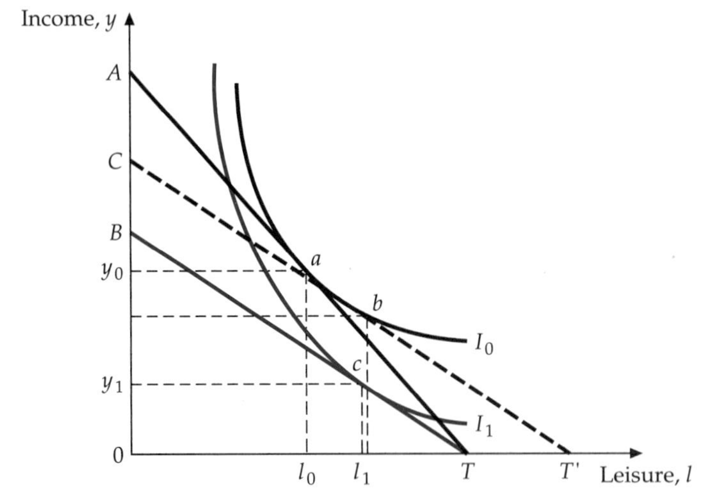

In order to view the two effects, we must add a bit more detail to the leisure-income figure we have been considering. Figure 12.3 illustrates the same situation as Figure 12.2, except that we have added a new budget line CT' parallel to the original budget line but tangent to the original indifference curve I_0. If the person's income were supplemented so that she suffered no reduction in utility, staying on indifference curve I_0 she would move from point *a* to point *b*. This change is the pure substitution effect. It illustrates how she would substitute leisure for income as the price of leisure is reduced. In reality, however, there is no such income supplement keeping her as well off as before the wage reduction. Hence, the income effect is illustrated by the parallel shift in the budget line CT' to BT that results in the movement from point *b* to point *c*. The total effect of the wage reduction is the movement from point *a* to point *c*, made up of two distinct subeffects: the substitution effect (the move from *a* to *b*) and the income effect (the move from *b* to *c*). Because the wage has fallen and the corresponding price of leisure has fallen, the person wants to spend more time in leisure and wants to work less (the substitution effect). But, the wage reduction causes the person's income to fall, and this means the person will want less of all normal goods, including leisure, and will therefore want to work more (the income effect). In the particular case illustrated in Figure 12.3, the substitution effect involves a larger desired increase in leisure than the income effect's reduction in the desired amount of leisure, so the substitution effect is stronger than the income effect and the person reacts to the wage reduction by working less. The relative sizes of the substitution and income effects determine the net effect. If both effects are the same size, they cancel one another and the net effect is zero—no change in time allocation. If the substitution effect

FIGURE 12.4 Effects of a Wage Reduction When the Income Effect Dominates

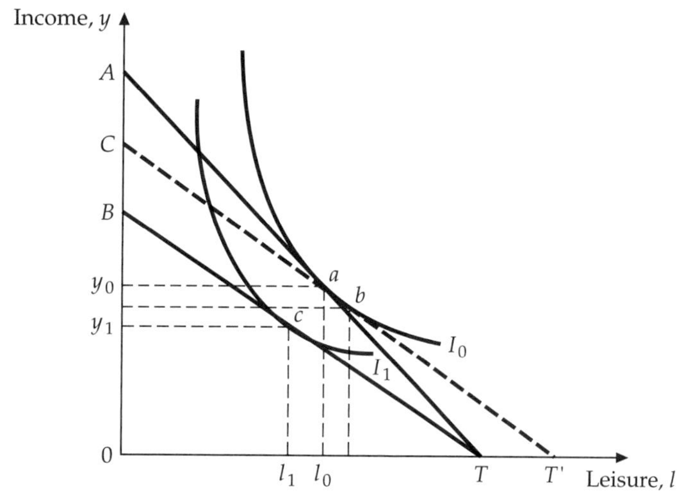

is stronger than the income effect, the person works less. If the income effect is stronger than the substitution effect, the person works more.

What would happen if the person's income effect were stronger than her substitution effect? Figure 12.4 illustrates a situation where the person's income effect is stronger than his substitution effect. Hence, he reacts to a wage reduction by working more. In this case, the substitution effect increases leisure (the move from *a* to *b*) by a smaller amount than the reduction in leisure due to the income effect (the move from *b* to *c*), so the person reacts to the wage reduction by taking less leisure and working more.

Every person confronted with a wage change will experience both substitution and income effects that arise from the wage change. For many people, the substitution effect will be stronger, resulting in a direct relationship between the wage and hours worked. As the wage increases, the person works more. For some, however, the income effect dominates, resulting in an inverse relationship between the wage and hours worked. As the wage rises, the person works less. The relationship between the percentage change in the hours of work and the percentage change in the wage rate is the **elasticity of labor supply.**[4] We expect that elasticity to be positive, reflecting a dominant substitution effect and an upward-sloping labor supply curve. As the wage rises, workers are willing to supply more hours of labor in the labor market. This is reflected in the normal upward-sloping supply curve of labor that assumes the substitution effect dominates the income effect for most workers in the labor market. If the income effect dominates, people respond to a higher wage by working less. This may actually happen at relatively high wage levels, causing the labor supply curve to bend back on itself, creating the so-called **backward-bending labor supply curve.**

Effects of a Tax on Wage Income

Now that we understand the essential issues involved in labor/leisure choice, we can model the effects of a tax on wage income. Suppose that a proportional tax of rate t is applied to wage income. Before the tax, the person has a wage income of $(T - l)w$. After the tax, the person is left with an income of $(T - l)\,w(1 - t)$. The tax has the effect of flattening the budget line, just as we saw in Figure 12.2. Because the tax reduces the wage, which is the price of leisure, it acts as any price change and induces both substitution and income effects. If the substitution effect dominates, the person will react to the tax by working less. In this case, the tax has the effect of reducing the labor supply. If the income effect dominates, the person will react to the tax by working more. In this case, the tax has the effect of increasing the labor supply. Hence, whether a proportional tax on wage income reduces or increases the labor supply depends crucially on whether substitution or income effects dominate in workers' preferences.

Keep in mind that the analysis above tells us how an *individual* worker may react to a tax on labor income. The labor *market* is composed of millions of individual workers, all of whom react to the tax on labor income. Some workers react by working less. Others react by working more. Still others don't react at all. The supply curve of labor combines the reactions of all the workers in the labor market.

Laffer Curve

If most workers have dominant substitution effects, then the tax causes them to work less than they otherwise would. A reduction in the tax rate would have the effect of inducing them to work more. With more labor supply, not only can we produce more but we will also generate more tax revenue, right? Could it be possible that we will actually generate more tax revenue at the lower tax rate? Will tax cuts pay for themselves? This is the hope of so-called *supply-side economists*. They believe that the substitution effect is dominant and strong enough to generate more revenue at lower tax rates. This requires a large elasticity of labor supply so that a reduction in the tax rate and a corresponding increase in after-tax wage leads to a very strong response in additional hours worked. The key to the supply-side view is that labor supply elasticities are assumed to be large (relative to 1—the usual benchmark for an elasticity). A noted supply-side advocate who popularized this concept in graphical form is Arthur Laffer, whose so-called **Laffer curve** is illustrated in Figure 12.5.

Starting from the origin, tax revenue rises with the tax rate, providing the conventional relationship whereby an increase in tax rate results in increased revenue. The conventional relationship changes, however, once we reach the top of the curve at tax rate t^*, which generates maximum revenue. From this point on, any further increases in the tax rate have the effect of reducing revenue. If the tax rate exceeds t^*, then a reduction in the rate will have the effect of increasing revenue. Supply-side economists believe that the economy is operating on this part of the Laffer curve so that revenues will actually rise when the tax rate is reduced. Such a view flies in the face of the conventional wisdom, however, that a reduction in

FIGURE 12.5 The Laffer Curve

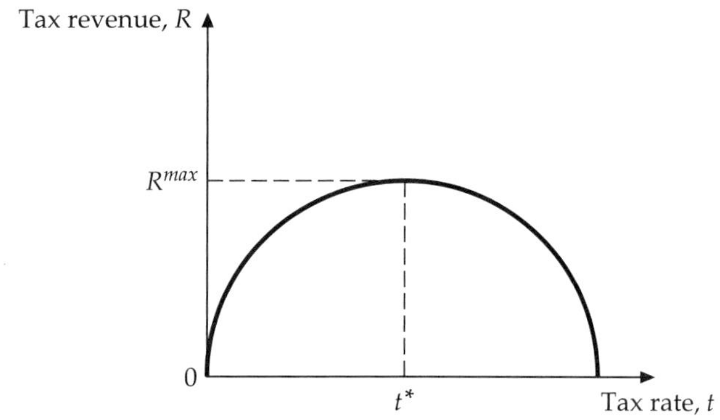

the tax rate will result in less revenue. Essentially, the difference of opinion is on whether the current tax rate exceeds t^*. If so, the supply-side view is valid. If not, the conventional view is valid. The dispute can be settled by an appeal to the empirical facts. If most workers have dominant substitution effects, as mentioned previously, then a tax increase causes them to work less. Therefore, a tax reduction would have the effect of inducing them to work more and would therefore generate more tax revenue, if that relationship were highly elastic. The supply-side view is that the substitution effect dominates the income effect and does so in a powerful way. As the after-tax wage rises due to a tax cut, the hours worked increase more than proportionately, thereby raising tax revenue. Whether this view is correct depends on the relative size of the substitution and income effects.

Joel Slemrod (1996) has addressed the question of taxing the rich and argues that before we can consider whether we *should* tax the rich more, we must answer the logically prior question of whether we *can* tax the rich more. Perhaps it is the case that a higher rate of taxation applied to the rich yields no revenue. In other words, what if there is a high-income Laffer curve at work and we are beyond the revenue-maximizing point? At high levels of taxation the economic activity being taxed is discouraged so much that revenue falls. If high rates of taxation applied to the rich do not yield additional revenue, indicating that we are at or beyond the maximum of the Laffer curve, then only pure envy motivates calls for higher tax rates on the rich. No revenue, or even a reduction in revenue, is derived from such increases. As an alternative, perhaps it is the case that a higher rate of taxation applied to the rich yields some revenue but also induces strong behavior responses that bring with them large excess burdens. In that case, the added revenue may not be economically justified. For both reasons, it is important to understand how the rich react to changes in tax rates in order to know whether they *can* be taxed more and to inform our view of whether they *should* be taxed more. Slemrod summarizes his findings with this concluding statement:

> In sum, with respect to two aspects that differentiate the rich from the nonrich—the importance of capital income, and the flexibility of the form of compensation—

> I have uncovered no evidence of a significant behavioral response to the marginal tax rate. There is, however, evidence of a significant response of capital gains realizations to the tax on capital gains; exactly how substantial is the long-run elasticity of this response remains a controversial issue. Thus, in assessing the behavioral response of the affluent, it is important to consider separately the marginal tax rate on ordinary income and the effective tax rate on capital gains. (1996, 208–9)

Slemrod's result indicates that for ordinary wage and salary income, there does not appear to be a behavioral response to tax rates supporting the idea behind the Laffer curve, but for capital gains realizations, there is evidence of such an effect although the size of the effect is uncertain.

One way to examine the effects of tax rate changes on all forms of response is to consider the elasticity of taxable income (ETI). The tax base includes all forms of taxable income, as explained in Chapter 10, including wage and salary income, interest, dividends, capital gains, etc. In a recent survey of evidence on the elasticity of taxable income with respect to marginal tax rates, Saez, Slemrod, and Giertz (2009) find, "much evidence to suggest that the ETI is higher for high-income individuals who have more access to avoidance opportunities, including deductible expenses." They conclude that, "the essential insight underlying the EI remains valid: that income tax rates cause taxpayers to respond on a wide range of margins and, under some conditions, all of these responses reflect inefficiency, because they would not have been undertaken absent the tax rates."

Empirical Evidence on Taxation and Labor Supply

Hausman (1985) surveyed the results of empirical studies seeking to estimate elasticities of hours of work with respect to wages and income. His survey results are summarized in Table 12.2 for males in the labor force. That table reports results from a number of different studies using U.S., U.K., and Swedish data sets. The wage elasticities estimated in these studies range from a low of −0.13 to a high of 0.09. These results indicate quite clearly that the elasticity of hours of work with respect to the wage is approximately zero for

TABLE 12.2 Male Labor Supply Elasticities

Estimated Wage Elasticity Range	Estimated Income Elasticity Range
[−0.13, 0.09]	[−0.17, −0.04]
Implications:	**Implications:**
1. Hours worked are not very responsive to changes in the wage, i.e. the labor supply curve is effectively vertical	1. Work is an inferior good (and leisure is a normal good), i.e. prime-age men reduce their hours of work as their incomes rise
2. No efficiency cost due to taxation	2. This effect is not large, however

Source: Elasticity estimates compiled from studies reported in Hausman (1985).

males. The implication, of course, is that the supply curve is vertical for these men. As a result, there is no efficiency cost due to taxation. Men will continue to work the same number of hours regardless of wage changes and are not affected by taxation that alters the net wage. The elasticity of hours worked with respect to income is estimated to be negative in all studies, although the size of the elasticity is close to zero, ranging from −0.04 to −0.11. As a result, we know that work is an inferior good. That is, prime-age men reduce their hours of work as their incomes rise. The effect is not large, however.

For married women, the empirical evidence is quite different. Table 12.3 summarizes a number of studies investigating the behavior of married women in the United States, the United Kingdom, and Canada. The elasticity of hours of work with respect to the wage ranges from −0.30 to 2.30 in the studies. Some studies clearly find that married women are much more responsive in their hours of work as the wage changes than are their husbands. As a general rule, the evidence has been interpreted to indicate that married women are much more responsive to wages than are prime-age men. The efficiency implication is that taxation may cause a good deal of excess burden by inducing married women to change their work behavior in response to the tax. As a result, there is a high efficiency cost of taxation for married women.

The estimated income elasticities for married women reported in Table 12.3 are negative and small (in absolute value). As a result, married women's behavior appears similar to men's behavior with respect to income. As income rises, they work fewer hours. This evidence confirms that leisure is a normal good for both men and women.

More recent evidence on female labor supply has questioned the conclusion that wage elasticities are much larger for women than for men, however. Triest (1996), for example, replicated the Hausman (1981) study using the same model of married women's labor supply. When he included nonparticipants in the data set, he found wage elasticities of approximately 0.90, but when he used only observations for women with positive hours of work, the

TABLE 12.3 Married Women's Labor Supply Elasticities

Estimated Wage Elasticity Range	Estimated Income Elasticity Range
[−0.30, 2.30]	[−0.50, −0.05]
Implications:	Implications:
1. Hours worked are much more responsive to changes in the wage than for prime-age men, i.e. the labor supply curve is much more likely to be upward sloping 2. There is a high efficiency cost due to taxation	1. Work is an inferior good (and leisure is a normal good), i.e. married women reduce their hours of work as their incomes rise 2. This effect is not large, however

Source: Elasticity estimates compiled from studies reported in Hausman (1985).

wage elasticity fell to approximately 0.27. Triest concludes his discussion of elasticity estimates saying:

> Overall, recent work on female labor supply has called into question the assumption that women's hours of work are highly responsive to economic incentives. In simulating the efficiency cost of progressivity, using low to moderate wage and income elasticities seems most reasonable. (1996, 142–43)

Burtless (1987) also points out that research based on experimental data tends to find much smaller elasticities, in the range of −0.04. Thus, it appears that wage elasticity estimates are quite sensitive to model specification. Recent research by Kimmel and Kniesner (1998) confirms the basic pattern of results where women are found to be more responsive than men, but less responsive than early evidence indicated. Furthermore, Kimmel and Kniesner improve previous estimates of labor supply elasticities by distinguishing between the effects of wage changes on employment status and the effects of wage changes on hours worked. The former describes how people respond in terms of their willingness to enter or exit the labor force while the latter describes how they change their hours worked assuming they are in the labor market.

One of the most important issues in considering the difference between male and female labor supply response is that women are much more likely to enter and exit the labor force than men. Kimmel and Kniesner (1998) find that single women have an elasticity of employment status of +2.41 and an elasticity of hours worked of +0.69, whereas married women have an elasticity of employment status of +1.85 and an elasticity of hours worked of +0.67. This evidence can be compared to that for men in their study. Single men have an elasticity of employment status of +0.65 and an elasticity of hours worked of +0.44 while married men have an elasticity of employment status of +1.08 and an elasticity of hours worked of +0.40. This evidence indicates that the elasticity of hours worked is less than 1 for both women and men but is somewhat larger for women. The elasticity of employment status is clearly larger for women than men, however, with the women's elasticity being 2.39 for all women (single and married) compared to the men's elasticity of 0.86 (single and married). The elasticities of hours worked are inelastic for both men and women, however. The hours worked elasticity for women (single and married) is 0.66, whereas that for men (single and married) is 0.39. Women's hours worked are somewhat more sensitive to wage changes than men's hours worked, but both are inelastic.

By way of summary, Meghir and Phillips (2010) provide an exhaustive review of labor supply and taxes and conclude that, "hours of work are relatively inelastic for men, but are a little more responsive for married women and lone mothers. On the other hand, participation is quite sensitive to taxation and benefits for women."

TAXATION AND SAVING/BORROWING

Another important area of life where taxes may affect people's decisions relates to consumption and savings (or borrowing) decisions. If a tax is applied to the interest earned on savings, the net return is reduced. Isn't it logical to expect that people will save less due to the effect of the tax? So, too, if the tax system permits interest paid by a borrower to be deducted from taxable income, isn't it logical to expect that people will borrow more? As it happens, there is more to the story to consider, just as there was in the case of labor supply.

Life Cycle Model of Consumption and Saving

We begin consideration of a person's saving or borrowing behavior by developing a model of the person's choice of resource allocation over time. The model we use to investigate such behavior is a **life cycle model** that presumes there are two periods across which resources can be allocated: the present and the future. The decision that must be made is how to allocate consumption and saving over the two periods. Lifetime income consists of current income y_0 plus future income y_1, both of which are taken as given. We cannot simply add the two incomes together to get lifetime income, however, because the units of income measurement are different. A dollar of future income is not equivalent to a dollar of current income due to the opportunity cost of money. The present value of lifetime income can be computed by discounting future income, putting it in terms of current income, and summing:

$$y_0 + y_1/(1 + r). \tag{12.1}$$

The discount rate r accounts for the opportunity cost of money between the present and future. The person would be indifferent between a dollar today and $1 + r$ dollars in the future. Hence, to convert a dollar of future income into today's value, we invert that process and divide the future income by $1 + r$. In similar fashion, lifetime consumption can be written as

$$c_0 + c_1/(1 + r), \tag{12.2}$$

where c_0 is current consumption and c_1 is future consumption. The person's lifetime budget constraint requires that lifetime consumption be equal to lifetime income:

$$c_0 + c_1/(1 + r) = y_0 + y_1/(1 + r). \tag{12.3}$$

We can solve this lifetime budget equation for c_1 as a function of c_0:

$$c_1 = [(1 + r)y_0 + y_1] - (1 + r)c_0. \tag{12.4}$$

In other words, future consumption is a function of lifetime income, present consumption, and the interest rate.

Figure 12.6 illustrates the lifetime budget constraint. Suppose that the person has an **income endowment** (y_0, y_1), or a given amount of wage income in the two periods. If no saving or borrowing were possible, the person would be constrained to operate at that point. Present consumption would exhaust present income and future consumption would have to equal future income; that is, he would have to consume his current income exactly today and consume his future income exactly tomorrow. But, of course, if it is possible to save and borrow, the person has other possibilities. He is not limited to a consumption pattern over time that equals his income pattern.

FIGURE 12.6 The Lifetime Budget Constraint

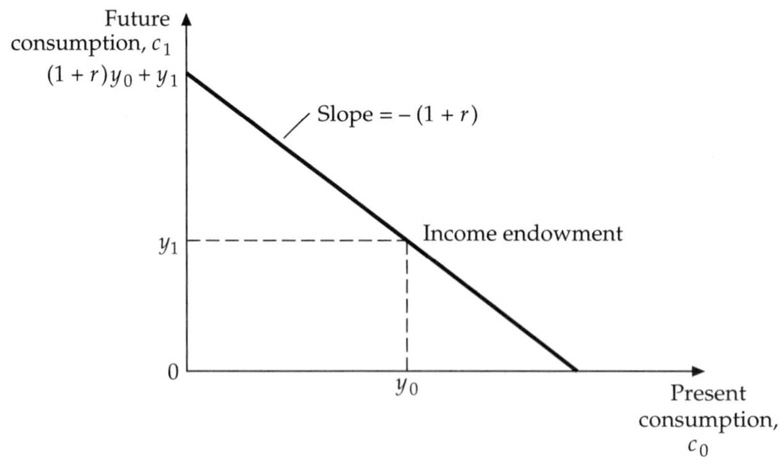

If he chooses to consume less than his current income and save some of it for future consumption, he moves northwest along the budget line from the income endowment point. He saves an amount equal to the difference between his current income and his current consumption: $s = y_0 - c_0$. That savings pays interest at the rate of r, so in the future period he has his income endowment of y_1 plus interest income on his savings of $r(y_0 - c_0)$. The savings allow him to have future consumption that is larger than his future income. The slope of the lifetime budget constraint is $-(1 + r)$, indicating that a dollar of forgone consumption in the present will provide $1 + r$ dollars of future consumption. The reason, of course, is that the dollar not consumed today is saved and earns interest at the rate of r between now and the future. On the other hand, it is possible for the person to borrow in the present and pay off the debt in the future. That enables her to have consumption in the present that is larger than her income. She pays back what she borrowed with interest in the future. A borrower is a person who moves southeast from the income endowment point along the budget line. She can consume more in the present than her present income by borrowing and paying interest at the rate r. Her future consumption is reduced as a result of the need to pay back what she borrows with interest.

The person has preferences over present and future consumption given by the utility function $u(c_0, c_1)$. Some people have a strong preference for present consumption over future consumption. That type of person is willing to give up a large amount of future consumption in order to be able to consume more today. Other people are more patient and are more willing to forgo consumption today in order to have greater consumption in the future. Whatever the person's preferences, the problem is to maximize utility subject to the lifetime budget constraint. The optimal consumption plan over the life cycle is the one where the budget line is tangent to the indifference curve, as

FIGURE 12.7 Life Cycle Model of Consumption and Savings

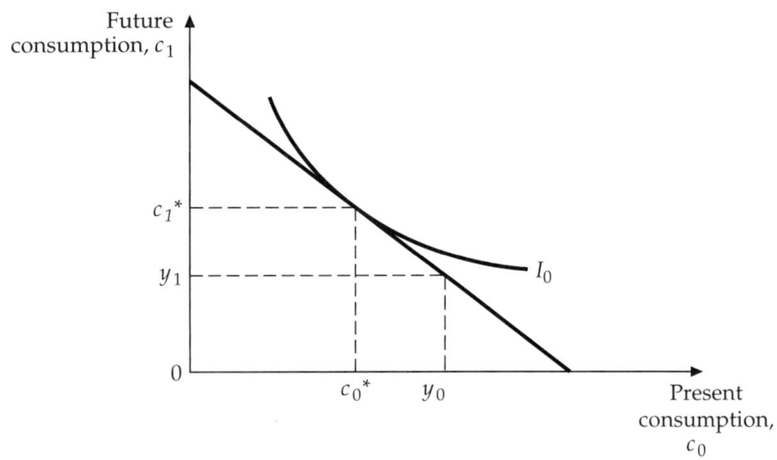

illustrated in Figure 12.7. That requires the slope of the budget line to be equal to the slope of the indifference curve. The slope of the budget line is $-(1+r)$ and the slope of the indifference curve is minus the marginal rate of substitution (MRS) between present and future consumption: $MRS = mu_{c_0}/mu_{c_1}$. Setting these two slopes equal, we have the optimality condition: $MRS = mu_{c_0}/mu_{c_1} = (1+r)$.[5] At this point, the person's willingness to trade present for future consumption (and maintain the same total utility) is exactly equal to the rate at which present and future consumption can be traded in the marketplace (at the interest rate r on saving and borrowing). The result is that the person's saving or borrowing is determined in such a way as to maximize lifetime utility subject to lifetime income.

Effects of a Tax on Savings

What effect does a tax have on the amount of savings? It would seem that a tax that reduces the return to savings would discourage savings, right? As is so often the case in economics, there is more to the story than meets the eye. A tax reduces the price of present consumption and therefore has both substitution and income effects, like any price change. It reduces the return to savings, thereby reducing the price of present consumption, and has a substitution effect that encourages present consumption and discourages savings. There is also an income effect to consider because the tax reduces lifetime income.

A tax applied to savings has the effect of reducing the return from a dollar of savings from the interest rate r to the after-tax rate of interest $(1-t)r$. If we make this substitution in the lifetime budget constraint we have

$$c_1 = y_0[1 + r(1-t)] + y_1 - c_0[1 + r(1-t)]. \tag{12.5}$$

FIGURE 12.8 Effect of a Tax on the Lifetime Budget Constraint

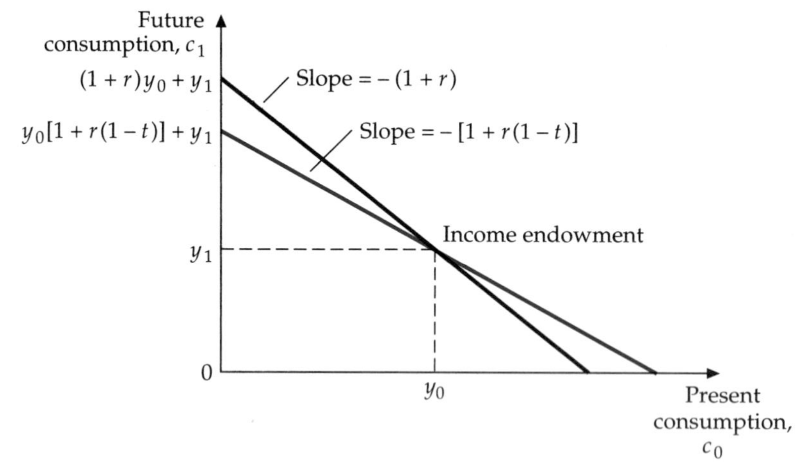

Comparing this expression with the expression for the budget line in the absence of a tax on savings indicates that the vertical intercept and the slope are both reduced. That is, the tax has the effect of rotating the budget line in a counterclockwise fashion around the income endowment point, like an airplane propeller spinning. Figure 12.8 illustrates the effect of the tax on the lifetime budget constraint. The tax clearly has the effect of limiting consumption possibilities for savers as it shifts the budget line downward.

For borrowers, however, the tax has the effect of shifting the budget line upward, enhancing consumption possibilities. Why the difference? Well, the reason lies in the way the tax law treats two types of interest: interest earned by savers and interest paid by borrowers. A saver has present consumption less than present income, operating to the left of the income endowment point. For any given level of saving, however, the tax reduces the rate of return to saving since the tax is applied to interest income earned by the saver and thereby reduces the future consumption that is possible. A dollar saved today earns interest and becomes $(1 + r)$ dollars tomorrow. But the interest earned is taxable, reducing the amount available tomorrow to the dollar saved plus the after-tax interest rate applied to that dollar: $1 + r(1 - t)$. Thus, the lifetime budget line must be lower to the left of the endowment point.

The story for a borrower is different, however, and involves the tax treatment of interest paid. When a person borrows in order to have present consumption in excess of present income and operate to the right of the income endowment point, the interest payments on the loan may be deductible from taxable income. With deductibility of interest payments, the tax reduces the cost of borrowing and enhances consumption opportunities. Borrowing a dollar today requires payment of $1 + r$ tomorrow. But if that interest paid is

TABLE 12.4 Effects of a Tax on Consumption/Saving Behavior

Substitution Effect	Income Effect	Total Effect
Tax reduces return to savings.	Tax reduces return to savings.	
Price of present consumption falls relative to future consumption.	Tax reduces lifetime income.	Tax reduces the price of present consumption and reduces lifetime income.
At lower price of present consumption, person desires more present consumption and *saves less.*	At lower income, person desires less of all normal goods, including present consumption, and *saves more.*	Effect on saving depends on relative strengths of the substitution and income effects.

deductible, as in the case of mortgage interest for homeowners in the United States, the net amount that must be paid back tomorrow is the dollar borrowed plus the after-tax interest due: $1 + r(1 - t)$.[6] If the interest paid is not deductible, as in the case of credit card interest paid in the United States, then the budget line of the borrower is unaffected by the presence of the tax.

So what effect does the tax have on saving and borrowing behavior? Two effects of this price change: substitution and income effects. The effects are summarized in Table 12.4, where once again the effects are opposite in sign. Hence, the net effect of a tax on saving is ambiguous in theory, depending on the relative sizes of the substitution and income effects.

Knowing how the tax affects the budget line, we can now analyze the effect of the tax on saving or borrowing behavior. First, consider a saver, as illustrated in Figure 12.9. This person reduces his savings as a result of the

FIGURE 12.9 Saver Responds to a Tax by Saving Less

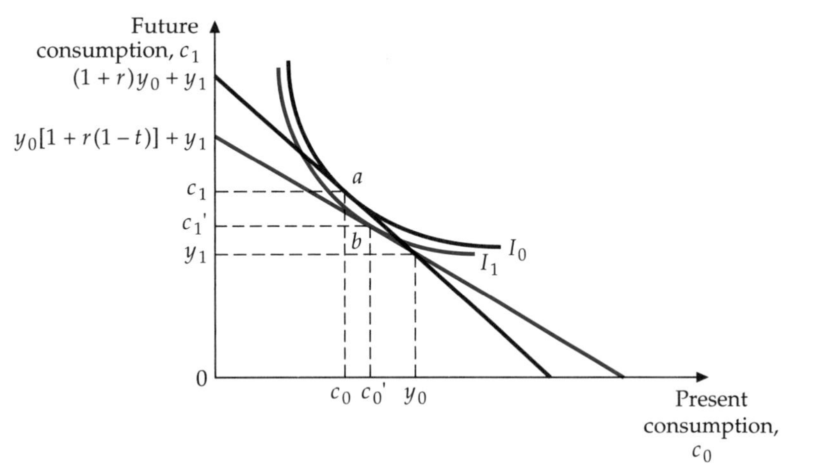

tax. The saver is initially at point *a* with coordinates (c_0, c_1), saving the amount $y_0 - c_0$. The introduction of a tax on interest income and the corresponding deductibility of interest paid rotate the budget line counterclockwise around the income endowment point to the dashed budget line illustrated. With this new flatter budget line, the saver moves to the new optimum point *b* with coordinates (c_0', c_1'), where present consumption is larger and therefore the amount saved is smaller. This move from point *a* to point *b* involves both the substitution effect and the income effect, but the substitution effect of the tax is dominant for this person. This is a saver who says to himself, "If the government taxes away part of my interest income, it's just not worth saving as much. I might as well enjoy consuming more of my income now." Because the price of present consumption is reduced relative to future consumption, this person wants more present consumption and decides to save less. The effect of the tax reducing his lifetime income and therefore encouraging him to consume less present consumption, a normal good, and save more is just not as important to this person. Because effect is more powerful for this person, he decides to save less. For a person such as this, a reduction in the rate of taxation would have the effect of stimulating him to save more. This is the person policymakers, who advocate reduced income tax rates in order to stimulate savings, have in mind.

Of course, not all savers are like this. Figure 12.10 illustrates the case for a saver whose income effect is dominant. She will react to a tax by saving more. For her, the income effect is more powerful than the substitution effect. The saver is initially at point *a* with coordinates (c_0, c_1) saving the amount $y_0 - c_0$. The introduction of the tax rotates the budget line counterclockwise around the income endowment point to the dashed budget line illustrated. The saver moves to the new optimum point *b* with coordinates (c_0', c_1') on

FIGURE 12.10 Saver Responds to a Tax by Saving More

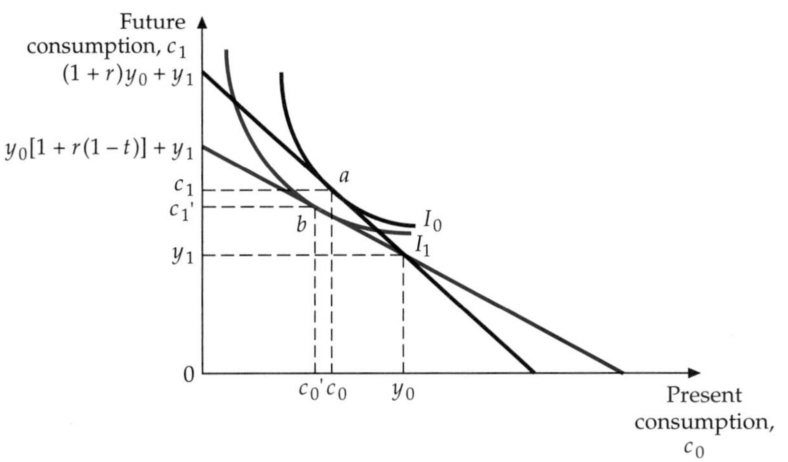

the flatter budget line where present consumption is smaller and therefore the amount saved is larger. This move from point *a* to point *b* involves both the substitution effect and the income effect as before, but in this case the income effect of the tax is dominant for this person. She reacts to a tax on savings by saying, "If the government taxes away part of my interest income, I have to consume less now and save more in order to preserve my future consumption plans." For a person such as this, a reduction in the rate of taxation would have the effect of stimulating her to save less. This is definitely not the type of person policymakers, who advocate reduced income tax rates in order to stimulate savings, have in mind.

Effects of a Tax on Borrowing

How does a tax affect a borrower? Well, the same two effects are at work, but in the case of a borrower, the tax reduces the price of borrowing due to the deductibility of interest payments on loans. Hence, the price of present consumption is reduced relative to future consumption, and by the substitution effect he will be encouraged to borrow more. There is also an income effect as the tax treatment of interest paid reduces interest payments on loans and increases his real income. As a result of the increase in income, he wants to have more present consumption, a normal good, and for this reason he will borrow more. Note that in this case there is an unambiguous effect. The tax treatment of interest paid by borrowers encourages them to borrow more. Figure 12.11 illustrates this case. The borrower is initially at point *a* with coordinates (c_0, c_1) borrowing the amount $c_0 - y_0$. The introduction of a tax on interest income and the corresponding deductibility of interest paid rotate the budget line counterclockwise around the income endowment point to the

FIGURE 12.11 Borrower Responds to a Tax by Borrowing More

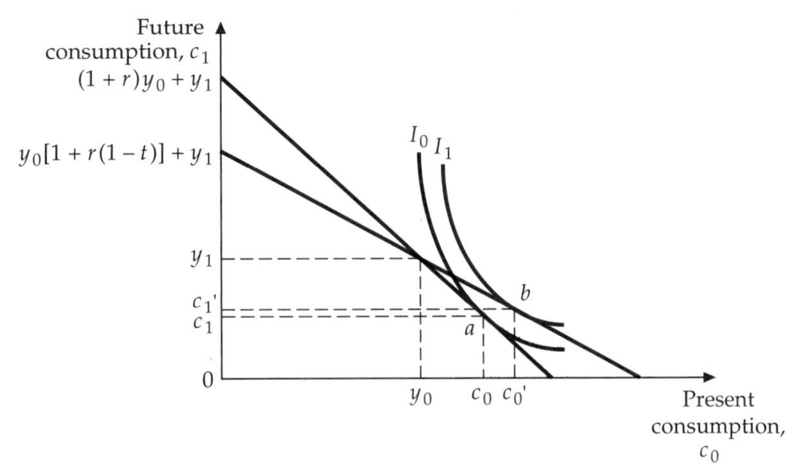

dashed budget line illustrated. With this new flatter budget line, the person moves to the new optimal point *b* with coordinates (c_0', c_1'), where present consumption is larger and therefore the amount borrowed is greater. This move from point *a* to point *b* involves both the substitution effect and the income effect. In this case, however, the two effects work in the same direction; both encourage the borrower to borrow more.

Empirical Evidence on the Effects of Taxation on Savings

The empirical evidence on the effects of taxation on savings indicates that taxes are probably not an important determinant of nonretirement savings but may affect pension savings substantially. Because the Individual Retirement Account (IRA) has been at the center of recent policy debates over saving incentives, we will focus on the literature related to that particular incentive. **Individual Retirement Accounts**, or IRAs as they are known, are savings accounts into which people can deposit funds and receive favorable tax treatment. Traditional IRAs provide a deduction for savings deposited on this year's income tax but require that future withdrawals from the account be taxed. If you look back at the U.S. income tax Form 1040, Figure 10.1, you will find that an IRA deduction can be taken on line 32—an adjustment to income. Premature withdrawals from IRA accounts are taxable with a penalty, and this is reported on line 15a as a form of taxable income. The advantage of putting money into such an account is twofold. First, after retirement you may have lower income and therefore be in a lower marginal tax bracket. Thus, your savings would be taxed at a lower rate in the future. Second, even if your tax rate is the same in the future, by putting money in an IRA account you can defer the tax due in the future and that is valuable. Another type of IRA account known as the **Roth IRA** does not provide the immediate tax deduction but rather makes the future withdrawals of both principal and interest tax free. In this case your savings grow at the before-tax rate of interest.

Early work on traditional IRAs by Venti and Wise (1986, 1987, 1988) and Feenberg and Skinner (1989) indicated that IRA incentives increased private savings substantially during the period from 1982 to 1986. Later research by Engin, Gale, and Scholz (1994, 1996) and Gale and Scholz (1994) found that IRA limit increases lead to a very small net increase in private savings. People apparently simply move other savings into IRA accounts and receive the tax benefit, but do not increase their net savings appreciably. This finding is confirmed by Long (1990). As a result, there is no clear evidence that private savings are very sensitive to the marginal tax rate. The policy implication is that a reduction in the income tax rate is unlikely to induce much new private retirement saving. This issue is the focus of a policy study at the end of the chapter.

Most recently, research on saving has focused on the question of employer matching in savings plans and the default setting. Insights provided from the field of ***behavioral economics*** have led investigators to consider the way savings plans are designed. Companies have offered many variations on employer-sponsored savings plans over the years. Most plans involve an employer match of some percentage along with employee saving. Furthermore, most plans have been opt-in plans by which the employee was required to take the initiative to sign up in order to obtain the benefit of the plan. Experimentation with opt-out programs by which employees were automatically included in the program unless they chose to opt out has resulted with much higher participation and savings. The studies by Choi et al. (2002, 2004), for example, provide strong evidence that the automatic enrollment increases savings plan participation by younger, low-tenure, and lower-income employees. Beshears et al. (2007) find that the matching rate provided by the employer has a modest effect on opt-out rates. They find, for example, that moving from a typical match of 50 percent on up to 6 percent of pay contributed to the plan, to no match at all, reduces participation under an automatic enrollment plan by just 5 to 11 percent.

TAXATION AND RISK TAKING

In this section we will investigate the ways in which taxation may affect people's willingness to take risks, or engage in economic activity with an uncertain outcome. Because this activity is at the heart of a capitalistic economic system and is necessary for economic growth and well-being, it is essential that the tax system not stifle the entrepreneur. Joseph Schumpeter's vivid description of the important role of the entrepreneur in a capitalistic economic system provides a good reminder why it is essential that an economy have people willing to take risks:

> The function of entrepreneurs is to reform or revolutionize the pattern of production by exploiting an invention or, more generally, an untried technological possibility for producing a new commodity or producing an old one in a new way, by opening up a new source of supply of materials or a new outlet for products, by reorganizing an industry and so on.... This kind of activity is primarily responsible for the recurrent "prosperities" that revolutionize the economic organism and the recurrent "recessions" that are due to the disequilibrating impact of the new products or methods. (1942, 132)

According to Schumpeter, entrepreneurial activity is primarily responsible for both economic prosperity and recession. Thus, it is essential to consider what role the tax system may play in fostering entrepreneurial activity. The essence of the entrepreneurial role is to take risks, do things that no one else would think of doing or be brave enough to attempt. Schumpeter describes what the risk taker does this way:

> To undertake such new things is difficult and constitutes a distinct economic function, first, because they lie outside of the routine tasks which everybody understands and, secondly, because the environment resists in many ways that vary, according to social conditions, from simple refusal either to finance or to buy a new thing, to physical attack on the man who tries to produce it. To act with confidence beyond the range of familiar beacons and to overcome that resistance requires aptitudes that are present in only a small fraction of the population

> and that define the entrepreneurial types as well as the entrepreneurial function. This function does not essentially consist in either inventing anything or otherwise creating the conditions which the enterprise exploits. It consists in getting things done. (1942, 132)

So, if we want people in the economy who take risks and get things done, as described by Schumpeter, we need to assure that the tax system does not get in the way. At first blush, it would seem that a tax would reduce the return to entrepreneurial activity and therefore reduce the incentive to engage in such activity. If so, the clear policy implication is to get rid of taxation in order to unleash the entrepreneurial spirit. This view is true, so far as it goes, but there is more to the story of how a tax system affects risk-taking behavior of entrepreneurs. A tax system also typically permits an entrepreneur to deduct losses if things turn out badly. In that way the tax system encourages risk taking since it implicitly subsidizes losses. If that is true, then the tax system may encourage entrepreneurial activity and fuel the engine of growth in the economy.

Fundamentals of Risk and Return

Consider the consequences of alternative acts by an entrepreneur and states of nature in the matrix illustrated in Table 12.5. The rows of the table correspond to acts taken by the economic agent (person or firm) while the columns correspond to states of nature. The acts correspond to the alternatives of taking risk or not taking risk, while the states of nature correspond to low and high returns earned. The returns are both zero in the case where the entrepreneur does not take risk. No risk, no return. Nothing ventured, nothing gained. If the entrepreneur takes the risk, however, there are two possible outcomes. If she is lucky, she will earn a high return. On the other hand, if the venture turns out to be a bust, her return is small or even possibly negative—a loss. Suppose that consequence c_1 is strictly smaller than the consequence c_2: $c_1 < c_2$. In fact, c_1 may be negative, reflecting a loss. Of course, the nature of taking a risk is that the outcome is not certain. We do not know which state of nature will occur. Suppose that the probability of earning a high return when taking a risk is denoted p. The corresponding probability of earning a low risk is then $1-p$. The expected consequence (or expected value EV) of the risky venture is then

$$EV[c] = (1-p)c_1 + pc_2. \tag{12.6}$$

TABLE 12.5 Risk and Return

	States of Nature	
Actions	***Low Return (Probability 1 − p)***	***High Return (Probability p)***
Do not take risk	0	0
Take risk	c_1	c_2

This expected value represents the weighted average of the two possible consequences, where the weights are the probabilities of each consequence. Of course, the weights add up to 1 because one of the two events must occur.

The expected utility of the risky venture is given by the weighted average of the utilities that would arise from the two potential consequences:

$$EU[c] = (1 - p)u(c_1) + pu(c_2), \tag{12.7}$$

where $(1 - p)$ and p are the probabilities of each event and $u(c_1)$ and $u(c_2)$ are the utilities that result from the two consequences associated with those events. Using the expected utility, we can compute the entrepreneur's marginal rate of substitution for this risky venture as

$$MRS = [(1 - p)mu(c_1)]/[(p)mu(c_2)] \tag{12.8}$$

which is the ratio of marginal utilities of the two consequences where each marginal utility is multiplied by the probability of that outcome. We could call this the *expected marginal rate of substitution*. As with any marginal rate of substitution, this *MRS* represents the rate at which the entrepreneur is willing to trade one consequence for the other, holding constant her expected level of total utility.

The effect of an income tax on the expected value of a risky venture can now be considered. First, note that the tax reduces the size of both consequences proportionately. If the tax rate is *t*, then the two after-tax consequences are $(1 - t)c_1$ and $(1 - t)c_2$. Because $c_1 < c_2$, we know that the after-tax relationship between the two consequences is preserved: $(1 - t)c_1$, $(1 - t)c_2$. Consider the effect of the tax on the expected value of the outcome of the risky venture, or the mean return. The expected value becomes

$$EV[(1 - t)c] = (1 - p)(1 - t)c_1 + p(1 - t)c_2, \tag{12.9}$$

which can be compared to the expected value $EV[c]$ before the tax was introduced. In order to compare, we can simplify the above expression and write it as

$$EV[(1 - t)c] = (1 - t)EV[c]. \tag{12.10}$$

This expression makes it clear that the tax reduces the expected value of the risky venture and reduces it by the amount of the tax times the expected value of the venture. With a reduction in the expected return, it is natural that an entrepreneur would be less likely to take a given risk involved.

We have to consider another important effect of the tax. Because the tax is symmetric and losses are deductible, just as positive returns are taxable, the tax has the effect of reducing the riskiness of the venture. This would encourage an entrepreneur to take more risk, other things being equal. A tax system that permits full deductibility of losses is said to have full **loss offset.** If the tax system does not allow any deductibility of losses, it is said to have no loss offset. An intermediate possibility is a tax system that permits some part of losses to be deducted but not the full loss. In that case the tax system has partial loss offset. Whether a tax system permits loss offset turns out to be very important in determining how that tax affects risk taking by entrepreneurs.

We can measure the riskiness of a project in several ways. The simplest measure is the range, or the difference between the maximum outcome and the minimum outcome. In our simple case there are two outcomes and the range is simply $c_2 - c_1$. The effect of the tax is to reduce the range and therefore reduce the riskiness of the venture. The after-tax range is $(1 - t)c_2 - (1 - t)c_1$, which is equal to $(1 - t)[c_2 - c_1]$. A more sophisticated measure of the riskiness of a venture is the standard deviation, which is the positive square root of the variance in the outcomes. Suppose that we denote the variance of the potential consequences as VAR[c]. When a tax including full loss offset is introduced, the variance of the potential after-tax consequences can be written as $\text{VAR}[(1 - t)c] = (1 - t)^2\ \text{VAR}[c]$. This result relies on the properties of the variance of a linear transformation of a random variable, as you may recall from your statistics course. In any case, it is clear that the tax has the effect of reducing the variance and thereby reducing the riskiness of the venture. We usually use the standard deviation SD[c] rather than the variance, because the standard deviation has the same units of measurement as the consequences c (rather than squared units as with the variance). Taking the square root of the above variance relationship yields the result $\text{SD}[(1 - t)c] = (1 - t)\text{SD}[c]$. Hence, either way we choose to measure the riskiness of a venture, we have the result that a tax system with full loss offset reduces risk.

Notice, however, that the relative size of the after-tax consequences is unchanged by the tax. The ratio c_2/c_1 is unaffected by a tax that treats the two consequences proportionately. Multiply both potential consequences of the risky venture by 1 minus a tax rate, $(1 - t)$, to verify that the ratio is unchanged: $(1 - t)c_2/(1 - t)c_1 = c_2/c_1$. Thus, although a tax reduces the expected value of a risky venture, it does not affect the *relative* sizes of the potential outcomes. This result would indicate that there may be an income effect due to the tax but not a substitution effect. In order to investigate the impact of a tax, however, we must consider what happens to the entrepreneur's preferences as well. If marginal utility is declining, as usual, we then know that with a tax the marginal utility of c_1 still exceeds the marginal utility of c_2, $MU[(1 - t)c_1] > MU[(1 - t)c_2]$, but what matters is the relative size of the two marginal utilities. The tax reduces the consequences c_1 and c_2 proportionately, but because marginal utility is declining at a decreasing rate, the marginal utility of the second consequence rises by more than that of the first consequence. The effect of the tax is therefore to reduce the ratio of the marginal utilities, or the *MRS*, making the entrepreneur less willing to take the action leading to the risky high-return consequence.

Consider an example of these effects from the point of view of a firm contemplating a risky investment. If the firm makes the risky investment, it must spend \$100 million up front. Then, if things go well (with probability 0.6), the firm will earn \$300 million, but if things go poorly (with probability of 0.4), the firm will lose the whole \$100 million invested in the venture. If the firm does nothing, it earns nothing. Table 12.6 illustrates the potential outcomes for the firm. The expected value of the risky venture is computed as $EV = 0.6(300) + 0.4(-100)$, which is equal to \$140 million. Hence the

TABLE 12.6 A Risk-Taking Example

	States	
Acts	***Low Return (Probability 0.4)***	***High Return (Probability 0.6)***
Do not take risk	0	0
Take risk	−100	+300

firm's expenditure of $100 million is expected to provide an expected return of 40 percent. A simple measure of the risk involved in this venture is given by the range of potential outcomes: from +300 to −100, or a range of $400 million. As the firm considers whether this venture is worthwhile, it will compare the return and the risk involved with this project to that with other potential projects. For a given level of risk, the firm prefers the project with the highest return. For a given return, the firm prefers the project with the least risk. In general, there is a trade-off between risk and return. The firm will have to accept more risk in order to earn a larger return.

Now, suppose that there is a 25 percent corporate income tax with full loss offset that permits the firm to deduct all losses from taxable income. In order to determine how the tax may affect the firm's willingness to take risk and spend money on highly uncertain ventures, we need to carefully examine how the tax affects both the return to a project and the risk involved. If the venture described above is successful, the firm earns $300 million, which is taxed at the rate of 25 percent, leaving an after-tax income of $225 million. On the other hand, if they lose everything, they can write off a $100 million loss on their corporate tax return and the government will reduce their tax liability by $25 million. Thus, their net loss is just $75 million. We can now recalculate the expected return to this venture, in the presence of a 25 percent tax. The expected value of the firm's return to the risky venture is now $EV = 0.6(225) + 0.4(-75)$, which is $105 million, or a 5 percent expected after-tax return. It is clear that the tax has the effect of reducing the expected return on the project from $40 million (40 percent) to just $5 million (5 percent). There is no question that the tax reduces the expected return to business activity. If there were no change in risk, the firm would then be less willing to engage in this risky activity and the tax could be said to discourage risk taking.

But there is still more to the story. Consider the effect of the tax on the riskiness of the project. Using the range as an estimate of risk, we see that originally the range was $400 million. What is the risk of the project in the presence of the tax? Well, we can recompute the range in the presence of the tax as $225 + $75 = $300 million. Compare that to the range of $400 million in the absence of the tax and you will see that the tax has the effect of reducing the range and therefore reducing the riskiness of this venture.[7] What is it about the tax system that reduces risk? The tax system reduces both the positive return if the project is successful and the negative loss if the project fails. Hence, the range of potential outcomes is reduced and the riskiness of the project is lessened. The tax therefore has the effect of encouraging the firm to engage in risk taking. In effect, the government is acting as a silent partner in the business who is willing to subsidize losses but then expects to share in gains. In this way, business activity can be considered a public-private partnership.

Notice an important principle regarding the effect of taxation on risk taking. The tax has the effect of reducing the return to business activity, which by itself would reduce risk-taking activity. But the tax also has the effect of reducing risk, which by itself has the effect of increasing firms' willingness to engage in risky activity. On balance we cannot determine whether the tax has a positive or negative effect on the risk-taking behavior of business firms without additional information and insight. On the face of it, it is not clear that the tax system has an effect on risk taking. The naive view that taxation reduces risk taking may in fact be incorrect as the tax system can reduce risk, thereby encouraging risk-taking behavior.

A Portfolio Model

Consider a household or a firm with given initial wealth w that they want to divide between two available assets. A risky asset provides a random rate of return ρ whose expected rate of return is distributed over the interval $[-1, +\infty)$. At the low end, the household or firm could lose its entire wealth, indicated by a rate of return of -1. At the high end, it could earn a nearly infinite rate of return. Consider two possible outcomes, called *state one* and *state two*, where the return to the risky asset is high in state one but low in state two. The rate of return in state one exceeds that in state two: $\rho_1 > \rho_2$. As an alternative, the household or firm can put its wealth into a safe asset that provides a certain (nonrandom) return of r. Regardless of what state eventuates, the rate of return r is certain. (Notice that the certain return to the safe asset is denoted r, whereas the random return to the risky asset is denoted ρ.) Let a be the amount of wealth the household or firm invests in the risky asset. The final wealth, denoted y, after realization of the random return to the risky asset, is then given by the expression

$$y = (w - a)(1 + r) + a(1 + \rho). \tag{12.11}$$

The first term on the right-hand side is the wealth the household or firm put into the safe asset, $(w - a)$, and its return, whereas the second term on the right-hand side is the wealth it put into the risky asset, a, and its return.

Figure 12.12 illustrates the portfolio choice problem the household or firm confronts. If they put their wealth in the safe asset, they earn a certain return of r, regardless of which state transpires. Point b is a point on the 45-degree line, reflecting perfect certainty where the household puts all of its wealth into the safe asset. At this point the household has certain wealth of $w(1 + r)$, regardless of whether state one or state two occurs because they put everything into the safe asset. On the other hand, if the household put all of its wealth in the risky asset, they have wealth $w(1 + \rho_1)$ if things

FIGURE 12.12 Portfolio Choice

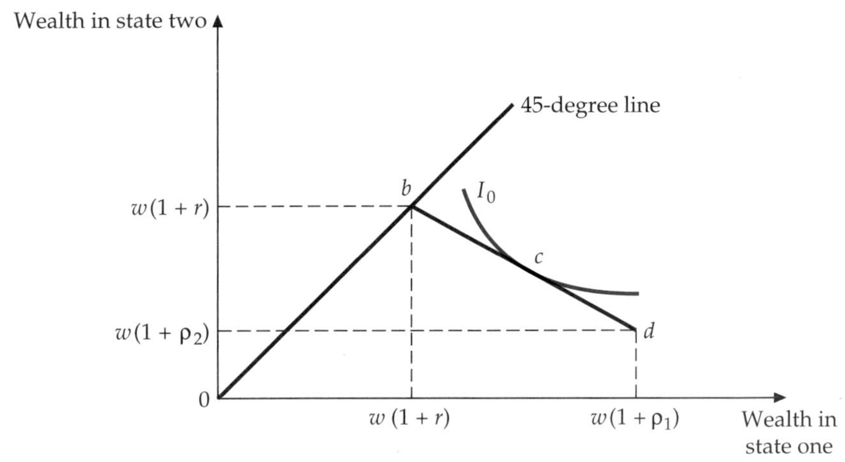

turn out well and state one occurs or wealth $w(1 + \rho_2)$ if things turn out badly and state two occurs. This is the combination labeled point *d* and reflects the portfolio choice where the household puts all of its wealth into the risky asset. Of course, the household can diversify its portfolio and allocate part of their wealth to the safe asset and part to the risky asset, located at a point along the line segment between endpoints *b* and *d*. The lower (higher) the proportion of wealth allocated to the risky asset, the closer the household is to point *b (d)*. This line segment represents the budget line on which the household must operate. Movement along the budget line segment from point *b* to point *d* reflects both increasing risk and increasing return. At point *b* the expected value of wealth is the certain quantity $w(1 + r)$. At point *d* the expected value of wealth is the risky combination of $w(1 + \rho_1)$ in state one and $w(1 + \rho_2)$ in state two. The expected value of the portfolio when they put all their wealth in the risky asset is $EV = pw(1 + \rho_1) + (1 - p)w(1 + \rho_2)$.

The slope of the budget line reflects the rate at which the household or firm can accept increasing risk and be compensated with an increasing expected return. Household or firm preferences over wealth in the two states are illustrated in the downward-sloping indifference curve in Figure 12.12. The shape of this indifference curve reflects the usual convex preferences over wealth in the two states. The optimal portfolio choice for the household or firm is illustrated at point *c* where the indifference curve is tangent to the budget line. The proportion of wealth invested in the risky asset is line segment *bc* divided by line segment *bd*, or the ratio *bc*/*bd*. Thus, we have a model that predicts how much of its wealth a household or firm will invest in the risky and safe assets, given the certain rate of return to the safe asset, the random rate of return to the risky asset, and their preferences for risk.

If the household or firm had steeper indifference curves, reflecting a greater preference for risk, a larger share of their wealth would be allocated to the risky asset as the point of tangency would be closer to point *d*. On the other hand, if the household or firm had flatter indifference curves, reflecting a greater preference for certainty, the point of tangency would occur closer to point *b* as the household or firm would allocate a smaller share of their portfolio to the risky asset. With this portfolio model in hand, we can now examine the effects of taxation, considering both a wealth tax and an income tax.

Effects of a Wealth Tax on Risk Taking

What is the effect of a tax on wealth? A wealth tax has the effect of moving points *b* and *d* in Figure 12.12 back toward the origin and shifting the budget line *bd* in a parallel fashion. The higher the rate of taxation, the closer in toward the origin the budget line shifts. Figure 12.13 illustrates the effect of a wealth tax applied at two rates. The lower tax rate shifts the budget line in to *b′d′*, whereas the higher tax rate shifts the budget line in farther to *b″d″*. For each budget line there is a point of tangency with a household indifference curve that determines the optimal portfolio choice. A wealth portfolio ray is traced out by the optimal portfolio choice points *c*, *c′*, and *c″* that result from the three different budget lines reflecting three different levels of taxation. The wealth portfolio ray demonstrates that the share of wealth allocated to the risky asset is constant when the wealth elasticity of demand is constant. If the wealth elasticity of demand exceeds 1, the ray traced out bends downward, away from the wealth portfolio ray. If the wealth elasticity is less than 1, the ray traced out bends upward from the wealth portfolio ray.

FIGURE 12.13 Effects of a Wealth Tax on Portfolio Choice

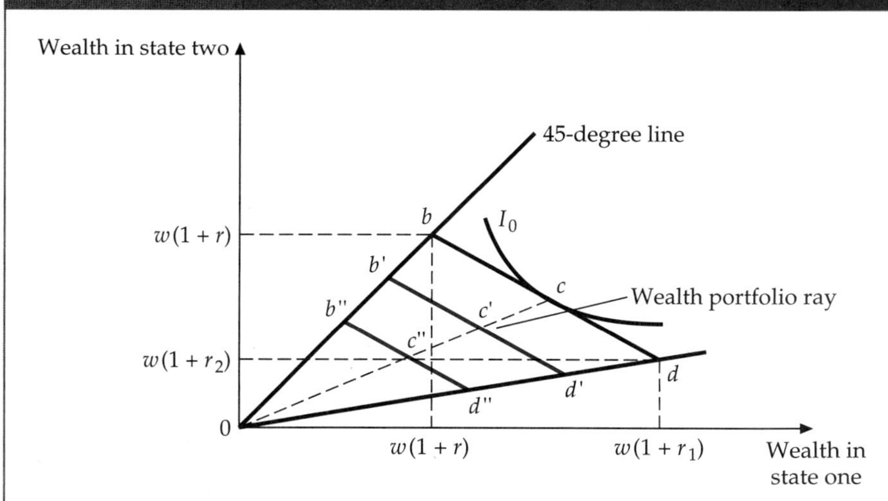

Effects of an Income Tax on Risk Taking

Now, consider the effect of an income tax, rather than a wealth tax. As mentioned previously, two effects of an income tax must be considered. An income tax reduces the rate of return to a risky asset; hence, people will be less willing to take less risk. But, an income tax also subsidizes risk taking through loss offsets, making people more willing to take risks. The net effect of an income tax depends on the strengths of these two effects. With full loss offset, and a zero return to the safe asset, it can be shown that the amount of wealth invested in the risky asset a rises with an increase in the tax rate.[8] This result holds as long as the family holds some of its wealth in the risky asset ($a > 0$). Hence, with full loss offset, the income tax *encourages* holding risky assets. The amount of wealth held in the risky asset increases as the rate of income tax increases. With partial loss offset, the issue is more complex and is not addressed here.

Consider the simplest case of an income tax when the return to the safe asset is zero, $r = 0$, as illustrated in Figure 12.14. In this special case, the initial point b lies at coordinates (w, w) where the household puts its wealth in the safe asset that provides no return. The introduction of an income tax does not affect point b because there is no interest income being earned. At the other extreme, point d represents the household portfolio allocation where all wealth is put into the risky asset. The effect of an income tax in this case is to shift point d inward to d' because the tax reduces the return from r_1 to $r_1(1-t)$. The household's holding of the risky asset is now a larger share of the portfolio because $bc/bd' > bc/bd$. Hence, the income tax has the effect of increasing risk taking as the household allocates a larger share of its portfolio to the risky asset.

FIGURE 12.14 Portfolio Choice with a Zero Return to the Safe Asset and an Income Tax

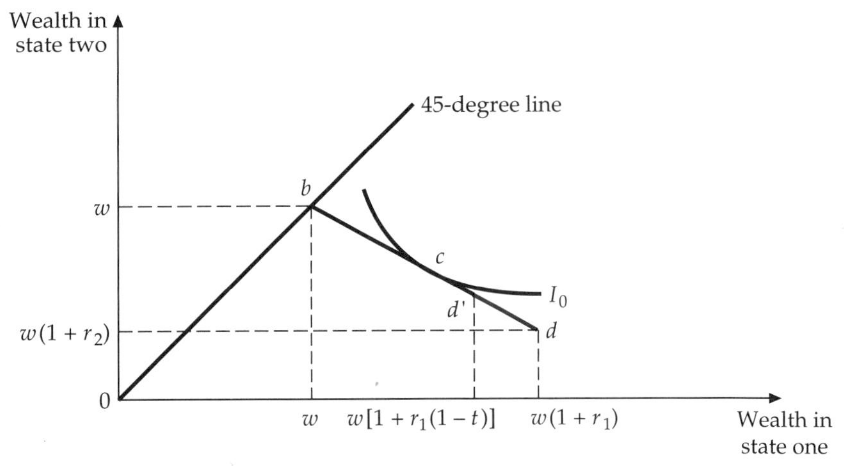

Harley Schwadron. Used by permission of Cartoonstock.com

This simple model can be generalized to the case where there is a positive return to the safe asset, $r > 0$, and an income tax. With a positive return to the safe asset, point b moves out along the 45-degree line to $w[(1 + r(1 - t)]$. This complicates the analysis of the effects of an income tax. The tax alters both points b and d and the net effect of the income tax is ambiguous. A change in the tax rate creates an income (or wealth) effect and a substitution effect, with the two effects having opposite directions of impact. As a consequence, the effect of an income tax on risk taking is ambiguous, depending on the relative sizes of the two effects.

TAX EVASION

Another context in which taxation provides an incentive effect worthy of analysis is the case of tax evasion. In fact, the model introduced previously can be used directly in this context to analyze evasion as a portfolio allocation problem.

The taxpayer with no moral compunctions may choose to underreport income (not reveal the full amount of income earned to the tax authorities), overstate deductions (claim deductions larger than is justified), or fraudulently claim credits in order to reduce his tax liability. All of these activities are forms of **tax evasion**. Tax evasion is illegal activity. It is perfectly legal to avoid taxes by earning income in nontaxable forms rather than taxable forms (for example, earning a larger share of compensation in the form of nontaxable benefits rather than taxable wages). But tax evasion activity is illegal. Despite its illegality, some taxpayers engage in tax evasion. Think of the decision to evade taxes as a two-step problem. The first step is to answer the moral question: Should I evade taxes? If the answer is "no" based on your moral standard and the moral standard embodied in the law, then you stop and do not evade taxes. If your answer is "yes," or "maybe" under certain circumstances, then you proceed to consider the second question: How much should I evade? This second question is a purely economic question. Using the model developed previously, in the tax evasion context, you can think of holding a tax-reporting portfolio. Income that is reported honestly is a safe asset with a certain tax liability, but income that is not reported is a risky asset because there is a chance that the tax authority will discover your underreporting and assess not only the tax but also penalties. The problem for the tax evader is to determine the proper balance of reporting and nonreporting—safe and risky forms of income disclosure.

Portfolio Model of Tax Evasion[9]

A taxpayer who is predisposed to dishonesty may consider opportunities to act in his best interest and pay less than the full tax he is obligated to pay to the government. This taxpayer has no scruples. He considers the tax system as a lottery. A probability p exists that his evasion activity will be detected and punished, and therefore a probability $1 - p$ that he will not be detected. His fixed gross income y is taxable at the rate t. For each dollar of income he receives, he is able to consume $1 - t$ dollars after he pays the tax due if he declares his income honestly. If he conceals that dollar of income from the tax authority and is not detected, he is able to consume the full dollar of income. If his evasion is detected, he must pay the tax plus a surcharge s, leaving him with $1 - t - ts$.

Figure 12.15 illustrates the taxpayer's situation. The axes in the diagram measure the taxpayer's after-tax income if not caught (the horizontal axis) and after-tax income if caught (the vertical axis). If he is perfectly honest, he operates on the 45-degree line, reporting his entire

FIGURE 12.15 The Tax Evader's Problem

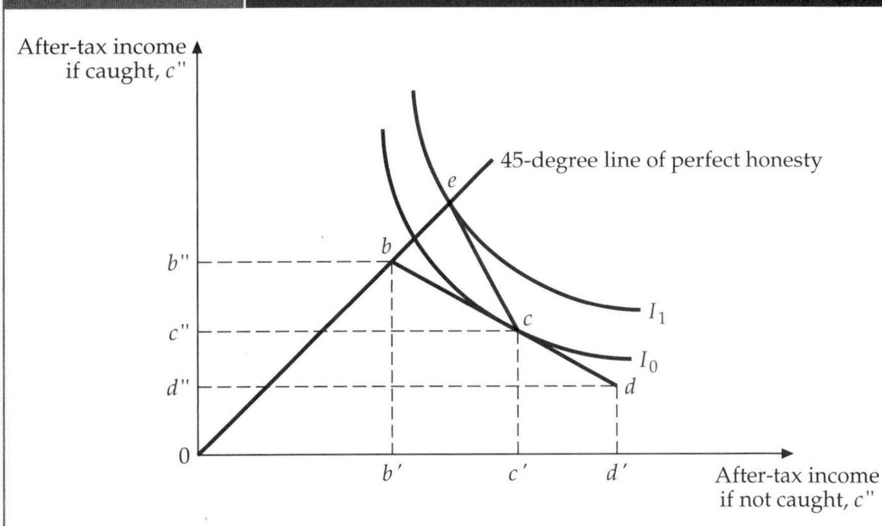

income. In this case, his income is identical whether he is caught or not. Suppose we start at point b where the taxpayer honestly reports all of his income y and pays tax on that reported income. The coordinates of point b are $([1 - t]y, [1 - t]y)$. If the taxpayer were to underreport his income, he would move along the line segment bd toward point d. When he underreports his income, his after-tax income will be larger if he is not caught (designated as amount c') than if he is caught (designated as amount c''). If he conceals his entire income from the tax authority, he is at point d, the point of blatant dishonesty. The coordinates of point d are $(y, [1 - t - ts]y)$. The slope of the line segment bd is $-s$, minus the surcharge rate. Thus, the budget set for the immoral tax evader is given by the area $0bdd'$. With normal convex preferences, the tax evader's optimum is at the point of tangency denoted point c. Notice that this model is exactly like the portfolio model of the previous section. The tax evasion problem is essentially a portfolio allocation problem for the dishonest taxpayer. He has two assets available: a safe asset (reporting his income honestly) and a risky asset (underreporting some or all of his income). The question he must answer is what portion of income to declare and what portion to underreport. The problem of determining the optimal amount of income to underreport is like the problem of determining the optimal amount of a portfolio to hold in a risky asset.

The tax evader's after-tax income is not a certain consequence, because we do not know whether he will be caught, but rather is a random variable denoted c:

$$c = (1 - t)y + \rho te, \tag{12.12}$$

where ρ is the risky return to a dollar of tax evasion (underreported income), denoted e. The random variable ρ takes on the value 1 with probability $1 - p$ and the value $-s$ with probability p. Hence, the expected return (ER) to a dollar of tax evasion is $ER = (1 - p)(1) + p(-s) = 1 - p - ps$, or $1 - p(1 + s)$. Notice that the expected return to evasion is reduced with an increase in the probability of detection or an increase in the surcharge. Table 12.7 illustrates the potential payoffs for the taxpayer.

The optimal amount of income for a dishonest taxpayer to underreport is the quantity associated with point c in Figure 12.15, where the person's indifference curve I_0 is tangent to the budget line segment bd. At that point, he is evading tax on the proportion of his income bc/bd. The

TABLE 12.7 Tax Evasion Outcomes

	States	
Acts	***Detected (Probability p)***	***Not Detected (Probability 1 − p)***
Do not evade	1	1
Evade	$-s$	1

taxpayer has gross income Od', on which he pays a tax equal to the amount $c'd'$ and evades tax in the amount of $b'c'$. His after-tax income is Oc' in this case. If he is caught, however, he must pay the tax $b'c'$ plus the surcharge $b''c''$. His after-tax income in this case is Oc''. The taxpayer's expected consumption, therefore, is somewhere between Oc' and Oc''. We can illustrate his expected after-tax income as point e in the graph. The slope of the line segment ce, which is tangent to the higher indifference curve I_1 at point e, is equal to minus the odds of not being caught.[10] The greater the probability of detection, the lower the odds of not being detected in tax evasion, the flatter the slope of this line segment, and the smaller the potential gain from tax evasion.

Effects of Changes in Income and Tax Rate

First, consider the effect of a change in the taxpayer's income. The effect of an increase in pretax income is to shift the budget line segment bd outward in the northeasterly direction, maintaining the same slope and proportionately increased line segment length. What happens to tax evasion depends on the nature of the taxpayer's utility function. In order to obtain a clear-cut result, we must assume that the taxpayer is risk-averse so that the new equilibrium point c is northeast of the original equilibrium point.[11] The result is that the absolute amount of tax evasion increases, although we cannot draw a firm conclusion about the proportion of underreported income. Hence, we have the result that increased income causes increased tax evasion.

Second, consider the effect of a simple reduction in the marginal tax rate t, with no change in the penalty surcharge or the individual's pretax income. The effect of a marginal tax rate reduction is similar to that of an increase in income, with an important difference. A reduction in the tax rate shifts the budget line segment bd upward, with the left-hand point b moving up the 45-degree line, but the right-hand point d moves vertically in this case. Hence, the bd line segment is shortened. The new equilibrium point will be northeast of point c, so tax evasion increases.

Finally, an increase in progressiveness of the tax system, an increase in the marginal tax rate t, accompanied by a lump-sum income transfer that keeps expected utility constant, has the effect of keeping the person at point c. Point b and the slope of the line segment bd are unchanged. The amount of evaded tax stays the same as the marginal tax rate rises. Hence, the amount of unreported income must fall. Thus, tax evasion is reduced.

Limiting Tax Evasion

The effect of increased enforcement on the tax evader is easy to determine by considering Figure 12.15. The slope of the tax evader's indifference curve is given by

$$-[(1-p)mu(c')]/[pmu(c'')], \tag{12.13}$$

which is minus the odds ratio of not being detected times the marginal rate of substitution (the ratio of the marginal utilities of c' and c''). In equilibrium, the slope of the indifference curve must equal the slope $-s$ of the budget line. Now, if the probability of detection increases, reflecting more vigorous auditing on the part of the tax collection agency, then the odds ratio $(1 - p)/p$ will decrease as the odds of *not* being caught fall. In order for the slope expression to remain constant, the tax evader will adjust so that the marginal rate of substitution rises. That requires that c' falls and c'' rises. Hence, the tax evader will move up the budget line closer to point b and will evade less tax. Similarly, an increase in the surcharge s will have the effect of making the budget line steeper. As a result, the tax evader will move to a steeper point on his indifference curve, requiring that he evade less tax. In this way, both increased enforcement and a higher surcharge on evasion will be effective in reducing tax evasion.

POLICY STUDY

Do IRAs Increase Private Savings?

Saving incentives of various types have been introduced into the U.S. income tax code by Congress over the past two decades in order to induce greater private savings. One of the most visible and popular forms of saving incentives has been the Individual Retirement Account (IRA), which was greatly expanded in the early 1980s. More taxpayers were made eligible to make IRA contributions, and the maximum contribution allowed was increased. The tax advantage of making a traditional IRA contribution is that the money deposited into an IRA savings account is not initially subject to federal and state income taxation. For example, if you deposit \$1,000 in an IRA account and you are in a combined federal and state marginal tax rate of 40 percent, that deposit will reduce your tax liabilities by \$400. In addition, the interest you earn on the IRA savings account grows tax deferred. You defer paying tax on that interest until you make withdrawals from the account when you retire.

The important policy question to consider is whether IRA provisions stimulate savings. Some studies have suggested that IRA provisions seem to induce new savings. However, more recent evidence suggests that IRA contributions may simply reflect the movement from existing savings into IRA accounts.

In order to determine what factors influence IRA contributions, Long (1990) examined the behavior of a large number of taxpayers, using IRS tax return data. The IRA provisions had been expanded in the prior several years and contribution limits had been raised. Long's findings are based on tax year 1983 for three types of taxpayer households: two-earner couples, one-earner couples, and single persons. The results indicate that the combined marginal tax rate (federal and state) is an important determinant of IRA contributions for all types of taxpayer households. For two-earner couples, for example, the results indicate that a 1 percent increase in the marginal tax rate has the effect of inducing an additional \$209 IRA contribution. A one-earner couple contributes less, \$119, in response to a 1 percent increase in the marginal tax rate, whereas a single person contributes an additional \$212. Long's study indicates that taxpayers are responsive to marginal tax rates. The higher the marginal tax rate, the greater the IRA contribution. This result confirms the substitution effect of economic theory. The higher the marginal tax rate, the lower the price of savings. The lower the price of savings, the more of it is demanded by the person, other things being equal.

The effect of income on IRA contributions is positive for all three types of taxpayer households. As a result, we know that IRA contributions are normal goods: as income rises people contribute more to IRA accounts, other things being equal. Long determined, however, that for two-earner couples, IRA contributions rise at an increasing rate with income, but for one-earner couples and single persons, IRA contributions rise at a decreasing rate. The effect of income is clearly nonlinear and the marginal effect of income is positive for two-earner couples, whereas it is negative for one-earner couples and single persons.

Households with more dependents, including children and others, contribute less to IRA accounts in Long's study. Apparently, the presence of additional dependents brings with it other demands on the household budget than IRA contributions. KEOGH savings (tax-advantaged savings for self-employed persons) appear to be complementary with IRA contributions. Households that make greater KEOGH contributions also make larger IRA contributions, although the statistical significance of this result is not as strong as that for the other variables in the model.

Finally, the coefficient estimate for the tax owed variable is very revealing. This variable captures the effect of a tax return having a positive liability, requiring that the taxpayer make a payment. The alternative is a negative liability in which case the taxpayer would receive a refund check. The strong positive result indicates that taxpayers who owed tax at the end of the tax year made much larger IRA contributions than those who were eligible for refunds. This result sheds some light on the policy question of whether IRA incentives induce new savings.

Think for a moment about filling out your 1040 form. As you complete the form, you see that you have a remaining tax liability of $1,200. Your withholding does not cover your liability, so you owe money. But you really do not want to pay $1,200 in tax. You know that an IRA contribution can reduce that liability. In fact, you know that a contribution to an IRA account as late as April 15, the tax filing deadline, can be applied to the previous tax year. If you have a combined 40 percent marginal tax rate, an IRA contribution of $2,000 reduces your tax liability by $500. You still owe tax to the IRS, but much less than you would owe without making an IRA contribution. All you have to do is move $2,000 out of your ordinary savings account and put it in an IRA account and your taxes are reduced by $500.

Long's evidence appears to provide some support for the suggestion that IRA contributions may, in part, reflect the movement of existing savings into IRA accounts rather than the inducement of new savings.

PROBLEMS

1. True, False, or Uncertain. Explain.
   a. Federal deductibility of home mortgage interest payments causes an income effect, but no substitution effect.
   b. An increase in the income tax rate causes a substitution effect, but no income effect.
   c. An increase in the income tax rate discourages risk taking.

2. Many states have introduced so-called 529 savings plans in recent years in order to encourage families to save money to fund their children's college education. Under these plans a family can set aside savings for higher education with a tax advantage. Interest earned on college savings in this plan is not taxed by the state. Use a graphical life cycle model to illustrate and analyze the program's efficiency effects.
   a. Demonstrate and explain how the savings plan affects a family's budget line.
   b. Demonstrate and explain how the savings plan affects a family's savings.
   c. Explain the conditions under which a family will save more for college as a result of this program.
3. President Bush's income tax cuts enacted in 2001 have come under increasing scrutiny due to the federal government's subsequent budget situation with an anticipated deficit for the next several years. Critics are suggesting that the income tax rate reductions should be repealed, at least partially. Use a labor/leisure choice model in graphical form to analyze the likely impact of raising an income tax rate on labor supply.
   a. Illustrate and explain the effect of raising the income tax rate on a worker's budget line.
   b. Illustrate and explain the effect of raising the income tax rate on a worker's labor supply.
   c. Explain the conditions under which a worker would react to the tax rate increase by working less.
4. Suppose that Hudson Meats is engaged in the business activity of supplying hamburger patties to major U.S. fast-food chains. A new business opportunity is presented to the firm. They have the opportunity to supply Burger Tsar with hamburger patties for all their franchises in Russia. The meat-processing business is inherently risky, however. Even with careful precautions, an outbreak of *E. coli* bacteria in this new venture can cause major losses to the firm by damaging its reputation. The new venture will necessitate an expenditure of $50 million. Then, the expected payoffs are as follows:

	States	
Acts	***Low Return***	***High Return***
Do not take risk	0	0
Take risk	−$50 million (probability 0.7)	+$200 million (probability 0.3)

   a. Compute the expected return to this venture.
   b. Compute the range of the outcomes as a measure of risk associated with this venture.

c. Now suppose that a tax of 35 percent is imposed (with full loss offset). Recompute the expected return to the venture and the range of outcomes. Explain what effects the tax is likely to have on Hudson Meats's decision to enter the Russian market.

5. True, False, or Uncertain. Explain.
A person who reacts to a reduction in a proportional income tax by saving more has an income effect that is larger than her substitution effect. (Graph required.)
6. True, False, or Uncertain. Explain.
A person who reacts to a reduction in a proportional income tax by working less has an income effect that is larger than his substitution effect. (Graph required.)
7. Mortgage interest paid by a homeowner is deductible but consumer credit interest paid on a car loan is not deductible under current income tax law in the United States. Draw a diagram like Figure 12.11 and explain why homeowners have an incentive to finance the purchase of a new car with a home equity loan rather than with a car loan.
8. The labor/leisure choice model discussed in this chapter presumes that there is just one source of income: labor income. Explain how the graphical model would be altered to include a second source of lump-sum income that is unrelated to hours of labor (a cash welfare transfer from the government, for example). Use the model to explain why a cash welfare transfer may cause a disincentive to work.
9. The life cycle model discussed in this chapter presumes that the income tax system taxes interest income received by savers and permits deductibility of interest paid by borrowers. Suppose that the income tax system has asymmetric treatment of interest, with interest payments by borrowers not deductible (as in the case of consumer interest). Explain how the graphical model would be altered to account for the asymmetric treatment. Explain the behavioral implications of the asymmetric treatment.

REFERENCES

Beshears, John, James J. Choi, David Laibson, and Briggite C. Madrian. "The Impact of Employer Matching on Savings Plan Participation Under Automatic Enrollment." NBER Working Paper 13352, 2007.

Bosworth, Barry, and Gary Burtless. "Effects of Tax Reform on Labor Supply, Investment, and Savings." *Journal of Economic Perspectives* 6 (1992): 3–25.

Burtless, Gary. "The Work Response to a Guaranteed Income: A Survey of Experimental Evidence." In *Lessons from the Income Maintenance Experiments*, edited by Alicia Munnell. Boston: Federal Reserve Bank of Boston, 1987.

Choi, James J., David Laibson, Brigitte C. Madrian, and Andrew Metrick. "Defined Contribution Pensions: Plan Rules, Participation Decisions, and the Path of Least Resistance." In James Poterba, editor, *Tax Policy and the Economy* 16, 2002, pp. 67–114.

Choi, James J., David Laibson, Brigitte C. Madrian, and Andrew Metrick. "For Better oir For Worse: Default Effects and 401(k) Savings Behavior." In *Perspectives in the Economics of Aging*, edited by David Wise. Chicago: University of Chicago Press, 2004, pp. 81–121.

Cowell, Frank A. *Cheating the Government.* Cambridge, MA: MIT Press, 1990.

Engin, Eric M., William G. Gale, and John Karl Scholz. "Do Saving Incentives Work?" *Brookings Papers on Economic Activity*, 1994, 85–151.

Engin, Eric M., William G. Gale, and John Karl Scholz. "The Illusory Effects of Saving Incentives on Saving." *Journal of Economic Perspectives* 10 (1996): 114–38.

Feenberg, Daniel, and Jonathan Skinner. "Sources of IRA Saving." In *Tax Policy and the Economy*, edited by Lawrence Summers. Cambridge, MA: MIT Press, 1989.

Gale, William G., and John Karl Scholz. "IRAs and Household Savings," *American Economic Review* 84 (1994): 1233–60.

Hausman, Jerry A. "Labor Supply." In *How Taxes Affect Economic Behavior*, edited by Henry J. Aaron and Joseph A. Pechman. Washington, DC: Brookings Institution, 1981.

Hausman, Jerry A. "Taxes and Labor Supply." Chapter 4 in *Handbook of Public Economics*, Vol. 1, edited by Alan J. Auerbach and Martin Feldstein. New York: North-Holland, 1985.

Keynes, John Maynard. *The General Theory of Employment, Interest, and Money*. New York: Harcourt, Brace and World, first Harbinger ed. 1964 [1935].

Kimmel, Jean, and Thomas Kniesner. "New Evidence on Labor Supply: Employment Hours Versus Hours Elasticities by Sex and Marital Status." *Journal of Monetary Economics* 42 (1998): 289–301.

Long, James E. "Marginal Tax Rates and IRA Contributions." *National Tax Journal* 43 (1990): 143–54.

Meghir, Costas, and David Phillips. "Labour Supply and Taxes." Chapter 3 in *Dimensions of Tax Policy*, edited by J. Mirrlees, S. Adam, T. Besley, R. Blundell, S. Bond, R. Chote, M. Gammie, P. Johnson., Oxford, UK: Oxford University Press, 2010.

Myles, Gareth. *Public Economics*. New York: Cambridge University Press, 1996.

Saez, Emmanuel, Joel Slemrod, and Seth H. Giertz. "The Elasticity of Taxable Income with Respect to Marginal Tax Rates: A Critical Review." Unpublished manuscript, 2009. Forthcoming in the *Journal of Economic Literature*.

Schumpeter, Joseph A. *Capitalism, Socialism, and Democracy*. New York: Harper, 1942.

Slemrod, Joel. "On the High Income Laffer Curve." Chapter 6 in *Tax Progressivity and Income Inequality*, edited by Joel Slemrod. New York: Cambridge University Press, 1996.

Triest, Robert, K. "The Efficiency Cost of Increased Progressivity." Chapter 5 in *Tax Progressivity and Income Inequality*, edited by Joel Slemrod. New York: Cambridge University Press, 1996.

Venti, Steven F., and David Wise. "Tax-Deferred Accounts, Constrained Choice, and Estimation of Individual Saving." *Review of Economic Statistics* 53 (1986): 579–601.

Venti, Steven F., and David Wise. *Have IRAs Increased U.S. Saving? Evidence from Consumer Expenditure Surveys*. Cambridge, MA: National Bureau of Economic Research (NBER) Working Paper No. 2217, 1987.

Venti, Steven F., and David Wise. "Individual Retirement Accounts and Saving." In *Taxes and Capital Formation*, edited by Martin Feldstein. Chicago, IL: University of Chicago Press, 1988.

NOTES

1. *Survey of Current Business*, January 2011, Table 1.12.
2. The formal problem is to maximize the utility function $u(y, l)$ subject to the budget constraint $y = (T - l)w$. Substituting the budget constraint into the objective function, we can solve the problem as an unconstrained problem, choosing the quantity of leisure l. The first-order condition for a maximum is obtained by taking the partial derivative with respect to l:
$$\partial u/\partial l = (\partial u/\partial y)(\partial y/\partial l) + \partial u/\partial l,$$
and setting it equal to zero. Doing so provides the optimality condition:
$$(\partial u/\partial l)(\partial u/\partial y) = w.$$
This condition specifies that at the optimal allocation of time to leisure and work the marginal rate of substitution is equal to the wage.
3. Recall the definition of a normal good. A normal good is a good that a person wants more of as the person's income rises. An increase in income shifts the demand curve for a normal good to the right. An inferior good is a good that a person wants less of as the person's income rises. An increase in income shifts the demand curve for an inferior good to the left. A classic example of an inferior good is Spam, a canned meat product that is an inferior good for most people, except in Korea where it is considered a delicacy and is a normal good.
4. If the hours of work are written as $T - l$, the elasticity of labor supply can be written as
$$[\partial(T - l)/\partial w]/[(T - l)/w].$$
5. The formal optimization problem is to maximize the utility function $u(c_0, c_1)$ subject to the budget constraint
$$c_1 = [(1 + r)y_0 + y_1] - (1 + r)c_0.$$

Substitute the constraint into the objective function, making utility a function of c_0 alone, then take the derivative of utility with respect to c_0:

$$du/dc_0 = \partial u/\partial c_0 + (\partial u/\partial c_1)/(\partial c_1/\partial c_0).$$

Setting this derivative equal to zero results in the first-order necessary condition that the marginal rate of substitution must equal the slope of the budget line (in absolute value):

$$(\partial u/\partial c_0)/(\partial u/\partial c_1) = 1 + r.$$

6. If interest paid on loans were not deductible, the budget line would have a kink at the income endowment point. We would follow the new flatter budget line left of the income endowment point, but then follow the original steeper budget line to the right of the income endowment point. The slope of the budget to the left of the income endowment point would be -1 plus the after-tax rate of interest, $-[1 + r(1 - t)]$, whereas the slope to the right of that point would be -1 plus the before-tax rate of interest, $-[1 + r]$. Recall that it is often the case that people cluster at kink points. That could occur in the saving/borrowing context as well. Because people's indifference curves are downward sloping, there will be a wide range of slopes for those indifference curves that will be consistent with the optimal choice of the income endowment point, with no saving or borrowing. In other words, many people with differing preferences over present and future consumption will all find that their best plan is to neither save nor borrow but simply live from paycheck to paycheck, spending all the income earned in each period.
7. If we use the standard deviation as a measure of the risk, denoting it by the Greek symbol σ that is typically used, we find that in the absence of the tax the standard deviation is $\sigma = 196$, but with the tax system in place, affording full loss offset, the standard deviation is $\sigma = 147$. Thus the standard deviation measure of risk also indicates that the tax system reduces risk. Notice that σ is reduced by the factor $(1 - 0.25)$, as indicated in the text.
8. Myles (1996) demonstrates that the share of wealth allocated to the risky asset rises with the tax rate. That is, the partial derivative of the amount of risky asset held with respect to the tax rate is $\partial a/\partial t = a/(1 - t)$, which is strictly positive.
9. This model is adapted from Cowell (1990).
10. This can be verified by noting that the expected after-tax income is $E[c] = (1 - p)c' + pc''$. Solving for c'' yields the slope of $-(1 - p)/p$, which represents the odds of not being detected.
11. Technically, the required condition is that of decreasing absolute risk aversion. See Cowell (1990, 59).

Radius Images/Getty Images

CHAPTER 13

Equity Aspects of Taxes and Expenditures

LEARNING OBJECTIVES

1. Discuss the incidence of taxation—who bears the ultimate economic burden of a tax?
2. Analyze the incidence of taxes.
3. Discuss the concepts of fairness or equity in taxation.
4. Analyze the aspects of equity in a tax system.

When the new property tax assessments are mailed out by the County Assessor, we often hear the response of an irate homeowner: "This just isn't fair!" With this cry, with perhaps a few expletives deleted, we are hearing an expression of distress over a tax situation that the homeowner thinks violates a fundamental sense of what is fair and equitable. The United States was founded, in part, on the basis of tax protest in the face of unfair treatment by the British government. The most famous tax protest in the history of our country was the Boston Tea Party where the cry was "No taxation without representation." In that case, citizens thought it unfair to be required to pay taxes to King George when they had no political representation. Indeed, they thought the situation so unfair that they were willing to take up arms and fight for their convictions. History is replete with examples of tax-induced rebellions because people have an innate sense of fairness, which when violated, evokes strong responses.

In the world of taxation and expenditure policymaking, we also care about what is fair and equitable. Not only do we want a tax system that is efficient, but we also want a tax system that is rooted in our sense of fairness as well. If my neighbor's house is assessed at $120,000 while my identical house is assessed at $135,000, something is wrong with the property tax assessment system in my community. Our government expenditure programs should similarly be fair in their implementation. Nothing undermines the credibility of government faster than expenditure programs that appear to be unfairly available to some while unavailable to others or to provide benefits in a capricious manner. Tax reform efforts in the former Soviet republics illustrate this reality in vivid fashion. It is proving to be very difficult to build a climate of compliance with the tax laws instituted because independence in many of those republics is due to the long legacy of distrust that remains from the Soviet era.

In this chapter we consider equity or fairness issues in both expenditure programs and tax systems. Although it is difficult to define the concept of fairness with precision, there are nonetheless several ways to specify standards of equity that can help guide our assessment of expenditure and tax systems.

Keep in mind that the two benchmarks by which we judge the quality and appropriateness of any government tax or expenditure program are the standards of efficiency and equity. Equity is just as important as efficiency. Balancing both objectives in such a way as to please voters is, however, difficult if not impossible. Perhaps Edmund Burke was right when he penned the line, "To tax and to please, no more than to love and to be wise, is not given to men."

THE INCIDENCE OF TAXES

The concept of **tax incidence** has to do with who bears the burden of a tax. We are concerned about the burden of the tax and on whom that burden falls. Things are not always as they appear in the world of tax policy, so we are concerned with who *really* bears the burden of a tax. We should not be fooled by appearances. The law may require a firm to pay a tax, for example, but the firm may pass the tax along to its customers in the form of higher prices or to its employees in the form of lower wages or to its shareholders through lower dividends. Those really bearing the burden of the tax may not be the ones the law specifies must pay the tax. Hence, there is a distinction between statutory incidence and economic incidence of a tax.

Economic versus Statutory Incidence

When we consider the burden of a tax, we must distinguish between the burden as it is specified in the tax law and the true economic burden. **Statutory incidence** refers to tax incidence required by legal statutes. Of course, it is not possible to specify true economic incidence in law, but that does not stop lawmakers from trying. Consider a simple example. The U.S. Social Security payroll tax requires that employers and employees split the tax, each paying one-half of the total. Hence, the statutory incidence of the tax is that half the tax falls on the employer and half falls on the employee. The current 12.4 percent tax for social security in the United States is split in half, with the employer and employee each legally obligated to pay 6.2 percent of the payroll. But, the true economic incidence of the payroll tax is quite different. The employer has some ability to adjust the employee's wage and pass the employer's half of the tax on to the employee. In fact, the employee may bear the entire tax. Of course, the extent to which the employer can pass the tax on to the employee depends on the labor supply elasticity of the employee; that is, the willingness of the employee to accept a lower wage and supply the same, or nearly the same, quantity of labor. Recent evidence in Gruber (1997), based on the Chilean payroll tax, for example, suggests that workers bear most of the burden of any increase in the tax rate.

Statutory incidence is not always aimed at making tax burdens equal. In some cases, legal statutes specify who should pay the tax with an eye toward making the tax collection process less costly for government agencies. For example, most state sales tax statutes require the seller of the product to pay the state sales tax rather than the buyer. Although you might think that you pay the state sales tax on your purchase at Wal-Mart, that is not so. Wal-Mart is simply collecting an amount from each purchaser so that the company can then pay its state sales tax liability. Wal-Mart is required by law to make the state sales tax payment. That makes tax collection much simpler because Wal-Mart can write one check to the state revenue department, rather than the law requiring thousands of Wal-Mart customers to individually make small sales tax payments to the state revenue department. This procedure also makes tax enforcement much easier as the state revenue department has just one company to audit for tax compliance, rather than thousands of individual customers. If state law makes the retailer legally liable to pay the sales tax on goods sold, it would appear that the incidence of the tax is on the retailer. Indeed, the statutory incidence of the sales tax is on the retailer. But, as Wal-Mart customers, you and I both know that the retailer asks us to pay some part of that sales tax. It appears as though the retailer requires us to pay the whole sales tax, simply adding the tax to our bill, but the reality is that the retailer may still bear a part of the tax burden implicitly through a lower price received on the product than would be charged in the absence of the sales tax. After all, you and I are not completely price insensitive. We shop at Wal-Mart because we like low prices, right? (It is not for the yellow smiley face sticker handed to us at the door by a friendly senior citizen!) The true economic incidence of the tax is likely to be shared between the retailer and the customer. This is the incidence about which we care.

Economic incidence is concerned with how the burden of the tax is distributed among economic agents (producers, consumers, employees, and shareholders) *as determined by market forces, not by the law*. It is one thing to specify in law that the sales tax be collected and paid by Wal-Mart, for example, but it is quite another matter to determine how Wal-Mart then passes some portion of the tax burden along to its customers, workers, and owner-shareholders, depending on the economic forces at work in each of these market contexts. Economic incidence is the pattern of tax burden as it is distributed by supply and demand forces in each of these markets. The production and sale of a taxed commodity involve both inputs and outputs, so we will have to consider the economic effects of the tax in both input (factor) markets and product markets.

Tax Incidence in a Single Market

When we examine the economic incidence of a tax, we start with the analysis of a single market in which the tax is directly imposed. If the tax is applied to a product, for example, we begin the analysis by considering the effects of that product tax on the equilibrium price and quantity of the good. By comparing the before-tax situation to the after-tax situation in the market, we

FIGURE 13.1 Effect of a Unit Tax on Demand

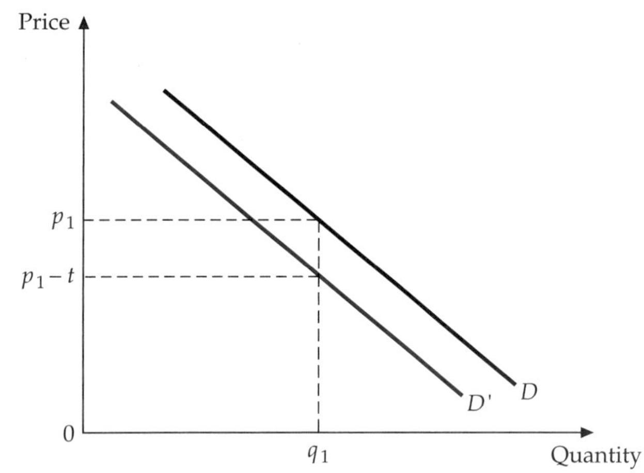

obtain a comparative static view of the effect of the tax and can judge the incidence of the tax. This analysis involves just a single market, so we call this type of analysis **partial equilibrium analysis.** With partial equilibrium analysis we are only looking at part of the picture. We only examine the market in which the tax is directly applied. Implications in other markets are ignored. If we widen our view to consider how a tax applied in one market has economic effects in other markets for both related products (substitutes and complements) and factors of production, we use **general equilibrium analysis.** With general equilibrium analysis of tax incidence, we consider the effects of a tax generally—in all markets simultaneously.

First, let us consider the partial equilibrium economic incidence of a unit tax collected from consumers. Figure 13.1 illustrates the market demand curve for a good, where quantity q_1 is demanded by all consumers at the price p_1 prior to the imposition of the tax. The tax is applied to consumers, so we model the impact of the tax on the market demand curve. From the point of view of consumers, p_1 is the maximum price they will pay for quantity q_1 of the good. If the good is subject to a unit tax of t, they are still willing to pay just p_1 for the q_1 units of the good, so they are now willing to pay $p_1 - t$ for the good plus the tax t for a total of p_1. The modified demand curve D' illustrates the consumers' demand in the presence of a tax. Notice that the unit tax has the effect of shifting the demand curve downward in a parallel fashion by the amount of the unit tax.

Now, in order to examine the economic incidence of a unit tax, that is, who actually pays the unit tax—consumers or producers—we must include the supply curve and see what happens in the market when the tax is applied and shifts the demand curve downward. Figure 13.2 illustrates this example. The new equilibrium price and quantity in the market are p_2 and q_2. The tax clearly reduces the quantity of the good produced and sold in the market.

FIGURE 13.2 Incidence of a Unit Tax Applied to Consumers

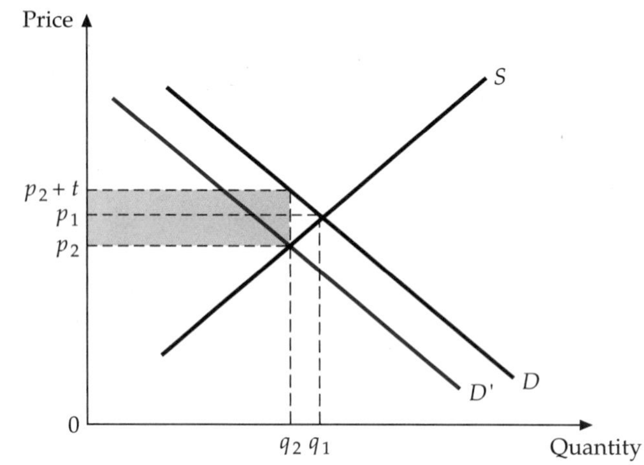

As for tax incidence, consider that the consumers paid the price p_1 prior to the tax and now pay the higher price $p_2 + t$; thus the consumers bear some of the tax burden. But notice that the increase in price paid by consumers, $(p_2 + t) - p_1$, is less than the tax t. The vertical distance between the demand curves D' and D is the tax, but the price paid by consumers has gone up by less than the amount of the tax. Although consumers bear a part of the tax burden, the tax burden also falls partially on the producer of the product. To see why, consider that the producer received the price p_1 prior to the imposition of the tax. After the tax is imposed on the consumers, the producer receives the price p_2, which is less than p_1. The shaded area in Figure 13.2 is the amount of tax collected. That area is made up of the amount actually borne by consumers—the upper part of the shaded area—and the amount borne by producers—the lower part of the shaded area. Although the tax law requires that consumers pay the tax, a portion of the tax burden is actually borne by producers. Consumers bear a burden that is less than the total amount of the tax and force producers to bear some of the tax burden. This is the essence of how the economic incidence of the tax differs from the statutory incidence of the tax.

Table 13.1 summarizes the partial equilibrium economic effects of the unit tax applied to consumers. The first column describes the situation before the tax is applied, whereas the second column describes the situation after the tax is applied and the final column on the right shows the difference between the before-tax situation and the after-tax situation.

Next, consider a unit tax collected from the producers of the good, rather than from the consumers. Figure 13.3 illustrates the impact of a unit tax applied to the producers of the product. In the absence of the tax, producers are willing to supply quantity q_1 at price p_1. If they are then asked to pay a tax of t on each unit produced, they will only be willing to provide quantity

TABLE 13.1 Effects of a Unit Tax Applied to Consumers

	Before the Tax	After the Tax	Difference
Producers	Price p_1	Price p_2	Price $p_1 - p_2$
	Quantity q_1	Quantity q_2	Quantity $q_1 - q_2$
	Revenue p_1q_1	Revenue p_2q_2	Revenue $p_1q_1 - p_2q_2$
Consumers	Price p_1	Price $p_2 + t$	Price $(p_2 + t) - p_1$
	Quantity q_1	Quantity q_2	Quantity $q_1 - q_2$
	Expenditure p_1q_1	Expenditure $(p_2 + t)q_2$	Expenditure $p_1q_1 - (p_2 + t)q_2$
		Tax paid tq_2	

q_1 at the price $p_1 + t$. This is true for any quantity we may consider. Hence, the supply curve is shifted upward in parallel fashion from S to S' as a result of the unit tax. The producers of the product are willing to supply the same quantities at the old price plus the amount of the tax. They would like to shift the entire burden of the tax to the consumers. But, to determine the economic incidence of the tax and the extent to which producers may be able to shift some part of the tax burden to consumers, we must also have the demand curve in the analysis.

Including the demand curve, as illustrated in Figure 13.4, permits us to examine the economic incidence of the unit tax applied to producers of the product. The tax causes the equilibrium quantity in the market to fall from q_1 to q_2 and the equilibrium price to rise from p_1 to p_2. The new equilibrium price p_2 is the price paid by consumers and received by producers.

FIGURE 13.3 Effect of a Unit Tax on Supply

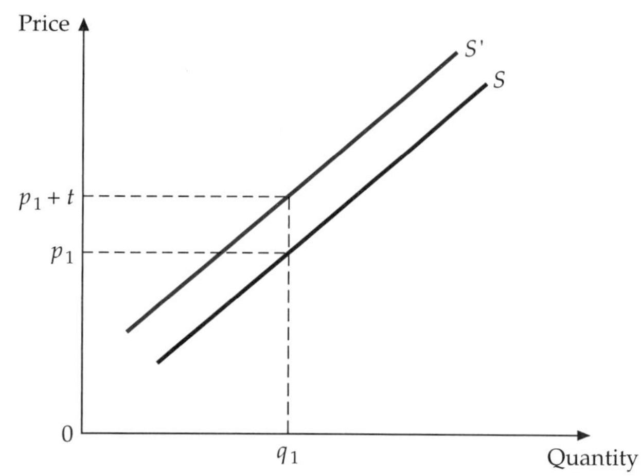

Richard Levine/Alamy

Who really bears the burden of a tax on consumer goods?

FIGURE 13.4 Incidence of a Unit Tax Applied to Producers

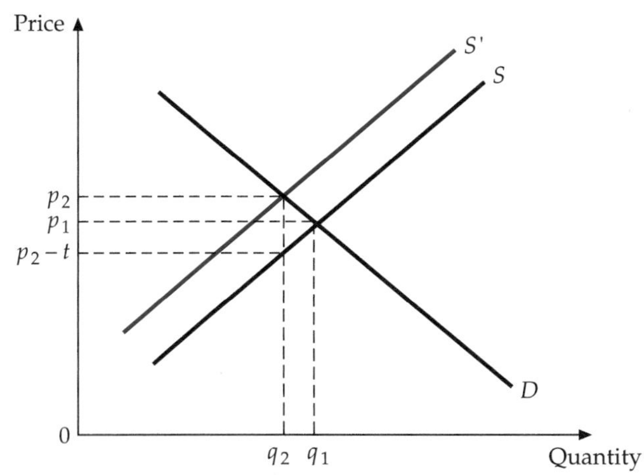

The producers must then send the tax payment to the government. The producers are required to pay the tax of t per unit of the good that they sell; this leaves them with the after-tax price $p_2 - t$. Producers are able to raise the price but by less than the full amount of the tax. In doing so, they are able to shift some of the tax burden onto the consumers, but they still bear a portion of the tax burden themselves. The total tax that producers pay to the government is the amount tq_2, shown as the shaded area in Figure 13.4. The burden of that tax falls partly on consumers and partly on producers. For the producers of the product, the price they receive net of the tax is reduced from p_1 to $p_2 - t$; hence they bear a tax burden of $[p_1 - (p_2 - t)]q_2$. The producers' tax burden is the lower part of the shaded area in Figure 13.4. Consumers bear the remainder of the tax burden, $(p_2 - p_1)q_2$, illustrated as the upper part of the tax burden in Figure 13.4. The reader may check to see that these two quantities add up to the total tax. Table 13.2 provides a summary of the effects of a unit tax applied to producers. The tax burden borne by consumers plus that borne by producers is given by the sum $[p_1 - (p_2 - t)]q_2 + (p_2 - p_1)q_2$, which is equal to tq_2, the total amount of the tax. In other words, the sum of both of the shaded areas in Figure 13.4 is the total amount of the tax collected. Here again, although the statutory incidence of the tax is placed on the producers, because the law requires them to pay the tax, the economic incidence is quite different. Despite the fact that the law says the tax must be collected from producers, the true economic incidence of the tax is shared partly by producers and partly by consumers.

The reality is that you cannot legislate the economic incidence of a tax. Market forces determine economic incidence, despite what the law says. In fact, if you compare Figures 13.2 and 13.4, it appears that the economic incidence of a tax is the same, regardless of whether the law requires the consumer or producer to pay the tax. That is true, in general. Economic incidence is determined by market forces independently of the law. For this reason, good tax policymaking requires both the expertise of the tax lawyer who can write the law properly and the insight of the tax policy economist who can provide insight on the economic incidence of the tax.

TABLE 13.2 Effects of a Unit Tax Applied to Producers

	Before the Tax	After the Tax	Difference
Producers	Price p_1	Price $p_2 - t$	Price $p_1 - (p_2 - t)$
	Quantity q_1	Quantity q_2	Quantity $q_1 - q_2$
	Revenue p_1q_1	Revenue $(p_2 - t)q_2$	Revenue $p_1q_1 - (p_2 - t)q_2$
		Tax paid tq_2	
Consumers	Price p_1	Price p_2	Price $p_2 - p_1$
	Quantity q_1	Quantity q_2	Quantity $q_1 - q_2$
	Expenditure p_1q_1	Expenditure p_2q_2	Expenditure $p_1q_1 - p_2q_2$

Incidence of an Ad Valorem *Tax*

An *ad valorem* tax is a tax applied to the value of the commodity, usually expressed as a percentage of the value. As a result, the *ad valorem* tax is a small tax when the price of the good is low, but a large tax when the price of the good is high. Figure 13.5 illustrates the effect of an *ad valorem* tax applied on the supply side (on producers of the product). At the low price p_1, the tax applied at rate t raises the price to $p_1(1 + t)$, where the tax required of the producer is p_1t. At the high price p_2, the same tax rate t is applied, making the price rise to $p_2(1 + t)$. The tax rate is expressed as a constant percentage of the price of the commodity, but the tax required of the producer at the higher price is much larger: p_2t. Hence, the effect of the *ad valorem* tax is to shift the supply curve upward in a nonparallel fashion. The supply curve shifts up by a small distance at low prices but by a large distance at high prices.

The analysis of tax incidence for an *ad valorem* tax proceeds in the same manner as that for a unit tax. Figure 13.6 illustrates the incidence of an *ad valorem* tax applied on the supply side. The incidence of the tax falls partly on the consumer and partly on the producer. The consumer bears a burden of $(p_2 - p_1)q_2$, which is represented by the upper part of the tax revenue rectangle, whereas the producer bears a burden of $[p_1 - p_2(1 - t)]q_2$, which is represented by the lower part of the tax revenue rectangle. The sum of those burdens is $(p_2 - p_1)q_2 + [p_1 - p_2(1 - t)]q_2$, which is equal to $p_2q_2 - p_1q_2 + p_1q_2 - p_2q_2 + p_2q_2t$, or simply p_2q_2t, the amount of the tax revenue collected.

What Determines the Producers' and Consumers' Incidence?

As illustrated in Figures 13.2, 13.4, and 13.6, the economic incidence of a tax appears to be shared equally by consumers and producers. In each figure the

FIGURE 13.5 Effect of an *Ad Valorem* Tax on Supply

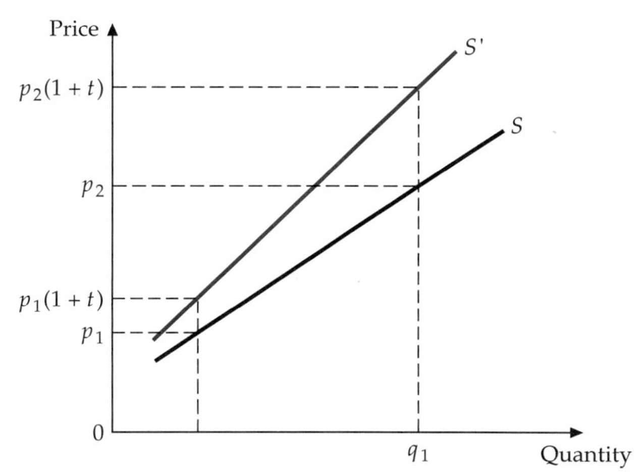

FIGURE 13.6 Incidence of an *Ad Valorem* Tax Applied to Producers

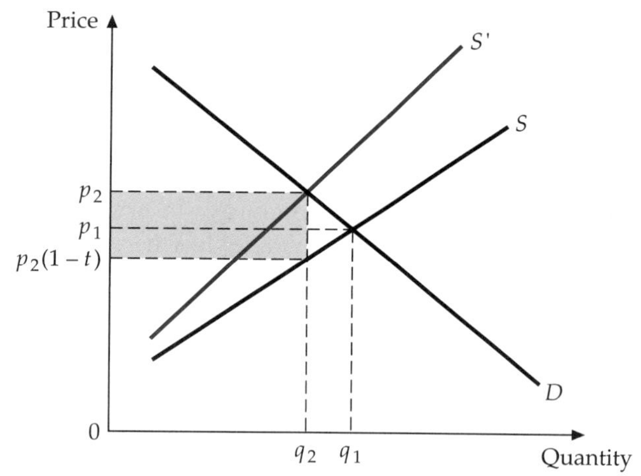

upper part of the shaded area representing the consumer portion of the burden appears to be half of the total area, as does the lower part of the shaded area representing the producer share. Consumers pay half of the tax and producers pay the other half. But is that always the case? If not, what economic forces determine the actual shares of tax burden borne by consumers and producers?

Let's examine conditions under which the consumers or producers may bear a disproportionate share of tax burden. Figure 13.7 illustrates the effects of a unit tax applied on the supply side, under two different demand

FIGURE 13.7 The Incidence of a Unit Tax Depends on the Elasticity of Demand

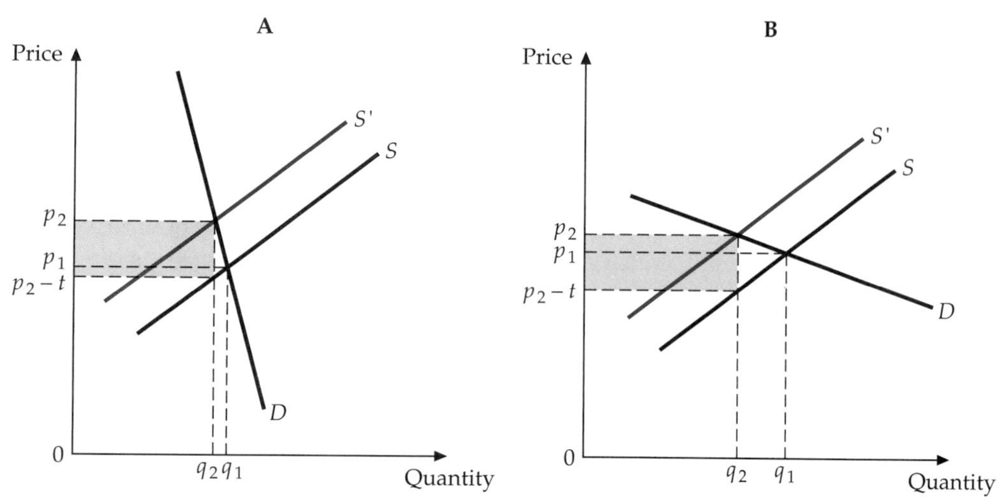

conditions. Panel A of the figure illustrates application of the tax when consumers are relatively unresponsive to changes in price, whereas the right-hand panel illustrates the case where consumers are very responsive to price changes. Notice that in panel A where consumers are relatively unresponsive to price, the share of the tax borne by consumers is large, illustrated by the upper portion of the shaded area demonstrating the tax burden. Of the total tax revenue tq_2, consumers bear most of the burden, $(p_2 - p_1)q_2$, whereas producers bear a small share of the burden, $[p_1 - (p_2 - t)]q_2$. Because they are relatively unresponsive to price, the consumers are forced to bear most of the tax burden. In panel B, where consumers are more responsive to price, the consumers bear a small share of the tax burden and producers bear most of the burden. Again, the upper part of the shaded area representing the total tax burden is the share borne by consumers and the lower part is borne by producers. In this case, it is clear that the responsiveness of consumers causes producers to bear more of the tax burden.

As a general rule, the unresponsive economic agent bears most of the tax burden. The notion of responsiveness to price is quantified by economists in the concept of price elasticity, of course. The less price elastic the demand for the commodity, the more of the tax burden is borne by consumers. The more price elastic the demand for the commodity, the less of the tax burden is borne by consumers.[1] Consider the case of the excise tax on gasoline, for example. Since consumer demand for gasoline is quite inelastic in the short run, with a price elasticity in the range of 0.15, consumers bear most of the tax burden. Conversely, consider the case of the special excise tax on imported Japanese television sets. The demand for television sets is quite price elastic, with a price elasticity in the range of 1.5 as is typical of consumer durables in general, so the producer bears most of the burden of the tax.

It is also important to consider the effect of the elasticity of supply on tax incidence. Figure 13.8 illustrates two cases. Panel A illustrates the case where supply is relatively steep so that the elasticity of supply is relatively small in comparison with the elasticity of demand. In this case, the incidence of a tax falls primarily on the producer. Panel B illustrates the opposite case where supply is relatively elastic in comparison to demand. In that case the consumer bears most of the burden of the tax. Once again, the general rule is that the economic agent with the relatively inelastic response ends up bearing most of the burden of the tax.

It is also important to consider the tax effects on quantity. Figures 13.7 and 13.8 illustrate that a tax reduces the equilibrium quantity cleared in the market. But notice that the quantity reduction is not the same in each case. In Figure 13.7, where we applied a unit tax on the supply side, the quantity reduction is small in the left-hand panel of the figure where demand is relatively inelastic. In the right-hand panel where demand is relatively elastic, the quantity reduction is larger. In general, we can expect that a tax will reduce output in a market to a greater extent the more elastic is demand and will reduce output to a lesser extent the less elastic is demand. For this reason, we would expect that the excise tax on gasoline (where market demand is

FIGURE 13.8 The Incidence of a Unit Tax Depends on the Elasticity of Supply

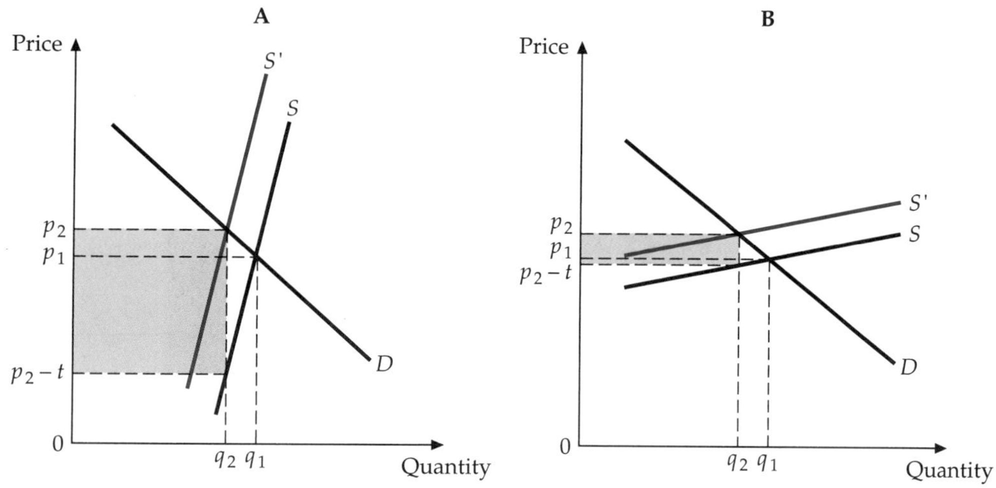

relatively inelastic) would not reduce the amount of gasoline cleared in the market by very much, but the special tax on Japanese television sets (where market demand is relatively elastic) would reduce the equilibrium quantity a relatively large amount.

This difference has important policy implications. Consider a public policy debate in which our objective is to reduce the production and consumption of a good, as in the case of cigarettes, for example, as a matter of public health policy. Will a tax on cigarettes be effective in reducing the production and consumption of the good? Well, a tax will be quite effective in the case of a good with relatively elastic demand and quite ineffective in the case of a good with relatively inelastic demand. In the case of cigarettes, we know that the demand for the product is quite price inelastic, as illustrated in panel A of Figure 13.7. Thus, we would expect that a tax on cigarettes would not be very effective in reducing the production and consumption of cigarettes. A tax may be quite effective in raising revenue, but the relatively inelastic demand for the product will inhibit the effectiveness of the tax in reducing the equilibrium quantity.

Similarly, the price elasticity of supply has an effect on the quantity reduction caused by a tax. The market equilibrium quantity reduction due to a tax will be greater when the price elasticity of supply is greater, as in panel B of Figure 13.8. Now consider the effects of a labor income tax. Think about the incidence effects of the tax and the impact on the quantity of labor supplied in the market. If the labor supply of men is relatively inelastic, as illustrated in panel A of Figure 13.8, we would expect the tax incidence to fall primarily on the supplier of labor, that is, the worker, and the impact of the tax on the equilibrium quantity of labor in the market to be minimal. Recall that in this case the labor services supplier is the worker and the labor

TABLE 13.3 Summary of Elasticity Effects on the Incidence of a Tax

	Demand Relatively Inelastic (e.g., Cigarettes)	Demand Relatively Elastic (e.g., Televisions)	Supply Relatively Inelastic (e.g., Land)	Supply Relatively Elastic (e.g., Personal Computers)
	Consumers-Demanders			
Incidence: share of tax burden borne	Large share	Small share	Small share	Large share
Price effect: relative effect on price paid by consumer	Large price increase	Small price increase	Small price increase	Large price increase
Quantity effect: relative effect on quantity demanded by consumer	Small quantity reduction	Large quantity reduction	Small quantity reduction	Large quantity reduction
	Producers-Suppliers			
Incidence: share of tax burden borne	Small share	Large share	Large share	Small share
Price effect: relative effect on price received by producer	Small price reduction	Large price reduction	Large price reduction	Small price reduction
Quantity effect: relative effect on quantity supplied by producer	Small quantity reduction	Large quantity reduction	Small quantity reduction	Large quantity reduction

services demander is the firm hiring workers. The men keep working for the most part. On the other hand, if the women's labor supply is more elastic, as in panel B of Figure 13.8, the incidence of a tax falls more heavily on labor services demanders—firms hiring workers—and the effect of the tax on the equilibrium quantity of labor is much larger. Hence, a public policy whose objective is to reduce production and consumption of a good will be more effective when the price elasticity of supply of the good is greater. In this case, the tax causes more women to withdraw their services from the market. Here again, the general rule is that the tax incidence tends to stick with the supplier who has a more inelastic supply.

Tax Incidence Effects in Multiple Markets

So far, we have only considered the effects of a tax in a single market, or partial equilibrium analysis. But, a tax applied to a good in one market may have effects on goods in other markets as well. We need to consider the general equilibrium effects of a tax in order to get the full picture. Consider the example of a unit tax applied to cigarettes and the corresponding impacts

FIGURE 13.9 Tax Effects on Related Goods

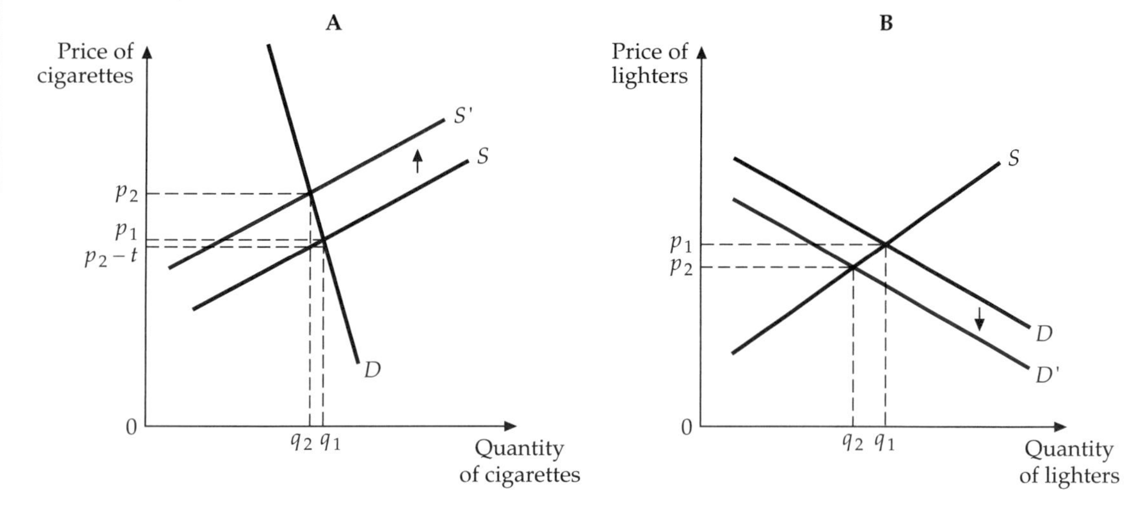

on the market for lighters. A unit tax applied to cigarettes has the effect of reducing the quantity of cigarettes cleared in the market and raising the price of cigarettes, as illustrated in panel A of Figure 13.9. The cigarette tax also has an impact on the market for cigarette lighters, however, as illustrated in panel B of the figure. Cigarettes and lighters are complements, so the cigarette tax has the effect of shifting the demand for lighters downward, causing their price to fall and the quantity cleared in the market to reduce. Hence, the cigarette tax has impacts in both markets. A general equilibrium view of the impacts of the tax takes into account the effects in all the markets for related goods, which includes all markets for substitutes or complements. In the case of a substitute good, such as chewing tobacco, a cigarette tax will shift the demand curve for chewing tobacco upward, causing price and quantity to rise.

Another aspect of the general equilibrium arises when we tax a good in one sector of the economy but do not tax the same good in other sectors. Consider the case of capital—machinery and equipment. The corporate income tax is really a tax on capital applied in the corporate sector of the economy. In the United States, capital in the form of buildings, factories, machinery, and equipment used by businesses with the legal status of proprietors or partnerships is not subject to the corporate income tax. Only firms that are incorporated are liable to pay the corporate income tax. Figure 13.10 illustrates the impact of taxing capital in the corporate sector of the economy while not taxing capital in the noncorporate sector of the economy.

Consider the case of mobile capital in the form of machinery and equipment. Personal computers used in a business, for example, are mobile in the

FIGURE 13.10 General Equilibrium Effects of Taxation of Capital in the Corporate Sector

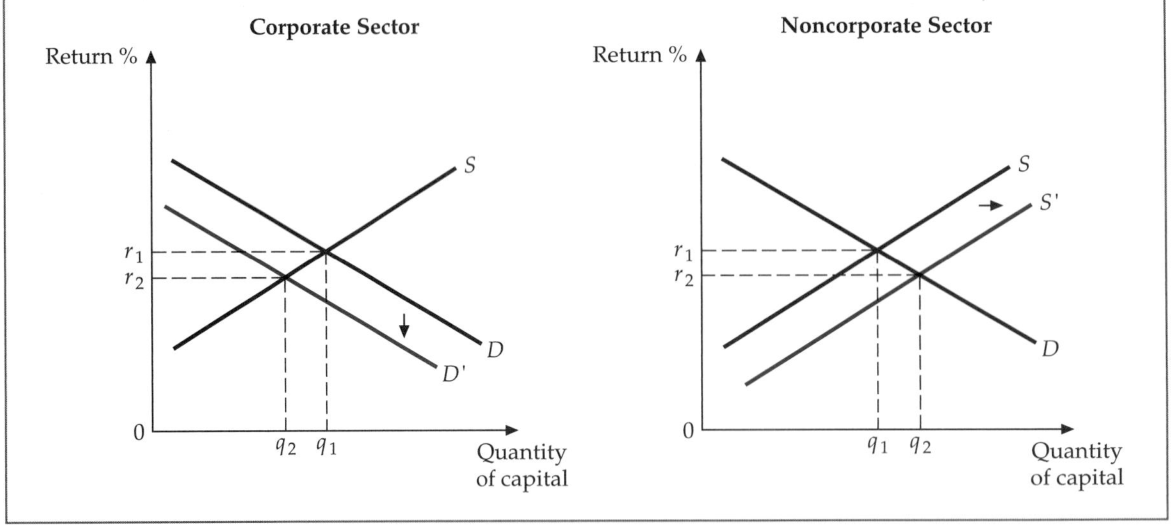

sense that the company can easily put them in a truck and move them to another location. Assuming that capital is mobile, a competitive equilibrium requires that the rate of return earned by capital be the same in the two sectors. After all, if it were possible to earn a higher rate of return in the other sector, mobility assures that capital will move out of the sector with a low rate of return and into the sector with a high rate of return until the rates of return are equalized in the two sectors. Begin with initial equilibrium where the rate of return is r_1 in both the corporate and noncorporate sectors of the economy. When a tax is applied in the corporate sector, the demand curve shifts downward from D to D' in the left panel of Figure 13.10, reducing the rate of return to r_2 and causing $q_1 - q_2$ units of capital to flee from the corporate sector. That capital migrates over to the noncorporate sector of the economy, causing the supply curve to shift outward from S to S', as illustrated in the right panel of Figure 13.10.[2] How is this accomplished in a practical sense? The corporation, realizing that it is paying a tax on every personal computer in its offices, decides that it can easily move those computers and the work done on them into a separate business that is legally organized as a partnership. The corporation forms a new business and buys the information processing services provided by the new business entity. The new business is formed as a partnership, so it does not pay the corporate income tax. Thus, the corporation can ultimately avoid the corporate income tax on that portion of its business and do so legally. As a result of the capital migration out of the corporate sector into the noncorporate sector, the rate of return to capital in the noncorporate sector falls to r_2. The full effect of the capital tax in the corporate sector is not only to cause the return to capital to fall in that sector but also to cause the rate of return to capital to fall in the noncorporate sector. As a result, capital owners in both sectors bear the burden of the tax, even though the tax is only applied in the corporate sector. The general equilibrium effect of the capital tax in the corporate sector has effects that are quite different from what we would have believed looking only at the partial equilibrium effects. The partial equilibrium analysis indicates that the tax is borne by users of capital in the corporate sector. The general equilibrium analysis indicates, however, that capital users everywhere, not just in the corporate sector, bear the burden of the tax in the corporate sector. With this realization our view of the effects of a capital tax is very different.

EQUITY CONCEPTS

Equity in taxation and government expenditure programs has two distinct aspects. First, we care about equal treatment of equals, or so-called **horizontal equity**. Comparing two taxpayers of equal position, we expect that they should pay equal taxes. Recall the example where my house is assessed at \$135,000 for property tax purposes, whereas my neighbor's *identical* house is assessed at \$120,000. The property tax due is the assessed value multiplied by the tax rate; the higher the assessment, the higher the effective rate of taxation. That situation seems fundamentally wrong because the houses are identical and we would expect each to have the same assessed value, and therefore the same tax. Similar homes should have similar assessments, right? That would seem to be a self-evident rule that any tax assessor should follow. Well, that standard of fairness is called horizontal equity. Second, we care about unequal treatment of unequals, or so-called **vertical equity**. Consider the property tax example again, but this time think of the assessed value of the mansion at the end of the block owned by the wealthiest business mogul in town. What if you were to find out that his mansion has the same assessed value for property tax purposes as your humble abode? That situation violates our sense of what is right, as we would expect the mansion to be valued higher than a modest home. In this case, we are expecting that unequal homeowners should be treated unequally. We expect that low-income families with modest homes should pay low property taxes, whereas wealthy families with ostentatious mansions should pay higher property taxes. This concept of fairness is known as *vertical equity*, because we are comparing taxpayers in two very different positions with respect to the tax base and fully expect that the higher a taxpayer's position, the higher should be his tax.

Horizontal Equity

The concept of horizontal equity is applied within the context of a tax system based on ability to pay. A tax is horizontally equitable if it requires the same tax of individuals with the same income. The adjective *horizontal* refers to the positions of the taxpayers on the income ladder. If two people are at the same level of income, they should pay the same tax. Consider the following thought experiment. Tim and Tom are twins, both of whom attend California

Polytechnical University, majoring in mechanical engineering. Both of the twins have annual incomes of $6,000 earned at their part-time jobs working for Gemini Carpet Cleaners. If we tax on the basis of their ability to pay, and both have equal incomes, we would conclude that the tax system should require the same tax payment for the two students. In legal terms, similarly situated persons should be treated similarly. This is the concept of horizontal equity. Although no one will argue with the concept of horizontal equity at this level of generality, when we become more specific about the definition of equals we run into difficulty. We will see that it is by no means obvious how to define equals.

Defining Equals: Income, Wealth, or Consumption?

Notice that the discussion so far assumes that the tax is applied to income, but there are other ways to measure taxpayers' ability to pay, of course. For example, you and your grandmother may both have incomes of $6,000. Your income is derived from a part-time job at In-and-Out Burgers, whereas your grandmother's income is derived from interest earned on bonds she inherited. That is, grandma has a great deal of wealth that generates a modest income, whereas you have no wealth and the same modest income. Which person has the greater ability to pay? Clearly, grandma does. But that conclusion is motivated by a consideration of wealth, not income. Our sense of how to define *equals* may require us to consider broader measures of ability to pay than simple income measures. It may make a difference in our thinking about a tax equity, depending on whether the basis for comparison is income or wealth. Furthermore, it may make a difference in our thinking, even if we confine our thinking to income taxes, whether the income taxed is derived actively from labor market activity or passively from capital income in the form of interest and dividends. Another case where the income-wealth distinction crops up is in farming. Farmers typically have a great deal of wealth tied up in their land but may generate a low income per acre due to low commodity prices. On the basis of their income they appear to be poor, but they are really very wealthy. On what basis should farmers be taxed: income or wealth? Your sense of whether a property tax system, for example, is fair and equitable will depend on whether you consider wealth as the more accurate indicator of ability to pay than this year's income.[3]

You can measure equals in other ways, however. Consider the case of the sales tax, which taxes people on the basis of their consumption of goods subject to the sales tax. Even if the definition of *taxable goods* is broad, covering all goods imaginable, the sales tax only assures that people with equal consumption are taxed equally. We could have a situation where frugal Frederick spends a small portion of his income and spendthrift Samuel spends every last dime of his income. Assume both fellows have the same income. On the basis of their incomes, they have equal ability to pay. But, on the basis of their consumption, they are very different. Which is the better measure of ability to pay? Income is the broader measure, so we should conclude that it is the better ultimate measure of ability to pay. Yet, for purposes of evaluating the horizontal equity of the sales tax, we will be content to check whether people with equal consumption pay equal taxes. Ultimately, however, our sense of whether a system of taxation is fair is probably tied to a broad measure of ability such as income or wealth.

Vertical Equity

The concept of vertical equity, in the specific context of an ability-to-pay tax, involves considering two taxpayers on different rungs of the income ladder. If Bill Gates is above Warren Buffet on the income ladder, we would expect Bill to pay a larger tax than Warren. We would expect both of them to pay more than you or me. The essence of vertical equity in taxation is that unequals are treated unequally. The greater a person's ability to pay, the more we expect him to pay. Vertical equity does not require a graduated tax rate structure, however. A proportional tax is sufficient to assure that as income rises, the tax rises and vertical equity results. For example, a flat-rate income tax of 20 percent would satisfy the requirement of vertical equity because it requires a larger tax of the person with a higher income. Yet, our sense of vertical equity may be stronger than that, requiring a progressive rate structure. The degree of vertical equity in a tax system can be a contentious issue. People differ in their opinions over the extent to which unequals should be taxed unequally.

Conflicts Between Horizontal and Vertical Equity

A conflict often arises as we attempt to design programs that meet both standards of equity, however. Consider a simple example. The U.S. income tax provides a personal exemption to each person. The personal exemption was $3,650 in the year 2010, for example. Thus, each qualifying taxpayer's first $3,650 of income was exempt from income taxation. However, for several years prior to 2010 the personal exemption was subject to a high-income phaseout for taxpayers with very high incomes in order to make the income tax system more progressive. A personal exemption for each person meets the standard of horizontal equity. Each taxpayer is treated equally, with everyone's first $3,650 of income being exempt. A high-income phaseout meets the standard of vertical equity as high-income taxpayers are required to pay more than low-income taxpayers. But, the combination of a personal exemption and a high-income phaseout results in a conflict. If we desire to make the income tax more progressive, enhancing vertical equity, we cause the tax system to be less equitable horizontally. Similarly, if we attempt to enhance the horizontal equity of the income tax by modifying the high-income phaseout of the personal exemption, making only the very wealthiest taxpayers subject to the phaseout, we reduce the vertical equity of the tax.

In the policy world, we are often in a situation where a policy change that enhances one form of equity in a tax system or expenditure program has the effect of reducing the other form of equity. As a result, we must often make a choice over which form of equity is more important.

INCIDENCE EFFECTS OF THE TAX/EXPENDITURE SYSTEM

We can investigate more specifically the effect the tax and transfer system has on the distribution of income. Research reveals that the impact of the tax and transfer system is to shift the Lorenz curve slightly upward, as illustrated in Figure 13.11. The extent to which the tax and transfer system works to reduce income inequality is modest, however. To quantify the difference, it is useful to compare the Gini coefficients of the U.S. income distribution before and after federal taxes and transfers. Recall that the Gini coefficient ranges from zero, indicating perfect equality in the income distribution, to 1, indicating perfect inequality.

Evidence on the Effect of the U.S. Tax and Transfer System

Table 13.4 provides a view of how taxes and transfers in the United States affect the income distribution. By comparing the distribution of income using the traditional money income definition with alternative income definitions we can examine the impact of government taxes and transfers.

The U.S. Census Bureau uses the money income definition along with three alternative income measures, defined as follows:

- Money income: all cash income received before deductions for taxes and other expenses
- Market income: includes money income less government cash transfers (social security, SSI, public assistance, and other transfers); adds imputed rental income from owner-occupied housing (return on home equity) and imputed net realized capital gains; subtracts work expenses such as child care

FIGURE 13.11 Effect of Tax and Expenditure System on the Income Distribution

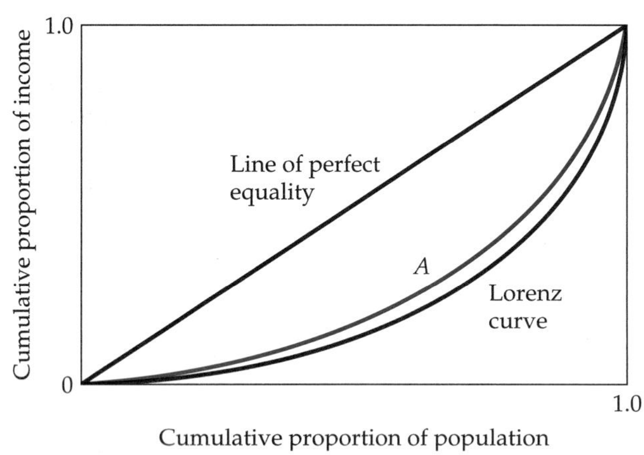

TABLE 13.4 Share of Aggregate Household Income by Quintile, Various Income Definitions, 2005

Quintile	Money Income	Market Income	Post-Social Insurance Income	Disposable Income
First	3.42	1.50	3.24	4.42
Second	8.79	7.26	8.59	9.86
Third	14.42	14.00	14.33	15.33
Fourth	23.02	23.41	22.80	23.11
Fifth	50.34	53.83	51.03	47.28
Gini Index	0.450	0.493	0.447	0.418

Source: U.S. Census Bureau (2007), Table 3.

- Post-social insurance income: includes money income plus imputed net realized capital gains and implicit rental income; subtracts government means-tested cash transfers; differs from market income by adding back non-means-tested government transfers, most importantly social security
- Disposable income: includes money income plus imputed net realized capital gains and rental income; subtracts work expenses; subtracts federal payroll taxes, federal and state income taxes, and property taxes; adds in the value of non-cash transfers including food stamps, subsidized housing, and free or reduced-price school lunches

The first column of the table indicates that the U.S. Census Bureau's official definition of money income yields an estimated Gini coefficient of 0.450 for the income distribution in the United States in 2005. Income shares rise from 3.42 percent of money income earned by the bottom 20 percent of households in the income distribution to 50.34 percent of money income earned by households in the top quintile. Broadening the definition of income to market income, which includes imputed capital income but excludes government cash transfers, we see that the overall Gini index rises to 0.493, indicating a somewhat less equal income distribution. Notably, the share of income earned by the bottom three quintiles of the income distribution is smaller, and the share of income earned by the upper two quintiles is larger. The third column of the table illustrates the specific effect of the social insurance system. The impact of the social insurance system is to lower the Gini coefficient to 0.447, making the income distribution somewhat more equal. Notice that the social insurance system raises the share of income in the first three quintiles while reducing the share in the fourth and fifth quintiles. Finally, we can see the impact of the tax system by considering the income distribution using the disposable income definition in the fourth column of the table. Using this definition of income, the Gini coefficient falls further to 0.418. Hence, the tax system has the effect of making the income distribution more equal, reflected in the smaller value of the Gini coefficient. Income shares rise for the first four quintiles, but falls for the top quintile. This evidence reflects the progressive nature of the U.S. tax system, which redistributes income from the top 20 percent of income earners to the remaining 80 percent of the population. Although the tax and transfer system clearly shifts the Lorenze curve upward, as illustrated in Figure 13.11, it does not shift the curve very much as the magnitude of the changes is relatively modest.

Evidence on the Incidence of U.S. Government Expenditure Programs

Aside from the issue of the incidence of tax and transfer programs, it is important to consider who benefits from government expenditure programs. To what extent do government expenditure programs differentially benefit the poor, or the rich for that matter? That is, what is the incidence of government expenditure programs? Sometimes the expenditure incidence of government programs is surprising. For example, McClelland and Skinner (1997) investigated the expenditure incidence of the U.S. Medicare program and found that the program has resulted in net transfers from the poor to the wealthy. The causes of that unexpected result are due to the relatively regressive financing mechanisms used in the program and the higher expenditures and longer survival times of wealthier program beneficiaries.

Another example of expenditure incidence analysis of a government program is the case of child care. Blau (2000) reports analysis of the data from the National Child Care Survey. His analysis reveals that federal subsidies for child care are concentrated among low-income households. Among households with annual income less than $5,000, 24.2 percent of the households received a subsidy for child care. That percentage falls as you move up the income distribution. Among families with annual household income in excess of $25,000, only 0.9 percent (less than 1 percent) receive a subsidy for child care. In this case, the incidence of the expenditures for child-care subsidies is clearly focused on relatively low-income households.

Although some selected government programs like Medicare and child-care subsidies have been analyzed from the point of view of their expenditure incidence, most government programs have not received such careful analysis. The United States does not have a regular comprehensive review of the expenditure incidence of government programs. This important policy question was analyzed in a one-time comprehensive study by Menchik (1991). Using data available from the Congressional Budget Office (CBO) and other federal agencies, he estimated the expenditure incidence of federal programs in the United States. Despite the importance of this issue, the Menchik study remains the only comprehensive study of federal program expenditure incidence to date. Even though there have been substantial changes in federal programs since the Menchik study, it is still useful to consider his results.

Table 13.5 reports Menchik's estimates of the distribution of program expenditures by quintile for major federal welfare programs. He calls these

TABLE 13.5 Distribution of Income and Expenditure Incidence of Federal Transfer Programs

	Share of Income by Household Quintile				
	1	*2*	*3*	*4*	*5*
Distribution of disposable pretransfer income (including health insurance), 1989	0.0136	0.0941	0.1741	0.2622	0.4528
Outlay Category (CPS Programs)	Expenditures by Quintile				
OASDI	0.436	0.274	0.144	0.078	0.068
Workers' comp.	0.227	0.253	0.203	0.173	0.145
Unemployment comp.	0.096	0.265	0.241	0.230	0.167
Medicare	0.472	0.257	0.133	0.073	0.066
AFDC	0.770	0.134	0.054	0.020	0.011
SSI	0.725	0.125	0.074	0.050	0.027
Medicaid	0.678	0.178	0.077	0.041	0.026
Food stamps	0.767	0.188	0.036	0.060	0.030
Other nutrition programs	0.608	0.200	0.091	0.055	0.045
Housing assistance	0.834	0.125	0.029	0.011	0.001

Source: From "The Distribution of Federal Expenditures" by Paul A. Menchik in *National Tax Journal* 44 (1991): 271, 273. Reprinted by permission of National Tax Association.

programs CPS programs because his analysis of the incidence of these programs is based on data from the Current Population Survey (CPS). For reference, the first row of the table reports the distribution of disposable pretransfer income in 1989, the year of the study, including an estimate of the value of employer-provided health insurance. If federal transfer payments were distributed in proportion to market income, we would expect to find incidence similar to that reported in the first row of the table. That is clearly not the case. Although just 1.36 percent of income was earned by households in the first quintile of the income distribution, those households received 43.6 percent of the social security payments (OASDI), 47.2 percent of the Medicare payments, 77.0 percent of the Aid to Families with Dependent Children (AFDC) payments, 76.7 percent of the food stamps, and 83.4 percent of the housing assistance.[4] As you look across any given row of Table 13.5 you see that declining shares of expenditure are allocated to higher-income households. At the high end of the income distribution, households in the fifth quintile earn over 45 percent of the income but receive very small shares of federal program expenditures, generally in the range of 1 to 6 percent. The two exceptions to that generalization are workers' compensation and unemployment compensation where top quintile households receive 14.5 and 16.7 percent of the payments, respectively. Menchik's estimates indicate that the cash transfer programs like AFDC and SSI are highly focused on low-income households. Seventy-seven percent of the AFDC expenditures went to households in the first quintile of the income distribution. For SSI, 72.5 percent of the expenditures go to households in the first quintile.

Federal in-kind transfer programs vary somewhat more in the income distribution of their recipients. Medicare and Medicaid provide a good contrast. Medicaid is the federal program providing medical care to the poor, whereas Medicare assists the elderly. Medicaid expenditures are more highly concentrated in the first quintile (0.678) compared to Medicare (0.472). Indeed, all across the income distribution, Medicaid expenditures are more focused on the poor, by design. Food stamp and other nutrition expenditures go primarily to households in the first quintile (0.767 for food stamps and 0.608 for other nutrition programs). Housing assistance is the most highly concentrated federal program with expenditures to households in the first quintile accounting for 83.4 percent of all expenditures.

Table 13.6 reports Menchik's estimates of the distribution of benefits for a wide range of other federal programs, called non-CPS programs, arranged by budget category. Again, for reference, the first row of the table reports the income distribution. The second row summarizes the share of these non-CPS programs analyzed. Although households in the first quintile earned just 3.8 percent of the income, they are estimated to have received 35.7 percent of the benefits of the programs listed in Table 13.6. At the top end of the income distribution, households earned 46.8 percent of the income but received just 21.6 percent of the program benefits. Individual programs provide widely varying benefit patterns, however. In the area of agricultural programs, for example, the Farmers Home Administration Rural Housing Insurance Fund provides benefits that accrue to low-income households: 75 percent goes to households in the first quintile and 25 percent to households in the second quintile. But the Commodity Credit Corporation provides benefits that accrue mostly to very high-income households with 71 percent of the benefits going to households in the top quintile and another 22 percent going to households in the fourth quintile. The national forest system is estimated to provide benefits that are much more evenly distributed with about 20 to 25 percent of the benefits received by each of the upper four quintiles and 10 percent of the benefits received by the first quintile.

Financial aid to postsecondary students provides benefits that accrue disproportionately to households in the first quintile. Much of the financial aid is need based, so that is to be expected. As you move up the income distribution quintile by quintile, less and less of the benefits is received. The top-quintile households receive just 2 percent of the benefits. Substantial new grants and tax credits for higher education have been introduced since the Menchik study that provide funding for higher-income families. Still, most aid for higher education is means-tested, including Pell Grants, which provide over $6 billion in funds to more than 3 million college and university students at more than 6,000 schools and federally subsidized Stafford loans that account for another $3.8 billion in expenditure.[5] The incidence of the expenditure benefits of these means-tested programs are not confined to students

TABLE 13.6 Distribution of Income and Federal Program Expenditure Incidence by Budget Category

	Money Household Income by Quintile				
	1	*2*	*3*	*4*	*5*
Share of household income	0.038	0.095	0.158	0.240	0.468
Share of non-CPS programs	0.357	0.184	0.106	0.124	0.216
Selected programs					
Agriculture					
Farmers Home Administration Rural Housing Insurance Fund	0.75	0.25	0.00	0.00	0.00
National Forest System	0.10	0.20	0.25	0.23	0.22
Commodity Credit Corporation (direct payment by net cash income on farms, not total household income)	0.04	0.06	0.08	0.22	0.71
Education					
Student financial aid, postsecondary, by student income	0.46	0.22	0.14	0.16	0.02
Higher education to schools with low-income students	0.67	0.25	0.08	0.00	0.00
Special services for disadvantaged students	0.50	0.45	0.05	0.00	0.00
Energy					
Energy assistance grants for weatherization	0.50	0.35	0.10	0.05	0.00
Health and Human Services					
Foster care and adoption assistance	1.00	0.00	0.00	0.00	0.00
Housing and Urban Development					
FHA mortgage insurance fund	0.04	0.08	0.35	0.42	0.13
Interior					
Fish and wildlife service	0.20	0.18	0.19	0.19	0.24
Bureau of Indian Affairs	0.35	0.25	0.25	0.10	0.05
Labor					
Community service employment for older Americans	1.00	0.00	0.00	0.00	0.00
Training and employment services	1.00	0.00	0.00	0.00	0.00
Black lung disability	0.80	0.20	0.00	0.00	0.00
Transportation					
FAA commercial air carrier	0.03	0.05	0.10	0.14	0.52
FAA general aviation	0.00	0.00	0.05	0.10	0.85
Recreational boating	0.07	0.15	0.19	0.27	0.32

TABLE 13.6 Distribution of Income and Federal Program Expenditure Incidence by Budget Category (continued)

	Money Household Income by Quintile				
	1	2	3	4	5
Amtrak subsidies	0.11	0.12	0.17	0.22	0.39
Urban mass transit	0.27	0.24	0.20	0.18	0.11
Federal highway administration	0.12	0.18	0.24	0.25	0.21
Veterans Affairs					
Medical care	0.89	0.08	0.02	0.01	0.00
Legal Services Corporation	0.95	0.05	0.00	0.00	0.00

Source: From "The Distribution of Federal Expenditures" by Paul L. Menchik in *National Tax Journal* 44 (1991): 271, 273. Reprinted by permission of National Tax Association.

from families in poverty. Rather, the expenditure incidence is spread widely across the income distribution. Furthermore, new tax credits for higher education expenses, including the HOPE Scholarship tax credit and the Lifetime Learning tax credit, provide benefits to families across the income distribution, although both credits are phased out for high-income families. Once fully phased in, the combination of these two tax credits is expected to benefit over 13 million students, many of whom will come from middle-class families.[6]

In the Health and Human Services area, 100 percent of the benefits of the foster care and adoption assistance program go to households in the first quintile. For the Housing and Urban Development area, the benefits of FHA mortgage insurance are received primarily by households in the third and fourth quintiles, each receiving 35 and 42 percent of the benefits, respectively. Benefits of Department of Interior fish and wildlife programs are quite uniformly distributed across the income distribution, whereas Bureau of Indian Affairs programs benefit the poor disproportionately.

The transportation budget category provides some interesting contrasts. Federal Aviation Administration (FAA) programs for commercial air carrier and general aviation provide benefits that accrue to higher-income households. Urban mass transit programs do just the opposite, benefiting lower-income households. Amtrak railroad programs have expenditure incidence that lies between the aviation and mass transit programs. Finally, medical care and legal services provided to veterans generate benefits primarily for low-income households.

Again, the overall incidence of these programs is summarized in the second row of Table 13.6: 35.7 percent of the benefits go to households in the first quintile, 18.4 percent to those in the second quintile, 10.6 percent to those in the third quintile, 12.4 percent to those in the fourth quintile, and 21.6 percent to households in the fifth quintile.

POLICY STUDY

Evaluating the Equity Effects of a Tax Reform

Tax systems are reformed in order to achieve a number of policy objectives, including both efficiency and equity. In this policy study we examine the equity implications of one of the most substantial tax reforms in modern U.S. history, the Tax Reform Act of 1986 (TRA86). Indeed, Eugene Steuerle has called the TRA86 "the most comprehensive reform of U.S. tax laws ever undertaken" (1992, 1). The TRA86 was a landmark tax reform that broadened the tax base of the personal income tax more substantially than any tax reform in modern history. As a result, TRA86 has been subjected to detailed analysis of its many provisions. In this policy study, we consider the comprehensive review of the vertical and horizontal equity implications of TRA86 in Gravelle (1992). Although many provisions of TRA86 have been undone to some extent in subsequent years, with both the executive and legislative branches of government involved in narrowing the tax base, that landmark tax reform provides the clearest opportunity we have to examine the effects of changes in the tax base and rate structure on the equity of the tax system.

Effects of the Tax Reform Act on Vertical Equity

The TRA86 was designed, in part, to increase the progressivity of the U.S. income tax. The Act removed approximately 6 million families from the income tax roles by increasing the standard deduction and personal exemption and expansion of the earned income tax credit. Although the Act also reduced the top marginal tax rate, giving the appearance of making the tax system less progressive, we know from previous chapters that things are not always as they appear in the tax policy world. The more important changes, in terms of making the income tax system more progressive, are the expanded personal exemption, standard deduction, and earned income tax credit. It is useful to note that TRA86 followed two previous pieces of tax legislation that both had the effect of reducing the progressivity of the income tax. The Economic Recovery Tax Act of 1981 (ERTA) included reductions in marginal tax rates that were substantial. The payroll tax was also increased in 1983 legislation to fund the social security system. That tax is proportional up to an income ceiling, after which the rate falls to zero, so the increased rate was regressive in its effect.

Official documents of the time indicated that TRA86 had the effect of redistributing income from higher-income individuals to lower-income individuals. Information from the Congressional Joint Tax Committee indicates that as income levels increased, the percentage change in tax liability due to TRA86 decreased. Although the overall reduction in liability was 6.11 percent, individuals with income less than $10,000 experienced a reduction of 65 percent, whereas those with income in excess of $200,000 experienced just a 2.43 percent reduction.

Judging tax legislation on the basis of proportional changes in tax liability is not a very meaningful yardstick, however. It is more insightful to consider percentage changes in after-tax income. Individuals at the low end of the income distribution experienced an increase of 1.12 percent in after-tax income, whereas those at the top of the income distribution experienced about half that rate of increase, 0.65 percent.

We have not discussed two essential aspects of TRA86, however. The Act substantially broadened the personal income tax base and increased the corporate income tax. Both of these changes had the potential to reduce the progressivity-enhancing effects covered previously.

In addition, two other aspects of the TRA86 require clarification. First, a number of the Act's provisions were transitory, involving short-term transition provisions. Second, a number of the provisions on the corporate income tax side are more appropriately classified as changes in excise taxes or labor income provisions. If those changes are reclassified and the transitory changes are properly accounted for, the apparent effects of TRA86 are modified. Studies by the Congressional Budget Office (CBO) and Wallace, Wasylenko, and Weiner (1991) have addressed these measures. According to the CBO estimates, TRA86 increased after-tax income by 0.22 percent in the first income decile. The effect was larger in the second and third deciles, whereas it was smaller in the fourth decile and continued to decline through the seventh decile. The percentage change in after-tax income jumps up in the eighth decile and falls again to a low level in the ninth and tenth deciles. The Wallace, Wasylenko, and Weiner estimates indicate that individuals in the first income decile experienced a reduction in after-tax income, whereas individuals in other income deciles experienced increases in after-tax income. The apparent pattern of increases rises in the second and third deciles then falls through the seventh decile, rising in the eighth decile and falling to lower levels in the ninth and tenth deciles.

Overall, this pattern of TRA86 effects is not one of major shifts in after-tax income. The Act had only modest effects on the vertical equity of the income tax system. Individuals at the upper end of the income distribution experienced relatively small increases in after-tax income, in comparison with all but those at the very bottom of the distribution. TRA86 did not have a large impact on the vertical equity of the income tax, however.

An important qualification to these results should be noted as well. Consider an example from the realm of portfolio choice that illustrates a general principle of policy analysis. Suppose that initially all taxable bonds are held by lower-income individuals, whereas all tax-exempt bonds are held by higher-income individuals. Of course, higher-income individuals must accept a lower rate of return on the tax-exempt bonds, equivalent to an implicit tax, in exchange for the tax savings they enjoy. The combination of a lower pretax rate of return combined with the tax savings makes the nonmarginal individual better off than she would be holding taxable bonds. Now, suppose that base broadening on the income tax facilitates marginal tax rate reductions. With a lower tax rate, the tax savings are no longer sufficient to compensate higher-income individuals for holding tax-exempt bonds. They will move into taxable bonds, and the return on tax-exempt bonds will rise, whereas the return on taxable bonds will fall. In a competitive market, the after-tax returns must be equal in the two markets. The before-tax return on tax-exempt bonds will increase, however, for higher-income individuals who are not at the margin. Similarly, the before-tax income of lower-income individuals who are not at the margin will fall. A policy study that does not take these changes into account will understate the extent to which higher-income individuals benefit from the tax rate reduction. It will also overstate the extent of the benefits to lower-income individuals.

Effects of the Tax Reform Act on Horizontal Equity

In assessing horizontal equity effects of the tax reform, Gravelle stated:

> Horizontal equity is a difficult concept to assess: it poses the problem of defining what characteristics the tax system should consider in defining equity. Two families with the same level of income incur different tax liabilities for a number of reasons: family characteristics, sources of income, and disposition of income. (1992, 36)

Her analysis of the horizontal equity implications of TRA86 considered each of these reasons why families with similar income may pay different taxes: family characteristics, sources of income, and disposition of income.

Family Characteristics

Many characteristics of families affect tax liability, including marital status, distribution of earnings among family members, number of children, and other factors. Primary among those characteristics affecting tax liability, however, is the marital status of the family and its corresponding choice of filing status. The TRA86 included a number of changes related to family characteristics: the two-earner deduction was eliminated, the standard deductions were increased, and a number of other changes were made.

Table 13.7 provides estimates of tax rates for various types of families, adjusting for the value of time available to a nonworking spouse. The top panel of the table

TABLE 13.7 Effective Tax Rates by Filing Status and Family Size

	1986 Tax Law			Tax Reform Act of 1986		
Family Size	***Two Earner***	***One Earner***	***Head of Household***	***Two Earner***	***One Earner***	***Head of Household***
A. Median income						
2	10.6	7.0	12.9	10.2	6.7	10.2
3	11.0	7.7	13.5	9.7	6.8	10.2
4	12.1	9.4	14.9	10.0	7.3	11.6
5	12.9	10.6	16.0	11.0	7.5	12.3
6	13.6	11.4	16.7	11.4	8.1	12.5
B. Twice median income						
2	15.9	13.8	19.3	14.7	11.5	15.9
3	17.6	15.5	21.0	15.3	12.6	16.3
4	20.0	18.1	23.3	16.2	14.1	17.0
5	21.6	20.0	24.8	16.7	14.8	17.3
6	22.5	21.1	25.7	16.9	15.3	17.5

Source: From "Equity Effects of the Tax Reform Act of 1986" by Jane G. Gravelle in *Journal of Economic Perspectives* 6, No. 1 Winter 1992: 38. Reprinted by permission of American Economic Association.

provides estimates for families of various sizes at the median of the income distribution. For example, a two-person family is assumed to have an income of $30,000 per year, a three-person family an income of $36,000, a four-person family an income of $45,300, and so on. These income amounts were developed using a concept of equity requiring that families with the same before-tax standard of living have the same after-tax standard of living. The lower panel of Table 13.7 gives effective tax rates for higher-income families of various sizes. In this case the two-person family has an income of $60,000, whereas the three-person family and four-person family have incomes of $72,000 and $90,600, respectively.

Effective tax rates are listed in Table 13.7, showing that families of various characteristics face different effective tax rates. The table reveals that TRA86 substantially increased equity among families of different sizes within a tax-filing status category, making their effective tax rates more nearly equal. The range of effective tax rates by family size in any given column of Table 13.7 is much smaller after the introduction of the TRA86. The Act also reduced differences in effective tax rates between two-earner couples and single-adult-headed families. One-earner married couples continued to enjoy lower effective tax rates after the Act was introduced. This occurs in part due to the nontaxation of imputed income for the secondary earner in the family. The results of Gravelle's estimates indicate that TRA86 made important advances in treating different-sized families of varying circumstances in a more equitable fashion.

Sources of Income

The sources of one's income can affect the tax owed. A most-glaring example of this situation is the case of fringe benefits. If fringe benefits are not taxed, whereas wage and salary income is taxed, then effective tax rates can depend on sources of income even though total income is identical. The TRA86 did little to remove this problem, although a couple of changes were made. First, TRA86 removed fully deductible Individual Retirement Account (IRA) contributions for those taxpayers with an employer-provided retirement plan. This change helped improve horizontal equity. Dividends were taxed more heavily than capital gains from corporate stock, and corporate equity in general was taxed more heavily than noncorporate equity and corporate debt. The TRA86 helped remove some of the difference in effective tax rates on various types of equity income by broadening the tax base, lowering the tax rates, and making capital gains fully taxable (a portion of capital gains had previously been excluded from taxation). As a result, there was probably some improvement in equity across families with different sources of income.

Disposition of Income

Finally, there can be differences in effective tax rates depending on families' disposition of income. Of course, differences in disposition of income are based on differences in consumption behavior. A family that chooses to spend a large proportion of its income on tax-deductible mortgage interest may have a very different effective tax rate than a family with the same income that spends its income on other taxable goods and services. Of course, TRA86 did not affect the deductibility of mortgage interest (it left mortgage interest deductible, although early drafts of the reform suggested removal of this deduction). In this way, TRA86 did not do much to change effective tax rates based on disposition of income.

A differential tax can be applied to various types of capital, however, resulting in different prices for goods produced by that capital. For example, goods produced by capital that is lightly taxed will have lower prices than goods produced with heavily taxed capital. Estimates indicate that before TRA86, tax rates on capital in different industries ranged from 34 to 52 percent. Even if the oil and gas industries are excluded from the comparison, the rates ranged from 40 to 47 percent. Differences in tax rates across industries have the effect of excise taxes on the prices of those industries. In this regard, TRA86 played an important role in reducing the differences in effective tax rates across industries, and thereby making the tax system more equitable.

Life Cycle and Intergenerational Equity Effects

A final way to examine the equity effects of TRA86 is to consider the effects of the Act on different age groups in the population. Table 13.8 provides Gravelle's estimates of the effects of TRA86 on different age cohorts' consumption. The main conclusion one draws from Table 13.8 is that TRA86 had little effect on intergenerational redistribution. Workers who are younger benefit from the Act because wage income is a larger fraction of their lifetime income and the Act reduced wage taxation. Older workers also gained more than the average because of advantages in the value of existing capital. However, the table estimates positive changes in consumption for all age cohorts,

TABLE 13.8 Effects of the Tax Reform Act of 1986 on Different Age Cohorts

Age	***Percentage Change in Consumption***
20–24	0.50
25–29	0.40
30–34	0.27
35–39	0.14
40–44	0.04
45–49	0.01
50–54	0.02
55–59	0.08
60–64	0.20
65–69	0.36
70–74	0.56

Source: From "Equity Effects of the Tax Reform Act of 1986" by Jane G. Gravelle in *Journal of Economic Perspectives* 6, No. 1 Winter 1992: 38. Reprinted by permission of American Economic Association.

reflecting the fact that the Act was a revenue loser. If that revenue loss is recovered in some way in the future, distributional effects across generations may result.

Summary

In her overall summary of the equity effects of TRA86, Gravelle stated:

> Despite studies which suggest that the Act redistributed income from higher-income individuals to lower-income individuals, it seems more likely that higher-income individuals will gain relative to lower-income individuals in the long-run. This gain is due to the transient nature of many of the capital income tax increases and the favorable effects on utility of portfolio adjustment. The Act did appear to achieve some gains in horizontal equity, in part by shifting the tax burden away from large families. There also appears to be some gains in horizontal equity due to the more uniform treatment of capital income. There appears to be little redistribution among generations, with both younger and older cohorts gaining somewhat more than middle-aged cohorts. (1992, 42)

Gravelle's assessment of the equity effects of TRA86, the most substantial tax reform in U.S. history, is that the Act probably made the income tax system somewhat more horizontally equitable, perhaps shifting some of the tax burden away from large families in particular. In terms of vertical equity effects, however, TRA86 may be responsible for some part of the increasing disparity in the distribution of income experienced in the United States over the past 15 years, with high-income households gaining relative to low-income households.

POLICY STUDY

The Incidence of Local Development Fees and Special Assessments

Local governments are increasingly concerned with providing services needed by new residents of their communities, yet they are mindful that community residents do not wish to have a property tax rate increase. With state tax limitations, many communities are already at the maximum property tax rates permitted by law; hence, new infrastructure needed to accommodate new community residents must be paid for by some other means. Many communities are now using development fees and special assessments as a means by which to finance new streets, sewers, water lines, and other infrastructure. Development fees are required of the land developer at the time that land is developed in order to pay for infrastructure provision. Special assessments are *ad valorem* charges, much like property taxes, that are applied to property for the provision of particular public services.

The interesting question that arises in the application of these financing mechanisms is, Who bears the burden of these assessments and fees? If new residents bear the burden of these charges, they may act as benefit charges. New residents benefit from the provision of public services in their neighborhoods and pay the cost of those benefits they enjoy through special assessments and development fees. On the other hand, if some part of the special assessment or development fee is actually borne by existing community residents or landowners, then these charges may not be benefit charges at all, because the burden of these charges falls more generally on community residents. So, the question of whether development fees and special assessments are really benefit charges boils down to the question of their incidence. Economist John Yinger (1998) has investigated this question and provides insight useful for answering the question of the incidence of these charges.

Development Fees

Yinger begins by assuming that households are mobile in an urban area and that housing markets are competitive. Further, he assumes that the infrastructure investment under consideration is worthwhile, evidenced by a benefit-cost ratio of at least 1. Armed with these working assumptions, he develops a model of the burden of development fees on landowners relative to the gross burden of the fees on home buyers. For the development fees to be pure benefit charges, we would expect the relative burden to be zero. That is, the landowner bears none of the burden relative to the home buyer who bears all of the burden of the fees.

The main result of Yinger's model is that even if a development fee meets the benefit/cost test, providing positive net benefits, that fee has the effect of reducing the price of land. Consequently, all landowners bear the burden of the fee, not just those in the new development. Firms in the business of building homes bear no burden because competition and free entry/exit in the construction industry assures zero long-run profits. New home buyers bear a large share of the burden of the fee in the form of higher house prices, but they also bear no net burden when we consider the infrastructure benefits they receive. Due to the mobility of households, there is no net burden. The economic intuition of this result is important to understand. Added infrastructure in the community raises the price of housing, because people are willing to pay more for houses with paved streets, municipal sewers, and water. The increase in price is subject to the property tax in the community, however. As a result, housing prices rise by less than the full amount of the value of infrastructure services provided. The development fee is equal to the full value of the service, so house prices rise by an amount less than that needed to compensate developers for the development fee. Hence, the price of land must fall to preserve zero long-run economic profit in the development industry.

Yinger estimates the burden of a development fee under varying assumptions for the parameters of his model. Consider the case of an infrastructure project where the benefit-cost ratio is unity, providing benefits equal to the costs of the project. When the new houses, equal in value to existing houses in the community, account for 5 percent of total house value in the community and the effective property tax rate is 1 percent, Yinger estimates a burden ratio of $b = 0.241$. With this ratio, we know that homeowners bear $1/(1 + b)$ of the burden, whereas landowners bear $b/(1 + b)$ of the burden of the development fee. In this case, with $b = 0.241$, the homeowner burden is 80.5 percent of the development fee and the landowner burden is 19.5 percent. As a result, we see that development fees are imperfect in playing the role of benefit charges in this situation, because existing landowners are forced to pay nearly one-fifth of the burden of the fees relative to the new home buyers. At a higher effective property tax rate of 3 percent, the burden ratio rises to 0.711. That burden ratio implies homeowners bear 58.4 percent of the development fee burden, whereas landowners bear 41.6 percent of the burden. Both of these burden ratios are slightly smaller when the new houses account for a larger share of house value in the community. The burden ratios are yet slightly smaller when the new houses being built are twice the value of existing houses in the community. The burden ratios are slightly larger when the value of new homes is 80 percent of the value of existing homes in the community.

Yinger points out that the lowest burden ratio implies that landowners bear 16.4 percent of the burden of a development fee, whereas the highest ratio implies that they bear 41.8 percent of the burden. The primary factor accounting for the difference in burden is the property tax rate. That makes sense because it is the property tax rate that creates a difference between the increase in the price of housing and the size of the development fee that the community applies.

Yinger also notes that these results imply that existing residents receive a capital gain from the development fee. New infrastructure raises the price of new houses relative to existing houses and thereby expands the property tax base. A community-wide reduction in property tax rate is then possible, keeping revenue constant, and the value of existing houses then rises due to the tax rate reduction. As a result, a development fee not only insulates existing house owners from added costs of new infrastructure but also grants them a capital gain.

In the case of a benefit-cost ratio of 2, Yinger determines that the burden ratios are negative. That implies the homeowner will bear a burden in excess of the fee, whereas the landowner will bear a negative burden, or a benefit. When Yinger evaluates the case where the benefit-cost ratio is less than 1, or 2/3, the burden ratios are higher than in the cases previously discussed, indicating that the homeowner share of the burden is smaller and the landowner share is larger.

Special Assessments

In the case of a special assessment, the results are different. Both the benefits and the costs of the infrastructure have an impact on the price of houses. Improved infrastructure raises house prices and that effect is offset by the decreased house price resulting from the special assessment. These two effects are exactly offsetting, so there is no impact on house price. Consequently, there is no effect on land prices and hence no burden to landowners. The whole burden of the special assessment falls on the new residents who receive the full benefit of the infrastructure improvement. Hence, the special assessment is a pure benefit charge, entirely neutral in its effect.

PROBLEMS

1. Suppose that the demand for a good is given by the inverse demand function $p = 10 - 3q$.
   a. Plot the demand curve on a graph.
   b. Compute the price at which 2 units of the good will be demanded.

c. Suppose that a unit tax of 1 is introduced. Plot the new demand curve.
d. What is the price at which 2 units will be demanded after the tax is imposed?
e. If supply is perfectly elastic at the price of 5, what is the equilibrium quantity of the good before the tax is imposed? What is the effect of the tax on price and quantity? Explain.
f. How much revenue is generated by this tax?
g. Who bears the burden of this tax?

2. Suppose that the demand for a good is given by the inverse demand function $p = 10 - 3q$, whereas the supply of the good is given by the inverse supply function $p = 2 + 2q$.
   a. Plot the demand and supply functions on a graph.
   b. Set the two price equations equal and solve for the equilibrium quantity.
   c. Using the equilibrium quantity, determine the equilibrium price.
   d. Now suppose that a unit tax of 1 is imposed, shifting the supply curve upward, increasing the intercept by 1 unit.
   e. Recompute the equilibrium quantity and price and determine the incidence of the tax. Explain who bears what shares of the tax.
   f. Calculate the elasticities of demand and supply at the original equilibrium point (before the tax) and describe the relative elasticities. [Recall that the elasticities are given as (1/slope)(p/q).]

3. The U.S. Food Stamp program provides monthly allotments of food stamps to families of various sizes, on the basis of their income. The following table lists the gross monthly income standards (130 percent of poverty level in the year 2002) and the maximum monthly food stamp allotment.

Household Size (Persons)	Gross Monthly Income Eligibility Standard (130 Percent of Poverty Level) ($)	Maximum Monthly Food Stamp Allotment ($)
1	931	135
2	1,258	248
3	1,585	356
4	1,913	452
5	2,240	537
6	2,567	644
7	2,894	712
8	3,221	814
Each additional member	+328	+102

Source: Food Research and Action Center, http://www.frac.org/html/federal_food_programs/programs/fsp_limits2002.html.

a. Compute the maximum monthly food stamp allotment as a fraction of the gross monthly income eligibility standard for households of various sizes listed in the above table.
b. Explain the pattern of Food Stamp program benefit incidence across households of various sizes revealed in the fractions computed in part a.
c. Compute the change in maximum allotment with a change in gross income for households of various sizes listed in the above table.
d. Explain the pattern of marginal food stamp benefit incidence across households using the ratios computed in part c.

4. Use a labor/leisure choice model such as that developed in Chapter 12 to analyze the incentive effect of a government program targeted at low-income households. Suppose, in particular, that the government provides a grant g_0 for households with income less than some threshold y_0. Once household income reaches the threshold y_0, however, the household is no longer eligible for the grant and receives nothing.
   a. Draw the household budget line and analyze the work incentive effect of the government grant program.
   b. Suppose, instead, that the lump-sum grant of g_0 is reduced as household income rises, with the grant formula: $g = g_0 - g_y y$. The term g_y is the marginal rate at which the grant is reduced as income increases. Once income reaches the level $y = g_0 / g_y$ the household no longer qualifies for the grant and receives nothing. Draw the budget line under this grant program and explain the work incentive effects of the grant program.

5. True, False, or Uncertain. Explain.
   a. A tax imposed on a good with relatively inelastic demand is borne primarily by the consumer.
   b. A tax imposed on a good with relatively elastic supply is borne primarily by the producer.
   c. A tax imposed on a good with zero elasticity of demand is borne entirely by the producer.
   d. A tax imposed on a good with zero elasticity of supply is borne entirely by the producer.
   e. A tax imposed on a monopolist is borne entirely by the consumers of the product.
   f. A tax imposed on a good with relatively inelastic demand will be effective in reducing the quantity of the good produced and consumed.
   g. A tax imposed on a good with relatively elastic supply will be opposed more vigorously by industry lobbyists than by consumer advocates.

6. The State of Aksarben has a problem. The state supreme court has just ruled that the state's method of taxing property is unconstitutional. Rather than suffer the revenue shortfall that would occur in the absence of legislative action, Senator Wahoo reacts by introducing legislation that would provide a new tax surcharge to be applied to capital used in the agricultural sector, while leaving capital taxation unchanged in the rest

of the economy. Set up a diagram like Figure 13.9 in which you can analyze the effect of an increase in the rate of taxation on capital in the agricultural sector and explain the effects of the tax increase.

7. Senator Beatrice is concerned that one of the state's major industries, food processing, is hampered by a high rate of taxation applied to capital. She has introduced legislation that would provide a substantial tax reduction for capital used in the food processing industry, while leaving capital taxation unchanged in the rest of the economy. Set up a diagram like Figure 13.9 in which you can analyze the effect of a reduction in the rate of taxation on capital in the food processing sector and explain the effects of the tax reduction.

8. Iona is a retired schoolteacher whose pension income is $18,000 per year. She also receives social security income of $12,000 per year. Jay is a young man who does not choose to work. He inherited $600,000 from his Aunt Midge which he invested in a bond fund that provides a 5 percent return, generating $30,000 income per year. If we are concerned about the horizontal equity of taxation, should we consider these two people equals and tax them equally? Explain why or why not.

REFERENCES

Blau, David. *The Economics of Means-Tested Child Care Subsidies.* Cambridge, MA: National Bureau of Economic Research (NBER), conference paper, 2000.

Gravelle, Jane G. "Equity Effects of the Tax Reform Act of 1986." *Journal of Economic Perspectives* 6 (1992): 27–44.

Gruber, Jonathan. "The Incidence of Payroll Taxation: Evidence from Chile." *Journal of Labor Economics* 15 (1997): S72–S101.

McClelland, Mark, and Jonathan Skinner. *The Incidence of Medicare.* Cambridge, MA: National Bureau of Economic Research (NBER), Working Paper 6013, 1997.

Menchik, Paul. "The Distribution of Federal Expenditures." *National Tax Journal* 44 (1991): 269–76.

Steuerle, C. Eugene. *The Tax Decade.* Washington, DC: Urban Institute, 1992.

U.S. Census Bureau. *The Effect of Taxes and Transfers on Income and Poverty in the United States: 2005.* U.S. Department of Commerce, Economics and Statistics Administration, 2007.

Wallace, Sally, Michael Wasylenko, and David Weiner. "The Distributional Implications of Reforming the Personal and Corporate Income Taxes." *National Tax Journal* 44 (1991): 181–98.

Yinger, John. "The Incidence of Development Fees and Special Assessments." *National Tax Journal* 51 (1998): 23–41.

NOTES

1. The reader should note that elasticity and slope of the demand curve are not the same thing. Although we have illustrated relatively inelastic demand with a steep demand curve and relatively inelastic demand with a flat demand curve, the reader should recall that along a linear demand curve the slope is changing. As you move up along a given linear demand curve, the elasticity of demand increases. The elasticity of demand is given as

$$\epsilon = (\partial q/\partial p)\,(p/q).$$

   The first term is the inverse of the slope of the demand curve (inverse because we plot p on the vertical axis and q on the horizontal axis). Hence, for a given (q, p) point, the steeper the demand curve, the greater the slope (in absolute value) and the smaller the elasticity (in absolute value). But for a given slope, as we move up along the demand curve, p rises and q falls, making the ratio (p/q) rise and the elasticity (in absolute value) increase (in absolute value).
2. We are assuming that the total quantity of capital is fixed. The capital that flees the corporate sector migrates to the noncorporate sector and the total amount of capital in the economy is unchanged.
3. Ultimately there is a direct link between income and property value. The value of an acre of land is the present discounted value of the future net income stream generated by the land. The dichotomy between income and wealth as a standard for evaluating vertical equity in taxation is due to a false comparison between a short-term measure of income and a long-term measure of wealth.
4. The AFDC program was replaced by the TANF program.
5. Committee on Ways and Means (2000).
6. The Hope credit provides up to $1,500 for expenses during the first two years of college. The tax credit is for 100 percent of the first $1,000 of tuition and fees plus 50 percent of the second $1,000 of tuition and fees. The credit is phased out for single filers with income between $40,000 and $50,000 and for joint filers with income between $80,000 and $100,000. The phase-out range was indexed starting in 2002. The Lifetime Learning credit is for students beyond the first two years of college and provides a 20 percent credit for the first $5,000 of tuition and fees (expands to $10,000 in the year 2003 and thereafter). This credit has the same phase-out range as the HOPE credit. For tax years 2009 and 2010 the American Opportunity Tax Credit modified the Hope credit: the maximum credit amount was increased to $2,500, the credit was extended to cover the first four years (rather than two) of postsecondary education, the modified AGI income limit was increased, qualified expenses were broadened to include course materials, and 40 percent of the Hope credit was made refundable. For more information on these tax credits, see the IRS website: *http://www.irs.gov/publications/p970/ch02.html*.

Radius Images/Getty Images

PART FIVE

Particular Taxes and Policy Issues

CHAPTER

14

Radius Images/Getty Images

Income and Payroll Taxes

LEARNING OBJECTIVES

1. Discuss deductibility and its economic effects.
2. Explain the design of the U.S. income tax system, including the taxable unit, marriage bonuses and penalties, earned income tax credit, and other issues.
3. Discuss how a payroll tax system is designed.
4. Identify different tax reform proposals.

The income tax is the cornerstone of the federal government revenue structure and serves as a major source of revenue for many states as well. Such was not always the case, however; the U.S. Constitution was originally written to forbid direct federal taxes that were not strictly proportional to the nation's population (see Section 9, Article 1, of the Constitution). Indeed, the constitutional framers did not conceive of the thought of using **direct taxation** such as a personal income tax at the federal level. They were more accustomed to **indirect taxation** in the form of excise taxes and duties on imports. Although the nation employed temporary income taxes during the Civil War and other wartimes, it was not until the adoption of the Sixteenth Amendment to the U.S. Constitution in 1913 that the federal income tax was given a firm constitutional basis. That amendment specifically provided for a federal income tax. Since that time, the role of the income tax has grown, making it the most important source of revenue for the federal government. The income tax stands squarely atop the ability-to-pay principle, based on the idea that those individuals with more income are capable of paying more to support the provision of public goods and services. Yet in many ways it is a curious and complicated tax, drawing much criticism.

DEFINING THE INCOME TAX BASE

The ideal measure of income that captures most fully the concept of ability to pay is the Haig-Simons definition of income. According to that definition, we should construct a broad income tax base following the rule that:

> All accretion to wealth should be included, whether it is regular or fluctuating, expected or unexpected, realized or unrealized. No consideration should be given to how the income is used, i.e. whether it is saved or consumed. (Musgrave and Musgrave 1989, 332)

Source: © The New Yorker Collection 1997 Roz Chast from cartoonbank.com. All Rights Reserved.

An Ideal Definition of Taxable Income: The Haig-Simons Definition Again

According to the Haig-Simons definition of income, an income tax should be applied to a very broad measure of income including not only wage and salary income but also capital gains (both realized and unrealized) and forms of wealth accretion such as the implicit rental value of a home or automobile. Further, the income tax should permit no deductions based on how the income was spent. This form of income tax would achieve the goal of a true ability-based tax, as nearly as possible. Of course, the actual structure of the U.S. income tax differs from this ideal, primarily due to the fact that other policy objectives are also incorporated into the design of the tax. Keep in mind that the current U.S. income tax is not a pure ability-based tax. Indeed, no real-world tax is a pure form of any particular tax ideal. In this regard, it is useful to recall the Platonic concepts of the *ideal* and the *particulars*. Although a Haig-Simons definition of income is the ideal for an income tax, we will be looking at the particulars of the U.S. income tax base definition. The two concepts differ quite substantially, but by knowing the ideal, we have a benchmark by which to judge the particular tax under consideration.

The U.S. Income Tax Definition of Income

The U.S. income tax is based on a measure of income that includes both wage and salary income, capturing labor income, as well as some forms of interest and dividends, capturing capital income. The attempt is to tax most forms of income, whether they are derived from labor or capital. It should be noted, however, that the U.S. income tax is not a pure income tax in the Haig-Simons sense. Since the 1980s the tax base has been modified in numerous ways that have moved in the direction of a consumption tax base. By providing tax-advantaged savings incentives and differential tax rates for capital gains, the effect has been to make the U.S. income tax a hybrid income-consumption tax. Nonetheless, we will continue to refer to it as an income tax.

Adjusted Gross Income (AGI)

We begin by recalling the concept of *adjusted gross income* (AGI), the gross income measure used as a starting point on the U.S. personal income tax. It is composed of both labor income in the form of wages and salaries plus capital income in the form of interest and dividends. It also includes capital gains and business income. A simplified definition of AGI that abstracts from a number of complexities in the tax code is:

$$\begin{aligned}\text{Adjusted gross income} = {} & \text{wages} + \text{salaries} + \text{tips} + \text{interest income} \\ & + \text{dividend income} + \text{capital gains} \\ & + \text{net business/farm income} - \text{adjustments.}\end{aligned}$$

Notice that AGI includes most labor income since the taxpayer is required to add in wages, salaries, and tips. Capital income is also included to the extent of adding in interest income, dividends, and capital gains. Then, net income from either business or farming activity is added as well. In this regard, the individual income tax also covers the business activity of individuals, insofar as it includes noncorporate business activity. Finally, a number of adjustments are permitted for specific purposes. Although this may appear to be a relatively comprehensive definition of income, there are important omissions.

Excluded Forms of Money Income

Adjusted gross income omits a number of important forms of money income. For example, interest on state and local bonds is often tax exempt, so the taxpayer does not pay tax on that interest. As a result, it is important for taxpayers to consider how to invest their savings—in taxable or nontaxable securities. A taxpayer with $10,000 to invest in a financial asset may purchase a private company's bond that pays 10 percent interest. The taxpayer would then have $1,000 in taxable interest income each year. If the taxpayer is in the 28 percent marginal tax bracket, her after-tax interest earnings are $720 and her after-tax rate of return is 7.2 percent. As an alternative, the taxpayer could purchase a municipal bond that pays 8 percent interest that is not taxable. In this case, the taxpayer would have nontaxable interest earnings of $800 and an after-tax rate of return of 8 percent. Obviously, this taxpayer is better off if she buys the municipal bond than the taxable security. Another taxpayer who is in the 15 percent marginal tax bracket would be better off with the taxable security, however. He would earn $1,000 in taxable interest, pay a tax of $150, and be left with after-tax interest earnings of $850, or an after-tax rate of return of 8.5 percent.

Taxpayers in high marginal tax brackets, where their marginal tax rate is higher than the average effective tax rate, benefit from tax-exempt interest, whereas those in low marginal tax brackets should avoid tax-exempt securities. Tax-exempt securities pay a lower rate of interest than taxable securities, and financial markets operate in such a way as to assure that the after-tax rates of return are equal for the average taxpayer.

Employer contributions to benefit plans are also generally not taxable. Medical, dental, and optical insurance benefits, as well as life and disability insurance and other benefits, may not be taxable as current income. Consider two employees, Jay and Iona. Jay works for Alpha Inc. and receives all of his compensation in the form of salary in the amount of $50,000 per year. Iona works for Beta LTD where she receives $40,000 in salary and $10,000 in medical, dental, and life insurance benefits. Which employee is better off? If they both face a flat 20 percent income tax, Jay will pay $10,000 in tax, whereas Iona will pay $8,000. Clearly, Iona has the potential to be better off in comparison with Jay. That requires an assumption that Iona values the benefits she receives, but it is quite possible that she will be substantially better off than Jay as a result of the tax exempt status of her benefits, as compared with the taxable status of wage and salary income. The modern trend toward increasing benefit packages as part of an employee's compensation is in part due to the different tax treatment of wage and salary income compared to that of benefits.

Contributions to retirement savings plans may also be exempt from taxation. When an employer provides contributions to a retirement plan, for example, that income is not subject to the income tax in the year it is earned. As a result, there are incentives for employees to take their compensation in the form of retirement benefits rather than immediate salary. Suppose that Kay earns $50,000 in salary a year working for Gamma Inc., whereas Elle earns $45,000 in salary and $5,000 in retirement contributions from Delta LLC. In the presence of a flat 20 percent income tax, Kay will pay $10,000 in tax, whereas Elle will pay $9,000. Clearly, by receiving some of her compensation in the form of retirement benefits, Elle can be better off than Kay.

Taxable Income

Once we have defined AGI as the starting point in defining income for tax purposes, the income tax provides exemptions and deductions and then defines taxable income. Taxable income is defined as adjusted gross income minus exemptions and deductions:

Taxable income = adjusted gross income − personal exemptions − deductions.

Thus, the income to which we apply the income tax is a relatively narrow measure of income, AGI, further narrowed by the subtraction of both personal exemptions and deductions.

Exemptions and Deductions

Personal exemptions are provided for the taxpayer, spouse, and dependents. Under year 2010 tax law, for example, the personal exemption is $3,650 per person. A family of four would have four personal exemptions amounting to $14,600 (4 times $3,650) of income exempt from taxation. The personal exemption is indexed for inflation, so it rises each year along with the general cost of living as measured by the consumer price index (CPI). For high-income taxpayers, the personal exemption is sometimes phased out. Taxpayers that are 65 years of age or more, and those who are blind, are given an additional personal exemption, regardless of income.

Taxpayers are also permitted to make certain deductions. These include deductions for medical expenses, some taxes paid to state and local governments, mortgage interest on homes, charitable contributions, and others. All taxpayers are provided a standard deduction (or default amount) that may be taken without itemization, that is, without any explanation or verification that the taxpayer actually incurred the expenses. The year 2010 standard deduction was $5,700 for a single taxpayer, $8,400 for a head of household, and $11,400 for a couple filing jointly. Here again, the deduction amounts are indexed and change annually. Indexation preserves the real value of the deduction over time. Otherwise, a deduction that is fixed in nominal terms erodes in value over time with inflation. If the taxpayer has deductions that can be verified in excess of the standard amount, the taxpayer may itemize those deductions on Schedule A of the Form 1040, listing the qualified expenditures. Itemized deductions are permitted for medical expenses (in excess of 7.5 percent of AGI), state and local taxes (property and income taxes, but not sales taxes), mortgage interest, charitable contributions, unreimbursed job expenses, and other miscellaneous deductions. Table 14.1 lists the 2010 personal exemption and standard deductions for three types of taxpayers.

Like personal exemptions, itemized deductions are sometimes also subject to a high-income phaseout once a threshold level of AGI is reached. For 2010 the limit on itemized deductions expired. Under current law, however, the limit is slated to return in 2011 at pre-2006 levels.

The phaseouts on itemized deductions and personal exemptions are intended to add more progressivity to the income tax structure. Although they

TABLE 14.1 Personal Exemptions and Standard Deductions, 2010

	Single Filer	Married Couple Filing Jointly	Family of Four
Personal exemption(s)	$3,650	$ 7,300	$14,600
Standard deduction	$5,700	$11,400	$11,400
Total	$9,350	$18,700	$26,000

Source: U.S. Tax Form 1040, 2010.

may accomplish that goal, it would be far simpler to build progressivity into the tax rate structure directly than to do it indirectly through high-income phaseouts. In recent years Congress has preferred to flatten the rate structure, reducing the apparent progressivity of the income tax, while at the same time adding high-income phaseouts that increase the progressivity of the tax. This is one area of tax policy where simplification has certainly taken a backseat to other policy objectives, like raising revenue while giving the appearance of lowering tax rates.

Taxable Income Thresholds

The effect of personal exemptions and the standard deduction is to provide a taxable income threshold that must be met in order for a taxpayer to have a tax liability. The last row of Table 14.1 provides the taxable income threshold for each type of taxpayer in the year 2010. A single filer, for example, was not required to pay income tax unless her taxable income was above $9,350. A married couple filing jointly that year had a taxable income threshold of $18,700. A family of four had a taxable income threshold of $26,000. These taxable income thresholds are actually underestimates of the true thresholds because they do not take into account other features of the tax code to determine the level of income that must be exceeded in order to have a tax liability. Income tax credits likely to be used by taxpayers make additional income effectively exempt from taxation. Those credits can include the Earned Income Tax Credit (EITC), Making Work Pay tax credit, child and dependent care tax credits, and other credits. Thus, the true taxable income thresholds are likely to be higher than those listed in Table 14.1.

INCOME TAX RATE STRUCTURES

William Simon, former secretary of the Treasury, has said that "There appears to be a widespread consensus that an element of progression is desirable in the tax structure." Mr. Simon is quite right, but there is always a lively debate over just how much progression! Indeed, the political debate leading up to the 2008 presidential election and the subsequent political rhetoric on both sides have served to highlight this reality. Over the years since 1913, the U.S. income tax rate structure has always been progressive, although the degree of progression has varied widely. For example, in the 1950s a family with one-half the median income faced a marginal tax rate of zero, whereas a family at twice the median income faced a marginal tax rate of 22 percent. By the early 1990s, however, those marginal tax rates were 15 and 28 percent, respectively.[1] A more dramatic example of changing views of appropriate progression in the income tax is that of changes in the top marginal tax rate applied to the highest income bracket. Prior to 1981, the top marginal tax rate was 70 percent. That rate was reduced by the Economic Recovery Tax Act of 1981 (ERTA81) to 50 percent and was reduced further by the Tax Reform Act of 1986 (TRA86) to 28 percent. Since that time, the top marginal rate was increased to 39.6 percent with the 1993 Omnibus Reconciliation Act (OBRA93), and then reduced to 35 percent with the 2001 Economic Growth and Tax Relief Reconciliation Act (EGTRA) rate reductions.

Graduated Tax Rate Structure

The structure of income tax rates in the United States is graduated, with the marginal tax rate rising as taxable income rises. Table 14.2 provides the tax rates for the year 2010 as a recent example of the tax rate structure. This is a rate structure with five distinct rates ranging from 10 to 35 percent. As taxable income rises, higher rates are applied. For a single person, taxable income up to the amount $8,375 was taxed at the rate of 10 percent. Income in excess of that amount, up to $34,000, was taxed at the rate of 15 percent. Income above that amount, up to $82,400, was taxed at the rate of 25 percent. Still higher income, but less than $171,850, was taxed at the rate of 28 percent. Above that level, up to $373,650, income was taxed at 33 percent. Finally, all income in excess of $373,650 was taxed at the rate of 35 percent.

A married couple filing a joint return follows a different tax rate schedule. The same tax rates apply, but the income break points where the tax rates change are different. Table 14.2 reports that the couple paid a tax rate of 10 percent on taxable income up to $16,750 in 2010. Then, the 15 percent tax rate was applied on income in excess of that amount, up to $68,000. The 25 percent rate was applied on income in excess of that amount, up to $137,300. The 28 percent rate was applied on income in excess of that amount, up to $209,250. Beyond that level, the 33 percent rate was applied on income up to $373,650. Income in excess of that amount was taxed at the 35 percent rate.

In order to illustrate how these rate structures are applied, the following example is provided. It is important to understand that these tax rates are *marginal* tax rates, applied to income within each of the taxable income brackets specified. That is, each tax rate is applied only to taxable income within the income range specified for that rate.

TABLE 14.2 Tax Rates for U.S. Income Tax, 2010

Schedule X—If your filing status is Single

If your taxable income is: Over—	But not over—	The tax is:	of the amount over—
$ 0	$ 8,375	......10%	$ 0
8,375	34,000	$837.50 + 15%	8,375
34,000	82,400	4,681.25 + 25%	34,000
82,400	171,650	16,781.25 + 28%	82,400
171,850	378,650	41,827.25 + 33%	171,850
373,650	......	108,421.25 + 35%	373,650

Schedule Y-1—If your fling status is Married filing jointly or Qualifying widow(er)

If your taxable income is: Over—	But not over—	The tax is:	of the amount over—
$ 0	$ 16,750	......10%	$ 0
16,750	68,000	$1,675.00 + 15%	16,750
68,000	137,300	9,362.50 + 25%	68,000
137,900	209,250	26,687.50 + 28%	137,300
209,250	373,650	46,833.50 + 33%	209,250
373,650	......	101,085.50 + 35%	373,650

Source: IRS Form 1040 Instructions, 2010, p. 98.

Tax Computation Examples

Suppose that Bob is a single fellow and has a taxable income of $30,000. His tax is computed as 10 percent of the first $8,375 of income plus 15 percent of the remainder of his income: Tax = 0.10($8,375) + 0.15($30,000 − $8,375). His tax liability is $4,081. Notice that although his marginal tax rate is 15 percent, his average tax rate is ATR = $4081/$30,000 = 0.136, or 13.6 percent.

Now consider Elizabeth who is single and has taxable income of $157,000. Her tax is 10 percent of the first $8,375, plus 15 percent of the income up to $34,000, plus 25 percent of the income up to $82,400, plus 28 percent of rest of her income: Tax = 0.10($8,375) + 0.15($34,000 − 8,375) + 0.25($82,400 − 34,000) + 0.28($157,000 − $82,400). Her tax liability is $37,699. Although she is in the 28 percent marginal tax bracket, her average tax rate is 24.0 percent ($37,699/$157,000).

Figures 14.1 and 14.2 illustrate the 2010 tax rate structures for single filers and married couples filing jointly. Each of the tax rates is illustrated on the vertical axis, with the rates plotted as a function of taxable income on the horizontal axis. The tax rate structure looks like a staircase when it is plotted. As a result, we call this a *step function*. Each tax bracket plots as a step. The width of the step's *tread* is determined by the taxable income amounts

FIGURE 14.1 Tax Rates for Single Filers, 2001

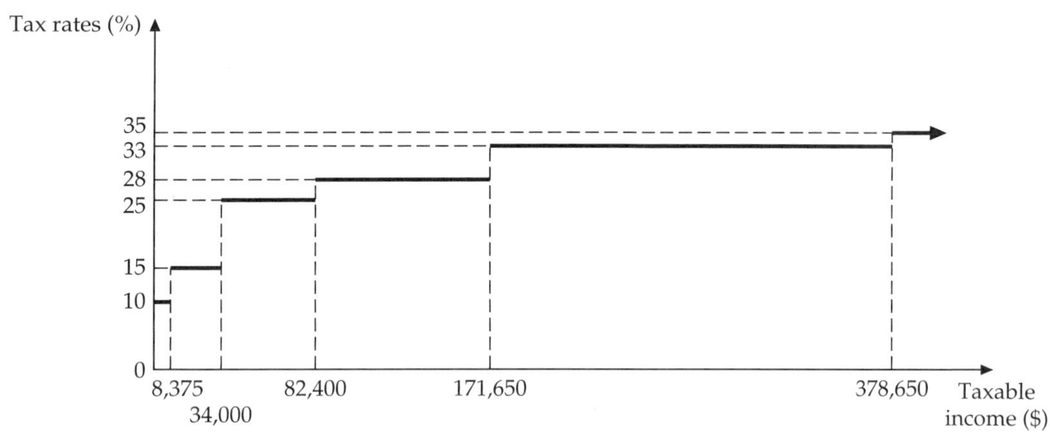

FIGURE 14.2 Tax Rates for Married Couples Filing Jointly, 2001

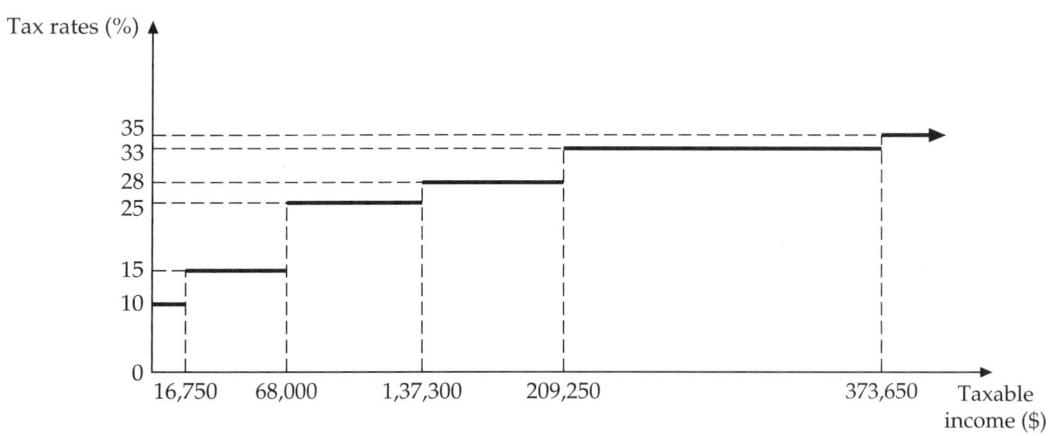

specified for that bracket. The height of the *riser* is determined by the increase in marginal tax rate applied as income rises. Notice that the risers in the step function look the same for the married couple, but the treads are wider. They are not, however, twice as wide. That is, a couple is not treated as two individuals.

DEDUCTIBILITY AND ITS EFFECTS

Income taxes at both the federal and state levels permit deductibility of various types of expenditures. Taxpayers are allowed to deduct certain expenditures from their taxable income, thereby reducing their tax liability. The effect of deductibility is to lower the after-tax price of any good or service that is deductible. For example, if expenditures on medical care are deductible and the marginal tax rate is 28 percent, a deduction of $100 for a laboratory test reduces tax liability by $28. Thus, the effective price of the laboratory test is $72. If the state income tax also permits a deduction for medical expenditures and the state marginal tax rate is 5 percent, the cost of the laboratory test is reduced by another $5, bringing the cost down to $67. Because the after-tax price of goods and services is reduced due to deductibility, the effect is to subsidize expenditures on those goods and services.

Deductibility at the Federal Level

Every taxpayer has the opportunity to itemize deductions, although most taxpayers simply take the standard deduction ($5,700 for a single filer or $11,400 for a couple filing jointly in 2010). If you have deductible expenses in excess of the standard deduction, you may itemize those deductions on your tax return and subtract them from your income in determining your taxable income. Taxpayers may elect to take the standard deduction, however, without itemization even if their actual expenditures are less than the standard deduction. No questions are asked for those electing the standard deduction. Itemizers may be asked for proof of expenditures claimed in their deductions if they are audited by the IRS.

What Is Deductible?

For those taxpayers electing to itemize, a wide range of expenditures are deductible on the U.S. income tax. Schedule A of Form 1040 permits a taxpayer to itemize expenditures for the following items:

1. Medical and dental care (Expenses in excess of 7.5 percent of AGI may be deducted.)
2. Taxes paid
    - State and local income or sales taxes
    - Real estate taxes
    - Personal property taxes
    - Other taxes

3. Interest paid
   - Home mortgage interest
   - Investment interest
4. Gifts to charity
   - Cash gifts
   - Other than cash gifts
5. Casualty and theft losses
6. Job expenses (Expenses in excess of 2 percent of AGI may be deducted.)
   - Unreimbursed employee expenses
   - Job travel
   - Union dues
   - Job educational expenses
   - Tax preparation fees

The taxpayer then adds the total of all itemized deductions and subtracts the total of itemized deductions from AGI in computing taxable income. Expenditures on any of the above items are effectively reduced by the marginal tax rate times the expenditure. For example, a taxpayer in the 25 percent marginal tax bracket who pays $5,000 to his state government for income taxes will have his federal tax liability reduced by $1,000 (0.25 times $5,000), making his net state income tax just $4,000. In this way, federal deductibility subsidizes state income tax–financed activity.

What Is the Effect of Deductibility on the Effective Tax Rate?

Deductibility has the effect of reducing the price of deductible goods and services. Medical and dental care, state and local income and property taxes, charitable contributions, and other deductible goods are all made cheaper as the result of deductibility. The extent of the reduction in price, of course, depends on the marginal tax rate. The higher the marginal tax rate, the more deductibility reduces the price. If the marginal tax rate is 25 percent, for example, deductibility of dental care expenditures reduces the price of dental care by 25 percent. If a six-month checkup and cleaning at your dentist's office costs you $100, deductibility reduces that price to $75. As a result of the lower price, you are likely to demand more dental care. Deductibility reduces the price and thereby increases the quantity of the good or service demanded. How much more is demanded depends on the price elasticity of demand and the income elasticity of demand. Recall that any price reduction creates a substitution effect and an income effect, so the response depends on both the price elasticity of demand and the income elasticity of demand.

By reducing tax liability, deductibility also reduces the effective rate of income taxation. Suppose, for example, that your income is $50,000 and your tax liability in the absence of itemization (just taking the standard deduction) is $10,000. That means your effective tax rate (average) is 20 percent (10,000/50,000). Now, if instead of taking the standard deduction you itemize your deductions, resulting in a reduced tax liability of $8,000, your effective tax rate is also reduced to 16 percent (8,000/50,000). Deductibility has reduced your average effective tax rate.

State Deductibility and Reciprocal Deductibility

States with income taxes also sometimes provide **state deductibility** for selected goods and services. For example, a state may make medical care expenses deductible. If that state has a 5 percent marginal income tax rate, a dollar of medical care expenditure results in a $0.05 reduction in state tax liability. That may come in addition to the reduction in federal income tax liability due to federal deductibility. Aside from state deductibility for specific types of expenditures, it is important to recognize that states may also permit general deductibility for all federal income taxes paid, just as the federal government permits deductibility of state income taxes and local property taxes paid. With each level of government permitting the taxes paid to the other level of government to be deducted from its tax base, there is a combined reduction in the effective tax rate.

Federal and state income tax systems may permit **reciprocal deductibility**. In this case, the federal income tax paid is deductible on the state income tax and the state income tax paid is deductible on the federal income tax. The effect of reciprocal deductibility is to provide a kind of compounded reduction in the combined rate of taxation. Federal deductibility reduces the effective rate of state taxation. State deductibility reduces the effective rate of federal taxation. The combined rate of taxation is reduced in a compounded way because each level of government provided deductibility for taxes paid to the other level of government.

In order to illustrate the effects of combined federal and state marginal tax rates, depending on the nature of deductibility, Table 14.3 illustrates the combined tax rates in the absence of deductibility and in the presence of two deductibility regimes. The second column of the table provides the general expression for the combined tax rates under the various regimes. Columns

TABLE 14.3 Effects of Deductibility on Combined Federal and State Tax Rates

Tax Structure Characteristic	General Case	Example 1	Example 2
Federal marginal tax rate	t_f	0.28	0.28
State marginal tax rate	t_s	0.05	0.10
Combined marginal tax rate with no deductibility	$t_f + t_s$	0.33	0.38
Combined marginal tax rate with state tax deducted against federal tax only	$t_f + t_s(1 - t_f)$	0.32	0.35
Combined marginal tax rate with reciprocal deductibility	$[t_f + t_s(1 - 2t_s)]/[1 - t_f t_s]$	0.31	0.33

Source: From FISHER. *State and Local Public Finance* with InfoTraC®, 3E. © 2007 South-Western, a part of Cengage Learning, Inc. Reproduced by permission. www.cengage.com/permissions.

three and four provide specific numerical examples. In the first example, listed in column 3 of Table 14.3, we see that a federal marginal tax rate of 0.28 combined with a state marginal tax rate of 0.05 would yield a combined tax rate of 0.33 in the absence of deductibility. With the state tax deductible on the federal return, however, the combined tax rate falls to 0.32, a reduction of 1 percent. With reciprocal deductibility, the combined tax rate falls another percentage point to 0.31. The second example simply raises the state marginal tax rate in order to illustrate the more powerful impact of deductibility in the presence of higher tax rates. When the state tax rate is raised to 0.10, the effect of federal deductibility is to reduce the combined tax rate from 0.38 to 0.35, a three-percentage-point reduction. With reciprocal deductibility, the combined tax rate falls to 0.33, a full five percentage points lower than the combined rate in the absence of deductibility. These two examples illustrate the powerful effects deductibility has on the effective combined marginal tax rate in a federal-state system of taxation.

Economic Effects of Deductibility

Deductibility changes prices and therefore has both efficiency and equity effects that must be considered. Efficiency effects have to do with how deductibility changes the quantity of the good demanded. Equity effects have to do with how deductibility redistributes tax burdens. These effects result from the substitution and income effects due to changes in the price. Because deductibility reduces prices, there is a substitution effect as taxpayers substitute deductible expenditures for nondeductible expenditures in their budgets. An income effect also arises because deductibility raises the purchasing power of the taxpayer's income, causing more of all normal goods to be demanded.

Efficiency Effects

The efficiency effect of deductibility is based in part on the elasticity of demand for the goods and services made deductible by federal and state governments. As with any reduction in price, the effect of that reduction depends on the elasticity of demand. The greater the price elasticity of demand, the larger the effect deductibility will have on the quantity demanded of the good or service. The greater the effect on quantity demanded, the larger the efficiency effect.

A service like medical care has a small price elasticity of demand. Most patients are not very sensitive to price when they need medical care—how much do you shop around for a low price when you need an appendectomy? As a result, such services will see very little increase in quantity demanded as a result of deductibility. Of course, some medical services are more sensitive to price. When the medical procedure does not involve a life-and-death situation, patients may be willing to shop around for providers that have lower prices. Patients may be quite responsive to the price of liposuction services. In this case, deductibility may have the effect of increasing the quantity demanded by a large amount. In the world of managed care, HMO (health maintenance organization) managers are very sensitive to price. Hence, patients are made more price-sensitive than they would be otherwise. As a result, we expect that deductibility plays an important role in increasing the demand for deductible services relative to nondeductible services.

An efficiency effect due to deductibility may be beneficial in the case of a public good like research and development. In that circumstance, we know that the private market will allocate too few resources to research and development because there is a positive externality that is ignored. If a pharmaceutical firm invests in the development of a new drug to treat a disease and in the process generates new knowledge of the disease and its effective treatment, there is no way for the firm to fully capture the benefit it generates. The improvement in general medical knowledge is a public good. Hence, a deduction for research and development expenditures by such firms can be efficiency enhancing, encouraging them to engage in activities that generate positive external benefits, as we discussed in Chapter 4. The deduction can act as a Pigouvian subsidy to encourage firms to produce the socially optimal output rate rather than the smaller privately optimal output rate. On the other hand, the efficiency effect of deductibility may be detrimental as in the case of medical expenditures for cosmetic purposes that have no positive externalities. In that situation, deductibility stimulates a larger quantity demanded and results in too many resources being allocated to provision of the service.

Equity Effects

Equity effects of deductibility occur as the after-tax prices of goods and services are altered and the burden of taxation is distributed accordingly. If the goods and services subject to deductibility are all consumed by high-income taxpayers, for example, the effect is to reduce the tax liability of those taxpayers relative to low-income taxpayers and also to reduce the progressiveness of the income tax system. Hence, the pattern of *who* takes advantage of the opportunity to itemize is important to analyze. Although you might think that the rich itemize and the poor take the standard deduction, thereby implying that deductibility makes the tax system less progressive than it would be otherwise, that is not necessarily the case. Although itemizers do tend to have higher incomes than nonitemizers, the amount of their deductions does not tend to rise proportionately with income. That is, the amount of their deductions *as a fraction of their income* falls. As a result, deductibility does not entirely undo the progressiveness of the income tax. For any particular good or service, however, the pattern of deductibility must be analyzed, as the demands for those goods and services each have unique income elasticities to consider.

U.S. INCOME TAX DESIGN AND POLICY ISSUES

The foundational issue of tax system design is defining the taxable unit. What is the essential social unit responsible for paying the income tax, individuals or families?

Taxable Unit

Prior to 1948 the **taxable unit** for the U.S. income tax was the individual, regardless of whether that individual was single or married. Furthermore, the individual's tax liability was independent of marital status. Under that regime, a husband and wife filed separate returns and each person paid tax on his or her own income. In this way, they were no different from single individuals. Beginning in 1948, however, the taxable unit was changed to be the family, rather than the individual, and **income splitting** was permitted.[2] Income splitting allows a married couple with an income of $50,000, for example, to be treated as two individuals with income of $25,000 each. The joint tax liability for a married couple is computed as twice the tax liability on half of their joint income. In terms of Figure 14.1, describing the tax rate structure for a single person, income splitting stretches the treads on the tax rate step function, making them twice as wide for a married couple. That has the effect of reducing the rate of progression in the tax structure for married couples. That reduction in progression is a tax advantage given to married couples. The reduction in tax can be considered a **marriage bonus** provided by the income tax system to married couples, compared to single persons with the same income.

Income splitting was justified on the argument that husbands and wives typically share their combined income equally. Their combined family income is used to pay for consumption expenditures required for the family, with savings set aside for the enjoyment of the children or in some other way used for the whole family. From this perspective, it would seem appropriate that married couples with the same income should pay the same income tax—a logical application of horizontal equity; that is, the division of income earned between the spouses should not matter. Couple A with income of $50,000, where the husband earns all the income and the wife earns no income, should be treated equally with couple B, where husband and wife each earn $25,000. This conclusion is firmly established in U.S. tax policy and is not challenged. Another implication of the income splitting view is that the tax liabilities of married couples should be computed by treating them as two individuals, each with half of the family income. Opinions on the wisdom of this tax policy differ. Should couple A be treated as an individual with income of $50,000 subject to a higher marginal income tax rate, or as two individuals each with income of $25,000 subject to lower marginal income tax rates? Here, we have a question of vertical equity where people's opinions differ due to their views on the appropriate degree of progression that should be embodied in the income tax. The introduction of income splitting caused the tax burdens of single persons and married couples with the same income to be different. The extent to which they differ depends on the degree of progression in the tax rates.

By 1969 changes in the tax law had made it possible for the tax liability of a single person to be as much as 40 percent higher than that of a married couple with the same income. Responding to pressure to remedy this situation, Congress adopted a new tax rate schedule for unmarried individuals.

According to that schedule, a single person's tax liability was limited to no more than 20 percent higher than that for a couple with the same income. As a consequence, it became possible that a person's tax liability could rise when he or she married (filing jointly instead of two single returns). Couples with earnings divided approximately 75 percent due to one spouse and 25 percent due to the other spouse, or more equally divided than that, could face a tax increase when they married. This created the so-called **marriage tax.** In 1981 the **two-earner deduction** was introduced in order to reduce the marriage tax. This was a deduction of 10 percent of the earnings of the spouse earning less. The effect of the deduction was to reduce the marriage tax. In 1986 the two-earner deduction was eliminated as it was deemed unnecessary as a result of the marginal tax rate reductions in the Tax Reform Act of 1986 (TRA86). Recent proposals to reduce or eliminate the marriage tax have suggested that the standard deduction be increased for married couples filing jointly. Resolution of the policy dilemma requires more than a simple increase in the standard deduction for married couples filing jointly, however, as we will see.

Marriage Bonuses and Penalties

A couple who marry may find that their income tax liability is affected quite dramatically. In most cases, their joint tax liability will be less than it was when they were single. But, for an increasing number of couples, their joint tax liability may rise. These so-called marriage bonuses and penalties are an interesting and difficult area of income tax policy. The issue is interesting because it raises the prospect that a couple may consider the tax consequences of their relationship in addition to the pure matters of the heart.[3] The issue is difficult because resolving the problem of marriage penalties involves contradictory policy effects. That is, to resolve one policy aspect of the issue makes another aspect of the policy issue worse.

First, let us consider an example of a couple who experience a marriage bonus and a couple who experience a marriage penalty. Table 14.4(A) provides a simple example of a couple where the husband has income of $75,000 per year and the wife has no income. In this case, their joint tax liability as a couple is $3,965 less than the sum of their individual tax liabilities, as illustrated in the table detail. Hence, the couple experiences a rather substantial marriage bonus. They pay less in tax because they are married. Notice why their tax liability is smaller as a couple. They have a lower taxable income and more of their income is taxed at lower rates. In contrast, Table 14.4(B) illustrates the case of a couple who experience a marriage penalty. This couple has the same total income, $75,000, but each spouse earns half of the income. Their joint liability is $1,525 more than the sum of their individual liabilities. Hence, their tax is higher when they file as a married couple than if they were to file as two single individuals. This couple is subject to a marriage penalty. Notice why they pay more as a married couple. Although their taxable income is the same, more of their income is taxed at higher rates. These examples not only illustrate the effect of marriage on tax

TABLE 14.4A A Marriage Bonus Example

	Husband	Wife	Couple
Adjusted gross income	$75,000	0	$75,000
Less personal exemptions	$ 2,900	0	$ 5,800
Less standard deduction	$ 4,550	0	$ 7,600
Equals taxable income	$67,550	0	$61,600
Taxable at 15%	$27,050	0	$45,200
Taxable at 27.5%	$39,500	0	$16,400
Taxable at 30.5%	$ 2,000		
Tax liability	$15,255	0	$11,290
Marriage bonus			$ 3,965

Source: Computed from data in Tables 14.1 and 14.2.

TABLE 14.4B A Marriage Penalty Example

	Husband	Wife	Couple
Adjusted gross income	$37,500	$37,500	$75,000
Less personal exemptions	$ 2,900	$ 2,900	$ 5,800
Less standard deduction	$ 4,550	$ 4,550	$ 7,600
Equals taxable income	$30,050	$30,050	$61,600
Taxable at 15%	$27,050	$27,050	$45,200
Taxable at 27.5%	$ 3,000	$ 3,000	$16,400
Tax liability	$ 4,882.50	$ 4,882.50	$11,290
Marriage penalty			$ 1,525

Source: Computed from data in Tables 14.1 and 14.2.

liability for two types of couples, they also illustrate a more general point that the distribution of earnings between spouses has important implications for tax liability. Couples with more equal earnings are more likely to be subject to marriage penalties.

The distribution of both marriage bonuses and marriage penalties by adjusted gross income for the tax year 1996 was analyzed in a major study by the CBO (1997). Their analysis found that a majority of couples with AGI less than $20,000 benefit from marriage bonuses (63 percent) or are unaffected (25 percent). Only 12 percent of the returns in this income class have a marriage penalty. At higher income levels, however, the number of returns with penalties rises to 44 and 54 percent. Of couples with income between \$20,000 and \$50,000, 44 percent of the returns have penalties, whereas 55 percent have bonuses. For couples with incomes above \$50,000, those figures are reversed with 54 percent of the returns with penalties and 44 percent with bonuses.

How big are these marriage bonuses or penalties? The CBO analysis found that the average penalty is 2.0 percent of AGI, whereas the bonuses average 2.3 percent of AGI. The size of the marriage bonuses and penalties varies inversely with AGI, when measured as a percentage of AGI. The income tax confers marriage bonuses amounting to a total of \$32.9 billion, whereas it inflicts penalties amounting to \$28.8 billion. The net effect is a \$4.1 billion net marriage bonus. Hence, on balance, the income tax pays couples more in marriage bonuses than it requires in marriage penalties. Most of the bonuses and penalties are in the higher AGI classes.

The distribution of marriage bonuses and penalties is not random, however. Predictable circumstances exist under which a couple can expect either a bonus or a penalty. Most marriage bonuses occur when the couple has one spouse earning all of the income. Among couples with a marriage bonus, 77 percent have one spouse earning all of the couple's income. Marriage penalties occur for couples with a more equal distribution of earnings among the spouses.

The issue of marriage bonuses and penalties is a difficult problem to solve because there are inherent policy conflicts involved with the income tax and marital status. Table 14.5 illustrates those conflicts. In the first row of the table we have two couples with equal family income of \$60,000. Couple A is married and each spouse earns \$30,000 per year. Couple B is also a married couple, but one spouse earns \$60,000 and the other spouse has no income. A reasonable policy objective to apply to these couples is to assure horizontal equity so that they pay the same tax. A second policy objective to consider is marriage neutrality. If a tax system is marriage neutral, a couple pays the same tax, regardless of their marital status. This objective is illustrated in the first and last columns of Table 14.5. The tax system would treat couple A in the same manner regardless of whether they are married (as in row 1) or not

TABLE 14.5 Policy Conflicts and Marriage Bonuses/Penalties

Couple A: Married with each spouses earning \$30,000	Policy objective: Same tax (horizontal equity, equal treatment of married couples)	*Couple B:* Married with one spouse earning \$60,000
Policy objective: Marriage neutrality (horizontal equity)		Policy objective: Marriage neutrality (horizontal equity)
Couple A: Not married, each spouse earning \$30,000	Policy objective: Progressive tax (vertical equity)	*Couple B:* Not married, one spouse earning \$60,000

Source: Modified from CBO 1997.

married (as in row 3). In similar fashion, the tax system would treat couple B in a neutral way, whether they are married (as in row 1) or not married (as in row 3). Finally, another important policy objective is that of applying a progressive rate of taxation to income. As income rises, a progressive income tax would have a rising marginal tax rate. This policy objective is illustrated in row 3 of Table 14.5. Under a progressive income tax couple B, with a combined income of $60,000 per year, pays a higher marginal tax rate than couple A, who each earn $30,000 per year.

The fundamental difficulty in marriage tax policy is that these three policy objectives cannot be met without creating marriage bonuses and penalties for some couples. If we are willing to give up any one of the three policy objectives, marriage bonuses and penalties can be eliminated. As long as we wish to attain all three policy objectives, however, we will necessarily have marriage bonuses and penalties in our income tax system. Recent proposals to remedy the problem of the marriage tax have emphasized increasing the standard deduction for married couples filing jointly. Although that partially resolves the problem, depending on the size of the increase, it does not completely harmonize the contradictory policy objectives we are trying to achieve in the U.S. income tax. Advocates of a flat tax point out that under their proposal the marriage tax goes away. That is correct, but they achieve that outcome by eliminating progressive tax rates and that violates the goal of vertical equity desired by others.

There is just no way around the policy obstacle that you must live with violation of one of the three policy objectives. Take your pick. You can have any two, but only two, of the following three outcomes:

- Horizontal equity
- Marriage neutrality
- Progressive tax rate structure

The only real solution to the problem is to distinguish among taxpayer units by varying the size of personal exemptions according to the number of people in the family and the family income level. Pechman points out that "This procedure could be used to achieve almost any desired degree of differentiation among families while avoiding the anomalies produced by income splitting" (1987, 105). The tax rates for single persons and married couples could be made equal by making the tax rate advantage of income splitting available to single individuals or by forcing married couples to use the same tax rates as single individuals. This would reduce tax revenues, which would have to be made up by overall tax rate increases.

Earned Income Tax Credit

The earned income tax credit (EITC) is a mechanism in the income tax structure that is designed to provide assistance to low-income working households. As a refundable credit, the EITC provides a reduction in tax for those with a tax liability or an outright payment for those with no tax liability (or a liability less than the credit for which they qualify). Steuerle (1990) traced the origins of the

EITC and points out that the credit was originally designed as a mechanism to encourage Aid to Families with Dependent Children (AFDC) recipients to work. As such, the credit can be considered a work incentive program more so than a welfare program.[4] The EITC was created in the Tax Reduction Act of 1975.

In order to qualify for the credit, a taxpayer must be working and have positive earned income. A taxpayer with two children and earned income of $9,000 in 2010 for example, would have qualified for a credit of $3,600 reflecting a credit rate of 40 percent. The maximum credit that the taxpayer with two children could earn that year was $5,036. Three separate credit schedules are used for the EITC, depending on the number of dependents in the family. Once the maximum credit is reached, additional income has no effect on the credit amount over a certain range of income as the credit is constant over that range. At higher income levels the credit is phased out and eventually the household may have income too high to qualify for the credit. For a family with two children, the credit phaseout begins at an income of $16,450 in 2010 and the credit is fully phased out by the time income reaches $40,363.

An important feature of the EITC is that the credit is **refundable**. This means that a qualifying taxpayer can receive the full amount of the credit even if the taxpayer has an income tax liability that is smaller than the credit. The difference is refunded. For example, if the taxpayer owes $1,200 in taxes and qualifies for a credit of $3,200, the taxpayer receives a check for $2,000 from the IRS. In addition, the refundable credit is also **frontloaded**. An advance payment option permits a taxpayer to receive the credit in her paychecks during the year, rather than wait until the end of the year after filing her tax return. The EITC provides substantial assistance to low-income families. In 2009, for example, the IRS reported that a total of 25.9 million households received credits totaling $57.9 billion, implying an average credit of $2,235.[5]

Figure 14.3 illustrates the EITC, plotting the credit as a function of earnings. A household with zero earnings receives no tax credit, so the graph of

FIGURE 14.3 Earned Income Tax Credit Design

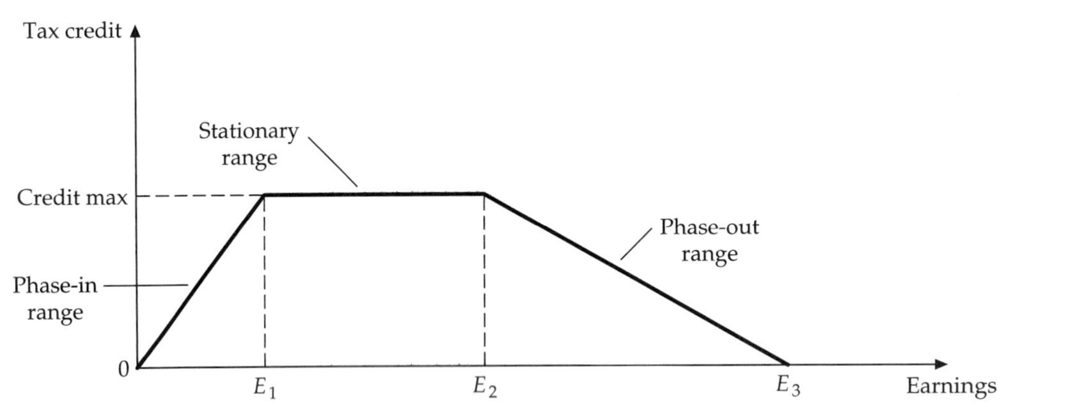

the credit begins at the origin. As earnings rise, the tax credit initially rises as well. Over this phase-in range, the taxpayer receives a credit equal to a portion of earnings. The credit reaches a maximum amount when earnings are equal to E_1 in Figure 14.3. Over the range of earnings from E_1 to E_2 the credit remains at the maximum amount. This range of earnings is called the *stationary range* because the credit amount does not change with earnings. Once earnings reach E_2, however, the credit begins a phaseout. From E_2 to E_3 each additional dollar of earnings reduces the credit amount. At earnings level E_3, the household receives no credit. Its income has risen to the level where it no longer qualifies for the credit.

The values of the parameters E_1, E_2, and E_3; the credit maximum; and the slopes of the phase-in and phase-out ranges are all adjusted periodically by Congress. Table 14.6 reports the 2010 EITC parameter values for single filers. A filer with two children, for example, receives a credit rate of 40 percent of earnings up to a maximum credit of $5,036. Families are eligible for the maximum credit with earnings of E_1 = $12,590. A phase-out rate of 21.06 percent applies over the phase-out range with a beginning earnings level of E_2 = $16,450 and continues up through earnings of E_3 = $40,363. The EITC parameter values are somewhat more generous for married couple filers, but the basic structure of the credit is the same. Earnings levels E_1, E_2, and E_3 are indexed to the inflation rate and are adjusted annually.

Taxpayers are not eligible to receive the tax credit if their income from interest (both taxable and nontaxable), dividends, net rent and royalty income (positive), capital gains (net, positive), and net passive income (positive) that is not self-employment exceeds $3,100. This income is called *disqualified income* for the purposes of computing eligibility for the EITC.

The Tax Policy Center (2007) analysis of the EITC revealed that about 15 percent of all taxpayers receive benefits from the EITC, with more than 87 percent of the benefit going to taxpayers with income of $30,000 or less. The average benefit for taxpayers with income of less than $10,000 was

TABLE 14.6 Earned Income Tax Credit Parameters, Single Filers, 2010

					Phase-Out Range	
Number of Children	Credit Rate (Percent)	Minimum Earnings for Maximum Credit (E_1)	Maximum Credit	Phase-Out Rate (Percent)	*Beginning Earnings (E_2)*	*Ending Earnings (E_3)*
0	7.65	$ 5,980	$ 457	7.65	$ 7,400	$13,460
1	34.00	$ 8,970	$3,050	15.98	$16,450	$35,535
2	40.00	$12,590	$5,036	21.06	$16,450	$40,363
3 or more	45.00	$12,590	$5,666	21.06	$16,450	$43,352

Source: Internal Revenue Service.

\$288, representing 125 percent of the tax they paid; that is, the credit is larger than their tax. For those with income of at least \$10,000 but less than \$20,000, the average credit was \$741, representing 113 percent of their tax.

Interaction with the Income Tax Structure

Once a family is in the phase-out range of the EITC, there is an interaction with the positive income tax that must be considered. Figure 14.4 illustrates this interaction. As income rises from zero to E_1 the household pays no tax and receives the credit. Once income reaches E_1, the credit is at its maximum. Further increases in income result in no tax and no additional credit. After income reaches the level E_2, however, the credit begins a phaseout. In this range, the household still pays no tax, but their EITC is reduced as their income rises. Once the household income reaches E_t, the income tax threshold has been reached and the household must begin to pay positive income tax. Of course, their EITC is larger than their income tax liability, so they still receive a check from the IRS. There comes a point, however, where their income tax liability begins to exceed their EITC. That income level is labeled E_v in Figure 14.4 and represents a break-even point where positive tax liability first exceeds the EITC amount. Beyond this point, the credit is phased out and income tax liability rises. Once income reaches the level E_3, the household no longer qualifies for the EITC. At this point the household is out of the credit program and in the normal income tax system.

Households are confronted with four different tax rates over the income range from zero to E_3. For income levels between zero and E_1, there is no tax but an EITC credit rate that results in a combined effective marginal tax rate equal to minus the credit rate. For income levels from E_1 to E_2, there is no tax and a constant credit, yielding a combined effective marginal tax rate of zero. For income levels from E_2 to E_t, there is no tax but an EITC credit phase-out rate is applied, resulting in a combined effective tax rate equal to

FIGURE 14.4 Earned Income Tax Credit and the Income Tax Structure

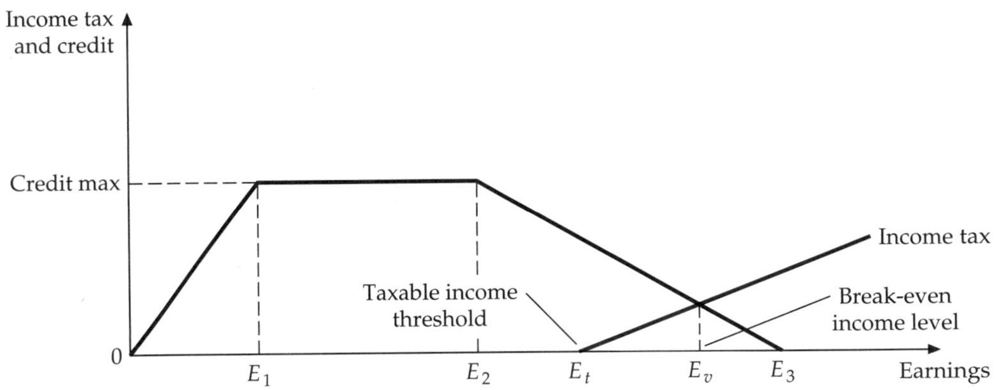

the credit phase-out rate. For income levels from E_t to E_3, both a marginal income tax rate and an EITC phase-out rate are applied. The effective combined marginal tax rate is the sum of these two rates.

A family of four in 2010, for example, began to pay income tax once their income exceeded $26,000 (the sum of four personal exemptions of $3,650 and a standard deduction of $11,400; see Table 14.1). The marginal tax rate applied to income was 10 percent. A family with income in this range is also eligible for the EITC, albeit at a phase-out rate, so there is an important interaction to consider. On the margin, income is taxed at the 10 percent rate above the income threshold of $26,000. But at that level, the EITC phase-out rate was also 21.06 percent. Thus, each additional dollar of income above $26,000 was taxed at a 10 percent rate and subjected to an EITC phaseout at a 21.06 percent rate. The EITC phase-out acts as an implicit tax. The combination of the income tax rate and the implicit tax due to the EITC phaseout yields a combined tax rate of 28.95 percent. Thus, households with income in this range were subject to very high marginal tax rates. Indeed, the rate applied to these low-income families exceeded the maximum income rate of 28 percent that was applied to high-income taxpayers with incomes in excess of $209,250 (see Table 14.2). This is just one example of the reality that some of the highest tax rates in the United States are paid by low-income families.

Interaction with Other Means-Tested Assistance Programs

How is the EITC counted when a family's income is evaluated for other welfare support? Well, the EITC a family receives is *not* counted as income for purposes of qualifying for other means-tested assistance programs such as TANF, Medicaid, SSI, food stamps, and low-income housing programs. Furthermore, the EITC credit amount is not counted in the computation of benefit levels in these programs. This has been the case since 1990, but prior to that time, the credit was counted as part of the eligibility standard.

Changes in U.S. Income Tax Policy

Over the past 20 years there have been a number of major legislative changes to U.S. tax law. Table 14.7 provides a brief summary of selected provisions of the implemented tax acts.

PAYROLL TAXES

Payroll taxes are a related form of taxation that have a more narrow base than income taxes. Rather than tax a broad range of income, a payroll tax typically applies only to wage and salary income. There are no deductions or credits and no return is filed. Payroll tax is withheld from each paycheck by the employer. If the taxpayer contributes more payroll tax than is required by law, the difference is returned via an income tax credit. This is the principal form of tax used for the social security system and Medicare at the federal

TABLE 14.7 U.S. Tax Acts, 1981–2010

Act	Provisions
Economic Recovery Act of 1981 (ERTA81)	▪ Phased in a 23% reduction in individual tax rates: top rate reduced from 70% to 50% ▪ Indexed individual tax parameters (beginning in 1985) ▪ Created a 10% exclusion for two-earner married couples (subject to $3,000 cap) ▪ Allowed all working taxpayers to establish IRAs ▪ Expanded provisions for employee stock ownership plans (ESOPs) ▪ Replaced $200 interest exclusion with 15% net interest exclusion ($900 cap) (begin in 1985)
Tax Reform Act of 1986 (TRA86)	▪ Reduced individual income tax rates: top rate reduced to 28% ▪ Repealed capital gains exclusion ▪ Increased personal exemption from $1,080 to $2,000 ▪ Increased standard deduction from $3,670 to $5,000 (joint filers) ▪ Repealed second earner deduction ▪ Repealed sales tax deduction for individuals ▪ Established a 2% floor for miscellaneous itemized deductions
Omnibus Budget Reconciliation Act of 1990 (OBRA90)	▪ Created new 31% individual tax rate ▪ Capped capital gains tax rate at 28% ▪ Temporarily limited itemized deductions (through 1995) ▪ Temporarily phased out personal exemptions (through 1995)
Omnibus Reconciliation Act of 1993 (ORA93)	▪ Created 36% and 39.6% tax rates for individuals ▪ Increased taxable portion of SS benefits ▪ Permanently extended phaseout of personal exemption and limit on itemized deductions ▪ Created 35% tax rate for corporations
Tax Relief Act of 1997 (TRA97)	▪ Established $500 child credit ▪ Established HOPE and Lifetime Learning education tax credits ▪ Phased in estate tax exemption equivalent from $600,000 to $1 million (in 2006) ▪ Reduced capital gains tax rate from 28% to 20% ▪ Established Roth IRAs; increased income limits for deductible IRAs ▪ Established education IRAs
Economic Growth and Tax Relief Reconciliation Act of 2001 (EGTRRA)	▪ Phased in reduction in individual tax rates: top rate reduced to 35% (through 2010) ▪ Created new 10% tax rate bracket ▪ Phased in increase in child tax credit to $1,000 (through 2010) ▪ Phased in marriage penalty relief provisions (through 2010) ▪ Phased in repeal of limit on itemized deductions (through 2010) ▪ Phased in increase in IRA contribution limit to $5,000 (through 2010) ▪ Increased individual AMT exemption to $49,000 ($35,750) for joint (single) returns (through 2004) ▪ Phased in repeal of limit on personal exemptions (through 2010) ▪ Created above-the-line deduction for higher education expenses (through 2005) ▪ Increased education IRA contribution limit to $2,000 (through 2010)

TABLE 14.7 U.S. Tax Acts, 1981–2010 (Continued)

Jobs and Growth Tax Relief and Reconciliation Act of 2003 (JGTRRA)	▪ Lowered top individual income tax rate on dividends to 15%/5%/0% (through 2008) ▪ Accelerated the 2006 tax cuts from EGTRRA ▪ Accelerated marriage penalty relief provisions from EGTRRA (through 2004) ▪ Accelerated child tax credit increase to $1,000 (through 2004) ▪ Increased individual AMT exemption to $58,000 ($40,250) for joint (single) returns (through 2004) ▪ Reduced top tax rate on capital gains to 15%/5%/0% (through 2008)
Tax Relief, Unemployment Insurance Reauthorization, and Job Creation Act of 2010	▪ Temporary extension of 2001 EGTRRA tax rates for all taxpayers ▪ Temporary extension of 2003 JGTRRA tax relief on dividends and capital gains ▪ Temporary 2% reduction in employer's portion of payroll tax ▪ Earned income tax credit modification and simplification ▪ Temporary AMT relief

Source: Author, updated compilation based on Tempalski (2006).

level in the United States and many other countries. At the state and local levels, some states apply a form of income tax that is essentially a payroll tax and some cities apply a form of payroll tax called an **occupational tax.**

Payroll Tax Base and Rates

The U.S. federal payroll tax is used to fund two distinct sets of programs: Old-Age, Survivors, and Disability Insurance (OASDI) and Medicare Hospital Insurance (HI). Workers covered by the social insurance programs are subject to payroll taxes, with separate aspects of the programs applying separate rates. Wage and salaried workers are subject to the taxes under the Federal Insurance Contributions Act (FICA) of Chapter 21 of the Internal Revenue Code. Self-employed workers are subject to the tax, as specified in the Self-Employed Contributions Act (SECA) contained in Chapter 2 of the Internal Revenue Code. These two payroll taxes are often called by their acronyms FICA and SECA.

Table 14.8 illustrates the essential features of the payroll tax base. Both employer and employee pay a tax of 7.65 percent, making the total tax of

TABLE 14.8 FICA and SECA Tax Rates and Maximum Taxable Earnings, 2010

Rates Paid by Both Employer and Employee						
OASI	*DI*	*OASDI*	*HI*	*Total*	*Self-Employed Rate*	**Maximum OASDI Taxable Earnings**
5.30%	0.90%	6.20%	1.45%	7.65%	15.3%	$106,800

Source: Social Security Administration, http://www.ssa.gov/oact/progdata/taxRates.html.

15.3 percent of payroll. The tax base is defined as adjusted gross income plus tax-exempt bond interest plus one-half of social security benefits. Above certain income thresholds workers are required to include part of their social security benefits. The total tax rate of 7.65 percent paid by employer and employee is made up of several components for specific purposes. The OASI tax rate is 5.3 percent and the disability insurance (DI) tax rate is 0.90 percent, making a combined total of 6.2 percent for OASDI. Wage and salary income is taxable under the OASDI portion of the tax up to an income limit that is indexed for inflation. The income limit in the year 2010 was $106,800. Beyond that level, wage and salary income is not subject to the OASDI portion of the payroll tax. As a result, the maximum tax that the employee and employer each pay is $6,622, for a total of $13,243. Another component of the total tax is the Medicare HI tax rate of 1.45 percent. Adding the OASDI and HI components gives the total tax rate of 7.65 percent. Under the HI portion of the payroll tax, all wage and salary income is subject to tax. Employed workers and their employers each pay half the tax. Because there is no limit on the income subject to tax on the HI portion, there is also no limit on the amount of tax.

The taxes are similar for self-employed workers, although there are some small differences. For both parts of the payroll tax, OASDI and HI, self-employed workers are required to pay the total amount, 15.3 percent, including both employer and employee halves. Self-employed workers may, however, deduct 7.65 percent of their net earnings before they compute their social security tax. In addition, they may deduct half of their social security tax paid as a business expense on their income tax. These two provisions are designed to make the tax treatment of employees and self-employed workers equivalent. Employees do not pay FICA tax on the value of the employer's FICA tax or the employer's income tax on the value of the employer's FICA tax, so self-employed workers are permitted the same treatment.

Social Security Benefits and Income Taxation

Social security benefits are reduced for some recipients with an income above a threshold level known as the *retirement earnings test exempt amount*. The earnings test exempt amount varies with the age of the social security recipient. In 2010, a retiree who had attained the normal retirement age (NRA) had an annual retirement earnings test amount of $37,680. If the retiree takes early retirement and has not yet attained NRA, the total exempt amount is $14,160. The Social Security Administration withholds $1 in benefits for each $2 of earnings exceeding the lower exempt amount (an implicit 50 percent tax) and $1 in benefits for each $3 of earnings in excess of the higher amount (an implicit 33.33 percent tax). For social security recipients of age 70 and older, there is no earnings test exempt amount.

Because social security benefits paid to individuals may also be subject to income tax, it is important to consider the income tax treatment of benefits. Table 14.9 lists the tax treatment of benefits. An individual with an income from $25,000 to $34,000 or a couple with an income from $32,000 to

TABLE 14.9 Income Taxation of Benefits

Income	Percent Taxed	Filing Status
$25,000 to $34,000	Up to 50%	Individual
$32,000 to $44,000		Joint
over $34,000	Up to 85%	Individual
over $44,000		Joint

Source: Social Security Administration, http://ssa-custhelp.ssa.gov/app/answers/detail/a_id/493.

$44,000 must pay income tax on up to 50 percent of the social security benefits received. A higher portion of benefits is subject to income tax for those with higher income. An individual with income over $34,000 or a couple with income over $44,000 must pay income tax on up to 85 percent of the benefits received. These income thresholds for taxation are not indexed, so an increasing number of beneficiaries are subject to taxation on a portion of their benefits each year. Projections by the CBO indicate that about one-third of all recipients of social security benefits are taxed to some extent by the federal income tax.[6] In addition, some states with income taxes also tax social security benefits.[7]

POLICY STUDY

Tax Reform Proposals

The old saying attributed to Benjamin Franklin is that nothing in life is sure, but death and taxes. But, over the past decade one might reasonably modify that old saw to say nothing is more sure than talk of tax reform. A number of plans for fundamental tax reform have been proposed in recent years. In this policy study we examine a national sales tax (NST), a value-added tax (VAT), the Hall-Rabushka Flat Tax, the progressive consumption tax, and two proposals offered by the 2005 President's Tax Panel.

National Sales Tax (NST)

The federal government could adopt a retail sales tax (RST) in much the same way that 45 states currently apply retail sales taxes. An *ad valorem* tax would apply to the value of final goods, and possibly services as well. Only final goods are usually taxed by a sales tax, exempting intermediate goods from taxation. The reason for this exemption is to avoid the problem of the cascading tax, with very high rates of taxation accumulating throughout the production processes where intermediate goods are passed on from firm to firm for additional finishing. A uniform tax rate would be applied to sales made anywhere in the country. This is the quintessential consumption tax. Consumption expenditures rise at a decreasing rate with income, however, so the sales tax is quite regressive. The effective rate of taxation (tax paid divided by income) falls as income rises. States generally relieve the regression by exempting essential commodities such as food (for home consumption), prescription drugs, and in some cases clothing.

One example of an RST proposal is the Fair Tax (see FairTax.org). According to its proponents, that proposal would replace the income tax, social security payroll tax, Estate tax, Medicare payroll tax, Alternative Minimum Tax, and other taxes with a 23 percent RST. Advocates also claim that the IRS could be eliminated. To relieve the regressivity of the RST, most proposals include a cash grant that would be paid to individual taxpayers. The FAIR tax proposal, in particular, would provide the cash grant as an up-front monthly rebate, or so-called *prebate*.

The 2005 President's Tax Panel considered a national retail sales tax alternative, but found several weaknesses of such a proposal. Their initial concern was that the RST would be quite regressive, as indicated previously. Beyond that they had additional concerns. First, they concluded that, even adopting favorable assumptions, in estimation the required tax rate would be at least 34 percent. Second, the federal administrative cost of the RST would be similar to the present tax system, offering no real savings in administrative cost. Two sources of administrative cost would be involved: collection cost and the cost of tracking personal information to provide each taxpayer's monthly cash grant. Third, the Panel found that taxpayers would likely have to continue to file state income tax returns (in all but nine states which do not have comprehensive state income taxes), limiting the simplification gains from replacing the federal income taxes with an RST.

A related issue worth considering is the manner in which tax rates are computed as they differ between income taxes and RST proposals. An income tax rate is quoted on a **tax-inclusive** basis, whereas a sales tax rate is quoted on a **tax-exclusive** basis. The difference can be illustrated with a simple example. Suppose you purchase a product for the price of $100. If a sales tax applies a 34 percent tax rate to that purchase, you must pay tax of $34, reflecting a tax-exclusive rate of 34 percent. If we were to calculate the tax-inclusive rate for that purchase we would take the $34 tax and divide by the tax-inclusive price of $134, yielding a rate of 25 percent. The two rates are equivalent in the sense that you paid $34 in tax either way, but they differ in whether the tax itself is excluded or included in the denominator when computing the tax rate. When you think of an income tax you are accustomed to think in terms of a tax-inclusive rate. If your income were $134, of which you had to pay $34 in tax, the tax rate is 34/134 = 0.25.

Value-Added Tax (VAT)

A value-added tax (VAT) taxes the value added of a business at each stage of production. Value added amounts to a firm's gross sales receipts less expenses for raw materials or intermediate goods purchases. Three variants of the VAT exist, distinguished by their treatment of depreciation and investment. The gross income type of VAT allows no deductions for depreciation or investment. The net income type of VAT allows a deduction for depreciation of capital equipment and plants. The consumption type of VAT allows a deduction for investment expenditure, which is equivalent to expensing. VATs are very broad-based taxes. As a result, they can generate large amounts of revenue at very low rates. This has led some to call the VAT a "money machine," although

Keen and Lockwood (2006) report finding evidence of a weak form of this impact of VAT adoption.

In order to relieve the regressivity of VATs, countries often zero rate certain commodities considered essential. **Zero rating** simply means that the tax rate applied to those commodities is zero. For example, many countries zero rate agricultural products, permitting producers to claim credits for VAT paid on inputs they used in production, but not taxing the goods at final sale. VATs are very common taxes around the world with about 130 countries now having a VAT, but not in the United States.

Recent tax reform discussion in the United States has focused on the possibility of implementing a national VAT in order to generate additional revenue. For example, the Bipartisan Policy Center in Washington, DC, has proposed a 6.5 percent national Debt Reduction Sales Tax (DRST), essentially a VAT packaged in the more familiar sales tax language, as part of its package of recommended tax and expenditure reforms (for details see http://bipartisanpolicy.org/projects/debt-initiative/about).

Hall-Rabushka Flat Tax

The flat tax proposal of Hall and Rabushka (1995, 2007) is another tax reform concept that continues to receive consideration. The tax is best thought of as a consumption-type value-added tax that would be applied in two pieces. A consumption-type VAT taxes gross sales, less the cost of raw materials and intermediate goods, less investment. The deduction of investment expenses for new machinery, equipment, and facilities is what makes this version of a VAT a consumption-type VAT. In terms of simple national income accounting, national income or product Y is made up of the components C, consumption expenditures, and I, investment expenditures: $Y = C + I$. If investment expenditure is deducted, we are left with consumption expenditures. This consumption-type VAT is then applied in two parts. First, a tax is applied at the household level on wages, salaries, and pension benefits. Second, a tax is applied to all businesses on their gross sales less wages, pension contributions, raw materials costs, and investment.

Progressive Consumption Tax

Economist David Bradford (1986, 2003) has suggested a progressive consumption tax, which he dubbed the X-Tax, as an alternative to the existing income tax system in the United States. This form of taxation is essentially a two-tiered consumption tax, providing a degree of progressivity. Under this form of taxation, and similar to the Hall-Rabushka proposal, there is a business tax and a compensation tax. The business tax applies to all businesses regardless of their legal structure (corporations, partnerships, sole proprietorships), which pay tax at a single rate. The business tax base is gross receipts minus purchases from other businesses. Importantly, payments to employees are deducted from the business tax base. Individuals are taxed under the compensation tax. Their tax base is the sum of all payments for labor services. A progressive tax rate structure is applied to the compensation tax base, with a zero bracket amount and a top marginal tax rate equal to the business tax rate.

Bradford (2003) identifies two key advantages of this tax reform proposal. First, it provides, "a tightly coordinated treatment of the tax base of companies and the earnings of workers." Second, "in determining the company level tax base and in motivating the form of integration of company and worker taxation, consumption replaces the accrual income ideal that, in principle, underlies so much of the present tax design." The result is a much simpler tax system that still embodies a degree of progressivity.

Income Tax Reform

In 2005 President Bush appointed a blue-ribbon tax panel to conduct a comprehensive review of the U.S. income tax system and recommend proposals to fix the system. They recommended two alternative proposals: the Simplified Income Tax (SIT), whose major improvement would be to greatly simplify the tax code and streamline tax forms, and the Growth and Investment Tax (GIT), which was a more substantive reform proposal that would have moved the income tax further in the direction of a consumption tax. Although the circumstances at the time proved inhospitable to a major tax reform, these proposals embody important ideas for fundamental tax reform. Budget circumstances in the wake of the great recession of 2008–09 make it much more likely that fundamental tax reform may be feasible in the near future. Consequently, it is useful to consider these proposals for tax reform ideas.

Both proposals simplify the income tax by combining personal exemptions, standard deductions, and the child credit into a single Family Credit. They also streamline the EITC mechanism into a simpler Work Credit. The marriage penalty is also reduced under both plans. Deductions are limited in several ways as well. The home mortgage interest deduction replaced with a credit for 15 percent of interest paid, capped at the average regional house price. Charitable giving is only deductible in excess of 1 percent of income. State and local taxes are not deductible. The current medical deduction is replaced with a provision permitting taxpayers to pay for health insurance with pre-tax dollars, up to the amount of the average premium. Several features of both plans provide for simplification for individual savings and retirement. Dividends and capital gains are both tax-favored with lower effective rates under both proposals. For small businesses, simplification is provided in the accounting methods used. Under the SIT proposal a simplified cash accounting method is proposed, whereas under the GIT proposal the business tax is converted to a cash-flow tax. Under both plans investment is expensed. For large businesses, investment is either provided accelerated depreciation under the SIT proposal or expensed under the GIT proposal. In terms of international business activity, the SIT proposal would switch to a territorial system of taxation, whereas the GIT proposal would make the business tax a destination-based tax with border adjustments. Table 14.10 provides a summary of the main features of each proposal.

So, which of these alternatives would be better than the current U.S. income tax system? Well, the answer to that question is Harry Truman's nightmare. He is the president who said he wanted a one-armed economist so that he would not hear explanations that follow the formula: "On one hand, … but on the other hand." In this case, there are a number of effects of tax reform plans to consider.

Distributional Effects of Tax Reform Plans

Aaron and Gale (1996) estimate the distributional effects of the major alternative systems.

Although the average effective tax rate is virtually identical for all four alternative tax systems, the distribution of effective rates by income is very different across the

TABLE 14.10 2005 President's Tax Panel Proposals

How the Tax Code Would Change		
Provisions	**Simplified Income Tax Plan**	**Growth and Investment Tax Plan**
Households and Families		
Tax rates	Four tax brackets: 15%, 25%, 30%, 33%	Three tax brackets 15%, 25%, 30%
Alternative Minimum Tax	Repealed	
Personal exemption Standard deduction Child tax credit	Replaced with Family Credit available to all taxpayers: $3,300 credit for married couples, $2,800 credit for unmarried taxpayers with child, S1,650 credit for unmarried taxpayer, $1,150 credit for dependant taxpayers, additional $1,500 credit for each child and $500 credit for each other dependent	
Earned income tax credit	Replaced with Work Credit (and coordinated with the Family Credit); maximum credit for working family with one child is $3.570; with two or more children is $ 5,800	
Marriage penalty	Reduced; tax brackets and most other tax parameters for couples are double those of individuals	
Other Major Credits and Deductions		
Home mortgage interest	Home Credit equal to 15% of mortgage interest paid; available to all taxpayers; mortgage limited to average regional price of housing (limits ranging from about $227,000 to $412.000)	
Charitable giving	Deduction available to all taxpayers (who give more than 1% of income) rules to address valuation abuses	
Health insurance	All taxpayers may purchase health insurance with pre-tax dollars, up to the amount of the average premium (estimated to be $5,000 for an individual and $11,500 for a family)	
State and local taxes	Not deductible	
Education	Taxpayers can claim Family Credit for some full-time students; simplified savings plans	
Individual Savings and Retirement		
Defined contribution plans	Consolidated into Save at Work plans that have simple rules and use current-law 401(k) contribution limits; AutoSave features point workers in a pro-saving direction (Growth and Investment Tax Plan would make Save at Work accounts "prepaid" or Roth-style)	
Defined benefit plans	No change	
Retirement savings-plans	Replaced with Save for Retirement accounts ($10,000 annual limit) available to all taxpayers	
Education savings plans Health savings plans	Replaced with Save for Family accounts ($10,000 annual limit); would cover education, medical, new home costs, and retirement saving needs; available to all taxpayer; refundable Saver's Credit available to low-income taxpayers	

(continued)

TABLE 14.10 2005 President's Tax Panel Proposals (Continued)

	How the Tax Code Would Change	
Provisions	**Simplified Income Tax Plan**	**Growth and Investment Tax Plan**
Dividends received	Exclude 100% of dividends of U.S., companies paid out of domestic earnings	Taxed at 15% rate
Capital gains received	Exclude 75% of corporate capital gains from U.S. companies rate {tax rate would vary from 3.75% to 8.25%)	Taxed at 15% rate
Interest received (other than tax exempt municipal bonds)	Taxed at regular income tax rates	Taxed at 15% rate
Social Security benefits	Replaces three-tiered structure with a simple deduction. Married taxpayers with less than $44,000 in income ($22,000 if single) pay no tax on Social Security benefits; fixes marriage penalty; indexed for inflation	
Small Business		
Tax rates	Taxed at individual rates (top rate has been lowered to 33%)	Sole proprietorships taxed at individual rates (top rate lowered to 30%); Other small businesses taxed at 30%
Recordkeeping	Simplified cash-basis accounting	Business cash flow tax
Investment	Expending (exception for land and buildings under the Simplified Income Tax Plan)	
Large Business		
Tax rates	31.5%	30%
Investment	Simplified accelerated depreciation	Expensing for all new investment
Interest paid	No change	Not deductible (except for financial institutions)
Interest received	Taxable	Not taxable (except for financial institutions)
International tax system	Territorial tax system	Destination-basis (border tax adjustments)
Corporate AMT	Repealed	

Source: President's Advisory Tax Panel on Federal Tax Reform (2005).

alternatives. The flat tax and VAT are both less progressive than the current tax system. Both would increase the effective rate of taxation for low-income households. However, in comparison to the current tax system, the VAT increases the effective tax rate for households up to $90,000 of taxable income and reduces the effective tax rate for households with income higher than that. Clearly, the VAT would reduce the overall progressivity of the tax system substantially. The flat tax is essentially a VAT, which we would expect to be much more regressive than the current tax system, but its effective tax rates are less regressive than a typical VAT due to the liberal exemptions it incorporates. Although a VAT could be designed to be less demanding of low-income households, most of the current proposals for a federal VAT would be quite threatening to the poor.

The flat tax is the next most progressivity reducing proposal. Compared to the current tax system, the flat tax would increase effective tax rates for households with taxable incomes up to $99,000 and reduce them substantially for households with higher incomes. It is important to note that the flat tax raises the effective tax rate substantially at low income levels but raises effective rates only slightly for middle-income households.

Direct Effects

The distributional properties of each of the tax reform plans described previously represent the direct effects expected. The Aaron and Gale microsimulation model is a static model; hence dynamic effects are not included. Static effects are those that occur at a single point in time, presumably at the initial point at which the proposal is implemented. Dynamic effects occur over time, starting when the proposal is implemented but continuing beyond that time. In order to simulate dynamic effects, however, you must make assumptions about the likely responses to tax reform. How will individuals and firms change their behavior? Depending on the elasticities you assume, you may get very different simulated effects. The issue of static versus dynamic simulation in tax policy modeling is controversial not so much because of genuine differences of opinion regarding the effects involved but because of the potential to bias the results of dynamic simulations with appropriately selected elasticities.

Indirect Effects

Fundamental tax reform may have indirect effects on macroeconomic variables to consider as well. For example, proponents of the flat tax such as Hall and Rabushka (1995) believe that pretax interest rates would fall by 2 percent following the introduction of a flat tax. Auerbach (1996) estimates that the flat tax would lower pretax interest rates by about 1 percent. Others, such as Gentry and Hubbard (1997), believe that the adoption of a flat tax would raise pretax interest rates. Of course, the effect of a flat-rate tax on pretax interest rates depends crucially on household saving behavior in response to the tax. Research provides mixed evidence on the sensitivity of the saving response to tax changes. As a result, we cannot know with any degree of certainty the direction of such indirect effects, much less their magnitude. Although indirect effects will occur, it is not wise or prudent to build one's case for tax reform on those effects.

Other Effects

The prospect of fundamental tax reform brings with it concern for a number of other effects that should be considered. For example, transition issues and effects are very important. If we were to adopt a tax plan that eliminates the mortgage interest deduction, for example, we would expect that the demand for owner-occupied housing would shift leftward, reducing prices and quantities cleared in housing markets, other things being equal. Owner-occupied homes are the primary source of wealth for most families, so this tax policy change would result in a reduction in wealth for many of them. Those effects could be substantial. As a result, the transition from the current system to the flat-tax system would be fraught with difficulties, each with distributional effects worthy of consideration.

Evaluation of Fundamental Reform Proposals

Each of these reform proposals has its merits and flaws. If we evaluate the plans from the policy viewpoint of a concern for equity, there are clear differences among the proposals in their distributional impacts. The Pechman plan for modifying the income tax and the savings-based USA tax are clearly preferable. Both the VAT and flat tax (in any of its variants) are inferior. If we evaluate the plans from the policy viewpoint of concern for efficiency, however, we may come to different conclusions. Consumption-based taxes such as the VAT, USA tax, or flat tax have certain efficiency advantages that may be worth some sacrifice in equity. Evaluation of tax reform proposals involves a complex set of issues.

Concerns for simplicity must be weighed carefully, when Form 1040EZ, which most taxpayers file, could easily be reduced to the size of a postcard like the proposed return for the flat tax (see Figures 10.5 and 10.6). In fact, increasing numbers of taxpayers now file their tax return on the telephone in a matter of minutes or electronically via computer. They do not even send a form to the IRS. In fact, there are a number of proposals for moving to an entirely return-free income tax system, even with retention of the current income tax.

What about other aspects of simplicity? One objective of tax law is simplicity; another is minimizing tax liability. Consider a simple example of a homeowner with a mortgage. Under the current income tax law, the homeowner may either file the simple Form 1040EZ with a standard deduction or the more complex Form 1040 along with including Schedule A itemizing deductions, including mortgage interest and local property taxes paid on the house. For most homeowners, these Schedule A deductions exceed the standard deduction, thereby reducing tax liability. But, of course, the taxpayer has a choice. If the taxpayer prefers simplicity, he can take the standard deduction. Most homeowners willingly forgo simplicity in exchange for a lower tax liability, however. Simplicity isn't all that it's cracked up to be. In fact, the transition issues involved in moving from an income tax system to a consumption-based tax system would be the most complex change in the history of U.S. tax policy. How do you hold harmless the generation of savers who built their savings on the basis of an income tax system that taxed income regardless of its use and also taxed interest paid on savings while moving to a new system that does not tax income saved or income from savings? Even though the new tax system may be simpler, the transition from here to there is very complex.

The current income tax system can be greatly simplified without moving to a completely new tax system. Congress has the opportunity to simplify the tax system in every session. Other policy objectives usually win out over simplicity, however, and the tax code becomes more and more complex over time. For example, former commissioner of the IRS, Margaret Miller Richardson, has said that "We cannot lose sight of the fact that complexity is the result of our struggle for fairness." Her comment makes clear that we may sometimes prefer a less simple tax code if in exchange we have a tax system we believe to be more fair. As always, there are policy trade-offs. Simplicity has its price, and it has been considered too high in previous policy debates.

Isn't the attractiveness of a single tax rate a powerful feature of the flat-tax proposal? Actually, this is one of the most trivial aspects of that proposed plan. Some people seem to believe that the computation of tax liability is simpler when there is just one rate rather than a progressive rate structure. Keep in mind that published tax tables along with the tax forms make tax liability computations very simple. Taxpayers do not need to compute their tax owed on income in each bracket separately. Rather, the taxpayer simply looks up taxable income in the tax table and finds the total. Could it really be any simpler? If you believe that it is simpler to ask taxpayers to compute the tax owed as 17 percent of their taxable income, an extremely large number of taxpayers will get the math wrong.

The more important aspect of moving to a single tax rate is the removal of a difference between the tax rate applied to personal income and the tax rate applied to corporate income. The tax rates charged to U.S. corporations differ from the rates charged to individuals. Any difference between the rates charged of the two types of taxpayers can lead to tax avoidance behavior. With a difference in rates, taxpayers have an incentive to transform one form of income into another form of income in order to take advantage of the lower rate. Suppose, for example, that a consultant earns \$200,000 per year in his consulting activity. He may report that income as corporate income for his consulting company, which is subject to a marginal tax rate of 35 percent. On the other hand, he may be able to report that income as business income on his personal tax return, using Schedule C, where it is subject to a marginal tax rate of 33 percent. The difference in marginal tax rates of 2 percent provides an incentive to convert corporate income into personal income. A reform moving away from a tax on income to a consumption-type VAT would reduce the differential in rates on personal and corporate income. It could also be accomplished without major reform. Indeed, the U.S. Treasury Department has well-developed proposals for integration of the two taxes that have been ignored by Congress for many years because policymakers have not considered the gains from integration sufficiently attractive to pursue.

Additional issues with transition costs deserve mention. Marginal changes in the current income tax system have relatively small marginal costs associated with them. Reform proposals that switch to a completely different tax base will result in very large transition costs. Not only are different accounting systems required, but there are also large costs associated with hold-harmless provisions of a major reform. Any major reform creates groups of winners and losers. Losers will lobby for special provisions to hold them harmless from the negative effects of the reform (in comparison to the status quo). Those provisions will be very expensive for the remaining taxpayers. Consider one small example. Suppose that a tax reform were to remove the tax-exempt status of interest earned on municipal bonds. That would hurt taxpayers who currently hold municipal bonds in their portfolios. A hold-harmless provision might be included in the tax reform that would continue to provide a tax exemption for existing municipal bond holders but subject others to taxation of the interest on such bonds. That hold-harmless provision would be expensive, costing an amount equal to the present tax expenditure projected into the indefinite future.

What are the prospects for tax reform? Perhaps humorist Dave Barry said it best when he reflected on the prospect of adopting a flat tax:

> If Congress were to pass a "flat" tax, you'd simply pay a fixed percentage of your income, and you wouldn't have to fill out any complicated forms, and there would

> be no loopholes for politically connected groups, and normal people would actually understand the tax laws, and giant talking broccoli stalks would come around and mow your lawn for free, because Congress is NOT going to pass a flat tax, you pathetic fool.[8]

It is too soon to know whether discontent with the income tax is sufficiently strong to induce Congress to adopt a completely different form of taxation. It is not too soon to know, however, that whatever alternative is considered will have both supporters and detractors. Dave Barry's point is that there are strong vested interests in maintaining the status quo. Although humorists are not usually very good economists, he certainly has that issue pegged.

PROBLEMS

1. Fred and Ethel are married with two children and plan to file jointly.
   a. Their taxable income sources were as follows.

Wages and Salaries	$ 42,381
Interest and Dividend Income	$ 1,215
Capital Gains	$ 3,092
Net Business Income	$ 7,824

   Compute their adjusted gross income.
   b. Compute their taxable income, given their personal exemptions and assuming that they take the standard deduction listed in Table 14.1.
   c. Compute their tax liability using the tax rates in Table 14.2.
2. For each of the following households, use the tax rate schedules in Table 14.3 to compute liability and average tax rate.
   a. Miriam is single and has a taxable income of $40,000.
   b. Robin is single and has taxable income of $173,000.
   c. Fred and Wilma are married filing jointly with taxable income of $123,000.
   d. Boris and Natasha are married filing jointly with taxable income of $451,000.
3. Suppose that Jimmy and Roslyn are married and have the following adjusted gross incomes. Compute their tax liabilities individually and as a couple. Determine whether they receive a marriage bonus or are subject to a marriage penalty. Use the 1998 personal exemptions, standard deductions, and tax rates.

	Jimmy	Roslyn	Couple
Adjusted gross income	$87,000	$37,000	
Less personal exemptions			
Less standard deduction			
Equals taxable income			
Tax liability			
Marriage bonus or penalty			

4. Bob and Elizabeth have the following wage and salary incomes. Bob is self-employed and Elizabeth has an employer. Compute their payroll taxes using the tax schedule in Table 14.10.

	Bob	Elizabeth
Wage and salary income	$48,000	$92,000
OASDI		
Employer		
Employee		
HI		
Employer		
Employee		
Total		

5. Consider the effect of deductibility on combined federal and state tax rates.
   a. Fill in the blanks of a table patterned after Table 14.3, but using the federal marginal tax rates of 15 and 32 percent.
   b. Explain the economic incentives that deductibility provides for taxpayers in the 32 percent marginal tax bracket, compared to those in the 15 percent marginal tax bracket.
6. Loretta is a single mom with two children who works at the Montgomery County Clerk's Office and earns $20,000 per year in salary.
   a. Compute the EITC that Loretta is qualified to receive. Use the EITC parameters from Table 14.6.
   b. What is the phase-out rate to which Loretta is subjected?
   c. Determine the combined effective tax rate that Loretta faces from the income tax rate (Table 14.2) and the phase-out rate (Table 14.6).
7. George and Lara live in a state that currently relies heavily on local property taxes to fund public education. They own a home valued at $125,000 and pay local property taxes of $2,200. Their combined income puts them in the 30.5 percent marginal tax bracket on the federal income tax, and they itemize their deductions. A politician in their state

has proposed a change in the state's tax structure that would reduce reliance on local property taxes for education and increase reliance on the state sales tax. For George and Lara the proposed change would reduce their property tax bill by $850 while increasing the amount they pay in state sales tax by the same amount.

a. Explain how the politician's proposal would affect George and Lara's federal tax bill.
b. Should they support the tax shift proposal?

REFERENCES

Aaron, Henry J., and William G. Gale. *Economic Effects of Fundamental Tax Reform*. Washington, DC: Brookings Institution, 1996.

Alm, James, Stacy Dickert-Conlin, and Leslie Whittington. "Policy Watch: The Marriage Penalty." *Journal of Economic Perspectives* 13(1999): 193–204.

Alm, James, and Leslie Whittington. "For Love or Money? The Impact of Income Taxes on Marriage." *Economica* 66(1999): 297–316.

Auerbach, Alan J. "Tax Reform, Capital Allocation, Efficiency, and Growth." Chapter 2 in Aaron and Gale, eds. *Economic Effects of Fundamental Tax Reform*. Washington, DC: Brookings Institution, 1996.

Bradford, David F. 1986. *Untangling the Income Tax*. Cambridge, MA: Harvard University Press.

Bradford, David F. 2003. "The X Tax in the World Economy." Princeton University Center for Economic Policy Studies, CEPS Working Paper No. 93.

Committee on Ways and Means. *Green Book*. Section 1. Social Security: The Old-Age, Survivors, and Disability Insurance (OASDI) Programs. Washington, DC: U.S. House of Representatives, 2000.

Congressional Budget Office. *For Better or for Worse: Marriage and the Federal Income Tax*. Washington, DC: U.S. Congress, 1997.

Ellwood, David T. "The Impact of the Earned Income Tax Credit and Social Policy Reforms on Work, Marriage, and Living Arrangements," *National Tax Journal* 53(2000): 1063–105.

Eissa, Nada, and Hilary Hoynes. *The Earned Income Tax Credit and the Labor Supply of Married Couples*. National Bureau of Economic Research Working Paper 6856, 1998.

Fisher, Ronald C. *State and Local Public Finance*. Glenview, IL: Scott Foresman, 1996.

Gentry, William M., and Hubbard R. Glenn. "Implications of Introducing a Broad-Based Consumption Tax," in James M. Poterba, ed. *Tax Policy and the Economy*, Volume 11, Cambridge, MA: MIT Press, 1997.

Hoffman, Saul D., and Laurence S. Seidman. *The Earned Income Tax Credit*. Kalamazoo, MI: W. E. Upjohn Institute for Employment Research, 1990.

Hall, Robert E., and Alvin Rabushka. *The Flat Tax*, 2nd ed. Stanford, CA: Hoover Institution, 1995, 2007 available at: http://www.hoover.org/publications/books/8329.

Joint Committee on Taxation. *Estimates of Federal Tax Expenditures for Fiscal Years 2002–2006*. Washington, DC: U.S. Government Printing Office, 2002.

Keen, Michael, and Ben Lockwood. "Is the VAT a Money Machine?" *National Tax Journal*, 59(2006): 905–28.

Musgrave, Richard A. and Peggy B. Musgrave. *Public Finance in Theory and Practice, Fifth Edition*. New York: McGraw-Hill, Inc., 1989.

Pechman, Joseph A. *Federal Tax Policy*, 5th ed. Washington, DC: Brookings Institution, 1987.

President's Advisory Tax Panel on Federal Tax Reform. 2005. *Simple, Fair, and Pro-Growth: Proposals to Fix America's Tax System*. Available at: http://govinfo.library.unt.edu/taxreformpanel/final-report/index.html.

Steuerle, C. Eugene. "Tax Credits for Low-Income Workers with Children." *Journal of Economic Perspectives* 4(1990): 201–12.

Steuerle, C. Eugene. *The Tax Decade*. Washington, DC: Urban Institute, 1992.

Tempalski, Jerry. "Revenue Effects of Major Tax Bills." Office of Tax Policy (OTA) Working Paper 81, U.S. Department of Treasury, 2006.

Tax Policy Center. Distribution of the Tax Benefits of the Earned Income Tax Credit (EITC) by Cash Income Class, 2007. Table T07-0109, available at: http://www.taxpolicycenter.org/numbers/displayatab.cfm?DocID=1518.

Whittington, Leslie, and James Alm. "Tax Reductions, Tax Changes, and the Marriage Penalty." *National Tax Journal* 54(2001): 455–72.

NOTES

1. Steuerle (1992, Table A.3).
2. Pechman (1987) provides interesting historical background on the introduction of income splitting. The adoption of income splitting in the United States grew out of a situation where eight states had community property laws that equally divided income between a husband and a wife. Couples in those states had been splitting their income and filing separate federal income tax returns. Of course, couples in those eight states paid a different amount of tax than couples in other states with the same income. This violated the principle of horizontal equity. After World War II a number of other states adopted or threatened to adopt community property laws in order to provide the same tax advantage for married couples in their states. Congress responded to this situation by universalizing income splitting in 1948.
3. See Alm and Whittington (1999); Alm, Dickert-Conlin, and Whittington (1999); and Whittington and Alm (2001) for insightful research on how the marriage tax may affect behavior.

4. See Eissa and Hoynes (1998) for research evidence on the effectiveness of the EITC as a work incentive. The EITC may provide incentives other than the one to work. See Ellwood (2000) for a description of the EITC incentives regarding labor supply, marriage, and cohabitation. See Hoffman and Seidman (1990) for general background on the EITC.
5. Joint Committee on Taxation (2002).
6. This estimate is reported in the Committee on Ways and Means (2000, 28).
7. Furthermore, state income tax systems may also tax some portion of social security benefits. In 2010, 28 states with income taxes exempt social security benefits from taxation; 4 states exclude some portion of benefits from taxation, 3 states provide a general retirement income exclusion or credit, 1 state taxes benefits on the same basis as the federal income tax using a modified income measure (Montana); and 6 states apply their income taxes to benefits following the federal income tax procedure (Minnesota, Nebraska, New Mexico, North Dakota, Rhode Island, and Vermont). Source: Minnesota House of Representatives, House Research, "Taxation of Social Security Benefits." Available at: *http://www.house.leg.state.mn.us/hrd/issinfo/sstaxes.htm*.
8. Dave Barry. "Why the Flat Tax Is a Fluke," *Miami Herald*, February 25, 1996.

Radius Images/Getty Images

CHAPTER 15

The Corporate Income Tax

LEARNING OBJECTIVES

1. Identify the types of taxes applied to firms, including the corporate income tax.
2. Explain how taxes affect the cost of capital and the behavior of firms.
3. Discuss the incidence of the corporate tax.
4. Discuss global business and taxation issues.

The Wal-Mart Stores Corporation sits atop the *Fortune* 500 list of the United States's largest corporations. Its revenues were \$408 billion and its profits \$14.3 billion in the year 2010.[1] The Exxon-Mobil Corporation is second on the list, with revenues of \$285 billion and profits of \$19.3 billion. Following are Chevron, General Electric, Bank of America, and so on. The list is the quintessential who's who of U.S. business. Even further down the list the corporations are household names such as Hewlett-Packard, Berkshire Hathaway, Verizon, and a host of others. These are the United States's largest corporations and the income they generate is huge. It is one thing to tax the income of the individuals working for these corporations and the shareholders receiving dividends from these corporations, but what about taxing the corporations themselves? That is the issue we address in this chapter.

CORPORATE INCOME TAX

The corporate income tax accounts for a rather small share of revenue currently in the United States, somewhat less than 10 percent of federal revenues, but the presence of the corporate income tax also helps preserve personal income tax revenue. It is a necessary part of having a system of income taxation, including both personal and corporate components. Indeed, in order to understand how income taxation works, one must have insight on the interactions between personal and corporate sources of income and the interplay between the forms of taxation applied to each source. Income generated by a corporation may be retained by the firm or may be distributed to shareholders in the form of dividend payments, for example. If only personal income were subject to taxation, there would be an incentive for shareholders to accumulate wealth in corporations and avoid taxation. On the other hand, if there were only corporate income taxation, there would be an incentive to distribute corporate income to shareholders in order to avoid taxation. Although there are a multitude of other interactions to consider, this simple example illustrates the fact that personal and corporate income taxes must be considered hand in hand. The Enron debacle in the 1990s illustrates the extreme measures that some corporations may take in order to avoid corporate income taxes. Analysis of the Enron case demonstrates how that is done and reveals the linkages between forms of taxation. Preservation of personal income tax revenue turns out to be a strong practical rationale for the corporate income tax, as we will see.

The corporate income tax was instituted in the United States in 1909, four years before the personal income tax. In order to avoid a constitutional problem with this new tax, however, Congress defined the tax as an excise tax on the privilege of doing business as a corporation.[2] The tax was challenged on constitutional grounds, but the Supreme Court upheld the tax as constitutional and concurred that corporate profits are an appropriate measure of the privilege of doing business as a corporation. In the years leading up to World War II, the corporate income tax usually generated more revenue than the personal income tax. In recent years, however, the tax has accounted for a small and declining share of federal government revenues.

Organizing a Business

Put yourself in the shoes of Charles Walgreen who bought a drugstore in 1901 on the South Side of Chicago. If you start out on your own with no partners or stockholders, you are called a **sole proprietor**. You operate the business, perhaps with employees, keep the profits earned, and pay taxes on those profits. This form of business is relatively easy to start and is subject to few restrictions, so it is well suited for a small firm starting out with an informal organizational structure (perhaps just the boss and a couple of employees). Most importantly, however, if you start your business this way, you must realize that you bear all the risk of the company should it not be able to pay its obligations and you personally bear **unlimited liability**.

If, instead of starting off on your own, you start your business with several friends, pooling your expertise and resources you may form a **partnership**. Your partnership agreement specifies how the company is managed and how its profits are divided among the partners. Each partner takes his or her share of the profits generated by the company and pays individual income tax on those profits. Like a proprietorship, a partnership has unlimited liability. As the business grows and the stakes rise, you may become concerned about the unlimited liability aspect of the venture and you may decide to incorporate, or become a **corporation**. The main advantage of incorporating is the benefit of limited liability. A lawsuit against the corporation can take the assets of the corporation, but not your personal assets. Although you as an owner of the company might lose some wealth tied up in the corporation, you can retain your home and personal assets. What makes a corporation different for tax purposes, however, is that the corporation is a legal entity that is separate and distinct from any of the individuals who own or work for the corporation, and therefore it is required to pay the corporate income tax. The corporation is a separate legal creature with the ability to retain earnings that are not paid out to owners or workers in the company. Because the corporation is a separate legal entity, it is taxed separately from the people who own it or work for it. In Europe, for example, it is common to speak of **legal persons** as a way of distinguishing corporations from individuals, or physical persons.

If only businesses with the legal status as corporations are subject to the corporate income tax, why would any business choose that legal form? Why not operate the business as a sole proprietorship or a partnership and avoid the corporate income tax altogether? Well, the answer to that question lies in the issue of limited liability. To get limited liability, you have to pay the price of subjecting the business to corporate income taxation. Several hybrid forms of business organizations try to enable business owners to have their cake (limited liability) and eat it too (avoid corporate income taxation). One option is a limited partnership under which the general partners actually manage the business and have unlimited personal liability, but other partners called *limited partners* are liable only to the extent that they have contributed to the business. Some U.S. states permit an organizational form called a **limited liability partnership** (**LLP**) or a **limited liability company** (LLC). This organizational form permits partnerships where all the partners have limited liability. That provides the tax advantage of a partnership with the limited liability advantage of a corporation. Although this might seem like the ultimate business organizational form, it is not well suited to very large firms where there is widespread ownership among shareholders and it is essential to keep ownership and management of the company separate. Doctors, lawyers, accountants, and other professionals often use the organizational form of a **professional corporation** (**PC**). By organizing their business this way, the business has limited liability although the individuals can be sued personally for malpractice.

Rationale for Corporate Taxation

So why are corporations taxed anyway? After all, people pay taxes, not corporations. Any tax that is applied to a corporation will ultimately be borne by a combination of the workers, customers, and shareholders. So why tax the corporation? Why not directly tax workers, customers, and shareholders? Groves (1946, p. 166) said long ago that:

> The rationale of a tax may seem to be of little consequence. Its incidence and economic effects may appear much more important. However, the effects of a tax depend somewhat upon the reasonableness of its imposition. Arbitrary taxes are likely to be injurious to morale.

If the corporate income tax is to have a solid basis, being supported with high morale and not being viewed as arbitrary and capricious, it must have a firm theoretical foundation. The rationale for a corporate income tax matters, and it begins with consideration of the benefits received by the corporation and the corporation's ability to pay.

Corporations are legal entities that provide rights beyond those belonging to the people involved. The corporation exists because its owners desire limited liability for their business activity. If that were not the case, they could easily avoid the corporate income tax by operating their business as a proprietorship or a partnership. By incorporating, however, they gain the benefit of limited liability and incur the cost of potentially having to pay the corporate income tax. Corporations are legal entities, or legal persons, that have rights under the law, which exist independently of the workers, customers, and shareholders of the corporation. Consequently, there is justification to tax those legal entities. A second and more practical consideration is that the corporate income tax is necessary in order to guard the integrity of the personal income tax. In the absence of the corporate income tax it would be quite easy for taxpayers to shift some of their income from the individual income tax to the corporation and evade taxation.

The **classical system** of income taxation is based on the rationalization that firms that benefit from incorporation are properly the subject of taxation. Hence, the corporate income tax is viewed as a benefits tax. The tax liability of the corporation is treated as distinct from that of individual shareholders. As a result, the net income, or profit, of the corporation is taxed at the corporate income tax rate. Dividends are taxed at the individual income tax rate, depending on the marginal rate that applies to the shareholder receiving the dividend. Bondholders are taxed on their interest earnings at their individual marginal tax rates as well. As a result, in the classical system there can be three distinct tax rates: the rate of taxation applied to corporate net income t_c, the rate of taxation applied to interest payments to bondholders, which is the personal tax rate t_p, and the rate of taxation applied to capital gains, t_g. Differences in these three rates of taxation can cause distortions due to **tax arbitrage**, or the alteration of economic activity based on differences in tax rates with the purpose of minimizing the tax liability. If, for example, the tax rate applied to capital gains is less than that applied to personal income, $t_g < t_p$, there is clearly an incentive for shareholders to ask the firm to retain earnings rather than pay dividends.

The classical system of taxation used in the United States is often criticized, however, as it can be considered to subject dividends to **double taxation**. Because dividends are not deductible from net income for the corporation, they are effectively taxed. Shareholders receiving the dividend payments are also liable for individual income taxation of those dividends. Consequently, dividends are taxed twice. In that case, shareholders might well prefer the corporation to retain earnings and not pay them out in dividends. Hence, the firm may prefer debt financing to equity financing.

The problem of double taxation of dividends is handled differently among countries with corporate income taxes. In the United Kingdom, for example, a different system of taxation is used. There, an **imputation system** is applied in an effort to avoid the double taxation of dividends. Under that system the corporate income tax and the individual income tax are integrated. Shareholders receive a credit for the tax paid by the corporation on that portion of its profit. The shareholder then is liable for any difference between the rate of taxation implicit in the imputation (the rate paid by the corporation on its profits from which dividends were paid) and the individual's personal income tax rate. Another option is that used by Germany and Japan who use a **two-rate system** to avoid double taxation. Under this type of system, distributed profits (paid out in dividends) and undistributed profits are taxed at two different rates. Undistributed profits of corporations are taxed at a higher rate than distributed profits. For more on the integration of personal and corporate income taxes, see the policy study at the end of this chapter.

Effects of Profit Taxation

In order to consider the potential effects of profit taxation on the firm, let's begin with the simple model of a profit-maximizing firm operating in a competitive industry. The firm buys labor L at the wage w and capital K at the price r. It sells its output at price p. Assume that the production function $Q = F(K, L)$ describes the transformation of input quantities of K and L into output Q, where this function is concave (so that we have constant or decreasing returns to scale). We can write the economic profit of the firm as

$$\pi = pQ - wL - rK. \tag{15.1}$$

Now, taxes may affect the firm in either of two ways. They may affect the output price p and hence the output quantity Q, or they may affect input prices w or r and hence input quantities L and K. As we noted in Chapter 2, there are efficiency effects to consider in the case where any of these parameters are affected by taxation. But, in the case of profit taxation, none of these parameters is affected. Hence, there is no efficiency effect from pure profit taxation. To show why, we can put a profit tax at the rate t_c and write the firm's after-tax profit as

$$\pi' = (1 - t_c)[pF(K,L) - wL - rK]. \tag{15.2}$$

Because the tax does not affect the output price or the input prices, it simply reduces the profit of the firm and has no efficiency effect. None of the efficiency conditions of the firm are affected by the tax. The tax falls on pure economic profit, so it is essentially a tax on the return to entrepreneurship.

The problem with applying this view to the corporate income tax is that it is misleading. The corporate income tax does not tax economic profit. It taxes accounting profit. Consequently, there are important efficiency considerations that we must examine and we will do that after we first examine what is really taxed by the corporate income (the tax base).

TAX BASE AND RATES

The corporate income tax is applied to the net income of corporations. In defining the tax base as net income, we might be tempted to think this is equivalent to the corporation's profit, but that would be a mistake. Net income, computed for tax purposes, bears little resemblance to the profit the corporation lists in its annual report to shareholders. It also bears little resemblance to true economic profit.

Net Income—The Tax Base

The corporate income tax base is net income. Figure 15.1 illustrates the U.S. corporate income tax return, Form 1120, on which the tax base, called *taxable income* (line 30), is clearly developed. The starting point is gross receipts (line 1) minus the cost of goods sold (line 2), resulting in gross profit (line 3). Then other forms of income (lines 4 through 10) are added to gross profit to obtain total income (line 11). Then various deductions are permitted for compensation of officers, salaries and wages, repairs and maintenance, bad debts, rents, taxes and licenses, interest paid, charitable contributions, depreciation, depletion, advertising, pension and profit-sharing plans, employee benefit programs, other deductions, and **net operating loss** (**NOL**). The NOL deduction permits the corporation to carry forward a previous loss that was incurred. Here is a summary of the essential components of the tax base:

$$
\begin{aligned}
\text{Gross profit} &= \text{gross receipts} - \text{cost of goods sold}\\
\text{Total income} &= \text{gross profit} + \text{dividends} + \text{interest} + \text{gross rents}\\
&\quad + \text{gross royalties} + \text{capital gain net income}\\
&\quad + \text{other income}\\
\text{Taxable income} &= \text{total income} - \text{total deductions}\\
\text{Total deductions} &= \text{compensation of officers} + \text{salaries and wages}\\
&\quad + \text{repairs and maintenance} + \text{bad debts}\\
&\quad + \text{rents} + \text{taxes and licenses} + \text{interest}\\
&\quad + \text{charitable contributions} + \text{depreciation}\\
&\quad + \text{depletion} + \text{advertising}\\
&\quad + \text{pension, profit-sharing, etc., plans}\\
&\quad + \text{employee benefit programs}\\
&\quad + \text{domestic production activities deduction}\\
&\quad + \text{other deductions}\\
&\quad + \text{net operating loss (NOL) deduction}
\end{aligned}
$$

Several important things should be noticed about the list of deductions permitted. First, employee compensation of all forms is deductible. It does not matter whether the corporation pays its employees in the form of cash wages, health care benefits, or pension contributions; the cost to the firm is deductible. Second, capital costs in the form of interest paid are deductible. When the firm borrows money to finance the purchase of capital equipment, for example, the interest paid is deductible, reducing the cost of borrowing. Third, notice that depreciation is deductible. Machinery and equipment used by the firm in producing its products or services wears out over time. The process of production uses up inputs, including capital inputs. Depreciation is the process whereby a portion of the value of a machine or piece of equipment is deducted each year in acknowledgment that the economic cost of production includes using up capital equipment. Specific pieces of machinery and equipment are assumed to have a useful lifetime of n years; for example, $1/n^{\text{th}}$ of the acquisition cost is deducted each year. Fourth, notice the NOL deduction, which permits a **carry-forward** of past losses. If the firm lost \$10 million last year but its taxable income was only \$7 million, it can carry forward the remaining \$3 million to

FIGURE 15.1 U.S. Corporate Income Tax Return—Form 1120

Form **1120**
Department of the Treasury
Internal Revenue Service

U.S. Corporation Income Tax Return

For calendar year 2010 or tax year beginning ______, 2010, ending ______, 20 __

▶ See separate instructions.

OMB No. 1545-0123

2010

A Check if:	Print or type		
1a Consolidated return (attach Form 851) ☐		Name	**B Employer identification number**
b Life/nonlife consolidated return ☐		Number, street, and room or suite no. If a P.O. box, see instructions.	**C** Date incorporated
2 Personal holding co. (attach Sch. PH) ☐		City or town, state, and ZIP code	**D** Total assets (see instructions) $
3 Personal service corp. (see instructions) ☐			
4 Schedule M-3 attached ☐	**E** Check if: **(1)** ☐ Initial return **(2)** ☐ Final return **(3)** ☐ Name change **(4)** ☐ Address change		

Income

1a	Gross receipts or sales ______ **b** Less returns and allowances ______ **c** Bal ▶	1c
2	Cost of goods sold (Schedule A, line 8)	2
3	Gross profit. Subtract line 2 from line 1c	3
4	Dividends (Schedule C, line 19)	4
5	Interest	5
6	Gross rents	6
7	Gross royalties	7
8	Capital gain net income (attach Schedule D (Form 1120))	8
9	Net gain or (loss) from Form 4797, Part II, line 17 (attach Form 4797)	9
10	Other income (see instructions—attach schedule)	10
11	**Total income.** Add lines 3 through 10 ▶	11

Deductions (See instructions for limitations on deductions.)

12	Compensation of officers (Schedule E, line 4) ▶	12
13	Salaries and wages (less employment credits)	13
14	Repairs and maintenance	14
15	Bad debts	15
16	Rents	16
17	Taxes and licenses	17
18	Interest	18
19	Charitable contributions	19
20	Depreciation from Form 4562 not claimed on Schedule A or elsewhere on return (attach Form 4562)	20
21	Depletion	21
22	Advertising	22
23	Pension, profit-sharing, etc., plans	23
24	Employee benefit programs	24
25	Domestic production activities deduction (attach Form 8903)	25
26	Other deductions (attach schedule)	26
27	**Total deductions.** Add lines 12 through 26 ▶	27
28	Taxable income before net operating loss deduction and special deductions. Subtract line 27 from line 11.	28
29	**Less: a** Net operating loss deduction (see instructions) — 29a	
	b Special deductions (Schedule C, line 20) — 29b	29c

Tax, Refundable Credits, and Payments

30	**Taxable income.** Subtract line 29c from line 28 (see instructions)	30
31	**Total tax** (Schedule J, line 10)	31
32a	2009 overpayment credited to 2010 — 32a	
b	2010 estimated tax payments — 32b	
c	2010 refund applied for on Form 4466 — 32c ( ) **d Bal ▶** 32d	
e	Tax deposited with Form 7004 — 32e	
f	Credits: **(1)** Form 2439 ______ **(2)** Form 4136 ______ — 32f	
g	Refundable credits from Form 3800, line 19c, and Form 8827, line 8c — 32g	32h
33	Estimated tax penalty (see instructions). Check if Form 2220 is attached ▶ ☐	33
34	**Amount owed.** If line 32h is smaller than the total of lines 31 and 33, enter amount owed	34
35	**Overpayment.** If line 32h is larger than the total of lines 31 and 33, enter amount overpaid	35
36	Enter amount from line 35 you want: **Credited to 2011 estimated tax ▶** **Refunded ▶**	36

Sign Here

Under penalties of perjury, I declare that I have examined this return, including accompanying schedules and statements, and to the best of my knowledge and belief, it is true, correct, and complete. Declaration of preparer (other than taxpayer) is based on all information of which preparer has any knowledge.

▶ Signature of officer — Date ▶ Title

May the IRS discuss this return with the preparer shown below (see instructions)? ☐ **Yes** ☐ **No**

Paid Preparer Use Only

Print/Type preparer's name	Preparer's signature	Date	Check ☐ if self-employed	PTIN
Firm's name ▶			Firm's EIN ▶	
Firm's address ▶			Phone no.	

For Paperwork Reduction Act Notice, see separate instructions. Cat. No. 11450Q Form **1120** (2010) the next taxable year and deduct that portion of last year's loss from this year's taxable income. Finally, notice what is not on the list of permissible deductions. Most prominent in this regard is dividends paid to shareholders. If the corporation chooses to pay dividends to its shareholders, it is not permitted to deduct those payments from its taxable income. Hence, the corporation pays tax on the income it uses to pay dividends. Of course, the shareholders receive those dividend payments as income, which is taxable to them on their personal income tax returns. This is the source of double taxation. A portion of corporate income—that part paid in dividends—is subject to both corporate and individual income taxation. Furthermore, consider the fact that interest paid is deductible, whereas dividends paid are not deductible. This asymmetry of treatment means that the corporation may have an incentive to borrow money to finance its activities, incurring debt, rather than use its retained earnings that have accumulated in the form of equity. This may lead the corporation to prefer debt to equity financing.

Profits: Economic and Accounting

The corporate income tax is applied to the net income of corporations. Notice that the tax base is called *net income* rather than *profit*. This distinction is not merely semantic. It is tempting to call the difference between a corporation's revenue from sales and its costs profit, but we must be more careful to distinguish the type of profit with which we are dealing. **Accounting profit** is the simple difference between revenue generated by sales and costs incurred for inputs. Recall that **economic profit**, in contrast, is the difference between revenue and cost, including **opportunity cost of capital**. The important opportunity cost to include when contemplating corporate activity is the next-best alternative use of the corporation's capital. The economist views profit as the return to an activity over and above the return that would have been earned in the next-best alternative, given comparable risk. We only consider a corporation's return beyond the opportunity cost of its capital as true profit. If the tax base of the corporate income tax were economic profit, there would be no efficiency loss due to the tax. That is, there would be no excess burden of taxation in that setting. Of course, we know that in a competitive industry the long-run equilibrium results in zero economic profit. Hence, in this context, a corporate income tax applied to economic profit will generate no revenue whatsoever.

In the short run the corporate income tax could generate some revenue due to the existence of short-run profits. In an industry with imperfect competition (a monopolistically competitive industry, an oligopoly, or a monopoly) long-run economic profits are earned. In that case, we could expect a corporate income tax on economic profit to generate revenue. In reality, however, corporations are not taxed on the basis of their economic profits. Rather, they are taxed on their accounting profits. Because accounting profit differs from economic profit, the corporate income tax has efficiency effects that must be carefully examined.

If the tax base of the corporate income tax were economic profit, then the tax would be perfectly efficient, creating no excess burden. That would make it

FIGURE 15.2 Competitive Firm Profits

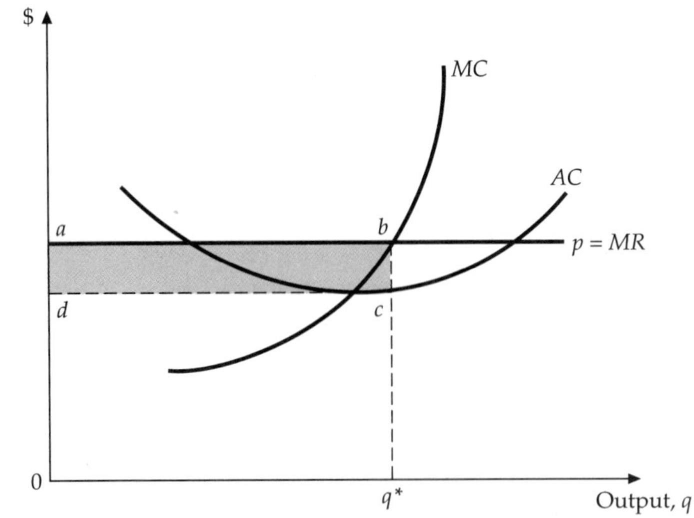

a very attractive tax because revenue could be generated without concern for the distortionary effects of taxation. Figure 15.2 provides a reminder of the situation for a perfectly competitive firm (a price-taker with horizontal demand curve). The profit-maximizing firm will produce q^* units of output and earn profits equal to the rectangular area labeled *abcd*. When the firm reports that profit for tax purposes, the corporate income tax simply takes a portion of the profit without affecting the price of the product or the firm's costs (*MC* and *AC*). Therefore, a tax on economic profit has no effect on the firm's output or input decisions and consequently has no efficiency effect. Keep in mind, however, that this economic analysis is short run in its time horizon.

The long-run equilibrium in a perfectly competitive industry involves no economic profit whatsoever. Free entry into the industry assures that the presence of economic profit in the short run will induce new firms to enter, shifting the industry supply curve rightward, lowering the equilibrium price in the market, and shifting downward the price-taking firm's demand curve. In the long run we expect that all economic profit will be competed away, leaving only **normal profit** reflecting the opportunity cost of capital. Economic profit is the return over and above normal profit. Normal profit reflects the opportunity cost of capital—the value of the next-best alternative—or the return to capital that would normally be expected in the market, given risk. The good news is that a tax on pure economic profit would be efficient. The bad news is that in the long run it would not generate any revenue.

What if the industry is not perfectly competitive and economic profit exists in the long-run equilibrium? Would a corporate income tax be a viable means of capturing some of the pure economic profit earned by a firm with market power, perhaps even monopoly power, in an efficient way? Figure 15.3 illustrates

FIGURE 15.3 Monopolist Profit

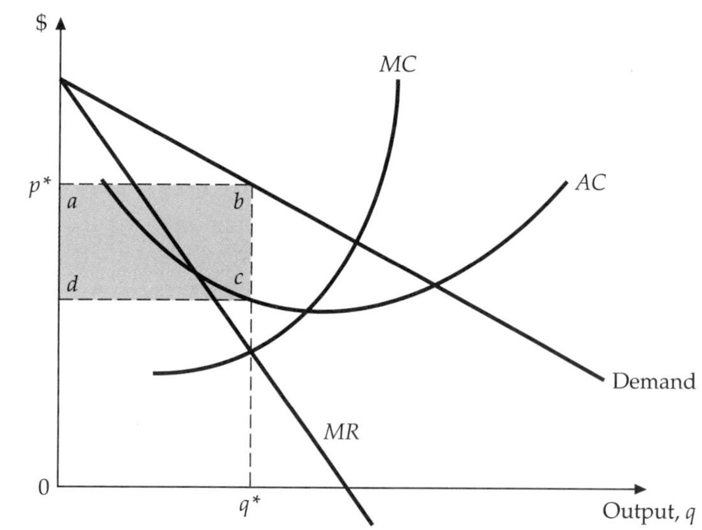

the case of a monopolist producer of a product, with a downward-sloping demand curve. The profit-maximizing monopolist will produce quantity q^* (where $MR = MC$), sell that quantity at the monopolistic price p^*, and earn profits equal to the area labeled *abcd*. In this case, a tax on profit will once again not affect the firm's marginal revenue (MR) or marginal cost (MC) and therefore not affect the profit-maximizing output rate. Although the monopolist will earn a smaller profit due to the tax, she will not change her output or price. In this case, a tax on economic profit would be perfectly efficient and would generate revenue because profit persists even in the long run.

The reality of the corporate income tax, however, is that it is not a tax on pure economic profit, whether applied to competitive corporations or noncompetitive corporations. Let's pause for a moment and consider whether the definition of net income for tax purposes is equivalent to the economist's definition of profit. The definition of net income for tax purposes does not permit a deduction for the opportunity cost of capital; it includes both normal profits and economic profits. Thus, the corporate income tax taxes not only economic profit but also normal expected return to capital. In this regard, the corporate income tax base is too broad. Net income for tax purposes might not be too far off the mark if depreciation were defined as true economic depreciation. That would permit the corporation to deduct a portion of its capital cost reflecting the rate at which the capital is used up in the production process. But, alas, that is not the case.

Several methods are used to compute depreciation for tax purposes, none of which is true economic depreciation because that is very difficult to measure. If the corporate income tax depreciation schedules captured true economic depreciation, then the true cost of capital would be taken into account and net income would reflect the proper extent to which the corporation is using up its capital equipment. If depreciation schedules permit faster write-off or more than true economic depreciation, however, then corporations are able to deduct an amount in excess of the true cost of capital.

Corporate Income Tax Rates

U.S. corporate income tax rates are graduated. The tax rate structure is given in Table 15.1. Marginal tax rates range from 15 to 35 percent, depending on the level of taxable income, with the typical firm paying the marginal 35 percent rate.

In an international context, corporate income tax rates vary widely across countries. Among the most industrialized countries, represented by the OECD, rates range from a low of 8.5 percent in Switzerland to a high of 35 percent in the United States. Figure 15.4 illustrates corporate income tax rates for OECD countries in 2010. The left (blue) bar for each country is the central government corporate tax rate and the right (red) bar is the combined central government rate plus any sub-central government rate. In the case of the United States, for example, the combined rate includes the average state corporate income tax rate for a combined rate of nearly 40 percent. At this point in time, the U.S. central government corporate tax rate of 35 percent is the highest among the OECD countries. For more on the U.S. tax system in international perspective see Chapter 5 of Council of Economic Advisers (2006).[3]

TABLE 15.1 U.S. Corporate Income Tax Rates, 2010

If Taxable Income (Line 30, Form 1120) Is

Over	*But Not Over*	*Tax Is*	*Of the Amount Over*
$ 0	$ 50,000	15%	$ 0
$ 50,000	$ 75,000	$ 7,500 + 25%	$ 50,000
$ 75,000	$ 100,000	$ 13,750 + 34%	$ 75,000
$ 100,000	$ 335,000	$ 22,250 + 39%	$ 100,000
$ 335,000	$10,000,000	$ 113,900 + 34%	$ 335,000
$10,000,000	$15,000,000	$3,400,000 + 35%	$10,000,000
$15,000,000	$18,333,333	$5,150,000 + 38%	$15,000,000
$18,333,333		35%	$ 0

Source: *Instructions for Form 1120* (Washington, DC: Department of the Treasury, Internal Revenue Service, 2010, page 18).

FIGURE 15.4 Corporate Income Tax Rates for OECD Countries, 2010

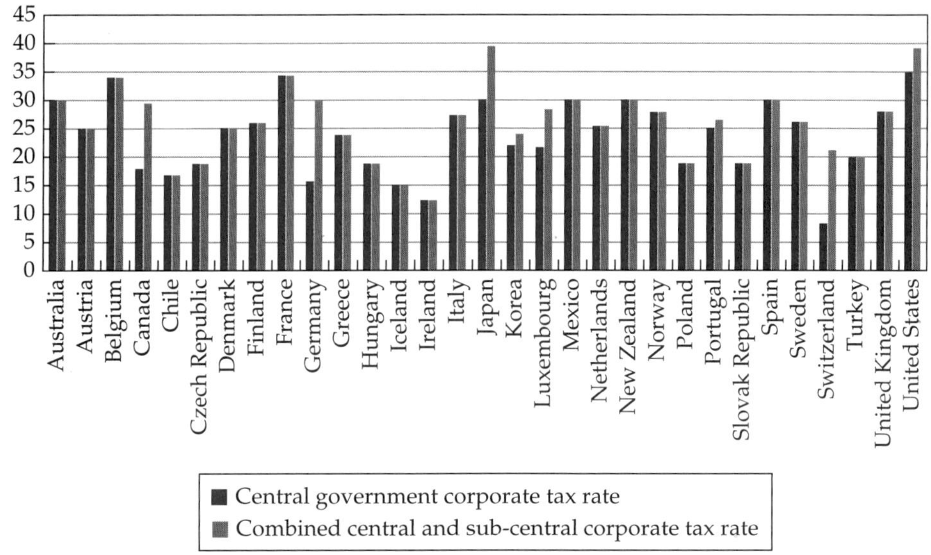

Source: OECD Tax Database, available at: http://www.oecd.org/document/60/0,3746,en_2649_34533_1942460_1_1_1_1,00.html

INCIDENCE OF THE CORPORATE INCOME TAX

In 1968 Arnold Harberger, a pioneer of modern incidence analysis, wrote that "The incidence of the corporation income tax has long been the subject of debate among economists, a state of affairs which is likely to continue for some time."[4] He was right. After more than thirty years the debate continues to rage. Who are the usual suspects to round up as we try to identify the bearers of the corporate income tax burden? That is, who could conceivably bear the burden of the corporate income tax? The traditional trichotomy holds that the tax falls on stockholders, consumers, workers, or some combination of these three groups. Indeed, Harold Groves warned long ago that "In the last analysis, all taxes come out of the income or capital (actual or potential) of individuals. Tax burdens cannot be borne by inanimate objects."[5] Harberger points out, however, that three errors are involved in this traditional trichotomy. First, there is an error in the use of the term *stockholders*. More correctly, we should consider owners of capital. Second, the distinction between consumers and workers is difficult as most consumers are workers and most workers are consumers. Third, there is also the problem implicit in this traditional view of those on whom the tax burden falls, that none of these groups could actually benefit from the imposition of the tax.

Incidence of a Partial Factor Tax

The corporate income tax is a **partial factor tax**. It is a tax applied to one factor of production—capital—in one sector of the economy—the corporate sector. Its effect in this context is to raise the cost of capital from r to $r + t$ in the corporate sector of the economy, leaving the cost of capital unchanged in the noncorporate sector. Under a certain set of assumptions, we can analyze the impact of the corporate income tax on the demand for capital.[6] Introduction of a corporate income tax has two effects on the demand for capital: a **factor substitution effect** and an **output effect**.

First, consider the effect of the tax on the use of inputs and how the input mix will change as a result of the factor substitution effect. Suppose that the corporate sector of the economy is designated as the X sector, with the noncorporate sector designated as the Y sector. Introduction of a tax on capital in the corporate X sector has the effect of raising the price of capital in the X sector relative to the price of labor (the other important input used in production). The increase in the cost of capital results in a reduction in the amount of capital demanded by firms in the corporate sector of the economy. This occurs as long as the technology used by firms is flexible, allowing them to substitute labor for the now more expensive capital.

Second, consider that the introduction of a tax on capital in the corporate X sector also has an impact on the output of the firm and hence affects the demand for capital. With an increase in the cost of capital in the corporate sector there will be an increase in the relative price of good X produced in this sector. The price of that good, p_x, rises relative to the price of the good produced in the noncorporate sector, p_y. Hence, the price ratio p_x/p_y rises. When this occurs the output of X in the corporate sector will fall relative to the output of Y in the noncorporate sector as markets adjust in response to the change in relative prices. As output of X is decreased and output of Y is increased, the demand for capital is affected.

Two possible effects exist, however. First, consider the case where the X sector of the economy is relatively labor intensive, reflecting a production process that requires larger amounts of labor relative to capital in the X sector as compared to the Y sector. In this case the demand for capital will rise. This occurs because the scale-back in output of X relative to Y reduces the demand for labor (X sector is relatively labor intensive) while increasing the demand for capital (Y sector is relatively capital intensive). Second, consider the case where the X sector is relatively capital intensive. By similar logic it follows that the demand for capital will fall. The conclusion is that a tax on capital in the X sector will cause the demand for capital to rise or fall depending on whether the X sector is relatively labor intensive or capital intensive. Table 15.2 summarizes these effects.

The net effect of a tax on capital in the corporate X sector causes the demand for capital to fall through the factor substitution effect but causes an ambiguous effect on the demand for capital through the output effect. Hence, the net effect of the tax on capital is uncertain. If the corporate X sector is relatively capital intensive we have a clear result: the corporate tax causes the demand for capital to fall. If the corporate X sector is relatively labor intensive, however, we have an uncertain effect. The factor substitution effect and the output effect are of opposite signs, and the net effect will depend on the relative sizes.

TABLE 15.2 Effects of a Corporate Income Tax on the Demand for Capital

Cost of Capital Rises in the X Sector		
Output Effect		Factor Substitution Effect
Relative price p_x/p_y *of X rises.*		*Quantity of capital demanded falls.*
Output of X Falls Relative to Y		
X sector relatively labor intensive. *Quantity of capital demanded rises.*	X sector relatively capital intensive. *Quantity of capital demanded falls.*	

Evidence on Incidence

The earliest research on the incidence of the corporate income tax is that of Harberger (1962). His path-breaking incidence analysis applied to the U.S. corporate income tax, and concluded with the following summary statement:

> It is hard to avoid the conclusion that plausible alternative sets of assumptions about the relevant elasticities all yield results in which capital bears very close to 100 percent of the tax burden. The most plausible assumptions imply that capital bears more than the full burden of the tax. (p. 234)

ON THE WEB

For more on corporate income tax equity, see the Policy Study "Who Bears the Burden of the Corporate Tax in an Open Economy?" on the companion website. (www.cengage.com/international).

On the basis of this conclusion, we would expect that the corporate income tax is borne entirely by capital, with none of the burden shifted to labor. Apparently capital is forced to bear the burden of the corporate income tax, with none of the burden shifted to labor. For more analysis of the incidence of the corporate income tax, this time in the context of an open economy with trade, see the Policy Study on the web, highlighted in the box at the left. That Policy Study provides evidence that most of the long-run incidence of the tax is borne by domestic capital, not domestic labor or landowners. Furthermore, in those cases where the tax incidence is not borne by domestic capital it appears to be exported rather than being borne by labor.

TAXATION AND GLOBAL BUSINESS

Increasing globalization of business has important implications for the taxation of business income (or other tax bases).

Globalization

International trade is increasing throughout the world with a larger share of many nations' GDP coming from the net exports component. With increased openness of many economies, including the U.S. economy which has been relatively closed in the past, business firms have the opportunity to not only produce products for international markets but also have the opportunity to operate in a multinational context producing and distributing products globally. Many firms now produce products for global markets rather than simply for the domestic market where the firm is located. **Globalization** refers to the increasing tendency of business firms to operate across national borders or combine with firms in other countries in mergers or strategic alliances. It also refers to the reality that most product markets and factor markets are now global rather than local. When a firm looks for a supplier of an input, it no longer is content to consider just local providers. The firm is more likely to search for suppliers globally, setting strict quality and performance standards, then putting the supply opportunity up for bid among all globally qualified suppliers. International capital markets provide the firm's capital needs, not just domestic capital markets. Labor markets are also increasingly global, although labor proves to be less mobile in many ways. Although certain specialized workers such as management consultants (with translators) may be globally mobile or workers in a region such as Western Europe may be more mobile across national boundaries because the European Union has made it easier to work in a country other than one's own, there are still many impediments to labor mobility including familial ties and language limitations. Nevertheless, even labor is increasingly mobile in the international context.

What are the implications of increasing globalization of business for taxation? Does increasing international competition mean that the opportunities for governments to collect revenue from firms in their jurisdictions are now more limited because taxation may drive the firm away? Put in more colorful terms, we might recall the advice of Jean-Baptiste Colbert to Louis XIV. He said that the art of taxation consists in so plucking the goose as to obtain the largest possible amount of feathers with the smallest possible amount of hissing. In the global economy, we may have to worry not so much about the hissing as the goose flying away!

Does the increasingly footloose nature of firms' globalization of business mean that governments must commit to a tax **race to the bottom**, lowering their tax rates faster than other nations in order to retain business firms? Not entirely, although keeping a competitive tax system is more important than ever. Research on firm location behavior has shown that low taxes are not all that firms care about. They also need public services and are willing to pay for them. Good transportation and communication networks are also very important for firms. Governments that provide favorable combinations of the public services that firms need and competitive tax systems will find that firms are more easily retained and attracted.

Taxation and Trade Issues

Trade agreements are becoming increasingly important and the removal of unfair trade restrictions is facilitating trade. Along with these agreements is increasing concern about unfair tax policies, however. The World Trade Organization (WTO), for example, exists to facilitate world trade and is responsible for coordination of trade policies among nations in order to increase global trading. Although the WTO exists to reduce trade barriers and facilitate trade, it has recently become involved in tax issues as well. For example, the European Union complained that foreign sales corporations were a means by which illegal export subsidies were provided to firms by the U.S. government, and the WTO agreed, concluding that they violate WTO rules.

Foreign sales corporations (FSCs) are shell companies in offshore tax havens that U.S. firms used to avoid taxes. The U.S. firms sent foreign income through the FSCs in order to avoid taxation. Some 6,000 U.S. firms were reported to use this mechanism with Boeing saving $130 million in tax in 1998 and General Electric saving $150 million.[7] The FSCs also benefited foreign subsidiaries of U.S. firms abroad. In Britain the firms British Petroleum, ICI, and Unilever benefit from FSCs. In Germany BASF, Daimler Benz, and Hoechst benefit. In France Elf-Aquitaine and Rhone-Poulenc benefit. The U.S. response is that FSCs simply offset the tax advantages that EU-based firms enjoy. Eventually, however, the World Trade Organization (WTO) ruled FSCs unacceptable and they were abolished by the American Jobs Creation Act (AJCA) of 2004. The U.S. income tax subjects firms' worldwide income to taxation (subject to honoring existing bilateral agreements for avoidance of double taxation), whereas EU tax policy does not. European value-added taxes (VATs) are applied on a destination basis; hence, exports are not subject to what is typically a 20 percent tax. That type of tax advantage was identified by U.S. supporters of FSCs (although the comparison is fully accurate since on the one hand we are considering a U.S. income tax and on the other hand an EU member state VAT). European firms also use sales subsidiaries in offshore tax havens. In fact, the Organization for Economic Cooperation and Development (OECD) has spearheaded a drive to reduce the number of offshore tax havens.[8] This debate is not new, but its resolution is both more important and more difficult in the context of increasingly global business activity.

Taxation of Foreign Income

In order to consider international taxation issues, it is useful to start with a basic description of the tax liability of corporations operating globally. A U.S. corporation that directly conducts its business in another country must pay U.S. tax on its net income earned in that country. If the U.S. corporation separately incorporates its foreign business operation, the foreign subsidiary is not subject to U.S. tax on this foreign source income. In general, a U.S. parent corporation is not subject to U.S. tax on the net income of its foreign subsidiaries unless and until that income is repatriated via dividend distributions (subject to certain restrictions and anti-deferral regime applications).

Most countries of the world tax income generated by economic activity exclusively within their borders. This approach to taxation is called **territorial taxation**. A few countries, such as the United States, however, apply their income taxes on a **worldwide** basis and also tax the foreign income of their residents.[9] Other countries taxing on a worldwide basis include Greece, Japan, Norway, and the United Kingdom. In order to avoid double taxation countries applying their income tax on a worldwide basis provide a **foreign**

tax credit for taxes paid to foreign governments. The tax credit reduces tax liability in the home country. For example, suppose a U.S. resident earns $1,000 in foreign income in a country with a 10 percent income tax. A tax payment of $100 is paid to the foreign government. Because the U.S. corporate tax rate is 35 percent, the U.S. resident must pay $350 in U.S. corporate income tax, less a foreign tax credit of $100, resulting in a net tax payment to the United States of $250. In the year 2007, for example, there were 6,675 U.S. corporate income tax returns filed with claims for foreign tax credits. The total U.S. income tax owed by the firms filing these returns was $292.3 billion, which was reduced by $86.5 billion in foreign tax credits claimed.[10]

The classic model of Richman (1963) indicates that countries have an incentive to tax the foreign income of their residents, allowing for tax deductions for foreign taxes paid. That model does not suggest limiting the deduction, however. The maximum amount of foreign tax credit permitted under the U.S. corporate income tax cannot exceed the amount that would have been owed under the U.S. tax system. This constraint is inconsistent with the Richman model. Hines (2005) points out that by taxing foreign income and permitting foreign tax credits, the U.S. tax system reduces the incentive for U.S. firms to earn income in low-tax countries because lower foreign tax liability is offset by higher U.S. tax liability. However, a U.S. firm can benefit from locating some portion of its operation in a foreign location in two situations. The first situation occurs when a U.S. firm can defer repatriation of foreign profits, it can also reduce the present value of its U.S. tax liability. The second situation is where a taxpayer has excess foreign tax credits that can be used to reduce U.S. taxes on lightly taxed foreign income. Hines asserts that the combination of these two situations is attractive for a sufficient number of U.S. firms to make, "investors in the aggregate highly sensitive to foreign tax rate differences."

The evidence on multinationals and their responses to international tax rules indicates that they are very responsive in three distinct ways.[11] First, tax avoidance is a natural response to taxes. Tax avoidance behavior shows up in several forms. Firms operating internationally engage in **transfer pricing** of goods and services. When one part of the company provides products or services to another part of the company, there is an explicit or implicit price at which that transfer occurs. When the price is explicit, the issue is straightforward, but if there is no explicit price an implicit price must be estimated. That implicit price must be made explicit for the purpose of computing each division's profit or loss. When setting that price there may be tax implications to be considered. The essence of transfer pricing is that the company prices the goods or services transferred within the firm between their U.S. and international operations in such a way as to minimize their total tax burden. Dworin (1990) provides a general definition of transfer pricing that refers to, "the broad range of issues that relate to the determination of both the amount and the characterization of the income reported by an entity doing business in one country that buys goods or services from a related entity located in another country."

TABLE 15.3 Transfer Pricing Examples

	External Market Exists and Arm's-Length Price is Available	No External Market Exists so no Arm's-Length Price is Available
Division to which the product is sent sells the product as a final product	Wal-Mart Corporation transfers slow-selling snowsuits from stores in Alabama to stores in North Dakota where they are selling like hotcakes	Microsoft Corporation transfers a patented software product from its subsidiary in Ireland to the United States for final marketing and sale
Division to which to product is sent uses it as an input in the production of a final product	ADM Corporation transfers corn from its acquisition unit in Illinois to one of its ethanol production units in Nebraska	General Motors Corporation imports auto parts produced by a subsidiary in Mexico for use in auto final assembly in Michigan

Table 15.3 provides four examples of transfer pricing situations. In cases where there is an external market that reveals arm's-length prices for the good being transferred, there is no problem with market-based transfer prices. The market sends the appropriate signals regarding scarcity and value. The corporation's incentives align perfectly with the market signals and efficient allocation of resources results. The tax authority can observe those prices and assure that the corporation's tax return reflects appropriate prices used in determining the profit of each division, and thereby reports the proper amount of income for tax purposes. In cases where there is no external market price observable, however, the lack of arm's-length transactions provides the corporation an opportunity to report transfer prices designed to minimize the tax burden rather than fully reflect actual, if only implicit, prices. The result is misallocation of resources and inefficiency.

One of the clues that something has gone on with transfer pricing is that the substantial increase in direct foreign investment by U.S. firms around the globe has not been associated with a similar increase in reported net income (profit) of the U.S. subsidiaries. Dworin (1990) notes that, "when measured by their net income … their apparent rate of return has been rather anemic." Of course, lack of profitability is not conclusive evidence of problems with transfer pricing.[12]

Another form of tax avoidance has to do with **dividend repatriation.** Foreign subsidiaries are foreign corporations owned by U.S. corporations. The income earned by a U.S. corporation via a foreign subsidiary is not taxable in the United States unless and until that income is returned to the U.S. corporation. Net income earned by the foreign subsidiary is taxable by the foreign government and not taxable in the United States unless it is repatriated to the U.S. parent corporation in the form of dividends. Repatriation of dividends to the U.S. parent company triggers U.S. corporate income tax. Hence, as long as the net income is retained in the foreign subsidiary those retained earnings are beyond the reach of the U.S. tax system. This feature of the tax system provides a potential deferral of U.S. taxation, which is valuable to the corporation.The value of this deferral depends on the two tax rates involved. If the tax rate applied in Country X is higher than that applied in the United States, say 40 percent for example, then there is no additional U.S. tax due (the foreign tax credit provides up to the amount of U.S. tax, but not more) and there is, therefore, no benefit to deferral. But this case is not currently relevant as the U.S. tax rate is the highest among OECD countries. On the other hand, if the corporate income tax rate in Country X is below that in the United States as is the case more generally, then there is a benefit to the corporation from deferral. If Ireland applies a 12.5 percent corporate income tax rate, as it currently does for example, then there is a potential deferral associated with the 22.5 percent of the Irish subsidiary's net income that is not taxed in the United States. The longer the U.S. parent corporation waits to repatriate those profits, the less the amount of the tax in present value terms. Tax deferred is tax saved. Deferral is a common feature of tax systems that tax foreign income. Desai, Foley, and Hines (2003, p. 64) report that this method is also used by Canada, Denmark, France, Germany, Japan, Norway, Pakistan, and the United Kingdom.

Consider an example of a U.S. corporation with a foreign subsidiary that earns $500 million in net income in a country with a corporate income tax rate of 20 percent. The subsidiary must pay $100 million in tax to the foreign government. Of its $400 million after-tax income, it might remit $100 million in dividends to its U.S. parent corporation and retain $300 million. The U.S. parent corporation must pay tax on the $100 million in dividends received, less its foreign tax credit. The foreign tax credit is $25 million, or the product of foreign taxes paid by its subsidiary ($100 million) times the ratio of the subsidiary company's dividends to after-tax profits: ($100/$400). This computation reflects the fact that dividends are treated as U.S. source in proportion to the U.S. source earnings and profits of the U.S. owned foreign corporation The U.S. corporation pays no U.S. tax on any of the $300 million earned by the subsidiary and unremitted to the parent company. If the subsidiary pays a dividend to the U.S. parent company the following year, the company must pay U.S. tax, net of foreign tax credit.

Desai, Foley, and Hines (2001) have analyzed the economic effects of the U.S. system and found that dividend remittances from incorporated foreign affiliates are sensitive to taxes. Their results indicate that a 10 percent higher repatriation tax is associated with 10 percent lower dividends. Their work also indicates that if the United States were to adopt a territorial tax system that would increase aggregate dividend payouts by 12.8 percent, with widely varying effects between affiliates in different tax situations. What is clear is that repatriation taxes reduce economic efficiency, with strong incentives to remit dividends from some foreign affiliates (in higher tax countries) rather than others (in lower tax countries). The loss of economic efficiency has the distributional and incentive effects of an extra tax imposed on U.S. multinational firms. Estimates indicate that the annual efficiency loss due to dividend repatriation taxes is 2.5 percent of dividends.

As part of the American Jobs Creation Act (AJCA) of 2004 the U.S. Congress granted a one-time opportunity in 2005 to repatriate dividends in order to stimulate the U.S. economy. The tax rate applied to repatriated dividends was 5.25 percent (15 percent of the usual tax rate of 35 percent). Such a tax holiday is most likely to induce a one-time shift of overseas dividends back to the United States, not a permanently higher stream of repatriated dividends. Because the stock of dividends with the potential of being repatriated is fixed, inducing a greater flow this year may provide temporary tax revenue, but it may not induce a larger permanent flow of capital back to the United States.

A final form of tax avoidance is in the location of intangible property; for example, patent transfers. All of these forms of tax avoidance result in wasted resources as they are dedicated to rearranging profits internationally. Empirical evidence cited by Desai (2005), for example, indicates that a 10 percent tax rate differential has the effect of changing reported profits by 2.3 percent. Second, ownership patterns of firms are affected by taxes, which may alter the way joint ventures are configured, the pattern of expatriations, and the form of mergers and acquisitions. Finally, investments made by firms are affected by taxes. Taxes have an impact on investment across countries, and between the home country and abroad. Both where the firm invests and the amount of investment may be affected. Desai (2005) cites empirical evidence indicating that a 10 percent difference in tax rates is associated with a 10 percent difference in the quantity of investment—a unitary elastic response.

Neutral Taxation of Foreign Income

Because international tax rate differences can create an inefficient allocation of global economic activity, economists have developed several proposed methods of foreign income taxation that are "neutral" in some sense. We consider three approaches to neutrality, following Hines (2008). First, under a system of capital export neutrality (CEN), an investor's income is taxed at the same rate regardless of where in the world it is earned. A home country adopting a CEN tax system provides firms an incentive to locate their economic activity wherever it can maximize its pretax profits. Under certain circumstances, this approach leads to a globally efficient allocation of capital. Hence, this approach is generally advocated as the appropriate way to tax foreign income, with the provision of foreign tax credits, as in Richman (1963). A CEN system is commonly thought to promote efficient production. When countries actually implement such tax regimes, however, they typically place a limit on the foreign tax credit and they also allow deferral of taxation for unrepatriated income. Consequently, the efficiency properties of this approach are not fully realized.

A similar but distinct approach is to implement a tax system with national neutrality (NN) by which the home country taxes the foreign income of their resident firms, permitting only a deduction for foreign taxes paid (a deduction, not a credit as with a CEN system). This approach discourages firms from engaging in foreign investment as it imposes a form of double taxation on them. The foreign taxes paid are treated like any other expense of doing business.

Another approach is to implement a capital import neutrality (CIN) tax system. In this type of tax system the return to capital is taxed at the same total rate, regardless of where the capital investor lives. Hines (2008) notes that a pure source-based tax system with tax rates that differ by location can be consistent with the CIN principle. That occurs because the various investors are taxed at the same rate on the same capital income. But, such a system also requires that personal income tax rates be harmonized across countries so that the combined tax burden on savings and investment in each country is identical. A CIN tax system is commonly described as promoting the efficient level of saving.

The final neutrality concept to consider is capital ownership neutrality (CON). This neutrality concept is motivated by the reality that a large proportion of foreign investment is for acquisitions of existing assets by new owners. CON is achieved when every country taxes foreign income in the same way, avoiding tax clienteles (i.e., groups of investors with the same preferences for particular assets that minimize their tax liabilities). Hines (2008) notes that the same situations that make a CON system desirable (in terms of maximizing world welfare) also imply that each individual country has an incentive to exempt foreign income from taxation. That occurs regardless of the tax regime selected by other countries. Hence, tax systems that completely exempt foreign income from taxation are said to be neutral in the CON sense.

Altshuler (2011) sates, "Our current system for taxing the income earned abroad by U.S. firms is very complex, induces inefficient behavioral responses, and leaves both companies and policy analysts dissatisfied." Given the inefficiencies caused by the current U.S. tax treatment of cross-border income, what can be done to reform the system? Options designed to end deferral include repeal of deferral, and taxation of all foreign income currently at a lower tax rate. Options to reform cross-border income taxation suggested by Gruber and Altshuler (2008) include the exemption of dividends from active business income abroad and a switch to a burden-neutral worldwide tax system.

Apportionment Issues

Another approach to international taxation (or state taxation within a federation) is to apportion the income to the various jurisdictions in which it was earned and let each jurisdiction apply its tax rate to the income earned in that jurisdiction. The European Commission has recently proposed using formula apportionment for taxing corporate income in the European Union. Devereaux and Loretz (2007) analyze the potential effects of such a policy, demonstrating that total tax revenues are likely to rise by more than 8 percent, making most European countries better off. They also investigate the sensitivity of the results to the specification of apportionment factors in the formula.

Formula apportionment has a substantial history in the United States, used to apportion income among the states. Consider a multinational firm such as the Ford Motor Company. The firm is based in Michigan in the United States, but it produces its products in factories all over the country and sells its automobiles around the world. How much of the net income of Ford should be taxed in Michigan, and how much of it should be subject to tax in the other jurisdictions where Ford operates? These are the issues of apportionment of net income to the taxing jurisdictions involved.

The traditional method of apportionment is a **three-factor method** that taxes the net income of a firm on the basis of its payroll, property, and sales factors. This system of apportionment was developed as part of the Multistate Tax Compact (MTC) in 1967 in the United States as part of an effort to increase uniformity in state tax laws.[13] Within the MTC, Article IV the Uniform Division of Income for Tax Purposes Act (UDITPA) specified a three-factor apportionment scheme for states that voluntarily joined the MTC. Most states initially adopted the equally weighted three-factor apportionment formula. Since that time 29 states have deviated from that formula method, placing half or more weight on sales. Just 13 states currently use the three-factor equally weighted formula.[14]

Suppose that we designate the firm's payroll, property, and sales in jurisdiction i as P_i, R_i, and S_i, respectively. The firm's total payroll, property, and sales are denoted P, R, and S. Hence, the three factors (shares) in jurisdiction i are written as P_i/P, R_i/R, and S_i/S. The traditional three-factor apportionment method is to allocate a share of the firm's net income from all its activities where the share allocated to jurisdiction i is the average of the payroll, property, and sales fractions. The amount of income apportioned to jurisdiction i is given by

$$A_i = \left[\frac{P_i}{P} + \frac{R_i}{R} + \frac{S_i}{S}\right]/3. \tag{15.3}$$

Suppose, for example, that Ford has 60 percent of its payroll, 80 percent of its property, and 3 percent of its sales in Michigan. In this case $P_i/P = 0.60$, $R_i/R = 0.80$, and $S_i/S = 0.02$. The amount of net income apportioned to Michigan would be

$$A = (0.60 + 0.80 + 0.02)/3 = 0.4733. \tag{15.4}$$

Hence, Ford would pay tax to Michigan on 47.33 percent of its worldwide net income.

The advantage of all taxing jurisdictions using such an apportionment scheme is that all of the net income of the firm will be taxed by some jurisdiction but no more than all of its net income will be subject to taxation. Without some agreement among taxing units such as this, it is possible that some part of the firm's net income may not be taxed or that its net income may be subject to taxation by multiple jurisdictions.

The disadvantage of an apportionment method such as this is that it is somewhat arbitrary. After all, why allocate net income to taxing jurisdictions on the basis of a simple arithmetic average of payroll, property, and sales factors? Payroll and property are input measures, but sales is an output measure. The three-factor formula is an average of two input measures and an output measure, all equally weighted. But, does that formula really capture the share of net income of the firm representing its ability to pay properly? Probably not. But then, what is the alternative?

In recent years several U.S. states have modified the traditional three-factor formula. Iowa started the trend toward sales-only apportionment. Under this apportionment scheme, only one factor is used in the apportionment formula—the sales factor. Why would a state make this change in its apportionment formula? Consider the impact of this change on the Ford example discussed previously. If the payroll and property factors are relatively high proportions and the sales factor is a relatively low proportion, the impact of sales-only apportionment is to dramatically reduce the firm's taxable income in the state where it is headquartered. In the hypothetical Ford case, the change is to tax just 2 percent of its worldwide net income, rather than 47.33 percent. Multinational corporations headquartered in the state receive a very large tax reduction. On the other hand, firms that sell all of their product in the state in which they are headquartered receive no tax reduction.

The essential issue with apportionment is whether the state corporate income tax will in fact be a partial factor applied to capital and/or labor or will be a general tax on sales. Choice of the factors in the apportionment formula and their weights can configure the corporate income tax in a variety of ways, either emphasizing the taxation of production (by taxing inputs) or emphasizing the taxation of sales (perhaps without production in the state, by taxing sales).

ON THE WEB

For more on cross-border taxation, see the Policy Study "The Weighting Game: Formula Apportionment" on the companion website. (www.cengage.com/international).

The effect of the change to sales-only apportionment is to lower taxes on multinational or multistate firms relative to those who sell domestically (within the state). States such as Iowa and Nebraska that have moved to sales-only apportionment justify the change as a means of retaining and attracting multinational firms. The argument in favor of heavily weighting the sales factor is that in the presence of mobile inputs, such as capital, an apportionment formula that taxes capital will drive it away. States believe that heavier weighting on sales has the advantage of retaining and attracting capital. Whether this in fact is true, of course, depends on a number of other factors as well. A Policy Study on the website for this chapter provides evidence that in the presence of fixed factors, the effect of a heavier weight on the sales factor is ambiguous. Consequently, some states may find it advantageous to stay with the traditional equally weighted three-factor formula, whereas others may find it advantageous to weight the sales factor more heavily.

Other states have adopted an intermediary method of double-weighting the sales factor. Under this method, payroll and property factors each count one-quarter of the total and the sales factor counts one-half. Now, what happens to the overall system of apportionment which was formerly based on an agreement to use the three-factor formula? When one or more states move to a different method of apportionment, there is no longer any assurance that the firm's total net income will be taxed once and only once. Net income allocated to the states no longer adds up properly. Table 15.4 summarizes the various methods of apportionment used by states in the United States.

TABLE 15.4 Formula Apportionment Systems Used in the United States

Weighting System	States	Frequency
Equal-weighted sales factor	Alabama, Alaska, Delaware, Hawaii, Kansas, Louisiana, Mississippi, Montana, North Dakota, Oklahoma, Rhode Island, Utah, Vermont	13
Double-weighted sales factor	Arizona, Arkansas, Connecticut, Florida, Georgia, Idaho, Illinois, Indiana, Kentucky, Maine, Maryland, New Hampshire, New Jersey, New York, North Carolina, Ohio, Oregon, Pennsylvania, South Carolina, Tennessee, Virginia, West Virginia, Wisconsin	23
Sales factor at least 50 percent	Iowa, Massachusetts, Michigan, Minnesota, Nebraska, Texas	6
Elective	California, Colorado, Missouri, New Mexico	4
None	Nevada, South Dakota, Washington, Wyoming	4
Total		50

Source: From "The Weighting Game: Formula Apportionment as an Instrument of Public Policy," by Bharat N. Anand and Richard Sansing in *National Tax Journal* 53, No. 2 (2002): 190. Reprinted by permission of National Tax Association.

POLICY STUDY

Less Than Zero: Enron's Corporate Income Tax Payments, 1996–2000

The spectacular failure of the Enron Corporation in late 2001 and early 2002 brought into public view one of the most common forms of tax avoidance (perhaps evasion) used by corporations. That is the creation of offshore tax havens such as those in Bermuda, the Cayman Islands, and other locations. Analysis of the corporate income tax situation for Enron over the period from 1996 through 2000 by Citizens for Tax Justice (CTJ) reveals that the corporation effectively used more than 800 such tax havens along with stock options and other tax loopholes to reduce its tax liability substantially. In fact, the CTJ analysis illustrates that Enron paid tax in only one year and was effectively able to reduce its corporate tax liability to less than zero. Table 15.5 lists Enron profits before federal taxes for the years 1996 through 2000 and computes the taxes that would have been due in the absence of stock options and tax savings from other loopholes. The bottom line of the table illustrates that only in 1997 did Enron pay a positive corporate income tax. In the other years, it received payments from the U.S. Treasury, despite the fact that the company was profitable.

This example illustrates how a profitable corporation may use tax shelters to reduce its taxable income and thereby reduce its tax liability. This is certainly not the way the corporate income tax system is designed to work, but it shows how the system can be manipulated. Despite the favorable tax situation for Enron, the company went belly-up, demonstrating that taxes are not the sole determinant of a corporation's success!

TABLE 15.5 Enron Corporate Income Tax Payments, 1996–2000 ($ millions)

	2000	1999	1998	1997	1996	1996–2000
U.S. profits before federal income taxes	618	351	189	87	540	1,785
Tax at 35 percent corporate rate	216	123	66	30	189	625
Less tax benefits from stock options	−390	−134	−43	−12	−19	−597
Less tax savings from other loopholes, etc.	−104	−94	−36	−1	−173	−409
Federal income taxes paid (+) or rebated (−)	−278	−105	−13	+17	−3	−381

Source: Citizens for Tax Justice January 17, 2002. Reprinted by permission of Citizens for Tax Justice.

POLICY STUDY

Integration of Personal and Corporate Income Taxes

A key issue with income taxation is the question of whether and to what extent to integrate the personal and corporate taxes. This involves an unavoidable set of policy questions that must be answered by any country with an income tax system. The U.S. Treasury Department (1992) reports on a number of integration proposals developed at Treasury. The most comprehensive integration proposal was their Comprehensive Business Income Tax (CBIT). That proposal was designed to accomplish three objectives: (1) equate the treatment of debt and equity, (2) tax corporate and noncorporate businesses alike, and (3) reduce the tax distortions between retained and distributed earnings. In order to accomplish these objectives, the CBIT prototype was based on the following changes to the tax system:

- Disallowing deductions for dividends or interest paid by the corporation,
- Excluding from income any dividends or interest received by shareholders and debt holders,
- Apply the tax to all but the smallest businesses, including corporations, partnerships, or sole proprietorships.

The result of these changes is that one, and only one, level of tax is collected on capital income earned by a business.

Table 15.6 provides a summary of the three major approaches used by countries with income tax systems: a classical approach, an imputation system, and a two-rate system.

TABLE 15.6 Three Approaches to Personal-Corporate Tax Integration

	Classical System	Imputation System	Two-Rate System
How the system works:	The corporation (a so-called legal person) benefits from rights that are distinct from any rights granted to any individual or group of individuals, so it is liable to pay tax on its net income, with no deduction for dividends paid out to shareholders. The tax liability of the corporation is treated as distinct from that of the individual.	Shareholders receive a credit for the tax paid by the corporation on that portion of its profit. The shareholder is then liable for any difference between the rate of taxation implicit in the imputation (the rate paid by the corporation on its profits from which dividends were paid and the individual's personal income tax rate).	Distributed profits (paid out in dividends) and undistributed profits are taxed at two different rates. Undistributed profits of corporations are taxed at a higher rate than distributed profits.
Tax rates applied to dividends:	All corporate net income is taxed at the corporate rate t_c and dividends paid to shareholders are taxed again at the personal rate t_p.	The corporation pays its tax on net income paid out in dividends, t_cD, and the individual potentially pays an additional tax on the dividend income if the individual is in a higher tax bracket, $(t_p - t_c) D$.	There are two distinct tax rates on undistributed and distributed dividends: t_u and t_d, with $t_u > t_d$.
Economic effects:	Corporations have an incentive to engage in debt finance rather than equity finance since interest paid on loans is deductible, but retained earnings are taxable. Corporations have an incentive to buy back shares and increase the value of the firm rather than pay dividends. Corporations also have an incentive to engage in mergers and acquisitions.	A full imputation system eliminates double-taxation of dividend income, but less-than-full imputation does not fully eliminate double taxation. Economic effects present in the classical system also arise in the case of less-than-full imputation systems.	Depends on the relative sizes of the two tax rates. Economic effects present in the classical system also arise in the case of two-rate systems, to the extent that the rate on undistributed dividends exceeds the rate on distributed dividends.
Countries that use this system:	United States, Belgium, Hong Kong, Ireland, Netherlands, Sweden, Switzerland	Australia, Canada (partial), France, Italy, United Kingdom (impure imputation system—shareholder relief scheme)	Germany (through 2001), Japan

Source: Country systems are from OECD Contact Group on Asset Prices, 2002. "Turbulence in Asset Markets: The Role of Micro Policies," pp. 8–9.

PROBLEMS

1. Draw a graph of a firm in a monopolistically competitive industry illustrating demand, marginal revenue, marginal cost, average variable cost, and average total cost. Identify the firm's profit in the diagram. Now, explain the impact of a tax on profit. Does the tax affect the firm's output? Does the tax affect the price the firm charges for its product?
2. How does a corporate income tax affect firms that operate in a perfectly competitive industry? Are the conclusions reached in the previous question applicable in this situation?
3. Galactic Industries has experienced a very good year with an increase in profit of $32 million this year. Using Equation 15.1, explain the potential implications for dividends and investment.
4. ProAgra Inc. had net income of $550 million in the year 2010. Use the corporate income tax rate structure in Table 15.1 to compute the tax liability of the company.
5. EndRun Inc. had net income of $12 million in 2010. Use the corporate income tax rate structure in Table 15.1 to compute the tax liability of the company.
6. Consider a tax imposed on labor in a labor-intensive industry and not on other sectors of the economy. An example is Britain's Selective Employment Tax that was applied to labor-intensive service industries. Explain the impact of that tax on the demand for labor, being sure to explain the factor substitution effect, the output effect, and the net effect.
7. Senator Maize from Iowa has recently submitted a bill in the state legislature that would reduce the rate of taxation applied to capital in the agricultural sector of the economy. He believes that this bill will not only be good for corn producers but will also increase the demand for farm implements. As a policy analyst working for the legislative fiscal office, you are given the assignment of writing a summary of the likely impact of this piece of legislation. Use what you know about the general equilibrium effects of a partial factor tax and explain the likely impacts of this tax reduction. (You will have to make an assumption about the factor intensity of the agricultural sector of the economy.)
8. Suppose that OZ Inc. is a large multinational firm based in Kansas (producing brains, hearts, and courage) with annual worldwide net income of $60 million. OZ has 75 percent of its payroll and 90 percent of its property in Kansas but just 1 percent of its sales.
   a. Compute the amount of net income that would be taxable in Kansas using the three-factor apportionment formula.
   b. Compute the amount of net income that would be taxable in Kansas using a double-weighted sales apportionment formula.
   c. Compute the amount of net income that would be taxable in Kansas using a sales-only apportionment formula.
   d. Explain what factors policymakers in Kansas should consider as they debate what apportionment formula to apply.

REFERENCES

Anand, Bharat N., and Richard Sansing. "The Weighing Game: Formula Apportionment as an Instrument of Public Policy." *National Tax Journal* 53 (2000): 183–99.

Altshuler, Rosanne. "Testimony of Dr. Rosanne Altshuler before the Senate Committee on the Budget, Hearing on Tax Reform: A Necessary Component for Restoring Fiscal Responsibility." U.S. Sendate Committee on the Budget, February 2, 2011.

Atkinson, Antony B., and Joseph E. Stiglitz. *Lectures on Public Economics*. New York: McGraw-Hill, 1980.

Auerbach, A. J. "Wealth Maximization and the Cost of Capital." *Quarterly Journal of Economics* 93 (1979): 433–46.

Auerbach, A. J. "Taxation, Corporate Financial Policy and the Cost of Capital." *Journal of Economic Literature* 21 (1983): 905–40.

Auerbach, A. J., and M. A. King. "Taxation, Portfolio Choice, and Debt-Equity Ratios: A General Equilibrium Model." *Quarterly Journal of Economics* 97 (1983): 587–609.

Council of Economic Advisers. "The U.S. Tax System in International Perspective." Chapter 5 of the *Economic Report of the President*. 2006. Available at: http://www.gpoaccess.gov/eop/download.html.

Desai, Mihir A., C. Fritz Foley, and James R. Hines, Jr. "Repatriation Taxes and Dividend Distortions." *National Tax Journal* 54 (2001): 829–51.

Desai, Mihir A., and James R. Hines, Jr. "Evaluating International Tax Reform." *National Tax Journal* 56 (2003): 487–502.

Dworin, Lowell. "Transfer Pricing Issues." *National Tax Journal* 43 (1990): 285–91.

Gordon, Roger H., and James R. Hines, Jr. "International Taxation." In Alan J. Auerbach and Martin Feldstein (eds.), *Handbook of Public Economics*, volume 4. Amsterdam, Netherlands: Elsevier, 2002.

Groves, Harold M. "Personal Versus Corporate Income Taxes. *American Economic Review* 36 (1946): 241–49.

Grubert, Harry, and Rosanne Altshuler. "Corporate Taxes in the World Economy: Reforming the Taxation of Cross-Border Income." Chapter in John W. Diamond and George R. Zodrow (eds.), *Fundamental Tax Reform: Issues, Choices and Implications*. 2008.

Harberger, Arnold. "The Incidence of the Corporation Income Tax." *Journal of Political Economy* 70 (1962): 215–40.

Harberger, Arnold. "Corporation Income Taxes." In *International Encyclopedia of the Social Sciences*. New York: Crowell Collier, 1968. Reprinted in *Taxation and Welfare*. Boston: Little, Brown, 1974.

Hines, James R., Jr. "Taxation of Foreign Income." In Lawrence E. Blume and Steven N. Durlauf (eds.), *The New Palgrave Dictionary of Economics*, Second Edition, Palgrave Macmillan, 2008. Also available online at *The New Palgrave Dictionary of Economics Online*, Palgrave Macmillan, 2011. http://www.dictionaryofeconomics.com/dictionary.

Hines, James R. Jr. "Do Tax Havens Flourish?" In *Tax Policy and the Economy*, volume 19, edited by James M. Poterba, Cambridge, MA: National Bureau of Economic Research, 2005.

Kotlikoff, Laurence, and Laurence H. Summers. "Tax Incidence." Chapter 16 in the *Handbook of Public Economics*, edited by Alan J. Auerbach and Martin S. Feldstein. Amsterdam: North-Holland, 1987.

Mintz, Jack. "Corporation Tax: A Survey." *Fiscal Studies* 16 (1995): 23–68.

Modigliani, F., and M. H. Miller. "The Cost of Capital, Corporation Finance and the Theory of Investment." *American Economic Review* 48 (1958): 261–97.

Pechman, Joseph A. *Federal Tax Policy*, 5th ed. Washington, DC: Brookings Institution, 1987.

Richman, Peggy Brewer. 1963. *Taxation of Foreign Investment Income: An Economic Analysis*. Baltimore, MD: Johns Hopkins Press.

Slemrod, Joel, and Jon Bakija. *Taxing Ourselves*, 4th ed. Cambridge, MA: MIT Press, 2008.

U.S. Department of Treasury. Report of the Department of Treasury on Integration of the Individual and Corporate Tax Systems: Taxing Business Income Once, Chapter 4, "Comprehensive Business Income Tax Prototype," 1992, pp. 39–60.

NOTES

1. Fortune magazine website at *http://money.cnn.com/magazines/fortune/fortune500/2011/full_list/*.
2. See Pechman (1987) and Slemrod and Bakija (2008) for useful historic perspectives on the corporate income tax.
3. The author of this textbook served as senior adviser for public finance at CEA and was the lead author for this chapter of the *Economic Report of the President 2006*.
4. Source: Harberger (1968). For more on the incidence of the tax, based on Harberger's model and its extensions, see Kotlikoff and Summers (1987).
5. Groves (1946).
6. The assumptions are: (1) The tax is introduced at an infinitesimally small rate in a setting where there is no preexisting tax, (2) the tax revenue is redistributed back to taxpayers in the form of lump-sum grants, and (3) consumer preferences have the property that they depend only on the ratio of the goods consumed (known as homothetic preferences).
7. Specific examples in this paragraph are from "A Tussle Over Tax," *The Economist*, March 2, 2000. Article is available at *www.economist.com/PrinterFriendly.cfm?Story_ID=330370*.
8. For more information, go to the OECD list of uncooperative tax havens at the OECD website: *http://www.oecd.org/document/57/0,3343,en_2649_33745_30578809_1_1_1_37427,00.html*.
9. Modern analysis of taxation of foreign income derives from Richman (1963) who was first to model the problem and suggest that countries have incentives to tax the foreign income of their residents, allowing for tax deductions for foreign taxes paid. The key issue is the allocation of capital between domestic and foreign locations. In order to illustrate the argument, consider that firms produce foreign output Q^* with the production function,

$$Q^* = F^*(K^*, L^*),$$

where output is produced using foreign capital and labor. Firms also produce domestic output Q using domestic capital and labor using the production function,

$$Q = F(K, L).$$

For simplicity we can assume that the price of output is unity and that all investments are equity financed. The foreign government taxes profit earned in that country at the rate t_c^* reflecting the relative rate of taxation in the foreign country relative to the home country. The total return earned on foreign investment of capital is then,

$$[F^*(K^*, L^*) - w^*L^*](1 - t_c^*).$$

And the return earned on domestic investment of capital is,

$$F(K, L) - wL.$$

Assuming that there is a fixed stock of capital $\overline{K}$ that can be allocated to production either at home or in the foreign country, we have the constraint $K^* + K \leq \overline{K}$. The optimization problem is to maximize the total return, combining the two preceding expressions, subject to the capital constraint. Doing so yields the first-order condition

$$\frac{F_K}{F_K^*} = (1 - t_c^*).$$

In order to establish the principle that the home country must tax foreign profit, net of foreign tax, at the same rate as it taxes domestic profit, suppose that the domestic tax rate applied to domestic profit is t_c and the tax on foreign profit is a residual tax rate t_c^r. Then the firm receives the amount

$$[F^*(K^*, L^*) - w^*L^*](1 - t_c^* - t_c^r)$$

from its foreign activity. Using this expression along with that for its domestic activity, we can derive the first-order condition as,

$$\frac{F_K}{F_K^*} = \frac{(1 - t_c^* - t_c^r)}{(1 - t_c)}$$

This expression is only consistent with the original first-order condition if $t_c^r = t_c(1 - t_c^*)$. This condition requires that the domestic tax applied to foreign profit must be equal to the tax rate applied to domestic profit, net of the foreign tax applied to that profit. This derivation follows that of Gordon and Hines (2002).

10. IRS Statistics of Income Division, Total Assets, Income, Taxes and Credits, and Foreign Income, Deductions, and Taxes by Major and Selected Minor Industry, 2007. *http://www.irs.gov/taxstats/bustaxstats/article/0,id=210069,00.html.*
11. The three causes of tax avoidance are based on a presentation by Mihir Desai of Harvard University before the President's Advisory Panel on Federal Tax Reform, San Francisco, CA, March 31, 2005.
12. For more on transfer pricing, with specific information by country see: *http://www.transferpricing.com/.*
13. For more information, go to the MTC website at *http://www.mtc.gov/.*
14. Anand and Sansing (2000).
15. This strong result is partly due to the restrictive assumptions on which the MM model of the corporation is built. For an extension of the basic model into a dynamic context, see Auerbach (1979). For more on corporate taxation and its impacts see Auerbach (1983), and Auerbach and King (1983).

CHAPTER 16

Sales and Excise Taxes

LEARNING OBJECTIVES

1. Describe the nature and use of excise taxes applied to specific goods.
2. Discuss efficiency and equity aspects of excise taxes.
3. Analyze the efficiency and equity of sales tax systems.
4. Identify different issues in sales taxation, including the taxation of traded goods, smuggling, harmonization of sales tax systems, taxation of e-commerce, and other policy issues.

Which tax has been responsible for revolts, revolutions, and other assorted skirmishes in world history? Without a doubt it is the excise tax. When applied to common goods purchased by the general populace such as salt, tea, and whiskey, such taxes cause great resentment and often rebellion against the government instituting the tax. One of the first known taxes is the tax on salt, dating back to 2200 B.C. in China under emperor Hsia Yu.[1] Since that time, other rulers have also taxed salt with disastrous consequences. For example, Charles of Anjou, king of Naples and Sicily starting in 1266 and also known as Charles I, placed a tax on salt called the *gabelle* in order to finance his military campaigns in France. That tax was one of the factors eventually leading to the French Revolution in 1789. The British monarchy relied on salt taxes but found that smuggling was a serious problem. In the United States the Erie Canal connecting the Great Lakes with the Hudson River was financed in part by a tax on salt. In fact, the canal became known as "the ditch that salt built." Why has salt been a favorite target of taxation and why have such taxes been so unpopular? These are the issues that we investigate in this chapter.

In this chapter we consider taxes applied to both specific goods, called **excise taxes**, and taxes applied broadly to goods (and sometimes services) in the form of a retail **sales tax**. These taxes are both forms of consumption taxation. In the case of excise taxes, the express purpose of the tax is often to discourage consumption of the taxed good. For example, an excise tax might be placed on tires during wartime for the additional purpose of reducing civilian consumption of tires as well as for raising revenue to support government expenditures. In the case of cigarettes, alcoholic beverages, and gaming, excise taxes (so-called *sin taxes*) are applied in order to discourage consumption of these goods and services, which are considered detrimental.

When taxes are applied broadly to all retail goods in the form of a sales tax, the purpose is to generate revenue from a broad-based consumption tax. The point of taxation here is not to discourage consumption of particular goods but rather to generate revenues to support state and local government activity through a broad-based tax on consumption, reflecting ability to pay. General retail sales taxes are used by nearly all U.S. states as a primary financing mechanism to support state and local government services. They are an increasingly important revenue source for state and local governments, and there are fascinating policy issues that arise in regard to their application.

EXCISE TAXES

The U.S. history of excise taxes is long and colorful.[2] These taxes have frequently, but not always, been associated with wartimes. The pattern has been that excise taxes have been created and employed as revenue-raising devices when the nation entered into armed conflict. After the adoption of the Constitution, an elaborate system of excise taxes was implemented. Taxes were applied to carriages, liquor, snuff, and items purchased at auction. Public reaction was that these taxes were unfair because a disproportionate portion of the tax burden fell on the poor. Public discontent with excise taxes flared, for example, with the Whiskey Rebellion of 1794 when a federal excise tax as high as 30 cents per gallon was levied on whiskey. The burden of this tax fell primarily on grain farmers and distillers in western Pennsylvania who saw the new federal tax as a serious threat to their economic livelihood. Resistance to the tax was organized and federal revenue agents were tarred and feathered. President George Washington put down the rebellion in what became an important test of the authority and power of the federal government. The Jefferson administration abolished all federal excise taxes in 1802, except for the tax on salt. During the War of 1812, federal excises were revived but were eliminated again in 1817. It was not until the Civil War that federal excises were again implemented. This return to excise taxes fits the general pattern: they have been created and employed as revenue-raising devices during wartimes in U.S. history. Consequently, we can trace the development and demise of various federal excise taxes using the historic benchmarks of U.S. wars.

Excise Taxes and War

During the Civil War taxes were placed on liquor and tobacco products. Those taxes have remained a permanent part of the federal excise tax system ever since. In addition, taxes were placed on manufactured goods, gross receipts of transportation companies, advertising, licenses, legal documents, and financial transactions.

World War I brought a variety of additional taxes—taxes placed on specific occupations, theater admissions, telephone calls, jewelry, toiletries, and luggage. After World War I, tobacco and stamp taxes on legal documents

© Bettmann/Corbis

The Whiskey Rebellion of 1794 was a reaction to a new federal excise tax.

were retained as the major federal excise taxes. Liquor taxes remained in place through the Prohibition.

In the 1930s Depression Era, federal excise taxes were placed on automobiles, trucks, buses, appliances, and other consumer durables. These taxes remained in place until 1965 when comprehensive excise tax reform took place. During World War II the tax rates were raised for most federal excise taxes, and new taxes were placed on furs, jewelry, luggage, toilet preparations, local telephone service, and both passenger and freight transportation. New taxes on wagering and diesel fuel were added during the Korean War. Existing excise tax rates were raised as well.

In the postwar era, a pattern has developed in which excise taxes have been earmarked and new excise taxes implemented for specific purposes. In 1956 a major innovation occurred as the federal Highway Trust Fund was established to facilitate construction of the interstate highway system. Existing taxes on gasoline, diesel fuel, special motor fuels, trucks, and tires were earmarked to that fund. In addition, new excise taxes on tread rubber and the use of heavy trucks and buses on the highways were implemented. In 1970 a similar innovation funded the Airport and Airway Trust Fund with existing taxes on passenger tickets, air freight, gasoline, tires, and tubes used in aviation earmarked to the fund. New taxes on international air travel and annual aircraft user taxes were added. Again in 1980 a similar model was followed in forming the Hazardous Substances Superfund to clean up chemical pollution from unidentified sources. Taxes on crude oil and an array of 42 hazardous, waste-creating chemicals were implemented.

After the Korean War ended, a long process of reducing federal excise taxes began. Rates were lowered one by one and excise taxes were repealed. This process resulted in a limited number of federal excise taxes, generating relatively little revenue. Federal excises in the United States have fallen to the point where they accounted for just 3.1 percent of total receipts in fiscal year 2010.[3]

One excise tax of special note is the windfall profits tax on domestically produced crude oil, enacted in 1980 by Congress as part of its program to deregulate the oil industry. The tax was applied to the difference between the selling price of oil and the price in May of 1979, that difference being called *windfall profit*. This tax was subsequently eliminated.

Efficiency of Excise Taxes

The application of an excise tax on a good with relatively inelastic demand, such as cigarettes and gasoline, has predictable consequences, given our previous study of the efficiency effects of taxation. Figure 16.1 illustrates the case of a unit tax applied to a good with relatively inelastic demand, reflected in the steepness of the demand curve relative to the supply curve. In the absence of the tax, the equilibrium price and quantity in the market are given by p_0 and q_0. When a unit tax of T is applied to the good, the supply curve shifts to S' and a new equilibrium is established at price p_1 and quantity q_1. As we would expect, the tax has the effect of reducing the equilibrium quantity cleared in the market. The reduction in quantity is given by the amount $q_0 - q_1$. Hence, the tax does have the effect of reducing consumption of the good. But, the size of that reduction is small when the demand for the good is relatively inelastic. As a result, it is difficult to say that the excise tax applied to a good with price-inelastic demand is effective in reducing consumption. It does reduce consumption but not by much. The reason for the tax's weak effect on quantity is the inelastic demand for the good—consumers are simply not very sensitive to the price of the good. Even though the excise tax has the effect of raising the price from p_0 to p_1, due to the steepness of the demand curve, the equilibrium quantity cleared in the market is not reduced by very much.

FIGURE 16.1 A Unit Excise Tax Applied to a Good with Relatively Price-Inelastic Demand

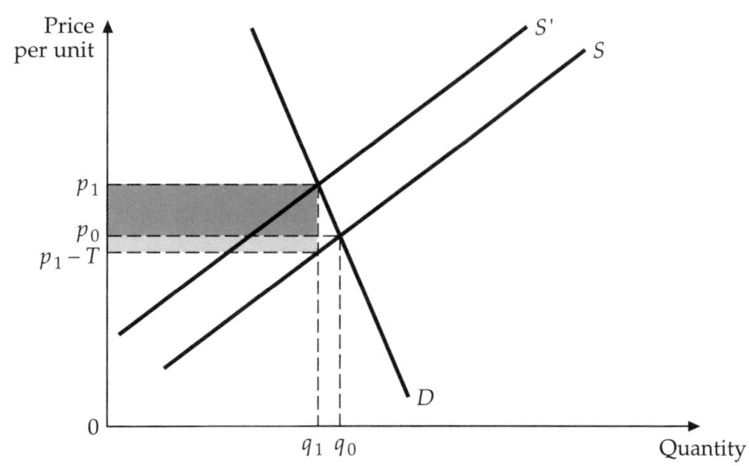

Excise taxes applied to goods with relatively inelastic demand have small excess burdens. That makes them relatively efficient taxes. When the compensated price elasticity of demand for a good is small, the excess burden of an excise tax on that good is small. Hence, excise taxes placed on cigarettes, alcoholic beverages, gasoline, and similar goods that have small price elasticities also generate relatively little excess burden. As a result, these excise taxes are relatively efficient. Of course, that says nothing of the equity of this form of government finance.

Recall the Ramsey rule from our study of optimal taxation. In order to obtain a given amount of revenue with the least excess burden, commodity excise tax rates should be set so that they are inversely proportional to the compensated price elasticity of demand for the goods. Goods with relatively inelastic demand should be taxed at relatively high rates. Coincidentally, many excise taxes are applied to commodities whose demand is relatively inelastic. As we have said, gasoline, cigarettes, alcoholic beverages, and other goods typically taxed with excises all have relatively inelastic demand. Although the reasons for these taxes are not entirely motivated by application of the Ramsey rule by any stretch of the imagination, it is reassuring that this pattern of taxation is probably less distorting than many other alternatives.

Excise taxes can also be used as Pigouvian taxes, resulting in efficiency enhancements as we discussed in Chapter 4. For example, the gasoline excise tax could be used specifically as a tool to reduce air pollution in major urban areas plagued by high pollution levels, such as Los Angeles, Houston, and Denver. In the presence of negative externalities, an excise tax can be efficiency-enhancing, resulting in the socially optimal use of gasoline rather than the privately optimal use of gasoline. Research by Krupnick, Harrington, and Alberini (2001) investigates the feasibility of using excise taxes in this way and indicates that voters may even support a plan where they are charged a pollution fee based on their vehicle's emissions, especially if the increased revenues from that fee are used to reduce the sales tax or vehicle license or registration fees.

Equity of Excise Taxes

As early as the Whiskey Rebellion in 1794 in the United States, people have realized that excise taxes often come with an incidence that falls heavily on the poor. In fact, the unpopularity of excise taxes such as the salt tax going back much further in history is founded on this reason. The fundamental reasons for that incidence are rooted in two important facts. First, consumers bear most of the burden of the excise tax because the tax is generally applied to goods with relatively inelastic demand. Second, consumption expenditures for the specific goods typically taxed do not rise proportionately with income.

The incidence of excise taxes generally falls primarily on the consumer. Figure 16.1 illustrates the case of a unit excise tax applied to a good with relatively inelastic demand. Notice that the tax T falls primarily on the consumer as the price increase paid by the consumer is $p_1 - p_0$, a large proportion of the tax. The part of the tax borne by the producer is $p_0 - (p_1 - T)$, which is a relatively small proportion of the tax. As a general rule, excise taxes applied to goods with relatively price-inelastic demand have incidence that falls primarily on the consumers.

The other issue to consider relates to the pattern of consumption as it is affected by income. Excise taxes applied to consumption goods also fall more heavily on relatively low-income consumers because consumption as a fraction of income falls as income rises. Take whiskey, as an example. We might expect that as income rises, a person would increase expenditures on whiskey, but we do not observe whiskey consumption rising proportionately. Do you expect that a person with $100,000 income will consume five times more whiskey than a person with income of $20,000? Probably not. Suppose that person A with income of $20,000 buys three bottles of whiskey at $15 per bottle, spending $45 per year on whiskey. Suppose further that person B with $100,000 income buys five bottles of whiskey, spending $75 per year. The higher-income person spends more on whiskey but not proportionately to income. As a result, whiskey expenditures as a fraction of income fall as income rises. In this example, the percentage is 0.225 percent at income level $20,000 but falls to 0.075 percent at income level $100,000. Now, suppose further that the excise tax on whiskey is 10 percent. As a result, taxes paid on whiskey also fall as a fraction of income as income rises, making the average tax rate fall with income. At income level $20,000 the tax is 0.0225 percent of income, whereas at income level $100,000 the tax is 0.0075 percent. Tax paid as a fraction of income falls as income rises, so the tax is regressive. That is so even though the high-income person pays more in tax.

Table 16.1 illustrates expenditures on tobacco, alcoholic beverages, and motor fuels as a percentage of posttax family income. These goods are all subject to federal and state excise taxes and represent the types of goods generally taxed. Expenditures on tobacco products as a percentage of posttax family income account for 1.1 percent of income for all families in the United States. But the distribution of expenditures across the income distribution is quite revealing. Families in the bottom quintile of the income distribution spend 4.0 percent of their income on tobacco products, whereas families in the top quintile spend just 0.5 percent of their income on tobacco products. Hence, a tax on tobacco products hits families in the bottom quintile eight times harder than families in the top quintile. Of course, this judgment is based on a particular measure. That measure is consumption as a percentage of income. As long as we agree that consumption as a percentage of income is a reasonable measure on which to base our consideration of tax burden, there is no doubt that an excise tax on tobacco products is very regressive. Low-income families pay a larger share of their income in tobacco taxes than do high-income families.

The same regressive patterns are clearly visible for alcoholic beverages and motor fuels. Although families in general spend 2.0 percent of their posttax income on alcoholic beverages, the percentage is much higher: 3.7 percent for families in the bottom quintile and much lower, 1.6 percent, for families in the top quintile. For motor fuels, the overall average is 2.7 percent, but

TABLE 16.1 Expenditures on Tobacco, Alcoholic Beverages, and Motor Fuels as Percentages of Posttax Family Income

	Percentage of Posttax Income			Percentage of All Expenditures		
	Tobacco	*Alcoholic Beverages*	*Motor Fuels*	*Tobacco*	*Alcoholic Beverages*	*Motor Fuels*
All Families						
Posttax family income	1.1	2.0	2.7	1.1	2.0	2.7
Bottom quintile	4.0	3.7	6.9	1.6	1.5	2.8
Second quintile	2.1	2.3	4.2	1.5	1.7	3.1
Third quintile	1.6	2.2	3.5	1.4	2.0	3.1
Fourth quintile	1.1	2.2	2.9	1.1	2.2	2.9
Top quintile	0.5	1.6	1.5	0.7	2.3	2.3
Age of Head of Family						
Under 30	1.5	3.0	3.4	1.3	2.8	3.1
30 to 44	1.2	2.1	2.8	1.2	2.1	2.7
45 to 59	1.3	1.9	2.8	1.3	1.9	2.8
60 to 74	0.9	1.7	2.4	0.9	1.9	2.5
75 and over	0.5	1.1	1.6	0.5	1.2	1.7
Census Region						
Northeast	1.1	1.9	2.1	1.1	2.1	2.2
Midwest	1.3	2.2	2.7	1.3	2.2	2.7
South	1.1	1.9	2.8	1.1	1.9	2.8
West	0.9	2.1	2.5	0.8	2.1	2.4
Rural	1.4	2.0	3.9	1.4	1.9	3.7

Source: Congressional Budget Office 1990.

families in the bottom quintile spend 6.9 percent of their posttax income on motor fuels, whereas top quintile families spend just 1.5 percent. As a result of these expenditure patterns, excise taxes applied to alcoholic beverages and motor fuels are quite regressive, with lower-income families paying a higher tax as a percentage of income than that paid by high-income families.

The remainder of Table 16.1 provides information on the distribution of consumption expenditures by age of family heads and by region of the country. The information on age distribution of household head indicates that excise taxes applied to tobacco products, alcoholic beverages, and motor fuels tend to hit younger families harder than older families. As for regional patterns, we find that tobacco and alcoholic beverage excise taxes hit midwestern residents hardest, whereas motor fuel excise taxes hit southern and midwestern residents hard. Both tobacco and motor fuel taxes hit rural residents harder than urban residents. From an equity, or fairness, point of view, there are clearly several dimensions for concern about excise taxes as they differentially burden people by income level, age, and region.

Consumption patterns vary widely around the world, having important implications for sales and excise tax burdens. Figure 16.2 illustrates the percent of household final consumption expenditures spent on food, alcohol, and tobacco consumed at home in 2008. U.S. consumers spent 6.8 percent of their total consumption on food, and 1.9 percent on alcoholic beverages and tobacco. As a consequence, taxes that are applied to these commodities represent a relatively small burden when compared to the rest of the world. The maximum food consumption expenditure share was 48.5 percent in Azerbaijan. In general, the food consumption share is less than 10 percent in highly developed countries and 30 to 40 percent in less developed countries. The share of consumption expenditures for alcoholic beverages and tobacco products is smallest in Qatar where it is just 0.3 percent, and largest in Hungary where it is 8.1 percent.

Federal Excise Taxes

Federal excise taxes can be classified into two broad categories: **general excise taxes** and **dedicated excise taxes**. The feature that differentiates the two types of excise taxes is whether the revenues generated by the tax are dedicated to specific trust funds out of which expenditures are made for specific purposes. Table 16.2 provides a listing of each federal excise tax, the amount of revenue generated by the excise, and the proportion of all federal excise tax revenue generated by each. The most important federal excise taxes are those applied to transportation fuels, alcoholic beverages, and tobacco products. General excise taxes are applied to alcoholic beverages, tobacco products, telephone services, transportation fuels, and other products. The taxes on alcoholic beverages and tobacco products are sometimes called **sin taxes** because of the normative judgment that use of these products is sinful. Despite that historic judgment, people choose to consume alcoholic beverages such as beer, wine, and distilled spirits and use tobacco products such as cigarettes and cigars, snuff, and chewing tobacco. Excise taxes on these goods are well accepted because they are considered unnecessary goods. Because these products are addictive, they also generate stable revenue. Excise taxes on transportation fuels cover gasoline, diesel fuel, and jet fuel. Revenue from these excises can be considered a form of user fees for federal highways and airport facilities. There is a direct correspondence between a driver's use of the roads and the amount of excise tax paid on gasoline. The more one drives, the more one uses the highways. The more one uses the highways, the more gasoline one purchases. The more gasoline one purchases, the more excise tax one pays. As a form of user fee, such excises are very effective mechanisms as benefit charges. The more one benefits from use of the public good, the more one pays for that benefit.

FIGURE 16.2 Percent of Household Consumption Expenditures Spent on Food, Alcohol, and Tobacco, Selected Countries, 2008

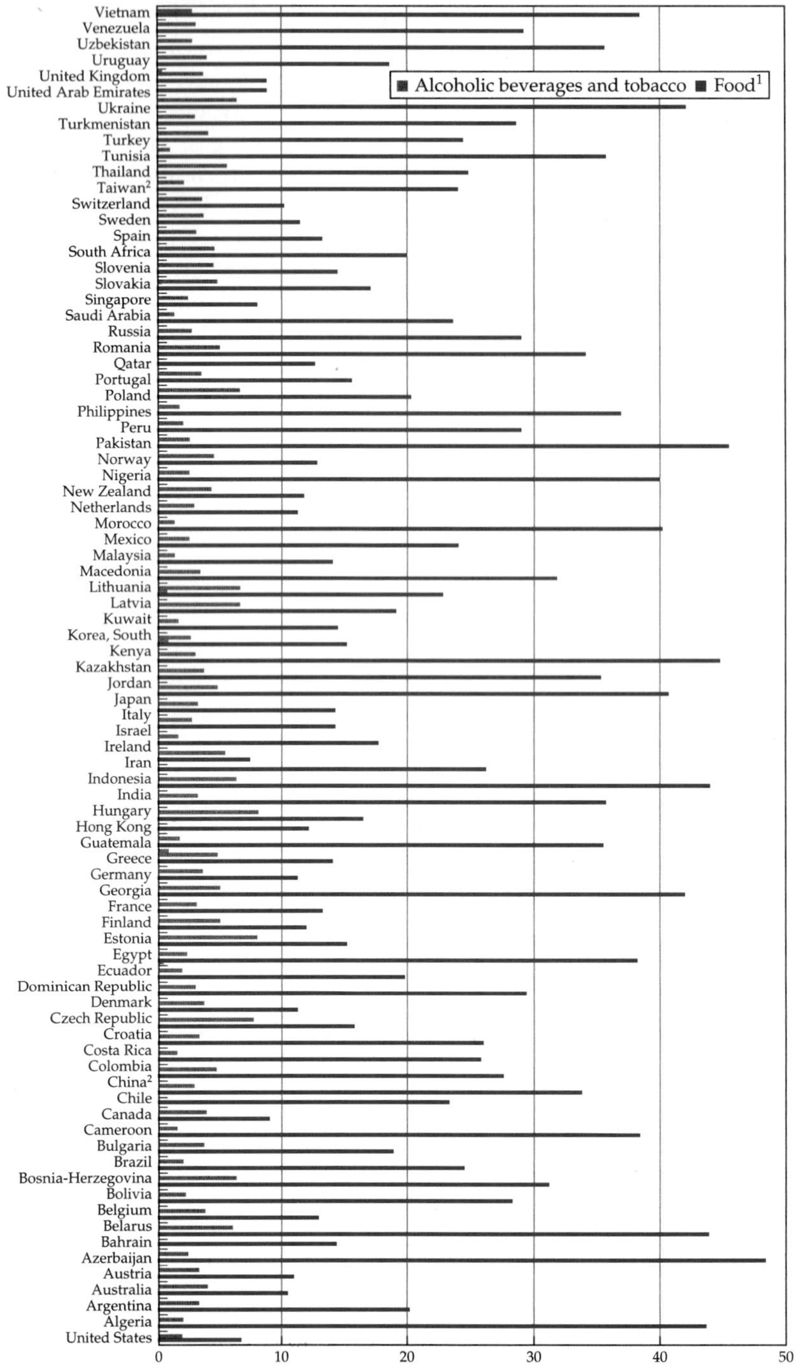

[1] Includes nonalcoholic beverages.
[2] With the establishment of diplomatic relations with China on January 1, 1979, the U.S. government recognized the People's Republic of China as the sole legal government of China and acknowledged the Chinese position that there is only one China and that Taiwan is part of China.

Source: U.S. Department of Agriculture, Economic Research Service; "Food, CPI, Prices and Expenditures: Expenditure Tables," July 2010. For more information: www.ers.usda.gov/Briefing/.

TABLE 16.2 U.S. Federal Excise Taxes, 2010

Source	Revenue ($ millions)	Revenue as a Percent of Total
Federal Funds		
Alcohol	9,637	12.893
Tobacco	18,613	24.902
Telephone	705	0.943
Transportation fuels	–6,741	–9.019
Other	153	0.205
Total	22,367	29.924
Trust Funds		
Highway	37,535	50.217
Airport and airway	11,697	15.649
Black lung disability	670	0.896
Inland waterway	86	0.115
Oil spill liability	412	0.551
Aquatic resources	587	0.785
Leaking underground storage tank	193	0.258
Tobacco Assessments	960	1.284
Vaccine injury compensation	238	0.318
Total	52,378	70.076
Total excise taxes	74,745	100.000

Source: Budget of the United States Government: Historical Tables Fiscal Year 2010, Table 2-4. Available at: http://www.gpoaccess.gov/usbudget/fy10/hist.html.

Some federal excise taxes are also dedicated specifically to trust funds in order to finance specialized compensation programs, listed in the lower panel of Table 16.2. Those excises provide funds for highways, airports, black lung victims (miners), inland waterways, oil spill liability, aquatic resources, leaking underground storage tanks (generally gasoline station tanks), tobacco assessments, and vaccine injury compensation. Dedicated taxes such as these are also called **earmarked taxes.**

State Excise Taxes

Table 16.3 lists the common excise taxes applied by states in the United States; taxes on gasoline, cigarettes, and alcoholic beverages are the most prominent excise taxes. Like the federal government, states also apply excise taxes to gasoline and other motor fuels, often dedicating the revenues generated to highway funds. Table 16.3 indicates that there is wide variation in the level of state gasoline excise taxes. States such as Alaska, Georgia, New Jersey, New York, Pennsylvania, and Wyoming have very low gasoline excise taxes, in the range of $0.08 to $0.13 per gallon. At the other end of the gasoline tax distribution is Rhode Island with a tax of $0.28 per gallon. There are 20 other states with gasoline excise tax rates in excess of $0.20 per gallon.

All of the states apply excise taxes to tobacco products, as does the federal government, but the state tax rates vary widely. Table 16.3 provides information on cigarette excise taxes for the states. Tobacco-growing states in the South tend to apply very low rates of taxation. For example, Kentucky applies a tax of just $0.03 per package, whereas the tax in North Carolina is $0.05 and that in South Carolina is $0.07. Obviously, these states do not wish to reduce the output of an important industry in their economies; hence they apply low tax rates. Of course, we know that the incidence of an excise tax applied in a market where the demand is relatively inelastic falls primarily on the consumer rather than the producer of the product. Although an excise tax is not likely to reduce output by very much in this type of market setting, these states are apparently particularly sensitive to any policy that affects output.

On the other hand, many states apply very high rates of taxation to cigarettes, most notably Rhode Island at $3.46, Connecticut at $3.00, New York at $2.75, New Jersey at $2.70, and Hawaii at $2.60 per package. In recent years a number of health policy initiatives at the state level provide medical care for the uninsured and health services for children and the poor, funded in part by higher cigarette taxes. The interesting question that arises in this policy situation is whether the large increases in excise taxes may actually result in the collection of *less* revenue. As we move up the demand curve, price elasticity is increasing. At very high prices we may reach a point where the price elasticity of demand begins to exceed unity, and beyond that point any further increase in price leads to a reduction in the quantity demanded that is proportionately greater, resulting in less revenue.

State excise taxes on alcoholic beverages include taxes on beer, wine, and spirits. Readers of this text may be most familiar with beer, so we will begin with that beverage. Excise tax rates on beer range from a high of $1.07 per gallon in Alaska to a low of $0.02 in Wyoming, as illustrated in Table 16.3.[4] States with major breweries, such as Missouri, home of Anheuser-Busch, and Colorado, home of Adolph Coors, tend to have very low excise taxes on beer.

Taxes on table wine are typically higher on a per gallon basis than taxes applied to beer. Looking down the next-to-last column in Table 16.3, you see that wine taxes may be as much as 10 times the rate applied to beer. One justification for higher tax rates on wine is that the alcohol content of wine is higher than the alcohol content of beer. If wine typically has four to five times the alcohol content of beer, perhaps tax rates should be four to five times higher if what is being taxed is the alcohol. Tax rates applied to wine also vary widely from state to state. Louisiana has the lowest tax rate at $0.11 per gallon and California and Texas have the next lowest tax rate of $0.20 per gallon. Alaska has the highest tax rate of $2.50 per gallon. Three

TABLE 16.3 Sales, Gasoline, Cigarette, and Alcoholic Beverage Tax Rates by State, 2010

State	General Sales and Use Tax (%)	Gasoline Tax ($/gal)	Cigarette Tax ($/pack)	Spirits Tax[b] ($/gal)	Wine Tax ($/gal)	Beer Tax ($/gal)
Alabama	4.0	0.16	0.425	[a]	1.70	0.53
Alaska	0	0.08	2.00	12.80	2.50	1.07
Arizona	5.6	0.18	2.00	3.00	0.84	0.16
Arkansas	6.0	0.215	1.15	6.60	0.75	0.23
California	8.25	0.18	0.87	3.30	0.20	0.20
Colorado	2.9	0.22	0.84	2.28	0.28	0.08
Connecticut	6.0	0.25	3.00	4.50	0.60	0.19
Delaware	0	0.23	1.60	5.46	0.97	0.16
Florida	6.0	0.04[d]	1.339	6.50	2.25	0.48
Georgia	4.0	0.075	0.37	3.79	1.51	0.32
Hawaii	4.0	0.17	2.60	5.98	1.38	0.93
Idaho	6.0	0.25	0.57	[a]	0.45	0.15
Illinois	6.25	0.19	0.98	8.55	1.39	0.235
Indiana	7.0	0.18	0.995	2.68	0.47	0.115
Iowa	6.0	0.21	1.36	[a]	1.75	0.19
Kansas	5.3	0.24	0.79	2.50	0.30	0.18
Kentucky	6.0	0.227	0.60	1.92	0.50	0.08
Louisiana	4.0	0.20	0.36	2.50	0.11	0.32
Maine	5.0	0.295	2.00	[a]	0.60	0.35
Maryland	6.0	0.235	2.00	1.50	0.40	0.09
Massachusetts	6.25	0.21	2.51	4.05	0.55	0.11
Michigan	6.0	0.19	2.00	[a]	0.51	0.20
Minnesota	6.875	0.271	1.23	5.03	0.30	0.15
Mississippi	7.0	0.18	0.68	[a]	0.35	0.4268
Missouri	4.225	0.17	0.17	2.00	0.30	0.06
Montana	0	0.27	1.70	[a]	1.06	0.14
Nebraska	5.5	0.268[d]	0.64	3.75	0.95	0.31
Nevada	6.85	0.24	0.80	3.60	0.70	0.16
New Hampshire	0	0.18	1.78	[a]	[a]	0.30
New Jersey	7.0	0.105	2.70	5.50	0.875	0.12
New Mexico	5.0	0.17	0.91	6.06	1.70	0.41
New York	4.0	0.08	2.75	6.44	0.30	0.14

(Continued)

TABLE 16.3 Sales, Gasoline, Cigarette, and Alcoholic Beverage Tax Rates by State, 2010 (Continued)

State	General Sales and Use Tax (%)	Gasoline Tax ($/gal)	Cigarette Tax ($/pack)	Spirits Tax[b] ($/gal)	Wine Tax ($/gal)	Beer Tax ($/gal)
North Carolina	5.75	0.303	0.45	(a)	0.79	0.53
North Dakota	5.0	0.23	0.44	2.50	0.50	0.16
Ohio	5.5	0.28	1.25	(a)	0.30	0.18
Oklahoma	4.5	0.16	1.03	5.56	0.72	0.40
Oregon	0	0.24	1.18	(a)	0.67	0.08
Pennsylvania	6.0	0.12	1.60	(a)	(a)	0.08
Rhode Island	7.0	0.30	3.46	3.75	0.60	0.10
South Carolina	6.0	0.16	0.07	2.72	0.90	0.77
South Dakota	4.0	0.22	1.53	3.93	0.93	0.27
Tennessee	7.0	0.20	0.62	4.40	1.21	0.14
Texas	6.25	0.20	1.41	2.40	0.20	0.20
Utah	4.7	0.245	0.695	(a)	(a)	0.41
Vermont	6.0	0.19	2.44	(a)	0.55	0.265
Virginia	5.0	0.175	0.30	(a)	1.51	0.26
Washington	6.5	0.375	2.025	(a)	0.87	0.261
West Virginia	6.0	0.205	0.55	(a)	1.00	0.18
Wisconsin	5.0	0.309	2.52	3.25	0.25	0.06
Wyoming	4.0	0.13	0.60	(a)	(a)	0.02

[a]This state is a liquor control state. As a result, it may have an implicit tax hidden in the price and may apply a tax as well. The mean markup rate for liquor control states is 48 percent, whereas private retailers apply an average markup rate of approximately 25 percent.

[b]Several states have multiple excise tax rates on distilled spirits, depending on the alcohol content. In those cases, the maximum rate is listed in this table.

[c]Florida gas tax rate varies by county. The counties may also apply their own tax of 12.6 to 18.6 cents plus a 2.2 cent pollution tax.

[d]Nebraska gas tax rate is a combination of a fixed rate plus a rate that varies by quarter.

Source: Federation of Tax Administrators 2010.

states apply differential rates to domestic wine produced in their state and foreign wine produced elsewhere. Both Alabama and Rhode Island apply a lower tax rate to domestic wine, whereas Colorado applies a higher rate to domestic wine.

Tax rates applied to distilled spirits are also reported in Table 16.3. These beverages include whiskey, vodka, rum, scotch, bourbon, and similar drinks. Notice that the tax rates applied to these beverages are much higher than those applied to wine and beer. Again, this can be justified on the basis of a higher alcohol content in these beverages. A notable feature of the market for spirits is that a number of so-called control states have liquor control commissions that strictly regulate marketing of these products. In these states, the government sets the markup rate applied to the beverages and thus build an implicit tax into the price. As a result, it is misleading to compare the tax rates in control states with those in noncontrol states. Table 16.3 does not list tax rates on spirits for control states.

SALES TAXES

Rather than tax individual commodities, as is done with excise taxes, state and local governments may apply an *ad valorem* tax broadly to all consumer goods purchased in the economy. This form of tax is known as a sales tax and is applied by 45 of the U.S. states. As usual, we begin with a consideration of the definition of the tax base and then proceed to consideration of tax rates for state and local sales taxes.

Tax Base

State and local sales tax bases are typically made up of the value of final goods sold in the jurisdiction. By taxing only final sales, states usually leave out taxation of intermediate goods. The reason for not taxing intermediate goods is to avoid cascading of the sales tax. Although state and local sales taxes have historically been applied primarily to goods only, there is increasing interest in applying them to services as well. As the economy shifts more heavily toward the production of services, goods output accounts for a shrinking share of total output. If required government services are proportional to the total output of the economy, reliance on a goods-based sales tax will fall increasingly short of providing the revenue necessary to support government services. Consequently, many states are moving in the direction of broadening their sales tax bases to include some services, especially professional services required of businesses.

Tax Rates

Table 16.3 lists the state sales tax rates for U.S. states in 2010. Forty-five states have sales taxes, whereas 5 states have no sales tax (Alaska, Delaware, Montana, New Hampshire, and Oregon). State tax rates range from a low of 2.9 percent in Colorado to a high of 8.25 percent in California. Many states also permit local government units such as cities, counties, or school districts to levy sales taxes as well. As a result, combined state and local sales taxes are higher in those states.

Effective tax rates are affected by exemptions and exclusions, which all states provide. In order to relieve the regressiveness of the sales tax, many states implement exemptions or exclusions for goods considered necessities. The most common exemption is for food purchased at the grocery store. Because all people need approximately the same quantity of food in order to sustain life and therefore spend about the same amount on food, exemption of food from the sales tax has the effect of making the tax less regressive. Although food expenditures do rise with income, they rise less than proportionately to income. Hence, a food exemption reduces a low-income family's sales tax more than a high-income family's, making the tax less regressive. Some states also exempt prescription drugs and clothing.

Administration of Sales Taxes

Sales taxes are typically collected from retailers rather than from consumers. The reason for using this method is to reduce the cost of tax revenue collection. Rather than ask thousands of Kmart customers each day to each fill out a tax form and submit a check for the sales tax on their purchase to the state revenue department, it is far easier and less costly to require Kmart to submit one check at the end of the month for the sales tax on all retail sales during the month. The incidence of the sales tax is unaffected by the statutory requirement (tax paid by retailer rather than consumer), but the cost of collection and enforcement may be substantially lower by levying the tax on the retailer.

Origin or Destination Tax?

Sales taxes can be applied as either origin or destination taxes. An **origin-based tax** is applied to sales that originate in the jurisdiction with the tax, whereas a **destination-based tax** is applied in the jurisdiction where the good is purchased by the consumer. Consider an example of a local city sales tax applied in Metro City. Suppose that you are not a resident of Metro City but live in the nearby suburb of Westville. As you shop for a new washing machine, you find a great deal on an Eddy machine (something like a Whirlpool, but smaller) at Crazy Sam's Appliance Mart in Metro City. Now, if the Metro City sales tax is applied on an origin basis, you will have to pay the tax, because the transaction will take place in Metro City. But, if the city sales tax is applied on a destination basis, all you need to do is to purchase the machine COD (cash on delivery) and arrange for delivery to your home in Westville. The destination of the machine is Westville, so you will not be charged the Metro City sales tax.

Nexus

Retailers are required to collect the state and local sales tax as long as they have a presence in the jurisdiction called **nexus**. A retailer with a storefront certainly has a clear presence and therefore has nexus and must collect the tax. But, a retailer in another state who has no outlets in this state has no nexus and is therefore not required to collect the tax. Intermediate cases are more difficult, however. What about a retailer based in another state who vigorously pursues sales through direct marketing in this state? Does that retailer have nexus in this state? Each state's sales tax law must define the terms on which nexus is determined and clearly establish what activities result in taxable nexus.

Taxing Electronic Commerce

When I purchase software to run on my computer, I have several choices of places to buy that software. I can drive down to the local Staples or Best Buy retail store and purchase the software. If I do that, I will pay state and local sales tax on my purchase. An alternative is to jump on the web and find a site where I can download the software, using my credit card to pay. Increasingly, people are finding it much more convenient to use the web and other electronic means of making purchases. In the process, sales tax laws designed with the presumption that purchases take place at local retail establishments are increasingly outdated. One of the most pressing problems in the realm of state and local tax policy is the issue of whether and how to tax electronic commerce. The advent of mail-order sales brought some of these issues forward, but there are more issues of greater complexity associated with electronic commerce.

Sales taxes were developed in order to tax local merchants selling manufactured goods. They work well in that context, but commerce is increasingly facilitated by the use of computer networks. Those networks are used to help produce, distribute, and sell goods and services. Sales taxes are generally applied to tangible goods and are not applied to intangible goods or services, but electronic commerce involves both of these to a heavy extent.

Table 16.4 is a taxonomy of commerce characteristics. Traditional retail and service commerce is conducted with tangible goods publicized at the

TABLE 16.4 Characteristics of Various Types of Commerce

Activity	***Product***	***Publicity***	***Role of Customer***	***Purchase***	***Payment***	***Delivery***
			Traditional Commerce			
Retailing	Tangible	Local	Active	Face to Face	Face to Face	Face to Face
Services	Services	Local	Active	Face to Face	Face to Face	Face to Face
			Disintermediated Commerce			
Mail order	Tangible	Mail	Passive	Mail/phone/ fax	COD/MO/ check/card	Common carrier
TV/ telemarketing	Tangible	TV/ telephone	Passive	Mail/phone/ fax	Check/card	Common carrier
Web order	Tangible	Online	Passive	Phone/online	Online	Common carrier
Electronic commerce in content	Intangible	Online	Active	Online	Online	Online

Source: From "Electronic Commerce, State Sales Taxation and Intergovernmental Fiscal Relations" by Charles E. McClure, Jr. in *National Tax Journal*, 50, No. 4, 1997: 735. Reprinted by permission of National Tax Association.

local level with the customer taking active part in a face-to-face transaction consummated with payment and delivery. Newer forms of disintermediated commerce, however, have one or more distinguishing characteristics. Mail-order commerce, for example, takes place with mail publicity, a passive consumer role, where the purchase takes place via mail, telephone, or fax, with payment made by cash on delivery (COD), money order (MO), check, or credit card. Delivery is accomplished by a common carrier such as United Parcel Service (UPS) or Federal Express (FedEx). Television and telemarketing channels also sell tangible goods using the television or telephone for publicity and involve a passive consumer making the purchase through the mail or via telephone using a check or credit card and receiving the product via common carrier. Web commerce takes place online for tangible products. The consumer takes an active role in the transaction, however, with the purchase being made online or via telephone and payment made online. Delivery takes place via common carrier. Finally, electronic commerce in content introduced additional new characteristics. When a person purchases music, a video game, or software by downloading that product from the Internet, a whole new form of commerce takes place. The product in this case is intangible, consisting of a set of zeros and ones in some form of database. Publicity for the product takes place online, as does the purchase, payment, and delivery.

How do the new characteristics of goods and services exchanged via electronic commerce affect the role of sales and excise taxes? Although it is relatively easy to apply taxes to tangible goods sold in local markets with face-to-face transactions, it is increasingly difficult to tax electronic sales of goods that may be intangible, originate out of state, and involve payment mechanisms that the government finds difficult to observe.

As a general principle, we desire a uniform tax system, treating all goods and taxpayers the same way. A traditional sales or excise tax does this, subjecting all purchasers of the good to taxation at the same rate. But, uniformity suffers once we move away from traditional commerce. In the case of mail-order sales, for example, you can buy your jacket from the L. L. Bean catalogue and avoid paying sales tax on the purchase. Although many states apply a use tax to such purchases, enforcement of that tax is so lax that most people are unaware of its existence. Hence, your jacket purchase is free of state and local sales tax. If you went to the local mall and purchased a similar jacket, that purchase would be subject to tax. This situation clearly violates the uniformity principle we would like to see applied in a tax system. If we exempt web purchases from state and local sales and excise taxes as well, we just make the uniformity problem worse. The alternative, of course, is to attempt to tax all such purchases. The U.S. Supreme Court has blocked application of state and local sales taxes to out-of-state mail-order sales, however, ruling that under the commerce clause of the Constitution, states cannot impose taxes on out-of-state vendors unless they have a physical presence in the state (known as nexus).[5]

A further problem with uniformity arises due to a blurring of the distinction between tangible and intangible goods and services that electronic commerce introduces. For example, if you purchase a CD performed by Lady

Gaga at a local store at the mall, the good is tangible and a sales tax is applied. Most state sales taxes do not apply to intangible goods and services, however. So, if you purchase a ticket to a live Lady Gaga concert, you have purchased a service that is not taxable under most state sales taxes. (Some states apply a separate entertainment tax, however.) Similarly, if you purchase the same Lady Gaga music online and receive it via the Internet, the good you have purchased is intangible and likely to be nontaxable under state tax law. As a result, we have three different forms of the same music subject to two different tax treatments.

The Supreme Court has ruled that a vendor may have a taxable nexus in a state if it uses agents to make sales or provide service to customers. If that were to include Internet service providers (ISPs), for example, then all electronic commerce taking place where the ISP has a physical presence in the state might be subjected to taxation. This interpretation may go too far, however, if ISPs are more like common carriers. It remains to be seen whether states will be successful in applying agency to electronic commerce.

Streamlined Sales Tax

The complexities of administering state and local sales tax systems, especially in light of the increasing prevalence of cross border sales and electronic commerce, has led most U.S. states to voluntarily work in cooperation to streamline their tax systems to enhance collections and enforcement. The Streamlined Sales and Use Tax Agreement, developed in recent years, provides a degree of commonality among disparate state sales tax systems. Here is the governing board's description of the agreement and its purpose:

> This Agreement is the result of the cooperative effort of 44 states, the District of Columbia, local governments and the business community to simplify sales and use tax collection and administration by retailers and states. The Agreement minimizes costs and administrative burdens on retailers that collect sales tax, particularly retailers operating in multiple states. It encourages "remote sellers" selling over the Internet and by mail order to collect tax on sales to customers living in the Streamlined states. It levels the playing field so that local "brick-and-mortar" stores and remote sellers operate under the same rules. This Agreement ensures that all retailers can conduct their business in a fair, competitive environment.
>
> Source: Streamlined Sales Tax Governing Board web site: http://www.streamlinedsalestax.org/index.php?page=faqs

Smuggling and Border Effects

Where there are substantial differences in sales tax rates across political borders, there is the potential for smuggling and other illegal activity. Cigarettes are a notorious case where the vast differences in state excise tax rates induce a great deal of smuggling activity. Suppose that you buy a truckload of cigarettes in North Carolina where the tax rate is $0.05 per package. You then drive your truck to New York where the tax is $1.11 per package. The

FIGURE 16.3 Share of U.S. Cigarette Market by Type of Cross-Border Activity, 1960–1997

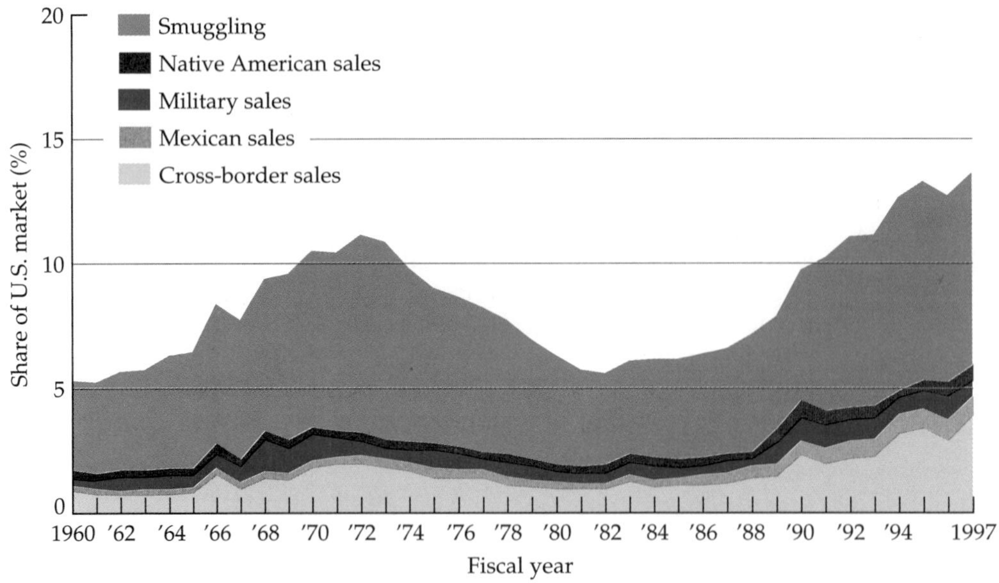

Source: From *How Excise Tax Differentials Affect Interstate Smuggling and Cross-Border Sales of Cigarettes in the United States* by Patrick Fleenor, Tax Foundation Background Paper #26, October 1998, p. 16. Reprinted by permission.

going price for cigarettes in New York reflects the high tax applied to cigarettes in that state. But if you can sell cigarettes at that high price and get away with not paying the tax, you can make very large profits on the smuggled cigarettes from North Carolina. Figure 16.3 illustrates the trend in smuggling cigarettes over the period from 1960 to 1997. According to these figures compiled by the Tax Foundation, smuggling more than doubled over this period as excise tax rates in northern states were increased relative to the rates in southern states. This figure also illustrates the trend in cross-border sales over the period 1960 to 1997. With the increasing divergence between cigarette excise tax rates across states, there is clearly an increasing number of cross-border sales. The greater the difference in price across state lines, the greater the incentive for consumers living near the border to cross the border to the low-tax state and purchase cigarettes.

This problem is not unique to the United States. Smuggling cigarettes is a huge business in Europe as well, where there are well-established smuggling routes.[6] In fact, cigarette smuggling has become one of the primary sources of wealth in Eastern and Central Europe, including some transition economies, where people have learned to make a living by smuggling and other directly nonproductive activities. The first major route runs by road from Belgium into Switzerland. From there the cigarettes leave the European Union jurisdiction (and are subsequently outside EU law and regulations) and go to destinations in Central and Eastern Europe or one of the former Soviet republics.

The second major smuggling route involves cigarettes taken from port warehouses to various regional airports in Belgium or the Netherlands. They are then flown by aircraft to destinations in Eastern Europe. From there they are transported by truck to Italy or Germany. Then the cigarettes are smuggled in small quantities in private cars and vans supplying the Italian market and the markets in other EU countries. Cigarettes bound for Italy also arrive by way of Albania and the republics of the former Yugoslavia. These cigarettes arrive on fast boats that cross the Adriatic Sea, which is a traditional and well-known smuggling route.

The third route runs through Gibraltar and Andorra, where cigarettes are smuggled from northern European ports via sea. Although the documentation accompanying these cigarettes indicates that they are headed for destinations in Africa, the sea route goes close to the territorial waters of Spain and the cigarettes are off-loaded and sent via fast boats to ports along the Spanish coast.

Use Taxes

In order to safeguard the integrity of the sales tax, all states with sales taxes also have **use taxes**. A use tax is equivalent to a sales tax, with the difference that it applies to goods not covered by the sales tax. The use tax is applied at the same rate as the state sales tax. A Vermont consumer who wishes to evade his state sales tax on the purchase of a new SUV may drive across the border and purchase the vehicle in New Hampshire where there is no sales tax. On returning to Vermont, however, the consumer owes a use tax equal to the state sales tax on his use of an SUV in Vermont. In this way, states are able to reduce the border effects that arise due to differences in sales tax rates. Collection and enforcement of the use tax is not visible or effective, however, and most consumers are unaware of the existence of use taxes.

Another example of use tax liability arises in the case of mail-order sales. When a hunter in Wisconsin orders a new pair of duck boots from L. L. Bean in Maine, he may think that he can legally avoid paying a sales tax on that purchase. In reality, however, he owes a use tax in Wisconsin equal to the sales tax that would have otherwise been applied. In reality, however, despite the fact that he owes the tax, it is unlikely to be collected from him. Most states are ineffective in collecting use taxes, except in cases where the tax is very large.

HARMONIZATION OF INDIRECT TAXES IN A FEDERATION OF GOVERNMENTS[7]

When a number of governments rely on indirect taxes such as excise taxes and also exist within a federation, a number of issues arise regarding harmonization of the tax rates. Such is the lot of the United States or countries in the European Union. Although each state may wish to apply its own tax rates to goods within its borders, economic effects arise from differences in the rates applied across borders and are important to consider.

Suppose that we have two states (provinces, or countries) with identical demand curves, as illustrated in Figure 16.4. The world price of the commodity is given at P. In the first state the excise tax is initially set at t_h, whereas in the second state the excise tax is set at t_l, where $t_h > t_l$. The excise taxes create excess burdens in each state, as usual. The excess burden of the excise tax t_h in the high-tax state is measured by the area *abc,* whereas the excess burden of the excise tax t_l in the low-tax state is given by *ade.*

Now, suppose that the excise tax rates are harmonized at a common rate equal to the average of the two rates: $0.5(t_h + t_l.)$. The tax is reduced in the high-tax state and increased in the low-tax state. As a result of the tax changes, the quantity demanded increases by the amount $q - q_1$ in the high-tax state and decreases by the amount $q_2 - q$ in the low-tax state. In both states there is a change in the excess burden of the tax. A reduction of excess burden in the high-tax state equals the area *bcfg.* In the low-tax state there is an increase in the excess burden of taxation of *defg,* but this amount is smaller than the reduction for the high-tax state. As a result of harmonization, the total excess burden of taxation in the two states is reduced by the amount *bcfg* – *defg.* Why does this occur? Recall that the excess burden of an excise tax rises with the square of the tax rate (assuming linear demand). As a result, a tax reduction in the high-tax state will reduce excess burden by a larger amount than the same tax increase raises excess burden in the low-tax state. In this simple example we see that harmonization of tax rates may well be welfare-enhancing.

FIGURE 16.4 Efficiency Gain from Harmonization of Indirect Taxes

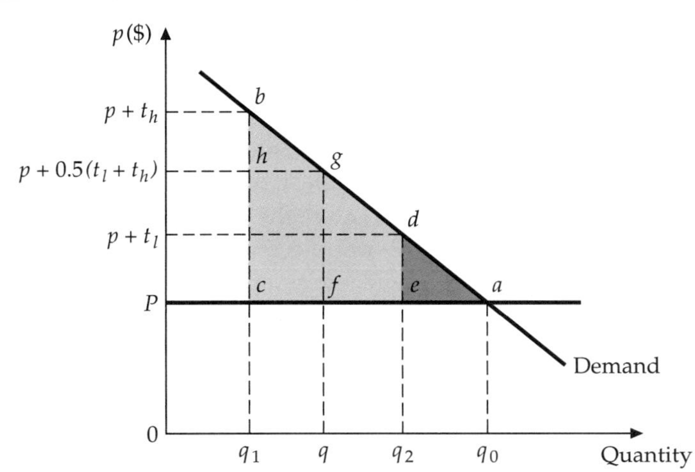

Why would harmonization of indirect taxes be a policy concern? Consider the case of unleaded petrol (gasoline) in the European Union (EU). Table 16.5 lists the excise duty in each member state along with the VAT rate applied. A great deal of variation exists in the rates applied by EU

TABLE 16.5 Excise and VAT Taxes on Unleaded Gasoline in the European Union, 2009

EU Member State	Excise Duty (Euros per 1,000 Liters)	VAT (%)
Belgium	613.5701	21.00
Bulgaria	350.24	20.00
Czech Republic	505.11	20.00
Denmark	566.70	19.00
Germany	669.80	19.00
Estonia	422.77	20.00
Greece	670.00	23.00
Spain	670.00	23.00
France	606.90	19.60
Ireland	543.17	21.00
Italy	564.00	20.00
Cyprus	359.00	15.00
Latvia	379.78	21.00
Lithuania	434.43	21.00
Luxembourg	464.5846	15.00
Hungary	444.02	25.00
Malta	459.38	18.00
Netherlands	713.99	19.00
Austria	442.00	20.00
Poland	451.09	22.00
Portugal	451.09	22.00
Romania	349.04	24.00
Slovenia	484.51	20.00
Slovakia	514.50	19.00
Finland	627.00	23.00
Sweden	542.74	25.00
United Kingdom	627.87	17.50

Source: From *Excise Duty Tables* Ref 1031 rev. 1, July 2009 Part II—Energy products and Electricity, from European Commission, Directorate General, Taxation and Customs Union.

member states. The excise duty applied to unleaded gasoline ranges from a low of 348.04 euros per 1,000 liters in Romania to a high of 713.99 in the Netherlands. With such a wide variation in rates, there may be substantial scope for welfare-enhancing harmonization. The member states of the EU also apply their VAT to gasoline. There is additional variation in VAT rates across EU member states, although the degree of variation in these rates is smaller than that with the excise duties.

POLICY STUDY

What do Littered Cigarette Packs on the Streets of Chicago Tell Us about Tax Avoidance?

Recently, a novel approach has been used to investigate cigarette excise tax avoidance. By examining the littered packs of cigarettes on the streets of Chicago, Merriman (2010) found that there is a high degree of tax avoidance. Each package of cigarettes sold in the City of Chicago require that a stamp be affixed to the package showing that the State of Illinois and joint City of Chicago and Cook County excise taxes have been paid. The wholesalers of the cigarettes must put the tax stamps on each package showing that the tax has been paid before distributing those packs to retailers who then sell them to consumers. By visually examining street litter in Chicago, it is clear whether the necessary tax stamps, including both the State of Illinois stamp and the Chicago stamp are affixed to the packages.

Large tax differentials across a relatively small geographic area provide both incentive and opportunity for cigarette consumers to engage in tax avoidance. There is substantial variation within Cook County where the City of Chicago is located. All cigarettes sold in Cook County are liable for a \$2.00/pack county tax. Within the county the municipalities of Berwyn, Cicero, Chicago, Evanston, and Rosemont also levy city excise taxes. The municipal taxes in Cook county range from a low of \$0.05/pack in Rosemont to a high of \$0.68 in Chicago. In nearby DuPage, Lake, and Will Counties of Illinois where there is no county or municipal excise tax the total tax is \$1.37. In the bordering State of Indiana there is a state excise tax of \$0.555/pack and no county or municipal excise taxes. Hence, in the metro Chicago area the combined taxes are just \$0.945/pack for cigarettes purchased at outlets in Indiana, rise to \$1.37/pack for cigarettes purchased in Illinois counties surrounding Cook County, and range from \$3.38/pack to \$4.05/pack for cigarettes purchased from outlets in Cook County depending on the municipal tax rate. Merriman (2010) estimates that for a pack-a-day smoker purchasing cigarettes in Indiana rather than Chicago saves approximately \$1,100 per year. Hence, there is ample incentive for a Chicago smoker to purchase cigarettes in Indiana and avoid purchases in Chicago.

Data collectors found a total of 2,391 littered cigarette packs with 1.147 of those (nearly 48%) with cellophane still attached so that tax stamps were identifiable. A total of 59% of the packs found in Chicago had Illinois stamps while 29% had Indiana

TABLE 16.6 Cigarette Excise Taxes in Metro Chicago Area, 2007

	Indiana	Illinois Cook County	Illinois DuPage, Lake, and Will Counties
Federal excise tax ($)	0.39	0.39	0.39
State excise tax ($)	0.555	0.98	0.98
County excise tax ($)	0.00	2.00	0.00
Municipal excise tax ($)	0.00	0.00 to 0.68	0.00
Total ($)	0.945	3.38 to 4.05	1.37

Source: Merriman (2010).

stamps. Five percent of the packs found had stamps from other states and seven percent had no stamps (indicating either purchase at Native American reservations where due to sovereignty no federal, state, or local taxes are collected, or purchases from illegal sources on the internet or elsewhere). Just 25% of the littered packs in Chicago had a Chicago tax stamp. A somewhat higher percentage of packages, 36%, had a Cook County stamp. Overall, Chicago littered packages were more likely to have an Indiana stamp than a Chicago stamp. Furthermore, Merriman (2010) examined the spatial distribution of littered packs and found clear statistical evidence that as you move farther away from a jurisdictional boundary with a substantial tax differential, the incidence of tax avoidance diminishes. That makes sense as the transportation cost involved in tax avoidance increases with distance, reducing the incentive to engage in avoidance behavior. Altogether, littered cigarette packs on the streets of Chicago tell a compelling story that smokers are sensitive to tax-based price differentials and respond accordingly. A very substantial proportion of the Chicago smoking population avoids the high cigarette excise tax in Chicago by purchasing smokes in nearby jurisdictions with lower taxes. Compliance rises geographically as avoidance costs rise with distance and as tax differentials decrease.

This evidence raises a number of interesting policy questions. For example, we might want to consider whether the City of Chicago may be taxing cigarettes at a rate that exceeds the revenue maximizing point on the demand curve (where the price elasticity of demand is unity). If so, a reduction in the city portion of the tax might actually raise revenue. This evidence also suggests that efforts to understand and measure tax avoidance can be very useful in the design of tax policies and the administration of tax systems.

For more on international perspectives on smuggling of tobacco products, see the Merriman chapter of the World Bank *Economics of Tobacco Toolkit* edited by Yurekeli and de Boyer.

POLICY STUDY

The Incidence of Gasoline Excise Taxes

Proposals to increase the gasoline excise tax have been suggested for a number of reasons including the reduction of air pollution and alleviation of global warming attributed to automobile and truck emissions. Despite the fact that combined federal and state excise taxes on gasoline in the United States are approximately one-fifth of the taxes applied in Western Europe, there is stiff resistance to increasing the excise taxes in the United States. That resistance appears to be rooted in the belief that excise taxes on gasoline are very regressive, requiring low-income households to pay a larger share of income in tax than is required of high-income households. Indeed, cross-section estimates of the incidence of gasoline excise taxes have indicated that the taxes are regressive.

Tax policy analysts have suggested, however, that if we were to consider the lifetime incidence of gasoline excise taxes, we might find a very different outcome. They argue that incidence analysis based on a single year's data is misleading because most people with low incomes are only temporarily poor. If gasoline consumption is based on expected lifetime income rather than current income, then the computation of tax burden based on a single year's data will give tax burdens for the poor that are higher than they would be if the burden were calculated on the basis of permanent income. In order to determine whether the incidence of gasoline excise taxes is very different based on current or permanent income, Chernick and Reschovsky (1997) conducted a study based on panel data. They used the Panel Study of Income Dynamics (PSID) data for the years 1976 to 1986. Table 16.6 provides their estimates of gasoline expenditure burdens by household income decile. The left-hand panel of the table provides estimates based on a single year's data, 1982. The incidence pattern revealed is regressive as the percentage of annual income spent on gasoline rises from 6.4 percent in the first decile to 7.3 percent in the second decile, then falls monotonically thereafter, reaching a low of 3.1 percent in the tenth decile. The increase in percentage from the first to the second decile may not be fully accurate as individuals in the first decile often report negative, zero, or very small incomes.

The right-hand panel of Table 16.6 provides Chernick and Reschovsky's estimates of gasoline expenditures using an 11-year average of expenditures and income. Although the percentage of income spent on gasoline falls in all deciles, the basic pattern is the same as that estimated from a single year's data. Gasoline expenditures account for 3.9 percent of income in the first decile, rising to 5.3 percent in the second decile, and falling thereafter. A gasoline excise tax applied to these expenditures would be similarly regressive.

Chernick and Reschovsky also compared three alternative measures of income and gasoline tax burden: annual, 5-year average, and 11-year average. Measuring annual income against annual gasoline tax burden indicates a regressive tax. Moving to 5-year and 11-year averages, respectively, data for both gasoline expenditures and income shows the tax as only slightly less regressive at each step.

Chernick and Reschovsky also consider what happens to the distribution of annual gasoline expenditure if we rank individuals by their average income rather than their annual income. Considering annual burden against average income over incrementally

TABLE 16.7 Gasoline Expenditure Burdens

1982 Family Income Decile	Gasoline Expenditures as a Percentage of Annual Income: 1982 Data from PSID	1976–1986 Average Family Income Decile	Average Family Gasoline Expenditures 1976–1986 as a Percentage of Average Family Income 1976–1986
1 (lowest)	6.4	1 (lowest)	3.9
2	7.3	2	5.3
3	6.7	3	5.1
4	5.8	4	5.0
5	5.7	5	4.6
6	5.2	6	4.3
7	5.0	7	4.0
8	4.6	8	3.8
9	3.9	9	3.4
10 (highest)	3.1	10 (highest)	2.5

Source: From "Who Pays the Gasoline Tax?" by Andrew Reschovsky in *National Tax Journal,* 50, No. 2, 1997, p. 241.

longer time periods, we observe that income reranking reduces the regressivity of the excise tax on gasoline. Here's why: some individuals in the sample with high annual gasoline expenditures move up in the income distribution. As a result, the measured regressivity of the tax falls.

However, we find the opposite result as we examine the average gasoline expenditure burdens ranked by alternative ability-to-pay measures: 5-year and 11-year average incomes. As we rerank individuals by their average incomes, we see a greater regressivity in the tax. This result is due to the fact that the calculation of intermediate-run burdens tends to reduce burdens for those individuals with exceptionally high annual burdens and low annual incomes and increase burdens for those individuals with exceptionally low annual burdens and high annual incomes. Individuals who are mobile within the income distribution and have low annual income and low average burden move up in the income distribution as we move to the intermediate-run measure of income. Individuals with high annual income and moderate or high average burden tend to move down the income distribution as we move to use of the intermediate-run measure of income. As a result, there is an increase in the regressivity for the excise tax.

Chernick and Reschovsky conclude that the use of measures of long-run tax burdens without corresponding ranking of individuals by long-run measures of ability to pay has the effect of overstating the magnitude of the annual income bias.

PROBLEMS

1. Answer the following questions about the sales tax in the state where you reside:
   a. What is the tax rate?
   b. Is grocery store food subject to taxation?
   c. Are prescription drugs subject to taxation?
   d. Is clothing subject to taxation?
   e. Is there a local government (city, county, or school district) sales tax also? If so, what is the combined state and local tax rate?
2. Answer the following questions about excise taxes in the state where you reside:
   a. What is the rate of taxation applied to beer?
   b. What is the rate of taxation applied to wine?
   c. What is the rate of taxation applied to gasoline?
   d. What is the rate of taxation applied to cigarettes? Has this rate changed recently? If so, why?
3. Find your home state in Table 16.3 and note the excise tax rate applied to beer, wine, and spirits.
   a. How does the tax rate on beer compare with the rate in contiguous states?
   b. How does the tax rate on wine compare with the rate in contiguous states?
   c. Is your state a control state? If so, how is state control likely to affect the market for spirits? Explain.
4. Find your home state in Table 16.3 and note the excise tax rate applied to cigarettes.
   a. For each of the states contiguous with your home state, look up their excise tax rate on cigarettes.
   b. Determine whether there is an economic incentive to cross the state line in order to purchase cigarettes in a nearby state.
   c. If there is an economic incentive to purchase cigarettes in a nearby state, how does the cost of transportation affect that incentive? Explain.
5. Suppose that you had information that consumption expenditures for a particular good were a function of income, given by the relationship $C = \$1{,}200 + 0.3Y$, where C is consumption expenditure and Y is after-tax income. The legislature of your state is considering application of a 5 percent tax on this good.
   a. Complete the following table of information.
   b. Write a one-page policy briefing paper on the incidence of the proposed tax.
6. State A has a sales tax of 4 percent that it applies to all goods and services. Consider the following households composed of four persons each

Income	Consumption	Tax	Tax as a Percentage of Income
$10,000			
$30,000			
$50,000			
$70,000			
$90,000			

located in state A. The Richardson family has an annual income of $20,000 and purchases $4,000 yearly from grocery stores. The Kubeks have an income of $50,000 a year and spend $8,000 at grocery stores. Neither family saves any of its income.

a. Calculate the amount of sales tax each family pays for grocery store items and the amount of total sales tax they pay.
b. Calculate the fraction of income each family allocates to sales tax payment.
c. The governor of state A says that taxing food is unfair to low-income families and she will propose that the state exempt grocery store food from taxation. Evaluate the governor's proposal in terms of cost, effectiveness, and progressivity.
d. A state senator agrees with the governor that low-income families need help but says a tax credit will be more effective in providing relief. He proposes that the state continue to tax food but grant a $50 per person tax credit for sales taxes paid on grocery store food (regardless of what anyone really spent). Evaluate this proposal in terms of cost, effectiveness, and progressivity.

REFERENCES

Chernick, Howard, and Andrew Reschovsky. "Who Pays the Gasoline Tax?" *National Tax Journal* 50 (1997): 233–59.

Congressional Budget Office. *Federal Taxation of Tobacco, Alcoholic Beverages, and Motor Fuels*. Washington, DC: U.S. Government Printing Office, 1990.

European Commission. *Excise Duty Tables* Ref 1031 rev. 1, July 2009 Part II—Energy products and Electricity, from European Commission, Directorate General, Taxation and Customs Union. Available at: http://ec.europa.eu

Joossens, Luk, and Martin Raw. "Cigarette Smuggling in Europe: Who Really Benefits?" 1998. Available at http://www.jstor.org/stable/20207457

Keen, Michael. "The Welfare Economics of Tax Coordination in the European Community." *Fiscal Studies* 14 (1993): 15–36.

Krupnick, Alan, Winston Harrington, and Anna Alberini. "Public Support for Pollution Fee Policies for Motor Vehicles with Revenue Recycling: Survey Results." *Regional Science and Urban Economics* 31 (2001): 505–22.

McClure, Charles. "Electronic Commerce, State Sales Taxation, and Intergovernmental Fiscal Relations." *National Tax Journal* 50 (1997): 731–49.

Merriman, David. "The Micr-Geography of Tax Avoidance: Evidence from Littered Cigarette Packs in Chicago." *American Economic Journal: Economic Policy* 2 (2010): 61–84.

Pechman, Joseph A. *Federal Tax Policy*, 5th ed. Washington, DC: Brookings Institution, 1987.

Yurekli, Ayda and Joy de Beyer. *World Bank Economics of Tobacco Toolkit*, Tool 7. Smuggling by David Merriman, "Understand, Measure, and Combat Tobacco Smuggling." World Bank, Washington, DC.

NOTES

1. The historical facts in this paragraph are taken from Rowena Bolin, "Salt of the Earth," *Courier Journal*, February 26, 2001.
2. The historical overview provided here is based on Pechman (1987).
3. This figure is computed based on information in *Economic Report of the President 2011*, Table B-81.
4. In order to compare these taxes in terms that are more familiar to beer drinkers, recall that a six-pack of beer consists of 72 ounces, whereas a gallon consists of 128 ounces. Thus, a six-pack of beer is 72/128 of a gallon, or 0.5625 gallons. Multiply the tax listed in Table 15.3 by 0.5625 to obtain the tax per six-pack.
5. This decision came in the National Bellas Hess case.
6. Joossens and Raw (2001).
7. The material in this section is adapted from Keen (1993).

CHAPTER 17

Radius Images/Getty Images

Property Taxes

LEARNING OBJECTIVES

1. Discuss property tax systems.
2. Describe different approaches to property valuation.
3. Explain incidence and equity aspects of property taxation.
4. Discuss the capitalization of property taxes and local public services.
5. Identify methods of providing property tax relief.

Property taxes are *ad valorem* taxes based on the value of property such as land, homes, shopping centers, and factories. They are the primary source of funds for local governments in the United States, as well as in many industrialized nations of the world. Dating back to colonial times, local governments in the United States have relied primarily on property taxes in order to raise the funds necessary to provide local public education, roads, and other local services.[1]

Table 17.1 illustrates that local governments in the United States currently derive approximately 72 percent of their own-source tax revenue from the property tax. This makes the property tax the primary source of local own-source tax revenue. Notice, however, that property taxes grew less important in the overall state and local revenue picture during the nearly 60-year period covered in Table 17.1. During this period most state-level property taxes were eliminated, and many local governments now rely increasingly on revenues transferred from their state governments. In fact, the property tax currently accounts for just 28 percent of total local revenues. Although there has been dramatic shifts in the sources of funds used to finance local government in the United States over the past half decade, the property tax still is the single most important source of local government tax revenue.

The property tax is an important tax revenue source for local governments, so it is paradoxical that it is also universally reviled. Surveys of taxpayer attitudes regularly report that taxpayers hate the property tax more than any other tax. Why is such an important tax so disliked?

The property tax applies to property. But, what counts as property? This is no trivial issue. We must begin by classifying types of property and we start

TABLE 17.1 Trends in Local Government Property Tax Reliance, 1950–2008

Year	Property Tax ($ Millions)	Total Own-Source Taxes ($ Millions)	Total Revenue ($ Millions)	Property Tax Share of Own-Source Tax Revenue	Property Tax Share of Total Revenue
1950	7,042	7,984	14,014	0.88	0.50
1955	10,323	11,886	21,092	0.87	0.49
1960	15,798	18,081	33,027	0.87	0.48
1965	21,817	25,116	47,528	0.87	0.46
1970	32,963	38,833	80,916	0.85	0.41
1975	50,040	61,310	14,6307	0.82	0.34
1980	65,607	86,387	232,452	0.76	0.28
1985	99,772	134,473	354,146	0.74	0.28
1990	149,765	201,130	512,322	0.74	0.29
1995	193,933	261,430	757,400	0.74	0.26
2000	228,453	315,833	952,330	0.72	0.24
2005	324,437	447,901	1,160,467	0.72	0.28
2008	396,995	548,764	1,401,341	0.72	0.28

Source: U.S. Census Bureau, Census of Governments, State and Local Government Summary Tables by Level of Government, various years.

with the distinction between real and personal property. **Real property** consists of such things as land and structures (buildings), whereas **personal property** consists of machinery, equipment, furniture, and financial assets. Within each of these categories of property, however, we can make a distinction between **tangible** and **intangible** forms of property. Table 17.2 illustrates this two-way categorization of property and provides examples of each. Land, buildings, and improvements are classified as tangible real property. For a business, the value of a firm's goodwill, or the going-concern value, is considered intangible. Further, a state-granted license or privilege, such as a liquor license, creates an intangible asset that may be considered part of property value for a business. Business equipment and machinery are personal property. For households, an automobile and household furniture are considered tangible personal property. Most states permit their local governments to tax tangible real property, including land and buildings. States also attempt to tax intangible real property, when they apply the property tax to railroads, utilities, airlines, pipelines, and other such firms, but it is very difficult to estimate the value of the intangibles. Although most local governments included personal property in the tax base a hundred years ago, that is no longer the case. For households, tangible personal property is typically exempt from property taxation. The exception to that rule is that some states apply a personal property tax to automobiles, but most states apply a registration fee

TABLE 17.2 A Taxonomy of Property

Tangible Property		Intangible Property
Real property	Land	Stocks
	Buildings	Bonds
	Improvements	Bank deposits
		Mortgages
		Cash value of insurance policies
		Patents
		Copyrights and trademarks
		Goodwill or going-concern value
		Licenses and other state-granted privileges
		Computer software
Personal property	Machinery	
	Equipment	
	Automobiles	
	furniture	

that is not directly related to the value of the vehicle. Finally, some states apply an intangibles tax to the value of a household's portfolio of assets, including stocks and bonds.

A property tax is also distinct from a **land value tax** (**LVT**) under which a local government taxes the value of land only, and not the value of improvements. LVTs have potential efficiency properties that are superior to property taxes since the supply of land is completely inelastic, hence taxation of land is nondistortionary. For more on LVTs see Dye and England (2009). Another variant of the property tax is the **split-rate property tax** or the **two-rate property tax.** Under these variants of the property tax different rates are applied to land and improvements, with the land rate typically higher than the improvements rate. For more on split rate taxes, see Anderson (1993).

For a comprehensive source of information on the various property tax systems and their features employed in the United States see the Lincoln Institute of Land Policy website: http://www.lincolninst.edu/subcenters/significant-features-property-tax/.

PROPERTY TAX BASE

In order to begin our investigation of property taxes and how they are computed based on property value, we must first clarify how this type of tax base differs from those we have considered previously.

Stocks and Flows: An Important Distinction

The property tax base is unlike other tax bases we have analyzed previously. We have considered taxation of income, consumption, and other economic tax bases measured in dollars per unit of time, such as a year. These measures are flows in economics because they involve measurement in dollars per unit of time. In the case of the property tax, however, we are not taxing an economic flow. Rather, when we tax the value of property, we are taxing an economic stock. A stock variable is simply measured in units without regard for time. For example, wealth is a stock variable and is measured in dollars; hence, the distinction between the flow variable income and the stock variable wealth is a distinction based on our time perspective. The property tax is a major form of taxation that is applied to an economic stock—the current value of property. Of course, property often generates a flow of income over time. For example, a rental house may generate a flow of net income for its owner each month. Yet, what determines the value of the rental house is the present discounted value of the future rental income stream. Hence, property value is a stock concept, but it is related to an economic flow in an important way. Although we could consider the property tax as a wealth tax, we should keep in mind that it is not a broad-based wealth tax because it applies to just one form of wealth—real property—or real estate in particular. An alternative form of wealth tax that also applies to a broader stock of wealth is the **estate tax**, which is applied to the entire value of an estate left by a wealthy person who dies, including the real estate that the person may have owned.

Market Value of Property

The process of determining the value of property for tax purposes is called **assessment**. The state or local government appoints or elects a person called the **assessor** whose job it is to assign a value to all property subject to the property tax. The essential concept at the heart of the property tax is the market value of property, so the assessor must determine the market value of all the properties in the jurisdiction. That means the assessor must determine what price the property would command in the real estate market with a willing buyer and a willing seller in an **arm's-length transaction**, or a transaction between parties unrelated in either a familial or economic sense. The point is that the assessor wants to know the true market value rather than the value a father might place on a piece of land sold to his son or the value a corporation might place on property bought from its subsidiary company.

When an assessor considers a particular parcel of property, he must ask himself, "What is the **highest and best use** of this property?" After all, market value should reflect the value of the property when used in its most productive use, not necessarily its current use. Consider the example of a paved parking lot in the center of a large city, surrounded by skyscrapers. The value of the land under the parking lot pavement is very high, not because the parking lot generates a large stream of net income for its owner but because the lot also carries with it the option of being converted into a developed land use that can generate even more net income. The highest and best use of that lot is probably a high-rise building with a vast amount of developed commercial space. Hence, the assessor should value the lot in that use, rather than in its current use as a parking lot. This requires the assessor to make an assumption about the best potential use of the land, given the economic conditions in the real estate market. The parking lot owner would rather have the assessor value the lot in its current use as a parking lot, but that would be inappropriate. Here is one of the sources of people's discontent with the property tax. Determination of highest and best use is subjective. The property owner may disagree with the assessor on the highest and best use of the property. In some cases, the current use of the property is its highest and best use, but in other cases the current use is far below the highest and best use.

Property Rights and Property Value

The value of a piece of property also depends on the bundle of rights that accompany the property. Normally, the owner of the property has **fee simple rights**, a legal term meaning that the owner can do whatever she wants with the property. Sometimes the bundle of rights is reduced, however, with one or more rights of ownership omitted. For example, the local utility company may have an **easement** for a right-of-way over a strip of the property in order to maintain a power line, telephone line, or underground cable. The easement gives the utility company the right to access the property for the purpose of improving and maintaining the services provided. Another form of easement is the *conservation easement*, whereby the landowner agrees to forgo the right to develop the property so that it will be retained in a natural state. Another example of a right of ownership that is often separated from the standard bundle of rights is the rights to mineral resources. A landowner can sell the mineral rights on his property to an oil company or natural gas company. The value of the property depends on the bundle of rights that accompany the property. Removing one or more rights will lower the value of the property.

Consider an example of how property rights affect property value. Suppose that you own 200 acres of undeveloped land on the north side of a growing metropolitan area. With brisk development occurring, the value of your land is rising at a fast pace and your wealth is increasing. You expect to sell your property soon to a developer who will build a large shopping center complex and a residential community surrounding a golf club. It is only a matter of time and you will be filthy rich. Then, one day an unexpected event occurs. The Environmental Protection Agency (EPA) discovers the presence of the near-extinct variegated prairie dog on your land. In order to save this last remaining piece of habitat and preserve the species, the development rights to your land are taken by a county government decree. All of a sudden, your land is nearly worthless and you are virtually penniless. The land has not changed in any way, but the simple removal of one right has caused a drastic change in its value. Property rights and property values are inexorably linked.

Clive Sawyer PCL/SuperStock/Corbis

The property tax base is the value of land and structures.

Fundamentals of Land Value

When valuing a piece of real estate, consider two important components. One is the value of the buildings and improvements and the other is the value of the land. Although the structure value is important, oftentimes the land value is far more important. Consider a simple example of two homes in the Bay Area of California. A 50-year-old three-bedroom home with 1,600 square feet of living space built on a standard city lot with dimensions 60 by 120 feet might have a value of $250,000 in Daly City, California, whereas a similar home with the same living space and lot size in San Francisco might be worth $1,250,000. What is the difference? It is certainly not the value of the structure. It is the value of the land. Hence, it is essential to take a closer look at what determines land values.

Land value in an urban area can be characterized as including four distinct aspects of price, depending on the location of the land in relation to the central business district (CBD) and the land's state of development, and is illustrated in Figure 17.1.[2] At distances closer than z^*, the urban periphery, the price of developed land has four component parts: the value of accessibility, the cost of land conversion, the value of expected future rent increases, and the value of agricultural land rent. The value of accessibility diminishes with increasing distance from the CBD. By the time land is at least z^* miles from the CBD, the value of accessibility has declined to zero. The cost of conversion of agricultural land to developed use is assumed to be independent of the location of the land. Notice that the presence of conversion cost implies that land prices jump at the edge of the city. At distance z^* there is an upward discontinuous jump in price. The third component of land price is the value of expected future rent increases after development of the land. This value is constant within z^* miles of the CBD but is declining with distance out past z^*. The farther out the land, the lower the expected future increase in rent. The presence of this component of price implies that agricultural land that is still in use but lies relatively close to the urban boundary will command a premium in its price due to the present value of expected future increases in rent that will occur after development. The size of that premium depends on distance to the urban perimeter. Finally, the land has a pure agricultural value that is invariant with respect to distance. Regardless of its location, a parcel of land is presumed to have a certain value in agricultural use. The overall pattern of land prices with respect to distance is declining. The farther from the CBD, a parcel's location, the lower its price, other things being equal.

This model of land value is based on a monocentric view of the urban area, assuming that there is a single CBD. Many urban areas are composed of multiple business districts, each with a land value gradient as illustrated in Figure 17.1. Urban areas are certainly more complex in reality than the situation we have pictured in Figure 17.1, the essentials of land value determination are nevertheless captured in that view.

The implications of land value fundamentals are critical to understanding the market value of property. You can take a given building and put it on different parcels of land at varying locations in the urban area, and it will have vastly different market value due to the variation in land value depending on location. The realtor's favorite saying is that there are three factors that determine the value of property: location, location, and location. That aphorism is true in the sense that the property's land value depends critically on location.

Valuation Methods

The objective is to determine the market value of properties for tax purposes, so we need only observe their prices in real estate markets, right? That sounds pretty simple and straightforward. Hold on partner, it isn't that easy. Some properties change hands in real estate markets, but most properties are not bought and sold regularly in market transactions. For most properties, we

FIGURE 17.1 Fundamentals of Land Price

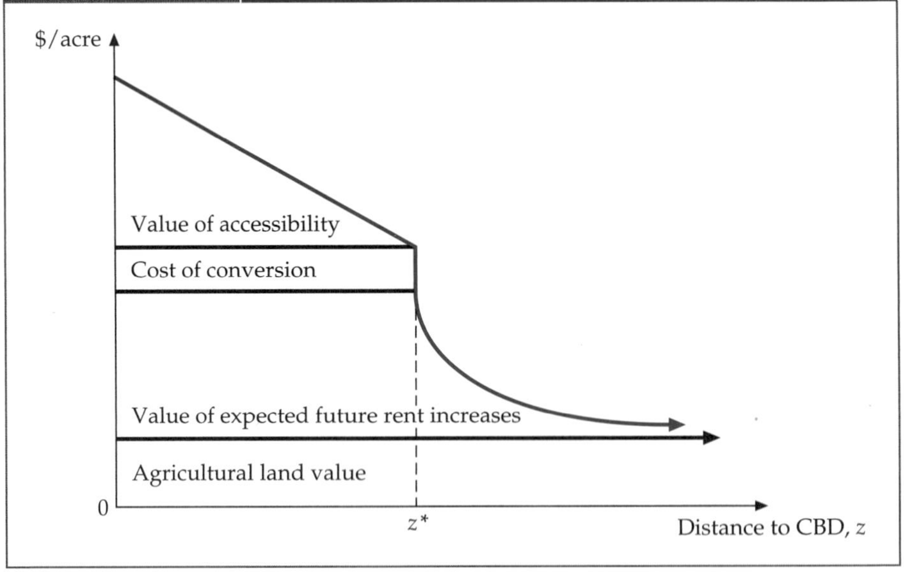

must estimate market value without the benefit of having market transactions to observe. Three established methods are used for property valuation: the **market comparison approach**, the **income capitalization approach**, and the **replacement cost approach**.

For single-family homes, the assessor will typically use the market comparison method in order to assign a value to each home. This method relies on a comparison of the subject home and its characteristics to other similar homes that have sold recently in the market where prices have been established by the interaction of supply and demand forces. By using prices for similar homes, called *comparables*, the assessor can establish an appropriate price for the subject home, after making adjustments for differences in characteristics. For example, the assessor may need to assess a three-bedroom, two-bath home in a particular neighborhood. The assessor checks the sales data for similar homes in that neighborhood and finds eight homes have sold in the last year. The average price of the eight similar homes was $88,500. The subject home is comparable to the other eight in all respects, except that the subject home has a fireplace that the other homes lacked. The assessor then adjusts the value to account for that difference in characteristics. The subject home may be assessed at $92,500, reflecting the fact that a fireplace adds $4,000 to the value of a home. The application of the market comparison method requires a sufficient number of similar properties so that the assessor can get an accurate view of the market's valuation of such properties. In the absence of sales data for similar properties, the method cannot be used.

The income capitalization method is appropriate for properties that generate a stream of income over time. It is used for commercial properties or multifamily housing units. Suppose that an apartment generates a net income (gross income net of expenses) of $200 per month. The expected life of the facility is 30 years and the discount rate (reflecting the opportunity cost of capital) is 7 percent. The value of the property is computed by figuring the discounted present value of the income stream, in this case $30,061. The assessor then assesses this property at this amount for tax purposes. In another example, a retail establishment on Main Street may be expected to generate a net income stream of $150,000 per year for the next 20 years. At the same discount rate of 7 percent, the value of the establishment is given by the discounted present value of the income stream: $1,589,102. This method is typically used when net income data is available. The problem, of course, is that many private firms do not wish to release net income information to the assessor. That makes the use of the income capitalization method difficult. The assessor may have to estimate the net income stream, and then use that estimated stream to compute the discounted present value.

In the replacement cost method, the assessor computes the cost of replacing a facility and then subtracts depreciation reflecting the present age of the facility. This method is most often used for manufacturing facilities and other unique properties where the market comparison method and the income capitalization method cannot be used. Suppose that a local manufacturer of jet skis has a facility that must be valued for property tax purposes. No data is available on comparable sales, because no similar production facilities have been sold in the market in recent years. Similarly, no data is available on the manufacturer's net income. As a result, the assessor must resort to computing what it would cost to build a similar production facility, and then depreciate that figure. If the manufacturing plant consists of 400,000 square feet of space and the cost of building such space is currently $80 per square foot, it would cost $32 million to build a similar facility. But the existing facility is 8 years old and has an expected 30-year life. Using a simple straight-line depreciation method, the remaining life of the facility is 22/30 = 73.33 percent of the total life; hence the value of the facility can be approximated as 73.33 percent of $32 million, or $23.5 million.

In theory, all three methods should yield the same, or approximately the same, answer. A thorough assessment or appraisal will provide estimates of value using all three approaches and an overall opinion on the value of the property. A private fee **appraiser** will typically employ all three methods in computing the value of a property. In practice, the tax assessor may be limited to using just one method due to data limitations. The difference between an assessor and an appraiser is that the assessor values property for taxation purposes, whereas the appraiser values property for other purposes such as real estate brokerage or insurance company purposes.

Once the assessor has placed a value on all properties in the local government unit (county or city), higher levels of government often implement an equalization process in order to assure that there is equity across local government units. Whenever local governments provide services across various assessment districts, it is necessary to make sure that assessments are similar in each district in order to assure fairness for taxpayers.

Property values are important because as property value varies with location, so too will assessed value and property taxes. Herein lies an important distinction, however. A jurisdiction with many properties with high assessed value can generate large property tax revenue with a relatively low tax rate. On the other hand, a jurisdiction with low-value property must apply high rates of tax in order to generate even a modest level of revenue per resident of the community. This issue is critical for understanding why the property tax is under attack as a poor financing mechanism for public education in inner-city areas, for example.

PROPERTY TAX RATES

Once property values are determined, the tax owed by the property owner is determined by the tax rate. For example, if a home is assessed at $100,000 and the tax rate is 2 percent, the homeowner owes a property tax of $2,000 to the local governments. The tax is determined by the product of the tax base (property assessed value) and the tax rate (usually expressed as a percent). Of course, not all property is assessed at full market value.

Defining Tax Rates

The property tax is very complex due to the fact that there is no single property tax rate. Actually, the property tax rate is a combination of a whole host of local government property tax rates. Table 17.3 provides a view of the property tax rate for a hypothetical community. This community applies a total property tax rate of 1.86 percent of property value. That rate is not a single rate, however. It is the combination of rates applied by the school district, city, county, library district, community college district, and other local government units. Each local government unit sets its tax rate in an independent fashion. The sum of the rates is then applied to property values.

TABLE 17.3 Property Tax Rates in a Hypothetical Community

Local Government Unit	Tax Rate (%)
School district	1.20
City government	0.30
County government	0.20
Library district	0.05
Community college district	0.08
Other local government units	0.03
Total	1.86

If citizens are concerned about the property tax rate in their community, they must voice that concern to all of the local government units that use the property tax to fund the provision of their services. Of course, the local public school district accounts for the largest share of the property tax in most communities. For that reason, education funding is particularly sensitive to taxpayer concern regarding property tax rates.

Some states require that local assessors value land at its full market value. In these states assessed value and market value are equal. Many states, however, require that the assessed value be some proportion of market value, mandating that assessed value be less than full market value. For example, Georgia and Michigan require that property be valued at 50 percent of its true market value, New Mexico at 33.33 percent, and West Virginia at 60 percent. Some states specifically permit differing assessment ratios, depending on the class of property. For example, Tennessee requires that residential real property be assessed at 25 percent of market value, whereas commercial and industrial real property is assessed at 40 percent and telecommunications and utility property is assessed at 55 percent of market value. In all of these cases, the **assessment ratio**, the ratio of assessed value (AV) to market value (MV), $r = AV/MV$, is less than one. The consequence of having an assessment ratio less than one is that the effective rate of property taxation is less than the nominal rate of taxation. Oftentimes, taxpayers like the idea that the assessed value is less than market value, believing that their tax is lower as a result. But, that belief is incorrect. The state may permit assessors to cut market value in half for the purpose of assessment, but then the local property tax base is one-half what it would otherwise be. As a result, the tax rate applied to that tax base is doubled, resulting in the same tax payment as would otherwise be required. State statutes that require assessment ratios less than one are ill advised because they fuel a kind of tax illusion that is not beneficial.

Because land and real estate may be valued at less than their full market value for property tax assessment purposes, a distinction arises between the nominal tax rate and the effective tax rate for property. In order to understand that distinction, we must develop a simple model of the property tax as it relates to the market value of the property. Suppose that T is the total property tax collected by local governments, MV is the market value of property in the jurisdiction, and AV is the assessed value of property in the jurisdiction. The relationship between market value and assessed value can be written $AV = rMV$, where r is the assessment ratio. Suppose that the local property tax rate is t. Then the total tax collected is given by $T = tAV$. We can then express the tax rate as $t^n = T/AV$. This tax rate is known as the nominal tax rate because it is applied to the nominal (or statutory) value of the property. The nominal tax rate in the community is the total tax people pay on their property divided by the assessed value of their property.

In order to highlight the important role of the assessment ratio, it is useful to rewrite this expression as $t^n = T/rMV$, using the definition of the assessed value. If we multiply both sides of this expression by the assessment ratio r, we obtain an expression for the effective tax rate: $t^e = t^n r = T/MV$. This tax rate is known as the **effective tax rate** because it relates the tax paid to the market value of the property and provides a rate of taxation in comparison to the property's actual market value, hence giving us an effective tax rate. It is important to notice that the effective tax rate depends on both the nominal tax rate and the assessment ratio. The higher the assessment ratio, the higher the effective tax rate, other things being equal (like the total tax T and the market value of the property MV). The lower the assessment ratio, the lower the effective tax rate, other things being equal. Unless we know both of these factors, we cannot know the effective tax rate. Similarly, if all we know is the nominal tax rate and not the assessment ratio, we can have no accurate idea of the effective rate of tax applied to property in our city. For example, if the nominal tax rate is $t^n = 0.02$, while the assessment ratio is $r = 1$, there is an effective tax rate of $t^e = 0.02$, whereas if the assessment ratio is $r = 0.33$ while the nominal tax rate is 0.02, the effective tax rate is $t^e = 0.0066$. That difference in the assessment ratio means a difference between an effective tax rate of 2 percent and an effective tax rate of 0.67 percent—a vast difference! Of course, what matters for resource allocation is the effective tax rate applied to property, not the nominal tax rate.

Classified Tax Structures

Real property is subclassified into residential, commercial, industrial, agricultural, forest, and other classes. Although some states require that property taxes be uniform among these classes, other states permit, indeed require, that they not be uniform. States that permit nonuniform property taxes are said to have **classified property tax systems.**

Classified tax systems can be designed in either of two fundamental ways. First, the rate structure can be classified. In this case, the law permits different tax rates to be applied to properties in different classes, but the assessment ratio is the same across all classes. For example, Massachusetts permits local governments to place higher taxes on commercial and industrial property than they place on residential property. As a result, the effective property tax rate applied to commercial and industrial property can be twice as high as that applied to residential property. Proposition 2.5 was passed in the 1970s in Massachusetts in order to assure that the average property tax rate in communities would not exceed 2.5 percent of market value, but the law permits a classified property tax system with rates in excess of 2.5 percent applied to commercial and industrial property, and rates below 2.5 percent applied to residential property. Only the average must be 2.5 percent or less.

Most states that permit classification, however, use a method of designing a classified tax that uses the same tax rates across property classes but permits the use of different assessment ratios among the property classes. In this method, the state permits local governments to apply the same nominal tax rates to property classes where the assessed values are determined with different assessment ratios. For example, New Jersey assesses residential real and personal property at 100 percent of market value, whereas commercial/industrial and telecommunications or utility real property is also assessed at 100 percent, but personal property in those classes is taxed at 50 percent of value. Preferences are often given to agricultural property. For example, Nebraska requires that uniform tax rates be applied to agricultural and other property, but the assessment ratio is 75 percent for agricultural property while it is 100 percent for all other classes of property. The difference in the assessment ratio produces a 25 percent difference in the effective tax rate for agricultural property as compared with other property classes.

PROPERTY TAX ADMINISTRATION

Because the property tax is primarily a local tax, the administration of the tax is carried out at the local government level. Assessment is the responsibility of the local tax assessor whose job it is to value properties for tax purposes. The assessor may be an elected official or an appointee of a local government official or board (such as the board of county supervisors). Increasingly, however, the essential work of the assessment function is being carried out by private firms that specialize in estimating property values. The estimated property values provided by such a private firm are then officially adopted by the local government units and designated as assessed values.

In order to check the quality of the assessment process, states usually require that studies be conducted to determine how close to market value are the assessor's assessed values. To do this, states conduct **sales-ratio studies** in which they collect a sample of sales data and compute the ratio of assessed value to market value. The state government will typically specify a level of precision in the sales ratio that is acceptable and will require assessors whose assessments are systematically low to make adjustments.

Collection Administration

The property tax is a collection of many local government taxes, so the county treasurer or some comparable local government official typically acts as the collector of the property tax on behalf of all of the local governments that rely on the property tax for funding. Using the hypothetical example provided in Table 17.3, we can imagine the county treasurer collecting a 1.86 percent tax on all property parcels in the county. Then, the treasurer must allocate property tax payments to each of the local government units, such as the school districts, cities, and other units, with specific revenue based on each of those local government unit's property tax rates times the assessed value of each parcel.

Certain classes of property are sometimes subject to either a centralized property tax collection method or a state-level property tax. For example, railroad or pipeline property that runs across a state may be subject to a state-level property tax, which is then allocated back to local government units. A centralized property tax mechanism helps a large number of local assessors avoid the complexity of assessing real and personal property in their jurisdictions. Utility properties are also often subject to central assessment by states. It is simpler for the state to assess all nuclear power plants in the state, for example, than to have a number of local assessors each dealing with the complexity of valuing such properties.

Equalization Mechanisms

Property tax systems also require equalization mechanisms in order to assure fairness. The property tax is generally administered at the local level, so there may be differences in the practices used by local tax assessors. The assessor in city A may be valuing property at 90 percent of full market value, whereas the assessor in city B is valuing property at 100 percent of full market value. What difference does that make? Well, differences in the assessment ratio across local jurisdictions can result in different effective rates of taxation. A nominal 1 percent tax applied in each city will yield different amounts of revenue, depending on the assessment ratios in the cities. If the cities simply care about funding a given level of public expenditure, it does not really matter that they have different assessment ratios. City A could apply a higher nominal tax rate than city B and derive the same revenue, despite having the lower assessment ratio, for example. But, for other situations it may matter very much how property is assessed.

Consider the case of a natural resource district extending over a wide area of a state. A property tax is applied in the district in order to finance environmental improvement projects. Suppose that the assessor in city A has undervalued properties, whereas the assessor in city B has followed the state statutes that call for full market valuation of property. In this case, the state must make sure to equalize the values or the residents of city B will pay an unfairly higher share of the taxes for the natural resource district. If the assessor in city A systematically undervalued properties by 10 percent on average, then the state can equalize the valuations by applying a 10 percent increase to all assessments in city A. This equalization method is required for equity purposes but is also important when state aid to local districts is distributed on the basis of local property values. For example, if state aid to local public schools depends in part on local property values, with more aid being allocated to school districts with low property values per pupil, then underassessment of property has the effect of increasing state aid to schools as well. This creates an inequity in school aid funding. Some states carry out equalization at both the county level and the state level. First, a county equalization process assures that all properties in the county are assessed similarly; then a state equalization process assures that values are determined similarly across counties. Equalization is an important but contentious process.

We can write the tax revenue generated in each city as $T^A = t^A r^A MV^A$ and $T^B = t^B r^B MV^B$, where the superscripts indicate the city. Now, suppose for a moment that we wish to raise the same property tax revenue in each city and that they have the same market value of property. We could then set these two expressions equal to one another and derive the relationship $t^A r^A = t^B r^B$. This expression indicates that the cities will generate the same revenue as long as the products of their nominal tax rates and assessment ratios are equal.

If we insert the assessment ratios $r^A = 0.9$ and $r^B = 1.0$, we derive the relationship $t^A(0.9) = t^B(1.0)$, or $t^A = t^B/0.9$, or $t^A = (1.11)t^B$. Hence, city A simply must apply a nominal tax rate that is 11 percent higher than city B in order to generate the same revenue. It would appear that there is no problem at all by letting each city select its own assessment ratio and nominal tax rate. A city that chooses a low assessment ratio will simply have to apply a higher nominal tax rate to generate a given level of revenue.

State-level equalization may be required, however, because local assessments are also important determinants of state aid to local governments, as noted earlier. For example, suppose that there is a state aid formula that provides state aid to local school districts, with the aid amount determined at least in part by the assessed value of property in the district. The state provides more aid to school districts that are relatively poor, as reflected in lower property value per pupil. This type of state aid formula is quite common not only for school aid but also for aid to cities and counties. In that case, a school district with relatively low assessed value due to underassessment will appear relatively poor compared to other school districts, not because it really is poor but because the assessor is simply undervaluing property in that district. Hence, the undervalued school district will receive more than its fair share of the state aid monies. As a result of this type of state aid mechanism, it is essential that properties be valued similarly for property tax purposes in all local jurisdictions. Hence, there is a need for state equalization of property values to assure fairness.

State equalization processes are usually carried out by the state department of revenue or treasury department. State officials in a property tax division of that state agency then carry out studies of the assessed values in each county in the state to assure that the assessed value of each county is the same proportion of market value; that is, to assure that the assessment ratios are the same across counties. A county that is found to have a low assessment ratio is then told to correct the situation. If the county does not fix the problem, the state will apply an **equalization factor** to the county in order to bring its assessments up to the proper level. For example, if the state equalization process were to find that a particular county was undervaluing property by 10 percent, the state could apply a factor of 1.1 multiplied to that county's assessed values in order to correct the situation.

Property Values and the Housing Crisis

With the bursting of the housing price bubble in the United States and many other parts of the world from 2006 to 2009, we might have expected property values to fall dramatically and therefore find property tax revenues to plummet correspondingly. That has not happened. Lutz et al. (forthcoming) report that U.S. house prices rose 64 percent in the four years leading up to the peak in the first quarter of 2006, then fell almost 30 percent in the following four years. That decline in overall U.S. house prices is unprecedented. Although state and local government revenues have fallen steeply, it is not because of sharply reduced property tax revenue.

Lutz et al. (forthcoming) trace five channels by which the housing market affects state and local tax revenue: (1) a decline in property tax revenues, (2) a reduction in real estate transfer taxes due to fewer transactions, (3) a reduction in sales tax revenues related to materials used in new house construction and existing house renovation, (4) an indirect negative effect on sales tax revenues from a decline in household consumption more broadly due to the decline in household wealth, and (5) a reduction in personal income tax revenues due to reduced employment related to construction and real estate. Their analysis indicates that property tax revenues do not decrease significantly following house price declines. That is due to very significant lags in the assessment process and the tendency of policymakers to compensate for lower assessed values by raising property tax rates. The other four channels have only a small impact on revenues. The overall conclusion is that the reduction in state and local tax revenue following the bursting housing bubble was due primarily to the 2007 to 2009 recession rather than the housing market crisis.

Other Aspects of Administration

The administration of the property tax system requires resources. It is neither a simple nor inexpensive system to administer. The complexity and expense of administering the system derive from the necessity to value property, assigning assessed values. The integrity and quality of any property tax system is based on the quality of the assessment process. Local tax assessors must be well educated in property valuation methods and must be completely impartial in applying generally accepted valuation methods. Assessments must be updated regularly in order to accurately reflect true economic value.

The property tax administration system must also provide for an appeals mechanism to provide property owners with the opportunity to challenge assessments that they believe are inaccurate or mistaken. Most appeals processes provide for an appeal to the local assessor first, with the assessor required to provide an explanation of the assessment on the property for the owner who questions the assessment. Most assessment disputes are resolved at this level, as the property owner receives information on how the assessed value was determined. Assessments are sometimes lowered as the assessor is provided with additional information on the property that justifies a lower value. An unresolved dispute between the assessor and the property owner, however, is then carried on to higher levels of government for resolution. Most states have some form of tax court as their highest level of review for property tax disputes. The most contentious and difficult cases usually involve very complex properties in the areas of manufacturing, utilities, railroads, airlines, and other such properties.

PROPERTY TAX INCIDENCE

The incidence of the property tax is one of the most contentious issues in public finance. Three views of the incidence of the property tax exist.

Traditional View

According to the **traditional view** of the incidence of the property tax, the tax is applied in the local housing market. The tax is essentially an excise tax on occupancy rights for land and/or housing. Using partial equilibrium analysis and the assumptions of a small open economy, this approach considers the impact of an increase in the property tax on housing and land prices. The rate of return to capital under this view is fixed at the national level. That results in a horizontal, or perfectly elastic, supply of capital.

The major conclusion of this view is that the property tax is for the most part passed forward to consumers of housing in the form of higher prices. Viewed as an ordinary consumption tax, the property tax can be analyzed as a garden variety excise tax. Consumers of housing bear the burden of the tax in proportion to their respective quantities. It is important to recognize that housing consumption, in particular, rises with income but at a rate that is less than proportionate. If housing consumption as a fraction of income declines as we move up the income distribution (because additional income may be saved or allocated to other forms of consumption), then the property tax will be a declining share of income as income rises. Hence, the property tax is regressive, requiring a larger share of income from low-income households than from high-income households.

Property comprises both land and capital; hence we must distinguish the two impacts of property taxation. First, local land bears the burden of the property tax according to the traditional view, because land is a fixed supply. Landowners bear a burden of taxation in accordance with their landholding. Second, the larger portion of the property tax applies to houses and other structures that are forms of capital. Under this view of the property tax, the supply of capital adjusts in such a way as to maintain a constant after-tax rate of return to capital. With a perfectly elastic supply of capital, as illustrated in Figure 17.2(a), local capital owners bear no burden of the tax. Capital migrates out of the community if the tax rate is increased. The after-tax rate of return to capital is unaffected, however, and there is no tax burden borne by capital.

The traditional view of the property tax considers the incidence of the tax in a partial equilibrium framework where the residential sector of a single city has a capital stock that is negligible in relation to that of the entire country. The effect of this framework is to assume that the community's supply of capital is infinitely elastic at the fixed national rental rate of capital. The other factor of production, land, is assumed to be totally inelastic in supply. Although both capital and land aspects of the problem are important, capital accounts for the largest share of property value, perhaps 80 to 90 percent of total property value on average for residential homes, and is more important.

The long-run effects of the property tax in this framework are illustrated in Figure 17.3, where S_0 denotes the original long-run supply curve of housing in the city and S_1 is the supply curve after imposition of the property tax. The demand for housing is given by D and the initial equilibrium price and quantity

FIGURE 17.2 Special Cases for the Supply of Capital

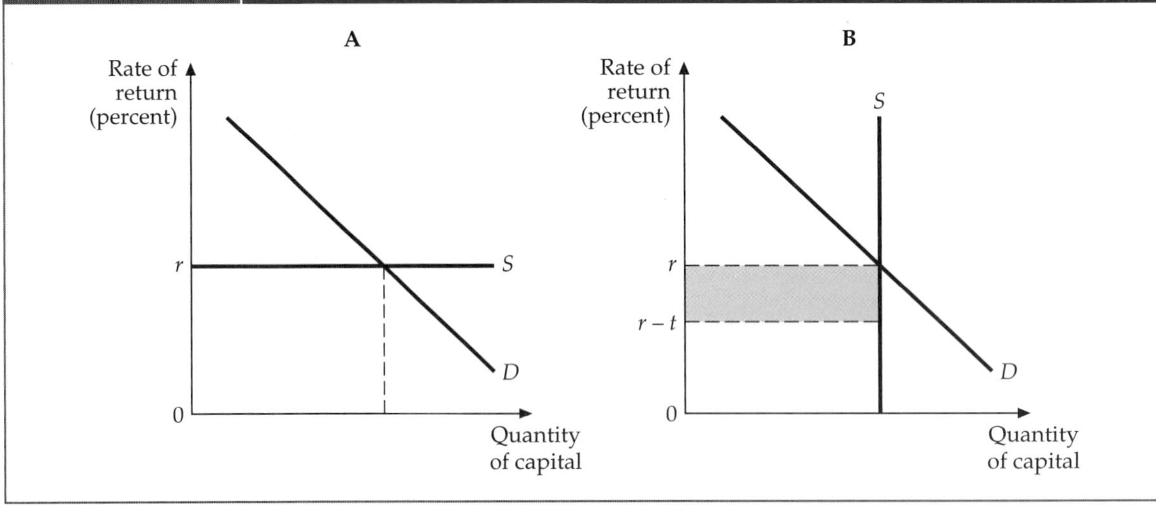

are denoted p_0 and q_0. The effect of the property tax is to increase the equilibrium price to p_1 and reduce equilibrium quantity to q_1. The incidence of the tax is shared by producer and consumer of the housing because p_1 exceeds p_0 by less than the amount of the tax t. The actual shares of tax borne by each are determined by the relative elasticities of demand and supply. The excess burden of the tax is represented by the triangle *abc* in Figure 17.3.

For the housing producer, the reduced return from housing production has the effect of reducing demand for both the factors of production. In the

FIGURE 17.3 Effects of a Property Tax

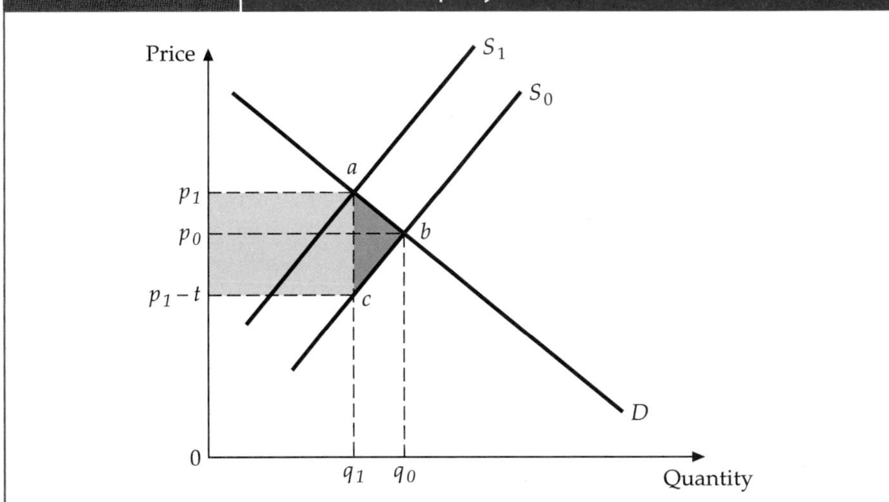

traditional view, however, the supply of capital is perfectly elastic, resulting in the implication that capital owners bear none of the tax burden because there is no effect on the rate of return to capital. Figure 17.2(a) illustrates this effect. Land, the immobile factor, does bear some of the burden of the tax, however, because the return to landholding declines. Hence, land bears the entire burden of the property tax, on the production side. (On the consumer side there are further considerations of incidence.) These results come directly from the assumption that the locally lower rate of return to capital, which drives out capital due to its mobility, has no effect on national rates of return to capital.

Capital Tax View

More recently, economists are looking at the property tax in a very different way. They are starting to consider how the tax distorts resource allocation in a general equilibrium framework. If the tax is really a tax on capital, then the presence of the tax causes a misallocation of resources as capital is moved from high-tax jurisdictions to low-tax jurisdictions. Capital may bear the burden of the average rate of property tax applied in all jurisdictions. As a result, capital owners bear the burden of the tax. Local deviations around the national average tax rate cause further distortions. High-tax communities will see capital fleeing to low-tax communities. As a result of the capital movement, there are additional effects to consider. This view of property tax incidence is called the **capital tax view**.

The principal difference in the capital tax view is a general equilibrium setting, which recognizes that all municipalities levy property taxes, thereby affecting the national rate of return to capital. Capital owners will bear the burden of the national average property tax rate, but local deviations around the national average rate will be borne locally by landowners and consumers. According to this view, a tax on the reproducible capital part of real property has several different incidence effects.

Consider three specific effects: a capital tax effect, an excise tax effect, and a factor immobility effect. First, consider the **capital tax effect** of the property tax. For a given urban area, the quantities of land and capital are fixed in supply, implying zero elasticities of supply. The capital market is illustrated in Figure 17.4. The fixed supply of capital and the downward-sloping demand for capital result in a rate of return of r percent on capital. If capital is mobile within the area, yet the tax per unit of reproducible capital is identical throughout the area, the impact of the tax is to reduce the rate of return earned by capital by the amount of the tax t. As a result, profits are reduced by the amount of the tax. This is the capital tax effect of the property tax.

Second, consider the **excise tax effect** of the property tax. As tax rates vary between areas, mobile capital may shift from high-tax areas to low-tax areas. Of course, in equilibrium the after-tax rate of return must be equal in both jurisdictions, indeed, everywhere. The difference between the uniform before-tax rate of return on capital and the uniform after-tax rate of return is the capital tax effect, as discussed previously. In addition, because the

FIGURE 17.4 Capital Tax and Excise Tax Effects of Property Taxation

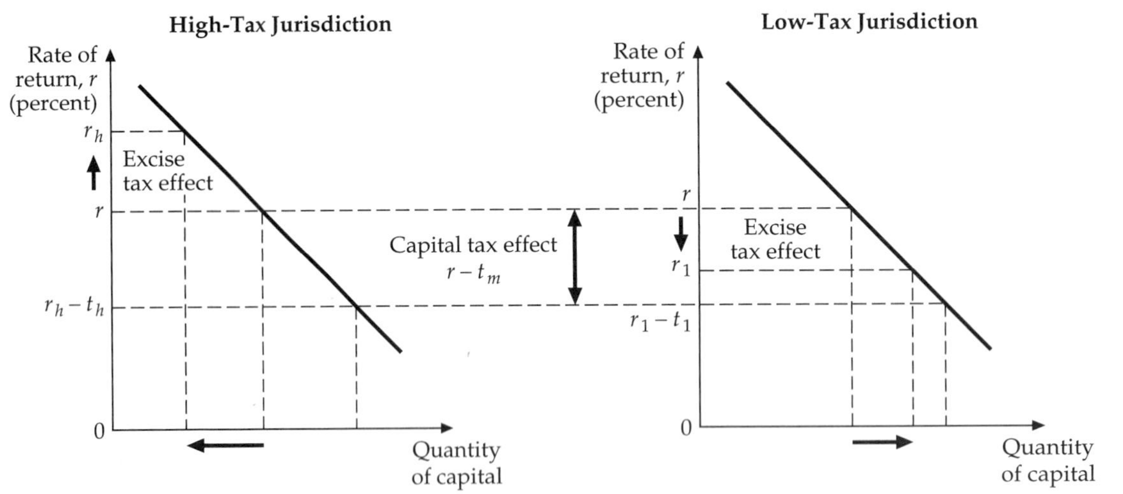

gross price of capital rises above the pretax price in the high-tax jurisdiction and falls below the pretax price in the low-tax jurisdiction, we have excise tax effects as well.

Figure 17.4 illustrates the case for two communities: a high-tax jurisdiction and a low-tax jurisdiction. Initially the rate of return to capital is r in both communities. Now, suppose that taxes are imposed in the two communities with $t_h > t_l$. The mean, or average, tax rate is $t_m = (t_h + t_l)/2$. As a result of the high tax, capital flees the high-tax jurisdiction, raising the rate of return earned by remaining capital to r_h, shown in the left panel of Figure 17.4. Net of the high tax, however, the after-tax rate of return is reduced to $r_h - t_h$. The excise tax effect is the original rate of return r adjusted for the difference between the mean tax rate and the community's high tax rate: $r_h = r - (t_m - t_h)$. Because the tax rate in the high-tax jurisdiction is larger than the mean tax rate for the two communities, the difference $t_m - t_h < 0$; that is, it is negative. Subtracting this negative difference results in a higher rate of return. Hence, the excise tax effect is reflected in a higher rate of return in the high-tax jurisdiction. In the low-tax jurisdiction shown in the right panel of Figure 17.4, capital is attracted, and the additional capital reduces the rate of return earned by capital in that community. The excise tax effect is the original rate of return r adjusted for the difference between the mean tax rate and the community's low tax rate: $r_l = r - (t_m - t_l)$. The tax rate in the low-tax jurisdiction is smaller than the mean tax rate for the two communities, so the difference $t_m - t_l > 0$; that is, it is positive. Subtracting this positive difference results in a lower rate of return. Hence, the excise tax effect is reflected in a lower rate of return in the low-tax jurisdiction. The excise tax effect captures the effects of deviations around the average tax rate.

The capital tax effect is the difference between the before-tax rate of return r and the after-tax rate of return in both communities: $r_h - t_h = r_l - t_l$. Of course, this difference is the same for both jurisdictions because capital is freely mobile and equilibrium will be established with the same after-tax rate of return in both communities. The after-tax rate of return falls by the amount t_m in both communities, compared to the original rate of return r. The capital tax effect captures the effect of the average rate of property tax applied in both jurisdictions.

Finally, a **factor immobility effect** arises from consideration of the impact of the property tax on factors of production with various degrees of mobility. If, for example, capital is mobile in a community but labor is not mobile, then we would expect that the relatively immobile factor would bear the incidence of the tax. A local property tax that falls primarily on residential housing in a community with relatively immobile labor can be expected to be borne by workers in the form of lower wages. If the tax causes some residents to migrate out of the community so that labor is partially mobile, then land values in the community with higher taxes will fall and some of the tax burden will fall on landowners. As a general rule, the tax will be borne to a greater extent by the relatively immobile factor of production.

Benefit View

Local governments use the property tax to fund services provided to the community residents. Because the tax funds the provision of local services, which are largely provided in proportion to the amount of property owned, the tax is a benefits tax, and there is a clear link between the tax paid and the benefits received. As a result, the **benefit view** of the incidence of the tax is that incidence is not particularly important. After all, we do not care about the incidence of expenditures on Big Macs because the expenditure is directly related to the benefits received by the customer. In a similar fashion, if local governments provide services proportional to property holding, then the incidence of the property tax is just not very important. The tax is borne by the property owner, but that is not an important issue.

Suppose that the property tax is perfectly capitalized into property value. Property owners in a high-tax community, receiving high-quality local public services, experience the capitalization of the high taxes into lower property values, other things being equal. Hence they pay for the high public service level by bearing the burden of the high tax in the form of lower property value. If the property tax works this way, perhaps it is simply a benefit tax, falling on those who benefit from the public services provided.

In order to make this work, it is necessary that households be mobile and have many community choices available to them. They can move to the community that provides a package of services and tax rates that suit them. Households sort themselves among communities according to their demands for local public services. The result is homogeneity within communities and heterogeneity across communities. Within a given community the residents are similar in their tastes and preferences for local public goods and taxes.

Across communities, however, we would expect to find very different service-tax packages offered due to sorting. Zoning regulations on minimum lot size, or some other constraints, are necessary to make this model work. Such constraints limit the number of residents per unit of land in the community.

The implications of this view are that the property tax is simply a benefits tax, with no effect on the distribution of income worth considering. Those who benefit from the local public services pay the cost of those services, bearing the burden of the property tax. As with any benefits charge, we are not concerned with incidence. As for efficiency concerns, the property tax under this view is nondistortionary. Hence there is no efficiency effect with which to be concerned.

Table 17.4 provides a summary and overview of these three views of property tax incidence. Both the assumptions underlying each approach and the implications for economic incidence are included.

Capitalization

Considering real property as an income-producing asset facilitates understanding of the capitalization of property taxes. In the following example, the income capitalization approach is used to value an asset. Suppose that we have a property that produces R dollars in net income per year in perpetuity. If the discount rate is r, then the value of the property is simply $V = R/r$. Now, if a property tax is applied to the property in the amount of T dollars per year, the value of the property is reduced to $V = (R - T)/r$. We can break this value expression into two pieces: $V = R/r - T/r$. Hence, we see that the value of the property is reduced by the capitalized value of the tax liability. In this sense, the tax is capitalized into the value of the property. Table 17.5 provides a simple example. In this example, the property tax has the effect of reducing the value of the property from \$100,000 to \$80,000. That reduction is simply the capitalized value of the property tax stream: \$1,000/0.05 = \$20,000.

In the more general case where the asset is not infinitely lived with a constant income stream, we can write the value of the property as

$$V = \sum_{i=0}^{n} \frac{R_i}{(1+r)^i}, \tag{17.1}$$

where R_i is the net rent earned in year i and the property has a life of n years. Now, if we incorporate a tax of T_i in year i, the value of the property becomes

$$V = \sum_{i=0}^{n} \frac{(R_i - T_i)}{(1+r)^i}. \tag{17.2}$$

Or, if we split apart the two components of the property value, we can write this expression as

$$V = \sum_{i=0}^{n} \left[\frac{R_i}{(1+r)^i} - \frac{T_i}{(1+r)^i} \right]. \tag{17.3}$$

TABLE 17.4 Three Views of Property Tax Incidence

	Traditional View	Capital Tax View	Benefit View
Source	Simon (1943)	Mieszkowski (1972)	Hamilton (1975)
	Netzer (1966)	Zodrow and Mieszkowski (1983)	Fischel (1975)
			White (1975)
Focus	A local housing market is considered in which the effect of increasing the tax in a local housing market is analyzed.	The property tax is viewed as a distortionary tax on the local use of capital, resulting in a misallocation of the national capital stock across localities.	Consumer mobility (voting with their feet) and interjurisdictional competition are sufficient to provide efficiency in the provision of local public goods.
Assumptions	Partial equilibrium model of local housing market.	General equilibrium model of capital.	Individuals are sorted into local jurisdictions according to their demands for local public goods.
	Small, open economy assumptions.	Fixed national capital stock.	There are enough localities to accommodate all tastes.
	National return to capital is fixed.	Free mobility of capital across jurisdictions.	Local jurisdictions are homogeneous in house values, and there are enough jurisdictions to accommodate all desired housing/government service combinations.
			Zoning constraints, in the form of minimum lot sizes, exist in all communities.
Implications	Local capital bears none of the burden of the local property tax because capital migrates out until the local after-tax rate of return equals the national rate.	Burden of the average rate of property tax is borne by all owners of capital throughout the nation. This is called the capital tax effect.	Perfect capitalization converts the property tax into a benefits tax. Hence the property tax is essentially a user charge for local public services.
	The tax burden is borne by local factors and/or consumers in the form of higher house prices. The tax burden is borne in proportion to housing consumption; hence it is a regressive tax.	Capital owners in high-/low-tax jurisdictions bear the burden of the difference between the local tax rate and the national average. This is an excise tax effect.	As a benefit tax, there are no impacts on the distribution of income to consider. Hence, there are no equity effects of concern.
	Property tax inefficiently reduces the size of the local housing stock.	An inefficient allocation of capital across jurisdictions results.	The tax is nondistortionary and has no efficiency effect.

Source: Adapted from Zodrow 2001.

TABLE 17.5 Tax Capitalization Example

	No-Tax Case	Property Tax Case
R	\$5,000	\$5,000
R	0.05	0.05
T	0	\$1,000
V	*V* = \$5,000/0.05	*V* = (\$5,000 − \$1,000)/0.05
	= \$100,000	= \$80,000

Here, we see clearly that the value of the property is composed of the discounted present value of the net income stream minus the discounted present value of the property tax stream. The value of the property is reduced by the present value of the property tax stream.

Property taxes are usually expressed as *ad valorem* taxes, so we need to modify the property value expression. Suppose that the property tax is $T = tV$. If we make this substitution in the case of a perpetuity, we have the property value expression: $V = R/(r + t)$. For example, we can verify the result in Table 17.6 by computing the value of the property given that the tax is $t = \$1{,}000/\$80{,}000 = 0.0125$. Then $V = \$5{,}000/(0.0125 + 0.05) = \$5{,}000/0.0625 = \$80{,}000$. If we make the same substitution $T = tV$ in Equation 17.2 and solve for V we will have[3]

$$V = \sum_{i=0}^{n} \frac{R_i}{(1+r+t)^i}. \tag{17.4}$$

These expressions indicate that the effect of including an *ad valorem* property tax is equivalent to increasing the discount rate by the amount of the tax.

TABLE 17.6 Evidence on Property Tax Capitalization

Study	Estimated Tax Capitalization (Assuming a 3 Percent Discount Rate and Infinite Horizon)
Dusansky, Ingber, and Karatjas (1981)	22 percent
Richardson and Thalheimer (1981)	15 percent
Ihlanfeldt and Jackson (1982)	66 percent
Lea (1982)	26 percent
Goodman (1983)	65 percent (intrajurisdictional)
	25 percent (interjurisdictional)
Gabriel (1981)	36 percent
Rosen (1982)	22 percent

Source: Yinger et al. 1988, 32–36.

During the early 1980s a number of studies were conducted to determine the extent of property tax capitalization. The evidence reported varied widely across studies, depending on the city and time period examined, as well as on whether the studies considered intrajurisdictional or interjurisdictional capitalization. Table 17.6 reports representative empirical results from those early studies of capitalization.[4] What is notable about these early results on property tax capitalization is that they indicated taxes are less than perfectly capitalized into house price. Later studies would use more sophisticated statistical methods and more careful attention to the institutional aspects of property tax system administration, but the evidence for less than full capitalization was confirmed. The policy study at the end of this chapter provides later evidence based on more sophisticated analysis by Yinger et al. (1988).

Just as property taxes are capitalized in the value of property, the value of local public services provided are also capitalized into value. When a family pays property taxes T each year, its members receive in return a whole set of local public services that are of value to them. The major service received is public education, of course, which benefits the family not only directly but also indirectly as the education level provided in the community has beneficial effects for all community residents. In addition, libraries, public safety, and other services are available that the family finds valuable.

Suppose that the value of public services provided in period i is denoted S_i. Incorporating those services into the property value is accomplished by adding the discounted present value of the service value stream over time. The following expression provides the modified value of the property, taking into account the capitalized value of public services:

$$V = \sum_{i=0}^{n} \frac{R_i - T_i + S_i}{(1+r)^i}. \tag{17.5}$$

An equivalent expression, breaking the property value into its three components, is given by:

$$V_i = \sum_{i=0}^{n} \frac{R_i}{(1+r)^i} - \frac{T_i}{(1+r)^i} + \frac{S_i}{(1+r)^i}, \tag{17.6}$$

where we see that the value of the property is the present discounted value of the net income generated by the property, adjusted for both taxes and public services. It is important to note that the tax is capitalized negatively, whereas the public service value is capitalized positively. If the value of public services provided is equal to the tax used to fund that public service provision, the last two terms on the right-hand side of Equation 17.6 are equal in size and of opposite sign, and hence cancel one another. As a result, the value of the property is simply the discounted present value of the net income stream it generates. Of course, it is possible that the local units of government provide services less valuable than the tax required to pay for them: $S_i < T_i$. In that case, the value of the property is reduced. The general principle to note is that taxes are negatively capitalized into value, whereas services are positively capitalized into value. Both sides of the budget must be considered when attempting to evaluate the effect of property taxes on property value.

DISCONTENT AND RELIEF MECHANISMS

So why is the property tax so reviled and hated? We have identified several sources in the chapter so far. They include:

- Subjectivity in assessment and assignment of market value for tax purposes due to the fact that relatively few properties are traded in markets
- Lack of uniformity in assessment causing horizontal inequities across property owners
- Incidence of the tax on land borne by the landowner, causing agricultural landowners to bear the burden of the property tax
- Lack of a direct link between income and property value resulting in property owners with valuable property being required to pay high taxes despite having low income
- Incidence of the tax on capital borne by capital owners throughout the economy, causing capital to flee high-tax communities
- Inequality in the distribution of property value across communities resulting in high tax rates in poor communities and low tax rates in wealthy communities
- Property tax liabilities sensitive to the rate of inflation, rising at a fast pace during periods of general price inflation

These problems with the property tax have resulted in a great deal of criticism over the past decades and numerous attempts to reduce reliance on this method of taxation.

Reduce Expenditure

The place to begin, if we wish to reduce property taxes, is with ways to reduce local government expenditure. After all, if the local government units spend less, then property taxes can be reduced. If school districts can find ways to cut expenditure, while providing quality educational experiences for students, then the school district portion of the property tax can be reduced. If the city council can find ways to reduce city expenditures, while providing the services city residents deem necessary, then the city portion of the property tax can also be reduced. The fundamental place to begin considering ways to reduce property taxes is to consider each unit of local government and attempt to find ways in which expenditure can be reduced while providing necessary services of acceptable quality.

Once this is done, and there is still further desire to reduce property taxes relative to other taxes, a number of additional mechanisms have been devised.

Homestead Exemptions

One property tax relief mechanism popularly used in many states is the homestead exemption. With this mechanism, an exemption is provided for some part of the value of the property used as a household's primary home: its homestead. For example, a state can provide an exemption for the first

$20,000 of property value on homesteads. A household living in a home assessed at $60,000 that is subject to a 2 percent combined property tax rate would ordinarily pay a property tax of $1,200. If the first $20,000 of assessed value is exempt from tax, however, the property tax is reduced to $800. Hence, the household receives a reduction of $400 in its property tax bill. The $400 reduction in tax is the tax that would have applied to the $20,000 of value, which is now exempt from taxation.

Homestead exemptions work this way. The local government or the state makes a decision to exempt some portion of assessed value from taxation. Note that the adjective *homestead* makes it clear that the exemption applies only to households' primary residences. Homestead exemptions do not apply to commercial or manufacturing property. On a farm, the homestead exemption only applies to the part of the farm used for the homestead, not the land used for production agriculture.

Homestead exemptions can be further restricted to apply only to the elderly or the poor. Some states provide such exemptions only for those at least 65 years of age or for those whose annual income falls below a certain level. Indeed, there is a very broad range of homestead exemptions used by the states. Each of these restrictions is designed to narrow the application of the exemption to those who really need it, while minimizing the revenue loss to the local government units. The problem with a restriction that the homestead exemption only apply to the elderly, for example, has the flaw that not all elderly are poor and unable to pay property taxes. Is it fair that the tax required be related only to age, disregarding ability to pay? Probably not. As a result, those means-tested homestead exemptions, tied in some way to ability to pay, are more appropriately designed.

Preferential Assessment

The most common form of property tax reduction is provided to agricultural landowners in the form of preferential assessment. Most U.S. states permit agricultural land to be assessed differently than other types of property. By valuing agricultural land in its current use, rather than its highest and best use, a tax advantage is provided. **Use value** assessment is the most common form of preferential assessment, and it provides a substantial tax reduction to agricultural land near urban areas. Recall from Figure 17.1 and our discussion of the fundamentals of land value that the value of land in agricultural use is low and invariant with respect to location. By permitting agricultural land to be valued in its current use, ignoring potential developed use, a significant reduction in assessed value is provided. Of course, the size of the reduction in value depends on location. The closer the land to the urban center, the larger the reduction by permitting use value assessment rather than market value assessment. In rural areas with no urban influence, there should be no difference between use value and market value because agricultural use of the land is its highest and best use.

Preferential assessment, particularly that applied to agricultural land, is designed to reduce the effective rate of property taxation. By reducing the assessment ratio, the effective tax rate is reduced, thereby diminishing the tax burden borne by landowners. What are the effects? First, it may be that the property tax reduction helps to preserve agricultural land in agricultural use, delaying development uses. That effect has the advantage of slowing the development process and preserving open space that may provide positive externalities for city folk. In the face of fast-paced urban development, however, it is unlikely that preferential assessment will delay development very long. The landowner is unlikely to forgo rapidly accelerating development opportunities in exchange for somewhat reduced holding cost in the form of lower property taxes on her undeveloped land. Another factor to consider is that the reduced property tax is capitalized into higher land value, other things being equal. By providing a reduction in property taxes, the local governments are causing land values to jump higher still. That confers a wealth transfer to landowners.

One of the earliest and most important programs of preferential assessment is the California Land Conservation Act of 1965, commonly called the **Williamson Act**. That preferential assessment program allows local governments to contract with private landowners in order to restrict specific parcels of land to remain in agricultural use or open space. In exchange for limiting the property rights of the landowner, the property tax assessment is reduced by assessing the land based on its farming and open space use rather than on its full market value. Local governments then receive a payment from the state government for the forgone property tax revenues under the California Open Space Subvention Act of 1971.

Property Tax Limitations

The mid- to late 1970s were years of accelerating inflation and growing concern over property values and property taxes. In California, where property values were growing at a record pace due to the general rate of inflation and other economic forces, disaffection with the property tax system resulted in a 1978 statewide ballot proposition to reduce property taxes known as the Jarvis-Gan Amendment, or **Proposition 13**. Under the proposition, property values were rolled back to their 1975 levels and the rate of increase in assessed value was limited to 2 percent per year thereafter as long as ownership did not change. Updating the assessment on a given property was restricted to take place only when the property changed ownership. The property tax rate was also restricted to no more than 1 percent of the property value. This mechanism was designed, in part, to deal with the rapid rate of property value inflation that caused property tax bills to rise at dramatic rates. Of course, local governments could have rolled back property tax rates proportionately and kept property tax bills constant, but that did not happen.

The effect of Proposition 13 was to convert the property tax mechanism in California from a traditional property tax based on the market value of property to an **acquisition value tax**. What is now taxed in California is not the current value of property. Rather, the value of property *when it was last acquired* is the tax base. Consider the following example. Mr. Smith purchased a home in Palo Alto in 1972, paying $80,000 for the home at the time of acquisition. The home is now worth $400,000. Ms. Martinez purchased an identical home in Palo Alto last week and paid $400,000 for the home at the time of her acquisition. Smith's tax base is $80,000 and Martinez's is $400,000, for two homes of equal value. The way the property tax is applied in California since Proposition 13 clearly causes vast inequalities. Similar homes are taxed at very different rates.

With a tax system that works this way, there is a clear incentive not to sell the property in order to avoid reassessment. As a result, homeowners are more likely to retain the property and rent rather than sell. Although there have been claims that such a tax system violates fundamental principles of equity in taxation, such as a violation of horizontal equity because similar homes can be taxed at very different rates if the ownership tenure differs, the courts have upheld the constitutionality of this method of taxation. The legal case establishing this principle was the **Nordlinger Case**.

At the same time California voters approved Proposition 13, Massachusetts voters approved a tax limitation amendment known as **Proposition Two and a Half.** This proposition limits local Massachusetts governments to a combined property tax rate of no more than 2.5 percent of fair market value. The proposition also limits annual increases in property tax levies to no more than 2.5 percent. Although the proposition limits the total property tax rate to no more than 2.5 percent, it also permits classification of property taxes, with higher rates of taxation applied to commercial and industrial properties compared to residential properties. It is the total weighted average of the rates that is constrained to be no more than 2.5 percent.

Circuit Breaker Mechanism

A circuit breaker is a mechanism that provides a state income tax credit for selected taxpayers with high local property tax burdens. It is a targeted means of providing property tax relief. The term **circuit breaker** is adapted from the common home electrical device that trips when an electric circuit is overloaded. In similar fashion, a property tax circuit breaker is designed to trip, providing relief, when a taxpayer is overloaded with property tax burden.

The credit mechanism is defined by specifying two parameters. First, we must define what is meant by being overburdened with property taxes. Circuit breakers do that by specifying a threshold proportion of income taken by the property tax beyond which the taxpayer is presumed to be overburdened. Second, the size of the tax credit must be specified as some share of the property tax in excess of the threshold proportion of income. Note that the circuit breaker mechanism presumes an ability to pay that is reflected by the taxpayer's income. When the property tax is high relative to income, the taxpayer is considered overburdened and deserving of relief.

The general form of a circuit breaker credit mechanism can be described as a credit C for which the taxpayer qualifies when her property tax liability

TABLE 17.7 Circuit Breaker Example

Income Y	Property Tax P	Credit C	Net Property Tax After Credit $P - C$
\$20,000	\$1,000	\$0	\$1,000
\$20,000	\$1,500	\$250	\$1,250
\$20,000	\$2,000	\$500	\$1,500
\$40,000	\$2,000	\$0	\$2,000
\$40,000	\$3,800	\$900	\$2,900

P exceeds some threshold proportion b of income Y. The credit is specified as a fraction a of the property tax in excess of the proportion of income bY:

$$C = \begin{cases} a(P - bY) & \text{if } P > bY. \\ 0 \text{ otherwise} \end{cases} \tag{17.7}$$

For example, a state can specify the circuit breaker as providing a 50 percent credit for property taxes paid in excess of 5 percent of income. In that case $a = 0.50$ and $b = 0.05$. If a taxpayer's property tax bill exceeds 5 percent of income the taxpayer qualifies for the credit. If the property tax bill is less than 5 percent of income, the taxpayer does not qualify and receives no credit. The credit is then 50 percent of the property tax liability in excess of 5 percent of income: $C = 0.5[P - 0.05Y]$. Table 17.7 lists the credit amount for several hypothetical taxpayers with income Y and property tax liability P.

A taxpayer with income of \$20,000 first qualifies for the credit when property taxes exceed \$1,000 (5 percent of income). Hence, a taxpayer with income of \$20,000 and property tax liability of \$1,500 would qualify for a credit of \$250 (50 percent of the difference between \$1,500 and \$1,000). The credit then reduces the effective property tax from \$1,500 to \$1,250. If the property tax were to rise to \$2,000, the credit would increase to \$500, reducing the net property tax liability to \$1,500.

Similarly, a taxpayer with income of \$40,000 first qualifies for the credit when property tax liability exceeds \$2,000 (5 percent of \$40,000). A taxpayer with such income and a property tax bill of \$3,800 would qualify for a credit of \$900 (5 percent of the difference between \$3,800 and \$2,000), reducing the property tax bill to \$2,900.

Both homeowners and renters can be included in a circuit breaker program. In the case of renters, a share of the rent paid to the landlord is assumed to be allocated to paying the property tax. That share of rent is counted as property tax payment to local governments. The circuit breaker then applies, as in the case of a homeowner.

The state can specify a maximum credit to be earned. For example, the credit ceiling could be \$1,000. Regardless of the taxpayer's property tax liability in relation to income, no more than a $1,000 credit is provided. The state can also specify several different sets of parameters a and b in the previous general formula. For example, the credit could be more generous for the elderly with $a = 1.0$ and $b = 0.03$. In that case, an elderly taxpayer would qualify for the credit when the property tax liability first exceeds 3 percent of income and the credit would be a full 100 percent of the property tax in excess of 3 percent of income.

A primary advantage of this form of property tax relief is that state resources are targeted specifically to those taxpayers most in need of property tax relief. If the state has $100 million it can spend on providing local property tax relief, that sum will be more effectively used when it is targeted to specific taxpayers than if it is spread across all property owners. Alternative mechanisms of providing property tax relief such as a homestead exemption spread the relief across all homesteads. The state's resources are not targeted to those most in need. Of course, defining an overburdened taxpayer is a problem. Although a person whose property tax bill exceeds 5 percent of income may indeed be overburdened with local property tax, it may also be the case that the person simply has chosen to spend an extremely large share of income on housing. Housing expenditures generally fall as a share of income as income rises, but exceptions do exist. Circuit breaker mechanisms define need in terms of property tax relative to income. In order to eliminate relief to very high-income taxpayers or to those with exceptionally large housing expenditures, a phase-out mechanism for high-income taxpayers or a cap on the credit can be applied.

A fully refundable credit makes the state's income tax more progressive, regardless of the tax rate structure. With a fully refundable property tax credit, a taxpayer without income tax liability can file a return, claim the credit for property taxes, and receive a check from the state. Some states have a single flat income tax rate, yet have progressive income tax systems due to their reliance on a circuit breaker mechanism. For convenience of property tax payment, it is sometimes the case that the credit is front loaded. That is, the state credit is received before the property tax bill is due the local government.

Because the circuit breaker mechanism provides *state* income tax relief for *local* property taxes paid, the state government is making an indirect commitment to fund local government activity. The precise working of a given state's circuit breaker mechanism should, therefore, be considered in tandem with that state's method of distributing state resources to local governments. Revenue sharing formulas, aid distribution formulas, grants, and equalization mechanisms are all methods states use to facilitate local government provision of public goods and services.

Approximately 35 U.S. states have adopted circuit breakers since the mid-1960s. The parameters of the circuit breakers vary widely from state to state. In some cases the circuit breaker provides a small amount of aggregate property tax relief to a narrowly targeted group of taxpayers. In other cases, hundreds of millions of dollars of property tax relief are provided to large numbers of taxpayers. Homeowners, renters, the elderly, and disabled are all provided property tax relief in varying degrees by the circuit breaker mechanism.

Two states use the circuit breaker mechanism to provide property tax relief for agricultural property owners: Michigan and Wisconsin. Although most states provide preferential treatment for agricultural property through use value assessment or a classified property tax system as discussed previously, these two states have chosen to employ a circuit breaker mechanism on the state income tax. Farmers whose property taxes are high relative to their income receive a credit on the state income tax for some portion of the property tax they pay to local governments. In exchange for this tax relief, farmers enter into contracts that limit their land development rights, similar to the Williamson Act mechanism.

Incentive effects of circuit breakers are a potential concern. If, on the margin, a taxpayer pays only 50 percent of the property tax, the price of local public goods like education is reduced significantly. The taxpayer may then be more likely to vote for additional local public goods, increasing demand for those goods and putting upward pressure on property tax rates. In theory this potential effect is worth consideration, but in practice the demand for local public goods is quite inelastic (unresponsive to price). Besides, only a fraction of the taxpayers receive the benefit of the circuit breaker credit. The others face the full price of local public goods, not subsidized by the credit. Thus, the effect of the circuit breaker is not likely to raise property tax rates.

Capitalization of the circuit breaker tax relief is also worth consideration. To the extent that the circuit breaker reduces the property tax, we would expect the market value of property to reflect the reduced tax liability. Tax relief is expected to be at least partially capitalized into higher property values.

Erosion of the Property Tax Base

The growing prevalence of tax abatements, exemptions, assessment limits, and other features intended to reduce the property tax burden has resulted in a general erosion of the property tax base. As the base shrinks, higher tax rates are necessary in order to generate any given level of revenue need to fund local government service provision. Consequently, there is growing concern that the erosion of the property tax base is partly to blame in the continuing upward pressure on property tax rates. Augustine et al. (2009) provide a comprehensive overview and analysis of the trends, causes, and consequences of this phenomenon.

Replacing Property Tax Revenues with Other Revenue Sources

Local government reliance on property taxes for revenue has been declining for a long period in the United States. Table 17.1 provides an overview of property tax reliance over the second half of the twentieth century: 1950 to 1999. During that period, property taxes as a share of own-source tax revenues fell from 88 percent in 1950 to 72 percent in 1999. That reduction indicates that property taxes have become less important relative to other own-source tax revenues over time. That is, other local government tax sources have been replacing the property tax in generating revenues. A more general measure of the reliance on property taxes comes from a consideration of property taxes as a share of total revenue. By that measure, property taxes fell from 50 percent of total revenue in 1950 to 24 percent in 1999. This reduction indicates that relative to all other sources of revenue, both own-source revenue and other-source revenue, such as state and federal revenue sharing funds, property tax reliance has fallen substantially over the past 50 years. State and local governments are relying more on sales and income taxes together with intergovernmental transfers. This is a long-term trend that is likely to continue.

POLICY STUDY

Property Taxes and House Values: Estimation of Tax Capitalization in Massachusetts

In order to test the extent to which property tax differences across homes within a city are capitalized into house prices (intrajurisdictional capitalization), Yinger et al. (1988) conducted an extensive study that represents the best research methodology on this topic to date. They used data on repeat sales for homes in Massachusetts communities where there was a significant community-wide revaluation of all property. Table 17.8 reports the results of their estimation for three Massachusetts cities. Table entries are the percentage rate at which property tax changes in each community are capitalized into changes in the sales price of homes. The *t*-statistics indicate whether the tax capitalization rate is significantly different from zero (i.e., there is a positive capitalization rate). When the *t*-statistic is larger than 1.96 (assuming a large sample was used in

TABLE 17.8 Capitalization Rates Estimated for Massachusetts Communities

City	Tax Capitalization Rate (%) and *t*-Statistics
Waltham	21.1
	(5.0)
Brockton	15.8
	(9.6)
Barnstable	33.1
	(2.9)

Source: Yinger et al. 1988, 99.

estimation) we can reject the null hypothesis that taxes are not capitalized and conclude that the capitalization rate is positive and significantly different from zero. These results indicate that the degree of capitalization is positive and ranges from a low of 15.8 percent in Brockton to a high of 33.1 percent in Barnstable. Given the *t*-statistics reported, we know that we can reject the hypothesis that there is no capitalization in these three communities. Hence, we have clear evidence of property tax capitalization.

The notable aspect of these results, however, is that the degree of capitalization is less than 100 percent. Approximately one-sixth to one-third of a change in property tax is capitalized into the sales price of properties in these communities. The natural question to ask is why these results are less than 100 percent. That is, why would differences in property taxes be less than fully capitalized into the value of the houses? Yinger et al. believe that the reason for less than full capitalization is that households do not expect pre-revaluation tax differences to persist—even before revaluation is announced (Yinger et al. 1988, 124). If households do not expect differences in taxes due to differences in assessment for similar homes to persist, then those differences are not fully capitalized into value. If households believe that differences in value are due to assessment errors that will be corrected over time, then the differences in tax are not fully capitalized.

PROBLEMS

1. For each of the following pieces of property, explain whether the property is real or personal:
   a. A personal computer
   b. A mainframe computer
   c. Computer network wiring in the walls and ceiling of a building
   d. The office building for a computer marketing firm
2. For each of the following properties, explain which method of valuation is most likely to be used and why (based on data availability):
   a. A McDonald's franchise store in suburban Washington, D.C.
   b. A cornfield somewhere in the middle of Iowa
   c. A General Motors assembly plant in Flint, Michigan
   d. The lavish home of Bill Gates in suburban Seattle
3. Suppose that a property is assessed at $AV = \$120{,}000$ for tax purposes, whereas its market value is $MV = \$150{,}000$. The nominal property tax rate is $t^n = 0.02$.
   a. Compute the effective tax rate t^e.
   b. Explain the difference between the nominal and effective tax rates.
   c. Suppose that a reassessment occurs that raises the assessed value to $AV = \$130{,}000$. Explain the effect of the reassessment on the effective tax rate.
4. Suppose that property can be considered a perpetuity, generating a perpetual income stream R_i each year forever. Assume that the constant

discount rate is r. In the case of a perpetuity, the value of the property is simply $V = R_i/r$.

a. Assume that $R_i = \$4{,}000$ and $r = 0.05$. Compute the value of the property.
b. Assume that $R_i = \$4{,}000$ and $r = 0.06$. Compute the value of the property. Explain the effect of a higher discount rate on the value of the property.
c. Assume that $R_i = \$5{,}000$ and $r = 0.06$. Compute the value of the property. Explain the effect of a higher net income stream on the value of the property.
d. Assume that $R_i = \$5{,}000$ and $r = 0.06$. Assume further that there is a property tax $T_i = \$1{,}000$ per year and public service provision value of $S_i = \$800$ per year. Compute the value of the property. Explain the effects of the property tax and public services on the value of the property.

5. Most states permit assessments for agricultural land based on the value of the land in its agricultural use, ignoring potential developed uses for the land.
   a. Using a graph like that in Figure 17.1, explain the difference between agricultural use value and market value for agricultural land.
   b. Explain the forgone revenue to local government units due to use value assessment.
6. In 1992 the state of Nebraska changed property tax law in a way that lowered the rate of taxation on capital in the nonresidential sector of the economy, whereas the rate of applied on residential capital was unchanged. (This policy change was known as Amendment One.)
   a. Analyze the effects of such a policy change in the context of a two-sector general equilibrium graphical model and explain the capital flows that result and the incidence of the tax reduction.
   b. Explain who benefits from the reduction in capital taxation of nonresidential capital.
7. Suppose that a citywide property reassessment has just been conducted. The last comprehensive reassessment occurred 30 years ago. The effect of the recent reassessment was to raise the citywide assessment ratio from 0.3 to 0.9.
   a. Explain the impact of such an increase in the assessment ratio on the effective rate of taxation.
   b. Won't the tax rates simply be adjusted by the local government units to generate the same revenue?
   c. What equity issues arise in this situation? Explain.
   d. What difference does it make that school aid is distributed to districts partly on the basis of property wealth per pupil? Explain.
8. The Clemente family lives in Wasatch County, whereas the Law family lives on adjacent land in San Pedro County. The parcels of land the families occupy are both in the Murtaugh School District and happen to have identical market values of \$500,000. The property tax rate for the school district is 2 percent of assessed value.

a. Identify the equity issue regarding these land parcels if the Wasatch County assessor assess land at 100 percent of market value, whereas the San Pedro County assessor assess land at 80 percent of market value.
b. Calculate the property tax paid by each family if the equity issue is not addressed and if it is addressed.

REFERENCES

Anderson, John E. "Two-Rate Property Taxes and Urban Development," *Intergovernmental Perspective* 19, 3 (summer, 1993): 19–20, 28. U.S. Advisory Commission on Intergovernmental Relations (ACIR), Washington, DC.

Anderson, John E. "Circuit Breaker." In the *Encyclopedia of Taxation and Tax Policy*. Washington, DC: Urban Institute, 2000.

Augustine, Nancy Y., Michael E. Bell, David Brunoiri, and Joan M. Youngman. *Erosion of the Property Tax Base*. Cambridge, MA: Lincoln Institute of Land Policy, 2009.

Bowman, John H. *Taxation of Business Property: Is Uniformity Still a Valid Norm?* Westport, CT: Praeger, 1995.

Bowman, John H., George E. Hoffer, and Michael D. Pratt. "Current Patterns and Trends in State and Local Intangibles Taxation." *National Tax Journal* 43 (1990): 439–50.

Capozza, Dennis R., and Robert W. Helsley. "The Fundamentals of Land Prices and Urban Growth." *Journal of Urban Economics* 26 (1989): 295–306.

Dye, Richard F. and Richard W. England. *Land Value Taxation: Theory, Evidence, and Practice*. Cambridge, MA: Lincoln Institute of Land Policy, 2009.

Fischel, William A. "Fiscal and Environmental Considerations in the Location of Firms in Suburban Communities." In *Fiscal Zoning and Land Use Controls*, edited by Edwin S. Mills and Wallace E. Oates. Lexington, MA: Lexington, 1975.

Fischel, William A. "Homevoters, Municipal Corporate Governance, and the Benefit View of the Property Tax." *National Tax Journal* 54 (2001): 157–73.

Fisher, Glenn W. *The Worst Tax? A History of the Property Tax in America*. Lawrence: University of Kansas Press, 1996.

Hamilton, Bruce W. "Zoning and Property Taxation in a System of Local Governments." *Urban Studies* 12 (1975): 205–11.

Hamilton, Bruce W. "A Review: Is the Property Tax a Benefit Tax?" Chapter 4 in *Local Provision of Public Services: The Tiebout Model After Twenty-Five Years*, edited by George R. Zodrow. New York: Academic, 1983.

Holland, Daniel M. *The Assessment of Land Value*. Madison: University of Wisconsin Press, 1970.

Lincoln Institute of Land Policy. Significant Features of the Property Tax®. http://www.lincolninst.edu/subcenters/significant-features-property-tax/

Lutz, Byron, Raven Molloy, and Hiu Shan. "The Housing Crisis and State and Local Government Tax Revenue: Five Channels." *Regional Science and Urban Economics*, forthcoming.

Mieszkowski, Peter. "The Property Tax: An Excise Tax or a Profits Tax?" *Journal of Public Economics* 1 (1972): 73–96.

Netzer, Dick. *The Economics of the Property Tax*. Washington, DC: Brookings Institution, 1966.

Simon, Herbert A. "The Incidence of a Tax on Urban Real Property." *Quarterly Journal of Economics* 59 (1943): 398–420.

U.S. Census Bureau. *Government Finances 1998–99*. Washington, DC: U.S. Government Printing Office, 2001.

Wassmer, Robert W. "Property Taxation, Property Base, and Property Value: An Empirical Test of the 'New View.'" *National Tax Journal* 46 (1993): 135–60.

White, Michelle. "Firm Location in a Zoned Metropolitan Area." In *Fiscal Zoning and Land Use Controls*, edited by Edwin S. Mills and Wallace E. Oates. Lexington, MA: Lexington, 1975.

Yinger, John, Howard S. Bloom, Axel Börsch-Supan, and Helen F. Ladd. *Property Taxes and House Values*. San Diego, CA: Academic, 1988.

Zodrow, George W. "The Property Tax as a Capital Tax: A Room with Three Views." *National Tax Journal* 54 (2001): 139–56.

Zodrow, George W., and Peter Mieszkowski. "The Incidence of the Property Tax: The Benefit View Versus the New View." Chapter 5 in *Local Provision of Public Services: The Tiebout Model After Twenty-Five Years*, edited by George R. Zodrow. New York: Academic, 1983.

NOTES

1. See Fisher (1996) for a description of the colorful history of the property tax in the United States.
2. Capozza and Helsley (1990).
3. The derivation of this expression involves the solution of a difference equation and hence is omitted.
4. Although there were some studies that reported finding more than 100 percent capitalization, Table 17.6 omits those studies since they are not considered fully reliable.

Radius Images/Getty Images

PART SIX

Multilevel Government and Intergovernmental Relations

CHAPTER

18

Radius Images/Getty Images

Deficit Finance, Government Budgets, and Borrowing

LEARNING OBJECTIVES

1. Analyze government budgets, including budget concepts, budget processes, and historical trends.
2. Explain the mechanisms and impacts of government borrowing.
3. Discuss deficit finance.

Current revenues do not always match current expenditures by governments. As a result, there may be either a surplus or deficit, depending on whether revenues exceed or fall short of expenditures. In the case of a deficit, the government is spending more during a particular period than it is receiving revenues from taxes and other sources; hence, it must borrow in order to support those expenditures. The government could raise taxes in order to fully fund expenditures but may in fact choose to use a combination of taxes and borrowing. The government debt is the accumulation of all prior deficits and surpluses. The deficit is a flow concept, based on a time dimension such as a fiscal year, annual year, or quarter, whereas the debt is a stock concept with no time dimension.

GOVERNMENT ACCOUNTING, BUDGETS, AND BUDGET PROCESSES

Things are not always as they seem. The Enron debacle that transpired in the early 2000s brought that reality home with a vengeance and illustrated that mundane private sector accounting matters are not so mundane after all. Later, the audit discovery of a seemingly obscure accounting misclassification of $3.8 billion in costs at WorldCom brought that huge corporation to its knees and an eventual historic bankruptcy (the largest bankruptcy in history at the time). Budgets and audits are essential to proper functioning of modern enterprises, both private and public. Nowhere is the maxim that things are not always as they appear more relevant than in the world of government budgeting and accounting. Government budgets are different from private sector budgets in some very fundamental ways. We consider some of the foundational concepts of public budgets and several fundamental differences between public sector accounting methods and private sector accounting methods in this section.

Budget Terminology

The discussion of government budgets involves the use of specialized terminology that we should clarify at the outset of our excursion into the carnival world of budgets. Table 18.1 provides a summary of brief definitions for key budget concepts. These terms will be used in the material to follow on the budget process, deficits, and markets for debt. **Outlays** are monetary disbursements by the government, including funds transferred to other units of government. If we net out those transfers to other government units, we have **net outlays**, which can also be called **expenditures. Revenues** include net receipts of the government from parties outside the government, primarily from taxes but also from fees and other sources. A budget **deficit** occurs when government outlays exceed revenues. Government **debt** is the sum of all past deficits minus the sum of all past surpluses plus trust fund balances. Trust funds have been created for specific purposes such as Social Security and environmental protection. The purpose of those funds is to bank surpluses generated in early years in order to facilitate deficit spending in later years. Hence, we must include those trust fund balances if we wish to have a complete picture of government debt. The distinction between a deficit and debt is the distinction between an economic flow and a stock, once again. A deficit is a flow measure and debt is a stock measure. The trust fund balances must be added because increases in the fund balances are used on an annual basis to reduce the size of deficits.

Government Accounting

Government accounting is not like private sector accounting in some very fundamental ways. First, governments usually account for revenues and expenditures on a **cash basis** rather than an **accrual basis** as is more typical

DILBERT reprinted by permission of United Features Syndicate, Inc.

TABLE 18.1 Definitions of Budget Terms

Term	Definition
Outlays	Monetary disbursements by the U.S. government, or by agencies within the government, including funds transferred between agencies.
Net outlays	Net outlays of the U.S. government to parties outside of government, such as private citizens and corporations, which exclude interagency transfers of funds. Net outlays are always in the form of cash (or check) disbursements. When used in the context of the overall budget, the term *outlays* normally refers to *net* outlays and is equivalent to net expenditures.
Expenditures	Equivalent to net outlays, and probably a more appropriate term, but virtually all government documents refer to spending as outlays rather than expenditures.
Revenues	Net receipts of the U.S. government from parties outside the government, typically via taxes. Receipts are always in the form of cash (or equivalent).
Budget deficit	Budget deficit = outlays − revenues, when outlays are greater than revenues.
Budget surplus	Budget surplus = revenues − outlays, when revenues are greater than outlays.
Balanced budget	Revenues = outlays, given some specified tolerance, such as within \$100 million.
Debt	Debt = $\sum$deficits − $\sum$surpluses + trust funds.
Marketable debt	Securities sold by the U.S. Treasury in order to fund deficits:
	U.S. Treasury Bills with maturity of 13, 26, or 52 weeks, sold at discount
	U.S. Treasury Notes with maturity of 2 to 10 years, with interest paid by coupon
	U.S. Treasury Bonds with maturity of 30 years, with interest paid by coupon
Nonmarketable Debt	Securities not sold by the U.S. Treasury, including trust funds and other securities held by the Federal Reserve System, foreign central banks, and others.

Source: Tables 1.1 and 1.2 from *Red Ink: The Budget, Deficit, and Debt of the U.S. Government* by Gary R. Evans.

of private firms. With cash accounting, the government books receipts and outlays when they actually occur. In the private sector, firms using accrual accounting book receipts and outlays when the obligations related to them are incurred.

The difference in the two accounting approaches has a substantial effect, permitting governments to adjust their budget situation more fluidly than can occur in the private sector with accrual accounting. Consider the situation of a state government that has fiscal difficulty during a recession. The state may anticipate a deficit of $100 million but be required by the state constitution to balance the budget. How can that be done? It is an easy two-step process. First, the state can delay some of its payments that would otherwise have been made in the last quarter of the fiscal year into the first quarter of the next fiscal year. Second, the state can require tax payments that would otherwise have been paid in the first quarter of the next fiscal year to be accelerated into the last quarter of this fiscal year. The combination of the two adjustments makes the deficit disappear. Of course, there has been no real deficit reduction. There has only been a budget-driven timing game played. This can easily be done when the state is using cash accounting. If the state were using accrual accounting, no such budget game could be played. As a general rule, very few government agencies use **Generally Accepted Accounting Practices (GAAP)**. Those that do are unusual, and fiscally responsible.

What about the auditing function, critical to the integrity of budgets and public finance? The Enron situation with its auditor, Arthur Andersen, illustrated that independent audits are absolutely essential to the integrity of an enterprise. Who plays the important role of auditor for the U.S. federal government? The answer to that question is the **General Accountability Office (GAO)**. That agency is charged with the responsibility of auditing federal agencies and reporting to Congress.

Operating and Capital Budgets

The federal government budget differs from private firm budgets in another fundamental respect. Although private firms keep separate operating and capital budgets, the federal government has just one budget: mixing operating and capital expenditures. Normally, firms account for capital expenditures separately from operating expenditures. The reason for the distinction, of course, is based on the longevity of the capital. If a private firm purchases an expensive piece of productive capital equipment, it expects that equipment to provide a flow of services over the economic life of the equipment. No expectation exists that this year's expenditure be covered with this year's revenue. Rather, the long-term stream of revenues over the years is expected to cover the expense incurred today.

The federal government budget does not work that way. Because there is no distinction in the federal budget between capital and operating expenses, the federal budget may appear to be out of balance because a current expense is not covered by current revenues. Suppose that the federal government builds a new federal building this year, for example. The expense of constructing that facility is fully included in this year's budget, and the operating expense of running the facility is included in each subsequent year's budget. Because the expense category of the federal budget includes both capital expenditures and operating expenditures, we should not necessarily expect current revenues to cover current expenses.

If the federal government has a separate capital budget, it would also need to account for depreciation of that capital stock. An expenditure of $100 million on a federal highway project is accounted separately from operating expenses of maintaining highways. But accounting for the capital expenditure separately would also require us to estimate the annual depreciation of the federal highways. Although this can be done in theory, it would be difficult in practice, and therein lays one of the obstacles to formulating a separate capital account in the federal budget.

Fiscal Years

The U.S. federal government operates on a fiscal calendar that begins October 1 of each year and runs through September 30. Although most private firms operate on a July 1 to June 30 fiscal year calendar, the federal government finds it advantageous to shift the fiscal year forward one quarter. Congress typically finishes its budget debate during the summer, so it is helpful to have the new fiscal year begin in the fall. Hence, each federal fiscal year consists of one quarter in calendar year n and three quarters in calendar year $n + 1$. For example, the 2011–12 fiscal year will begin October 1 of the calendar year 2011 and run through September 30 of the year 2012. The last quarter of 2011 and the first three quarters of 2012 make up fiscal year 2011–12. Although fiscal years span two calendar years, the naming convention is to use the calendar year in which the fiscal year ends.

State governments differ in the fiscal year definitions they employ. Some states follow the federal fiscal year, whereas others follow the traditional private sector fiscal year from July 1 through June 30. Local governments also differ in the fiscal year they follow, generally adopting the fiscal year of the state government.

Federal Budget Process[1]

The federal budget process takes place in three interrelated stages: formulation of the president's budget, congressional action on the budget, and execution of the budget.

Formulation of the President's Budget

First, the president formulates a budget reflecting the spending priorities of his administration for the next fiscal year as well as the following three years (a four-year horizon). For example, the 2011 budget covers spending plans out through 2015. The budget also traditionally includes information on the most recently completed fiscal year so that budget estimates can be compared with actual expenditure data. The president's State of the Union address, delivered to a joint session of Congress in January, is used in part to preview those spending priorities. The president then transmits the proposed budget to Congress between the first Monday in January and the first Monday in February.

The process of formulating the budget for a given fiscal year begins no later than the spring of the prior calendar year, a full 18 months before the fiscal year begins. The president and his administration determine the broad outlines of the budget, specifying general budget and fiscal policy guidelines. The **Office of Management and Budget (OMB)** then works with each federal agency to establish policy directions and planning levels for the agency that are consistent with the president's budget guidelines. By the fall of the year, the federal agencies submit their budget requests to OMB. After analysis of the budget requests and extensive discussion with the agencies, the budget proposals are finalized by the end of the calendar year (December).

Budget plans are heavily influenced by estimates of general economic conditions in the country and anticipated changes in those conditions. Estimates of the rate of growth of output, employment, prices, interest rates, and other key macroeconomic variables are critical in formulating the budget. Those forecast conditions directly influence estimates of the likely receipts the government will have in the upcoming budget years. Forecast error is also an important factor in the budget planning process. Even a small deviation between expected and actual receipts can have a dramatic effect on the actual budget balance realized. An unexpected economic shock of significant magnitude can have a devastating effect. For example, the FY 2011 federal budget document includes an estimated deficit of $1,267 billion for FY 2011, in contrast to the projected FY 2011 deficit of $183 billion in the FY 2007 budget document. The budget situation deteriorated dramatically with the depth of the unanticipated recession of 2008 to 2009. The overall balance projected in the federal budget is driven by the expectation of economic conditions. If those expected conditions do not materialize, the budget projections can be way off. Because budget plans hinge critically on economic conditions, a great deal of attention is paid to forecasts of economic conditions in each year's budget document. The budget projections in any given budget document must be understood as conditional on the realization of the economic conditions built into the projections.

Congressional Action on the Budget

Congress then takes the president's proposed budget; debates its provisions; and approves, modifies, or disapproves of each provision. Funding levels can be changed, programs can be added or eliminated, and revenue-generating provisions can be altered. Congress does not enact a budget per se. Rather, it adopts a budget resolution whereby it agrees on appropriate expenditure levels and revenues. That budget resolution provides the framework within which congressional committees formulate appropriations bills and receipts legislation. Then appropriations acts throughout the year provide the specific mechanism by which the budget is implemented.

Congressional review of the president's proposed budget begins after its transmittal in January or February. According to the rules established by the

Congressional Budget Act of 1974, Congress begins by considering budget totals before moving to consider individual appropriations. Each of the standing committees of the House and Senate must recommend budget levels and report legislative plans to the Budget Committee of each body. The two Budget Committees then concurrently engage in resolution activities, setting appropriate levels for total receipts and budgetary authority and expenditure outlays by functional category of the budget. Deficit or surplus levels are also set, along with the debt. The budget resolution includes an explanatory statement that allocates budgetary authority and outlays to functional category totals to committees with jurisdiction in those areas. The House and Senate Appropriations Committees then allocate budgetary authority and outlays among subcommittees. Although the budget resolution is scheduled for adoption by Congress by April 15, in practice, passage of the resolution is usually delayed until later in the spring or summer.

Controlling the size of the budget is a major issue recently in the United States. The Budget Enforcement Act of 1990 (BEA) set the ground rules under which the budget process proceeded for much of the 1990s. The BEA included a mechanism that constrained spending and receipts. Spending programs were divided into **discretionary spending** and direct spending. Discretionary spending included salaries and operational expenses of federal agencies and was controlled through annual appropriation acts subject to caps that constrained outlays. Direct, or mandatory, spending included outlays for programs such as Medicare, Medicaid, unemployment insurance, and farm price supports. Spending for these programs was controlled by permanent laws. If the amount of budget authority included in the appropriations acts exceeded the cap on discretionary spending or the amount of outlays expected to result from the budget authority, the BEA included a process of **sequestration**. In order to reduce spending, funds were sequestered by reducing program spending by a uniform percentage across all program areas subject to the sequestration process. Although many program areas were subject to potential sequestration, some programs were exempt from the sequestration process. Mandatory spending and receipts were controlled through the use of a **pay-as-you-go** (PAYGO) mechanism. Under this budget provision, any proposal that would increase spending or reduce receipts was required to also include a provision paying for the increased spending or replacing the lost receipts. Congress enacted the **line item veto** in 1996, which authorized the president to cancel any item of discretionary or direct spending and/or to limit tax benefits. The president is required to send a special message to Congress within five days of signing the Act containing the provisions vetoed. Although President Clinton used the line item veto after it was made available, it was declared unconstitutional by the Supreme Court in 1998.

More recently the U.S. federal budget process has not been implemented with these controls. Congress has struggled to find effective mechanisms to control spending. One perennial issue is the **debt ceiling** that constrains the total amount of federal government debt through a cap on the amount that the Treasury Department can borrow. At present the U.S. federal debt is approximately $14 trillion. As the debt approaches the debt ceiling, debate in Congress often heats up with rhetoric about controlling spending, but typically Congress raises the debt ceiling without serious threat of substantial changes in its fiscal behavior. In recent years the practice of including **earmarks** in congressional spending bills has been very contentious. Under this practice, a Congressperson adds a special provision in a law (perhaps entirely unrelated) that provides funding for a particular purpose (typically in the Congressperson's home district). If the bill is adopted and signed by the president, it becomes law and the expenditure is implemented without the usual budget oversight. The OMB defines earmarks as,

> Earmarks are funds provided by the Congress for projects, programs, or grants where the purported congressional direction (whether in statutory text, report language, or other communication) circumvents otherwise applicable merit-based or competitive allocation processes, or specifies the location or recipient, or otherwise curtails the ability of the executive branch to manage its statutory and constitutional responsibilities pertaining to the funds allocation process.
>
> source: http://earmarks.omb.gov/earmarks-public/

Execution of the Budget

The budget is carried out, or executed, by the president who delegates authority for this responsibility to the OMB. Table 18.2 provides a calendar by

TABLE 18.2 Federal Budget Calendar

Date	Budget Action
Between the first Monday in January and the first Monday in February	President transmits the budget.
Six weeks later	Congressional committees report budget estimates to Budget Committees.
April 15	Action to be completed on congressional budget resolution.
May 15	House consideration of annual appropriations bills may begin even if the budget resolution has not been agreed to.
June 10	House Appropriations Committee to report the last of its annual appropriations bills.
June 15	Action to be completed on "reconciliation bill" by Congress.
June 30	Action on appropriations to be completed by House.
July 15	President transmits Mid-Session Review of the budget.
October 1	Fiscal year begins.

Source: *Analytical Perspectives, Budget of the U.S. Government, Fiscal Year 2011*, p. 116.

which the U.S. federal budget process takes place each fiscal year. The president transmits his budget, reflecting the administration's spending and taxing priorities for the coming year, to Congress during the month of January. Presidents typically use the State of the Union Address in January as the public forum in which to highlight the spending priorities that are in the budget proposal to the American people. Reconciliation of the president's budget and congressional budget priorities takes place during the period from mid-March to mid-April. Then, between May 15 and June 30 the House considers specific appropriations bills. It is the appropriations process that actually implements the budget. Congress does not directly adopt spending bills. Rather, it approves budget authority by which outlays can be implemented by executive branch units.

Funds are apportioned to federal government agencies by quarters during the fiscal year. If changing circumstances require, or a natural disaster occurs, Congress may enact **supplemental appropriations**. If the originally appropriated funds prove to be more than needed due to cost savings or improved efficiency, the Impoundment Control Act of 1974 provides a procedure by which the president may withhold funds. Congress may also pass a law permanently canceling budget authority—a so-called **recision**.

On-Budget/Off-Budget Items

The budget provides information on all of the federal government's agencies and programs. Some federal laws prevent the receipts and outlays of certain funds from being included in the budget totals and from the computed surplus or deficit. Those funds are also excluded from Budget Enforcement Act provisions. The funds excluded are two of the social security funds (the Federal Old-Age and Survivors Insurance fund, and the Federal Disability Insurance trust funds) and the Postal Service fund. Activities in these funds are called **off-budget** because these transactions are excluded from budget totals by law, distinguishing them from other federal programs that are **on-budget**. The on-budget and off-budget totals are combined to construct a **consolidated budget** in order to obtain a full view of the financing of the federal government's activity. For example, the federal budget in fiscal year 2011 shows a unified budget deficit of $1,267 billion, with that deficit made up of a larger on-budget deficit of $1,363 billion and an off-budget surplus of $96 billion. Table 18.3 illustrates the relative magnitudes of on-budget and off-budget categories in the estimated figures for fiscal year 2011. The president's budget indicates that the on-budget items will provide for outlays of $3,834 billion and receipts of $2,567 billion, leaving an anticipated unified deficit of $1,267 billion. The total unified deficit is comprised of the **primary deficit** plus interest expense on the debt. For fiscal 2011 the total unified deficit consists of a primary deficit of $1,016 and an additional $251 billion in net interest.

So what? Who cares where the surplus comes from? Does it really matter? Well, it actually matters quite a lot. If we do not have an appropriate picture of both on- and off-budget balances, we really have no accurate view

TABLE 18.3 On-Budget and Off-Budget Categories for the U.S. Federal Government

Budget Category	Estimates for Fiscal Year 2011 (Billions of Dollars)
Total outlays	3,834
Total receipts	2,767
Unified deficit	−1,267
On-budget deficit	−1,363
Off-budget surplus	+96
Primary deficit	−1,016

Source: Budget of the United States Government, Fiscal Year 2011.

of the budget at all. It could well be the case that the on-budget expenditure categories are seriously in deficit but that the situation is obscured by surpluses generated in off-budget categories. Does that matter? If the surplus funds for off-budget programs like social security are being diverted in order to reduce deficits in other parts of the budget, there may be serious consequences. Congress may simply be raiding off-budget funds intended for future use, in order to spend beyond the nation's current means. Worse yet, those off-budget funds may then be dry in the future when they are needed. This is an important current policy issue with respect to the social security system. Although the social security system is primarily a pay-as-you-go system with current tax revenues funding current benefits paid to retirees, several trust funds, such as the two off-budget funds noted above, accumulate current balances for future use.

Neither the on-budget nor the off-budget categories listed above include the financing of government-sponsored enterprises. For example, activities of the Federal National Mortgage Association (Fannie Mae) are not included anywhere in the budget figures. These organizations are privately owned and operated corporations created to accomplish specific public policy purposes. The federal government budget includes appendix material on the financial aspects of these enterprises, but the budget does not include such enterprise activity. In addition, the net earnings of the Federal Reserve System, although transferred directly into the U.S. Treasury, do not appear in either the on-budget or off-budget totals.

Unified Federal Government Budget

So, what is in the unified federal budget? Table 18.4 provides a breakdown of the unified budget (including both on-budget and off-budget items) over the years 1980 to 2010 with the major categories of spending listed. Budget data for fiscal year 2010 are estimates. The largest spending category in the 2010 budget is social security, accounting for 19 percent of total outlays of the

TABLE 18.4 Budget of the U.S. Federal Government, 1980–2010

	Net Outlays (Billions of Current Dollars)						
Government Function	***1980***	***1985***	***1990***	***1995***	***2000***	***2005***	***2010 (est.)***
National defense	134.0	252.7	299.3	272.1	294.5	495.3	719.2
Human resources							
Education, training, employment, social services	31.8	29.3	38.8	54.3	53.8	97.6	142.5
Health	23.2	33.5	57.7	115.4	154.5	250.5	372.3
Medicare	32.1	65.8	98.1	159.9	197.1	298.6	457.2
Income security	86.6	128.2	147.1	220.5	253.5	345.8	685.9
Social security	118.5	188.6	248.6	335.8	409.4	523.3	721.5
On-budget	0.7	5.2	3.6	5.5	13.3	16.5	37.6
Off-budget	117.9	183.4	245.0	330.4	396.2	506.8	683.9
Veterans benefits	21.2	26.3	29.1	37.9	47.1	70.1	124.7
Physical resources							
Energy	10.2	5.7	3.3	4.9	−1.1	0.4	19.0
Natural resources and environment	13.9	13.4	17.1	22.1	25.0	28.0	47.0
Commerce and housing credit	9.4	4.3	67.6	−17.8	3.2	7.6	−25.3
On-budget	n.a.	n.a.	66.0	−15.8	1.2	9.4	−31.7
Off-budget	n.a.	n.a.	1.6	−2.0	2.0	−1.8	6.4
Transportation	21.3	25.8	29.5	39.4	46.9	67.9	106.5
Community and regional development	11.3	7.7	8.5	10.6	10.6	26.3	28.5
Net interest	52.5	129.5	184.2	232.2	223.0	184.0	187.8
On-budget	54.9	133.6	200.4	265.5	282.8	275.8	306.2
Off-budget	−2.3	−4.1	−16.0	−33.3	−59.8	−91.8	−118.4
Other functions							
International affairs	12.7	16.2	13.8	16.4	17.2	34.6	51.1
General science, space, technology	5.8	8.6	14.4	16.7	18.6	23.6	33.0
Agriculture	8.8	25.6	12.0	9.8	36.6	26.6	26.6
Administration of justice	4.6	6.3	10.0	16.2	28.0	40.0	55.0
General government	13.0	11.6	10.7	13.8	13.3	17.0	29.3
Undistributed offsetting receipts	−19.9	−32.7	−36.6	−44.5	−42.6	−65.2	−79.7
On-budget	−18.7	−30.2	−31.0	−38.0	−34.9	−54.3	−64.8
Off-budget	−1.2	−2.0	−5.6	−6.4	−7.6	−10.9	−14.9

(Continued)

TABLE 18.4 Budget of the U.S. Federal Government, 1980–2010 (continued)

	Net Outlays (Billions of Current Dollars)						
Government Function	*1980*	*1985*	*1990*	*1995*	*2000*	*2005*	*2010 (est.)*
Total outlays	590.9	946.4	1,253.2	1,515.7	1,788.8	2,472.0	3,720.7
On-budget	476.6	769.6	1,028.1	1,227.2	1,458.1	2,069.8	3,163.7
Off-budget	114.3	176.8	225.1	288.7	330.8	402.2	557.0
Total receipts	517.1	734.1	1,032.0	1,351.8	2,025.2	2,153.6	2,165.1
Budget surplus (+) or deficit (−)	−73.8	−212.3	−221.2	−164.0	236.4	−318.3	−1,555.6
On-budget	−72.7	−221.7	−277.8	−226.4	+96.6	−493.6	−1,633.8
Off-budget	−1.1	+9.4	+56.6	+62.4	+149.8	175.3	78.2

Source: Budget of the United States Government, Fiscal Year 2011, *Historical Tables.*

federal government. The second-largest spending category is national defense, accounting for another 19 percent of total outlays. Income security programs (including federal employee retirement and disability, unemployment compensation, and other programs) account for 18 percent of outlays, whereas health and Medicare each account for 10 and 12 percent of budget outlays, respectively. Net interest payments are the sixth-largest category of spending, accounting for 5 percent of total outlays.

Over the decade of the 1980s there were dramatic changes in the federal budget. Social security net outlays increased from $118.5 billion in 1980 to $248.6 billion in 1990, more than doubling. Keep in mind that these budget figures are in *current dollars,* so they include the effect of inflation. Nevertheless, a near doubling of outlays for social security represented a substantial real increase in expenditure. National defense outlays increased even more substantially over the decade, increasing from $134.0 billion in 1980 to $299.3 billion in 1990, more than doubling. Net interest payments by the federal government rose by an astonishing factor of 3.5 during the decade, from $52.5 billion in 1980 to $184.2 billion in 1990. Interest payments rose for two reasons. First, the size of the federal debt grew due to increasing deficits. Second, high interest rates at the time caused interest payments to accelerate. Income security program spending also increased substantially during the decade of the 1980s as net outlays went from $86.6 billion to $147.1 billion. Finally, the decade saw dramatic increases in health care expenditures as well with Medicare outlays more than tripling from $32.1 billion to $98.1 billion, whereas other health expenditures rose from $23.2 billion to $57.7 billion.

The decade of the 1990s witnessed a substantial further increase in social security, net interest, income security, Medicare, and health net outlays. The rate of increase in these expenditures slowed during the decade, however.

National defense outlays were reduced as the cold war ended, providing a so-called **peace dividend**. Most recently, however, the federal budget has increased national defense expenditures dramatically due to new security concerns related to the War on Terrorism. Interest payments fell substantially during the 1990s as deficits were brought under control, reducing the size of the federal debt, and as interest rates fell. Agricultural expenditures rose sharply in the 2000 budget, after reductions in the early 1990s. The Freedom to Farm Act of 1996 was intended to reduce federal subsidies for agriculture, but with drought, low commodity prices, and hard lobbying in the late 1990s and early 2000s, agricultural support increased substantially and effectively ended this policy approach. Another budget area with substantial growth in recent years is the administration of justice. This category includes not only outlays to administer the federal court system but also outlays for federal prisons.

During the first decade of the twenty-first century, the federal budget total outlays more than doubled in nominal terms with most categories of spending increasing substantially. The severe recession of 2008 to 2009 resulted in total receipts in 2010 that were nearly identical to those of 2005, but total outlays increased dramatically. As a consequence, the budget deficit skyrocketed from $318.3 billion in 2005 (which was trending down in 2006 and 2007) to a record-breaking $1,555.6 billion in 2010. Even taking into account growth in the size of the economy over time, the 2010 deficit was 10.6 percent of GDP, well above the 50-year historic average of 2.4 percent and second only to the deficit in 1943 of 30.3 percent of GDP.

WHAT DETERMINES THE SIZE OF THE FEDERAL DEFICIT?

The federal government deficit is determined by a combination of two factors: federal government expenditures and taxation, and fundamental economic conditions in the country. Although the size of the deficit is affected by tax and expenditure policies, those policies are built on top of fundamental macroeconomic conditions that are considered by Congress and the president during the budget process.

Macroeconomic Determinants of the Federal Deficit

During a period of strong economic performance within the United States, revenues flow into the Treasury and the demand for public assistance programs like welfare and unemployment compensation is reduced, making the budgetary picture much brighter. A recession, on the other hand, has the effect of reducing revenues and increasing federal expenditures, resulting in larger deficits.

National revenue systems in most countries are typically income elastic; as national income rises, revenues increase by an even larger amount. The elastic response of revenues to income changes is primarily due to the progressive income tax system. As income rises, income taxes rise more than proportionately under a progressive system. Not all taxes have this elastic response. Sales taxes, for example are not so elastic. As income rises, consumption expenditures rise less than proportionately (some of the increased income is saved); consequently, sales tax revenues are less elastic with respect to income. On the expenditure side of the budget, numerous federal government programs are highly countercyclical. Programs that provide unemployment benefits, welfare assistance, and other such benefits are all examples of highly countercyclical programs: as national income rises, expenditures fall, and as national income falls, expenditures rise.

Combining both of these factors means that during an economic boom revenue growth is strong and expenditure needs are relatively weaker, making it easier to balance the budget or produce a surplus. During a recession, however, revenues fall more than proportionately, whereas expenditure needs increase. Under this set of circumstances budgets are typically in deficit.

Historical Trends in the Federal Deficit

Table 18.5 provides a long-term view of the U.S. federal budget. The left-hand side of the table reports receipts, outlays, and surplus or deficit as well as the debt held by the public in terms of billions of current dollars. The right-hand side of the table reports the same magnitudes as percentages of GDP. Figure 18.1 illustrates federal government receipts and outlays in current dollars over time. The graph shows dramatically rising federal receipts and outlays, but keep in mind that these data are in current dollars so they have inflation in them. Even more important, do not forget that the size of the U.S. economy grew dramatically over this period of time as well. Recall that measures of the size of government such as this can be misleading. We would expect that federal government receipts and outlays would grow along with growth in the economy. It is more insightful to plot receipts and outlays over time as a percent of GDP, as shown in Figure 18.2. This figure demonstrates clearly that federal receipts and outlays have stabilized at a level of just about 20 percent of GDP over the past 30 years.

Except for the effect of World War II in the 1945 data, the federal government ran either a small surplus, usually less than 1 billion dollars, or a modest deficit of less than 3 billion dollars up through 1970. After 1970 consistent deficits grew in magnitude through 1990, a reduction in the federal deficit followed in 1995, and then another reversal occurred to a surplus in 2000. Two periods of significant deficits, measured as a percent of GDP, clearly show up in Figure 18.2. First, the period extending from the Great Depression in the 1930s through World War II was marked by large deficits, especially during the war. Notice that the deficit in 1945 was $47.55 billion, which at the time was a whopping 21.9 percent of GDP. Debt held by the public at that time was 108 percent of GDP, meaning that federal government debt exceeded the output of the economy in that year. Of course, that comparison is tricky because it contrasts debt, a stock, with GDP, a flow. Nevertheless, federal debt was extremely high due to the war effort, and the public was willing to buy and hold war bonds, trusting that

TABLE 18.5 Historic U.S. Federal Budget Data

	In Billions of Dollars				As Percentages of GDP			
Year	***Receipts***	***Outlays***	***Surplus (+) or Deficit (−)***	***Debt Held by Public***[a]	***Receipts***	***Outlays***	***Surplus (+) or Deficit (−)***	***Debt Held by Public***[a]
1930	4.06	3.32	0.74	15.40	4.1	3.3	0.7	15.9
1935	3.61	6.41	−2.80	28.10	5.1	9.1	−4.0	40.9
1940	6.55	9.47	−2.92	42.77	6.7	9.7	−3.0	43.7
1945	45.16	92.71	−47.55	235.18	20.8	42.6	−21.9	108.2
1950	39.44	42.56	−3.11	219.02	14.5	15.6	−1.1	80.2
1955	65.45	68.44	−2.99	226.62	16.5	17.3	−0.8	57.2
1960	92.49	92.19	0.30	236.84	17.8	17.8	0.1	45.6
1965	116.82	118.23	−1.41	260.78	17.0	17.2	−0.2	37.9
1970	192.81	195.65	−2.84	283.20	19.1	19.4	−0.3	28.0
1975	279.09	332.33	−53.24	394.70	18.0	21.4	−3.4	25.3
1980	517.11	590.95	−73.84	709.84	19.0	21.7	−2.7	26.1
1985	734.17	946.50	−212.33	1507.36	17.7	22.9	−5.1	36.4
1990	1031.97	1253.20	−221.23	2411.83	18.0	21.8	−3.9	42.1
1995	1351.83	1515.84	−164.01	3603.80	18.5	20.7	−2.2	49.1
2000	2025.22	1788.83	236.39	3410.12	20.6	18.2	2.4	34.7
2005	2,153.6	2,471.97	−318.3	5,592.21	17.3	19.9	−2.6	36.9
2010	2,165.12	3,720.70	−1,555.58	9,297.65	14.8	25.4	−10.6	63.6

[a]Figures for debt held by the public for the years 1930 and 1935 are not comparable with later figures.

Source: *Budget of the U.S. Government Fiscal Year 2011, Historical Tables.* Tables 1.1, 1.2, and 7.1.

the federal government would pay them back in the future. Second, a period of persistent federal deficits extended from 1965 through 1995, approximately. The annual deficits during this period were relatively large in current dollars, rising to $221 billion in 1990, but as a percentage of GDP those deficits were typically less than 5 percent. Comparing deficits measured in current dollars over time does not make any sense. When comparing annual deficits over a long period of time, it is important to use deficits relative to GDP.

The explosion of federal government deficits and debt due to the financial crisis and recession of 2008 to 2009 is also apparent. The record-breaking 2010 deficit of 10.6 percent of GDP was due to both a reduction in receipts and a dramatic increase in outlays. Debt held by the public exploded from $4.6 trillion in 2005 to $9.3 trillion in 2010. As a percentage of GDP, the debt increased from 36.9 percent to 63.6 percent, a level not seen since

FIGURE 18.1 U.S. Federal Receipts and Outlays in Current Dollars ($1,000), 1930–2011

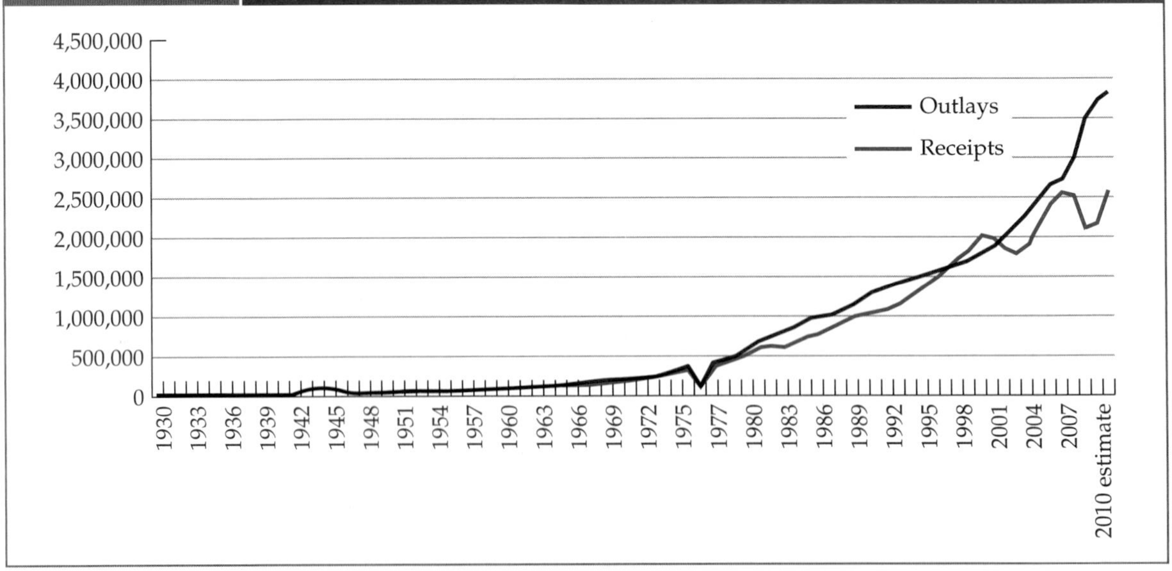

Source: *Budget of the United States Government, Fiscal Year 2011, Historical Tables*, Table 1.1. http://www.gpoaccess.gov/usbudget/fy11/hist.html.

FIGURE 18.2 U.S. Federal Receipts and Outlays as a Percentage of GDP, 1930–2011

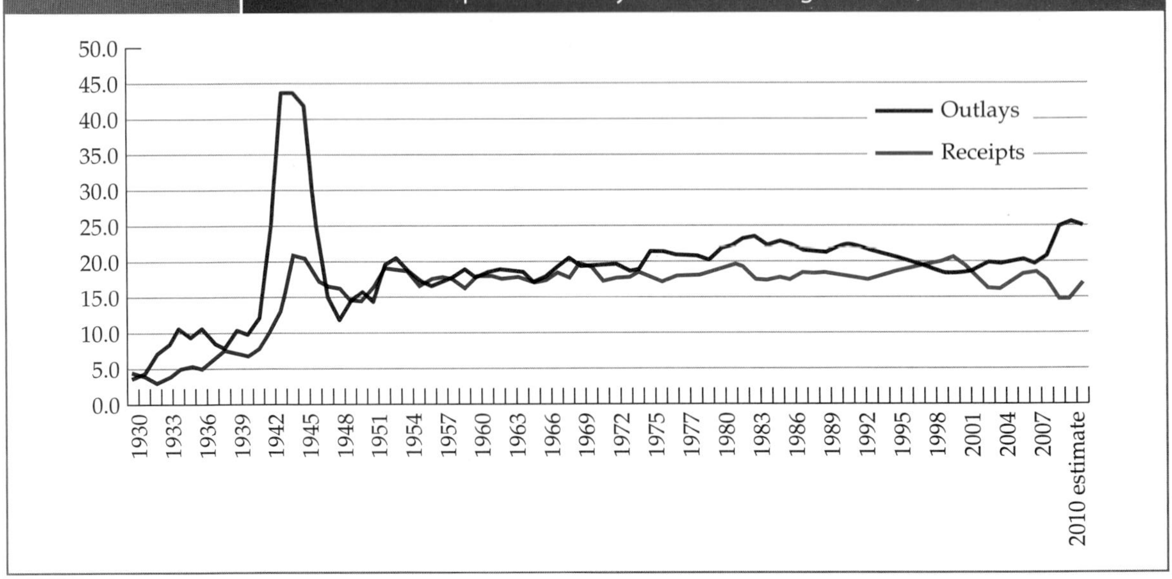

Source: *Budget of the U.S. Government Fiscal Year 2011: Historical Tables*, Table 1.2. http://www.gpoaccess.gov/usbudget/fy11/hist.html.

the immediate post–World War II era. Taking a long view, we see that over the period from 1950 to 2010 the historic average for receipts was 17.8 percent of GDP and for outlays was 20.0 percent. That means on average the deficit was 2.2 percent of GDP. In that light, the 2010 deficit of 10.6 percent of GDP can be viewed as extremely high by historic

"Our deficit-reduction plan is simple, but it will require a great deal of money."

Robert Weber/Cartoon Bank

standards. The CBO has presented its **baseline budget** outlook based on current law. CBO estimates that President Obama's budget plan will increase federal outlays to approximately 23.3 percent of GDP over the decade from 2011 to 2020, representing a very substantial increase by historic standards. With revenues estimated to come in at 20.1 percent of GDP over that same decade, CBO is forecasting a return to deficits in the range of 3 percent of GDP, but that deficit is forecast to occur atop a new larger size of the federal government with both outlays and receipts substantially larger than their historic averages.

As a general rule, the size of the federal deficit is clearly affected by macroeconomic conditions. A recession in 1975 was partly responsible for the then precedent-setting deficit of $53 billion. The double-dip recessions of the early 1980s were also definitely part of the reason for ballooning deficits from 1980 to 1985. Improving economic conditions in the late 1980s and early 1990s were responsible for moderating and declining deficits. The return to federal budget surpluses in the late 1990s and early 2000s after decades of deficits also reflects fundamental economic conditions. With a very strong economy over much of the decade of the 1990s, revenue growth caught up with expenditures and a surplus resulted in 1998 for the first time since 1969. Although politicians would like to claim credit for fiscal discipline, reining in spending, the primary reason for the surplus was the strength of revenue growth. Of course, with even less spending discipline, the size of the surplus could have been smaller. This fundamental relationship between macroeconomic conditions and the federal government deficit should make it clear that the deficit is fundamentally a product of economic conditions, rather than the other way around.

STATE AND LOCAL GOVERNMENT DEBT

State and local governments routinely use debt to finance construction of new capital projects such as schools, highways, bridges, sewer and water systems, and a host of other projects. They also use debt to smooth over the revenue flow during the year, because taxpayers may make one or two lump-sum payments of tax, but the government must provide its service continuously throughout the year. For these and other reasons, state and local governments rely on municipal bond markets for a part of their public finance. The federal government permits state and local governments to issue municipal bonds that pay interest free of federal income taxation. Because the interest paid on municipal bonds is tax-free, the state and local governments issuing the bonds can pay a lower rate of interest. As a result, state and local governments can finance their capital programs at lower interest cost than if they had to issue taxable bonds.

Municipal Bond Market

Let's consider how the municipal bond market works by asking the question: Who should buy tax-exempt bonds? Everyone? Why would any person want to hold a taxable bond when a tax-exempt bond is available? Well, with just a bit of reflection, it becomes clear that tax-exempt bonds are not appropriate for everyone. In fact, they are only appropriate for certain families with a particular characteristic. Suppose that you have a choice between a taxable bond that pays 7.5 percent interest and a municipal bond that pays tax-exempt interest of 5.5 percent. If you purchase the taxable bond, your after-tax return depends on your marginal tax rate. Assuming that you are in the 28 percent marginal tax bracket, your after-tax return on the bond is 0.72 times the rate of interest 7.5 percent. That product (0.72)(0.075) is 0.054, or 5.4 percent. Compare that to a tax-free municipal bond that pays 5.5 percent, and you see why it may be sensible to purchase a municipal bond.

FIGURE 18.3 Public and Private Sector Bond Markets

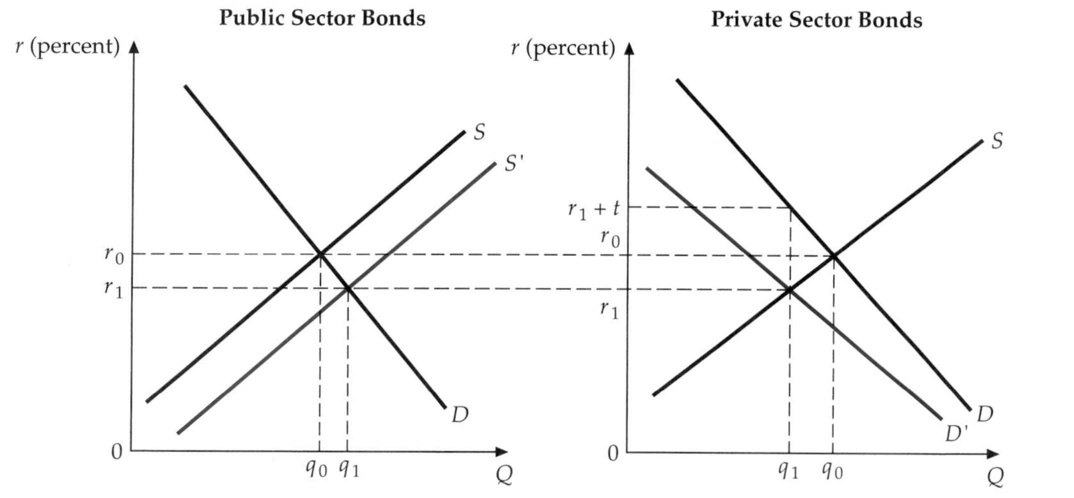

Before you leap to the conclusion that tax-free municipal bonds are for everyone, however, consider how the outcome may be different for a taxpayer in a lower marginal tax bracket. Suppose that the 15 percent marginal tax rate applies to your interest income from the bond. In that case, the taxable bond pays you an after-tax rate of return 0.85 times the interest rate of 7.5 percent. That product is 0.85 times 0.075,which is 0.06375, or 6.375 percent. Compare that to the 5.5 percent rate paid by the tax-free municipal bond and you see why municipal bonds are not for everyone. Some people are able to buy taxable bonds, pay the tax, and be left with a rate of return that is higher than the rate paid by tax-exempt bonds. It all depends on your marginal tax rate.

The rate spread between the rate of interest paid by taxable bonds and the rate of interest paid by tax-exempt bonds is important to consider. The difference in the rates is an implicit tax rate, which should approximately equal the average marginal tax rate of bondholders, making the after-tax borrowing cost the same on taxable and tax-exempt bonds. Figure 18.3 illustrates the markets for bonds. The left panel illustrates the market for public sector bonds, whereas the right panel illustrates the market for private sector bonds. Suppose that initially the rate of interest paid in the two markets is identical at r_0. Now, introduce an income tax t applied to interest in the private sector bond market. The effect of the tax is to shift the demand curve downward to D' and cause the before-tax interest rate to rise to $r_1 + t$. Of course, the after-tax interest rate paid by these private sector bonds falls to r_1. The tax has the effect of reducing the equilibrium quantity of bonds in the private sector, shifting funds into the public sector. That shift causes the supply curve in the public sector to shift rightward to S', causing the equilibrium interest rate to fall to r_1. Notice that the after-tax interest rates paid in the two sectors are identical. Private sector bonds pay the rate $r_1 + t$, whereas

FIGURE 18.4 Net Returns to Bondholders

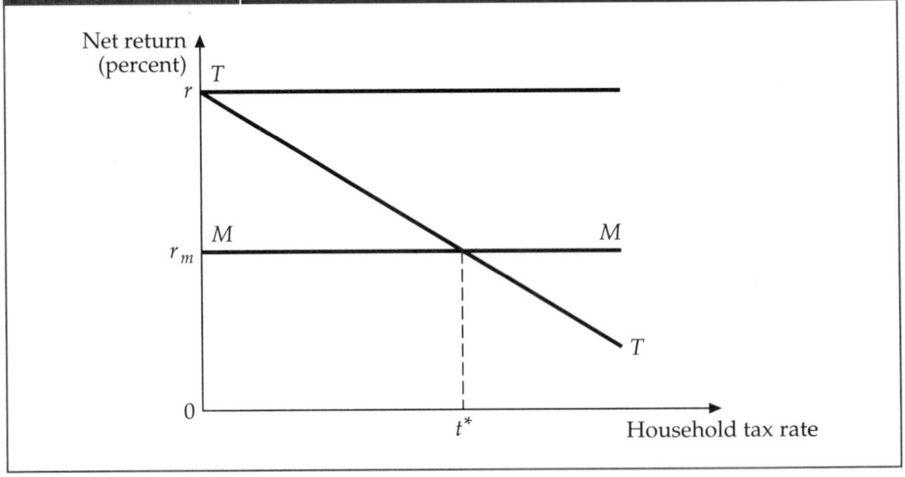

public sector bonds pay the rate r_1. After-tax, however, private sector bonds pay r_1, which is identical to the public sector rate. The difference in interest rates paid in the two sectors is an implicit tax rate, which we can denote t^*. The interest rate spread in the two markets can then be written as $r(t^* - t)$, where t is the tax rate paid by a particular bond-holding household, whereas t^* is the implicit tax determined by the bond markets.

Now, who should hold tax-exempt bonds? A household whose income tax rate is above the implicit rate t^* will find it advantageous to hold tax-exempt bonds. The tax advantage is more valuable than the forgone interest. On the other hand, a household whose tax rate is below the implicit rate t^* will find it advantageous to hold taxable bonds because the higher interest rate paid by taxable bonds is worth more to that household than the tax advantage.

Figure 18.4 illustrates the situation.[2] Line TT illustrates the net return on taxable bonds, which is declining with the household's marginal income tax rate. The net return to tax-exempt bonds is given by the line MM. This return is independent of the household's marginal income tax rate, and is therefore horizontal. Any household with a marginal tax rate greater than t^* will earn a greater after-tax return with tax-exempt bonds. In fact, such households have a clear incentive to engage in arbitrage activity, borrowing funds at the taxable rate, deducting the interest payments on their income tax return, and using the money borrowed to purchase tax-exempt bonds.[3]

> **@ ON THE WEB**
>
> *For more on municipal bonds, see the Policy Study "Bond Market Conditions and State-Local Capital Spending" on the companion website (www.cengage.com/international).*

This story has another side as well. Households with marginal tax rates below t^* have an incentive to purchase taxable bonds and could gain further from borrowing at the tax-exempt rate and then using the money borrowed to purchase taxable bonds. Of course, individual households cannot borrow at the tax-exempt rate, but the municipality in which they reside can do that. The municipality should do so until the costs of further arbitrage just equal the tax benefit. The municipal bond market may therefore operate to provide benefits to both high- and low-tax households, with households in between receiving no benefit.

TANs, BANs, and GANs

State and local governments use borrowing mechanisms frequently in order to facilitate the provision of services. A local school district may receive its property tax revenues twice a year when winter and summer taxes are collected by the county treasurer. However, the district must pay teachers, administrators, and staff, as well as pay utility bills and other expenses, on an ongoing basis all year. In order to smooth over the problem of the *lumpiness* of tax collections, local districts can use **tax anticipation notes (TANs)**. TANs are short-term debt issued for the express purpose of permitting the school district to borrow against its anticipated tax revenues. By using TANs, districts can spend in advance for six months, then pay off the debt with the property tax receipts that arrive with the next payment from the county treasurer. Of course, this method of financing the school district has its price. That price is the interest expense involved in continual borrowing. Nevertheless, TANs are widely used and very useful financing mechanisms.

Similar mechanisms are used in anticipation of bond revenue, where a municipality may issue **bond anticipation notes (BANs)**, borrowing short term in expectation of revenues to come from the sale of bonds. The same mechanism can also be used to borrow short term in expectation of grant revenue coming from the federal government. Local governments can use **grant anticipation notes (GANs)** in order to get a project underway before the actual grant monies are received.

Build America Bonds (BABs)

The American Recover and Reinvestment Act of 2009 (ARRA) included a temporary two-year innovative infrastructure financing tool for state and local governments. Build America Bonds (BABs) were provided for state and local government issuers that typically use municipal bond financing for infrastructure projects. With the financial crisis in 2008 the municipal bond market had all but seized up, so it was difficult for state and local government bond issuers to proceed with their bond-financed projects. The introduction of BABs was intended to jump-start the nearly comatose market for municipal capital and provide governments greater access to capital. As explained in Krueger (2010), BABs are taxable bonds, unlike municipal bonds, on which the U.S. Treasury Department pays a 35 percent direct subsidy to the bond issuer in place of the typical tax exempt status provided by municipal bonds. As a result, the interest cost of debt for the government issuing a BAB is reduced by 35 percent.

With a 35 percent subsidy provided to reduce the BABs interest expense for state and local governments, the net cost of borrowing may be even lower using BABs than using traditional municipal bonds. Tax exempt munis have an interest rate that is lower than the taxable market rate for comparable risk by the amount of the average marginal tax rate of the muni bond purchasers. At current tax rates, that average is below 35 percent, so BABs enable governments to borrow at a lower cost.

The Obama administration has proposed that BABs be extended with a lower 28 percent subsidy rate. The Treasury Department estimates that at this rate the BABs program would be revenue-neutral. It remains to be seen whether Congress will enact this program extension.

TAX OR BORROW: COMPARING TAX FINANCING AND DEFICIT FINANCING OF GOVERNMENT

To tax or to borrow? That is the question. Whether, 'tis nobler to finance government programs with current tax revenues than with borrowing against future tax revenues, that is the question. With apologies to William Shakespeare, we pose the essential question that state and local government units often confront. A given project the government wishes to implement may be financed either out of current tax revenue or out of borrowing through a bond issue. We need to consider the factors that affect the choice between taxing and borrowing as finance mechanisms for government services and projects.

Nature of the Project

The very nature of a project may determine whether it is appropriate to use current taxes or to borrow. Capital projects lend themselves to borrowing rather than tax financing because the benefits of the project are spread over a long period of time into the future. Rather than burden current taxpayers with the full tax burden of the capital project, it is reasonable to spread the burden over the full life of the project by borrowing up front, then paying off the debt with taxes over the life of the capital project financed. This is the method most often used, for example, to build schools, water and sewer systems, airport facilities, and other capital projects. In general, infrastructure projects such as these are likely financed with government borrowing rather than taxation.

Optimal Debt

If the nature of the project does not constrain the method of financing, and the government has access to both credit markets and tax instruments, then the question the government must consider is the optimal combination of taxes and borrowing to employ. Barrow (1994) provides helpful insight regarding optimal debt management. He suggests that the question of the optimal combination of taxation and borrowing be considered in three stages. First, if we simply have lump-sum taxes that are nondistortionary and the other conditions of Ricardian equivalence are satisfied, then the allocation of government financing between borrowing and taxation does not matter. Ricardian equivalence is a theorem based on an idea first suggested by David Ricardo in the 1800s: consumers take into account the government's budget constraint as they plan their consumption plans over time, making irrelevant whether the government taxes or borrows to fund the provision of public goods. According to this theorem, when consumers see the government borrowing to fund current expenditures, they realize that in the future taxes will be raised, hence they adjust their consumption accordingly.

Second, Barrow suggests that if taxes are distorting, due to excess burden, the timing of taxes does matter. Consequently, it is advantageous to smooth tax rates over time to minimize the excess burden of taxation. Consider the situation where the tax is applied to an individual's labor income or consumption. With either of those tax bases, an excess burden of taxation is proportional to the tax rate for reasons explained in detail in Chapters 11 and 12. Consequently, the timing of taxes over the business cycle matters. Rather than implement a countercyclical pattern of tax rates over time, it may be better to smooth the tax rates over time and supplement taxes with borrowing during the downtimes. Economic theory provides this guidance that is helpful, but it is not so precise as to specify the exact composition of government debt by maturity, however.

Third, if future real interest rates, GDP, or government expenditures are uncertain then the correspondence between tax rates and economic conditions will matter. The kinds of debt issued by the government will matter. Barrow suggests, for example, that the government may want to structure the maturity of its outstanding debt in order to protect its cost of financing from changes in real interest rates.

Interest Rates and Borrowing Constraints

Interest rates on government borrowing have an impact on the choice of funding. Of course, the cost of borrowing is primarily influenced by the rate of interest that must be paid on the capital borrowed. If interest rates on government borrowing are relatively high, there is an incentive to use tax financing of projects rather than to incur the high cost of interest expenses. Other things being equal, we expect that the lower interest rates, the more attractive deficit finance is, compared to tax finance.

Borrowing constraints are also a factor to consider. Some governments have limited access to capital markets. Laws against borrowing by subnational governments in some countries exist, especially in less developed countries. Even where borrowing is permitted, there are effective limits to the amount of borrowing that is permitted by the credit markets. In other cases, the creditworthiness of the local government limits its access to capital markets.

POLICY STUDY

Build It and They Will Come—Sports Stadia and Municipal Bond Financing

All across the United States communities have recently built or are in the process of building new stadia for professional sports teams playing baseball, basketball, and football.[4] Dennis Zimmerman (1998), a noted public finance expert with the Congressional Research Service, reported that about $6.5 billion in tax-exempt bonds were issued for new stadia over the period from 1985 to 1998. He analyzed the financing for those stadia and found that tax-exempt bonds were issued to finance about 60 percent of the construction cost; that required about $8 billion in future taxes to pay principal and interest. State and local government funds were also used to help subsidize operating costs in some cases. Is that right? Should state and local governments provide publicly funded stadia for private sports franchises? What is the public benefit? This is a fascinating example of the contemporary use of municipal bonds. Further, the public finance economist has much to contribute to the debate over public financing of new stadia.

Table 18.6 reports five principles suggested by Zimmerman for guiding the use of public funds related to stadia. First, he suggests that because a large component of the benefits provided by a stadium are private benefits enjoyed by those who attend the games, the largest share of subsidy cost should be generated from a ticket tax and other revenue sources related to the stadium. In addition, television and radio fees could generate substantially to the public subsidy provided. This set of suggestions applies the benefits principle. Those who benefit from the stadium should pay for it.

Second, in a sense, a stadium is a public good enjoyed by everyone in the community. Indeed, you will notice that some communities use sports stadia as a kind of community logo. Everyone recognizes Pittsburgh as home of Three Rivers Stadium, Saint Louis as home of Busch Stadium, Baltimore as home of Camden Yards, and so on. If there is a public good aspect to the benefits provided by a stadium, then some portion of the public subsidy should be provided through a broad-based tax such as a property tax. It may be the case, however, that citizens who attend games in the stadium get a lot more civic pride from the community playing host to a franchise than those who do not care to attend the games. If that is the case, we are back to suggesting ticket taxes and other stadium-use fees as an appropriate method of finance.

Third, although the stadium may be located in city A within the metropolitan area, the public and private benefits flow to residents throughout the attendance area that extends well beyond the city limits. Therefore, tax bases should be tapped that cover the entire geographic area, not just the host city.

Fourth, if we consider who may benefit most from stadium-related income generated, we will conclude that real estate and restaurant interests, job recipients, and businesses using the luxury skyboxes are likely beneficiaries. This identification of beneficiaries suggests taxation of real estate and restaurant owners whose property

TABLE 18.6 Suggested Principles for Stadium Financing

Principle Number	Principle Statement
1	The largest share of subsidy costs probably should be raised from a substantial ticket tax and other stadium-related revenue and from cable television and radio fees. The incidence of these taxes and fees would fall on stadium attendees and fans and on owners and players. These are the groups that receive private benefits from viewing the games or from increases in their private income.
2	Most citizens probably attach some value to the public consumption benefits from the stadium. A broad-based tax that touches all citizens, such as a property tax, might be appropriate. If, however, these benefits are valued much more by those who view the games, one might wish to consider additional stadium-related use charges such as a higher ticket tax and a tax on cable TV fees.
3	Because private and public consumption benefits are enjoyed by taxpayers in all jurisdictions within the metropolitan area, tax bases selected should cover the entire geographic attendance area.
4	Gains from the sources side of income are probably fairly concentrated among real estate and restaurant interests, those who receive the few jobs created, and businesses using their luxury boxes for business entertainment. This might argue for a special taxing district if substantial appreciation in property values is expected, and for an additional tax on tickets associated with luxury boxes to account for their source-of-income benefits (as distinct from their use-of-income benefits).
5	Large cash payments should be avoided. Debt finance will minimize intertaxpayer subsidies across time.

Source: From "Public Subsidy of Stadiums," by Dennis Zimmerman in *NTA Forum*, No. 30, March 1998, p. 4.

and businesses are directly impacted by the new stadium. In addition, taxation of skybox tickets may be justified.

Finally, Zimmerman's most important piece of advice is that large cash payments should be avoided. Whatever state and local governments do, they should not make cash payments from teams or stadium developers. Use of debt finance over a long period of time helps to minimize the intertaxpayer subsidies over time.

Now, we may ask how these principles hold up when we consider how new stadia were actually financed. The Baltimore Ravens and the Seattle Seahawks built new stadia financed primarily with lottery revenue. The problem with this financing mechanism is that the incidence of the lottery tax has no relationship to the public or private benefits provided by the stadia. In the case of the Ravens' stadium, a large proportion of the funding has been provided by preexisting lottery revenue. That means that today's taxpayers are paying a very high proportion of the cost in relation to future taxpayers. If the stadium benefits are generated over the next 30 years, why ask today's taxpayers to pay most of the public contribution?

In both Seattle and Dallas, hotel and rental car taxes were used. The problem with this policy is that those taxes are borne primarily by consumers of hotel rooms and rental cars who do not attend games at the stadium. Further, the hotel and rental car company owners and workers bear some of the burden of the tax as well. Is it fair to ask them to pay? Is their business directly related to stadium use? Probably not.

The Milwaukee Brewers stadium was financed by a five-county general sales tax. This has the advantage of matching the area taxed to the likely attendance area, but it has the disadvantage of not being appropriately focused on the private consumption beneficiaries. Furthermore, the general sales tax is quite regressive. Is it fair to ask the low-income citizens to fund the largest share of the tax burden?

Popular new sources of revenue include the so-called *personal seat license* (PSL), naming rights, and pouring rights. The PSLs require ticket consumers and skybox businesses to pay for the right to purchase tickets. Naming and pouring rights require businesses to pay substantial fees to have their name attached to a facility or to have their product exclusively sold at the stadium.

POLICY STUDY

The Balanced Budget Amendment

In 1995 the 104th Congress Joint Resolution 1 proposed a balanced budget amendment to the U.S. Constitution. The resolution read as follows:

> Resolved by the Senate and House of Representatives of America in Congress assembled (two-thirds of each House concurring therein), that the following article is proposed as an amendment to the Constitution of the United States, which shall be valid to all intents and purposes as part of the Constitution when ratified by the legislature of three-fourths of the several States within seven years after the date of its submission to the States for ratification:
>
> Article. 1A
>
> Section 1. Total outlays for any fiscal year shall not exceed total receipts for that fiscal year, unless three-fifths of the whole number of each House of Congress shall provide by law for a specific excess of outlays over receipts by a roll call vote.
>
> Section 2. The limit on the debt of the United States held by the public shall not be increased, unless three-fifths of the whole number of each House shall provide by law for such an increase by a roll call vote.
>
> Section 3. Prior to each fiscal year, the President shall transmit to the Congress a proposed budget for the United States Government for that fiscal year in which total outlays do not exceed total receipts.
>
> Section 4. No bill to increase revenue shall become law unless approved by a majority of the whole number of each House by a roll call vote.
>
> Section 5. The Congress may waive the provision of this article for any fiscal year in which a declaration of war is in effect. The provisions of this article may be waived for any fiscal year in which the United States is engaged in military conflict, which causes an imminent and serious military threat to national security and is so

declared by a joint resolution, adopted by a majority of the whole number of each House, which becomes law.

Section 6. The Congress shall enforce and implement this article by appropriate legislation, which may rely on estimates of outlays and receipts.

Section 7. Total receipts shall include all receipts of the United States Government except those derived from borrowing. Total outlays shall include all outlays of the United States Government except for those for repayment of debt principal.

Section 8. This article shall take effect beginning with fiscal year 2002 or the second fiscal year beginning after its ratification, whichever is later.

Criticism of the Amendment

Professor Gary Evans in his book *Red Ink: The Budget, Deficit, and Debt of the U.S. Government* (1997) points to four serious flaws in this proposed amendment:

1. There is no enforcement provision. If the conditions are not met it is not clear what must be done by whom. If the Supreme Court would end up in a role of enforcement, a constitutional crisis could easily result.
2. Section 2 requires that "the limit on the debt of the United States held by the public shall not be increased." This requirement is vague. At present, there is no limit on the debt held by the public. The statutory limit on debt presently applies to total debt, not that held by the public.
3. The federal government will run a deficit in any year for which the economy is in recession. This will occur due to the recession's impact on taxes. The proposed amendment makes no provision for this occurrence. The difficult question raised is whether outlays must be cut by some automatic procedure in the middle of the recession, making the recession worse.
4. Economic policy of this type is not typically included in the same document containing the Bill of Rights. It may not be wise or prudent to place such specific economic policy into the Constitution.

History of Attempts to Pass the Amendment

The version of the amendment provided here passed the House of Representatives on January 26, 1995. The vote in the Senate failed by one single vote. In another attempt in the Senate the following year, it failed again. The same issue was raised yet again in a vote in the Senate in March of 1997 and failed to gain enough support. Over the period from 1998 to 2001 federal deficits turned to surpluses and concern for balancing the federal government budget dissipated. Although the period of surplus was brief, with the federal budget returning to a deficit in 2002 and deficits experienced in subsequent fiscal years, the intense concern for balancing the federal budget has heated up as unprecedented fiscal deficits have been experienced in 2010 and 2011.

The history of attempts to force the federal government to balance its budget is replete with gimmicks and politically motivated mechanisms. The reality of the constitutional framework is that Congress has the responsibility to act in a fiscally prudent manner. Although that is difficult, given political pressures to grant favors in the form of expenditures and tax breaks to constituents, the balance of powers between the executive and legislative branches of the U.S. federal government stipulated in the Constitution is designed to provide an adequate degree of flexibility without putting the government into a straightjacket. When the economy slips into a recession, these realities are brought home once again.

POLICY STUDY

State Rainy Day Funds

An important innovation in state budgets for the past 25 years is the so-called *rainy day fund* that many states have implemented. Based on the old adage that one should set something aside for a rainy day, these funds are a means by which states can set aside some of the revenues they receive during strong periods of revenue growth in order to tide the state over during a subsequent period of weak revenue performance of the state's economy. In market-based economies inevitably boom and bust periods occur, yielding something of a cycle of ups and downs in the output and income of the economy. That cycle in output and income leads to a similar cycle in tax revenues received by the state government, illustrated in Figure 18.5.

But government services are required on a regular basis. The state prison system and the university system, to name just two expenditure needs, must operate on a predictable basis across the cycle of ups and downs in the revenue flow. The linear upward trend in Figure 18.5 illustrates the desired expenditure path. Hence, it is sensible for the state to take the revenue in excess of the desired expenditure path between point *a* to point *c* in the business cycle and place that revenue in a fund, protected from current use. At a later time when revenues are declining due to a recession, between points *c* and *e*, the state can then use the fund balance to supplement the weak revenue flow and keep funding state services along the desired growth path.

Figure 18.5 illustrates a second round in the process, with one slight difference. The revenues set aside between points *e* and *g* are not sufficient to fund the expenditure requirement of a more serious recession between points *g* and *i*. That is a reality all rainy day funds must struggle to overcome. The revenue set aside during good times may not be sufficient to smooth over the next round of bad times. Yet, ultimately the state is in much better shape than if it had set nothing aside. A difficulty also arises as revenues are declining during a recession while desired expenditures are

FIGURE 18.5 Rationale for a Rainy Day Fund

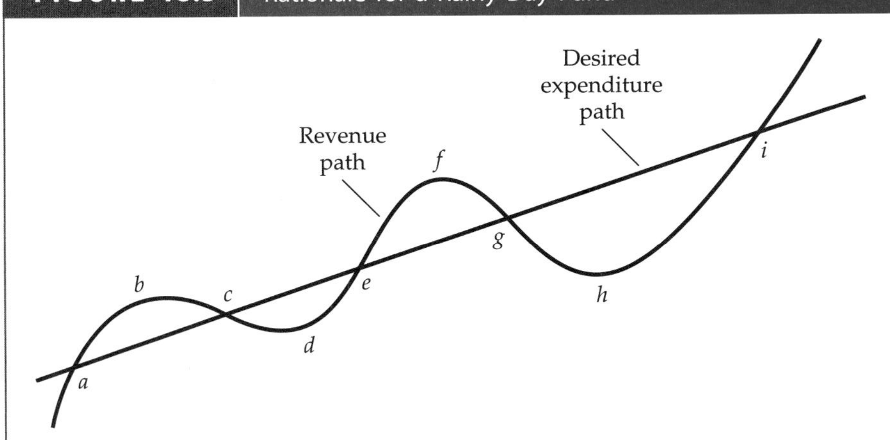

rising. For example, from point *b* to point *d* in the cycle revenues are on a downward trajectory while desired expenditures continue to rise. The political reality in this circumstance is that legislators become nervous and uncomfortable continuing to spend the revenues socked away over the part of the cycle from point *a* to point *c* while revenues appear to be in a downward freefall.

The real political problem with rainy day funds is that they are attractive targets when the balance grows large. It is difficult for some politicians to sit back and let the fund work as designed. When the balance in the fund grows to a reasonably large amount in the first boom time, it is tempting to propose a tax cut or a new expenditure program to use those funds. If the state falls prey to such shortsighted thinking, there is nothing left in the rainy day fund for the rainy day. As a result of such political opportunism, some state rainy day funds are totally inadequate for even a light sprinkle, much less a real downpour.

PROBLEMS

1. Explain how each of the following events would affect the federal government budget deficit, as it is measured by the government. Be sure to distinguish between one-time effects and permanent effects, if appropriate.
   a. Congress decides to sell the Grand Canyon to a consortium of private investors who will operate private tourist enterprises.
   b. Congress appropriates $500 million for construction of a new bridge next year. Toll revenue will result in $10 million per year during the 50-year life of the bridge.
   c. Congress passes a bill to privatize the National Park Service, granting rights to the Marriott Corporation to run the park service in all national parks.
   d. Congress decides to completely privatize the social security program, removing all federal government involvement with payroll taxes, provision of benefits, and trust fund balances.
2. Suppose that a local government has a choice between financing the construction of a new facility with an excise tax of 5 percent applied to the taxed commodity in the year 2000 or a series of 1 percent taxes for each of five years from 2000 to 2004. On the basis of the excess burden created by these two options, which is preferable?
3. Using a two-sector model, as illustrated in Figure 18.3, demonstrate the effects of an increase in the income tax rate. Explain what implications you would expect in the private and public sector bond markets.
4. Using a two-sector model, as illustrated in Figure 18.3, demonstrate the effects of a federal government policy change that limits the quantity of municipal bonds that can be issued by state and local governments. Explain what implications you would expect in the private and public sector bond markets.

5. Many states have capital budgets as well as operating budgets. As you have learned in this chapter, the federal government does not.
   a. It is frequently noted in discussions of the federal budget and national debt that most states are prohibited from having budget deficits, and therefore the federal government should also be able to "live within its means" and have an annually balanced budget. Evaluate this argument in light of this difference in the budget systems of the federal government and the states.
   b. Identify some items that might be included in a federal government capital budget if such a system were adopted.
6. The Caldwell family is in the 28 percent federal income tax bracket. They are discussing the relative merits of using some of the household savings to buy a bond for a city water plant project that will pay 5.5 percent tax-free interest versus the alternative of buying a bond offered by the local electric power company that will pay 8 percent interest that is taxable. Which investment will provide the higher after-tax return for the Caldwells?
7. Suppose that r is the rate of growth of desired expenditure in Figure 18.5, whereas p is the growth rate along the actual revenue path.
   a. Explain the relationship between r and p at points a, b, c, and d in Figure 18.5.
   b. As explained in the text, a rainy day fund can accumulate a positive balance from point a to point c in the business cycle to use from point c to point e in the cycle. An alternative design for the fund is to accumulate funds as long as the rate of growth of revenue p exceeds the desired rate of growth in expenditure r. Explain how that type of fund would work in terms of Figure 18.5.
   c. Suppose that your state government is at point f in Figure 18.5. Explain what newspaper accounts will say about state revenues from point f to point h. What will the stories say about the state government as it continues to spend along the desired expenditure path?

REFERENCES

Barrow, Robert J. "Optimal Debt Management." National Bureau of Economic Research (NBER), Cambridge, MA. Working Paper 5327, 1995.

Evans, Gary R. *Red Ink: The Budget, Deficit, and Debt of the U.S. Government.* San Diego, CA: Academic, 1997.

Gordon, Roger H., and Gilbert E. Metcalf. "Do Tax-Exempt Bonds Really Subsidize Municipal Capital?" *National Tax Journal* 44 (1991): 71–79.

Holtz-Eakin, Douglas. "Bond Market Conditions and State-Local Capital Spending." *National Tax Journal* 44 (1991): 105–20.

Krueger, Alan B. Testimony before the Senate Banking, Housing and Urban Affairs Committee, September 21, 2010. Available at: http://www.treasury.gov/press-center/press-releases/Pages/tg863.aspx.

Office of Management and Budget, 2011. Budget of the United States Government, Fiscal Year 2011. Washington, DC: U.S. Government Printing Office, 2011.

Zimmerman, Dennis. "Public Subsidy of Stadiums." *NTA Forum* 30 (1998): 1–2, 4–5.

NOTES

1. Material in this section is based on "The Budget System and Concepts," *Budget of the United States Government, Fiscal Year 2011*, Washington, DC: U.S. Government Printing Office, 2011.
2. This figure and the accompanying arguments are adapted from Gordon and Metcalf (1991).
3. For more on this topic see Gordon and Metcalf (1991).
4. A few notable examples are privately funded, AT&T Park in San Francisco, for example.

Radius Images/Getty Images

CHAPTER 19

Multilevel Government Finance

LEARNING OBJECTIVES

1. Explain the framework for analyzing relationships between federal, state, and local governments.
2. Discuss expenditure and tax assignment to levels of government.
3. Explain the economics of grants, mandates, and fiscal disparities.

Put yourself in the shoes of Rick Scott, governor of Florida. You are the chief public official in a state of 18.5 million people, larger than many countries of the world, yet your state is not sovereign.[1] It is 1 of 50 states in a federation where each state's rights are limited by the terms of the federation. A federal government is above you and 1,623 local governments below you, including 66 counties, 411 municipalities, 95 school districts, and 1,051 special district governments.[2] Your state government generates nearly $36 billion in state tax revenue, whereas local governments generate over $37 billion in revenue. The federal government provides nearly $20 billion in intergovernmental transfers to your state government and another $489 million to local governments in your state. In turn, your state government sends about $22 billion in intergovernmental transfers to local governments in the state.

Think of the systems of governments in the state, the many questions that have been answered in the development of these systems, and the remaining fiscal relations between governments that require attention. How many local governments should there be in the state? Do the residents of Hollywood have a different demand for public services than the residents of Miami? Should some of the smaller school districts consolidate in order to provide schooling at lower cost? What taxes should the state use? Does it make sense that Florida relies on sales taxes for three-quarters of its tax revenue, and not have a personal income tax at all? Should differences in spending between a high-spending school district in wealthy West Palm Beach and a low-spending district in less wealthy Clewiston be equalized in order to assure students have equal access to education? Did the election fiasco of 2000 reveal fundamental problems with county election services that require a state mandate in order to assure more fair and equitable elections? These and many other questions are at the heart of government finance in the presence of a multilevel U.S. government system, and they are the stuff of fiscal federalism.

In this chapter we consider the special reasons for and problems stemming from multilevel government. In the United States there is a federal government structure below which state governments operate. Each state has counties, townships, cities, and villages. Within any one of those local government units, there are library districts, water districts, school districts, and a whole host of other local governments. We want to examine the reasons why multiple levels of government exist and also consider the financing problems that arise from that situation.

In Chapter 1 we discussed the federation form of government. The comparison between the United States and the European Union (EU), for example, reflects two different conceptions of the role and importance of a central government. In the United States, the 50 states cede certain powers to the central, or federal, government but retain certain powers for themselves. The U.S. Constitution lays out the powers of the central government and explicitly leaves all other powers to the states. The central government is granted sufficient powers to enable it to act in the interests of the people in providing adequate defense and engaging in international affairs, but the states carry the primary burden of educating the people, providing public safety, and administering justice. In the European Union (EU), however, a collection of 15 sovereign states are currently groping for some form of central government. At this point, they have agreed to cooperate in a monetary union and reduce barriers to economic cooperation. They have yet to form a central government with significant powers, however. The European Commission and the European Parliament may someday be vested with significant powers, but for now the EU is a loose confederation of states reminiscent of the early U.S. states prior to the adoption of the Constitution. At the heart of the issue is the fiscal relationship between the central government and lower-level governments in a federation, or confederation, of states. The fiscal relationship among states at various levels in a federation is called **fiscal federalism**. The nature and scope of that relationship depends critically on the cultural and institutional setting involved, but the essential features of the fiscal relations between central and lower-level governments are common to all federations.

In federations and other forms of government, there are important issues regarding relationships and responsibilities among the governments at different levels. Although U.S. and other federation public finance economists typically refer to this set of issues as fiscal federalism, the issues of multilevel government finance apply just as directly in other contexts. Governments can be categorized by their level and reach. First-level governments include villages, towns, and cities. Sometimes the first-level governments have subdivisions. For example, the City of New York is composed of five boroughs: Manhattan, the Bronx, Queens, Brooklyn, and Staten Island. New Orleans is made up of parishes, a name for submunicipal level government taken from the British church-based unit of government. Although these are distinct units of government, they are subdivisions of the city government. Also at the first level are townships and counties. Second-level governments are a step higher in aggregation and include states, as in the United States, or provinces, as in Canada. The third-level government is typically the central, or federal, government.

FISCAL FEDERALISM: A FRAMEWORK FOR ANALYSIS

Wallace Oates, a leading economist who has conducted pioneering research on fiscal federalism, defines a **federal government** as one with:

> A public sector with both centralized and decentralized levels of decision-making in which choices made at each level concerning the provision of public services are determined largely by the demands for those services of the residents of (and perhaps others who carry on activities in) the respective jurisdiction. (1972, 17)

Subnational, or local, governments have been justified in the U.S. federal system for two primary reasons.[3] First, representative democracy seems to work best the closer the government is to its constituency. The presumption is that a local government will be better at perceiving the desires and demands of its constituents for public services than a distant centralized government. For this reason, transition economies and government systems around the world are currently undergoing a process of **decentralization**, pushing responsibilities and resources to lower levels of government than was typical in the highly centralized systems of the past. Second, subsets of people in the country have the right to demand different types and quantities of public goods and services. It is unnecessary for a uniform menu of public services or a fixed level of those services to be provided nationally. Indeed, clear benefits exist from allowing subsets of national residents to demand different arrays of services. This principle lies at the heart of so-called **states' rights** that have been an important policy issue since pre–Civil War days. The issue with states' rights involves the relative powers of the states versus the central government. The debate is an old one, going all the way back to the formation of the United States. In the debates over the nature and function of governments, it was Alexander Hamilton who advocated a relatively strong central government and Thomas Jefferson who favored relatively powerful states. During the extended debate over the U.S. Constitution, it was the Anti-Federalists who argued in favor of the Bill of Rights in order to assure state sovereignty—protecting from the federal government the rights already assured by the states.[4] From their point of view, there would have been no need for a Bill of Rights if the Constitution properly assigned power to the states in a loose form of confederation with a weak central government. James Madison proposed an institutional structure of checks and balances among the branches of the central government in order to rely on "opposite and rival interests" among the legislative, executive, and judicial branches of government.

George Stigler (a Nobel Prize–winning economist) concludes that these principles imply we should ". . . give each governmental activity to the smallest governmental unit which can efficiently perform it . . ." (1957, 219). In other words, using the Musgravian framework, decision making should occur at the lowest level of government that is consistent with the twin goals of allocational efficiency and distributional equity. Indeed, Stigler saw strong local governments ". . . a basic ingredient of a society which seeks to give to the individual the fullest possible freedom and responsibility" (1957, 219). From Stigler's perspective, one could ask why anything *but* local government is needed. However, Stigler's rule also indicates that national government is required in some cases in order to achieve allocational efficiency or distributional equity.

Perfect Correspondence

Stigler's principle was formalized and became the foundation for thinking about fiscal federalism when Wallace Oates defined the concept of **perfect correspondence**. Perfect correspondence exists in a system of multilevel governments when there is one level of government for each subset of the population over which the consumption of a public good is specified. The jurisdiction that provides that public good and determines the amount of its provision includes exactly those individuals who are consuming that public good. Each level of government has complete and perfect knowledge of the wishes of its constituents and acts in such a way as to maximize their welfare. By having such a perfect correspondence in the system of governments, the benefits from the provision of each public good are enjoyed by those in the community and there are no externalities. This outcome assures the Pareto-efficient provision of public services. The public services would then be financed through a system of benefit pricing whereby each resident would pay in accordance with the benefits received. A perfect correspondence also limits the size of each government unit. The government is no larger than required in order to provide the public good to its constituents. The limits of geography and the output range over which public good provision can be provided naturally limit government size. The question that arises, however, is whether local decision making is necessary in order to provide perfect correspondence. Couldn't a national government recognize the situations that require local variation in the provision of public goods and implement provision mechanisms that take this into account? Theoretically, it could.

Decentralization Theorem

A compelling argument for a federal system of governments is not based solely on the concept of perfect correspondence. A further justification is provided in Oates's **decentralization theorem**, stated as follows:

> For a public good—the consumption of which is defined over geographical subsets of the total population, and for which the costs of providing each level of output of the good in each jurisdiction are the same for the central or the respective local government—it will always be more efficient (or at least as efficient) for local governments to provide the Pareto-efficient levels of output for their respective jurisdictions than for the central government to provide *any* specified and uniform level of output across all jurisdictions. (1972, 35)

An important policy arena in which we see the implications of the decentralization theorem clearly revealed is public education. The rallying cry in the realm of K–12 local public education is for "local control." Although there may be clear fiscal incentives for consolidation or equity bases for reducing the disparities across school districts, the desire for local control is strong and receives voice in public debates. Because subsets of the population have quite different demands for local public education, they rightly perceive that they would be worse off with a given fixed level of education provided by a central government. People want the right to select the quantity of public education locally.

Consider a simple example with two communities: Central City and East Pointe. The demand for schooling in each community is illustrated in Figure 19.1. The residents of East Pointe clearly have a greater demand for schooling at any given price than do the residents of Central City. This is caused by their higher income. The marginal cost of producing schooling is assumed to be the same in both communities and is denoted *MC*. The efficient levels of education to provide in the two communities are those where the communities' demand for schooling equals the marginal cost of producing schooling (recall that the reason for this is the Samuelson rule) and are denoted S^*. As you can see, the efficient level of schooling that should be provided in Central City is less than that in East Pointe. We would expect, therefore, to observe the two school boards responding to community desires for education and providing two distinctly different schooling levels.

If a central government were to step in and provide a uniform level of schooling *S* in both communities, the residents in both cases would be made worse off. The residents of Central City would be made worse off by the amount of the triangle *abc*, and those of East Pointe would be made worse

FIGURE 19.1 Decentralization Theorem Example

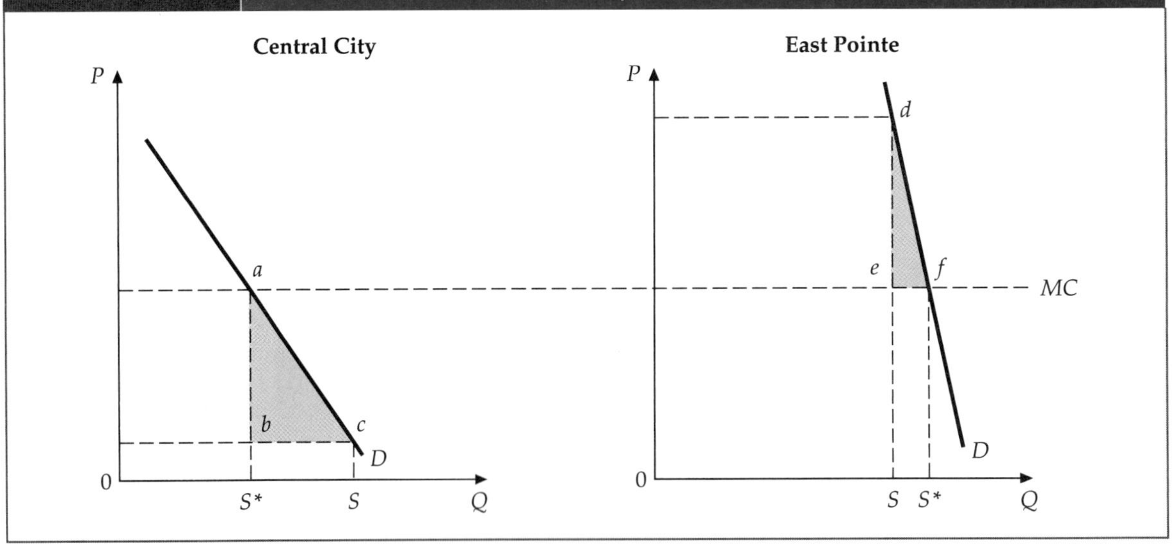

off by the triangle *def*. In both cases these triangles measure the welfare loss to the residents over and above the change in the total value of schooling provided. (Recall that we made this same argument when discussing the Samuelson rule in Chapter 3.) Residents of Central City are forced to accept a higher level of schooling than they desire for their children, and the value they place on that welfare loss is greater than the cost of providing the additional schooling. Similarly, East Pointe residents are forced to accept less schooling than they desire for their children, and the value they place on that reduction is greater than the cost savings of the reduced schooling. The decentralization theorem holds that it is more efficient for the two communities to provide the efficient levels of schooling than for a central government to provide a uniform level of schooling.

Several implications of the decentralization theorem deserve highlighting. First, welfare losses increase with heterogeneity and decrease with homogeneity. The more different, or heterogeneous, the two communities, the greater the welfare loss from providing a uniform level of the public good. If communities are identical, or homogeneous, then the welfare loss from providing identical public service levels disappears. Second, the size of the welfare loss depends on the price elasticity of demand: The more inelastic the demand, the smaller the welfare loss. In Figure 19.1 the demand for education in East Pointe was drawn as less elastic than the demand in Central City (compare the relative slopes). The steeper the demand curve, the smaller the welfare loss triangle for any given change in the quantity of public good provided. Third, if economies of scale are in the production of the public good, the optimal jurisdiction size will be larger. Economies of scale result in declining costs, and hence it is efficient to provide the good in larger quantities. In that case, the two communities could consolidate and provide schooling at lower cost per pupil, saving resources.

Measurement of Decentralization

We measure the extent to which a country's system of governments is decentralized by computing the decentralization ratio: the proportion of government revenues received or expenditures made by subnational governments. For example, if the central government spends \$6.5 billion while subnational governments spend \$3.5 billion, the decentralization ratio is 0.35 (3.5/10.0). The decentralization ratio can be computed in two ways, depending on whether one uses revenue data or expenditure data.

Some countries such as Egypt, Ethiopia, Japan, Korea, New Zealand, and Pakistan have completely centralized systems where the central government accounts for 100 percent of all government expenditures.[5] In those cases the decentralization ratio is zero. Other countries have more decentralized fiscal systems where subnational governments account for at least 30 percent of total government expenditures, yielding a decentralization ratio of at least 0.30 or more. Those countries include Brazil, Canada, Germany, Sweden, Switzerland, and the United States. For example, the U.S. decentralization ratio is approximately 0.35, indicating that subnational governments are responsible for 35 percent of total government expenditure.

Figure 19.2 illustrates World Bank measures of decentralization for selected countries in Eastern and Central Europe in the 1990s during a significant period of transition. This figure reports subnational expenditures as a share of total government expenditures. These shares are computed two ways in Figure 19.2: blue bars report the subnational share of total government expenditures, and gray bars report the subnational share of adjusted expenditures where national defense expenditures have been removed. All of the countries listed in the chart were formerly highly centralized owing to their political regimes. In recent years, all of these countries have been engaged in decentralization to some extent. Most of these countries now have subnational governments responsible for about 20 percent of all government expenditures. Belarus and Russia are higher at about 40 percent, and the

FIGURE 19.2 World Bank Measures of Decentralization for Transition Countries[7]

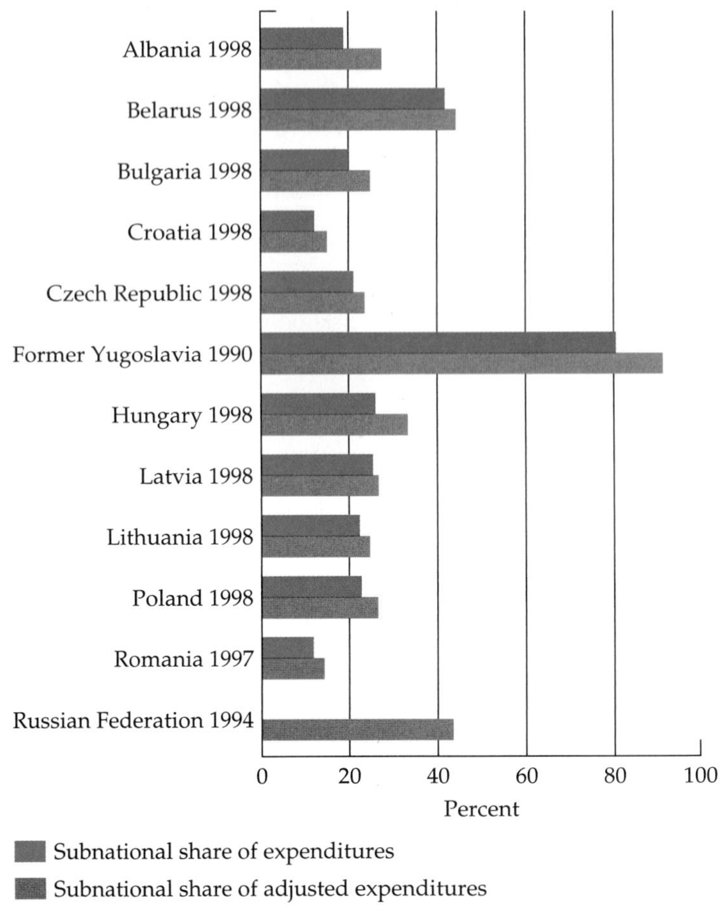

Source: IMF, Government Finance Statistics, 2001. Reprinted by permission of International Monetary Fund.

former Yugoslavia tops the chart at about 80 percent.[6] Evidence provided in DeMelo (1999) indicates that decentralization in transition economies has had the effect of increasing the size of subnational governments.

EXPENDITURE AND TAX ASSIGNMENT

The assignment of expenditure functions to levels of government in a federal system should be based on a clear set of criteria so that sensible sets of responsibilities are given to federal, state, and local governments. Although it would be nice to be able to say that such a clear set of criteria exist and are assiduously followed, that is not the case.

Expenditure Assignment

In general, we can say that the federal government is assigned responsibilities where significant externalities or redistribution are involved. For example, the federal government has the responsibility to provide national defense, because positive externalities are involved in making a single federal defense program much more efficient than 50, state defense programs. In the area of environmental policy we would also expect the federal government to take the lead in policy-making because each region would otherwise have an incentive to simply dump its waste and encourage activity that degrades the environment of other jurisdictions. State and local governments should be given responsibilities to oversee the provision of local public goods, consistent with the decentralization theorem.

Tax Assignment

In similar fashion, the responsibility for taxation should be allocated to levels of government in a federal system in such a way that the most highly redistributive taxes are levied at the federal level and other taxes are levied at the subnational level. That would mean, for example, that although both federal and state governments might tax income, the state income taxes should be less progressive than the federal income tax. Musgrave and Musgrave's summarization of their classic recommendations for tax assignment is given in Table 19.1. At the central government level, taxes should include a progressive income tax (if progressivity is desired, this is the place for it), estate or inheritance taxes, and taxes on natural resources (things like oil, natural gas, coal, and uranium). State or provincial governments should use income taxes (less progressive than the central government's income tax) and retail sales taxes. In addition, they should tax income earned by factors of production (labor and capital) that are owned abroad but originate in the state. For example, the state should tax the net income of a foreign corporation when that income is generated by a factory it owns in the United States. The Kawasaki factory that makes jet skis in Lincoln, Nebraska, should be taxed under the Nebraska state income tax. States should also use origin-type product taxes as benefit charges. For example, Florida could implement an orange tax applied to all oranges and orange juice produced in the state, regardless

TABLE 19.1 Tax Assignment

	Taxes			
Central government	Progressive income tax	Death/estate taxes	Natural resource taxes	
State/provincial government	Income tax on individuals	Income tax on factors of production owned abroad but originating in the jurisdiction	Retail sales tax	Origin-type product tax as a benefit charge
Local government	Real estate property tax	Payroll tax	Benefit charges	

Source: Musgrave and Musgrave 1989, 470.

of where it is consumed (origin-type tax rather than destination-type tax, as discussed in Chapter 16). The purpose of the tax would be to provide state services that benefit the orange-growing industry, such as research on developing blight-proof and frost-resistant breeds of oranges. At the local government level, the appropriate taxes are property taxes, payroll taxes, and benefit charges. Property taxes belong at the local level because as ability-based taxes they are used to provide benefits for local property owners. Street and curb improvements, for example, directly enhance the value of property in the city and should be financed with a tax on property owners. Similarly, the payroll tax belongs at the local level as it is used to provide public safety. Workers in the city earn wage payments as a result of their employment in the city, which provides them with police and fire protection at their places of employment. Benefit charges are appropriate at the local level in order to fund specific services provided. For example, it is appropriate for Naperville, Illinois, to charge a fee for the privilege of depositing trash in the city's landfill. That fee is a direct benefit charge and belongs at the local level.

When multiple levels of government use the same tax base, such as income, it is important to consider the role of deductibility. Which taxes paid at one level should be made deductible at other levels? Should the taxes paid at the local level be deductible from taxable income at the federal level, and vice versa? George Break has summarized the basic argument for income tax deductibility as follows: In a multilevel government setting where governments use the income tax, each government should tax on the basis of income minus the ability-to-pay-based taxes of the other government units. In order to accomplish that outcome, deductibility is needed. Consider the case of income tax deductibility. Because a state income tax is ability based, it should be deductible on the federal income tax. Local property taxes are more likely benefit-based taxes; hence, deductibility for property taxes is not justified. The state and local sales tax is a hybrid combination of an ability-based tax and a benefit-based tax, so no clear conclusion is drawn regarding its deductibility at the federal level.[8] Table 19.2 provides examples of both

TABLE 19.2 Tax Classification

Ability-Based Taxes ⟵		⟶ Benefit-Based Taxes
Income tax	Sales tax	User fees
Consumption tax		Tolls
Wealth tax		Complementary goods taxes (e.g., gasoline excise tax)
Payroll tax		Property tax

Source: Break 1986.

ability-based taxes and benefit-based taxes. Consider the first row of the table as a continuum from ability based on the left to benefit based on the right. The income tax, consumption taxes (such as VAT), wealth taxes, and payroll taxes are all ability based. At the other extreme are benefit-based taxes such as user fees, tolls, taxes on complementary goods such as the gasoline excise tax used for road maintenance, and the property tax. In between is the sales tax, which is neither purely ability based nor purely benefit based.

GRANTS

Grants are an important means by which central governments transfer funds to subnational governments in order to facilitate decentralization of services while maintaining centralization of tax collection.

Taxonomy of Grants

Grants are categorized by three main characteristics. First, the type of grant depends on whether the funds provided by the grant are restricted to certain spending categories or are unrestricted. Second, the type of grant depends on whether the amount of the grant is open-ended or closed-ended. Third, the type of grant depends on whether the grant requires matching by the local government. Table 19.3 provides a taxonomy of grants with examples of each type. The economic effects of grants vary with the characteristics of the grants, as delineated in Table 19.3.

Categorical Versus Noncategorical Grants

A **categorical grant** provides funds with a restriction that the money be used for a specific purpose, or category of spending, whereas a **noncategorical grant** is an unrestricted grant that can be spent on anything. Noncategorical grants are also called **revenue sharing**, because they are used by the central government as a means to share revenue it collects with subnational

TABLE 19.3 Economic Taxonomy of Grants, with Examples

	Noncategorical (Unrestricted)		Categorical (Restricted)	
	Open-Ended	***Closed-Ended***	***Open-Ended***	***Closed-Ended***
Matching	Aid to Families with Dependent Children (AFDC)		Medicaid School aid provided through district power equalization	Federal transportation grants to states for highway construction
Nonmatching		Temporary Assistance for Needy Families (TANF) Community development block grants		State grants to local governments for gambling addiction programs

governments. Because noncategorical grants are unrestricted in their use, they have an effect similar to that of winning the lottery (a pure income effect with no price changes). Imagine being the lucky recipient of \$1 million. What would you do with the money? Spend it, save it, or do some of both? Let's consider a unit of local government that has just been notified that it has been selected to receive a large noncategorical grant from the federal government. The local unit of government purchases goods and services in the amount g in order to provide the local public goods and services that its citizens desire. It purchases those goods and services at price p_g. Residents of the community also purchase private goods and services in the amount of c at price p_c. Their total expenditure on public and private goods is given by

$$E = p_c c + p_g g. \tag{19.1}$$

If we graph this budget constraint in g-c space, we find that the budget set is the triangle formed by the axes and the line

$$C = E/p_c - (p_g/p_c)g, \tag{19.2}$$

where the c intercept is the term E/p_c and the slope is $-p_g/p_c$. The c intercept represents the maximum amount of private consumption possible if nothing is spent on the public good g. If the community moves away from that point (in the southeasterly direction), they can purchase units of g by giving up units of c. The relative price of g as compared to c provides the trade-off the community may follow as it exchanges units of private good consumption for the public good.

Now, if the community receives a grant in the amount of G from a higher-level government agency, it has available all of its prior expenditure E plus the new grant monies G. The budget equation becomes

$$E + G = p_c c + p_g g, \tag{19.3}$$

which can be solved for viewing in g-c space and written as the budget line

$$c = (E + G)/p_c - (p_g/p_c)g. \tag{19.4}$$

The effect of the grant is to shift the budget line outward, parallel to the original budget line. The c intercept increases from E/p_c to $(E + G)/p_c$ and the g intercept increases from E/p_g to $(E + G)/p_g$. The slope is unaffected by the grant because the grant does not alter either price p_c or price p_g.

Figure 19.3 illustrates the effect of a noncategorical, nonmatching grant. The original budget line is shifted out to the new budget line. The grant simply causes a parallel shift of the budget line outward. How does the community respond to the receipt of the grant? As with any increase in income, resulting in a parallel shift of the budget line, the community will increase its consumption of both private goods c and public goods g (as long as both goods are normal goods—goods whose consumption is increased when income rises). Given the community's preferences, captured in the indifference curves illustrated, the grant will result in an increase in the provision of the public good from g_1 to g_2 and will also enable consumption of other goods to increase from c_1 to c_2.

The effect of the grant is to enable the community to operate on the higher (blue) budget line and increase community welfare by moving out to a higher indifference curve. If the community moved rightward from a point on the old budget line to a point on the new budget line, maintaining consumption of other goods at c_1, it maintains the private consumption level of its residents, but enables residents to have more of the government-provided public good. Thus the grant provides added public goods with no change in private consumption or in taxes paid to fund the local government. On the other hand, the community could choose to move straight upward from a point on the old (black) budget line to a point on the new (blue) budget line, maintaining the level of public good provision at g_1. In this case, the grant has the effect of providing no additional public goods but enables residents to purchase more private goods. This can easily occur as the grant enables the government to reduce its taxes for a given level of public good provision. Thus, we see that a grant can result in the provision of increased public goods or reduced taxes or some combination of the two. If the community moves in a northeasterly direction from a point on the old budget line to a point on the new budget line, as illustrated in Figure 19.3, a combination of more public goods and more private goods, funded through tax reductions, can occur.

Now, suppose that the grant is categorical and must be spent on a particular category of expenditure. For example, the grant is provided by the state department of education for specific types of educational expenditures. If we modify Figure 19.3 so that education is measured on the horizontal axis and a composite private good is measured on the vertical axis, we can see the effect of the categorical nature of the grant in Figure 19.4. The categorical grant has the effect of shifting the budget line outward in a parallel fashion, but the portion E/p_c of the budget line above the c intercept is not available to the community. Because the grant funds must be spent on education, no increase in consumption goods is possible beyond E/p_c. The budget line is

FIGURE 19.3 Noncategorical Grant

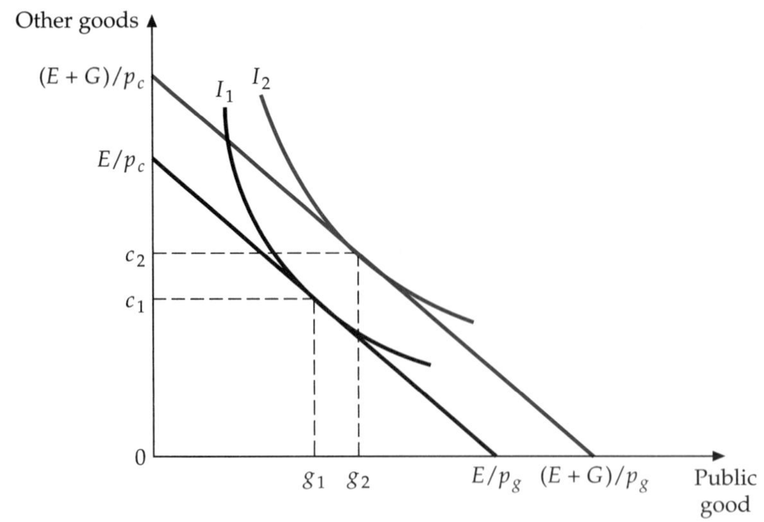

FIGURE 19.4 Categorical Grant

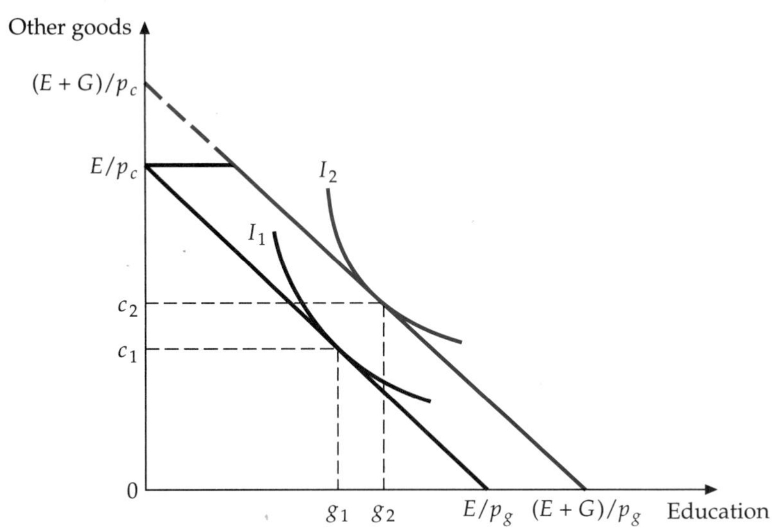

made up of the horizontal line segment from E/p_c to the point G/p_g units to the right, followed by the downward-sloping budget line segment to the g intercept $(E + G)/p_g$. The larger the grant, the greater the rightward shift in the budget line.

What is the economic effect of the categorical grant? Figure 19.4 illustrates that the local government will move out to the new combination of goods g_2 and c_2. That is, the local community moves northeast from combination (g_1, c_1) to combination (g_2, c_2). The local community does not simply move easterly (rightward) retaining its noneducational spending at the original level c_1 while increasing its education spending by the amount of the grant. The grant induces the local school district to spend more on schools, but the increase in education spending is less than the amount of the categorical grant. So, education spending rises but by less than the amount of the grant. How is that possible, because the categorical grant requires that the money spent go for education? Well, the local government does spend the categorical grant on education, as required, but they reduce the amount of spending that they would have otherwise allocated for education, making the combined total increase by less than the amount of the grant. This situation reveals the **fungibility** of funds. New money can substitute for old money, and do so perfectly. In fact, the change caused by a categorical grant illustrated in Figure 19.4 appears identical with the change in spending induced by a noncategorical grant as illustrated in Figure 19.3. One of the important conclusions about the economic effects of grants is that specifying that the grant must be spent on a certain type of program has no binding effect. Because of the fungibility of funds, local governments cannot be forced into spending all of the grant on a specific purpose.

One of the anomalies related to categorical (nonmatching) grants is the so-called **flypaper effect**. According to the theory presented previously, a categorical grant will be spent partly on more of the public good but also on more of other goods. On the basis of this theory, we would expect that categorical grants should increase education spending by substantially less than the amount of the grant. Evidence on the behavior of grant-receiving governments, however, indicates that they increase spending on the public good by more than this theory indicates. The grant money tends to stick where it hits, hence the term *flypaper effect*. Why would that sometimes happen? The situation depicted in Figure 19.4 describes the case where the local government wants to spend amount g_1 on the local public good prior to the grant program. The amount of the categorical grant is relatively small in relation to that desired level of spending by the local government in the absence of the grant.

In order to understand the flypaper effect, consider a somewhat different case where the desired level of spending on the public good is small in the absence of the grant, as Figure 19.5 illustrates. In this case, the local government has a very small desired level of spending g_1 prior to the grant. The categorical grant is large in relation to that desired level of spending, shifting the budget line outward to the right. If the grant were not categorical, the local government would want to increase spending to g_2' but the categorical nature of the grant forces the local government to increase spending by a larger amount, out to g_2. The effect is to induce the local government to increase spending on education by an amount almost equal to the grant, so the flypaper effect is apparent. What makes this example work in illustrating the

FIGURE 19.5 Flypaper Effect of a Categorical Grant

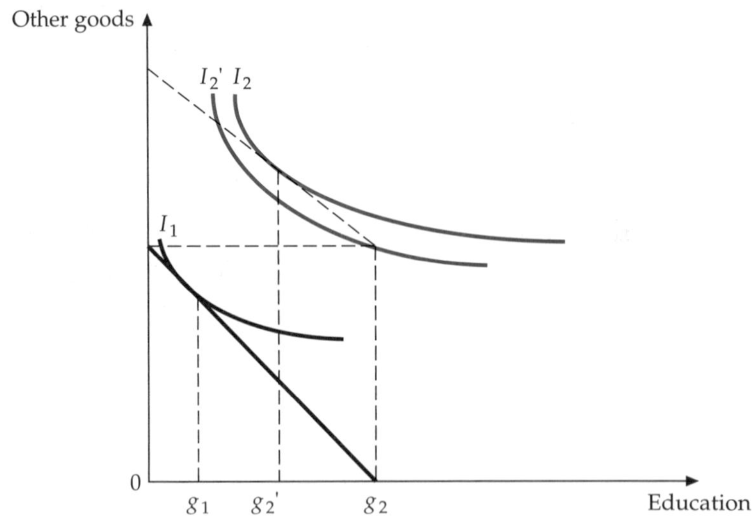

flypaper effect is that the local government's desired level of spending is small in the first place and the indifference curves are relatively flat, reflecting a low marginal utility of education relative to other goods. Under these circumstances, we can expect a categorical grant to stick where it hits.

Matching Versus Nonmatching Grants

Many intergovernment grants require matching on the part of the lower-level government receiving the funds. For example, U.S. federal highway funds for the construction of interstate highways require the state government to contribute $1 for each $9 received from the federal government. That means that out of each dollar of expense for interstate highway construction, the state government pays one-tenth of the cost, whereas the federal government pays nine-tenths of the cost. The federal government also uses matching grants to distribute Medicaid funds to the states using the Federal Medical Assistance Percentage (FMAP) that is determined according to a formula taking into account the average per capita income for each state relative to the national average. Poorer states receive higher FMAPs. In 2010 the federal government paid FMAPs between 61.59 percent and 84.86.[9] That means it cost the states just 15 to 38 cents per dollar of increased spending on their Medicaid program's covered health care.

The effect of such a matching grant is illustrated in Figure 19.6, with particular reference to the highway application. The matching grant has the effect of reducing the slope of the budget line, because it reduces the relative price of the government-provided good measured on the horizontal

FIGURE 19.6 Matching Grant

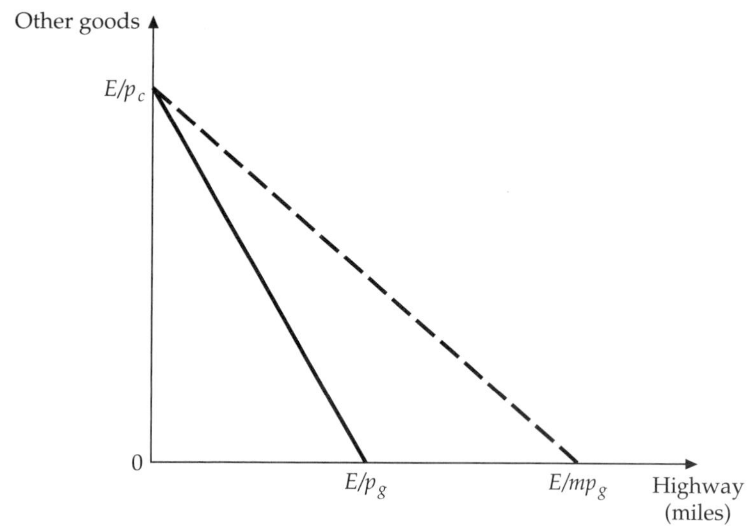

axis ($0 \leq m \leq 1$). If we denote the matching rate as m, the budget constraint that the state government faces as it allocates resources to the provision of interstate highways g and other services c can be written as

$$E = p_c c + m p_g g, \tag{19.5}$$

where E is the total expenditure of the state, p_g is the price of highways, and p_c is the price of other services. Solving this relationship for c in terms of g provides the equation of the budget line:

$$c = E/p_c - (m p_g / p_c) g. \tag{19.6}$$

The effect of the matching rate is to reduce the relative price of highways, reducing the slope of the budget line (in absolute value) from p_g/p_c to mp_g/p_c. The c intercept remains the same as it was before the grant, E/p_c, whereas the g intercept increases from E/p_g to E/mp_g.

The matching grant changes the relative price of highways, so the grant causes both a substitution and an income effect. The substitution effect follows from the price of highways being reduced. The state government will purchase more highway construction because it is now relatively cheap compared to all other goods it purchases. An income effect also results, because the price reduction has the impact of increasing the purchasing power of the state's total budget, enabling the state to purchase more of all (normal) goods in its budget, including highways. For both of these reasons, the matching grant has the effect of stimulating expenditure on highways. Of course, the community response will depend on the preferences of community residents. Those preferences are characterized by the indifference curves drawn for the community.

Closed- Versus Open-Ended Grants

The amount of grant monies available from the higher unit of government may be limited to some maximum amount. If so, the grant is said to be closed-ended because there is a finite upper limit on the amount of the grant. An open-ended grant has no such limit. Matching grants involve a variable amount of money being sent to the lower unit of government. The amount sent depends on the matching amount provided by the lower level of government. The total amount that the higher level of government may wish to make available can be capped at the amount G_0. Then the amount of the grant G will be confined to the interval $[0, G_0]$, and the specific amount sent to the lower unit of government will depend on the match rate and the expenditure on the public good. We can write the amount of the grant to the lower unit of government as

$$G = (1 - m)p_g g \leq G_0. \tag{19.7}$$

The more units of the public good g purchased, the greater the grant until we reach the closed end of the grant at G_0. Once we reach that limit, the lower unit of government can continue to purchase additional units of the public good but must pay the full price p_g. That is, the matching rate goes to zero. The effect of the closed-ended nature of the grant is to put a kink in the budget line at the point where the matching rate falls to zero. Figure 19.7 illustrates a closed-ended matching grant.

If a grant is closed-ended, the slope of the budget line reverts to the non-matching slope at the point where the grant runs out. In Figure 19.7, the flatter slope of the budget line from the c intercept to the point corresponding

FIGURE 19.7 Closed-Ended Matching Grant

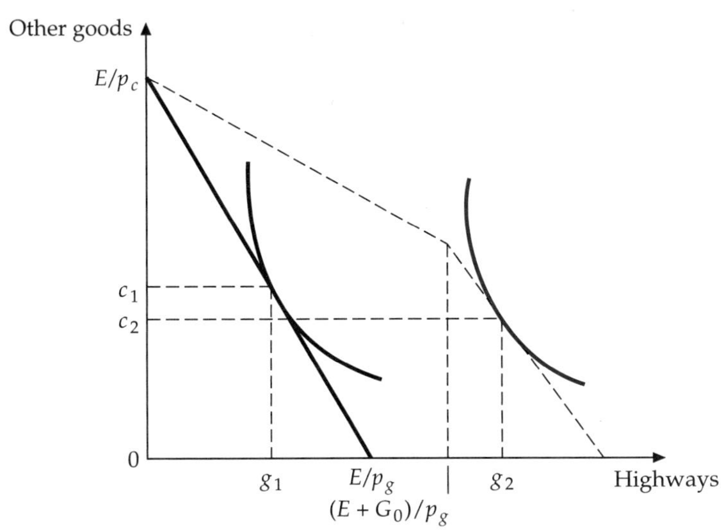

to the end of the grant, at highway expenditures of $(E + G_0)/p_g$, reflects the relative price ratio including the matching rate. But once the grant runs out, the slope switches to the steeper ratio that prevails when the matching rate is zero, and the lower unit of government must pay the full price of the public good.

If the lower unit of government purchases fewer than $(E + G_0)/p_g$ units of the public good, the closed-ended nature of the grant is nonbinding. The match still applies on the last unit of the public good purchased. If, however, the lower unit of government purchases more than $(E + G_0)/p_g$ units of the public good, the match applies to all the units prior to $(E + G_0)/p_g$ but not to those after. In this case, the closed-ended nature of the grant is a binding constraint.

Empirical Evidence on the Economic Effects of Grants

Fisher and Papke (2000) have reviewed the behavioral responses to education grants and found that there is substantial evidence that grant funds are fungible and substitute for other categories of spending. For example, Gold and Lowenstein (1996) found that a dollar's worth of federal grant money for education had the effect of raising spending on the aided service by anywhere from $0.20 to $0.90, depending on the service. Stotsky (1991) also found that federal nonmatching categorical grants for education had the effect of raising state education spending by 40 percent of the amount of the grant. That result indicates grant money is fungible, with at least a portion of the grant funding channeled either into other public services or into tax relief. The evidence also suggests that categorical matching grants stimulate more spending at the state and local level than do other forms of grants. It is also clear that open-ended matching grants stimulate more spending than do closed-ended matching grants. Economic analysis of grant effects also indicates that there is substitution of one current expenditure for another in many cases. Craig and Inman (1982) examined state government response to federal welfare and education grants and found that $1 of additional lump-sum federal education aid to states raised state education expenditure by $0.43. But the federal education grants also had the effect of raising state welfare expenditures by $0.23, of which $0.09 was state matching expenditure, reducing state taxes by $0.39 and raising other state spending by $0.09. Their research demonstrated similar substitution patterns arising from federal welfare grants. An additional $1.21 in open-ended federal welfare grants generated $0.34 additional state welfare spending. It also generated $0.54 less in state education spending and $0.78 more in other state spending. Although the precise magnitude of these effects has likely changed over the years since the study was conducted, the economic effects are very likely to still be associated with federal grants.

MANDATES

Fiscal relations between levels of government are also affected by requirements that may be passed from a higher level of government to a lower level of government. For example, when the federal government requires that highways must be built to certain design standards, state and local governments engaged in road-building activity must comply. In so doing, their cost of road construction may be higher than it would be otherwise. As a result, a fiscal impact accompanies a mandate. The state government in this case faces the situation where it must pay for the federally mandated road requirements, but the federal government has sent no additional funds to cover those expenses. Mandates have become contentious in recent years as they have become more common. State and local governments claim that they have been increasingly burdened with requirements of the federal government with no accompanying fiscal resources provided. The Americans with Disabilities Act (ADA) is an example where a federal regulation mandates handicap access meeting specific federal requirements be provided in public facilities. State and local governments, including cities, counties, school districts, libraries, universities, and other public agencies, must assure that their buildings meet ADA requirements. In some cases the cost of compliance with ADA requirements is very high due to the need for ramps and elevators. The federal mandate that handicap access meet specific requirements provides no funds for expensive renovations required at the state and local government levels. State and local governments are left to fund the expensive remedies required by the federal mandate.

Economics of Mandates

The U.S. election in the year 2000 provides a compelling example of mandates and their potential economic effects. That election revealed serious weaknesses in state and local election procedures, most notably in Florida where differences in voting technology (optical scanning of ballots versus mechanical reading of punch-card ballots) and the accompanying differences in error rates became very important in the closest presidential election in history. In the wake of that experience there have been a number of state-level election procedure reviews conducted in order to assure that future elections will be fair and accurate. Suppose, for example, that a state reviews its election procedures and recommends that all counties in the state move to optical scanning technology in future elections. County election boards are notified that they must comply with a new state mandate that optical scanning equipment be used in future elections. If a county is currently using the older punch-card ballots and readers, it must make arrangements to replace that equipment with new optical scanning equipment. Most importantly, the county elections board has to figure out how to pay for the conversion to new election equipment and procedures. The state mandate is designed to assure more fairness and equity in voting processes, but it provides no funding and therefore places the burden of implementation at the local government level.

Figure 19.8 illustrates the case where a state mandate requires a county election board to increase election services provided. Initially, the county government is providing e_0 level of election services and c_0 level of other services to county residents. The state mandate requires the county to provide a higher level of elections services e_1. The county government now has two

This man examines hanging chads in the 2000 Florida election.

FIGURE 19.8 State Mandate Requires County Elections Board to Increase Election Services

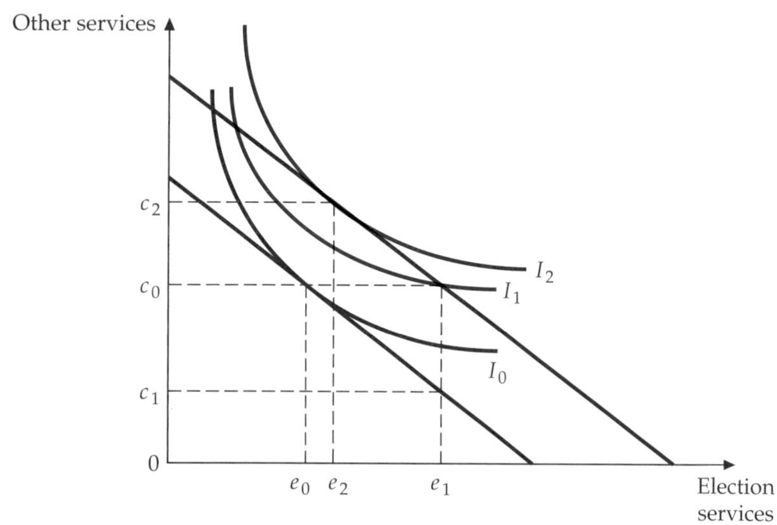

choices in its response. It can provide the higher level of election services by reducing other county services and move to point (e_1, c_1). That puts the county on a lower indifference curve, making people worse off, but at least the county meets the mandate and avoids whatever sanction the state threatens to impose in the absence of county compliance. The other choice is to continue providing the same level of other services, c_0, and simply increase the level of elections services to e_1. Of course, the combination (e_1, c_0) is on a higher budget line, requiring greater county government expenditures. County residents are better off at this point, because they are now on indifference curve I_1.

In order to provide that combination of services, however, the county will have to raise taxes. Worse yet, if the county were to raise taxes and spend that additional amount, moving out to the new budget line, it could do so in a way that would be more acceptable to residents. In the absence of the mandate, the county could move out to the point of tangency (e_2, c_2) with indifference curve I_2. That would make county residents even better off than the mandate. That combination involves a smaller increase in election services, however. This is the dilemma of the lower level of government when confronted with a mandate from a higher level of government.

Taxonomy of Mandates

Table 19.4 provides a taxonomy of federal mandates with their rationales, and examples of each type. One rationale for mandates is to reduce negative externalities. Examples of mandates for this purpose are clean air standards,

TABLE 19.4 Economic Taxonomy of Federal Mandates

	Rationale for Mandate		
	Reduce Negative Externalities	***Impose National Standards***	***Reflect National Norms***
Requirement that states must:			
Produce some good	Clean air	Assure that highways are built appropriately for large trucks.	Provide unemployment insurance program.
Produce in a specified way	Specific tests for drinking water	Set a uniform speed limit on rural interstate highways.	Require that union wages be paid in government construction projects.
Regulate firms and consumers (or refrain from regulation)	Handgun purchase waiting period	Establish educational testing standards.	Set alcoholic beverage drinking age at 21.

Source: From "Federalism and Reductions in the Federal Budget," by John M. Quigley and Daniel L. Rubinfeld from *National Tax Journal* 49, No. 2, 1996: 291.

such as those in the U.S. Clean Air Act, or EPA standards for drinking water quality (e.g., nitrate level) or a handgun waiting period such as that required under the Brady Bill. In each of these cases there is a negative externality that the mandate is intended to eliminate or reduce. Another rationale for mandates is to impose national standards. For example, national highways are required to meet certain standards in order to accommodate interstate truck commerce. Another example is the Corporate Average Fuel Economy (CAFE) standard for fuel economy required of manufacturers by the U.S. Department of Transportation. According to those standards, the manufacturers' fleet of vehicles must meet minimum fuel economy standards in order to encourage production of more efficient vehicles. Educational testing standards, which have been hotly debated in recent years, are an example of a mandate intended to regulate producers of education. The intent is to assure minimum educational quality across school districts. A third rationale for mandates is to reflect national norms. In this case we can point to the requirement that employers provide unemployment insurance for their employees. This mandate assures that all employees have proper coverage in case they become unemployed. Another mandate that government-funded projects must pay union wages in construction projects is intended to assure that such projects are produced using union labor or at least pays the equivalent of union wages. The final example of a mandate reflecting national norms is a national drinking age, requiring anyone purchasing an alcoholic beverage to meet a minimum age standard.

Whether mandates are effective in accomplishing their intended purpose is another question altogether. Take the CAFE standards, for example. Although the fleet-wide standard of 27.5 miles per gallon is specified by the law, there is a different standard for light trucks of 20.7 miles per gallon. The light-truck standard applies to pickups and sport-utility vehicles. At least part of the reason for the extreme popularity of light trucks in recent years in the United States is that those vehicles face a lower CAFE standard. One aspect of the CAFE mandate relates to the weight and safety of vehicles. In order to increase fuel economy in automobiles and meet the CAFE standard, manufacturers reduced the weight of automobiles. Although that improved fuel economy, it also made those vehicles less safe. When involved in a collision, a light car is more likely to result in damage to its occupants than a heavy car. Therefore, some consumers reacted to the increased risk of driving an automobile by trading it for a sport-utility vehicle. The heavier sport-utility vehicles are much safer, but they get far lower gas mileage. The result of the switch from cars to trucks may have actually caused gasoline consumption to rise rather than fall, as intended by the original CAFE standards instituted in 1975. This problem is sometimes called the **law of unintended consequences.** A mandate passed in order to fix a policy problem sometimes has unintended consequences that make the situation worse.

Consider a state-level mandate and the complications that arise with a mandate in combination with other state regulations. Car insurance premiums paid by drivers in New Jersey are among the highest in the country, averaging $1,200 per driver per year. One reason for the high premiums is the state's mandate that all car insurance companies selling insurance in New Jersey must accept all applicants. Faced with the mandate to provide coverage, insurance companies must accept high-risk drivers, and therefore they must charge high premiums. The state insurance commission caps premiums, however, in order to force the insurance companies to charge less. As a result of the combination of mandated coverage and regulated premiums, major insurers are leaving the state. State Farm Insurance Company, for example, left New Jersey, dumping 780,000 customers.[10] The state implemented the coverage mandate to assure that every driver can get insurance, but when that mandate is combined with regulated premiums, the result is unacceptable to the insurers who decide that it is in their interests to forgo business in the state altogether. This example illustrates the complex interactions that must be considered with mandates.

FISCAL DISPARITIES[11]

The concept of fiscal disparities among local government units is prominent in public finance. In its most crude and intuitive form, the term *fiscal disparities* refers to "differences in fiscal outcomes between central city and suburb." For example, if a suburban city government spends $1,000 per resident per year on parks and recreation programs, whereas an inner-city government spends $500 per year, the difference can be called a *spending disparity*. Similarly, if the suburban city can accomplish its parks and recreation spending with a 0.25 percent property tax while the inner-city government must use a 0.50 percent property tax rate to generate its revenue, we have a disparity in tax rates. In this example, disparities exist in spending per resident and in tax rates. These disparities can be considered outcome disparities because we observe differences in the fiscal outcomes in the jurisdictions. Outcomes differ for several reasons, but concern over fiscal disparities highlights the differences in tax bases that may cause the disparities.

William Oakland (1994) cautioned that outcome disparities should be viewed critically, however, because they may reflect differences in tastes as well as differences in opportunities. The suburban city may spend more per resident on parks and recreation because community residents have a stronger demand for neighborhood parks and youth recreation programs, quite aside from any differences in tax bases. This concept of fiscal disparity is more satisfying in the case of public services for which there is an explicit equality goal, such as in the case of public education. We care about spending disparities in public education because they have profound implications for fairness and equality of opportunity in our society. In other situations, however, the concept of outcome disparities is probably not adequate.

A more well-defined concept of fiscal disparity has been suggested by Bahl, Martinez, and Sjoquist (1992). They define fiscal disparity as the relative resource requirements gap between local government jurisdictions. The gap is the difference between the revenues provided by identical local tax efforts applied in each jurisdiction and the cost of providing a fixed package of local public services. If a city, for example, has a positive resource requirements gap, it is in relatively good fiscal condition compared to other cities. It can set its tax rates at lower levels, or it can provide a higher level of public services than other cities can. Cities with negative resource requirements gaps are in relatively poor fiscal condition and must implement higher tax rates, provide lower-quality services, or both.

What causes fiscal disparities? Some disparities are due to differences in the cost of providing local public services. The cost of providing local public services varies across cities due to variations in input costs such as wages. It simply costs more to provide a given level of service in a city with higher prevailing wages. Some populations are also more costly to serve than others because a given amount of input, such as labor, results in less output of local public service. Consider public safety services provided by a police department. A city that hosts a large transient population of commuters, for example, will have higher costs of providing a given level of public safety. In a similar way, cities in cold climates with significant snowfall will have higher costs of providing a given level of transportation services.

Disparities also arise due to differences in access to revenue-generating resources. Communities with high income or wealth have a superior ability to generate tax revenues by applying a given tax structure than communities with low income or wealth. Because most tax bases are directly correlated to income or wealth in the community, higher income results in a greater tax base which permits revenue generation at lower tax rates. Another resource factor resulting in disparities is the uneven distribution of natural resources across communities. Natural resources include mineral resources, climate, location, and other features. Oil- and gas-rich communities, for example, may apply property taxes on the value of real estate or severance taxes on the oil and gas in order to generate revenue to fund local public good provision. Communities without such oil and gas resources have fewer resources from which to fund local public good provision.

We care about fiscal disparities because we care about equity and efficiency considerations. Disparities due to variations in the cost of providing public services violate our sense of fairness. Is it fair that the cost of providing public safety depends on where one lives? Most of us would say it is not fair. As a result, we have implemented mechanisms that reduce the fiscal disparities due to cost differences. The most common form of mechanism designed to reduce fiscal disparities is a system of intergovernmental grants. A state government can provide grants to local communities in such a way that high-cost communities receive disproportionately more in state financial assistance; this has the effect of reducing the disparities across communities.

We also care about fiscal disparities because we care about efficient allocation of resources. The allocation of a productive resource should result in equal net marginal social product of the resource across spatial locations. Labor, for example, should have the same net marginal social product in Chicago that it has in Denver. If not, workers should migrate until the net marginal social product of labor is the same in both cities. If the marginal product of labor were higher in Chicago than in Denver, we could increase total welfare by moving workers from Denver to Chicago. The added social product of those workers in Chicago is larger than the lost social product in Denver. Spatial neutrality of this sort requires that tax rates on such resources be location neutral. Location choices should not be influenced by differences in tax rates.

Should Fiscal Disparities Be Eliminated?

Although it may appear as though all disparities are loathsome and deserving of swift elimination, that is not actually the case. Consider a fiscal disparity based on cost differences across communities. If the cost difference is due to varying labor costs, should we work to eliminate the disparity? Perhaps so, but consider the possibility that the reason wage rates vary across communities is due to differences in the productivity of workers. Higher wages result from greater productivity. If that is the case, we would be foolish to attempt to eliminate the difference with a system of grants equalizing the cost of providing public services. Similarly, we would be foolish to attempt to eliminate disparities resulting from community characteristics such as climate or topography.

Cost-induced disparities due to population characteristics are more problematic. The case for reducing disparities is compelling when the population characteristic is not subject to control by the residents of the community. For example, the higher costs of providing library access to handicapped patrons results in a spending disparity that should be reduced, perhaps by means of a state grant to local library districts that reduces the cost of providing handicap access. However, if spending disparities arise due to higher costs related to behavior under the control of community residents, reduction of fiscal disparities is more difficult to justify. A higher cost of providing library books to patrons more prone to mutilating those books, for example, makes it difficult to justify a grant system to reduce the higher cost.

Population heterogeneity causes difficulties in designing appropriate mechanisms to reduce fiscal disparities. Consider two communities with equal average income. Community A consists of residents all with the same income. Community B has equal numbers of high-income residents and low-income residents. A policy to reduce fiscal disparities that is based on average income would treat both communities equally. The high-income residents of community B would then have an incentive to relocate to a high- or average-income community where their taxes would be lower. Attempts to compensate for income differentials across communities result in creating incentives for homogenization of those communities. Although equity arguments remain for reducing disparities based on income or wealth differences across communities, equalization mechanisms may be a poor method of accomplishing that purpose. An equalization mechanism, such as a grant system, may be a crude instrument for accomplishing worthwhile equity goals. It may provide windfall gains to high-income residents of a community with low average income and consequently not be a very effective mechanism for redressing fiscal disparities. Oakland concludes that the efficiency case for reducing fiscal disparities due to differences in natural resources is actually much stronger than differences due to income or wealth. That is because grants designed to reduce disparities rooted in differences in natural resource endowments cannot change the endowments. With no change in endowments, there is no efficiency cost. This logic harkens back to the logic of the efficiency effects of taxes and subsidies we discussed in Chapter 10.

Intergovernmental Aid Mechanisms[12]

Two main methods of equalization are used in federal systems of government: foundation aid and power-equalizing aid. The fundamental difference between these two forms of intergovernmental aid programs is that the power-equalizing aid program provides aid based on the level of expenditure chosen by the local jurisdiction, while the foundation aid program provides aid based on the foundation level of expenditure chosen by policymakers at the higher level of government. A foundation aid mechanism sends aid in the amount A_j to jurisdiction j (city, county, school district, or other unit of local government), where

$$A_j = \begin{cases} F - t^* V_j & \text{if } t^* V_j < F, \\ 0 & \text{if } t^* V_j \geq F, \end{cases} \tag{19.8}$$

where F is the foundation level of spending per resident in the district, V_j is the per resident property value, and t^* is the foundation tax rate that is applied to each community's tax base to determine its required contribution to financing the foundation spending level for all communities. The foundation aid program can be seen to fill the gap between the community's need, defined as F dollars of expenditure per resident, and its available local revenue per resident measured by $t^* V_j$. If the jurisdiction's available revenue falls short of the foundation level of expenditure required, the jurisdiction receives aid equal to the difference between the foundation level and the revenue it can generate at tax rate t^*. On the other hand, if its tax revenue exceeds the foundation level of spending, the jurisdiction receives no aid.

Policymakers in the higher level of government designing this foundation aid program must select values for F and t^*. The number of lower-level government units that receive aid and the amount of aid provided depends on the values of F and t^* chosen. The higher the foundation level of expenditure F, the greater the number of communities that will qualify for aid and the more aid will be distributed by the foundation aid program. The higher the tax rate t^*, the fewer communities receive aid and the smaller the amount of aid distributed.

In contrast, a power-equalizing aid program is one that assures that all jurisdictions have equal revenue-raising ability compared to a base, or reference, jurisdiction. The aid formula is given by

$$A_j = \begin{cases} t_j(V^* - V_j) & \text{if } V_j < V^*, \\ 0 & \text{if } V_j \geq V^*, \end{cases} \tag{19.9}$$

where V^* is the per-resident tax base in the reference jurisdiction (perhaps the jurisdiction with the largest V_j), t_j is the jth jurisdiction's actual tax rate, and

V_j is its actual property value per resident. This mechanism assures that each jurisdiction can realize at least as much revenue from applying a given tax rate as in the reference jurisdiction. This assures, for example, that an inner city can raise as much from a 2 percent property tax as a suburban city, despite the fact that the suburban city has much higher property value per person. As a result, power-equalization mechanisms are sometimes said to provide a guaranteed tax base or a guaranteed yield.

The tax rate that applies in a jurisdiction will depend on its per-resident spending level E_j. The tax rate will be $t_j = E_j/V^*$. If we substitute this expression in the previous formula for power-equalizing aid, we obtain an equivalent formula:

$$A_j = \begin{cases} E_j(1 - V_j/V^*) & \text{if } V_j < V^*, \\ 0 & \text{if } V_j \geq V^*, \end{cases} \tag{19.10}$$

The given tax base and expenditure level chosen in the jurisdiction determine the amount of aid it will receive from the higher level of government. The more it chooses to spend, for a given tax base, the more aid it will receive. The smaller its tax base, for a given level of chosen expenditure, the larger the amount of aid the jurisdiction will receive. The power-equalizing aid program works just like a matching grant where the matching rate is $1 - V_j/V^*$. For example, if a school district has a property tax base that is 80 percent of the reference district amount, it receives a grant with a match rate of 20 percent. For each dollar it spends on education per pupil, it receives 20 cents in aid from the state.

Education Aid

Let's consider two examples of how states use equalization mechanisms in the context of education finance. Wisconsin uses a district power-equalizing method of distributing state aid to local public school districts. Reschovsky and Wiseman (1994) provide an example of how the system works for a mythical district—the Badgertown district. The property tax base in Badgertown is \$150,000 per pupil, and the district applies a tax rate of 30 mills, or 3 percent.[13] At that rate of taxation, the Badgertown district can spend \$4,500 per pupil per year (0.03 times \$150,000). Now suppose that Wisconsin introduces a district power-equalization program that provides a guaranteed tax base of \$300,000 per pupil. If Badgertown keeps the same level of expenditure, they can reduce their property tax rate to 15 mills, or 1.5 percent. The power equalization program acts like a matching grant with a match rate of 1 − 150,000/300,000, or 0.5. For each dollar that the Badgertown school district spends, it receives \$0.50 in aid from the state of Wisconsin. The effect of such a mechanism could be an increase in education spending, a reduction in tax rate, or a combination of both.

Iowa uses a foundation aid program to provide assistance to local public school districts. The foundation aid formula is

$$A_j = F - 0.0054\, V_j, \tag{19.11}$$

where the foundation property tax rate is 5.4 mills, or 0.54 percent (0.0054). State foundation aid is designed to fill the gap between the revenue yielded at that rate in district j and the foundation level of spending.[14] If the state set the foundation level of expenditure at F = \$5,000, for example, a district with property value per pupil of V_j = \$200,000 would receive a grant of \$3,920 per pupil, whereas a district with V_j = \$500,000 per pupil would receive a grant of \$2,300 per pupil. Districts with more than \$926,000 (5,000/0.0054) per pupil in tax base would receive no grant from the state.

POLICY STUDY

Effects of Changing the Federal Speed Limit Mandate

In 1987 the U.S. federal government changed an existing mandate that states set the maximum speed limit on rural interstate highways at 55 miles per hour (mph), permitting the states to raise their speed limits to 65 mph. In response, 40 of the 47 states with rural interstate highways raised their speed limits within a year. During that subsequent year, the fatality rate on rural interstate highways rose dramatically, leading policy analysts to conclude that the higher speed limits were responsible for more fatalities.

Lave and Elias (1997) examined the data, however, and questioned whether that simple interpretation was correct. They conjectured that the full effect of raising the speed limit to 65 mph was to cause drivers and police to reallocate their resources. Specifically, they thought that the higher speed limit on rural interstates caused drivers to switch from driving on dangerous side roads to the relatively safer interstate highways, taking advantage of shorter travel times (the price of travel is reduced on rural interstates, causing drivers to demand more rural interstate travel). They also thought that the higher speed limit freed the police from speed enforcement and allowed them to allocate more of their effort to activities with greater impact on safety (perhaps inspections, warnings, and other activities directly enhancing safety). These effects would reduce fatalities on noninterstate highways in rural areas and other roads patrolled by state police. The net effect of the higher speed limit statewide would then be ambiguous. The Lave and Elias statistical data showed evidence that vehicle miles traveled increased from 1986 through 1988 on rural interstate highways, as they predicted. They presented anecdotal evidence on state trooper reallocation activities, but such evidence is not compelling. Finally, they provided statistical evidence that the introduction of the 65-mph speed limit was associated with statewide fatality reductions. Their conclusion was that the higher speed limits reduced fatalities on a statewide basis.

More recently, Greenstone (2002) has reexamined the data and come to the conclusion that the impact of raising the speed limit to 65 mph was to cause statewide fatality rates to decline modestly. That overall reduction, however, is composed of a sharp increase in fatality rates on rural interstate highways and a large reduction in fatality rates on urban noninterstate highways. Greenstone was unable to find any evidence, however, of the reallocation of drivers and state troopers, as supposed by Lave and Elias. Using several rigorous statistical tests, he was unable to find statistically significant evidence that drivers switched to using rural interstates or that state troopers allocated more of their effort to safety-enhancing activities other than writing speeding tickets. His conclusion is that the effect of raising the speed limit on rural interstate highways increased fatality rates on those highways.

PROBLEMS

1. U.S. local governments are sometimes criticized for being Balkanized, or being a crazy quilt pattern of overlapping jurisdictions of different sizes and purposes. In light of the concept of perfect correspondence, briefly discuss the desirability of this pattern of local governments.
2. Examine the graphs of demand for schooling presented in Figure 19.1.
   a. Explain how per capita income is taken into account in the analysis.
   b. What is the effect on welfare losses due to an enforced uniform level of schooling in the two districts if per capita income in the districts is relatively large?
   c. Using a graph, explain how economies of scale would lead to lower costs per pupil and provide an incentive for the two districts to consolidate.
3. Assume that Cherry County has an initial budget line and indifference curves for the public good miles of highway and a composite good representing all other private goods.
   a. Indicate graphically what will happen to demand for the two types of goods if the county receives an open-ended matching grant from the state for highways.
   b. Indicate what will happen to demand for the two types of goods if the county receives an unrestricted nonmatching grant from the state for highways where the size of the grant is such that the budget line goes through the optimal allocation based on the open-ended matching grant in part a.
   c. Compare the likely outcomes in parts a and b. Is Cherry County better off with one or the other type of grant program? If so, explain.
4. Consider the World Bank measures of decentralization in Figure 19.2.
   a. Using the blue decentralization measure, find the top three countries with centralized government.
   b. Using the gray decentralization measure, explain how eliminating national defense expenditures affects the decentralization pattern.
5. Consider the case of two school districts in a state that uses a power equalization school aid formula, as described in Equation 19.10. The state has set $V^* = 200{,}000$. Alpha district has property value per resident $V_\alpha = 150{,}000$ and expenditure per pupil of $E_\alpha = 6{,}000$. Beta district has property value per resident $V_\beta = 400{,}000$ and expenditure per pupil of $E_\beta = 9{,}000$.

a. Compute the state aid that each district will receive per pupil.
b. Explain the economic effects provided each district by the school aid formula.

6. Specify whether each of the following taxes or fees is ability based or benefit based:
   a. Automobile fee based on value of the vehicle
   b. Automobile fee based on weight of the vehicle
   c. Inheritance tax
   d. FICA tax
   e. Excise tax on alcoholic beverage
   f. Excise tax on telephone service
   g. Airport departure tax
7. Classify each of the following mandates, using the taxonomy in Table 19.4:
   a. Requirement that each community have an EPA-approved landfill
   b. Requirement that railroad lines in all states have the same gauge (i.e., same width between rails)
   c. Requirement that all public drinking water must have nitrate content of less than 10 parts per billion
   d. Requirement that all public school teachers must pass a competency examination in their discipline
8. The election services example in Figure 19.8 assumes that additional election services can be purchased at a constant price. Suppose instead that the mandate requires new technology that has a higher price relative to other services the county provides.
   a. Illustrate how the higher price affects the county budget line.
   b. Explain the choices that now confront the county government.
9. The American Recovery and Reinvestment Act of 2009 (ARRA) provided substantial funding for local public schools to retain teachers in the wake of the 2008 to 2009 recession.
   a. Analyze the impact of ARRA on the likely spending of a local school district, including the adjustment process necessary when ARRA funding ends in 2012.
   b. Check the federal government website recovery.gov to see the recovery funds received in your home state.

REFERENCES

Bahl, Roy, Jorge Martinez-Vasquez, and David Sjoquist. "Central City-Suburban Fiscal Disparities." *Public Finance Quarterly* 20 (1992): 420–32.

Break, George F. *Proceedings of the Annual Meeting of the National Tax Association.* Columbus, OH: National Tax Association, 1985.

Craig, Steven, and Robert Inman. "Federal Aid and Public Education: An Empirical Look at the New Fiscal Federalism." *Review of Economics and Statistics* 64 (1982): 541–42.

DeMelo, Luiz. *Fiscal Federalism and the Size of Government in Transition Economies: The Case of Moldova*. Washington, DC: International Monetary Fund, Working Paper WP/99/176, 1999.

Downes, Thomas A., and Thomas F. Pogue. "Accounting for Fiscal Capacity and Need in the Design of School Aid Formulas." In *Fiscal Equalization for State and Local Government Finance*, edited by John E. Anderson. Westport, CT: Praeger, 1994.

Fisher, Ronald C., and Leslie E. Papke. "Local Government Responses to Education Grants." *National Tax Journal* 53 (2000): 153–68.

Gold, Steven D. "Issues Raised by the New Federalism." *National Tax Journal* 49 (1996): 273–87.

Greenstone, Michael. "A Reexamination of Resource Allocation Responses to the 65-mph Speed Limit." *Economic Inquiry* 40 (2002): 271–78.

Lave, C., and P. Elias. "Resource Allocation in Public Policy: The Effects of the 65-MPH Speed Limit." *Economic Inquiry* 35 (1997): 614–20.

Musgrave, Richard, and Peggy Musgrave. *Public Finance in Theory and Practice*, 5th ed. New York: McGraw-Hill, 1989.

Oakland, William H. "Recognizing and Correcting for Fiscal Disparities: A Critical Analysis." In *Fiscal Equalization for State and Local Government Finance*, edited by John E. Anderson. Westport, CT: Praeger, 1994.

Oates, Wallace E. *Fiscal Federalism*. New York: Harcourt Brace Jovanovich, 1972.

Oates, Wallace E. An Essay on Fiscal Federalism. *Journal of Economic Literature* 37 (1999): 1120–49.

Quigley, John M., and Daniel L. Rubinfeld. "Federalism and Reductions in the Federal Budget." *National Tax Journal* 49 (1996): 289–302.

Reschovsky, Andrew, and Michael Wiseman. "How Can States Most Effectively Meet Their School Financing Responsibilities?" In *Fiscal Equalization for State and Local Government Finance*, edited by John E. Anderson. Westport, CT: Praeger, 1994.

Sandel, Michael J. *Democracy's Discontent: America in Search of a Public Philosophy*. Cambridge, MA: Belknap Press of Harvard University Press, 1996.

Stigler, George. "The Tenable Range of Functions of Local Government." In *Federal Expenditure Policy for Economic Growth and Stability*, Joint Economic Committee, Subcommittee on Fiscal Policy, 213–19. Washington, DC: U.S. Government Printing Office, 1957.

Stotsky, Janet G. "State Fiscal Responses to Federal Government Grants." *Growth and Change* 22 (1991): 17–31.

Tresch, Richard. *Public Finance—A Normative Theory*, 2nd ed. New York: Academic Press, 2002.

NOTES

1. Florida statistics in this paragraph are from the *U.S. Census of Population* 2010 and the *Census of Governments* 2008.

2. U.S. Census Bureau, *Statistical Abstract of the United States: 2000*, 299, Table 409. Washington, DC: U.S. Government Printing Office, 2000.
3. These justifications are based on Stigler (1957) and Tresch (1981).
4. See Sandel (1996, 35) for a good discussion of the historical debate over rights of the state.
5. The decentralization measures in this paragraph are computed by the author using data from the International Monetary Fund, *Government Finance Statistics Yearbook*. Washington, DC, 1999.
6. Yugoslavia no longer exists, having disintegrated into separate countries including Croatia, Bosnia-Herzegovina, Macedonia, Slovenia, and most recently Serbia and Montenegro.
7. *http://www1.worldbank.org/publicsector/decentralization/fiscalindicators.htm.*
8. Break (1986).
9. For a list of the state matching rates see *http://www.statehealthfacts.org/comparetable.jsp?ind=184&cat=4.*
10. *Wall Street Journal*, April 2, 2002.
11. The material in this section is based on Oakland (1994).
12. The material in this section is adapted from Downes and Pogue (1994).
13. A mill is $1 of tax per $1,000 of property value, or an effective tax rate of 0.001 (0.1 percent).
14. See Downes and Pogue (1994) for more on this topic.

CHAPTER

20

Radius Images/Getty Images

The Economics of Local Governments

LEARNING OBJECTIVES

1. Describe the nature of clubs and club goods.
2. Explain how local public goods are a type of club good.
3. Discuss the Tiebout model of household sorting in a spatial setting.

People have grouped together in associations and communities since the very first human settlements. Furthermore, they have found mutually advantageous benefits from association with one another in a wide variety of associations. One motivation for associating with others is to reduce production costs. Farmers, for example, have learned to cooperate with one another, forming so-called co-ops, in order to reduce the costs of shipping their products to markets. It is far cheaper to truck your grain to the local co-op from where it will be shipped via railcar to a large metropolitan area, than to incur the cost of getting the grain to market on your own. Another motivation for association with others is the fact that you may derive some tangible benefit from that association. For example, Hungary has recently decided that there are benefits from close association with other European Union countries, and hence it has decided to join NATO, the North Atlantic Treaty Organization. By associating with NATO members, Hungary hopes to gain benefits for its national defense and economic strength.

Why did Spanky and Alfalfa form the Woman Haters Club in the old *Spanky and Our Gang* movies? (And after forming the club, why did they both defect to obtain Darla's attention?) Why have consumer membership clubs such as Sam's Club become so popular in recent years? Obviously, members of Sam's Club perceive a benefit from association with others in the form of lower prices on the goods they wish to purchase. In this chapter we investigate how and why clubs are formed and how they can solve some fundamental problems that plague the market. If clubs are capable of providing public goods to their members, there may be no need for government provision of public goods. But, the solution of this problem using the institution of a club also has its limitations.

In this chapter we will look at communities and their governments as a particular type of club. Local governments provide public goods to citizens who live within a defined geographic area. The local government provides a public good, but it is exclusively available to those people who live in the community. As Stiglitz (1983) puts it, the public library in Princeton, New Jersey, provides no benefits to the residents of Houston, Texas. The interesting question is whether the fundamental theorems of welfare economics covered in Chapter 3 apply to this particular type of public good—a local public good. Recall that the First Fundamental Theorem of Welfare Economics states that under certain circumstances the market allocation is efficient, whereas the Second Fundamental Theorem states that any given Pareto optimal allocation can be achieved by the market mechanism. Do these results still hold when the good being allocated is a public good, and not just any public good but one that is provided over a specific geographic area? That is the question. The short answer is: It may be possible, but it is not likely. The fundamental theorems may apply, but if they do, they do only in special circumstances that are unlikely to occur.[1]

CLUBS AND CLUB GOODS

What do Sam's Club, Oprah's Book Club, and the North Atlantic Treaty Organization (NATO) have in common? They are clubs that provide benefits to their members. More particularly, a **club** is:

> A voluntary group of individuals who derive mutual benefit from sharing one or more of the following: production costs, the members' characteristics, or a good characterized by excludable benefits. (Cornes and Sandler 1996, 437)

Key aspects of this definition include: voluntary club membership and members derive benefits from either sharing costs, association with one another, or from consuming a public good. A **private club** is one where production costs are shared and the good involved is purely private, hence rivalrous. In this situation, if club member characteristics differ and motivate sharing of the club good, then club membership fees will differ across members. In this case, the fees are *nonanonymous,* because the fees are directly related to the identity and characteristics of the members. Consider the example of a social club that provides access to an exclusive restaurant, for members only. Club members share in the cost of providing the restaurant facilities and staff, but each member differs in his distinct tastes and patronage patterns. Food and service provided in the restaurant are private goods. Fees paid by members will have two components: a flat fee to share in the expense of the restaurant and additional fees that reflect the member's usage of the restaurant and the food and drink consumed. In general, club theory applies to the situation where members share an excludable public good that is subject to congestion called a *club good.*

Characteristics of Club Goods

Six characteristics of club goods are important to recognize in order to distinguish between club goods and pure public goods. First, club goods are provided in the context of a club with *voluntary membership.* We assume a costless exit so that any member wishing to exit the club may do so without economic penalty. This is not always the case for pure public goods. Often no costless exit is available for a pacifist who does not wish to participate in a country's system of national defense. On the other hand, if you do not want the club goods provided by Netflix, you can withdraw your membership without cost.

Second, club goods are *subject to congestion* or *crowding*. Whether the purpose of the club is to provide sharing of an impure public good or the desirable attributes of fellow members, inevitably a problem of rivalry occurs as membership increases. Increased membership causes both the cost of providing the club good and the benefits derived from the club good to increase. On the cost side, congestion costs arise from increased membership. On the benefit side, increased membership means that the costs of club good provision are being shared by a larger number of members, reducing the per member cost. Consider the case of a neighborhood swimming pool in a growing subdivision where new homes are being built. The additional neighborhood residents will help reduce the per family cost of the pool, but they will also make it more difficult to swim laps at the time you are most likely to want to use the pool!

Third, it is important to distinguish whether the entire population is *partitioned* into clubs or not.[2] In the case of a pure public good, there is no crowding or congestion and all members of a society can be accommodated. In the case of a congestible public good, however, an exclusive club may be formed with a limited membership. What do nonmembers do in this situation? They can either join another club that provides the same club good, or they can simply be nonmembers of any club and not receive the club good. If every member of society is a member of a club (and only one club), the population is *partitioned*. Otherwise, the population is not partitioned and some members of society are not members of any club. Consider the case of national defense for European nations during the cold war era. Your country could have been a member of NATO (as was France) or a member of the Warsaw Pact (as was Poland) or a member of no defense organization (as was Switzerland). When the population is partitioned, the issue of the number of clubs becomes very important. In the cold war national defense example, the fact that there were two defense clubs was critical, but why only two? Why not three or four defense clubs? In similar fashion, consider the case of K–12 education in a community. What determines the number of private schools formed in the community as alternatives to the public schools?

Fourth, an *exclusion mechanism* enables the club to provide the club good to members and exclude its provision to nonmembers. Sam's Club will stop you at the door and prevent you from buying anything in the store if you do not have your membership card. United Airlines Mileage Plus frequent flyer club will not log your miles without your membership number. Netflix will not give you access to a video unless you log in with a membership number. These are all examples of exclusion mechanisms that effectively exclude nonmembers from using the club services.

Fifth, *simultaneity* occurs in the two decisions a club must make: the decision of how much of the club good to provide and the decision on the membership size of the club. The club must decide how much of the club good to provide, but that decision is not independent of the decision that must also be made on membership size. The more members admitted to the club, the smaller the per member share of the club good. The smaller the per member share of the club good, the fewer members want to join the club. Sam's Club, for example, must simultaneously determine how many and which products to stock on the shelves along with the number of members admitted to their merchandise club.

Sixth is an issue of *optimality*. In the case of pure public goods, we know that the market mechanism will typically provide too little of the public good—a suboptimal situation. For this reason, government intervention is usually required in order to provide enough of the public good. In the case of club goods, however, clubs can collect payment for the club good using an exclusion mechanism, thereby providing the Pareto optimal quantity of the club good. If this can be done, government provision of the public good is not needed. Gold's Gym solves the problem of allocating recreational services without government intervention, for example. They have devised an exclusion mechanism, requiring membership and payment in order to use the facilities provided.

Taxonomy of Clubs[3]

Two important attributes of clubs help us distinguish the various types of clubs that are observed in practice. First, the nature of the club membership is important. If all club members are identical in their preferences and other attributes, most importantly their endowments such as wealth, the membership is *homogeneous*. Differences among members in their preferences result in *heterogeneity*. If the population is partitioned, then every person is a member of a club and no person belongs to two clubs that provide the good in question. Second, the good provided may either be fixed in supply for all club members or be variable in supply. If the good is variable, some type of visitation rate is involved that may be measured by the number of visits or the length of time spent in visits, for example. Table 20.1 provides a taxonomy of clubs, characterizing them by homogeneity/heterogeneity of membership and by fixed/variable utilization of the club good.

Club Model

In order to understand the voluntary association involved in clubs, let's begin with a simple example from Buchanan (1965), the formation of a swim club. Suppose that we have individuals with identical tastes for both public and private goods. We take the size of the pool to be fixed and the associated cost is denoted as F. Figure 20.1 illustrates the marginal benefits and marginal costs for an additional member of the swim club.

Consider the marginal benefit of added club members first. With a total cost F, a club consisting of one member will involve that member bearing the

TABLE 20.1 Taxonomy of Clubs

Membership Characteristics	Utilization of the Club Good: *Fixed*	*Variable*
Homogeneous (population partitioned)		
Homogeneous (population not partitioned)	NATO	Country club (golf)
	Local private schools	Racquet club (tennis)
	Faculty club at the university	Church/synagogue/mosque
	Lions Club	Blockbuster Video
	Rotary Club	Airline frequent flyer club
	Kiwanis Club	Baseball card club
	Tiger Woods Official Fan Club	Coin collectors club
	Unofficial Studebaker Drivers Club	Stamp collectors club
	Mercedes-Benz Club of America	Ham radio club
	Second Wives Club	Oprah's Book Club
		Microbrewed Beer of the Month Club
		Premium Cigar of the Month Club
		International Wine of the Month Club
		Boca Raton Resort and Club
Mixed (population partitioned)	National defense	
	Local public schools	
Mixed (population not partitioned)		Sam's Club
		Diner's Club

full cost of the pool. If costs are shared equally among club members, a second club member will reduce the cost per member to $F/2$; hence the marginal benefit to the first club member is the reduction in per-member cost of $F/2$. Increasing club size to $n = 3$ will provide a marginal benefit of $F/3$ to each of the first two club members. In similar fashion, we can show that the marginal benefit of adding the nth club member is F/n for the first n members. Hence, the marginal benefit curve in Figure 20.1 illustrates decreasing marginal benefits (MB) per club member with increasing membership size.

Now consider the marginal cost of added club members. This cost is the psychological cost that results from adding members. For example, if swim club members prefer to swim alone, the psychological marginal cost of added club members will be positive over the full range of possible membership

FIGURE 20.1 Swim Club Size

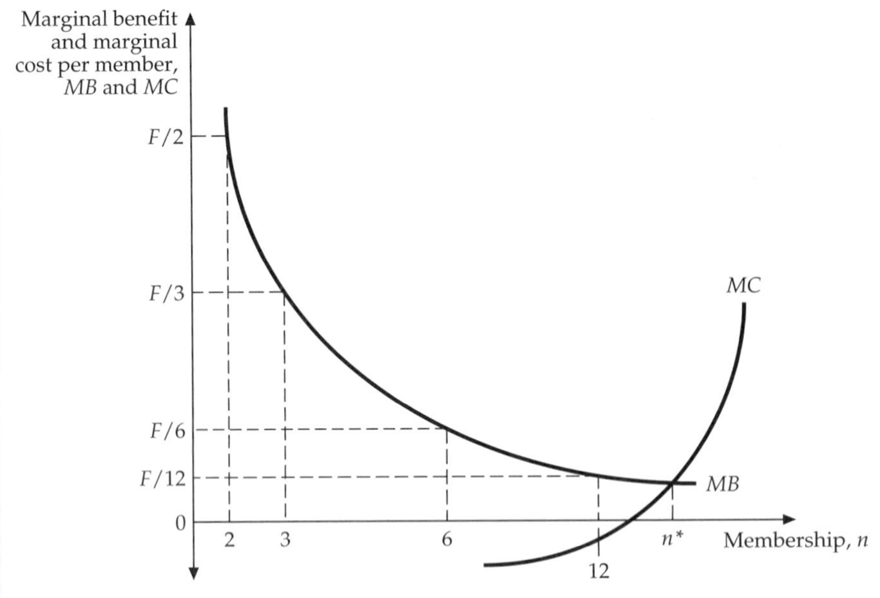

sizes. Each additional member admitted to the club raises the psychological marginal cost. It is possible, however, that club members prefer to have companionship as they swim. If so, the marginal cost of added members may be negative at low levels of membership, as illustrated in Figure 20.1. A club with just a few members may provide both the opportunity to swim and colleagues with whom to share the experience. But eventually, as membership rises, the marginal cost becomes positive and continues to increase. Although a swimmer may enjoy the company of a couple of colleagues with whom to share the experience, she does not enjoy sharing the experience with a large school of flailing swimmers. For sufficiently large membership, the marginal cost is bound to turn positive because the pool becomes crowded and the added members get in the way of the existing members. For these reasons, we draw the marginal cost (MC) curve as rising with membership size n. Optimal swim club membership is that membership n^* where the marginal benefit equals the marginal cost: $MB = MC$. The marginal cost of the last member admitted, causing crowding for the existing members, is just equal to the marginal benefit that the added member brings as the required club member dues are spread thinner over the membership.

Recall that in the case of a pure public good, no crowding exists because no rivalry exists. In that case, the marginal cost is zero for all membership sizes and the optimal club size is infinite. At the other extreme, a pure private good is subject to rivalry. A second person sharing the pure private good introduces crowding. If the first person derives any consumer surplus from consuming the good, sharing half of it with a second person involves forgone utility that exceeds the marginal benefit of sharing its cost. The optimal club size in this case is 1. Hence, we have the two polar cases of a pure public good where optimal club size is infinite and a pure private good where optimal club size is 1. In between, we have the case of a congestible public good where the optimal club size is greater than 1 but less than infinity.

The essence of a club lies in the fifth characteristic identified previously. It must solve two simultaneous problems: optimal quantity of the shared good to provide and optimal club membership.

Optimal Quantity of the Club Good

Figure 20.2 illustrates the problem of determining the optimal quantity of the shared good x to provide, holding club membership n constant. For simplicity, we assume constant costs in the production of the shared good, resulting in a linear cost curve $C(n)$. For example, assuming membership size n_1, the benefits and costs per person in the club are illustrated by $B(n_1)$ and $C(n_1)$. Of course, optimal quantity is determined where the marginal benefit equals the marginal cost, illustrated at quantity $x_1{}^*$ where the slopes of $B(n_1)$ and $C(n_1)$ are equal. For a different and larger club size, say n_2, the benefit and cost curves are lower, as illustrated in $B(n_2)$ and $C(n_2)$. These lower curves reflect the fact that a given quantity of the shared good will have lower benefits and costs per club member with more members. With the larger club size, the optimal quantity of the shared good that should be provided by the club is increased to $x_2{}^*$.

FIGURE 20.2 Optical Club Good Provision

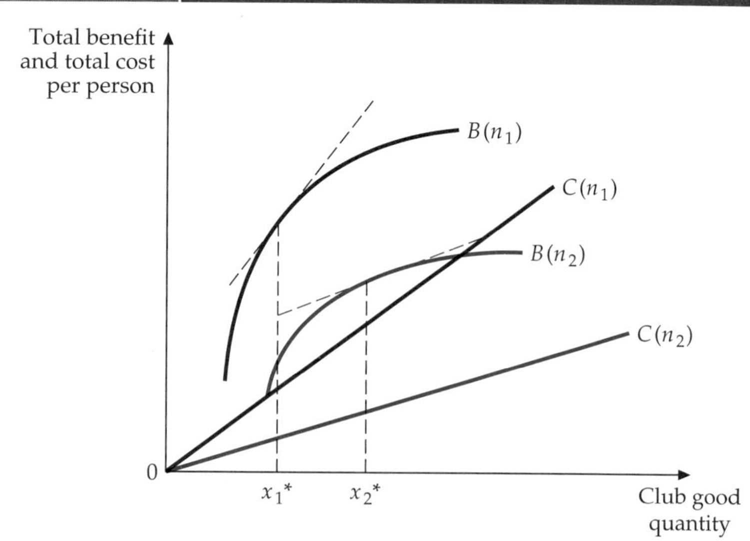

Optimal Membership Size

The other problem is determining optimal club membership, given the quantity of the shared good provided by the club. Figure 20.3 illustrates the determination of optimal club membership n. Total benefit and total cost per person are graphed, assuming a given quantity of the shared good x. The curves $B(x_1)$ and $C(x_1)$ illustrate how the total benefit and total cost per person vary with club membership, given a fixed quantity x_1 of the shared good. The optimal club membership is determined where the marginal benefit equals the marginal cost, at the point where the slopes of the curves are equal. Club size $n_1{}^*$ is the optimal membership when the quantity of the shared good is x_1. If the quantity of the shared good is increased to x_2, both the benefit curve and the cost curve shift upward. The optimal club membership for the larger quantity of shared good is then $n_2{}^*$.

For a given size park, the larger the community size, the smaller the membership fee required of residents. But, as community size grows, so do congestion costs. The optimal size community is found by expanding up to the point where the membership fee just equals the per person marginal increase in congestion costs. For a given number of residents in the community, the more public good provided, the greater the benefits and the costs of provision. But, for a given quantity of public good, the larger the community size, the lower the benefits and the costs. Park size should be expanded up to the point where each member's marginal benefit just equals the per member marginal cost.

FIGURE 20.3 Optical Club Membership

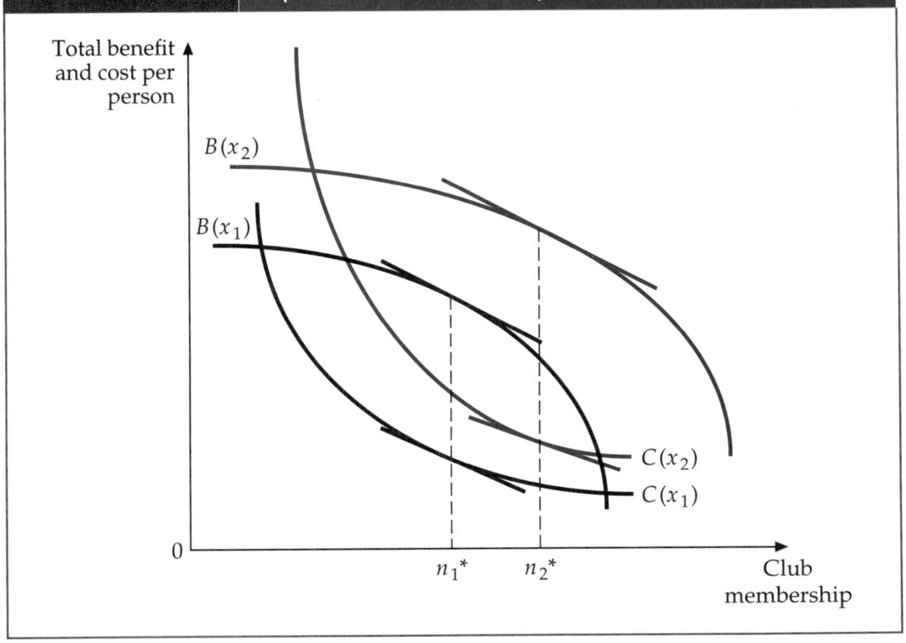

Simultaneous Solution

Consider a community struggling to determine the amount of land to allocate to parks. We know that for a given park size, the larger the community size, the smaller the membership fee (otherwise known as tax) required of residents. But, as community size grows, so do congestion costs. With more people comes more softball teams using the fields and more family reunions scheduled to use the pavilions, not to mention more joggers, cyclists, and skateboarders on the paved pathways.

Of course, another way to look at the problem is to assume a fixed city size with park space and think about how many people to permit to live in the city. The optimal size community is found by expanding population up to the point where the membership fee (tax) just equals the per person marginal increase in congestion costs. This approach may seem a bit odd, but many communities do just this. Boca Raton, Florida, is a good example. Boca is now a very prestigious city along Florida's Gold Coast with extremely high property values. Part of the reason is that during its formative years in the 1960s, the city restricted the number of new building permits to 500 per year, thereby limiting the number of people who could move into the city. This is only part of the reason—a supply-side factor. Demand-side factors like income and wealth also played a part. If families demanding homes in Boca had greater income or wealth than families demanding homes in other communities, their demand curve was further to the right, given the position of the supply curve, causing a higher equilibrium home price in Boca.

Another local government policy approach that has become popular in recent years is the **urban growth boundary**. The idea is to reduce urban sprawl by forcing development to occur within the boundary, resulting in higher-density development and lower per capita costs of providing local public goods. This too is a supply-side approach to managing the problems every community faces. Portland, Oregon, is currently restricting growth using an urban growth boundary, and its home prices are rising rapidly.

In general we know that for a given number of residents in the community, the more of the public good provided, the greater the benefits and the costs of provision. On the other hand, for a given quantity of public good, the larger the community population size, the lower the benefits and costs. The amount of the public good provided (park space, for example) should expand up to the point where each member's marginal benefit just equals the per member marginal cost. These principles apply to the United Airlines frequent flyers club, the Jockey underwear frequent buyers club, and the city of Los Angeles.

LOCAL PUBLIC GOODS

We have studied the theory of public goods, and we have just examined the theory of club goods that are congestible public goods. Now we turn to consider **local public goods**, which differ from other public and quasi-public goods because they are fixed in geographic location. Households must simultaneously choose the location, community services, and amount of private housing they wish to consume.

Optimal Provision of Local Public Goods[4]

Suppose that the total output Y of a community can be used for either of two purposes—private consumption of X per person or a public good G provided in a fixed quantity for all community residents. Output Y is produced with technology in such a way that Y increases with population N at a decreasing rate. We can write $Y = f(N)$. Assuming that all residents of the community are identical, the community's aggregate output will be the sum of private good production plus public good production. Now, the private good production is the product of per person output and the population; hence, we can write the aggregate output of the community as

$$Y = XN + G = f(N). \tag{20.1}$$

For a given community population N, this expression defines the consumption opportunity set and is illustrated in Figure 20.4. Consider the trade-off between private good X and public good G. Because $Y = XN + G$, we can solve for X as a function of G, obtaining $X = (Y - G)/N$. Then we can see that the trade-off between X and G involves the ratio $1/N$.[5] For each additional unit of X we want, we must give up one-*n*th of G.

Consumers find satisfaction in having both the private good X and the public good G; hence, we write their utility function as $U(X, G)$ and illustrate an indifference curve with the usual shape in Figure 20.4. If the local government selects the amount of the public good G to maximize the utility of the consumer, for a given population N, the point of tangency illustrated in Figure 20.4 is the optimal combination. The point of tangency represents the

FIGURE 20.4 Community Opportunity Set for a Fixed Population

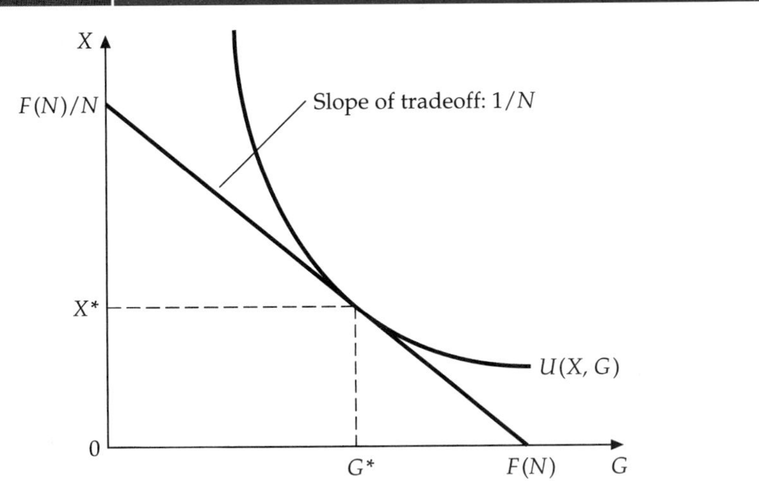

combination of private and public goods that maximize consumer utility given community population. At this point the slope of the indifference curve (*MRS*) is equal to the slope of the opportunity set (*MRT*). We can write

$$U_G / U_X = 1 / N, \tag{20.2}$$

where U_G is the marginal utility of the public good and U_X is the marginal utility of the private good. Rearranging this expression, we can write the optimality condition as

$$NU_G / U_X = 1, \tag{20.3}$$

which is simply a restatement of the Samuelson rule for optimal public good provision. The sum of the marginal benefits for all residents must equal the marginal cost of public good provision. Because community residents are identical, the sum of their marginal benefits is the sum of their marginal rates of substitution, or N times the *MRS* for one person—the left-hand side of Equation 20.3. The marginal cost of providing the public good is the marginal rate of transformation, or the marginal rate at which private good production can be transformed into public good production. Because the aggregate output of the community is the sum of private good production plus public good production, the *MRT* is simply 1.

Now what happens if the population of the community is changed? Suppose that we increase N. This causes output, including the maximum possible quantity of the public good, to rise, but the maximum consumption per capita falls. The ratio $f(N)/N$ declines because $f(N)$ rises at a decreasing rate with N. Hence, a population increase causes the opportunity set illustrated in Figure 20.4 to change. As N rises, the slope of that opportunity set falls (because the slope is minus the inverse of N). If we vary N over the full range of possible population sizes, we can trace out the envelope curve representing the opportunity set for variable population size illustrated in Figure 20.5.

FIGURE 20.5 Effect of Population on Opportunity Set of Community

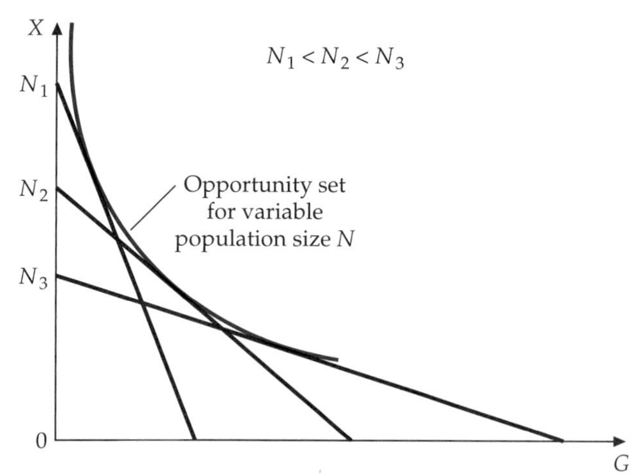

The envelope curve illustrated represents the best possible combinations of private and public goods the community can attain, assuming variable population. We can think of this by taking a fixed value of the public good $\dot{G}$ and then varying population N in order to maximize private good X consumption. Writing the quantity of X as

$$X = (f(N) - G) / N, \tag{20.4}$$

the maximization of X with respect to N for a given G requires that

$$f'(N) = [f(N) - G)] / N = X. \tag{20.5}$$

The expression $f'(N)$ on the left-hand side of Equation 20.5 is the marginal product of labor. As we would expect, this condition requires that for the last person added to the community, the marginal product of labor must equal the per capita output of X (the right-hand side).

Henry George Theorem

Rearranging Equation 20.5 provides another important perspective. We can equivalently write the condition for optimal population in terms of the public good G as

$$G = f(N) - N f'(N), \tag{20.6}$$

which implies that at the optimal population the quantity of the public good provided (the left-hand side) will equal aggregate output minus wage payments if workers are paid their marginal product. Now, think about that expression on the right-hand side of Equation 20.6. It represents total output minus labor payments. That difference can be considered economic rent—the return over and above factor payments. This expression implies that rents will equal public goods expenditure. Stiglitz (1977) has called this result the **Henry George theorem**, named after the famous New York City mayor and advocate of the single tax on land. George advocated abolishment of all forms of taxation except for a single tax on land that would be nondistortionary and sufficient to pay for all needed public services. The land tax would take all of the economic rent earned by the fixed factor land in a perfectly efficient manner, causing no distortion or efficiency effect (no excess burden), and would provide resources to pay for the public goods and services provided by government.

Social Optimum

So far we have considered variations in the quantity of the public good G and variations in population N. Now we need to put the two together and characterize the social optimum, including both the optimal quantity of the public good and the optimal population. If we plot the variable population opportunity set for the community and the indifference curves, we get the diagram illustrated in Figure 20.6. Point S represents the social optimum because it identifies the optimal combination of private and public goods, as well as implicitly determines the optimal population. The curves in Figure 20.6 show

FIGURE 20.6 An Interior Social Optimum

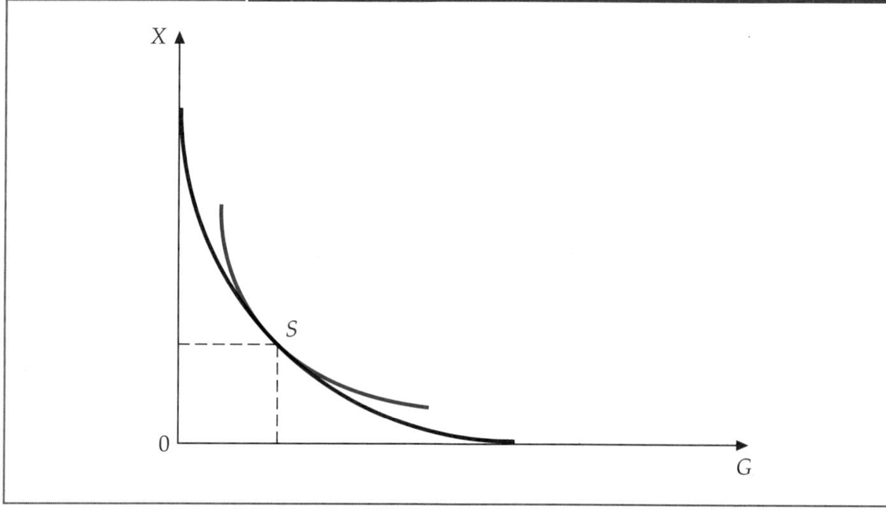

a nice interior optimum. Life is not always lived at interior optimum points, however! Consider what happens if the community indifference curve is relatively flat. In that situation, we will have a corner solution S on the vertical axis where the community population approaches zero. On the other hand, if the indifference curve is relatively steep, we will have a corner solution S on the horizontal axis and that solution will require an infinite population.[6]

Optimal Number of Communities

> **ON THE WEB**
> *For more on the economics of local governments, see the Policy Study "The Number of Local Governments in an Urban Area" on the companion website (www.cengage.com/international).*

So far we have assumed implicitly there is sufficient land to form any required number of optimally sized communities to accommodate the total population. You just find the right N^* defined in Figure 20.6 and build sufficient communities of that size to house the entire population of the state, region, or nation. What happens, however, when the total population you seek to accommodate is not an integer number times N^*? This is a familiar problem from the literature on clubs. For example, what do you do when the optimal size of NATO is 6 nations, but you have 12 nations that want to belong? Furthermore, in the context of local public goods, community formation may be limited by scarcity of land. While thinking about forming new optimally sized communities is no problem in Wyoming where there is plenty of open space, it may well be a problem in Delaware which has very limited open space.

Market Equilibria and Optimality

Let's consider the potential outcomes that may occur in a market situation where people are freely mobile. Suppose that we have total population of $2N^*$ to allocate to two communities. Let N_i be the population of community

i, and V_i be the maximum utility level that can be attained in that community with population N_i, assuming the quantity G_i of the public good in that community is chosen optimally. We expect the V_i functions to begin at a low level, because a very small community does not provide much by way of local public goods, and rise with population N_i. As we approach very large N_i, however, we expect that the V_i functions will fall due to crowding. With an egalitarian social welfare function, we can write total social welfare as the sum of the welfare attained in each of two communities:[7]

$$SW = N_1V_1 + N_2V_2. \tag{20.7}$$

Should we form two communities of equal population, with $N_1 = N_2$, or should the communities be different sizes? Figure 20.7 illustrates one possibility where the equal-sized communities solution is not the social welfare–maximizing solution. Neither community is large enough to reach its optimum size in this case. By having two communities of different size, we could increase social welfare. Enlarging one community to its optimal size while shrinking the other community to a level well below its optimal size provides greater social welfare. The $N_2 > N_1$ solution illustrates that possibility. By moving away from the $N_1 = N_2$ solution to the $N_2 > N_1$ solution, we gain a net increase in social welfare in the amount of triangle (approximately) *abc*. The larger community is able to attain maximum welfare, whereas the smaller community falls short of its maximum. The gain from reaching maximal welfare in the larger community is greater than the loss in the smaller community, however.

But that solution is not stable either, because social welfare will be even higher if we move all the way to $N_2 = 2N^*$ and $N_1 = 0$ labeled point *d*. This equilibrium is stable, but it is Pareto inferior to the equilibrium allocation at

FIGURE 20.7 Market Equilibrium with Two Communities

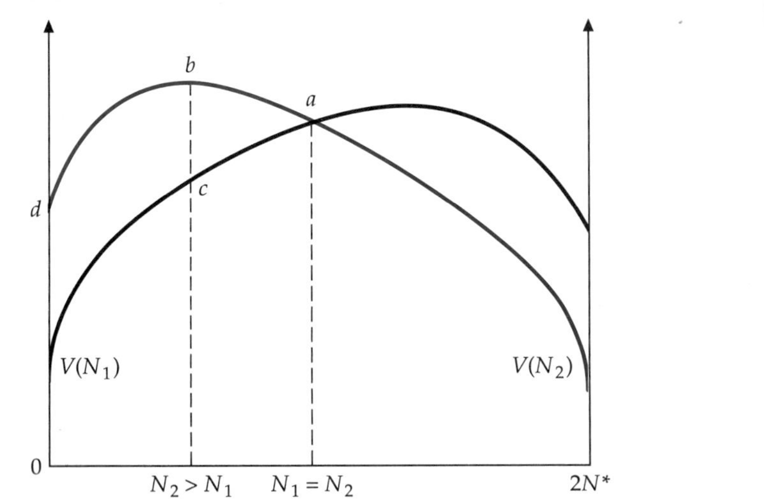

point *a*. (The argument is perfectly symmetric for the $N_1 = 2N^*$ and $N_2 = 0$ solution as well.) It is better to have one large community, even though it is beyond the optimal size, than to have two equally sized communities. We should consider other possibilities, but it is sufficient to make the point that the market equilibrium with free mobility of population may provide an outcome that is not social welfare maximizing.

Stiglitz (1983) has shown that there may be conditions under which a local public good's competitive equilibrium is Pareto efficient, thus establishing that the First Fundamental Theorem of Welfare Economics applies in this context, but that it may not be fulfilled. He has also shown that the Second Fundamental Theorem of Welfare Economics may not hold in the case of local public goods. Can every Pareto efficient allocation be supported by a decentralized market mechanism? Stiglitz has shown that not every Pareto efficient allocation can be decentralized. Four problems are involved with trying to decentralize:

- *There may be just one community*. With a pure public good, the marginal cost of provision to an additional resident is zero. This leads to the strong possibility that there will be a single community.
- *The public good must be local in the sense that its benefits do not spill over to other communities*. If benefits cross jurisdictional lines, each community has an incentive to underprovide public goods. This limits the scope over which the Tiebout decentralization mechanism may be effective.
- *The Pareto optimal allocation cannot involve subsidies provided by residents of one community to residents of another community*. The Second Theorem of Welfare Economics holds that every Pareto optimal allocation can be supported by a decentralized competitive economy with appropriate lump-sum transfers used to redistribute income. In the local public goods context, that would require redistributions to not depend on the community in which the individual has chosen to locate.
- *If the total population is not an integer multiple of the optimal community size, then in the presence of community entrepreneurship, the Pareto optimal allocation may not be supported*. The equal-sized (and equal utility) community equilibrium in Figure 20.7 involves both communities being smaller than the efficient size. An entrepreneurial community leader might suggest forming a third community with the optimal size. The developer of the new community could extract as rents an amount making households indifferent between staying and moving into the new community. This means that the Pareto optimal allocation cannot be sustained.

In the next section we consider a more explicit market model where people are freely mobile and migrate to the community that provides the public goods and services along with taxes that they desire. We cannot be assured, however, that the decentralized market mechanism will assure the Pareto efficient allocation. Clearly, regional and national governments have roles to play in order to internalize externalities and provide proper incentives. In this sense, a system of local, state, and national government units is required. Still, there are strong reasons to favor decentralization of public service provision as much as possible (fiscal federalism, Chapter 19). Those reasons include greater responsiveness of local government to citizen-voter desires and opportunities for local participation (exit, loyalty, and voice options, Chapter 6). The real issue is how to use the decentralized market mechanism to gain as much advantage in the provision of local public goods, despite the fact that we cannot be assured of the Pareto optimum.

COMMUNITIES AS SPATIAL CLUBS: THE TIEBOUT MODEL

Efficiency conditions in economic theory tell us that private goods will be allocated optimally by decentralized markets. The fundamental theorems of welfare economics apply to the case of private goods. Because the goods provided by local governments are public goods or congestible public goods, those efficiency results do not apply, right? For optimal provision of a public good, the Samuelson rule requires that the sum of the marginal benefits for all community residents must equal the marginal cost of providing the public good. A decentralized market economic system results in each individual consumer purchasing the quantity of a good where her marginal utility equals the price, which fulfills the efficiency condition for private goods but does not fulfill the efficiency condition for public goods. Hence, a decentralized price system will fail to provide the proper (efficient) quantity of the public good. That was the thinking in the economics profession, until an important article by Charles Tiebout (pronounced tee-bow) appeared in 1956.

Tiebout challenged the conventional wisdom of the time and developed a theory that led to the conclusion that competition among decentralized local governments could actually provide the same efficiency result as was known to hold for private goods in markets. The essence of the Tiebout model is that people select among the many community packages of public services and taxes, choosing to live in the community that provides their desired quantity of public goods and taxes.

People Vote with Their Feet

Tiebout argued that the problem of local public good provision is potentially solved by having a large variety of communities and **interjurisdictional mobility** of residents. He observed that the problem of determining the efficient level of public goods might be difficult at the federal level but was potentially solvable at the local government level because people "vote with their feet," moving to the community that provides the public good and tax package that most nearly suits their preferences. Tiebout said it this way:

> The consumer-voter may be viewed as picking that community which best satisfies his preference pattern of public goods. This is a major difference between central and local provision of public goods. At the central level the preferences of the consumer-voter are given and the government tries to adjust to the pattern of

> these preferences, whereas at the local level various governments have their revenue and expenditures patterns more or less set. Given these revenue and expenditure patterns, the consumer-voter moves to that community whose local government best satisfies his set of preferences. The greater the number of communities and the greater the variance among them, the closer the consumer will come to fully realizing his preference position. (1956, 418)

If the Tiebout conception of the world is accurate, families sort themselves spatially among the various communities in a metropolitan area. If you live in Southern California, for example, you can determine whether Santa Monica, Los Angeles, Anaheim, El Monte, or some other community best suits your preferences and ability to pay for public goods and taxes. A local government that provides high-quality public services, such as public schools, will attract families that want quality schools for their children and are willing to pay for those quality schools. Other families, who are more concerned with low taxes or have lower income, can find a community with low taxes and correspondingly low-quality public services.

The outcome of the Tiebout voting-with-your-feet process is that the population is sorted into communities where residents have similar preferences for local public goods and taxes. Within a community, people will be relatively homogeneous in terms of their preferences. Across communities, however, we would expect to see a great deal of variation, or heterogeneity, in public service provision levels and tax rates.

Implications of the Tiebout Model

Two fundamental implications follow from the Tiebout model:

- Homogeneity exists within communities with residents having similar tastes for public services and taxes.
- Heterogeneity exists across communities with different service/tax packages offered in different communities.

If the Tiebout model is correct, we would expect to find that urban areas have a good deal of heterogeneity across communities but a remarkable degree of homogeneity within communities. We would expect to find some communities with very high-quality public schools and other public services, whereas other communities in the urban area have very low-quality public schools and other public services. We would expect to find that within the high-quality communities most of the people are from the same upper slice of the income distribution. They all drive new Lexus SUVs, drink Chardonnay wine, and play golf at the country club. On the other hand, we expect that in the low-quality community most of the people are from the same lower slice of the income distribution. They all drive oil-burning 1972 Chevys with serious body damage, drink Budweiser beer, and play the lottery at the local Gas-N-Shop. Of course, both of these characterizations are dangerous stereotypes, but you get the idea. People sort themselves into communities that provide the public good–tax package that they want. The result is heterogeneity across communities (they look very different) with homogeneity within each community (they all look alike).

Assumptions of the Tiebout Model

As with any economic model, it is important to question the assumptions on which the model is built in order to determine whether the predictions of the model are likely to be relevant. Here are Tiebout's seven assumptions:

- No externalities arise from local government behavior.
- Individuals are completely mobile.
- People have perfect information with respect to the public services they receive in each community and the taxes that are required.
- There are enough different communities that each individual can find one with the public services meeting her demands.
- The cost per unit of public goods and services is constant.
- Public services are financed with a proportional property tax.
- Communities can enact exclusionary zoning laws.

We must ask ourselves whether these assumptions are accurate descriptions of the actual situation families face. First, is it likely to be the case that local governments generate no externalities? Hardly. At the very least, *fiscal externalities* are likely generated. Fiscal externalities are monetary benefits or costs imposed on others through the tax system. Consider the example where people have sorted themselves into two communities: a low-crime community and a high-crime community. The high-crime community may confer a fiscal externality on the low-crime community. For example, in the high-crime community drug users seeking to steal electronic equipment in order to get drug money may target homes in the low-crime community near the border. The increased cost of police patrols causes higher taxes in the low-crime community than they would be otherwise.

Second, is it true that families are perfectly mobile? Hardly. We all know how difficult it is to move away from family. All right, I know that some of us cannot wait to move away from family, but in general, people have ties to communities and regions that make them less than fully mobile. Although you might like to get away from Mom and Dad, you may be reluctant to move 3,000 miles. In part, your reluctance has to do with the transaction costs involved. Moving a household is an expensive proposition, measured in time costs, aggravation, and emotional stress. There may be a community across the state that more closely fits your desired profile of public goods and taxes, but it is difficult and expensive to move to that location. You are not perfectly mobile.

Third, do people really have perfect information about the quality of local public schools and other local public services? Hardly. Tell me, if you can, how the mean achievement score for students in the school district in which you live differs from those in contiguous school districts (not to mention all of the districts that are not contiguous with yours). Do you have perfect information about schools? How about the libraries, sewer systems, parks, and other public goods? What is the tax rate of each of the units of local government in the communities in your urban area? Do you know the tax rates applied by the cities, counties, school districts, library districts, and sewer districts? You probably have quite imperfect information.

Fourth, are there enough communities from which to choose that you can find one that closely approximates your ideal community? This may be the case if you live in metropolitan New York, Boston, Washington, DC, Dallas, or Los Angeles. But if you live in Omaha, your choices are restricted to a handful of communities, and you may not be able to find one that is close to your desired ideal. Worse yet, what if you live in Slippery Rock, Pennsylvania; Broken Bow, Nebraska; or Lame Deer, Montana? You may have one and only one choice. So much for voting with your feet.

Fifth, is it likely that the unit cost of public service provision is constant? That is, does the unit cost of providing the public good or service remain constant as the local government scales up the quantity? Given the pattern of questions and answers so far, this one may surprise you. Empirical evidence indicates that there are approximately constant unit costs over a fairly wide range of output levels for many local public goods. Of course, at extremely small or large scales, that is not likely the case. Most long-run average cost curves for local public goods are U-shaped, but they have a wide, flat bottom on the U. This means that there are roughly constant unit costs of provision, except at very small or very large levels of provision. Consequently, the cost of provision over a wide range is approximately constant as required by the Tiebout model.

Sixth, are all local public goods financed with proportional property taxes? Certainly not. Some are financed with local sales taxes or local income taxes. Others are financed with user fees. The portfolio of taxes and fees used by local governments is very broad, including a wide range of fiscal instruments.

Finally, do all communities have exclusionary zoning laws? Many do and some do not. A notable example of a large community without zoning is Houston, Texas. Since the 1920s most large communities have adopted zoning laws that restrict land use, designating some areas for industrial use (factories and warehouses), other areas for commercial use (stores, restaurants, and offices), and other areas for residential use (homes and apartments). Even among communities with zoning laws, however, we could question the effectiveness of the laws. It is often easy for developers and citizens to get a variance, or an exception to the zoning law, and use the land in a way inconsistent with the community's plan.

In summary, a number of good reasons exist to question the underlying assumptions of the Tiebout model. In his original paper, Tiebout calls this model an extreme case, indicating that even he thought these were extreme assumptions. Given the assumptions, the conclusions of the model are refutable hypotheses that can be subjected to empirical testing. Do urban areas demonstrate heterogeneity across communities and homogeneity within communities? Well, it seems to be the case that this is true virtually everywhere. Despite the fact that some of the model's assumptions are questionable, the model seems to predict rather well. Of course, there are exceptions, but for the most part the model provides a picture of urban areas that is amazingly accurate.

Tests of the Tiebout Model

Since Tiebout's original article, a whole literature has sprung up with hundreds of articles written to relax one extreme assumption or another. Zodrow (1983) provides a good summary of the first 25 years' worth of research. One of the first empirical tests of the implications of the Tiebout model was from Oates (1969). The results of that initial research confirmed the implications of the Tiebout model, as Oates found evidence that variation in public service provision across communities was capitalized into real estate prices. This seminal research was discussed in more detail in the Policy Study "Property Taxes and House Values" in Chapter 16. Following Oates, a large number of studies were published with varying approaches used to test whether public service provision was capitalized into property value.

A later contribution to this literature that provided a more satisfying modeling approach was that from Brueckner (1979). Brueckner developed an estimation procedure that is capable of determining whether public goods are efficiently provided by local governments. His empirical results, using Oates's original data (1960), showed that local governments in northeastern New Jersey were overproviding public goods. Brueckner's methodology is important and worthy of additional explanation. His approach was to jettison Tiebout altogether and simply ask whether local governments were providing the efficient level of public services—efficient in the Samuelson rule sense. This question is not unrelated to the Tiebout model, but it is the more fundamental question that underlies the notion that people in an urban area sort themselves among communities according to their income and preferences for public services and taxes.

Suppose that we denote the value of a given property as v, which we may take to reflect the value of a house (including the land). We will denote the quantity of a public good provided by the local government as z. Brueckner's

FIGURE 20.8 Model of Property as a Function of the Quality of a Local Public Good

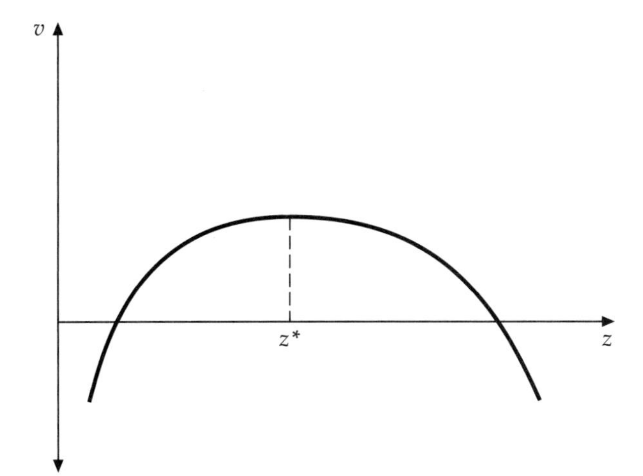

theory says that additional units of the local public good increase the value of the property when the local public good is not overprovided but reduce the value of the property when the local public good is overprovided.[8] Figure 20.8 illustrates the relationship. To the right of z^*, the local public good is overprovided and additional units of z reduce property value (the slope of the v function is negative). The marginal value per additional unit of z is negative. When z is underprovided, we are left of z^*, where additional units of z increase property value (the slope of the v function is positive).

This idea makes sense when you consider, for example, what happens in the situation where the city government is underproviding picnic tables at the municipal parks. Assuming underprovision, additional picnic tables are valued by city residents, and the additional public good makes property in the city more valuable. The situation is different, however, if the city is already providing more picnic tables than residents want. In this case, additional picnic tables provided by the city government reduce property values because the additional cost of providing the public good requires higher taxes and the public goods provided are not valued positively.

Brueckner regressed median house values on a number of control variables and measures of expenditures on local public services. Table 20.2 reports his estimates for two models that differ only in the specification of the expenditures for local public services. Model 1 assumes that local governments produce a composite public good. Model 2 assumes that communities produce two separable public goods: education and other municipal services. In both

TABLE 20.2 Brueckner's Tests of Efficiency in the Provision of Local Public Goods

Variable	Model 1	Model 1
Constant	26.0607[a] (21.474)	26.3405 (21.209)
Median number of rooms in all housing units	0.1717[a] (1.871)	0.1901[b] (1.462)
Median household income ($)	0.2167[a] (6.388)	0.2170[a] (5.686)
Total community expenditures	20.1858[a] (22.22)	
Education expenditures		20.2675[b] (21.391)
Other municipal service expenditures		20.1383[b] (21.364)
Distance to downtown Manhattan (linear distance in miles)	20.0786[a] (21.958)	20.0832[a] (21.780)
Population in 1960	0.1550[b] (1.481)	0.1703[b] (1.313)
Sales of retail, wholesale, and service establishments in 1963 (proxy for business profit)	0.0227 (1.199)	0.0307 (1.137)
Percentage of structures built before 1950	20.0499[a] (22.221)	20.0544[a] (21.992)
Percentage of families with incomes below $3,000	0.1184 (0.888)	0.0898 (0.587)
Adjusted R squared	0.9111	0.8896

Source: Brueckner 1979.
[a]indicates significance at the 5 percent level. [b]indicates significance at the 10% level.

cases the dependent variable is the median value for all homes in a community and the models are linear. He used Oates's original cross-section data (1960) on 53 communities in New Jersey. Table 20.2 reports the estimated coefficient estimates and t statistics.

Brueckner's estimated coefficient on public good expenditures (rows 4 to 6 in the table) was nonpositive (negative or not significantly different from zero) in each case. Hence, his evidence was consistent with the explanation that the communities represented in the sample were overproviding public services, with $z \cdot z^*$ as illustrated in Figure 20.8.

A more recent study of Tiebout model implications is from Nechyba and Strauss (1998), who used a discrete choice framework in their modeling approach. This approach to modeling assumes that households make choices about which community they will locate to, given their housing demand and household characteristics that determine their demand for local public services. The particular application of Nechyba and Strauss is the selection of school districts by households in New Jersey. They combine tax data and property data to construct a rich data set from which they can estimate the probability that a household will select any of six different school districts in close geographic proximity to one another. Table 20.3 reports the estimated elasticities of the probabilities for the six school districts. A probability elasticity in this type of model is the percentage change in probability of locating in a community divided by the percentage change in some factor that affects the probability of location.

Per pupil spending has an estimated elasticity that varies from 1.651 to 3.058 across the school districts in the sample. An elasticity of 1.651 means that a 1 percent change in per pupil spending has the effect of increasing the probability of location in that school district by 1.651 percent. These estimated probability elasticities mean that school district choice is quite responsive to per pupil spending in the districts. The higher the spending per pupil, the greater the probability that households will choose to locate in a school district, other things being equal.

TABLE 20.3 Nechyba's and Strauss's Estimated Elasticities of Community Selection Probabilities

Community	Per Pupil Spending	Private Consumption	Violent Crime	Commercial Activity	Distance from Central City
Cherry Hill	1.651	0.723	20.145	1.273	0.377
Collingswood	3.058	1.340	20.225	1.314	0.552
Gloucester	2.938	1.287	20.144	2.036	0.460
Haddon	2.829	1.239	20.145	1.224	0.626
Haddonfield	2.893	1.268	20.102	1.147	0.703
Pennsauken	2.315	1.014	20.422	2.465	0.245

Source: From "Community choice and local public services: A discrete choice approach," by Thomas J. Nechyba and Robert P. Strauss in *Regional Science and Urban Economics* 28 (1998): 51, p. 68. Copyright 1998 by Elsevier Science.

The second variable in Table 20.3, private consumption, is included to measure community "entry" prices. The idea here is that you may have to be able to afford a 10,000-square-foot house, a Mercedes, and a Town and Country minivan in order to enter some communities. A 1 percent increase in the average household private good consumption—due to either high taxes or high housing prices—is interpreted as an entry price to live in that district and has the effect of increasing the probability of locating in that district by anywhere from 0.7 to 1.3 percent. The violent crime variable has an estimated probability elasticity that is negative in all districts, reflecting the fact that higher violent crime has the effect of reducing the probabilities of location in all districts. Estimated probability elasticities for commercial activity and distance to the central city are positive, with the elasticities larger in the case of commercial activity.

These results provide additional support to the Tiebout hypothesis that households will sort themselves into communities that provide public service and tax packages that are consistent with their demands.

Although the literature on Tiebout models is extensive and results vary from study to study, it is fair to say that there is a good deal of evidence that households do vote with their feet. Thus, the essential idea of the Tiebout model seems correct.

POLICY STUDY

The Nebraska Corn Board as a Club[9]

Nebraska corn farmers hate taxes, yet they voluntarily agree to pay the equivalence of a tax to the Nebraska Corn Board. The board is engaged in marketing activities to stimulate sales of corn-based products ranging from organic corn chips to ethanol-based fuels. In order to fund the activities of the corn board, farmers pay a fee (alias tax), called a *checkoff*, that is based on their output per bushel of corn produced to the corn board. Given the amount of whining and complaining about property taxes and state income taxes, this is an amazing situation! Why is it that Nebraska corn farmers are willingly paying this fee when they are so reluctant to pay taxes to the government?

The answer to this paradox lies in understanding the nature of the corn board as an association or club using club theory. To gain insight on the purposes of the board, here are the mission and vision statements for the Nebraska Corn Board:

> **Mission:**
> The mission of the Nebraska Corn Development, Utilization and Marketing Board is to enhance the profitability of the corn producer by developing, carrying out and participating in programs of market promotion, research and education.
>
> **Vision:**
> Nebraska Corn—The first choice for a consistent supply of quality corn by global customers and by Nebraska value-adding industries who process the equivalent of 100 percent of corn produced in Nebraska, with greater farmer participation in all related industries and through broad-based cooperation.

The board works to promote both domestic and international programs to accomplish these objectives. Domestic initiatives include:

Corn on the Hoof Livestock production continues to be the largest consumer of Nebraska corn—some 40 percent of the state's corn crop is fed to livestock in the state. Combined, corn and beef make up nearly 75 percent of all Nebraska farm cash receipts.

A Sweet Story Corn sweeteners command more than half the nutritive sweetener market in the United States—using over 700 million bushels of corn each year. Sweeteners are a mature market, so the efforts of the Nebraska Corn Board in this area have primarily dealt with consumer awareness and promotion.

Nebraska-Brand Corn Nebraska corn is known as some of the best in the world, and the Nebraska Corn Board is looking to capitalize on that reputation—investigating ways in which the identity and integrity of Nebraska corn can be preserved to get producers a premium price for our premium product. Specialty corn is another promising market for Nebraska producers. Growers are looking to specific types of corn for specific applications, and the opportunity for increased profits is very real.

Ethanol: Nebraska's Homegrown Fuel Nebraska is fast becoming a leader in ethanol production. The state is home to seven ethanol plants in Blair, Hastings (2), Columbus, York, Sutherland, and Aurora, with two more plants being proposed. Combined, Nebraska's ethanol plants produce over 350 million gallons of ethanol annually. When the proposed plants are built, that number will increase to over 400 million gallons of ethanol per year! Typically, an ethanol plant will increase the value of corn grown in the area by 5 to 20 cents per bushel.

Cornstarch: The Promise of Plastics Rapid advancements in research are allowing cornstarch to be used in plastics—up to 99 percent in some products! The University of Nebraska—with significant funding from the Nebraska Corn Board—has become one of the leading centers for the development of cornstarch-based plastics, including polylactic acid (PLA), which will be produced at the Cargill plant in Blair.

International initiatives include:

Export Market to the World Just how important is export markets to Nebraska? Nearly one out of every four acres of corn we grow is exported, and the Nebraska Corn Board is active in promoting further exports.

The *U.S. Grains Council* Nebraska corn producers are represented in the world marketplace by the U.S. Grains Council, a non-profit organization with 11 international offices. The Council received substantial checkoff funding from the Nebraska Corn Board.

The Mexican Market Nebraska corn checkoff dollars are being used to fund efforts aimed at transporting Nebraska corn directly by rail to buyers in Mexico. The goal is to garner a premium price for the high-quality corn we grow in Nebraska.

Corn Exports Through Livestock One of the best ways of exporting Nebraska corn is in the value-added form of red meat. In fact, every pound of red beef exported represents the equivalent of seven pounds of corn exported.

The Nebraska Corn Board distributes checkoff funds to the *U.S. Meat Export Federation* for the development of red meat exports.

U.S. grain-fed pork and beef exports account for nearly 200 million bushels of corn.

Foreign Visitors See the Quality of Nebraska Corn The Nebraska Corn Board regularly hosts trade teams from other countries to let them see first-hand the quality and abundance of Nebraska corn.

Teams from Japan, South Korea, Taiwan, Indonesia, Malaysia, Bulgaria, Poland, Turkey, Egypt, the former Soviet Union, Mexico, and many other nations have visited.

Using the framework of club theory we can see that such an association is a classic example of collective action that is beneficial to the participants. The total cost of the board's market development activities is divided among the farmers who produce and pay the checkoff. All corn producers have an interest in market development that provides a collective benefit. But, they would prefer that others pay the cost of such activity, just as they would prefer that someone else fund the cost of local public education. So, how is this fundamental problem of a public good overcome?

We can use Mancur Olson's explanation. First, we state his condition under which the collective good will be provided:

> The collective good will be provided if the cost of the collective good is, at the optimal point for any individual in the group, so small in relation to the gain of the group as a whole from the collective good, that the total gain exceeds the total cost by as much as or more than the gain to the group exceeds the gain to the individual. (1965, 24)

Then, we can edit that explanation to fit the Corn Board application. The key in this explanation is the relative proportions involved. The collective good is provided because the cost of the board's marketing activity is small in relation to the gain to all corn farmers from such marketing activity. At the optimal amount of marketing activity for any particular corn farmer, the total gain to corn farmers exceeds the total cost. And, that amount is larger than the excess of the gain to the group of corn farmers over the gain to a particular corn farmer.

POLICY STUDY

The European Monetary Union as a Club[10]

Seventeen of the 27 nations of the European Union (EU) are also members of the European Monetary Union (EMU), which has introduced the euro to replace each nation's domestic currency. As part of the agreement to joint the EMU, each nation committed itself to strict budgetary limits, promising to keep its domestic financial house in order for the good of the union. Member states found it relatively easy to keep those promises during the booming economic time of the mid- to late 1990s. As the dawn of the euro currency introduction drew close in 2001, however, in the context of a weaker economic environment, the strains of fiscal discipline became clearly evident.

When the Italian government announced that it would run a larger deficit than that to which the previous government had committed itself, there was a sharp reaction among other EMU member states. If the Italian government breaks its commitment and runs larger deficits than permitted under the EMU agreement, who cares? Well, the rest of the member states *all* care. Because Italy's fiscal policy has direct economic consequences for the rest of the union members when they are linked with a common currency, they all care *very* much. Expansionary fiscal policy in Italy might cause a negative spillover effect in the rest of the EMU by driving up the overall deficit of the euro zone and sparking inflation. In the face of this development, the European Central Bank would have a difficult time keeping interest rates low (contractionary monetary policy to fight inflation would drive interest rates upward and slow economic growth). The real fear is that the self-disciplined countries would pay an economic price in terms of slower growth and/or inflation because of the spendthrift habits of undisciplined countries (like Italy in this case).

Another recent example of undisciplined behavior causing EMU members frustration is the case of Ireland, which cut taxes in the midst of an economic boom. This behavior is certainly unconventional fiscal policy and caused great consternation and a degree of jealously as well among member states.

Actually, three EMU countries in addition to Italy were recently identified as being in danger of breaching their fiscal promises: Germany, France, and Portugal. Those promises include limiting the size of their deficits to 3 percent, which if not done, results in fines imposed by the European Commission in Brussels. The difficulty is that deficit cutting is much tougher in the weak economic environment that these countries currently face. As their economies weaken, revenue growth slows and expenditure growth accelerates. Their desire to run larger deficits is natural but not conducive to stability in the EMU.

Most recently in the wake of the 2008 to 2009 recession and the global financial crisis the economies of Portugal, Ireland, Greece, and Spain (the so-called PIGS) were severely stressed. The crucial policy question was whether the relatively strong economies of

FIGURE 20.9 European Monetary Union Members

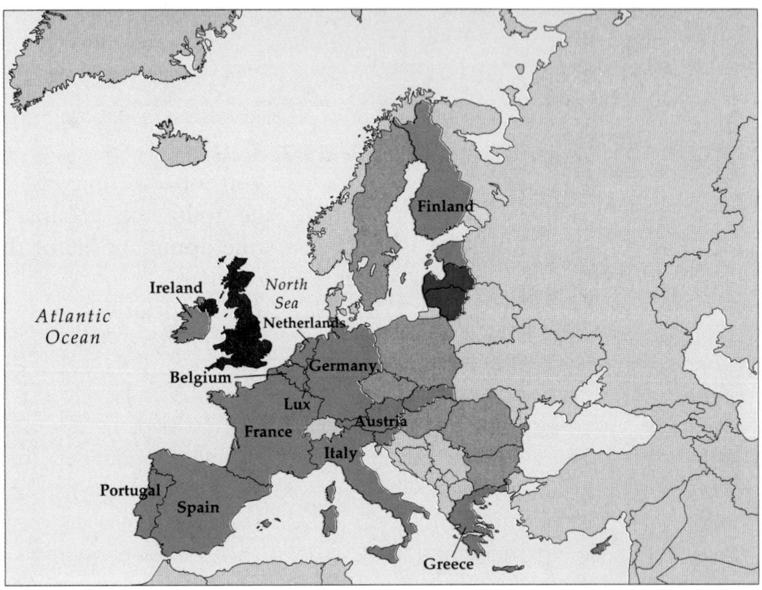

Germany, France, and the United Kingdom would be willing to provide bailouts for the PIGS to avoid severe impacts to the broader euro zone economy and the euro currency.

So why would European countries want to give up their autonomy to join the EMU? Each member state in the EMU must agree to give up two important tools for managing its economy in exchange for the benefits that club membership brings. First, EMU members must give up the ability to manage their own interest rates. Second, they must give up the ability to set their exchange rates and thereby their currency value. Of course, each member must make the decision about whether the benefits of membership are worth the cost of membership when they make the decision to join the EMU. Ten of the 27 EU nations have decided that the costs are greater than the benefits, including the United Kingdom, Denmark, and Sweden. They have refused to be part of the monetary union, although they joined the EU. Figure 20.9 illustrates both member and nonmember states.

PROBLEMS

1. Many states permit agricultural producers to form a voluntary market association to promote their commodities. For example, a corn producers association may be formed to promote consumption of corn-based products including corn chips and ethanol-based fuel. To fund these marketing activities, these associations often require a so-called checkoff, which is a per unit production fee (alias tax) required of producers. Why would individual corn farmers join such an association and be willing to pay the checkoff fees for such services? Explain using the club theory.
2. Mancur Olson states in his book *The Logic of Collective Action* that "the larger the group, the farther it will fall short of providing an optimal amount of a collective good" (1990, 35). Explain why this may be so in light of the theory of club goods.
3. The definition of a club says that members derive benefits from either sharing costs, association with one another, or consuming a congestible public good. For each of the following groups, specify which of these three benefits is likely to be the dominant factor that encourages membership:
   a. Blockbuster Video club
   b. Iowa Pork Producers Association
   c. Unofficial Studebaker Drivers Club
   d. First United Methodist Church
   e. AARP
   f. American Civil Liberties Union (ACLU)
4. Suppose that in Figure 20.1 the cost of the swim club is $F = \$350{,}000$ and the marginal cost is $MC = 100n^2$, where n is club membership.
   a. Compute the optimal membership size for the club.
   b. Suppose that the marginal cost rises to $MC = 200n^2$. Explain the impact on the optimal membership.

5. What happens in Figure 20.7 if the V functions for both communities are constantly rising, rather than peaking and then falling as drawn? Explain the implications for community formation in this situation.
6. The following data depict the fiscal characteristics of two school districts in a metropolitan area, each composed of identical single-family houses with one pupil per household.

Wolverine School District	Characteristic	Spartan School District
\$250,000	Per pupil property value	\$50,000
2%	Property tax rate	10%
\$5,000	Per pupil expenditure	\$5,000

7. The voters who have chosen to live in each district desire educational expenditures of \$5,000 per pupil. Each district then finances education with a property tax, but because the Spartan District has small houses (with low value) and the Wolverine District has large houses (with high value), the tax rate in the Wolverine District is much lower.
   a. Would a voter in the Spartan District prefer to live in a small house (\$50,000) in the Wolverine District? (Assume that the tax rate is unchanged at 2 percent.) Explain.
   b. Suppose there is a third district, the Buckeye District, to choose from with an equal number of big and small houses so that the per pupil value is \$150,000. What tax rate is required in the Buckeye District in order to spend \$5,000 per pupil on education? If small houses cost \$50,000 in this district, are small-house consumers better off here or in the Spartan District? If big houses cost \$250,000 in this district, are big-house consumers better off here or in the Wolverine District? Explain.
   c. Given your answer in part b, what do you expect will happen to the demand for big and small houses in the Buckeye District? What will happen to the prices of these houses in this mixed district with both big and small houses?
8. Explain the economic issues involved in NATO expansion as countries such as Albania and Croatia potentially approach membership in the defense organization. Specifically, how will admission of new members affect the costs and benefits provided to existing members? What are the issues related to public good provision when the good is defense?
9. Consider club membership in the European Union. How would the decision to join the EU be different if membership required that the country also join the EMU? Explain in the context of club theory.

REFERENCES

Buchanan, James M. "An Economic Theory of Clubs." *Economica* 32 (1965): 1–14.

Brueckner, Jan. "Property Values, Local Public Expenditure and Local Economic Efficiency." *Journal of Public Economics* 11 (1979): 223–45.

Cornes, Richard, and Todd Sandler. *The Theory of Externalities, Public Goods and Club Goods,* 2nd ed. New York: Cambridge University Press, 1996.

Fisher, Ronald C., and Robert W. Wassmer. "Economic Influences on the Structure of Local Government in U.S. Metropolitan Areas." *Journal of Urban Economics* 43 (1998): 444–71.

George, Henry. *Progress and Poverty.* New York: Henry George, 1879.

Martinez-Vazquez, Jorges, Mark Rider, and Mary Beth Walker. "Race and the Structure of School Districts in the United States." *Journal of Urban Economics* 41 (1997): 281–300.

Nechyba, Thomas J., and Robert P. Strauss. "Community Choice and Local Public Services: A Discrete Choice Approach." *Regional Science and Urban Economics* 28 (1998): 51–73.

Oates, Wallace W. "The Effects of Property Taxes and Local Public Spending on Property Values: An Empirical Study of Tax Capitalization and the Tiebout Hypothesis." *Journal of Political Economy* 77 (1969): 957–71.

Olson, Mancur. *The Logic of Collective Action.* Cambridge, MA: Harvard University Press, 1965.

Stiglitz, Joseph E. "The Theory of Local Public Goods," in *The Economics of Public Services,* edited by M. S. Feldstein and R. P. Inman. Macmillan, London, 1977.

Stiglitz, Joseph E. "The Theory of Local Public Goods Twenty-Five Years After Tiebout: A Perspective." Chapter 2 in *Local Provision of Public Services: The Tiebout Model after Twenty-Five Years,* edited by George R. Zodrow. New York: Academic, 1983.

Tiebout, Charles M. "A Pure Theory of Local Expenditures." *Journal of Political Economy* 64 (1956): 416–24.

Zodrow, George R., ed. *Local Provision of Public Services: The Tiebout Model after Twenty-Five Years.* New York: Academic, 1983.

NOTES

1. On this point see Stiglitz (1983, 18–19).
2. The concept of a partition in set theory requires that the entire set be divided into subsets, the union of which is the entire set.
3. This material is adapted from Cornes and Sandler (1996, 355).

4. The basic model in this section is adapted from Atkinson and Stiglitz (1980).
5. The derivative provides the trade-off: $\partial X/\partial G = -1/N$.
6. Other possibilities exist as well. It is possible that the community indifference curve is less convex than the variable population opportunity set for the community. The two curves could be coincidental, in which case there are an infinite number of optimal combinations. Other possibilities arise if the community indifference curve has less curvature than the community variable population opportunity curve.
7. Recall the discussion of social welfare functions when we considered the optimal income distribution in Chapter 5. We use the same Benthamite social welfare function here to represent the egalitarian case. Other cases such as those described in Chapter 5 could be considered.
8. In mathematical terms, $\partial v/\partial z > 0$ when $z \leq z^*$, but the derivative may be ambiguous in sign when $z > z^*$.
9. This material is taken from State of Nebraska Executive Budget, 2009–2011 Biennium, available at: http://budget.ne.gov/das_budget/budget09/20092011.htm.
10. This policy study is based on the *Economist* article "Trust or Mistrust the Euro Neighbor?" July 21, 2001, 41–42.

Radius Images/Getty Images

CHAPTER 21

Policy Analysis and Policymaking

LEARNING OBJECTIVES

1. Describe the taxation and expenditure policymaking process.
2. Identify the key players and institutions in the taxation and expenditure policymaking arena.
3. Identify opportunities and careers in public finance and policy analysis.

Markets are much like Alice in Wonderland. When they are good, they are very, very good, but when they are bad, they are horrid. Markets allocate goods in a very efficient manner, but they may also fail to allocate resources properly, as we studied in the cases of public goods (Chapter 3), externalities (Chapter 4), and income distribution (Chapter 5). That being understood, we now want to consider how the policymaking process works when it becomes clear that there is a market failure and a need for government action. In particular, we want to understand the interplay between economic theory, as we have studied in this text, and the real world of the policymaking process.

Sheffrin (1993, 7) says that "silence is the first casualty when the public cares about markets that fail to work." We all know that the squeaky wheel gets the grease, so we know that it is important to be loud in order to make our needs known. The political system is designed to be sensitive to the volume of noise being generated in current policy debates and to reward loud volume with more careful attention. Given that reality, the political system then produces a demand for action on the part of policymakers. Whether we like it or not, the demand for action will most likely be met with a purely political response. "Raw politics rears its head when markets fail to work," as Sheffrin (1993, 9) says. Heads of important legislative committees protect the interests of their constituents at the expense of broader collective welfare. Rent-seeking behavior becomes all too apparent as lobbyists turn down the screws and special interest money is directed to influence crucial votes. Sheffrin reminds us that the carousel on the capitol mall in Washington, DC, is not just an entertaining pastime for schoolchildren on holiday. Rather, he says (1993, 9), "The circular flow of funds takes a detour through the Washington money-go-round." Sheffrin has reflected on the interplay between markets and politics in the realm of public policy and concluded that:

> Our economic problems appear to be more profound and no longer the type that can be cured by simple solutions proposed by policy technicians. No ivory tower economist or policy analyst can offer the magic solution to our difficulties. Our economic problems today are inseparable from the political and regulatory environments that surround them. Solutions to our crises today necessarily involve the messy and seemingly intractable world of politics and social change. (vii)

If that is true, then we must pay attention to the policymaking process and understand the actors who play important political roles. An old saying in the policy world states the two things you do not want to watch being made: sausage and tax policy. Each is a ground-up concoction of various bits and pieces, some respectable but others we would rather not identify.

This book has been telling a story, since the opening page. We have learned much about the plot (expenditure and tax issues in public finance), various subplots (equity and efficiency aspects of expenditure and tax issues in public finance), and elements of intrigue (tax evasion and smuggling, for example). But, for the most part, we have not yet met the specific actors who play important leading roles in the theatrical production of public finance implemented in public policymaking. Here's an example of the theater involved in public finance, and why it is essential to understand the cast of characters, including important institutions, that play leading roles in the theatrical production of policymaking.

A few years ago in a midwestern U.S. state, there was a governor and like-minded political leadership in the legislature who wanted to substantially reform the state's tax system in order to enhance both equity and efficiency goals of their administration. They sought tax policy advice from learned economists and eventually developed a set of proposals for tax reform. The economists, having studied a textbook like the one in your hands, advised the governor to broaden the income tax base, removing certain exemptions and special tax breaks for limited groups of taxpayers, thereby permitting personal exemptions to be raised and improving the fairness of the income tax system both horizontally and vertically. The proposals were revenue-neutral overall, not changing the level of taxation. Of course, there was political opposition that sought to defeat the governor's proposals. Rather than debating the tax reform issues directly, however, the process of policymaking involved a series of public hearings around the state on the governor's proposals. The state senate finance committee held the hearings because that committee was responsible for tax legislation in the state senate. The chair of that committee was in political opposition to the governor, so the hearings were used as a platform from which to criticize the tax reform plan and the governor. At each of the venues selected for hearings, in various locations around the state, the chair of the committee and his staff would identify particular taxpayers who might be characterized as hurt by the governor's proposals.

The public hearings provided a wonderful theatrical opportunity to present taxpayers who would be victimized by the tax reform proposals, all in front of the local media cameras there to record the events of the public hearing for the Channel 8 *Eyewitness News* coverage at 6:00 and 10:00 P.M. An insurance company executive might appear before the committee and explain how his company would be put out of business if it lost the special tax treatment targeted for elimination in the governor's plan. A group of farmers might be trotted out in front of the committee and explain how the governor's plan would wreak havoc for their family farm businesses. Of course, the governor's advisers, knowing that the purpose of the hearings was to criticize their plan, made sure that members of the public would show up at the hearings and advocate policies consistent with the governor's plan. They would arrange for testimony, for example, that most of the insurance companies in the state paid no state tax at all, violating any reasonable sense of equity in taxation, and should be required to pay their fair share of state taxes. Although the essential issues of tax policy were part of the plot being portrayed in the hearings, what mattered most for public consumption was the theatrical aspect of the hearing process. In order to understand the production being observed, as carefully choreographed as a Balanchine ballet, however, the viewer needed to know the players involved and have a guide to understanding their roles in the play. An uninitiated observer simply watching and listening to the public hearing was as blissfully ignorant of what was really going on as an opera viewer who does not know the plot of the opera. It was essential to know that state senate finance committee approval was required for the governor's proposals to come up for vote in the full legislature. Furthermore, it was critical to understand that the chair of the committee holding the hearings was a political opponent of the governor and wanted to be governor himself (and eventually became governor). Whatever the merits of the plan before the committee, there was political intrigue mixed in healthy doses with public finance policy.

The point of this example is that public finance policy is made within a context that must be understood in order to appreciate fully the policy-making process. It is essential to know the actors, both institutional actors such as government agencies and committees, as well as individual actors, such as the committee chairs. To this point, we have focused on economic principles and their use for the development of public finance policy. We know, for example, how to design sales and excise taxes that will distort the economy as little as possible while generating a given amount of revenue. The fundamental economic principles and the ensuing tax policy suggestion are important for the design of public policy. But, how is the policy actually made? Who are the important players in the policy arena? What are the public institutions that make tax and expenditure policy? Because the individual actors change constantly in this theatrical context, we will focus on the institutional players (government entities and private sector actors).

POLICYMAKING INSTITUTIONS

It is the actors in the policymaking theater who give reality to the principles of public finance we have examined in this text. In this section, we identify the key institutions that play a part in the fiscal policymaking process, both in the United States and to a greater extent in other parts of the world.

Expenditure Side

It is the U.S. president who formulates the nation's budget in consultation with the advisers and department heads (Labor, Defense, Education, Health and Human Services, Transportation, Commerce, Treasury, and others) and the Office of Management and Budget. The budget is then submitted to Congress. In Congress, the president's budget is debated in committees and modifications are made to the budget plan before approval is granted by both houses. Recall that Congress does not adopt a budget per se. Rather, Congress adopts a budget resolution within which it will later formulate appropriation bills and receipts legislation. The appropriations bills are the vehicle through which Congress actually spends money during the session.

The important institutional players in the process of expenditure policymaking are the people, committees, agencies of the administration, and Congress. In the administration, the president, cabinet members, Council of Economic Advisers, department heads, Office of Management and Budget, and Treasury Department are the key players. In Congress key committees in both the House and Senate are the forums where policy debate on taxation and expenditure take place. Congress also has important support agencies that assist in research and policy design. The additional key function of auditing budgets falls to the General Accountability Office (GAO), an independent agency outside of the executive branch with direct responsibility to Congress.

At the state level, the list of key players in expenditure policymaking varies with the institutions of the state government. As a result, it is not a consistent set of institutions or names for key offices and agencies. In every state, however, the governor works with department heads to develop a budget plan and submits that plan to the legislature. The legislature debates and modifies the governor's budget plan and then adopts budget resolutions and provides appropriations to implement the budget plan. Policy is forged as the result of executive and legislative deliberation. The executive departments, as in the national government, then have the responsibility to implement the programs.

Local governments operate in similar fashion, with the mayor, city manager, or county supervisor proposing a budget, which is then subjected to scrutiny by the policymaking board of the local government unit that then makes appropriations. Whether a city has a professional administration with a city manager or is run by a mayor responsible for day-to-day operations, the essential relationships are similar. City council makes a policy and the administration carries out that policy. At the county level, a county board typically makes policy and the county supervisor carries out the policy plans.

Tax Side

At the federal government level, several sets of key players play a role in tax policymaking, including key committees in both houses of Congress. In the House of Representatives, the Committee on Ways and Means is the very important committee where all bills relating to taxation begin. In the Senate, the Senate Finance Committee considers all bills relating to taxation. In addition, the Joint Committee on Taxation (JCT), a joint House-Senate committee, is responsibility for tax policy.

Suppose the president has an idea for a change in tax policy. That change must follow a series of steps in order for the tax policy to become law for the administration to implement. First, the Treasury Department takes the idea and has its tax attorneys draft a bill that is then submitted for consideration in the House Ways and Means Committee. All tax legislation must begin in the Ways and Means Committee, according to the Constitution. After the bill has been debated and passed by the committee and voted on and passed by the full House, it goes to the Senate Finance Committee for consideration. After debate and a positive vote in the committee and then in the full Senate, where in both committee and full Senate the bill may have been changed substantially, the bill goes to a conference committee for reconciliation. Reconciled and passed, the bill becomes law. The job of administering the tax policy then falls to the Internal Revenue Service (IRS). The IRS is a bureau within the Treasury Department, an agency of the administration.

Executive Support Agencies

The executive branch of government has a number of support agencies that assist in the formulation of tax and expenditure policy. We will consider the Office of Management and Budget (OMB) and the Department of the Treasury.

Office of Management and Budget

The OMB has the primary responsibility to assist the president in the preparation and execution of the federal budget. It also supervises the administration of all of the executive agencies headed by cabinet members. As it assists in the formulation of the president's spending plans, the OMB also plays a role in the evaluation of the effectiveness of programs, policies, and procedures. It assesses the many competing funding demands from executive agencies and helps to set funding priorities. The OMB also attempts to ensure that reports, rules, testimony, and proposed legislation from the various agencies are consistent with the president's budget and with overall administration policies.

In addition, the OMB has the responsibility to oversee and coordinate administration policies in the areas of procurement, financial management, information, and regulatory policy. The OMB role in these areas is to help improve administration and management, to assist in the development of better performance measures and mechanisms of coordination, and to find ways to reduce unnecessary governmental burden.

AP Photo/Charles Dharapak

President Obama presents his budget proposal.

Council of Economic Advisers

Under the Executive Office of the President (EOP) an important group of economic advisers exists at the Council of Economic Advisers (CEA). The Council consists of three members nominated by the president and confirmed by the Senate. The chair of the Council is joined by two additional members, usually one specializing in macroeconomics and the other in microeconomics, with the purpose of providing the president with objective economic policy advice. A group of 8 to 10 senior advisers rotates through CEA, each with expertise in a subfield of economics (e.g., international trade, labor economics, environmental economics), including a senior adviser in public finance. Typically, the members and senior advisers are noted economists from academe, think tanks, or government agencies. They usually are on leave from their home base and serve at CEA for one year and then return.

In addition to providing day-to-day policy advising for the White House, the CEA members and staff compile the annual *Economic Report of the President* (ERP). The *ERP* contains both timely chapters on the most pressing current economic policy issues as well as a comprehensive set of data tables. The *ERP* is one of the best single sources of economic data and includes a set of tables on government finances covering both revenue sources and expenditure categories.

Treasury Department

The Treasury Department is the government agency charged with the responsibility of managing federal finances, including the payment of bills and the collection of taxes, duties, and other payments to the federal government. The department is organized into two major components: offices and bureaus. Bureaus make up 98 percent of the Treasury employees who carry on the day-to-day operations of the department. Treasury offices are headed by assistant secretaries who are responsible for policy formulation and department management.

In addition to these duties, the Treasury has other important responsibilities:

- Producing the nation's postage stamps, currency, and coinage
- Managing government financial accounts and the public debt
- Providing supervision of national banks and thrift institutions
- Providing advice on domestic and international financial, monetary, economic, trade, and tax policy
- Enforcing federal finance and tax laws
- Investigating and prosecuting tax evaders, counterfeiters, forgers, smugglers, illicit spirits distillers, and gun law violators
- Protecting the president, vice president, their families, candidates for those offices, foreign missions residing in Washington, and visiting foreign dignitaries

Within the Treasury Department, the Office of Tax Analysis (OTA) conducts the analysis of the revenue impact of proposed changes in taxes. The OTA is staffed with professional economists and lawyers who are armed with extensive databases and econometric models. They are able to provide detailed projections of the potential impacts of a change in tax policy. For example, when a new president comes into office and establishes an agenda for income tax reductions, it is the OTA that runs computer simulations of various alternative rate structures and their distributional revenue implications. Because OTA is within the Treasury Department, an executive branch department, it is subject to the direction of the president and advisers.

If the idea for a change in tax policy comes from a legislator, the process is identical with the exception that the bill is initially drafted by staff of the Committee on Ways and Means or other legislative drafters. The Treasury Department staff is not the first to work on the bill, although they will examine the bill and comment on its merits and weaknesses during the process of committee hearings on the bill. A Treasury spokesperson will provide the administration's view on the bill, but the bill is drafted by congressional staff and introduced by a member of Congress in an appropriate committee for consideration.

Table 21.1 provides an overview of the tax and expenditure institutions of the federal government. Both legislative and executive branch agencies and committees are identified.

Congressional Support Agencies

Congress has a number of support agencies that assist in the formulation of tax and expenditure policy. We will consider the Congressional Budget Office, the Congressional Research Service, and the General Accounting Office.

Congressional Budget Office

If you were looking for an analysis of the federal government budget, with estimates of the likely size of the deficits over the next five years, where would you

TABLE 21.1 Tax and Expenditure Institutions of the Federal Government

	Legislative Branch		Executive Branch
	House of Representatives	***Senate***	***Administration***
Expenditure	House Ways and Means Committee	Senate Finance Committee	President works with agency heads to develop and propose a budget.
	Congressional Budget Office (CBO) provides budget analysis. General Accounting Office (GAO) performs audits of budget accounts. Congressional Research Service conducts research necessary for the design of policy.		Office of Management and Budget (OMB) provides analysis of spending proposals and makes revenue forecasts for the administration.
Taxation	Committee on Ways and Means is the place of origin for all legislation having to do with taxation.	Senate Finance Committee deals with tax policy issues in the Senate.	Treasury Department Office of Tax Analysis (OTA) provides analysis of tax proposals and works with the administration in developing new tax policy.
	Congressional Joint Committee on Taxation (JCT) provides analysis of all tax legislation proposed and makes revenue forecasts for Congress.		

Source: Musgrave and Musgrave 1989 and Pechman 1987.

look? You could examine the president's budget proposals, but they are likely tainted by political interpretations, because the executive branch is controlled by a single political party in power. If you wanted information that takes into account both sides of the current political debates, you could turn to an analysis conducted by the Congressional Budget Office (CBO). As an advisory agency for members of Congress, the CBO must take into account political influences on all sides. Although it is not a nonpartisan agency (there is no such thing in Washington, in reality), it is at least subject to political influence from both sides of the aisle (Democrats and Republicans).

The CBO was created by Congress in 1974 and began operation in 1975. Its creation was part of the 1974 Congressional Budget Act that provided comprehensive reforms in the federal budget process and institutions. Economist Alice Rivlin was appointed as the first director. The CBO's mission is to "provide the Congress with objective, timely, nonpartisan analyses needed for economic and budget decisions and with the information and estimates required for the Congressional budget process." The office accomplishes that mission by providing services in four categories: assisting Congress in formulating the budget plan, helping Congress to fulfill the budget plan, helping Congress to consider the impact of federal mandates, and assisting Congress as it considers policy issues related to the budget and to national economic policy.

The CBO's mission is rather narrow in comparison with the other congressional support agencies: the Congressional Research Service and the General

Accounting Office. Despite its more narrow focus, however, its role in the budget process gives it wide influence because nearly all important matters of the federal government ultimately involve the budget.

Support work for House and Senate committees on the budget is the primary activity of the CBO. It is the responsibility of those committees to enable Congress to set targets for revenues and expenditures, and consequently the deficit or surplus as well. Furthermore, those committees establish the distribution of federal spending according to broad expenditure categories.

In order for the CBO to be effective, it must operate in a professional and nonpartisan manner. The CBO does not make policy recommendations. A nonpartisan position is required in order to preserve its independence and enhance the credibility of its analysis. The analysis itself must fully disclose the assumptions made and the analytic methods used. Nothing kills the credibility of policy analysis faster than the appearance of partisanship or methodological sleight of hand.

The CBO conducts some of its activities in response to statutory mandates. Other activities are in response requests from congressional committees. The CBO gives first priority to requests from the House Committee on Ways and Means and the Senate Finance Committee because they are the two appropriations committees. It then responds to requests from other congressional committees and provides cost estimates for bills introduced by individual members of Congress, as it has resources available.

Congressional Research Service

If you were a member of Congress and saw a critical need for an in-depth policy analysis of an important issue, where would you turn for policy analysis? Suppose, for example, that questions were being raised about retirement benefits for members of Congress and your investigative committee needed concrete answers to questions on what retirement benefits members receive, how those benefits compare to private sector benefits, and how member benefits have changed over time. The answer is that you would turn to the Congressional Research Service (CRS). The CRS is a support agency located within the Library of Congress whose purpose is to provide Congress with research, analysis, and information. The CRS describes its history and mission as follows:

> **History**
> In 1914, Congress passed legislation to establish a separate department within the Library of Congress. President Woodrow Wilson signed the bill into law, and CRS, then called the Legislative Reference Service, was born to serve the legislative needs of the Congress. With the Legislative Reorganization Act of 1970, Congress renamed the agency the Congressional Research Service and significantly expanded its statutory obligations. The services provided today by CRS are a direct result of congressional directives and guidance.
>
> **Mission**
> CRS serves the Congress throughout the legislative process by providing comprehensive and reliable legislative research and analysis that are timely, objective, authoritative, and confidential, thereby contributing to an informed national legislature (http://www.loc.gov/crsinfo/about/history.html).

General Accountability Office[1]

If you were looking for a study of the progress that has been made to date in improving homeland security in the United States since the September 11, 2001, tragedy, where would you look? If you needed to know the latest information on U.S. policy tools for combating weapons of mass destruction, where would you turn? If you wanted information on the manufacturing process for the anthrax vaccine, where would you search? The answer to all three of these questions and many more is the General Accountability Office (GAO). The GAO reports provide information on the economic impacts of military base closures, cost-effectiveness analysis of privatization of government services, nuclear attack submarine issues, and a host of other government program issues. Furthermore, consider the recent accounting scandal with Arthur Andersen and the Enron Corporation. With some 11 congressional committees conducting investigations of what happened and why, who do you suppose is providing the background information and analysis for members of Congress and conducting audits of both firms? The GAO, of course.

The GAO was established in 1921 as an independent arm of Congress with responsibility for auditing government agencies in all matters related to the receipt and disbursement of public funds. The U.S. controller general is in charge of the GAO. That person is appointed by the president, subject to congressional approval, for a term of 15 years. The GAO's major responsibility is to support Congress, and it fulfills that role by conducting audits and evaluations of government programs and activities. Specific congressional requests for review are acted on, with requests from committee chairs of either political party given equal status. Requests from individual members of Congress are also acted on, as resources permit. In some cases, reviews are mandated by law.

With the broad responsibility of reviewing all government functions, the GAO must have a multidisciplinary staff capable of conducting any type of analysis required. Consequently, the GAO staff includes accountants, lawyers, economists, experts in public administration and business administration, and scientists of various types. The GAO is organized by subject area. That enables the staff to develop in-depth knowledge of their subject and makes them more effective in analyzing the effectiveness of government programs.

In the area of accounting and information management policy, the GAO works to ensure that Congress has current, accurate, and complete financial management data. In order to accomplish this task, the GAO conducts the following three primary activities:

- Prescribing accounting principles and standards for the executive branch
- Advising other federal agencies on fiscal and related policies and procedures
- Prescribing standards for auditing and evaluating government programs

In the area of legal services, the GAO provides legal assistance to the federal government as it carries out the expenditure plans of Congress. Assistance is provided through a number of specific services, including:

- Providing advice on legal issues related to government programs and assisting in drafting legislative proposals for members of Congress

- Advising Congress on issues related to budget recisions and deferrals of federal funds
- Resolving bid protests challenging government contracts
- Assisting government agencies in legal aspects of implementing expenditure plans
- Adjudicating legal claims related to government programs
- Conducting special investigations

Finally, the GAO provides reports of its reviews and investigations. Those reports take various forms, including congressional testimony, briefings, and written reports. Unclassified reports are made available to the public. A list of GAO reports issued during the past month is provided to members of Congress. Beyond Congress, GAO reports are made available to researchers, the press, nonprofit organizations, and the public in general.

Think Tanks or Policy Shops

In recent years, private think tanks or policy shops have become increasingly visible as part of the policy scene in Washington. Indeed, a large number of state and regional think tanks have been developed as well. These institutions are privately funded research and policy advocacy organizations. They receive money from donors willing to fund research on particular policy issues, conduct the research, and then often play a role in informing policymakers on the issue or advocating on behalf of a particular policy.

In the field of tax policy, the best-known Washington, DC, think tank is the Tax Policy Center (TPC), which is a joint effort of the Brookings Institution and the Urban Institute. The TPC has developed highly sophisticated databases and microsimulation models that enable its analysts to simulate tax policy changes in a more complete and timely way than other think tanks outside of the government. For more on the TPC and their latest tax policy simulations see their website at http://www.taxpolicycenter.org/.

Two of the better-known general interest think tanks are based in Washington, DC: The Brookings Institution and the American Enterprise Institute.[2] Both of these think tanks have gained widespread respect for their research and contributions to public policy debates. Each has a staff of highly qualified economists, lawyers, policy analysts, and other professionals engaged in ongoing policy analysis. Both institutions provide very valuable policy analysis that is used by members of Congress, their staff, government agencies, and others engaged in policy debates. One of the most interesting developments in policy debate over the past 20 years has been the increasingly vital role played by think tanks in public policy debate.

The statement of institutional purpose for each institute is given below.

> **Brookings Institution:** A private, independent, nonprofit research organization, Brookings seeks to improve the performance of American institutions, the

effectiveness of government programs, and the quality of U.S. public policies. It addresses current and emerging policy challenges and offers practical recommendations for dealing with them, expressed in language that is accessible to policy makers and the general public alike.

American Enterprise Institute: The American Enterprise Institute for Public Policy Research is dedicated to preserving and strengthening the foundations of freedom—limited government, private enterprise, vital cultural and political institutions, and a strong foreign policy and national defense—through scholarly research, open debate, and publications.

Notice that both think tanks see themselves as working to improve the quality of public policy in the United States. They engage in research in order to inform policy debates. The results of that research are then communicated to the policy community through publications, briefings, and other means.

Although each institution would claim to be objective, and these two institutions in particular have reputations for sound research, all such institutions have a philosophic or political viewpoint that is transparent to informed observers. The Brookings Institution, for example, tends to take a more liberal view than the American Enterprise Institute, which is relatively conservative. That does not diminish the quality of the work produced by either institution. But, the interested policy observer should know the viewpoint of the institution in terms of political and economic philosophy up front before buying the policy advice. Although some think tanks exert great effort in conducting top-quality economic analysis and engage some of the best economists in the world to conduct that analysis, others simply provide convenient cover for politicians whose policy initiatives may not be based on sound economic grounds. In this realm, as in many others, the watchword is *caveat emptor* (buyer beware).

Other Washington, DC, think tanks include:

- CATO Institute
- Center for Strategic and International Studies
- Center on Budget and Policy Priorities
- Economic Policy Institute
- Heritage Foundation
- Institute for Policy Studies
- Progressive Policy Institute
- Urban Institute

Other notable think tanks outside Washington, DC, include:

- Conference Board
- Council on Foreign Relations
- Hoover Institution at Stanford University
- Hudson Institute
- National Bureau of Economic Research (NBER)
- Rand Cooperation

WORLD INSTITUTIONS

During the fall of 1999 the streets of Seattle, Washington, normally occupied by serious coffee drinkers on their way to work or school, were the site of demonstrations by thousands of protesters upset with a heretofore little-heard-of organization—the World Trade Organization (WTO). The success of antiglobalization protests in Seattle was followed in subsequent years with similar serious protests at each site of annual meetings of the World Bank and the International Monetary Fund (IMF) as well. Both Washington, DC, and Genoa, Italy, saw violent protests when international institutions met. Water cannon tanks, tear gas grenade launchers, and gas masks would hardly seem appropriate tools for policymaking! But, interest in and concern over the policy advice provided by these world institutions reached a fever pitch.

For most of our country's history, matters of public finance have been considered domestic issues, with tax policy issues in particular viewed as parochial and domestic. Since the end of World War II, however, worldwide institutions have been formed that directly influence the public finance policies of many nations. Now, institutions such as the World Bank and the IMF place external forces on countries. If Greece, for example, wants IMF assistance with its latest international monetary crisis, it must satisfy IMF conditions in order to receive aid. Those conditions include specific requirements forcing the Greek government to put its fiscal house in order. That may require spending reductions or tax increases. Or, what if Ethiopia requests World Bank assistance in developing small-scale agricultural cooperatives to assist farmers in marketing their products? The World Bank may require a review of the Ethiopian spending programs and forms of taxation that have a bearing on small-scale agriculture. In these ways, public finance is now an integral part of the role played by world institutions as they have become increasingly important in stabilizing the world financial system and advancing economic development.

The IMF and the World Bank have become increasingly visible players in the world of tax policy as they have been involved in assisting countries around the world in reforming their economies and their fiscal structures. Developing countries and transitional economies all over the world are being advised by IMF and World Bank advisers to reform their fiscal structures. The IMF and the World Bank were both established shortly after the close of World War II as economic institutions to expedite recovery after the war, provide for stability in the international monetary system, and facilitate economic development among countries. The design of these institutions took place at extensive policy discussions in Bretton Woods, New Hampshire. Here are short descriptions of each institution and explanations of their respective roles.[3]

World Bank

At Bretton Woods the international community assigned to the World Bank the aims implied in its formal name, the International Bank for Reconstruction and Development (IBRD), giving it primary responsibility for financing economic development. The bank's first loans were extended during the late 1940s to finance the reconstruction of the war-ravaged economies of Western Europe. When these nations recovered some measure of economic self-sufficiency, the bank turned its attention to assisting the world's poorer nations, known as developing countries, to which it has since the 1940s loaned more than $330 billion. The World Bank has one central purpose: to promote economic and social progress in developing countries by helping to raise productivity so that their people may live a better and fuller life. World Bank projects run the gamut from water projects in desert areas of Africa providing clean water access to electric meter installation projects in Eastern European apartment buildings. At the most recent annual meeting of the World Bank, a policy decision was announced that primary education programs would have highest priority in the coming years. The economic development rationale for this emphasis is that enhancing human capital pays large dividends.

Part of what promotes economic and social progress, raises productivity, and provides a better life for people are a well-designed tax policy and appropriate public expenditures. As a result, the World Bank has clear opinions on what makes for sensible public policy with regard to tax and expenditure aspects of public finance.

International Monetary Fund

The International Monetary Fund (IMF) describes its mission and purposes as follows:

(i) To promote international monetary cooperation through a permanent institution which provides the machinery for consultation and collaboration on international monetary problems.

(ii) To facilitate the expansion and balanced growth of international trade, and to contribute thereby to the promotion and maintenance of high levels of employment and real income and to the development of the productive resources of all members as primary objectives of economic policy.

(iii) To promote exchange stability, to maintain orderly exchange arrangements among members, and to avoid competitive exchange depreciation.

(iv) To assist in the establishment of a multilateral system of payments in respect of current transactions between members and in the elimination of foreign exchange restrictions which hamper the growth of world trade.

(v) To give confidence to members by making the general resources of the Fund temporarily available to them under adequate safeguards, thus providing them with opportunity to correct maladjustments in their balance of payments without resorting to measures destructive of national or international prosperity.

(vi) In accordance with the above, to shorten the duration and lessen the degree of disequilibrium in the international balances of payments of members.[4]

(Source: http://www.imf.org/external/pubs/ft/aa/aa01.htm)

You can see that the IMF mission not only involves the international payments system but also gives it reason for concern about public finance issues in member countries as well. As a result, the IMF routinely provides specific policy advice on expenditures and tax systems, making it an important player in international public finance. Table 21.2 provides a summary of the tax policy advice generally advocated by the IMF. The tax policy advice listed in that table is solid and sound. After reading this text, it should sound very familiar.

So, why are IMF actions so controversial? First, realize that the IMF does not simply provide advice for the sake of providing advice. The advice is a carrot intended as an appealing set of policy proposals in its own right. But, a stick exists as well. If a country would like the financial assistance of the IMF, it better follow this advice. As a result, many countries around the world are adopting the IMF (and World Bank) advice on reforming their public sectors. In doing so, the recipient country must often implement painful fiscal restraint that can be considered onerous. Is that unreasonable? Hardly. A lender has a direct interest in assuring that a loan will be repaid. The rub, in this instance, is that the borrower may not be creditworthy in the first place. Critics claim that by providing loans to countries without reasonable expectation of repayment, the lending agencies are indenturing the countries to which they provide assistance. The debt forgiveness movement made popular by the band U2 and Bono was based on this view and has pushed both the IMF and the World Bank and other lenders to forgive large amounts of debt. Of course, the IMF (and World Bank) maintain that they lend in situations if the country prudently follows their policy advice and will be able to repay the loans.

This is really an issue of market failure, once again. If world financial markets fail to allocate resources properly, perhaps due to imperfect information, government has a role to remedy the market failure and provide assistance to support economic development. Critics on the political Right claim that the inability to borrow in normal capital markets is a clear indication that the country is not creditworthy and international lending agencies are foolish to make loans to that country. Critics on the political Left claim that impoverished countries are systematically shut out of world financial markets and denied access, requiring international agencies to provide access. The current debates about debt relief and the appropriate roles of the IMF and World Bank are all about market failure and government intervention that can potentially correct for that market failure.

Organization for Economic Cooperation and Development

Another important world institution is the Organization for Economic Cooperation and Development (OECD). The OECD has its roots in the establishment of the Organization for European Economic Cooperation (OEEC) in 1947, which was created to facilitate the distribution of U.S.-financed aid for rebuilding Europe after World War II. In 1960, Canada and the United States joined OEEC members to form the OECD. Since then, the OECD has grown into an important world institution with a substantial focus on public finance issues. The OECD is a very useful source of country-specific and comparative information on tax systems and expenditure programs.

TABLE 21.2 IMF Tax Policy Advice

Tax	Recommendation
Overall tax revenue	Most countries rely on taxes as the main source of public sector funding. The size of the public sector is positively related to per capita GDP in the country. Hence, the amount of overall tax revenue generated in a tax system will depend on the GDP per capita in the country, reflecting the citizens' desires for public goods and services, and their ability to pay for those services.
Domestic consumption taxes	The objective of domestic consumption taxes is to tax the consumption of a broad base of goods and services at a low rate, so that maximum revenue is obtained and the burden of the tax is spread widely. Efficiency in taxation is achieved with equal treatment across economic sectors and types of activity. Because the VAT is superior to turnover taxes and retail sales taxes, the IMF recommends a VAT with a single rate in the range of 10 to 20 percent. Zero rating of export goods is recommended. Only a few exemptions are recommended on the basis of the difficulty of administering a VAT: rental income from housing, financial services, and the agricultural sector. Otherwise, the IMF recommends taxing all other goods and services, including construction materials, professional and personal services, sales of new buildings, and purchases by government and other public and nonprofit entities. The IMF recommends a consumption-type VAT, exempting investment. Further, the IMF recommends a destination-based VAT, taxing goods and services based on their destination, rather than origin. As for method of application, the IMF recommends a credit-invoice method whereby the firm pays a tax based on its gross sales, and then receives credits for taxes paid on inputs and intermediate goods. Excise taxes should cover goods that can generate revenue with little excess burden due to the tax, as well as correct for externalities and vertical equity. The IMF recommends a five-point excise tax reform program. 1. Limit the list of goods excisable to a short list such as tobacco products, alcoholic and nonalcoholic beverages, petroleum products, and perhaps vehicles and some luxury goods. 2. Replace specific taxes with *ad valorem* taxes in order to prevent erosion of the tax base with inflation. 3. Select excise tax rates that are internationally competitive. 4. Tax imports and domestic production, so there is no tax disadvantage to domestic production. 5. Apply the VAT to the value of goods and services exclusive of excises.
International trade taxes	The IMF recognizes that successful growth strategies for developing countries have generally involved being outward oriented. That involves lowering trade barriers, removing disincentives for exporting, and making the country's currency convertible. The IMF generally advises against reliance on import and export taxes. On the import side, the IMF recognizes the potential role of import taxes to protect infant industries or industries undergoing restructuring. The IMF policy advice is to simplify and rationalize the structure of import taxes, eliminate ad hoc exemptions, set a uniform minimum tax on all imports that is generally well below the existing rates in those countries, adopt *ad valorem* taxes, and value imports on the basis of market values.

(Continued)

TABLE 21.2 IMF Tax Policy Advice (continued)

Tax	Recommendation
	The IMF strongly advises against taxes on exports, believing that the burden of such taxes is shifted back to producers. The IMF also discourages export subsidies.
Income Taxes	The IMF recognizes that income taxes, both personal and corporate, are the mainstay of tax revenues in industrialized countries but are less important in developing countries. Personal income taxes in particular are an important part of a balanced tax system, although they require a greater tax administrative capacity than is present in many developing countries.
	As for tax structure, the IMF recommends de-emphasizing graduation in the rate structure, broadening the tax base by limiting deductions, exemptions, and preferences. The IMF-recommended tax structure has no more than three rates with a maximum rate of 40 percent or less. In order to remove low-income people from taxation, the IMF recommends raising the taxable income threshold through higher standard deductions and personal exemptions. In some Western countries, the IMF has advocated lowering the taxable income threshold by limiting deductions, in order to expand the tax base. The IMF also recommends indexing the tax structure (brackets, credits, standard deduction, and other nominal amounts in the tax code) in order to eliminate effects of inflation. Taxation on an accrual basis (rather than a cash basis) is also recommended.
	On the corporate side, the IMF recommends a single-rate tax of 30 to 40 percent. It also recommends making the top tax rates identical on the personal and corporate taxes.
	The IMF views tax incentives as largely ineffective. As a result, it recommends a broad-based corporate income tax with few deductions. It also recommends uniform treatment of domestic industries (private and state enterprises) and uniform treatment of domestic and foreign enterprises.
Payroll taxes	Payroll taxes to finance social programs should have broad bases, including all forms of compensation (in-kind and monetary). The rate structure should be simple and internationally competitive.

Source: Stotsky 1995.

Current OECD membership includes 34 countries: Australia, Austria, Belgium, Canada, Chile, Czech Republic, Denmark, Estonia, Finland, France, Germany, Greece, Hungary, Iceland, Ireland, Israel, Italy, Japan, Korea, Luxembourg, Mexico, Netherlands, New Zealand, Norway, Poland, Portugal, Slovak Republic, Slovenia, Spain, Sweden, Switzerland, Turkey, United Kingdom, and the United States.

The OECD mission is "… to promote policies that will improve the economics and social well-being of people around the world." To accomplish this mission, the OECD provides a forum for member country governments to share experiences and work together toward solutions of common problems. This cooperation involves:

- Work with governments to understand what drives economic, social, and environmental changes
- Measurement of productivity and global flows of trade and investment
- Analysis of country data to predict future trends

- Setting of international standards on all sorts of things, from the safety of chemicals and nuclear power to the quality of cucumbers
- Analysis of how much people pay in taxes and social security and how much leisure time they can take
- Comparisons of how countries' school systems are readying their young people for modern life, and how different countries' pension systems will look after their citizens in old age

(Source: OECD web page, http://www.oecd.org/pages/0,3417,en_36734052_36734103_1_1_1_1_1,00.html)

POLICY ANALYSIS AND POLICYMAKING

Policy analysis is becoming an increasingly important aspect of policymaking in advanced democratic economies. Administration agencies have in-house policy shops that produce policy analysis to support their initiatives. Congressional committees have support staff that provides analysis to inform policy debate. Private think tanks produce policy analysis that is used by various interest groups in public policy debate. Specific interest groups commission consulting firms and academics to provide policy analyses of issues of particular import to the interest group. Interests on all sides of an issue provide policy analysis that enlightens policymakers on the aspects of the policy debate.

Policy Analysis for High-Stakes Issues

A direct correspondence often exists between the policy issue stakes and the resources expended in producing policy analysis. A potential change in tax law that affects a few taxpayers and involves just a few million dollars in revenue will probably generate just a modest amount of policy analysis. But a major tax policy initiative that affects large numbers of taxpayers and involves billions of dollars in revenue will generate a plethora of policy studies that will be used in the policy debate. The Tax Reform Act of 1986 (TRA86) is a good example. That reform effort generated the largest flow of policy analysis in the history of tax policymaking.[5] It was a high-stakes tax reform that created significant numbers of winners and losers. A contemporary example can be found in the present public policy debate surrounding the flat tax and fundamental tax reform efforts.

Is There a Link Between Theory and Policy?

With all of the effort put into policy analysis, one might ask to what extent is there a link between theory and policy? That is, does public finance theory really have the ability to directly inform policy debates? Or, is it merely an academic exercise that provides partisans on all sides a convenient cover for their initiatives motivated by factors wholly other than the desire to make good public policy? Well, one can be cynical to the point of despair in any aspect of life. Aside from that extreme position, which we dismiss, there is reason to believe that fundamental principles of public finance play an important role in shaping public policy debates. In most cases, the real issues at hand boil down to questions of equity and efficiency—the essential stuff of public finance. At their heart, most policy debates are driven by concern for fairness or a desire to make the system more efficient in its operation. As such, public finance principles can be used to inform public policy debate.

Good policymaking requires solid policy analysis. When the policymaking process is functioning well, it relies on comprehensive, thoughtful, and insightful policy analysis of the issue at hand. That requires economic analysis of the issue, with careful attention paid to both equity and efficiency aspects of the issue. In this respect, the economic analysis of public finance issues discussed throughout this text is absolutely essential to sound policymaking. We would be naive, however, if we thought that sound economic analysis is all that goes into policymaking. As we saw in the beginning of this chapter, policymaking also involves politics and theater. Politics is a necessary part of the process in a democracy because it is the principal means by which issues are raised and interest groups express their concerns. Competing interests are balanced against one another in the political process, yielding a collective choice. Theater is just part of that political process by which collective choices are ultimately made. For a good introduction to the public policy process and public policy analysis, see Wheelan (2011).

As Sheffrin said in the long quote at the beginning of this chapter, however, "Our economic problems appear to be more profound and no longer the type that can be cured by simple solutions proposed by policy technicians." Although sound policy analysis is necessary for good policymaking, it is not sufficient. Yes, a link exists between economic theory and policy. The link is that in order to have good policy you must begin with sound economic theory and solid policy analysis. Complexity in the modern democratic policy arena requires a challenging depth of insight that requires increasingly penetrating analysis. For that reason, the role of the economist and the policy analyst is becoming more important. Yet, we know that the modern policymaking process in a democratic context involves other factors. The policy wonk does not act alone to implement solutions.

PROBLEMS

1. The president usually announces major policy initiatives in the State of the Union Address in January. Those initiatives are often not formulated with all the details worked out. In fact, the proposals are often very sketchy concepts with no substantive form whatsoever.
   a. Explain why this may be the case, given the timing of the State of the Union Address and the remaining process of budget formulation.
   b. Explain why this may be the case, given the institutional process of budget development.
   c. Explain why the State of the Union Address is a highly political statement, given your answers in parts a and b.
2. The House Ways and Means Committee and the Senate Finance Committee are the two most important congressional committees from the point of view of formulating tax policy in the United States.

a. Name the current chairs of these two committees.
b. Most state legislatures have corresponding committees in the two chambers of the state legislature. Find out the names of your state committees and their chairs.

3. Go to the Policy.com website; find the link to additional think tanks.
   a. Follow three links to think tanks and obtain their statement of purpose.
   b. Examine those statements of purpose.
   c. Is there evidence of a particular political or economic point of view evident in the statement? If so, explain.
   d. Compare the statements to those of the Brookings Institution and American Enterprise Institute. What similarities and differences do you see? Explain.
4. Given what you know of U.S. taxes, explain whether U.S. tax policy is consistent with the IMF policy advice in Table 21.2. If not, explain why not.
5. Given what you have learned about the elements of good tax policy in this text, evaluate the IMF policy advice given in Table 21.2. Identify areas of consistency between the text and the IMF advice. Identify areas of conflict between the text and the IMF advice.
6. Go to the CBO website (http://www.cbo.gov) and download a recent policy study relating to a tax issue. Skim over the study and write a paragraph explaining the basic policy advice provided.
7. Go to the CEA website (http://www.whitehouse.gov/administration/eop/cea/) and download a recent policy study relating to a tax issue. Skim over the study and write a paragraph explaining the basic policy advice provided.
8. Go to the IMF website (http://www.imf.org/external/ns/cs.aspx?id=29) and download a World Economic Outlook Report. Skim over the report and write a paragraph summarizing the public finance aspects highlighted in the report.
9. Go to the IMF website (http://www.imf.org/external/country/index.htm) and find a country of interest to you. Download a recent Article IV Consultation report and write a brief summary of the current conditions in that country's economy, including fiscal conditions.

REFERENCES

Musgrave, Richard A., and Peggy B. Musgrave. *Public Finance in Theory and Practice,* 5th ed. New York: McGraw-Hill, 1989.

Pechman, Joseph A. *Federal Tax Policy,* 5th ed. Washington, DC: Brookings Institution, 1987.

Sheffrin, Steven M. *Markets and Majorities: The Political Economy of Public Policy.* New York: Free Press, 1993.

Steurele, Eugene. *The Tax Decade: How Taxes Came to Dominate the Public Agenda.* Washington, DC: Urban Institute, 1992.

Stotsky, Janet. "Summary of the IMF Tax Policy Advice." In *Tax Policy Handbook,* edited by Parthasarathi Shome. Washington, DC: International Monetary Fund, Fiscal Affairs Department, 1995.

Wheelan, Charles. *Introduction to Public Policy.* New York: W.W. Norton and Company, 2011.

NOTES

1. This material on the GAO is adapted from the *U.S. Government Manual*.
2. A convenient link to many think tanks is available on the web at *www.policy.com*.
3. IMF website.
4. Text excerpt from IMF Articles of Agreement: Article 1, Purposes (*http://www.imf.org/external/pubs.ft/aa/aa01.htm*) IMF © 2002. Reprinted by permission.
5. Steuerle (1992) chronicles the tax reform efforts of this era.

APPENDIX TO CHAPTER 3

Efficient Provision of Public and Private Goods

We can also demonstrate the efficient provision of both the public and private goods and the allocation of the private good to the two consumers in the diagram in Figure 1.[1]

1. The production possibilities frontier (*PPF*) is given. That means we take resources and technology as given. This frontier traces out the combinations of public and private good quantities that the economy is technically capable of producing, assuming full utilization of resources and given production technology.
2. Take the utility level of person 2 as given, illustrated by the indifference curve u^2.
3. Trace out the consumption possibilities frontier (*CPF*) for person 1. To do that, we assume a given level of x and label it x_g. We then observe how much of the total amount y_g that can be produced corresponding to x_g, and allocate the amount y_k of y to person 2 that is necessary to put person 2 on indifference curve u^2. Then plot the amount remaining, $y_g - y_k$, as a point y^j on the consumption possibilities frontier for person 1. Doing this for all possible quantities of x traces out the *CPF* illustrated.
4. We then maximize utility for person 1, subject to the consumption possibilities frontier (which holds the other person's utility constant; note that we are applying the Pareto criterion here). Any point on the *CPF* is feasible (given the *PPF* and fixed utility for person 2), but the question is which point on the *CPF* would give the maximum utility for person 1? We can imagine a set of indifference curves for person 1 drawn in the diagram, and from there we can find the highest level of utility possible for person 1. Point *h* represents that level.
5. Determine the optimal point of production on the *PPF* (x^*, y^*). Given *h* on the *CPF*, we can trace back to point *m* on the *PPF* and find the optimal combination of the two goods.
6. Given the optimal combination of x and y to be produced, we then determine the allocation of *y* to each individual. Person 1 should

[1] Figure 1 is adapted from Oakland (1987).

receive y^1 units of y, whereas the remainder $y^* - y^1$ should be allocated to person 2. That is, $y^2 = y^* - y^1$.
7. Both consumers receive the same level of the public good X* due to the nonrival nature of the public good.
8. Notice that the Samuelson condition holds at this allocation of goods. The slope of the *PPF* at point *m* is MRT_{xy}. That slope equals the sum of the marginal rates of substitution for the two consumers, $MRS^1_{xy} + MRS^2_{xy}$, which are illustrated by the slopes at points *h* and *l*. This condition is assured because the construction of the *CPF* results in its slope being the slope of the *PPF* minus the slope of person 2's indifference curve.

FIGURE 1 Providing the Proper Combination of Public and Private Goods

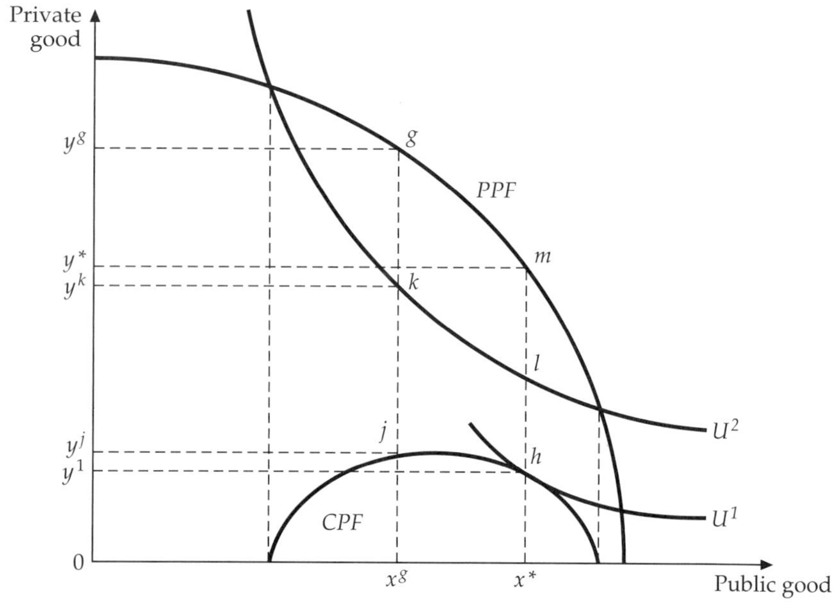

APPENDIX TO CHAPTER 5

Top Incomes in the United States, France, and the United Kingdom over the Twentieth Century

Research on the distribution of income and the causes of observed changes in the distribution provides important insight. A recent study by Piketty and Saez (2007) takes a long view of history and examines changes in the income distribution not only in the United States, but also in France and the United Kingdom.

Their analysis reveals a U-shaped pattern over the century for the top income and wage shares. Figure 1 illustrates their estimates for the extremely wealthy top 0.1 percent of the income distribution in all three countries. The U.S. pattern clearly reveals a U-shaped share of income earned by those in this top income category, falling from about 8 percent during World War I to a low of approximately 2 percent in the 1960s, and then rising to about 6 percent at the end of the century. The patterns in France and the United Kingdom fall throughout the century, with a more modest rise at the end of the century.

Piketty and Saez also examine the sources of income earned over the century, finding that the composition of income sources changed dramatically. Figure 2 illustrates two snapshots of the top decile of the U.S. income distribution in 1929 and 1999. In 1920, wage income as a source of total income declined from 60 percent of income in the 90th to 95th percentile to 10 percent in the 99.99th percentile. The mirror image of that decline is seen in the increasing share of capital income, rising from 20 percent in the 90th to 95th percentile bracket to 70 percent at the top of the income distribution. Entrepreneurial income was a relatively flat 20 percent source of income. By 1999 the sources of income had changed dramatically with wage income accounting for a larger share at all of the upper-income brackets, falling from 90 percent in the 90th to 95th percentile bracket to 60 percent in the top bracket. Capital income accounted for a much smaller share in all of the upper-income brackets and entrepreneurial income accounted for a rising share of income across the top income brackets.

FIGURE 1 Top 0.1% Income Shares in the United States, France, and the United Kingdom,1913–1998

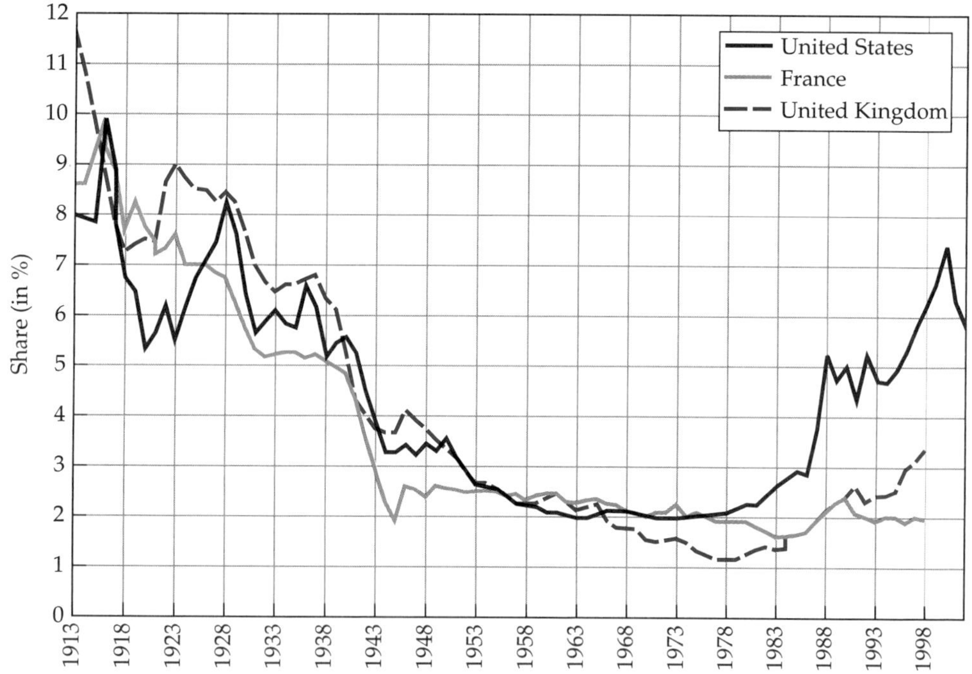

Source: Piketty and Saez (2007), Figure 12.

FIGURE 2 Income Composition of U.S. Top Groups within the Top Decile, 1929 and 1999

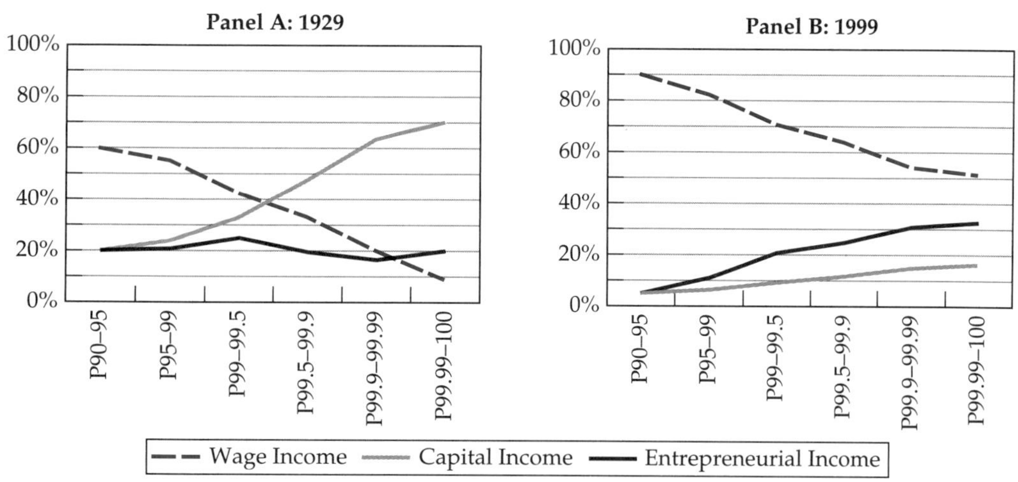

Source: Piketty and Saez (2007), Figure 4.

APPENDIX TO CHAPTER 6

Rational Voters

RATIONALITY IN VOTING

Suppose that there is a proposal on the ballot that would reduce taxes.[1] If the ballot measure passes, you will have after-tax income of y_2, whereas if the proposal fails, you are left with income y_1, your current after-tax income. Let us suppose that there is a probability p that the ballot measure will pass without your vote. Thus, your expected income is $py_2 - (1 - p)y_1$. This expected income is a weighted average of the two potential outcomes, where the weights are the probabilities associated with each event.

We can also consider your expected gain. If the ballot measure passes, your expected increase in income is $y_e - y_1$, which is a probability-weighted average of the two outcomes: $y_e - y_1 = (1 - p)0 + p(y_2 - y_1)$, or $y_e - y_1 = p(y_2 - y_1)$. We can rearrange this expression to illustrate the probability of the ballot measure passing as $p = (y_e - y_1)/(y_2 - y_1)$. The probability of passage equals the expected income gain over the total income gain.

Now, let's consider whether it is worth going to the polls and voting for a ballot measure. The process of voting is costly. It takes time and effort. Suppose that the transaction cost involved is c. As a result, your potential net incomes y_1 and y_2 will be reduced to $y_1 - c$ and $y_2 - c$ if you choose to vote. Will it be worth the trouble required to vote? Certainly, one more vote for the proposal will help it pass, increasing the likelihood of realizing the proposal's benefit. But, on the other hand, there is the cost of voting to take into account.

If the person does not vote, the expected income is y_e, as described previously. If the person does vote, the expected income is y_e' and the expected increase in income is $y_e' - (y_1 - c)$ times the probability of success *with the person's vote,* which we will denote as q. This expression is a probability-weighted average of the two outcomes: $y_e' (y_1 - c) = (1 - p)0 + q[(y_2 - c) - (y_1 - c)]$, or more simply, $y_e' (y_1 - c) = q[(y_2 - c) - (y_1 - c)]$. Here again, we can rewrite this expression to isolate the probability q on the left-hand

[1]This material is adapted from Jones and Cullis, 1986, "Is Democracy Regressive? A Comment on Political Participation," *Public Choice* 51: 101–7.

FIGURE 1 Expected Utility of Voting

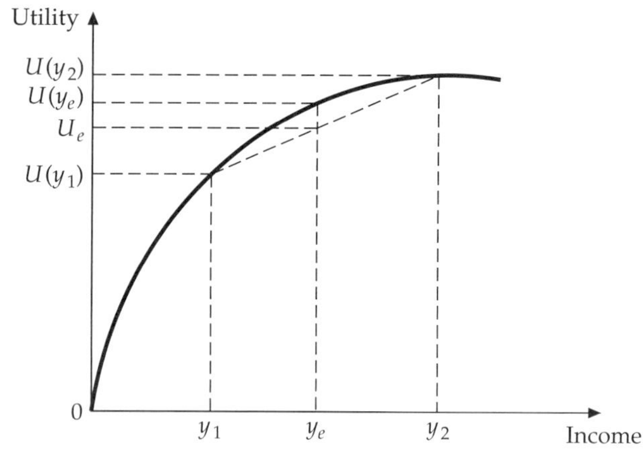

side: $q = [y_e' - (y_1 - c)]/[(y_2 - c) - (y_1 - c)]$. It is worth voting if the probability of success *with my vote* is at least q.

Now, the decision on whether to vote hinges on whether q is greater than p, that is, whether the probability of the measure passing increases with my vote by enough to compensate me for the trouble of voting. The decision to vote must increase the probability of the measure passing by enough to justify the cost involved with voting.

If we consider the graphical presentation, we can see that in Figure 1 the implicit probability of the ballot measure passing is $p = 0.5$ because y_e is halfway between y_1 and y_2. In Figure 2, the probability q appears to be more than one-half since the ratio of $y_e' - (y_1 - c)$ to $(y_2 - c) - (y_1 - c)$

FIGURE 2 Expected Utility of Voting with Transactions Cost

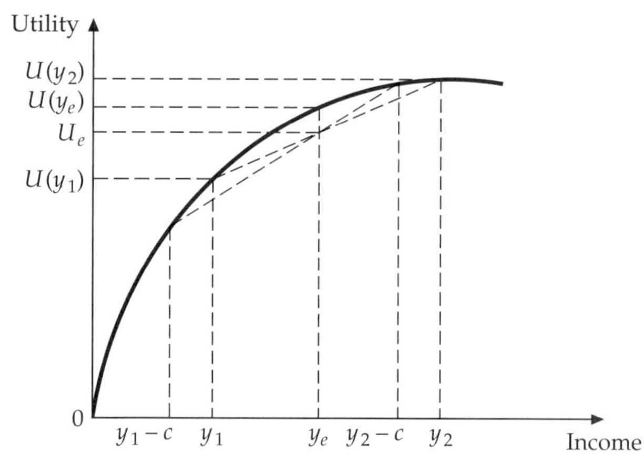

is clearly greater than 0.5. As a result, the voter confronted with this situation will vote.

RATIONAL VOTER IGNORANCE

Have you ever noticed how many voters seem woefully ignorant of the issues they will face on a ballot? Are such voters just intractably ignorant, or is there a good reason to be ignorant? From the economist's point of view, there may be good reason to be ignorant when becoming informed is costly. A clear cost exists in obtaining information on the issues that will appear on the ballot. A potential benefit exists in obtaining that information and using it to affect the outcome of the vote. But only when the expected marginal benefit is at least as great as the marginal cost of obtaining information is it economically sensible to become informed. Thus, there is such a thing as rational ignorance.

APPENDIX TO CHAPTER 8

Production and Cost Functions

Chapter 8 relies on concepts of production and cost from the principles of a microeconomics course. The appendix provides a review for those students who need a refresher or who need a quick overview of the concepts.

PRODUCTION FUNCTIONS

The first problem to address in the production of a public good or service is the technical aspect of converting factors such as land, labor, and capital into the output. Physical quantities of these factors are used to produce a physical quantity of the output. For example, the police department of the city government must solve the technical problem of how many police cruisers and officers are needed and how they should be combined to provide a specific level of public safety. In this particular case the production technology is readily apparent. They combine two officers with one police cruiser. The remaining economic issue to solve is how many such combinations are needed to provide the maximum level of public safety given the police department's limited budget. The mathematical description of the relationship between the minimum quantities of each input required to produce a given quantity of the output is known as the production function. This is the critical starting point for analyzing the production of public goods and services.

Figure 1 illustrates the concept of a production process which takes inputs of land, labor, and capital and combines them in producing outputs such as schooling, housing, or medical care. The mathematical description of

FIGURE 1 The Production Relationship

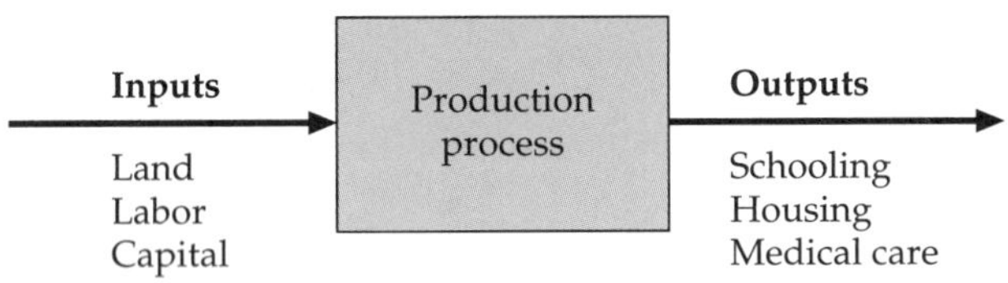

FIGURE 2 Total and Marginal Product

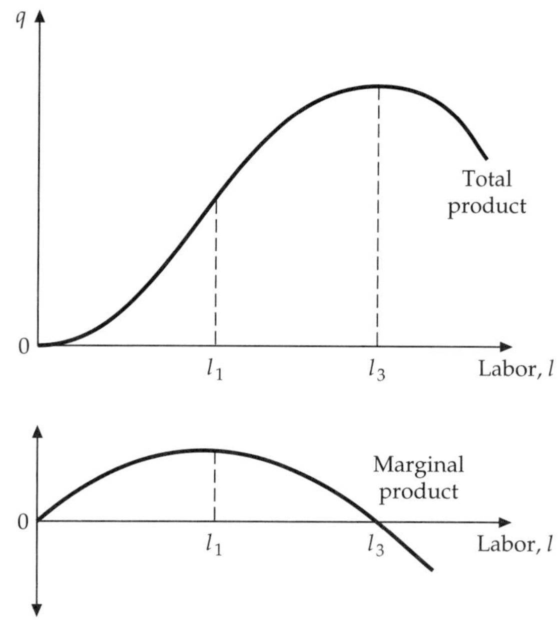

the maximum quantity of output that can be derived from given quantities of the inputs, taking technology as given, is the production function. We can express the production function as $q = f(k, l, n)$, where q is the quantity of output and k, l, and n represent quantities of the inputs capital, labor, and land.

Let us begin by concentrating on a simple case where the quantity of land is fixed and the quantities of labor and capital are variable inputs. Hence we have one **fixed input,** land, and two **variable inputs,** labor and capital. Because one of the inputs is fixed in supply, we are taking a short-run view of the problem. In the **long run,** unlike the **short run,** all inputs are variable. Suppose that q measures the quantity of the public good to be provided, l measures the quantity of labor, and k measures the quantity of capital. The production function is then written as $q = f(l, k)$. We will not specify a particular functional form for the function f. We can draw a two-dimensional graph of the relationship between one of the variable inputs and the output of the public good, as illustrated in Figure 2.

TOTAL, MARGINAL, AND AVERAGE PRODUCT

Plotting the total output q as a function of the variable input labor gives the **total product** curve, which shows how output increases with increased usage of the input. A change in the quantity of the input used leads to a change in the quantity of output produced, the ratio of which is called the **marginal**

product of the variable input. The total product and marginal product of a variable input such as labor are illustrated in graphically in Figure 2. The top panel of the figure illustrates the total product of a public good that can be produced with various quantities of the variable input labor. Two important quantities of labor are labeled: l_1, where the total product curve has an inflection point, and l_3, where total product reaches its maximum. The **inflection point** occurs where the total product curve switches from being concave to being convex (or switches from rising at an increasing rate to rising at a decreasing rate).[1] The total product reaches its maximum with variable input quantity l_3. If our objective were to maximize output, we would use l_3 units of labor, combined with the fixed inputs in order to obtain the largest possible output of the public good.

Using a smaller quantity of labor would not enable us to produce as much of the public good because we are combining that labor with a fixed amount of capital. With too little labor, our output suffers. Consider the example of the police department producing public safety using officers and cruisers. Suppose that the cruisers are designed to be operated by two officers—one to drive and the other to operate the radar detector and eat powdered sugar doughnuts. If we want to maximize the output of public safety, there is a number of officers l_3, which, when combined with the number of cruisers in the department's motor pool, will produce the greatest number of fully functional units on the streets. In similar fashion, a larger number of officers, greater than l_3, would not produce as much public safety since we are constrained to a fixed number of cruisers. The additional officers do not produce public safety without additional cruisers. In fact, with extra officers sitting in the back seats of cruisers eating powdered sugar doughnuts and distracting the officers in the front seat of the cruiser, the production of public safety is reduced.

The corresponding marginal product curve is illustrated in the lower panel of Figure 3. The marginal product is rising initially but reaches its maximum at the quantity of labor l_1. Because the marginal product is the rate of change in the total product with a change in labor, we can think of it as the slope of the total product curve.[2] For quantities less than l_1, the marginal product is rising, and for quantities greater than l_1, it is falling. Hence, the marginal product is at its maximum at l_1, the same point where the second derivative of the total product changes sign—the inflection point.

Additional units of labor initially provide increasing returns as each additional unit of labor employed results in increased output and the rate at

[1] Using terminology from differential calculus; that is the point where the second derivative changes sign from positive to negative.

[2] Marginal product is the first derivative (or slope) of total product, $\partial q/\partial l$; hence it makes sense that the marginal product reaches it maximum at the quantity where the total product has its inflection point—where the total product curve switches from increasing at an increasing rate to increasing at a decreasing rate. The derivative (slope) is positive for quantities of labor up to l_3, although the derivative (slope) is initially rising and then falling. For quantities of labor up to l_1, the second derivative $\partial^2 q/\partial l^2$ is positive, but thereafter it is negative.

FIGURE 3 Relationships Between Total, Marginal, and Average Product

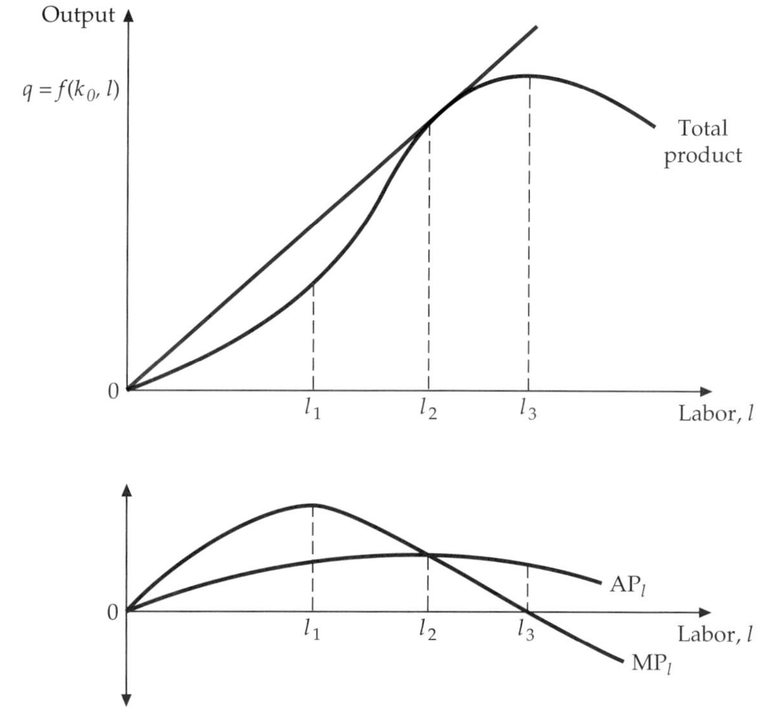

which output increases is rising. That experience ends once we have employed l_1 units of labor. After l_1 units of labor, each additional unit of labor employed adds to output but at a decreasing rate. That is true of all units of labor employed up to l_3, where the marginal product reaches zero. For units of labor employed in excess of l_3, the marginal product of labor is negative, reducing total product.

The **average product** of a variable input is the amount of output that results from using a unit of the input *on average,* over all of the units of input employed, not just the last unit employed as in the case of marginal product.

THE RELATIONSHIP BETWEEN AVERAGE AND MARGINAL PRODUCT

The relationship between the marginal and average product of a variable input is important to know. The easiest way to understand that relationship is to reflect on some marginal and average relationships you use all of the time yourself. Take, for example, your grade point average (GPA). Because this measure of your academic performance is an average, it is like the concept of an average product. Your GPA is computed by dividing your total number of honor points (or whatever your college or university calls them) by the number of credit hours of course work you have taken. For example, suppose that you have taken 48 credit hours of course work and you have earned 120 honor points. Your GPA is then GPA = 120/48 = 2.5. This is a measure of your overall performance in the 48 hours of course work. Now, your performance in courses this semester will involve a change in the number of credit hours taken and a corresponding change in the number of honor points. Suppose that you take 12 credit hours this semester and earn grades of B in all of those credit hours. That will add 36 honor points to your total. Your semester GPA is 3.0. This is your marginal GPA, the increase in honor points corresponding to an increase in credit hours taken. Notice that because your marginal performance in courses this semester is above your average performance to date, your cumulative GPA will increase. You have a total of 156 honor points now over the 60 credit hours you have taken, so your GPA will rise to 2.6. Your marginal performance is above your average, so your average is rising. Similarly, if your marginal performance were below your average, your average would be falling.

The average product of labor, when capital is fixed at the level k_0, is $AP_l = q(k_0, l)/l$. The average product is defined in this way, and the average product of labor will increase if q rises faster than l and decrease if q rises slower than l. This can be seen in Figure 4 by considering several points along the total product curve, defined as $q = q(k_0, l)$. Using l_a units of labor results in q_a units of output. Increasing labor input usage in the interval $(0, l_b)$ results in increasing returns to the variable input. Here we find that each additional unit of labor used in the production of the public good creates an increasing quantity of additional public good. Point b is the inflection point, however, after which the returns to the variable input are decreasing. This point is called the **point of diminishing marginal returns (PDMR).**

FIGURE 4 Returns to a Variable Input

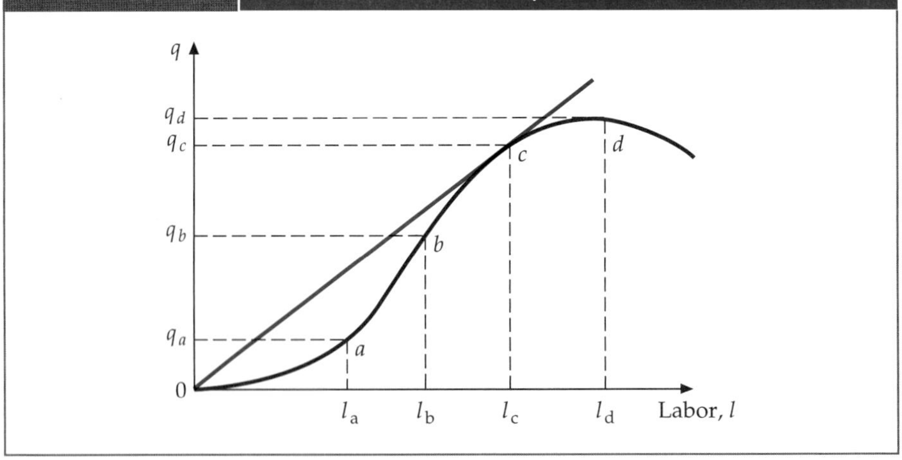

Over the range (l_b, l_c) additional units of labor create more output of the public good but at a decreasing rate. Point c is the point where the average product of labor is maximum. This point is called the **point of diminishing average returns (PDAR).** For units of labor employed in excess of l_c, the marginal product is positive, but the average product is declining. Point d represents the point at which the marginal product is zero. Beyond this point, added use of labor actually decreases output.

Notice that the production function has been drawn with output which is initially rising at an increasing rate (from the origin to point a), followed by a range over which output is increasing at a constant rate (the nearly linear segment before and after point b), followed by another range over which output is increasing at a decreasing rate (from point c on). Eventually, output is decreasing with increased use of the variable input. This pattern reflects the most general production case where we have increasing, constant, and decreasing returns to the variable input.

The marginal product of an input is the added amount of output derived from an incremental increase in the amount of the input employed in production. If we are considering discrete units of the input capital, for example, the marginal product of capital is $MP_k = \triangle q/\triangle k$, where the symbol $\triangle$ indicates a discrete change.[3] Of course, we are changing the quantity of capital while holding the amount of labor fixed; as a result, the marginal product gives us the productivity of capital on the margin, or for the last unit of the capital employed in the production process. Figure 4 illustrates the graph of a typical marginal product curve for a variable input.

Additional amounts of each of the inputs are initially expected to produce more output. Hence, the marginal products of an input are initially positive. There may come a point, however, where there is so much of the input that additional amounts of the input cause output to decline, making the marginal product negative. The average product of a variable input is the total amount of output divided by the quantity of input. For example, the average product of capital is given by $AP_k = q/k$. The average product of capital gives us the average productivity of capital, for all the units of capital used in the production of the output.

The important relationship between marginal and average measures of the productivity of an input must be recognized. When marginal product is above average product, average product is rising. When marginal product is below average product, average product is falling. The combination of these two relationships implies that the marginal product must intersect the average product at its minimum. Hence, the graph of marginal and average products must be drawn with the marginal product curve cutting through the average product curve at its minimum.

[3] In the continuous case where we consider infinitesimally small changes, the marginal product of capital is given by the partial derivative $MP_k = \partial q/\partial k$. A partial derivative measures the effect of a change in one variable while holding all else equal. In this case we are holding constant the quantity of the other input, labor. Hence, the marginal product of capital, as measured by the partial derivative, gives us the increase in output due to an increase in a single variable input, holding all other variable inputs and fixed inputs constant.

COST FUNCTIONS

The cost of producing a public good or service is a function of the output rate. As the quantity of the public good we wish to produce varies, the cost of producing it will vary as well. At its most basic level, cost depends on two factors: production technology, as described in the production function, and factor prices that must be paid for the land, labor, and capital that go into making the public good.

FIXED AND VARIABLE COSTS

Costs associated with the use of variable factors are called **variable costs,** whereas the costs associated with fixed factors are called **fixed costs.** Returning to our school example, if a public elementary school occupies five acres of land, the cost of the land is fixed since a change in the quantity or quality of education provided in the school has no impact on the required amount of land, and hence no impact on cost. The costs associated with the variable inputs, labor and capital, depend on the quantities of each that are used in the production process. The more labor and capital employed, the greater the cost per unit of schooling produced. Hence, the variable costs are those costs associated with the employment of variable inputs. Total cost is the sum of fixed costs and variable costs.

If we denote **total cost** as ***TC*,** **total fixed cost** as ***TFC*,** and **total variable cost** as ***TVC*,** the relationship between the three concepts can be written as $TC = TFC + TVC$. Total cost is the sum of total fixed and total variable costs. We can illustrate these cost concepts graphically, as in Figure 5. Total fixed cost *TFC* is constant at the same level regardless of the output. That is the nature of a fixed cost. Total variable cost *TVC* rises initially at a decreasing rate due to increasing returns to scale, but that pattern changes to just the opposite once decreasing returns sets in. Total cost *TC* is just the sum of *TFC*

FIGURE 5 Total Cost as a Function of Output

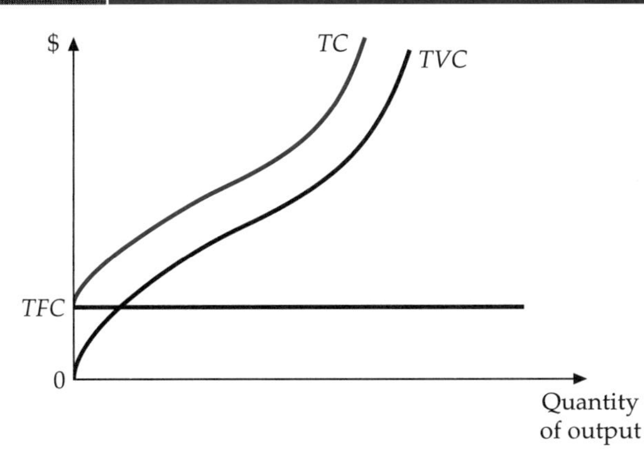

and *TVC*; hence the *TC* curve lies above the *TVC* curve by a fixed amount, reflecting *TFC*.

AVERAGE COST

If we spread our total cost over all of the units produced, we obtain average cost. Average cost indicates how much units of production cost to produce, on average. **Average total cost** (*ATC*) is defined as total cost divided by output: $ATC = TC/q$. Because total cost (TC) can be subdivided into total fixed cost and total variable cost, $TC = TFC + TVC$, we can similarly subdivide average total cost into average fixed and average variable cost: $ATC = AFC + AVC$. **Average fixed cost** (*AFC*) is defined as $AFC = TFC/q$ and **average variable cost** (*AVC*) is $AVC = TVC/q$.

MARGINAL COST

Although average cost tells us what units of production cost on average (an average over all of the units produced), **marginal cost** tells us what the last unit of production costs to produce. The adjective *marginal* refers to a change in the total cost of production that results from a *change* in the number of units produced. Marginal cost is defined as $MC = \triangle TC/\triangle q$, or the change in total cost associated with a change in the quantity of the good produced. (The Greek letter $\triangle$ is used to indicate a discrete change.)[4] Marginal cost indicates the additional cost associated with additional output. It tells us how much it costs to produce the good, *on the margin*. Typically, marginal cost is rising with the output level, as illustrated in Figure 6, indicating that as we produce more of the good, the additional cost of each unit of production is rising.

FIGURE 6 Marginal and Average Cost

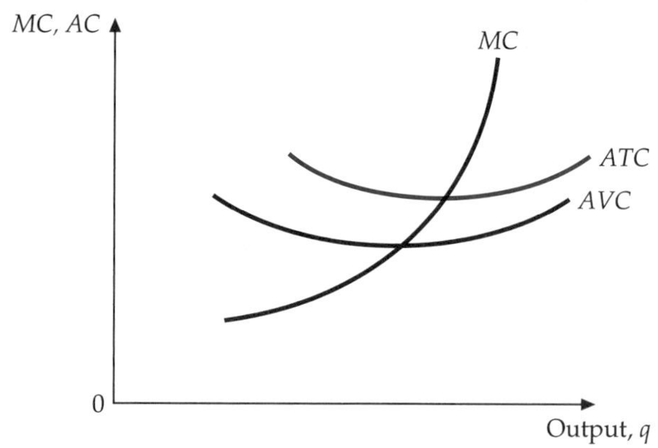

[4] If we let these changes become infinitesimally small, we have the derivative concept from mathematics and the marginal cost is defined as $MC = dTC/dq$.

RELATIONSHIP BETWEEN AVERAGE AND MARGINAL COST

Average and marginal cost concepts are distinctly different, yet they are intimately related. To understand the relationship, put yourself in the knee socks of Chipper Jones, who plays third base for the Atlanta Braves. You are playing the Los Angeles Dodgers tonight at Dodger Stadium in Chavez Ravine. Your current batting average is 0.300, indicating that you have gotten a hit 30 percent of your times at bat over the season so far. This is your average performance. Tonight will be your marginal performance. If you get four hits in your four times at bat, your marginal performance will be 1.000 and your season's average will rise. But, on the other hand, if Hideo Nomo strikes you out three times, your marginal performance will be 0.250 and your season's average will fall. Notice that when your marginal performance is above your average, your average rises, but when your marginal performance is below your average, your average falls. The same is true for student grade point averages discussed earlier and costs of producing public education, health care, and national defense. Figure 6 also illustrates the relationship between average and marginal cost. When marginal cost is below average cost, average cost is falling. When marginal cost is above average cost, average cost is rising. Consequently, the marginal cost curve cuts through the average cost curves at their minimum points. It is important to draw the curves with this essential characteristic.

LONG-RUN AVERAGE COST

In the long run there are no fixed inputs. All inputs are variable. Therefore, there is no need for the distinction between fixed and variable inputs in long-run analysis, and we focus exclusively on average cost. For any given level of the fixed input in the short run, we can draw a short-run average cost curve, but that is also true for every possible level of the fixed input. If we are free to vary the fixed input, there is an infinite number of short-run average cost curves possible, each one corresponding to a different level of the fixed input.

If we trace out all of the short-run average cost curves and pick the lowest one for any given level of output we may wish to produce, we trace out the envelope curve known as the long-run average cost (*LRAC*) curve. Figure 7 illustrates the long-run average cost curve. This curve shows the lowest average cost that can be attained in producing any given level of output when we are free to vary the fixed input.

THE RELATIONSHIP BETWEEN PRODUCTION FUNCTION ANALYSIS AND COST FUNCTION ANALYSIS

The production function tells us the maximum output that is attainable from given quantities of the inputs: $q = q(k, l)$. One way to think of the optimal input combination is to think of maximizing the output of the public good subject to a budget constraint represented by the isocost line. We want to

FIGURE 7 Long-Run Average Cost

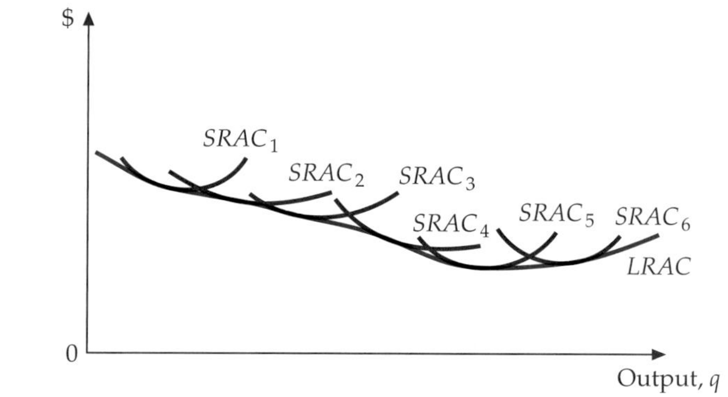

reach the highest possible isoquant while simultaneously being on a given isocost line. The point of tangency between the isoquant and the isocost line provides that optimal point. Alternatively, we could think of producing a given level of output and minimizing the cost of producing that level of output. That would require operating on a given isoquant and finding the isocost line closest to the origin that enables us to product that output. If we know the output level we wish to attain, q^0, the minimum cost necessary to attain at least that level of output gives us the cost function: $c(r,w,q^0)$, where r and w are the prices of capital and labor, respectively. The identical optimal input combination is found by either thought experiment. One useful advantage of the cost minimization approach is that factor demand functions are derived from the cost function by simply differentiating with respect to each factor price.

We can also see the implications of returns to scale when we observe the *LRAC* curve. If there are economies of scale in the production of the public good or service, the *LRAC* curve is falling. Greater output levels can be produced with less than proportionate scaling of input quantities, so the average cost per unit of output falls. On the other hand, if the production of the public good or service is characterized by decreasing returns to scale, the *LRAC* curve is rising with increases in output. In the case of constant returns to scale, the *LRAC* curve is horizontal.

APPENDIX TO CHAPTER 9

The Basic Economics of PAYGO

In this appendix we consider the basic economics of a PAYGO system, as described in Feldstein and Liebman (2002). Suppose we have L_t workers at time t, each earning a constant wage w. Suppose further that the number of workers grows over time so that $L_{t+1} = (1+n)L_t$. Each working generation pays a fraction θ of their earnings to the retirees who were workers in the previous generation. The total amount of tax paid by the workers at time t is $T_t = \theta w l_t$. The benefit that the working generation will receive when it retires is B_{t+1} and is computed as the tax paid by the next generation, $B_{t+1} = T_{t+1} = \theta w l_{t+1}$. With this information we can compute the ratio of the benefits received by the retirees in the system to the taxes those same retirees paid during their working careers:

$$B_{t+1}/T_t = T_{t+1}/T_t = L_{t+1}/L_t = (1+n). \tag{1}$$

Hence, the retirees receive a rate of return that reflects the rate of growth in the number of workers over time.

If there is technological progress causing the economy to grow at the rate g, then the wage rises with that progress so $w_{t+1} = (1+g)w_t$. The ratio of benefits received by retirees to taxes paid is given by,

$$B_{t+1}/T_t = T_{t+1}/T_t = \theta w_t L_{t+1}/\theta w_t L_t = (1+g)(1+n). \tag{2}$$

Hence, the implicit rate of return is approximately $n+g$.

A PAYGO system like this is attractive because it provides a positive rate of return to each generation of retirees; plus it grants a one-time windfall to the first group of retirees when the system is implemented. In a political economy sense, this type of system is politically attractive. Of course, if the rate of growth in the number of workers is negative or if the rate of technical progress slows, the PAYGO system is much less attractive.[8]

APPENDIX TO CHAPTER 11

WELFARE COST OF A TAX

Consider the welfare cost of a tax on good X. Initially the prices of the two goods X and Y are p_x and p_y and you have a fixed money income m_0. Suppose that at these prices and income level you initially buy x_0 units of X and y_0 units of the other good Y. You are on the initial indifference curve I_0 at the point of tangency with your budget line. The tax increases the price of X, from p_x to $(1+t_x)p_x$, rotating the budget line as indicated to the steeper blue budget line. You react to the tax by buying fewer units of X and more units of good Y, reflected in the new quantities x_1 and y_1. You are clearly worse off as a result of the tax as you are now on the lower indifference curve I_1.

In order to illustrate these effects of a tax (or a tax increase) we use the concept of the *equivalent variation* (EV) of the tax, which is a measure of the welfare cost of the tax. The EV is the amount of money that would have to be given you to have exactly the same effect on your welfare as that caused by the tax. Because the tax causes a welfare loss, this is alternatively the amount you would be willing to pay to avert the tax. The EV measure of your welfare loss is generally larger than the amount of tax you actually pay, so the excess burden of the tax is the difference between the EV and the amount of tax you pay. Thus we can decompose the impact of the tax on you into two components: (1) the tax you pay on the amount of good X you buy that makes you worse off, and (2) an additional amount by which you are made worse off, called the *excess burden of the tax*, that is due to the fact that the tax has caused you to change your consumption behavior.

Figure 1 illustrates the tax revenue and the excess burden. The original budget line has the slope $-\frac{p_x}{p_y}$, whereas the new steeper budget line (in blue) reflects the tax and has the slope $-\frac{(1+t_x)p_x}{p_y}$. The vertical distance between the original budget line and a new hypothetical budget line with the original slope that is tangent to the new lower indifference curve I_1 is the EV. This is the vertical distance illustrated as *ac*. Of that amount, the vertical distance between the original budget line and the steeper budget line reflecting the new relative prices with a tax on good X, is the amount of tax revenue paid

FIGURE 1 Welfare Effects of a Tax on Good X

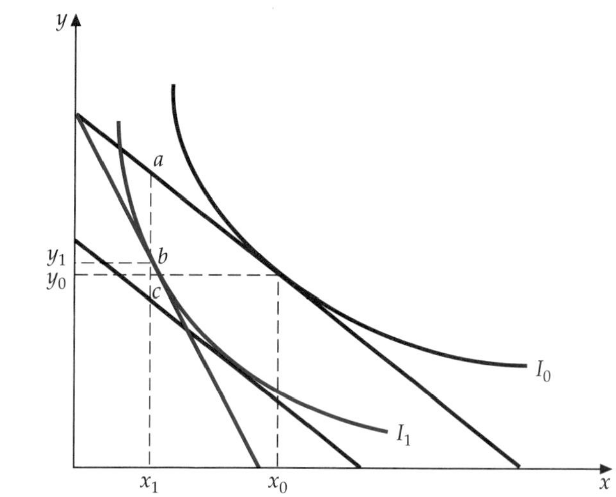

to the government, illustrated as *ab*. The remaining vertical distance in EV is the excess burden of the tax, illustrated as *bc*.

We can also use the expenditure function commonly used in microeconomic theory to define EV. The expenditure function $E(P, u)$ defines the minimum amount of expenditure necessary at the prices $P=(p_x, p_y)$ to attain the given utility level u. The equivalent variation for a move from the initial situation with no tax on X to the new situation with a tax on X is given by

$$EV = E(P^0, u^1) - E(P^0, u^0). \tag{1}$$

Notice that EV takes as its reference point the final utility level, not the original utility level.

WELFARE COST OF A SUBSIDY

Consider the welfare cost of a subsidy applied to good X. Suppose that you initially buy x_0 units of good X and y_0 units of the other good Y. You are on the initial indifference curve I_0. The subsidy reduces the price of X, rotating the budget line as indicated in the flatter blue budget line. You react to the subsidy by buying more units of X and fewer units of good Y, reflected in the new quantities x_1 and y_1. You are clearly better off as a result of the subsidy as you are on the higher indifference curve I_1.

In order to illustrate the effects of the subsidy we use another way to measure the welfare effect, this time using the **compensating variation** (CV). The CV is the amount of income we would have to take away from you to exactly negate the effect of the subsidy, making you as just as well off as you were before the subsidy. Because the subsidy causes a welfare gain, this is

FIGURE 2 Welfare Effects of a Subsidy on Good X

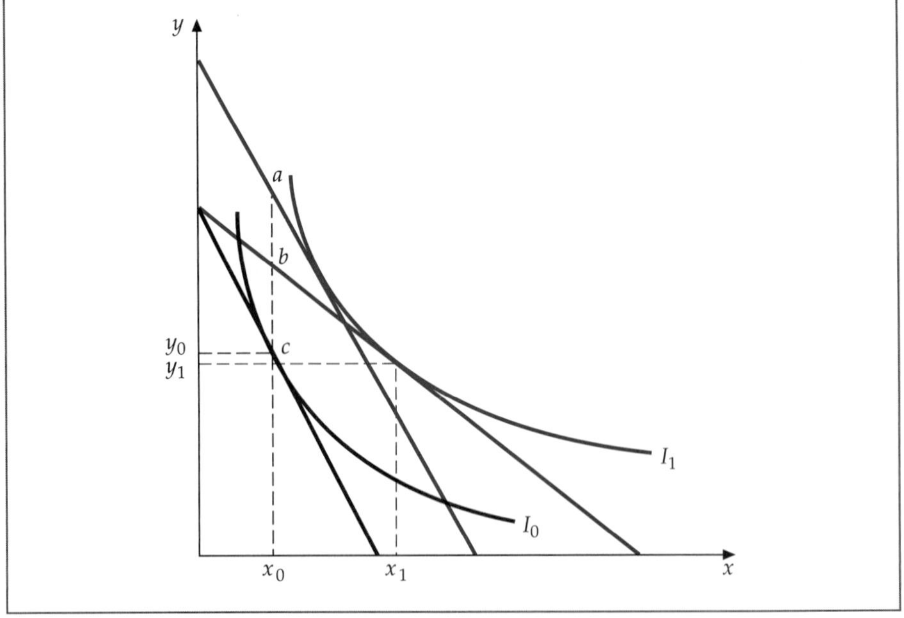

alternatively the amount you would be willing to pay for the change. The CV is generally larger than the actual subsidy you receive, so the excess burden of the subsidy is the difference between CV and the amount of subsidy received. We can decompose the welfare effect of the subsidy into two components: (1) the subsidy you receive based on the amount of X you buy that makes you better off, and (2) an additional amount by which you are made worse off, called the *excess burden of the subsidy*, that is due to the fact that the subsidy has caused you to change your consumption behavior.

Figure 2 illustrates the subsidy and the excess burden. The original budget line has the slope $-\frac{p_x}{p_y}$, whereas the new flatter budget line (in blue) reflects the subsidy and has the slope $-\frac{(1-s_x)p_x}{P_y}$, where s_x is the subsidy rate applied to good X. The vertical distance between the original budget line and a new hypothetical budget line with the new flatter slope that is tangent to the new higher indifference curve is the CV. This is the vertical distance, measuring in terms of good Y, illustrated as *ac*. Of that amount, the vertical distance between the original budget line and the steeper budget line reflecting the new relative price with a tax on good X, is the amount of subsidy received, illustrated as *bc*. The remaining vertical distance in CV is the excess burden of the subsidy, illustrated as *ab*.

Using the expenditure function, we can write CV as

$$CV = E(P^0, u^0) - E(P^1, u^0). \tag{2}$$

In contrast to EV, CV takes as its reference point the original value of utility, not the final value. This welfare measurement concept is originally due to economist John Hicks and was also employed by Nickolas Kaldor in his proposed method for welfare measurement. The Hicks-Kaldor welfare compensation criterion was mentioned in Chapter 3, footnote 11.

For normal goods EV > CV, but for inferior goods the reverse is true. For goods with no income effects, EV = CV. The main difference between the EV and CV measures of welfare change is that EV uses the original prices, whereas CV uses the new prices. For additional information on EV, CV, and measurement of the welfare costs of taxes and subsidies, see Cornes (1992) and Johansson (1991).

APPENDIX TO CHAPTER

TAXATION, INVESTMENT, AND THE CAPITAL STRUCTURE OF THE FIRM

The corporate income tax is fundamentally a tax on capital, so we need to consider in more detail how the tax affects the cost of capital and therefore how the tax affects the firm's financial structure and investment decisions. The firm's choice of alternative forms of long-term financing is called its **capital structure**.

Capital Structure of the Firm

In order to examine the ways that the corporate income tax may alter the way the corporation finances its activity, we must consider the corporation's receipts and disbursements more carefully. On the receipts side, there are three important sources. First, there is the corporation's gross profit in period *t*, denoted π_t, which is the difference between revenue and factor costs for labor and capital:

$$\pi_t = P_t Q_t - w_t L_t - r_t K_t. \tag{1}$$

Second, the firm may generate revenue from the sale of new bonds issued. If we denote bonds outstanding at the beginning of period *t* as B_t, then new bonds issued in the next period are $B_{t+1} - B_t$. Third, the firm may issue new equity in the form of stock. If we denote equity at the beginning of period *t* as E_t, then new equity issued in the next period is $E_{t+1} - E_t$.

On the disbursement side, the firm also has three sources of potential expenditures. First, the firm may pay out dividends to shareholders. We can denote dividends paid in period *t* as D_t. Second, the firm may pay interest to bondholders. In this case, the disbursement depends on both the interest rate and the quantity of outstanding bond debt. Hence, the interest expense to the firm is written as rB_t, where *r* is the interest rate. Finally, the firm may purchase new equipment and machinery, thus engaging in fixed investment denoted I_t. Note that this is called *fixed investment,* reflecting the fact that the firm is buying new productive buildings, machinery, and equipment. This is not financial investment such as the purchase of securities in financial markets.

Having identified the major sources of receipts and disbursements, we can write the fundamental accounting relationship for the firm. In period t, firm revenues must equal disbursements:

$$\pi_t + (B_{t+1} - B_t) + (E_{t+1} - E_t) = D_t + rB_t + I_t, \tag{2}$$

where the left-hand side of this equation sums the three sources of receipts (profit, new bonds issued, and new equity issued) and the right-hand side of the equation sums the three disbursements (dividends paid, interest paid on bonds, and investment). Notice that the basic accounting identity of the firm in Equation 2 implies that at least two financial variables must be changed at a time, one on each side of the equation. For example, a decrease in the firm's profit this period (on the left-hand side) must be balanced by some reduction in dividends paid or new fixed investment (on the right-hand side). Also, there are intertemporal implications in Equation 2 that the firm must consider. For example, if the firm sells new bonds today (an increase on the left-hand side), there will be an increase in the firm's interest payments in the future (on the right-hand side). Table 1 summarizes the sources of corporate receipts and disbursements.

The firm's **retained earnings** are those profits earned by the corporation that are not paid out in dividends or interest. We can write the firm's retained earnings as $\pi_t - D_t - rB_t$. Using this definition, we can see that the firm's investment must be financed out of one of three potential sources: retained earnings, borrowing in the form of new bonds issued, or new issues of equity shares. Thus, we can express investment as:

$$I_t = (\pi_t - D_t - rB_t) + (B_{t+1} - B_t) + (E_{t+1} - E_t). \tag{3}$$

If there are no taxes, the net financial flow from the firm to shareholders and bondholders, denoted Y_t, can be written as

$$Y_t = D_t + rB_t - (B_{t+1} - B_t) - (E_{t+1} - E_t). \tag{4}$$

This equation says that dividends and interest paid to people are balanced against new bonds issued and new equity shares created. This financial flow is also equivalent to the difference between profit and investment. The important implication of this result is that the flow of financing to individuals is determined by the real variables in the model and is not affected by the firm's financial structure. The real variables measure the firm's **real assets**—assets used to produce goods and services (in contrast to

TABLE 1 Firm Receipts and Disbursements

Firm Receipts	Firm Disbursements
Gross profits: $\pi_t = p_tQ_t - w_tL_t - r_tK_t$	Dividends paid: D_t
New bonds issued: $B_{t+1} - B_t$	Interest paid to bond holders: rB_t
New equity issued: $E_{t+1} - E_t$	Investment: I_t

financial assets or securities, which are claims to the firm's income generated by its real assets). This result is known as the **Modigliani-Miller (MM) theorem**, named after the two economists who discovered the result. The MM theorem says that in the absence of taxation and bankruptcy, corporate financial policy is irrelevant and has no effect on the value of the firm. The implication of the MM theorem is that the firm is indifferent to its choice of financial policy, or capital structure. It makes no difference whether the firm finances new investment from the issuance of bonds or new equity. If financial policy has no impact on the value of the firm, it simply does not matter how the firm is financed. Of course, the presence of a corporate income tax may change this result, as we will see.[15]

Tax Effects on the Firm's Capital Structure

So what happens when we put taxation into the model of the corporation? Do the MM theorem results hold or are they turned on their head? We will answer that question, but first we must put taxes into the model of the corporation, making sure that we clearly distinguish among the various taxes that are applied. We begin by making the following assumptions of a classical income tax system:

- A corporate tax on net income is applied at the rate t_c.
- Interest payments made by corporations are deductible on the corporate income tax at the rate t_c.
- Interest payments made by individuals are deductible on the individual income tax at the rate t_p.
- Both dividends and interest received by shareholders and bondholders are subject to individual income taxation at the rate t_p.
- Realized capital gains are taxable at the rate t_g, which is less than the personal income tax rate that applies to other sources of income; that is, $t_g < t_p$.

In the presence of this tax system, the financial identity of the corporation can be written as

$$\pi_t(1 - t_c) + (B_{t+1} - B_t) + (E_{t+1} - E_t) = D_t + r(1 - t_c)B_t + I_t. \tag{5}$$

The corporate income tax applies to the corporation's profit and the interest rate paid on bonds. Because there is also a tax liability for the individuals who are bondholders and shareholders, the financial flow of the corporation to individuals, after taxes, becomes

$$Y_t = (D_t + rB_t)(1 - t_c) - (B_{t+1} - B_t) - (E_{t+1} - E_t) - t_g G_t, \tag{6}$$

where G_t, is realized capital gains in period t.

Now, consider how taxation may affect the firm's capital structure. First, consider the effect of a change in the way funds are transferred to households. Suppose that the firm reduces its dividends paid to households by \$1 and also reduces its outstanding equity by \$1. In effect, the firm is taking a dollar of its net income and using it to buy back a dollar's worth of outstanding shares rather than paying out a dollar in dividends. In so doing, the firm is not paying out dividends directly to shareholders but is rather increasing the value of shareholders stock. That is, $\Delta D_t = -1$ and $(E_{t+1} - E_t) = -1$. What is the impact on households? The reduced dividend results in an after-tax loss of income of $1 - t_p$ to the household. On the other hand, the reduced equity outstanding benefits the household by the amount $1 - t_g$. Recall that the tax rate applied to capital gains is generally less than that applied to ordinary income: t_g, t_p. If that is the case, this change benefits the household that owns stock in the firm. Bondholders are unaffected. Hence the corporate repurchase of stock is beneficial to some households and harmless to the rest—on balance, an improvement.

So why do firms pay dividends rather than repurchase stock? As long as the tax rate on capital gains is less than that on ordinary income, it makes sense for the firm to buy back shares rather than pay out dividends, even though this generates capital gains. Even so, many corporations still pay dividends. But, why would they? This is one of the major puzzles of corporate finance. One reason often given for why a firm might pay out dividends regularly is that such payment might be an attempt by the firm to signal its real value in financial markets. As a result of regular dividend payments, investors come to believe that the firm is sound financially and are therefore willing to pay more for shares in the firm. If dividend payment is viewed as a signal, then consider how the firm's repurchase of outstanding equity shares can also be considered a signal. It is not clear that dividend payment is a better signal of firm financial health than share repurchase. Laws in some countries limit firms in repurchase of shares, however. Also, in some countries (including the United States), the repurchase of shares may be considered equivalent to a dividend payment by the tax authority. If that is so, what are the alternatives?

An alternative to the repurchase of shares is the **acquisition** of another firm. The increasing frequency of mergers and acquisitions is due, in part, to tax policy. Suppose that firm A is in the position to pay out \$100 million in dividends. As an alternative, suppose that firm A can buy firm B for \$100 million. Shareholders benefit from the acquisition because firm A is now worth \$100 million more than it was before. Hence, shareholders have a potential capital gain that is taxed at a preferential rate, as compared to dividend income. Hence, the two alternatives (paying out dividends and buying another firm) are equivalent in terms of the impact on shareholders. It might seem like that equivalence only holds when the two firms are owned by the same person or group of people, but it holds more generally. As long as there is another firm in the world with the same riskiness as the one making the acquisition, the equivalence still holds. The key is that shareholders adjust their portfolios.

Consider another possible change in financial policy on the part of the firm. Suppose that the firm increases dividends in the current period by borrowing. Of course, the loan has to be paid back in the future with

TABLE 2 Impacts on Shareholders and Bondholders from Firm Borrowing to Pay Dividend

	Shareholders	Bondholders
Period 1	$+ (1 - t_p)$ due to dividend	1 due to lending
Period 2	$- (1 - t_p)[1 + r(1 - t_c)]$ due to dividend	$+ [1 + r(1 - t_p)]$ due to repayment of principal with interest

Source: From *Lectures on Public Economics*, edited by Anthony B. Atkinson and Joseph E. Stiglitz, p. 38.

interest. Table 2 provides a summary of the impacts on shareholders and bondholders in a simple two-period model where the tax rate on capital gains is zero. Shareholders' gain in period 1 is due to the fact that the firm pays a dividend of $1. Of course, the net benefit to the shareholder is the after-tax dividend. In period 2 there must be a reduction in dividends, however. The amount of that reduction is $1 plus the after-tax interest rate (reflecting the firm's marginal tax rate) that the firm must pay for its borrowing. The net impact on the shareholder in period 2 is the after-tax reduction in the dividend (reflecting the shareholder's marginal tax rate). For bondholders there is a reduction of $1 in period 1 due to their lending to the firm. Then in period 2 they are repaid with interest. The net benefit in period 2 to bondholders reflects the after-tax interest earnings on their lending.

What is the effect of this corporate financial policy change on the household? Well, that depends crucially on the household's discount rate reflecting its opportunity cost of funds. Suppose that we write the household discount rate as $r(1 - t)$. Recall that the discount rate of a given household depends on that household's marginal tax rate. Of course, the marginal tax rate that applies also depends on the household's use of the funds. If the household uses the increased dividend to reduce its level of borrowing or increase its level of lending, then the marginal tax rate that should be used in the discount rate is simply the personal income tax rate: $\tau = t_p$. The household could, alternatively, use the increased dividend payment to increase its pension fund savings for retirement in which case $\tau = 0$ because pension contributions are not taxable. In this case, the discount rate should simply be r.

A shareholder will benefit from the increased borrowing by the firm when the benefit due to the higher dividend in period 1 exceeds the discounted cost due to the lower dividend in period 2:

$$1 - t_p \geq \frac{(1 - t_p)[1 + r(1 - t_c)]}{1 + r(1 - \tau)}. \tag{7}$$

This condition will hold as long as $\tau \leq t_c$; that is, as long as the shareholder's marginal tax rate is not greater than the marginal tax rate that applies to the firm, the shareholder will benefit.

The essential aspect of this policy change is that the individual can substitute corporate borrowing for personal borrowing. Whether this is advantageous depends on the after-tax cost of borrowing for the two entities. When the firm can borrow at a lower after-tax cost than the individual, the policy makes sense. For a given interest rate, the after-tax rate will be lower for the entity with the higher tax rate. With the corporate tax rate at least as large as the rate that would apply in the household's discount rate (reflecting its particular opportunity cost of funds), $t_p \leq t_c$ makes sense for the household to substitute corporate borrowing for its own. In the situation where $\tau = 0$, there is no question but that corporate borrowing is clearly better from the shareholder's point of view. So, if the use of the increased dividend is to fund additional tax-free pension contributions, the shareholder will want the firm to borrow, pay dividends, and put the money into pension funds.

So far, we have been considering the change in corporate financial policy from the point of view of a single shareholder. A representative shareholder will desire the firm to borrow and pay dividends as long as the corporate income tax rate is at least as large as the household's personal income tax rate. If we move to consider a group of shareholders, however, what matters in the collective choice of the shareholders will be the median tax rate. Recall from Chapter 6 on collective decision making that the median shareholder will be decisive (Median Voter Model). Hence, there may be a group of shareholders with high marginal tax rates that oppose such a corporate financial policy change at the same time that there is another group of shareholders who support such a change. Whether the financial policy change is sensible for the entire group of shareholders depends upon the marginal tax rate of the median shareholder.

Bondholders benefit from the increased firm borrowing as long as the loss in period 1 is no greater than the discounted gain in period 2:

$$1 \leq \frac{1 + r(1 - t_p)}{1 + r(1 - \tau)}. \tag{8}$$

That will be the case as long as $\tau \geq t_p$; that is, as long as the bondholder's marginal tax rate used in her discount rate is at least as large as her personal income tax rate, the increased borrowing by the firm is beneficial. If, however, $\tau < t_p$, the increased borrowing by the firm is not beneficial to the bondholder.

Capital Gains and Market Value of the Firm

The previous analysis is based on the assumption that the capital gains tax rate is zero: $t_g = 0$. This was done in order to assure that the tax rate on capital gains was lower than the rate applied to dividends. We should consider briefly how modification of the model to include a positive capital gains tax rate would affect the predictions of the model. Atkinson and Stiglitz (1980) have shown that a corporate financial policy change involving borrowing to pay dividends will raise the value of the firm as long as $\tau < t_c + (1 = t_c)t_g$. This inequality involves a comparison between the tax rate used in the discount rate of the household (the left-hand side) and the total tax burden placed on the return to equity that is taken as a capital gain (the right-hand side). The total tax burden on equity taken as a capital gain involves both the corporate income tax and the capital gains tax on the net income. In the special case of no capital gains taxation that we considered earlier, $t_g = 0$, this condition collapses to the familiar $\tau < t_c$ requirement.

If the tax rate on capital gains is not zero, however, we may have a different result. Consider the case where $t_g = t_p$ and capital gains are taxed at the ordinary personal income tax rate. In this case borrowing will certainly be beneficial if $\tau = t_p$. In reality, the tax rate applied to capital gains is typically somewhere between zero and the full personal rate. Because the effective tax rate applied to accrued capital gains is relatively low, our results from the simple model are probably about right. Hence, taking a positive capital gains tax rate into account does not affect the basic conclusion of the model.

TAXATION AND INVESTMENT

The previous analysis pertained to the financial decisions of the firm—its so-called *capital structure*. Now we turn to a real decision that the firm must make: how much to invest in new equipment, machinery, tools, and structures.

Fundamentals of Depreciation

Capital assets such as building, machinery, and equipment generate income streams over time. Those assets wear out over time also. If we are concerned with the net stream of income generated by these assets, we need to reduce the gross income stream they generate by some measure of the extent to which they wear out each year. This is the process of deducting **depreciation.** If we could deduct **true economic depreciation**, the actual replacement cost of the physical wear and tear on the asset, then the process of allowing depreciation deductions would not affect the investment behavior of the firm. The depreciation method would be neutral in this sense, having no impact on investment. How would we determine true economic depreciation? Well, if there were perfect capital markets for these assets, we would have no difficulty in determining true economic depreciation. Market prices for assets would inform us of the value of physical wear and tear. We could compare the market value of a 5-year-old stamping machine with a similar 6-year-old stamping machine and obtain an accurate estimate of the extent of depreciation in the sixth year for such an asset. The problem is that markets for such capital assets are typically imperfect; hence we cannot typically obtain such information.

As an alternative, tax systems usually permit approximate methods to be used in determining depreciation for capital assets. Some common depreciation methods include the following. **Straight-line depreciation** is a method whereby a fraction of the capital expenditure is permitted in each period. For example, an asset with a lifetime of 10 years is depreciated over that period with one-tenth of the value of the asset deducted each year. This is a linear pattern of depreciation, so it is called straight-line depreciation. Depreciation tables are specified in tax laws with classes of property identified by their depreciable life. Machinery and equipment may be listed as 5-year property, for example, whereas buildings are listed as 30-year property. Straight-line depreciation is computed by taking the number n of years for the listed property and deducting $1/n$ of the initial capital expenditure each year for a total of n years. Another method sometimes used is **declining balance depreciation**. Under this method a fraction of the capital expenditure is deducted in each period with the fraction fixed, but the value of the capital investment is written down over the life of the asset. For example, an investment of $1 million worth of machinery may be written off over a 10-year period, with one-tenth of the value deducted each year. The value of the machinery is reduced over the 10-year life, however. A third method sometimes used is the **sum-of-digits method** of depreciation. Under this method a fraction of the capital expenditure is deducted in each period with the fraction declining linearly over time. For example, a 10-year asset is written off over time with 10/55 of the investment deducted in year 1, 9/55 deducted in year 2, 8/55 deducted in year three, and so on, until 1/55 is deducted in year 10.

In some cases, tax laws permit the ultimate in accelerated depreciation, a method called **expensing** (sometimes called **free depreciation**). In this case the entire value of the asset is deducted in the year in which the investment is made. With such a large deduction it is often the case that the taxpayer's tax base is wiped out, leaving no tax liability. In fact, if the deduction for investment exceeds the tax base, the taxpayer is often permitted to carry forward the excess amount and use the investment against the subsequent year's tax base. It is not unusual for tax law to permit carryforward for up to 10 years. None of these methods captures true economic depreciation. All of these methods distort economic depreciation for tax purposes and cause net income reported on the firm's corporate income tax return to differ from profit. This is one of the fundamental reasons why the corporate income tax is not a tax on profit.

The U.S. corporate income tax currently provides a method of depreciation known as the **modified accelerated cost recovery system (MACRS)**. This depreciation method permits higher tax deductions in early years of an asset's life and lower deductions in later years. Real assets are put into one of six categories of asset life ranging from 3 years to 20 years. For example, an asset with 7-year life is depreciated using the following percentages starting in year 1: 14.29, 24.49, 17.49, 12.49, 8.93, 8.93, 8.93, and 4.45 percent. Eight years are listed in the 7-year asset life because the asset is assumed to be placed in service midway through year 1 and continue in use through the midpoint of year 8. The depreciation percentage is lower in the first year because the asset is assumed to be in service for just half the year. The MACRS pattern is one of declining depreciation percentages over the years.

It is important to know that large corporations routinely and legitimately keep two sets of books for two distinct purposes. One set of books is kept for financial reporting to stockholders. For those books, the corporation will usually employ a straight-line depreciation method. The other set of books is kept for the IRS tax purposes. For those books, the corporation will use the MACRS depreciation schedule to take advantage of the accelerated depreciation permitted by tax law. These tax books contain the relevant information needed for capital budgeting (investment) purposes.

Bond-Financed Investment

We can also consider the case where the firm chooses to finance its investment with bond financing rather than with borrowing. In years when investment exceeds retained earnings, the firm borrows, but in years when retained earnings exceed investment, the surplus can be used to reduce the firm's debt. In this situation, the marginal cost of capital is $r(1-t_c)$, reflecting the after-tax interest cost, assuming that interest is deductible.

Suppose that the competitive firm selects quantities of capital K and labor L in a profit-maximizing manner. We want to consider the effect of a one-time increase of a dollar of investment for additional capital K. If there is no tax, the firm's profit will rise with a dollar's worth of investment if

$$pMP_k > r + \gamma, \tag{9}$$

where γ is the true rate of economic depreciation. That is, profit will rise if the value of the marginal product of the additional capital (product price times marginal product of capital, the left-hand side of the inequality) is greater than the cost of the additional capital including both the interest cost r and depreciation γ (the right-hand side of the inequality). Now, if there is a corporate income tax with true economic depreciation, the firm's profit will rise as long as

$$(1-t_c)pMP_k > r(1-t_c) + \gamma(1-t_c) \tag{10}$$

The firm will be making the optimal investment by purchasing that quantity of capital where the left-hand side of Equation 10 is equal to the right-hand side of Equation 10, replacing the inequality with an equality. Comparing the inequality in Equation 10 with the inequality in Equation 9, it is clear that the presence of the corporate income tax has no effect. Because the

TABLE 3 Corporate Financial Policy and the Cost of Capital Net of Depreciation

	True Economic Depreciation	Expensing
Debt financing:		
Interest deductible	r	$r(1 - t_c)$
Interest not deductible	$r/(1 - t_c)$	r
Retained earnings	$[r/(1 - t_c)(1 - \tau)]$	$r(1 - \tau)$

Source: Adapted from Atkinson and Stiglitz 1980, 147.

$(1 - t_c)$ terms can be canceled out, the inequality of Equation 10 is identical to the inequality of Equation 9. Hence, the tax has no effect on investment. This is an important benchmark case: A corporate income tax has no effect on investment when the tax law allows interest deduction and permits true economic depreciation.

If the tax law permits expensing of investment, this conclusion must be modified. Expensing reduces the price of a dollar's worth of capital from $1 to $(1 - t_c)$ dollar because the full cost of the capital is deductible from taxable income. Suppose further that a fraction of interest is deductible. Denote that fraction as d. The condition for optimal investment in this case is

$$pMP_k = r(1 - \delta t_c) + \gamma, \tag{11}$$

indicating that the firm should purchase that quantity of capital where the value of the marginal product (the left-hand side of the equation) is equal to the after-tax cost of capital including depreciation.

We can now consider the special cases of no deductibility ($\delta = 0$) and full deductibility ($\delta = 1$). In the case of no deductibility, the right-hand side of Equation 11 reverts to $r + \gamma$, as we had in Equation 9. With full deductibility, however, the right-hand side of Equation 11 becomes $r(1 - t_c) + \gamma$. Table 15.5, found on page 488, summarizes these cases. Expensing of investment provides a powerful incentive for firms. It can reduce the cost of investment below that in the no-tax situation. By making investment cheaper than it would be in the absence of a corporate tax, the tax system can stimulate investment. Consider an example of full expensing in a country with an income tax that permits full deductibility ($\delta = 1$) of interest. Suppose, for example, that the interest rate is $r = 0.10$ and the marginal corporate income tax rate is $t_c = 0.50$. In this case the right-hand side of Equation 11 can be computed as $0.10(1 - 0.50)$, which is equal to 0.05. The effect of the tax system is to reduce the marginal cost of investment from the 10 percent that would prevail in a world without the income tax to 5 percent. The effect of permitting expensing of investment is to convert the corporate income tax into a tax on pure economic profit, which is entirely neutral.

Of course, expensing is an extreme case of **accelerated depreciation.** There are intermediate cases that we could consider that permit depreciation in excess of true economic depreciation but fall short of full immediate expensing. Many states and countries permit various forms of accelerated depreciation on their corporate income taxes in order to stimulate investment. From the firm's point of view, accelerated depreciation involves a trade-off between more generous depreciation deductions in the early years but less generous depreciation deductions in later years.

Investment Financed from Retained Earnings

If the firm funds its investment with retained earnings rather than borrowing or bonds, the situation differs. Suppose that a fraction ϕ of investment can be expensed while the rest is depreciated at the rate of true economic depreciation. Consider the firm making a \$1 investment in new capital. The shareholders of the firm are responsible for financing $1 - \phi t_c$ of that dollar of investment, whereas the government, through its tax system, is responsible for financing ϕt_c. In this sense, the government is a partner in the investment of the firm. By using retained earnings, the firm causes shareholder dividends to be forgone in the near term in exchange for higher dividend payments in the future. The opportunity cost to the shareholder is $r(1-\tau)$, the personal income after-tax interest rate. In this case, the optimal amount of capital for the firm to purchase is given by the condition

$$pMP_k = \frac{r(1-\tau)(1-\phi t_c)}{1-t_c+\gamma}, \tag{12}$$

which is a modification of our previous condition. The effect of the corporate income tax on the optimal quantity of capital depends on whether the term

$$\frac{(1-\tau)(1-\phi t_c)}{1-t_c} \tag{13}$$

is greater than or less than 1. That, in turn, depends on the degree (f) of expensing permitted in the tax law and the opportunity cost to shareholders. If there is no expensing permitted (only depreciation by true economic depreciation), then the effect on investment depends on whether t_c is greater than or less than t. That is, the effect on investment depends on whether the corporate income tax rate is greater or less than the personal income tax rate. If the corporate rate is greater, investment is reduced. In the absence of a personal income tax, $\tau = 0$, the cost of capital to the firm is raised by the corporate tax system if $\phi < 1$. On the other hand, the effect of corporate taxation is completely offset if $\phi = 1$. Hence, expensing can negate the effect of the corporate income tax.

What are we to make of all this? Well, the tax system may either raise or lower the cost of capital to the firm, depending on the values of the parameters. For a country with a corporate income tax rate of $t_c = 0.25$, the net cost of capital may be either cut to one-quarter or quadrupled. The subsequent impact on investment could be either to greatly stimulate or to reduce the amount of new capital that the firm wishes to finance out of retained earnings. Table 15.5, found on page 488, summarizes this case as well as the previous cases considered.

Taxation and Market Imperfections

Models of firms that act so as to maximize profit or stock market value such as those described previously are informative but certainly not exhaustive of the possibilities. What is the effect of taxation on firms in oligopolistic or monopolistic industries? What about the effects of market imperfections? What happens if we take account of the irreversibility of investment? These and other issues are important to consider, although we do so in a brief, less technical way in this section. Our intent is to suggest ways in which the basic model can and should be extended.

First, consider the case of imperfect competition. A firm operating in an imperfectly competitive industry faces a downward-sloping demand curve rather than a horizontal demand curve as is the case for a perfectly competitive firm. It is not difficult to replace the value of the marginal product of capital discussed in the previous model with the marginal revenue product. Then, we can compare the marginal cost of capital to the marginal revenue product, including the effects of the corporate tax system's depreciation and deductibility characteristics as before. That simple extension enables us to develop results for monopolies or firms in monopolistically competitive industries. The case of firms in an oligopolistic industry is more difficult, however. There is no simple extension of the competitive result to that situation.

Second, consider the effect of imperfect information in capital markets. So far, our model of firm investment has been cast in the context of full information and certainty. What happens if the firm has imperfect information or there is risk? The original MM theorem result does not require the absence of risk. In fact, the original MM result permitted various risk classes, and that has been extended to even more general conditions of uncertainty. The MM result does, however, require that no **bankruptcy** can exist. No bankruptcy also implies that individuals can issue riskless bonds in unlimited quantities at a given interest rate. For example, a person with no assets can invest a large amount (unlimited in theory) in a firm that everyone else is certain will generate zero profit. This is clearly unrealistic. Allowing for bankruptcy means that bonds become risky assets with the amount of risk depending on the amount borrowed. That means the capital market becomes imperfect. With an imperfect capital market, the expected returns to lender and borrower differ. The expected receipts of the lender may be less than those of the borrower, and the difference may increase with the size of the amount borrowed. The cost of capital to the firm may depend on the size of the firm. Furthermore, the amount of investment may depend not only on the cost of capital but also on the availability of financing. In that case, even a neutral corporate income tax may affect investment.

With uncertainty comes a fundamental problem in identifying the objective of the firm. Consider the publicly owned firm with shareholders. Even in the case of perfect certainty the shareholders may have very different marginal tax rates and therefore very different views of the appropriate policies of the firm. Add to that the possibility of different views of the future and different attitudes toward risk (and hence different discount rates applied) reflecting uncertainty, and you have a more complex situation. The problem of collective choice for a group of shareholders can become quite difficult. They may not be able to agree on the appropriate objective for the firm. Whether the firm pursues the objective of profit maximization, sales maximization, market share maximization, or some satisfying objective is indeterminate.

Third, consider what happens when there are adjustment costs. A complication exists that adjusting the capital stock of the firm may not be costless, as assumed in the basic model. There may be constraints on the ability of the firm to change its capital stock. If investment is totally irreversible, the cost of reducing the capital stock may be essentially infinite. In reality, markets exist for used machinery, equipment, and structures, so the assumption of complete irreversibility may be inappropriate. That means adjustment costs are not likely to be infinite. Even so, adjustment costs are probably positive, not zero as assumed in the basic model. More advanced models of investment sometimes include an adjustment cost that is convex (increasing at an increasing rate).

Models with adjustment costs highlight the fact that the firm is making a decision not only on the amount of capital it uses but also on the time path of that capital use; both the quantity and the timing are important. If the firm expects current capital prices to continue into the future, it may select a constant time path for capital investment. As a result, the firm adds to its capital stock at a steady rate over time, reaching its goal in a steady or gradual manner. This trajectory reduces the adjustment costs. On the other hand, if the firm expects that capital prices will fall in the future due to some favorable policy change such as an investment tax credit or other incentive, the firm may delay investment.

Finally, consider the impact of changes in firm expectations. The basic model described previously assumes that firms have static (unchanging) expectations. If, instead, firms have dynamic expectations that change over time, the basic model is inadequate. Consider the model presented earlier where there is a corporate income tax in which a fraction f of firm investment can be expensed, true economic depreciation is applied to the remaining investment, and a fraction d of interest is deductible. Now, suppose that the firm expects the permissible fraction of expensing to change to ϕ^* in the next period, with all other parameters unchanged. In this scenario the optimal amount of capital for the firm to purchase in the current period is given by the condition

$$pMP_k = \frac{r(1-\delta t_c)(1-\phi t_c)}{1-t_c} + \gamma + \frac{(1-\gamma)(\phi^* - \phi)t_c}{1-t_c} \tag{14}$$

This condition no longer assures the neutrality result presented earlier. Consider the special case where we have full expensing ($\phi = 1$) and no deductibility of interest ($\delta = 0$). That set of conditions assured us that the optimality condition was independent of the income tax rate t_c in the basic model, but in this case no such result occurs. Hence, the neutrality condition no longer holds.

Notice that an expected future reduction in the investment allowance (share of investment expensed) makes the term $\phi^* - \phi$ negative; this reduces the current cost of capital relative to the future cost. Consider the situation where the firm expects the share of investment subject to expensing to fall in the future from the current level $\phi = 0.50$ to the future level $\phi^* = 0.40$; that is, the firm expects the share of investment that can be expensed will fall from 50 to 40 percent. In the presence of a tax rate $t_c = 0.50$ and a deductibility parameter $\delta = 0.15$, the cost of capital will fall by 8.5 percent (obtained by substituting parameter values in the last term on the right-hand side of Equation 14). In the face of such a reduction in the cost of capital, we would expect firms to invest more in the present period.

Expectations of policy changes can result in sharp changes in firm behavior, even if the policy regime is temporary. If firms expect that a capital subsidy will be introduced in the future, they may curtail current investment quite substantially and increase investment during the subsidy regime. Of course, we would also expect that investment would fall sharply at the end of the subsidy regime. The general rule that temporary policies are less powerful than permanent policies may not be fully accurate in this sense. The response of firms may be quite elastic in the short run when policy regime changes are involved.

Empirical Studies of Taxation and Investment

Do taxes affect investment? That is a fundamental question regarding corporate income taxes, an important policy question for the design of a tax system, and the subject of a large empirical literature in economics. Mintz (1995) has identified three approaches to modeling investment in the literature: the accelerator model, the neoclassical model, and the *Q* model. The accelerator model links investment to changes in aggregate demand (not changes in relative factor prices such as labor). Changes in aggregate output measured by GDP or national income have an effect on investment in the multiplier-accelerator context. Because investment is determined by changes in output only, taxes can only affect investment insofar as they affect aggregate output. The neoclassical model of investment assumes that firms are profit-maximizing entities that employ labor and capital up to the point where the value of the marginal product of the last unit of each input equals its price. The demand for capital therefore depends on output and the price of capital and other factors of production. Taxes can affect relative prices, so they can have a direct impact on investment as well as an indirect effect through their effect on output. The *Q* model approach is based on the idea that firms will invest in capital as long as the value of the project for which they are buying the capital is at least as great as the cost of purchasing the capital. The ratio Q is the market value of the firm's equity and debt liabilities, which can be thought of as the present value of the firm's future returns, divided by the replacement cost of capital. As long as Q is greater than 1, the firm will invest, but if Q is less than 1, it will divest.

Glossary

Ability-to-pay principle: the principle that a tax should be based on the taxpayer's ability to pay as judged by income or wealth.

Absolute measure of poverty: a measure of poverty based on an absolute measure of income per capita, expenditure per capita, or some other measurement.

Accelerated depreciation: any method of depreciation that is faster than straight-line depreciation.

Accounting profit: the difference between revenue generated by sales and the costs incurred for inputs. No account is taken of the opportunity cost of the firm's activity.

Accrual basis: a method of accounting by which receipts and outlays are recognized when the obligations are incurred.

Acquisition: the purchase of one firm by another.

Acquisition value tax: a property tax based on the value of the property when it was acquired.

***Ad valorem* tax:** a tax applied to the value of a good. For example, a sales tax applied at the rate of 7 percent of the price of a good.

Additive method: the method of defining the VAT tax base that involves adding all the components of tax base including wages, profits, interest payments, etc.

Adjusted gross income (AGI): a measure of income used on the U.S. personal income tax, equal to total income minus adjustments.

Adverse selection: a problem in the realm of insurance under which those most likely to need the insurance coverage elect to have coverage and those least likely to need the coverage opt out.

Agenda control: manipulative behavior by a government agency with monopoly power to control the choices put before voters on a ballot in order to obtain the outcome desired by the government agency.

Allocation: the act of allocating scarce resources to competing uses in an economy, especially in public finance the question of producing private and public goods.

Alternative budget: in federal government budgeting, a budget based on current policy, as distinct from a baseline budget which is based on current law.

Alternative hypothesis: a hypothesized statement of what we hope to prove which is then tested using statistical methods.

Annuity: a financial asset that pays a fixed amount each year for a specified period of time.

Apportionment: the method of allocating the total net income of a corporation to each of the taxable locations (states or countries) in which it operates.

Appraiser: an expert who specializes in estimating the value of property for private purposes.

Arm's-length transaction: a transaction between parties that are unrelated in either a familial or economic sense.

Assessed value: the value of a property for tax purposes as determined by the tax assessor.

Assessment: the process of determining the value of property for tax purposes.

Assessment ratio: the ratio of the assessed value of a property divided by the market value of the property.

Assessor: the government official whose job is to assign a value to all property subject to the property tax.

Asymmetric information: a situation in which buyers and sellers in a market have different sets of information.

Average fixed cost (*AFC*): total fixed cost divided by output; $AFC = TFC/Q$.

Average tax rate (*ATR*): the average rate of taxation applied to all the units of taxable base—the total tax paid divided by the tax base. The *ATR* represents the share of the total tax base taken in tax.

Average total cost (*ATC*): total cost divided by output; $ATC = TC/Q$.

Average variable cost (*AVC*): total variable cost divided by output; $AVC = TVC/Q$.

Averaged indexed monthly earnings (AIME): in the U.S. social security system, the average monthly earnings used to determine the benefit paid, or primary insurance amount (PIA).

Backward-bending labor supply curve: a labor supply curve that has the traditional upward slope at relatively low wage levels, but bends backward (like a backward letter C) on itself becoming downward sloping at higher wage levels.

Balanced budget: a government budget where outlays equal revenues.

Bankruptcy: the process by which a failed corporation is liquidated and its assets are distributed among creditors.

Base year: in the context of a price index, the year in which the index takes on the value of 100.

Baseline budget: a budget based on expenditures required by current law, as distinct from an alternative budget that is based on current policy.

Behavioral economics: a field of economic study which incorporates insights from psychology in drawing on social, cognitive, and emotional aspects of human behavior in analyzing economic decision making.

Benefit-cost analysis: economic analysis of an activity or program that determines whether the benefits of the activity or program exceed the costs, in which case the activity or program may be economically feasible.

Benefit-cost ratio: a ratio computed in benefit-cost analysis where the total benefits are divided by total costs. If the ratio exceeds 1, the benefits are larger than the costs and the activity or program is economically feasible.

Benefit view of the incidence of the property tax: a view of the incidence of the property tax that holds that local governments provide services to property owners in proportion to the amount of property owned; hence the tax is a benefits-based tax.

Benefits-received principle: a principle of financing the provision of public goods and services based on the concept that those persons who receive direct benefits of the public good or service should pay in proportion to the benefits received.

Bill of Rights: the first ten amendments of the U.S. Constitution, specifying fundamental rights of citizens.

Bond anticipation notes (BANS): short-term government debt issued in anticipation of the receipt of funds from a government bond issue.

Borda Rule: a collective decision-making rule whereby each voter ranks all of the alternative candidates or proposals.

Budget constraint: a limitation on economic activity due to a limited monetary budget with which to buy the goods and services desired.

Capital export neutrality (CEN): a form of neutral taxation of foreign income by which an investor's income is taxed at the same rate regardless of where in the world it was earned (requires a credit for foreign taxes paid).

Capital import neutrality (CIN): a form of neutral taxation of foreign income by which the return to capital is taxed at the same rate regardless of where the capital investor lives.

Capital ownership neutrality (CON): a form of neutral taxation of foreign income by which every country taxes foreign income in the same way, avoiding tax clienteles.

Capital structure of the corporation: the financial structure of the corporation reflecting its choices of alternative forms of financing, including the issuing of bonds and shares of equity.

Capital tax effect of the property tax: a general equilibrium view of the incidence of the property tax whereby capital owners throughout the economy bear a burden due to property taxation in the form of a reduced rate of return to capital.

Capital tax view: a view of the incidence of the property tax that considers the tax to be a tax on capital.

Carry-forward: the ability to carry into the future an operating loss from the past.

Cascading of a sales tax: the process whereby the effective rate of taxation of a sales tax grows through multiple stages of production as the tax is applied on top of the tax at each stage, just as a waterfall cascades over a brink, becoming broader and broader the farther the water falls.

Cash basis: a method of accounting whereby receipts and outlays are recognized only when actually received or paid.

Cash transfer: a transfer from the government to a person in the form of cash.

Cat bond: a bond issued by to insure against catastrophic losses.

Catastrophic insurance: insurance to cover a catastrophe such as a tsunami, earthquake, or hurricane.

Categorical grant: a grant that provides funds with a restriction that the money be used for a specific purpose, or category of spending.

Circuit breaker: an income tax credit that provides property tax relief to taxpayers whose property taxes are high relative to their income.

Classical tax system: a system of corporate income taxation under which firms that benefit from incorporation and limited liability are the subjects of taxation (a benefit-based tax system).

Classified property tax system: a property tax system in which different classes of property (residential, agricultural, commercial, industrial) are taxed at different rates.

Club good: a public good that is subject to exclusion and congestion.

Coase Theorem: a result in economic theory that says the assignment of liability for an externality does not affect the efficient allocation of resources in an economy.

Comparability: a property of preferences that assures all possible combinations of goods can be compared with one another.

Compensated demand curve: a demand curve along which income is held constant (not utility as in an ordinary demand curve), illustrating substitution effects of price changes, but no income effects.

Concave preferences: a property of preferences that means the person prefers an extreme combination of goods to a mean combination of goods.

Condorcet Rule: a collective decision-making rule whereby the winner is the candidate chosen by considering all possible pairwise comparisons.

Congressional Research Service (CRS): a research unit within the U.S. Library of Congress that conducts economic analysis of government programs and taxation.

Consolidated budget: a combination of on-budget and off-budget items.

Constant dollars: measurement of an economic quantity over time where each year's measurement is converted into a base year's dollars in order to eliminate the effects of inflation.

Constitution: a system of fundamental principles, maxims, or laws embodied in a legal document that serves as the legal basis for a society.

Consumer surplus: the amount consumers are willing to pay for a given quantity of a good, but do not have to pay at the going market price.

Contingent valuation methodology (CVM): a method of eliciting survey respondents' willingness to pay. The respondent is confronted with a situation, contingent on a number of explicit factors such as cost, and then is asked to state how much he or she would be willing to pay.

Contract curve: a curve in an Edgeworth-Bowley Box Diagram that illustrates all of the points of Pareto optimality.

Convex preferences: a property of preferences that means the person prefers a mean combination of goods to an extreme combination of goods.

Corlett-Hague rule: a rule in optimal taxation that says taxes that are least distortionary are those taxes which apply to goods or services complementary with leisure.

Corporate welfare: a pejorative term used for tax expenditures granted to corporations.

Corporation: a form of business organization whereby the business is owned by stockholders who are not personally liable for the business's liabilities.

Cost-benefit Analysis: *see* benefit-cost analysis.

Cross-price elasticity: the price elasticity of a good with respect to a change in price of a related good (substitute or complement).

Current dollars: measurement of an economic quantity over time where each year's measurement of the quantity is in the dollars of the year in which the entity was measured; hence inflation is included.

Deadweight loss: an alternate term for the excess burden of a tax.

Debt: the sum of all past government deficits minus the sum of all past surpluses plus trust fund balances.

Debt ceiling: a legislated limit on total government debt permitted.

Decentralization: the process of pushing responsibilities and resources to lower levels of government within a multilevel government setting.

Decentralization theorem: a result in economic theory that says the provision of a public good that is defined over geographical subsets of the population will always be more efficient (or at least as efficient) for local governments to provide the efficient levels in each area than for the central government to provide any uniform level across all local jurisdictions.

Decile: a 10 percent grouping of the income distribution. The first decile represents the bottom 10 percent of the income distribution, whereas the second through tenth deciles represent the succeeding 10 percent groupings.

Declining balance depreciation: a method of computing depreciation for tax purposes by which a fraction of the capital expenditure is deducted in each period with the fraction fixed, but the value of the capital investment is written down over the life of the asset. For example, an investment of one million dollars' worth of machinery may be written off over a 10-year period with 1/10th of the value deducted each year. The value of the machinery is reduced over the 10-year life, however.

Dedicated excise tax: an excise tax applied to a commodity whose revenue is allocated to a specific purpose (e.g., gasoline excises are often dedicated to a highway trust fund).

Deductibility: a feature of an income tax system that permits the deduction of an expense from taxable income (*see also* state deductibility and reciprocal deductibility).

Deduction limitation: a limitation on tax deductions for high-income taxpayers having the effect of raising the effective tax rate.

Deductive reasoning: reasoning from knowledge of a known population to the likely characteristics of a sample drawn from that population.

Deficit: a government budget imbalance where outlays exceed revenues.

Defined benefit plan: an insurance plan under which specified benefits are paid out of the plan; payments into the plan must be sufficient to fund the defined benefits that are paid out.

Defined contribution plan: an insurance plan under which specified contributions are paid into the plan; payments out of the plan are then paid out of the contributions plus interest earned.

Depreciation: the process used for deducting a portion of the value of real assets such as machinery and equipment each year, reflecting the fact that the asset is used up over time as it is employed in the production process.

Deregulation: the process of reducing regulations that control the behavior of firms in an industry.

Destination-based taxation: a system of indirect taxation under which the tax is applied in the jurisdiction where the good is purchased by the consumer.

Development fees: fees charged of land developers for the purpose of paying for public infrastructure such as streets, sewers, and lights.

Direct taxation: taxation of income, both personal and corporate, where the initial incidence of the tax is directly on the taxpayer.

Discount rate: the interest rate used in the discounting process, reflecting the time value of money.

Discounting: the process of converting future benefits and costs into today's dollars.

Discretionary spending: government spending where the amount of spending is under the control of a government oversight body (legislative or executive) and subject to that body's discretion.

Distribution: the process of allocating resources in an economy with the purpose of altering the distribution of income or wealth.

Dividend repatriation: net income earned by the foreign subsidiary of a home country returned to the parent company in the form of dividends, usually triggering tax liability in the home country.

Double-peaked preferences: voter preferences characterized by two relative maximums or most preferred options.

Double taxation: the practice of taxing corporate income that is used to pay dividends to shareholders who are also liable to pay personal income tax on the dividends received.

Duty: a tax applied to imports.

Earmarked taxes: taxes whose revenues are dedicated to specific trust funds in order to finance particular programs.

Earmarks: special expenditure provisions included in legislative bills (typically unrelated to the substance of the bills) that have the purpose of directing government spending to the home district of a legislator.

Earned income tax credit (EITC): a credit on the U.S. personal income tax designed to eliminate the work disincentive of welfare programs.

Easement: a legal restriction on the use of a specific portion of real property (e.g., the utility company may retain the right to travel along the land underneath its power lines).

Economic incidence of tax: tax incidence resulting from market forces.

Economic profit: profit computed as the difference between revenue from sales and the cost of inputs, including the opportunity cost of capital (i.e., profit in excess of the opportunity cost of capital).

Economic rent: the return to a factor of production that is fixed in supply, over and above the amount that would be required to draw that factor into the market.

Edgeworth-Bowley Box Diagram: a diagram in economic theory illustrating indifference curves for two individuals and the exchange opportunities afforded the pair.

Education programs: public programs providing schooling and educational opportunities.

Effective property tax rate: the product of the nominal tax rate and the assessment ratio.

Effective tax rate: the rate of taxation that applies taking into consideration exemptions, deductions, and credits.

Elasticity of labor supply: a measure of the sensitivity of workers' labor supply decisions to changes in the wage rate. The elasticity is computed as the percentage change in the hours of work divided by the percentage change in the wage.

Elasticity of substitution: a measure of the sensitivity of the capital/labor ratio used in production to changes in the relative price of capital to labor. The elasticity is computed as the percentage change in the capital/labor ratio divided by the percentage change in the capital/labor price ratio.

Empiricism: the philosophical school of thought that argued truth is discovered through our sense perceptions by making empirical observations based on those perceptions.

Endowment point: the point in a life cycle model of consumption that represents the assumed levels of current and future income.

Entrepreneur: a person who reforms or revolutionizes the pattern of production for producing a new commodity or producing an old commodity in a new way through the introduction of an invention or an untried technology, by opening up a new source of supply of materials or a new outlet for products, or by reorganizing an industry.

Epistemology: the philosophical study of how we know what we know.

Equalization factor: a multiplicative adjustment applied to property values in a jurisdiction in order to assure that all properties have the same assessment ratio.

Estate tax: a tax applied to the value of an estate upon the death of the estate owner.

Euro: monetary unit of the European Monetary Union (EMU).

European Monetary Union (EMU): countries of the European Union that participate in using the single currency, the Euro. Note: Currently there are 17 EMU member countries, with 10 of the EU countries choosing to adopt the Euro, most notably the United Kingdom, Denmark, and Sweden.

European Union: An association of 27 European countries established to foster a single economic market, common foreign policy, and closer economic and political cooperation.

Excess burden of a tax: the welfare loss caused by the imposition of the tax, over and above the revenue the tax generates.

Excise tax: a tax applied to the manufacture, sale, or consumption of a commodity within a country.

Excise tax effect of the property tax: a view of the impact of local variations in property tax rates whereby properties in relatively high tax jurisdictions bear an additional burden of the tax and properties in relatively low tax jurisdictions bear a smaller burden of the tax.

Exemption phaseout: a reduction in the amount of an exemption permitted for taxpayers with income above a threshold level. The amount of the exemption is reduced in proportion to the amount of income the taxpayer has in excess of the phase-out threshold level. Such a phaseout has the effect of raising the effective rate of taxation.

Existence value: value of an object reflecting consumers' knowledge that the object merely exists, regardless of whether they ever use the object.

Exit: a strategy option for an individual in a community: the person can leave the community because the type and quantity of public goods provided are unacceptable.

Expansion path: the set of all optimal input combinations (points of tangency between isoquants and isocost lines) as output is scaled up.

Expenditure: spending.

Expenditure tax: a tax applied to expenditures, or consumption, rather than income.

Expensing: a method of depreciation that permits 100 percent of the value of the asset be deducted in the year in which the asset was acquired and put into use.

Externalities: benefits or costs imposed on one economic agent by another economic agent when that effect is external to the working of the market.

Factor immobility effect of a property tax: an effect of property taxation by which immobile factors of production such as land and fixed structures bear a portion of the tax burden.

Factor substitution effect: the economic effect of a partial factor tax that causes factor substitution due to the change in the relative price of the factor.

Factor taxes: taxes applied to factors of production, or inputs, such as land, labor, and capital.

Factors of production: inputs used in the production process such as land, labor, and capital.

Federal government: a federal government system is one where government authority is diffused among the various levels of government (central, state, and local governments).

Fee simple rights: a legal term for the full set of property rights, permitting the property owner to do whatever the property owner wishes to do with the property.

FEMA: the U.S. federal emergency management agency.

First Fundamental Theorem of Welfare Economics: a statement of the result in economic theory that competitive markets will provide an efficient allocation of resources under certain circumstances.

Fiscal disparities: differences in fiscal outcomes (expenditure or taxation levels) between cities and suburbs.

Fiscal externalities: costs or revenues conferred on other government jurisdictions that are not a party to the decisions made by those within a given jurisdiction.

Fiscal federalism: a term used to describe fiscal relationships among states at various levels in a federation.

Fixed input: an input constrained in the short run to a constant or fixed amount.

Flat-rate tax: a tax whose average tax rate *(ATR)* is constant over the income distribution.

Flat tax: a proposed consumption-type value-added tax (VAT) split into two components, one paid by businesses and the other paid by workers, with a single marginal tax rate applied to value-added by either type of taxpayer.

Flypaper effect: an anomaly related to categorical grants whereby the grant money is spent to a larger extent than expected on the restricted category of spending. The money "sticks where it hits."

Food stamps: coupons redeemable for food at grocery stores—given to low-income families that meet government income guidelines.

Foreign sales corporations: shell companies in offshore tax havens that firms use to avoid taxes.

Foreign tax credit: a tax credit providing (full or partial) relief from double taxation of income earned and taxed in a foreign country.

Free depreciation: *see* expensing.

Free market economy: an economy in which markets are free to allocate resources without interference from government.

Free rider: a person who enjoys the benefits provided by a public good, but who does not want to pay for that public good.

Front-loaded tax credit: a tax credit that is provided prospectively, rather than retroactively.

Fungibility: a property of money in a budgeting context by which it is capable of being moved and replaced.

GDP: gross domestic product. A measure of value of all final goods and services produced domestically during a year.

GDP deflator: a price index used to measure the overall price level for all goods and services included in GDP.

General Accounting Office (GAO): the investigative arm of the U.S. Congress that conducts auditing and economic analysis of policy issues for Congress.

General equilibrium analysis: economic analysis of equilibrium in all markets simultaneously (as distinct from partial equilibrium analysis in which only one market is analyzed).

General equilibrium tax incidence: economic incidence of a tax considering the effects in all markets generally.

General excise tax: an excise tax applied to a general class of commodities.

Generally accepted accounting practices (GAAP): a recognized set of accounting practices in widespread use.

Gini coefficient: a numerical measure of the concentration of the income distribution taking on values from zero (indicating a perfectly equal income distribution) to one (indicating a perfectly concentrated income distribution).

Glasnost: Russian term for the new openness, voicing, or making public of things formerly forbidden that was embraced during the time of Mr. Gorbachev and the demise of the soviet system in the 1980s.

Globalization: the increasing tendency of business firms to operate across national borders or combine with firms in other countries in mergers and strategic alliances.

Graded property tax: a property tax system with different tax rates applied to land and improvements (also called a *split-rate* or *two-rate property tax*).

Graduated tax rate: a tax rate structure in which the marginal tax rate rises as the tax base increases.

Grant anticipation notes (GANs): short-term government debt issued in anticipation of grant revenues that are used to pay off the debt.

Grants: a means by which central governments transfer funds to subnational governments.

Haig-Simons definition of income: a broad definition of income used by economists as the ideal against which to judge income tax systems.

Harmonization of taxes: a process of making tax bases and tax rates similar for jurisdictions within a federation.

Henry George theorem: a result in economic theory that holds that in a local public goods equilibrium land rents will just equal expenditures on public goods.

Hicks/Kaldor compensation criterion: a concept of welfare improvement that says a re-allocation from one person to another is welfare enhancing if the gain to one person is larger than the loss to the other person.

Highest and best use: the use of a property, either current or potential, that would maximize the value of the property.

Homestead exemption: a property tax exemption provided to property owners who use their property as their home.

Horizontal equity of taxation: concern for fairness, or equity, in taxation with a focus on how the tax treats equal taxpayers; sometimes summarized as "equal treatment of equals."

Housing assistance: public programs that provide housing assistance to families in the subsidized rent, mortgage interest, or other forms.

Imperfect competition: a condition of a market in which there is less than perfect competition, meaning that buyers or sellers have some degree of control over the price.

Imperfect information: a condition of a market in which there is less than perfect information, meaning that either buyers or sellers have less information on which to make their decisions.

Impossibility theorem: a result in collective decision theory that says under a certain set of reasonable assumptions about what makes for a good collective decision-making rule, it is impossible to find a decision-making rule that is consistent with all of the properties of a good rule.

Impure public good: a public good that is not a pure public good, also called a *congestible public good* because use of the good is subject to congestion.

Imputation system: a method of integration of the corporate and personal income tax systems whereby shareholders receive a credit for the tax paid by the corporation on a portion of its profit. The shareholder is then liable for any difference between the rate of taxation implicit in the imputation (rate paid by the corporation on its profits from which dividends were paid) and the individual's personal income tax rate.

Imputed income: income earned by a taxpayer, not realized explicitly in the form of cash income, but earned implicitly through an increase in wealth.

In-kind transfer: a transfer from the government to a person in the form of goods or services such as housing, education, medical care, or insurance.

Incidence of a tax: a description of the pattern of tax burden and on whom the burden of the tax falls.

Income capitalization approach: an approach to the valuation of property that computes the present value of the future net income stream generated by the property.

Income distribution: table, graph, or equation illustrating shares of income earned by groups of households in an economy, from lowest to highest income.

Income effect: the effect of a price change that induces a person to alter consumption of goods due to the fact that the price change has affected the person's real income.

Income elasticity: a measure of the responsiveness of demand to a change in consumers' income; the percentage change in quantity demanded divided by the percentage change in income.

Income endowment: a given allocation of income in both the present and the future in a life cycle model of consumption and savings.

Income splitting: a feature of an income tax system whereby the tax for a married couple is twice the tax liability on half their joint income.

Indirect taxation: taxation applied to goods and services using excise taxes, sales taxes, and value-added taxes where the incidence of the tax is not directly on a particular taxpayer, but rather is indirectly applied to producers and consumers.

Individual retirement account (IRA)—Roth IRA: a savings account into which a person can deposit money that is not tax exempt in the year of its deposit, but withdrawals from the account after retirement are tax exempt.

Individual retirement account (IRA)—traditional IRA: a savings account into which a person can deposit money that is tax exempt in the year of its deposit, although withdrawals from the account after retirement are taxable.

Inductive reasoning: reasoning from knowledge of a known sample and its characteristics to the likely properties of a population.

Intangible benefits: benefits of a program or activity arising from intangible aspects such as security, safety, opportunity, aesthetic beauty, or the option value of an irreversible action.

Intangible property: property consisting of stocks, bonds, bank deposits, mortgages, cash value of insurance policies, patents, copyrights, trademarks, goodwill, licenses, and other forms of intangible property.

Intergovernmental aid mechanisms: formula mechanisms for transferring aid from higher-level governments to lower-level governments in a multilevel government setting.

Interjurisdictional mobility: mobility between local government jurisdictions.

Internal rate of return: the implicit rate of interest on a project with known net benefit stream equal to zero.

International Monetary Fund (IMF): an international agency created after World War II with the purpose of stabilizing world currency markets.

Isocost: the set of input combinations that have the same cost.

Isoquant: the set of input combinations physically capable of producing the same level of output; also a contour of the production function for a given level of output.

Job training programs: public programs to assist potential workers in preparing for employment either by providing training in job-seeking skills, work skills, or both.

Jurisdictional level: the level of a government in a multilevel government system, as in first-level (local government), second-level (township, county, province, or region), or third-level (central government).

Jurisdictional reach: a term referring to the breadth of activity carried on by a government in a multilevel government system.

KEOGH: a retirement savings plan for self-employed workers with tax advantages.

Kink point: a point on the boundary of a budget set where there is a kink in a line segment of the set.

Labor-leisure choice: a model of a person's choice between spending time in working earning income and in leisure.

Laffer curve: a relationship between the tax rate and the revenue generated by a tax in which the revenue initially rises with increases in the tax rate up to a point and then falls with further increases in the tax rate.

Land Value Tax (LVT): a property tax system in which the tax base is the land value only, ignoring the value of any improvements on the land.

Law of unintended consequences: a general rule in the policy world that holds that policy actions or decisions often have consequences that were not intended, in addition to or instead of those intended.

Legal person: a term used to identify a corporation as a legal entity, distinct from a physical person.

Lemon law: a law that grants legal rights and recourse to consumers who have purchased goods that have subsequently proven to be defective or unreliable (so-called lemons).

Leviathan hypothesis: the economic hypothesis that government intrusion into the economy should be smaller the greater the extent to which taxes and expenditures are decentralized.

Life cycle model: an economic model of the allocation of consumption over time, given lifetime income.

Limited liability: legal liability of a business that is limited to the assets of the business.

Limited liability company (LLC): a hybrid form of business organization under which the owners of the company have limited liability.

Limited liability partnership (LLP): a hybrid form of business organization under which the partners have limited liability.

Lindahl equilibrium: an equilibrium allocation for public goods whereby each individual is charged a tax price reflecting his or her demand for the public good.

Lindahl prices: custom prices for public goods to be charged of individuals as determined in a Lindahl model.

Line item veto: a budget control device by which the president had authority to change a single line item within a larger package of appropriations approved by Congress.

Lobbying: the act of exerting influence in order to affect the voting behavior of public officials.

Local public goods: public goods provided in a fixed geographic area (city, county, school district).

Logrolling: the process of vote trading in a representative democracy.

Long-run: a time horizon in economics long enough that there are no fixed commitments, so all inputs are variable.

Lorenz curve: graphical plot of the income distribution with share of population on the horizontal axis and share of income on the vertical axis.

Loss offset: a provision in the income tax law that permits a business to deduct losses from taxable income, at least partially.

Loyalty: a strategy option for an individual in a community; the person can stay in the community and remain loyal to the community leadership.

Maastricht Treaty: the treaty that provides the fundamental pillars upon which the European Union is built, named after the city in the Netherlands where the negotiations took place.

Majority rule: a collective decision-making rule whereby the winner is the candidate or proposal receiving the majority of votes cast in an election.

Mandates: requirements of a higher level of government regarding service provision by a lower level of government, with no funds transferred to pay for the costs of that provision.

Marginal benefit: the additional benefit derived from an additional unit of a good or service.

Marginal cost: the additional cost of producing another unit of output.

Marginal cost pricing: a pricing policy whereby the price of a good or service is set equal to its marginal cost of production.

Marginal damages (*MD*): the additional external damages caused by the provision of an additional unit of a good or service.

Marginal excess burden of a tax: the additional excess burden that arises from an increase in a tax.

Marginal external benefit (*MEB*): the marginal benefit conferred by production of a good that generates an external benefit.

Marginal private benefit (*MPB*): the marginal benefit of production to a private producer.

Marginal private cost (*MPC*): the marginal cost of production to a private producer.

Marginal rate of substitution: the rate at which a person is willing to substitute one good or service for another while holding constant her level of economic well-being.

Marginal rate of transformation: the rate at which the production of one good or service can be transformed into the production of another good or service while holding constant resource use and technology.

Marginal revenue: the additional revenue derived from the sale of an additional unit of good or service.

Marginal social benefit (*MSB*): the marginal benefit of production to society, including both the marginal private benefit to the producer and the marginal external benefit of that production: $MSB = MPB + MEB$.

Marginal social cost (*MSC*): the marginal cost of production to society, including both the marginal private cost to the producer and the marginal damages of that production: $MSC = MPC + MD$.

Marginal tax rate (*MTR*): the rate of taxation applied to an additional unit of tax base—the change in tax divided by the change in tax base. The *MTR* represents the share of an additional unit of tax base that is taken in tax.

Marginal utility: the additional utility a person derives from consuming one more unit of a good or service.

Market comparison approach: an approach to the valuation of property that uses sales values of comparable properties to establish the value of a subject property.

Marriage bonus: the reduction in income tax for a married couple that results when their joint tax liability from filing as a couple is less than the sum of their individual tax liabilities would have been had they filed as single persons.

Marriage tax (or marriage penalty): the increase in income tax for a married couple that results when their joint tax liability from filing as a couple is more than the sum of their individual tax liabilities would have been had they filed as single persons.

Means-testing: a mechanism of limiting recipients of a welfare program to those with low income.

Median income: income level of the middle household in the income distribution.

Median location: the middle element of an array along a line of political opinion, desired level of public expenditure, or other continuum of measurement.

Median voter theorem: a result in collective decision making that says under certain circumstances the candidate or proposal chosen by majority rule will be the median option.

Medicaid: an in-kind transfer program providing medical care to low-income families in the United States.

Medicare: an in-kind transfer program providing medical care to the elderly in the United States.

Missing markets: the absence of markets for some goods or services (e.g., a student cannot buy unemployment insurance to guard against the possibility that when he finishes college the job he wants will be available).

Mixed market economy: a mixed market economy relies on a mixture of markets and government actions to allocate resources.

Modified accelerated cost recovery system (MACRS): the accelerated depreciation method currently used in the U.S. corporate income tax.

Modigliani-Miller Theorem: a fundamental result in corporate finance proving that under certain conditions the flow of financing to individuals by a corporation is determined by real variables and is not affected by the firm's capital structure.

Money income: income in the form of cash.

Moral hazard: a problem in the realm of insurance by which an insured individual, by his/her own actions, can change the odds of the insured event occurring.

Nash equilibrium: an equilibrium concept in economic theory whereby agent A's strategy is optimal given agent B's choice, and agent B's strategy is optimal given agent A's choice.

National neutrality: a form of neutral taxation of foreign income by which the home country taxes the foreign income of their resident firms, permitting only a deduction for foreign taxes paid (not a credit as with a CEN system).

National sales tax: a single sales tax system applied on a national basis, as distinct from the U.S. system of independent state sales tax systems.

Negative externalities: an event that inflicts an appreciable damage on some person or persons who were not fully consenting parties in reaching the decision or decisions that led directly or indirectly to the event in question.

Net operating loss (NOL): the operating loss of a corporation for tax purposes.

Net outlays: outlays minus transfers of funds to other units of government, also called *expenditures*.

Net primary benefits: primary benefits minus direct costs.

Net secondary benefits: secondary benefits minus secondary costs.

Nexus: the legal definition of presence in a state with which comes the requirement to collect and pay state sales taxes.

Nominal measures: monetary measures of economic entities such as revenues and expenditures that are in current dollars, not adjusted for changes in the price level.

Nominal tax rate: the tax rate applied to a tax base, ignoring the effects of exemptions, deductions, and credits.

Noncategorical grant: a grant that may be spent on any category of spending; sometimes called *revenue sharing*.

Nonexcludable: a characteristic of public goods indicating that if the good is provided to anyone, it is available to everyone.

Nonpoint source pollution: pollution that originates from many diffused sources.

Nonrefundable tax credit: a tax credit that can only be used up to the amount of the taxpayers' liability.

Nonrival: a characteristic of public goods indicating that consumption of the good by one person does not diminish the amount available for others to consume.

Nonsatiation: a property of preferences that means a person cannot be simultaneously satiated with all goods. Satiation means the person has so much of the good that his marginal utility of the good has been driven to zero and additional units of the good are useless to him.

Nordlinger case: the Supreme Court case establishing the constitutionality of California's Proposition 13.

Normal good: a good which people buy more of as their income rises (as distinct from an inferior good which people buy less of as their income rises).

Normal profit: profit equal to the opportunity cost of capital reflecting the normal rate of return to capital, given risk.

Normative analysis: a description of the way things ought to be in the public sector.

Null hypothesis: a hypothesized statement of what we do not expect to be true which is then tested using statistical methods.

Occupational tax: a payroll tax applied to certain occupations, typically levied by a city or local government.

Off-budget activities: government activities whose receipts and outlays *are not* reflected in the budget of the government agency.

Office of Management and Budget (OMB): an office within the U.S. government executive branch that prepares and oversees the federal budget process.

Office of Tax Analysis (OTA): an office within the U.S. Treasury Department dedicated to conducting tax policy analysis.

On-budget activities: government activities whose receipts and outlays *are* reflected in the budget of the government agency.

Opportunity cost of capital: the value of the next-best alternative use for capital equipment that is forgone due to its present use.

Optimal commodity taxation: *see* Ramsey rule.

Optimal income taxation: an excess burden minimizing income tax derived from a model in which labor supply is affected by taxation and society has a taste for redistribution, thus combining both efficiency and equity considerations.

Option value: value of an object reflecting its irreversible nature; may be considered a risk premium that some consumers are willing to pay to assure that the object will be available in the future.

Ordinary least squares (OLS) method: a method of estimating a regression line through a scatter of data points in statistics in which the line is fit by minimizing the sum of squared vertical distances from the observed data points to the estimated line.

Origin-based taxation: a system of indirect taxation under which the tax is applied in the jurisdiction where the good is produced.

Outlays: monetary disbursements by the government including funds transferred to other units of government.

Output effect: the effect of a partial factor tax on the level of output of the firm.

Own-price elasticities: price elasticities of demand or supply that measure the responsiveness of the quantity demanded or supplied to a change in the goods' own price (as opposed to a change in the price of a related good such as a substitute or complement).

Parameters: prices, income, or other entities in an economic model that can be varied in order to observe changes in behavior.

Pareto efficient: a concept of efficiency in the allocation of resources which holds that an allocation is efficient if one person cannot be made better off without making someone else worse off.

Partial equilibrium analysis: economic analysis of equilibrium in a single market (as distinct from general equilibrium analysis in which only all markets are analyzed simultaneously).

Partial equilibrium tax incidence: economic incidence of a tax considering a single market in which the tax is introduced.

Partial factor tax: a tax applied to a factor of production (an input) in one market, but not other markets (e.g., a corporate income tax under which capital is taxed in the corporate sector, but not in the noncorporate sector).

Partnership: a form of business organization whereby at least two persons pool expertise and resources to start and run the business, splitting business profits between them.

Pay-as-you-go (PAYGO): a government program financing method whereby current contributions into the program provide sufficient revenues to pay the cost of providing benefits to current beneficiaries.

Payroll tax: a tax on wage and salary income earned (not a broad income tax that applies to both labor income and capital income).

Peace dividend: a freeing up of budgetary resources resulting from the end of military expenditures related to war.

Peak-load problem: the problem that arises when demand shifts over time, perhaps over a 24-hour period or over the course of a week/month/year, and the peak demand exceeds the capacity of the supply system.

Per capita: per person.

Perestroika: Russian term for the reconstruction of society that was embraced during the time of Mr. Gorbachev and the demise of the soviet system in the 1980s.

Perfect correspondence: a situation in a multilevel government setting where there is one level of government for each subset of the population over which the consumption of a public good is specified.

Perpetuity: a financial asset that has an infinite life providing a perpetual income stream.

Personal property: property consisting of machinery, equipment, furniture, and financial assets.

Phaseout: a provision in tax law by which a deduction, exemption, or credit is reduced as the taxpayer's income rises.

Pigouvian tax or subsidy: a tax or subsidy designed to correct for an externality.

Plurality: the number of votes received by the leading candidate or proposal in an election.

Point source pollution: pollution that originates from discrete sources such as factory smokestacks or effluent pipes.

Pollution abatement: the process of abating, reducing, or withdrawing pollution.

Portfolio choice: the economic problem of allocating assets in a portfolio among various levels of risk.

Positive analysis: a description of the way things are in the public sector.

Positive externality: an event that confers an appreciable benefit on some person or persons who were not fully consenting parties in reaching the decision or decisions that led directly or indirectly to the event in question.

Poverty gap: a measure of the depth of poverty given by the distance from a poor family's income up to the government-designated poverty line.

Poverty line: an absolute measure of poverty specifying a level of income below which a person or family is considered to be impoverished.

Prebate: a front-loaded (prior) rebate.

Preferential assessment: any of several ways in which the assessed value of property is given preference in a property tax system, as in the case of use-value assessment or with a tax abatement.

Present value: today's value of a future monetary sum.

Pressure groups: social groups that engage in efforts to pressure elected officials to pass legislation that is favorable to them.

Price discrimination: a pricing scheme used by a monopolist whereby higher prices are charged to customers with a low price elasticity of demand and lower prices are charged to customers with a high price elasticity of demand.
Price elasticity: a measure of the responsiveness of demand to changes in the price; the percentage change in quantity demanded divided by the percentage change in price.
Primary insurance amount (PIA): in the U.S. social security system, the monthly benefit payments paid to recipients.
Prisoners' Dilemma: a classic positive-sum game.
Private club: a club in which membership is controlled and access to club goods is limited to club members only.
Private good: a good which is rival in consumption and excludable.
Private information: information available only to a select individual, not available publically to all who may care to know; a cause of market failure.
Producer surplus: the amount producers are paid for a given quantity of a good produced over and above that which would be necessary in the market to induce them to produce that quantity.
Product taxes: taxes applied to products that are produced, or outputs.
Production function: a mathematical summary of the technical relationship between the quantities of inputs used to produce a good or service and the maximum amount of output that can be obtained using those inputs.
Professional corporation (PC): a form of business organization commonly used by doctors, lawyers, and other professionals that provides limited liability although the individuals can be sued personally for malpractice.
Progressive tax: a tax whose average tax rate *(ATR)* rises as income rises.
Property rights: legal rights that govern the use and disposition of property.
Property tax capitalization: the process by which property prices adjust in markets in response to the property taxes associated with those properties.
Proposition 13: a property tax limitation law passed in California in 1978.
Proposition Two-and-a-half: a property tax limitation law passed in Massachusetts.
Public economics: the economic study of the public sector.
Public finance: the set of issues that centers around the revenue-expenditure process of government.
Public good: a good which is nonrival in consumption and nonexcludable.
Public service commission (PSC): a state regulatory agency with responsibility for regulating the activities of utility companies.
Pupil-teacher ratio: the number of pupils in the school or class divided by the number of teachers.
Pyramiding of a sales tax: *see* cascading of a sales tax.

Quintile: a 20 percent slice of the income distribution. The first quintile represents the bottom 20 percent of the income distribution, whereas the second through fifth quintiles represent the succeeding 20 percent groupings.

Race to the bottom: a competitive process whereby governments compete with one another in reducing tax rates or expenditure levels.
Ramsey Rule: a rule for commodity taxation that minimizes excess burden for a given level of revenue generated, implying that taxes on commodities should be inversely proportional to the elasticities of demand.
Rate of technical substitution: the rate at which one input can be substituted for another input in the production of a good or service, while holding the quantity of output constant.
Ratio progressivity index: a measure of tax burden defined as the average burden in deciles seven through nine, divided by the average burden in deciles two through four. The lower this ratio, the more regressive the tax. The higher the ratio, the more progressive the tax. A value of one indicates perfect proportionality of the tax.
Rationalism: the philosophical school of thought that argued truth is discovered through pure intellectual reasoning or rational thought.
Real assets: assets of a corporation that are used to produce goods and services, as distinct from financial assets.
Real measures: monetary measures of economic entities such as revenues and expenditures that are in constant dollars, adjusted for changes in the price level.
Real property: property consisting of land and structures.
Reciprocal deductibility: a feature of federal and state income tax systems whereby each level of government permits the deduction of tax paid to the other level of government from taxable income.
Recission: cancellation of budget authority in the form of a law passed by Congress cancelling previously approved appropriations.
Redistribution pessimism: pessimism regarding the efficacy of redistribution of income through the tax system based on the belief that the marginal excess burden of taxation is large.
Refundable tax credit: a tax credit which is fully usable, even if the amount of the credit exceeds the tax liability.
Regression line: an estimated line representing the relationship between two economic variables that is determined using the statistical method of regression.
Regression model: a statistical model of an economic relationship estimated using the method of regression.
Regressive tax: a tax whose average tax rate *(ATR)* falls as income rises.
Relative measure of poverty: a measure of poverty that defines being poor in relation to other people in an economy (e.g., poverty defined as one-half of the median income level).
Rent: the economic return to a factor of production like land, labor, or capital that is over and above the return required to draw that factor into productive use in the market.

Rent seeking: economic activity aimed at capturing some of the rents generated due to monopoly power or control.

Replacement cost approach: an approach to the valuation of property that computes the cost of replacing the structure.

Republic: a government based on the rule of law, usually embodied in the context of a constitution, rather than the exercise of unconstrained power by a few individuals.

Retained earnings: earnings or net income of a corporation that are retained and not distributed as dividends to shareholders.

Returns to scale: a long-run relationship between the quantity of inputs used and the amount of output produced. If a proportionate increase in the use of all inputs yields the same proportionate increase in output, the production process is said to have constant returns to scale. If the output increase is less than proportionate, there are decreasing returns. If the output increase is more than proportionate, there are increasing returns.

Revenue sharing: *see* noncategorical grant.

Revenues: net receipts of government from parties outside the government, primarily from taxes but also including fees and other sources.

Risk-taking: actions taken by an economic agent (person, household, or firm) leading to an expected payoff with a probability of success that is less than one.

Rivalrous: a characteristic of an economic good or service by which one person's use of the good or service precludes use by others.

Rule of Law: a method of organizing a society by which the final arbiter is the law, embodied in a constitution.

Sales-ratio studies: studies of the sales prices of real estate properties that compute the ratio of assessed value to market value.

Sales tax: a tax applied to the final sales of goods (and sometimes services).

Samaritan's dilemma: an economic situation where the rich cannot help but provide assistance after a disaster to the poor that leads to a misallocation of resources.

Samuelson rule: a rule in economic theory that describes efficiency in the provision of a public good. The Samuelson rule requires that the sum of all persons' marginal benefits of a public good or service must equal the marginal cost of providing the public good or service.

Scientific method: the modern method of discovering truth, combining rational thought and empirical analysis.

Seasonal pricing: a pricing scheme whereby prices change with seasonal fluctuations in market activity.

Second Fundamental Theorem of Welfare Economics: a statement of the result in economic theory that any given allocation of resources can be achieved by competitive markets under certain circumstances.

Secondary benefits: benefits not directly associated with a project that arise due to the existence of the project.

Sequestration: a process of government budget spending control whereby funds are held or reduced.

Short-run: a time horizon in economics over which there are fixed commitments, resulting in fixed quantities of some inputs.

Sin tax: a tax applied to a good or service that is traditionally considered harmful (e.g., cigarette or alcoholic beverage excise tax).

Single-peaked preferences: voter preferences characterized by a single maximum or most-preferred option.

Social welfare function: a mathematical function describing the economic welfare of a society as dependent on the welfare levels of individuals in the society.

Sole proprietor: a person who owns and operates a business with no partners or stockholders.

Special assessments: *ad valorem* charges, much like property taxes, that are applied to property for the provision of particular public services.

Spillover benefits: secondary benefits.

Split-rate property tax: a property tax system that applies two different tax rates to land and improvements (also called a *two-rate property tax* or a *graded property tax*).

SSI: Supplemental Security Income—a government welfare program providing cash assistance.

Stabilization: the process of implementing economic policies in an attempt to stabilize the economy.

State deductibility: a feature of a state income tax system that permits the deduction of certain expenses from taxable income.

States' rights: a policy position that emphasizes the rights of states to provide the level and quality of public services they desire rather than that prescribed by the central, or federal, government.

Statutory incidence of a tax: tax incidence specified in law, or statute.

Statutory tax incidence: tax incidence as defined in legal statue.

Statutory tax rate: a rate of taxation specified in law or statute.

Stockholders: people who own shares of stock in a corporation.

Straight-line depreciation: a depreciation schedule whereby a $(1/n)$th of the value of a real asset with life of n years is deducted each year.

Student-*t* distribution: a probability distribution used in statistical analysis when sample size is too small to approximate with the normal distribution.

Subnational government: a government at a level below the national level (i.e., a state or local government).

Substitution effect: the effect of a price change that induces a person to substitute away from purchasing the more expensive good in favor of the less expensive good.

Subtractive method: the method of defining the VAT tax base that involves starting with gross receipts and subtracting payments for inputs.

Suits Index: a measure of the distribution of tax burden. It is an index number in the interval [21, 11], where a value of 21 indicates a completely regressive tax, 11 indicates a completely progressive tax, and a value of zero indicates a neutral tax.

Sum-of-digits method: a method of computing depreciation. Under this method a fraction of the capital expenditure is deducted in each period with the fraction declining over time. For example, a 10-year asset is written off over time with the fraction 10/55 of the investment expense deducted in year one, the fraction 9/55 deducted in year two, 8/55 deducted in year three, and so on until 1/55 is deducted in year 10.

Supplemental appropriations: midterm appropriations in addition to those appropriations approved at the beginning of the budget period.

TANF: Temporary Assistance to Needy Families—a government welfare program.

Tangible material benefits: measurable material benefits of a program or activity arising from the use of the products or services of the program or activity.

Tangible property: property consisting of real and personal property.

Tariff: a list or menu of taxes, prices, or charges for public goods and services.

Tax anticipation notes (TANs): short-term debt issued by a government that is paid back with tax revenues that are known to be arriving at a certain date.

Tax arbitrage: the practice of exploiting differences in tax rates by altering economic activity in order to minimize tax liability.

Tax avoidance: legal actions by a taxpayer to reduce tax liability.

Tax base: the definition of what is taxed by a tax system.

Tax brackets: ranges of tax base over which specific marginal tax rates apply.

Tax credit: a provision in tax law that gives a taxpayer a credit against the tax due, as if the taxpayer had already paid the amount specified in the credit.

Tax deduction: a specification in tax law that certain expenditures may be deducted from taxable income.

Tax evasion: illegal actions of a taxpayer to reduce tax liability.

Tax-exclusive tax rate: tax rate computed as the tax paid divided by tax base excluding the tax paid.

Tax exemption: a specification in tax law that a certain class of taxpayers or a certain class of activities that would normally be taxable are exempt from paying the tax.

Tax incidence: analysis of the tax burden and on whom that burden falls.

Tax-inclusive tax rate: tax rate computed as the tax paid divided by tax base including the tax paid.

Tax liability: the amount of tax owed by a taxpayer, or the amount the taxpayer is liable under law to pay.

Tax Reform Act of 1986 (TRA86): a landmark income tax reform law adopted in the United States that broadened the tax base of the personal income tax.

Taxable income: income subject to taxation under an income tax system.

Taxable unit: the social unit to which an income tax is applied, typically either the individual or the family.

Territorial taxation: an approach to taxation by which a country taxes all of the income of its residents and firms earned within the country's territory (and does not tax the income earned elsewhere in the world).

Theory of the second best: economic theory of the optimal allocation of resources in the situation where the first-best optimal allocation is not possible.

Three-factor method: a method of apportionment under which three factors are used: property, payroll, and sales.

Tiebout model: an economic model of the way people "vote with their feet," selecting the community that provides the combination of local public goods and taxes that most closely matches their desires.

Time endowment: the total amount of time a person is endowed with in a labor-leisure choice model.

Time of day pricing: a pricing scheme whereby the price charged varies inversely with demand throughout the day.

Toll: a tax or charge for a privilege, especially for permission to use a highway or a bridge.

Total cost (*TC*): the sum of total fixed cost plus total variable cost; $TC = TFC + TVC$.

Total fixed cost (*TFC*): the total cost of fixed inputs.

Total income: a measure of income used on the U.S. personal income tax, equal to labor income (wages, salaries, and tips) plus capital income (interest and dividends) plus business net income.

Total variable cost (*TVC*): the total cost of variable inputs.

Traditional view of the incidence of the property tax: a partial equilibrium view of property tax incidence that contends that the property tax is for the most part passed forward to consumers of housing in the form of higher prices.

Transactions costs: costs associated with carrying out an economic transaction (buying or selling).

Transfer pricing: determination of the amount and characterization of income reported by a business entity doing business in one country that buys or sells goods or services from a related business entity in another country.

Transitivity: a property of preferences that assures a kind of consistency. If x_a is preferred to x_b and x_b is preferred to x_c, then x_a is preferred to x_c.

Trilemma: a situation requiring a choice between three equally difficult or unpleasant alternatives.

True economic depreciation: a depreciation schedule that reflects the true rate at which a real asset loses its economic ability to produce.

Two-earner deduction: a feature of an income tax system designed to reduce the size of the marriage tax whereby a couple in which both spouses have earned income is permitted a deduction from taxable income.

Two-part tariff: a scheme of pricing or taxing whereby users are required to pay two fees, a flat fee for the privilege of using the public facility or service, and a second variable fee that is proportional to the amount of usage.

Two-rate income tax system: a method of integration of the corporate and personal income taxes under which distributed profits paid out in dividends and undistributed profits retained by the corporation are taxed at two different rates. Undistributed profits of the corporation are taxed at a higher rate than distributed profits.

Two-rate property tax: a property tax system that applies different tax rates to land and improvements (also called a *split-rate property tax* or a *graded property tax*).

Type I error: the error one makes when rejecting a true null hypothesis.

Type II error: the error one makes when not rejecting a false null hypothesis.

Unanimity: a collective decision-making rule requiring all voters to be in agreement.

Unit tax: a tax applied per unit of the good taxed (e.g., a cigarette excise tax that is applied in dollars per package of cigarettes).

Unlimited liability: legal liability of a business that is not limited to the assets of the business but includes all assets of the business owner, including personal assets.

Urban growth boundary: a geographic boundary within which urban growth is confined by law.

USA tax: a proposed consumption tax that would permit deductions for deposits into savings accounts—an unlimited savings allowance.

Use tax: a tax equivalent to a state or local sales tax that is applied to goods not subject to the sales tax, based on the use of the good in the jurisdiction.

Use value: value of an object reflecting its current direct use, ignoring other potential uses, as distinct from market value.

User fee: a fee charged of a public good or service user.

Utilitarianism: a school of philosophy in which the value of an object or an action is determined by its utility or its usefulness.

Utility possibilities frontier (*UPF*): a graphical illustration of the combinations of utilities for two persons in an economy where one person's utility is maximized holding constant the other person's utility.

Value-added tax (VAT): a tax applied to the value added at each stage of production.

Variable input: an input used in the production process whose quantity is freely variable, not fixed.

Vertical equity of taxation: concern for fairness, or equity, in taxation with a focus on how the tax treats taxpayers of unequal ability; sometimes summarized as "unequal treatment of unequals."

Voice: a strategy option for an individual in a community: the person can remain in the community and voice clear opinions about public goods in order to influence the type and quantity of public goods provided.

Voting paradox: a contradiction in voting outcomes whereby voters with transitive preferences have a collective preference that is intransitive.

Welfare: measurement of the economic well-being of people in the economy.

Williamson Act (California Land Conservation Act of 1965): one of the earliest and most influential programs of preferential assessment for property tax purposes.

Willingness to accept (WTA): in contingent valuation methodology WTA is the amount the survey respondent would be willing to accept in exchange for an undesirable situation.

Willingness to pay (WTP): in contingent valuation methodology WTP is the amount the survey respondent would be willing to pay for some public good or service.

World Bank: an international agency created after World War II with the purpose of advancing economic development in less developed nations.

Worldwide taxation: an approach to taxation by which a country taxes all of the income of its residents and firms regardless of where in the world the income was earned.

Zero rating: the process of applying a zero tax rate to a specific commodity or group of commodities under a value-added tax (VAT).

Index

U.S. State Government General Revenue Sources, 2007

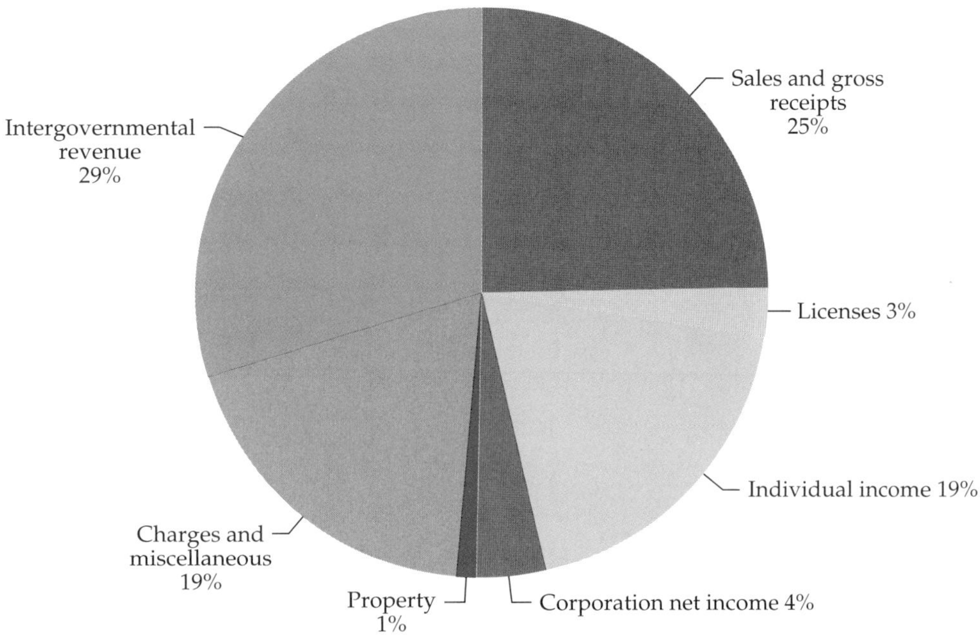

U.S. State Government General Expenditures by Category, 2007

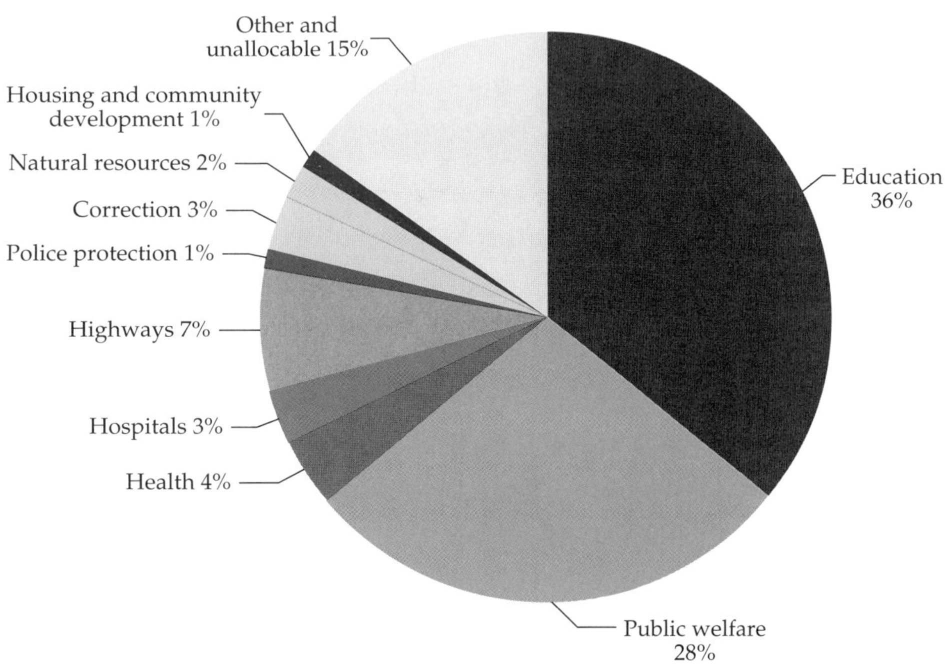

U.S. Federal Government Receipts by Source, 2010

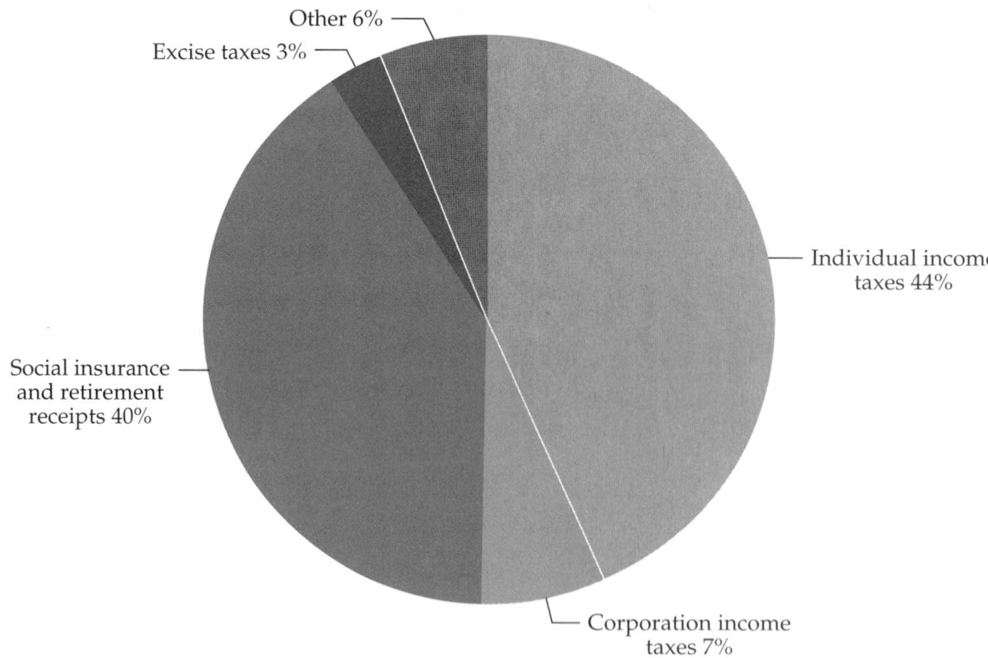

U.S. Federal Government Outlays by Detailed Function, 2010

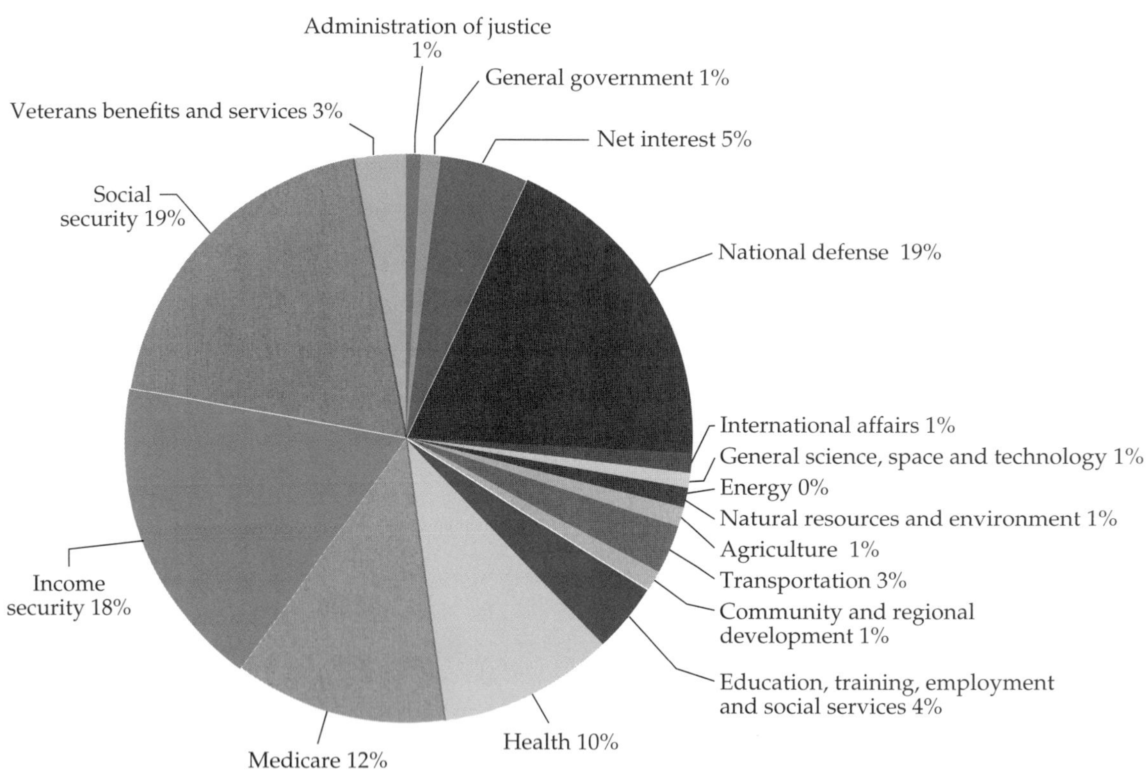

Central Government Debt as a Percent of GDP OECD Countries, 2009

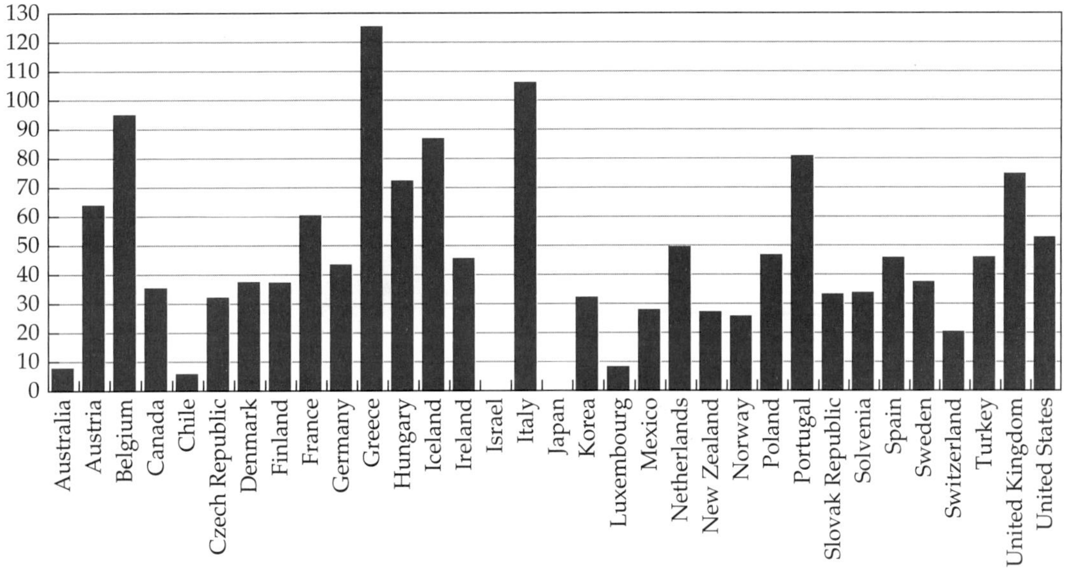

Individual and Corporate Income Tax Rates (%) OECD Countries, 2009

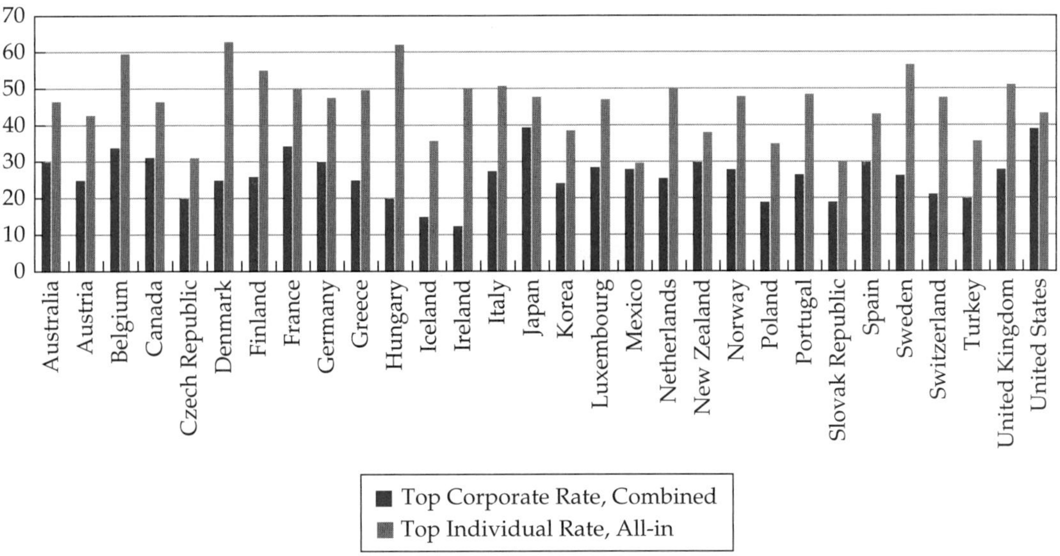

U.S. Federal Government Receipts, Outlays, and Deficits (billions of current dollars), 1960–2010

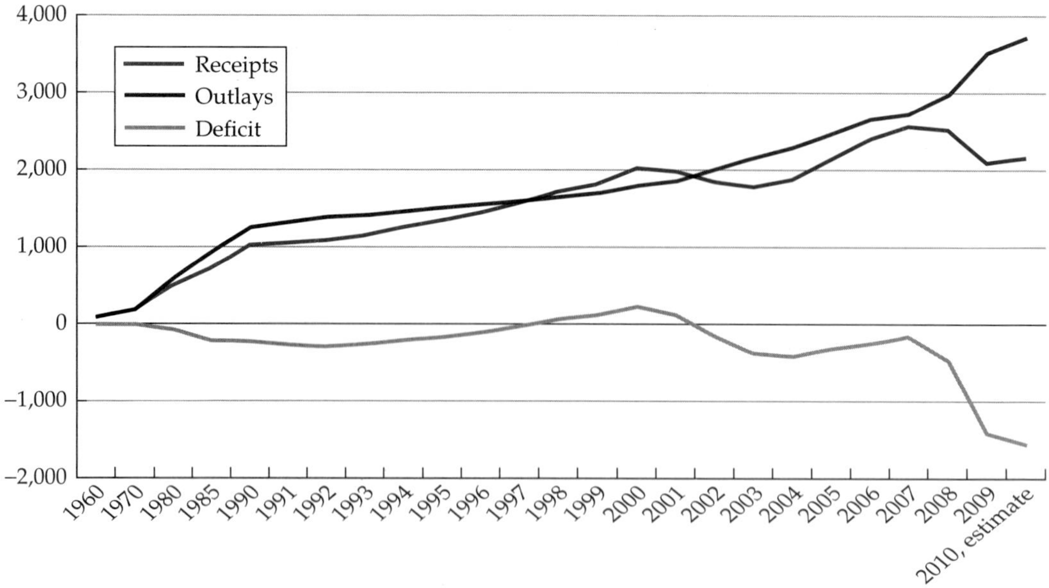

U.S. Federal Government Receipts, Outlays, and Deficits (percent of GDP), 1960–2010

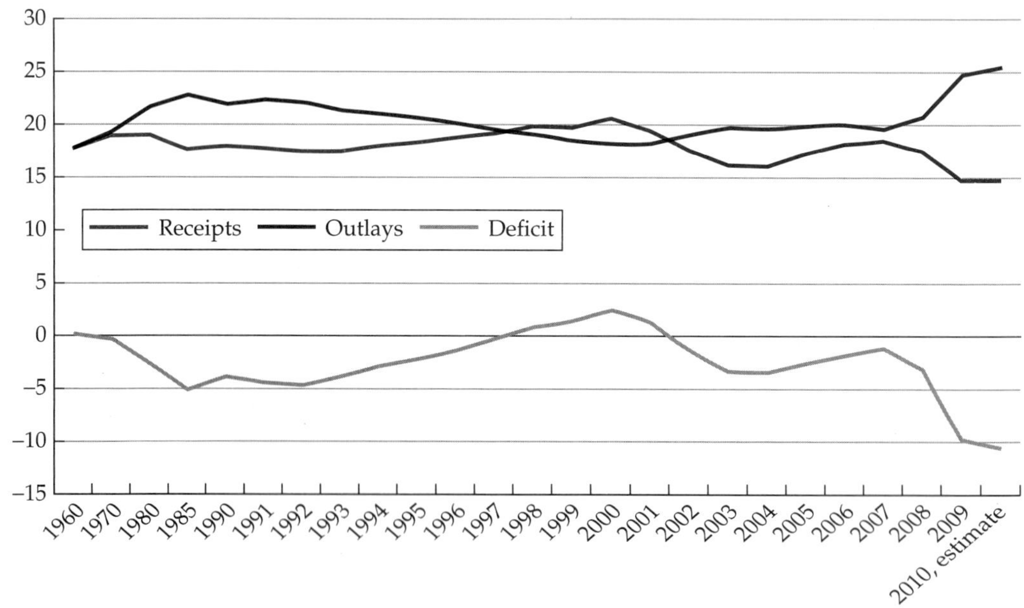